Psychology

John C. Ruch, Mills College

PSYCHOLOGY The Personal Science

Wadsworth Publishing Company
Belmont, California
A Division of Wadsworth, Inc.

Psychology Editor: Kenneth King
Production Coordinator: Sally Schuman
Interior and Cover Design: MaryEllen Podgorski
Copy Editor: Judith Hibbard
Illustrations: J&R Services
Photo Research: Mollie Hughes, Lindsay Kefauver and Jean O'Korn
Cover Photos: The Bettmann Archive, Inc., Darwin Museum, Dr. Albert Bandura, Mark Godfrey/Archive Pictures, Inc., Bell Labs, Harper & Row Publishers, Inc., The Gorilla Foundation, Kanehara & Co., Ltd.

Printed in the United States of America

1 2 3 4 5 6 7 8 9 10–88 87 86 85 84

ISBN 0-534-02672-9

Library of Congress Cataloging in Publication Data

Ruch, John.
    Psychology: the personal science.

    Bibliography: p.
    Includes index.
    1. Psychology.   I. Title. [DNLM: 1. Psychology.
BF 121 R899pc]
BF121.R78 1984   150   83-6679
ISBN 0-534-02672-9

Brief Contents

Contents

Contents

Preface

My goal in writing this text has been to direct the interest students have in their own behavior and in the behavior of others into the scientific discipline of psychology. I see psychology as a quantitative experimental science. It is a particular kind of science, however, because most of the topics psychology studies are of personal interest or concern to all of us: why as individuals we eat, sleep, and think, why in interaction with others we talk, fight, and make love, why in social groups we support our friends and confront our enemies. I have tried throughout the book to present the science of psychology without sacrificing its *personal* meaning. In seeking to achieve that goal, I have sought to make the book comprehensive, scholarly, integrative, thematic, current, and teachable.

To make it *comprehensive*, I have included a broad range of concepts and terms—but not so many as to overwhelm students. I have tried to cover all major topics in a consistent fashion, with an appropriate level of detail, avoiding both superficial coverage and excessive details that can obscure meaning.

To make the book *scholarly* and *integrative*, I have provided more historical background and more thematic unity than the usual "eclectic" introductory text. For example, Chapter 1 includes the work of Wundt, Fechner, and James and the role of structuralism and functionalism in the development of psychology. I describe five major questions with both historical and contemporary implications, including the nature/ nurture and mind/body questions. And seven major psychological perspectives are introduced, including their founders as well as their major views. I note the attempts of theorists to combine perspectives as well as the relationship of psychology to other sciences. I thus try to present psychology as a particular way of thinking, with a substantial past, a multi-faceted present, and future goals.

To further the *thematic* integration, I use both the classic questions and the major perspectives throughout the book. The "human-as-animal" question and the ethological perspective, for example, are further elaborated in the discussion of evolution in Chapter 3, then picked up in the contexts of motivation, sensory sampling of information, consciousness, language, and elsewhere. The cognitive perspective is covered both in Chapters 10 and 11 on language and thinking and within other chapters, such as the social cognition discussion of Chapter 17. Some themes are developed primarily within a single chapter (for example, the theme of survival in Chapter 4), and others span several chapters. Hemisphere-differences research is described in Chapter 2, then further noted in several later chapters, including those on consciousness, language, and thinking.

The text is *current* in its overall orientation, its topic coverage, and the research it draws on, based on a variety of journals, periodicals, and books. The emphasis on cognitive approaches in many chapters, for example, reflects a major trend in the field. Particular developments noted include not only those of psychology itself—such as new approaches in learning theory, recent arguments about ape language, the Kaufman Assessment Battery, DSM-III, and research on loneliness—but also developments relevant to psychological research, such as the nuclear magnetic resonance technique for exploring brain function. (I have not, however, included some topics that I feel are faddish or not yet well supported by evidence, such as near-death experiences or ESP.)

In keeping with psychology's ongoing concern with gender roles, the entire text is gender-balanced in language use and choice of examples, and it consistently identifies female researchers as such.

To enhance *teachability*, I have set formal concepts in a context of student interest and relevance. The chapter-opening vignettes, for example, are based on real experiences and are further developed in the body of the chapter. Topics of particular interest are included throughout, not merely for interest but as integrated parts of the chapter—Chapter 10, for example, includes discussions of animal language research, black English, bilingualism, sex differences in speech patterns, spoonerisms, and fortune tellers. Examples and applications include the Personal Application boxes, which focus on particular applications of the chapter's content; other applications occur throughout the prose. The Notable Quotes, the Patient Quotes of Chapter 15, and the quotations included with illustrations of famous psychologists all provide a first-person immediacy. Even the statistics appendix emphasizes thought processes, not computations.

Various structural features are also designed to aid the teaching of this text. In addition to standard features such as boldfacing of key terms, boxed examples, chapter summaries, further readings, and an extensive bibliography, the book has a combined glossary/index, so that students can get both page references and key definitions in one place. I have tied all illustrations and boxes to the relevant text discussion by means of square "bullets" (■), thus enabling students to easily relate prose and illustrative materials; illustration references always occur at the ends of paragraphs.

The ancillaries include a study guide, prepared by Jay Braun of Arizona State University, and a detailed instructor's manual, prepared by David Volckmann of Whittier College and Jean Volckmann of Pasadena City College. Almost 2000 multiple-choice test items, a large percentage of which are conceptual in nature, are available both in printed form and through Wadsworth's testing program for mainframe and micro computers, including the testing services offered through its area-code-800 testing service.

ACKNOWLEDGMENTS

No text is the work of just one person. I feel genuinely indebted to a number of people; without their help this text either would not exist or would not be what it is.

First, I thank my wife Connie for her unending support and good humor, even when the pressure of deadlines turned me into something of a grouch and despite the demands of her own work. I could not have written this book without her help.

Second, I thank two professors for my inspiration and training in psychology: Dr. B. F. Skinner and Dr. E. R. ("Jack") Hilgard. Of all the courses I took as an undergraduate, Dr. Skinner's course still seems the most interesting and significant. When I finally attended graduate school after ten years in another career, I had the good fortune to become one of Jack Hilgard's students. I thank Dr. Skinner for his inspiration, even though it took some years to reach fruition. And I thank Dr. Hilgard not only for all that he has helped me to do but even more for being an inspiring role model.

I am also grateful to many people at Wadsworth; they include Ken King, the psychology editor. He offered me the chance to write this book and stood by me through the travails of turning my ideas into a finished manuscript. Once the project began, Mary Arbogast showed me how much I still had to learn about writing. Her unique combination of editorial skills and insight into what I was trying to say were invaluable in trimming and polishing the manuscript through repeated rewrites. Judith Hibbard's keen editorial eye helped keep all the many details consistent. Mollie Hughes and Jean O'Korn's search for photos and Marion Hansen's pursuit of permissions were both persistent and inspired. Wendy Calmenson skillfully oversaw the extensive art program. MaryEllen Podgorski's design for the book brought everything together into a beautiful package. And Sally Schuman coordinated the complex and difficult production of the book.

My thanks also to David and Jean Volckmann for their fine instructor's manual and to Jay Braun for his outstanding study guide.

I also owe a considerable debt to those professors and researchers who took time out of their busy schedules to read various drafts and to point out where what I was saying was too much or too little, or where I was in error. For their help, I am grateful; any errors that may remain are, of course, my responsibility. Those reviewers include:

Nadine R. Anderson, Wilson College

Linda Baker, University of Maryland

James H. Butler, James Madison University

Stephen F. Davis, Emporia State University

Randy L. Diehl, The University of Texas at Austin

Ernest Doleys, DePaul University

John R. Donahoe, University of Massachusetts, Amherst

Bernard S. Gorman, Nassau Community College

Robert J. Gregory, University of Idaho

Alfred E. Hall, The College of Wooster

Ralph W. Hansen, Augustana College

Steven Hinkle, Miami University

John R. Hovancik, Seton Hall University

John E. Kello, Davidson College

Richard A. King, The University of North Carolina at Chapel Hill

Daniel S. Kirschenbaum, University of Wisconsin

John M. Knight, Central State University

Kenneth O. McGraw, The University of Mississippi

Steven Penrod, University of Wisconsin

Glenn Shean, College of William and Mary

David C. Solly, Radford University

W. Scott Terry, University of North Carolina at Charlotte

Jerry W. Thornton, Angelo State University

Jeffrey S. Turner, Mitchell College

Jean Volckmann, Pasadena City College

Patricia Walsh, Loyola Marymount University

Writing this text has been thoroughly enjoyable, but it has also been an effort that only other authors can truly appreciate. Now that it is finished, I present it to you as a parent presents a child: I am certainly proud of it, but you must decide what you think of it. If you have any comments on my progeny that you would like to share with me, please do—at Mills College, Oakland, Calif. 94613.

John C. Ruch

Psychology

Part I

The Science
of Psychology

You go to a party given by some friends, where you are introduced to someone described to you as a "psychologist." What are your immediate expectations about this person? Do you have any idea what he or she studied to become a psychologist, or what he or she is likely to do every day to earn a living? Do you assume that this person is a therapist, spending each day trying to understand and help disturbed people? Are you just a little concerned as to what you say, and a little uncomfortable lest such daily practice at uncovering unconscious motives allow this psychologist somehow to uncover your innermost thoughts? If you don't, you're unusual. If you do know that most psychologists are *not* therapists, do you know what else they do? What would you expect this person to be interested in? Our first task in studying psychology is to answer some of these questions, to examine just what psychology is and what psychologists do.

Many people think of psychology primarily as a profession that helps mentally disturbed people. Many practicing psychologists *are* therapists, but most are not; psychologists work in industry, in schools, and elsewhere, and perform a wide variety of tasks. Psychology is also the scientific discipline behind these applications. Research psychologists seek to add to the basic understanding that practicing psychologists can apply.

Psychologists often find that issues they confront are variants of a few very old philosophical questions, and most must take some position on these questions to carry out their work effectively; we will note five such classic questions. As psychology developed in the late 19th century, the approach taken to these classic problems by the early psychologists helped determine the form and content of contemporary psychology, so we will briefly consider these historical approaches.

Since its inception, psychology has grown and changed, so an overview of seven current perspectives will help lay the groundwork for the rest of the text. Finally, psychology as a science utilizes several accepted methods of gathering its basic data; some understanding of these methods is also necessary for the chapters to follow.

PSYCHOLOGY AS SCIENCE AND PROFESSION

The psychology we will focus on is a scientific discipline that seeks to understand human behavior (Monte, 1975; Schultz, 1970). But psychology is also a profession aimed at improving the quality of life (Miller, 1969, 1980). Applied psychology may involve therapy, but more frequently involves quite different

Chapter 1

What Is Psychology?

activities: the arrangement of job rules or the design of aircraft cockpits, for example, to make the activities carried out within them easier, more efficient, and safer (Chapanis, 1953). Although most of our emphasis will be on the science of psychology, we will occasionally look at some of the applied professional uses (Fox et al., 1982).

Psychology as a Science

A **science** is a structured form of study of some range of phenomena (Goldstein, 1980). Before looking at that structure, which is called the *scientific method*, let us examine the general content of psychology, its classic questions, and the historical and contemporary approaches to them.

Defining Psychology The word *psychology* combines the Greek words for mind (psyche) and study (logos) and thus means "the study of the mind." It has also been frequently defined as the science of behavior. But psychologists who use this definition include mental activities as a kind of behavior; to them, if you "think" of something, you are still behaving, even though you may show little activity on the outside. Other psychologists, however, wish to give hidden behavior more specific emphasis. To emphasize that both are included, we define **psychology** as the science of behavior and mental activity.

The goals of psychology are the goals of any science: to describe, explain, predict, and control the phenomena that are its subject matter. The case of John W. Hinckley, Jr., for example, demonstrates some of the problems faced by psychology as well as the society of which it is a part. ■ Figure 1.1

How can psychologists (or judges, or jurors) describe Hinckley: as misguided, psychotic, a cunning liar, or . . . ? How can we explain how he came to be this way? Could we have predicted his attack on the president or can we predict if he would kill again if released? How could we have controlled Hinckley so that whatever led him to kill was prevented, and how can we best control him now so that he is not a continuing danger?

Most psychologists would accept our definition and goals of psychology, though each would no doubt wish to add qualifiers. Perhaps the most controversial part is the meaning of the word *control*, largely because of its complex moral and ethical implications. Note, however, that control simply means "make effective change"; this is the sense in which most practicing psychologists seek to control behavior, whether they are therapists, teachers, or industrial consultants. All seek to make some effective change in behavior; if no one's behavior changed as a result of what psy-

chologists did, their work would be ineffective. In a similar sense, we all seek to make effective changes in our own behavior: this is *self*-control.

Psychology and Other Sciences Psychology is one of several disciplines that focus on human behavior. It is usually grouped with the behavioral sciences or social sciences, which include disciplines closely related to psychology, such as sociology and anthropology, along with others such as economics, linguistics, and political science (Prewitt, 1981; Simon, 1980). Psychology is also sometimes considered one of the natural sciences, which also include biology. Since psychologists approach questions in such varied ways, they sometimes seem closer to these other disciplines than they do to other psychologists. A social psychologist may seem more like a sociologist, for example, and a physiological psychologist may seem more like a biologist than they seem like each other.

But psychologists share many commonalities, including assumptions, training, and language, that help to define them. Psychologists, for example, share a focus on the *individual* and on *behavior*. A social psychologist thus focuses on the individual within a social context, whereas a sociologist focuses on the social group as a whole. A physiological psychologist concentrates on physiological explanations of behavior, whereas a biologist studies all aspects of physiology.

Basic and Applied Research Whatever their area of interest, some psychologists focus on **basic research,** seeking to understand underlying rules or mechanisms (Handler, 1979). These psychologists may choose simplified or specialized problems with little obvious practical significance. Other psychologists are more interested in **applied research;** they study very realistic problems, seeking to develop appropriate applications of what has been understood through basic research.

Both basic and applied researchers may be interested in memory, for example. Basic researchers might study how people memorize lists of words, something few of us do in daily life, or even how memory works in a species remote to us, such as flatworms. Applied researchers would be more likely to study problems such as those children have in remembering schoolwork.

A Technology of Behavior? The set of rules for carrying out some procedure may be called a *technology*. Although technologies can develop out of direct experience, they are more efficiently developed from scientific understanding. The technology of cannon building grew up through trial and error, for example, but modern physics and metallurgy allow much more

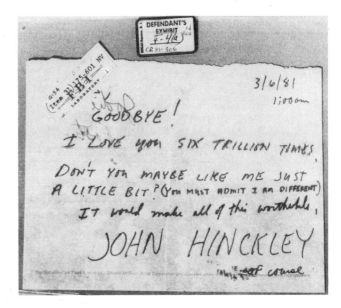

Figure 1.1 ■ John W. Hinckley, Jr., in a self-portrait, and one of his letters to Jodie Foster. Obsessed with Foster after seeing her in the movie *Taxi Driver*, Hinckley sought to demonstrate his love by trying to assassinate President Reagan. In one of the most publicized and controversial uses of the insanity defense, he was declared not guilty by reason of insanity and sent to a mental institution—from which he sends letters to the media discussing his case. Hinckley's case is unusual, but it poses the same questions psychology asks about all of us: Who are we? Why do we do what we do?

(Wide World Photos)

efficient design of any metal device. In the biological sciences, understanding of how organisms reproduce and grow has led to striking technological advances, from laboratory manipulation of DNA (the molecular basis of heredity) to surgery on fetuses.

Psychology has not yet provided the kinds of technological applications that the physical sciences have. Technological offerings from the behavioral sciences are not likely to be new machines or laboratory techniques. Instead, they will be more subtle: a **technology of behavior.** This phrase may seem a bit bizarre if you think of technology in terms of products, but remember that technology refers not to products, but to the rules for building them. Any technology, including a technology of behavior, offers a set of practical rules that may be easily applied to concrete problems; these may derive from scientific principles, but can be applied by almost anyone.

Some psychologists have offered the beginnings of such a technology (Skinner, 1968), but a broad and effective technology for application to human behavior is yet to be developed. The relative newness of the behavioral sciences, the complexity of their subject matter, ethical questions, and other reasons have kept this from occurring—at least for now. The technology that therapists and other professional psychologists now use is a mixture of scientific findings and methods developed through trial and error. Their work is as much art as technology.

However, psychology *has* demonstrated that some of the rules that everyone learns from society are, in fact, true—and perhaps more importantly, that some others are false. ■ Personal Application: Did Your Society Tell You the Truth About Behavior?

Although there might be some disagreement on detail interpretations, psychologists consider *all* of the statements listed in the box on p. 6 to be false. Even after taking introductory psychology, most students continue to believe these myths, which are very resistant to change. (As we study the relevant topics, the reasons why these statements are false should be evident.)

Psychology as a Profession

Soon after the formal founding of psychology in 1879, psychologists began to get together to share their interests. When the American Psychological Association (APA) was founded in 1892, it had fewer than 20 members, but progress thereafter was increasingly rapid; as of 1978, there were over 47,000 members (Dorken & Webb, 1981; McKinney, 1976).

This explosion in numbers occurred for practitioners of all sciences and in all countries in the 20th century, and both psychology and the United States have been strong participants. It is often said that 90% of all scientists who ever lived are alive today; for psychology, the percentage is at least 90%. Although psychology began in Germany, the center of the discipline

Did your society tell you the truth about behavior?

More than 50% of beginning psychology students believed the following statements to be true (Vaughan, 1977). Do you agree?

1 To change people's behavior toward members of ethnic minority groups, we must first change their attitudes.

2 Memory can be likened to a storage chest in the brain into which we deposit material and from which we can withdraw it later if needed. Occasionally, something gets lost from the "chest" and then we say we have forgotten.

3 Personality tests reveal your basic motives, including those you may not be aware of.

4 The basis of the baby's love for his mother is the fact that his mother fills his physiological needs for food, etc.

5 By feeling people's faces, blind people can visualize how they look in their minds.

6 The more highly motivated you are, the better you will do at solving a complex problem.

7 The best way to ensure that a desired behavior will persist after training is completed is to reward the behavior every single time it occurs throughout training (rather than intermittently).

8 A schizophrenic is someone with a split personality.

9 Blind people have unusually sensitive organs of touch.

10 Fortunately for babies, human beings have a strong maternal instinct.

11 Biologists study the body; psychologists study the mind.

12 Unlike man, the lower animals are motivated only by their bodily needs—hunger, thirst, sex, etc.

13 Psychiatrists are defined as medical people who use psychoanalysis.

14 Children memorize much more easily than adults.

15 The ability of blind people to avoid obstacles is due to a special sense which develops in compensation for their absence of vision.

16 Boys and girls exhibit no behavioral differences until environmental influences begin to produce such differences.

17 "The study of the mind" is the best brief definition of psychology today.

18 Genius is closely akin to insanity.

19 The weight of evidence suggests that the major factor in forgetting is the decay of memory traces with time.

20 The unstructured interview is the most valid method for assessing someone's personality.

21 Under hypnosis, people can perform feats of physical strength which they could never do otherwise.

22 The more you memorize by rote (for example, poems) the better you will become at memorizing.

23 Children's IQ scores have very little relationship with how well they do in school.

(Eva D. Vaughn, *Teaching of Psychology*, 4, No. 3, Oct. 1977, 138–141.)

---

soon shifted to the United States, where it remains: Two-thirds of the world's psychologists are American.

Working in Psychology To be a psychologist, a person must earn an appropriate higher degree, perhaps be certified, and then get a job using these credentials. Two critical steps thus are training and occupation; a third way of categorizing psychologists is by their continuing interests.

A psychologist usually is the holder of a Ph.D. degree in psychology. Many schools offer M.A.'s, but there is substantial argument within the field as to whether holders of these ought to be regarded as full-fledged psychologists—whether they should be licensed for independent practice, for example, or be eligible for medical insurance payments for therapy. For research or teaching, the Ph.D. is virtually a necessity. For some applied fields, however, especially therapy, there are other acceptable specialized degrees. A Doctor of Psychology degree (Psy.D.), for example, qualifies a person to be a therapist, but is not as appropriate a degree for teaching or research as the Ph.D. Whatever the degree, however, a psychologist must specialize in some area. ■ Figure 1.2

The largest single area of specialization in training (Figure 1.2a) is clinical psychology, or therapy, but this area still accounts for less than one-third of the total. Its relative popularity may account, however, for the general impression that all psychologists are clinicians.

Psychologists may also be categorized in terms of what they do and for whom (Stapp et al., 1981). Figure 1.2b summarizes what they do. Note that an even smaller percentage of psychologists earn their living as clinicians (15%) than were trained as clinicians (29%) (Schneider, 1981). Not shown is for whom psychologists work—for example, whether the clinical work is an independent practice or for a state mental hospital.

Psychologists also differ in their interests; one way of representing these is by the Divisions of the APA. APA divisions sponsor meetings, publish specialized journals, and in other ways represent different interest groups; many psychologists belong to several divisions

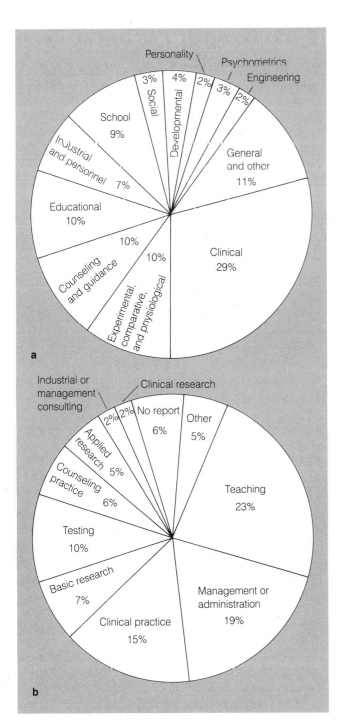

a

Personality
3%

Social
3%

Psychometrics
2%

School
9%

Developmental
4%

Engineering
2%

Industrial and personnel
7%

General and other
11%

Educational
10%

Counseling and guidance
10%

Experimental, comparative, and physiological
10%

Clinical
29%

b

Industrial or management consulting
2%

Applied research
2%

Clinical research

No report
6%

Other
5%

Counseling practice
5%

Testing
10%

Teaching
23%

Basic research
7%

Clinical practice
15%

Management or administration
19%

Counseling practice
6%

Figure 1.2 ■ Areas within psychology. (a) The percentage of psychologists who studied and took degrees in each area. (b) The percentage of psychologists who make their living in each area.

at once. As new topics become of concern to enough psychologists, they may become APA divisions or may be organized outside of the APA. The latter include organizations of black psychologists, gay and lesbian psychologists, and psychologists organized for political lobbying. ■ Table 1.1

Table 1.1 ■ Divisions of the American Psychological Association

1. Division of General Psychology
2. Division on the Teaching of Psychology
3. Division of Experimental Psychology
5. Division on Evaluation and Measurement
6. Division on Physiological and Comparative Psychology
7. Division on Developmental Psychology
8. Division of Personality and Social Psychology
9. The Society for the Psychological Study of Social Issues
10. Division of Psychology and the Arts
12. Division of Clinical Psychology
13. Division of Consulting Psychology
14. Division of Industrial and Organizational Psychology
15. Division of Educational Psychology
16. Division of School Psychology
17. Division of Counseling Psychology
18. Division of Psychologists in Public Service
19. Division of Military Psychology
20. Division of Adult Development and Aging
21. The Society of Engineering Psychologists
22. Division of Rehabilitation Psychology
23. Division of Consumer Psychology
24. Division of Philosophical Psychology
25. Division for the Experimental Analysis of Behavior
26. Division of the History of Psychology
27. Division of Community Psychology
28. Division of Psychopharmacology
29. Division of Psychotherapy
30. Division of Psychological Hypnosis
31. Division of State Psychological Association Affairs
32. Division of Humanistic Psychology
33. Division on Mental Retardation
34. Division of Population and Environmental Psychology
35. Division of the Psychology of Women
36. Psychologists Interested in Religious Issues
37. Division of Child and Youth Services
38. Division of Health Psychology
39. Division of Psychoanalysis
40. Division of Clinical Neuropsychology
41. Division of Psychology and Law

Note: There is no Division 4 or Division 11.

Psychologists' Ethics Some of the interventions that psychologists might make into peoples' lives, both research subjects and psychotherapy patients, could conceivably cause them psychological distress. Because of this risk, and in keeping with the self-administered ethical rules of other professions, the APA has developed and administers a set of ethics for psychologists that applies both to research and to applied techniques, primarily psychotherapy (APA, 1981). The standards for research, for example, call for informed consent of subjects or their legal representatives, minimal use of deception, and appropriate follow-up procedures. Research standards are typically administered through committees made up of, or at least including, members of other disciplines. All universities and many colleges have such committees to monitor faculty research, and each study must be approved before it proceeds. Such committees can and do suggest changes to studies or may refuse them outright.

This does not mean that all ethical problems can be avoided (Kimmel, 1979). Consider the concept of informed voluntary consent (Loftus & Fries, 1979). Just exactly what does it mean? Should legal guardians be able to consent for all groups, including the very young, the retarded, and the psychotic? Can prisoners ever truly volunteer, since they stand to gain in a variety of ways if they do? Some decisions that medical research cannot be done in prisons because prisoners cannot truly volunteer have been loudly criticized by prisoners' groups. They claim that such research breaks up the monotony, may provide pocket money through fees paid, and allows them to contribute to society. They argue that they are more penalized by the prohibition of research than by its presence.

Another problem with informed consent is the frequent need for deception, especially in social psychology experiments. For subjects to behave normally and not try to influence the results, they frequently must be misled about the purpose of the experiment. However, if they don't know what is to be done, can they offer *informed* consent? Another problem is that the researcher may not know all the consequences of the study in advance. But how can subjects be informed if the experimenter doesn't know what will happen? There are ways to handle these problems, but not all observers agree on the decisions that have been made.

Many ethical problems are avoided by the use of animal models. Researchers can breed them and then control their diet and experiences in ways that could never be ethical for humans. However, animals also have rights, so there are also ethical issues with animals: they should not be used in research unless the experiment cannot be done otherwise, they ought not to experience unnecessary pain or suffering, they ought not be sacrificed unnecessarily, and so forth.

Other ethical issues more directly involve society as a whole. Such questions include what research ought to be allowed for military purposes and how the results should be used.

Research findings add to the base of knowledge of the society and the use of that knowledge is under the same social constraints as the use of any other knowledge. Is it ethically responsible to leave all decisions on the use of techniques for affecting behavior to the society or its chosen representatives—or must individual researchers consider the potential consequences of their work, including possible misuse? Psychologists are no more united on such questions than are atomic scientists, who face similar questions; but in general all scientists, although they feel both personal and social responsibilities, prefer to seek truth as far as possible. They are reluctant to self-censor, preferring to encourage responsible social control of scientific findings.

THE QUESTIONS

It is our task in this text to examine what psychology is, why it does what it does, what it is finding out about our behavior, and where it may lead us in the future. Examining its focus on five ancient and difficult philosophical questions is one way of introducing psychology. We will then briefly consider how these problems have been approached over the history of psychology, and then examine the perspectives of contemporary psychologists.

As we have already seen, psychology is barely a century old (Hearst, 1979). The problems it addresses, however, are ones that philosophers have wrestled with for centuries. They may be named and stated as follows:

1　*Free will or determinism?* Are you "free" to choose your own behavior or is it somehow determined by natural laws?

2　*Are humans merely animals?* If so, how do they differ from other animals? If not, what are they?

3　*The nature/nurture problem.* Does a particular behavior reflect innate patterns or has it been learned from experience?

4　*The mind/body problem.* Is your mind separate from your body? If so, what is it? If not, why do we talk about it?

5　*Developmental or situational causes?* Does a particular behavior reflect past influences that shaped you or present ones that tell you what to do?

The problems that research psychologists study may often seem far removed from these old and difficult questions, or from your daily concerns, but each such problem represents a small piece of the larger picture. Rats in boxes, goldfish in mazes, or details of nerve-cell physiology may be discussed only in a line or paragraph in this text; they may occupy months, years, or a lifetime for some psychologists. Psychologists' studies may involve small acts of behavior, special laboratory situations, or peculiar measurements. But all of this, from minds to goldfish, is psychology.

These problems also pervade every aspect of our personal, social, and political lives. The answers to them are so relevant to so many specific questions that humans have been confronting them for as long as we have *been* humans. The exact statement of each problem has changed over time, but each remains a contemporary one on which any psychologist must take a position.

Whether you have ever specifically considered these questions or not, you probably had ready answers to the questions when you read them. Your answers have been subtly shaped by your cultural training, and they help you direct your approach to your own and others' behavior.

But don't be too quick to take a stand. Although the answers to these problems may seem immediate, obvious, and unquestionable to you now, try to consider them with a fresh perspective as you read. By the time you have finished this text, you may find that answers that once seemed obvious no longer satisfy you. You may even find that you no longer agree with the way the problems are stated. If so, good; problems as ancient and as complex as these are not easily solved.

1. Free Will or Determinism?

Perhaps the most basic of these questions is whether human behavior is "caused" at all, that is, whether it follows natural laws akin to the laws of astronomy or physics. This problem is often stated in terms of **free will** versus **determinism.** If humans have free will, they can choose to do whatever they wish. But if behavior is determined by natural laws, then every act is the inevitable outcome of what has happened before and humans do not choose to act any more than a dropped rock chooses to fall to the ground.

All of us, of course, *feel* that we are free to choose, and thus we seem to have free will. But in admitting that there are limits on this freedom, we recognize ourselves as subject to some natural laws. No human can fly unaided by machinery, for example, and only the appropriate previous experience allows you to speak Chinese. Obviously, free will doesn't really mean being completely free to do anything. But can we be partly free and partly determined? Or do we simply tend to label as the product of free will any behavior whose causes are unknown?

Consider how we have come to understand *any* causes in the natural world. Early humans once assigned all activity—whether movement of the planets, objects, animals, or themselves—to the whim of gods or fate; these could be neither understood nor controlled. Much of the development of human thought, especially scientific thought, has involved the shifting of phenomena from this realm of the unknown to the realm of the understood, or lawful.

As a science, psychology asks whether human behavior also follows natural laws, even though we may remain largely ignorant of them. If it does, behavior is in that sense determined as much as a satellite's orbit. Psychologists take a variety of positions regarding this problem. Most (though not all) feel that if psychology is a science, it *must* assume that natural laws do determine behavior. According to this view, it simply does not make sense to try to understand something unless you assume that such understanding is possible. And for a scientist to "understand" a phenomenon means to discover the natural laws that govern it. ■ Notable Quote: Carl Sagan on Science

2. Are Humans Merely Animals?

At some point in the dim and distant past, humans began to wonder who they were and why they were there. That some things were alive, including themselves, was probably immediately obvious. That other things were not alive was less obvious; many of our ancestors believed that living forces moved even the rocks and winds. But what our ancestors' relationship was to other living creatures probably didn't seem obvious to them. As the many religious traditions developed, humans continued to ask whether we are similar or dissimilar to other animals.

Our ability to even ask such questions, and to manipulate the natural world, seems to set us apart from animals. Yet our physical limitations—our birth and death, and the eating, drinking, fighting, and sex that occur in between—show clear parallels to the activities of animals.

Different religious and philosophical views have dealt with this question in different ways. Some

---

NOTABLE QUOTE
Carl Sagan on science

❝Science is a way of thinking much more than it is a body of knowledge. Its goal is to find out how the world works, . . . to penetrate to the connections of things—from subnuclear particles, which may be the constituents of all matter, to living organisms, the human social community, and thence to the cosmos as a whole. Our intuition is by no means an infallible guide. Our perceptions may be distorted by training and prejudice or [by] the limitations of our sense organs. . . . Even so straightforward a question as to whether in the absence of friction a pound of lead falls faster than a gram of fluff was answered incorrectly by Aristotle and almost everyone else before the time of Galileo. Science is based on . . . an openness to see the universe as it really is. Accordingly, science sometimes requires courage—at the very least the courage to question the conventional wisdom.❞
Sagan, 1974, p. 13

Eastern views place humans firmly in the natural world, though clearly special. Other traditions, including the Judeo-Christian one that underlies many of our cultural beliefs, set humans apart from animals in some way, perhaps differentiating between an "animal instincts" part of us and a "higher" part.

The human/animal question became prominent in psychology with Charles Darwin's theory of evolution because it implied a closeness between humans and animals based on common ancestry. Now, most psychologists accept some form of evolutionary similarity between humans and other species, although how important they believe the similarities to be varies substantially.

One major way in which this problem recurs in psychology concerns the use of animals in examining human issues. Whether you believe that anything discovered about how a rat learns has relevance to how a human learns, for example, depends on what you believe to be the similarities between humans and rats. The perspectives of psychologists vary widely on this issue, as on many others, but each has some opinion on it.

3. The Nature/Nurture Problem

It is obvious to the most primitive of human groups that newborn babies are already young humans and not members of some other species. The differences between one tribal group and another are also likely to be obvious. But why the habits or languages of groups differ, or why individuals differ from one another, may not be understood. As questions about these differences are raised, two major classes of answers are obvious possibilities. Humans may be different because of something about their *nature,* or innate makeup; racial groups may differ in skin color and individuals may differ in eye color. Or they may be different because of something in their *nurture,* or upbringing; different groups speak different languages. These two types of answers must have become evident relatively early in human development, and various forms of the **nature/nurture problem** have long been posed, each asking whether a behavior of interest is the result of innate factors or learning.

The nature/nurture problem is a continuing and exceptionally thorny one. As you begin to understand the factors involved, the problem itself splits into a set of related problems. The first difficulty concerns how to categorize certain influences. If nature means "innate" and nurture means "learning," how should we categorize such factors as diet, drugs, or injury? These affect the body directly, rather than through learning, but they are not innate. They are considered a special type of nurture.

A more serious problem is the fact that nature and nurture causes **interact,** that is, they require not just one factor but specific combinations of both actually to cause behavior. Asking whether light or water keeps a plant alive, for example, is a foolish question. Obviously, both light and water are required if the plant is to stay healthy; the plant is said to require the interaction of light and water, as no amount of one can compensate for a lack of the other. The important question for a botanist is how much water is best for a certain amount of light.

Similarly, interaction is usually the reasonable approach to answering questions about human development. Normal language development, for example, reflects an interaction of nature and nurture: It requires both a physically growing human brain (nature) and the right learning situation (nurture). Thus the nature/nurture problem is no longer simple; no behavior can result entirely from nature or entirely from nurture. In contemporary form, the question is rephrased to ask which factor is more important in a given behavior, or which gives rise to the greater differences between individuals. (Chapter 3 explores the interaction of nature and nurture in human development further.) ■ Figure 1.3

4. The Mind/Body Problem

The **mind/body problem** asks what relationship mind has to body; it is at the very heart of psychology, but is nevertheless sometimes difficult even to see as a problem (Feigl, 1960). Let's examine what the problem is, and also how easy it is to avoid, through a look at a contemporary procedure called biofeedback. **Biofeedback** consists of hooking up a person to an apparatus that amplifies some measure of body functioning to help the person learn to control that function (Schwartz, 1975).

Skin temperature, for example, may be measured and fed back to the subject, who then seeks to change it (Pew, 1979). Typically a light or tone is connected to the temperature sensor in such a way that increasing temperature increases the brightness of the light or loudness of the tone. Without the information provided by the light or tone, the subject probably could not discriminate small changes in skin temperature well enough to know when it was being raised or lowered successfully. But by trying different strategies and noting their effect on the light or tone, the subject may learn to control the temperature. Using biofeedback, the subject might increase hand temperature, for example, by dilating capillaries to increase blood flow to the hand, doing so through a mental image of the hand burning up.

Now comes the problem. How can a *mind* event

(mental image) change a *body* process (capillary action)? You may answer that this simply shows the power of the mind to influence the body; this mind over-body concept is a basic one in our culture and our language, but notice that in a sense it avoids facing the problem. What exactly is the mind and how does it differ from the body? If the mind is different, how does it influence the body? Is *mind* approximately the same as *person*, so that "My mind learns" means "I learn"? Or is a mind something each of us possesses? If so, who or what am "I" that possesses it? In contemporary terms, the mind/body problem is often treated as a mind/brain problem (Sperry, 1982). Is this terminology easier for you to understand or harder? What are the differences, for you, among "I learn," "My mind learns," and "My brain learns"?

If you find yourself beginning to get confused, you are probably making progress; this is a confusing issue. We may resolve it somewhat by looking at two traditional philosophical positions: dualism and monism (Reeves, 1958). **Dualists** say mind and body are dual or somehow different, then offer some proposal as to how these influence each other. Dualism is commonly accepted in our culture, and thus mind-over-body explanations are familiar to you. **Monists** say that mind and body are one, a single unified system. They see no useful separation between mind and body (or usually now between mind and brain).

A contemporary version of the monist position, called the **double language view,** suggests that it may be convenient to use *mental* terms some times and *body* (or brain) terms at other times, as long as it is clear that these are only two languages for one kind of activity. A sunset, for example, remains the same event whether you describe the beauty of its colors or whether you describe it in terms of light refraction in an oxygen–nitrogen atmosphere. Similarly, to a monist a mental event can be a powerful subjective experience but may also be described with equal accuracy in terms of body/brain activities (Fodor, 1981).

You can now recognize that the mind-over-body description of biofeedback is dualistic. But what would a monist description be? First of all, at one level, *mental imagery* would be an acceptable term for discussing procedures; but if asked what that means, the monist would say that it refers to activities of the brain. To the monist, the imagery of a hand burning up is just as much a body event as the resulting capillary action. The question of how biofeedback works becomes: "How does one part of the body, the brain area that generates imagery, influence a different part of the body, the circulatory system?" The question may still not be easy to answer, but the rephrasing suggests ways of going about it. Since the question is now phrased in body/body terms, it might be answered by

Figure 1.3 ■ An American man of northeastern European ancestry and a Fijian woman. Some of the differences between them, such as skin color, reflect nature; others, such as clothing, reflect nurture. Still others, perhaps the male or female roles they play in their respective cultures, are the result of both factors interacting in complex and subtle ways.

(Reproduced by permission from *Heredity, Evolution, and Humankind* by A. M. Winchester. Copyright © 1976 by West Publishing Company. All rights reserved.)

tracing the nerve connections between the brain and the circulatory system.

You don't have to be a monist to be a psychologist, but you probably ought to give the problem some serious thought before deciding what you believe. The ease with which a dualist position may be taken in our culture does not necessarily make it the best one.

5. Developmental or Situational Causes?

It may not have occurred to you earlier that both nature and nurture often refer to events that have happened in the past. But if we seek all of the causes of human behavior, we must consider more than these **developmental causes** that have shaped an individual up to the moment of interest. We must also consider **situational causes** acting at that moment on the individual.

This comparing of past and present is a different way of analyzing the causes of behavior than asking about nature and nurture; together these two questions split contributions to behavior into four possible

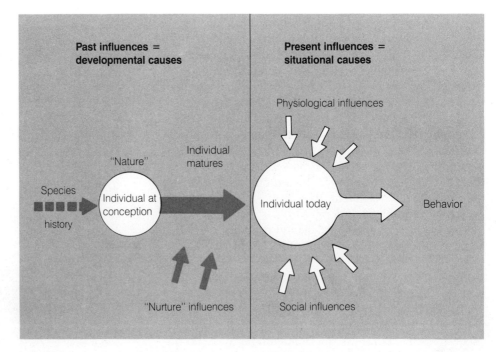

Figure 1.4 ■ The pattern of interactions that contribute to any act of behavior includes both past and present influences as well as both nature and nurture influences.

categories. But here also interaction is the rule. It sometimes makes sense to consider developmental and situational factors separately to try to see which is more important, but these can never be truly separated. Developmental factors influence who a person is, but that person must have some situation in which to behave. Similarly, situational factors influence present behavior, but any person in that situation must also have some developmental history. ■ Figure 1.4

These five questions will recur throughout the text in one form or another. They had already been stated by the time psychology began to develop as a new science, and the early psychologists often defined their tasks in terms of one or more of these questions.

HISTORICAL APPROACHES

The current status and perspectives of psychology are more understandable if we know something about its past. That past is filled with interesting and sometimes outrageous personalities and issues, but we hardly have space to do justice to these. For some insight into them, see Crutchfield and Krech (1962) and the work of the foremost historian of psychology, E. G. Boring (1950a).

The Founding of Psychology

Psychologists usually date their discipline to 1879, when **Wilhelm Wundt** (1832–1920) founded the first laboratory of psychology at the University of Leipzig, Germany. The questions that psychology concerns itself with are much older, and the active development of the scientific discipline began some years before 1879 and continued for years after. Wundt's laboratory is important because it marked a critical turning point from a general development of trends to a named, laboratory-based discipline at a world center of learning.

Wundt was an ideal person to be a founder. He contributed no special theories or findings to psychology; innovation was not his style. "He never said a foolish thing or a brilliant one," said one historian (Heidbreder, 1933, p. 92). But Wundt was an excellent organizer, spending his 63-year career at "the endless writing of the ponderous tomes which eventually did so much to give him his place in history" (Boring, 1950a, p. 317). This was just what psychology needed at the time: a compiling and organizing of many other researchers' work. Heidbreder noted that in doing so "at times he strongly suggests the careful housewife, industriously picking up after a growing science that had not learned—and has not yet learned—to be neat" (1933, p. 96).

Wundt was not the only founder of psychology, however. Although many others were involved, the other leading contender is **Gustav Fechner** (1801–1887), like Wundt a Leipzig professor. Fechner had wrestled for years with his particular version of the mind/body problem: How can the subjective experiences of consciousness be reconciled with the laws that govern the physical world, including our bodies? Fechner was so torn between his allegiance to his scientific training and his personal questioning of it that for years he wrote both serious scientific papers under his own name and satirical attacks on such papers under a pen name. He switched professions from medicine to physics and mathematics, then began research on sensation. But he seriously injured his eyes by looking directly at the sun to study the resulting afterimages, and he felt increasing despair at not being able to resolve his quandary. By 1840, he had become "a nervous invalid with neurotic depression, hypochondriacal tendencies, and thoughts of suicide" (Schultz, 1980, p. 47).

Yet on the morning of October 22, 1850, an insight occurred to Fechner that so revived him that he left his sickbed and began a whole new career. What insight could have had such an effect? Admittedly, it is hard for most of us to understand it in the same way that it affected Fechner, but his insight was that stimuli from the physical world give rise to perceptions in the mental world according to *mathematical laws.* To Fechner, this meant that the mind could be studied scientifically by measuring the physical stimuli brought into it, even though it could not be measured directly, and he spent much of the rest of his life testing and exploring this lawfulness (Woodward, 1972).

To contemporary research psychologists, Fechner's recognition of the lawfulness of mental phenomena marks the true beginning of scientific psychology. Some of them even celebrate October 22 as Fechner Day, more or less seriously, to commemorate his insight. As Boring puts it, "Fechner, because of what he did and the time at which he did it, set experimental quantitative psychology off upon the course which it has followed" (1950a, p. 294–295).

From Fechner's insight came the field of **psychophysics,** or roughly the physics of psychological experience (Boring, 1961). Like Wundt, the early psychophysicists sought to explore the direct experience of the world through perception, but they used careful measurement of stimuli and simple responses to them, rather than seeking to measure their mental effects. Psychophysicists might present a variety of stimulus intensities to their subjects, for example, and all the subject has to do is report whether he or she sees anything. The brass instruments with which the early psychophysicists made their measurements have long since given way to complex instruments and computers, but the trend of psychophysics remains an important one in psychology.

The Zeitgeist of the 19th Century

Major achievements in culture and technology occur not as isolated events, but in a context; they build on what has come before and are noted later because of what they led to. In some cases, the necessary conditions build up so that a particular development seems virtually inevitable; if one person doesn't do it, another will. This intellectual and technological context is the **Zeitgeist**, a German word meaning "spirit of the times." In 1875, for example, Alexander Graham Bell reached the United States Patent Office with his patent application for the telephone only a few hours ahead of a competitor (Hounshell, 1981). In contrast, if an exceptionally independent thinker offers something revolutionary and the Zeitgeist is not ready for it, it will simply be ignored.

In the 19th century, psychology was in the air, and its founding was probably inevitable. The 17th, 18th, and early 19th centuries had seen a surge of interest in the physical sciences, resulting in a wonderful series of discoveries and inventions. At the same time, there was growing interest in how a similar scientific approach might be applied to human behavior. Medicine and physiology already existed as human-oriented sciences, but these were sciences of the body, not of the mind.

Philosophy had long been the approach to problems of the mind, but its techniques were not those of science; philosophers had no laboratories, made no measurements, wrote no equations—in short, provided no observable, repeatable evidence. Their working tools were those of intuition, structured by formal logic and often superimposed on religious teachings. One famous German philosopher, Immanuel Kant, even insisted that there could never be a science of psychology because it was impossible to measure or to experiment with phenomena of the mind.

Fechner was raised and trained in this Zeitgeist; we can see why the mind/body problem so troubled him, and why he found his insight so satisfying. We can also see how, now that the Zeitgeist was ready for it, a scant 29 years later Wundt could found a laboratory-based science.

Introspection

For Wundt, the only appropriate subject matter for a science of psychology was the conscious experience of an intelligent adult. This was to be approached through a study of the simple elements that made up complex perception. Higher level thought, Wundt felt, was beyond scientific study, at least for the foreseeable future. Also, because only the perceiver could describe perception, Wundt's psychology excluded the young, the retarded, or others unable to offer such descriptions. Finally, his science was to be a "pure" one; it was not to be concerned with application of its findings.

The sole method of study, according to Wundt, was to be **introspection.** This did not mean what it often does today, a kind of general looking inside yourself, but was a technical term for a special procedure requiring substantial training (Boring, 1953). An observer using introspection was to report not particular objects perceived, but rather the sensory elements that were thought to make them up. Thus if you looked at this text and called it "a book," that would be a serious mistake; you had to report the sensations of color, line, and angle that made up the perception of *book*.

Despite their rigid training and supervision, however, Wundt's introspectionists were never able to agree on what the elements of perception were; much of later psychology developed as a rejection of this approach. But a negative against which to rebel is nevertheless an influence, and so Wundt's introspection did have an impact—even though not the one he intended (Blumenthal, 1977).

Historical Schools of Psychology

Many English words, *school* among them, have several more-or-less related meanings. A school of fish, for example, has limited similarity to a grade school for humans. A **school of psychology,** however, is a major theoretical movement, typically with a name, a founder, and a group of followers (Woodworth & Sheehan, 1964). In the sense that it provides terminology and guidance for its members, a school of psychology is a form of education. Or, if you prefer, in the sense that all of the followers tend to cluster together and to behave more like each other than like members of other schools, it is akin to a school of fish.

The perspectives we will consider a bit later represent current major schools of thought in psychology. But two historical schools—structuralism and functionalism—have been important in the development of psychology.

Structuralism Wundt's psychology was termed **structuralism;** his search for the basic elements of perception through introspection is considered a search for the structure of consciousness. Wundt was both the founder of structuralism and its major proponent. Structuralism flourished for a while in Germany and also in the United States; here it was established and led by a devoted student of Wundt's, E. B. Titchener (Titchener, 1921). Structuralism substantially influenced American psychology, although it did not outlast Titchener's own productive life (Evans, 1972).

Functionalism In contrast, **functionalism** asked what function consciousness served—specifically, how it contributed to the survival of the individual who had it (Heidbreder, 1969). Functionalism derived largely from the work of Charles Darwin; his theory of evolution, published in 1859, focused on how differences among members of a species gave some a better chance of survival than others (Russett, 1976). (See Chapter 3.)

With the death of structuralism, functionalism flowered as the first uniquely American school of psychology, drawing strength from the American Zeitgeist. The United States prided itself on its rough-and-ready frontier democracy, in which individual characteristics, not who your ancestors were, determined what you became. Thus a concern with the functioning of consciousness to aid survival fitted in well with the American Zeitgeist (Boring, 1950b).

Unlike Wundt's structuralism, functionalism deliberately focused on individual differences, including those of the young, the retarded, and the psychotic, and it deliberately sought to apply its findings—to educational psychology, for example. In phrases that repeat the mind/body problem, Boring said of American psychology that "it had inherited its physical body from German experimentalism, but it had got its mind from Darwin. American psychology was to deal with mind in use" (1950a, p. 506).

William James and American Psychology There was no single American founder of functionalism, but there was one person who was broadly influential in the development of American psychology (Allport, 1966b). **William James** (1842–1910) was the premier American psychologist: one of the first, most important, best known, and most flexible in outlook (Allen, 1967). James was generally a functionalist, but not exclusively a disciple of that or any other school. He was logical in thought and generally scientific in approach, but was still willing to pursue interesting problems that were difficult to measure; one of his better-known books is *The Varieties of Religious Experience* (1902). James referred as much to his own far-ranging interests as to any generalized American character when he said of Wundt's introspection that it "taxes patience to the utmost, and could hardly have arisen in a country whose natives could be *bored*" (1890, p. 192). James's introductory psychology text (1890) has recently been reprinted (1981), and still seems contemporary in many of its observations (Adelson, 1982). ■ Figure 1.5

Although structuralism and functionalism are no longer current schools of thought in American psychology, their influence continues to be felt. Several other major schools of thought in psychology are currently important, and new ones continue to be developed. Seven current approaches that recur throughout this text are described below as *perspectives*. Another major school, Gestalt psychology, has been more important in Europe than in the United States; we will look at it primarily in the context in which it developed, the study of perception.

CURRENT PERSPECTIVES

Suppose you ask some physicists why a dropped object falls, some meteorologists why the weather changes, or some chemists how plastics are made. Although they might disagree over details, experts in any one of these fields would, in general, give you consistent answers. But suppose you ask several psychologists why some parents abuse their children. The answers you get will vary greatly, depending on which psychologists you ask; some of the answers will seem to be related, but others will seem entirely contradictory. Disagreement among psychologists is a continuing and sometimes heated activity. We will try to strike a balance in this text between assuming that psychologists are all in agreement, which is almost never true, and assuming that psychologists agree on nothing, which is equally untrue.

Perhaps the best way of looking at these differences for our purposes is to consider them as differences in perspective, or in the way of focusing when looking at behavior. A psychologist's **perspective** is the set of beliefs that guide his or her approach to all issues in psychology; it suggests what to look at and how, in seeking answers to questions about behavior.

Perspectives as Lenses

All of us use some perspective to help focus on particular aspects of behavior. You already have a perspective, for example, whether you realize it or not, given to you by your parents, friends, schools, television, and other representatives of your culture. The difference between your perspective and a formally defined perspective in psychology is that yours may not be very exactly defined and probably is inconsistent, offering one comment on behavior at one time and a different one another time. This happens because our culture tends to absorb and combine bits and pieces of both

Figure 1.5 ■ William James (1842–1910). America's premier psychologist, whose small laboratory at Harvard University preceded Wundt's formal founding of psychology by four years. James was interested in nearly everything, including the stream of consciousness and the development of emotion. *"Consciousness, then, does not appear to itself chopped up in bits. Such words as 'chain' or 'train' do not describe it fitly as it presents itself in the first instance. It is nothing jointed; it flows. A 'river' or a 'stream' are the metaphors by which it is most naturally described. In talking of it hereafter, let us call it the stream of thought, of consciousness, or of subjective life"* (James, 1890, p. 239).

(Photo from The Bettmann Archive)

folklore and professional psychological perspectives and then presents them in a variety of forms more or less continuously. The same newspaper or magazine often includes items that reflect quite different perspectives, but typically these differences are not even pointed out, much less identified.

A recent item on the radio described how you dream and why dreaming is necessary. It included information that is data-based and widely accepted by psychologists, such as the fact that you dream approximately every 90 minutes of a night's sleep. But the item also bluntly stated that you dream to work out emotional problems you could not deal with during the day; *that* is a perspective statement, and many psychologists disagree with it. Tomorrow, the same station may carry another statement about dreaming that reflects a different perspective; how you reconcile them is apparently up to you. Their political statements carry a disclaimer that "The preceding message reflects the speaker's perspective and not necessarily the view of this station." No such disclaimer is presented for a psychologist's statements, but one probably should be.

Described in this way, a perspective might seem to be a kind of bias. In fact it is, but it seems to be a necessary one. Suppose you set out to be an unbiased psychologist. Whatever behavior you seek to explain, you find that you can't watch everything that occurs or measure everything that changes. You *must* be able to select the important parts of the problem, the ones that will tell you what's happening and why. But how will you know how to focus on the right things?

In psychology, a perspective provides your focus. It acts as a lens, through which you peer closely at some aspects of the problem, seeing those clearly and others dimly or not at all. Another psychologist may focus so differently that the two of you cannot agree on much of what you see. So you seek out others whose lens is akin to yours; you join organizations, attend meetings, read professional journals, and talk to friends who share your focus, while elsewhere other groups of psychologists are sharing their different focus. In doing so, you have become biased, not necessarily in a negative sense but biased nonetheless.

A theory is a special sort of perspective; only some of our perspectives are also theories. A **theory** is a formal statement of what someone believes to be true about a class of problems, including the natural laws involved and the relationships among those laws. Laws summarize facts and theories in turn summarize laws. This summarizing of many separate facts in an easily understood way is a major function of a theory.

But an equally important function of a theory is to direct the search for further laws, based on facts that have not yet been collected. When you summarize what is known, the summary often implies that other things *ought* to be true that have not yet been looked at; this function of directing the search is what makes a theory a lens. Theories thus stand in the middle between past facts and future facts, compiling the former and predicting the latter. The more predictions that are found to be facts, the more believable and useful the theory is; if predictions do not work out, however, the theory must be modified or even given up entirely.

There are a variety of perspectives in psychology. In one sense, there are as many as there are individual psychologists, but we only need to consider seven views. The first three are usually considered *the* major theories in psychology: psychoanalysis, behaviorism, and humanism. We will consider them in that order, the sequence in which they reached prominence. We will then consider four other important perspectives of American psychology: the social learning, cognitive, ethological, and physiological perspectives.

The three major perspectives differ about as much as perspectives can. They look at different problems, propose different mechanisms to explain behavior, accept different kinds of evidence, and thus predict quite different outcomes for particular situations. In some cases, the differences between them may only be one of focus and each may be true. In other cases, their theoretical positions may not be reconcilable, and at least one of them must be wrong.

The other four perspectives tend to be primarily different lenses for different purposes, each focusing only on some parts of the total question of why humans behave as they do. It is possible that these four perspectives may eventually be reconciled and synthesized to yield a more complete picture of human behavior than any one of them taken separately. In general, we will assume that each of the seven perspectives has something useful to offer, even if some of its aspects eventually turn out not to have been correct.

Psychoanalysis

Psychoanalysis was founded by Sigmund Freud early in this century. It was developed and has been used more as an applied technique of therapy than as a school of academic/experimental psychology. Psychoanalysis suggests that much of our daily behavior results from conflicts between powerful innate tendencies toward sex and aggression and learned ways of dealing with these conflicts (Freud, 1933, 1935, 1938). Psychoanalysis also says that these conflicts may occur at an unconscious level. As an approach to behavior, psychoanalysis thus focuses on sexual and aggressive tendencies and childhood experiences relating to them. As a therapy, it seeks to explain an individual's current problems as the unconscious expression of conflicts not resolved in childhood.

Founder Psychoanalysis was developed by **Sigmund Freud** (1856–1939) in the late 1800s and early 1900s. Freud grew up in Vienna, Austria, and attended medical school intending to become a scientist and researcher. After graduation, however, financial pressures caused him to enter private practice as a clinical neurologist (we would now call such a person a psychiatrist). Freud used his practice to explore the whys of behavior as well as to directly help his patients. He experimented first with hypnotic techniques learned from the great French psychiatrist Jean Charcot, but eventually developed his own methods. His theory of behavior and his application of it to therapy thus developed simultaneously out of his clinical practice (Clark, 1980).

At first, Freud was attacked for his views, but by the early 1900s his approach was attracting international attention. Over the next 30 years, Freud revised and added to his theory, shifting from an initial emphasis on sexuality toward increased emphasis on forces leading to violence and death. His ideas were being increasingly accepted and he was still at work when he died in 1939 at the age of 83.

According to the scientific approach, all theories are to be tested on their merits, and why a person develops an idea is not itself evidence for or against the idea. But it is often useful in understanding a concept to know the context from which it came. To understand Freud's ideas, it is important to understand both his experiences and the Zeitgeist.

Freud grew up in a time of relative peace and provincialism, of "large patriarchal families who took long summer vacations and lived in overfurnished rooms" (Wilson, 1964, p. 90). This period is called the Victorian era after Queen Victoria, who ruled England from 1837 to 1901 and whose conservative ideas of propriety set the tone for much of the age. Thus *Victorian* has also come to represent moral severity or hypocrisy, middle-class stuffiness, and pompous conservatism. In the Victorian era, the notion of sex was so forbidden that even pianos had "limbs" rather than "legs."

In such a time the public admission of sexual activity is unthinkable, and the private admission of sexual desire, even to yourself, is almost so; it is not surprising that many of Freud's patients felt confused and guilty about sex. Whether sexuality *always* plays such a role in human behavior is arguable; that it did so then seems almost inevitable. Nor is it surprising that Freud's attempts to tell what he had learned subjected him to rejection and ridicule. He was considered risque: "Ladies blushed when you mentioned his name," said a former student (Wilson, 1964, p. 101). To suggest that humans, in addition to having sex, thought about it a lot, that it influenced their other behaviors, even that children were interested in it, was perhaps more shocking to the Victorians than anything we can imagine could shock us today.

Perhaps less shocking, but equally in opposition to the Victorian view, was Freud's suggestion that many behaviors are controlled by unconscious forces. Victorian society prided itself on rational control, on humanity overcoming nature, including its own. It was almost as offended by Freud's suggestion that irrational behavior existed as it was by the suggestion that such behavior reflected sexual motives. ■ Figure 1.6

Freud's later emphasis on a death instinct seems also to be related to his experiences. In the post-

Figure 1.6 ■ Sigmund Freud (1856–1939). The founder of the psychoanalytic perspective, responsible for demonstrating how much of our behavior may be unconscious and/or irrational. *"He that has eyes to see and ears to hear may convince himself that no mortal can keep a secret. If the lips are silent, he chatters with his finger-tips; betrayal oozes out of him at every pore. And thus the task of making conscious the most hidden recess of the mind is one which is quite possible to accomplish"* (Freud, 1905, pp. 77–78).

(Photo from Pictorial Parade)

Victorian period, he watched the awful course of the First World War, in which the world lost its innocence as the drawn-out butchery of trench warfare decimated an entire generation. Then, as a defeated Germany struggled with enormous postwar problems including galloping inflation, Freud, a Jew, watched the rise of Nazism; it eventually drove him to exile in England a year before he died. For the last 16 years of his life, he was sick and in pain from a progressive and painful cancer of the jaw and throat. He underwent 33 operations for it, and by the end his speech was nearly unintelligible. With Freud's experiences and in such a Zeitgeist, we ought not to be surprised that his later ideas seem so pessimistic.

Freud has become one of the most important contributors to the Zeitgeist of the 20th century (Shakow & Rapaport, 1964). His ideas, once rejected by the public, now permeate the media, and popular concepts of why people do the things they do—including, no doubt, some of yours—are frequently those he originally proposed: rare is the movie or television villain whose motives do not turn out to be those that Freud proposed.

Basic Concepts As with each of the major perspectives, psychoanalysis has been added to and

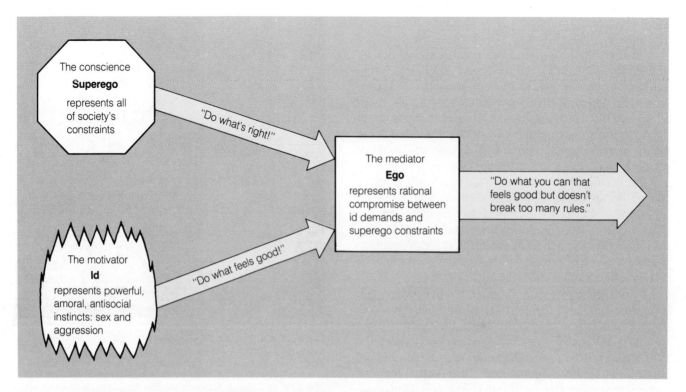

The conscience
Superego
represents all of society's constraints

"Do what's right!"

The mediator
Ego
represents rational compromise between id demands and superego constraints

"Do what you can that feels good but doesn't break too many rules."

The motivator
Id
represents powerful, amoral, antisocial instincts: sex and aggression

"Do what feels good!"

Figure 1.7 ■ Freud thought of human behavior as reflecting relationships between three forces; id, ego, and superego. Successful personality integration represented a balance between these; abnormal behavior might result from several kinds of imbalances.

changed since its founding. We will consider some of the changes later, together with some of the "neo-Freudians" who developed them (Roazen, 1975). According to Freud:

1 Most human behavior is strongly influenced by how individuals deal with two basic powerful instincts, a **life instinct,** reflected primarily in a drive for sexual gratification, and a **death instinct,** reflected primarily in various forms of aggression.

2 Personality develops through five **psychosexual stages,** in which the two primitive instincts are gradually brought under control. Each stage provides a different kind of sexual gratification and can lead to different problems of adjustment.

3 All behavior reflects the relationships among three forces, which are ways of summarizing tendencies within us. The **id** represents both life and death instincts, which it seeks to gratify in an extremely selfish way; if unchecked, the id can lead to criminality, violence, and war, as well as uncaring sexual gratification. The **superego** represents the internalized social constraints we call conscience; it is designed to counteract the id's demands. The **ego** is our rational intelligence; it seeks to find acceptable compromises between the demands of the id and the constraints of the superego. ■Figure 1.7

4 Ideal balance among id, ego, and superego yields psychological health, and imbalance yields psychopathology. Much of this balancing occurs outside our awareness, in the unconscious. **Unconscious motives** include some we have never been aware of and others that we have **repressed,** or hidden because they made us anxious.

Focus Each perspective focuses on certain aspects of any situation. The psychoanalytic perspective believes that adult behavior is critically determined by powerful instincts, brought under control through lengthy development of strategies that begin in childhood. In considering any behavior of interest, then, it focuses on the search for powerful, hidden motives and for childhood problems.

Psychoanalysis is typically more of a clinical approach—that is, a form of therapy—than an experimental approach, as Freud's own use of it was. Although some of the concepts of psychoanalysis have been experimentally tested, the results have not given the theory much support (Fisher & Greenberg, 1977). This need not mean that the concepts are incorrect, however, since they do not lend themselves well to such testing.

Figure 1.8 ■ John B. Watson (1878–1958). The founder of behaviorism, shown here as a comparatively young man. He was 35 when his founding paper was published and left psychology only seven years later. *"Psychology as the behaviorist views it is a purely objective experimental branch of natural science. Its theoretical goal is the prediction and control of behavior. . . . The behaviorist, in his efforts to get a unitary scheme of animal response, recognizes no dividing line between man and brute. The behavior of man, with all of its refinement and complexity, forms only a part of the behaviorist's total scheme of investigation* (Watson, 1913, p. 158) *. . . . If you will grant the behaviorist the right to use consciousness in the same way that other natural scientists employ it—that is, without making consciousness a special object of observation—you have granted all that my thesis requires"* (p. 175).

(Photo from Culver Pictures)

Behaviorism

Behaviorism was founded in 1913 by John B. Watson. Watson's **behaviorism** was to be the study of overt, observable behavior; the rationale was that only such behavior could be measured and objectively examined. Watson expected it to be a science of the relationship among reflexes, but quit as a theorist and researcher so soon after founding the perspective that he had little influence over its actual development. Much of this resulted from the work of others, in particular B. F. Skinner, who has used animal models to find basic laws of learning. These laws are examined for possible implications for human learning, on the assumption that most human behavior is learned (Skinner, 1974). This emphasis on learning is reflected in an alternate term for the behavioral perspective, **learning theory.** The focus is on the environmental conditions that originally teach behavior and on those that later sustain it, in both cases by rewarding or punishing each act.

Founders John B. Watson (1878–1958) is traditionally named as the founder of behaviorism, even though he contributed little beyond the founding act itself (D. Cohen, 1979). After receiving his Ph.D. in 1903, Watson taught and carried on research. Like many others in the early 1900s, he became convinced that structuralism and its method of introspection was a dead end and that Darwinism and functionalism were the direction of the future. In seeking a new direction, Watson encountered the work on reflexes in dogs of some Russian researchers, including Ivan Pavlov. The Russian work seemed to show how basic reflexes could be developed into learned responses to the environment, and this provided the approach Watson was seeking. In a famous paper, he called for a new psychology of behaviorism (Watson, 1913).■Figure 1.8

Watson's behaviorism was to be a functionalist approach, asking what useful purpose behavior served, and it was to examine only behaviors that could be directly observed; no introspection or other internal technique was to be used. Watson expected it to find that behaviors were primarily learned on the basis of innate reflexes. It was to include a wide range of subjects not considered appropriate by the structuralists—animals, children, the retarded, the insane—and it had a distinctly optimistic flavor: If behavior was mostly learned, all you had to do to solve any behavioral problem was to teach appropriate behavior (Watson, 1919).

Watson had given expression to ideas that had been accumulating in the United States, and psychologists rushed to call themselves behaviorists. Before he could elaborate his theory, however, Watson became involved in a scandal along with Rosalie Rayner, his research assistant, and was divorced by his wife. Even though he later married Rayner and stayed married to her, the scandal ended his academic career in 1920, only seven years after he founded the movement. Watson continued to write popular books on behavioral psychology (1925) and thus continued as a force in the Zeitgeist, but his own theoretical contributions had ended.

Behaviorism then took its course under the direction of others. Many theorists and researchers have played important roles in the development of behaviorism, but the best-known contemporary behaviorist is B. F. Skinner.

B. F. Skinner (1904–) was only nine years old when Watson published his famous paper, but the timing was nearly ideal for influencing his career (Skinner, 1976a). While Skinner was attending college, Watson was spreading the word about behaviorism. Skinner, who graduated as an English major, planned to be a professional writer, but he soon found that he didn't have much to write *about*. Around the same time, he encountered Watson's writings, which had such a powerful effect on him that he went back to school, graduating from Harvard in 1931 with a Ph.D. in experimental psychology. After time in research and teaching elsewhere, he returned to Harvard and remained until his retirement in 1976 (Skinner, 1979). He continues to live and work in Cambridge, Massachusetts.

Skinner's nearly 50 years of careful professional work has had a significant effect not only on psychology but on the course of 20th century thought (Evans, 1968). This infuence has come through positive and negative reactions. He has been honored by those who agree with him (he was named Humanist of the Year in 1972 and received the APA Distinguished Scientific Contribution Award in 1958 and Lifetime Career Award in 1976) and vilified by those who disagree, having received perhaps the worst press of any theorist since Darwin. Many critics reject Skinner's work without understanding it, often without even reading it. They imagine what they think he must mean and what they think that must lead to, and attack these nonexistent positions more than his own.

Part of this frequent ill-informed criticism of Skinner arises from a paradox in his work. His own research always used animals, particularly rats and pigeons, but he always sought to apply the results of this research to human behavior (Skinner, 1953, 1978). Other researchers have tested whether ideas obtained from rats and pigeons are relevant to humans; often it seems that they are. Yet the very idea of such a connection between human and animal is so repugnant to many that they personally condemn Skinner for suggesting it. ■ Figure 1.9

Watson intended to be a founder and was a remarkably successful one. He pulled together the elements of behaviorism and gave it clear methods, goals, and ideals. As a popularizer, Watson's success is also unquestioned; both during his brief academic career and for many years thereafter, his books and articles have attracted attention. Skinner has fulfilled a different role, fleshing out behaviorism into a comprehensive, scientific perspective. His lengthy and careful collecting of data has been the opposite of Watson's work, though his willingness to move quickly from animal data to human possibilities has frequently earned him the same criticisms.

Basic Concepts Watson's theoretical contributions were minimal, but he was an effective popularizer of his views. They have become so embedded in the popular consciousness that many writers today criticize Skinner and other contemporary behaviorists in terms that show they are really criticizing Watson but don't know it. According to Watson:

1   The only appropriate methods for a scientific psychology involve measurement of **overt behavior,** or behavior observable by others. Nonobservable or **covert behavior** might be measured indirectly, however. First, verbal behavior is observable, even though you can never test in a direct behavioral way what lies behind it. Thus you can note that a subject claims to have a mental image, even though you can never measure the image directly. Second, some forms of internal behavior may be potentially measurable. For example, you may be able to measure one form of thought through covert speech, literally talking to yourself, with throat movements so reduced in magnitude that no sound results. (Such movements do occur, as do hand movements in deaf individuals who "speak" in sign language, but measuring them doesn't seem very useful as an approach to measuring thought.)

2   When such approaches are used, human behavior will be found to be nearly entirely learned, rather than innate or instinctive, and to be based on a few innate reflexes. This is usually summarized as an **S-R position,** for "stimulus-response"; any input from the environment, such as a sight or sound, can be the stimulus, and any behavior that results is the response.

3   Because humans have few innate behavior patterns, they can almost be considered a **tabula rasa,** or "blank slate," on which the environment writes to create personality. Although frequently seen by nonbehaviorists as cruelly manipulative, this strong nurture position is a positive and optimistic statement. It implies, for example, that crime and other undesirable activity can be completely eliminated: Because criminals are made, not born, you have only to find out how this happens and rearrange the learning. (Quite obviously, this is easier said than done, for both technical and ethical reasons, but Watson was stating what he thought might eventually be possible.) ■ Notable Quote: John Watson on Creating a Specialist and on the Optimism of Behaviorism.

4   Psychology would be able to be, and ought to be, a practical applied science. Because you can measure observable behavior, you can deal with individuals unable to give verbal cooperation. Because behavior is learned, you can eliminate undesirable behavior and create desirable behavior, once you understand the laws of learning.

Skinner shares Watson's focus on measurable overt behavior, on a strong learning or nurture position, and on the positive implications of learning theory. The major difference in Skinner's view—and it is

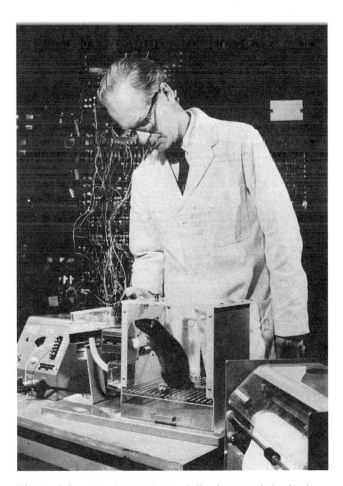

Figure 1.9 ■ B. F. Skinner (1904–). The foremost behavioral psychologist, responsible for much of the content of the behavioral position that Watson is credited with founding. He is shown here with a typical research subject. *"The practical problem in continuing the struggle for freedom and dignity is not to destroy controlling forces but to change them, to create a world in which people will achieve far more than they have ever achieved before in art, music, literature, science, technology, and above all the enjoyment of life. It could be a world in which people feel freer than they have ever felt before, because they will not be under aversive control. In building such a world, we shall need all the help a science of behavior can give us. To misread the theme of the struggle for freedom and dignity and to relinquish all efforts to control would be a tragic mistake"* (Skinner, 1975, p. 47).

(Nina Leen, LIFE MAGAZINE, © 1952, Time, Inc.)

a very important one—is in the proposed form of learning. According to Skinner:

1   Some human behaviors result from the kind of association of stimulus and response that Watson suggested. This is involved in some kinds of emotional learning, for example, such as learning to be afraid of dogs because of being bitten.

2   Most learning, however, takes place in a different way: An animal or person actively behaves and learns through the consequences that follow the behavior (Skinner, 1981). These consequences both shape behavior and sustain it throughout life.

3   Several kinds of good and bad consequences may follow acts, and these consequences can be arranged to assist learning. The best arrangement is to follow appropriate behavior with a reward or **reinforcer.** Many animal trainers have long used rewards, but they may be equally applicable to humans.

It is probably this position that polarizes people. Skinner's supporters feel that the emphasis on learning through benevolent techniques—rewards rather than punishment—make his a positive approach to human problems. Critics feel that the comparison to animal training is intrinsically degrading to humans, and that applying Skinner's approach would necessarily result in less personal freedom and dignity. However, Skinner, in his book *Beyond Freedom and Dignity* (1971), states his belief that much of our apparent freedom is simply hidden control and that greater true freedom will result from recognizing this fact (see the quote in Figure 1.9).

Focus   The first questions a behaviorist asks about any behavior concern the rewards that follow it in the present. The first suggestions for change—in therapy, for example—concern rearranging those rewards.

Behaviorists may ask about a person's history, but only to help define what is going on in the present. They don't necessarily expect to find the roots of today's problems in childhood; they assume that even if such problems began then, today's rewards keep them going. Behaviorists feel that rearranging current conditions will encourage, or if necessary teach, appropriate behavior. Behaviorists would lay the blame for inappropriate behavior not on innate instincts as Freud would, but on environmental arrangements outside the person (Skinner, 1954, 1963). This difference has important implications; in legal terms, for example, if the environment arranges behavior, can *anyone* be considered personally responsible and thus guilty?

Humanism

Humanistic psychology includes several somewhat different approaches that share some beliefs: that humans, unlike animals, are characterized by an awareness of themselves as unique beings of great potential, and that they strive to fully develop that potential. Two major humanist views are identified with particular founders: Abraham Maslow and Carl Rogers. Maslow's **humanism** emphasizes presumed innate human tendencies to self-actualize: to develop so as to maximize human capacities for self-expression, love, creativity, and other positive values (1968, 1971). Maslow called his position a "third force," to mark his rejection of both psychoanalysis and behaviorism. The instinctive tendencies Maslow's humanism proposes are weak positive ones, rather than the strong negative ones proposed by psychoanalytic theory. In contrast to behaviorism, Maslow's humanism focuses on uniquely human characteristics rather than animal research. Unlike the strong determinism of both psychoanalysis and behaviorism, Maslow's humanism suggests that humans have both the ability and the duty to make choices (although it recognizes some effects of both childhood experiences and later environment).

Rogers's work is best known in the context of psychotherapy, but his ideas supplement Maslow's to yield a general humanistic approach. Rogers focuses on defining the self, if necessary through a therapy that seeks the client's (patient's) own views of problems and possible solutions.

Founders   **Abraham Maslow** (1908–1970) developed his form of humanism in the mid-1900s. Maslow, like Freud, lived through the First World War, but as a young child and, although a Jew in a non-Jewish neighborhood, distant from the actual fighting. The postwar United States in which he grew up, unlike the defeated Germany of Freud, was a confident and booming country. Perhaps as a reflection of this Zeitgeist, his theory of human development is positive and optimistic.

Like Skinner, Maslow became an early proponent of Watsonian behaviorism, but he soon rejected Watson's views as too animal-focused and too mechanical. Maslow shared Watson's optimism, however, and perhaps reflecting Watson's influence included more environmental influences in his views than is sometimes realized.

Carl Rogers (1902–) was born about the same time as Skinner and Maslow and thus grew up in the same Zeitgeist. His career has focused on counseling and therapy programs, first at several universities, then later, as he became well known, at special study institutes—most recently one he founded in La Jolla, California, called the Center for Studies of the Person.

Basic Concepts   Maslow's contributions to psychology have included a new approach to obtaining information as well as a new theory of personality and motivation. According to Maslow:

1   In seeking to understand people, psychologists ought to focus on the "good" people, those who are successful achievers yet retain other positive qualities. Such **self-actualizers** show us what humans can be when conditions permit. This focus on self-actualizers was a response to Freud's development of a general theory based on patients who had psychological problems. Maslow's idea of seeking out and measuring successful people rather than disturbed ones is usually considered a worthwhile methodological contribution apart from its results.

2   All people have an innate tendency to **self-actualize,** or to become the best people that they can be. In terms of the nature/nurture problem, this is a nature statement; it has a very positive quality, however, in contrast to Freud's instincts, which lead to negative behavior unless carefully controlled.

3   Because all people seek self-actualization, Maslow's theory is a motivational one (1970). Basic survival motives are the most powerful. But when they have been served—when you have enough to eat and other survival needs have been met—higher motives come into play, with self-actualization being the highest, most human, motive. ■ Figure 1.10

4   The development of personality is primarily the learning of ways to satisfy the several levels of motives. If the environment is supportive, or at least permissive, a person moves toward self-actualization. But if the environment is too harsh, the person may spend all of his or her time on survival needs, and may even continue to focus on them if the environment improves.

A repressive environment thus can easily stunt and distort a person's personality. Self-actualizers are in practice much rarer than cruel, petty, or otherwise

Figure 1.10 ■ Abraham Maslow (1908–1970). The founder of the third force in psychology, the humanist perspective, with its central concept of self-actualization. *"So far as motivational status is concerned, healthy people have sufficiently gratified their basic needs for safety, belongingness, love, respect and self-esteem so that they are motivated primarily by trends of self-actualization (defined as ongoing actualization of potentials, capacities and talents, as fulfillment of mission (or call, fate, destiny, or vocation), as a fuller knowledge of, and acceptance of, the person's own intrinsic nature, as an unceasing trend toward unity, integration or synergy within the person)"* (Maslow, 1968, p. 25).

(Photo by Ted Polumbaum)

inhumane people. This idea of human development has been called a "developing flower" view: A flower needs some environmental support, such as air, water, and a place to grow, but given those minimum needs it grows simply because it is a flower, developing along built-in guidelines. Maslow's view of human development obviously parallels this description.

Rogers agreed with many of Maslow's concepts; both theorists, for example, emphasize innate human tendencies to develop positively toward self-actualization, if and when possible. But there are some differences, and Rogers has added some additional elements. According to Rogers:

1   It can be useful to draw on what one learns from patients (called clients by Rogers). Rogers, like Freud, developed his theoretical views simultaneously with his therapy procedures in the course of years of counseling and clinical work (1959). But unlike Freud, he designed careful research studies to document and quantify those insights.

2   A useful way to consider a person is in terms of his or her perceived self (1961). The **self** is the sum total of the person you believe yourself to be; it is based on your history and influences your future possibilities.

3   Seeking to define our selves, including seeking our full potential or self-actualization, is what we all do—or ought to be doing.

4   Rogers's therapy is called **client-centered therapy** (1951), to indicate that the situation is *not* medical. Calling it client-*centered* notes that it tries to help clients clarify their own problems and possible solutions, rather than imposing the therapist's views.

5   Rogers puts great emphasis on the individual's point of view being *the* one for him or her. This emphasis on accepting the world as you perceive it to be is called **phenomenology**. Other perspectives in psychology emphasize phenomenology to some extent, but it is central to Rogers's approach.

Focus   Maslow felt that humans are innately good, with built-in tendencies to self-actualize when the environment allows it. Answering questions about human behavior thus requires looking at the current environment in terms of its potential for encouraging growth or at past environments in terms of growth that they have or haven't permitted.

Rogers's focus is similar to Maslow's, with slightly different emphases. In examining any behavior, Rogers looks at who the people involved believe themselves to be and what they think is happening. If two people have quite different views of their mutual interaction, Rogers would say that *each* is correct, in phenomenological terms. He might seek as a therapist to get them to recognize the other's point of view, but not in the sense that only one was "right."

Social Learning Theory

Social learning theory is based on the behavioral or learning theory approach, but emphasizes learning based on social factors. It shares many concepts with behaviorism, but has not replaced it. Also, social learning theory emphasizes some concepts that Skinner and other behaviorists do not use. For these reasons, and because of its growing popularity in psychology, we will treat it separately.

Founder Although others have contributed to its development, social learning theory is usually attributed to **Albert Bandura,** (1925–), a professor at Stanford University. Bandura was among those in the 1960s who began to feel that the behavioral position was limiting as an approach to human behavior. They believed that Watson's emphasis on overt behavior had gone as far as it could, and wished to investigate covert behavior. They also felt that Skinner's emphasis on learning from the direct consequences of actions had limitations for human learning, and that Watson and Skinner had focused too narrowly on single individuals without enough consideration of social factors. Bandura became the voice of these elements of the Zeitgeist in creating social learning theory (Bandura, 1977b).

Basic Concepts The social learning view basically accepts the suggestions made by Skinner, but adds several elaborations felt to be especially important in human learning (Bandura, 1974). According to social learning theorists:

1 Like animals, humans learn by association and even more by direct reinforcement (reward), as Watson and Skinner had noted.

2 In addition, humans learn a great deal of their behavior, perhaps most of it, from observing other humans. They need not actually behave, or receive any direct reinforcing or punishing consequences, to learn. Humans can learn simply by seeing others behave and seeing what happens to them. The concepts of **vicarious reinforcement** and **vicarious punishment** emphasize the idea that you can, in a sense, share other people's rewards and punishments by watching their behavior and its results.

3 The people whom you watch for guidance in behavior are important; they are called **models** and the process

of learning from them is called **modeling** (Bandura, 1971).

4 Direct reinforcement and modeling may often be combined in learning. A model, for example, may demonstrate behavior to be imitated, and then the imitation may be reinforced either by the model or by direct consequences of the behavior. In this case, two things are said to be learned: the particular behavior modeled and imitated and the general tendency to imitate.

Focus Because its basic concepts are shared with the behavioral approach, the social learning view also asks about present rewards for a given behavior and perhaps the history of reward that taught it. It places a special emphasis on modeling and vicarious reinforcement in both the current situation and the past one. What role is being played and where did it come from? What reinforcements for that role has the person seen modeled in the past? Because the social learning view is that we come to be what our particular society teaches us to be, for better or worse, it will ask these questions about all social institutions that teach people how to behave (Bandura & Walters, 1963).

Cognitive Perspective

Cognition means "thought," and the **cognitive perspective** focuses on the characteristics that many people believe most separate our species from others: thinking, problem solving, and creativity.

Founder The cognitive perspective has no single founder. It represents the work of a number of theorists, many of whom are adding a cognitive focus to their work in a particular specialty, such as memory.

Basic Concepts Although its basic concepts reflect the work of many researchers, there is nevertheless a consistency to the cognitive perspective:

1 Humans can best be characterized as **information-processing** organisms. In seeking to understand why people behave as they do, the processes that are most relevant to examine are how people take in information through their senses and how they process it to yield any behavior: in short, how they think about the world.

2 Learning and storage in memory of what is learned provide the basis for thinking. But how learning progresses may reflect innate human tendencies interacting with a given environment.

3 One way of characterizing thinking is to consider it to be problem solving; this allows types of problem solving to be used as models for thought processes in general. Many, but not all, of the problems studied in this way are verbal and logical.

4 Computers can help to specify what competent human thought is like. Ideas about how humans think may be

imitated in computer programs, with the results compared to real human problem solving to see how good the original ideas were. Or you may simply attempt to build problem-solving computers without trying to imitate humans directly. This may turn up ideas about how thinking could be done, even creative thinking, that can be relevant to learning how humans think.

Focus You have probably already thought about the focus of a cognitive psychologist. Of course: Given any situation, each of us must think about how to solve the problems that situation presents. We process the information presented, make decisions, and move on—into new situations. This perspective does not directly contradict any of the others; all agree that thinking is something we do. But the cognitive focus is a narrowing from focusing on all behavior to focusing specifically on thinking behavior.

Ethological Perspective

The **ethological perspective** focuses on our millions of years of evolutionary history, asking how we came to be what we are as a species and what evolution can tell us about our current behavior. The basis of this view, *ethology*, is a branch of biology that focuses on the behaviors characterizing particular species; its founders are biologists, not psychologists (Eibl-Eibesfeldt, 1970). It becomes a psychological perspective when psychologists adopt ethological techniques and concepts for examining human behavior.

Founder Ethology became a discipline largely through the work of **Konrad Lorenz** (1904–). Lorenz took the position that behavior, like body structure, aids survival of the species, and that thus the typical behavior of a species represents the end product of evolution (1958, 1974). He looked at a wide variety of animal species in their natural surroundings, seeking to understand both their behavior and what survival purpose it served (Evans, 1975b). Lorenz was so successful that he has been called "the father of modern ethology" (Tinbergen, 1965, p. 18). Together with two other ethologists, Lorenz was awarded a Nobel Prize in 1973 (Marler & Griffin, 1973).

Functionalism provided a fertile ground for the ideas of Lorenz and the other European ethological biologists. As their work became known in the United States, it developed into a perspective that looks at the behavior of one particular animal species—the one to which you belong.

Basic Concepts From the European biologists we have gotten concepts with relevance for psychology,

but because these are derived from work on nonhuman species they offer only the *possibility* that humans may behave similarly. Ethological concepts deal with survival behaviors such as eating, mating, rearing young, and aggressive patterns.

Perhaps best known is the concept of **imprinting.** Some species of birds hatch without knowing who and what *mother* is, but with the predisposition to imprint on a moving, sound-making object in their immediate vicinity: they build in, through a special kind of learning, what is to be "mother" for the rest of their lives. The nearest moving object in the wild usually *is* mother, but Lorenz showed that it could also be a dignified, gray-bearded Austrian professor; photographs of Lorenz and his "children" are among the most widely published of any in science. ■ Figure 1.11

The evolutionary ties between birds and humans are very distant, and humans do not imprint in the same way these birds do. Possibly, however, human infants become emotionally attached to whomever cares for them at a crucial early period and perhaps this attachment in turn affects their later development. Attachment and similar issues are being studied in humans by ethologically oriented psychologists. According to them:

1   The human species, like all others, reflects a long evolutionary history in which some behaviors are better suited for survival than others.

2   The study of the probable course of that evolution through whatever means are available, including comparison with other species, can help us understand who we are and why we do what we do.

3   The study of any species, including ours, is best carried out in its natural surroundings, moving to experimental work in laboratories only to check a particular idea derived from the naturalistic observation.

4   What will probably be found, as human behavior is studied in this light, is some pattern of *interaction* of nature and nurture, or of genetic code and environment. For example, the nature of Lorenz's goslings is to learn about *mother* at a critical time, but it is the interaction of nature with what the environment provides as a mother—whether a goose or an ethologist—that determines the final behavior.

Focus In examining behavior, an ethological psychologist considers what relation it might have to behavior patterns of our remote ancestors. What survival value would it have had? Is the behavior "natural" or "unnatural," that is, is it similar to what our ancestors might have done or does it fly in the face of such patterns? Can a problem be solved by arranging the circumstances to be more what our species evolved to do?

Figure 1.11 ■ Konrad Lorenz (1904–). The Austrian biologist who founded ethology, with some of the young geese who imprinted on him shortly after hatching and then, in effect, believed him to be their mother. *"To anyone tolerably versed in biological thought, it is a matter of course that learning, like any function of comparably high differentiation and survival value, must necessarily be performed by a very special mechanism built into the organic system in the course of evolution. The indubitable fact that every learning mechanism is phylogenetically evolved is in no way contradicted by the other fact that a learning mechanism is evolved to exploit individual experience"* (Lorenz, 1965, p. 13).

(Nina Leen, LIFE MAGAZINE, © 1964, Time, Inc.)

Physiological Perspective

Physiology is the study of body structure and how it functions; like ethology, it is a part of biology, not psychology. The **physiological perspective,** however, turns this biological focus to psychology's repeated question: Why does anyone behave as he or she does? Answers to this question that refer to our species' history are ethological ones. Answers that refer to our physical structure and functioning—the results of our species' history—are physiological ones. All aspects of physiological functioning are important to biologists; physiological psychologists focus on brain function and influences of certain glands.

The physiological perspective thus investigates the "body" half of the mind/body problem, seeking answers to why we behave in terms of the structures and functions that compose us. This focus on *mechanisms* is compatible with any of the other perspectives; it is like a zoom lens that sweeps us up to and within the behaving organism to see just how it works.

Founder The German psychophysicists are one line of founding; they sought to explain how the body processes sensory input. For another line, physicians who explored the mechanisms of the brain surgically are the founders. One figure of critical importance in the development of physiology as a contemporary perspective was the Canadian neurosurgeon, **Wilder Penfield** (1891–1976). Penfield charted, literally mapped, the surface of the human brain during a career that spanned more than 50 years and hundreds of operations in which the exposed brains of conscious people were electrically explored (Lewis, 1982; Penfield, 1958; Penfield & Roberts, 1959). Each operation was for that patient's benefit, typically to relieve epileptic attacks. But the accumulated knowledge about brain function that these operations provided has been useful for psychologists as well as neurologists.

Basic Concepts The basis of the physiological perspective is a monist view of the mind/body problem. This perspective also generally accepts an evolutionary explanation for human attributes. Several basic concepts follow from these key assumptions; others develop from the ensuing research. According to physiological psychologists:

1   Humans are animals. Our species is different in many respects from others, but an animal species nonetheless; it has evolved from simpler forms and thus shares both history and mechanisms with other species. (This is basically the ethological assumption.)

2   All human behavior is the result of or reflects physiological activity, even if we can't currently specify exactly what it is. (This is the monist position.)

3   Because humans are animals, the study of other animals can tell us something relevant to humans. Thus animals may be used to study a wide variety of human behaviors, just as they may be used by medical researchers to explore human diseases.

4   Because behavior is the result or reflection of physiological activity, questions concerning any behavior, however elaborate and "human," can be explored in terms of underlying mechanisms and processes. It might even be reasonable to seek the physiological basis of such human abilities as creativity.

5   Body processes can be shown to generate a wide variety of normal and abnormal behaviors. Particularly important are areas of the brain and a network of body glands; these glands affect both the body's structures as they grow and the processes that these structures carry on throughout life.

6   In both normal and abnormal behavior, the linkage between behavior and physiology operates in both directions: Not only does physiology yield behavior, but behavior affects physiology. Whatever we see, do, or think about is not only itself physiological, but has further physiological consequences, including the stress diseases (such as ulcers or high blood pressure) that can result from psychological distress.

Focus   The focus for this perspective is to ask about the mechanisms or processes that underlie any behavior. If you want to explore the causes, you do so experimentally in animals. Perhaps, when it is considered ethical, you then apply the findings to research with humans, maybe even eventually to routine practice with them. Beneficial interventions developed in this manner, including ways to influence behavior through drugs or surgery, are already in wide use.

Combining Perspectives

Social learning theory in some ways represents a trend to combine elements of prior perspectives in the elusive search for the best compromise. Social learning theory as a whole is substantially different from each of the other approaches and offers its own new concepts. But its emphasis on the social environment is somewhat like Maslow's, its consideration of "natural" human social learning arrangements is reminiscent of the ethological perspective, and its consideration of covert processes is related to the cognitive perspective.

In recent years other theorists have proposed different combinations. **Behavioral humanism**, for example, seeks to combine humanist goals and behavioral techniques (Mahoney & Thoresen, 1974; Thoresen, 1972).

Cognitive behaviorism remains behavioral but accepts even more covert behavior than the social learning approach (Meichenbaum, 1977). In its emphasis on an individual's phenomenological world, it also sounds like Rogers's humanism.

A reconciliation between psychoanalysis and behaviorism might seem even less likely than these combinations, but a psychoanalyst has offered one (Wachtel, 1977). Wachtel suggests that psychoanalysts should pay more attention to their own behavior and that of their patients and that behaviorists should pay more attention to patients' basic motives.

We should not let these few offered combinations distract us from the substantial differences that still exist among the major perspectives. They do suggest, however, that there is room for more views and more combinations than have been tried so far. An intermediate position may eventually turn out to be the best one, at least for some tasks. In the meantime, seeking the ideal compromise keeps psychologists aware of each other's views.

Choosing and Using Perspectives

These then are our seven perspectives: three major theories offering quite different and frequently conflicting views, and four other focuses that each emphasize some particular set of concepts. ■ Table 1.2

As we look at different topics in this text, we will sometimes emphasize one of these perspectives, sometimes several. Each of these views has demonstrated its value as a way of looking at behavior, but no one could *always* apply *all* of them. How someone decides on which perspectives to use differs according to who the person is and what his or her goals are.

Professional researchers often choose to focus narrowly within a single perspective, both to organize their research and in hopes of contributing to knowledge and to the perspective. Many practicing professional psychologists are not researchers, however, and will not need to apply so narrow a focus. Yet both training and professional needs require that some perspective be taken; the demands of their particular jobs will determine how many perspectives they find useful and how these are fitted together. A professor teaching developmental psychology, for example, must be able to present all major theories of development. A therapist, in contrast, may choose to adopt a particular view as narrowly as its originator or may draw on a variety

Table 1.2 ■ Summary of Perspectives

Perspective	Founder	Summary
Psychoanalysis	Sigmund Freud	Proposes powerful instinctive drives toward sex and aggression that must be brought under control by learned constraints. Major concepts include id, ego, superego, and unconscious motives.
Behaviorism	John B. Watson, B. F. Skinner	Focus on overt behavior. Strong nurture view of a relatively neutral child learning virtually all behaviors, primarily through their environmental consequences. Major concepts include reinforcers.
Humanism (third force)	Abraham Maslow, Carl Rogers	Developing flower view of innately positive human nature needing only a nonpunishing environment to allow it to grow. Focus on phenomenology. Major concepts include self and self-actualization.
Social learning theory	Albert Bandura	Accepts behavioral view but adds focus on learning from the behavior of others and the consequences they receive. Also more willing to consider covert behavior. Major concepts include vicarious reinforcement and punishment, modeling.
Cognitive perspective	Several founders	Information-processing focus on how human thinking develops and functions. Major concepts include computer models of problem solving.
Ethological perspective	Konrad Lorenz	Views the behavior of our species as biologists view others, seeking evolutionary roots of survival-related behaviors such as child rearing and aggression. Major concepts include imprinting.
Physiological perspective	Wilder Penfield (and others)	Focus on the mechanisms of behavior, primarily the brain and key glands. Major concepts include brain mapping.

of approaches for different patients and different problems.

There is no rule saying that a psychologist must stick to one view. In practice, however, most have one basic perspective with which they most identify; they may then have one or two others that they either shift among or seek to combine with it. This reflects several factors, primarily training and practical limitations. Most psychology graduate schools teach primarily a single perspective; most practicing psychologists associate with others who share their perspective and tend to focus all their own work through them, including their teaching. (Some instructors make it a point to explain their own perspective to students. You might wish to ask your instructor to do so.)

Virtually all professions have similar arrangements of training and specialization that lead to members communicating mainly with their professional counterparts. To outsiders, all of these seem intentionally restrictive and the technical language is often termed *jargon*, implying that its only function is to conceal simple ideas from nonmembers. In fact, technical language is usually intended to be both concise and precise; it is specialized, however, and will be obscure if you don't know it.

One major function of any introductory course is to demystify the technical terminology in a discipline. Even if you never take another psychology course, at the end of this one you should not only be able to understand popular media items about psychology, but may even be able to read some professional journals (at least well enough to follow what they are

discussing). But before you can follow the perspectives you will encounter, or can interpret a comment that does not explain its perspective, you must know something about each. Therefore, in this very first psychology course you will study the full range of psychological perspectives, even though if you go on in psychology you will probably specialize increasingly.

We've considered some of psychology's problems, history, perspectives, and current status. We need now to consider its methods before spending the rest of the text on its findings.

METHODS

One of our greatest achievements as a species is that we have been able to develop objective methods of determining what is true about the world, even though we ourselves remain subjective, emotional creatures. This set of objective procedures for understanding the world, for finding what is true, is the scientific method. And any particular set of topics to which that method is directed is a science (Shen, 1975).

The key to the scientific method is that all statements must be explicit ones based on repeatable public observations. A claim can be called scientific only if it is stated in such a way that someone else can check it, to see if it is true. Thus it is designed as the scientist's protection against his or her own mistaken beliefs as much as those of others (Radner & Radner, 1982).

In psychology, as in other sciences, different methods of collecting and evaluating data are available (Borkowski & Anderson, 1977). Each must be based on repeatable and public procedures, but there are substantial differences in the difficulty of carrying them out and the value of the data obtained. *Observational techniques* are among the easiest and most common methods in psychology, but they can only provide limited information. *Correlations* are computed from observations; they can help predict events but cannot reveal their causes. Only the *experimental method* allows causes to be uncovered.

Observational Techniques

One problem with simply observing behavior is that people rarely behave normally when they know their behavior is being examined. They seek to behave intelligently, or in socially appropriate ways, or even to help the researcher by acting as they believe he or she wants them to act. These biases may be deliberate, but often are not. Subjects who know they are being watched may not be able to behave as they usually do, despite their best intentions. Similar biases operate when a researcher asks about previous behavior. Again, some people deliberately lie, or at least selectively report, to make themselves look good, but more of them just misremember their actions. (Aren't you more likely to remember the occasions you acted well than those you didn't—or to modify events a bit so you come off a little better?)

Psychologists have developed ways to correct for some of these biases, but still often find it necessary to use subterfuge or misdirection in obtaining data through observation. They may use passersby as subjects who never know they have participated in a study, or use data collected by others. One study, for example, examined public records of plane crashes and related these to major news stories of murders and suicides, asking whether the news reports encouraged people to commit suicide in the guise of an accident (Phillips, 1978). (The author argues that they did.)

Surveys　**Surveys** are organized versions of what you might do if you wanted answers to a question: They ask the question of a number of people and summarize the answers, choosing people to represent some particular population and summarizing their answers with the help of statistics. The form of survey probably most familiar to you is the public opinion poll, often used for political or advertising purposes as well as for scientific ones. Surveys have some obvious difficulties, however. Some people refuse to answer, or bias their answers to make themselves look good. There is also

"I think you should be more explicit here in step two."

© 1977 by Sidney Harris—American Scientist Magazine

the problem of how the subjects are obtained. If you use an on-the-street interview, for example, you get people who are out on the streets at that time, not others who are sleeping or working.

Scientific polls plan ahead of time who ought to be represented and where they may be found, and then seek to get them. But even this strategy has problems concerning who is to be reached and whether they will talk to the interviewer, what questions are to be asked, and how the answers are to be analyzed. Anyone who understands how people's question-answering biases work can easily develop a biased poll that will seem to support his or her own position. Privately sponsored polls that have some axe to grind, such as those done for advertisers, are thus always especially questionable. Interpreting and summarizing the many different answers people give is a potential difficulty under the best of conditions, and another possible source of bias in less carefully controlled studies.

Overall, surveys are comparatively inexpensive, can sample large populations, and can be done quickly. However, their many problems are hard to deal with at best, and may lead to biased or entirely erroneous conclusions at worst. A careful look at a few people may better answer some questions, and more exact control of the questions and answers may better handle others. These latter techniques are those of case histories and tests, respectively.

Case Histories   In the treatment of the mentally disturbed, the case history describes events and behaviors of a patient's past that may have a bearing on his or her current condition. But more broadly, a **case history** is any detailed compilation of data about a single individual. As the term *history* implies, the intent is always to know about the individual's past as well as his or her present, but the data are often acquired long after the events happened. They usually come from the individual's personal recollections, especially for clinical cases, but may come from other people's memories or objective records.

The focus on the individual is both the strength and weakness of the case-history technique. You can get a much better understanding of how things fit together by studying a single person in depth than you can in questioning many people briefly, as in a survey. But you cannot be sure that the person has reported what really happened, and you cannot be sure that you have fitted events together correctly; given a mass of data about an individual, different evaluators make different interpretations. Furthermore, you cannot directly apply the findings about this person to anyone else; this may be the only individual who behaves in just this way. And you cannot easily combine separate cases to obtain some average. The range of differences among individuals always makes such grouping difficult and the conclusions questionable.

Overall, case histories may be useful in showing what *can* happen in certain circumstances, at least presuming that you believe all of the pieces and the way they are assembled. Case histories are frequently fascinating, as most of us seem to relish a peek into another person's life, especially some of the unusual people who become the subjects of case histories. But their utility must always be carefully analyzed.

Tests   **Tests** are techniques for measuring characteristics of people in a standardized way so that their performances can be numerically compared to the results for other test takers (Kaplan & Saccuzzo, 1982). You presumably know them in the context of school exams, but there are many other kinds of tests. You may also have taken one or more IQ tests, for example, and perhaps personality, creativity, or job interest tests.

In most tests, often called *instruments* by psychologists, answers to standardized questions are chosen from a limited set, as in multiple-choice exams. But tests can take other forms. Tests of physical fitness, for example, usually require you to perform some action and then measure a parameter such as your heart rate for comparison to other people's under the same circumstances.

The advantages of tests derive from their standardized procedure and scoring. *If* a test has been carefully developed and standardized, and *if* it has been correctly given to the intended population and correctly scored, then the results offer a good measure of that which is being tested, a measure that is probably both believable and useful. As we will see in Chapter 14, however, if any of these procedures is *not* properly followed, the results become less worthwhile, perhaps useless. But correctly administered tests offer greater control over the situation and scoring as well as a built-in reference to other people, both significant advantages over survey and case-history methods. Tests (even correctly administered ones) also have disadvantages. By the time you have specified both the conditions of the test and its scoring, you have made many decisions and have eliminated far more possibilities than you have retained. For each decision you have made, others will argue with you, often on good grounds. Applied tests, especially IQ tests, are also criticized because the results may be misused. For example, a person who scores low on an IQ test may be inappropriately assigned to a class for the retarded. But applied tests are a form of technology, and must be used with care, not discarded because they can be misused.

Correlation

Correlation is a way of numerically specifying how closely related are any two sets of numbers. Correlation offers more possibilities than do observational techniques, because it allows the researcher to compare or correlate data that have not been compared before. Correlating these data may help find out how they are related, and when new relationships are found may allow prediction of further events. But correlation's major failing, and the reason experimental techniques are superior, is that it can never tell *how* or *why* the numbers are related—that is, it can never establish *cause*. Correlation can help show where to look for causes, but only experiments establish what causes what.

Scatter Plots   One way of comparing two sets of numbers is to plot them. Often what you plot in psychology are two sets of scores on the same subjects. Imagine the committee that reviewed your own college admissions application, for example; for each applicant, they probably had a high-school grade-point average (GPA) and a Scholastic Aptitude Test (SAT) score. What might they have found if they had plotted these two values for a group of applicants? Most students might do equally well on both measures, but a plot of many scores will show some "scatter" about a

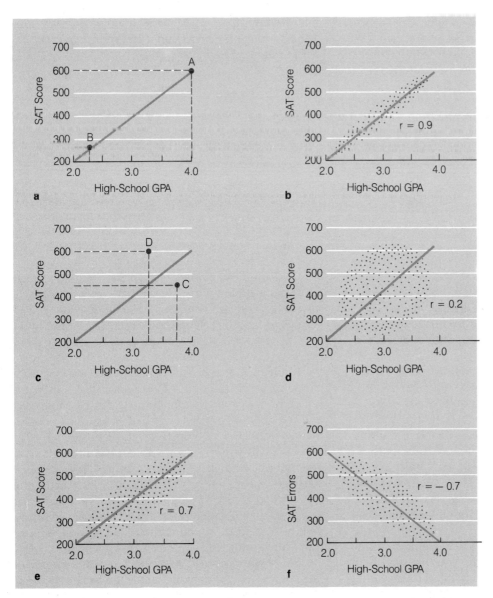

Figure 1.12 ■ Scatter plots and correlation. (a) Hypothetical scores of two students who did about as well in their high school GPAs as their SATs: Student A did well in both and student B did poorly in both. (b) Hypothetical scores of two other students: C did proportionally better on GPA, D on SAT. (c) A plot of many such scores, called a *scatter plot*. The extent of scatter about the diagonal line is measured by the coefficient of correlation, r. Here r = 0.7 shows a reasonably high correlation. (d) Higher values of r indicate less scatter, as in this plot of r = 0.9. (e) Lower values of r indicate more scatter, as in this plot of r = 0.2. (f) A negative sign indicates the direction of the correlation. Here SAT *errors* are plotted against GPA. The scatter, and correlation magnitude, are the same as in (c), but the plot slopes from upper left to lower right, as negative correlations do.

diagonal line. Such a plot is called a **scatter plot.** ■ Figure 1.12

Coefficient of Correlation A shorthand way of representing the degree of relationship shown in a scatter plot is called the **coefficient of correlation** **(r).** The same values as those in the scatter plot are used in an equation that generates a single summary number ranging from zero to one. Larger correlations (higher numbers) represent better fits to the diagonal lines (less scatter), and smaller correlations represent worse fits (more scatter).

Now suppose we had plotted high-school GPA against errors on the SAT. Because SAT errors and SAT scores offer the same information (800 − errors = score), the extent to which errors are related to GPA should not differ from the extent of relationship of scores and GPA. But a high SAT score equals a low error score. The scatter diagram of GPA and SAT errors would have the same shape as before, but would run from upper left to lower right (Figure 1.12f). A falling plot like this has a negative slope; the correlation equivalent to such a scatter plot has a negative (minus) sign, even though its *magnitude* is the same as before.

The plus sign on a positive correlation thus tells you only that a high number in one group is associated with a high number in the other. If a high number in one group is associated with a low number in the other, the correlation is negative. Because the same basic information can yield either a positive or negative correlation (as with SAT scores or errors), you must always know just what numbers have been correlated to know what a positive or negative correlation implies.

Nothing about any correlation, however, tells you what has *caused* what, however obvious the relationship looks to you. If two variables are correlated, all you know about cause is that variable *A* may cause variable *B*, or variable *B* may cause variable *A*. But it's also possible that another variable may cause both of them, directly or through some complex linkage.

Suppose you look for biological differences between normal people and a group of hospitalized schizophrenics (a common and serious problem discussed in Chapter 15). And suppose schizophrenia is correlated with some difference, say a chemical in the blood. Now consider the problem: You don't know if having schizophrenia causes this chemical to appear in the blood (*A* causes *B*), if the chemical causes schizophrenia (*B* causes *A*), or if something else causes both. If you compared the hospitalized schizophrenics to nonhospitalized normals, for example, something about the hospital—perhaps the diet or lack of exercise—might cause the blood chemical. Thus the chemical might be related to schizophrenia only because the schizophrenics were in a hospital.

Such complex relationships abound in psychology and one must always be careful in interpreting them. Any apparently simple correlation might be thought of as something like a small window in a large aquarium, offering a limited view of what's happening. Other windows offer different views, but the whole is never clearly visible all at once; it must be figured out, a bit at a time. Many thousands of computed correlations in psychology thus offer tantalizing glimpses into the complex reality of our behavior, but cannot by themselves allow us to understand it fully. To seek such understanding we must adopt the more powerful experimental techniques.

The Experimental Method

Experimental techniques are not defined by the use of gleaming laboratories and precision apparatus; it is the general approach that is critical. Experiments may be brief and informal or may be exquisitely complex and costly. They may use whatever falls to hand or may require millions of dollars worth of equipment. It is *what* experiments do that is crucial, not the place in which they are done or the devices that may be used (Ray & Ravizza, 1981).

Confounded Variables Scientists call any measurable dimension of the world that varies over time a **variable.** The problem in establishing what causes what is to find the relevant variables. The world, however, is filled with overlapping and interrelated variables. When we ask what causes something to happen, we often find dozens or even hundreds of variables changing at the same time. We typically do not know which one, or which combination, caused the event, and which were related in other ways or were completely unrelated. Scientists speak of this problem as one of **confounded variables.** For example, suppose you have a cold. If you take aspirin, drink chicken soup, go to bed, and perhaps take a cold remedy, the cold will go away. But did *any* of these treatments do any good? If so, which one(s)? The variables of drugs, diet, and so forth are all confounded, overlapping so that you cannot tell which, if any, was helpful.

The **experimental method** is a way of controlling confounded variables. The ideal experiment seeks to arrange a situation so that only a few variables are allowed to change, and to do so in a specified way; all others are held constant. If what you're looking for occurs, you can then say that the changed variables actually caused it to occur. This ability to establish cause gives experimentation its superiority over observation and correlation techniques.

In an effort to simplify complex problems, scientists often make use of a **model,** some simplified form of the problem under study. In engineering, a small physical model may take the place of a large one, as when a wooden model of an airplane is tested in a wind tunnel. In psychology, various forms of animal models are used, in which the physiology or behavior of some species is studied, rather than its more complex human equivalent. Researchers in the physiology of memory, for example, have used goldfish as animal models. But even in such seemingly simple creatures,

RESEARCH CONTROVERSY

Do goldfish learn better in the winter?

Some of the research controversies we will look at have broad implications or are surrounded by emotional arguments. Many such controversies have not been resolved to the participants' satisfaction. This one, however, is typical of the minor controversies that arise in research, are debated briefly, and are then resolved. It thus offers insight into the scientific process itself.

You read earlier in the chapter that goldfish learning was one of the unlikely activities of interest to psychologists and that there were many problems involved in doing research to tease out the causes of behavior. Consider an example of both points from the pages of *Science*, an important journal that publishes research from a variety of fields.

In an article entitled "Seasonal Changes in the Learning and Activity Patterns of Goldfish," Harvard researcher Shashoua (1973) reported this striking finding: "In studies of the biochemical changes that occur in the brain during learning, the ability of goldfish to learn new swimming skills was found to vary with the season of the year" (p. 572). (This work was a replication and extension of a similar 1968 finding by other researchers.) The rest of the report gave the sort of details that the scientific method requires, for example, "Goldfish (7 to 8 g. comet variety from Ozark Fisheries, St. Louis, Missouri) were used" (p. 573). Handling, water, training procedures, and

so forth, were described in detail. Then Shashoua advanced a number of tentative hypotheses about why this seasonal variation might exist: first possible irrelevant causes such as stress from being shipped, then possible relevant ones, such as seasonal hormonal changes. In classic fashion, Shashoua concluded that "additional experiments are required before any definitive...."

Somewhat later a Danish researcher replied, stating that in four years of work with goldfish he had observed no such seasonal effect, even though some of his fish came from the same Ozark Fisheries (Fjerdingstad, 1974). He suggested that Shashoua might be treating the fish differently depending on the time of year.

Shashoua defended his procedures and noted that Fjerdingstad's goldfish all seemed to be learning equally poorly and may·have "had a low level of arousal in both summer and winter," perhaps because their water had not been properly aerated (Shashoua, 1974, p. 1321).

Finally, the University of Michigan authors of the original 1968 report were heard from (Agranoff & Davis, 1974). After chastizing Fjerdingstad about minute details of fish-handling and training procedures, they suggested that a hidden source of bias had existed, despite all the previous careful work, and that seasonal learning changes did not, in fact, exist. New goldfish were used for each study; these were presumed to be equal random samples of the goldfish population

at Ozark Fisheries. The researchers always got untrained fish of the same size, 6 to 7 cm in body length. Now comes the hidden problem: Goldfish only breed once a year, so fish 6 to 7 cm long can be anything from five months to more than two years old. Agranoff and Davis proposed that, "beginning in May or June, an increasing number of the fish we receive are the slower-growing individuals of the previous year" (1974, p. 65). The summer fish learned more slowly because they were the runts of the litter, who had reached shipping size months later than their faster-learning (and growing) siblings. They proposed that such differences in rate of growth might occur because of innate metabolic differences or deliberate breeder crowding to hold down size (so as to have some to sell later in the year).

Four highly trained researchers at three major universities in two countries had spent months studying a learning phenomenon that turned out not to exist! One of their assumptions, though it had seemed a good one, was faulty. Now the researchers can proceed—by buying the "smarter" winter fish and keeping them until summer, they suggest. But who knows how many other problems still lie hidden in all the feeding and water aeration and training procedures? Every dramatic finding you read about is matched by enormous efforts that have turned out to be blind alleys. It's too bad there isn't a quicker way, but nature does not give up its secrets easily.

---

sorting out the confounded variables can be difficult.
■ Research Controversy: Do Goldfish Learn Better in the Winter?

Hypotheses The first step in the experimental method is the stating of a **hypothesis** (plural, hypotheses), a tentative statement of what some relationship might be. Any possibility that is subject to empirical testing can be the basis of a hypothesis, but the more important hypotheses are those that concern causes.

Once a hypothesis has been stated, the experimenter uses it to generate a prediction that can be tested experimentally. The prediction must be **falsifiable,** that is, it must be phrased in such a way that if the prediction is incorrect the experiment will show it to be incorrect. This is a subtle point, but an important one. Unless the possibility that the experiment can disprove the prediction exists, it isn't worthwhile to bother testing it. But if the experiment *could* have shown the prediction to be wrong *and* does not, the correct prediction is said to confirm or support (not prove) the hypothesis.

The more times each hypothesis is supported, the more solid it is. Any experimentally oriented theorist thus builds a theory by generating a related set of hypotheses that in a sense are the theory and by testing each of them experimentally.

Operational Definitions To apply the experimental method, you must define every relevant variable in an unambiguous way. This is done by specifying all key aspects of a study in terms of an **operational definition,** one phrased in terms of the operations or procedures necessary to obtain it. If you wanted to use anxious subjects in an experiment, for example, you would state the operations used to make them anxious. You could threaten your subjects with lowered grades, random electric shock, or any one of a number of unpleasant possibilities that might make them anxious. But whichever procedure you used would be, for that study, the operational definition of anxiety.

Operational definitions are basic and necessary if scientists are to understand each other and if their results are to be public and repeatable. But they also have many problems. One problem is that different operational definitions may yield different results, even when each definition might be a reasonable one. A more severe problem, however, is that some operational definitions have such serious flaws that the outcome means nothing. In extreme cases, they so miss the mark that the results are ludicrous.

One government study, for example, set out to study urban "distressed areas." It defined them operationally through a set of measures that specified no industry, few jobs per person, static or declining population, and so forth. This definition identified some of the known distressed areas—but it also listed some of the wealthiest areas in the country. The authors had neglected to include a variable such as average income that would eliminate these exclusive areas. Of course, multiacre old-money estates don't have much industry or increase in population!

Control of Variables The heart of the experimental method lies in its careful control of all relevant variables. Operationally defining all variables and procedures is a necessary part of this control, but it is only the first step. A typical experiment takes a group of subjects, splits them into two groups, treats them differently, and compares the results. ■ Figure 1.13

First the intended **population** must be defined, that is, who you wish your actual subjects to represent. Ideally you'd like to have your results apply to all people. But technically you are allowed only to generalize to the specific population from which your subjects were selected, and then only if your subjects have been randomly chosen from it. In fact, these most stringent conditions are rarely met because volunteer subjects are typically used and it's hard to know the extent to which these subjects represent nonvolunteers, even within the same population.

After you have a group of subjects, you must split them; this is a crucial step. Each subject must be assigned to a group randomly, without any bias in the assignment procedure. The intent is to insure that the two groups do not differ in any regular way so the separate subgroups will represent the original combined group equally well. It's difficult to do this correctly and exact procedures have been worked out to ensure that subject assignments are truly mathematically random.

In some cases, you may use a mixture of selection and randomization, but it is the randomization that is critical. To ensure that both groups had equal numbers of males and females, for example, you would collect and split a group of one sex, then do the same with the other sex. But within each sex group the assignment would still have to be random.

One of the resulting groups, the **experimental group,** receives what you think will be an effective procedure, the **experimental treatment.** They get the drug, the psychotherapy, or whatever procedure is to be examined. (If you are comparing several treatments, you could have several experimental groups, but for simplicity we'll stay with one.) The measurement of what happens to this experimental group would answer your question, except for one major problem. Many other things can happen to your subjects in addition to the experimental treatment, especially in studies that may cover days or weeks of periodic testing. Suppose one of these other things affects the subjects—perhaps a difficult midterm, food poisoning in the dining hall, or even something in the national news. You would have no way of separating any such effects from the effects of the experimental treatment.

The function of the **control group** is to control for such variables by being equally susceptible to them. Because the two groups are equal samples of the original population, whatever affects the experimental group should equally affect the control group, *except for* what you think is the *critical* part of the procedure.

A presumably ineffective procedure given to the control group is usually called a **placebo;** the classic placebo for drug studies is the sugar pill, which looks like the real thing but has no physiological effect. A major reason for using placebos is that supposedly ineffective drugs or procedures can have some effects. Such placebo effects can be powerful ones; for many

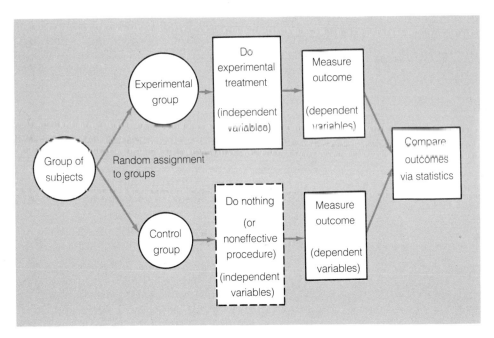

Figure 1.13 ■ A general experimental plan. A group of subjects is randomly split and subjected to two different procedures under carefully controlled conditions. Any difference between the measured outcomes is a measure of the effectiveness of the experimental treatment.

subjects, sugar pills can be as effective in relieving pain as morphine. To have true value, any drug or procedure must be more effective than a placebo.

Thus the control group may be given a procedural placebo, a sugar treatment rather than a sugar pill. If a particular film is thought to be effective at changing subjects' emotional reactions, you might give the control group some other kind of film, one that you think won't be effective. Whatever the form of the placebo, the same rule holds: Unless the experimental treatment is more effective than a placebo, you don't really have anything.

Researchers have also found that it is not enough that the *subjects* be deceived by the placebo. If the person giving it to them or the person observing them for effects knows who is receiving the real drug, these people may unintentionally bias the results by treating the subjects in each group slightly differently or by interpreting their behavior differently. Proper experimental design requires that those administering procedures and taking measures not know who is getting what; they are said to be blind to the procedures. Because the subjects must also be blind, this procedure is called a **double-blind** test. Obviously, someone must know who gets what, but it is usually possible to minimize this person's direct involvement in the procedures.

Two special kinds of variables are named in Figure 1.13: independent and dependent variables. **Inde-**

pendent variables are the measures of the experimental treatment. If the study is administering drugs, for example, the major independent variable might be the strength of the drug received. **Dependent variables** "depend on" what was done; they measure outcomes of the procedures. The dependent variable of a drug study would be a measure of the expected effect, such as a reduction in pain. If you remember that independent variables are independent only in the sense of being the beginning or input ones, and that dependent variables depend on what you do, you will not forget which is which.

A comparison of the dependent measures for the two groups then allows you to assess whether your experimental treatment was effective. If you obtain significantly more effect for the experimental group than for the control group, you may legitimately claim that your treatment *caused* the effect.

Statistical Significance   The term *significant* in the description of experimental results does not simply mean "important." It refers to a specialized way of avoiding capitalizing on chance, or taking advantage of an accident. These specialized techniques are called tests of **statistical significance;** they are a means of calculating mathematically the probability that a particular finding might occur by chance. Only if the outcome of your research is unlikely to occur by chance are you scientifically justified in believing it.

"IT WAS MORE OF A 'TRIPLE-BLIND' TEST. THE PATIENTS DIDN'T KNOW WHICH ONES WERE GETTING THE REAL DRUG, THE DOCTORS DIDN'T KNOW, AND, I'M AFRAID, NOBODY KNEW."

© 1983 by Sidney Harris

The basic computations of significance only tell you how likely the finding is to be real. You must also decide how likely it must be that the results are real before you will accept them. The decision to accept results is stated in terms of the highest acceptable probability of a chance result. It would be too risky to stake your reputation on a result with as high as a 20% probability of being a chance result, for example.

For psychology, the cutoff point customarily accepted is the **.05 level:** Any consequence more likely than .05 (5 possibilities in 100 that it occurred by chance) must be rejected (Cowles & Davis, 1982). More than 5% probability that the finding occurred by chance is too high; researchers cannot legitimately interpret or publish such results. Note that the result could still be a chance one, even if the calculated probability is less than .05. It just is more than 95% likely to be real and less than 5% likely to be chance.

It is possible to get more significant findings. You may see a significance level of .01 (1 chance in 100) or sometimes .001 (1 chance in 1000 that the result is accidental). The original studies cited in this text report some such value for their data; it will usually appear in a footnote as, for example, $p < .05$, which indicates that the probability has been calculated as less than .05.

You may feel that careful research would give exact results and the need for such computations might be eliminated. It is true that the better the control exerted over the data collection process the less random "noise" is introduced into the outcome. But there are always chance factors that you cannot know about or control, so that statistical computations are always necessary. If you have carefully controlled the study, the statistical tests will give you a better (lower) value of the chance probability.

One final comment on statistical significance. Probability computations only tell the likelihood that the numbers are "real" or "believable"; they are never an indication of the *importance* of the finding. A finding that one group averages one-half inch taller than another might be statistically significant at the .001 level, yet be trivial and uninteresting. "I believe it, but I don't care," might be your response. Of course, what is important depends on the observer. ■ Research Controversy: Is Studying Love a Golden Fleece?

CHAPTER SUMMARY

1   Psychology is both a science of human behavior and a profession with many subspecialties.

2   One way of defining psychology is in terms of five old and difficult questions that often play a role in psychological issues. These ask questions about free will, humans as animals, nature/nurture, mind/body, and developmental or situational causes.

3   Psychology dates itself to the founding of Wundt's laboratory in 1879, but in a more general sense psychology as a science was part of the Zeitgeist of the late 19th century.

4   Wundt's structuralism, the first school of psychology, was followed by functionalism, which drew strength from Darwin's theory of evolution. William James, America's foremost early psychologist, shared many beliefs of functionalism but was in a sense his own school.

5   Current perspectives in psychology may be considered analogous to lenses; they focus attention on certain aspects of behavior as a way of narrowing the possibilities to a manageable few.

6   Seven current psychological perspectives will recur throughout the text. The first three—psychoanalysis, behaviorism, and humanism—differ substantially. The other four—social learning theory and cognitive, ethological, and physiological perspectives—offer specific emphases on behavior that may not disagree as much as focus differently.

7   Professional psychologists use one or more perspectives, depending on the needs of their jobs. In the process,

Is studying love a Golden Fleece?

United States Senator William Proxmire regularly offers a Golden Fleece Award, a way of singling out what he considers some spectacular waste of public funds. These awards have frequently been given to behavioral science studies, though this may happen less often now that several recipients have successfully sued him for his derogatory remarks (Kiesler & Lowman, 1980). In one case, Proxmire's Golden Fleece Awards to the research done by Ellen Berscheid and Elaine Walster included comments that many have felt were outstanding examples of ill-informed and confused criticism of behavioral science—and the courts apparently agreed (Shaffer, 1977).

Berscheid and Walster were studying the concept of *love*, seeking to specify just how people define this notion and what effects it has on them. These researchers felt that *love* is a central concept in many human activities, including those in which government plays a part, such as the care or abuse of children. Proxmire had several criticisms of this research, some of which exactly contradict others. We can't possibly study topics such as love, he said (apparently refusing to accept the possibility of a science of behavior). Besides that, we already know all we need to know. And finally, if we *could* find out, he preferred not to know (a call for retaining ignorance in the name of mystery). At the risk of belaboring the obvious, let's note a couple of the problems with his arguments. Either he already knows all about love or he doesn't. If he does, what doesn't he want to know? If we can't study love, how can we know all about it already? Or, ... It's certainly obvious that Proxmire doesn't like the studies, but it's not at all clear from his statements just why not.

Behavioral scientists, of course, have quite a different view of the value of psychology. They point out that it offers society three benefits in return for money and time spent in research: (1) some scientific facts, or findings, about why behavior really occurs, whether or not this agrees with generalized cultural knowledge; (2) some applied technology for dealing with behavioral issues, for example, in education or therapy; and most importantly, (3) a set of special techniques for finding answers to whatever new behavioral questions may be raised. This third benefit, for example, may be applied to major social questions, such as how to reduce racism or to avoid mistaken eyewitness identifications of the innocent (see Chapter 18).

---

some help develop combinations of existing perspectives.

8 Psychologists utilize several forms of observation techniques, including surveys, case histories, and tests.

9 Correlation offers a mathematical summary of the degree of relationship between two variables that is often useful. But it cannot specify the causes of any relationships found.

10 The experimental method, through its careful control of variables, is the technique most able to specify the causes of events, including human behavior.

Further Readings

The APA publishes a number of interesting books and pamphlets, including *The Psychology Major* (Woods, 1979), *A Career in Psychology* (1975), *Preparing for Graduate Study in Psychology* (Fretz & Stang, 1980), and *Graduate Studies in Psychology* (annual), a detailed description of all United States graduate programs. The APA also publishes several divisional journals, the *APA Monitor* (a newspaper), and *American Psychologist* (a journal that goes to all APA members and most libraries). For a complete list of APA offerings, write to them at 1200 17th Street NW, Washington, DC 20036. For some highly readable essays on science see Sagan's collection, *Broca's Brain* (1974). (The title refers to one of the essays, his thoughts as he discovered the preserved brain of a famous scientist in a museum collection.) Some issues concerning psychology as a science are included in a collection edited by Schultz, *The Science of Psychology* (1970). A small but valuable book on the difference between science and pseudoscience is Radner and Radner's *Science and Unreason* (1982). In addition to the standard reference for the history of psychology, Boring's *A History of Experimental Psychology* (1950a), see his later *History, Psychology, and Science* (1963). Historical issues are also discussed in a collection edited by Hearst called *The First Century of Experimental Psychology* (1979) and in Wertheimer's *A Brief History of Psychology*, (1970). *Psychology in the Making* (1962), a collection edited by Postman, also has many fascinating tales of people and episodes in the history of psychology. For a review of current perspectives, see Woodworth and Sheehan's *Contemporary Schools of Psychology* (1964). For further information about methods, see a contemporary text such as Ray and Ravizza's *Methods toward a Science of Behavior and Experience* (1981). Finally, for some of the most frequently cited works in psychology, see Solso's article "Twenty Five Years of Recommended Readings in Psychology" (1979).

Part II

Origins
of Behavior

You visit a hospital neurological ward on a class visit. While there, you are introduced to a patient who seems perfectly normal. Watching from behind a one-way mirror as some tests are run, however, you see her fumble and make mistakes at trying to assemble a simple block puzzle. "It's too bad she can't do that. But block puzzles aren't an important part of life anyway," you think. Just then she reaches out with her left hand, which had been out of sight in her lap. Literally pushing away her own right hand with her left, she deftly begins to arrange the blocks, but the therapist stops her. She then sits on her left hand and begins again the laborious and largely unsuccessful effort with her right hand. Astounded and perplexed, you ask a doctor about her. "Oh, yes, that's not uncommon for a hemispherectomy patient," says the doctor. "We had a man a while back who tried to strangle his wife with his left hand and could only fight himself off with his right. The two halves of such patients' brains are no longer as integrated as they used to be. They act as if they had two minds in a single body, each with one hand to call its own." As you leave, the doctor doesn't hear you mutter under your breath, "I had enough trouble with the mind/body problem. But two minds?"

In this chapter we will explore the physiology of behavior, or of "mind," if you prefer. We will focus primarily on the brain and associated structures, asking how these function to yield both overt behavior and consciousness. In doing so, we will review some of the major concepts and findings of the physiological perspective. This will give you a grounding in the structure and functioning of two major systems that underlie behavior: the **nervous system,** made up of the brain, spinal cord, and peripheral nerves, and the **endocrine system,** a set of specialized glands.

BRAINS AND BEHAVIOR

In examining the nervous system, we will first ask why brains have evolved at all and what relationships there are between complex brains and minds—in animals and humans. We will next look briefly at how brain functioning is studied and then turn to the details of structure and function.

Input—Brain—Output

Simple organisms, such as the single-celled ones living by the millions in a puddle of water, draw nourishment from the fluid around them without needing complex behaviors to do so. The same cell performs both "sensing" and "behaving" functions.

More elaborate organisms develop specialized cell systems for different purposes, but this complexity also

Chapter 2

Physiology of Behavior

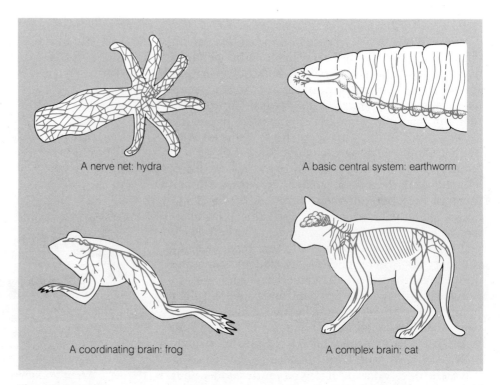

A nerve net: hydra

A basic central system: earthworm

A coordinating brain: frog

A complex brain: cat

Figure 2.1 ■ Four nervous systems of increasing complexity, corresponding roughly to stages in the evolution of our own nervous system. Each step allows greater processing to occur between input and output and thus provides for more flexible and adaptive behavior.

brings the problem of choosing behavior appropriate for each situation. Information about the environment is first provided as input, then one or more layers of cells process the information before other cells yield an output, which is often a movement (Kandel, 1979; Epps, 1982). In more complex species, an increasingly greater proportion of nervous-system cells do *central processing*, the combining and manipulating of information that in humans is the basis of "thinking" (Jerison, 1976). For us, 99% of the cells in our nervous systems do central processing; 1% or fewer handle the input and output. Many animals with simpler nervous systems than ours have superior sensory input systems and many are more agile in muscular output. Our superiority, we believe, lies in the central processing for which our brain is most specialized. This central processing gives rise to—or *is*—thought, according to a monist perspective.

The needs of a simple organism can be represented in a mechanical model. One such model was the "Hopkins beast," which had input, output, central processing, and even a kind of motivation. Although it could not reproduce, it could seek out and acquire the necessary "nutrients" to keep it "alive." Its only motive was survival and its specialized camera eye continually sought out what it needed: electrical power. It rolled

along the corridor on its wheels (output), "looking for" electrical outlets. When it found one, it plugged itself in and charged its batteries. It did this indefinitely until something broke, and it "died" (Raphael, 1976).

The wiring that linked input and output in the Hopkins beast is analogous to the nervous system of a simple organism. A simple nervous system merely links one part of the organism's body with another so these parts respond in a unified way (Stent & Weisblat, 1982). Such a nerve net is found in the hydra, a tiny freshwater animal. When any of its tentacles touches prey, the others swing toward the first to trap that prey, but there is no central coordination; if two tentacles are touched simultaneously, the hydra cannot "decide" what to do. ■ Figure 2.1

The earthworm's centralized nervous system is an enormous advance over a nerve net. The earthworm has a front end with basic sensors, a string of input and output nerves running down its body, and cerebral ganglia (clumps of cells that represent the beginnings of a centralized brain) to put together the inputs and outputs.

The frog represents the next logical development: it has a true brain that receives inputs, coordinates them, and commands outputs by means of a spinal cord. The frog's behavior can thus be more varied and flexible than an earthworm's, but it still does not seem to "understand" much. The frog normally strikes accurately with its tongue at flying insects, for example, but if you surgically change its eye position slightly, it never adapts. Humans quickly adapt to visual changes created by prism goggles, but the frog will continue to strike in the wrong place indefinitely (Sperry, 1956). The cat's nervous system represents the more complex and rapid mammalian system; cats' visual adaptations are much superior to frogs' and more like those of humans.

As we look at nonhuman species with increasingly complex brains, we find increasingly complex behavior. Some psychologists argue that with complex brains comes the possibility of some form of mind. Others strongly deny that any nonhuman species can possibly have a mind. Still others prefer not to use the term *mind* at all—even for humans. ■ Research Controversy: Do Animals—or Humans—Have Minds?

Studying the Brain

For most of human history, people did not recognize the brain's role as the physiological seat of the mind. The ancient Greeks, for example, saw the brain as a simple heat radiator; they felt the mind or soul was centered in the heart. The Egyptians agreed, carefully mummifying the hearts but discarding the brains of the dead. (It is probably these traditions that underlie the concept of giving your beloved your heart on Valentine's Day.) Only within the last few hundred years has the general role of the brain been understood, and even now, most techniques for exploring its function remain crude compared to the complexity of the brain itself. Research in brain function is a booming field, however, and many new techniques are now being developed.

Observed correlations between brain injuries and later performance deficits probably form the basis of understanding the brain's role in all cultures. This approach continues to be useful, with information from autopsies now used to determine the exact extent of the damage (Krech, 1962). The first functional area of the brain to be correctly identified, Broca's area (discussed later in the chapter), was specified in this way.

By the early part of this century, animals were being used to explore the effects of brain damage. The animal is tested on some task, a specific area of damage called a **lesion** is created, and then the animal is again tested on the task, sacrificed, and its brain examined. The brain is quick-frozen, sliced very thin with a special cutting tool, and examined under the microscope. Special techniques selectively stain different kinds of tissue to make them visible. The functional problems noted in the second test are then compared with the exact area of brain damage found, to try to specify the relationships between particular brain areas and particular behaviors. Lesioning can thus be used to trace complex systems; damage in one area causes associated cells to die and a series of stained slices allows these connections to be traced throughout the brain (Heimer, 1971).

Another useful source of information comes from exploration of human brains during surgery. The earliest known brain surgery simply bored holes in the skull; surprisingly, some of these patients survived for a while. Only in this century has brain surgery been done with any scientific basis and with much hope of helping the patient. The exposure of the brain for surgery also allows exploration of brain function by direct electrical stimulation of the surface. During surgery, a mild electrical current is applied to different areas of the exposed brain of a conscious patient. The patient's actions or verbal reports can then be compared to the location of the stimulus (Penfield, 1958; Penfield & Roberts, 1959). Stimulation in one area might cause the patient to make a sound, for example, or to move a hand.

Recently, electrodes have been pushed deep into the brain both to monitor and to stimulate other areas. This has been done largely with animals, but there has been some work with humans. Some techniques even allow single brain cells to be monitored on a long-term basis (Chase, 1978). Brain function can also be studied by injecting chemicals through a previously implanted tube, causing direct chemical stimulation, although this form of research has only been done with animals (Fisher, 1964).

The first technique for measuring the brain's function without intruding upon it was the **EEG** (*e*lectro-*e*ncephalo*g*ram), commonly known as the brain wave. The EEG is a rapidly varying low-level electrical potential that is a mixture of many frequencies; it is obtained from electrodes pasted to the scalp. Different frequency components within the EEG have been assigned Greek-letter names, beginning with the most easily seen wave, named *alpha*. Alpha waves are associated with a relaxed, nonfocused state for most subjects.

Brainwaves are useful in diagnosing major brain problems such as epilepsy, in categorizing states of sleep, and in exploring the functions of the two halves of the brain. But just *what* the EEG measures remains unknown. It must reflect the activity of very large numbers of cells and thus is an overall measure at best. (Varying magnetic fields have also been found to characterize brain function, but this approach has so far yielded little actual data; Brenner et al., 1978.)

Do animals—or humans— have minds?

Some psychologists believe that our nearest biological relatives, the chimps and gorillas, are also akin to us in being able to use a simple form of language and even being able to "think" (Gallup, 1979; Griffin, 1981). Others disagree, saying that such behavior is complex but still lacking in understanding, more like a flexible version of frog behavior than true language or thought (Terrace et al., 1979).

This argument can be turned around, however. Chimps and at least one gorilla can solve problems that some young or retarded humans cannot. So where is the dividing line between mind and non-mind? If chimps have simply learned complex behavior but don't really have minds, why can't the same thing be said of some humans—or even of all humans?

Some behaviorally oriented psychologists adopt a position like this: If learning can account for a given behavior, why attribute that behavior to an unseen mind? But for most of us, our own mental experiences is too direct, too powerful, for us to be comfortable with that. We'd rather grant minds to chimps than give them up for ourselves. The problem then becomes how

to reconcile what we know of evolution and physiology with our perceived sense of mind.

Consider just one problem with the view that mind is separate from body. When light has entered the eye and processed information has been sent to a visual area of the brain, how does the visual image get to the mind? And with what does the mind process it? It is easy to think of the mind as being inside the head and as "looking at" the image from the eyes—until we realize that it would have to look at that information with something (Crick, 1979). With what? Its own little eyes?

A double-language monist view of the mind/body problem offers one possible way of reconciling such difficulties. It allows us to admit the reality of our thought and to speak of it in experiential terms. Yet we can also recognize our mental experiences as being the workings of our brains, and discuss them in physiological terms (Bindra, 1980). According to this reasoning, an earthworm or frog is a biological Hopkins beast, responsive but unknowing. A cat or chimp is also a biological machine but one complex enough to have some comprehension of itself and the world. Humans are then also biological machines, but are complex enough to understand that they are. And they see with their brains more than with their

eyes. By adopting this monist approach, we can use mind as a term for the brain process that sees.

Many lines of evidence support the concept of brain as mind, but they add up to one general finding: Our impression of a unified mind actually reflects the summary of many separate components. One kind of evidence for specific functional areas of the brain comes from the behavioral alterations that result from brain damage.

Different brain areas are important in different behaviors. People whose brains are damaged become unable to do something that they had done before, with the type of functional loss corresponding to the location and extent of damage (Gardner, 1975). Although brain damage can occur in many ways, in one notable case it is intentionally inflicted. In boxing, the stated intent is a knockout, a rendering unconscious through bruising the brain by repeated blows to the head. Boxers not infrequently die from such blows (over 350 have died since 1945). For the majority who survive, the repeated impacts take their toll in gradual generalized brain damage, causing them to lose competence in virtually all human performances. The wide variety of symptoms displayed by aging boxers is almost an index of the kinds of brain damage that can occur. ■ Figure 2.2

A brief change in the brainwave may be evoked, or made to happen, by the presentation of a single stimulus, but the effect is lost in the rest of the EEG. If the stimulus is presented repeatedly, however, and the results averaged by a computer, other waves cancel out and the evoked response becomes clear. This technique of **average evoked potential** has provided interesting results and no doubt will be more useful in the future (Regan, 1979). It has already been able to show differences in what might be considered mental events. An identical visual stimulus, for example, yields different average evoked potentials when the subject perceives it as having different meanings (Johnston & Chesney, 1974).

The CAT scan (for computerized axial tomography) uses an X-ray machine that circles the head while feeding its results to a computer. The computer calculates what a cross section of the head would look like and presents it as an image on a screen; for the observer, it is like looking at a slice across the head at any point (Kety, 1979). Now used primarily as a medical diagnostic device, the CAT scan also has research potential. One study, for example, used it to examine the brains of chronic alcoholics and compare them to normal controls, seeking evidence of brain deterioration (Carlen et al., 1978). ■Figure 2.3

One new technique takes advantage of the brain's flexible use of blood-carried oxygen. A radioactive isotope added to the blood gives off low levels of radioactivity that increase as greater blood flow occurs to

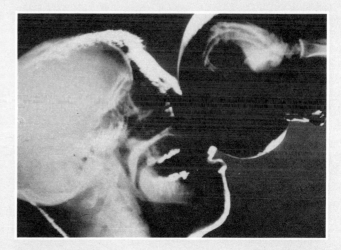

Figure 2.2 ■ Boxing punches bounce the brain around within the skull, bruising it enough to render it partially nonfunctional and the person unconscious. The long-term effect, according to a study of 16 professional boxers, is widespread destruction of cortical tissue. All of the boxers exhibited increasing physical and mental symptoms after they quit boxing, including slurred speech, drooling, tremors, faulty gait, even a variety of psychiatric syndromes.

(left, United Press International; right, Howard Sochurek/Woodfin Camp & Associates)

This chapter (and, implicitly, the rest of the text) assumes that no behavior, however slight or brief, occurs without equivalent physiological activity. Although it may be convenient to use the language of mental events—"I see" or "I think"—such events are presumed to be equally accurately described in the language of physiology: "I have nervous system activity in my eyes and brain" (Bunge, 1980). This language of physiology is gradually being developed for many behaviors, but is still incomplete (Caplan, 1980). It is also more complex than its mental equivalents, and is unlikely to replace our ordinary language for many purposes. But for those who seek to understand in detail what such terms as *see* mean, it often becomes the necessary language.

Not all psychologists agree with this double language view, however. And even some who agree that brain areas are important in human behavior would not take this as requiring a monist position on the mind/body problem. Whatever your view, however, it must be able to reconcile somehow such observations as the complex behavior of some animals and the selective loss of function that accompanies human brain damage.

more active areas of the brain. A scanner beside the head feeds radiation readings to a computer, which displays the results as a colored map of the areas that are most and least active; someone watching the screen can see areas of the brain change color as the person tries different tasks (Lassen et al., 1978).

Another new technique currently receiving much attention is the PET scan (for *p*ositron *e*mission *t*omography). It uses the same computer-calculation approach as the CAT scan, but uses radiation for the information from which cross sections are computed (Ter-Pogossian et al., 1980). A radioactive tracer is added to a substance used in the body, such as oxygen or glucose; as the marked substance is metabolized, the PET scan shows the patterns of its use. More or less use of glucose in the brain, for example, may indicate problems such as tumors. But the PET scan is also sensitive enough to show differences during normal brain function; it changes noticeably when the eyes are open or shut, for example (Phelps et al., 1981).

An even newer and more exotic technique is nuclear magnetic resonance imaging (NMR) (Shulman, 1983). The NMR technique not only provides computed cross-sectional images of various parts of the body; it may also be better able to distinguish between healthy and diseased tissue. NMR involves applying a magnetic field and measuring its effects on the rotation of atomic nuclei of some element in the body. So far, only hydrogen nuclei have been used, because these are present in the water that makes up 75% of our

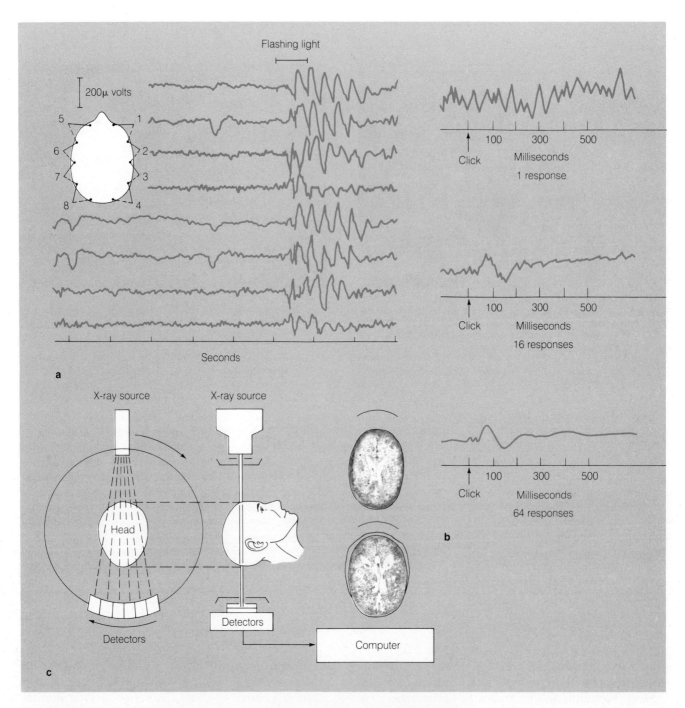

Figure 2.3 ■ Some nonintrusive measures of brain function. (a) EEG traces from eight locations all show the onset of an epileptic attack triggered by a flashing light. This seven-year-old boy sometimes suffered attacks while watching television and these tracings confirm the diagnosis. (b) A single evoked potential in the EEG can be brought out from the background by averaging a series of repeats of the same stimulus. Here the stimulus was an auditory click, delivered at the time marked by the arrow. (c) The CAT scan uses a moving X-ray beam and a computer to determine the comparative density of tissue and presents the results as if they were a cross section of the head. Two actual scans are shown: a normal brain (at the top) and one with several problems, including general atrophy, enlarged ventricles (white spaces in the center), and stroke damage (below).

(**a**, from *Clinical Electroencephalography*, 3rd ed., by L. G. Kiloh, A. J. McComas, and J. W. Osselton. London: Butterworth, 1972. Reprinted by permission; **b** and **c**, from *Left Brain, Right Brain* by S. P. Springer and G. Deutsch. Copyright © 1981 by W. H. Freeman and Company. All rights reserved. Reprinted by permission.)

"MY PROBLEM HAS ALWAYS BEEN AN OVERABUNDANCE OF ALPHA WAVES"

© 1977 by Sidney Harris—American Scientist Magazine.

bodies, but the technique could be used with other nuclei. NMR is so new that it is not known just what it will be able to show, but it seems to be a very promising technique.

The future may see even more dramatic techniques. Preliminary attempts have been made, for example, to keep alive brain tissue that has been removed in surgery. If such tissue could be made to grow and function in the lab, it might allow measurements impossible with an intact brain. And transplants of brain tissue from one animal to another have already shown promise both of helping researchers to understand brain development and perhaps of offering a form of therapy (Marx, 1982; Kolata, 1982b).

To fully understand the workings of the brain is unquestionably the greatest single challenge our species has ever undertaken. You will certainly see great advances in your lifetime, but not full understanding.

BASIC UNITS OF THE NERVOUS SYSTEM

The brain is made up of subsystems, each composed of large numbers of specialized nerve cells (Hubel, 1979). We turn now to a close-up look at those specialized cells and the interactions between them. Then we can assemble them into subsystems and consider how these fit together in the brain.

The specialized cells that make up our nervous systems are called **neurons.** The points at which neurons interact with each other are **synapses.** The interactions of these cells make up the central processing on which we pride ourselves.

Neurons

A neuron, like all body cells, consists of a cell membrane filled with fluid, within which are structures that sustain the cell and help carry out its particular task (Stevens, 1979). Different types of cells carry out many different functions; the neuron's sole function is to convey information. Most of the estimated 100 billion neurons in our nervous system convey information to other neurons (Hubel, 1979). Typical neurons connect to between 1000 and 10,000 others, and some may connect to as many as 100,000. A relatively small number of neurons (perhaps 1%) receive information from our sense organs and convey information to our muscles. Neurons in different systems have different shapes, even though all convey information. ■ Figure 2.4

A neuron conveys information in only one way: It **fires,** or sends a single pulse out along its **axon,** a specialized projection of the cell that carries the information to other cells (Baker, 1966). The neuron can convey information only through the *rate* at which it fires; this rate varies from occasional irregular pulses when the neuron is relatively inactive up to several hundred per second when it is maximally activated. The complexity of our behavior arises from the large number of neurons and the ways in which they are combined; at the cellular level, each one can only fire or not fire at any given time. This process has been likened to the functioning of a digital computer; each of the computer's many elements can only be on or off, but in combination they yield complex information processing.

Information travels in *only one direction* in a neuron. The cell body itself or the projecting branches called **dendrites** receive information (firings) from other neurons. If the sum of the information the neuron receives is sufficient, it fires out along its axon. At specialized ends of the axon called **synaptic knobs,** or buttons, the information represented by the firing is passed across the synapses to other neurons.

The axons of most human neurons are wrapped in fatty white tissue called the **myelin sheath,** which wraps around the axon as a kind of insulator (Morell, 1979; Morell & Norton, 1980). Firing along an axon is a shorthand term for an exchange of charged ions between the fluids inside and outside the axon. (The movement of these chemical ions into and out of the axon creates the electrical change called a firing; thus

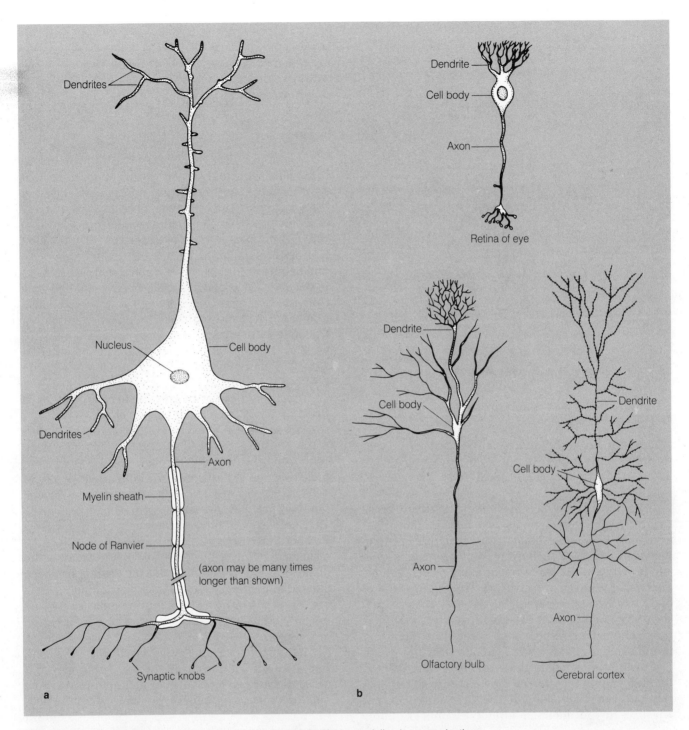

Figure 2.4 ■ (a) A schematic diagram of a single neuron, one of the specialized communication cells that together make up the nervous system. (b) Three of the many different shapes of neurons found in the nervous system.

(**b**, from *From Neuron to Brain* by S. W. Kuffler and J. G. Nicholls. Copyright 1976 by Sinauer Associates, Inc. Reprinted by permission.)

the process is termed an *electrochemical* one.) The myelin insulation prevents this exchange except at regular intervals where there are breaks in the myelin called **nodes of Ranvier.** The myelin sheath forces the firing to jump from node to node rather than traveling uniformly down the axon.

This jumping form of conduction is much faster than that which occurs along unmyelinated axons—perhaps 130 m/sec compared to .5 m/sec—and represents a significant evolutionary development. Whereas an increase in brain size makes possible more neurons and more synapses connecting them, this form of con-

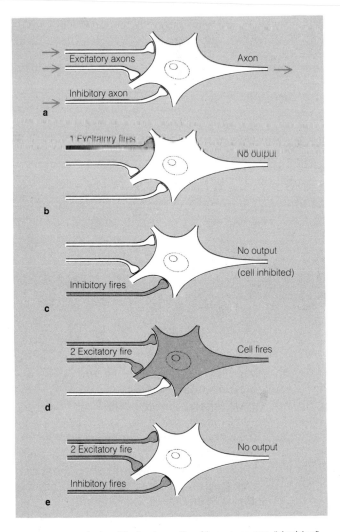

Figure 2.5 ■ A simplified schematic of how a neuron "decides" whether or not to fire (see discussion in text).

(Adapted from "The Synapse" by Sir John Eccles, *Scientific American*, January 1965.)

duction speeds up the rate at which neurons can interact (Keynes, 1958). These two developments make possible the flexibility of function of mammalian brains compared to smaller and slower brains such as the frog's.

If each neuron excited others that in turn excited still others, the brain would "blow up," or self-stimulate until all neurons were firing at their maximum rate. (Something similar occurs in a grand mal epileptic seizure or in electroshock therapy for depression.) For the brain to work in a balanced fashion, there must be a form of brake, a way of slowing activity as well as speeding it up. A continuous balancing occurs between braking or inhibitory inputs and speeding-up or excitatory inputs. This balancing begins with the synapses at which neurons connect.

Some of the many axons coming to each neuron

end in **excitatory** synapses; their message is "Fire!" But other axons are **inhibitory** ones. They fire in the same way as other neurons, but the message they carry to the following neuron is "Don't fire!" Each neuron continuously sums the total of the messages from other neurons, and fires only when that total is large enough (Eccles, 1965). ■ Figure 2.5

Although a real neuron has thousands of inputs, a simplified example with two excitatory and one inhibitory input illustrates the summing process. In Figure 2.5, if only one excitatory input fires, as in (b), it makes the receiving neuron more likely to fire; by itself it cannot actually cause the receiving neuron to fire. A single inhibitory firing (c) makes the receiving neuron less likely to fire, and there is still no output at the axon. Two excitatory firings (d) will cause the cell to fire. But if these two excitatory inputs (from two other neurons firing) are joined by one inhibitory one (e), the inhibitory input cancels one of the excitatory inputs and again the neuron does not fire.

Vast numbers of excitatory and inhibitory inputs are involved in any actual thought or movement. The summing process at any one axon is not as important as the total effect of millions of such summings, often carried out hundreds of times a second. The brain is almost more complex than we can imagine, and its activity continues unceasingly throughout a lifetime.

The firing of a neuron results in a change in electrical potential that travels along its axon toward the next neuron. An electrical potential is an electrical pressure measured in volts. The voltage in the brain is very low compared to electrical devices you are familiar with; whereas a flashlight battery is 1.5 volts (V), neuron electrical potentials are measured in millivolts (mV, or thousandths of a volt). ■ Figure 2.6

When the neuron is not firing, the inside of the axon is at −70 mV compared to the outside, a level called the *resting potential*. An excitatory impulse drives the cell's potential toward zero, and an inhibitory impulse pushes it farther from zero. The two excitatory inputs shown in Figure 2.5 would push the cell to the *threshold potential*, the voltage at which the cell will fire.

The firing itself is a sharp shift in voltage up past zero and back, often called a *spike* discharge because of the pointed shape when diagrammed. It is more formally called an **action potential,** a change in potential that represents the action of the neuron's firing. The action potential always has the same shape and size, no matter how many inputs it has summed up. The facts that the cell can only fire or not fire and that the discharge is always of the same size can be summed up as the **all-or-none rule:** If the cell fires, it gives all that it can give; if it doesn't fire, it gives nothing, even if thousands of other neurons are bombarding it. (Since the action potential is always the same, infor-

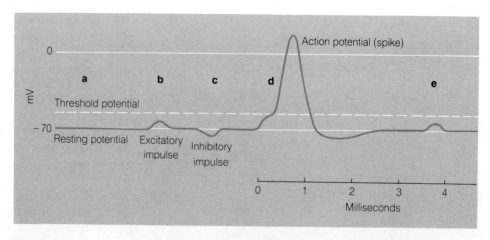

Figure 2.6 ■ Electrical equivalent of the several inputs of Figure 2.5. A single excitatory input (b) excites the neuron above its resting potential, but not enough to fire it. An inhibitory input (c) pushes it below the resting potential. Only the pair of excitatory inputs (d) cause the neuron to reach threshold. At that point, an action potential or spike is generated that represents the firing of the neuron. This potential begins at the axon hillock and travels down the length of the axon.

mation is conveyed only in terms of how often the neuron fires, as noted earlier.)

The conduction of the action potential down the axon may be likened to the burning of a fuse. If you attach one end of a fuse to an explosive and light the other end, the match ignites the first part of the fuse, which ignites the next, and so on until the explosive is finally set off by the last part. In the axon, each electrical change (represented by the spike) causes the next part of the axon to change, which affects the next. The action potential remains the same size throughout, just as the flame of the fuse does.

At the end of the action potential is a brief period when the cell voltage dips below its resting potential. The neuron is somewhat inhibited during this period, just as if it were receiving inhibitory inputs, and is thus more resistant to firing. Under continued normal stimulation, the neuron will fire repeatedly each time it returns to the resting potential and is again driven up to threshold. But very extreme stimulation can force the neuron to fire even during this relatively inhibited period; this allows for occasional bursts of intense activity when the demand is great.

Synapses and Neurotransmitters

All neurons work in similar fashion, and when connected into groups they yield nervous systems. But before we move to such groups, we need to look more closely at the synapses between neurons and the chemicals they utilize; anything that affects these affects the functioning of the entire system.

Synapses   The action potential moves undiminished down the axon and its branches to its many synapses with other neurons. But how does the action potential influence those other neurons, which are separate cells? Some neurons use a form of direct electrical influence; these "electrotonic" synapses are not yet well understood, however (MacVicar & Dudek, 1981; Schmitt et al., 1976). But most neurons interconnect at synapses where a form of chemical communication is used (Iversen, 1979). ■ Figure 2.7

The major features of the synapse are the two cell surfaces, the **presynaptic membrane** at the axon's synaptic knob and the **postsynaptic membrane** of the following dendrite. These membranes are separated by a gap called the **synaptic cleft** (Jones, 1981). Information conveyed by one cell must be transmitted across this cleft if it is to influence the next cell.

Neurotransmitters   Transmission across the gap is accomplished by a chemical called a **neurotransmitter** (Axelrod, 1974). The neurotransmitter is stored in packets called **vesicles,** clustered within the synaptic knobs like water-filled balloons. When an action potential reaches the synaptic knob, a vesicle blends with the presynaptic membrane, then ruptures and spills its neurotransmitter into the synaptic cleft. Once emptied, the vesicle becomes part of the membrane; replacements are created and refilled elsewhere in the cell.

The molecules of neurotransmitter released from the vesicle float through the intervening fluid toward the postsynaptic membrane. Those that reach it have their effect by nesting into special **receptors.** An analogy often used is a key in a lock: Each transmitter

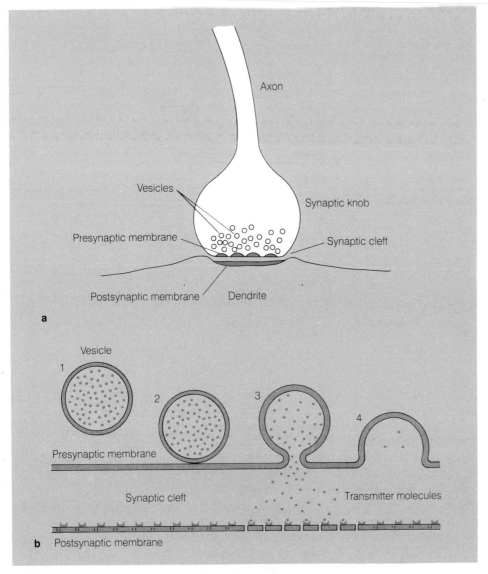

Figure 2.7 ■ (a) A simplified diagram of a synaptic knob and its synapse to the next cell. The important parts of the synapse are the pre- and postsynaptic membranes and the vesicles full of neurotransmitter. (b) A vesicle releasing its supply of neurotransmitter in response to an action potential down its axon. The transmitter crosses the synaptic cleft to modify the properties of the postsynaptic membrane.

molecule is a key that fits into and opens its receptor, or lock.

The neurotransmitter engaging in the receptor of the postsynaptic membrane creates a potential change in that membrane. An excitatory synapse's transmitter causes a potential change up toward threshold; the transmitter from an inhibitory synapse causes a potential change down from threshold. These changes cause continuous variations about the resting potential of the postsynaptic cell, above it one time and below it another. Any time they cause the cell's potential to reach threshold, the cell fires and the whole process moves to the next set of synapses.

Finally, the synapse is restored to its original condition. The neurotransmitter is removed from the postsynaptic membrane, along with any excess in the synaptic cleft, and is broken down, to be reassembled and put into new vesicles later. Other already-prepared vesicles move into place along the presynaptic membrane, ready for the next action potential (Schwartz, 1980). The entire process takes place in less than 3 milliseconds, or thousandths of a second.

Table 2.1 ■ Some Neurotransmitters

Neurotransmitter	Probable Synaptic Function(s)	Related Behavior
Norepinephrine (NE)	Inhibitory and excitatory	Wakefulness and behavioral arousal; emotional arousal; eating
Dopamine (DA)	Inhibitory	Voluntary movement; emotional arousal (schizophrenia?)
Serotonin or *5-hydroxytryptamine* (5-HT)	Inhibitory and excitatory	Sleep; temperature regulation; behavioral activity
Acetycholine (ACh)	Excitatory and inhibitory	Transmitter at neuromuscular junction; behavioral inhibition; drinking, memory
Gamma-aminobutyric acid (GABA)	Inhibitory	Motor behavior
Glycine	Inhibitory	Spinal reflexes and other motor behaviors
Glutamate	Excitatory	?
Aspartate	Excitatory	?
Peptides	Inhibitory and excitatory	Sensory transmission; pain

Adapted from *Physiological Psychology* by Mark R. Rosenzweig and Arnold L. Leiman, 1982, D. C. Heath and Company. Reprinted by permission of the publisher.

Some 30 different transmitters are known or suspected, and there are undoubtedly more (Snyder, 1980b; Stjärne et al., 1981). But this number is reasonably small compared to the many activities in which transmitters play a part. ■ Table 2.1

A class of neurotransmitters that has received a great deal of attention in recent years is the **endorphins,** short for "endogenous (internal) morphines." Endorphins are so named because of their chemical similarity to morphine and their apparent ability to act as a natural pain reliever (Snyder, 1977). In fact, morphine is now thought to be a pain reliever only because it mimics the action of these natural brain chemicals. Originally thought to be important largely because of their pain-relieving properties, endorphins have since been implicated in a variety of activities, including temperature regulation, control of breathing and heart action, and memory processes (Bolles & Faneslow, 1982; Gurin, 1979).

Neurotransmitters and Drug Effects   Because the preparation, release, and breakdown of neurotransmitters are central to synaptic function, whatever affects these processes affects the functioning of the nervous system. **Psychoactive drugs,** those that have effects on consciousness, are one major way of influencing behavior by influencing the synapses (Jacobs, 1979). ■ Figure 2.8

Psychoactive drugs may affect the production, the transport to the presynaptic membrane, the release, or the breakdown of transmitters (Julien, 1981). They may also block receptors by engaging them but not activating them, like the wrong key in a lock; such drugs are called false transmitters. Drugs may also directly activate the receptors, as if more transmitter had been released.

Druglike effects may even result from some foods. Some foods contain ingredients that are necessary precursors for important neurotransmitters (chemicals needing only small changes to become the neurotransmitters). Tryptophan, for example, is a precursor of serotonin, a neurotransmitter important in sleep and other functions. Tryptophan is found in a number of foods, including milk and cheese. Hence, a glass of warm milk before going to sleep may be a kind of natural sleeping pill; the warmth may not be helpful, but the tryptophan may be (Hartman, 1978).

Just as the combined effects of several drugs can be fatal, so can be the combination of some foods and some drugs. Psychic energizers ("uppers") of the class called MAO inhibitors, for example, work by inhibiting the breakdown of neurotransmitters. A lunch of beer and cheese, both of which are rich in tyramine, has proved fatal for some people taking MAO inhibitors. When the tyramine is not broken down (because of the MAO inhibitor), it affects synapses in peripheral nerve endings, leading to raised blood pressure, stroke, and death (McGeer, 1971).

Which synapses are affected by a drug depends on what transmitter is used at that synapse. A drug de-

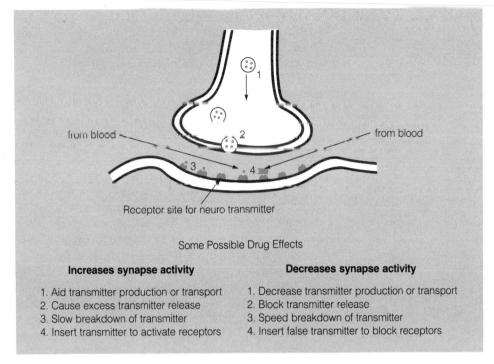

Some Possible Drug Effects

Increases synapse activity

1. Aid transmitter production or transport
2. Cause excess transmitter release
3. Slow breakdown of transmitter
4. Insert transmitter to activate receptors

Decreases synapse activity

1. Decrease transmitter production or transport
2. Block transmitter release
3. Speed breakdown of transmitter
4. Insert false transmitter to block receptors

Figure 2.8 ■ A summary of ways in which psychoactive drugs can affect behavior by affecting synaptic functioning. Note that the overall behavioral effect depends on the effect at the synapse *and* on what the synapse normally does.

signed to affect synapses that use a particular transmitter will affect *all* synapses using that transmitter, many of them in structures that are not the drug's intended target. Effects other than the desired one are side effects. A single drug may be used for a number of different problems. In one case, the intended effect will be A and the side effects B and C; the next time, the intended effect may be C, whereupon A and B are side effects. The overall effects of any drug also depend on the function of the affected synapses. Increasing the activity of an inhibitory synapse, for example, increases the inhibition of the next neuron and decreases its probability of firing.

Now it's time to look at the larger systems that are made up of neurons (Nauta & Feirtag, 1979). All such systems taken together make up the nervous system.

DIVISIONS AND FUNCTIONS OF THE NERVOUS SYSTEM

In examining the nervous system, we will summarize first its major structural subdivisions, then the major functions of these subdivisions. Then we can look at these subdivisions in somewhat more detail, beginning with the innermost and oldest structures.

Summary of Nervous System Divisions

Just as neurons are specialized cells for information transmission, the nervous system is the body's overall information system, linking skin, muscle, bones, organs, and senses into an integrated organism (Bullock et al., 1977). The major divisions of the nervous system are the central and peripheral systems.

The **central nervous system (CNS)** is made up of all of the nervous system that is encased and protected by bone: the **brain,** within the skull, and the **spinal cord,** running down the spinal column. The central nervous system develops prenatally as the elaboration of a hollow tube, called the **neural tube,** which by the third week of development runs the length of the embryo (Cowan, 1979). The top end of this neural tube develops bulges, then begins to fold back on itself, into a Z shape. The result is that the developing end bulge surrounds the structures developed from the other bulges, hiding them from view. (In the process, the end of the neural tube splits and folds down on each side of lower structures, yielding the two separate *cerebral hemispheres,* which we discuss later.) Further expansion and folding continue in the outer portion until it eventually takes on the wrinkled and grooved appearance of the adult brain (Jacobson,

"I STOPPED TAKING THE MEDICINE BECAUSE I PREFER THE ORIGINAL DISEASE TO THE SIDE EFFECTS."

© 1983 by Sidney Harris

1978). In the completed CNS, most of the length of the neural tube remains as the spinal cord. At the brain end, however, the folding and development of the tube result in a complex series of passages within the brain called *ventricles.* These ventricles and the space within the spinal cord form a single closed system, filled with pressurized cerebrospinal fluid that helps to support the soft tissue of the brain. Overall, the CNS is thus well protected, supported by fluid from inside and encased in bone on the outside.

All neurons outside the CNS make up the **peripheral nervous system.** The peripheral nervous system develops as a set of **nerves,** bundles of many axons similar to the bundles of wires that make up telephone cables. Nerves run from the spinal cord to all parts of the body, linking the nervous system into a functional unit. The peripheral system is usually further subdivided into somatic and autonomic systems; the logic of these divisions is shown in Figure 2.9. (Note that these divisions are somewhat arbitrary representations; the nervous system is actually a complex whole and any separation such as this tends to oversimplify its relationships.) ■ Figure 2.9

The **somatic system** is the body system (soma means "body"). It brings in sensory information about the position of the limbs, pressures on them, and so forth, and sends out motor commands to them. (Mo-

tor, in neurology, always refers to muscle control.) The **autonomic system** is the control system for body *organs* such as heart, lungs, and intestines. Both of the autonomic system's main divisions (the sympathetic and parasympathetic systems) are primarily command systems; the difference between them is in the type of commands they give.

The **sympathetic system** activates the body's internal organs to prepare themselves for violent, rapid physical activity, apparently as a survival mechanism. It signals the organs to prepare for a fight for survival. The heart speeds up, digestion halts while the intestines' blood flow goes to the brain and muscles, and so forth. This entire package of consequences is called the **fight-or-flight response** because it presumably prepared our ancestors to fight or flee.

The **parasympathetic system** balances the sympathetic; its commands represent the all-clear signal that returns all organs to their appropriate conditions for relaxed behavior. In the members of a wild baboon troop, for example, their parasympathetic systems help them return to eating, grooming, and sleeping after the sight of a tiger has briefly mobilized frantic action by activating their sympathetic systems.

Summary of Nervous System Functions

The functioning of the nervous system is so complex that it must be broken down into smaller units if we are to understand it. And the brain, the most complex part of the nervous system, also can be subdivided for study. One useful overview of the brain's structure and function is MacLean's concept of a "triune," or three-in-one, brain (Holden, 1979; MacLean, 1970). ■ Figure 2.10

MacLean suggests that we think of the brain as three superimposed layers. The **inner core,** or reptilian brain, evolved first, and is thus behaviorally primitive. According to this view, the inner core is a kind of survival machine, without consciousness as we understand it, but with stock responses to a few standard situations. Psychologists often use the term *alligator brain* for these systems.

The second layer, superimposed on the first, MacLean calls the paleomammalian, or "old mammalian," brain. It represents the evolved brain changes that mammals, unlike reptiles, share. Now more commonly known as the **limbic system,** this middle layer was once called the rhinencephalon, or "nosebrain," because it connects directly to the sense of smell. The limbic system is now thought to be a center of emotional behavior, but smell and emotion are closely related. You have only to watch a dog out for a walk to recognize the major role that scents play in its behavior, especially its emotional behavior; the dog lives in

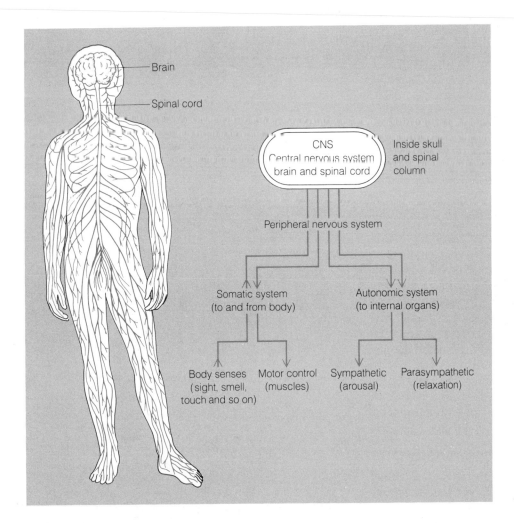

Figure 2.9 ■ Overall organization of the nervous system. (See text for details.)

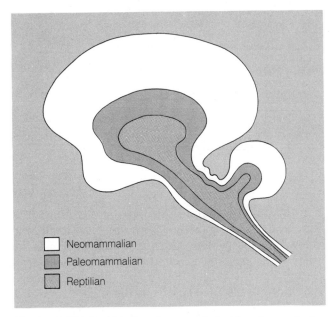

Figure 2.10 ■ Paul MacLean's concept of a triune human brain: We retain reptilelike survival mechanisms *and* early mammalian emotional systems, but have surrounded these with newer structures, most notably the cerebrum.

a world of scents, one denoting an enemy, the next a potential mate, the next a possible prey.

The third and final layer is the neomammalian, or "new mammalian," brain. This is the **cerebrum**—what we sometimes think of simply as *the* brain. Note that our evolution has not replaced the reptilian or old mammalian brains with the cerebrum, but has added it, leaving the older two systems functional. Many life-support functions, such as breathing and heartbeat, are still controlled by the reptilian system, leaving the cerebrum free to do other things.

Now that you've seen the overall organization, let's examine the major subsystems one at a time. We'll begin with the spinal cord and associated somatic system, showing how these function in basic reflexive behavior.

Spinal Cord, Cerebellum, and Muscular Control

The spinal column that encloses the spinal cord consists of a series of vertebrae, discs of bone stacked one atop the other with cartilage pads between them. Peripheral nerves from all parts of the body enter and leave the cord through passages in the vertebrae. Alongside the spinal column is a chain of ganglia (clumps of neuron cell bodies). These are part of the sympathetic portion of the autonomic system. ■ Figure 2.11

Spinal Cord   The nerves of the somatic system enter and leave the spinal cord in pairs, one at each vertebra. Sensory "roots" enter at the back of the cord and motor "roots" leave at the front; each goes to a particular body area.

Information brought in by the sensory nerves normally continues up the spinal cord to appropriate areas of the brain. Motor commands generated in the brain are then sent back down the cord and out to the muscles. This tells us why damage to the spinal cord can leave body parts below the damage both insensitive and paralyzed: The neural signals to and from the limbs cannot pass the point of damage. If the damage is relatively low in the back, only the legs may be affected. (Patients with such damage are called paraplegics.) But if the cervical vertebrae near the head are broken, as sometimes happens from a dive into shallow water, the resulting spinal-cord damage may leave no sensation or movement from the neck down. (Patients with such damage are called quadriplegics.)

Above the spinal cord, a specialized set of cranial nerves enters the brain at several locations. These are actually within the skull, above the last vertebra. Most cranial nerves either bring in sensory input from the head, including the senses of smell, sight, and hearing, or carry commands to muscles of the head and neck. One exception is the vagus nerve, which runs to many internal organs; the vagus nerve allows these organs—the heart, for example—to continue functioning even when spinal-cord damage has paralyzed the entire body.

If all input/output processing were done at the level of the brain, spinal-cord damage would eliminate all neural activity below that point. But in fact some simple responses remain: the **spinal reflexes,** input/output loops in which a stimulus leads directly to a motor response without involving higher centers. The arrangement of neurons in a spinal reflex is straightforward, but to understand its function you need to know a bit more about how muscles work.

Muscular Control   We are enabled to stand and move by a framework of rigid skeletal bones moved by muscles (Talbot & Humphrey, 1979). Muscles cannot push; to move a body part, you must pull it one way or the other (Huxley, 1965). Muscles are typically arranged in antagonistic pairs: one to pull in one direc-

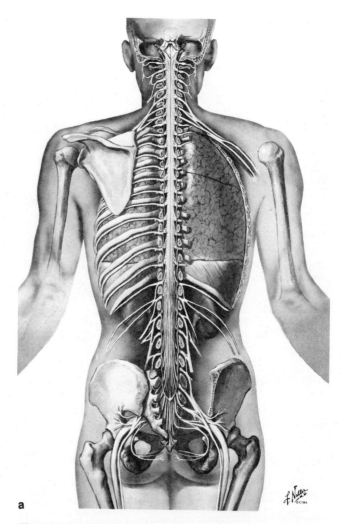

a

Figure 2.11 ■ (a) The spinal cord and peripheral nerves, which follow the general framework of the skeleton to reach all parts of the body. (b) A small section from the chest portion of the spinal cord shows details of how the peripheral nerves enter and leave the cord. (c) The sensory responsiveness of the body's somatic system is divided into strips as shown; each corresponds to a particular sensory nerve. Those at chest level run around the body in parallel strips, corresponding to nerves such as those shown in the detail of (b). Those for the limbs are more complex, as shown.

(a and c, adapted from an original painting by Frank H. Netter, M.D., from THE CIBA COLLECTION OF MEDICAL ILLUSTRATIONS, copyright by CIBA Pharmaceutical Company, Division of CIBA-Geigy Corporation. Reprinted by permission; b, from *Handbook of Anatomy* by J. Bevan, Simon and Schuster, 1978. Reprinted by permission from Mitchell Beazley International, London.)

tion, the other to pull in the opposite. An example is the biceps/triceps pair that pivots the forearm at the elbow. The biceps raises the arm by contracting as the triceps relaxes. (It is the contracted biceps that makes the bulge in the front of your upper arm.) In extending the arm, the biceps relaxes and the triceps contracts. This alternate relax/contract pattern is typical of antagonistic pairs all over the body. The body rigidity seen in some seizures is caused by tightening both muscles at

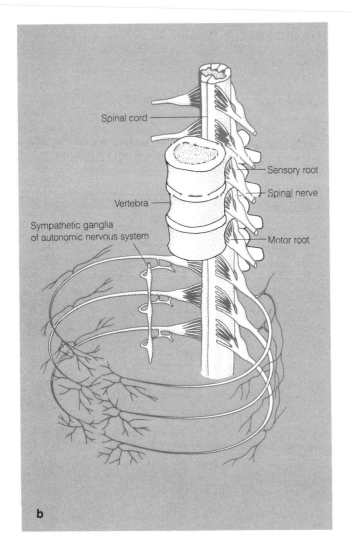

Spinal cord

Sensory root

Spinal nerve

Vertebra

Motor root

Sympathetic ganglia
of autonomic nervous system

b

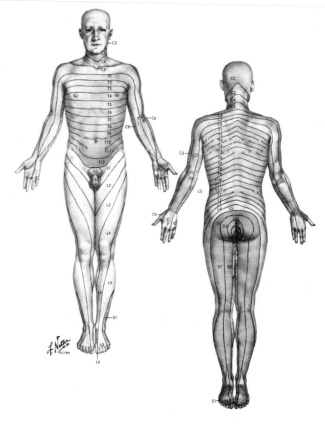

c

once so that no movement results. Stage hypnotists induce a similar effect to stretch someone's rigid body between two chairs. (Such demonstrations are both ethically questionable and physically dangerous, however.)

Skeletal muscles receive signals from motor neurons that synapse directly onto them at *neuromuscular junctions*, using the neurotransmitter acetylcholine (Lester, 1977). Each motor neuron controls or innervates a set of muscle fibers; major muscles, such as the biceps and triceps, are made up of many such sets of fibers. These fiber sets function through a muscular equivalent of the all-or-none rule: When a motor neuron fires, all of the muscle fibers that it innervates contract at once. Variations in the applied force of a muscle result from firing more or fewer neurons to add or subtract groups of muscle fibers within it. Body muscles, such as those of the legs or arms, have relatively large numbers of fibers innervated by each neu-

ron and are thus strong but not very precise. Delicate and sensitive muscles, such as those of the face, have very few fibers innervated by each neuron, and so can be very precisely controlled (Merton, 1972).

This arrangement also helps in prolonged use of the muscles. A muscle can apply a continuous force because alternating sets of muscle fibers are stimulated, letting some rest while others contract. Rarely in normal muscular activity are all fibers contracted at once. If such massive contraction is stimulated abnormally—by drugs or emergency activation of the sympathetic system—there are several problems. The contractions may be strong enough to break the bones, a problem that can occur in the user of the street drug PCP, or angel dust. If this does not happen, the result is at least rapid and deep fatigue, as typically follows an emergency activation.

Now that you know something about how muscles function, we can look at spinal reflexes. Reflexive

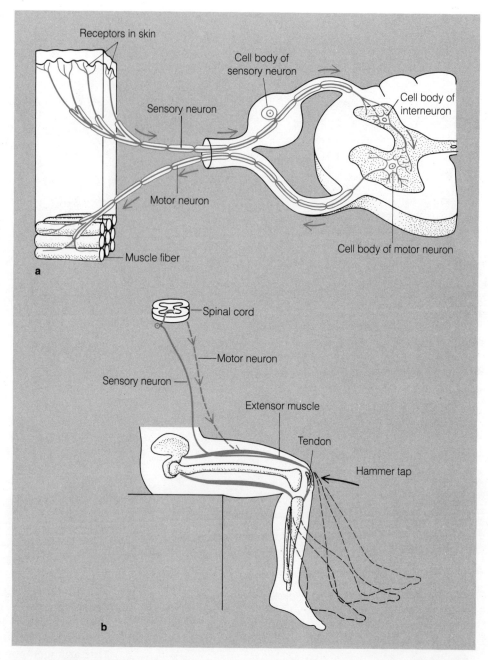

Figure 2.12 ■ (a) A spinal reflex consisting of one sensory neuron, one interneuron in the spinal cord, and one motor neuron. (b) The knee-jerk reflex: A doctor taps your knee with a rubber hammer to test the quality of your spinal reflexes.

muscle activation is an automatic feedback system that helps sustain body posture and simple activity. It relieves the need for higher centers to pay attention to minor postural adjustments, and by eliminating the time it takes for an action potential to go to the brain and back, it makes faster responses available in emergencies. These input/output loops seem to represent the form of sensorimotor arrangement that preceded the evolution of central (brain) processing. The fewest neurons that may be involved in a reflex are two: a sensory one in and a motor one out, though often there is another "interneuron" within the spinal cord. ■ Figure 2.12

The butterfly shape in the middle of the spinal cord (2.12a) represents the cell bodies and dendrites of spinal-cord neurons. The lighter areas in the outer part of the spinal cord represent myelin sheathing of other axons going up and down the cord.

One example of a simple (probably two-neuron) postural reflex is the one tested when a doctor taps your knee with a rubber hammer. The tap tests the speed and strength of the reflex that helps you to stand; the tap falls on the tendon that normally pulls your lower leg forward and thus stimulates the input received when the knee starts to bend. If you are standing and your knees begin to buckle, this reflex jerks you back upright; as tested, it simply results in a reflexive kick. This reflex can also demonstrate another aspect of motor control, however: Higher brain centers can influence reflexes. In doing this test, the doctor will ask you to relax and try to avoid any control of the leg. This means minimizing brain control so the pure spinal reflex can be seen. In normal muscular use the brain modifies and manipulates spinal reflexes, using them as subsystems to accomplish what it wants. A gymnast, for example, sends a series of commands for the body positions he or she wants next, and reflexive loops achieve them.

One technological innovation that follows from an analysis of motor-control systems is the brain-controlled prosthetic arm. It replaces muscles and bones with mechanical structures, which are controlled by the wearer's own neural signals to the now-amputated arm. All the wearer need do, for example, is intend to raise the arm and the mechanical biceps responds (Pines, 1978; Teresi, 1978). Such limbs now hook up to the remaining muscle, but there is no reason why they could not eventually be hooked up directly to the spinal cord or even to the brain.

Some researchers are also experimenting with technology to replace the neural signals rather than the limb. They use a microcomputer to sequence a series of electrical signals as commands to leg muscles in paraplegics. Several patients have been able to pedal an exercise bicycle, and one patient has even taken a few steps. Eventually, patients may be able to walk unaided, even though their spinal-cord damage means that they can neither feel nor directly command their legs.

Cerebellum At the base of the brain is the **cerebellum,** or "little brain," a special subsystem for smoothing and integrating motor commands to the muscles. A primitive version of the cerebellum is included in the reptilian brain, but like the cerebrum the cerebellum reaches its largest and most complex form in humans. It receives inputs from a number of other brain areas, including sensory areas and those that are planning what movements will occur next (Evarts, 1979). All these inputs are fitted together in a multi-layer network that makes up the outer portion, or cortex, of the cerebellum. (Cortex means "bark," as on a tree.) The result is the output of the large Purkinje cells, which send the actual motor commands down the spinal cord to the muscles. The Purkinje cells have the largest number of synapses per cell that have been found to date—up to 100,000 (Llinás, 1975). ■ Figure 2.13

The cerebellum makes rapid and complex movements possible. If it is damaged, a generalized clumsiness results; a patient with cerebellar damage can no longer perform rapid and precise acts such as playing the piano, and can walk only slowly and with great effort. The cerebellum's rapid and specialized motor-command system is needed because both nerve transmission and muscular contraction take time; the further the signals have to go, the greater the problem of responding soon enough. For example, one dinosaur species—the *Stegosaurus*—with its slower reptilian rate of transmission probably required nearly a minute for a sensation from its tail to reach its brain, 87 feet away. Its less-than-3-ounce brain probably could barely have controlled its 10-ton body at all were it not for a secondary minibrain in its pelvic region, at the bottom of the spinal cord (Ratkevitch, 1977).

We have developed the ability to move our legs with our central brain and to coordinate exceptionally rapid and delicate series of movements. We do so with the cerebellum, which must have so many inputs to be able to send the right motor commands at the right times. Any complex performance such as speech requires a continuous stream of commands, some of them on their way even while others are being carried out. Some commands must even be sent out of sequence, starting early toward a relatively slow-responding set of muscles. We thus ought not to be surprised that some people stutter or have difficulty coordinating their body parts. It is remarkable that so many of us perform such complex maneuvers so well (Towe & Luschei, 1981).

Brainstem and Survival

Where the spinal cord enters the brain lies the oldest and most basic of the inner core or "reptilian brain" systems, the **brainstem.** The brainstem includes a number of basic survival mechanisms that provide a base upon which the more complex brain systems are elaborated. The more complex structures control much of our behavior, but it is the brainstem mechanisms that sustain our lives by keeping the heart beating, the lungs breathing, and so forth.

These survival mechanisms may even sustain a kind of minimal life in those whose higher brains are dead. In some kinds of brain damage, for example, such as that caused by oxygen lack, the brain seems to die in approximately reverse order to its evolutionary

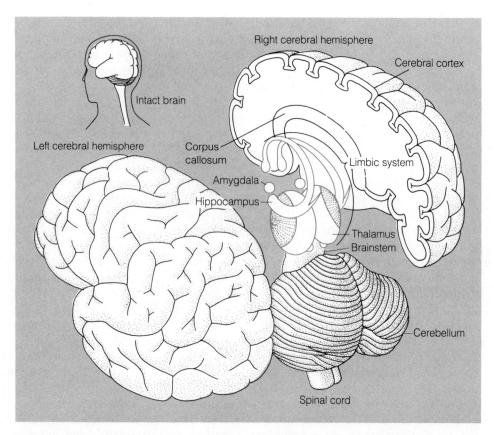

Figure 2.13 ■ The basic structures of the brain. The brainstem, a simple version of the cerebellum, and the thalamus are the reptilian portion. The limbic system is the early mammalian addition. The elaboration of the cerebellum and addition of the large cerebrum represent the new mammalian additions.

development. The cerebrum dies first; the older, simpler structures hang on longer. Because of this arrangement, drowning or poisoning victims who are resuscitated may be left, in the traditional cruel term, "vegetables." The well-known case of Karen Quinlan represents an extreme example, a condition sometimes called "brain death," although what is meant is cerebral death (Sun, 1980).

Karen Quinlan was a 21-year-old college student who fell into a coma after a drinking and drug-using party. Most likely she vomited, then inhaled and partially strangled on the vomit. She was found the next morning, still minimally alive but "brain dead." For a year she was on life-support machines, but her parents sued for and won the right to unplug them. Taken off the machines, she continued to breathe on her own, indicating that her brainstem mechanisms were still functioning. That was in 1976; she has remained in a fetal posture since, weighs less than 70 pounds, and requires constant care. There is no hope of her ever functioning as a human again, but her tough brainstem mechanisms survive (Keerdoja et al., 1980).

RAS and the Orienting Response   Karen Quinlan's condition also illustrates another brainstem function. At a touch or sudden sound her eyes open, though they remain blank and unseeing. Subsystems for alerting her to new inputs still work, though they no longer serve anyone. Comparable behaviors can be seen in anencephalic infants, those whose cerebrums failed to develop prenatally. Anencephalic infants are born with nearly empty skulls and typically die within a month or two. The fact that they live at all reflects the functioning of their brainstem survival systems, but researchers have found something even more remarkable: Anencephalic infants are *more* responsive to inputs such as sudden lights or noises than are normal infants. (The response is an alerting one, measured by a slowing of heart rate.) Apparently the normal infant's still-developing cerebrum partially overrides the older systems at birth, so that they cannot respond; the cerebrum itself is not complete enough for the alerting response to work well until some months later. The anencephalic infant, with no interference from a partially grown cerebrum, is thus more responsive than the normal child (Graham et al., 1978).

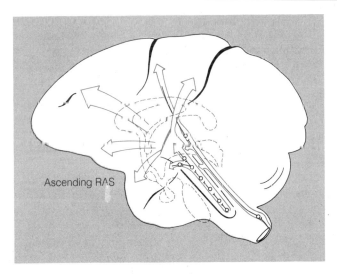

Figure 2.14 ■ The reticular activating system, or RAS, alerts the rest of the brain to changes in the pattern of incoming stimuli.

(From *Psychophysiology and Motivation* by D. B. Lindsley, in M. F. Jones (Ed.), *Nebraska Symposium on Motivation*, University of Nebraska Press, 1957. Reprinted by permission of the author.)

The responsiveness to sudden inputs of Karen Quinlan and anencephalic infants reflects the functioning of the **reticular activating system (RAS),** a network of nerve connections in the brainstem that is connected to many brain structures (French, 1957). (Its name comes from reticulum, meaning "net.") Inputs from portions of the body below the neck are brought up to the brain centers by the ascending RAS. Other connections perform the same function for the major senses. ■ Figure 2.14

Any sudden increase or decrease in a sensory input alerts all systems through the RAS; this mechanism causes us to pay attention to changes in the environment. The result is called the **orienting response;** it's what you feel when a sudden noise behind you causes you to jerk and blink. When activated, the orienting response temporarily improves all the senses: A sudden sound briefly improves visual processing as well as hearing.

Waking and sleeping are also controlled through brainstem systems, including the RAS. People who are *not* brain dead can remain indefinitely in comas because of damage to these mechanisms. The cerebrum may be intact and able to function, but if it is not awakened, they continue to "sleep," perhaps for years. Sometimes they awaken, but typically they do not.

The **thalamus** is a structure at the top of the reptilian brain that receives inputs from the sensory systems; it is generally considered to be a kind of sensory relay station, passing on to the cerebrum the sensory information it receives (Gaither & Stein, 1979). Some theorists, such as Penfield (1975), believe the thalamus

to be the seat of consciousness itself, but this role has not been established.

The thalamus may also have a role in such sensory behavior as peripheral vision and visually based orienting. The thalamus may be the basis of the phenomenon of "blindsight," for example. Seeing normally depends on activity in the cerebrum, but some people with cerebral damage that renders them blind still show some visually guided behavior. Although they claim not to see a thing, they may still flinch or blink if something is thrust at their eyes, and they may even be able to point to the direction that a light came from or to walk across a room without falling over furniture. Sensory input to the thalamus is probably reaching other systems to direct these movements, but the person is blind because the cerebrum cannot process the information (Hechinger, 1981).

Limbic System, Motivation, and Emotion

Above the inner core lies the limbic system. Tied in with both the inner core (especially the hypothalamus) and the cerebrum, it is physically, functionally, and evolutionarily in the middle. Although possibly involved in more complex acts, it is primarily the center of motivation and emotion.

Limbic System and Psychosurgery The limbic system is related to the sense of smell for lower animals. For us, it is involved in emotional behavior and some crucial aspects of memory. Limbic-system structures, like the cerebrum in which they are embedded, come in pairs, each structure having a right and a left version (see Figure 2.13).

The **hippocampus,** named for its supposed seahorse shape, is involved in the storage of new memories. The surgical removal of both the right and the left hippocampus in one notable case caused a patient to be unable to store any new memories, though he could continue to locate old ones (Milner, 1959). He is said to be able to read the same magazine indefinitely, not remembering by the time he reaches any article that he has read it before. The **amygdala** seems to play a major role in the patterning of aggressive behavior and thus has been the object of surgery designed to reduce violent outbursts.

Any surgery designed to alter behavior, called **psychosurgery,** is highly controversial (Delgado, 1969; Valenstein, 1973, 1980). Its opponents feel that deliberate brain damage for behavioral ends is too extreme and too permanent a procedure, but its proponents feel that it offers a useful technique for helping people who cannot otherwise be helped. A national commission to decide whether to ban psychosurgery in fact ended a year's study with an endorsement, apparently agreeing that its potential benefits outweigh its potential abuses (Culliton, 1976).

Violent spells can result from an unusual type of epileptic seizure. People with epilepsy are subject to periodic seizures, which result from a wave of abnormal excitatory activity in the brain. This activity often begins at an area of brain tissue scarred from a prior injury but spreads out until the entire cerebrum is involved in a grand mal seizure, a kind of "great storm." As the seizure begins, the person often senses something wrong, such as a peculiar smell or feeling, called an aura. The seizure spreads across the cortex, producing random motor activity and a sensory jumble and ending with unconsciousness. Memory processes are also interrupted, so the epileptic may have only a vague recollection of the aura.

But seizures may be both smaller (petit mal) or more specialized. In one well-known case, a young woman experienced spells of unprovoked violence that frightened her as much as they did those around her. She was diagnosed as having temporal-lobe epilepsy. (The temporal lobe is the portion of the cerebrum just inside the temple; part of the limbic system lies inside it.) Left to herself, she might have killed someone; she was examined because of an unprovoked attack. She was normal nearly all of the time, and to lock her up as mentally ill would have been cruel—but such an outcome was likely. Instead, surgery was performed to destroy the area of the amygdala that was triggering the seizures (Mark & Ervin, 1970).

Limbic System and Motivation Many motivations and emotions are affected by the limbic system. Reptiles carry out even life-and-death behavior with what we see as calm detachment. One reason for their apparent lack of emotion is their lack of facial expression, but, more importantly, they probably don't have the brain structures with which to experience it, at least to the extent that mammals do—typically in close association with motivated behaviors. Anger goes with aggression, sexual excitation with mating, and so forth.

In fact, we may think of emotions as being the coded values placed on various experiences that have utility for survival (Routtenberg, 1978). Finding and eating food, for example, is necessary for survival. We speak of the tendency to do this, a tendency that gets more urgent if we remain unfed, as a *motive;* we call it hunger. But closely associated with this motive is the set of positive sensations involved in smelling, tasting, and eating food. In general, the greater the food deprivation, the more hungry we become and the more rewarding the eating sensations become.

Some kind of emotional experience is associated with all motives, apparently as a way of directing the choices that become possible with a complex brain and the ability to learn a range of behaviors. The frog automatically strikes at flies, but cannot adjust its aim slightly to get them, much less plan or carry out behavior to seek them; if the flies don't come by its nose, it doesn't eat. But mammals develop elaborate and lengthy behavior patterns in their search for food. They do so where the frog cannot, partially because of the guidance offered by the limbic system.

Probably the most important structure for the direction of motivated behaviors is the **hypothalamus** (or structure "below the thalamus"). The hypothalamus is central to a wide range of basic motivations, is important in control of the autonomic system, and is central to the system of glands called the endocrine system. (We will discuss its functions in more detail at several points later in the text.)

Autonomic System and Emotional Arousal Humans experience many emotions that have little apparent relation to basic survival motives; this reflects the complexity of our cerebrum. These "higher" emotions may be thought of as being superimposed on the basic ones, just as the cerebrum is superimposed on the limbic system. Before examining the cerebrum, however, let's look a bit more closely at how body resources are mobilized during a state of emotional arousal through the two halves of the autonomic system. ■ Figure 2.15

The sympathetic or arousal portion of the autonomic nervous system includes a chain of spinal ganglia lying just outside and along the length of the spinal column; these are clumps of cell bodies of the neurons involved. Axons of these neurons run out to various organs, sometimes through other ganglia. When the sympathetic system is aroused, the fight-or-flight response sends commands to all these organs at once, as a unified response to danger. Some organs, such as the heart, are activated in the fight-or-flight response; others, such as the intestines, are deactivated. (If you don't survive the next 10 minutes, digestion won't be needed anyway; if you do, it can be done later.)

The parasympathetic or relaxation system differs in several ways. It has no spinal chain of ganglia, for example, and it reaches the organs from nerves at each end of the spinal cord rather than along the full length. And it does not work in as integrated a way as the sympathetic system. The fight-or-flight response is a crash package, and in recovery the various systems go back to their own business at their own pace.

All the neural systems we have examined so far may be thought of as support for the one to which we turn next, the only system we know of that continues to struggle to understand its own workings: the cerebral cortex.

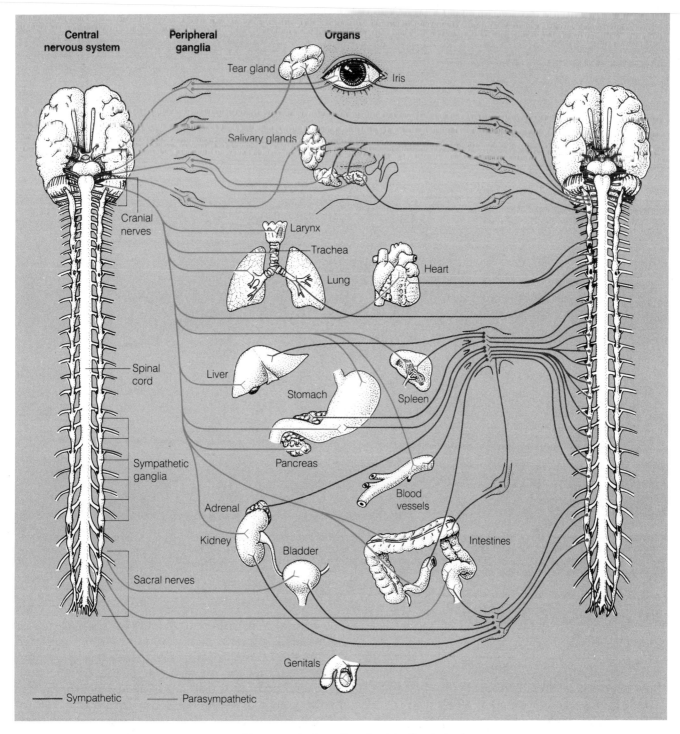

Figure 2.15 ■ The autonomic nervous system. The sympathetic portion stimulates the organs in a single, coordinated fight-or-flight emergency arousal; the parasympathetic portion returns them to conditions appropriate for quiet relaxed behavior.

Cerebral Cortex and Complex Behavior

The cerebrum is the most recent brain structure to evolve and the last to develop in an infant, reaching completion more than a year after birth. The complex-ity of the cerebrum makes possible consciousness or mind as we know it, based on the integration of many separate areas and subsystems (Cowan, 1979). Figure 2.16 shows some major landmarks of the cerebrum and Figure 2.17 shows how the cerebrum relates to other areas of the brain. You may want to refer back to

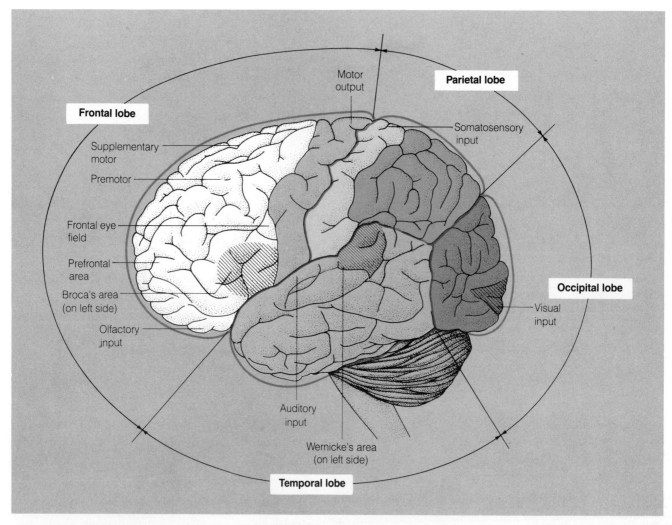

Frontal lobe

Motor output

Parietal lobe

Supplementary motor

Premotor

Somatosensory input

Frontal eye field

Prefrontal area

Occipital lobe

Broca's area (on left side)

Visual input

Olfactory input

Auditory input

Wernicke's area (on left side)

Temporal lobe

Figure 2.16 ■ Lobes of the cerebrum and some major functional areas of the cerebral cortex. The four lobes are defined by major fissures and are the same on both sides of the brain. The functional areas have generally parallel equivalents in the right hemisphere to those shown here for the left, except for the language-related ones, Broca's and Wernicke's areas.

these figures in the discussions that follow. ■ Figures 2.16 and 2.17

The Cerebrum and Its Cortex The outer layer of the cerebrum is called the **cerebral cortex** (Schmitt et al., 1981). The cerebral cortex is also known as gray matter for its pinkish-gray color. The cerebrum's synapses occur at the cortex, so this is where its actual communication takes place. The underlying part of the cerebrum is known as white matter for the white color of the myelin sheathing of the axons that make it up. These axons run from other parts of the nervous system up through the center of the cerebrum to the synapses in the cortex. From there, other axons go back down and out.

The **corpus callosum** is a band of tissue that joins the two halves of the cerebrum, known as the two

cerebral hemispheres (or, if the context is clear, just hemispheres). You see the corpus callosum in Figure 2.16 as it crosses from one side to the other, but within each hemisphere, on each side of this cross section, callosal neurons spread out to all areas of the cortex. The complete corpus callosum thus has a sort of double-fan shape, narrowest at the central point and flaring out on each side.

The most obvious features of the cerebrum's overall appearance are the complex folds and fissures (technically, gyri and sulci) that cover its surface. These folds and fissures develop prenatally as the brain grows and expands (Richman et al., 1975). Evolutionarily primitive mammals such as the opossum have smooth cerebrums, whereas more complex mammals have increasingly convoluted ones. The folding and fissuring increases the brain's surface area

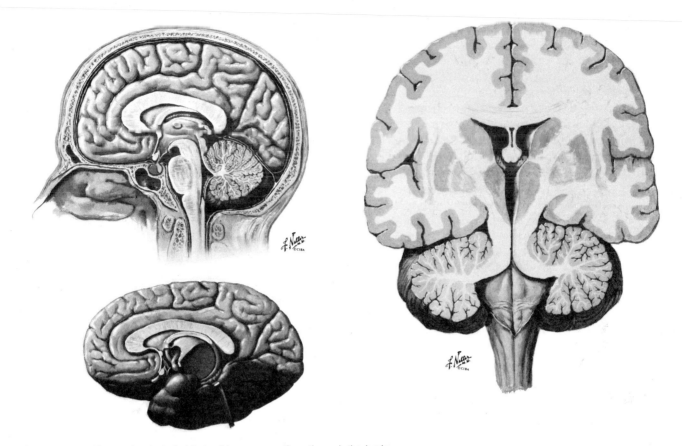

Figure 2.17 ■ Front-to-back and side-to-side cross sections through the brain.

(Adapted from an original painting by Frank H. Netter, M.D., from the THE CIBA COLLECTION OF MEDICAL ILLUSTRATIONS, copyright by CIBA Pharmaceutical Company, Division of CIBA-Geigy Corporation. Reprinted by permission.)

(the cortex) while minimizing increases in total volume, so the head does not become too big for the birth process. Flattened out, the cortex would form a sheet of about 24 by 36 inches.

The many blood vessels that supply the cortex lie both within it and along its surface. On the surface, they follow the fissures, making maximum use of all the space within the skull. This complex web of blood vessels brings the constant flow of nutrients and, more importantly, oxygen that the cerebrum needs: It uses 20% of the body's total oxygen use and will begin to die in two or three minutes if this blood flow is cut off. (Recent research suggests that the neurons of the cerebrum may not die this quickly, but that a change in artery walls occurs, such that restoring blood flow in the body after a few minutes may still not provide oxygen to the cerebral neurons; *Medical World News*, 1982.)

Discontinuing the supply of oxygen to the cortex causes problems such as strokes (also known as CVAs, short for cerebral vascular accidents). CVAs occur when a blood vessel ruptures or is blocked; reduced blood flow causes the cortex to malfunction, and inter-ruption kills it. The behavioral consequences of strokes are as varied as the functions of the cortex that they affect. Even comparatively minor strokes can be devastating (Dahlberg & Jaffe, 1977; Fein, 1978). Reduction of blood flow may also have other behavioral consequences. People faint sometimes if they stand up too suddenly because the blood flow is temporarily reduced. And the long-term reduction of blood flow caused by the buildup of deposits within the arteries is one cause of senile behaviors in the elderly.

Lobes and Functional Areas Traditionally, the cerebrum is divided into four major lobes or areas. Your **frontal lobe** fills your forehead; your **occipital lobe** lies at the very back of your head, just where your neck muscles join your skull. Your **temporal lobe** is just beneath your temple, and your **parietal lobe** makes up the rest.

In general, the more rearward and lower portions of the cortex serve sensory functions (Luria, 1970). Direct stimulation of these areas with an electrode may yield the sensation of a sight or sound, or may interfere with sensory processing. Information from the ears goes to the temporal lobe, that from the nose to the bottom of the frontal lobe, and that from the eyes to the occipital lobe (see Figure 2.16).

An important area for body control lies along each side of the central fissure that divides the frontal lobe from the parietal. Just to the rear of this fissure is a strip that receives **somatosensory** information: the position of limbs, touch, and so forth. Just in front of the fissure is a comparable strip for motor control of body parts. The cortex thus controls the somatic system by receiving inputs at the somatosensory strip and sending appropriate commands back down from the adjacent motor strip.

Only the left hemisphere is shown in Figure 2.16, but the right hemisphere has comparable somatosensory and motor strips. All four strips share a special arrangement of input and output information: Particular areas on the cortex correspond to particular areas of the body and areas adjacent on the body are also adjacent on the cortex. The hand somatosensory area, for example, is adjacent to that for the arm. Overall, the body is represented as if there were tiny human figures lying upside down on each of the four strips, with their feet tucked between the hemispheres and their heads down along the sides of the cortex (Geschwind, 1979).

■ Figure 2.18

Such a figure is called a **homunculus** (plural, homunculi); its shape is drawn so that the relative size of a homunculus part reflects the relative amount of cortex devoted to it. Animunculi, the comparable shapes for animals, show where sensory and motor emphasis lies for any species and are thus good clues to its behavior.

What does the shape of the homunculus tell us about our own species? Its enormous hands tell us that we can tell a great deal about an object by touching it with our hands, and much less with our elbows. And we can control our hands with delicate precision. People have inscribed lengthy prose passages on a grain of rice, using simple hand tools; with the aid of microscopes and special tools, neurosurgeons operate on brain structures too small to be seen easily with the naked eye. Such hand use is one of our major evolutionary advances, but it is the other important advance, the brain, that actually controls the hands.

And what of the enlarged face of the homunculus? Among other things it makes kissing a sensitive and pleasurable act, but that is only an incidental outcome. What is actually represented here is another major accomplishment of our species, that of complex speech. Not seen on the homunculus, but also represented by its large face, are internal structures such as the tongue and larynx. Using all these facial structures in speaking a sentence is one of the most complex motor acts you can perform.

Near the motor strip lie other motor-related areas (Figure 2.16). The premotor and supplementary motor areas help plan and carry out complex motor commands, and the frontal eye field helps coordinate head and eye movements, as in tracking objects while you are also moving.

Most other areas of the frontal lobe, as well as parts of other lobes, perform functions that are more difficult to specify and map. Direct electrical stimulation of such areas yields no perceptible effect—they have thus been called silent areas—but they certainly play an important role in our overall behavior. Some evidence from brain surgery and accidental brain damage suggests that the frontal lobes are important in at least some aspects of personality or mind.

One of the earliest forms of psychosurgery, for example, was one that you've probably heard referred to as a lobotomy. Technically called a prefrontal lobotomy, it separated the prefrontal area from the rest of the cortex, resulting in substantial changes in the patient's personality. Besides the intended reduction in aggressive behavior, the operation caused undesirable side effects, such as a reduction in other emotional behavior. (The person might not be as aggressive as before, but also might not seem as interested in *any* activity as before.) The point is that surgery in this area has effects on who the person is and in that sense on the mind. (See also Chapter 16.)

Other evidence shows that the frontal lobes are involved in making and carrying out plans, also a major part of what makes us who we are. Although many brain-damaged patients with severe performance deficits are able to make their way in the world, "frontal" patients may remain hospitalized for life (Gardner, 1975). Such patients may be capable of doing virtually all of the tasks they once did; but their will or initiative seems to be gone. They may not bother to do what they physically can do. They lie in bed all day, or if gotten up, they sit; to do anything else seems not to occur to them. In this sense, they are more tragically damaged than those with sensory or motor deficits, and their future seems more bleak. Obviously the frontal lobes are important, even if "silent" when electrically stimulated. It's just that what they do is too advanced to be easily noticed through stimulation.

Whether what you say is your own thought, or is read from a book, or is a repetition of what you have just heard, the same somatosensory and motor areas are involved. But other cortical areas are specialized for other speech functions. The most notable of these is the first cortical area to be correctly specified in terms of its function; it is named **Broca's area** after its discoverer (Geschwind, 1972). Damage to any of several brain areas can cause speech problems, but damage to Broca's area produces a characteristic pattern: The patient's speech is labored and halting, and in extreme cases, the patient is unable to speak at all. Broca was able, through autopsies, to find damage in this location in two such patients (H. Gardner, 1978). Another area involved in speech is **Wernicke's area;** we will discuss its function in Chapter 10.

The Split Brain and Its Implications

Most of us have had the experience of being confused for a second in a situation having to do with left or right, but we quickly recover. That brief confusion is a clue to a remarkable aspect of our nervous systems. The left and right sides of our bodies are each controlled primarily by one cerebral hemisphere. The apparent integration of our normal world is an achievement of cooperation between these two hemispheres, but we tend to be aware of the magnitude of this achievement only when it breaks down.

Integration of Left and Right Our bodies have three dimensions: top/bottom, front/back, and left/right. We are not likely to confuse the first two; our heads are different from our feet and our fronts from our backs. But in the right/left dimension we are symmetrical (Gardner, 1979). To move about successfully, we must maintain unambiguous control of these two symmetrical sides of our body. We could neither walk nor grasp were there any confusion about control of these sides, for they include both our legs and our arms (Corballis & Beale, 1976).

Difficulty in integrating the two sides seems to be characteristic of some behavioral problems, including those caused by brain damage or developmental difficulties. Children with **dyslexia,** for example, are those who show characteristic errors in reading that include letter reversals and other right/left problems. Such children often have difficulty coordinating the sides of their bodies and moving with respect to right/left in the world. They may have difficulty catching something thrown to them or may have bicycle accidents caused by turning toward an approaching car instead of away from it (Clarke, 1974). Dyslexia thus may reflect a failure to integrate left and right sides successfully (Witelson, 1977) (although not all researchers are convinced; Naylor, 1980).

Each area of the left cerebral hemisphere has a comparable area in the right hemisphere, to which it is connected by the corpus callosum. Comparable areas often have similar functions, but there are some important differences. One is that each hemisphere sees the *opposite* side of the world. The left half of the **visual field** (all you see that is to your left) goes to the right hemisphere, and the right visual field goes to the left

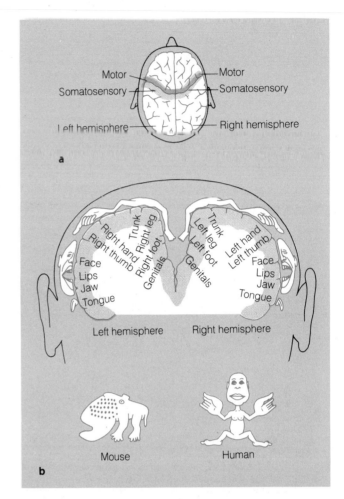

Figure 2.18 ■ (a) The somatosensory and motor strips of the cortex are arranged so that adjacent body areas are represented by adjacent cortical areas. The overall pattern of these cortical areas may be drawn as distorted shapes. (b) These animunculi and homunculi show how much cortical area is devoted to each body area. The mouse explores with its nose, and each whisker has its cortical area. We can use our hands for sensing, though we normally rely more on vision. The large face of the homunculus reflects the large cortical areas necessary for control of speech.

(**a**, reprinted with permission of Macmillan Publishing Company from *The Cerebral Cortex of Man* by W. Penfield and T. Rasmussen. Copyright © 1950 by Macmillan Publishing Company, renewed 1978 by Theodore Rasmussen; **b**, from *Mechanics of the Mind* by C. Blakemore, Cambridge University Press, 1977. Reprinted by permission.)

hemisphere. Only by communicating across the corpus callosum or by moving the eyes can both hemispheres see the entire field. ■ Figure 2.19

Other sensory inputs are also split, although not all show the same crossover from right to left. The right ear goes primarily to the left hemisphere, for example, but each nostril goes directly to the hemisphere on the same side. This may be because smell for us is not a sense that locates us in space the way vision and, to a lesser extent, hearing do (Kimura, 1973).

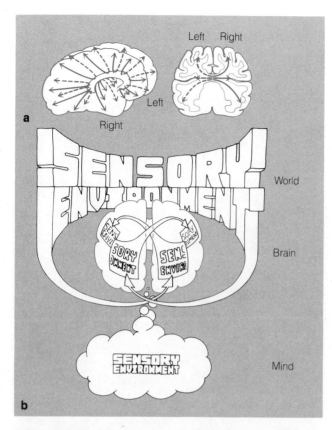

Figure 2.19 ■ (a) The corpus callosum connects each part of the left hemisphere's cortex with the comparable part of the right. (b) This arrangement allows each hemisphere to have access to the other hemisphere's visual half-field. We perceive an integrated world by somehow combining this information in our mind.

(Adapted from *The Integrated Mind* by M. S. Gazzaniga and J. E. LeDoux, Plenum Publishing Corp., 1978. Reprinted by permission.)

Each hemisphere also controls the *opposite* side of the body; nerve tracts cross over in the lower brainstem and then descend. The reason for the crossover remains unknown, but if vision crosses, so must motor control: The only way to control a hand accurately is to see where it is and what it is doing. The fact that visual *fields* cross over, not eyes, may be confusing—but just remember that the right hemisphere must see where the left hand is. In doing so it receives information from both eyes, which helps to give a three-dimensional view of the hand.

Not *all* body control, only primary or dominant control, crosses over. The major motor and somatosensory nerves that cross over are called *contralateral* or "opposite side" ones, but much weaker *ipsilateral* nerves run to the "same side." The ipsilateral connections allow the removal of one hemisphere in a young child, when medically necessary, without lifetime paralysis of the other side of the body; the ip-

silateral connections develop to allow full control of the body by the single remaining hemisphere.

The existence of these separate systems poses a problem: How is normal behavior integrated? One possibility is that the two hemispheres cooperate continuously, each moving one side of the body and keeping track of the other side through the corpus callosum. This doesn't seem very efficient, however. It is more likely that single-hemisphere control is used, at least when the whole body moves as a unit. This could be attempted through one hemisphere's contralateral and ipsilateral connections, but that also seems unlikely to yield a smooth performance. Perhaps the most likely possibility is that general action is commanded by one hemisphere but partially controlled by signals sent across the corpus callosum, with detailed motor commands sent from the other hemisphere.

Common usage in psychology refers to one hemisphere as "dominant"; this is usually the left hemisphere because most people show a preference for using their right hand. But the left hemisphere does not always command. For some performances it might not even play much of a role. The integration of hemispheres across the corpus callosum is normally so rapid and efficient that subtle tests are necessary to determine which hemisphere is active when. Such tests are only now being developed, and hemisphere research is still in its infancy.

The descriptions that follow give the roles of the hemispheres as they have been found for the average right-handed person with no prior brain injury or family history of left-handedness. For all others, including left-handers and the ambidextrous, the picture is more complex. Left-handers, for example, are *not* just right-handers with everything reversed. Their pattern of brain specialization is qualitatively different (Herron, 1979).

Splitting the Brain Most of what we know so far about the abilities of the right and left hemispheres comes not from studying normal, integrated people but from a small group of about 25 patients whose brains have been surgically "split" (Gazzaniga, 1975). Results of this research have become widely known—and widely misinterpreted; one writer has termed them the "fad of the year" (Goleman, 1977). Why are people so fascinated by these findings?

Severing the corpus callosum was originally undertaken as an experimental last-resort measure for the relief of epilepsy. None of the drugs that reduce seizure activity is completely successful, and some patients continue to suffer several life-threatening grand mal seizures a day. For such patients, almost any alternative that offers a possibility of relief, including surgery, is worth trying. One type of experimental surgery, first tried in the 1930s, was the severing of the corpus callosum in hopes of reducing the spread of the seizure from one hemisphere to the other.

The operation seemed to be successful, reducing the spread of the attacks sufficiently that drugs were able to suppress them. The first patients reported that they felt better than they had in years, and following a postoperative recovery period seemed able to function normally. By the 1940s, there had been a number of such operations, and neurologists were growing perplexed; the recovery seemed too good to be true. Millions of neurons had been severed and the patients seemed to show no functional loss. A perplexed humor was reflected in neurologists' response to the question of what the corpus callosum does: "It keeps the hemispheres from falling apart."

One researcher, Roger Sperry, began to look more closely at these patients, beginning in the 1960s (1964, 1968, 1982). What he found was remarkable, even shocking; his findings captured wide attention and led to Sperry's winning the Nobel Prize for Medicine in 1981 (Gazzaniga, 1981). The apparent "person" following callosal section turned out to be, he claimed, two different people inhabiting the same body at the same time (Springer & Deutsch, 1981)! Other researchers have since made the same claims (Gazzaniga, 1972), and the topic continues to be debated (Marks, 1981). What was it about these few **split-brain patients** that suggested so drastic a conclusion?

Sperry found that the patients' seeming normalcy was an illusion. Verbal responses were coming only from one hemisphere, typically the left; *it* reported itself to be just fine. But with appropriate testing, the right hemisphere could also be contacted—and it might disagree. How extreme the disagreement could be was shown when one split-brain man literally had to stop his left hand—by grappling with it with his right hand—from strangling his wife (Gazzaniga, 1970). All of us think sometimes that we are in internal conflict, but this is more like a horror movie than everyday life. Can such an aberration really tell us anything about ourselves? To decide, we must look more carefully at how such patients are tested and what has been found.

Testing Split-Brain Patients In a typical testing arrangement, the patient sits before a translucent screen with a narrow space below it. The researcher can project slides on the screen or can place objects in the patient's hands that the patient cannot see. Using this arrangement, one of the first things Sperry found was that one hemisphere no longer knew directly what the other was doing. If a slide was flashed so rapidly that the patient's eyes could not scan the whole screen, whatever was to the patient's left went only to the right hemisphere and vice versa. Without the corpus callosum to transfer information, each hemisphere knew only about its own half of the visual field. ■ Figure 2.20

Asked to point to something related to what he saw, a split-brain patient in this situation points simultaneously with both hands—at different pictures. *Each is correct because each is a valid interpretation of what was seen by the hemisphere that points the hand. But which of these apparently separate systems is "the patient"? The answer is a kind of paradox: both and neither. *Both* hemispheres together once made up the integrated patient who submitted to surgery. But separated, the hemispheres are in effect two people, each of which has half a body. *Neither* of them is exactly the person who submitted to surgery (though the left hemisphere comes closest).

How could the doctors—or the patients—have missed recognizing such a stunning outcome when the first operations were done? Why did the patients not awaken with a great sense of loss or separation? The answer lies in how we build our phenomenological world. Apparently, each of our hemispheres normally senses one half of the visual field and fills in the rest with information from the other hemisphere or by moving the eyes. Evidence for this comes from another split-brain finding. ■ Figure 2.21

Shown a portrait made up of halves of two faces, we see simply a grotesque image; if asked about it, we will describe it as such. If such an image is briefly flashed on the screen and a split-brain patient is asked to describe it, she will describe only the face the left hemisphere saw. But if asked to point with her left hand at what she saw, she points to the *other* face, the one that the right hemisphere saw (Blakemore, 1977). The patient does not verbally describe half a face, which is what her left hemisphere actually saw. She simply describes a face and reports nothing wrong with it. Her left hemisphere apparently assumes that the other half matches and somehow "sees" it as being present when it is not. Asked to explain why she pointed with her left hand to a different picture from the one she described, she may become confused or apologetic, but does not explain it as another experience having occurred to another brain or mind.

Apparently, then, this is why the patients never reported half of their selves as missing. This implies that they must not have directly sensed its presence before the operation, leading to the further suggestion that you don't either. You're simply not neurologically "wired" to experience the interchange between hemispheres.

A related finding with important implications concerns *cross-cueing*, one reason why the early patients

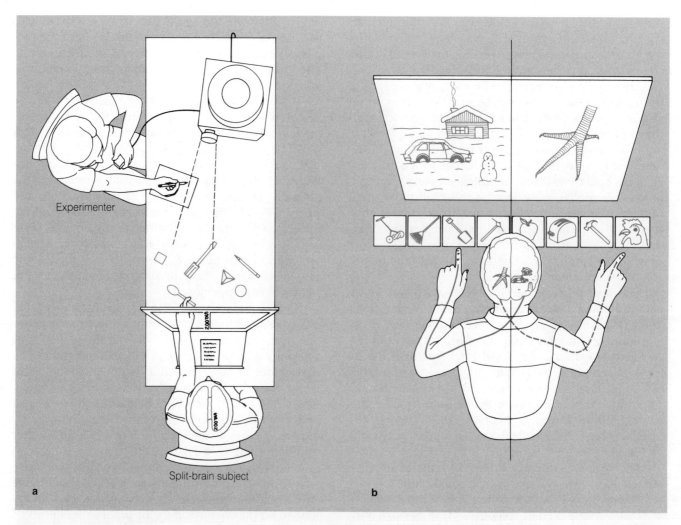

Figure 2.20 ■ (a) A general arrangement for testing split-brain patients. Slides may be projected on the screen in front of the subject; a hole below the screen allows objects to be handled but not seen. (b) A split-brain subject points at the drawing related to what he saw. Because the hemisphere received different drawings, the right and left hands point to different pictures, both of which are correct.

(Adapted from *The Integrated Mind* by M. S. Gazzaniga and J. E. LeDoux, Plenum Publishing Corp., 1978. Reprinted by permission.)

seemed so normal; their separated hemispheres quickly developed new ways of communicating. The hemisphere that knew the answer, for example, might point the eyes at it, because eye control is shared; the other hemisphere then could report what it was looking at. Other cueing seemed almost a nervous-system equivalent of kicking a bridge partner under the table: The left hemisphere would guess, then hesitate and say "No, I meant . . ." until its silent partner let it continue. Because only the cerebral hemispheres were separated, such communication might be conveyed by any of a number of lower systems. These could not convey detailed information as the corpus callosum had, but might transmit enough to convey a "yes" or "no" message in response to a guess.

The speed and ease with which cross-cueing develops attests to the behavioral flexibility of our nervous systems. But there is also an important mind/body implication. These cross-cueing systems were apparently *not* deliberate, nor even understood by the patients themselves; they would report things like "I just guessed" or "It seems like that might be the right answer." These adaptations worked on what you could loosely term an *unconscious* (or "out-of-awareness") level. Cross-cueing gives us an insight into how elaborate and adaptive behavior may be without needing to be conscious.

A further important finding is that the hemispheres differ in their skills and thought processes (Milner, 1975). The "two people" of a split-brain pa-

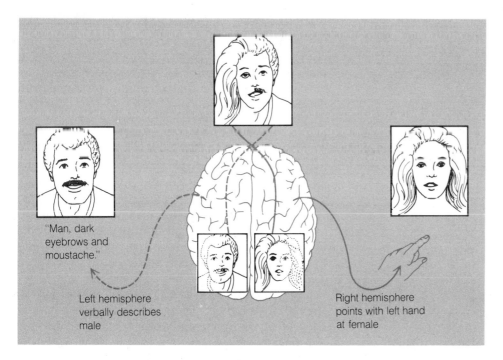

"Man, dark eyebrows and moustache."

Left hemisphere verbally describes male

Right hemisphere points with left hand at female

Figure 2.21 ■ A split-brain subject seems unaware of the missing half field, as if he or she were making up the missing half. The left hemisphere correctly describes the half face it saw, but describes it as if it were a whole face. The right hemisphere points with "its" left hand to what it saw.

tient have quite different capabilities. Each does well *some* of what the total person did before surgery, but each is incompetent at other performances.

In most people, the left hemisphere is the language specialist; it deals with most aspects of speech, especially the grammatical sequencing, and with nearly all aspects of reading and writing (Krashen, 1975). The left hemisphere also specializes in thought that is similar to language in some way, usually because it is specific, sequential, and orderly. The left is therefore the hemisphere of formal logic and any other step-by-step process. The right hand, operated by the left hemisphere, is typically used for skilled tasks.

Because the left hemisphere reports its thoughts verbally, it is easy to fall into the trap of thinking of it as the "real" person and the right hemisphere as a support structure. But simple tests show that even some tasks normally done with the right hand are directed by the right hemisphere. With the callosum sectioned, for example, the left hemisphere is unable to copy, with the right hand, even simple three-dimensional drawings such as a cube. The left hand, directed by the right hemisphere, produces drawings that are shaky from lack of practice, but correct.

The right hemisphere specializes in spatial arrangements (Witelson, 1976). It is basically the body-position-in-space expert. It also specializes in spatial thought; in addition to copying three-dimensional

drawings, for example, it recognizes faces (Blakemore, 1977). The right hemisphere also specializes in thought patterns that are similar to spatial ones: it is the hemisphere of intuitive logic and other nonlinear processes, seeking quick patterns and playing hunches (Nebes, 1975). ■ Figure 2.22

A sense of the right hemisphere as an organized entity comes from one of several examples of conflict between the hands in split-brain patients. One type of spatial puzzle requires arranging small colored blocks to match a pattern; this task is ideally suited to the right hemisphere and difficult for the left. When the left hemisphere was working on this task, the right hemisphere seemed to become so disgusted at the inability of the left to solve what for it was a trivial problem that it moved the left hand over, pushed the right hand out of the way, and took over the problem. The subject then sat on the left hand to restrain it.

The right hemisphere usually has a minimal understanding of language, apparently developed during the early language-learning days before the hemispheres developed their specialties. This allows it to be asked to "point at what you saw," for example, but it usually cannot speak or understand more complex requests. In only one case has there been an opportunity to question a right hemisphere about its thoughts. Gazzaniga and LeDoux (1978) described a boy whose left hemisphere wanted to be an accountant and whose

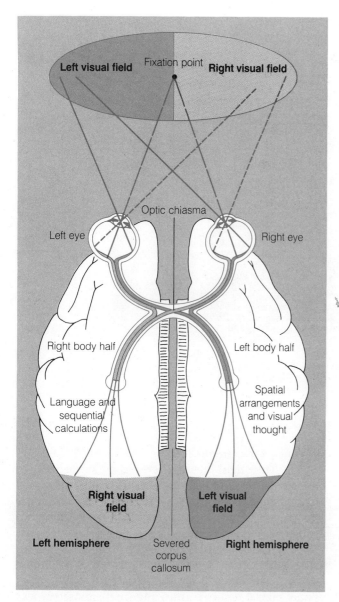

Left visual field   Fixation point   Right visual field

Optic chiasma

Left eye   Right eye

Right body half   Left body half

Language and   Spatial
sequential   arrangements
calculations   and visual
                          thought

Right visual   Left visual
field   field

Left hemisphere   Severed   Right hemisphere
                   corpus
                   callosum

Figure 2.22 ■ Summary of the specializations of the cerebral hemispheres.

right hemisphere wanted to be a race driver. These are, of course, excellent descriptions of the hemispheres' specialties. But, more important, this is the first "verbal" report from the right hemisphere, obtained by having it arrange letters to spell out words. Future work may tell us more about how it views the world.

The right hemisphere also has its own emotional responses; on one occasion when a slide of a nude woman was inserted into a sequence shown to the right hemisphere of a patient, she blushed and giggled.

But when asked why, she could only reply that something just seemed funny (Gazzaniga, 1970). The verbal reply, of course, came from the left hemisphere, which hadn't seen the picture. All it was aware of was the blush and giggle and the sensations associated with them.

Patients who have had the corpus callosum partially severed may show a variety of problems, depending on the location and extent of damage. One case has allowed partial disconnections to be studied when the damage was exactly known (Sidtis et al., 1981). It is the only case in which callosal sectioning was done in two stages: the rear portion of the callosum, which carries visual information between the occipital lobes, was severed first, but this was not enough to end the seizures, so the rest was cut. ■ Figure 2.23

When a word such as *knight* was presented only to the right hemisphere before the first surgery, the image of the word apparently simply transferred to the left hemisphere, which then read it aloud. After the partial section, that could not happen. Yet the patient was often able to figure out the correct word. Only when the sectioning was completed did the patient lose all ability to transfer information. What is remarkable about this case is the apparent transfer, across the front of the callosum, of processed information about the stimulus. It is as if the right hemisphere, which has seen the stimulus and apparently recognized it, is trying to explain it to the left by using associations, perhaps in the form of pictorial thought.

Taken as a whole, research with split-brain patients tells us that their two separated hemispheres function as quite different "minds," each with awareness of the environment, responsiveness to the experimenter, and emotional responses. These are quite remarkable findings, to be sure, but aren't such findings peculiar to brain-injured and surgically-altered patients? Our own minds are as integrated as our brains, aren't they? (See Robinson, 1982.)

Implications of Split-Brain Findings Split-brain research shows that particular behavioral specializations are physically located in different hemispheres. What it doesn't demonstrate is whether these hemispheres can function separately when the corpus callosum is intact. No one really knows yet just how the hemispheres of a normal person interact, but a provocative finding suggests that one hemisphere may have knowledge that is not accessible to the other, even with an intact corpus callosum. Injecting sodium amytal into the left carotid artery in the neck quickly puts the left hemisphere to sleep. Before the drug can put the right hemisphere to sleep, an object is placed in the left hand. On awakening, the patient cannot verbally describe the object, but can point it out with the left hand (Gazzaniga & LeDoux, 1978). Even granting that the input is highly abnormal—the brain does not normally sleep one half at a time—this implies that one hemisphere's knowledge may not be readily transferrable to the other. (See also Holtzman & Gazzaniga, 1982.)

Other research shows that the brain waves from the two hemispheres often differ in appearance. Researchers have been able to correlate one wave form, the alpha wave, with a relaxed or "idling" hemisphere. The relative amounts of this wave in the two brain waves change as different tasks are undertaken, apparently indicating which hemisphere is most involved in processing the task and which is relatively relaxed (Ornstein, 1978).

Such evidence argues strongly that the hemispheres can have different memories as well as different functional specialties even when the corpus callosum is intact. This evidence does not tell us how the mind integrates the different information or skills, but it offers a possible biological basis for many of the phenomena we experience, from handedness differences to intrusive thoughts (Kinsbourne, 1982). Future research may demonstrate which of the speculations that have been offered along these lines are factually based.

In the meantime, one major risk in interpreting these findings is oversimplifying them. Such shorthand labels as *language hemisphere* for the left hemisphere may obscure the fact that the right hemisphere typically has some language comprehension and may even be able to spell out words, whereas many lefthanders have substantial language use in both hemispheres.

But the total picture is even more complex, as we can see in the following example. The right hemisphere is typically the one concerned with music, in the sense of a tune as a pattern (Gardner, 1982b). And in normal speech, at the same time that Broca's area of the left hemisphere is commanding the string of words, the right hemisphere is adding the intonation pattern, the rising and falling "music" of speech. Right-hemisphere-damaged patients have been characterized as "talking computers," because they lose the intonation patterns (Gardner, 1975); they speak like Hal, the computer in Kubrick's film *2001*. Word commands from the left hemisphere and intonation commands from the right hemisphere must normally be integrated somehow, because they use the same muscles to produce one string of speech. Obviously, to attribute speech solely to the left hemisphere greatly oversimplifies the real situation. Only an under-

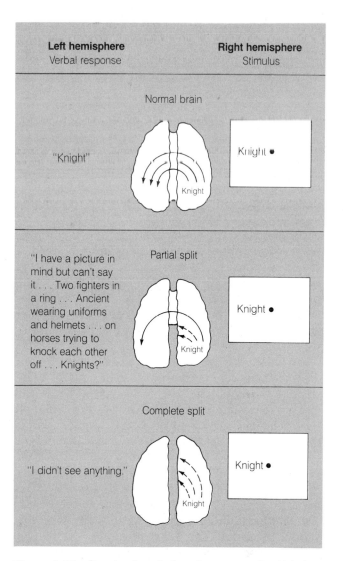

Figure 2.23 ■ Sample of results from the one case in which the callosum was sectioned in two separate operations, 10 weeks apart. With the rear of the callosum sectioned, visual information could not transfer, but some kind of processed information was apparently given to the left hemisphere by the right, perhaps through visual imagery.

(Adapted from "Cognitive Interaction after Staged Callosal Section: Evidence for Transfer of Semantic Activation" by J. J. Sidtis et al., *Science*, 1981, *212*, 344–346. Copyright 1981 by the American Association for the Advancement of Science. Used by permission.)

standing of such subtle relationships will allow correct interpretations of what actually happens.

People who stutter, for example, often sing without the least hesitation; one notable example is the award-winning country singer Mel Tillis. Apparently something about adding the right hemisphere's music control helps smooth the speech. Some therapists teach stutterers to "sing" their words, then to gradually reduce the "music." This may reflect a way of teaching them to use more right hemisphere speech control, or at least to integrate right and left control better. If the integration of hemispheres in normal speech control were better understood, it might suggest even more effective therapies.

The more that is learned about hemisphere differences, the more implications there will be for other areas of psychology. Many hemisphere differences, for example, seem to be learned, although these are probably superimposed on genetic bases. Right-handedness seems to be genetically controlled and left-hemisphere speech may very well be (Herron, 1979), but the ways in which children are taught to approach particular tasks is no doubt also important in how their brain specializations develop. Sex differences are often found in human performances and typically reflect a nature/nurture interaction. You ought not to be surprised, then, to find that sex differences in hemisphere specializations are an active area of current research (for example, deLacoste-Utamsing & Holloway, 1982; Goleman, 1978).

When it is understood when and how hemisphere differences develop, educational procedures to increase a variety of skills will follow (Bogen, 1975). But in the meantime, some well-intentioned attempts have been naive or misguided. One frequent misuse of the hemisphere data has been to think in terms of either/or. A criticism of what they see as the rigid, verbal thinking of the left hemisphere, for example, has led some people to advocate a shift to what they see as the more natural, loose, "creative" thinking of the right hemisphere. Such suggestions overlook what should be obvious but apparently isn't: the skills of both hemispheres are necessary; their balanced cooperation is desirable, not one or the other.

The right hemisphere *can* be creative when visual or intuitive thought is helpful, but it can also be wrong. Its quick pattern analysis is a kind of fast guess; it may reach a correct solution sooner than the plodding left hemisphere, but it may also jump to the wrong conclusion. So the left hemisphere must check the conclusion methodically and reject it if it's wrong. It has even been suggested that the right hemisphere may be the source of paranoid ideas, those that seem to see some plot against us. Hearing a sudden burst of laughter as we enter a room, for example, it may assume that people are laughing at us. Those people whom we consider "crazy" may include some who are unable to reject such right-hemisphere notions.

What you know now about the hemispheres may allow you to understand more about your own behavior—and maybe even to change it somewhat. ■ Personal Application: Can You Observe and Encourage Your Own Hemispheres?

ENDOCRINE SYSTEM

A **gland** is a body organ, a cluster of cells specialized to produce a chemical product. Some glands, such as the millions of sweat glands in the skin, secrete their products to the surface of the body; these are called exocrine glands, with the exo- signifying "outside." But another set of glands works closely with the nervous system. These glands secrete their products, called **hormones,** inside the body, usually directly into the bloodstream (Zuckerman, 1957). They are called **endocrine glands,** with the endo- signifying "inside" (Beach, 1975). Figure 2.24 shows the major endocrine glands, with a summary of their normal function and some possible malfunctions (Leshner, 1978). ■ Figure 2.24

The **pituitary gland** is enclosed in its own chamber within the skull, relatively isolated and exceptionally well protected. Known as the "master gland" because it produces many separate hormones and many of its hormones direct the output of other endocrine glands, the pituitary is actually two glands in one. Hormones produced by the anterior (front) lobe control the output of the adrenal cortex (the outer part of the adrenal gland), the thyroid, and the testes or ovaries. The posterior (rear) lobe receives hormones manufactured in the hypothalamus and brought to it through a connecting stalk, which it stores and releases as if they were its own. The posterior lobe also receives chemical releasing factors from the hypothalamus that control the release of at least some of the pituitary's anterior-lobe hormones.

The result of these arrangements is a complex interlocking of nervous system and endocrine system. The hypothalamus, a basic portion of the nervous system, is also an endocrine gland, producing hormones for use elsewhere and releasing factors for influencing the pituitary (Guillemin & Burgus, 1972). And the pituitary is a master endocrine gland that is also a storehouse for, and in some ways controlled by, the hypothalamus. It is thus not surprising that the search for the roots of behavior often leads from nervous system to endocrine system and back again (McEwen, 1976).

One example of nervous system and endocrine system interaction is *deprivation dwarfism.* Normal growth depends on growth hormone produced by the pituitary's anterior lobe. In some cases, however, children fail to produce enough growth hormone to achieve normal height. Normal growth can be achieved in these cases by injecting growth hormone (now being synthesized using recombinant DNA technology). Usually such failure to grow reflects a genetic problem, but sometimes children fail to grow for psy-

Can you observe and encourage your own hemispheres?

Even though evolution has not provided you with a way of sensing the interplay of your hemispheres directly, you may use your knowledge of their characteristics to seek them out. If you observe yourself carefully, you may be able to find things that you do with one or the other hemisphere, perhaps even at the same time.

Keep several things in mind as you try this. First, this is not a scientific experiment; it is a tentative exploration of how you function. But there is likely to be some truth to what you find, and the exploratory process itself may be useful as well as fun, focusing your attention on behaviors of which you may not have been aware. As you try it, keep in mind the major characteristics of the two hemispheres. For the average right-handed person, orienting the right visual field to a task, talking about it (even to yourself), or applying step-by-step logic probably reflects left-hemisphere activity. Orienting the left visual field or thinking about the problem in visual images or sudden "illogical" steps probably reflects right-hemisphere activity.

Left-handed or ambidextrous people may make the same observations, but probably won't find exactly the same patterns as right-handed ones. Visual fields and hand use will still represent the opposite hemisphere, but the packaging of skills by hemisphere may be different—not *opposite*, just different. Most left-handers still have speech centers primarily in the left hemisphere, for example, but most also have more speech development in the right hemisphere than do right-handers (Penfield & Roberts, 1959).

And what might you find when you carefully observe your own behavior, looking for hemisphere performances? I can only note some examples of what I have found. The trick seems to be to behave normally and then once in a while catch yourself doing something indicative. I have caught myself:

1 Driving to school with my left hand on the wheel and my line of sight pointed approximately at my rear-view mirror, so that my left visual field was centered on the road. My right hemisphere was thus apparently driving while my left hemisphere busily planned what I was soon going to lecture about.

2 Reading an article in *Science* while eating a hamburger and tapping in time to the restaurant's Muzak with only my left hand and left foot. My left hemisphere was apparently reading, my right bored and listening to the music. I don't know who was eating.

Some people have even claimed to be able to carry out two different tasks at once, such as practicing football while also studying (Haley, 1967). It's unlikely that you routinely experience this extreme a separation, but you may find that you do something like it.

Finally, you may want to try deliberately changing how you perform some tasks: for example, try some things with the left hand that you normally do with the right. One student who tried painting with her left hand found not only substantial changes in her style but also a kind of emotional release. It was as if part of her had been tied up and could now "come out," she said. After drawing with her left hand for some months, she not only felt less bound-up and more integrated, but also found she used her left hand for a variety of tasks for which she had not used it before.

The key to all of this is not to push too hard. Watch yourself and enjoy what you find, but don't be too concerned with whether it fits some pattern or whether you're doing it right. Similarly, if you try using your left hand, don't force it. If you really have a right hemisphere just itching to use that hand, it will feel comfortable to do so. If your left hand still seems relatively clumsy, that's fine. We all differ in many respects, and how we arrange our tasks by hemisphere is certainly one of them.

A final caution. The same rule holds for your treatment of others. If you are in charge of a child who prefers to use his or her left hand, let the child do so unless there are very good reasons to do otherwise. It is traditional in many cultures to force everyone to conform to the average right-hander's pattern, but this is now thought to be a possible cause of such problems as stuttering and even some forms of dyslexia. Gentle encouragement is the rule, with acceptance of what happens, both for yourself and others.

---

chological reasons. In cases of deprivation dwarfism, the ignoring or abusing of a young child affects the pituitary, presumably through the hypothalamus. The deprived child fails to grow, often seeming quite a few years younger than he or she actually is, and thus is "dwarfed" by experience. In a striking mind/body interaction, the child has responded to a lack of love with a change in body structure. A new environment with loving care has sometimes resulted in a dramatic resurgence of growth in these children without injected growth hormone (Gardner, 1972).

We will encounter other such interactions between behavior and the nervous and endocrine systems throughout the text. Given the physical linkages, such interactions might be expected to be the norm rather than the exception.

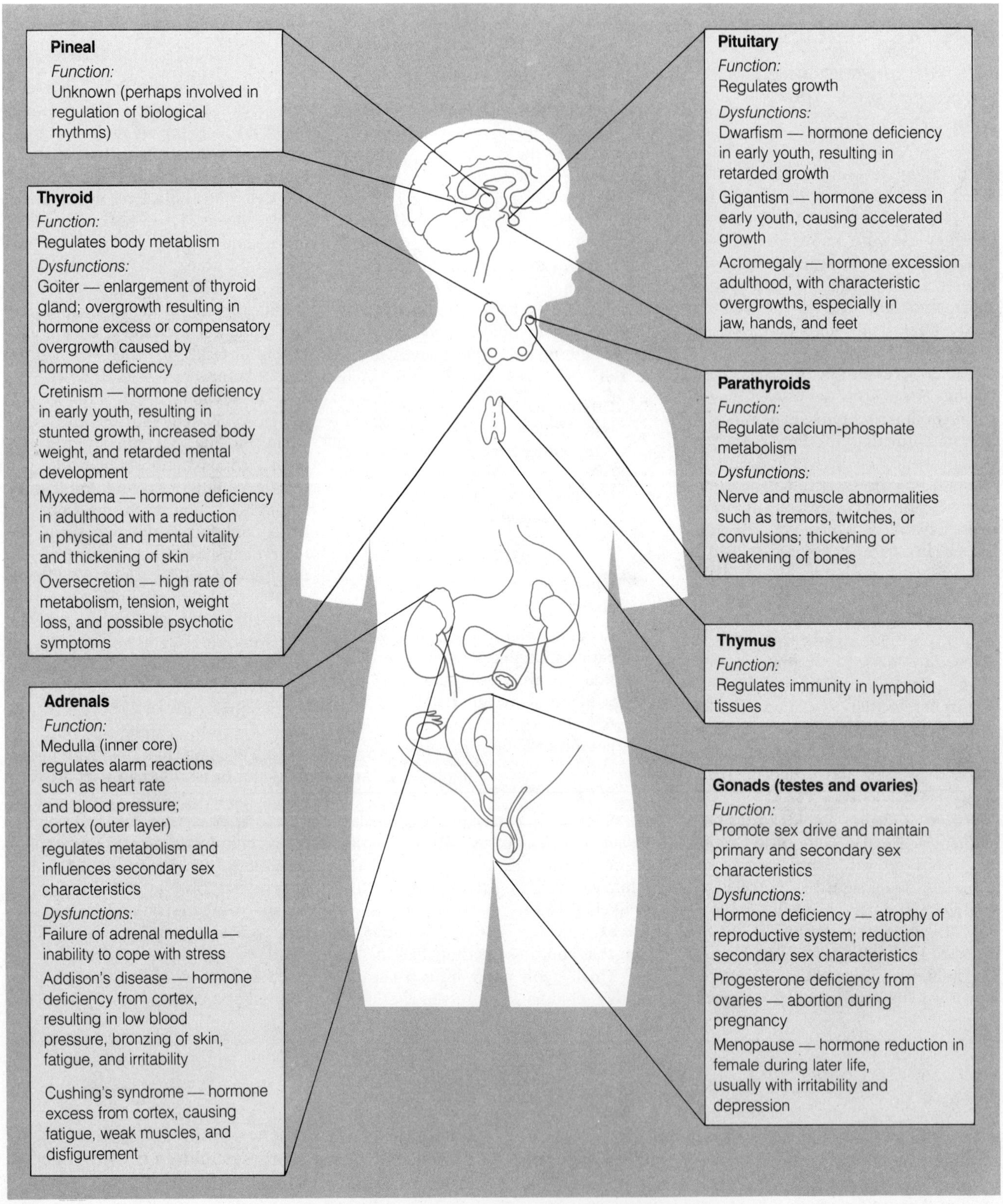

Pineal

Function:
Unknown (perhaps involved in regulation of biological rhythms)

Thyroid

Function:
Regulates body metabolism

Dysfunctions:
Goiter — enlargement of thyroid gland; overgrowth resulting in hormone excess or compensatory overgrowth caused by hormone deficiency

Cretinism — hormone deficiency in early youth, resulting in stunted growth, increased body weight, and retarded mental development

Myxedema — hormone deficiency in adulthood with a reduction in physical and mental vitality and thickening of skin

Oversecretion — high rate of metabolism, tension, weight loss, and possible psychotic symptoms

Adrenals

Function:
Medulla (inner core) regulates alarm reactions such as heart rate and blood pressure; cortex (outer layer) regulates metabolism and influences secondary sex characteristics

Dysfunctions:
Failure of adrenal medulla — inability to cope with stress

Addison's disease — hormone deficiency from cortex, resulting in low blood pressure, bronzing of skin, fatigue, and irritability

Cushing's syndrome — hormone excess from cortex, causing fatigue, weak muscles, and disfigurement

Pituitary

Function:
Regulates growth

Dysfunctions:
Dwarfism — hormone deficiency in early youth, resulting in retarded growth

Gigantism — hormone excess in early youth, causing accelerated growth

Acromegaly — hormone excession adulthood, with characteristic overgrowths, especially in jaw, hands, and feet

Parathyroids

Function:
Regulate calcium-phosphate metabolism

Dysfunctions:
Nerve and muscle abnormalities such as tremors, twitches, or convulsions; thickening or weakening of bones

Thymus

Function:
Regulates immunity in lymphoid tissues

Gonads (testes and ovaries)

Function:
Promote sex drive and maintain primary and secondary sex characteristics

Dysfunctions:
Hormone deficiency — atrophy of reproductive system; reduction secondary sex characteristics

Progesterone deficiency from ovaries — abortion during pregnancy

Menopause — hormone reduction in female during later life, usually with irritability and depression

Figure 2.24 ■ The major glands of the endocrine system interact with the nervous system in the development and maintenance of body structure and behavior.

(From *Abnormal Psychology: Current Perspectives,* Copyright © 1972 by CRM Books, 1972. Reprinted by permission of the publisher, Random House, Inc.)

CHAPTER SUMMARY

1 The evolution of brains, and thus of minds, reflects increasing central processing between sensory input and motor output, thereby allowing more flexible responses to the environment.

2 The brain has been studied in a variety of ways, including observation of injuries, surgery, and a growing number of noninvasive techniques.

3 The basic unit of the nervous system is the neuron, a body cell specialized for communicating information to other cells. A neuron conveys information by the firing of an action potential that travels out its axon toward the dendrites of another neuron and thus causes it to be more or less likely to fire.

4 Communication between neurons occurs at specialized junctions, the synapses. An action potential arriving at the synapse triggers release of a quantity of neurotransmitter, which acts as a key in a lock to influence the next neuron. Psychoactive drugs alter experience and behavior by interfering in various ways with synaptic transmission to increase or decrease its effects.

5 The nervous system is made up of many components; it can be discussed in terms of the central nervous system of brain and spinal cord versus the peripheral system, or in terms of further functional subdivisions.

6 The brain can be thought of as three layers: an inner core or reptilian brain that mediates survival and arousal, a superimposed limbic system or old mammalian brain that is important in motivation and emotions, and a further superimposed cerebrum or new mammalian brain.

7 Body movement is controlled by pulling on rigid bones with muscles in response to commands sent down the spinal cord and out over peripheral motor nerves to neuromuscular junctions on the muscles. The motor commands are integrated and smoothed through the cerebellum.

8 The two hemispheres of the cerebrum are joined by the corpus callosum; it links each area of cerebral cortex to the comparable area of the other hemisphere. Each hemisphere can be considered in terms of four major lobes, or in terms of specific functional areas, including those for sensory input and body control.

9 Split-brain patients, whose corpus callosa have been severed, have demonstrated differences in specializations of the cerebral hemispheres. These findings imply that all humans have similar specialized hemispheres that somehow integrate their capabilities to direct normal behavior. Understanding these hemisphere differences is a challenge, but one with significant potential implications.

10 The endocrine system, a set of glands that produce hormones, interacts with the nervous system in many body functions.

Further Readings

The best general introduction to a broad range of brain functions is Blakemore's *Mechanics of the Mind* (1977); done originally as a set of BBC lectures, it is very readable and has been beautifully illustrated. For overall information on the nervous system, see Bullock, Orkand, and Grinell, *Introduction to Nervous Systems* (1977). For separate articles on the brain, its development, functional areas, and so forth, see the special issue of *Scientific American*, September 1979, or the version of it reprinted as a book, *The Brain* (W. H. Freeman, 1979). Gardner's book on brain damage and its implications for psychology, *The Shattered Mind* (1975), although not quite as easy to read as Blakemore, is intended for a nontechnical audience; it offers many fascinating excerpts from case histories. Limbic system involvement in human aggression, including the use of psychosurgery to eliminate aggressive attacks, is thoroughly covered in Moyer's *The Psychobiology of Aggression* (1976). For coverage of split-brain patients and the implications of this work, see Gazzaniga and LeDoux's *The Integrated Mind* (1978) and Springer and Deutsch's *Left Brain/Right Brain* (1981). Those interested in handedness differences, including differences in hemisphere organization of left-handers, should see Herron's *Neuropsychology of Left-Handedness* (1979). For a thorough and well-illustrated text on all aspects of physiological psychology, see *Physiological Psychology* by Rosenzweig and Leiman (1982). For coverage of endocrines, see Leshner's *An Introduction to Behavioral Endocrinology* (1978).

Wandering through a museum, you pass a skeleton of a horse mounted in a dramatic rearing pose and are struck with how similar its bones are to human ones. Looking closer, you feel that you can find most of the same bones in the horse, although they are differently shaped and the feet are not like human feet. Wandering about the great hall, you look more closely at the other skeletons. With increasing excitement, you discover that many other mammals also share the same bones. With a shock you realize that the long and delicate wing bones in the fragile skeleton of a bat are finger bones, enormously elongated; the bat apparently flies with its hands! Suddenly you remember that whales are mammals, and you wonder. You peer at the great hanging skeleton of the sperm whale, one of the largest creatures ever to inhabit the globe. And, yes, there in its stubby flippers are the bones of a hand, the same bones as in the wings of the bat. And, you remember as you look down, the same bones as in your own hands. As you leave the shadowed hall, you wonder about the millions of years of evolution and your kinship with the other organisms whose bleached bones you saw. As you turn to go, a squirrel sits up on the grassy lawn and begins to eat a nut—holding it in paws that now look strikingly familiar.

This chapter explores some of the reasons why living creatures, including humans, look as they do and, more importantly, behave as they do. Later chapters will examine other reasons why we behave as we do; this one looks at humans as one of many species that have evolved over millions of years, and asks what that implies about our behavior.

EVOLUTION

Not only our hands, but all parts of our bodies have been shaped over millions of years by the process of **evolution**, the major unifying principle of contemporary biology. The principle of evolution states that the characteristics of all species—including our own—change to keep them fitted to their environments; species that fail to adapt die out. But unlike most species, which are specially adapted to particular environments, we have evolved to be generalists, able to live in a wide variety of environments. We are the species that most learns its behavior and is least constrained by built-in specifics.

But we remain a product of the millions of years of our history and of the species from which we evolved. We may learn to correct some problems medically, build mechanical limbs, create new senses, or make genetic manipulations. But we always do so with

Chapter 3

Evolution and Genetics

brains controlling hands in the service of motives—all of which have been shaped by evolution. We can no more escape our roots than a tree can. Our roots, however, are hidden in the remote reaches of prehistory, and the course of development of trunk and branches remains subject to debate.

In noting that we have evolved to be flexible, we are led inevitably to the nature/nurture problem: Our evolved nature fits together with the flexibility provided by nurture. The only appropriate resolution is in terms of interaction, the locking together of *both* nature and nurture to provide the actual outcome: humans are, it has been said, "100% nature *and* 100% nurture." We will therefore in this chapter go from consideration of our nature, as provided by evolution, to some elaboration of nature/nurture interactions. (Most other aspects of our development as individuals will be left to later chapters, especially Chapter 12.)

Processes of Evolution

Our understanding of how we came to be the species we are derives primarily from the work of one man, Charles Darwin. Some of the mechanisms of evolution, most notably genetics, were unknown to him, and the details of how some relationships develop remain currently arguable. But there is no question that the processes he described form the basis of evolution (Mayr, 1978).

Darwin's Theory of Natural Selection   **Charles Darwin** (1809–1882) was a young biologist of uncertain future when he was recommended in 1831 for the post of naturalist on the British exploration ship *HMS Beagle*. He was originally suggested as much because of his suitability as the captain's dinner companion as for any demonstrated skill as a naturalist, but the conclusions he drew from his observations on the five-year voyage have forever changed our view of ourselves.
■ Figure 3.1

Darwin's duties included collecting and sending to England samples of flora and fauna while the *Beagle* mapped the South American coast (Keynes, 1979). He also sent back many fossils, including some never before seen, but was most influenced by what he found in the Galapagos Islands. The Galapagos, off the coast of Ecuador, were a source of wonder to the young Darwin. Their fauna included some species not known elsewhere, but more impressive to him were the variations of common species, especially finches. Each island had one or more varieties that differed both from the finches of the other islands and from those with which Darwin was familiar. Each species was

definitely a finch, yet the shape of beaks and other parts and the behavior of each variety differed widely. How these differences could have come about, and why, greatly perplexed Darwin (Bingham, 1982).

For years after his return to England, Darwin struggled to put together what he had seen and wondered about on the *Beagle's* voyage: the incredible variation in plants and animals, including the special variations in the Galapagos; the fossils, some of them once ocean dwellers now located on high peaks; and the earthquake that notably altered the coastline where his boat was tied up. He also drew on Malthus's writings about population growth, English agricultural practice, and even the sport of breeding fancy pigeons (Mayr, 1977).

Darwin's conclusions were finally published as *On the Origin of Species by Means of Natural Selection* (1859). Only at the very end did he touch on human evolution, saying that the results of his work would have implications for it. But the uproar that followed publication centered on those very implications. "Descended from the apes! My dear, let us hope that it is not true," said the wife of the Bishop of Worcester, "but if it is, let us pray that it will not become generally known." Yet only in his later work did Darwin actually make the case for human evolution.

The central concepts Darwin proposed were as simple as the ensuing arguments were to be lengthy. Farmers and breeders of pigeons, he noted, shape the characteristics they wish their animals to have by **selective breeding**: selecting the members of the current generation most like the ones they want and breeding those. Beginning with the wild rock pigeon, English breeders had created over 300 exotic varieties. Similar selective breeding from a few originals had led to the varieties of agricultural plants and animals as well as domestic pets (Coppinger & Coppinger, 1982).

Darwin realized that a similar process might occur in the natural world without a human breeder to plan the outcome. His **theory of natural selection** proposed that natural forces could shape a variety of species from a common ancestor. The natural evolution of the Galapagos finches would thus be a parallel development to the deliberate breeding of the English pigeons (Grant, 1981). Darwin's proposal required only three basic elements: (1) variation, (2) selective life and death, and (3) lots of time. The variation of individuals is evident in all species; offspring are similar but not identical to their parents and each other (Ayala, 1978). Life and death in the natural world are also evident; its many dangers kill most wild animals while they are still relatively young. (The average life span of an animal in a zoo may be several times greater than in the wild.) The greatest danger is to the very young; in mammals, most of the young may survive, but in fish or crustaceans, one in hundreds or thousands may survive. But always, for all species, only some individuals of each generation live to be the parents of the next. And there has been plenty of time for even very slow processes to work. Darwin could see from the fossils he found, the earthquake he experienced, and other evidence that the earth must be many millions of years old, and not just a few thousand, as many of his contemporaries believed.

Darwin's proposal was simple but powerful. Of the many individuals in each generation, some will be better suited to the local conditions—which themselves change as the earth does—and on the average they will be more likely to survive. Over long times, the environment shapes, by life and death, the features of the creatures that inhabit it. The process is referred to as **selective pressure** on a trait, which is said to be "selected for" if it aids survival or "selected against" if it inhibits survival. Some species are altered by the process and others become **extinct**: they die out without leaving direct descendents (Ehrlich & Ehrlich, 1981).

In Darwin's time, the process of evolution was sometimes referred to as "survival of the fittest," but this phrase is no longer common because it is easy to misinterpret. For one thing, fitness here is defined by the environment. The ugliest creature or the one with the most disgusting habits, by our standards, may be "fit" in the sense that its life-style helps it to survive (Gould, 1982b). Beauty and grace work for some species, but others survive by their slowness and unattractive appearance. One tropical tree toad, for example, spends its entire day motionless on a leaf, imitating bird droppings, then carries on all of its active life at night (Tinbergen, 1965). This is not a very appealing life-style by our standards, but it does work.

Another problem with "survival of the fittest" is that it is not the sole mechanism for shaping species. Darwin's finches, for example, did represent adaptations to each island. But they also represented some chance factors; the characteristics of the first finches to reach a particular island also influenced the adaptation of their offspring. We will consider such accidental factors after looking at what Darwin emphasized: shaping by success.

Shaping by Success The concept of successful life-styles being passed on to the next generation was already part of the Zeitgeist of Darwin's time. But it was generally interpreted differently, in a way called Lamarckian after its major proponent, the French naturalist Jean Baptiste de Lamarck. To compare Darwin's and Lamarck's notions, consider the giraffe. An obvious adaptive characteristic of the giraffe is its height, including its long neck; this allows it to eat the tops of

Figure 3.1 ■ Charles Darwin (1809–1882) was a 22-year-old naturalist barely out of school when he set sail on the *HMS Beagle*. He is shown here at 31, four years after his return. *"Man with all his noble qualities, with sympathy which feels for the most debased, with benevolence which extends not only to other men but to the humblest living creature, with his god-like intellect which has penetrated into the movements and constitution of the solar system—with all these exalted powers—Man still bears in his bodily frame the indelible stamp of his lowly origin"* (1871, p. 920).
(Photo from the Royal College of Surgeons of England)

trees, which other animals cannot. Less visible are a host of other adapatations that support this neck, literally as well as figuratively. Arteries leading to the giraffe's head, for example, have special one-way valves to prevent blood draining back when it stands up suddenly, which would otherwise cause it to faint (Warren, 1974). How did the giraffe come to have such a neck?

Lamarckian evolution proposed the transmission to offspring of *acquired* characteristics. Each giraffe stretches its neck to reach the tops of trees, said Lamarck, and the necks of its young are longer because of the parent's neck-stretching. This is an intriguing idea that still recurs occasionally, but it is generally considered to be wrong (Lewin, 1981b).

Darwinian evolution, in contrast, proposes the transmission to offspring of approximately the parents' characteristics, but with variation. Then the best-adapted or fittest of the offspring survive, and the least fit die. The next generation again varies, but slightly differently. Each generation of giraffes would be of different heights, but if being taller aided survival, each new generation would be, on the average, slightly taller. The same rules apply to all features that affect survival; all species thus become adapted to their environments (Lewontin, 1978).

Attention has often been focused on the beauty and precision of the resulting adaptations. But one current theorist has emphasized some adaptations that are jury-rigged, yet effective (Gould 1978). It is most intriguing, he says, when the evolutionary process makes something that is less than perfect but nevertheless *works* well. Gould illustrates the point with the panda's thumb. The panda lives almost entirely on bamboo shoots, which it eats after stripping the leaves by pulling them between the main part of its paw and what seems to be a thumb. In fact, this "thumb," complete with its own muscles, is an overdeveloped sesamoid bone—a bone we also have but, for us, is small and hidden in the wrist. It might have been a better design to have used one of the panda's "fingers" as a thumb, as we do; but the evolution of the panda adapted the sesamoid bone instead. It may not be ideal, but it enables the panda to eat its fill of bamboo—and survive. Our own ears reflect a similar adaptation. They utilize the smallest bones in our bodies as part of their sound-transmission system, bones that evolved from part of our ancestors' jawbones (Crompton & Parker, 1978).

An especially striking example of adaptation is found among the anglerfish. What must originally have been a projecting bit of tissue for other purposes has evolved into a fishlike lure. The anglerfish uses it to attract other fish close enough so it can eat them—and survives (Pietsch & Grobecker, 1978). ■ Figure 3.2

Although adaptations that occurred in the past obviously cannot be experimented with today, this adaptation-by-success mechanism itself can be explored through both laboratory experiments and ongoing natural experiments. The most famous of the latter is the shift in the color of England's peppered moth over the last 100 years. The peppered moth comes in two varieties, mottled gray and black. Much of the moth's time is spent sitting on the bark of oak trees, where its mottled gray color is an excellent camouflage; black ones are quickly spotted by birds and eaten. During the industrial revolution, however, soot blackened the trees, so the black moths blended in and the gray ones lost their camouflage. As the birds

Figure 3.2 ■ The more than 200 anglerfish species have evolved flexible appendages used as lures combined with a body camouflaged to look like a rock. This particular species has a lure so fishlike that it has imitation fins which ripple as the lure is swept back and forth. Fish attracted to the lure as a seeming source of food are captured and eaten by the anglerfish.

(Photograph by David B. Grobecker. T. W. Pietsch and David B. Grobecker, *Science* Vol. 201, 28 June 1978. Copyright 1978 by the American Association for the Advancement of Science.)

ate more gray moths, gray became the rare color and black became common. In more recent years, as the pollution decreased, the colors have shifted back toward their original ratio (Bishop & Cook, 1975).

Similar adaptations cause continuing problems in species deemed pests. Where poison is regularly used, the few who are resistant survive to develop a new resistant population. Insects have thus become resistant to DDT and "super-rats" have become resistant to the poison Warfarin.

There is one subtlety of this success shaping that we need to note, lest we be misled when we compare human behaviors to those of other species. **Homologous parts** may differ in form, but they derive from the same common predecessor. The forefeet of most mammals, for example, contain essentially the same bones as do your hands, all apparently derived from a common ancestor. But these have since been adapted to many purposes (Lorenz, 1974). ■ Figure 3.3

Analogous parts, however, have evolved independently; they function similarly but have quite different antecedents. Thus, the panda's thumb is analogous to our own. And the human eye is similar to that of an octopus, but these eyes are also analogous; they reflect similar demands of the environment—the physics of light and the informational needs of organisms—rather than common ancestry. If we find

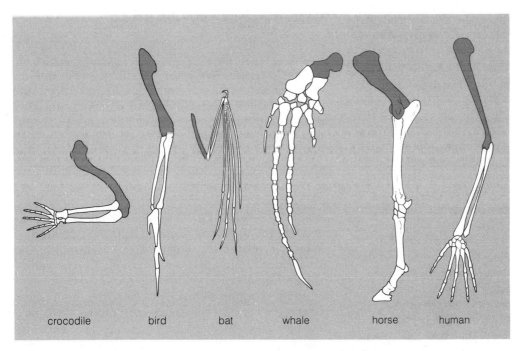

Figure 3.3 ■ These limbs are examples of homologous parts, ones that share a common ancestry. The crocodile is closest to the ancestral type, and in a sense we are more similar to its form than the others shown. The bird's and bat's wings, the whale's flipper, and the horse's hoof seem less similar to the crocodile, though all differ in many respects.

(Bat limb adapted by permission from *Heredity, Evolution and Humankind* by A. M. Winchester. Copyright © 1976 by West Publishing Company. All rights reserved. Other limbs from *Invitation to Biology*, 3rd ed., by H. Curtis and N. S. Barnes, Worth Publishers, New York, 1981, p. 478.)

an apparent similarity in structure or behavior between humans and another species, we need to know if it is a homologous or analogous one in order to know what the comparison can tell us about ourselves.

Although these examples focus on structures, remember that structure and behavior are always interlocked (Lorenz, 1958). A wing is not a wing unless its possessor flies with it, and an eye implies seeing; the behavioral repertoires of bats and whales differ as much as their "hands." But behavior leaves relatively few traces in the fossil record, and much of the study of evolutionary processes has focused on body structure. In living species, however, behavioral relationships can be found that are similar to those noted for body parts. Different species of ducks, for example, show mating behaviors that are homologous, derived from a common ancestor; penguins and seals swim in analogous fashion, reflecting the physics of moving in water.

The origins of *behaviors*, of course, are the important questions for a science of psychology. And *learning* to behave is characteristic of most complex species; not only do structures and behavior patterns evolve, but so does the ability to learn. The nature/nurture problem is not restricted to our species, but itself reflects our ties to other living beings.

Another point to remember is that limbs, brain, and behavior, including learning, all evolve together. Each generation must represent a successful package; a new step cannot be seriously maladaptive or no offspring would survive. "What good is half an eye?" it has been asked. The answer is that it was good for something else until it became capable of some sight, or at least it was *not* harmful.

Shaping by Isolation and Drift Many evolutionary theorists once assumed that all characteristics of an organism have been selected because they offered a survival advantage. But it has gradually been realized that many evolutionary changes, especially at the molecular level, may be neutral rather than advantageous (Kimura, 1979). They simply reflect chance factors.

A **species** is usually defined as a group of organisms that interbreed within the group but not outside it. Cross-species matings may occur under unusual conditions, but either the offspring are sterile or the occasions are so infrequent that the groups do not intermix. How then can one species give rise to two or more? What can separate a species into groups that no longer interbreed? The arguments over how many ways this can occur continue, but one accepted major cause is geographical isolation. Darwin's finches, for example, began with the finches that happened to reach the different islands, from wind currents or floating debris. The local conditions then shaped their descendants into different species (Boag & Grant, 1981).

Many slow and rapid earth changes act to separate groups of a species so that they develop separately. The continuous shifting in position of the earth's crustal plates over millions of years has split apart continents that were formerly united, creating a separation that leads to new species. Earthquakes may separate populations overnight.

If the separated groups are large enough, they may begin with essentially equal populations. But if only a few individuals are isolated, as with the finches, what the later species will be like depends in large part on what these few were like. In humans we find occasional similar examples; the native inhabitants of some Pacific islands, for example, share characteristics that reflect their few founders. There are also groups of people who all suffer from an inherited disease that can be traced to a single ancestor.

A final mechanism that may spread a characteristic in a population, independent of its adaptive character, is called "drift." Characteristics of some ancestors of a group drift across the whole population through random interbreeding. Such drift helps maintain variability in the species, which helps the species as a whole, but the particular characteristics need have no survival value for those who have them. Human blood types, for example, are not uniformly distributed around the world; some types are more recent than others and are more common in areas close to their presumed point of origin (Kan & Dozy, 1980). Large numbers of such characteristics are known. It has even been noted that the paths of conquest of famous armies can be traced through their physical characteristics in the populations of the conquered areas (Winchester, 1976).

We will look at the genetic basis for such characteristics a bit later. First let's look briefly at what is known about the evolution of one particular species, our own.

Human Physical Evolution

In evolutionary time, our species is exceptionally young. You often hear the dinosaurs disparaged as failures, yet they were the dominant organisms on earth for many times longer than we have been human, and their direct descendents remain as the birds (Bakker, 1975). Whether we will be more successful than they, in the sense of long-term survival, remains to be seen. We are, however, a unique species. A very large number of species have developed, flourished, and died on this planet, but none of them has ever developed such a brain as ours. The others have adapted by their basic physique, together with appropriate behavior. We are alone in using our intelligence to reshape the world to suit us, and in transmitting the knowledge of how to do so externally to later generations through culture.

In seeking to discover just how this uniqueness developed—and just what makes us unique—we have examined both living creatures and fossil remains. The probable evolutionary relationships we find are displayed in diagrams called evolutionary trees.

Evolutionary Trees   Some 4.6 billion years ago, our planet was born out of interstellar dust. Within the next billion years, life began in the seas of the new planet. The earliest life consisted of organic molecules that could reproduce themselves; similar molecules have been generated in the lab by passing electrical shocks (to simulate lightning) through a mixture of gases that represent the atmosphere above the early seas (Dickerson, 1978). Only during the last fifth of the total time of life on earth have multicellular organisms existed; but once they did, their evolution was comparatively rapid (Valentine, 1978).

The course of that evolution is usually studied by examining fossilized skeletal remains after dating them by a number of techniques (Shipman, 1979). Most frequently found are the hardest bones, the teeth, from which a striking amount of information can be obtained (T. White, 1981). For early humans, tools are also useful, as are the marks made on animal bones by those tools (Lewin, 1981a, 1981c). There are other rare finds, such as the 3.5-million-year-old footprints recently discovered (Hay & Leakey, 1982), and there are more exotic techniques. Coprolites (hardened excrement thousands of years old), for example, can be dissolved and analyzed, yielding such components as pollen grains; these can indicate what plants grew in the area and even the season of the year (Bryant & Williams-Dean, 1975).

Such analysis, however, soon yields more specific information than anyone can easily keep track of. One major conceptual technique for summarizing evolutionary relationships among species is the **evolutionary tree**; its roots are the early life forms and each branch is a separate species splitting off from the others. (Figure 3.4 shows such a tree, turned on its side for convenience.)

The tree diagram reminds us that all current species are equally evolved. Opossums, sharks, and cockroaches, for example, species often thought of as primitive ones, have been evolving for as long as we have. They may not have changed as rapidly as we, but that says that they were already successful as they were. The tree diagram also tells us that we did *not* "descend from the apes"; the apes and we have a common ancestry, but we have each gone our own way since we separated.

The general form of the evolutionary tree is widely accepted. But as you look closely at the relationship of the branches, especially those of the species that led to ours, you find more controversy (Holden, 1981). A number of theorists have proposed trees with different arrangements of branches. The available skeletal evidence is so slight that these alternate proposals all seem possible, and a single new find may suggest further rearrangements (Pilbeam, 1978). The picture of our past is becoming gradually clearer, but it may never be completely clear. We know we *had* ancestors and something about who they were, but they may never be more to us than the blurred photos in a family album found in the attic.

Looking at our immediate predecessors, the pictures become somewhat clearer, and we begin to obtain a few glimpses into their lives. With the Neandertals (formerly called Neanderthals), we find our first definite evidence of humanity: the grieving burial of a loved one—and interpersonal violence.

Neandertals   About 50,000 years ago, in a cave in what is now Iraq, a ceremonial burial took place, with the deceased carefully laid on a bed of branches and covered with flowers. The grave lay untouched until its discovery in this century. It contained no great riches, not even any simple artifacts, but it nevertheless was an important find: the earliest known example of an intentional and apparently loving burial. It is the earliest evidence we have of a cultural practice that seems to be exclusively human.

The deceased and those who buried him were not exactly humans as we think of ourselves, however. They were the same species as we, but a different subvariety, *Homo sapiens neandertalensis*; we are *Homo sapiens sapiens*. (*Sapiens* means "thinking.") They are usually called simply **Neandertals** after the Neander valley in Germany where their remains were first found.

The Neandertals were much more powerfully built

"I've been trying to trace my roots, but after a couple of generations, they go off into a different species."

(© 1980 by Sidney Harris–American Scientist Magazine)

than we are (Trinkaus & Howells, 1979), but their brains were as big as ours and their appearance probably not too different (Rensberger, 1981). The cave of the flower burial also showed us evidence of two other human abilities—the power to kill another person with weapons and the capacity to care for the helpless. Among the other skeletal remains in the cave was a rib that shows the mark of a spear, which killed the individual; it is the earliest unequivocal evidence for the killing of one person by another (Trinkaus, 1978). The skull of another male shows a flattened left temple, almost certainly the result of a powerful blow from a weapon swung by a right hand. Yet the skeleton of the head-injured one tells us about their compassion as well as their passion. He was partially paralyzed by the blow; his right leg and arm show the atrophy of disuse that resulted. He could never have survived on his own in such a condition, yet he lived a number of years after the injury; the only explanation is that the others must have fed and cared for him. If our distant past is a violent one, it is also a caring one. These skeletal remains tell of love as much as of murder.

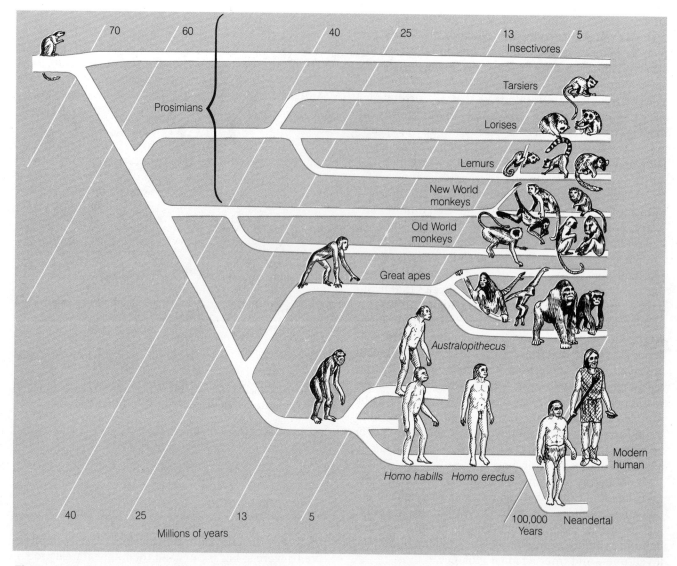

Figure 3.4 ■ An evolutionary tree for the four families of primates: prosimians, monkeys, apes, and us. This general form is widely accepted, although the details of dates and branches, especially of those for humans and apes, are still debated.

(From *Origins* by R. E. Leakey and R. Lewin, E. P. Dutton, 1975. Reprinted by permission of Rainbird Publishing Group, London.)

The place of the Neandertals in our family history is one of the arguments still going on. They may be a direct ancestor or they may be a parallel branch that died out. But some time around 40,000 years ago, our species became essentially what it is today. We have continued to develop varieties, (Howells, 1960), but all of these are variations on one species (Cavalli-Sforza, 1974). How did this happen? What did it take for us to become what we have become? We can begin with the relationships between ourselves and the great apes.

Primates, the Great Apes, and Us The primates evolved from more remote ancestors into four

"families," beginning about 70 million years ago (Leakey & Lewin, 1977b). The line leading to humans separated most recently, diverging from the line leading to the great apes (including the chimpanzees and gorillas); these are thus our closest relatives. ■ Figure 3.4

You might expect that we share few characteristics with the great apes after millions of years of separation—but you would be wrong. Studies of biochemical similarities among species have provided consistent and striking findings (for example, Yunis & Prakash, 1982). Despite superficial similarities between them, the great apes differ from monkeys more than they do from us! (This represents the longer separation time, as shown in Figure 3.4.) As Darwin remarked, "if man had not been his own classifier he would never have thought of founding a separate order for his own reception" (Washburn & Moore, 1974). ■ Notable Quote: S. L. Washburn and Ruth Moore on The Great Apes and Us

Among the biochemical analyses conducted have been comparisons of DNA (the basis of all heredity), blood chemistry, and immune reactions, all of which give similar answers. Consider the structure of hemoglobin, the oxygen-carrying protein of the blood, as an example. Hemoglobin comes in two forms, one with 141 amino acids strung together as a chain, the other with 146 units. Of these 287 amino acids, there are 43 differences between us and a horse, 12 differences between us and a monkey, 2 differences between us and a gorilla, and no difference whatever between us and a chimpanzee! (At least one young zoo chimpanzee has been saved by a transfusion of human blood.)

Studies of chimpanzees have also seemed to find some similarities to human behaviors; their ways of caring for infants, facial expressions, and aggressive behaviors can seem very humanlike (Van Lawick-Goodall & Hamburg, 1974). But Washburn, noting the biological similarities, has also pointed out the dangers in too-easy comparisons of ape and human behavior (1978b). The study of chimpanzees and other apes can tell us a great deal, but only if we are careful in the questions we ask and how we go about asking them.

Washburn and Moore also argue that 5 to 10 million years ago is a more likely time for separation than the often-quoted 20 million. But all such estimates include some assumptions that cannot easily be tested, and dates on proposed evolutionary trees differ as much as the branches do. In any case, 5, 10, or even 20 million years is a very short time in evolutionary history. Imagine a stop-action movie film, with one photo taken each year over the last 757 million years and the set of pictures then run, 24 each second, as a movie. The resulting film would take a year to show. Multicellular life would appear in April, plants in July, and amphibians in August. Dinosaurs would dominate for part of September, October, and part of November. Birds and mammals would begin to appear in November and would become dominant in December. The first primitive humans would not make an appearance until noon of December 31. It would be 11 P.M. when stone tools appear, and 11:55 before the first civilization. 1 A.D. would occur only 1 minute and 17 seconds before the end of the film. Compared to the dinosaurs' 2 months of supremacy, we have been in existence less than 12 hours, and in civilized form barely 5 minutes!

For those last minutes, we have probably been essentially the species we are now. Four important features differentiate us from our ancestors and from the great apes: (1) we have a fully upright posture and are bipedal (walk on two legs); (2) we have fully opposed thumbs and great hand dexterity; (3) we have an enormously enlarged brain; and (4) we have used the first three to develop a complex technological culture. The physical features seem to have evolved gradually to make us the species we are by 40,000 years ago (Washburn, 1978a). Their application to develop a culture began slowly, but as it built upon itself cultural development speeded up more and more rapidly. Once a certain pattern of chipped-stone arrowhead might have been made without change for generations; now each day brings changes that affect our lives. Once we survived and evolved by gradual body change, but we will live or die in the future by this invention of rapid cultural change.

Bipedalism seems to have been the first major change (Gould, 1979b). Monkeys live mostly in trees and all four limbs are adapted for climbing. Even some of the apes are remarkably adept at this; the gibbon, for example, can leap 30 feet from one branch to another and grab a bird in midflight. Chimpanzees can also climb, but they are less agile than gibbons. On the other hand (so to speak), they can briefly walk and run on two legs, even at times carrying objects in their hands. Their usual gait, however, is semi-bipedal with the back of their hands touched down for balance, called "knuckle walking." We humans do something like this when we line up to play football, but our

---

NOTABLE QUOTE
S. L. Washburn and Ruth Moore on the great apes and us

❝ Man and chimpanzee proved to be as close as sheep and goat, two species that had always been regarded as very close. Man and chimpanzee are more closely related than horse and donkey, cape buffalo and water buffalo, cat and lion, or dog and fox. Thus we are much nearer to the chimpanzees than to the monkeys many had believed to be our immediate ancestors. . . . Science long has known that all men basically are alike under the skin. The new genetics and molecular biology includes the anthropoid apes in this category of internal likeness and outer difference. The visible, widely advertised differences are turning out to be outer and relatively recent❞
Washburn and Moore, 1974, pp. 11–13, 23

a

b

c

Figure 3.5 ■ Our posture changed as we came out of the trees and began to walk upright. (a) A mother gibbon and baby swing through the trees. A chimpanzee walks upright for a short distance to carry food, but the knuckle-walk position (b) is more typical. (c) Chimpanzees can make and use simple tools, such as the stick shown here, used to probe a termite nest and pull out and eat termites.

(**a**, Field Museum of National History; **b**, Brian O'Connor; **c**, J. Moore/Anthro-Photo)

relatively short arms make it impossible for us to run that way; we have become fully upright. The advantages of upright posture are many; for example, the higher position of the head provides a larger field of vision. ■ Figure 3.5

The ability to carry objects allows food to be brought to places other than where it is found, perhaps to be shared with others (Isaac, 1978); this is a neces-

sary first step for a fixed-base village. Chimpanzees have a very limited ability to carry things; they move continuously, eating food where they find it and sleeping where they happen to be at dusk. With the forelimbs freed of the need to act as legs, the front feet could develop into hands, better adapted for grasping and carrying (Giacometti, 1978; Napier, 1980). As hands developed, carrying and using tools also became important (Butzer, 1977). Bits of stone and bone as much as 2 million years old are thought to be the early tools of our ancestors, though their simplicity makes it hard to tell the difference between naturally broken objects and deliberately made tools (Pfeiffer, 1980).

The ability to carry is also useful for tending relatively helpless infants, especially if you don't have much fur for them to hang on to (Lancaster, 1978). A baby gibbon can hold on while its mother swings through the treetops, and presumably so could our ancestors' infants. Human infants still show a form of grasping reflex, but they lack the strength and their mothers lack the fur, so they must be carried.

Once bipedalism and hand use set the stage, the major physical change that characterizes us occurred: the enlargement of our brains (Lewin, 1982). A gorilla skull, although much larger overall than ours, is mostly jaw, with a crest on top as a mounting point for the massive muscles of that jaw. The gorilla's brain volume is only about 500 cc, whereas that of modern humans is about 1400 cc; the fearsome appearance of a 400-pound gorilla thus hides a brain one-third the size of yours. Most of us are familiar with the science-fiction stereotype of big-headed humans of the future. But in comparison to our ancestors, we *are* the big-headed humans of the future (Jerison, 1973). ■ Figure 3.6

Before we could use these new brains to control our new hands and build a civilization, however, we had to survive a crucial problem. The upright posture of bipedalism works best with a narrow pelvis, like that of Lucy, the most complete australopithecine skeleton found to date (Johanson & Edey, 1981). But how can there be an enlarged brain and at the same time a narrow birth canal through which the infants' heads must pass? What happened was that the pelvis did get somewhat larger, especially for females (Figure 3.6b). But this was not nearly enough; to allow the increase in head size we actually achieved, another important change occurred. What seems to have happened is that the infants who survived to become our ancestors were those who were born early. As the brain got bigger, the birth had to be still earlier.

Yet premature infants are usually weaker, so both early and late births would have been risky. The delicate balance between these two risks—death from being too premature or death of both child and mother from a blocked birth—has no doubt long been an important evolutionary mechanism. The probability of problem births is a major reason for the many thousands of cesarean deliveries each year.

Over time, this balancing has produced a species whose infants are born, in comparison to those of the great apes, from seven to twelve months premature (Gould, 1976). The brain itself is incomplete at birth,

and a lengthy period of growth takes place outside the womb that in the apes takes place within it. Not only are we "premature," but our entire rate of growth is slow compared to the apes, and our adult face and head are more like those of a juvenile ape than an adult (S. J. Gould, 1975). Many of the most notable and striking differences between us and the apes thus involve not structural but timing differences (Lewin, 1981d). We are born premature, mature slowly, and live our long adult lives with relatively juvenile features, compared to our ape relatives.

The extended period of childhood that results from our slower maturation rate is complexly related to other evolutionary changes. On the one hand, the helpless infants *must* be carried and taken care of in order to survive. On the other, this extended childhood allows them to learn a great deal from parents and other group members, setting the stage for the transmission of increasingly complex cultural information.

Human Cultural Evolution

We can see the minimal beginnings of culture in the apes. One example of a cultural practice is the immersion of sweet potatoes in the sea, both to wash and to salt them, a practice invented by one Japanese macaque monkey and continued by the members of her group (Eaton, 1976). But there are relatively few such examples (Bonner, 1980). Our species is the only one to go beyond these minimal beginnings, and for us culture has become the primary mode of adaptation.

Our **cultural evolution**, the refinement and transmission of information outside our physiology, has now largely taken over from our biological evolution. Culture sets us apart from our ancestors, not physique; the first *Homo sapiens* tool user was probably physically little different from us. But cultural evolution is not independent of physical or behavioral evolution; it depends on the physiology that our ancestors had already evolved, including the larger brain, and on a developing ability to cooperate (Axelrod & Hamilton, 1981).

Currently, cultural evolution is also drastically altering the forces that structure physical evolution. Modern medicine is keeping alive many people who would have died in a nonindustrial society, and our outpouring of new chemical products, radiation, and other technologies may be increasing the rate of change of our physical characteristics. These changes are not likely to cause major problems for our species for a long time, but it is something that our cultural evolution will have to concern itself with in the future.

It is ironic that we have in this way made Lamarck correct. Cultural evolution, unlike biological evolution, is Lamarckian: what one generation struggles

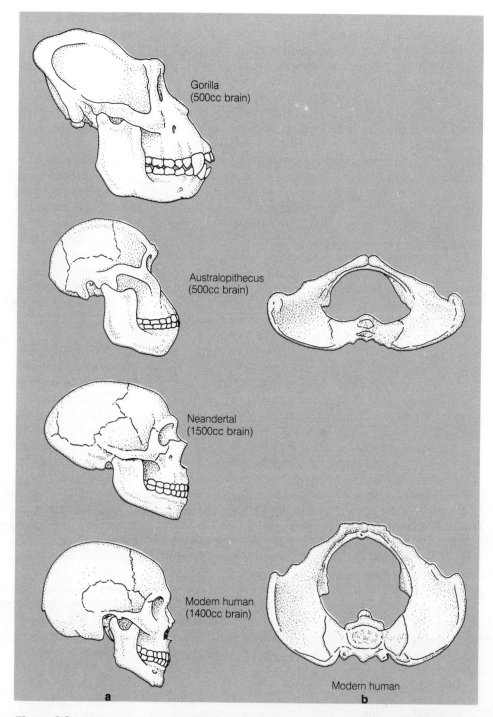

Figure 3.6 ■ (a) The skulls of a contemporary gorilla, two now-extinct ancestral species, and a modern human show the head and face changes that differentiate us. (b) The 3.5-million-year-old pelvis of Lucy, the most complete australopithecine skeleton found to date, compared to the pelvis of a modern human female. Analysis shows that Lucy walked bipedally but bore comparatively small-headed offspring.

to learn *is* transmitted to the next—not through body structure but through cultural information (Gould, 1979c). This ability to begin not from scratch but from what the last generation learned is the reason for the rapid growth of culture. We have become the species we are by Darwinian evolution, but we will survive or not by a new adaptation pattern, a kind of cultural Lamarckism.

When this cultural/technological world seems to overwhelm us, we may wonder if this is the best way.

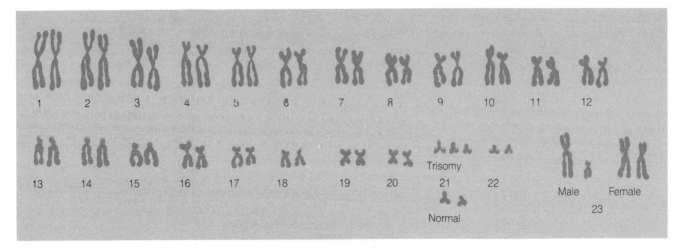

Figure 3.7 ■ A sample karyotype. The 21st chromosome pair shows a common problem: one too many chromosomes, called a trisomy. The 23d chromosome pair here shows both male and female versions; only one such pair would be found in a normal karyotype, of course.

But it's far too late to change our adaptation pattern, and few of us would truly want to change. The decimation of populations by disease, the constant struggle to obtain food and to avoid becoming some predator's food—these we can do without. But perhaps we can adjust our practices somewhat, to fit our cultural/technological evolution to our heritage from biological evolution better (Dobzhansky, 1960).

GENETICS

Genetics refers to the effects of **genes**, specialized molecular structures that carry the codes for building body structures, making enzymes, and so forth. The genes are the library of information about any species and thus are how the results of its evolution are stored and transmitted. We have added cultural evolution and outside-the-body information storage, but much of what our bodies become, and at least some of our behavior, is carried from one generation to the next in this same way (Dawkins, 1976).

Chromosomes, Genes, and DNA

If you had a magic tool at your command, part X ray and part microscope, and used it to look at your own body at ever-increasing magnifications, what might you find? As you focused on the skin of your hand, for example, it would seem increasingly rough, and the hairs on the knuckles would seem like telephone poles. At greater magnification, you would find the separate cells of your skin arrayed like a tile floor. If you peered into a single skin cell, you would find a number of structures scattered around a central nucleus. Finally, within that nucleus you would find some twisted, approximately **X**-shaped filaments; these are the **chromosomes** (Yunis, 1976).

Chromosomes are found in every cell in the body. Except for special arrangements in the reproductive cells—the eggs and sperm—they are the same in all cells; humans have 23 pairs of them. Although your magic machine does not exist, the technology to photograph and examine chromosomes does. The portrait of an individual's chromosomes is called a **karyotype**. ■ Figure 3.7

With the notable exception of the 23d pair, which differs in shape according to the individual's sex, or gross abnormalities (as in the 21st pair in Figure 3.7), the karyotype tells us little about the inheritance messages carried by the chromosomes; these require greater magnification. If you zoomed in on an individual chromosome and increased the magnification, you would find that it looks rather like a string of beads. These beads are the genes.

Some genes operate only early in development, and others function throughout life. Some may even specify aging processes, to get rid of you in favor of a new generation. Researchers are working on a complete human gene "map" of where each gene is and what it does; although far from complete, this map is now beginning to be filled in (McKusick & Ruddle, 1977). One of the uses of a karyotype is to spot damaged or missing chromosomes; knowing that a particular location is damaged may tell you what genes are missing and thus what problems that individual will have.

Finally, if you magnified a single gene, you would eventually be able to see the "double helix" of **DNA** (*d*eoxyribo*n*ucleic *a*cid)—a double spiral, something like a ladder twisted about its longitudinal axis. At this point, with a magnification of over 7 million times, you would have found the molecular structure of the genes, the true basis for heredity.

This DNA molecule contains millions of atoms strung together in very long chains. Each of your cells contains about three feet of DNA chains; the total DNA in your body is billions of miles long. All the information of heredity is encoded through the particular combinations of molecules that make up the chains; the sequences of molecules specify your species, race, sex, approximate height, shape of ear, and so forth. Your DNA is a vast library of information, summing up the environmental experience of your ancestors over millions of years.

Even though DNA is the actual basis for heredity, it usually makes more sense, at our current level of understanding, to talk about genes and chromosomes. So long as we remember that these three levels are superimposed—chromosomes include genes and genes are made up of DNA—we can consider whichever is convenient for a given analysis. Much of the rest of this chapter will refer to genes and chromosomes, but we will occasionally refer again to DNA.

The reproductive cells produced by the woman are called ova (singular, **ovum**) (colloquially known as eggs). Approximately every lunar month a single ovum becomes ready to be fertilized; fertilization, if it occurs, is accomplished by a single male **sperm**, one of millions produced daily (Karp, 1978). The process of duplicating an ordinary body cell normally duplicates the DNA in all chromosomes. But a special process arranges for the reproductive cells to have only one set of chromosomes. When one ovum and one sperm are put together to form a new individual, that new person will have the full complement of 23 chromosome pairs, with half of them coming from each parent. This separating and recombining process provides the continuous variation of Darwinian evolution—and explains why offspring typically resemble their parents but are not identical to them.

The fertilized ovum, containing chromosomes from both mother and father, is called a **zygote**. Any word that includes *zygote* (or *zygous*) has something to do with the fertilized ovum. Thus, identical twins are technically called **monozygotic (MZ) twins** and fraternal twins are **dizygotic (DZ) twins**. Identical (MZ) twins are genetically identical because they are the result of only one (*mono*) zygote; the split into separate but genetically equal individuals took place as that single zygote developed. Siamese twins, individuals joined together at birth, are MZ twins who failed to fully separate. Fraternal (DZ) twins, in contrast, result from two (*di*) separate zygotes, conceived close enough

together in time that both were carried to term; they are genetically no more alike than any other brothers and sisters. Because they share a common maternal environment before birth, both might be affected by drugs the mother takes or by other maternal factors, but genetically they are simply siblings.

Another use of *zygote* concerns the particular gene forms an individual has. Each gene often has two or more forms; thus, the gene controlling eye color includes a blue-eye form and a brown-eye form. Each sperm or egg carries one form of the gene, so each zygote receives two. If these two forms are identical, the individual is **homozygous** for that characteristic, meaning "zygote with the same form." That is, two brown-eye genes yield a brown-eyed person and two blue-eye genes yield a blue-eyed person. But what happens if a zygote receives two different forms—one blue-eye and one brown-eye, for example? Such a person is called **heterozygous** for that trait, meaning "zygote with different forms." Whether the person actually has blue or brown eyes depends on how the two forms work together.

Sometimes when genes combine, they average out, but for many characteristics one form overrides the other and you see only the effect of the first one. A gene that overrides an alternate form is called a **dominant gene**; one that is overridden is called a **recessive gene**. Only when no dominant gene is present to override it will the recessive characteristic be expressed (actually show up in body structure). A person's genetic pattern is called his or her **genotype**, and what the body actually expresses is called the **phenotype**. If both parents are carriers of a particular recessive gene, their children can be expected to express the dominant form three times out of four.

Eye color is an example of these relationships: The gene for brown eyes is dominant, and the one for blue eyes is recessive. A person who received one of each form of gene will have brown eyes, because brown is dominant. But that person is also a **carrier** for blue eyes, and will give the blue-eye gene, on the average, to half of his or her children. The only people who will have blue eyes, however, are those who are homozygous for them (have two blue-eye genes). There is one chance in four that a child of parents who were both carriers would have blue eyes. ■ Figure 3.8

The genetics of behavior, as they are gradually understood, will likely include more complex relationships than the simple dominant/recessive one of eye color. One such complexity concerns the number of genes involved; a single gene can control eye color or many other characteristics, but behavioral patterns are probably influenced by several genes, perhaps many.

Many genes (though not necessarily all) are present in a species in a pattern that reflects their sur-

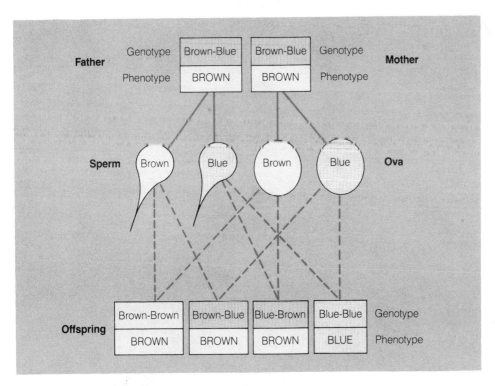

Figure 3.8 ■ When both parents carry the same recessive gene, they may statistically expect that dominant versus recessive characteristics will be expressed in their offspring in a ratio of 3:1. Eye color is shown, but the same ratio applies to any dominant/recessive pattern.

vival value; selection pressures balance each gene's value against other forms. But this is not the whole story. Genes may also allow for environmental shaping in the individual that fine-tunes the gene's effect to the immediate environment. Let's look at an example before we go on: the gene that controls production of melanin (Pawelek & Körner, 1982). Melanin is the pigment that darkens our skin, eyes, and hair, thus protecting us from the sun. Variations in melanin production determine the various skin colors and cause tanning and freckling. When the melanin-production gene is missing or inoperative, the result is an albino, a condition that seems to occur in all mammals (Witkop, 1975). ■ Figure 3.9

Normally, melanin production reflects both gene balancing over many generations and short-term adaptions. For the body to produce vitamin D, sunlight must penetrate the skin, but too much sun may cause the body to produce too much vitamin D, or may cause the skin to get sunburned—which would have made it hard for our ancestors to escape predators or find food. In contrast, with too little sun, you may get sick from vitamin D deficiency. The different selective pressures on melanin-gene forms over many generations have produced the skin coloration of various races. The very dark skin color of African blacks, for example, reflects

strong protection against the powerful tropic sun, and the very light complexions of Scandinavians are appropriate in the much-weaker northern sunlight.

For both groups, the skin color is fine-tuned through the further production of melanin, an effect we call tanning. Within limits, this allows both Africans and Scandinavians to adjust to greater sun exposure. But when technology allows people to move to another part of the world from that in which the gene forms became balanced, this adjustment may not be enough. Blacks living in Northern climates (including all of the United States) are healthier now, for example, than they were before vitamin D supplements were routinely added to milk. White hair as a sign of aging reflects the cessation of melanin production, which points out another kind of variation in genetically controlled traits: They can change over a person's lifetime.

How selection pressures have led to genetic control of our body structures remains only partially understood and relatively little is known about the genetics of our *behavior*. But there is every reason to suspect that our behavior has been subject to similar selection. As we examine some of the known genetic variations and diseases and the ways of dealing with them, remember that a wide variety of behaviors may also be

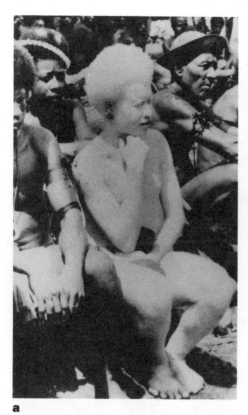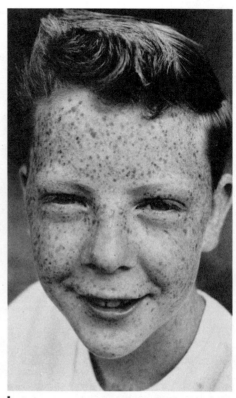

a b

Figure 3.9 ■ Melanin in the skin, eyes, and hair gives them their color and protects us against sunlight. (a) An albino such as this Melanesian tribesman suffers from a genetic inability to produce melanin. His squint is noticeable and extended exposure to the sun can produce not only terrible burns but skin cancer. (b) Freckles represent a different but related genetic trait in which spots of skin produce excessive melanin when exposed to the sun.

(**a**, Wide World Photos; **b**, Robert Kelley, LIFE MAGAZINE © 1958 Time, Inc.)

at least influenced by genetics, and these may also be subject to genetic variation and error. One such possibility that has already led to wide speculation is whether males with a particular genetic makeup are more prone to criminal behavior (Witkin et al., 1976; see Chapter 4). But you will no doubt see many others suggested in the years to come.

Genetic Variations and Diseases

Mutations and Combinations of Genes   The total of all the genes in the living members of a species is called the species' **gene pool**; it represents all of the current genetic possibilities for that species. Reassortment and combination of these genes is a major source of individual differences and of evolution, which operates on such differences. There are, for example, many hand variations in the human gene pool; some are shown in Figure 3.10. ■ Figure 3.10

Not all individual differences in each generation represent recombinations of existing genes. A variety

of natural—and, in our time, newly introduced—factors can cause changes, called **mutations**, in the DNA structure of the gene (Hook & Porter, 1981). Both solar radiation and medical X rays can cause mutations, as can some chemicals.

A mutated gene is a new entry into the gene pool, for better or worse. It may disappear immediately if it is a lethal mutation, one that is fatal to its recipient. Or it may have relatively little immediate effect if it is a neutral mutation, such as a new earlobe shape; it may disappear or randomly drift across the gene pool. A mutation may have more complex consequences, however; it may have different effects in the homozygous and heterozygous forms, for example, one perhaps being lethal but the other advantageous. In such a case the mutated gene may become an active part of evolution, changing frequency in the gene pool in a way that reflects selection pressures.

If you think of what the chances would be of improving any complex machine by randomly changing part of it, you will realize that most chromosomal changes and even many single-gene mutations are

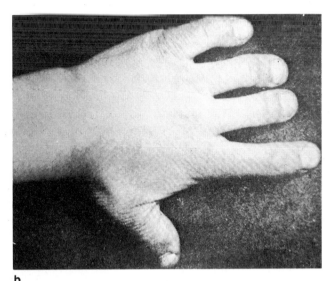

a

b

Figure 3.10 ■ Two genetic variations in human hands, somewhat extreme examples of the variation present in our species. (a) A boy with six fingers on each hand and six toes on each foot. (Many of his close relatives also have more than five digits.) (b) Fingers that are short because they have only two joints (brachyphalangy).

(**a**, Gabriel Benzur, LIFE MAGAZINE © 1945 Time, Inc.; **b**, reprinted by permission from *Heredity, Evolution, and Humankind* by A. M. Winchester. Copyright © 1977 by West Publishing Company.)

likely to cause severe problems. In fact, most such changes are lethal, causing spontaneous abortion of the genetically damaged zygote or fetus early in development—often so early that the woman never knows that she was pregnant.

The small percentage of infants who do survive chromosomal abnormalities such as the trisomy 21 shown in Figure 3.7 usually show severe body/behavioral deficits. These often include mental retardation, as in trisomy 21, which causes Down's syndrome (see Chapter 14). But if the change is a mutation within a single gene, the consequences may be less severe. Not all single-gene mutations are fatal, and some may remain recessive and not even be expressed in the phenotype. If so, the single "correct" gene may be able to provide the instructions for normal development. Then only individuals who are homozygous for the mutated gene will actually suffer the problem; heterozygotes will seem normal but will carry the gene.

If the mutated form of the gene does not reduce the survivability of the carriers, it may drift through a population and become part of the gene pool. Only if close genetic relatives breed is there a high chance of two carriers getting together; if they do, they are likely to have homozygous offspring with the problem. The difficulties that occur when close genetic relatives breed (**inbreeding**) are probably the basis for the strong prohibitions against incest found in most human cultures. Such prohibitions may be very old; avoiding inbreeding seems to be of paramount importance in determining which gorillas can belong to particular groups, according to one researcher (Veit, 1982).

Geneticists estimate that *each* of us carries four *lethal* recessive genes and many other detrimental ones. But the total number of such variations is large and the chances that you and your mate will have the same ones is slight, unless that mate is a close genetic relative. In first-cousin matings, for example, some genetic flaw is noticeable in half the offspring; in brother-sister matings nearly every child shows some genetic defect. Albinism, for example, is relatively uncommon in random matings; the odds are more than 20,000 to 1 against it. But when first cousins mate, even when no family record of albinism exists, the chances are 9 times greater. For brother/sister matings, the chances are more than 35 times greater, or 1 in only 568 (Winchester, 1976).

If incestuous inbreeding continues in a family, problems may become almost universal within the resulting family line. Among European royal families (a well-known example) a number of characteristics, including both trivial and serious ones, are known to have run in such families, often for hundreds of years. Because the only eligible mates were from other royal families, first-cousin marriages were common. The deleterious effects of damaging recessive genes became so frequent that many homozygous sufferers were born and most others were carriers. Hemophilia, faulty blood clotting that makes the slightest injury a threat to life through continued bleeding, ran in Queen Victoria's family. Of her nine children, four had hemophilia and four were carriers.

In populations with a limited gene pool, such problems can become much more common than in large gene pools. Albinism is much more common among the Navajos, a different pigmentation problem is common in some South Pacific islands, and six fingers are more common among American Amish than among groups with fewer restrictions in potential mates. Genetic defects are also notorious in some inbred animal strains, including dogs and cats as well as farm animals (Page, 1982b).

One way of overcoming the problems of inbreeding is to introduce quite different genes deliberately into the pool. Any mixture of different plant or animal varieties is called a **hybrid**. Many hybrids are both larger and stronger than either parent, a phenomenon called hybrid vigor; most current agricultural plants and animals are carefully combined hybrids. When the varieties are so far apart that they approach separate-species status, however, such hybrids may be very difficult to produce, or if produced may be sterile. Mules are a long-used hybrid of donkey and horse that are stronger than either parent but are infertile; farmers cannot breed a line of mules, but must always breed donkeys and horses. Hybrid primates are rare; the first known to have occurred is a gibbon-siamang hybrid (Myers & Shafer, 1979).

There is no reason, by the way, why hybrid vigor is not as important for humans as it is for other species. Geneticists once worried about the consequences of human racial mixing, but they now seem to lean toward a more favorable view of it (Provine, 1973). ■ Personal Application: Cataloging Your Own Genetic Characteristics

Genetic Diseases   There are hundreds of known human genetic diseases. The first of two examples we will examine is **Tay-Sachs disease**, a genetic disease that afflicts primarily Jews of eastern European ancestry. The higher frequency in this population presumably reflects drift within a mostly interbred population following some original mutation that is now untraceable. A number of such diseases affect primarily the ethnic or racial groups within which they originated (Mourant et al., 1978).

Tay-Sachs disease results from a single gene mutation that causes the lack of a particular enzyme; without it, harmful deposits build up in brain cells (Brady, 1976). As a result, an apparently healthy baby seems to slow and then reverse its development over the course of a year or two, with death inevitable in another few months to several years. The infant never really has a chance to live, and the parents are put through several years of agonized waiting for the end.

Like many genetic diseases, Tay-Sachs afflicts only the homozygous; heterozygous carriers seem perfectly normal. Thus a Tay-Sachs infant may be born only when both parents are carriers. In years past the probability of the parents being carriers had to be estimated from their family histories, a difficult and inaccurate process. A test now exists that will identify carriers with a high degree of certainty and Tay-Sachs screenings are frequently held. Two identified carriers now know that they have a 25% chance of any particular pregnancy resulting in a Tay-Sachs child.

If the only test were for carriers, those odds would put great strain on such prospective parents. But there are also ways of testing the fetus itself. **Amniocentesis** is a technique for obtaining and testing, including karyotyping, tissue samples from any fetus thought to be at risk (Fuchs, 1980). Many genetic diseases, including Tay-Sachs, can now be identified in the fetus, either by amniocentesis or by one of several other techniques (Epstein & Golbus, 1977). Consequently, amniocentesis is becoming increasingly common, especially among older mothers, who tend to have more children with birth defects than do younger ones. For a fetus with defects as severe as Tay-Sachs, many parents will chose an abortion. For less severe problems, however, the ethical questions involved in abortion become increasingly difficult.

Our second example, **sickle-cell anemia**, is one of the most widespread genetic diseases. Like Tay-Sachs, sickle-cell is primarily a disease of one identifiable population: blacks of African descent. Some 60,000 black Americans are estimated to have the disease and perhaps 2 million are carriers (Marx, 1978). It is named for the distorted shape the red blood cells sometimes assume in the afflicted homozygous individual. In the resulting sickle-cell "crisis," the cells tend to clot and not to move smoothly through the tiny capillaries; victims experience intense pain, often in the joints. Their overall life span is greatly reduced

Cataloging your own genetic characteristics

In writing this chapter, I found myself listing some of my own physical features that I have learned over the years are genetic ones; you might find it interesting to do the same. In my case, I'm a tall, dark-haired, brown-eyed male. I'm of mixed European ancestry, and the afflictions of some other racial groups are not mine. But I was born with severely inward-turned feet that required months in casts to reshape. And I have a newly discovered form of heart-valve abnormality—prolapsing mitral valve, for any medical students among you—that is more susceptible to infections; it is known to be a genetic variant that affects tall males. I also have a history of allergies and asthma-like problems and am nearsighted.

On the other hand, I've never had to worry much about excess weight gain, have rarely been seriously ill, have never broken a bone, and my family seems relatively free from strokes and heart attacks. And, although it doesn't really seem to have much use, I can roll the sides of my tongue up toward the center. All of these characteristics and many more are genetically controlled.

One reason why many adopted children have sought to find their biological parents in recent years is so that they can know something about their genetic history (Rosenfeld, 1981a). As susceptibility to allergic reactions, particular diseases, and so forth are increasingly shown to be genetic, proper medical care may demand knowing some family history. One old joke about how to live a long life suggests that you arrange to have long-lived parents. It's probably too late for you to manage that now, but knowing about their medical histories gives you some insight into possibilities for you. Remember, however, that the recombining of genes, mutations, environmental shaping within reaction ranges (discussed later), and so forth may all contribute to what you become. A family member's having a problem doesn't mean you will get it—just as their being free from problems doesn't mean you will avoid them.

You thus might find it both interesting and medically useful to catalog some of your own genetic characteristics. As you do, you will realize just how many of these there are and that anything approaching a complete catalog is impossible. But it will teach you a bit more about yourself and it's also fun. Try the tongue-roll for starters. And check your fingers. One sex-influenced characteristic is the relative lengths of index and fourth (next-to-last) fingers; males' index fingers tend to be shorter than the fourth and females' tend to be longer. But don't worry if yours don't fit that pattern; like the tongue-roll, this doesn't seem to mean much except to reemphasize that we're all different.

---

by accumulated damage from the poor blood flow in various organs. ■ Figure 3.11

Sickle-cell anemia results from a single incorrect molecule in the DNA of a single gene. Despite its destructive effect, sickle-cell's wide distribution reflects active selection pressure: Although the sickle-cell crisis of a homozygote is painful and even life-threatening, the slight sickling of a heterozygote carrier seems to help protect against malaria (Roth et al., 1978). Malaria has long been common in areas of Africa, and any protection against it offers such a powerful evolutionary advantage that, in effect, the homozygous individual has been sacrificed for the sake of the more numerous heterozygous ones. This effect is referred to as a **heterozygote advantage**. Many other genetic diseases may also reflect heterozygote advantages (Warga, 1980).

Note that the sickle-cell mutation should spread only as long as malaria is there to "help" it. Without the threat of malaria, it should gradually fade, as it may now be doing among American blacks (Maugh, 1981b). But remember that cultural, not biological, evolution is now our strong point. Work is under way not only to be able to test and predict sickle-cell and many other genetic diseases, but to cure them as well, perhaps even through direct genetic intervention.

Genetic Manipulations and Modifications

The suggestion that humans should be deliberately bred for desirable characteristics is called **eugenics**. First formally suggested by Sir Francis Galton, proposals that human breeding be controlled in some way have continued to recur sporadically in various guises since Galton's time. Suggestions have been made to limit the portions of the population considered undesirable and in some states, in the past, the mentally retarded were sterilized to serve this end. The most recent example of a plan to breed for desirable characteristics is a sperm bank recently set up. Women with high IQs can choose from the sperm of a number of carefully selected donors, supposedly including Nobel prize winners. To some people this is a rational way to plan a pregnancy; to others, it conjures up images of Nazi-like planning for a "super race." It remains to be seen if the idea will catch on.

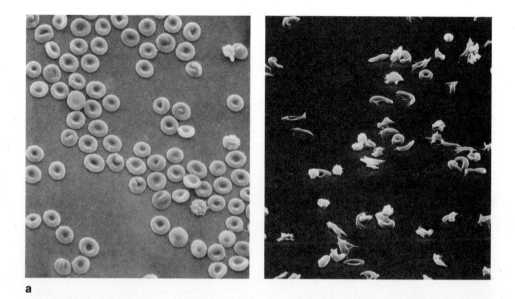

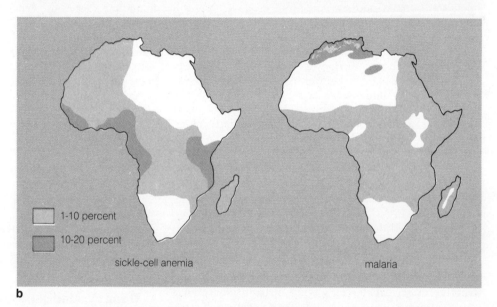

1-10 percent

10-20 percent

sickle-cell anemia   malaria

b

Figure 3.11 ■ (a) Normal red blood cells compared to the deformed ones that give sickle-cell anemia its name. (b) Maps of sickle-cell and malaria incidence in Africa, showing the spread of sickle-cell over the areas where malaria has been a major killer.

(**a**, Dr. Patricia A. Burke and Dr. Patricia N. Farnsworth, Department of Physiology, U.M.D.N.J., New Jersey Medical School, Newark, N. J.; **b**, from *Evolution and Human Behavior* by Alexander Alland, Jr. Copyright © 1967 by Alexander Alland, Jr. Reprinted by permission of Doubleday & Company, Inc.)

Specific advice to individual potential parents is called **genetic counseling**; it began prior to real genetic understanding, but now draws on a substantial bank of information and the ability to do genetic testing (Scriver et al., 1978). Unfortunately, there are still large holes in the information. And it is, of course, fraught with ethical questions (Omenn, 1978). Who should be told what and in what detail? Should abortions be allowed or encouraged, and if so ought they to be somehow limited (Chedd, 1981)? (There are fears

that some couples might abort for relatively minor problems, or even solely to get a child of desired sex now that the sex of the fetus can be determined by amniocentesis.)

For those children born with problems, the approach shifts to relieving, and ideally curing, the problem. The first level of response is symptomatic relief. Surgery may be needed, as it frequently is to repair holes in the hearts of Down's syndrome children. (Heart problems are the most common of genetic defects; Rosenfeld, 1981b.) Supplements may be used when hormones, such as growth hormones, are absent.

If the mechanism of the problem is understood, then sometimes more subtle interventions can offer dramatic relief. In **PKU** (*phenylketonuria*), for example, lack of an enzyme necessary to digest some foods leads to a buildup of toxic products in the brain; although not fatal, this causes severe mental retardation. Once PKU could not be treated at all; even now, if the retardation is allowed to occur it cannot be reversed. But now that the problem is understood, most infants are tested for PKU at birth. If they have it, they are put on a special diet that does not require the missing enzyme. The genetic fault remains, but the retardation does not develop (Brady, 1976). PKU is one of the best understood of the more than 150 such enzyme problems, but work is under way on many of them. Other researchers feel they are getting close to finding some environmental manipulation, perhaps a drug, that can reduce the sickling of the blood cells in sickle-cell anemia (Klotz et al., 1981).

One stage more direct—and more difficult—is the direct insertion of a gene into a patient's body so it will function in place of a faulty natural gene. Work to date has focused on the possibility of inserting genes into bone marrow to produce normal blood cells for those with sickle-cell or similar blood diseases. Such research has been successful in mice, but its use in humans is still some time away (Marx, 1980b). One researcher who attempted a clinical trial with humans was severely censured for acting too soon (Wade, 1981).

Obviously the ultimate manipulation would be to directly correct the faulty gene at some stage in the process: You might hope to alter the genes of the carriers, the zygote, the fetus, the newborn infant, or the adult. Such direct interventions would all fall under the heading of **genetic engineering**, although this term also includes other forms of genetic manipulation (Anderson & Diacumakos, 1981).

The most dramatic contemporary example of genetic engineering is **recombinant DNA** technology (also called "gene splicing"); it is the insertion of a new gene into the middle of a chromosome that did not have it before (Wetzel, 1980). The most successful work in recombinant DNA research so far has been the insertion of genes for the making of human hormones (such as insulin or human growth hormone) into bacteria. The rapidly growing bacteria then manufacture the human hormone according to the genetic instructions (Gilbert & Villa-Komaroff, 1980). (One important legal landmark here was the decision that newly-created life forms were patentable; Wade, 1980.) Inserting a functioning gene into a mammalian cell is a much trickier procedure, but work is progressing and it is very likely that you will live to see direct genetic modification of human genetic diseases.

Most of what we have looked at so far in this chapter has concerned genetic control of body structures. But to psychologists, the important questions concern the possible genetic influences on behavior.

Behavioral Genetics

Issues of how behaviors are genetically transmitted form the field of **behavioral genetics**, studied by both biologists and psychologists (Mayr, 1974; McClearn, 1962). The effects of behavioral genetics were actually being studied long before the concept of a gene was proposed. The similarity between parents and offspring of all species must have been obvious to early humans, and arranging to use that effect deliberately probably soon followed. Selective breeding of animals and plants, long a feature of agricultural practice, has also been a major source of information about the genetics of behavior (Benzer, 1973).

Consider a classic example, the breeding of maze-bright and maze-dull rats. If you run a group of young rats in mazes, some will be better at the task than others. (A maze for a rat is a runway with one or more turns, usually with a food reward waiting at the end.) This variation in maze performance reflects the individual differences that are a mainstay of evolution. But by selective breeding you may quickly develop separate breeds of rats that *consistently* differ in maze skills: You simply arrange to mate only the brightest and dullest of the rats (measured by speed and accuracy of maze performance), always mating bright with bright and dull with dull. (You would, of course, keep all other aspects of their treatment identical.) If you do this for many generations, the ability of the offspring gradually separates until none of the dull group is as good at mazes as the worst of the bright group (Tyron, 1940). ■ Figure 3.12

Results such as those in Figure 3.12 demonstrate that something about running mazes well or poorly is *inherited* in rats; this is a complex behavior, and different from the behaviors of their ancestors, but success at it is nevertheless inherited. You can see how Lamarck might have been misled into assuming that the parents' practice has affected the offspring, but it hasn't. You have simply selected for one aspect of their inherited behavioral repertoire that was mixed with others before. It might have to do with their sensory abilities, their learning abilities, or something else; all you know is that *something* about running mazes is inherited.

Many behaviors of various animal species have been studied to see to what extent they are inherited.

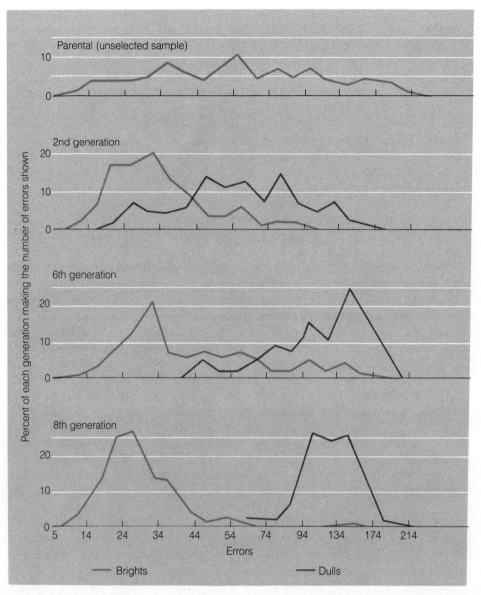

Figure 3.12 ■ Selective breeding can produce specialized populations, such as maze-bright and maze-dull rats. Maze-running scores overlap for a number of generations but eventually the two populations separate entirely.

(Adapted from "Genetic Differences in Maze-Learning Ability in Rats" by R. C. Tryon in *Intelligence: Its Nature and Nurture*, 39th Yearbook of the National Society for the Study of Education, 1940, Part 1, 111–119.)

(Other rat behaviors studied include alcohol preference and the tendency to explore open areas.) But to know if any human abilities are inherited requires different tactics. These include the study of family histories and separated twins, as well as direct studies of human genetics. Darwin's cousin, Sir Francis Galton, originated the study of families, examining ones (such as his and Darwin's) with unusually successful members. (Musicians among you may think of the Bachs and the Mozarts, for example.) Galton looked at well-to-do families with the elitism of a person of his social class and time and seemed to find support for this elitism. The successful were successful *because* they were especially able, he felt.

In the hands of Galton's less-intelligent contemporaries, this notion became *social Darwinism*, a kind of socioeconomic survival of the fittest. The poor, they felt, demonstrated how unworthy they were by being

"Somehow I was hoping genetic engineering would take a different turn."

(© 1983 by Sidney Harris)

GENETICS AND THE NATURE/NURTURE INTERACTION

In discussing genetics we occasionally touched on environmental factors, such as suntanning or the effects of diet for a PKU child, but we emphasized the genetic coding. There *are* human characteristics that are almost entirely genetically determined, such as eye color, but they tend not to be the important ones—especially the important behavioral ones. Many human physical traits and virtually all behavioral ones derive from some *interaction* of genetic code and environmental treatment, or nature and nurture.

You are, of course, already familiar with the concepts of nature and nurture, and know that they typically interact. But this is all too easy to forget when you consider a particular issue, and a finding that some behavior has a genetic basis may seem to mean things that it does not. It does *not* mean, for example, that such a behavior is inevitable, and it does *not* mean training and practice are unimportant. It simply means that *something* that genetics codes for is important in the behavior, perhaps providing the basis for it or limiting it in some way.

The complete genetic coding for an individual may be thought of as a library, with some of the information used on one occasion, some on another. But substantial amounts may never be used at all, either because newer information overrides it or because the environment never calls for it. Chickens, for example, have no teeth. But one study showed that they still retain the genetic codes for building teeth, which are normally prevented from being expressed (Kollar & Fisher, 1980).

Even genetic codes that are expressed interact with the environment in many ways. One major way is for the environment to specify one of several genetically coded possibilities. Consider lung development, for example. The volume of air your lungs can take in reflects not only the genetic codes you have for lung development but also the altitude at which you were raised (Perlman, 1980). Children growing up in Denver grow larger lungs, to cope with the thinner air at Denver's high altitude, than children growing up at sea level. Once they reach adulthood their lungs do not change in size, even if they move to a higher or lower altitude; adults compensate by changing how rapidly they breathe. So lung development is both genetically and environmentally controlled.

Reaction Ranges

In the total population, genetic variations are mixed with environmental variations; measuring a person's

poor. We now realize the failings of such a notion. A young Mozart gets—in addition to Mozartian genes—good food, leisure time, a piano, parental modeling and encouragement, and other help: the children of the poor are trapped by the limits of being poor. A potential Mozart born to a poor family of Darwin's day might never *see* a piano, much less compose on one.

Later, psychologists realized that some method of analyzing both the effects of inherited factors (nature) and environmental factors (nurture) was needed. Although family studies are still done for special purposes, most research has turned to the study of separated identical (MZ) twins. (Identical twins are called that, despite small differences that may exist between them, if they are genetically identical.) If you experimentally separated such twins and raised them under different conditions, you could examine how alike or unlike they were at the end; similarities despite different nurture might indicate inherited tendencies. Obviously it would be unethical to do so deliberately, but there are cases of twins who have been separated, usually by adoption; these offer a kind of poorly controlled natural experiment. Early findings from a major ongoing study of separated twins have been widely reported. The detailed similarities of some of these twin pairs have surprised some psychologists and have renewed debate about the role of genetics in behaviors long thought to be solely the product of learning. ■ Research Controversy: Do Genetics Code for Detailed Behaviors?

Research Controversy

Do genetics code for detailed behaviors?

The study of genetically identical individuals is one of the oldest techniques in psychology for looking at the nature/nurture problem. In an approach originated by Galton, psychologists examine both similarities and differences for several types of siblings: identical twins, fraternal twins, and other siblings (Holden, 1980a). One of the most important comparisons is between twins reared together and those reared apart (Rose, 1982). Dramatic similarities of behavior in twins reared apart are not hard to find. But how hard would it be to find *some* similarities among *any* two or three people of the same sex, age, size, and appearance? Such similarities in themselves are provocative but are not good *evidence* for nature factors. More careful study is needed to see if such evidence can be found.

A major research project is now under way at the University of Minnesota, studying as many identical twins reared apart as can be found; the researchers hope to study 20 pairs in detail (Holden, 1980c). The first few pairs studied show remarkable similarities, from ways of dressing to choice of cigarette brands. If these similarities really reflect genetic influences, psychologists may be forced to revise their thinking somewhat, as such behaviors have long been assumed to reflect only learning.

One of the first pairs of twins studied were the "Jim twins," Jim Springer and Jim Lewis of Ohio. The many similarities reported for them include not only their sons' names—James Alan and James Allan—but the fact that each was the only one in his neigh-

Figure 3.13 ■ Jim Lewis of Elida, Ohio, and Jim Springer of Dayton, Ohio, are one of the pairs of twins being extensively studied to see if behavioral similarities might be more genetically influenced than most psychologists have previously believed. The tree benches that each of the "Jim twins" built are among the many provocative similarities found for them.

(© Enrico Ferorelli/Wheeler Pictures)

borhood to build a white bench around a tree in the front yard (Jackson, 1980). Is it possible that building tree benches is somehow influenced by genetics? This seems impossible at first, but as the researchers keep finding such seemingly impossible commonalities among twin pairs who have never known each other, they are beginning to speculate on possible ways in which genetics *could* influence them. ■ Figure 3.13

We would never expect such behaviors as building tree benches—or wearing multiple rings on each finger, as a pair of English women twins did— to be genetically *controlled*. But a

person's genetics may turn out to influence subtly which choices that person makes from the possibilities available. We can safely assume that if one of the Jim twins had been raised in California where tree benches are virtually unknown, rather than the Midwest where they are common, he wouldn't have built one. But is there some possible genetic influence—perhaps manual dexterity—that would explain some of these remarkable coincidences? Or are they just that: Coincidences that you find when you look for similarities? Perhaps this research will tell us.

lung capacity cannot tell you the relative influence of genetics and environment. Sorting out genetics and environment becomes even more difficult when the questions concern more complex phenomena. A useful concept here is that of reaction range. A person's **reaction range** for a genetically influenced trait is the range of possibilities that the genetics allows; the envi-

ronment selects from within this range (Freedman, 1979). But the environment cannot cause the trait to go any further than the genetic boundaries of the reaction range.

Height, for example, is definitely genetically controlled. Tall parents, other things being equal, will have tall offspring. But what if other things are not equal?

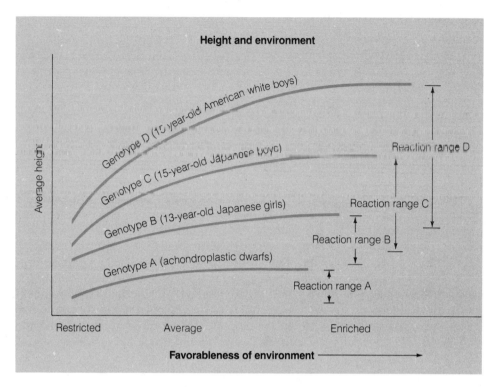

Figure 3.14 ■ Reaction ranges for four different genotypes. A favorable environment would make each genotype taller than an unfavorable environment, but the amount of variation caused by environmental differences varies with the different genotypes. Genotype A is limited by the genetic error that causes that type of dwarfism; for any but the most restricted environments, the genetic limit restricts the height. In contrast, substantial differences in height would occur in different environments for Genotype D. Note also that the reaction ranges overlap. In general, 15-year-old Japanese boys (Genotype C) would be taller than 13-year-old Japanese girls (Genotype B). But if such a girl comes from a much better environment, she could be taller. (Note: Reaction ranges refer to difference between maximum and minimum possible height.)

(From *Developmental Genetics and Ontogenetic Psychology* by I. I. Gottesman, University of Minnesota Press, 1974. Used by permission.)

Diet also influences height; a child on a near-starvation diet will grow slowly and mature into a rather short adult. If the diet has been as bad as possible while still allowing survival, the person's actual height will be at the bottom of his or her reaction range; let's say that's five feet tall. But if the diet had been optimal, perhaps that person could have been six feet tall. The reaction range for height would here be five to six feet. Those *limits* would be genetic ones, but the person's actual height would be somewhere in between, specified by diet.

Several things about this example also apply to more complex reaction ranges, including those for behavior. First, any actual height reached must have been genetically possible (within the reaction range), or it couldn't have happened. Second, this actual height alone does not tell you what else would have been possible. If you know that the diet has always been especially good or especially bad, you could *guess* that this might be near the top or bottom of the reac-

tion range, but you don't know. Third, two individuals of identical height may have had quite different reaction ranges. One five-footer might represent a five-to-six-foot reaction range, the other a four-to-five-foot one. ■ Figure 3.14

These relationships help explain such questions as why young Japanese after World War II often grew taller than their parents: Their different diets pushed them higher in the reaction range. But the tallest parents still tended to have the tallest children, even if all children were taller than all parents. Reaction ranges also explain why the average English and American young man has gradually grown taller since the 14th century. The difference of several inches (based on military records) is much too great and occurred much too fast to be an evolutionary change; it simply represents a gradual improvement of diet. But there must be a limit; no diet will cause the average young man to grow seven feet tall. In fact, the height limit may already have been reached; the data seem to suggest that this trend has leveled off (Tanner & Taylor, 1965).

Reaction range is only one of many interactions between genetics and environment. Even a relatively straightforward body characteristic such as height is controlled by more than basic height genetics and diet. An individual's sex, for example, influences it; males usually grow somewhat taller because of the influence of their hormones. And the genetics for other hormones can greatly expand the basic reaction range, causing some people to be very short or very tall—for example, three feet or eight feet. Through the technology provided by our cultural evolution, we now have the ability to provide substitute hormones or to alter their production surgically and thus make the would-be-very-short taller and prevent the would-be-very-tall from being so.

When these relationships are examined for a complex human *behavior* such as intelligence or schizophrenia, the situation becomes vastly more complex. Many genes may be involved, not just one or two, and they may interact with each other and with the environment in a variety of ways. To say that height is genetically controlled does not fully explain how a person comes to be a given height; to say that IQ is genetically controlled says even less about that person's intelligence.

One complex human performance that illustrates some of these time relationships is language. Our species is clearly genetically prepared in some way for language although the details aren't well understood (Lenneberg, 1967). But equally clearly, *what* language you speak, as well as your accent and other characteristics, are determined by environmental input. Just as the young gosling is prepared for imprinting (Chapter 1), the young human is prepared for language acquisition. And both gosling and human seem to show the influences of this special learning for life. Our very long childhood allows for a great deal of such environmental specifying and structuring within the range of our genetic possibilities. Then as adults we do other kinds of learning and adjusting that continue to adapt our behavior to our current environment; this learning is based on our genetics and prior environmental influence, but it allows further fine-tuning of behavior to fit our needs.

Heritability

Our genetic codes thus set up possibilities and limits, sometimes very broad ones, within which we are shaped by our environment. The differences between people therefore always reflect some combination of genetic and environmental differences. Is there a way to separate these effects quantitatively? There is, but you must be exceedingly careful lest you misuse or

misinterpret it. A variety of techniques, including twin studies, may be used to establish estimates of heritability. The **heritability** of a trait refers to the proportion of the variation in a particular population that is attributable to genetics. Now even stated simply, that's a mouthful. What does it mean? And equally important, what does it *not* mean?

Let's go back to our height examples. In a pre-World War II Japanese population that had been reared nearly identically, you would find a range of actual heights. Because environmental differences had been slight, most of the actual differences would probably be genetic; you could be fairly confident that *most* of the *variation* found was genetic. In this case, the heritability for height would be high, maybe 80 or 90%. But consider a randomly collected group of post-World War II Japanese whose upbringing during the war had varied widely. The heritability for height would be much lower, as much more of the actual differences seen would reflect environment. You could no longer be sure that the tallest individuals necessarily had the tallest genetic codes.

This example shows several critical dimensions of heritability. First, it is a *relative* index, relevant only to a particular population at a particular time. It does *not* say something fixed and definite—about height, for example—but reflects only a temporary state of some population. Second, it *changes* with environmental changes; as the environment becomes more uniform, for example, the heritability goes up. If environments for all members of a population had been perfectly equal, all of the difference among them would reflect genetics and the heritability would be 100%. (Of course it could never be this high for any real population.) Finally, heritability is only a *population* measure; it can never apply to any single individual. It is a measure of variation across a whole group, but cannot be applied to anyone in that group. Knowing that environments had been generally equal and heritability was high for a group, you would still *not* know that any particular person in the group was near his or her own genetic limit.

We will consider the processes of development in general in Chapter 12 and that of particular behaviors at numerous other points in the text. In all cases, we may expect the developmental causes of both structures and behaviors to be a complex interaction of nature and nurture, beginning with the history of our species and carried by genetics to individuals—whose personal development then reflects an interlocked chain of physical and social factors. Sorting out the factors will in each case be difficult. But acting as if such questions have simple answers would be to ignore all we have learned to date.

CHAPTER SUMMARY

1 All living species represent the current products of the process of evolution. Their structural and behavioral characteristics have been adapted to particular conditions by their ancestors' success in surviving and in rearing young.

2 Charles Darwin is known as the founder of evolutionary theory because of his theory of natural selection, in which the environment operates to select features of a species somewhat as a human breeder selects features of a domesticated species. Some characteristics are not selected through their success, but have been established through random factors such as isolation and drift.

3 Human evolution is characterized by an upright posture, hand use, and an exceptionally large brain. Some of the sequence leading to our species is known, and our close biological similarity to the great apes has been demonstrated, but the details of the branches of the primate evolutionary tree remain in debate.

4 One major difference between other species and our own is our development of culture, a pattern of information transmission outside our bodies. The continuing evolution of human culture parallels biological evolution but allows much more rapid change, and is now likely to be more important for our species' continued survival than is biological evolution.

5 Biological evolution operates by the transmission to offspring of the parents' physical characteristics through the mechanisms of genetics. By specifying the way in which body structures develop, genes code for both adult physical characteristics and at least some aspects of behavior.

6 The recombining of genes through sexual reproduction and the addition of occasional mutated genes provide continuous variation in all members of a species. This is useful for the natural selection process, but also is the basis of a variety of human genetic diseases.

7 Current research in genetic engineering seeks to alter genetic control of species characteristics deliberately. Recombinant DNA technology is already causing bacteria to produce human hormones, and genetic engineering to directly alter human genetic diseases is being studied.

8 Although the genetics of body structures are easier to specify, genetic influences on numerous behaviors have been demonstrated in animals. Some human behaviors are also known to be at least somewhat genetically influenced, and research continues to seek others.

9 The interaction of genetic constraints and environmental inputs that shapes any single individual's characteristics can be discussed in terms of reaction ranges, such as those for height.

10 The heritability of a particular trait indicates, for some particular population, how much of the variation in that trait results from genetic variations and how much results from environmental variations. But each individual within the population is the unique product of some particular set of genetic/environmental interactions, and these are not assessed by heritability.

Further Readings

Darwin's original works, such as *On the Origin of Species by Means of Natural Selection* (1859) and *Descent of Man* (1871), are still available in a variety of editions and remain quite readable. Evolution in animals and its importance as a unifying theme in contemporary biology can be explored in a good biology text such as Curtis' *Biology (3rd edition)* (1979). The relationships among evolution and genetics, with special reference to human implications, are the topics of Winchester's *Heredity, Evolution and Humankind* (1976). Some details of human evolution, especially the biochemical similarities between humans and the great apes, are provided in Washburn and Moore's *Ape into Man* (1974). Leakey and Lewin's *Origins* (1977b) is a beautifully illustrated discussion of human evolution (although its evolutionary trees present only one of the current views). Gould's monthly columns in *Natural History* magazine discuss a wide variety of evolutionary issues; some of the columns have been collected in three volumes: *Ever Since Darwin* (1977), *The Panda's Thumb* (1980), and *Hen's Teeth and Horse's Toes* (1983). The September 1978 issue of *Scientific American* is a special issue devoted to evolutionary topics; it has numerous relevant articles.

Browsing through some old newspapers one day, seeking unusual events for a class project, you are struck by some of the things people do to themselves and others and you find yourself repeating, "Why?" Several of the articles you notice concern people who have died because of their weight problems. A man, one of a pair of identical twins, has died from the complications of obesity: He and his twin each weighed over 700 pounds. "Why does anyone get that big?" you think. Another notes the fatal heart attack of a young woman, a popular singer, caused by years of self-starvation; the paper calls it anorexia nervosa. "Why would anyone choose to starve like that?" you wonder. "Didn't she realize what she was doing to herself?"

Several other items concern people who seem to be deliberately frightening themselves: A new roller coaster has opened at the amusement park and people are lined up to try it, horror movies are doing well at the box office, and the local skydiving club is sponsoring a weekend meet. A young man even skied directly over the edge of El Capitan in Yosemite National Park—to float by parachute to the valley floor. And when a filmmaker missed him the first time, he did it again. "Fear is supposed to be a bad thing," you think, "so why are all these people spending money and time to scare themselves?" The more articles like this you read, the more curious you become: "Why does anyone bother to do anything? Why don't we all just sit back and relax? People work hard all day, then run around in the evenings and on weekends, seeking . . . what?" Food and water you can understand, and of course sexual gratification. But why is there such variation in what seems to motivate people?

MOTIVES AND EMOTIONS

Why anyone behaves in any manner has long been wondered about, not only regarding unusual behaviors, but also common ones. Why do we eat, talk, go to work? Why do we breathe, sleep, fight? We do some things because they feel good, like eating tasty foods or engaging in sexual intercourse. We do others to avoid pain. Sometimes we do things merely because we have learned that we are expected to. There are many different kinds of behaviors and many reasons for doing them. Explaining these reasons and fitting them all together is the task of psychologists concerned with motivation.

Survival through Motives and Emotions

According to the ethological perspective, the reasons why organisms behave in particular ways—their

Chapter 4

Motivation and Emotion

motives—are best explained by the survival value of those behaviors. An animal that doesn't eat does not live to reproduce. One that lives but does not mate has no descendants, and one that does not aid its offspring may have no descendants. All living species descended from animals who ate, mated, and took care of their young; thus eating, mating, and parenting are strongly motivated behaviors. Other motives, possibly exclusively human ones, can also be considered in addition to basic survival motives.

Experiences called *emotions* often accompany motives: when the motive becomes especially important, when motivated behavior is carried out, or when the goal implied by the motive is achieved. Here we will emphasize motives, turning to emotions only toward the end of the chapter. But the two topics are closely related.

Defining Motives and Emotions

Formally, **motivation** refers to the reasons *why* any behavior occurs, or specifically, to the forces or processes that *initiate* the behavior, *direct* it, and contribute to its *strength*. **Motives** initiate and direct behavior toward particular goals, with varying degrees of strength. Hunger, for example, initiates food-seeking and consuming behaviors and directs these behaviors as necessary (Wong, 1976). The strength of a motive is indicated by the intensity and persistence of the seeking and consuming behaviors. An animal is said to be hungry when it goes where it has found food before and eats food that is available. It is said to be especially hungry if it actively persists in seeking food when it does not find any at the usual spot, or consumes unusual amounts when food becomes available.

Motives frequently direct an organism toward some object or event, as hunger directs behavior toward food. But motives can also direct behavior away from objects or events. Pain, for example, is highly motivating; it mobilizes escape from the conditions causing it. Fear also directs behavior away from objects or events (sometimes because these have previously been associated with pain).

An **emotion** is an affective experience, one that both causes body arousal and has meaning or value to the experiencer. Emotions are often closely associated with motives. Pleasurable emotions often mark the achievement of motivated goals, and anger or hurt may mark the frustration of motives. Rage may accompany aggression and fear may accompany fleeing from danger. This close association of emotional experience and motivation has long been recognized by philosophers. One of the oldest theories of why we behave is **hedonism,** the tendency to do what we find pleasurable and avoid what we find painful. A hedonistic view of motivation is often useful, but falls far short of a full explanation. The obvious next question, for example, is *why* some objects and events give pleasure and others pain.

Some motives serve the most basic survival needs. Holding your breath under water soon becomes painful and breathing again is pleasurable. Others help you organize your life for long-term survival, not only for yourself but for your family, your children, even your larger social group. Some motives may be little related to survival: the pleasure of mastering a musical instrument, of producing a work of art, or just of being as capable as you can be.

Discussions of human motives and emotions often include three quite different factors: biological ones, which we share with many species; learned ones, which we share with some species; and cognitive ones, which are primarily or exclusively human.

Biological Factors Biologically, motives and emotions are based on body structures. Most important are the nervous and endocrine systems, which are often involved in complex interactions over time, with behavior leading to hormonal changes which influence other behaviors. Sensory mechanisms are also important, bringing in information about the environment and the body, and motor outputs are involved in most motivated behavior. Central processing structures must also exist to sort and direct motivation-related inputs and outputs. If the central mechanisms of a very hungry organism have assigned food the highest priority, for example, the organism may ignore other normally enticing odors or sights and give up normally frequent behaviors until food is obtained.

One research finding that aroused widespread interest was the discovery by James Olds of a so-called **pleasure center** in the hypothalamus (Olds, 1956; Olds & Milner, 1973). At first, this location was thought to be a central structure in the biological organization of priorities for motives, the physical seat of the pleasure/pain rule of hedonism. We now know that hypothalamic involvement in motivation is more complicated than this, but the hypothalamus clearly plays a major role in many motives (Routtenberg, 1978).

Biological structures are developed according to genetic codes passed from generation to generation. Hence any discussion of biological factors must also involve evolutionary or ethological issues. If the hypothalamus assigns a higher priority to food than to sex for an animal under given circumstances, for example, this implies that such a priority helped that animal's ancestors survive.

Learning Factors For species in which adult behavior is determined entirely by biological structures built from genetic codes (some insects, for example), all motivated behavior can be explained in terms of evolutionary survival. But for many species, some learning contributes to each adult's pattern of behavior. In mammals—especially in our closest relatives, the great apes—substantial amounts of learning are involved.

We saw in Chapter 3 that the capacity to learn is a product of evolution. But each individual makes different use of this learning capacity. The flexibility of the human species has given us both the greatest capacity for and the greatest requirement for learning. With learning, we can accomplish more than any other species; without it, a child would probably be unable to survive. This means that all people differ in the way they sort various motives or respond to them. The response to motives will even differ from time to time for the same person as new learning changes the patterns of motivation.

Cognitive Factors Human motives are also affected by factors that we share with few if any other species: We can think about what we are doing and what utility our actions may have. Cognitive factors clearly depend on both biological structures and learned patterns of thinking, but are different from either.

Regardless of the sources of our ability to think, to analyze situations, and to make decisions, our ability to do these things affects how we respond to motives. It may even create entirely new motives. If you think of yourself as a particular kind of person, you may behave in ways that sustain your self-image, even when more basic motivational patterns might urge some other course. People who commit suicide to dramatize a political cause, for example, go directly against all built-in patterns of survival.

Current Issues Some current issues in the study of human motivation concern the relative importance of the biological, learned, and cognitive factors (Franken, 1982). These three categories correspond to the physiological, behavioral, and cognitive perspectives in psychology. Other major perspectives in psychology offer their own versions of motivation. The ethological perspective emphasizes evolutionary survival patterns. The social-learning perspective emphasizes learning from others. The psychoanalytic perspective proposes a special view of innate instincts that are shaped through particular kinds of learning. The humanist perspective agrees that survival motives are basic, but emphasizes higher, more human, motives.

Psychologists not committed to a single perspective may try to reconcile the different perspectives for each motivation of interest. How important are built-in motives resulting from our evolutionary history, parts of the brain, our learning capacity, or our cognitions? And how do all of these factors interact?

Consider the questions that might be asked about the problem of obesity in humans. Is a given person obese because of eating too much or because of genetic predispositions to a larger body? If overeating *is* involved, does it occur because of a too-strong hunger drive, learned patterns of food consumption, or innate preferences for the taste of some foods? Might the person think about being, and for some reason choose to be, obese?

In fact, any or all of these factors may be relevant to a single person. Japanese sumo wrestlers, for example, who often weigh several hundred pounds, are first selected from those children who are genetically large, then are fed special fattening diets for years (Tanner & Taylor, 1965). The wrestlers cooperate because they know that theirs is a respected and prestigious occupation in their culture. So sumo wrestler Wakamiyama weighs 390 pounds because of a unique combination of genetics, biology, learning, and cognition. ■ Figure 4.1

There are interacting causes for all motivated acts, and thus no single principle is applicable to all motivations. Furthermore, every person is unique and can change over time. The only way to understand any person's motivation is to study first the factors common to all people, then those that allow individuals to develop their own patterns.

MOTIVES FOR INDIVIDUAL SURVIVAL

The task for members of any living species is to survive for the next minute, day, winter, or decade—whatever it takes to mate and have offspring, and to arrange for them to survive to be independent. Each step depends on the preceding one: If you don't survive the next minute, all else is irrelevant. If you do, then you have to worry about surviving tonight, and next week. An active adult is often serving many survival motives at once, so that some are obscured by others. But considering short-term and long-term survival separately allows us to sort out some major motives.

Homeostasis and Short-Term Survival

Survival over the short term often depends on systems for balancing the body's physiology to keep it within

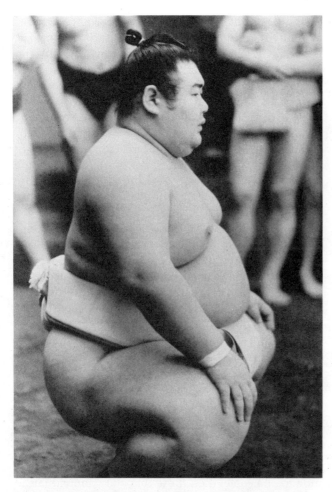

Figure 4.1 ■ Wakamiyama's 390-pound weight is large even for sumo wrestlers. Born a genetically large child, he has been fed over 5000 calories a day in huge meals followed by rest (to avoid burning up the calories). He is even buffered from problems by his trainers, lest he worry off a pound or two.

(T. Tanuma, LIFE MAGAZINE, © 1965, Time, Inc.)

allowable boundaries. The body is a complex biochemical machine, and it can only continue to function under certain conditions. The rapid and precise nervous system that allows you to read this line, for example, must be continuously supplied with oxygen if it is to keep functioning, and is exceedingly sensitive to the temperature at which it functions. A brief interruption in oxygen supply or a few degrees' change in temperature and it malfunctions or dies.

Oxygen Need: Survival over Minutes The brain's need for oxygen, via the lungs and the bloodstream, is powerful and basic. We live in an ocean of oxygen-rich air, which we breathe continuously under the guidance of mechanisms so evolutionarily old that we are hardly aware of them. Although our need for oxygen is so critical that we will die in minutes without it, we

only learn how powerful our motive for oxygen can be if breathing is interrupted. People frequently die of smoke inhalation in fires, for example, because they cannot keep from breathing for the few minutes needed to escape the smoke.

Temperature Control: Survival over Hours An increase or decrease of a few degrees from the normal human body temperature of 37°C will result in brain malfunction characterized by dizziness, confusion, and coma. Changes of a few more degrees will cause death. Even normal daily swings of a degree or two may cause measurable differences in nervous-system functioning (Marshall, 1982). As a species we are *endotherms*, organisms that regulate body temperature through internal mechanisms (Crawshaw et al., 1981). In contrast, reptiles are *ectotherms;* they regulate temperature using external factors, such as by lying in the sun or shade. Endothermy requires much more food, to burn as fuel to maintain body temperature, but it also allows a more efficient nervous system. In unusually hot or cold environments, however, our temperature mechanisms can only stave off the excess heat or cold for a few hours before we suffer heatstroke or hypothermia, body temperatures too hot or too cold for our nervous systems to function properly.

Temperature control, like breathing, is mostly accomplished by evolutionarily old mechanisms of which we are usually unaware (Satinoff, 1978). But more often than in oxygen motivation, the need to be warmer or colder results in general body activity and a conscious awareness of motivation. We move out of the sun, or put on a coat, knowing why we do so. In moving out of the sun, we simply add the lizard's ectothermic trick to our own internal mechanisms. But putting on a coat is a culturally transmitted activity of great significance. We evolved as a tropical species, with a high internal temperature as well as a relatively hairless skin and other systems designed for shedding excess heat. Yet as a species we live in a wider range of climates than any other mammal through our use of cultural techniques of housing and clothing. Eskimos, for example, survive in temperatures as low as −45°C by living in houses so well insulated that the internal temperatures may exceed 27°C (80°F). Even when they go outside, the layer of air trapped by their fur clothing keeps their skin at tropical temperatures (Crawshaw et al., 1981).

Homeostasis In many motivations, both internal body adjustments and overt behavior are directed according to a pattern called homeostasis. **Homeostasis** is the maintaining of a body variable within allowable boundaries by feedback loops that sense and correct deviations of the variable. For breathing, this means

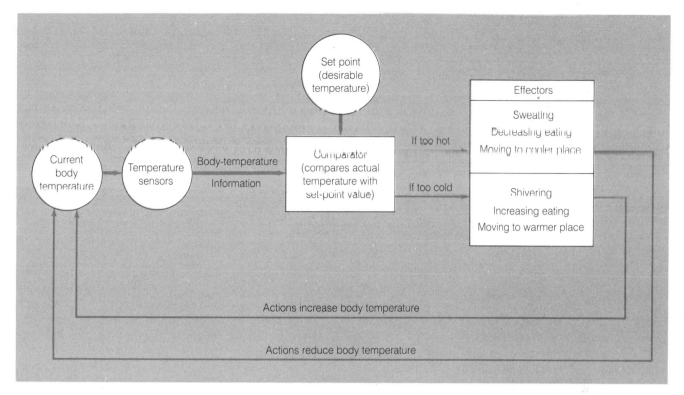

Figure 4.2 ■ Homeostasis as a feedback mechanism. All homeostatic mechanisms balance some body variable, such as temperature, by sensing the actual value of the variable, comparing that to an ideal or set-point value, and activating effector mechanisms to alter the variable as needed. This use of the sensed value to effect a change in that value is a feedback loop.

that when oxygen need increases, you breathe faster; when the need is reduced, you breathe more slowly (Perlman, 1980). Temperature control is another example of homeostatic mechanisms. ■ Figure 4.2

Homeostasis requires a particular arrangement of several components. The variable to be controlled, such as body temperature, must be sensed, and the sensed information compared to the ideal value called the **set point.** If the sensed value is above or below the set point, *effectors* must be activated to bring the body variable back to the set point. For body temperatures below the set point, automatic effectors include changes in blood flow to conserve heat and shivering, a form of muscle trembling that uses energy to create heat. Behavioral effectors include stamping the feet, moving into the sun, and putting on more clothes. For body temperatures above the set point, automatic effectors include sweating and blood-flow changes to eliminate heat. Some behavioral effectors are moving into the shade and fanning oneself. The relationships between temperature diverging from set point and actions to restore ideal temperature are called **feedback loops;** information about high or low temperature is

sent to effectors that modify temperature, and is thus fed back.

Many kinds of body adjustments are homeostatic. In hunger, for example, body sensors sensitive to metabolic fuels call for more food if reserves run low, less food if energy consumption is generating too much heat. But learned and cognitive factors are often superimposed on basic homeostatic mechanisms and can generate powerful motives even when no homeostatic adjustments are needed.

The set point for a homeostatic mechanism is usually quite stable, but it is often biologically alterable when it is useful to survival. One notable example in temperature control is fever. Long thought to be simply a negative consequence of illness, fever is now seen as a survival-enhancing adaptation (Kluger, 1979). In fever, the body is thought to elevate the set point as high as the nervous system can take, even high enough to result in temporary delirium, as a mechanism for killing the disease-causing bacteria. After the danger passes, the set point is reset to normal (in common terms, the fever breaks) and the person suddenly sweats profusely to get body temperature back down

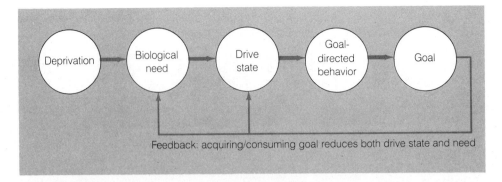

Figure 4.3 ■ A need-drive model of motivation is most appropriate to survival motives based on tissue needs, such as hunger or thirst, that increase with deprivation of some needed input. With increasing deprivation, tissue need builds up, leading to an active drive state that motivates actions toward an appropriate goal (such as food or water). Acquiring or consuming the goal reduces both need and drive until further deprivation reactivates the cycle.

to normal. (Postmenopausal hot flashes are apparently brief changes in set point caused by lower hormone levels; Crawshaw et al., 1981.)

Temperature set point can also be lowered, as it is in hibernation (Heller et al., 1978). The lowered set point reduces nervous-system activity so that the hibernating animal remains inactive and unaware, with such a low level of energy use that it need not eat for long periods of time (Musacchia & Jansky, 1981).

Understanding how natural set points are established and changed helps psychologists understand motivation. But it also has medical value. If fever is adaptive, using aspirin to lower a fever may not be in the best interests of the patient. But giving enough hormones to prevent hot flashes may be. And deliberate lowering of the set point for body temperature could be useful in surgery.

Needs, Drives, and Intermediate-Term Survival

If an organism can manage its immediate survival, somewhat less pressing motivations come into play. Most body tissues are largely water, and water loss through breathing, sweating, and urination must be made up or the body will become dehydrated. Furthermore, the energy used in metabolism and behavior must be made up through new food intake or the organism will starve. The motives resulting from these needs are what we call thirst and hunger.

One traditional way of describing motives such as hunger and thirst is in terms of needs and drives. A **need** is a tissue deficit of some kind that accumulates over time; the body develops needs for oxygen, water, and fuel, for example, over minutes, hours, and days. **Drive** is the general energizing of body activity that results from a tissue need. Needs can be measured directly, but drives can only be inferred. A drive is a

general arousal, and particular needs give rise to particular kinds of drive. **Hunger** is thus the drive that arises from the need for food, which in turn develops from food deprivation. ■ Figure 4.3

When a drive is aroused by a tissue need, the drive both energizes and directs behavior toward a goal that will satisfy the need. Acquiring the goal (eating food, in the case of hunger) reduces both the drive and the need. Note that this need–drive–drive-reduction sequence forms a feedback loop that seeks to return the drive to zero.

Thirst: Survival over a Few Days   A person lost in the desert must first be able to breathe, then to keep cool enough. The next critical need is water. With water, the person can last many days; without it, only a few. Hence, animals that have evolved to fit desert conditions often have specialized mechanisms for obtaining or retaining water. The camel, for example, has elaborate structures in its nose that both conserve water and reduce the temperature of the air it breathes (Schmidt-Nielsen, 1981).

All species need water to maintain necessary levels of fluids, both within body cells and between cells. Homeostatic mechanisms manage the total water supply so as to balance these two needs, but inevitable water losses must be replenished. **Thirst** is the drive that results from the need for fluid; it is a basic motive of most species (Rolls et al., 1980). We say that thirst directs the nervous system to find and consume water. But thirst is not found as an entity anywhere in the biological mechanisms of water need and water consumption. Biologically, what corresponds to thirst is activity in a set of **drinking circuits,** neural and hormonal linkages among tissues, organs, and the nervous system. These drinking circuits, like those of other motivations, are closely tied into the hypothalamus (Thompson et al., 1980) ■ Figure 4.4

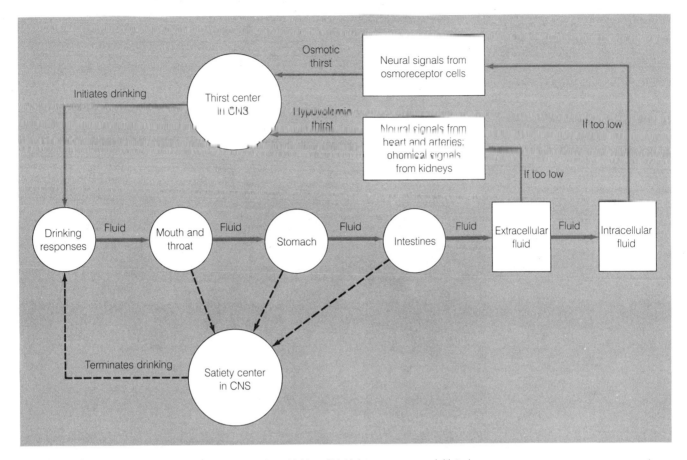

Figure 4.4 ■ Summary of the body circuits that regulate drinking. Drinking responses are initiated by thirst centers and terminated by satiety centers associated with areas of the hypothalamus. Thirst can be initiated in two major ways, based on too little fluid within the cells (osmotic thirst) or loss of body fluids such as blood (hypovolemic thirst).

As represented in Figure 4.4, changes in the amount of intracellular fluid (within cells) produce changes in cell-wall structure that are sensed as one type of thirst, called **osmotic thirst.** The information that the cells are low in water content is fed to a *thirst center* in the central nervous system (at least part of which is in the hypothalamus). That leads to finding and consuming water. As water is drunk, sensors in the mouth and throat report the water consumption to a *satiety center*, which stops the drinking when enough water has been consumed to make up the body's current needs. Shortly after that, sensors in the stomach, and later others in the intestines, also report that water has arrived. The water eventually reaches the cells, where it relieves the actual tissue need (Rosenzweig & Leiman, 1982).

Note that the mouth and throat sensors terminate drinking long before the water reaches the cells; this prevents unnecessary drinking. In the wild, drinking is often a time of great danger to an organism (predators often frequent water holes) and taking on excess water would add weight and require the kidneys to dispose of it. It is much more efficient to stop drinking when enough water has been consumed, even though the tissue need may not be relieved for some time. The sensors in stomach and intestines seem to be backup systems; if the mouth and throat sensors didn't terminate drinking, these later sensors would.

Figure 4.4 also shows another kind of thirst, caused by extracellular fluid loss, as for example, blood loss from a wound. This form of thirst, called **hypovolemic thirst,** results from neural signals from sensors in the heart and arteries that note the loss of blood volume, and from chemical signals from sensors in the kidneys (Andersson, 1971). But once the thirst center of the CNS is activated, the process of drinking to satiation is the same.

Hunger: Survival over Many Days Food is less critical for the short term than oxygen or water, because the body can begin to burn its own stored reserves of fat and even muscle; these can be replenished when food is finally available. People who have gone on water-only hunger strikes for political reasons have

"AS FAR BACK AS I CAN REMEMBER ALL THE GREAT MEALS
I'VE EVER HAD CONSISTED PRIMARILY OF ANTS."

(© 1983 by Sidney Harris)

survived for many days before dying; the effects on their brains become severe only in the last days, producing confusion and coma. This long-term brain survival occurs because homeostatic mechanisms allow the brain to "eat first"; any available energy is used first to maintain the brain, and what is left goes to the rest of the body.

Hunger is more complex than thirst in several respects. Whereas thirst is typically relieved by water, animals eat a wide variety of foods, many of which are potentially poisonous. Those foods provide an astounding array of vitamins, minerals (including trace elements), and other necessary inputs besides the basic energy fuel to maintain life. Hunger systems must encourage the eating of enough of the right kinds of foods to supply all of these needs while discouraging eating anything that could be harmful. Basic tastes and taste preferences of some species seem to have evolved to help them manage their food intake. In general, most species have preferences for the tastes of foods they usually eat and that are good for them.

The taste of sweet, which many mammals prefer even without prior learning, seems to be a guide to the

fruit sugars that are a useful energy source for many species (Wurtman & Wurtman, 1979). The taste of salt is also basic and preferred, at least in moderation; the sodium in sodium chloride plays a critical role in neural transmission as well as other body processes. Sour and bitter tastes, in contrast, are usually avoided, perhaps because they may imply food is spoiled and thus potentially dangerous.

Tastes also play a role in learned food preferences. A wide range of tastes is made possible by combinations of elementary tastes. With this array of tastes to guide it, an animal can learn not to eat foods again that produced illness the first time. Animals can also learn to prefer tastes that make them feel better over time. This ability is the probable basis of most **specific hungers,** cravings for particular tastes. Some specific hungers may reflect innate mechanisms, as when salt deficiencies lead to unusual consumption of salt, but others probably represent learned preferences (Zahoric et al., 1974). Learned adaptations to tastes thus maximize survival by helping the organism both avoid what it cannot tolerate and consume what it needs.

In its simplest form, hunger works like thirst. In a

Figure 4.5 ■ Each day, this 277-pound Munich carpenter consumes all the food and drink on the table. It is unlikely that much, if any, of this consumption is in response to hunger based on tissue need. No doubt much of it is in response to the incentive value of the foods and habit.

(Frank Scherschel, LIFE MAGAZINE, © 1963, Time, Inc.)

series of experiments, Dethier (1976) showed how the elements of hunger and eating in the blowfly form a simple feedback loop. As the fly encounters a sweet substance, it begins to ingest it; a stretch sensor in its abdomen tells it to stop eating when full. If the neural link from the abdominal sensor is cut, the fly will keep on eating, sometimes until it bursts.

Other species, including humans, use similar feedback loops, which become increasingly elaborate in more complex species. Learned factors are also added for many species and, for humans, a variety of cognitive and social factors. Humans eat or don't eat for many reasons, only some of which can be called hunger (Novin et al., 1976). We will look at some of these other factors later, in the context of long-term weight control.

As with drinking, eating is controlled by neural and hormonal loops that pass through the hypothalamus (Thompson, 1980). Two particular areas of the hypothalamus have been associated with hunger (Keesey & Powley, 1975). When first discovered, these areas were thought to be integration centers. The **lateral hypothalamus (LH)** was thought to receive sensory signals that indicated a body need for food and to turn on hunger. The **ventromedial hypothalamus (VMH)** was thought to receive sensory signals from food intake and to turn off hunger. This *dual-center* view of hunger summarized the results of many lines of research and is to some extent still accepted. But later researchers have described the mechanisms of hunger as a circuit that passes through these areas of the hypothalamus. The LH and VMH, according to this modified view, are important way stations for the processing of information but not exactly on or off centers.

Research continues on specifying the role of all the elements in these hunger feedback loops, from sensors to hypothalamic areas (Ritter et al., 1981). But how they are integrated, and how other social and cognitive factors are added to them, remains the subject of debate.

Motives for Long-Term Survival

Much greater flexibility of behavior is available to longer-lived species that are capable of substantial learning. For insects, whose lives are measured in days and whose brains are tiny, a single hunger feedback sensor and fixed behavior patterns make sense. But birds and mammals, with lives measured in years and relatively large brains, operate differently: They have both the time and the capability to learn complex patterns of behavior, as in finding and eating food. Even birds, though less flexible in general than mammals, show this kind of learning: for example, oyster catchers do not mate until they are three years old, apparently because it takes that much time for them to learn to pry open shellfish efficiently enough to be able to feed both themselves and their young.

Incentives One consequence of the flexibility provided by learning is that environmental stimuli can come to have motivational properties independent of the organism's current tissue needs. A stimulus is said to be an **incentive,** or to have incentive value, if an organism approaches it or avoids it because of some attribute of the stimulus itself, regardless of the organism's motivational state. A good-tasting food, for example, is a positive incentive, one that is approached; it may be eaten for its taste alone, whether the organism is hungry or not. Other tastes or smells are negative incentives and will be avoided. Incentives can be innate, as sweet tastes are, but many are learned, especially by humans. ■ Figure 4.5

A need-drive-incentive framework allows for more complex interpretation of motivated behavior than the need-drive model alone. A person may eat because of a food's good taste even when not hungry. Or he or she may eat a bad-tasting food because of need-drive hunger, despite its negative incentive value—but eat less of it than of a good-tasting food.

Curiosity and Optimal Arousal Even a need-drive-incentive model is insufficient for some motives, however. This became obvious to motivation researchers when they realized that *curiosity* acts in many ways as a motive: It can initiate and direct exploratory behavior, and a bored animal can be reinforced with a novel stimulus just as a hungry animal can be reinforced with food (Butler, 1954).

But curiosity cannot be fitted into a need-drive format. Boredom does seem to build up and be satisfied almost as hunger does, but no tissue need for novel stimuli can be found or is even likely. (No one is *really* ever bored to death.) And incentive is not enough of an explanation, because curiosity varies in ways apart from the novelty (incentive) value of the stimuli. So how are we to interpret curiosity as a motive?

From an evolutionary perspective, curiosity is a useful mechanism for encouraging exploration and incidental learning. Biologically, it might be a kind of set point for novelty; if nothing novel has been encountered the animal seeks it out, and if too much new has been happening the animal retreats to the comfort of the familiar.

This notion of a set point for novelty has been expressed more generally as an **optimal arousal** model of motivation (Berlyne, 1960, 1966). Where need-drive theory proposes that an organism seeks to return drive to zero, optimal arousal suggests that both too much and too little drive are undesirable. If hunger or thirst is strongly aroused, activity will be undertaken to reduce it. But when hunger is reduced, curiosity may take its place. The net effect will be to keep the animal active at tasks useful to survival, either fulfilling tissue-need drives or exploring the environment and learning about it in ways that could be useful later. ■ Figure 4.6

Fight or Flight Other motivated behaviors that help maintain survival are related to extreme arousal; these behaviors are associated with the fight-or-flight reaction of the sympathetic nervous system. It does little good for the species if an organism stays warm and well fed but then is killed by a rival, is eaten by a predator, or falls off a cliff through inattention. The active behaviors supported by the arousal of the fight-or-fight response are also motivated survival behaviors. ■ Figure 4.7

The fight-or-flight response itself is not a motive but a crash arousal of body resources for energetic and

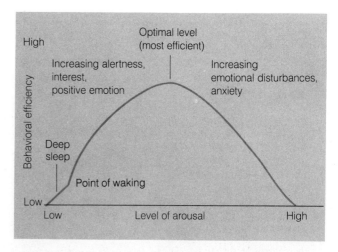

Figure 4.6 ■ Optimal arousal lies somewhere between the point of minimal awakening and the point of maximal arousal. The actual point of greatest efficiency differs somewhat for different kinds of tasks: A slightly higher level of arousal is best for well-learned tasks, a slightly lower level for comparatively new and complex tasks.

(From Hebb, 1955)

physically dangerous activity. What behaviors follow its arousal will be guided by other cues: An animal may flee a predator when it can, then turn and fight when cornered. A monkey whose arousal is triggered by brain stimulation from implanted electrodes may either fight or flee, depending on the monkey it is with; it is likely to attack its social inferiors but not its superiors (Delgado, 1967).

Humans fight or flee for learned and cognitive reasons as well as innate ones, but in life-or-death circumstances at least some of the same basic survival mechanisms come into play. During the fall of Saigon at the end of the Vietnam War, for example, the few helicopters leaving the city were mobbed by those desperate to leave before the arrival of the Viet Cong. Many would-be escapees were literally beaten back from the doors. (For more on "fight" behavior, see the discussion of aggression in Chapter 18.) ■ Figure 4.8

Long-Term Weight and the Causes of Obesity The short-term motive of hunger reflects the longer-term survival need of maintaining an appropriate body weight. In the short term, hunger is activated until enough food has been eaten; but in the larger view, how much is enough at a given time depends on numerous factors. An animal seeking to maintain a very heavy body weight, or one that metabolizes food inefficiently, might become hungry much more frequently than a lean or metabolically efficient animal.

What weight is appropriate depends on other factors. A fatter animal will be less able to catch prey or to escape predators, but will be better able to withstand

Figure 4.7 ■ This photograph of a leopard attacking a baboon has been called the best of its kind. It graphically captures both the effect of and the reason for the fight-or-flight response. Baboons rarely survive such encounters, and only the crash mobilization of all their body resources gives them any chance at all.

(John Dominis, LIFE MAGAZINE, © 1973, Time, Inc.)

Figure 4.8 ■ Frightened would-be escapees from Saigon, at the end of the Vietnam War, are beaten back by those already aboard a loaded evacuation helicopter. This life-or-death situation no doubt aroused the fight-or-flight response in all participants; their postures and expressions show the same desperation as Figure 4.7.

(United Press International Photo)

cold or temporary absence of food. Thus predators such as cougars or prey with plentiful food such as jackrabbits are typically lean and fast. Animals that must withstand cold or periodic food shortages are plumper, especially those that are neither predators nor prey—beavers, for example. When wide temperature changes occur annually, an animal may even drastically change its weight, as bears do before hibernating (Rogers, 1981).

Body weight may thus be considered a set-point variable that metabolic mechanisms and hunger/eating mechanisms seek to satisfy. If too much food is eaten, it may be burned off as heat; if too little food is eaten, the animal will become hungrier. This body-weight balance seems to be maintained by a balance between the neural circuits tied into the LH and the VMH (Keesey & Powley, 1975). ■ Figure 4.9

The LH has been considered an *on* center for eating because an animal tends to eat less if its LH is damaged. The VMH has been considered an *off* center because an animal tends to eat more if its VMH is damaged. But a more contemporary view is that the circuits in which these hypothalamic areas play important roles are part of a feedback system for maintaining long-term body weight. A VMH-lesioned rat does not eat indefinitely. The initial phase of rapid eating is somewhat analogous to the sweating when fever breaks: The rat eats rapidly to raise its weight to a new, higher set point, as sweating seeks to lower temperature to the newly reduced set point. Once the weight is reached, the rat adjusts its diet to maintain that weight, eating less if it is force-fed to a higher weight and more if it is deprived and loses weight. Similarly, a LH-lesioned rat maintains a lower body weight, but otherwise responds normally to deviations from that weight (Keesey, 1980).

This interpretation suggests that one cause of human obesity or unusually low weight might be a hypothalamic problem. In fact, some human hypothalamic tumors have been associated with unusual weight gain or loss (Beal et al., 1981). Furthermore, some animals seem to alter their weight set points routinely in response to other important survival needs such as hibernation, mating, or incubating eggs, so perhaps human weight set points might be artificially adjustable, if they were more fully understood (Margulies, 1979; Mrosovsky & Sherry, 1980).

Human weight levels are no doubt maintained by the interaction of biological, learned, and cognitive factors (Rodin, 1978). Consider just a few of the possible relationships. A naturally plump child is likely to be teased and harrassed in a society such as ours that puts a strongly negative value on obesity. That child may overeat as a way of passing time and providing pleasure, a practice our culture often encourages. After a

few years, the eating pattern may be habitual, maintained by routine cues. In fact, early childhood eating patterns may help establish the lifetime set point (Bennett & Gurin, 1982; Jones & Friedman, 1982). Trying to isolate the reasons any single human is obese is obviously not an easy task (Wolman, 1982).

One major theoretical suggestion that seems to account for many findings about obesity is Schachter's internal-external dimension. Based on many ingenious studies, Schachter (1971) suggested that the obese are less attuned to the internal cues that should stop their eating and more attuned to external cues for eating than are the nonobese. With so many cultural cues for eating, the obese might then continue to overeat even when not hungry. But one researcher has recently criticized Schachter's view (Rodin, 1981); the limits of Schachter's approach may only reflect the fact that many causes can lead to the same problem. Perhaps obesity will have to be considered a general description of many different conditions rather than a single condition (Stunkard, 1980).

Obesity *is* generally less healthy than normal weight. Sumo wrestlers, for example, are more susceptible to diabetes and to liver and kidney trouble, and their life spans are also some ten years shorter than the Japanese average (Tanner & Taylor, 1965). But the opposite problem of too little weight can be far more dangerous to health. People, usually teenage females, who suffer from **anorexia nervosa** (not eating for "nervous" reasons) often die of starvation, despite attempts to help them. ■ Research Issue: Why Do Anorexics Starve Themselves?

MOTIVES FOR GROUP SURVIVAL

Individual survival as an adult is not the only necessity for species continuity. Some motivated actions of adults serve to create and care for the next generation. Other motivated actions contribute to the survival of a social group, and thus contribute indirectly to the survival of individuals.

We will look first at child care, then at sexual motivation and some of the aspects of sexual development that lie behind it. Motives that specifically concern interactions in social groups will be considered later in the text.

Parenting

For most reptiles, the only care of offspring may be choosing a location to bury the eggs. But some reptilian species care for their young to a limited extent until

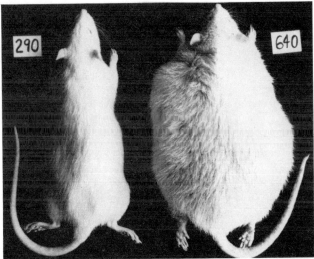

Figure 4.9 ■ Hypothalamic lesions in rats seem to raise or lower the set point for body weight. (a) An overweight rat compared to a normal rat. The obese rat has a lesion in the VMH. (b) The effect of the VMH lesion is to stabilize the rat at a higher weight. If the rat is fed even more and forced to gain more weight, it eats less when left on its own until it regains its stable overweight level. If it is deprived so that it loses some of the weight and then is left alone, it eats only enough to hold its overweight level. (c) Similarly, a rat with a lesion in the LH maintains its weight, as a normal rat does, but at a lower level.

(**a,** courtesy of Philip Teitelbaum; **b** and **c,** adapted from *Physiological Psychology* by Mark R. Rosenzweig and Arnold L. Loiman, D. C. Health and Company, 1982. Reprinted by permission of the publisher.)

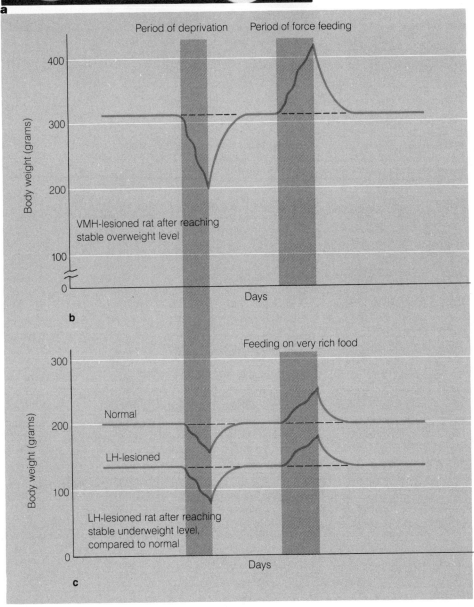

Why do anorexics starve themselves?

Despite all the innate mechanisms for maintaining weight, thousands of young women (and some men) in the United States are this minute apparently starving themselves voluntarily, often to death. As many as .5% of all girls in their late teens have been estimated to be anorexic (Crisp et al., 1976). Typically, children who seem to be developing normally change, in their teens or early 20s, to a virtual starvation diet. The change may begin with conventional dieting, but when the full pattern of anorexia begins, weight drops radically. One woman went from 120 pounds at age 18 to 47 pounds a few years later (Bachrach et al., 1965).■ Figure 4.10

Anorexia offers a perplexing problem of interpretation as well as a life-threatening medical problem (Bruch, 1978). The cause cannot be as simple as a set-point shift, because anorexics often report strong hunger. Yet if they give in and gorge themselves, they may then induce vomiting to get rid of the food lest it add weight. For some anorexics, this *binge-purge* sequence becomes habitual; some researchers have adopted the term *bulimia* to describe that pattern, considering it clinically distinct from anorexia.

Anorexics exhibit a bewildering variety of psychological and physical changes from normal. Their drastic weight loss causes a broad range of starvation-related body changes, including damage to major organs, cessation of menstruation, and alteration of hormone levels. Psychologically, anorexics seem aware of most aspects of reality but have a strangely distorted body image. A bikini-clad anorexic may observe her 50-pound body in a mirror and proclaim herself still too fat—even as her parents and doctor worry whether she will survive the week.

a

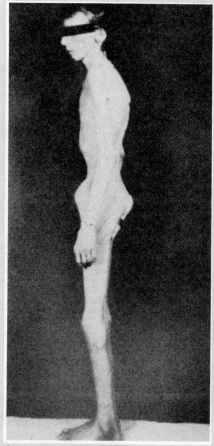

b

Figure 4.10 ■ (a) This Arizona newspaper reporter, afflicted with anorexia and bulimia (the binge-purge syndrome), has publicized her story in the hope of helping others who suffer from eating disorders. (b) This anorexic woman has reached a near-fatal point in her illness.

(**a,** Wide World Photos; **b,** Dr. Arthur J. Backrach, Dr. Leonard Krasner, Dr. Leonard Ullmann)

Anorexia often stops and reverses the body changes that come with puberty, eliminating menstruation, breast enlargement, and other signs of physical maturity. Some psychologists feel that this self-starvation is a rejection of sexuality or of adulthood in general (Levenkron, 1978). Others feel that the major hormonal changes associated with puberty, or with the initial dieting, may trigger some biological problem (Herbert, 1983a; Holt et al., 1981). About all that is clear about anorexia is that unless drastic intervention is undertaken the anorexic may die, as do 10% of those whose cases are severe enough to be reported to a physician.

The patient in Figure 4.10b was treated by behavior modification (a technique of rewarding desired behavior); she was taught to eat and maintain weight, apparently successfully. Other therapists suggest that long-term follow-up psychotherapy is needed to prevent recurrence, however, even when behavior-modification techniques have succeeded in maintaining a survival weight. As the many contributions to normal hunger and weight maintenance are better understood, perhaps anorexia will also be better understood (Levenkron, 1982).

Figure 4.11 ■ A female chimp plays with her infant. Primate mothers can be good parents if they have other experienced mothers to learn from. But they are often unable to behave appropriately without such learning and may kill the infant by neglect or mishandling.

(Co Rentmeester, LIFE MAGAZINE, © 1972, Time, Inc.)

they are old enough to have a chance of surviving on their own: Crocodiles show some minimal *parenting* behaviors, for example. Unlike newly hatched reptiles, mammalian young require extensive care to survive; human infants require the most care for the longest time. The need to care for offspring is thus an evolutionarily old and basic motive.

For any species that cares for its young, some form of parenting motivation thus seems necessary. Such a motivation has traditionally been called a *maternal instinct* because of an emphasis on the mother's care (e.g., Langman, 1982). But fathers of many species actively care for infants, so *parenting* is more general. As with other motivations, simpler species seem to carry out innate parenting behaviors in response to environmental cues. But more complex species, especially the great apes, must learn parenting behaviors. Harry Harlow, for example, found that monkeys raised in isolation make terrible parents (Harlow et al., 1971). Zoo-raised gorilla mothers have similar difficulties and must learn how to take care of their babies (Rock, 1978). A single zoo-raised female gorilla may be unable to handle her newborn safely, and may accidentally kill it. But if put with a group of experienced gorilla mothers, she will learn from them. ■ Figure 4.11

Some human parents are also unable to care for their children, or abuse them (Kempe & Kempe, 1978). Such child abuse often seems to be learned: Many child abusers were themselves abused as children (Starr, 1979). It is possible that humans retain innate patterns of responding to and caring for young: Many people have a positive emotional response to babies, or even to cartoon characters with similar facial proportions, such as large eyes (Eibl-Eibesfeldt, 1972; Gould, 1979a). (This probably reflects a mechanism that in other species encourages adults to take care of juveniles until their head shape reaches adult proportions.) But if humans do retain this responsiveness to young, it is not strong enough to prevent large numbers of those young from being battered (Belsky, 1980).

Sexual Motivation

Most species reproduce sexually: Two adults of different sexes behave in such a way as to create offspring that are a genetic mixture of both adults. Behaviors leading to mating are strongly motivated for all sexually reproducing species (Wickler, 1973). In animals, many of the mating patterns are innate, although some learning may be involved. In humans, any innate patterns that remain are strongly overlaid with learned and culturally regulated factors. ■ Figure 4.12

Sexual motivation in mammals is mediated through circuits that pass through the hypothalamus (Hutchinson, 1978). But instead of being triggered by body-tissue need, sexual arousal typically occurs in response to an environmental cue. The immediate cues usually come directly from an opposite-sex individual. The tendency for such sexual stimuli to be arousing, however, depends on other cues that, through hormonal changes, prepare the animal for mating (Adler, 1981). The length of daylight, daytime temperature, or another seasonal cue triggers hormonal changes from the gonads. These changes prepare both males and females for their respective roles.

In some species—ring doves, for example—an interlocked sequence of cues leading to behavior continues throughout mating and parenting (Lehrman, 1964). Once the doves are prepared for mating, each step in the sequence leads to further hormonal changes that make the next step possible. The sight of the opposite-sex dove prepares each for nest building, the act of nest building prepares them for copulating, copulating prepares the female for providing "crop milk" as a food for offspring, and so forth. Ring doves thus carry out their roles without having to learn them.

But in species that learn much of their behavior, sexual activity often includes learned components. In a series of experiments begun in the 1950s, Harlow (1973) showed that monkeys raised in isolation are often unable to mate successfully. When a male and female who have been raised without the opportunity to observe other monkeys mating and without themselves indulging in juvenile sex play are placed together, they may become sexually aroused and attempt to mate, but one or both may fail to adopt the body position needed for intromission.

The acquiring/consuming portion of sexually motivated behavior in mammals is intercourse. For the species the important outcome of intercourse is fertilization, but for individuals the important event is orgasm. In male mammals, orgasm occurs together with ejaculation of sperm, the key action in their reproductive role. It is likely that female mammals also experience orgasm, although it is not so directly tied to reproduction (Davidson, 1981); however, only recently has female orgasm in nonhuman species been carefully studied (Goldfoot et al., 1980).

The work of Kinsey and his associates (1948, 1953) and of Masters and Johnson (1966, 1970, 1975) on human sexual behaviors has been widely publicized. Hence human physiological responses in intercourse are reasonably well understood (Beach, 1977).

Intercourse has four major phases, as defined by measurable physiological changes: an initial phase of building general excitement, a plateau phase of maintained arousal, orgasm, and resolution (return to the unaroused condition). These phases show general similarities for males and females. One difference, however, is that males typically show a rapid resolution following orgasm and a refractory period (before further arousal is possible) lasting from minutes to hours. Females, in contrast, may show several patterns. Besides a pattern similar to that of males, they may also experience a prolonged plateau phase without orgasm followed by a slow resolution, or several orgasms in succession. ■ Figure 4.13

These physiological changes are influenced by innate patterns. But the sequence of behaviors that lead to them is probably largely learned (McGill et al., 1978). That is, once a couple is engaging in intercourse, their body responsiveness is probably similar to that of most humans. But who has intercourse with whom, and under what circumstances, varies according to a multitude of learned and culturally specified rules (Katchadourian & Lunde, 1980).

As with other motives, arousal mechanisms for sexual motivation are shared to some extent with many species, but the behaviors that the motive leads to may be exclusively human. As we may learn to get oxygen from a tank, to wear warm clothing, and to eat or drink novel substances, so we may learn to be sexually stimulated in a variety of ways. In this case, our flexibility as a species can be troubling for us. Mating patterns can sometimes show variations in animals—for example, both homosexual behavior and rape are reported in some animal species—but only humans show the astounding range of sexual responsiveness noted by mental-health professionals.

SEXUAL DEVELOPMENT AND IDENTITY

Males and females do not differ in most motivations, but for reproduction to take place males must be sexually responsive to females and vice versa. People often discuss the sources of this and other sex differences in extreme terms: For many years sex differences were thought to be givens of nature, and recently some people have argued that virtually all sex differences are learned. But both extreme nature and extreme nurture positions are wrong.

There are unquestionably genetic and innate physiological differences between the sexes. There may even be subtle innate behavioral differences, although the evidence for them is far less clear. It is *also* true that some differences long thought to be innate

Figure 4.12 ■ Mating of male/female pairs is a highly motivated behavior in all species that use sexual reproduction. Various other mammals show apparent affection and tenderness, in addition to explicit sexual arousal, in the mating sequence. But as with other human behaviors, human mating is to a large extent a culturally determined process, not just a biological one.

(Top left, Rene Burri/Magnum Photos; top right, Freelance Photographers Guild; bottom left, Robert Capa/Magnum Photos; bottom right, Stern/Black Star)

actually result from cultural training. But most important are the interactions between nature and nurture. As we look at these interactions, we will note how the topics we have studied so far are all involved: evolution, genetics, physiology, and motivation. (We will also refer to aspects of physical and personality development examined in more detail in Chapters 12 and 13.)

Sexual Selection in Evolution

The mechanism of sexual reproduction apparently evolved early as a useful system for rearranging and mixing genes in creating the next generation (Daly & Wilson, 1978). Sexual reproduction is now widespread throughout the animal kingdom and many aspects of behavior have evolved to aid it (Mitchell, 1979).

For successful sexual reproduction, the sexes must recognize each other and must both be interested in mating at the correct time. Hence **sexual selection,** the selecting of some mates and not others, becomes an important mechanism of evolution. Often sexual selection amplifies differences in appearance or behavior between the sexes (Kolata, 1977b). If the most noticeable males and females can most easily recognize each other and mate, sex differences will be strengthened in the gene pool (Darwin, 1871). Thus some sexual differences in appearance and behavior are to be expected (Searcy and Yasukawa, 1983).

Sexual Development

Human sexual structures and behaviors develop in what has been described as a series of nine prenatal and postnatal steps (Money & Ehrhardt, 1972). We will look at sexual development in terms of these steps, noting both normal development and some of the better-known variations from the norm. ▪ Figure 4.14

Chromosomes In humans, the 23d chromosome pair is composed of dissimilar *sex chromosomes:* Females have two **X chromosomes,** males one X chromosome and one **Y chromosome.** In reproduction, a mother gives her children one of her two Xs and a father provides either his only Y or his only X. Thus it is always the sperm that determines the sex of a child.

Sex-linked characteristics are coded by genes on the arm of the X chromosome that is missing from the Y. Because there is no matching arm on the Y, any recessive gene located on that arm of a male's X must be expressed. Many human genetic problems, such as color blindness, are sex-linked: Females are more often carriers than actual sufferers, but half their male offspring will tend to show the problem (those who get the recessive gene from the mother's X).

Several common genetic problems result from the loss or addition of sex chromosomes in an individual. In each case, the basic pattern of development will be female unless a Y chromosome is present; then the body type will be male. An XO pattern (where the O represents a missing chromosome) results in **Turner's syndrome;** the individual has normal female appearance, but she is quite short and may have other physical problems (J. G. Hall et al., 1982). An XXX count is sometimes called a *superfemale* because of the extra X, but there is no apparent increase in "female" behavior, however defined. A YO pattern is lethal. An XXY count, which can be considered as female plus a Y, yields **Klinefelter's syndrome;** the individual has a generally male body type but muscle distribution,

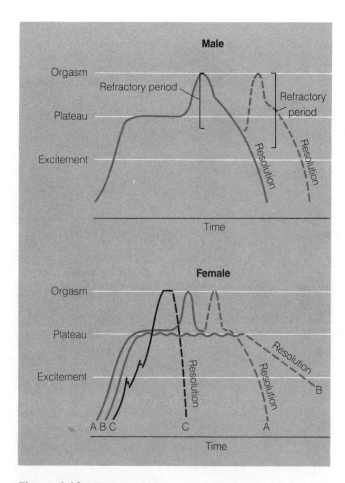

Figure 4.13 ▪ Patterns of human male and female sexual response, as measured by physiological changes. In males, orgasm leads to rapid resolution over a time interval, called a refractory period, before renewed arousal is possible. In females, other patterns are also noted, including an extended plateau phase without orgasm (curve B) and multiple orgasms without an intervening refractory period (curve A).

amount of body hair, and other characteristics are intermediate between male and female.

The sex-chromosome variation that has attracted the most interest is XYY, sometimes called a **supermale** because of the extra Y. XYY individuals show substantial male body development, typically being over six feet tall and well muscled. But it is an open question whether they show more "male" behavior.

There has been widespread debate about whether XYYs are more prone to aggression and violence, after a number were found in prison populations (Jarvik et al., 1973). Unfortunately, answering this question is hampered by the lack of good control data. It is not clear whether the XYY pattern is actually more common in prison populations, or whether it has just been easier to measure there. But even if XYY is more com-

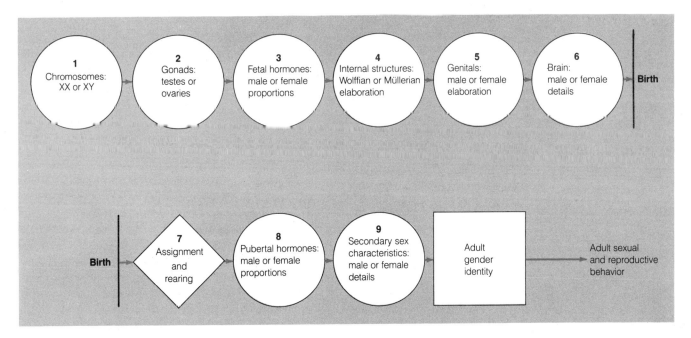

Figure 4.14 ■ The overall sequence of development of adult gender identity. Circles indicate physiological steps, and the diamond indicates assignment and rearing, the nurture or learning step.

(Based on Money and Erhardt, 1972)

mon in prisoners, this does not demonstrate that to be more "male" is to be more criminally violent. As with many genetic problems, the XYY pattern often yields mild retardation, and muscular but not very intelligent males might be likely to end up in prison for several reasons—being criminals is one of the few social choices open to them, they are more likely to be caught and convicted, and so forth (Witkin et al., 1976).

Gonads and Fetal Hormones The chromosomes' only direct effect in the developmental sequence is to cause the appropriate development of the **gonads,** the male testes or female ovaries (Gordon & Ruddle, 1981). Gonads develop from a pair of structures called *ovotestes.* Presence of a Y chromosome causes the inner cores of the ovotestes to begin developing into testes during the sixth week of development. If no Y is present, the outer portions of the ovotestes develop into ovaries a short time later.

The rest of the sexual-development sequence results from hormones produced by the gonads (Haseltine & Ohno, 1981). Male hormones are called **androgens;** the most notable is **testosterone.** Of the several female hormones, the most notable is **estrogen.** Both testes and ovaries produce both male

and female hormones, however; it is the relative proportions that differ, with testes producing more male hormones and ovaries producing more female hormones. Testosterone, in fact, though called an androgen, seems to be the *libido* or *sex-drive* hormone for both sexes.

Rare individuals develop one testis and one ovary; they are true **hermaphrodites** and develop characteristics of both sexes, possibly including the ability both to father and to bear children. More commonly, however, inappropriate prenatal hormones cause a mixed pattern of development; such individuals are technically called **pseudohermaphrodites,** but are often simply referred to as hermaphrodites (Mittwoch, 1981).

Internal Structures and Genitals At most prenatal steps, an androgen is necessary for male structural development. In its absence, female development occurs; no comparable female hormone is necessary. The first such step is development of the internal structures that transport sperm or ova from the gonads. By the second month of gestation, all fetuses have developed the beginnings of both systems. For male development, two androgens are necessary, one to develop the male system and another to suppress the female

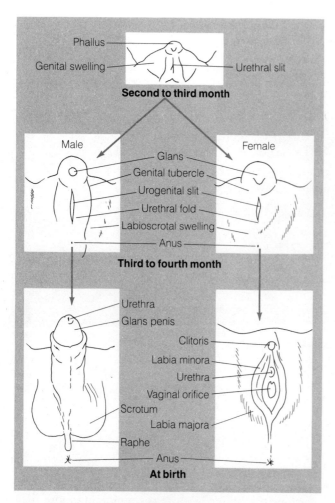

Figure 4.15 ■ In prenatal development of genitals, a single set of structures is elaborated into either the female or male pattern.

(From *Man and Woman, Boy and Girl* by J. Money and A. Ehrhardt, Johns Hopkins University Press, 1972. Used by permission.)

system. Female development occurs if neither androgen is present (Wilson et al., 1981).

Genitals, the body structures used in intercourse, are the last reproductive structures to develop. Here the presence of an androgen causes male genitals to develop. Without an androgen, the same "indifferent" structures will develop into female genitals. ■ Figure 4.15

Genital development is one of the steps most sensitive to developmental problems, and thus one of the least indicative of "true" sex. If testosterone, or something that acts like it, is present when the genitals are developing, the result will be male genitals; if it is not, the result will be female genitals—regardless of whether prior developmental steps have been male or female. Too small an amount of testosterone will only partially masculinize the genitals, yielding an ambiguous appearance. In the *adrenogenital syndrome*, an an-

drogen produced in excessive amounts by the mother's adrenal gland masculinizes the genitals of a female fetus. Masculinization can also be caused by drugs that the mother takes. The synthetic hormone diethylstilbestrol (DES), for example, was given to pregnant women in the 1940s and 1950s to prevent miscarriages, but later was found to have masculinized the genitals of some female fetuses (Seaman & Seaman, 1977). In the *androgen-insensitivity syndrome*, a genetic male's testes produce androgens, but body tissues don't use them and the genitals develop as female.

Brain   The brain is also a sexually differentiated organ (Arnold, 1980). Brain differentiation is the basis of the focus of sexual arousal toward one sex or the other in animals and probably to a large extent in humans. Its differentiation toward a male or female pattern may have more widespread consequences than sexual arousal, however; just how widespread these are for humans is the topic of current research (MacLusky & Naftolin, 1981). Some of the behavioral differences between the sexes no doubt reflect assignment and rearing, but others may represent subtle prenatal brain differentiation.

One of the best-established brain differences in other species concerns menstrual cycling in females and the lack of a similar cycle of hormonal outputs in males. Apparently, a prenatal androgen suppresses cycling in males by modifying an area of the brain. In rats, altering to the male pattern is accomplished by as little as a six-hour exposure to androgens. Furthermore, only a small amount of androgen is necessary: Female rats carried in the uterus adjacent to males showed partially masculinized behavior as adults, a result of the male hormone produced by their littermates (Meisel & Ward, 1981).

In nonhuman mammals, the menstrual cycle is also a "heat" or sexual-readiness cycle. The males of these species are responsive to the female's cycle and are prepared for intercourse whenever she is. This difference in sexual responsiveness seems to have evolved to maximize reproduction; the ovum's development is critical and intercourse is timed to fertilize it when it is ready, whereas males produce millions of sperm daily and always have some ready. So suppressing the male's cycling eliminates the need for males and females to come into heat at the same time and increases the chances of successful fertilization.

Brain structures must also be coded to tell males that they *are* males and to make them responsive to females—just as females must know who they are and seek out or accept males. Both sexes must also carry out any other sex-differentiated behaviors coded by their species' genetics, so these must also be built into their brains.

Do male and female humans also develop different brains as a consequence of prenatal hormones? The short answer is almost certainly yes—but the long answer includes many buts and maybes. Prenatal brain structuring may influence many human adult behaviors (Ehrhardt & Meyer-Bahlberg, 1981). But the flexibility of our species means that nurture factors may still outweigh genetics. Differences in brain structure can be amplified or suppressed by learning, especially social or cultural learning.

Most research on physiological brain differences has used animals, but until recently, no direct evidence had been found of relevant brain differences in humans. One study, however, claims to have found sex differences at autopsy in the structure of the corpus callosum (deLacoste-Utamsing & Holloway, 1982). If this finding holds up, it may be the first step in understanding the physiology of sex differences in behavior. (This still would not demonstrate that such differences were innate, because rearing practices might affect brain structure.)

Assignment and Rearing Most people think of a child's sex as a given of nature, but it is not; it is *assigned* to us at birth by someone who says "It's a girl!" or "It's a boy!" Massive treatment or rearing differences then follow. These nurture effects are potentially more important than all the givens of prenatal nature.

From the instant of assignment on, virtually everyone in a child's society will treat "him" differently from "her." Parents in particular will rear children in very different ways depending on sex assignment—even while they protest that they treat their children alike. Male and female children are held differently, talked to differently, and disciplined differently. One of the first things strangers ask is whether an infant is a boy or a girl; they do so not casually, but in order to know how to treat it. The effects of this differential treatment soon show up in behavior. John Money, a well-known researcher in this area, has suggested that a child's sense of self as male or female is so firmly established by the age of *three* that it is practically irreversible (Money & Ehrhardt, 1972).

If prenatal errors are discovered at birth, the infant can be assigned to the sex that will allow the best surgical and hormonal treatment. The effects of assignment and rearing are so powerful that an appropriate gender identity will follow.

One case of postnatal injury demonstrates this power of assignment and rearing. Monozygotic twin boys were being circumsized with an electric device when a malfunction destroyed the penis of one of them. Surgeons can build a sexually functional vagina but not a penis, so the boy was reassigned as a girl. The accident occurred at 7 months, the reassignment at 17 months, and reconstructive surgery for female appearance at 21 months. Within a few years, follow-ups found "her" to be a normal, happy girl, whose behavior differed in many ways from her brother's. These behavioral differences must have resulted from the different rearing, because the children were genetically identical and hormones play little or no role during childhood (Money & Ehrhardt, 1972). (At puberty, the girl will require further surgery and will receive hormonal replacements for life.)

Pubertal Hormones and Secondary Sex Characteristics During childhood the gonads are relatively inactive, but this changes with puberty. Physiological adulthood then occurs in response to a burst of hormones from the gonads when they become reproductively functional. Females begin to menstruate as their reproductive cycles begin, and males begin to have live sperm in their ejaculate. This hormonal surge also causes a wide variety of other physical changes, called **secondary sex characteristics;** these include differences in overall build, body fat and muscle distribution, breast development, patterns of body hair, and width of pelvis (and consequently in gait). Other differences include elaboration of the Adam's apple and other throat changes in males that cause lower voices. Both sexes' genitals become more prominent and both develop genital hair.

When errors in sex assignment are discovered later than at three years of age, it is easier to alter the body than to change the child's sense of self as male or female. This is especially true if the problem is discovered at puberty. Consider a female fetus whose development proceeded normally until an androgen from her mother's adrenal gland masculinized her genitals. If she spent 12 years assigned and reared as a boy, then she will think of herself as a 12-year-old boy. But at puberty her ovaries will produce a female hormonal balance and she will begin to develop breasts and other female secondary sex characteristics. She/he will like this no more than any other 12-year-old boy raised in a strongly gender-coded society (Ehrhardt, 1979). At this point the best treatment is to remove her ovaries, implant artificial testes (for appearance), and give a male balance of hormones, which will induce male secondary sex characteristics and support adult male sexual behavior.

If detected early, most hermaphrodites can be successfully assigned as either sex. But the body of an androgen-insensitive male will not use injected androgen any more than it uses his own. Hence the only option is to assign and rear him/her as a girl. The testes will be left in the abdomen; the low levels of female hormones they produce at puberty will trigger female secondary sex characteristics. Adult gender identity and body structure will be normal female, although she will not be able to bear children.

Adult Gender Identity   The term *sex* usually refers to sexual activity and reproduction; *gender* includes all other behaviors that a society differentiates by sex (Unger, 1979). Adult **gender identity** is thus the sense of self as a male or female, including both sexual and culturally coded sex-role behaviors. Gender identity is a complex result of *all* the preceding steps and their interactions, but the single most important input is assignment and rearing. **Gender role** is the total package of behaviors that society expects of each sex. Public gender role usually agrees with private gender identity, but in some cases does not. Gender behavior includes influences from the entire sequence of sexual development (Money, 1980).

Puberty marks physiological adulthood, but social adulthood may be delayed. The more industrialized the society, the later is the formal conferring of social adulthood—at the same time that better diet pushes the pubertal age earlier. In other mammals, role demands are directly associated with physiological changes; the new looks and smells associated with reaching maturity require that young mammals begin to behave as adults. For humans, however, a complex cultural overlay mediates the demands of adulthood, greatly modifying whatever nature is present. Society often demands mature behavior in some respects while seeking to prohibit use of the sexual organs themselves. An integrated adult gender identity under such circumstances is not a given; it is a fought-for prize, an accomplishment of no small value.

A multitude of experiences and hormonal influences can probably result in variations in gender identity. It is thus not surprising that a variety of reversed, mixed, or unusual roles have developed in most cultures. However, because the hormonal and brain bases for normal erotic response are not well understood, it follows that the causes for any variations—such as homosexuality and transsexualism—are not known (Bell et al., 1981).

Homosexuals are people who are erotically responsive only or primarily to their own sex. (*Homosexual* refers to both sexes, but *lesbian* is usually used for female homosexuals.) Homosexuality was once considered a sin or an intentional nastiness that to Victorians was "the love that dare not speak its name." Then, like other socially unacceptable behaviors, it came to be considered a mental illness. But in 1973 the American Psychological Association formally agreed that homosexuality in the absence of other problems was not a mental illness. So what is it?

Homosexuality is a complex mixture of behaviors that may or may not reflect prenatal, pubertal, or adult hormonal differences (Bell & Weinberg, 1978). It is learned behavior for some, rebellion against the status quo for some, political statement for others. It probably reflects as many complex interactions over time as the "normal" orientation, technically called **heterosexuality.** About the only thing you can be sure of is that homosexuality is *not* a simple outcome of any single factor, such as hormones or rearing.

Transsexuals are individuals whose gender identity seems opposite to their otherwise normal-seeming body physiology. Chromosomes, internal structures, genitals, and overall appearance may all be of one sex and gender-role behavior may be appropriate, yet the person has the opposite gender *identity*, considering him/herself to be really of the opposite sex. Jan Morris, for example, was reared as a boy and served in the British army, yet from the age of three or four felt like a woman trapped in a man's body. He underwent sex-change surgery at the age of 45 and has since reported being satisfied with the results (Morris, 1974). ■ Figure 4.16

The causes of transsexualism remain unknown. Sometimes there have been relevant social influences, such as parents dressing the child in opposite-sex clothing, but often there apparently have not been (Green, 1974). It is possible that transsexuals reflect a hermaphroditic variation in the brain-structuring step, rather than in the internal structure or genitals, but this is only speculation.

Therapy for transsexuals was once solely psychological. But in the early 1950s, the case of Christine Jorgensen—a former United States soldier who went to Denmark for a sex-change operation—brought surgical alterations to worldwide attention. Since then, a number of institutions in the United States have performed such operations. Transsexual therapy requires much more than surgery, however. To be convincing, transsexuals need retraining in many routine daily activities—to learn to stand, walk, and hold objects appropriately for their new sex, and even to speak appropriately (Chapter 10). Transsexual therapy has thus brought out some subtle effects of assignment and rearing that had not previously been noticed.

No doubt other important factors in the establishment and maintenance of gender roles will be discovered in the future. For now, the picture of how anyone comes to behave in gender-appropriate ways remains cloudy and sometimes seems contradictory.

Sex Differences in Other Behaviors   Two researchers at Stanford University have reviewed, analyzed, and attempted to synthesize all relevant research on sex differences in behavior. Eleanor Maccoby and Carol Jacklin's book (1974b) has become a standard reference work for those seeking to understand the development of sex or gender roles. Maccoby and Jacklin sorted traditional views of sex differences into three categories: (1) those the evidence shows to be myths, (2) those the evidence shows to be probably true, and (3) those for which the evidence remains ambiguous. Myths include differences between the sexes in analytic ability, type of learning, and suggestibility, for example. Real differences include greater aggression in males, superior verbal ability in females, and superior visual-spatial and mathematical abilities in males (Wittig & Petersen, 1979). Possible but undemonstrated differences include general activity level, competitiveness, and nurturance. (For a brief review of these categories, see Maccoby & Jacklin, 1974a.)

Note that the origins of true sex differences may still be partially or wholly cultural. Some differences are found so widely, in such different cultures, as to suggest that they may be innate. Other differences may have innate underpinnings but still be expressed differently, depending on the culture. Human females, for example, may tend to have more precise control of their fingers than males—but whether this digital dexterity is used in typing or neurosurgery is culturally determined. ■ Notable Quote: Maccoby and Jacklin on Sex Differences

HUMAN MOTIVES BEYOND SURVIVAL

So far, we have looked at a variety of motives that help ensure survival in many species. Humans also share many of those survival motives, even though they learn many of the behaviors that help to satisfy the motives. Many psychologists have suggested, however, that humans are also motivated by exclusively human motives unrelated to survival. Humans seem motivated to create objects and engage in events, for example, for the pure esthetic pleasure of them.

As a species, we sing, play musical instruments, and compose symphonies. We paint, write, and sculpt. We develop both our bodies and our brains through programs of exercise and practice. And all the while we think about why we're doing all this. It is not obvious that motives to create, to achieve, or to understand the world are related to survival. But it *is* obvious that such tendencies energize and direct large numbers of people. We will look at such human motives later, primarily in Chapters 12 and 13.

Another form of motivation we have not discussed at length is that which supports group survival—even at a possible cost to the individual; for example, parenting sometimes involves substantial risks to the par-

Figure 4.16 ■ Transsexual Arlene Lafferty, shown in her current female role following surgery. About the differences between male and female roles, well-known British transsexual Jan Morris writes: *"[Having] experienced life in both roles, there seems to me no aspect of existence, no moment of the day, no contact, no arrangement, no response, which is not different for men and for women. The very tone of voice in which I was now addressed, the very posture of the person next in the queue, the very feel in the air when I entered a room or sat at a restaurant table, constantly emphasized my change of status"* (Morris, 1974).
(Lester Sloan—Newsweek)

ents. Group-related motives help to direct behaviors of many species: giving alarm cries to warn of predators, defending weaker members of a group or the group as a whole, and hunting cooperatively. For some species—such as beavers—the only relevant social group is the family. For others, the group may include a dozen to many thousands of individuals: A single herd of buffalo of the early American West, for example, often covered miles of terrain. Whatever the size of the group, patterns of motivated behavior are common (perhaps even necessary) to maintain order, control the movements of the group, and provide for defense. We will consider motives specifically relevant to social groups in Chapters 17 and 18.

EMOTIONS

As noted early in the chapter, emotions are closely associated with motives, but psychologists often focus on emotions as a distinct topic. Subareas of research include emotional experiences, recognition of emotional expressions by outside observers, and attempts to develop integrated theories of how emotions occur.

Experiencing Emotions

There are many ways of describing emotional experiences. Some descriptions emphasize subjective factors, such as the pleasurable or unpleasurable nature of the experience or its intensity. Other descriptions seek to be more objective by measuring internal physiological changes or external behavior. Subjective, qualitative descriptions might seem to get most directly at the experience of emotion, and this view has been a traditional one. We seem to know that we are angry, sad, or elated on a given occasion because we experience these emotions directly. But more careful thought and observation suggest that this is an oversimplified view.

People are often confused about what they are feeling, for example. They may know they are emotionally aroused but be unable to specify the emotion they are experiencing. Sometimes a felt emotion shifts rapidly from one category to another, as fear sometimes yields to anger in soldiers, or as excitement can change to fear for roller-coaster riders or horror-movie viewers.

In their attempts to analyze emotions, researchers have divided them into three major components: (1) physiological arousal, (2) cognitions (often verbal labels) about emotions, and (3) overt emotional behavior, including facial expressions and body movements. Theories of emotion have often sought to relate these three components, asking which leads to the others and how. Such theories often begin with the most easily noted mark of emotions, facial expressions.

Expressing Emotions

Darwin's (1872) view of emotion was one early approach that did not seek to separate various components. Darwin simply noted the similarity of some human expressions to those of animals, and proposed that human emotional expressions had evolved from expressions that in animals conveyed behavioral intent. A tooth-baring threat expression would thus convey a probability of attack, and other expressions would indicate other probable actions. (For a contemporary view of the evolution of emotions, see Plutchick, 1980.) ■ Figure 4.17

If Darwin's view is correct, then humans should recognize each other's facial expressions as animals do, relatively independent of culture. Observations of those born blind have supported the possibility of some basic innate expressiveness; they often smile, laugh, frown, or even cover their faces in embarrassment, though they have never seen anyone else do so. Experiments have also suggested that basic emotional expressions are recognizable across broad cultural differences: A photo intended to represent happiness, for example, is chosen as such by nearly 100% of subjects (Ekman, 1973). But about half of such subjects do not agree on some expressions, even basic ones. As the emotions to be expressed become less obviously related to survival motives, Darwin's view becomes less applicable. Studies then find much more cultural influence and much less innate recognizability. One early but frequently quoted study of Chinese literature, for example, found such expressions as "they stuck out their tongues" (Klineberg, 1938). Few non-Chinese observers would know that this expressed surprise.

Body postures and gestures are also used to express emotions, and much the same pattern is found when these are examined. A shaken clenched fist is widely recognized, for example, but other gestures may be peculiar to a particular culture (Hall et al., 1978). In Chinese literature, "he drew up his leg and stood on one foot" also indicated surprise (Klineberg, 1938).

There is another difficulty with a direct evolutionary view of emotional expressions. Many natural expressions do not clearly indicate the nature of the

Figure 4.17 ■ Many mammals, especially the more aggressive males, express anger and threat by baring their teeth. Human aggressive expressions and actions are less stereotyped but may include some similar elements retained from common ancestors.

(Nina Leen, LIFE MAGAZINE, © 1962, Time, Inc.)

emotional experience, and thus would not convey the behavioral intent of the experiencer very well. People whose expressions seem to be those of terror may actually be excited, whereas those who appear distraught with grief may be enjoying themselves. ■ Figure 4.18

A physiological approach to analyzing facial expressions may also be useful (Grings & Davison, 1978). Several findings about the physiology of emotions concern hemisphere differences. It has been noted, for example, that the cerebral hemispheres cooperate in producing facial expressions, but that the left side of the face (controlled by the right hemisphere) expresses them more intensely (Sackeim et al., 1978). It is not yet clear, however, whether this effect represents a greater intensity of emotional experience in the right hemisphere, as is usually suggested. A more intense expression on the left side of a person's face might also represent a clearer emotional cue for an *observer's* left hemisphere, which might simply be a poorer judge of facial expression. (An experiencer's left facial side falls in the right visual field of an observer, and thus goes to the observer's left hemisphere). ■ Figure 4.19

The hemispheres have also been said to experience emotions differently, with the left hemisphere being more cheerful and the right hemisphere more depressed (Kinsbourne, 1981). The hemispheres may also react differently to emotions expressed by others.

People with damage to the right hemisphere have trouble matching an emotional expression on one face with a similar expression on other faces; people with damage to the left hemisphere have trouble verbally describing others' expressions (Kolb & Taylor, 1981).

Another physiological approach to emotion focuses on the extent to which emotional thoughts result in subtle facial expressions. Schwartz and others (1976) have found that asking people to think about a happy or sad occasion causes faint facial muscular patterns that are characteristic of those emotions. Schwartz has used these subtle facial expressions to study differences in patterns of emotional thinking. He has found, for example, that the responses of people who are depressed are measurably different from responses of people who are not depressed (Schwartz et al., 1976).

Theories of Emotion

The major theories of emotion have sought to explain the relationship of all three factors in emotions, relating physiological arousal and cognitive interpretations to emotional expression. One of the first and best-known interpretations was developed independently by William James (1884) in the United States and Carl Lange (1885) of Copenhagen; it is now

a

b

Figure 4.19 ■ What emotion is being expressed in each of these photos? (a) Some expressions seem universally interpretable, as does the pleasure shown by these Aborigine boys. (b) Other expressions seem recognizable, but do not necessarily indicate the nature of the situation. These apparently terrified people are riding a roller coaster. (c) Other expressions can be more seriously misleading. These apparently grief-stricken people are actually ecstatic at the sight of the Beatles in concert.

(**a,** Wide World Photos; **b,** The Boston Globe; **c,** United Press International)

c

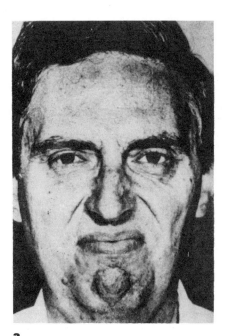

a

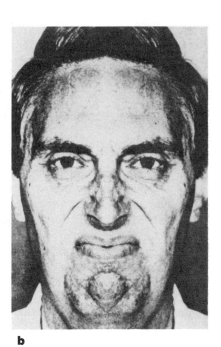

b

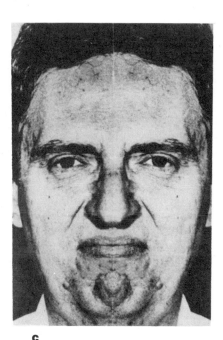

c

Figure 4.18 ■ Three photographs used in a study of hemisphere differences in emotional expression. The left photo (a) is a real one, and the other two are laboratory composites made up of two left halves of the face (b) and two right halves (c). Viewers felt that (b) displayed the greatest emotion in such composite photos. Because the left side of the face is controlled by the right hemisphere, this suggests a greater emotional expressiveness of the right hemisphere.

(H. A. Sackeim et al., *Science*, Vol. 202, pp. 434–436, *27*, October 1978. Copyright 1978 by the American Association for the Advancement of Science.)

known by both their names. The **James-Lange theory** of emotion is most often expressed in the phrase "we are afraid because we run." James and Lange reversed the sequence that we normally think of as occurring in emotion—of seeing a predator, for example, becoming afraid, and running because we are afraid. The James-Lange theory proposes instead that the most basic relationship is that of running in response to the predator. When a more conscious experiencing of emotion is added to the basic pattern, James argued, it *follows* running rather than being the cause of it. Thus we are afraid because we run, rather than the reverse.

The James-Lange view stimulated much discussion and research. It was important partly because it was the first to draw explicit attention to the physiological arousal component of emotion, but was later seriously criticized by a physiologist, Walter Cannon (1927). By severing some nerve connections in dogs, Cannon noted, they could be deprived of the body arousal that the James-Lange theory had said was a necessary step in emotion. Yet the dogs still seemed to respond emotionally—as do human quadriplegics who cannot be responding to visceral arousal. However, both the lesioned dogs and human patients could be giving learned responses to cues that *formerly* triggered visceral arousal. Some suggestion that emotions are different in quadriplegic patients comes from their reports that emotions are experienced as less intense in the absence of body arousal.

Another problem with the James-Lange view, said Cannon, was that visceral arousal is too vague and general to give rise to the range of emotions that we experience. Research since then has found some differences in arousal—between fear and anger, for example—but not nearly enough to account for the range of emotional experience. However, it is still possible that there are subtle differences in arousal that have not yet been measured.

Cannon proposed instead that the thalamus was central in processing stimuli that lead to emotions; this view was elaborated by Bard (1934). In the **Cannon-Bard theory,** stimuli to the thalamus result in simultaneous signals to arouse the body and to begin overt action. More recent research, however, has found that the hypothalamus and limbic system, not the thalamus, are important in emotional arousal. Furthermore, the time distinctions drawn by James and Cannon are no longer emphasized. Emotional experiences are recognized as events that occur over some time.

Two-Factor Theory   Recent research on emotions has stressed cognitive factors (Campos & Sternberg, 1981). One of the first and most important approaches was offered by Stanley Schachter. Schachter's **two-factor theory** proposes that both body arousal and cognitive interpretations are important in determining the experienced emotion. Emotional expression is then an accompaniment to the experienced emotion, with no emphasis placed on whether it precedes or follows arousal. Schachter's two-factor view interprets the James-Lange example of fleeing from a predator as follows: Sight of the predator goes simultaneously to mechanisms in lower brain centers that mediate arousal and to mechanisms in the cerebral cortex that lead to cognitive interpretations of the input. Visceral arousal and cognitive recognition of threat occur approximately simultaneously, with their *interaction* yielding the emotional experience of fear.

In the experimental arrangement that led to this view, Schachter and a colleague, Jerome Singer (1962) first injected subjects with adrenalin to produce a known arousal in all of them. While supposedly waiting for the injection to take effect, subjects waited, one at a time, in a room with another supposed subject who was in fact a confederate of the experimenter. Subjects in two experimental conditions were unaware of the injections' real effects, having been told that these would cause other symptoms than the rapid heart beat and other arousal effects that they did cause. In two control conditions, other subjects were told of the real effects of the injections.

The crucial part of the procedure concerned the emotional reactions of all four types of subjects when the confederates with them began acting emotionally. In one experimental and one control group, confederates acted lighthearted and carefree, joking and flying paper airplanes. In the other pair of groups, the confederates acted as if they were angry at the delay. The control subjects, who knew that their injections would create body arousal, did not become emotional with either type of confederate. But the experimental subjects reported themselves to have become either euphoric or angry, depending on the type of confederate they were exposed to. Schachter and Singer interpreted these results as indicating that unexplained arousal provided the activation of an emotion, and cognitive interpretation of situational cues added meaning to the arousal. Hence the same injection could make subjects either euphoric or angry, depending on the *cognitive label* assigned to the arousal, in response to situational cues.

Schachter's two-factor theory offers a way of explaining a number of aspects of emotions that are otherwise perplexing. One emotion could switch to another if the cognitive label changed, for example. Hence an excited roller-coaster rider could become truly frightened at the sight of a broken rail or other cognitive sign of real danger. And if arousal levels from different stimuli are additive, maybe one label can be applied to the total. Thus people who are sexually aroused in frightening circumstances could label all arousal as sexual and be *more* sexually aroused than they would be in less dangerous circumstances. People who had affairs during World War II bombing raids report an intensity to the experience that could be interpreted in this way. Alternately, they might label the entire arousal as frightening, thereby causing situations that should be sexually arousing to arouse only fear. Some sexual fears seen in therapy might be interpreted in this way.

The Schachter and Singer (1962) study that led to the two-factor theory has been criticized, however. Two attempts that sought to replicate the results by using hypnotically induced arousal found anger much easier to obtain than euphoria (Marshall, 1976; Maslach, 1979). These results have been interpreted to mean that any unexplained arousal is not truly neutral, but is itself irritating—thus easy to turn into anger, but perhaps not possible to turn into euphoria (Zimbardo et al., 1977).

Other contemporary approaches to emotion have again raised the question of what comes first in emotional experience, with some theorists arguing that cognitions are both necessary and sufficient to arouse emotions (Lazarus, 1982) and others disputing that sequence (Zajonc, 1980). Currently Schachter's two-factor theory remains a major framework for emotional research, but whether it will need further revision or will be replaced by an even more cognitive theory remains to be seen (Plutchik & Kellerman, 1980; Schachter, 1979).

Opponent-Process Theory   One view of emotional arousal currently receiving substantial attention is R. L. Solomon's (1980) **opponent-process theory,** which proposes that each emotion is matched by an opposite emotion and that activation of any emotion is followed somewhat later by automatic activation of its opposite. The major effect of such a sequence would be to allow an initial high level of emotion, but then to reduce the level of arousal to a more optimum level. If the emotion were fear, for example, the initial arousal might be extreme, but this would soon be reduced by activation of its opposite (perhaps elation), thus allowing the organism to cope better with the fear-producing situation.

Solomon also suggests that the opponent emotion takes some time to disperse after the original emotion ends, thus resulting in an overshoot in the opposite direction. If the source of fear arousal is removed, for example, the fear soon ends. But the opponent emotion temporarily remains, yielding a sense of relief and

even elation before it too fades, leaving the person back at neutral. Solomon and Corbit (1974) illustrated this effect with a reanalysis of Epstein's (1967) study of emotions in sports parachutists. They noted that the parachutists were extremely frightened during the jump, but once safely on the ground they seemed at first dazed, then were for a time quite elated.

Opponent-process theory offers a new approach to some emotional behaviors that have been difficult to explain. It suggests why people indulge in thrill-seeking activities such as parachuting, for example. Repeated experience with the same sort of stimulus typically results in a lesser emotional response, a form of adaptation to the environment. According to Solomon (1980), this adaptation occurs through a strengthening of the opponent response to a familiar situation until the strengthened opponent emotion nearly neutralizes the initial emotion. But note what this means for the period immediately after the end of the initial emotion: The overshoot will now be even stronger than before. Thus an accomplished parachutist or other thrill seeker might be less frightened during the activity and more elated afterwards. If this is generally true, it could explain why some people become addicted to activities that are intrinsically frightening.

Emotions and Lie Detection

One kind of emotional arousal is that involved in anxiety. Since most people can be assumed to be anxious when they lie, measures of arousal have been used as the basis of attempts to build lie detectors (Waid & Orne, 1982). The earliest and best-known form of lie detector is the **polygraph,** a device for simultaneously recording several physiological measures. Polygraphs are general-purpose laboratory instruments; they are often used in sleep research, for example. When a polygraph is used as a lie detector, the variables measured usually include respiration rate, skin resistance, pulse rate, and pulse amplitude. ■ Figure 4.20

A polygraph operator first asks the subject a series of neutral questions to establish a baseline, then a few emotionally distressing questions to establish how arousal changes the subject's physiological patterns. The operator then asks a series of questions, including some key ones about the event being investigated. The operator seeks to determine, from the differences in physiological responses to key questions and neutral questions, whether the subject is lying in his or her responses to the key questions.

The basic procedure is straightforward, but its reliability and validity are questionable. One problem is

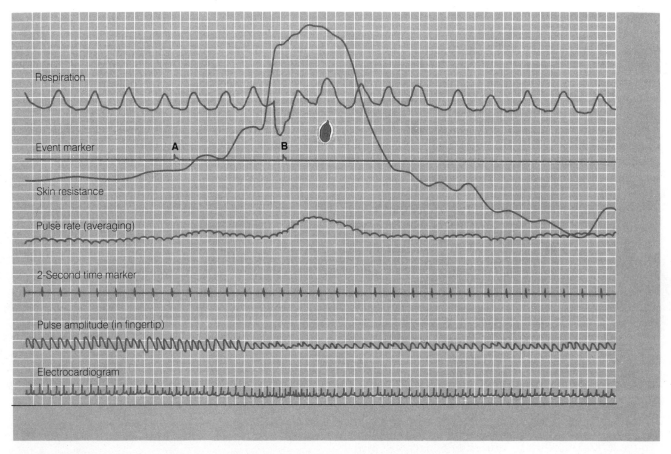

Figure 4.20 ■ A section of polygraph record. Electrodes transmit various physiological data to a series of pens; these make a continuous record on a moving paper tape for interpretation by the polygraph operator. A whispered conversation with the subject began at point A, resulting in some change in skin resistance. At B, an emotionally charged reference was included in the whispered conversation, resulting in substantial changes in skin resistance, pulse rate, and pulse amplitude, with transients also noted in respiration and heart rate (electrocardiogram).

(From *Psychology: The Frontiers of Behavior* by Ronald E. Smith, Irwin G. Sarason, and Barbara R. Sarason. Copyright © 1978 by Ronald E. Smith, Irwin G. Sarason, and Barbara Sarason. Reprinted by permission of Harper & Row, Publishers, Inc.)

that, even under the best of circumstances, a subject's lies may go undetected. The subjects may deliberately modify the baseline information, perhaps by tensing muscles to some questions to introduce variation into the traces. Drugs may also affect some responses (Waid et al., 1981). Some emotionally unresponsive subjects just do not become very anxious and thus do not show much change with the supposedly stressful questions. Conversely, truthful subjects may be so upset by these questions that they seem to be lying. Finally, the skill of the operators in interpreting the patterns varies and usually cannot be independently checked (Szucko & Kleinmuntz, 1981). Hence most scientific investigators are skeptical of polygraph lie detection, despite its widespread use.

Another technique that claims to use emotional responses to detect lying is the Psychological Stress Evaluator (PSE). The PSE examines the patterns of what are called *microtremors* in the person's voice. Proponents of the PSE claim to be able to detect lying—or at least emotional arousal—even from a telephone conversation or tape recording. If accurate, PSE would obviously be an important aid in criminal investigations, but so far it has not been accepted by the scientific community (Holden, 1975).

You may not want to rush out and get a PSE to monitor your conversations. But you probably will have reason to control your own emotional responsiveness, if only in self-defense. ■ Personal Application: Controlling and Manipulating Your Emotions

Controlling and manipulating your emotions

Your emotional responses are subject to a wide variety of influences, by both others and yourself. Other people often seek to manipulate your emotions for their own gain, whether to obtain your vote, your participation in warfare, or your money in exchange for a product.

And you are likely to learn to control your own emotional responses. Sometimes, this means you willingly join with others in their manipulative attempts, as when you pay to go on a roller coaster, or to see a horror movie or one that makes you cry. Other times you seek to harden yourself to resist emotional appeals; you learn not to be too easily manipulated by politicians, or those seeking funds, when they offer words or pictures designed to arouse you.

The overall task in learning to control your own emotions is to strike some happy medium for who you are and what you need to do. People who are too emotionally responsive for their circumstances will be drained and ex-hausted by them. But people who teach themselves to minimize their responses may lose the very real rewards that emotional experiences offer.

Some professionals are put in exceptionally difficult positions by the demands of their work. Physicians, for example, must learn to steel themselves to injury and death so they can efficiently help their patients. But each physician must try to do so without losing personal sensitivity, an exceptionally difficult line to tread. Psychotherapists have a similar problem, although they encounter different stresses. Therapists must remain distant enough from patients' emotional problems to operate efficiently, yet must also remain in touch with those emotions if they are to help their patients.

Learning to manage your own emotional responses is not always a matter of minimizing them, however. Some people engage in what has been termed *risk exercise*, sports or activities such as skydiving or mountaineering that arouse strong fear responses in a way that is exciting. But, perhaps because the fear is predictable and occurs in a controlled setting, or perhaps because of the opponent process described by R. L. Solomon (1968), the activity is perceived as exciting in a positive way. Not all people are thrill seekers to the same extent, for reasons that may be biological (Zuckerman et al., 1980). But for those who enjoy it, risk exercise may be healthy, stimulating the sympathetic system in the manner in which it was evolved to function: strongly but briefly.

Overall, our emotional responsiveness can be a blessing or a curse. Few of us would want to give up the emotional pleasures of such basic motivated activities as eating and sex. And those who do enjoy risk exercise seem to become addicted to it. Most of us would willingly forgo the more unpleasant emotional experiences, such as anguish or terror. But unfortunately, all of these emotions come as a package. The best you can hope for is to manage the package as rationally as possible, seeking out the positive emotions and avoiding the negative ones.

"VERY WELL. I'LL SHUT OFF MY VOICE-STRESS ANALYZER IF YOU'LL SHUT OFF YOURS."

CHAPTER SUMMARY

1 The study of motivation is the study of why an organism does anything: Motives initiate and direct behaviors toward particular goals. Emotions are affective experiences that often are associated with motivated behavior.

2 Some motives are associated with homeostatic mechanisms, feedback loops that act to keep some aspect of body physiology at an ideal set point. Temperature control is a notable example; homeostatic mechanisms control shivering or sweating and motivate behaviors that will warm or cool the body.

3 A need-drive model is descriptive of some motives necessary for intermediate-term survival: Thirst and hunger are notable examples. As a body tissue need builds up for water or fuel, the drives of thirst or hunger result. Drinking or eating reduce the drive, and eventually the need.

4 Hunger, thirst, and other motives are associated with areas in the hypothalamus. Once thought of as centers for motives, these hypothalamic areas are now considered to be important parts of complex circuits that link

eating or drinking with tissue need through feedback loops.

5 Incentives are stimuli in the environment that motivate behaviors, either toward them or away from them. The concept of incentive helps explain, for example, why people will eat good-tasting food even when they are not hungry.

6 Long-term weight control also depends on hypo-thalamic areas. But in humans a variety of other influences also contribute to weight maintenance, making the causes of obesity or anorexia difficult to understand.

7 Some motives, including parenting and sexual ones, help ensure survival of the species rather than of the individual. In primates, and especially humans, the behaviors in response to these motives are in large part learned.

8 Sexual development involves a series of prenatal and postnatal steps, all of which must be consistent if adult gender identity is to be integrated. This sequence begins with the sex chromosomes, but later steps are the result of hormones or of environmental treatment. A variety of problems can result from errors at any of these steps.

9 Emotional experience is made up of several factors, including body arousal, cognitions, and overt behaviors. Theories of emotion seek to establish the relationships among these factors.

10 Emotional expressions are in part innate and in part learned. The body arousal that is a part of anxiety may indicate when a person is lying, but results to date are ambiguous.

Further Readings

For motivation topics in general, see a good text such as Arkes and Garske's *Psychological Theories of Motivation* (1982) or Franken's *Human Motivation* (1982). *Theoretical Readings in Motivation* (1975), edited by Levine, offers a variety of theoretical views. For issues concerning hunger, see *Hunger: Basic Mechanisms and Clinical Implications* (1976), edited by Novin, Wyrwicka, and Bray, or Thompson's *Controls of Eating* (1980). Weight extremes are discussed in *Obesity* (1980), edited by Stukard, and in Levenkron's *Treating and Overcoming Anorexia Nervosa* (1982). For sexual issues in general, see the text *Fundamentals of Human Sexuality* (1980) by Katchadourian and Lunde. Recent work from the Kinsey Institute is presented in Bell, Weinberg, and Hammersmith's *Sexual Preference* (1981). For Masters and Johnson's work, see *The Pleasure Bond* (1975). A recent book of Money's, *Love and Love Sickness* (1980), summarizes his research and discusses all aspects of sexual development, gender identity, and erotic responsiveness. For sex differences, see Maccoby and Jacklin's *The Psychology of Sex Differences* (1974b). Theories of emotion are discussed in *Emotion* (1980), edited by Plutchik and Kellerman. How people judge expressions is the topic of Ekman, Friesen, and Ellsworth's *Emotion in the Human Face* (1972).

Part III

Perception and Consciousness

You wake up in the morning, open your eyes, and there's the world. You look in the mirror, and sure enough, it's you. You hear the water running, feel the rough towel on your face, taste your toothpaste. You dress yourself and bend over to pull on your shoes. An ordinary beginning to another day? Not really. These acts, however unexceptional they seem, are acts of skill that call on the resources of finely tuned and continuously adjusted systems. The world as you experience it is not just "there"; it is your own creation, one of staggering complexity. Yes, an objective world exists, as best we can tell. But what you experience is both less and more than that objective world. Less, in that you sense only a fraction of the information it offers. (Many other species, even insects, sense aspects of the world that you cannot.) And more, in that you actively sum up what has occurred in the past and predict what will happen next in building your phenomenological world (the world as you experience it). You thus know much more about what is happening at a given instant than you would from that instant alone.

Students in introductory psychology usually expect to learn about the mind, or at least about behavior. They are frequently perplexed to find themselves studying the eye and the ear. The eye seems of interest to biologists or medical students. But psychologists? Actually, it *isn't* the eye that is of primary interest to psychologists; it *is* behavior. But behavior is a response to the world an organism experiences, and for our species much of that world is based on what we see. "I see," we say, meaning "I understand." We even suggest that "seeing is believing." Psychologists are concerned with the visual mechanisms of eye and brain because behavior cannot be understood without some understanding of them. Vision and other sensory inputs not only tell you about the world, but their continued presence keeps it stable and allows you to behave.

Looked at in this way, studying the senses may seem more reasonable. They are the only way for the central nervous system to respond to the outside world. Without the information brought to it by sight, sound, taste, smell, or touch, your brain would be completely isolated within your skull. Even your own body would be unrecognized and inoperable, because other senses (the proprioceptive senses) monitor its position and movement.

This chapter focuses on the sensory mechanisms that bring us information about both the outside world and the state of our body. We will look at what senses exist, what information they are sensitive to, and where this information goes in the nervous system. Chapter 6 then examines how the sensed information

Chapter 5

Sensation

is used, in the process termed *perception,* to build our experienced world, particularly our visual world. **Sensation** refers to the basic experiences provided by sensory systems such as vision; a single visual sensation might be a patch of color. **Perception** further processes and adds meaning to sensations; we perceive colored objects rather than isolated patches of color. In perceiving objects, we combine information from more than one sense, we draw on memories, and we predict what we expect to find: "Oh, that's the book I was looking for." This sensation/perception distinction is artificial and is sometimes hard to draw because the process is an integrated whole, but the split is a traditional one in psychology and is often useful.

In keeping with our species' emphasis, both this chapter and the one that follows emphasize vision. But we do sense other kinds of information, through a number of sensory systems.

SENSORY SYSTEMS

The objective world is filled with unceasing activity. The planet on which we live is in a state of constant change: Its molten core boils out in volcanoes, earthquakes shake it, great weather fronts shift about its surface, and radiation from the sun falls unendingly. Each living being is surrounded by a wide range of environmental information, and each generates more information by its own activity. No organism can absorb all this information.

Sensory Sampling

Each species has evolved senses that inform the species of activity that is important for it; each organism **samples** only some of the total available information, sensing information useful to it and ignoring the rest. Sensing anything else would be wasteful of time, energy, and processing space in the brain (Dethier, 1971). Some species have developed hearing sensitive to particular sounds and others vision sensitive to low levels of light, but outside the range of stimuli to which each species responds, other information goes unnoticed. Some senses, such as vision, provide broadly useful information; hence vision is shared by many species and has even evolved independently more than once (Lorenz, 1974).

Some species show unusual sensitivity in otherwise common senses. Salmon, for example, can smell and taste the water in which they swim so precisely that they routinely return as adults to the stream in which they were spawned (Hasler et al., 1978). Bats generate 250 sound pulses a second at frequencies five times higher than we can hear, yet they hear the faint echoes so well that they can use them to catch a moth flying through trees in the dark (Simmons et al., 1979). Other senses, suited only to particular lifestyles, are rare: sharks can sense electrical fields generated by fish buried under the sand, and homing pigeons can sense the earth's magnetic field (Gould, 1980).

The more varied and flexible an animal's life-style is, the more likely it is to have several senses. The larger and more adaptable its brain, the more elaborate its perceptual processing of these senses can be. Even insects can have extremely sensitive sensory systems, but what they sense tends to control their behavior directly (Fenton & Fullard, 1981). A female wood tick can smell one component of mammalian sweat soon enough to drop off a tree and fall on the animal as it passes. We do not suppose that the tick "perceives" the approach of her dinner; she *must* respond to the sensed input. But a complex organism can combine information from several senses, analyze it, and select one of several possible responses.

Humans have no sense that is superior to those of all other creatures; on the contrary, many species have senses superior to ours. What we have that they lack, however, is the brain behind these senses. The retina of a ground squirrel's eye is more complex than ours— but its brain is *less* complex (Michael, 1969). Each of our senses feeds relatively unprocessed information to our large and complex brains. As a result, we perceive the world and its possibilities in ways far beyond other species, even though we may not sense parts of it as well as some of them.

Humans are traditionally said to have five senses: vision, hearing, smell, taste, and touch. The term *sixth sense* is often used to refer to some undiscovered sense, but we might say that we already have a sixth sense, one that responds to changes largely within the body rather than outside it. This sense, called **proprioception,** includes two components that could themselves be considered separate senses: the **kinesthetic sense** monitors the position of your limbs and joints and the tension of your muscles, and the **vestibular sense** responds to gravity and accelerations of your head. Together these senses tell you where your body is and what it is doing.

Each sense is better thought of as a **sensory system,** a set of structures working together to sample one type of environmental information. All sensory systems have similar structural and functional features. The information they bring in is processed at intermediate points in the brain and is finally integrated by the cerebral cortex. ■ Figure 5.1

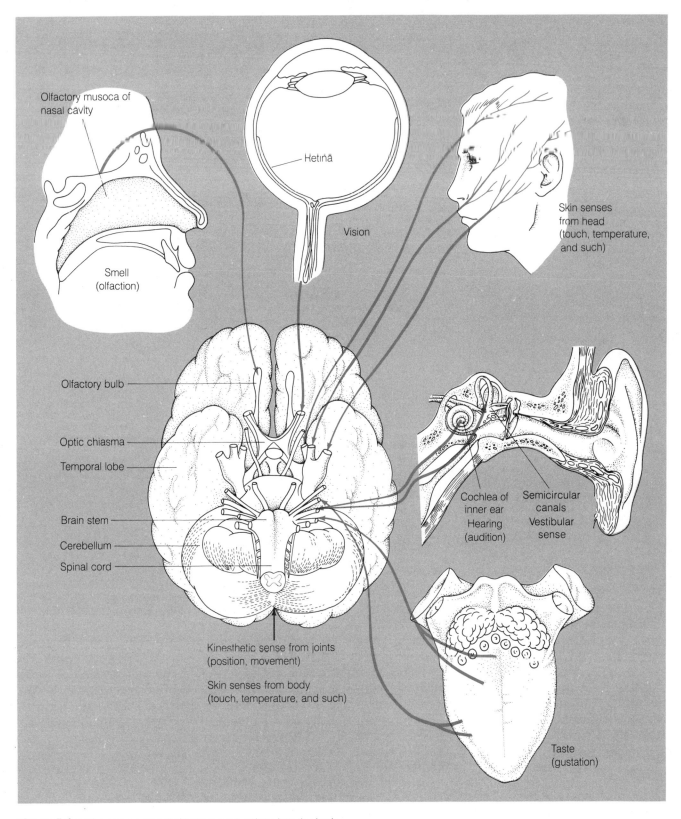

Figure 5.1 ■ The senses and their nerve connections into the brain.

(From *Essentials of Psychology*. Copyright © 1977 by Random House, Inc. Reprinted by permission of the publisher.)

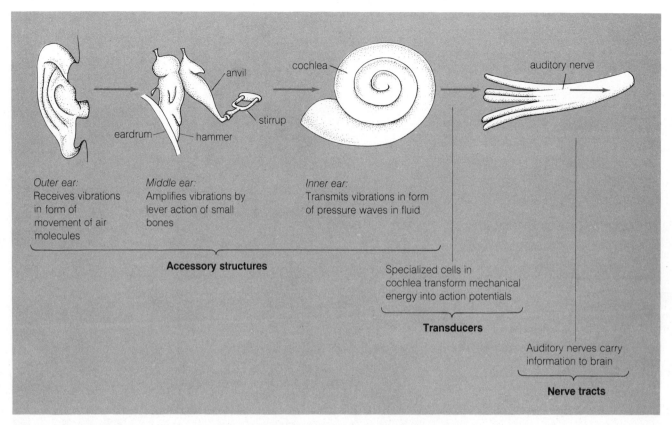

Figure 5.2 ■ Structural features of the hearing sensory system. In any sensory system, accessory structures manipulate the environmental information, leaving it in essentially original form. Specialized transducer cells alter the information from its original form to action potentials. Nerve tracts then carry the information to the cortex. In hearing, the outer ear, middle ear, and cochlea all transmit sound waves—first as air vibrations, then as pressure waves in fluid—before the transducers in the cochlea send action potentials up the auditory nerves.

Structures of a Sensory System

All sensory systems sample some available information and respond with activity in the nervous system (Ludel, 1978). The input could lead directly to a response—as do some reflexes, such as jerking a hand back from a hot stove. But most sensory inputs go to the brain for processing. The sensory systems that convey information to the brain have several common structural features. All sensory systems have specialized cells that respond to the sensed information by generating action potentials; these are called **transducers,** because they "transduce" or alter the form of the information (Loewenstein, 1960). (Such cells are sometimes called **receptors** because they "receive" information; Miller et al., 1961.) Sensory systems also include one or more **accessory structures,** which bring the information to the transducers, and a **nerve tract,** which carries the action potentials to the brain. ■ Figure 5.2

Functions of a Sensory System

Each sensory system responds to a limited range of stimuli, such as the radiation range sensed by vision (Figure 5.3 below). Even stimuli within that range, however, may not be sensed if they are too weak. The minimum amount of stimulus energy needed for an observer to detect the stimulus is called an **absolute threshold.** Absolute thresholds are commonly measured by presenting stimuli of varying intensity and noting when a stimulus reliably gives rise to a sensation. (Stimuli that are detected every time are clearly above threshold; ones that are rarely detected are considered to be below threshold. The exact value of the threshold is conventionally defined as the stimulus intensity that the subject accurately senses 50% of the times it is presented.) Absolute thresholds are not constant for a sense, but typically show differing sensitivity within the overall range. Hearing, for example, is less sensitive to both high and low sounds than it is to the middle range. Therefore the absolute threshold is lower for the middle range than for the extremes.

All stimuli that are sensed must then be interpreted and their meanings coded in the nervous system (Uttal, 1973). Seeing color, for example, means that part of the available visual information is being coded or interpreted as "color"; seeing shapes means that another code is being used. Each sense uses a different set of codes. We are not normally aware of these codes because we only experience what our senses provide us and the information that reaches the brain has already been coded by our sensory systems.

Some people experience **synesthesia,** a blending of the senses in which information in one code overlaps into another. For them a spoken word may also have a color, a texture, or perhaps a smell; in extreme cases, it may have all of these (Marks, 1978). Synesthesia demonstrates that sensory coding systems are important determiners of how we interpret what we experience. ■ Notable Quote: A Person with Synesthesia Describes the Experience

Another important aspect of sensory coding is the **difference threshold,** the smallest difference between two stimuli that will allow them to be sensed as different. This minimum stimulus difference is called a **just noticeable difference (JND).** The JND is not constant but depends on the level of stimulation already present; the more intense the existing stimulus, the larger the change must be to be noticeable. Adding a single candle is noticeable when only one is already burning in a dark room, but not when a hundred are already lighted. Obviously it is not the *amount* of additional light that is noticeable, but its *ratio* to existing light: adding a single candle to one already burning adds 100%, but with 100 existing ones it adds only 1%. Our visual system codes incoming light so that each JND represents this proportional increase in light, not an absolute increase.

Ernst Weber first noted this effect. He found that each sensory system responds to a constant proportional increase; the value of the proportion is **Weber's constant.** Weber's constant for visual brightness, for example, is $\frac{1}{60}$; this means that, for any level of stimulus intensity, a further increase of $\frac{1}{60}$ of that level is necessary for one JND. Thus 1 candle would yield one JND for a room with 60 candles already burning. If 120 were already lighted, 2 candles would be needed for a JND, and if 180 were lighted, 3 more would yield one JND. The same process works for all of the senses, though the values of Weber's constant differ substantially among them. (Because sensitivity varies across the range for each sense, Weber's constants apply only to midrange stimuli.)

Weber's law states that a constant fractional increase in physical intensity is needed to produce each additional JND. When he saw Weber's law, Fechner realized that it might be the key to his mind/body dilemma (Chapter 1): by stating how each JND was added, he could state how sensations were related to physical stimuli. The relationship Fechner derived is now called the **Weber–Fechner law;** it is stated as:

$$\Gamma = K \log I$$

or (perceived intensity) = (a constant) multiplied by (logarithm of stimulus intensity). The Weber–Fechner law describes the sensitivity of a sensory system in terms of the physical energy needed to activate it. But what does it mean in terms of how we sense the world? Because the relationship is logarithmic, we can sense a broad range of stimulus intensities without the lower values being overwhelmed by the higher ones. Our senses can thus respond both to very slight physical inputs and to intensities many thousands of times greater; these greater intensities will seem stronger, but not thousands of times stronger (Wasserman et al., 1979). This logarithmic compressing of a range of stimuli allows us to sense and respond to a wider range of environmental information. Under ideal conditions,

NOTABLE QUOTE
A person with synesthesia describes the experience

❝Presented with a tone pitched at 2,000 cycles per second and having an amplitude of 113 decibels, S. said: 'It looks something like fireworks tinged with a pink-red hue. The strip of color feels rough and unpleasant, and it has an ugly taste—rather like that of a briny pickle. . . . You could hurt your hand on this.' (p. 23)

'You know there are people who seem to have many voices, whose voices seem to be an entire composition, a bouquet. The late S. M. Eisenstein had just such a voice: listening to him, it was as though a flame with fibers protruding from it was advancing right toward me. I got so interested in his voice, I couldn't follow what he was saying.' (p. 24)

(After being asked if he could find his way back to the research institute:) 'How could I possibly forget? After all, here's this fence. It has such a salty taste and feels so rough; furthermore, it has such a sharp, piercing sound.' (p. 38) ❞

The Mind of a Mnemonist by A. R. Luria. Copyright © 1968 by Basic Books, Inc.

we can see an amount of light equivalent to one candle 30 miles away and can hear a sound equivalent to the ticking of a watch 20 feet away; yet we can continue to see in bright sunlight and to hear a jet aircraft fly overhead.

Sensory systems also share a tendency for **sensory adaptation,** the tendency to respond less to stimuli that continue without change. Constant sensory inputs provide no new information and the brain can better occupy itself with other activities. But changes in an adapted sensation *may* be important information. Hence the reticular activating system (Chapter 2) responds to any change in an adapted stimulus with an "alert," in the form of the orienting response.

One form of sensory adaptation results from repeated stimulation of the same receptors. Vision is so much our primary sense that we have developed ways of keeping its receptors from becoming adapted; our eyes continuously make tiny jiggling movements, which continuously change the receptors and prevent adaptation. If our eyes did *not* keep moving, we could stare at an object until we no longer saw it. Senses that cannot shift to different receptors, such as smell, quickly adapt. This is why we no longer notice a strong odor, such as glue or a cooking odor, after we have been in a room for a while.

Senses also differ in their sensitivity to rapid changes in stimuli. Events in the world happen at differing rates, and sensory systems have evolved to sample the most useful time ranges as well as types of stimuli. Because vision is so important to us, you might expect it to be particularly sensitive to rapid changes—but it is not. Rather, the sensitivity of a sense to rapid change seems to depend on how fast the useful part of its sensed information changes, and visual information rarely changes as rapidly as speech sounds. If our ears were no "faster" than our eyes, we would never be able to understand each other's speech. A movie with 24 still pictures presented each second easily deceives our eyes so that we see apparent motion, but our ears can accurately discriminate changes that occur in $\frac{1}{2000}$ of a second.

All sensory systems are sensitive to the same external world, but they sample different information at different rates. The brain must then reintegrate all the sampled information to represent the external world.

Integration of Sensory Systems

The fraction of the world that our senses sample still provides such a flood of information that managing it becomes a problem. We cannot possibly pay full attention to all sensed information all the time, so two subprocesses help us deal with it. One is that much processing occurs in structures other than the cerebral cortex and either never enters consciousness or does so only in summarized form. Also, information that reaches the cortex is used selectively and further sampled as needed to build up a phenomenological world.

Motor control of our bodies typifies the first kind of subprocessing. Information from the proprioceptive senses goes primarily to the cerebellum; it handles detailed information from the joints and muscles just as it handles detailed commands to them. The cerebral cortex receives only general information about body position and only sends general commands to adjust it. You are aware of your approximate position at this moment, for example, not the angle of each of your 268 joints or the tension of each of your hundreds of muscles. Commands must be continuously fed to all relevant muscles if any controlled body movement is to occur, but your cerebellum does this for you and leaves you blissfully ignorant of the details.

Sensory systems typically send offshoots to one or more lower brain centers to support cortical activity (Glickstein & Gibson, 1976; Gordon, 1972). These help in such sensory activity as keeping your eyes pointed at a target while both you and the target are moving (Sekuler & Levinson, 1977). Information from different sensory systems is also integrated at subcortical sites. Normally the senses agree, and all is well. But if they disagree there can be problems: When our vestibular sense and visual orientation are stimulated in certain ways, we get seasick; when an object we pick up is much lighter than it looks, we may practically fling it into the air. In such cases, our subsystems have not been able to handle the situation with the smoothness that normally makes them invisible.

You can only cortically process—or pay attention to—a limited number of sensory inputs at once. If you attend strongly to one sense, as you are now presumably attending to vision, you tend to leave out others. You probably haven't been noticing the touch of your clothing, for example; notice now how much touch, pressure, and texture information has been there all along.

This limitation on how much we can process at one time means that we cannot always pay attention to new sensory inputs. Instead, we build up a phenomenological world by selectively using sensory information as necessary. We shift attention now and then to update our world, but assume in between that things haven't changed. One researcher has studied this ability to integrate information from successive visual inputs; he found that subjects can easily build up a perception of an object that they can only view a piece at a time through a slit (Rock, 1981).

A magician often uses this phenomenon, drawing your attention to one part of the stage or to one movement. At that moment, something else can happen without your ever being aware of it, even though you feel you were aware of everything at all times. Some tricks, for example, depend on substituting one object for another that is in plain sight on a table. A dramatic sweep of the magician's hand to one side, especially if accompanied by a sound, the release of a live bird, or other distractor, draws everyone's visual attention; the magician can simply put down the new object and remove the old one in one motion.

Selective attention is only one way we build up our world rather than having an immediate awareness of all of it. You probably don't think of the visual world as partly clear and mostly vague, for example, but that's how you see it; only a small area is detailed at any one time. We think of the world as equally detailed in all areas; indeed, we seem to "see" it as such. But that is an illusion, kept alive because we move our eyes around to sample and update the world.

Each of us thus creates our own phenomenological world, a world built of perception and belief. No single sense is necessary—the blind and deaf each have their own perceptual worlds—but each sense that we do have contributes its part.

In examining the several senses that we integrate to build our world, we will first consider vision, the most important of our external sensing systems, and then hearing, only somewhat less important because of its role in language. Our other three external senses all respond to direct physical contact with the environment: the "chemical senses," smell and taste, respond to molecules of substances directly engaging special receptors, and several "skin senses" combine to make up the sense of touch. Finally, we will look at our internal proprioceptive senses. We will consider the environmental information sampled by each sense, then its accessory structures, transducers, coding, and nerve tracts.

VISION

Vision tells us about events as far away as the stars and as close as a few inches; it helps to keep us oriented in space, to sense movement, and to locate the sources of other sensory inputs, such as sounds. We may have the feeling that we merely open our eyes and the world is there, but it's not that simple. A remarkable series of both innate and learned processes must take place for us to see the most routine sight. The fact that we are unaware of all of these details shows how well they are integrated and how automatically they function.

Light as Environmental Information

The environmental information processed in vision is **light;** light is one form of radiation, energy waves that travel out in all directions from a radiation source such as the sun. The various types of radiation are characterized by the length of these waves. What we see as light (called the visible spectrum) is only a narrow band of this natural radiation, falling between the shorter ultraviolet and the longer infrared wavelengths. Other species can sense some of these other waves, and we can make them visible through technology. ■ Figure 5.3

Infrared radiation, known to us as heat, is a primary source of environmental information for a hunting rattlesnake, which is very sensitive to it (Newman & Hartline, 1982). For us, infrared can be made visible by technology (Conner & Masters, 1978). (One such device called the Sniperscope, originally devised to help soldiers see at night, is now used to help persons with bad night vision.) Other radiation lies far below (X rays) or far above (radio, television) our visible spectrum. These waves fill the air, as turning on a radio will show, but we are quite blind to them.

When light waves strike an opaque surface, they bounce or **reflect** off it. If the reflecting surface is very smooth, waves bounce off adjacent portions at the same angle and the surface acts as a mirror: we see a reflected image of the original light source. But most surfaces, even apparently smooth ones, have microscopic surface irregularities that reflect waves at a variety of angles. This breaks up the image of the original light source and eliminates the mirror effect, so we see only the object. Light also travels in a vacuum (as it must to reach us from the sun) and in media denser than air, such as glass or water. Within any transparent medium, light waves travel in straight lines, but at a boundary between two media of different densities they are bent.

In locating the position of objects, our visual system (eye and brain) "assumes" that light waves have traveled in a straight line from the object we see to our eye. In the world in which we evolved, this is usually a good bet. (It can occasionally fail, as in mirages, which are caused when light rays are bent by layers of air of different densities; Fraser & Mach, 1976.) But in a world of mirrors, this assumption can be very misleading, as magicians have long understood. The old phrase that magic is "all done with mirrors" is an oversimplification, but many perplexing tricks do rely on mirrors. If the mirrors are properly placed, our visual system is unable to differentiate between light coming directly from an object and light reflected one

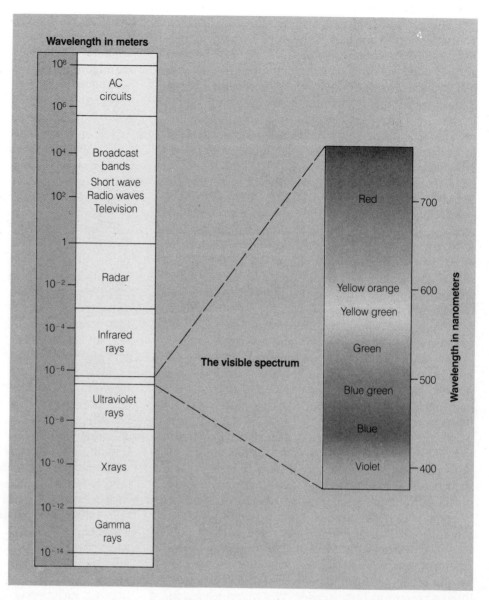

Figure 5.3 ■ Each sense samples only a small part of the potential information in the world. The radiation we see as light, for example, is a narrow section of a much wider band that also includes invisible X rays and radio waves. Most organisms with vision see approximately this same band, but the boundaries may differ. Bees, for example, see ultraviolet. A flower that looks uniform in color to us may have a clear pattern to the bee.

or more times. Thus, when a person is sawed in half in a magic act, the visible top half is one person and the visible bottom half is another. The unseen parts of both people are bent down below the box that is sawed, while mirrors give the illusion of empty space beneath the box.

Mirrors reflect nearly all light falling on them, but most objects reflect only some light and absorb the rest. The apparent brightness of an object represents how much light it reflects: Bright objects reflect most of the light, dark ones absorb most of it.

The color of an object also depends on how it reflects and absorbs light. Natural sunlight, called white light, is a mixture of all visible wavelengths. Any colored light is only a part of white light; a red light, for example, contains only the longer wavelengths we see as red (Figure 5.3). A prism generates a rainbow of colors by separating white light into its components (plate 1); a true rainbow is created by millions of moisture droplets in the air acting as multiple prisms (Fraser, 1981). What we see as the color of any object is the color of the light that it reflects to the eye, after it has absorbed the other colors; a red object is thus one that selectively absorbs all wavelengths except red. A white object reflects all wavelengths, while a black one absorbs all of them.

Wrapping all colors of the spectrum in a circle, leaving a space for some purples not in the spectrum, produces a **color circle** (plate 2). Any pair of colors opposite each other in the color circle are **complementaries;** if lights of these colors are mixed, they yield a neutral gray. Two major complementary pairs at about right angles in the color circle are red/green and blue/yellow.

The name we normally use to identify a color, such as *red*, is technically termed the color's **hue.** Hue is one of three **psychological dimensions** of color, ways in which we experience the physical properties of colored lights. A color's **brightness** results from the overall amount of light that reaches the eye. The color's **saturation** results from the proportion of the light reaching the eye that is a particular wavelength. A color low in saturation has a lot of neutral or gray mixed in and we see it as weakly colored; we might describe a low saturation red as "reddish." But a color high in saturation we see as a strong color; a highly saturated red might be used on a fire engine or race car. These three dimensions are represented simultaneously in a **color solid** (plate 3). What we consider the richest colors are the hues of high saturation and medium brightness around the circumference of the color solid.

Many colors that we see are not included in the basic spectrum, but result from combining two or more spectral colors in different proportions. There are two different ways of combining color, which work in different ways and yield different effects. These are called subtractive and additive mixtures.

When paints (or other colored objects such as chalk or crayons) are combined, the mixture is **subtractive:** each object absorbs or subtracts, from the light that strikes it, all of the spectrum but its own color. In subtractive mixture, the resulting color of the object is whatever is reflected after the other colors have been absorbed. Thus green paint mixed with red paint yields black; the red absorbs everything but red and the green absorbs everything but green, so together they absorb all colors.

A series of colored filters can also demonstrate subtractive mixture. If we shine white light through a blue filter, light in the green-blue-violet range passes through, but all other colors are blocked. Shining these remaining colors through a yellow filter blocks everything but green. (The yellow filter would also have passed yellow and orange, if these had been present.) Thus, in subtractive mixture, blue and yellow yield green.

In contrast, when different colors of light reach the eye, they are combined by the eye's mechanisms in a process termed **additive mixture.** In additive mixture, a blue light and a yellow light presented to the eye simultaneously yield gray (as do any complementary pair of colors). The added lights can be superimposed by shining separate beams of light through separate colored filters onto the same screen. But lights presented close together in either space or time also yield an additive mixture (as with a checkerboard pattern or a rapidly rotating circle made up of two colors; see plate 1). (We will examine the perception of color in more detail in Chapter 6.)

The Eye's Accessory Structures

Most of the structures of the eye are accessory structures; they bring the light rays in to the transducers, which are located at the back of the eye. The eye is often compared to a camera (Wald, 1950). A camera is a dark box with a convex lens in the only opening and light-sensitive film at the back. The amount of light allowed to enter is controlled by an iris, a variable opening in front of the lens that opens wider in relative darkness. A convex lens **focuses** light waves by bending them as they enter and leave the lens to bring them together at a point behind the lens. The collected light forms an inverted **image,** a representation of whatever is in front of the lens. The film chemically changes when struck by light, so the varying amounts of light in the image are recorded.

Your eyes are similar to a camera in many respects. Light passes first through the clear **cornea;** usually thought of as a window, it is also a fixed-shape lens that provides the major part of the eye's focusing. Once past the cornea, light passes through a fluid-filled chamber to the **iris,** which expands or contracts to control the amount of light passing through its opening, the **pupil.** The admitted light is then focused by an adjustable **lens** on the light-sensitive **retina** at the back of the eye. ■ Figure 5.4

Unlike a camera, however, which admits only a brief pulse of light for a single fixed picture, your eye constantly admits a changing flux of light and must continually develop its pictures. Looked at in this way, it's not so surprising that events faster than about $\frac{1}{24}$ of a second are too fast for the eye. Instead, perhaps we ought to be surprised that events that fast *are* visible, for as much as 100 years or more, on one self-renewing "pack of film".

The shape of the eye's lens can be altered to focus the images of objects at varying distances. For viewing distant objects, the lens is relatively flat, but to focus on near objects it is made thicker by muscles attached to it. A normal eye easily accomplishes this **accommodation,** or adjustment of focus for different distances, but differences in eye shape can cause problems. In a **nearsighted** eye, the eyeball is too long; the flattened

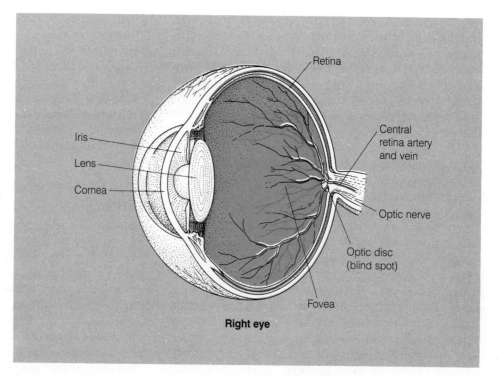

Figure 5.4 ■ A vertical section of a right eye. All available light passes through the clear cornea, which focuses it somewhat. The amount of light reaching the lens is controlled by the iris, which can open or constrict. Light admitted by the iris passes through the lens, which further focuses it on the retina at the back of the eye. Almost directly behind the lens is the fovea, the area of the retina most sensitive to detail. At the optic disc, or blind spot, blood vessels enter and leave the eye and the optic nerve leaves it.

lens then is appropriate for viewing close objects, but because it cannot flatten any further it cannot focus on distant ones. In a **farsighted** eye, the eyeball is too short, so the lens must be thickened just to focus on distant objects and cannot thicken further to focus on near ones.

The accommodation of the eye is measured by a variety of tests, the most common of which is the Snellen chart. With one eye closed, if you can just recognize letters that are defined as appropriate for 20 feet, you have normal or 20/20 vision in that eye. If you're a bit nearsighted and can see only larger letters that an average person could see at 30 feet, that eye has 20/30 vision.

It takes more than distance vision to be able to see well, however. You must also be able to change focus quickly to accommodate different distances, to track objects well despite sudden movements of your head, and to perform a number of other skilled acts. Many of these visual skills originate in the brain, not in the eye. Because simple tests such as the Snellen chart do not measure these other skills, they are inadequate as measures of visual competence. Children who have trouble learning to read, for example, may have 20/20 vision but still be unable to perform the precise short eye movements necessary in reading (Thacher, 1978).

The Retina's Transducers

The transducers of the eye are located at the back of the retina. To reach these cells, light must travel through the cornea and lens, the fluid-filled main chamber of the eye, and the network of blood vessels that nourish the eye. Then it must pass through several parts of the retina itself—the axons that make up the optic nerve and several layers of processing cells—before finally reaching the transducers at the back of the retina. Only about 10% of the light that enters the eye actually reaches the transducers; the other 90% is absorbed by the eye's structures (Gregory, 1966).

The transducers are of two types, called rods and cones because of their shapes. **Rods** are about 1000 times more sensitive to light than cones, but they do not sense variations in color as well as the more specialized cones; rods are thus useful to us mostly at night. **Cones** offer color vision and greater precision in daylight, but are less sensitive to low light levels than rods (Young, 1970).

Both rods and cones contain photosensitive chemicals that change structure, or "bleach," in response to being struck by light (Rushton, 1962). This chemical change triggers action potentials from the rods and cones and thus represents the transduction of light to nervous-system information. The chemical bleaching must then be reversed to restore that rod or cone to full sensitivity. This process takes some time, but the eyes are always moving and there are enough rods and cones that new ones are always ready to respond: about 124 million rods and 6 million cones per retina.

The distribution of transducers differs for different locations on the retina, and rod and cone distributions are quite different from each other. The oldest trans-

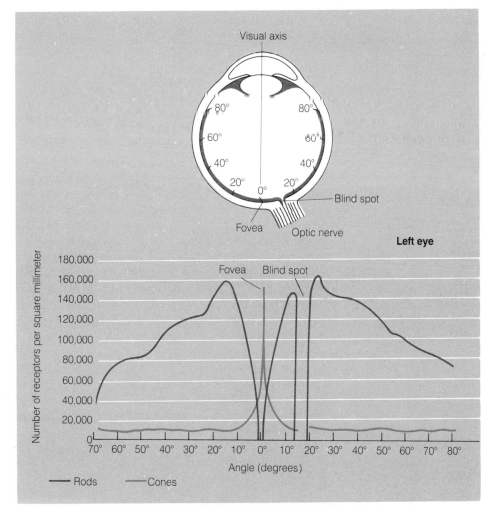

Figure 5.5 ■ The retina covers most of the back of each eye, but vision differs in different areas of the retina. Fewer rods furthest from the center yield the less-detailed peripheral vision. The fovea has a high concentration of cones and no rods, creating precision daylight vision. The area of retina adjacent to the fovea, where the rods are densest, provides maximum night vision. The blind spot has neither rods nor cones.

(After *Vision and the Eye*, 2nd ed., by M. H. Pirenne, Chapman & Hall, 1967. Used by permission.)

ducers, in evolutionary terms, are the rods, which we share with many other species. Rods provide general vision across the full visual field; they are densest near the middle of the retina and gradually diminish toward each side. Cones are concentrated in a single spot at the center of the retina, with a few distributed evenly but sparsely throughout the rest of the retina. These patterns are sharply interrupted at another spot, however, where the optic nerve leaves the eye and the blood vessels enter. At this optic disc, or **blind spot,** there are neither rods nor cones. ■ Figure 5.5

We do not notice our blind spots, however, for several reasons. One is that in normal vision images of different portions of the environment fall on the blind spots of the two eyes, so one eye always sees what the other does not. Another is that the eyes move around, providing information about the missing area that is automatically integrated. People who see with only one eye are also unaware of the blind spot. An object may disappear in the blind spot and then reappear with their eye movements, but they still don't "see" the blind spot itself—just as you do not see it with one eye closed. Our visual systems are "wired" to ignore the blind spots; instead of seeing a hole, we just don't see anything at all. (The brain automatically fills in the gap, using visual information available from the rest of the retina.)

Rods also are absent at the retinal spot where the number of cones rises sharply to a peak, the **fovea.** The fovea is also unique in not having blood vessels or

"Run, Spot, run."

(© 1983 by Sidney Harris)

other layers of cells in front of it; thus it receives incoming light more directly. These special arrangements in the fovea help to give it much greater detail resolution than the rest of the retina. The fovea is where you actually see the details of what you look at; in fact, to "look at" something really means to point the fovea at it. If we are especially interested in something, we automatically look at it, thus placing its image directly on the fovea. We have the impression that our vision is equally clear across a wide area. However, that overall clarity is a creation of the brain; each eye actually supplies only a small detailed center with much more vague surroundings.

At night, when light levels are too weak to stimulate your cones, only your rods provide vision; the fovea, with its dense concentration of cones, is no longer the source of best vision. If you catch a glimpse of something and turn to look directly at it, it will disappear, only to reappear when you look away. You must look slightly to the side of the object you wish to see; this puts its image onto the area of the retina with the most rods.

This technique will only work after you have been in the dark for a while, however, as it takes some time for the rods to become fully sensitive. In bright daylight, both rods and cones are being continuously bleached by the light and have lost some sensitivity. When you then go into a dark place, such as a movie theater, the rods and cones both adapt; it takes 20 or

30 minutes to become fully adapted. Cones adapt more quickly to the dark than rods, reaching maximum sensitivity in about 7 minutes. Rods are initially less sensitive than cones and adapt more slowly, requiring 20 minutes or more, but eventually become more sensitive. Thus, the total curve for **dark adaptation** has two parts, cone adaptation and rod adaptation, with a break in the middle. ■ Figure 5.6

Rods and cones also differ in the wavelengths they respond to and the information they encode. Cones, which are sensitive to all visible wavelengths, provide our sense of color as well as the most precise vision in good light. Rods adapt in the dark to become more sensitive, but do not code light into sensations of color at all. When it's dark enough that only the rods function, you see only in shades of gray. In addition, rods do not sense the longest waves of the spectrum, the red ones, at all; to rods, normal red light is invisible. Red lights can be used, as they are in photographic darkrooms, to allow rods to remain continuously dark-adapted. World War II flight crews took advantage of this effect by wearing red goggles while on the ground. By admitting only red light, the goggles allowed their rods to remain fully adapted. Once in the air, crews could remove the goggles and immediately have their eyes be as light-sensitive as possible. (They would still have to look to one side of objects to see them.)

Optic Nerves to the Brain

If the retinas were only sensory structures, information from their rods and cones would be sent directly up the optic nerves to the brain for processing. But in prenatal development the retinas grow as brain tissue that develops outside the brain. Before information reaches the optic nerves it is combined and processed within the retinas: The 130 million rods and cones in each eye are summarized to 1 million axons in each optic nerve. Information reaching the brain from the optic nerves is thus already somewhat refined, unlike the relatively raw information from the other sensory nerves.

Within the retina, rods and cones synapse on bipolar cells, which lead to ganglion cells. It is the axons of the ganglion cells that actually make up the optic nerve. This structural arrangement provides for the summation of information within the retina before the optic nerve leaves the eye. The degree of this summation differs substantially for different areas of the retina. In the periphery of the retina as many as 1200 rods may lead to a single ganglion cell, and thus to a single axon in the optic nerve. This summarizing of many cells provides only very general visual information. In areas closer to the center of the retina, fewer

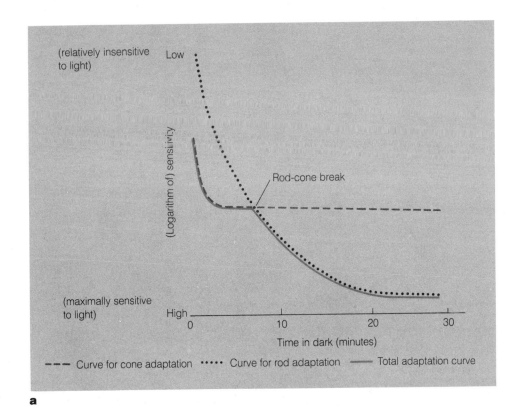

a

b

Figure 5.6 ■ (a) Rods and cones both adapt to dark by becoming more sensitive, but at different rates and to different extents. (b) Rods are insensitive to red light so red filters, such as this World War II flight crew is wearing, allow the rods to remain fully dark-adapted.

(United Press International photo)

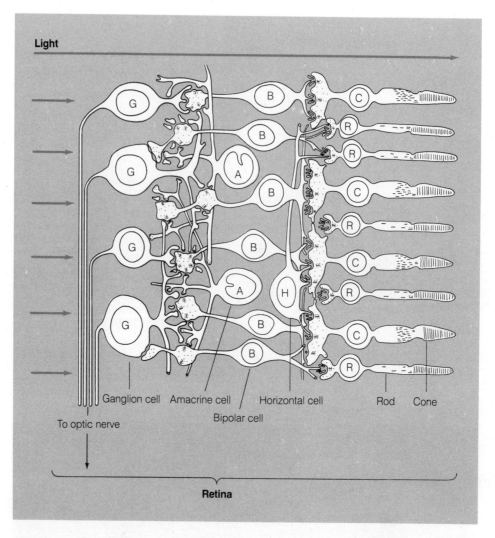

Light

Ganglion cell   Amacrine cell   Horizontal cell   Rod   Cone

Bipolar cell

To optic nerve

Retina

Figure 5.7 ■ The layers of the retina. Light reaching the light-sensitive rods and cones must first pass through the axons that make up the optic nerve, then through several layers of other cells. As the rods and cones are stimulated, their information is combined and processed in these other cells before being sent by the optic nerve to the brain. (Because the retina develops as remote brain tissue, this processing already is a kind of brain function.) Information from the rods and cones is first summarized by bipolar cells, which in turn are summarized by ganglion cells; the ganglion cell axons make up the optic nerve. Horizontal and amacrine cells form lateral connections across the other cells, as shown; the functions of these connections are still unknown.

rods or cones are summed for each ganglion cell, providing more detailed visual information. The summation for the rods of the periphery is 100 times greater than for the cones of the fovea. ■ Figure 5.7

In addition to this three-layer summarizing, horizontal and amacrine cells also interconnect laterally across groups of the other cells, linking them together further. The exact functioning of these connections is still being investigated, but such a richness of linkage among millions of cells obviously allows for substantial processing of the information (Werblin, 1973).

We noted earlier that a ground squirrel has a more complex retina than ours, and that this reflects a less complex brain. Now you can see why: The ground squirrel does more processing in its retina than we do, so its brain gets more finished information than ours. This simplifies and speeds up the squirrel's ability to react, but reduces its flexibility for learned visual adaptations (Michael, 1969).

The frog is a more extreme example of fixedness in visual processing; its visual information is fitted into a few fixed categories that are used to call for a few fixed responses (Lettvin et al., 1959; Muntz, 1964). If a small dark object moves across its visual field, the frog sees it as a bug and tries to eat it. A shadow that suddenly darkens the entire field must be a predator, and the frog leaps to avoid it. But the frog cannot modify these responses through learning; it will starve in the presence of food if the food doesn't produce an image moving across its retina at the correct speed. The frog and you thus represent quite different directions of evolutionary adaptation. It has a few immediate fixed responses, whereas you have a wide range of possibilities but may need years of visual experience to learn to manage them.

The processed information carried by the optic nerve then undergoes further rearrangement and passes through other brain areas before reaching the cerebral cortex. First the optic nerves blend and then split again at a special junction called the **optic chiasma.** The optic nerve information is rearranged at the optic chiasma so that information from the left half of each retina (information from the right visual field) goes to the left hemisphere and vice versa. The rearranged information then passes through an area of the thalamus before reaching the occipital cortex of each hemisphere.

The half-visual-field images are arranged on the occipital cortex upside down, as they are on the retina. (The lens inverts the image as it focuses it.) This might seem to imply that you should see the world upside down, but it does not; the brain makes this correction without difficulty.

The placement of visual information on the cortex approximates locations of the real world in that adjacent areas of the world fall side by side on the cortex. But the amount of cortex devoted to different areas of the world differs. The portion of the visual field that falls on the fovea is greatly emphasized, with peripheral areas receiving relatively little cortical representation (Frisby, 1980). Figure 5.8 schematically represents these arrangements. (It does not show the structures in their true proportions, but expands some of them for clarity of presentation.) ■ Figure 5.8

If an area of occipital cortex is damaged, that area will be unable to process information about its portion of the visual field. Information about that area of the visual field comes from both eyes, so the result will be a blind area in both eyes called **cortical blindness** (Teuber et al., 1960). People with cortical blindness are as unaware of these newly created blind spots as we are unaware of our natural ones. But they do notice peculiar effects that help to tell us how we see the world.

A cortically blind man may enter a room and see it as uniformly papered with a print wallpaper. As he turns his head, however, pictures on the wall that had been in his blind area suddenly pop up. His "view" of a uniform wall was a kind of visual assumption; he had extrapolated the portion of wall that he did see to cover the rest of the wall. Once the man has seen the pictures, he will continue to "see" them when he turns his head back to the original angle. He no longer sees them in the conventional sense because they are in his blind spot; but he has corrected his assumption, from a blank wall to a wall with pictures, so that is what he now "sees." If you sneaked up and removed the pictures he would still see them—until he again looked over and recorrected (Gardner, 1975).

Where in the brain is such a person "seeing" the pictures if he is blind at that point of the occipital cortex? It seems that other brain areas must be processing and storing information that fills in the damaged area. Similar processes must be taking place for our normal blind spots, to build up and hold a view of the world *based* on visual input but not identical to it. You thus "see" elsewhere in the brain, not in your eyes or even your occipital cortex.

This arrangement is the basis for experimental work on artificial vision. If the occipital cortex is stimulated directly, the person sees something, even though there has been no activity in retina or optic nerve; such stimulation might in the future allow vision in people whose eyes are totally nonfunctional (Dobelle et al., 1974).

We will continue investigating visual perception in the following chapter. But what you have already learned about your eyes will allow you to observe their functioning in new ways. ■ Personal Application: Seeing the Mechanisms of Your Own Eyes

HEARING (AUDITION)

We hear "sound." But just what is sound? A classic philosophical puzzle supposes that a great tree falls in a lonely forest. With no ear to hear it, does it make a sound? The answer is "yes and no." To solve this puzzle, we must separate the physical-event definition of *sound* from the sensation—**hearing,** or **audition**—that the event gives rise to; the first always occurs when a tree falls, but the second requires an ear.

Sound as Environmental Information

Fish have a lateral-line sense organ along each side of the body that senses pressure waves in the water. Imagine two fish swimming close beside each other; if

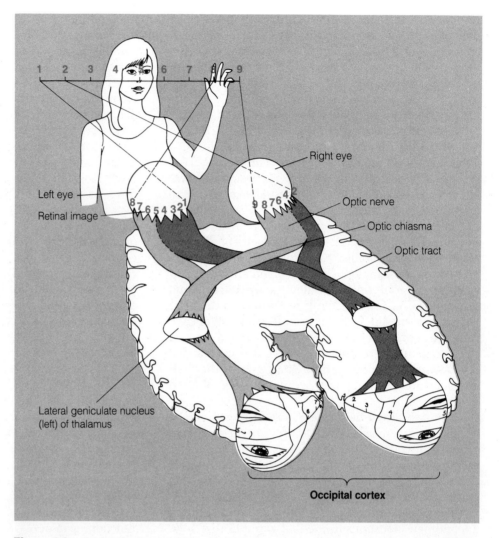

Figure 5.8 ■ Schematic diagram of how visual information reaches the brain. The numbers show how information from both eyes is rearranged at the optic chiasma so that each hemisphere sees only its visual field. Numbers 1 to 5 are in the observer's left visual field. They fall on the right side of each retina and the information from them goes to the right hemisphere, passing through the lateral geniculate nucleus of the thalamus on the way. Numbers 5 to 9 follow a comparable path from the right visual field to the left hemisphere. The distorted proportions of the image on the occipital cortex show the emphasis on foveal vision; an observer looking directly at the woman's face would see it in detail, but her hand would be seen only more generally.

(From *Seeing: Illusion, Brain and Mind* by John P. Frisby, Oxford University Press, 1980. Reprinted by permission of Roxby Press Limited.)

one swerves, the other's lateral-line organ senses the pressure change. This arrangement allows a school of fish to swim in close formation; movement of one fish raises the pressure for the next, which moves over and pressures the next, and the whole school turns (Partridge, 1982). Our hearing has evolved from lateral-line organs to a sensory system for use in air (Crompton & Parker, 1978). Any object vibrating in that air sends out a series of pressure waves in all directions, as pushed molecules transmit the pressure to others. One definition of sound is a series of such pressure waves in some medium. (Sounds can be transmitted through any medium in which pressure waves can be generated, including solid objects as well as water and air. But unlike light, sound cannot be transmitted in a vacuum; we see the sun but we do not hear it.) ■ Figure 5.10

The alternating compression and expansion of adjacent molecules in a repeating pressure wave is diagrammed as a smoothly rising and falling curve. A sound wave is described by its **frequency,** the number of complete cycles of compression/expansion per second; it is measured in **Hertz (Hz),** named after the German physicist Heinrich Hertz (1857–1894). (One

Seeing the mechanisms of your own eyes

Our blind spots are so well-adjusted-for that it might be hard to convince you of their existence—were it not for the fact that they are easily demonstrated. Some simple exercises will allow you to "see" the blind spots as well as other structures of your eyes. Once you find your blind spots you'll discover that they can be located in everyday vision. The size of a blind spot is just about big enough to remove the whole face of a person across a table, for example, leaving only a fringe of hair with nothing in the middle: just the thing to enliven lunch hour. ■Figure 5.9

You can also see other eye structures. You may already have seen small spots drifting down across your vision that move when you move your eyes. They are actually bits of natural debris, floating in the fluid that fills the main chamber of your eye (Walker, 1982). Left alone they will sink out of sight, but a sharp upswing of your eyes will toss them up so that they will drift down again, like snow in an old-fashioned paperweight.

You normally cannot see the blood vessels of your eyes because they always occupy the same position relative to the retina and the sensors behind them adapt. But you can see them under some special circumstances. After strong exercise or excitement, for example, when all arteries notably expand with each heartbeat, the eye capillaries become marginally visible. If you look at a neutral surface when your heart is pounding, you may see a kind of rippling effect, in time with your heartbeat. This is the pulsing of your eye vessels; as they expand and cover new retinal cells, they are made visible.

Another way to see these capillaries is with the narrow beam of a pen-light in a dark room. (The brighter the light the better, as long as the beam is narrow.) Shine the beam up into your eye at a steep angle from close beside the eye. You will have to keep moving the beam around, but at some point you will see a dark red pattern like the veining of a leaf; this pattern is the network of blood vessels of that eye. It is also possible to see individual blood cells moving through these vessels by staring at a clear blue sky with one eye closed. Careful observation will reveal specks moving across the visual field in time with your pulse rate.

Noticing the fovea is a different sort of problem; because you normally use it extensively, the problem becomes how to notice the difference between it and the vision in the rest of the retina. As with the blind spot, you just have to know how to look. First fix your gaze (fovea) on the period at the end of this sentence and hold it there; then try to see what else is around you, *without* moving your fovea off the period. Now look around. Notice how much detail pops up when you look directly at something that you didn't see before; this is detail that only the fovea can provide.

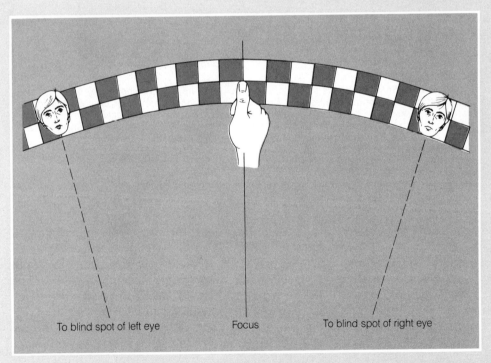

To blind spot of left eye   Focus   To blind spot of right eye

Figure 5.9 ■ Even with one eye closed or covered you will not notice your blind spot, but here is a way to find it. Using only one eye, look directly at the drawing of a thumb and move the text toward or away from you until the appropriate face disappears. The face image will then be exactly on your blind spot. (If you have trouble, check to be sure you're using only one eye and holding your gaze on the thumb; if you let your gaze turn toward the face, it won't work.) Once you can do this reliably, try it in the real world. Use your own thumb as an aid to hold your gaze straight ahead, if necessary.

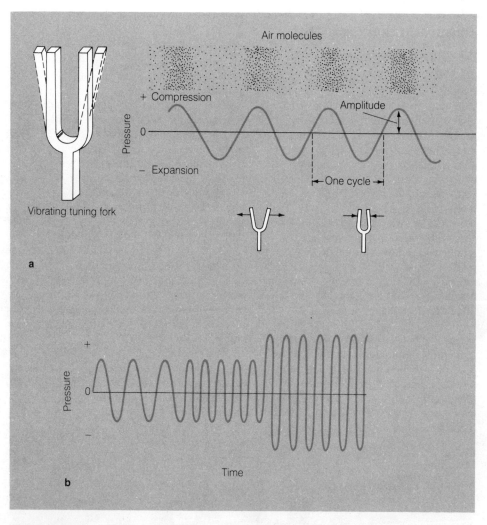

Figure 5.10 ■ What we hear as sound is a series of pressure waves in the air. (a) A tuning fork, by alternately increasing and decreasing the distance between the arms, sets up sound waves that can be represented by a curve as shown. The peak of the wave represents maximum compression of the air molecules and the bottom represents expansion of them. (b) This wave represents a sound that first decreases in loudness (smaller amplitude), then in pitch (slower frequency). (The first part of the wave to reach the ear is on the right.)

Hz is one cycle per second.) The **amplitude** of a wave is the vertical height of one peak.

New pressure waves will be formed as long as an object vibrates. A falling tree always generates such pressure waves, first as it breaks away, then as it hits the ground. In this sense, it makes a sound. But another definition of sound is something that is heard by an organism. The physical characteristics of a sound wave are transformed by an ear and brain into psychological dimensions of sound (Békésy, 1957). The frequency of a wave is the basis of the psychological dimension of **pitch;** the higher the frequency, the higher the pitch we hear. The amplitude of the wave is

the basis of **loudness;** the greater the amplitude, the louder the sound we hear (Wightman & Green, 1974).

Normally the frequency of the waves reaching your ear is the same as those leaving the object, but this is not true when the sound source is moving toward or away from you. Suppose that a car speeds past you as you stand on the side of the road. As the car approaches, its movement sends sound waves toward you that much faster; you hear this as a higher pitch than you would if you were moving at the same speed as the car. But as it passes you and moves away, the sound waves are "stretched apart"; you hear this as a lower pitch. The overall effect is a steady pitch as the

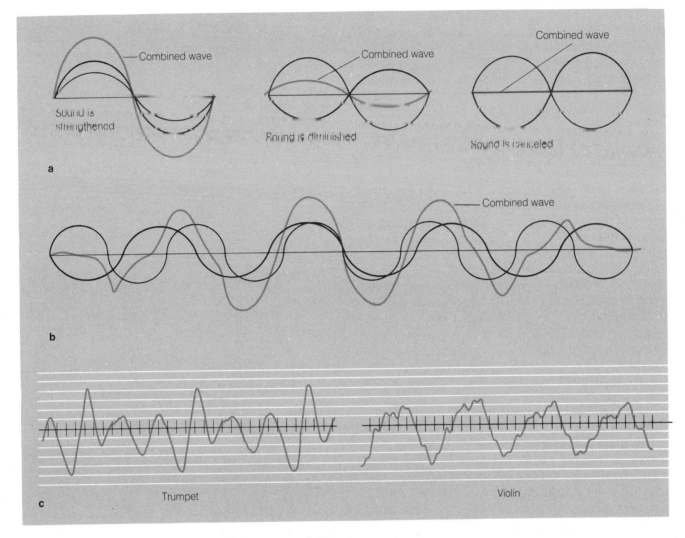

Figure 5.11 ■ Ordinary sounds are made up of a mixture of different waves. (a) Overlapping waves can either add to or subtract from each other. (b) Waves of different frequencies generate a complex output. (c) The same note played on different instruments. The major waveform of two different instruments playing the same note is the same, but the details—representing the overtones that give each instrument its characteristic timbre—are quite different.

car approaches, with an abrupt drop as it passes to a lower level that it then holds. This change of pitch of a moving object is called the **Doppler effect.**

The characteristics of sound described so far apply to any "pure" tone, or sound of only one frequency. Pure tones are rarely found in nature, however; mixed waves make up most ordinary sounds. ■ Figure 5.11

To see how sound waves combine, first consider two pure tones of the same frequency. When their peaks occur at the same time, they add up to increase the amplitude; this makes the sound louder. When peaks occur opposite each other, they reduce the net amplitude and thus reduce the sound; unlikely as it

may seem, two identical tones can thus cancel each other completely so that you hear nothing. When two waves of different frequencies are superimposed, parts of them add and other parts subtract to yield a complex wave.

Real sounds are often made up of many frequencies; the complexity of the resulting wave is interpreted by ear and brain as the **timbre,** or texture of the sound. Timbre allows us to differentiate between the same note played on different instruments. The note itself is produced by the dominant part of each wave, but **overtones,** additional higher frequencies, give the waves from various instruments distinctive detail structure. A trumpet and a violin, for example, generate quite different overtones for the same note; we hear them as having different timbre. Modern music synthesizers, from the home electronic organ to the instruments of a rock band, deliberately use overtones. A single tone at a given pitch yields a bland, rather unmusical sound, but by adding the appropriate overtones a synthesizer can imitate the pattern of any conventional instrument—or sound like no instrument ever heard before (Hilts, 1980a).

As more and more frequencies are added to a sound, it eventually loses any specific pitch and becomes **white noise,** which contains essentially all frequencies. (It is called white in an analogy to white light.) White noise sounds like a hiss rather than a tone—like the static sound of a radio between stations. White-noise generators are sometimes sold as sleep or study aids. Even at low volume, white noise masks irregular sounds that would otherwise disturb concentration; yet because it is relatively featureless and unchanging, people quickly adapt to it and pay it no attention. Some people wear portable white-noise generators like hearing aids, to mask the constant ringing in the ears (tinnitus) that can result from inner-ear damage.

The natural world is full of vibrations, from a few Hertz to many thousands, but we hear only those between about 20 and 20,000 Hz, and much of what we rely on falls in the middle of this range. (Notes on a piano range from 27.5 to 4180 Hz, although the overtones go up to 10,000 Hz.) Animals that use sound as a form of sonar, such as bats or dolphins, are sensitive to 100,000 Hz or more, but even animals without such specializations may be more sensitive than we are. Dog whistles are available that are higher than we can hear; animals with larger heads, like elephants, can hear lower sounds than we can.

Besides frequency (pitch), hearing also responds to the amplitude of sound waves, which we interpret as loudness. Loudness is measured in **decibels (db);** one decibel is one tenth of a bel, a unit named for Alexander Graham Bell, inventor of the telephone. Decibels measure a sound wave's maximum pressure (above atmospheric pressure) on a special scale. Zero decibels is defined as the pressure needed to reach threshold for a 1000-Hz tone; each 10-db increase represents a pressure *10 times greater* than the previous pressure. Higher decibel values are therefore many times greater than lower ones: thunder (or a rock band), at 120 db, is a million times stronger than ordinary conversation at 60 db. Since our hearing utilizes a similar scale for higher intensities (as shown by the Weber-Fechner law), we don't hear these sounds as a million times louder, but the ear is subjected to a million times greater pressure. ■ Figure 5.12

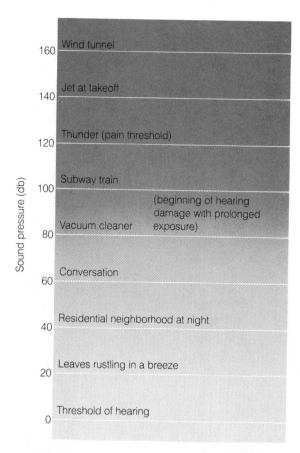

Figure 5.12 ■ The decibel values of some common sounds, together with some other critical levels. Hearing damage begins to occur well below the pain threshhold. Very high sounds, if sustained, can be so stressful that they kill laboratory rats. Continued sounds near this point may also cause stress problems for humans, as well as hearing loss.

This difference between objective pressure and experienced loudness has important consequences, including the fact that you will not know when your hearing is being damaged. Sounds that reach 120 db are experienced as painful, but this warns only of *immediate* damage. The ear can briefly withstand pressures between 90 and 120 db, which do not cause pain, but even these lower pressures soon begin to cause damage (Raloff, 1982). Prolonged exposure to sounds over about 90 db causes gradual hearing loss and eventual deafness. The amplified instruments of rock music have caused hearing loss in both musicians and listeners, high-speed drills have caused hearing loss for dentists, and so forth. People who work in extremely noisy environments, such as airline mechanics, now customarily wear special hearing protectors. For people who need to hear some sounds there are ear plugs that attenuate the strongest pressures without blocking other sounds.

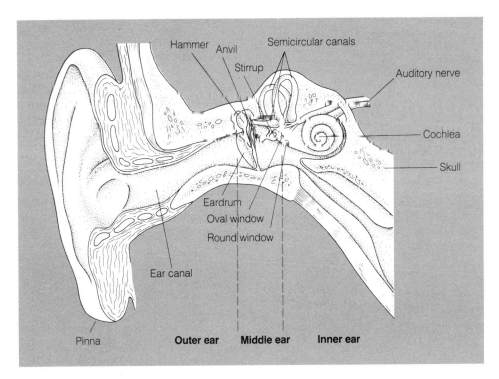

Figure 5.13 ■ The ear is conventionally divided into three portions. The pinna and the ear canal collect and amplify sound waves, which cause the eardrum to vibrate. The three bones of the middle ear transmit these vibrations to the fluid inside the cochlea of the inner ear. The semicircular canals contain the sensors for the vestibular sense.

Another useful attribute of sound waves is the direction from which they come. Because the head itself blocks sound waves, sound originating to one side of you will reach the ear on that side directly but will take longer to reach the other ear and will be weaker when they do. Thus whenever a sound source is not directly in front of or behind you, the sound waves reaching the two ears will differ in intensity and time delay. These differences are clues to the location of the sound, though you need to be able to move your head slightly to use this information effectively (Rosenzweig, 1961).

We are not normally aware of how we locate the source of sounds. In fact, vision is often used to specify a sound's location, even when hearing could do so more accurately. We see a movie or watch a ventriloquist without being aware of any sensory discrepancies; voices simply seem to come from the mouths of those whom we see speaking. But the sounds often come from a notably different location, one we could accurately point to if our eyes were closed. A movie speaker may be many feet from the screen, but your brain simply adjusts hearing to fit the visual location. Similarly, a ventriloquist cannot "throw" his or her voice, but just uses different voices and moves only the dummy's mouth for one of them; the listener's brain does the throwing.

The Ear's Accessory Structures

We may think of the ear as what we see on the side of someone's head, but that is only the **pinna,** or external portion of the **outer ear.** The pinna aids in collecting sound waves and channeling them to other accessory structures of the ear, but is not really necessary. Some animals, such as the bat-eared fox, have very large pinnas to help them hear faint sounds—it can hear termites moving beneath the ground—but others do quite well with little or no pinna. Just inside the head is the other part of the outer ear, the **ear canal,** a tube about an inch long. Sound waves resonate in the ear canal like the vibrations of an organ pipe; this resonance amplifies the incoming sound by about two times. At the end of the ear canal is the **eardrum,** a flexible membrane that is set in motion by the air vibrations. ■ Figure 5.13

The eardrum marks the outer boundary of the **middle ear.** Within the middle ear are the three smallest bones in the body, the **hammer,** the **anvil,** and the **stirrup,** which are set into motion by the movement of the eardrum. These bones further amplify the sound by two or three times through mechanical leverage built into their shapes before transmitting the vibrations to the inner ear. To help protect these delicate middle-ear structures, tiny tendons attached to the bones and eardrum can be pulled by equally tiny muscles to strap them down against the battering of strong sounds. If these muscles are given time to react they can protect the ear quite well, but unexpected loud sounds can rupture the eardrum, tear the bones apart, or cause the stirrup to damage the inner ear.

Long-term decreases in sensitivity may also occur as this entire system grows stiffer in a protective adaptation to continued loud sounds; this helps protect the ear, but also reduces its ability to respond to quiet sounds. To some extent, this adaptation may affect all who live in an industrialized environment. One researcher studied members of a Stone Age tribe in Ethiopia living in a remarkably quiet environment; the background noise in one of their villages was about one-tenth as loud as the hum of a refrigerator. Nearly all of the 500 adult males tested could hear a soft murmur across a clearing the size of a football field (Stevens & Warshofsky, 1965), probably the greatest sensitivity that would be practical. If the ear were much more sensitive it would sense the rush of blood in our veins and the creaks of our joints.

The **inner ear** consists of two major fluid-filled structures: the spiral-shaped **cochlea** containing the sound transducers and the **semicircular canals,** sensory structures for the vestibular sense. If we lived in water, we wouldn't need the structures of the middle ear; fish have none. For efficient hearing in air, however, the sound waves must be amplified to pass from air into the inner fluid without restricting the sensitivity of our hearing. To the amplification provided by the ear canal and middle-ear bones is added further amplification caused by the large size of the eardrum compared to the small point of attachment of the stirrup to the cochlea. Together, these features amplify the sound transmitted to the inner ear by up to 180 times.

The Cochlea's Transducers

The cochlea, though much smaller than a fingernail, is a complex structure; it may be the most efficient packaging of function in the entire body. The cochlea further conducts the amplified sound waves and the transducers within it extract the information that we sense as sound; only then do the vibrations of a falling tree finally become action potentials in a listener's nervous system.

The cochlea is a three-chambered tube wrapped in a coil and surrounded by the rigid temporal bone, the hardest in the body, to isolate the vibrations within it. Each of the three chambers is filled with a watery fluid similar to cerebrospinal fluid. Vibrations enter at the

oval window to which the stirrup is attached; at this point, the sound waves in the air have become pressure waves in the fluid of the vestibular canal. These pressure waves spiral up one of the three chambers, the vestibular canal, then back down another chamber, the tympanic canal. As the pressure waves travel down the tympanic canal they flex the **basilar membrane,** which forms one wall of the tympanic canal. (The third chamber, the cochlear duct, prevents the incoming vibrations in the vestibular canal from affecting the basilar membrane.) When the pressure waves reach the lower end of the tympanic canal, they cause the **round window** to vibrate, dissipating the energy of the waves back into the air of the middle ear. ■ Figure 5.14

The transducers for hearing are tiny **hair cells** located in a structure called the **organ of Corti,** after its discoverer. The organ of Corti is attached to the basilar membrane and flexes with it; the ends of the hair cells are attached to a rigid structure within the cochlear duct. As the basilar membrane flexes from the sound pressure waves, the hair cells are subjected to sideways or "shear" forces at their attachment points. This is the final mechanical action that represents the incoming sound; the shear on the hair cells causes them to fire action potentials up the **auditory nerve.** The hair cells thus alter the sound waves, brought all the way to them from the vibrating sound source, into nervous-system information (Hudspeth, 1983). ■ Figure 5.15

Auditory Nerves to the Brain

The basic question of sound coding for auditory-nerve transmission concerns how sound frequencies are turned into what we experience as differences in pitch. We have known for several hundred years that the cochlea performs this translation but it took much longer to discover how it codes the information (Békésy, 1960). It is now known that two different principles, once proposed as alternate theories, apply: the place principle and the volley principle.

According to the **place principle,** different places, or areas of the basilar membrane, respond to different sound frequencies. A pure tone maximally displaces the basilar membrane at one particular point; low frequencies are sensed toward the inner end of the cochlear spiral, and high frequencies nearer the round window. A complex wave displaces several areas of the basilar membrane, with the strongest frequencies causing the greatest displacement (Zwislocki, 1981). Once known as the place theory, the place principle is now known to be essentially true, although it is not the only code used.

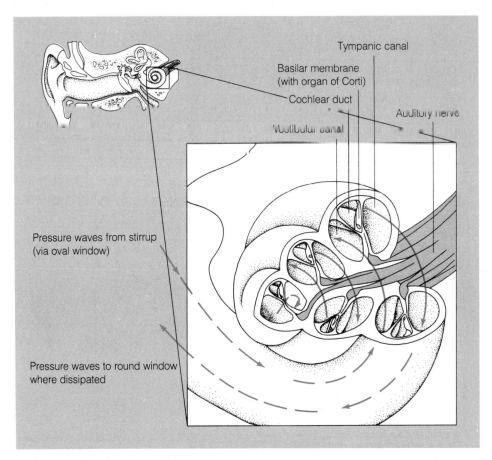

Labels on figure:
Tympanic canal
Basilar membrane (with organ of Corti)
Cochlear duct
Vestibular canal
Auditory nerve
Pressure waves from stirrup (via oval window)
Pressure waves to round window where dissipated

Figure 5.14 ■ Pressure waves caused by the vibrations of the middle-ear bones enter the cochlea at the oval window, spiral up the vestibular canal to the end, then spiral back down the tympanic canal to the round window where they are dissipated. As the pressure waves go down the tympanic canal, they flex the basilar membrane and the associated organ of Corti. The cochlear duct allows the basilar membrane to respond to waves in the tympanic canal without being affected by those in the vestibular canal.

Research on restoring hearing in some types of deafness includes experimental cochlear implants that make use of the place principle. Microsurgery is used to insert 8 or 10 electrodes into different locations within the cochlea. A microphone picks up sounds, which activate the electrodes and stimulate activity in the auditory nerve. The information sent to the brain is crude compared to normal hearing, but the person can hear sounds and make some discriminations among them. Researchers hope future versions will provide enough electrodes to make speech interpretable (Buys, 1982; Weintraub, 1980).

An alternate proposal to place theory was that the basilar membrane vibrates at the same frequency as the sound, and action potentials in the auditory nerve then match this frequency. When this idea was first proposed, there seemed to be a major problem: The maximum rate of firing for neurons is slower than the sound frequencies we can hear. (Tones of 20,000 Hz mean 20,000 pressure waves *per second*, and the hair cells of the organ of Corti cannot respond that fast.) For frequency matching to be possible there would have to be a mechanism for responding when the vibrations occur faster than the fastest response time of the hair cells.

In fact, there is such a mechanism, involving a number of neurons firing at once. Suppose 1 neuron can only fire fast enough to match every tenth cycle of the sound. Then 10 properly spaced neurons firing in sequence could match every cycle: 1 neuron would fire at the first cycle, another neuron at the second cycle, and so forth. By the time the eleventh cycle occurred, the first neuron would be ready to fire again. Thus the total information sent up the auditory nerve could match a high-frequency tone, even though each neuron could only respond at a slower rate. This concept of groups of neurons firing together to provide a frequency code is called the **volley principle.**

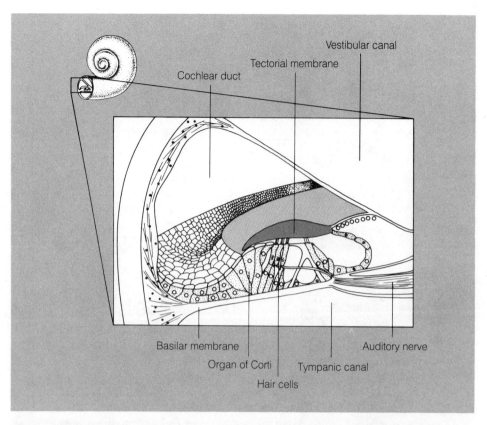

Figure 5.15 ■ As incoming pressure waves (representing sounds) travel down the tympanic canal, they flex the basilar membrane and thus the organ of Corti. Hair cells within the organ of Corti are the actual transducers for sound: They are also attached to the relatively rigid tectorial membrane, so the flexing applies a force to them, causing them to generate action potentials out the auditory nerve.

Another aspect of information that must be coded is intensity, which we hear as loudness. In the place principle, this can easily be done; the stronger the displacement, the louder is the tone. But intensity information can also be coded as loudness in the volley principle by increasing the number of neurons: 2 firing at every cycle rather than 1, for example. With around 30,000 neurons from each cochlea, there are certainly adequate numbers for group firing.

Overall both the place and the volley principles are used, although they are not equally applicable to all frequencies. For sounds below about 500–1000 Hz, the frequency principle applies. For frequencies above about 5000 Hz, the place principle applies. For the 1000–5000 Hz midrange, both seem to be used.

Coded information carried by the auditory nerves is then further processed at several intermediate points in lower brain centers before it reaches the auditory areas in the temporal lobes. Each hemisphere receives information from both ears, but the information is biased so that each hemisphere emphasizes the ear on the side of the body that it also controls. Thus, the left hemisphere, which operates the right hand, also emphasizes the right ear. The other ear's information is secondary; it is helpful for locating sounds, for example.

The cortex is where we truly hear sounds, that is, turn the sensed information into content. If a stimulus can somehow bypass the ear and stimulate the brain directly, it can be heard just as if it were a real sound. For example, at the touch of an electrode on the auditory cortex the patient may seem to "hear" a sound. A recent report suggests that the "sounds" of ringing in the ears called tinnitus are actually "the sounds of silence," a result of damage to the hair cells. The *lack* of signal from the damaged hair cells is interpreted by the brain as if it were a *continuous* signal, and the person hears a constant sound (Dunkle, 1982).

Another way of "hearing" sounds that don't come from the ear is to generate them from memory. We all do this to some extent: We can remember someone speaking to us in important memories. However, many people who hear sounds that are not really there are considered "crazy." In fact, hearing voices is one defining characteristic of schizophrenia (Chapter 15). The crucial difference between the kinds of experiences described earlier and "crazy" ones seems to be the interpretation put on the experience. A composer who "hears" music knows that it is being self-generated. But someone who hears music when no one else does may be considered by others—and may even come to think of him- or herself—as "crazy." Some people who once heard but are now deaf experience a memory replay of sounds they once heard. Now that this is known to happen, deaf persons who report hearing voices are not necessarily presumed to be mentally ill. They may simply be told to ignore the voices if there seem to be no other difficulties.

SMELL AND TASTE

Chemicals as Environmental Information

Molecules of various chemicals provide the environmental information for both smell and taste, which are therefore known as the chemical senses. Even very simple organisms respond to molecules in the fluid in which they live; these molecules directly stimulate cells on the surface of their bodies. In more complex organisms, only certain cells in special locations retain this sensitivity, and accessory structures have evolved to bring the molecules to them (Müller-Schwarze & Silverstein, 1980).

Smell, technically termed olfaction, extracts molecules from the air; taste, or gustation, extracts them from liquid solutions (Ziporyn, 1982). Smell and taste are both physically close and experientially linked; as you eat food, much of its taste is actually smell from molecules of food brought through the air to smell sensors. In some ways these two senses are as much alike as the separate skin senses that are grouped together under touch, but smell and taste are traditionally discussed separately.

Smell (Olfaction)

On a warm summer night, you smell a faint sharp odor and recognize it as that of a disturbed skunk. Just how did you become aware of that distant skunk? When frightened or angered, the skunk projects a few drops of a volatile and odorous liquid into the air from a scent gland. Those few drops rapidly dilute themselves in the air, spreading out over several miles to a concentration

of a few parts per million. Among those who smell this tiny residue is you: you sniff the night air, and turbulence within your nasal cavities forcibly deposits a few of these molecules onto a specialized mucus layer. Receptors in the layer respond to the molecules' presence with action potentials that travel up the olfactory tract to your brain, which recognizes them. ■ Figure 5.16

Accessory Structures and Transducers What for our remote ancestors was a sensitive skin is now a couple of inch-square patches at the top of our nasal passages; as air breathed in flows over these **olfactory mucosa,** molecules in the air are trapped in the mucus, where receptor cells respond to them. The actual reception sites are believed to be the cilia, dendritelike projections from the receptor cells that extend into the mucus layer. Sniffing the air improves sensitivity by setting up turbulence over the turbinate bones, which helps to force any available molecules directly into the mucosa. The nose thus includes several accessory structures that bring air in and extract the scent molecules before the information is altered by the transducers in the mucosa.

How the olfactory transducers code information is largely unknown (Cagan & Kare, 1981). One major theory, called the **stereochemical theory,** proposes that the shapes of receptor sites match the shapes of particular molecules (Amoore, 1970; Amoore et al., 1964). According to this concept, when a molecule of an odorous substance fits into a similarly-shaped site, it activates the smell receptors, somewhat as neurotransmitter molecules do. The theory proposes that combinations of a limited number of different shapes give our full range of smells. Although the general concept of several basic smells (ranging from putrid through floral to ethereal) is not unreasonable, work to date has been unable to agree on what they are.

Smell has been thought to be less precise than some of the other senses; people are commonly said to be able to identify only 6 to 22 odors. However, one researcher has found that, under the right conditions, subjects can identify up to 80 odors—apparently still without reaching a limit (Cain, 1979). Careful control of the odors used as test stimuli allowed subjects to demonstrate a sensitivity to odors at very low concentrations that was as good as that of the best chemical analyses (Cain, 1977).

Individual differences in smell sensitivity have often been considered to reflect genetic differences, but one study of twins found no evidence to support that conclusion. Instead, it found that a variety of environmental agents, including smoking and alcohol, contribute to differences in sensitivity (Hubert et al., 1980).

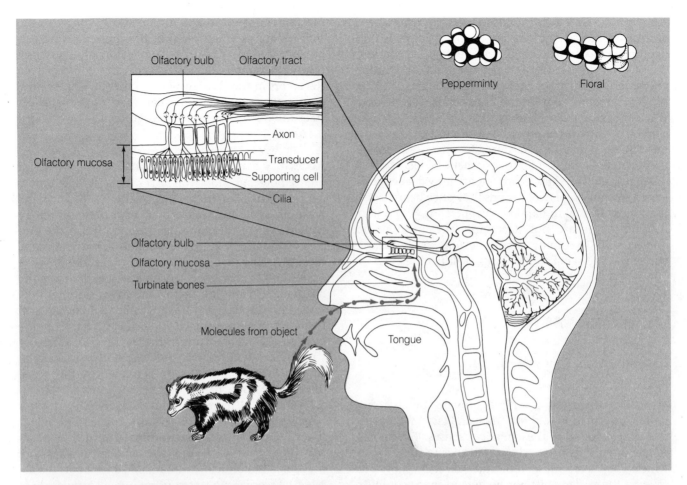

Figure 5.16 ■ In smell, odor molecules pass through the nasal passages and are trapped on the olfactory mucosa. Transduction may occur when molecules of different shapes fit into similarly shaped transducers on the cilia. Axons from these transducers synapse in the olfactory bulb, and the olfactory tract carries the information from there to the frontal cortex.

(Adapted from Amoore et al., 1964.)

Because the basic smells remain unknown, how they are coded for neural transmission also is unknown. The nerve tracts that carry the sensed information, however, are reasonably well defined. Transducers in the mucosa send their axons up through the base of the skull to synapse in two **olfactory bulbs** just beneath the brain. From the olfactory bulbs, parallel **olfactory tracts** carry information to several parts of the limbic system and to the frontal lobe of the cortex. Unlike the other senses, smell does not pass through the thalamus on its way to the cortex. Instead, the olfactory area of the frontal cortex is connected with the thalamic taste area. This arrangement is presumably related to the experiencing of smell as a part of taste, but the details are not clearly understood.

Pheromones The connections of smell to the limbic system are important for many species in the control of survival behaviors, including eating and reproduction.

(The limbic system has been called a "nose brain" because of these direct ties.) Scent messages called **pheromones** are a major form of communication for many species' survival behaviors. In insects, pheromones may direct many or all behaviors (Schneider, 1974; Wilson, 1963); they are often important in sexual behavior of non-human mammals (Shorey, 1976; Stoddard, 1980).

Whether pheromones play any role in human behavior remains unknown (Hassett, 1978). We do retain both odor-producing and odor-sensing capabilities: Sweat glands in groin, armpits, and chest produce a special output that bacteria act upon to generate odors, and the body hair in these areas may act as an antenna to disperse odors into the air. And though it is not known how they use the ability, humans *can* discriminate such odors: Infants, for example, can recognize their own mothers and adults can identify the sex of other adults (Russell, 1976).

One interesting recent finding about pheromones concerns their presence in truffles, a highly prized gourmet delicacy. Truffles grow wild, at about three feet beneath the ground; trained sows (female pigs) have long been used to dig for them, but one problem has been to keep the sows from eating them when they found them. German investigators have found that truffles contain a steroid that is known to be a sex pheromone of boars (male pigs). This, they say, "might explain the efficient interest of pigs in search of this delicacy" (Maugh, 1982a, p. 1224). Maugh also notes that this might explain why humans like truffles: The same steroid is synthesized in the testes of human males and secreted by auxiliary sweat glands.

Our sense of smell is far less sensitive than that of most other mammals and our behavior is far more directed by learned patterns, so we are less directly affected by pheromones. But it would be rash to assume that we are not affected at all (Hopson, 1979). The ways in which humans interact are often subtle and complex, and multiple influences may be at work simultaneously. Interpersonal likes and dislikes, including sexual ones, are frequently based on impressions that we cannot easily describe. The bases for these may include a variety of learned variables, but it is also possible that they include more primitive ones based on scent (D. White, 1981).

Taste (Gustation)

We taste substances by extracting molecules from solutions in our mouth and sensing them by transducers located primarily on the surface of the tongue. Three kinds of ridges called papillae, located around the sides of the tongue, contain **taste buds;** those in different areas are sensitive to different basic tastes. (The center of the tongue is not sensitive to taste.) Each of the 10,000 or so taste buds has up to 200 transducers within it that receive the solutions through a central pore. ■ Figure 5.17

The tongue, papillae, and taste buds are thus all accessory structures. Aided by salivary glands in the cheeks that help to moisten dry food, they provide information in the form of molecules to the transducers; these cells alter the information for neural transmission. (In this case, the transducers are not themselves neurons, but synapse onto the dendrites of sensory neurons.) Other cells adjacent to the transducers were formerly considered to be supportive cells, but are now believed to be transducers at a different stage in their life cycle. Bathing the transducers in chemical solutions that are sometimes quite acid or hot is hard on them, and their lifetime is only about 10 days; as they wear out, others take their place.

Coding rules for taste are somewhat better understood than for smell, but are still ambiguous, partly because it is hard to separate sensations of smell and taste. (People who lose their sense of smell report the loss of taste to be what they notice most.) It has long been thought that there are four basic tastes: sweet, salt, sour, and bitter. These do make sense evolutionarily. Correct salt concentrations are necessary for body functioning, and we share a taste for salt with many species (Dethier, 1977). Many mammals will travel miles to lick at a natural salt pocket, and salt was one of the earliest forms of money. Sweet tastes also seem to be innately desirable, probably because they are associated with fruit sugars, and sour or bitter tastes may warn against poisons. Just how these basic tastes combine to create the full range of tastes remains unclear, however, as does the influence of odors in creating tastes (Dethier, 1978).

We all show some combining of senses, in addition to taste and smell, that may be considered a kind of synesthesia. The color of a food can affect its taste, for example. (Have you ever eaten something dyed green for St. Patrick's Day? Did it taste normal?) This normal synesthesia may be at least partially learned. Patterns of taste preferences for cultural groups are largely learned and differ widely (Moskowitz et al., 1975); it is likely that at least some aspects of individual taste sensitivity are also learned. Other differences, including the ability to taste some substances, are inherited (Kalmus, 1952).

Why does a given substance have the taste it does? Some evidence supports the possibility that basic molecular shapes fit receptor shapes, as was proposed for smell. For example, flavor chemists have succeeded in matching some molecular shapes to taste sensations, creating new substances that mimic the sweet or salty taste of existing ones. Some of these are hundreds of times more effective in stimulating taste than natural substances (Acton & Stone, 1976).

SKIN SENSES

Most sensory systems give rise to a single class of sensation. Visual sensations, for example, are all of one sort and different from hearing ones. Furthermore, most senses use a single class of receptor cell, though receptors may vary slightly in what they respond to, as taste buds do. The sense we usually think of as "touch," however, includes a wide variety of both sensations and receptors.

Your approximately 18 square feet of skin is not simply a body cover. It is a complex, multilayered organ that serves many purposes (Montagna, 1965).

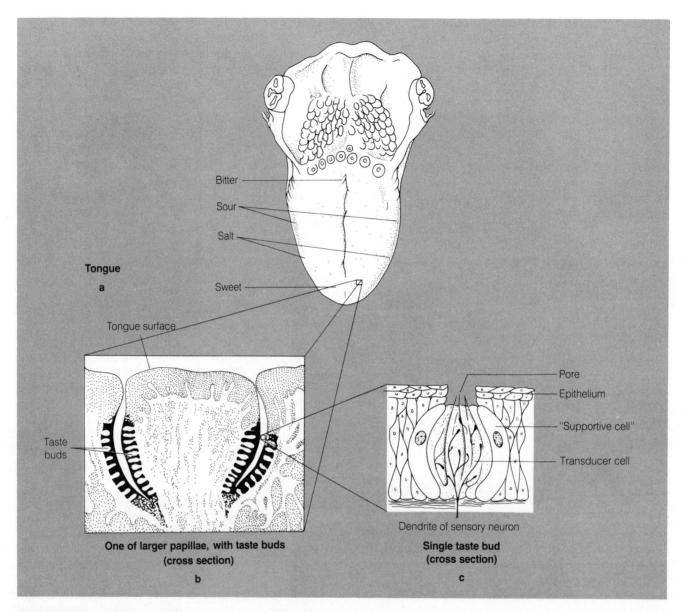

Figure 5.17 ■ (a) Taste, like smell, responds to molecules of the substance sensed, but taste extracts these molecules from solutions in the mouth. Taste buds in different areas around the edge of the tongue are responsive to different tastes. (b) Taste buds are located primarily on tongue papillae, though a few are located elsewhere in the mouth. (c) Each taste bud has a number of transducer cells within it that continuously replace others as they wear out.

Your skin protects the rest of your body from a variety of dangerous environmental agents and helps maintain a constant temperature. Injuries that damage large skin areas, such as burns, are frequently fatal, not through the injury itself but because of the loss of these skin functions (Lamberg, 1980). Skin is also the accessory structure for the multicomponent sense we usually call touch. But that name hardly does justice to the variety of sensations and the number of receptors that are included; all of these together are called the **skin senses.**

The three major skin sensations are usually said to be touch, temperature, and pain, but this is an oversimplification. Touch, for example, includes simple touch as well as pressure, vibration, itch, and tickle; it is not clear that these are all touch in the way that vision is always vision. Similar questions can be raised about temperature and pain. Are hot and cold the same sensation? Are sharp, sudden pains and slow, dull aches the same sensations? One way of seeking answers to such questions is to see if the receptors are similar and if they share nerve tracts.

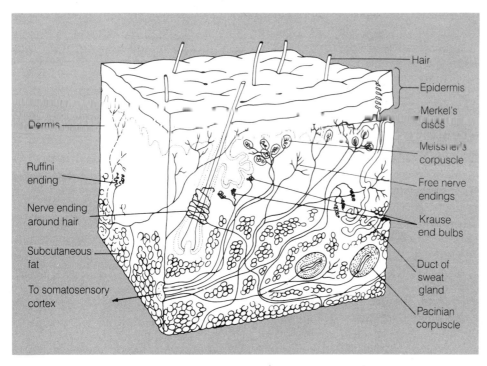

Figure 5.18 ■ Some of the many specialized transducers that contribute information to the skin senses. The exact function of most of these remains uncertain.

(From *Fundamentals of Neurology*, 6th ed., by E. Gardner, W. B. Saunders Co., 1975. Used by permission.)

Early research sought to identify particular receptors for touch, temperature, and pain, but it quickly became obvious that more than three sensations were involved. Microscopic studies now indicate that your skin contains about five million sensors of at least seven different types. Research has shown what stimuli activate some of them: Meissner's corpuscles seem to respond to touch, for example, and Pacinian corpuscles to stronger pressure; Krause end bulbs probably respond to cold. ■ Figure 5.18

But even these identifications remain somewhat uncertain. Part of the problem is that different study techniques don't necessarily yield the same answers. An area of skin that is especially sensitive to a particular input—cold, for example—may contain fewer Krause end bulbs than a less sensitive area. Another part of the problem is that the sensors may respond to simpler sensations than those we are used to thinking of: What we experience as a single sensation may actually be a combination of sensations from several different sensors. The sensation *hot*, for example, results not from special sensors for hot, but from simultaneous stimulation of two other sensors that separately sense warm and cold. (If two tubes of water, one warm and the other cold, are twisted together, the combined coil will feel hot when grasped.) This may not seem logical, but it is a way to code information with a relatively

limited number of sensors. Physically, the cold sensors respond either to hot or cold, but not to warm; thus, for increasing temperatures, first the cold sensors respond, then the warm sensors, and finally both.

Touch sensations may represent similar combinations. Some cells might respond to the onset of touch, for example, but not to continued touch; others might respond to any change in pressure above a certain value. Hence a "quick light touch" might be an interpretation of the sensations from several receptors. Future research may specify what stimuli each skin receptor responds to, but it is unlikely the answers will be as simple as touch or pressure.

Because the coding of skin sensors is unclear, the messages carried by the nerve tracts are also. It is known that they go to the somatosensory strips in the parietal cortex and to the cerebellum.

The skin senses complement the proprioceptive senses in maintaining an integrated awareness of where the body is and what it is doing. Consider how hard it is to walk with a foot that has gone to sleep, or how hard it is to chew or swallow after a dental anesthetic; commands can reach the muscles, but the lack of touch or pressure information causes any movement to be clumsy.

The great sensitivity of our finger tips (represented by the large hands of the sensory homunculi in Figure

2.18) is often useful, but thickened layers of epidermis typically keep us from extracting as much information as we might. People recovering from hand burns note that the new skin, before it builds up a layer of calluses, seems several times more sensitive than normal. A slightly rough surface may feel like sandpaper, and lukewarm water may seem hot.

Blind people, who cannot emphasize vision as others do, find that touch and hearing can provide more information than most of us normally use. Contrary to popular belief, the senses themselves don't change; the blind simply concentrate on them and learn to use the information more efficiently than most sighted persons.

Another way that touch and vision are connected is through pattern recognition. People who have been unable from birth to see patterns because of cataracts do not automatically integrate visual information even when the cataracts are surgically removed. They must spend time developing their vision through simultaneous use and comparison of it and their other senses. They may know what a square and a triangle feel like, for example, yet may be unable to recognize these shapes by sight until they have spent some time simultaneously looking at and touching them (Senden, 1960). Even then, when given some new object to examine, they may close their eyes and fall back on the familiar sense of touch.

Our ability to use touch information to comprehend the world also offers a basis for specialized sensory systems. One special use of touch is **Braille,** the raised-dot alphabet used by the blind. The skin senses can also take in information in other ways. A device called the Optacon can "read" ordinary print for the blind by scanning the letters and transforming them into vibration patterns to the fingertips (Craig, 1977). And the skin of the back has been used experimentally as a blackboard on which to write messages by vibration; volunteers have been able to receive Morse code messages as fast as skilled operators can by ear. Other researchers are trying to provide a form of visual input: Information from a television camera is turned into a spatial pattern on the subject's back. For practical use, the equipment would eventually be miniaturized and carried by a blind person, with the camera concealed in a pair of glasses.

This may seem like a peculiar way of seeing, but people can adapt remarkably well to different channels of information; it is likely that such a device could be used to great advantage. Blind children who grew up with it would probably structure their growing brains to suit its particular information and might become very adept with it.

We noted earlier that touch may represent complex interpretations of basic sensory data; this is especially true for the third of the classic touch sensations, that of pain. More complete understanding of pain would obviously have widespread practical benefits, but such understanding is turning out to be difficult to achieve.

Pain is so unpleasant that we tend to think of it as something we would happily do without. But pain is often a useful warning signal; it may prevent body damage by telling us to stop what we're doing, or may prevent further problems by telling us to be careful until an injury heals. The evolutionary advantage of this warning signal is apparent; hence the unpleasantness of pain is also its advantage. People who do not experience pain, either because they are congenitally insensitive or because of nerve damage, suffer frequent injuries and infections. The extensive crippling of leprosy victims' hands, for example, is often not the direct consequence of leprosy. Leprosy damages the nerves and thus removes the pain feedback, but it is the environmental hazards of everyday life that destroy the hands.

Not all pain is useful, however: Once you know that you're injured and get medical attention, you'd like the pain to go away, and some conditions generate long-term chronic pain that serves no useful warning function. But researchers seeking to eliminate pain have encountered complex relationships. ■ Research Issue: Just What Is Pain?

PROPRIOCEPTIVE SENSES

The five traditional senses tell you about the external environment and its direct interaction with your body. To these we may add two more senses, the **proprioceptive senses.** These keep track of primarily internal information about your body's position and movement through a combination of information from the kinesthestic and vestibular senses.

Like touch, **kinesthesia** uses a combination of transducers: ones in joints report the position of your bones, and ones in muscles and tendons report the tension in your muscles (Neutra & Leblond, 1969). These components are tied together at a basic level through spinal reflexes. Once in the spinal cord, the information goes on to the cerebellum, where more complex postural and movement sequences are coordinated. Finally, a summarized version goes to the cortex—so that you know this minute, for example, where your right foot is.

Kinesthesia tells you the position of body parts with respect to each other, but you also need to know the position of your body with respect to the world. You do this by sensing the forces of gravity and other accelerations through the **vestibular sense** (Parker,

Just what is pain?

Although called a basic touch sensation, pain may not be a sensation at all. If pain is a straightforward sensory system, research should be able to find the transducers, nerve tracts, and cortical areas for it; inactivating any of these should stop the pain. But it doesn't work that way (Melzack, 1961). Free nerve endings in the skin do seem to be a source of pain sensations—but areas of the body may hurt without these cells being present. Also, although nerves can be found that carry pain information, cutting them does not always eliminate the pain; cutting a spinal root may leave an area of the body completely insensitive to touch, yet still painful (Hilgard, 1969). And no single cortical area for pain has been located.

Furthermore, pain may be present even when there seems to be no sensory information—or the possibility of any. *Phantom limb pain* is pain felt in an amputated limb; it occurs in a substantial fraction of amputees, and for some can be excruciating. Yet this pain does not originate from the cut nerves in the stump, because the stump itself can be completely anesthetized without affecting the pain in the nonexistent limb (Melzack, 1970).

Techniques for relieving pain show still other complexities. Sometimes normally effective drugs will fail to relieve pain, but psychological techniques such as hypnosis may be able to relieve even severe pain (Hilgard & Hilgard, 1975).

No simple sensory system could yield such results. Pain must be more, some complex perception that we build up from inputs. Some inputs, such as those from the free nerve endings, may be direct sensations of tissue damage. Others may be information that we must interpret as pain; our nervous systems may be so wired that light inputs beyond a certain intensity, for example, are both recognized as light and interpreted as painful.

Considering pain as a perception may also help to explain some of its peculiarities. The confused and missing signals from an amputated arm, for example, might be interpreted by the brain as "pain." Such an interpretation might not respond to an anesthetic; indeed, the pain might get worse because the information available would then be even more distorted. And if pain is an interpretation, then reinterpreting the signals, or ignoring them, might relieve the pain. Any psychological technique that aids this reinterpreting might thus be able to reduce pain.

One major theory of how pain sensations are interpreted is Melzack's **gate-control theory** (1973). Melzack suggests that pain sensory messages are carried to the brain by one type of axon. Another type of axon that runs down from the brain to synapse with the first type supposedly interrupts the flow of pain messages to the brain, thus "closing the gate" (Melzack, 1974). According to the gate-control theory, the common mode for many ways of relieving pain would be activation of the second type of axons (Casey, 1973). Other techniques might work in other ways.

One technique for relieving pain that has received much attention is acupuncture, an ancient Chinese approach to pain relief and healing consisting of placing needles in the skin at traditional key points. Acupuncture unquestionably relieves pain for some people, but both its general effectiveness and its mode of operation have been widely questioned (Clark & Yang, 1974; Hassett, 1980). It may be a form of hypnosis, with the formal procedures of placing the needles acting as impressive window dressing, or it may have some direct physiological effect not yet understood. It seems virtually certain that acupuncture *can* have a hypnotic effect; the real question is whether it also does something else—perhaps directly activating the pain gates, for example (Hilgard, 1978b).

Another possible way acupuncture might work is through the stimulation of endorphins, or endogenous morphines. These neurotransmitters have received much attention as being potentially important in numerous human activities. Named for their resemblance to the drug morphine, they seem to be the brain's own natural drugs; in fact, drugs such as morphine may have the effects they do because they imitate these brain chemicals (Snyder, 1977). One area where the endorphins are thought to be potentially important is in pain relief. This has been demonstrated in laboratory animals (Gintzler, 1980; Miczek et al., 1982) and is thought to be true of humans (Akil et al., 1978; Willer et al., 1981). If so, then anything that triggers the release of endorphins will relieve pain. Endorphins may be discovered to be the common factor in a wide range of pain-relieving techniques, including those, such as hypnosis and acupuncture, whose mode of action is now unknown (Bolles & Faneslow, 1982; Gurin, 1979).

1980). The vestibular sensors lie within and at the base of the semicircular canals of the inner ear. The semicircular canals themselves sense acceleration in any direction, and the chambers at their base, the **vestibular sacs,** sense position with respect to gravity.
■ Figure 5.19

Gravity is sensed through tiny crystals, called **otoliths** or "ear stones," which are attached to hair cells within the vestibular sacs. Any shift in the position of the inner ear causes movement of these stones, which pulls the attached hair cells; the new input is read by the brain as a new position of the head.

Accelerations are sensed by hair cells within the semicircular canals; these canals lie at approximately right angles to each other in a three-dimensional array. Each canal is filled with fluid; under acceleration, the

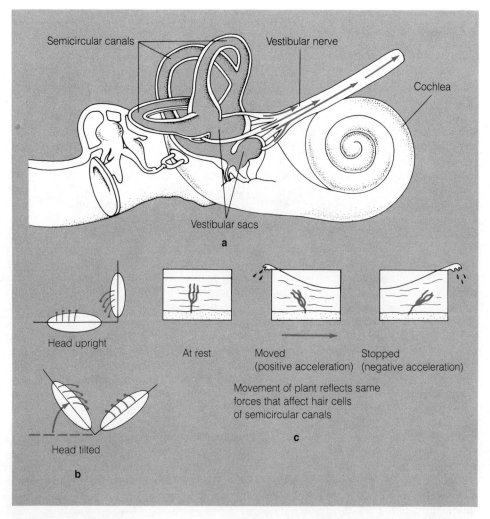

a

Head upright

Head tilted

b

At rest

Moved
(positive acceleration)

Stopped
(negative acceleration)

Movement of plant reflects same
forces that affect hair cells
of semicircular canals

c

Figure 5.19 ■ (a) The vestibular apparatus consists of the semicircular canals and the vestibular sacs at their base. Information from these travels up the vestibular nerve to be blended with kinesthetic, visual, and other information. (b) Ear stones in the vestibular sacs respond to gravity, moving the attached hair cells and thus providing information on head position. (c) Fluid within the semicircular canals moves in response to accelerations as the head speeds up or slows down along any axis. This fluid movement, sensed by hair cells, provides acceleration information.

inertia of the fluid causes it to change speed less quickly than the canals themselves. This applies shear forces to the hair cells.

An analogous effect is the movement of an aquarium with a plant in it. If the aquarium is moved, its initial acceleration tends to leave the water, and thus the plant, behind because of inertia. Once the system—aquarium, water, and plant—is moving at a steady speed, acceleration is zero and the water will level out. Stopping the aquarium then gives the opposite effect: The water and plant tend to continue in motion. The fluid in each semicircular canal responds similarly to accelerations in its own plane. The pattern of response of all three provides information about how much acceleration the head is experiencing and in what direction. As with the aquarium, movement at

a constant speed and direction is equivalent to sitting still; in this case, the semicircular canals report no acceleration.

In many activities, other senses are combined with information from the vestibular sense. A figure skater, for example, receives sensations from the semicircular canals only at the beginning and end of a spin (when the acceleration changes). But the skater is also constantly receiving information from the vestibular sacs, from the kinesthetic sense, and from the other senses, most notably vision. How is all of this successfully integrated?

A space vehicle keeps track of its position with an inertial platform, a device that is kept oriented by information from a set of three accelerometers mounted on it at right angles to each other; integration of these

a

b

Figure 5.20 ■ Organisms with inner-ear vestibular systems use their head orientation to keep track of body position. (a) A pigeon keeps its head level as its body is moved into different positions. (b) Professional motorcycle racers attempt to keep their heads level as they negotiate a turn. Because the forces applied by the motorcycles can easily cause accelerations in the same range as gravity, the riders must also use visual input from their upright heads to keep from becoming disoriented and crashing.

(a, Bernard Hoffman, LIFE MAGAZINE © 1949, Time, Inc.; b, James Huff/Photo Graphic Services)

accelerations over time provides both speed and position information. For comparison and updating, a telescope mounted on the platform provides visual-referent data such as star sightings. Because the location of the platform itself is always known, the position of the vehicle around it can always be determined.

This book is about psychology, not celestial navigation, so there must be a point to all this. There is: Your head is a natural inertial platform, kept oriented by its semicircular-canal accelerometers. With your head thus located, you can keep track of the rest of your body, piece by piece, through your kinesthetic system. Finally you use vision to check and update the other information (Monty & Senders, 1976). ■ Figure 5.20

A major reason for holding your head level is the need for a stable visual input. Technology may provide inputs that are so different from those for which our sensory systems evolved that the results can be disastrous. Accelerations of vehicles, for example, can cause a variety of problems, especially if visual inputs are also confused. One common example occurs when the irregular surges of ships lead to the nausea of seasickness; the effect is more pronounced if the person is below deck, where he or she senses the ship's surges but sees no movement.

Particularly dangerous situations are those where artificial accelerations are perceived as if they were gravity. When an aircraft is both banking and turning, for example, the balanced forces cause the pilot's vestibular apparatus to sense an upright posture. This is normally overcome by relying on visual orientation.

But one common combination of vestibular and visual misinformation so often led to fatal accidents that instrument training became a requirement for all pilots. In this "graveyard spiral," the pilot accidentally enters a turn and the plane begins to descend. The pilot realizes that the plane is descending but feels the wings are level, so he or she pulls back on the stick to pull up. This only tightens the spiral and the plane descends faster, eventually spiraling into the ground. Only by rigorous training and careful application can a pilot force him or herself to resist such sensations and follow correct instrument procedures. After all, the vestibular and visual systems are millions of years old, and airplanes less than a hundred.

If sensory conflict occurs rapidly, visual input may override all other senses. A gymnast walking a balance beam in a room in which all four walls can be moved slightly can be flipped off by a slight jiggle of the walls; kinesthetic, vestibular, and touch information are all overridden by the quick visual input. A similar effect is used in flight simulators, the imitation-aircraft devices used for training pilots. With appropriate visual jiggles from television screens masquerading as windows, the occupants seem to feel the simulator move.

Thus vision for us is both complexly interrelated with our other senses and dominant in these relationships. We will look more at these relationships in our next chapter, where we will see how sensations give rise to more complex perceptions.

CHAPTER SUMMARY

1 Complex organisms have evolved specialized sensory systems that sample relevant environmental information. Sensory systems typically include assessory structures that manipulate the information and bring it to transducers, which alter it to action potentials that are conveyed to the brain.

2 Appropriate stimuli more intense than the absolute threshold will stimulate a sensory system. Beyond the absolute threshold, the Weber-Fechner law applies; its relationships say that more intense stimuli are not sensed in direct proportion to their value but are compressed.

3 The several senses are integrated to provide a perceptual world unique to each perceiver, often with the aid of automatic mechanisms of lower brain centers.

4 Environmental radiation called light is sampled by the sense of vision. The eye contains numerous accessory structures that bring light to the rods and cones at the back of the retina. Some brainlike processing occurs in the retina before the optic nerves leave. That information is rearranged at the optic chiasma and passed through the thalamus to the occipital cortex.

5 Environmental vibrations called sound are sampled by the sense of hearing (audition). The ear is divided into outer, middle, and inner portions, all of which act as accessory structures to move the vibrations into the fluid of the cochlea. Transducers in the organ of Corti respond to the basilar membrane flexing and the information is carried by the auditory nerves to the temporal cortex.

6 Chemicals in the air are sampled by the sense of smell (olfaction). These are trapped in a mucus layer above the nose, where they stimulate transducers. The information travels by way of the olfactory bulbs to the limbic system and frontal cortex. The limbic system connections may be involved in motivational effects of odors acting as pheromones.

7 Chemicals dissolved in fluids are sampled by the sense of taste (gustation). These enter taste buds on the tongue and elsewhere, where they trigger responses, perhaps by engaging specially shaped receptor sites.

8 Several forms of environmental energy, including touch, pressure, and temperature, are sampled by the collection of senses termed the skin senses. Many potential receptors have been identified but their functions remain unclear; probably they act in multiple combinations to provide the skin senses we experience. Pain is often summarized as a skin sense but is actually a complex perception built up of many inputs.

9 Two proprioceptive senses help you maintain body position. The first, the kinesthetic sense, keeps track of the position of limbs and joints by means of transducers in the muscles and tendons. Much of this information is processed automatically by the cerebellum to maintain posture and to smooth body activity.

10 The second proprioceptive sense, the vestibular sense, keeps track of accelerations acting on the head. Transducers in the inner ear respond both to gravity and to other accelerations of the head in any direction. This information combines with that from the kinesthetic sense and other senses, especially vision, to provide a summary of where your body is and what it's doing.

Further Readings

For treatment of sensory systems in the general context of physiological psychology, see a good textbook, such as the well-illustrated *Physiological Psychology* (1982) of Rosenzweig and Leiman. For more detailed treatment, see a more specialized text such as Goldstein's *Sensation and Perception* (1984). For specific coverage of the eye and visual processes, see Frisby's *Seeing: Illusion, Brain and Mind* (1980); it offers many interesting graphics, both representations of how you see—Figure 5.8 was adapted from one of these—and examples of visual patterns and illusions. Gregory's books *Eye and Brain* (1966) and *The Intelligent Eye* (1970) are older but also rather easier to read. Also somewhat dated but readable and well illustrated is Stevens and Warshofsky's *Sound and Hearing* (1965), published as one of the Life Science Library series. Hypnotic pain relief is the primary emphasis of E. R. Hilgard and J. R. Hilgard's *Hypnosis in the Relief of Pain* (1975), but it also summarizes some of the problems of defining pain.

You glance up as you start to cross a street on your way to class, and immediately know that a green car is approaching too quickly for you to cross. In the same instant, you also recognize the car as one belonging to an acquaintance, and notice that someone else is driving it. You see that it has a newly damaged fender and a political bumper sticker. You are somewhat surprised at its being there, since there is usually no traffic at that time of day, and a bit angry that the car is traveling too fast for the conditions. Such rapid perceptual processing is routine for you, and you tend not to notice how much you are doing all at once. But such seemingly simple incidents are actually a summation of many aspects of perception. You see any object, for example, in terms of its color and brightness, its features (such as corners and lines), and its overall shape. You estimate its distance, its size, and its position. You assess its speed and the direction of its movement, if any, and then decide what meaning this has for you. To do so, you draw on many aspects of past experience, and predict what should happen now. Furthermore, you do all of this so quickly and easily that you are hardly aware of doing it.

You can *do* all this in an instant, but to understand how you can do so much so quickly, it is easier to consider your rapid perception in separate pieces. We will spend the rest of the chapter examining some aspects of *perception*, the comprehension of objects and events based on sensory information. In doing so, we will look first at some key questions and some general principles, including a brief consideration of those proposed by the Gestalt school. We will then examine a series of increasingly complex perceptions, beginning with the perception of color and working up to the perception of movement and events. We will emphasize visual perception processes throughout, in keeping with our species' emphasis on vision (Haber, 1978). But much of what we will cover is relevant to other senses as well.

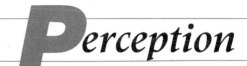

Chapter 6

Perception

PERCEPTUAL QUESTIONS AND PRINCIPLES

As you saw in Chapter 1, questions about perception have been important in psychology since its founding. These questions may be grouped into three main categories: How does perception develop? How does the mind perceive sensory information? How does perception function?

Perceptual Questions

How perception develops is a version of the nature/nurture problem. **Nativist theories** of perception emphasize nature factors; they suggest that perception is native or innate. **Empiricist theories** of perception emphasize nurture factors; they suggest that perception is empirical, obtained from interaction with the environment (Hochberg, 1962). As with other versions of the nature/nurture problem, purely nativist or empiricist views have yielded to more subtle interactive ones. Even if much of perceptual processing is built-in, at least some aspects must be learned: perceiving depth seems to some extent to be innate, but no one would argue that perceiving an object like an automobile is innate. Contemporary research on the nature/nurture or nativist/empiricist problem seeks to specify which aspects of perceptual processing are innate and how these are elaborated through experience to yield the perceptual capabilities of an adult.

Perception also leads to the mind/body problem: How does the mind use the information supplied by the senses? In some versions of dualism, the body was said to process sensory information up to a point and then to pass it on to the mind. But it was never clear just how the mind received visual information, for example. Did it "look" at it? If the mind "looks at" visual input, like a person looking at a television screen, the next question to be answered is what is behind the *mind's* eye (Crick, 1979).

Some psychologists have avoided directly confronting the mind/body problem. The approach of psychophysics—to present a stimulus and measure a response to it—may be thought of as an input/output or "black box" analysis (Blough, 1961). The term **black box** derives from engineering design, where it refers to any device that responds to a particular input with a particular output. In psychology it means that the performance characteristics of an organism are measured without asking what goes on inside the black box of the organism. The experimenter is not concerned with who perceives or with the mechanisms of perception (Riggs, 1976). You can find out, for example, how rapidly a series of separate photos must be displayed for a human subject to perceive smooth motion; the answer does not depend on knowing anything about how internal mechanisms yield a perception of motion.

Another major approach to the mind/body question in perception is to assume a monist position—that the brain perceives—and then seek the mechanisms by which it does so. This is the major concern of physiological psychologists. Their task is similar to that of engineers trying to understand a space vehicle constructed by an unknown builder: The general purpose of the device might be fairly obvious, but understanding *how* it operates may be exceptionally difficult. The physiological psychologist seeks to recreate the missing blueprints for the contents of the black box through careful step-by-step examination of the pieces found inside.

© 1983 by Sidney Harris

Both black-box and physiological approaches have been helpful in understanding perception. They provide different and often complementary information: A black-box approach establishes what the organism *can* do, and knowledge of the mechanism tells *how* the organism does it and may even allow repair of a malfunction.

Gestalt Principles

Gestalt is a German word meaning an "organized whole." **Gestalt psychology** was founded by three German psychologists in the early part of this century: Max Wertheimer, Kurt Koffka, and Wolfgang Köhler. It took the name because of its focus on "wholes" in perception (Ellis, 1967).

Part of the Zeitgeist at the time of psychology's founding was a search for smaller units in any complex problem. Sciences such as chemistry had been successful in seeking simple laws and ever-smaller particles, and various philosophers had proposed simple rules for human behavior. Wundt's search for the elements of perception through introspection (Chapter 1) was an attempt to find something like the newly discovered chemical elements.

The Gestaltists opposed this trend. They felt that attempting to cut up perception into elements would lose the phenomenon. In the phrase most associated with the school, they noted that "the whole is different from the sum of its parts." When separate elements were perceived as wholes, they felt, the experience was of the whole, not of the separate parts. ■ Figure 6.1

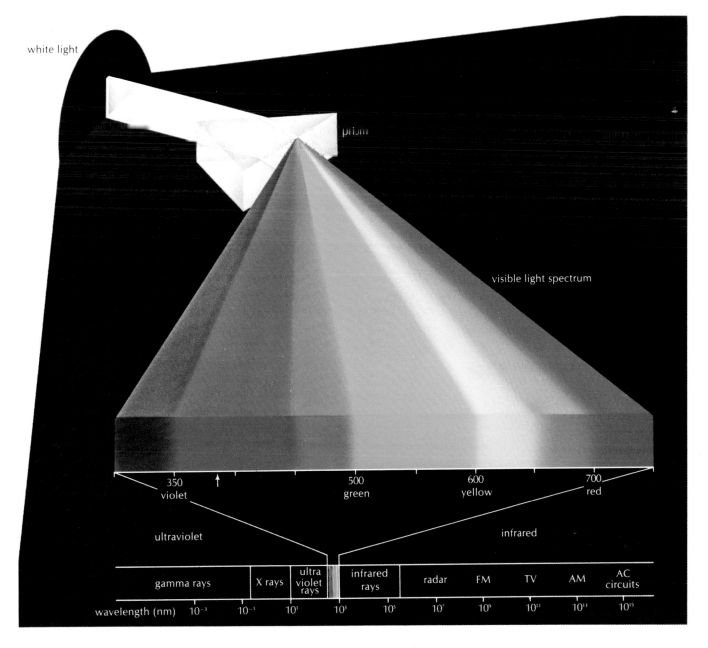

Plate 1 ■ Light waves of different wavelengths bend by different amounts in passing through a prism, which separates a beam of white light into its components. All of this visible light spectrum, however, is only a small fraction of the total range of electromagnetic radiation.

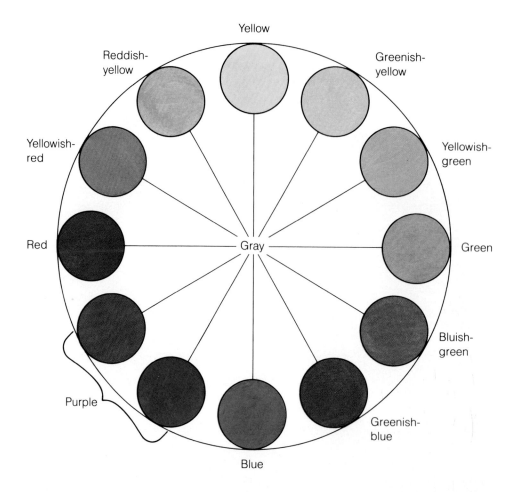

Plate 2 ■ The spectral colors can be arranged in a color circle, together with some non-spectral reds and purples. (These are not single-wavelength components of white light but combinations of other wavelengths.) Any two colors opposite each other on the color circle are complementaries; lights of such complementary color pairs combine to yield a neutral gray.

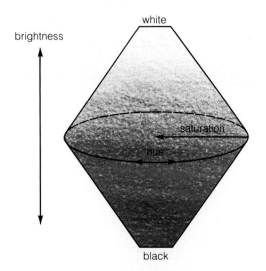

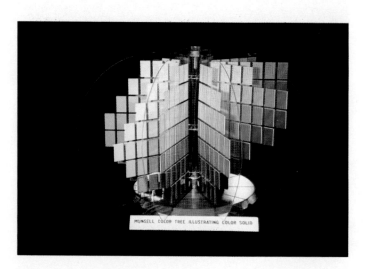

Plate 3 ■ The color solid represents all three psychological dimensions of color simultaneously. *Hue* varies around the solid, *brightness* from top to bottom, and *saturation* from its center outward. The richest colors are those around the periphery, which are of high saturation and medium brightness.

(Courtesy Munsell Color, 2441 N. Calvert St., Baltimore, MD 21218)

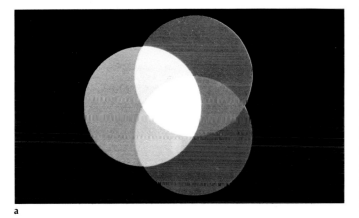

a   b

Plate 4 ■ The two types of color mixture. (a) Colored paints combine through *subtractive mixture*: Because each added color subtracts more wavelengths, adding more colors moves the mixture toward black. (b) In contrast, colored lights combine through *additive mixture*: Because each added color adds more wavelengths, adding more colors moves the mixture toward white.

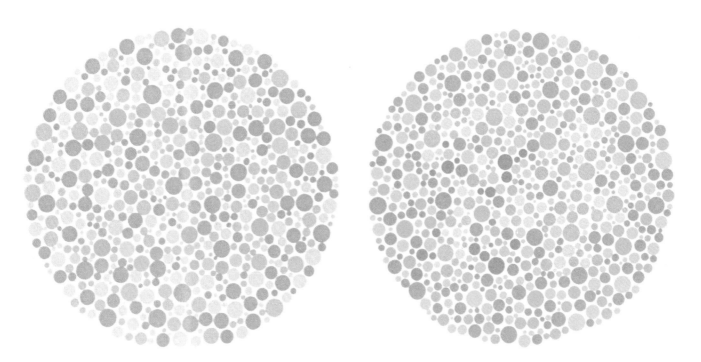

Plate 5 ■ "Pseudo-isochromatic" plates such as these are used to test for colorblindness. The two colors of dots in any plate are designed to appear identical to people who cannot distinguish between those particular colors; to such people, the plates appear "isochromatic"—the same color throughout—and thus they cannot read the numbers.

(From *Ishihara's Tests for Color Blindness*, Kanehara & Co., Ltd., Tokyo, Japan)

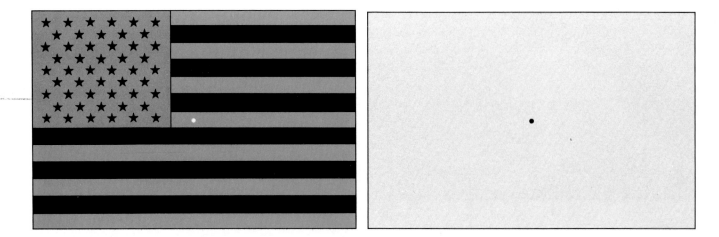

Plate 6 ■ A demonstration of negative afterimages. Stare at the dot in the center of the flag for about a minute, then quickly look at the dot in the middle of the blank area. You will seem to see a flag in the correct colors, which represent the negative afterimages of the colors in the printed flag.

Plate 7 ■ This "op art" work by Victor Vasarely is based on a series of Necker cubes. The overall pattern can seem to represent a number of different three-dimensional shapes as you look at it carefully, because the Necker cubes reverse their apparent positions.

(Courtesy of the artist and Gallery 1, San Francisco)

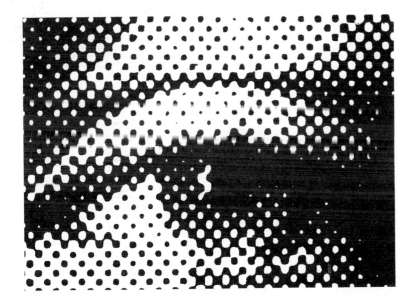

Figure 6.1 ■ Illustrations of the Gestalt principle that "the whole is different from the sum of its parts." The image of an eye becomes clear when you move the book away from you, but up close it remains a pattern of dots and blobs. Both the blobs and the eye are legitimate perceptions, according to the Gestaltists, but only one tends to be perceived at a time.

The primary founder of the movement was Max Wertheimer (1880–1943) (Asch, 1946b). In 1910, he had become intrigued with a stroboscope, a child's toy invented some 80 years earlier that seems to generate a moving picture from a series of still pictures flipped past the eye. It occurred to Wertheimer that the perception of motion either happened or it didn't. If the pictures were moved slowly, he perceived correctly a series of still pictures; if they were moved more rapidly, he perceived motion. In one sense, perceiving the still pictures was a "correct" perception and perceiving motion could be called an "incorrect" one. His point was that a perception is neither correct nor incorrect, but simply a perception. The whole—the perception—is different from, and more important than, the parts that make it up. He took the phenomenon into the laboratory for study, thus beginning the Gestalt approach.

The Gestalt view of perception emphasizes perceptual rules for organizing sensory input into meaningful wholes; six major ones are noted in Figure 6.2. Each of these Gestalt principles describes some features of perception, especially visual perception (Pomerantz & Kubovy, 1981). ■ Figure 6.2

The Gestalt psychologists studied many aspects of perception and were the first to note many of its characteristics (Hochberg, 1957). They also sought to apply the approach to other kinds of behavior, but here they were less successful. A contemporary form of therapy in the United States that uses the Gestalt name has little or no direct tie to the principles of the Gestalt school (Henle, 1978).

General Principles

Non-Gestalt psychologists have reinterpreted some Gestalt principles into other terms, including those of information processing (Garner, 1970; Julesz, 1965). But they do not necessarily agree that the Gestaltists' principles are the best way to describe perception. Most psychologists do agree, however, on some general principles of perception, beginning with our need to interpret what we perceive.

Interpretation The most basic principle is that all perception involves interpretation. When you see or hear anything, you have already interpreted sensory information on several levels. Some of these levels involve innate mechanisms such as the structure of the retina or cochlea. Others involve extensive learning and memory, as in recognizing particular people or objects.

Learning to interpret the incoming sensory barrage so as to perceive a stable and understandable world is a large task for a child and in a sense continues through adulthood. William James once suggested that the infant's world was a "buzzing confusion." Psychologists now know that infants perceive more than James thought they did, but the phrase reminds us how much we must learn if we are to perceive as we do.

People whose sight is surgically corrected, after they have been unable to see shapes since birth because of cataracts, tell us something about the learning

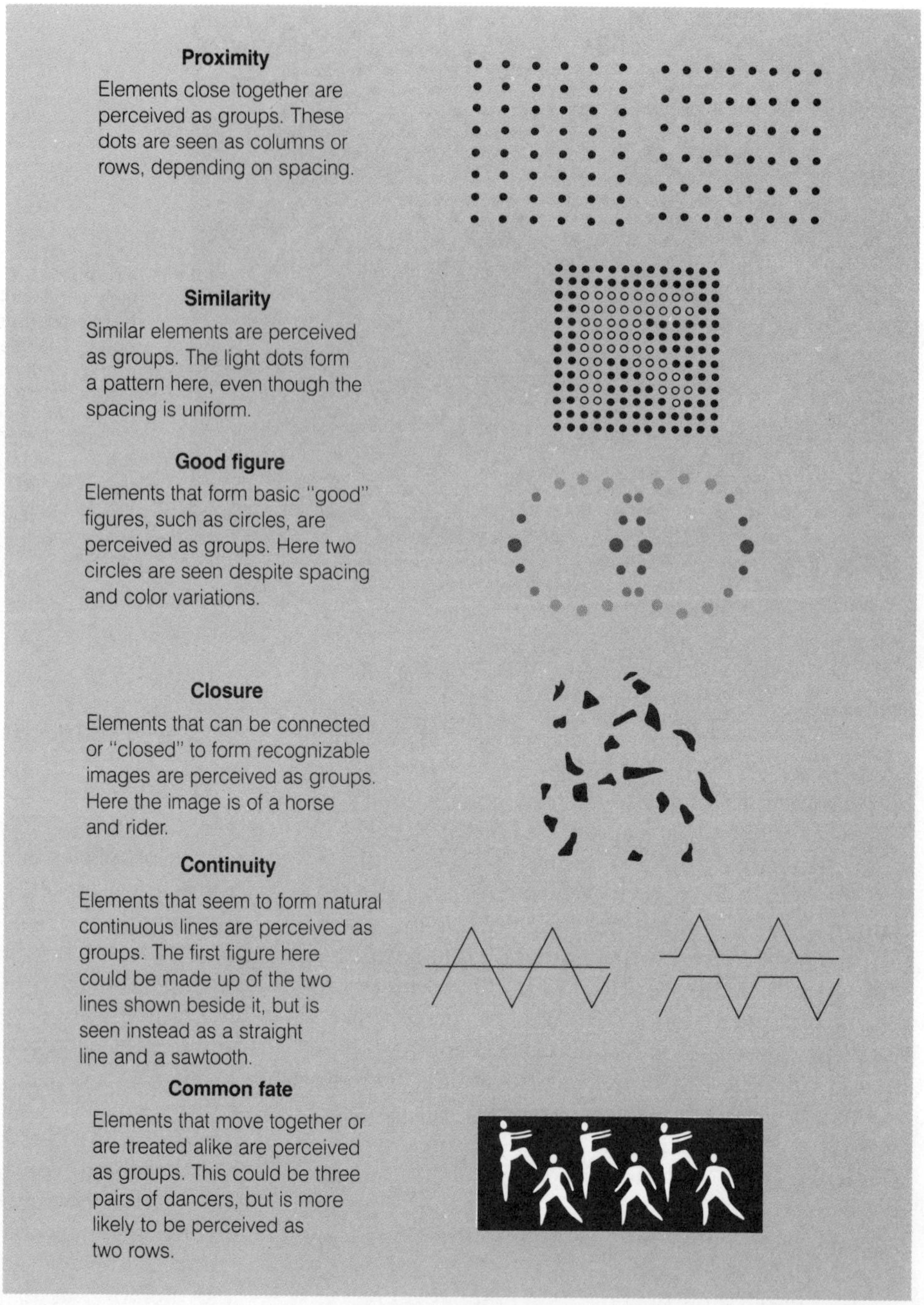

Proximity

Elements close together are perceived as groups. These dots are seen as columns or rows, depending on spacing.

Similarity

Similar elements are perceived as groups. The light dots form a pattern here, even though the spacing is uniform.

Good figure

Elements that form basic "good" figures, such as circles, are perceived as groups. Here two circles are seen despite spacing and color variations.

Closure

Elements that can be connected or "closed" to form recognizable images are perceived as groups. Here the image is of a horse and rider.

Continuity

Elements that seem to form natural continuous lines are perceived as groups. The first figure here could be made up of the two lines shown beside it, but is seen instead as a straight line and a sawtooth.

Common fate

Elements that move together or are treated alike are perceived as groups. This could be three pairs of dancers, but is more likely to be perceived as two rows.

Figure 6.2 ■ Some Gestalt principles of how sensory elements are organized into perceptual wholes.

involved. Even when they already know about objects, distances, and events, they find it hard to interpret the new visual inputs. They may, for example, look out of a second-story window and not know whether they could step out to the ground (Hechinger, 1981). It takes some time for them to learn to interpret what they are seeing in terms of the world they understand. An infant has the even harder task of learning *about* objects and depth at the same time as he or she learns to perceive them.

Even nonhandicapped adults continue to refine their perceptual interpretation processes. Navy sonar operators, for example, learn to distinguish the echoes made by a whale from those produced by a ship and even to tell whether the ship is approaching or receding (Cronbach, 1977). The cues they use, however, are

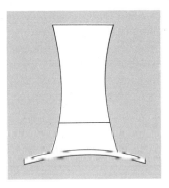

a

b

Figure 6.3 ■ Two examples of visual illusions. (a) The top hat illusion: the height of the portion above the brim is exactly equal to the width of the brim but seems taller. (b) Fraser's spiral: there is no spiral here, only concentric circles made of curved segments.

(**b**, From *Seeing: Illusion, Brain and Mind* by J. P. Frisby, Oxford University Press, 1980. Reprinted by permission of Roxby Press Limited.)

ones such as the peculiar beat of helicopter blades, and a myriad of other sensory inputs that people with different experiences would not be able to interpret.

The process of interpreting sensory inputs has been likened to the hypothesis testing of the scientific method (Chapter 1). A **perceptual hypothesis** is a tentative interpretation of sensory input that may or may not be confirmed by further information. As we go about our daily activities we continually create and test perceptual hypotheses. Usually our hypotheses are correct and we never realize that we have made and confirmed them. But sometimes we get a brief insight into the process when a hypothesis is *dis*confirmed.

Suppose, for example, that you have stopped your car at a stoplight and while you are waiting for the light to change, the car next to you begins to roll. In this case you may generate the perceptual hypothesis that *your* car is rolling and step hard on the brake to stop it. But the failure of this action to stop the movement or to give the sensation of braking disconfirms your hypothesis. You feel this disconfirmation as a kind of perceptual jolt in which you realize that you had not been moving after all.

Some sensory inputs tend to repeatedly yield incorrect perceptual hypotheses; both such sensory inputs and their effects may be called **illusions** (Coren & Girgus, 1978). Some illusions are so powerful that nearly everyone experiences them in the same way and so stable that they resist the correct interpretation even when it is pointed out; we'll look at some later in the chapter. The most common and best known of these illusions are visual; many of them consist of simple line drawings (Figure 6.3), but others can occur in the real world. In the moon illusion, for example, the moon seems much larger when it is just above the horizon than it does when it is high in the sky—even when you know intellectually that it occupies the same size on the retina in each case (Kaufman & Rock, 1962). Other illusions may be more individual, depending on something about the person experiencing them. These are often brief and unimportant, signifying only a failed perceptual hypothesis. You might seem to recognize a friend, for example, only to realize quickly that it was a similar-appearing stranger.
■ Figure 6.3

Illusions also occur in other senses than vision. Auditory illusions in both speech and music, for example, have been found to share some characteristics with visual illusions (Deutsch, 1975; Oster, 1973; Warren & Warren, 1970). A kinesthetic illusion of an impossible limb position can be created by stimulating a tendon with vibration (Craske, 1977); other illusions result from the absence of kinesthetic information created by a muscular-paralysis drug (Matin et al., 1982).

so subtle that the sounds are indistinguishable to those not trained to make this discrimination. In one sense, trained and untrained listeners hear the same sounds; however, they do not *perceive* the same sounds, because one listener has an ability to interpret the sounds that the other does not have.

Continued learning and interpretation are not limited to specialized situations; they are features of everyone's perceptual processing. We learn to interpret the everyday sounds of our own vehicles and the appearance and voices of friends, or more unusual

Patients whose limbs have been amputated may still have a kinesthetic sense of the limb, but it may seem to expand to fit an artificial limb, then shrink when the artificial limb is removed—perhaps to the sensation of a hand attached directly to the shoulder (Melzack, 1970). And the lack of vestibular input has led to some illusions for astronauts (Lackner & Graybiel, 1979; Parker, 1980).

Sometimes, however, an individual's incorrect perceptual hypotheses are more extreme, more long-lasting, and more likely to raise questions about the person experiencing them. **Hallucinations** are perceptual experiences that differ strikingly from what other people would experience in the same sensory situation (Siegel & West, 1975). Hallucinations are essentially "wrong" perceptual hypotheses, primarily the creation of the perceiver and bearing little relationship to the actual sensory input. For example, one person may see and hold a conversation with someone whom others do not see or hear. Perceptual hypotheses that are this extreme tend to indicate a malfunctioning perceptual system; the malfunction may be a temporary result of emotional distress, fatigue, lack of sleep, or drugs, or it may indicate long-term physiological or serious mental difficulties (R. K. Siegel, 1977). Some alcoholics have visual hallucinations, for example, and schizophrenics may "hear voices."

Perceptual interpretation may be such a general feature of our nervous systems that it continues even in the absence of sensory input, although the evidence is open to interpretation. **Sensory deprivation** studies have sought to minimize sensory input to subjects by having them lie down in soundproof chambers. Blindfolds, special arm cuffs, and other devices have been used to further isolate the subjects. These studies initially seemed to indicate that sensory deprivation produces mental confusion and hallucinations resulting from a lack of solid sensory input for interpretation (Heron, 1957). More recent studies have questioned the meaning of these results, however, suggesting that other aspects of the situation may have been important (Suedfeld, 1975). The releases signed by subjects, for example, may have acted as subtle suggestions that the situation would cause problems.
■ Figure 6.4

A contemporary version of sensory deprivation is seen in the flotation tanks that some people use as relaxation or meditation devices. Users float weightlessly in salt water, in the dark, inside a closed container like a bathtub with a lid. People have reported a wide variety of effects from extreme hallucinations to a blissfully blank experience, but these experiences are so colored by individual expectation, drug use, and other factors that they say little about the basic effects of sensory deprivation.

Whether or not it leads to sensory-deprivation hallucinations, perceptual interpretation *is* basic to many processes. It involves not only interpretations within one sensory system, but also the combination of several senses to yield the interpretation of a total situation. Several of the other perceptual principles that follow are details of how this overall interpretation process works.

Physiological Limits Many introductory psychology students believe that a blind person can visualize a face by touching it. But they cannot do it any better than a sighted person can; touch provides a different kind of information from what vision provides. And to people who have never been able to see, the concept of *visualizing* has no experiential meaning. They understand some basic aspects of vision, such as the fact that something behind another object can't be seen (Hechinger, 1981; Kennedy, 1983). But they cannot use abstract knowledge of visual rules to construct a visual image.

You can only experience perceptions for which you have physiological sensory and processing mechanisms. The position of the congenitally blind with respect to sight can only be explained by an analogy. It is as if someone else had a sense that you did not have and were to tell you to do as they did—that is, to "sniligize" carefully. But no description of a sniligal world would allow you to sniligize. You might imagine something of what it could be, but your imagining would be done in terms of the senses you *do* have and could never be the same as sniligizing.

This is not to say that people cannot be given something like new senses. If a device such as an artificial vision system can be implanted, people can learn to use it. But the device simply becomes a non-biological part of their physiological functioning, as an artificial kidney can perform kidney functions. It does not avoid the basic physiological limitation; it just expands the limit a bit by technology.

One experimental system, for example, has sought to provide a young boy with a sense somewhat like the audiolocating systems of bats or porpoises. Dennis was born three months prematurely and lost his sight soon after birth from complications of prematurity. When doctors realized that he was making clicking sounds at the age of six weeks, apparently as a way of exploring his environment, they designed a special device for him. The sonarlike device sends out sound pulses, receives echoes from objects, and feeds these echoes to Dennis through earphones. The sonic beam is narrowly focused in front of him and the resulting echoes are sensitive to the distance, direction, and texture of objects; by moving his head, he can sense where an object is, and something of what it is like. Dennis quickly learned to play a kind of peek-a-boo with it, turning first toward then away from his mother as sighted children do. He also learned to identify a number of objects with it, including his favorite toy (Clark and Agrest, 1975).

In learning to discriminate fine differences between echoes, Dennis is doing what the Navy sonar operators do—but in using it full-time while still a young child, he is developing his phenomenological world around it. When the device was first tested, Dennis's doctors planned to provide him with devices of greater range and more detail as he grew older. If this has worked out, he may now be the only human in the world with this particular audiovisual sense.

But Dennis remains as constrained by his own physiology, including the external hardware, as any of us—whether we use glasses, hearing aids, or only our natural physiological mechanisms. Sensory systems, natural or artificial, must accurately supply information, and perceptual systems must correctly interpret it, if we are to perceive the world without error.

Attention As a species, we are characterized by the large amount of processing that we are able to do between input and output. But there are substantial variations in how much of our brains' processing capabilities we actually apply to a given task on different occasions. Perception, although based on built-in mechanisms, is subject to attention variations (Wurtz et al., 1982). Whether the perception is of simple objects or involves a complex learned sequence like reading, we can either do it routinely while our attention is elsewhere or we can focus on it intensely. What we perceive is likely to vary widely as our attention varies between these extremes.

When our perception is functioning through routine mechanisms, what we perceive can often be in error. In casually glancing over newspaper headlines, for example, you may seem to read about very strange events. Only when you really pay attention do you realize that the headline says something quite different from what you read initially. This effect shows up in both deliberate and accidental manipulations. If you read either of the signs in Figure 6.5 correctly the first time you saw them, you were paying unusually close attention. ■ Figure 6.5

The opposite of routine or limited attention is fully focused attention. This function of the reticular activating system probably reaches its maximum in emergencies, especially those involving personal danger. Many people who experience accidents report that time seemed to slow down and they saw things with unique clarity and speed—watching the hood of a car buckle and fold in slow motion as they drove into the back of a truck, for example.

Figure 6.4 ■ A subject in a sensory deprivation study. Various devices are used to eliminate or make constant all sensory inputs.

Such experiences have been collected from individuals who have undergone near-fatal falls. Sometimes these people survived because they were able to move with rapidity and precision, saving themselves by grabbing something as they fell, like circus acrobats. This ability to respond successfully to threats is apparently adaptive and may be why perception seems to become so quick in emergencies. But events are typically seen with the same clarity and speed even when no action is possible, according to those who survived for other reasons.

Motivation Other motives besides survival also play a role in perception. When the situation is not immediately threatening, however, motivation does not speed up perception but directs or influences it.

When some particular motive is strongly activated, it may *direct* perception, causing you to pay attention to certain relevant cues. (Have you ever noticed how many restaurant signs you drive by when you're hungry?) Basic motives such as hunger, thirst, or sex orient

Figure 6.5 ■ A deliberate and an accidental test of attention in reading. The extra *the* and the misspelling of *Illinois* are easily overlooked unless you know that there is some problem with the signs.

(right, from St. Louis *Post-Dispatch*, Oct. 29, 1977. Reprinted by permission of the Pulitzer Publishing Company, St. Louis, MO.)

perceptual processes to aid in the search for what is needed (Herkenham & Pert, 1980).

Motives may also *influence* what you perceive, sometimes to the extent of creating illusions; when you're seeking food, other signs may be seen as restaurant signs, for example, or other smells may seem like food. The interpretation process seems to become biased, so that anything possible gets a "food" interpretation. Anecdotes suggest that under extreme conditions of deprivation people may even hallucinate, as with the stories of seeing water in the desert. But seeing water mirages may be more an optical effect than a motivation one (Fraser & Mach, 1976). Whether motives can really trigger hallucinations in otherwise healthy people is not clear.

Perception may also be affected by such motives as fear. In this case, you may tend to see what you *don't* want to; if you're walking home late at night from a horror movie, for example, the world may seem to be filled with threatening sights and sounds. It has even been suggested that television and newspapers may have a similar effect on people, especially the elderly, frightening them with stories of muggings until they see danger everywhere.

Fear or distress does seem to play a role in some people's disturbed thinking and perception. Both peculiar beliefs and hallucinations of mental patients may be related to the patients' fears. But the fear did not necessarily *cause* the mental problems and there is no evidence to suggest that even terror will cause otherwise normal people to hallucinate.

One way in which emotions can enter into hallucinatory perception is through the use of psychoactive drugs. A psychoactive drug is one that is said to have psychological or consciousness effects. Some psychoactive drugs alter perceptual processes, often making them more intense and vivid. The emotions of a person taking a drug such as LSD may easily create and direct

hallucinations ranging from peaceful wanderings to the most awful horrors. Because drug use can be severely punished under the law, users are often apprehensive when they take drugs and as a result may become acutely anxious and paranoid. Thus the drug law may ruin the "trip" even though the user isn't arrested.

Expectation   Another way of interpreting some of these examples is to call them the effects of "expectation" (Sekuler & Ball, 1977). The LSD user who expects to be pursued by the police, for example, may be pursued by hallucinations. But expectation also applies to other situations. ■ Figure 6.6

An **ambiguous stimulus** is one that is perceived differently depending on expectation, with the context providing the cues for expectation. In Figure 6.6a, the stimulus is a *B* when reading left to right but a *13* when reading top to bottom. The different perceptions of this identical figure can even be detected in the brain wave of the perceiver; the evoked potential is different when this figure is perceived as a letter or a number—in the *B/13* example, the source of the expectation is clearly the surrounding letters or numbers. But the examples in Figures 6.6b and 6.6c are somewhat more subtle. We read *The Cat* easily and immediately, even though the same shape is used for the middle *H* and *A* (Selfridge, 1955). In this case, the expectation is based on our implicit knowledge of the rules of the English language. Neither *tae* or *cht* is a likely English word, but *the* and *cat* are familiar from nursery school.

If this effect worked only for familiar block-printed words, we could explain it as simple memory for appearance; CAT is familiar but CHT is not. However, Figure 6.6c shows the inadequacy of a simple visual-familiarity explanation. You probably had no trouble reading the two sentences correctly even though the

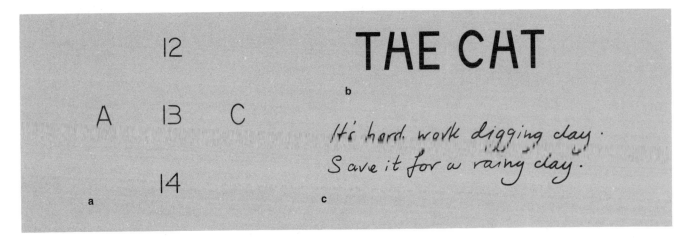

Figure 6.6 ■ Ambiguous stimuli. (a) The middle figure is seen as a *B* or as *13* depending on its position in a row of letters or a column of numbers. (b) The central letter is perceived as *H* or *A*. (c) The last word is perceived as *clay* or *day* depending on the word you expect to find there.

(**a**, from *Introduction to Psychology*, 7th ed., by Ernest R. Hilgard et al., © 1979 by Harcourt Brace Jovanovich, Inc. **b**, from O. G. Selfridge, "Pattern Recognition and Modern Computers," *Proceedings of the Western Joint Computer Conference.* © 1955 IEEE. Used by permission; **c**, after *Seeing: Illusion, Brain and Mind* by John P. Frisby, Oxford University Press, 1980. Reprinted by permission of Roxby Publications Limited.)

handwritten word at the end is identical for them. Here you are predicting the sort of word you expect to appear next because of your familiarity with English word sequences. This makes it easy to fit an ambiguous stimulus into your predictions. Throughout your day, you routinely see what you expect to see, hear what you expect to hear, and easily deal with the objects and events you encounter. One group of processes that help you maintain a constant perceptual world are the perceptual constancies.

Perceptual Constancies

In general, the world is a reasonably stable place: Large objects tend to stay in one place, and smaller ones and living organisms tend to move in reasonably predictable ways. Usually, neither objects nor organisms change size suddenly or transform themselves into other forms. Perceptual systems evolving under such conditions might be expected to rely somewhat on this constancy and in fact they do. Size, color, shape, and location are usually named as the four basic perceptual constancies, although we also show constancy in perception in other ways (Neisser, 1968). ■ Table 6.1

One basic perceptual constancy that obviously reflects the characteristics of our natural environment is **size constancy**, the automatic perceptual assumption that objects stay the same size despite differing-size retinal images. As an object approaches you its image on your retina grows many times larger, but you

see it as getting closer, not as inflating. Size constancy results from visual mechanisms, but these mechanisms presumably evolved to suit a physically stable world. If we lived where objects or creatures could suddenly expand by many times, we probably would not automatically interpret a growing image as coming closer. But in our world, size constancy is taken for granted.

When everyone has been exposed to similar learning experiences, it may be difficult to assess whether a perceptual constancy is largely innate or largely learned. Size constancy, for example, seems so basic that it's hard to believe that it isn't built-in; the experience of one anthropologist's Pygmy friend, however, strongly suggests that it is not (Turnbull, 1961). After spending his life in the dense forest, Kenge was unable to comprehend the sight of distant buffalo. With no prior visual experience for distances beyond a few feet, he seemed to have no size constancy. Instead, as they drove toward the buffalo, he responded to the increasing size of the retinal image as if the animals were growing before his eyes. ■ Notable Quote: Colin Turnbull Describes Kenge's Perception of the Insects/ Buffalo

We all probably suffer somewhat from the breakdown of size constancy in unusual circumstances. When looking down from great heights, for example, we are struck by the image of tiny people and cars, but we are worldly wise enough to understand intellectually that they are still their conventional size.

The light reaching your retina varies in both wavelength and intensity. Even light from a single object

Table 6.1 ■ Four Major Perceptual Constancies

Perceptual Constancy	Definition	Examples
Size constancy	Objects are perceived as having a constant size even though their retinal image changes for different distances.	Cars that approach you are seen to get closer, not bigger. People at a distance are seen as further away, not smaller. (This breaks down at unusual heights.)
Color constancy	Objects are perceived as having a stable color despite varying amounts or colors of illumination.	A white shirt looks white even in dim light and a black one looks black in bright light, even if the latter is actually reflecting more light.
Shape constancy	Objects are perceived as having a constant shape even though their retinal image differs for different viewing angles.	Round objects like wheels appear round even when their image is an ellipse. Rectangular objects like doors appear rectangular even when their image is a trapezoid.
Location constancy	Objects are seen correctly as being steady or moving despite irregular movement of their retinal images.	If you know you are moving, the objects you pass are perceived as stationary. (This may break down in vehicles, especially at high speeds.)

often differs substantially because of shadows on it or different angles or textures of its surface. And the light you receive may flicker and change as objects or light sources move. Yet we routinely maintain **color constancy**, in which objects are seen to be uniformly of one color despite differing amounts or different colors of illuminating light.

Even our perception of brightness or black and white takes into account what we know of the surrounding light and adjusts the perception accordingly. If we are shown a piece of black velvet in ordinary light, for example, we see it as black. We continue to see it as black in very bright light, even though much of the light is now reflected from it rather than being absorbed. If we receive no clues to the velvet's real color and to the intensity of the light, however, color constancy does not operate and we no longer see it as black. If the velvet is mounted inside a closed box with a peephole, we can see only the amount of light reflected from it and it seems to be white, not black (Gelb, 1929).

Colors are similarly adjusted for incident light: Our perceptions include a general expectation of white light similar to sunlight and tend to interpret all colors accordingly. You may have noticed that clothing seems a different color when you take it home than it did under the fluorescent light in the department store or that your face in the mirror seems pale under some lights. This happens because fluorescent bulbs have a different range of wavelengths than natural sunlight;

the apparently white light fools your correction mechanism and it cannot correct the colors. If you know that incident light is colored, however, you can often adjust remarkably well. You will be most successful with things you already know the color of, like an apple or your own clothes, but you may be able to hold constant any colors that you have once been able to see in white light. Under the colored lights at a party, for example, you may see a friend's clothing as the correct color, but be quite wrong about something worn by another guest.

The shapes that fall on the retina are also ceaselessly changing. We see objects as having fixed shapes only because of **shape constancy**, which interprets the changing retinal patterns in terms of the fixed shapes that give rise to them. ■ Figure 6.7

Round objects seen at an angle actually appear on the retina as ellipses and rectangular objects appear as trapezoids. But you routinely perceive them as circles and rectangles by interpreting them based on your experience. Some studies have suggested that frequent experience with rectangular objects is necessary for shape constancy to work for them; members of jungle tribes who see few rectangular objects may not see them as constant, just as the Pygmy Kenge did not have size constancy for unfamiliar distances (Derêgowski, 1972, 1980).

The pattern of movement on the retina offers clues to environmental movement, but these must also be interpreted. If you turn your head rapidly, for exam-

Figure 6.7 ■ Shape constancy helps you see this arch as a three-dimensional object based on rectangles and uniform curves. If you were to walk around it, its images on your retina would be quite distorted, compared to its actual shape, but chances are you wouldn't even notice. (The photograph also offers you the chance to apply other constancies, most notably size constancy for the people, cars, and buildings.)

(© Bohdan Hrynewych/Stock, Boston)

ple, the entire visual field is swept across your retina, yet the room does not appear to have moved. For most circumstances we are able to maintain **location constancy**, in which we and the objects we see are perceived in their appropriate locations despite movement on the retina.

However, unusual conditions may lead to a breakdown of location constancy. In a rapidly moving vehicle, for example, we have no body-movement cues such as occur when we run; this may sometimes cause us to feel that we are still and the environment is flowing by.

All of our separate perceptual constancies may be thought of as contributing to a **generalized object constancy**, a tendency to perceive the environment in terms of solid, stable, predictable objects. For the natural environment in which our species evolved, the perceptual constancies offer rapid and accurate interpretation of changing sensory input. Only under unusual

NOTABLE QUOTE
Colin Turnbull describes Kenge's perception of the insects / buffalo

"With typical Pygmy philosophy, he accepted what he could not understand and turned his back on the mountains to look more closely at what lay all around him. . . . Then he saw the buffalo, still grazing lazily several miles away, far down below. He turned to me and said, 'What insects are those?'

At first I hardly understood; then I realized that in the forest the range of vision is so limited that there is no great need to make an automatic allowance for distance when judging size. Out here in the plains, however, Kenge was looking for the first time over apparently unending miles of unfamiliar grasslands, with not a tree worth the name to give him any basis for comparison. . . .

When I told Kenge that the insects were buffalo, he roared with laughter and told me not to tell such stupid lies. . . .

The road led on down to within about half a mile of where the herd was grazing, and as we got closer, the 'insects' must have seemed to get bigger and bigger. Kenge, who was now sitting on the outside, kept his face glued to the window, which nothing would make him lower. I even had to raise mine to keep him happy. I was never able to discover just what he thought was happening— whether he thought that the insects were changing into buffalo, or that they were miniature buffalo growing rapidly as we approached. His only comment was that they were not real buffalo, and he was not going to get out of the car again until we left the park."

From *The Forest People,* copyright © 1961 by Colin M. Turnbull. Reprinted by permission of Simon & Schuster.

circumstances, often those created by recent technology, do they break down. But they can also fail to function in circumstances unfamiliar to us, even when these are a part of the natural environment, as with Kenge's misperceptions of depth. So the perceptual constancies must depend on learning as well as on evolved mechanisms.

BRIGHTNESS AND COLOR

Brightness and color for us are closely associated, and this association sometimes causes problems. One of the tasks of color constancy, for example, is maintaining a stable perception of color despite changes in brightness. But evolutionarily these are relatively new problems. For many species, color perception is no problem at all; they don't see color.

If you look for the simplest form of eye, such as our remote ancestors may have had, you find that many organisms are sensitive to light without eyes of any kind. Many plants, for example, open and close in response to daylight and night, grow toward light, or even move slowly during the day to track the sun.

In the evolutionary evidence from animals you begin to find systems that have become specialized as light sensors. In their simplest form these are a kind of pit in the skin, with especially sensitive skin cells at the bottom (Gregory, 1966). Such a pit, which admits light primarily from one direction, is the beginning of an oriented sense organ. As such pits became deeper with evolution, some species developed lenses at the top of the pit that would focus light rays on the sensitive cells below and thus evolved eyes. Our own eyes develop in a similar sequence, with an initial depression eventually growing into an eye cup, and then a closed eyeball.

Rod cells similar to ours are found in the retinas of many species. This suggests that these sensors are evolutionarily very old, as they must have first developed in ancestors common to all these species. Rods are sensitive to a wide range of wavelengths, though not to red light, but they report all of these wavelengths to the brain in terms of relative brightness, not color. The cone cells that allow us to distinguish color are a much more recent and much less widespread adaptation.

Human color perception, like brightness, seems to be largely innate, although we must learn to discriminate between similar shades of color or to name colors. This perception makes us somewhat unusual. Many species, including some fish, see in color to some extent (Jacobs, 1981; Levine & MacNichol, 1982), but even among daytime-adapted birds and mammals, few are as specialized for color vision as we are. Our color perception is based on the capabilities of a series of specialized cells, from the cones in our retinas through other retinal cells and into the cells of the visual cortex. How these cells work together has been debated for years (Beck, 1975; Gilchrist, 1979; Wallach, 1963).

Early physiologists discovered the cone cells in our retinas and noted their density in the fovea. But it has been much more difficult to determine how the cones' functioning differs from that of the rods, allowing us to see the wide range of colors we do. Current research suggests that two major theories are both partially correct. ■ Figure 6.8

One approach was first suggested by Thomas Young in 1801, then revised by the German physicist Hermann von Helmholtz in the mid-1800s. The **Young–Helmholtz theory** proposes three different types of color receptors (or transducers), each primarily sensitive to one of three colors: red, green, and blue. Different color sensations result from combining separate signals, from the three types of receptors, in the brain.

An alternate theory was proposed by Ewald Hering, a contemporary of Helmholtz. The **Hering theory** proposes that the light receptors are all the same but that analyzers higher in the system organize the receptors' information in terms of blue/yellow, red/green, and black/white. Hering's approach is also called the **opponent-process theory** because the color analyzers are said to be made up of opponent processes: The more blue an analyzer reports, for example, the less yellow it will report. The suggested analyzer color pairs supposedly cannot combine; blue "opposes" yellow and red "opposes" green. Hence if you see one color from a pair, you cannot see the other simultaneously at the same point on the retina. (Shades of gray can exist as a mixture of black and white.) (Note that this opponent-process theory of color combination is different from the opponent-process theory of emotions discussed in Chapter 4.)

Both color theories seemed equally able to explain the data of the early psychophysicists. But as studies began using microelectrodes to measure the responsiveness of separate living cells, it seemed as if Young and Helmholtz might have been right. As they had predicted, three types of cones were found, each type most sensitive to a different wavelength of light (MacNichol, 1964). Further work, however, found that opponent-process analyzers also exist. By the time information reaches the optic nerve, it has been recombined to a red/green plus blue/yellow form similar to that suggested by Hering. Both theories must therefore be partially true, and any complete explanation will require combining them in some way. Composite theories have been proposed that include both three-color and opponent processes, but a great deal still remains unspecified. ■ Figure 6.9

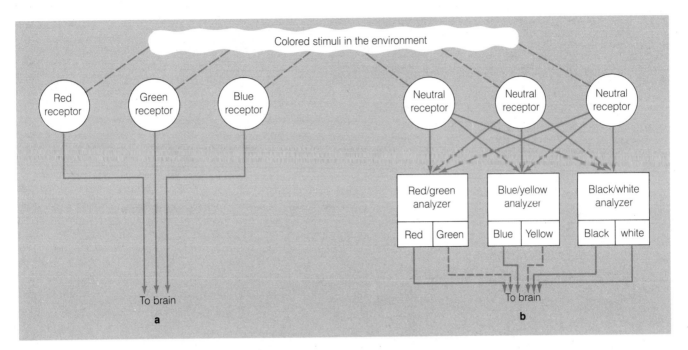

Figure 6.8 ■ The two classic theories of color perception. (a) The Young–Helmholtz theory proposes three kinds of retinal receptors, sensitive to blue, green, and red light. Their signals are combined in the brain to yield all colors. White, for example, would be coded by activity in all three receptors. (b) The Hering or opponent-process theory proposes nonspecialized receptors, with three types of analyzers further on. These would code some blue *or* yellow, some mixture of black and white and some red *or* green, which the brain would then process to yield the other colors. When red light is viewed, only the red portion of the red/green analyzer is stimulated. The green portion shuts down and does not send a green signal to the brain.

Not all people see color in the same way: **color blindness** is the inability to discriminate between colors as most people do (W. A. H. Rushton, 1975). Those who are color blind *see* colored objects, of course; they simply cannot make the same color discriminations that others do. They may confuse colors, but this is not a severe handicap in daily life. In fact, it is possible to be color blind and not even know that you are; specific tests, such as the Ishihara color plates (plate 5), are needed to determine whether someone is color blind.

There are three main forms of color blindness, defined in terms of the opponent processes of Hering's theory. By far the most common form is red-green color blindness; people with red-green color blindness cannot distinguish, for example, between a red and a green of similar intensity. Red-green color blindness is hereditary and sex-linked, carried by females but expressed in males. (About 8% of males but fewer than 1% of females experience some form of color blindness.) Yellow-blue color blindness is far less common and usually results from disease, and total color blindness is even more rare.

Color contrast effects and colored afterimages also provide evidence in favor of the opponent-process theory. **Simultaneous contrast** refers to the enhancement of one color by the adjacent presence of another; the most powerful effects are those of the four colors of opponent-process theory: blue/yellow and red/green. Each of these seems brighter when viewed alongside its complementary color. Some other contrast effects can also be demonstrated when the two colors are presented in sequence. A yellow seems brighter just after viewing blue; similarly, the blackest blacks are those that follow white and the whitest whites are those that follow black. Both forms of contrast suggest something special about the blue/yellow and red/green pairs, some relationship between the perception of them.

But the most direct evidence for an opponent process comes from *afterimages* (Brindley, 1963). If you look at a brightly colored area for a while and then at a white or neutral gray surface, you may see a brief **positive afterimage**, a kind of ghost image in the same color you have been looking at. Whether or not

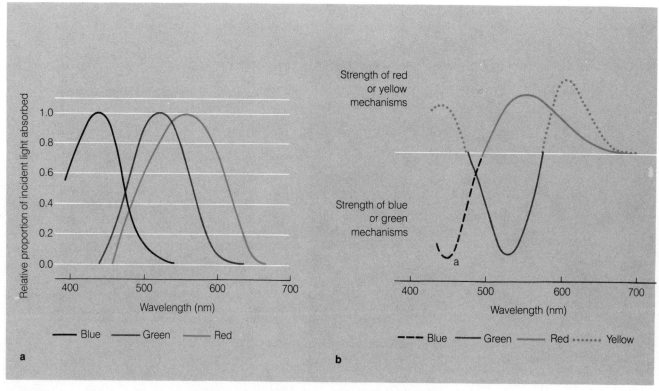

Figure 6.9 ■ Two sets of curves show the sensitivity of single cells in different portions of the visual system. (a) Three types of cones in the retina are maximally sensitive to different wavelengths. The color names represent the approximate area of greatest sensitivity. (b) Two kinds of cells in the optic nerve respond positively to one color but negatively to its complementary color.

(**a**, from G. Wald and P. K. Brown, "Human Color Vision and Color Blindness," *Cold Spring Harbor Symposium on Quantitative Biology*, 30, 345–359. Copyright 1965 by Cold Spring Harbor Laboratory. Used by permission; **b**, from Hurvich and Jameson, 1957)

you see a positive afterimage, you will definitely see a strong **negative afterimage**, a pattern of the same shape as you have been looking at but in the complementary color (Favreau & Corballis, 1976). The longer you stare at the original image, the stronger will be the afterimage. Something about the visual mechanism responds to the steady input by adapting to it. When the input is removed, the mechanism "rebounds" in the opposite direction, producing a negative afterimage. You can try this yourself using the green and yellow flag of plate 6. The plate itself may be strange looking, but the afterimage will be more familiar. (The afterimage will also show a size-constancy effect: The apparent size of the afterimage will change as you look at surfaces at different distances.)

The colored flag of plate 6 is, of course, not made up simply of color; it also includes a series of angles and lines that give it a defined shape. The real flag that it represents is even more complex; it has thickness, a position in three-dimensional space, and often movement. On occasions such as a ceremonial flag-raising it may have deep emotional significance. Your intro-

duction to perception will not be complete until we have considered these aspects of it.

FEATURES AND SHAPES

As early eyes evolved, the next step after simple light sensitivity probably was responsiveness to changes in overall brightness. But after that must have come sensitivity to some more specific feature of the environment, such as a rapid change in light or a shape of some sort.

Perceiving Features

Studies of the frog's visual system have given us some idea of what those early features might have been like. In a series of well-known experiments in the 1950s, microelectrode recordings from single cells in the frog's optic nerve were used to map the frog's visual world (Lettvin et al., 1959). It turned out that the frog's visual system is sensitive to four features of the environment. ■ Figure 6.10

Figure 6.10 ■ The frog's visual system responds to four features in the world (from left to right): contrast between light and dark, a moving edge of light or dark, a sudden decrease in overall light, and a small moving black spot.

(From *Psychology Today: An Introduction*, 2nd ed., by J. Braun et al. Copyright © 1972 by Random House, Inc. Reprinted by permission of the publisher.)

Feature Detectors   The frog responds to: (1) light/dark contrast, as between an object and its surroundings; (2) a moving edge of light or dark, as at the approach of an animal; (3) a sudden reduction in overall light, as with a sudden shadow; and (4) a small dark object moving across the visual field. The frog's responsiveness to these four features is said to reflect its having four kinds of **feature detectors**, visual-cell systems combined to yield information about these four features. The frog's "shadow" detector is simply a more rapid response than that of a plant to overall light changes. The others, however, involve some form of edge detection and two of them require moving edges.

All four feature detectors seem suited to the frog's survival needs. The first apparently offers the frog a minimal awareness of its surroundings, and the second and third signal the approach of possible predators; the frog will respond to them by jumping to escape. The fourth has become the most well known; it has been dubbed, for obvious reasons, a "bug detector."

These feature detectors were found in the optic nerve, so they do not tell us how the frog's brain responds to them or what further processing it may do. Other evidence, however, suggests that further processing is slight and that the frog's visual world is essentially what these feature detectors suggest. The frog will starve to death, for example, in the presence of bugs that don't move "correctly," but will try to eat anything that does.

The obvious question when these findings were published was whether the visual fields of other organisms, including humans, could be similarly mapped, and if so, whether we would have similar feature detectors. ■ Research Issue: Are our Heads Full of Pandemonium?

Simple and Complex Cells   Work with cats and monkeys has discovered some basic physiological mechanisms. Generally these mechanisms seem to operate by summing up of successive cell layers to yield increasing complexity. The rods and cones begin with a basic responsiveness to incoming light. Each higher processing layer in the retina and brain then sums and analyzes information from the previous layer. Pattern analyzers of the detail of a monkey hand cell are well up in this sequence, though presumably not the last step. There must also be cells or groups of cells further along that complete the perception, but only the lower steps in this sequence have been explored so far. ■ Figure 6.13

Information from rods and cones is combined by the ganglion cells in the retina. The fields of sensitivity for these ganglion cells have circular shapes, with a "center" and "surround" that respond in opposite ways (Hubel, 1963). Some ganglion cells are activated by a spot of light on the receptors that feed to their center and are inhibited by light from the surround; others have inhibitory centers and excitatory surrounds. The effect of the center/surround arrangement is to sharpen or emphasize edges. A ganglion cell with an excitatory center is maximally responsive to a spot of light that falls only on that center; light spilling over into the surround tends to inhibit the cell. In this way the cell can give the maximum response to its feature, a spot of light of a particular size and location. Similarly a cell with an inhibitory center is maximally stimulated by light surrounding a dark spot. Such cells could provide the basis for detecting a small dark object, as the frog's bug detector does.

These ganglion cells are then summed up to yield more elaborate features. A number of ganglion cells provide input to the simplest of the cerebral cortex visual cells, the **simple cell.** Simple cells have been found that respond to light bars or lines of differing orientation and location in the visual field.

Information from simple cells is further combined by **complex cells.** A series of simple-cell light lines may be added together by a complex cell, for example, to yield a response to a moving bar of light. Complex cells are typically sensitive to both shape and movement, often in particular directions; movement in one direction may yield a strong response, but movement in the opposite direction only a weak response. Complex cells, therefore, produce the response of the frog's "moving edge" feature detector. Information from complex cells is still further combined by **hypercomplex cells**, which may respond only to a light

Are our heads full of pandemonium?

Are you able to spot an approaching car so quickly because it triggers a "car detector," or to recognize a friend through the use of a "face detector"? The answer so far is "maybe," even "probably," but psychologists cannot yet say for sure. If you do have such detectors, they would have to have been specified through experience—unlike those of the frog, which are innate. The question of whether humans have feature detectors has been approached through both black-box and physiological techniques.

One black-box approach to such questions has sought to be more lively by referring to "demons" rather than boxes. Selfridge's *pandemonium model* of perceptual recognition proposes four sequential types of demons, a shorthand term for unknown physiological mechanisms: image demons, feature demons, cognitive demons, and decision demons (Selfridge, 1959). Image demons register incoming information and send it to the feature demons. (Physiologically, image demons might correspond to rods and cones, but in a black-box model you don't need to specify what mechanisms the boxes correspond to.) Feature demons are specialized to recognize their own features, such as angles or lines. When they recognize their features, they report them to the cognitive demons ■ Figure 6.11

Cognitive demons analyze these inputs seeking perceptual patterns that might be expected in the world, such as letters. When they receive enough feature information to think that they might have found their own perceptual patterns, the cognitive demons begin to yell. The better the match to their patterns, the louder they yell; this gives the model its name of *pandemonium*, which means "noisy chaos." Decision demons listen to the pandemonium and decide which cognitive demon is yelling the loudest, and therefore which pattern must exist in the world.

The pandemonium model is useful in hypothesizing different steps in the recognition process so that these may be considered separately. Like any model, it seeks to summarize what is known and suggest ways of exploring what is not yet known. But are the demons likely to correspond to actual physiological mechanisms?

Physiological psychologists have used nonhuman species to explore directly the mechanisms of perceptual recognition. In such research, an electrode is implanted into a single cell of an animal's visual system, in the occipital cortex or beyond. This electrode is hooked up to an oscilloscope that records the cell's individual action-

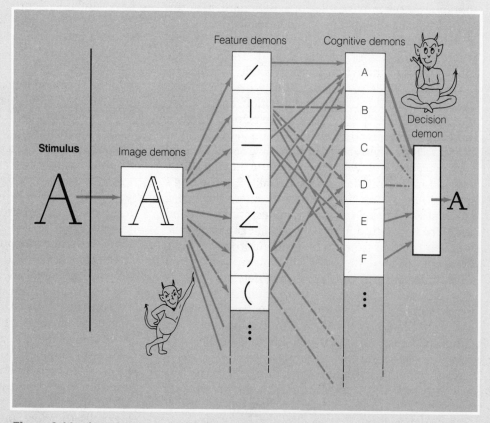

Figure 6.11 ■ A representation of Selfridge's pandemonium model of perceptual recognition processes, suggested by Selfridge's use of demon names for the boxes.

potential spikes; then varying visual stimuli are presented, and the cell's response to them is examined. Suppose the cell being tested is maximally sensitive to a single vertical line of light. A tilted light bar that falls on its receptive field will cause the cell to fire occasionally, as shown in Figure 6.12b, but a vertical light bar will cause it to fire almost continuously.

In one of the most dramatic findings from such studies, a cell was discovered in a monkey's cortex in an area adjacent to the occipital cortex, that responded best to a shape that approximated a monkey's hand (Gross, 1973). This monkey-hand cell suggests what primate feature detectors might be like. It has given rise to speculation that humans might have a range of such cells for visual recognition, an idea sometimes referred to as a "grand-mother-face" cell. If such complex pattern detectors do exist in our brains, they are relatively high up in the perception process. The light patterns falling on the rods and cones must have gone through a series of stages, such as those represented by Selfridge's demons, before getting to these special cells. The grandmother-face cell would be at least at the level of the decision demon, perhaps further.

a

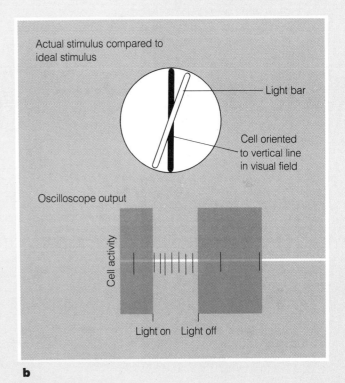

b

Figure 6.12 ■ (a) A partially anesthetized monkey being shown images on a screen. An electrode in its brain senses the firing of a single cell in response to the patterns presented. (b) Representation of a light bar on the screen only partially overlapping the ideal vertical-line field of one cell. The tilted bar causes the cell to fire weakly, as shown on the oscilloscope, but far less than a vertical bar would.

(**a,** Fritz Goro, LIFE MAGAZINE © 1971 Time, Inc.)

pattern of a particular shape, movement, *and* location (Hubel & Wiesel, 1962, 1979). These in turn are presumably followed by a series of still more complex cells, but little is known about them. (Hubel and Wiesel shared a Nobel Prize in 1981 for their work in specifying what we do know; Lettvin, 1981.) As noted earlier, the properties of these cells must be specified in some way through individual experience.

These hierarchical connections are not exclusive; each rod or cone may be part of the pattern of many ganglion cells, each ganglion cell may connect to many simple cells, and so forth. Complex and hypercomplex cells are both feature detectors, in a sense, and later cells might be called pattern detectors or object detectors. It now seems probable that our own visual system uses a similar set of detectors, though even less is known about their specific details than is known for cats and monkeys.

Several lines of evidence besides animal research suggest the presence of successively more complex layers of visual cells in humans. One is the necessity for some visual cells further forward than the rearmost

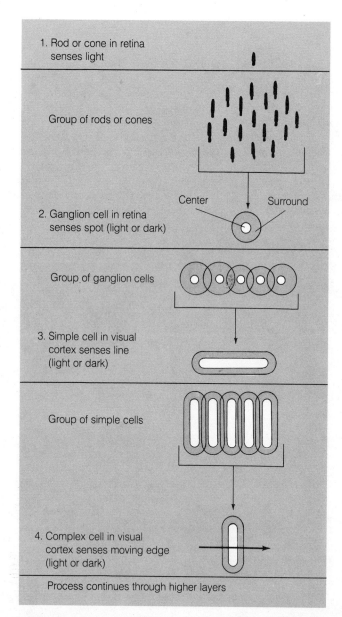

1. Rod or cone in retina senses light

Group of rods or cones

Center   Surround

2. Ganglion cell in retina senses spot (light or dark)

Group of ganglion cells

3. Simple cell in visual cortex senses line (light or dark)

Group of simple cells

4. Complex cell in visual cortex senses moving edge (light or dark)

Process continues through higher layers

Figure 6.13 ■ Visual processing operates by successively summing the input of cells at lower levels. The higher the level of processing, the more complex is the feature to which a cell responds.

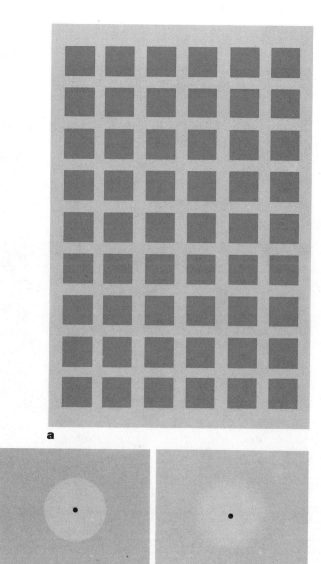

a

b

Figure 6.14 ■ Effects that depend upon feature detectors. (a) The Hering grid: accenting the edges between light and dark results in illusory gray spots at the intersections. These are not seen in the fovea, where vision is more detailed. (b) Without sharp edges a form is harder to see. If you stare with one eye at the black spot on the blurred disk, the disk gradually disappears; the sharp-edged disk remains visible under similar conditions.

(**b,** from *Visual Perception* by T. N. Cornsweet, Academic Press, 1970. Used by permission.)

occipital cortex, where the optic nerve tracts end: It is possible for a person to have normal eyes, and even normal evoked potentials in the back of the occipital cortex, yet still be cortically blind, from damage further forward (Bodis-Wollner et al., 1977). Some migraine headache sufferers see regular patterns called *fortification illusions*; these patterns may be caused by activation of particular feature detectors (Richards, 1971). Some other visual illusions also seem to result from the pattern sensing of our feature detectors; en-

hancement of lines and corners, for example, may cause us to "see" lines or spots that do not exist, and the absence of sharp contours may make other patterns harder to see. ■ Figure 6.14

Eye Movements and Feature Detection   A further complexity of our visual system is that all receptors quickly fatigue. In order to see anything for more than a few seconds, our eyes must move continuously. If you were to fix your gaze on an unmoving object

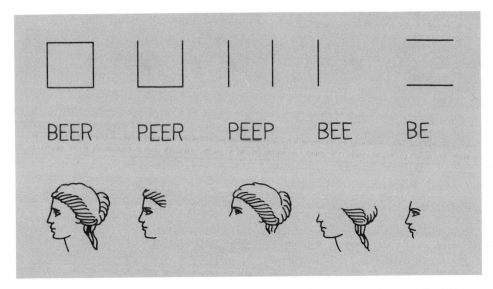

Figure 6.15 ■ Stabilized vision experiments show that when the same receptors are stimulated continuously, the image will disappear sequentially, feature by feature, as feature-detector cells show fatigue. The features lost may be simple lines, complete letters, or parts of complex forms.

(From "Stabilized Images on the Retina" by Roy M. Pritchard, *Scientific American*, June 1961. Copyright © 1961 by Scientific American, Inc. All rights reserved.)

and hold your eyes truly steady on it, a remarkable thing would happen: The object would soon begin to disappear, a feature or two at a time. Ordinarily this is impossible; to avoid this disappearance, caused by fatigue of visual system cells, your eyes are in constant slight jiggling motion (Fender, 1964). The light edges necessary for feature detection are thus continually being shifted to new receptors and you continue to see the features. (The blood vessels of the eye are not visible except through specialized techniques because they normally cast their shadows on the same receptors.) We know what would happen if you could stop this movement, however, because of an ingenious technique. Instead of trying to stop the eye, researchers arranged to have the image move with it (Pritchard, 1961). ■ Figure 6.15

A tiny slide projector was mounted on a contact lens, which moved with the eye; the image from the projector thus stayed on the same receptors. Within a few minutes, the image began to disappear, a feature at a time, suggesting fatigue at one of the feature detector stages. A square might lose one side at a time, for example, or a word might lose a letter at a time, as the feature detector comparable to a *cognitive demon* gave up. Even a complex pattern like a face in profile would disappear in logical segments, losing the hair or half the face at a time. Ordinary vision must therefore depend on many detectors for any feature, with rapid and tiny eye movements shifting the task among them so none becomes fatigued.

Overall, each more complex level of cells from receptors to brain sums up information from the previous level, so spots of light become lines, then moving edges, then more complex patterns. Eventually the result is shapes, particular forms that have meaning.

Perceiving Shapes

When certain features are assembled, the result is a *shape*. Shapes may be open patterns of lines, but are usually closed figures; they range from simple forms like triangles to complex outlines of real objects. At this higher level of processing, new problems can occur and new illusions can be demonstrated. ■ Figure 6.16

Some classic illusions are based on one set of lines influencing another set to distort the shape that is perceived. In the Zöllner illusion (Figure 6.16a), the small lines cause the larger ones not to seem parallel, even though they are. The perception of a simple closed shape such as a circle can be distorted in a similar way. (Figure 6.16b). Yet even though such distortions occur, the perception of shape often works remarkably well. You can pick out an actual complex shape from a confusion of inputs, for example, or perceive shapes that are only implied (Kanizsa, 1976). ■ Figure 6.17

Figure and Ground Examples such as those of Figure 6.17 also demonstrate a major tendency in the perception of shapes: We tend to pick out of the overall

Figure 6.16 ■ Shape-distortion illusions. (a) In the Zöllner illusion, the small bars distort the parallel pattern of the larger lines. (b) Even familiar, basic shapes can be distorted by other lines, as with the circle here.

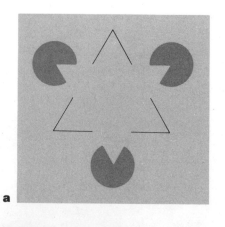

Figure 6.17 ■ Perception of shapes. In (a) you see a white triangle even though strictly speaking it is not there; the impression of edges is strongly suggested by the patterns that are present. (b) Our shape perception can function well despite confusing perceptual cues. The Dalmatian dog requires some effort to see at first but then becomes stable.

(**b,** © Ron James)

pattern, or texture, on the retina, some shapes as figures and others as background (Julesz, 1975).

The real world is filled with objects, each superimposed on a background made up of other objects. Perhaps as an adaptation to this, our perceptual systems strongly organize perceptions into figure and (back)ground. This tendency is so strong that we even organize some figures that do not seem to require it. One way of illustrating this tendency is with patterns designed to be reversible in figure and ground. ■ Figure 6.18

The goblet/faces drawing in Figure 6.18 is a classic illustration of reversible figure and ground. The perception of a white goblet on a dark background alternates with one of two faces in profile against a white background. A definite sense of figure and ground accompanies each perception, and this sense is so strong that it is very difficult to see both images at the same time. Concentrating on one tends to eliminate the other, and simply staring at the drawing usually yields spontaneous alternations between them.

Figure 6.18 ■ The goblet/faces drawing is the classic figure/ground image. The drawing spontaneously reverses for most people, the white goblet on a dark background alternating with two faces in profile.

Figure 6.19 ■ Two examples of alternate-perception drawings. (a) The rabbit/duck requires some effort to see but once seen tends to reverse spontaneously. (The rabbit faces to the right, the duck to the left.) (b) The old woman/young woman. Viewers generally see one of these alternatives initially and must exert substantial effort to break that pattern and see the other one. The smaller drawings should help you organize both perceptions.

Alternate Interpretations A special kind of reversible figure is one that can be interpreted in more than one way (Attneave, 1971). In such a figure, some key elements are emphasized for one interpretation, but when the figure reverses, these elements become relatively unimportant and other elements become critical. The resulting shift is something like that of figure and ground but more subtle. ■ Figure 6.19

Compared to the goblet/faces drawing, the "rabbit/duck" and the "old woman/young woman" figures in Figure 6.19 are less obvious and less likely to spontaneously reverse. The rabbit and duck are reasonably easy to see when you look for them, but the old woman/young woman is not easily seen in both forms. People may quickly see either the old or the young woman, but once this perception has been organized it tends to be stable. Seeing the alternative seems to require a deliberate shifting away from the first image and an active seeking of the other one. A nose must become a chin, perhaps, or an ear must turn into an eye; this requires breaking up a stable whole, or gestalt, and reforming it.

The arguments over the "real" image in this drawing that often occur when a group of people view it for the first time show how individual our views of the world must be. If a simple drawing can so easily give

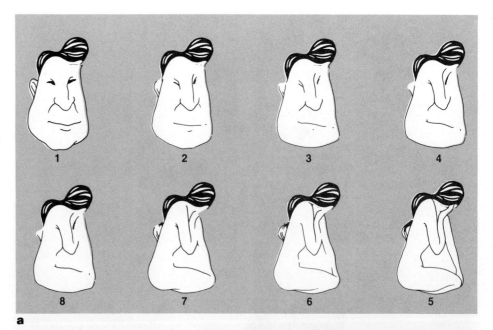

Figure 6.20 ■ (a) Expectations can influence your interpretation of a drawing. Drawing 4 seems to be a man's head if viewed in the order 1-2-3-4. Drawing 8 seems to be a woman if viewed in the order 5-6-7-8. Yet drawings 4 and 8 are the same; only the prior expectation aroused by the other drawings determines what each will seem to be. (b) *Day and Night* by M. C. Escher utilizes figure/ground patterns in the upper center, then leads into them from right, left, and below with three different expectations.

(**a,** from G. H. Fisher, *Perception and Psychophysics*, 1968, *4*, 189–192. Used by permission; **b,** © Beeldrecht, Amsterdam/ V.A.G.A., New York, Collection Haags Gemeentemuseum—The Hague, 1981. Image appears courtesy of the Vorpal Galleries, New York City, San Francisco, and Laguna Beach, California.)

rise to two different and firmly held views, it is not hard to understand how real objects, people, and events can be perceived very differently by different observers. "Beauty is in the eye of the beholder," we say. Perhaps it is actually in the cerebral cortex, but the differences in how we organize our perceptions are certainly real.

Differences in the perception of real objects and events often reflect predispositions of the perceivers. Familiarity with something or an expectation of some kind often predisposes us to perceive it in certain ways. The same play will no doubt be a different experience for those who have read glowing reviews of it than for those who have read critical ones. It will also be different for those who have read it or seen it performed elsewhere than for those who have not, and so forth.

The effect of expectation on perception can easily be demonstrated. ■ Figure 6.20

Features and shapes are useful perceptual organizations, but they are only the beginning. They would be important in perceiving the painted backdrop of that play, but to perceive the play itself we also need to perceive depth and three-dimensional objects, movement, and—most importantly—meaning.

DEPTH AND OBJECTS

In perceiving a shape on a page, you are frequently perceiving it as a representation of a three-dimensional object. But perceiving a world full of real objects at varying distances is a much more complex task. Perceiving objects and perceiving depth are closely related tasks, but we may separate them for the sake of discussing how we accomplish the perceptions.

Perceiving Depth

If we are to perceive the world visually as it is, we must perceive *depth*, the differing distances from us to the other people and objects we see. Some of the cues we use may be innate, but many are learned. Some are visible using only one eye, but others require both. Depth cues could be described in other ways, but it is usual in psychology to categorize them as monocular (one-eyed) or binocular (two-eyed).

Monocular Cues to Depth People who have lost vision in one eye are still able to perceive depth (Wernick, 1980). They have lost the use of those cues that require both eyes, but they can still interpret what they see by using **monocular depth cues**, aspects of the visual scene that indicate depth even to a single eye. ■ Table 6.2 ■ Figure 6.21

Several monocular depth cues are based on optical rules and the position of our eyes in comparison to other objects. Overlap (1 in Table 6.2 and Figure 6.21) results because light rays from far objects are blocked by closer ones. Height in plane (2) recognizes that we usually see faraway objects higher up toward the horizon, and nearer ones lower down toward the ground on which we stand. Other monocular cues are based on typical patterns found in the natural world. Both texture gradient (3) and relative size (4) reflect repetition in nature of similar-sized objects: rocks, trees, flowers, and so forth.

Still other monocular cues depend on a combination of optical rules and arrangements of the natural or artificial environment. Light and shadow patterns (5) represent an expectation that light comes from overhead, as well as indicating depth. (Some depth-reversal illusions can be created by shining light on objects from below.) Linear perspective (6) is found in natural circumstances, but is seen most clearly in human constructions that offer long parallel lines, such as roads or railroad tracks. Aerial haze (7) reflects the gradual reduction and color change in light as it passes through greater distances of the earth's atmosphere. Object familiarity (8) can reflect familiarity with either natural or artificial objects such as trees or telephone poles.

All of us use monocular depth cues, even though we may add binocular cues; the more information we have, the more accurate and stable our depth perception will be. Monocular cues are also important in another way, however: Painters, photographers, film-makers, and other artists working in two-dimensional media rely on them to represent the world. Some monocular cues, such as overlap and height in plane, have been used from early times by artists in many cultures, but others were only recognized much later (Hochberg & Brooks, 1978). For example, by the 17th century, the development of multiple vanishing points had allowed artitsts to imitate linear perspectives for any scene (Haber, 1980). ■ Figure 6.22

The impression of depth that linear perspective conveys is so powerful that it may cause illusions as well as improve paintings. Both two-dimensional and three-dimensional illusions seem to result from it. ■ Figure 6.23

In the Ponzo illusion (Figure 6.23a), for example, although the two horizontal lines are the same length, the upper one seems longer. This illusion seems to result from linear perspective cues, as any real objects that appeared as the rectangles do on the railroad-track photograph would be of different sizes. In applying a size-constancy rule, the brain automatically adjusts the same-size retinal images so that the more distant rectangle seems larger. In effect, it assumes that the same-size retinal image can result from a smaller object close by or a larger object further away. When a depth cue such as linear perspective implies that one image represents an object that is further away, the brain automatically sees it as larger (Gregory, 1968).

A more elaborate drawing can create an even more powerful illusion. The ovals in Figure 6.23b are seen as quite different in size, for example. Vanishing-point cues are strong depth indicators; this is probably the basis for the moon illusion. All of the real depth cues provided by looking toward the horizon tell us that the moon is very distant so its apparent size is perceived as huge. Further up in the dark sky no depth cues surround it, so we see it simply as the retinal image suggests, without correction (Kaufman & Rock, 1962).

Table 6.2 ■ Monocular Cues to Depth

1. Overlap	The shapes of near objects overlap or mask those of more distant ones.
2. Height in plane	Near objects are low in the visual field: more distant ones are higher up.
3. Texture gradient	A texture, such as the pattern of stones, is coarser for near areas and finer for more distant ones.
4. Relative size	If separate objects are visible that are expected to be of the same size, the largest ones are seen as closer.
5. Light and shadow	Patterns of light and dark suggest which objects are in front of which others.
6. Linear perspective	Parallel lines that run away from the viewer seem to get closer together.
7. Aerial haze	Distant objects seem increasingly hazy and bluish in color.
8. Object familiarity	Objects that seem to be familiar are assumed to be their usual size.

a

Figure 6.21 ■ Monocular cues to depth. See Table 6.2 and text for details.

(**a,** © Frank Siteman MCMLXXX, 136 Pond St., Winchester, MA 01890 (617) 729-3747/Stock, Boston; **b,** Dimitri Kessel, LIFE MAGAZINE, © 1960, Time, Inc.)

Taken together, the various monocular cues can provide strong and accurate indicators of depth for those with vision in only one eye, and in perspective drawings they make flat pictures more realistic. Additional important cues to depth, however, are provided by two eyes working together.

Binocular Cues to Depth The eyes of many mammals are located on the sides of their heads, so they have little or no binocular overlap; the right eye sees events to the right and the left eye those to the left. Neither eye looks straight ahead as ours do, and only the front peripheral fields of the eyes overlap. Thus, these animals see a much wider visual field than we do, one that can approach a full 360 degrees, but they must rely on monocular cues for perceiving depth.

Early in primate evolution, the eyes began to be located more toward the front of the head, reducing the overall visual field but improving depth perception. This modification may have helped primates' locomotion in the trees, or it may have helped in catching small prey, but such causes are difficult to establish from the fossil evidence. We do know that the amount of binocular overlap increased over time, so the great

apes and we now see most of the visual field with both eyes, a feature that provides powerful depth cues. (Some nonprimate species have also developed excellent binocular perception; one of the most notable is the falcon, with more sophisticated eyes than yours in a body of only a few pounds. Callahan, 1974; Fox et al., 1977.)

There are two important kinds of **binocular depth cues**, or visual indicators of depth that can only be utilized by two eyes working together (Ross, 1976). The two kinds of cues are a form of muscular feedback called *convergence*, and the slightly different views seen by the two eyes, known as *binocular disparity*.

When both eyes look at an object, they are oriented by eye muscles so that the image falls on both foveas. This results in the eyes being pointed somewhat toward the center of the visual field, or converged. The closer the object, the more sharply inward they must turn. This **convergence**, or turning inward of the eyes, offers a binocular cue to how close an object is through feedback from the eye muscles. You can experience convergence by holding a pencil at arm's length and focusing on it, then moving it toward your nose. As the pencil comes closer, you will find it

7. Aerial haze

8. Object familiarity

6. Linear perspective

b

a

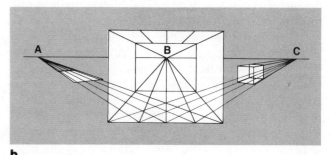

b

c

Figure 6.22 ■ With understanding of monocular depth cues came the ability to create more real-istic perspectives in art. (a) This 12th-century painting uses only overlap and height in plane. (b) The technique of establishing multiple vanishing points recreates linear perspective cues through mathematical rules. B is the vanishing point directly ahead of the viewer; each object to the side has its own vanishing point. (c) From the 18th century, Canaletto's "Stairs of Santa Maria della Salute" demonstrates the power of the multiple-vanishing-point technique.

(**a,** The Pierpont Morgan Library; **c,** Dimitri Kessel, LIFE MAGAZINE, © 1969, Time, Inc.)

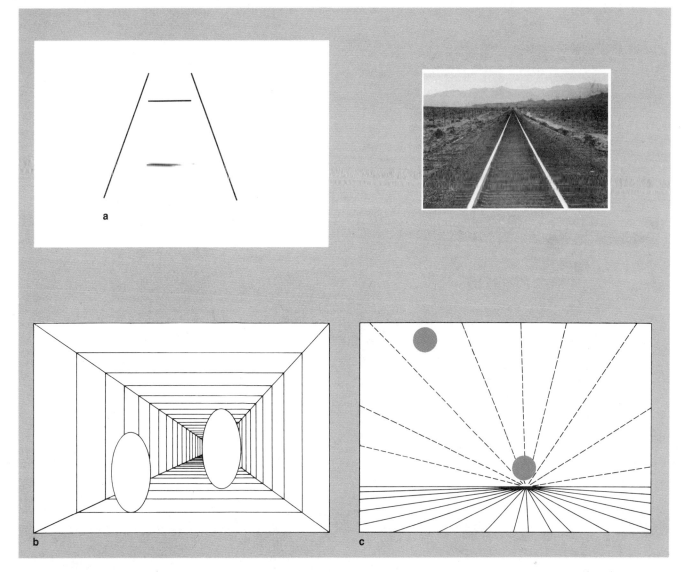

Figure 6.23 ■ The brain automatically adjusts the size of objects based on linear perspective depth cues. (a) The Ponzo illusion seems to result from the perceptual assumption illustrated by the railroad-track photo. (b) The ovals superimposed on the drawing are the same size, but if real objects were lying on the tracks, the far one would be substantially larger. (c) In the moon illusion, linear perspective cues show that the moon is very far away at the horizon, and thus huge. These cues are lacking when the moon is higher up, so it seems smaller.

(**a,** Dimitri Kessel, LIFE MAGAZINE, © 1960, Time, Inc.)

increasingly difficult to maintain a single clear image because of the extreme inward angle of convergence required. To an observer, you will appear almost crosseyed.

If you relax your efforts while the pencil is close to your nose, it will seem to split apart into two separated images. These somewhat different images demonstrate the most important binocular depth cue, **binocular disparity**, or "two-eyed difference." That is, because of the space between them, your two eyes see slightly different images of all but the most distant three-dimensional objects.

The two images produced by binocular disparity are fed to the brain, which integrates or fuses them into a single perception of an object in depth (Pettigrew, 1972). The process, called **binocular fusion**, results in a total perception that is different from the image seen by either eye. It has been compared to a zipper, smoothly linking the pieces from each side into an integrated whole (Julesz, 1974). ■ Figure 6.24

The perception of depth by binocular fusion can be simulated by presenting the eyes with two separate pictures taken from slightly different angles; the brain fuses them as if they were real views of a scene, and the person perceives depth. Stereoscopes, which did this, were very popular in the Victorian period. Binocular

Figure 6.24 ■ Powerful depth cues result from binocular disparity, or slightly different images being seen by the two eyes. 3-D movies simulate binocular disparity: The entire movie is shot in two versions by separated cameras. These two movies are projected on the same screen in different colors; colored filters in special glasses allow each eye to see only one of the images.

(J. R. Eyerman, LIFE MAGAZINE, © 1952, Time, Inc.)

fusion can also be simulated on film but it requires more complex hardware. Movies in 3-D were briefly popular in the 1950s and are trying a comeback in the 1980s (Stark, 1981b).

In stereoscopes and 3-D movies, the images presented to each eye actually have no depth. Everything in each picture lies in the same flat plane, so a single convergence angle allows you to see any part of the image. But in viewing the real world, you must focus on, and converge on, a particular distance. An object at that distance will be binocularly fused, but objects at different distances will be seen as double images. Normally we shift our attention when we shift our convergence angle, so we tend not to notice these double images, but they are quite easy to see if you try. Bring your pencil up toward your nose again, but stop when it is a foot or so away. While holding your gaze steady, focus first on the pencil, then on the desk or other surface a few feet behind it. Whichever you focus

on becomes a single image while the other separates. This occurs because the different convergence angles change the location of the images on the retina; the image of what you're looking at becomes correctly located for fusion, but other images do not. This always happens but we normally do not pay attention to it and thus do not perceive it.

Binocular fusion, like our other perceptual mechanisms, can also create illusions, but they are not easy to illustrate. However, here's an illusion you can try to create. Roll a tube out of a sheet of paper and hold it in your right hand, with the far end alongside your left hand. Look toward your left hand so that your right eye looks down the tube but the left focuses on your left hand. If you can fuse the two images, the binocular perception that results will seem to be a hand with a hole in it.

Both monocular and binocular cues are used in perceiving objects, as well as all the perceptual constancies. Putting these different systems together becomes an increasingly complex task for the brain, but a necessary one.

Perceiving Objects

As noted earlier, the perceptual constancies all contribute to a generalized object constancy. In addition, relationships among objects offer further cues for interpreting them (Gogel, 1978). But the integration of these cues in the perception of stable objects has its own special problems. One basic difficulty is that our foveas allow us to see clearly only one small area at a time. This limitation, as well as our need to converge at different angles for different depths, requires us gradually to build up our perception of complex objects and real scenes from a number of separate small images (Jonides et al., 1982). Apparently this is the reason that people can easily build up an integrated perception of an object seen only through a narrow slit, so they can never see more than a part of it at a time (Rock, 1981).

The fact that we put together our perceptions of objects one part at a time also means that an ingenious artist can draw objects that could never exist in three dimensions. **Impossible objects** are drawings that combine inconsistent perceptual cues to represent convincingly three-dimensional objects that could not exist. ■ Figure 6.25

The best known of the impossible objects is the "impossible triangle." It was designed to be logically consistent over small regions but not as a whole. Any single corner is a reasonable representation of a possible object. Even any two corners could exist, but the sides could never join at the third corner. The reason impossible objects look so convincing until you study

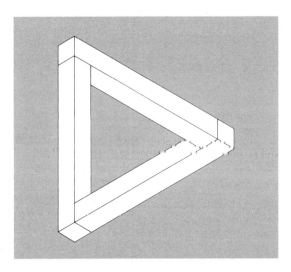

Figure 6.25 ■ The impossible triangle. Real objects have been built that look like this from one viewing angle, but they cannot actually meet at all corners.

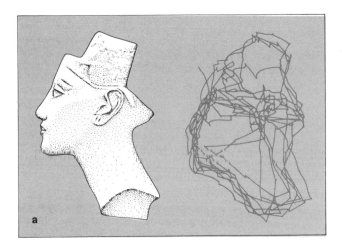

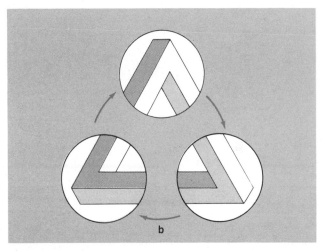

Figure 6.26 ■ Why impossible objects seem reasonable. (a) We rapidly scan an object that we look at, jumping from spot to spot along the contours and stopping at important features. (b) When we scan an impossible object in this way, a piece at a time, it seems reasonable.

(**a,** from *Eye Movements and Vision* by Alfred Yarbus, Plenum Press, 1967. Used by permission; **b,** from L. S. Penrose and R. Penrose, *British Journal of Psychology*, 1958, *49*, 31–33. Used by permission.)

them more carefully is thought to be the manner in which we sum up the details of an object. We do so by scanning them and adding up what we find. When we look at a scene, whether a real one or a two-dimensional representation, our eyes focus first at one spot then at another. They continue to follow a **scan path** as we look at the object, jumping from important feature to important feature (Noton & Stark, 1971). We may think we are looking at the entire object, but recordings of eye movements show the scan paths. ■ Figure 6.26

Scan paths primarily follow outlines, stopping at and frequently returning to features with perceptual or emotional importance. When an impossible object is scanned in this way it seems perfectly reasonable; repeated scans and careful analysis are required to spot its problems. As these relationships came to be understood, impossible objects began to be used as the basis for some striking art. ■ Personal Application: Seeing the Visual Illusions in Escher's Art.

Nature/Nurture in Perceiving Depth and Objects

The foveas of newborns are probably too incomplete to see well (Abramov et al., 1982). But at the age of 3 to 6 months, infants can begin to use binocular cues (Fox et al., 1980). Some research even suggests that infants can see as well as adults, in terms of how their eyes function when looking at a single fixed target. But the pattern of movements, called **saccades**, that adults use to build up an overall perception is apparently a learned habit; in a complex environment,

children's unpracticed saccades may limit the information they take in (Bahill & Stark, 1979; Kowler & Martins, 1982). In addition, they may not get as much out of what they do take in, because their immature brains cannot completely process the information their eyes provide (Bower, 1976).

The elements that go together to provide adult perception may require years to develop. In adults, for example, pictures are much harder to recognize when presented upside down than when right side up (Rock, 1974). But children as old as 10 may be able to see them as well; at least they remember them almost as well (Carey & Diamond, 1977).

Overall, we seem to be born with a predisposition to see depth, and perhaps objects, with the aid of both monocular and binocular cues. But a variety of life

Seeing the visual illusions in Escher's art

One artist known for his many works with perceptual themes was M. C. Escher (1898–1971). Escher liked to read about new findings of psychologists who were studying perception and often used these findings as the basis of his work (Ernst, 1976).

One of the perceptual phenomena he used was reversibility, as it occurs in the two-dimensional representation of a three-dimensional object. In the early 1800s, a Swiss naturalist named Necker was sketching the shape of a transparent crystal and noticed that it spontaneously seemed to reverse in depth. The cubical version that he devised in 1832 is now called a Necker cube. A Necker cube is shown in Figure 6.27a, with one side shaded for emphasis. As the figures reverse, the shaded side becomes alternately a front face or a rear face seen through a transparent cube; the small drawings of solid cubes show each alternative. (It has been suggested that about 5% of people cannot "see depth" in the Necker cube, for unknown reasons; Baird, 1980.) (See plate 7.)

The Necker cube became the basis for an "impossible crate," constructed by combining the two versions of the Necker cube. Seven corners of the impossible crate fit one interpretation of the Necker cube. The middle corner, however, is drawn like the other interpretation. The result is like a Necker cube frozen in midtransformation. ■ Figure 6.27

The impossible crate served as the model for one of Escher's best-known prints, *Belvedere*. To be sure that the point was not missed, Escher included both a Necker cube drawing on the floor and a man holding an impossible crate (Teuber, 1974). *Belvedere* is a good example of problems caused by our need to scan complex representations; it is sometimes hard for observers to see anything wrong with the building because all of the details seem so reasonable. But the top story is at right angles to the bottom and the pillars that support it go from one side of the bottom to the other side of the top!

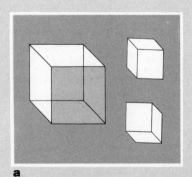

a

b

Figure 6.27 ■ Reversible objects and impossible art. (a) The Necker cube tends to reverse in depth spontaneously. (b) *Belvedere* by M. C. Escher. A Necker cube drawing is on the floor and an "impossible crate" is being examined by the seated man. Look at the figures on the ladder and compare upper and lower stories to see why this building is as impossible as the crate.

experiences can either complete or inhibit the use of the visual mechanisms. An adult's depth perception represents the end effect of a series of nature/nurture interactions. If all goes well, depth perception can be both rapid and accurate, but if there are either nature or nurture failures it can be weak or distorted.

One nature failure is amblyopia or "wandering eye." In this condition, a muscular-control problem present from birth keeps one eye from properly tracking and converging with the other. The result is two nonoverlapped images and the brain responds by ignoring one of them (Eggers & Blakemore, 1978). The

muscular problem can be corrected, but unless the surgery is done when the child is young it will not provide binocular fusion. If done too late, although both eyes converge, the brain continues to ignore one and the person must get by with monocular cues.

Assuming that our visual physiology works correctly, we seem to build up learned routines for processing inputs by extensive experience in the world. These routines work almost as automatically as if they were innate. One set of illusions, for example, seem to be based on experience with rectangular buildings (Gillam, 1980). ■ Figure 6.28

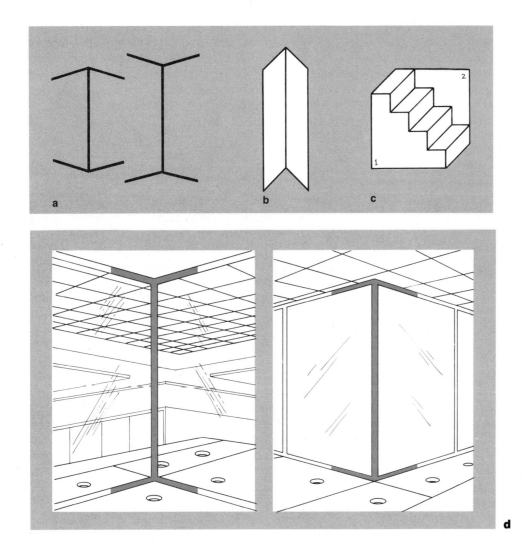

Figure 6.28 ■ Several classic illusions seem based on learned cues to depth that are based on experience with rectangular objects. (a) The Müller–Lyer illusion. (b) The probable explanation for the Müller–Lyer illusion: We have a learned tendency to adjust the apparent size of near or far corners. (c) The Mach reversible-card illusion. (It is probably based on the same cues as the Müller–Lyer illusion.) (d) The Schröder stairs are made up of a series of Mach cards and probably utilize the same cues.

In the Müller–Lyer illusion, reversing the direction of arrowheads changes the perceived length of equal vertical lines (Figure 6.28a). The most probable explanation for this effect is a size-constancy mechanism based on experience with rectangular building corners. Corners that project toward or away from us are similar in shape to the Müller–Lyer arrows. In correcting to maintain size constancy, the corner projecting toward us would be reduced and the corner away from us expanded. If the Müller–Lyer arrows are perceived as corners, this adjustment would cause the illusion.

In the Mach reversible-card illusion, a card folded like a tent and placed on a table seems to reverse in depth, as does a line drawing of it (Yellott, 1981). This illusion may also be related to the perception of rectangular corners (Gregory, 1970). Focusing on the top, where the card resembles a near corner, tends to make it project toward you; focusing on the bottom tends to push it away from you. The spontaneous reversals we see in just looking at the card may occur as we automatically scan from one end to the other. The Schröder stairs are another reversible-depth drawing; they are made up of a series of steps that are each the same shape as the Mach card. The stairs reverse in a way similar to the card.

Even though it seems to be learned, our tendency to adjust for rectangular buildings is obviously quite strong. What do you suppose would happen if it were set in opposition to another basic rule of constancy—that people stay the same size?

Comparing, Analyzing, and Synthesizing

The **Ames room** is a real three-dimensional room that is *not* rectangular, but provides powerful illusory cues suggesting that it is. The illusion of its being rectangular is so powerful that it even overcomes size constancy for people inside it. ■ Figure 6.29

If you peer through a peephole into an Ames room, you see only a simple rectangular room, but a person inside will appear much larger in one corner than in the other. The size illusion persists if two people move toward each other from opposite sides of the room: One shrinks before your eyes and the other expands. Figure 6.29 shows the room's true shape, but we must still ask why it has the effect it does. To answer that question requires considering how the brain integrates multiple sensory inputs and multiple constancy mechanisms.

We perceive a stable world partially because we keep rechecking one sense against another and one constancy against another. Normally, the cues we receive are redundant and we don't need to resolve conflict. Occasionally a perceptual hypothesis is wrong, however, as when the car next to you rolls and you think your car is moving; then kinesthetic feedback corrects the mistaken visual hypothesis and all is well again. Indications of how this sensory integration takes place, and how necessary it is, have come from animal experiments. ■ Figure 6.30

Early studies in visual perception showed that animals completely deprived of light develop abnormally; if kept in the dark too long, they will simply be unable to see when brought into the light (Riesen, 1950). Later studies provided light through translucent goggles, but varied the animals' exposure to patterns. This turned out to affect the development of feature detectors, biasing them in the direction of the kind of features the animals had experienced. A study using kittens in a merry-go-round apparatus (Figure 6.30) represents the next complexity. Their daily time in the merry-go-round was the kittens' only experience with patterns. One always walked and the other always rode. Only the walking kitten, which had been able to integrate muscular cues and visual patterns, developed normal depth perception. The passive kitten seemed almost blind to depth cues (Held, 1965). Exposure to visual input alone is not enough, apparently; the visual depth cues are given meaning by association with the other senses, including kinesthesis and touch.

Humans who have had their sight restored by the removal of lifelong cataracts report much the same effect; they can see but often cannot interpret patterns in terms of shape or distance until they have had experience with them (Hechinger, 1981). In a person whose visual development has been normal from birth, however, vision becomes so powerful that it can often override a conflicting cue, as from touch. Even though touch alone can accurately assess size, its message is rejected in favor of an incorrect visual input. In this sense, seeing is believing.

If something distorts one of your sensory inputs slightly, you usually adapt, perhaps without even knowing it. But not all species are so flexible. When young chicks wore distorting lenses, they seemed unable to adapt their pecks to accommodate the change (Hess, 1956). But humans adapt quickly to similar changes, apparently by adapting the kinesthetic feedback sense to match their vision (Kohler, 1962; Rock & Harris, 1967. We apparently retain this flexibility in sensory integration throughout life.

Now we can return to the question of why the Ames room produces its distorting effect. Both the rectangularity cues and the size cues are visual, so it can't be visual cues overriding others. What seems to happen in cases where the cues conflict is that the brain does the best it can with what it has. It analyzes what it receives and synthesizes a perception.

The brain's tendency to make the best compromise

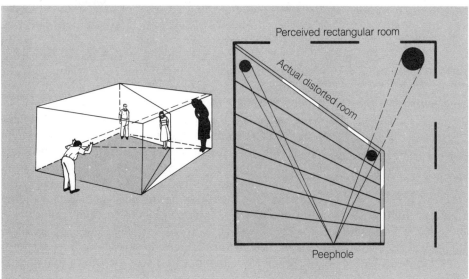

Figure 6.29 ■ The Ames room. The striking size distortions are seen from a peephole in one side. The room so strongly creates the illusion it is rectangular that it overcomes size constancy.

(Photograph by N. Rodger/© Exploratorium)

of multiple inputs has been termed **analysis by synthesis** (Neisser, 1976). The inputs are put together and a perception is built up or synthesized from them. Perceptual analysis of the world is thus an analysis by synthesis, and the Ames-room effect seems to be one result. Cues that seem to come from larger or more stable objects are generally given more weight, and cues to retangular rooms are especially powerful. In synthesizing the overall perception, then, cues from the room are given priority, and the room is perceived

as rectangular. But if the room is rectangular, then the people must be different sizes. And so we see them that way.

Suppose you retreat from the peculiarities of the Ames room and take solace in a movie. You walk to the theater, looking up once to see the moon "racing through the clouds," and finally settle down with your popcorn to watch the "moving pictures." Some of the events you saw were real—but the moon wasn't racing and the pictures don't move.

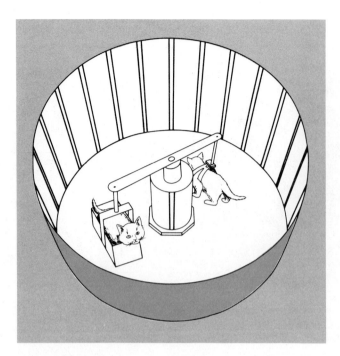

Figure 6.30 ■ Feedback from other senses is important in developing and maintaining visual perception. These kittens in a merry-go-round apparatus are both able to see the patterned wall, but the walking kitten develops more accurate visual perception than the one riding.

(From R. Held and A. Hein, *Journal of Comparative and Physiological Psychology,* 1963, *56,* 872–876. Copyright 1963 by the American Psychological Association. Adapted by permission of the author.)

MOVEMENT AND EVENTS

In a world where many things move, including you, you are faced with the constant task of sorting out what is moving and what is not. It's not surprising that you sometimes make mistakes; it's more surprising that you make so few of them.

Movement perception is based on images moving on the retina, but far more processing is required for us to perceive movement accurately (Regan et al., 1979; Regan & Beverley, 1979). Retinal images also move when the eyes or head moves, for example, and the brain must correct for this. (Regan & Beverley, 1982; K. D. White et al., 1980). To do so, it uses proprioceptive cues in addition to visual ones, so body and head movements can be related to movement of the images across the retina (Bizzi, 1974; Monty & Senders, 1976). Special neural circuits also help your eyes track a moving object independent of what the object looks like; you see the *object* with other neural systems, but these *movement* circuits keep it in sight (Sekuler & Levinson, 1977).

Relative movement between two parts of the envi-ronment poses another problem. Which is moving? A number of cues help you keep track of real movement. You automatically assume, for example, that large objects move less than small ones (Wallach, 1959). This assumption normally works well, though in artificial situations it yields illusions: in a darkened room, for example, if the frame around a spot of light is jiggled, you see the spot move, not the frame. This is what seems to cause the moon to race across the clouds; the moon is visually smaller, so it seems to move rather than the clouds.

To keep the world from swinging crazily every time you move your eyes, you automatically subtract the eye-movement commands from the resulting movement on the retina. So when you command a swing of the eyes to the right, you compensate at the same time, thus keeping the room stable. These compensation techniques provide you with rapid and accurate perceptions of motion under most circumstances. They may even be correct under highly unusual circumstances: In one case, untrained observers were able to interpret a set of lights moving in the dark accurately as people with lights on their arms and legs (Johansson, 1975).

But illusions of movement still occur. Apparent movement can even exist without any real movement at all when the cues are minimal or carefully calculated. The **autokinetic effect**—literally "self-moving" effect—is the apparent movement of a fixed light in a darkened environment; with no other cues to help keep it stable, the light seems to wander about. Pilots flying at night must guard against this effect altering their perception of beacon or warning lights. If they can arrange their view to include the plane's window frame, it will be enough to hold the light stable.

Moving-light advertising signs, such as those in New York's Times Square, are based on another form of apparent movement. The signs don't move; the small lights of which they are composed flash on and off, but when the timing is right, the perception of motion is very powerful. The moving-sign effect is based on the **phi phenomenon**, the first perceptual effect to be studied by the Gestalt psychologists (Kolers, 1964). The phi phenomenon is the basis for the toy stroboscope Wertheimer noticed. It is also the basis of our most dramatic form of apparent motion, the movies. Movie projectors are actually only rapid slide projectors; they project one picture, mask the lens so that no light escapes, advance the film, project another picture, and so forth, 24 times a second. The only movement is that which you synthesize from the still pictures; movies move in the brain, not on the screen.

Movies are probably one of the few industries built entirely on a perceptual illusion derived from a child's toy. Yet they have the power to amuse or frighten us, to stir our patriotism, or otherwise to affect us deeply. Illusions they may be, but they are more than movement; they are events.

All of our perceptual mechanisms are directed to one end—to tell us about *events*, what is going on in the world that we ought to know about. Perception is not just visual illusions and tricks; it is our way of comprehending a vast, subtle, and ever-changing environment. We sample the information from that environment with our sensory systems. We process the samples, compare them, refer them to memory for identification and emotional meaning, and finally synthesize from them . . . what? Our own unique view of the world and what is going on in it, our own complex creation.

We ought to be proud of this creation of ours, this perceived world full of meaningful events. But we often are blissfully ignorant of it. "Oh well, another dull day," we say. "Nothing special happening." But perception, even of ordinary events, is very special. It's certainly not all we're capable of, but it is a remarkable achievement. Perhaps after having read this brief glimpse into its workings you will be less likely to dismiss it so easily.

CHAPTER SUMMARY

1 Nativist theories of perception emphasize innate factors and empiricist theories emphasize environmental ones, but perception actually depends on an interaction of both kinds of factors.

2 Gestalt psychologists were the first to study many aspects of perception. Their insistence that the whole perception was different from the sum of its parts has continued to influence perceptual research.

3 Other general principles of perception include the need for interpretation of inputs through perceptual hypotheses and limits or influences on perception from physiological mechanisms, attention, motivation, and expectation.

4 Perceptual constancies of several kinds operate to keep the perceived world stable, despite varying patterns of input from light changes, movement, and so forth.

5 The most basic perceptions are of brightness and color. The Young–Helmholtz and the Hering theories both describe some aspects of how we perceive color and help us understand color blindness and afterimages.

6 Feature detectors build up more complex perceptions from simpler ones, with shapes being perceived when enough features have been assembled. Shapes are typically organized as figures set against a background; such figure/ground patterns are usually stable, but some special ones are reversible.

7 Numerous monocular cues make it possible to perceive depth with only one eye, but additional cues made possible by two eyes are useful.

8 Objects are perceived a piece at a time as the eyes follow some scan path from feature to feature. Drawings of impossible objects take advantage of this process, as in the art of M. C. Escher.

9 Adult depth perception is the end product of both innate attributes and extensive visual experience. Even in adults perception remains somewhat flexible and subject to further learning.

10 The perception of movement requires all of the prior processes and some further special mechanisms. The end product, perception of events, is a remarkable achievement.

Further Readings

Most of the books suggested for Chapter 5 are also relevant here: Goldstein's text, for example, is specifically titled *Sensation and Perception* (1984). Frisby's *Seeing: Illusion, Brain and Mind* (1980) is even somewhat more focused on perception than sensation, and Gregory's *The Intelligent Eye* (1970) is somewhat more relevant here than the earlier *Eye and Brain* (1966). For specific emphasis on perception as such, see Rock's *An Introduction to Perception* (1975) or *Perceptual Organization* (1981), edited by Kobovy and Pomerantz. If you are intrigued by Escher's work, Ernst's *The Magic Mirror of M. C. Escher* (1976) includes many preliminary sketches and working drawings that show how Escher used perceptual principles in constructing his works. If you'd like to try some of this yourself, see Ranucci and Teeters's *Creating Escher-Type Drawings* (1977).

The room is small, dimly lit, and filled with apparatus. Racks of equipment cover two walls, and against a third stands a complex device with what looks like a tabletop covered with graph paper jutting from it. The fourth wall is mostly window; on the other side lies a young man, sound asleep despite the electrodes glued to his face and head. Suppressing a yawn, you briefly envy him, as it's now about 2:00 in the morning. After a late-night study session you've dropped in to visit the sleep lab, where a friend is a research assistant on what she calls a "lucid-dream" investigation. Startled by a sudden rattling noise, you turn to see a burst of activity from the device with the graph paper. The paper is slowly unreeling along the table and onto the floor while hinged pens draw rapid squiggles on it. "What's happening?" you ask. "REM burst," she answers tersely. You decide to wait for a translation, as she seems very attentive to the sleeper and the apparatus. "There it is!" she exclaims, as one pen makes several quick marks on the paper. "There's what?" you can't resist asking. "The code marks from the subject. They indicate that he's dreaming—which we knew from the REM—*and* that he *knows* he's dreaming." You're impressed. Later, you'll have to ask her how the silent, unmoving sleeper in the dark room beyond the glass has reported, through all that equipment, that he knows he is dreaming.

In this chapter we will consider some aspects of what it means to be conscious and some of the variations on that consciousness, including sleep, dreams, hypnosis, and drugs.

CONSCIOUSNESS

Although consciousness is a commonly used term, it is difficult to define with precision. But only when we define consciousness can we ask what it does for us, what its major subdivisions are, and how altered states of consciousness differ from normal ones.

Defining Consciousness

You might think that distinguishing between consciousness and nonconsciousness is a trivial task: You are conscious, a rock is not. But there are many intermediate possibilities between an alert human and an inert rock. Are the primates, our closest living relatives, conscious? Many people say they are and, in fact, psychologists have studied language and problem solving by primates. Our pet dogs and cats? Well, maybe. Somewhere along the spectrum of living creatures, most of us will rebel; few of us consider earthworms conscious. But where do you draw the line—at rabbits, chickens, fish, lobsters?

And what about humans other than alert adults? Is a sleeping person conscious? Someone "unconscious" from a blow to the head, or from drugs? Someone so mentally disturbed that he or she is catatonic and sits unmoving for days, apparently unresponsive to the environment? A brain-damaged individual? A newborn infant? Does it change your answers to know that patients can sometimes remember what their surgeons said while they were anesthetized? That people think and experience in some sense throughout all stages of sleep? That catatonic patients may be fully aware of what goes on around them? That even newborns show more interest in some aspects of their environments than in others?

It turns out that you and a rock are easy to discriminate because you represent opposite ends of a continuum. But drawing a line on the continuum that will exactly separate consciousness from nonconsciousness is nearly impossible. In seeking to draw that line, we have three "languages" to choose from: subjective experience, physiology, and overt behavior. ■ Figure 7.1

Each of the three languages of consciousness suggests some ways of studying it (Hilgard, 1980; Webb, 1981). Humanistic psychologists emphasize subjective experience. Physiological psychologists focus primarily on physiology, but also use overt behavior as a reference point (Davidson & Davidson, 1980). Many behavioral psychologists do not wish to argue about consciousness at all, but some psychologists use overt behaviors as consciousness indicators. Stroke patients who have lost the ability to speak, for example, may respond to queries with movements that signal their awareness.

Problem solving is a special class of behaviors that may imply consciousness. Consider the behavior of chimpanzees in response to a particular kind of problem. The chimp is anesthetized and a red spot is placed on its face; when it awakens, it is given a mirror. The chimp typically stares at the mirror, then raises a hand to its face to try to rub off the spot. This behavior may imply that the chimp is aware of a number of relationships: that the mirror image is a reflection of itself, that the spot was not there before, and so forth (Gallup, 1979). Not all psychologists agree that such behavior implies consciousness, however. And most cognitive psychologists simply focus on the behaviors of information processing or problem solving, trying not to become mired in the question of whether these behaviors imply consciousness.

In general, psychologists are most confident of consciousness when it fits well into all languages; when these disagree, serious questions are raised. Some surgery patients whose pain is being relieved hypnotically, for example, may begin to squirm or grimace while reporting no pain. Are they or aren't they in pain? At present, no one can answer that question satisfactorily (although for practical reasons such patients are given drugs). The disagreement of indicators simply pinpoints a problem for future research.

For our purposes, we may define **consciousness** as a process of experiencing the external and internal environment in ways that separate immediate stimuli from immediate responses. This means that stimuli are processed and "understood" in some sense, rather than leading directly to mechanical responses. This definition is still inadequate; it doesn't, for example, tell us whether language-using primates or computers are conscious. To avoid such problems, we will specify that we mean *human* consciousness.

Functions of Consciousness

Many behaviors in response to stimuli, both of other species and of humans, do not require consciousness. In insects and reptiles, elaborate behavior in response to stimuli can be automatic and mechanical. If consciousness has evolved on top of an existing behavioral responsiveness, it must offer some utility beyond what can be accomplished by automatic responses. The nervous-system complexity that makes our consciousness possible probably allowed a behavioral flexibility that helped our ancestors survive. But it is less obvious whether consciousness was itself adaptive or simply was a side effect of a complex nervous system (Humphrey, 1982).

Most of us have had the sensation of being a bystander at some of our own actions. Someone poses a problem, for example; you pause briefly and then the answer pops into your head. You may be entirely unaware of the processes that solved the problem; they often take place "out of consciousness." Or consider the spontaneous development of cooperative strategies in split-brain patients (Chapter 2). Those strategies are also a kind of problem solving, yet the patients seemed not to be conscious of them.

Some psychologists believe that problem solving is what's important, not whether you are conscious of it. According to this view, consciousness is incidental to information processing. Other psychologists believe that consciousness is a powerful agent for controlling behavior that has evolved in its own right. Nonconscious problem-solving systems are then thought of as the servants of consciousness; they carry out automated routines but are guided and integrated by consciousness.

One way of approaching these issues is to consider varying divisions of consciousness. Perhaps problem

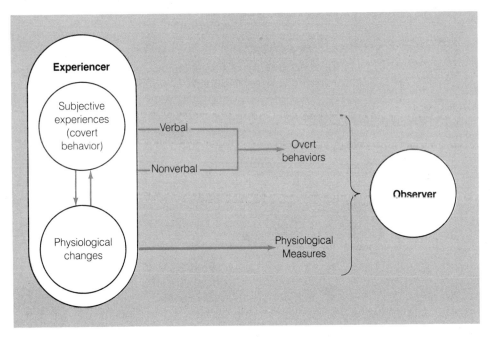

Figure 7.1 ■ There are three major indicators of consciousness. Subjective experiences are only available to the experiencer, but an external observer can assess the experiencer's consciousness through behavior (verbal and nonverbal) or physiological measures.

solving can be outside the awareness of one part of consciousness but inside the awareness of another.

Divisions of Consciousness

Many psychologists have proposed different divisions of consciousness (Hilgard, 1977a; Hirst et al., 1978). The best-known proposal is Freud's three levels of consciousness. In Freud's system, **conscious processes** are those in awareness at a given time; they correspond closely to what most people think of as consciousness. **Preconscious processes** are memories available to consciousness on demand but not presently in awareness. You probably think of them simply as memories, but Freud contrasted them to **unconscious processes:** memories that are *not* available for conscious recall but that nevertheless can affect behavior through dreams, mannerisms, or slips of speech. If such behaviors were properly interpreted, he believed, they provided clues to emotional memories of which people could not be consciously aware. (Freud has not been the only theorist to discuss concepts of the unconscious; Shevrin & Dickman, 1980.)

Where Freud used a depth or levels analogy for his different proposed types of consciousness, others have proposed side-by-side forms, such as Hilgard's **neodissociation theory** (1977b). According to this view, the consciousness that solves a problem may be *different* from the one that reports the solution, but not necessarily "lower" (Hilgard, 1978a; see Figure 7.12 below).

Neither Freud nor Hilgard has attempted to relate consciousness to neurology. But one form of side-by-side consciousness does seem likely to be related to brain structure: the differences in thought processes of the right and left cerebral hemispheres. Split-brain research indicates that alternate modes of thinking and problem solving are compartmentalized in the two hemispheres. These findings may offer a physiological basis for some kinds of alternate-consciousness proposals.

All proposed divisions of consciousness, whether based on physiology or not, seek only to capture the main features of the behaviors involved; they are not intended to be exact duplicates of reality. Some divisions of consciousness probably do correspond to older brain centers versus newer ones and others to right hemisphere versus left. The relationships between areas within a single hemisphere suggest other, even more subtle patterns of consciousness. Theoretical divisions of consciousness need not capture all of this complexity to be useful.

Normal and Altered States

The phrase *altered states of consciousness* includes many different states and a variety of ways of achieving them (Tart, 1972). The first task in defining altered states is to define any state of consciousness. Only then can you ask how states differ and which are normal ones, which altered ones (Ornstein, 1973, 1977).

People typically discuss their states of consciousness in experiential terms, using dimensions such as alertness or focus. One state might be alert and focused, in which processing is very rapid and events seem to unfold slowly: a person experiencing an automobile accident, for example. Another might be relaxed and nearly empty of content: the state that many meditational techniques seek to accomplish. For other purposes, such as understanding the effects of psychoactive drugs, it is desirable to discuss states of consciousness in physiological terms. Differing degrees of alertness, for example, might correspond to differing activity in the reticular activating system.

Any state of consciousness can then be defined in either experiential or physiological dimensions. Each dimension may have many values: you do not click from alert to relaxed like the throwing of a switch, but can be more or less alert. We can thus define **state of consciousness** as a set of values on one or more experiential or physiological dimensions. An "alert, focused, waking state," for example, could be described in terms of the degree of alertness and focus, expressed either as what each feels like to the experiencer or in terms of physiological activity.

Psychologists are more confident of the descriptions of a state of consciousness when dimensions agree than when they conflict. The physiological measures used in defining sleep, for example, usually correspond well to the experiences of the sleeper (as indicated by verbal reports). But a few people report that they were awake most of the night when the physiological measures indicate that they were asleep (Mitler et al., 1975). Such mismatches indicate that the two dimensions are not yet interchangeable, even if both are describing the same processes.

Normal states are then defined as common or routine sets of values. An **altered state** exists when any difference on one or more dimensions is large enough to seem different to the experiencer. By this definition, several waking states are normal for everyone, but sleep or the hyperalert state sometimes experienced in an accident are "altered" for everyone. Other states, such as hypnotic or drug-induced ones, are normal for some people in some cultures, yet unusual or unknown for others. We will explore several widely experienced states, beginning with the most universal ones—sleep and dreams.

SLEEP AND DREAMS

Sleep and dreams, although universal, are so different from waking that they seem a mysterious state. They have intrigued people of all times and cultures and have been thought to represent contact with the dead or gods. Contemporary psychology sees them in a different light; some of its findings, although not quite as exciting as contact with the dead, are nonetheless striking and unexpected (Webb, 1975; Arkin et al., 1978). One important aspect of sleep that is too little appreciated is its tie to biological cycles.

Sleep and Biological Cycles

No one stays in a single state of consciousness for very long; many shifts occur throughout the day. In particular, almost everyone spends about a third of each 24-hour day in a state of consciousness called sleep. We have some control over when sleep occurs, and may even be able to go without it for a night or two. But we have a powerful innate demand for sleep that becomes increasingly difficult to resist. After a few nights without sleep, people may literally go to sleep standing up. Some may even hallucinate (Dement, 1978).

What *is* sleep, and why is it apparently so important that our bodies demand it? Why can't we just decide to stay awake indefinitely? Or if we need sleep, why can't we just sleep a few hours here and there, as convenient, rather than sleeping at night? Unfortunately people who try to average out their hours of sleep over a number of days—the way Federal Aviation Administration regulations limit airline pilots' schedules—find that they are "fooling with Mother Nature," and must suffer the consequences. (One pilot on a passenger flight over the Pacific awoke to find all three of the other cabin crew members asleep—one of hundreds of such incidents.) Sleep is an activity that your body needs on a regular basis at the *same* hours of the 24-hour day. These hours can be adjusted slowly but not chosen arbitrarily each day. Let's see why.

Biological Cycles The earth's rotation on its axis, the basis of the 24-hour day, has been relatively regular for the billions of years that life has been evolving. The activities of a wide variety of species have become linked to this time span, called the **circadian cycle.** (The name is derived from the Latin for "about a day.") Mammals, invertebrates, and even plants regularly vary their physiology and overt behavior according to the time of day (Takahashi & Zatz, 1982). But we have only recently begun to understand the importance of circadian cycles in humans (Moore-Ede et al., 1982).

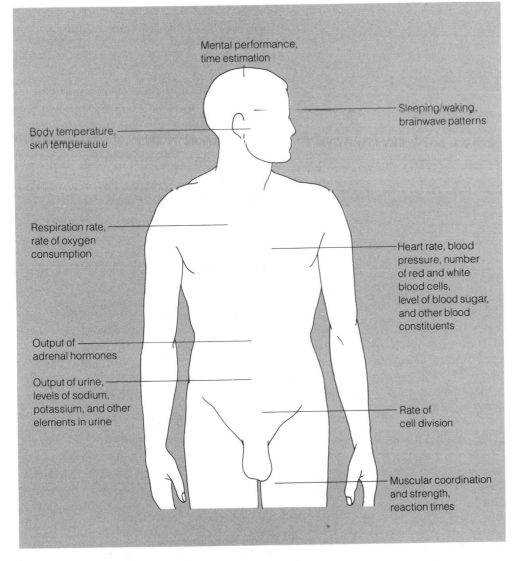

Mental performance,
time estimation

Sleeping/waking,
brainwave patterns

Body temperature,
skin temperature

Respiration rate,
rate of oxygen
consumption

Heart rate, blood
pressure, number
of red and white
blood cells,
level of blood sugar,
and other blood
constituents

Output of
adrenal hormones

Output of urine,
levels of sodium,
potassium, and other
elements in urine

Rate of
cell division

Muscular coordination
and strength,
reaction times

Figure 7.2 ■ Many aspects of human physiology show clear-cut circadian cycles, changing regularly over each 24-hour period. Some of the more important ones are shown here.

Most physicians, for example, are still unaware that human responsiveness to drugs may vary widely depending on the time of day the drugs are taken (Hilts, 1980b). ■ Figure 7.2

There are also both longer and shorter biological cycles. Women's menstrual cycles, for example, follow the 28-day lunar month, but men also show evidence of hormonal cycles (Palmer & Goodenough, 1978; Parlee, 1978). Many species also show yearly cycles, including those of mating and hibernation (Follett & Follett, 1981). An important shorter cycle is the **ultradian cycle,** which runs about 90 minutes. During sleep, the ultradian cycle marks regular changes in sleep patterns (as we will see later). But there may also be 90-minute cycles in waking activity level, daydreaming content, and so forth (Lavie & Kripke, 1975; Chase, 1979). It's possible that waking ultradian cycles may reflect a shift in balance between the two cerebral hemispheres. Subjects' performance on both verbal and spatial tasks varied on an approximately 90-minute cycle, but out of phase; when subjects were more efficient at verbal tasks, they were worse at spatial ones (Klein & Armitage, 1979).

The biological cycles of some organisms seem to be controlled by time cycles in the environment itself. The natural world is filled with information about the

"If we ever intend to take over the world, one thing we'll have to do is synchronize our biological clocks."

© 1983 by Sidney Harris

24-hour earth-rotation period, the 28-day lunar cycle, and annual cycles; such external sources of time information are called **Zeitgebers,** German for "time-givers" (Brown, 1972). An organism that is sensitive to such information can adjust its body rhythms to match. Some organisms, however, seem to have their own internal sources of time, called **biological clocks.** These biological clocks can be shown to exist in various ways—such as eliminating likely external Zeitgebers and seeing if the rhythms continue—but the actual biological structures that constitute the clocks are largely unknown. Studies of biological clocks have discovered, however, that the clocks are often not very precise and are synchronized by the Zeitgebers. The internal clock provides a basic value and the Zeitgeber corrects this value as necessary to keep the organism exactly synchronized with the environment.

Sunlight is a major Zeitgeber; its daily changes mark the circadian cycle and its longer-term changes indicate seasons (Wurtman, 1975). One major effect of light is to control the timing of variations in hormonal output of the pineal gland (Lewy et al., 1980). Pineal hormones, in turn, influence a variety of body cyclical activities (Binkley, 1979). An animal's eyes act as light sensors for this purpose, independent of their function in sight; the eyes of many blind people register enough light for the pineal to synchronize their circadian periods. If the eyes register no light at all, however, the blind person may find it difficult to study and work on a 24-hour day. Without light as a Zeitgeber, the human body tends to cycle on a built-in 25-hour period, so that each day it becomes less aligned with the earth's light and dark schedule. Researchers tested one blind student in the lab, controlling his activity cues by hav-

ing him eat and sleep on a rigid 24-hour cycle. Even after 26 days his other body rhythms continued on the 25-hour cycle (Miles et al., 1977).

Complex species may even utilize several biological clocks for different purposes. In mammals, one clock is now known to be located in an area of the anterior (front) hypothalamus called the suprachiasmatic nuclei (SCN) (Rusak & Groos, 1982). (The name means that it lies just above the optic chiasma.) In fact, there may be two interacting clocks in the SCN, one on each side (Pickard & Turek, 1982). And there is thought to be at least one other internal clock that acts in conjunction with the SCN clock(s), but its location is not yet known (Moore-Ede, 1982). Apparently some factor in the maternal blood sets the SCN clock(s) prior to birth (at least in rats) so that the young are born with their bodies already on local time (Reppert & Schwartz, 1983).

Cycles of Sleep The time when sleep occurs is closely tied to the circadian cycle. **Nocturnal** organisms, ones adapted for night living, have internal clocks with a basic period of about 23 hours; **diurnal** organisms, those adapted for daytime living, have clocks with a basic period of 25 hours. Both kinds of clocks are synchronized to the actual time of day by information from Zeitgebers. The net effect, the synchronized clock, determines when an organism sleeps. When living in a natural-light environment, diurnal species, including humans, tend to sleep through the darkest hours of the night. But they can adapt somewhat to unusual circumstances, such as continuous light or artificial lighting patterns longer or shorter than natural ones. Some animals can adjust to substantial changes in the length of their day, showing a strong reliance on light as a Zeitgeber. Studies with humans, however, have had mixed results.

In one of the first major studies, conducted in 1938, two men went deep into a cave and for 32 days attempted to live according to a 28-hour day. A number of measures were taken, including body temperature, which cycles regularly and usually reaches its lowest point in the early morning hours. (Temperature cycles are one of the standard measures of a person's circadian cycles.) The results of this study, shown in Figure 7.3, are also typical of later findings: One subject adjusted and the other didn't (Dement, 1978).
■ Figure 7.3

Because sleep is tightly locked to the circadian cycle, you cannot just do it when you get around to it. Sleeping at times of day when you don't usually sleep cannot "make up for" lost sleep; on the contrary, it probably disrupts behavior even more. Students commonly rearrange their sleep cycles, but this only means that a lot of students are less efficient than they could be. It's a toss-up whether you should lose sleep to study for the next day's exam, for example; you gain some new knowledge but become less efficient in using all of your knowledge (Goleman, 1982).

The phenomenon of **jet lag,** a cluster of symptoms that make world travelers uncomfortable and disoriented, results from disruption of circadian cycles. Jet lag actually has nothing to do with jet planes; they are just a way of putting you quickly into a new time zone. The problems ensue when you try to sleep and live by the new clock time (McFarland, 1975). The body's circadian cycles typically require a day to begin sorting themselves out, and up to two weeks to adapt completely to a several-hour shift. Travelers who use a few weeks before a trip to change their cycles gradually to the new time suffer no jet lag; neither do those who stay on their original time while traveling.

It should now be obvious that the worst thing you can do, in terms of circadian cycles, is to work a rotating shift (several weeks on days, then several on nights). A rotating shift virtually guarantees that employees will be in jet lag indefinitely, because each time they catch up they must change again (Hilts, 1980b). Yet about 27% of workers work on rotating shifts. (One study suggests that careful use of circadian principles may minimize the negative effects of shift work; Czeisler et al.; 1982.) You can also now see the problem with FAA rules for pilots: They specify amount of sleep over days, but say nothing about when that sleep occurs in the 24-hour day or how regular the sleep is (Czeisler et al., 1980). Flight crews often work for many hours then sleep whenever their shift is over. Hence they are almost always in the equivalent of jet lag. Further, they are often trying to fly at times when it is the hardest to stay awake. (Nearly a third of rotating-shift workers in one study reported that they had fallen asleep on the job in the last three months, so it is not surprising that some flight crews do; Rafferty, 1983.)

We will look at ultradian sleep cycles later. But before we leave the topic of biological cycles in general, a cautionary note is in order. The number and variety of biological cycles that *have* been scientifically established should not lead you to accept the currently popular pseudoscience of "biorhythms." ■ Research Controversy: Are "Biorhythms" Science or Pseudoscience?

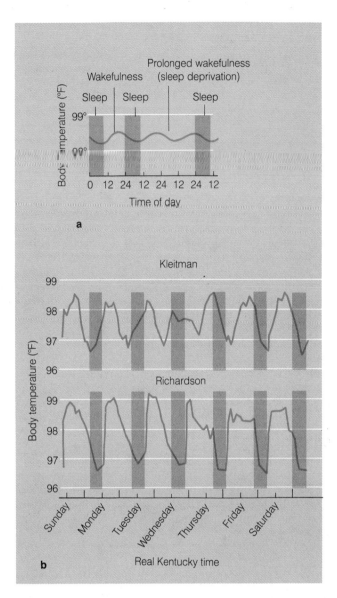

Figure 7.3 ■ Body temperature varies according to a clear circadian cycle. (a) Normally, temperature drops to a minimum in the late night or early morning hours, then peaks in the afternoon. (b) In 1938, two men spent 32 days in Kentucky's Mammoth Cave trying to adapt to a 28-hour-cycle. Richardson's temperature cycles became synchronized with the artificial night periods (marked by the colored bands), but Kleitman's stayed approximately in synchrony with real time outside the cave.

(**a,** reproduced from *Some Must Watch While Some Must Sleep* by William C. Dement by permission of W. W. Norton & Company, Inc. Copyright © 1972, 1974, 1976 by William C. Dement; **b,** adapted from *Sleep and Wakefulness* by N. Kleitman, University of Chicago Press, 1939. Used by permission of the author.)

The What, How, and Why of Sleep

Sleep is so literally an everyday occurrence that we sometimes take it for granted—but we shouldn't. Think about it for a moment as if you were a visitor from another planet, a member of a race that does not sleep. You observe that earthlings rush about for 16 hours or so (usually in the daylight but not always), then stop and lie down for 8 hours. No matter how busy they seem when awake, they spend approximately a third of their lives sleeping; think of how much more they could get done if they didn't sleep. A

RESEARCH CONTROVERSY

Are "biorhythms" science or pseudoscience?

All sciences share key assumptions and procedures. Careful observation of events is used as the basis for proposing hypotheses. These hypotheses are refined into quantifiable predictions and the predictions tested. Repeated support of these predictions strengthens a hypothesis; repeated disconfirmation weakens it. When several independent researchers have replicated and confirmed a hypothesis, it is usually accepted—but remains open to disproof or refinement indefinitely. Claims that fit well into what is already known may be accepted with more limited support than new claims, because they draw some strength from the other known findings. But claims that contradict other established results require exceptionally strong demonstrations before they will be scientifically accepted.

Pseudosciences imitate this scientific procedure without any of the underlying rigor (M. Gardner, 1981; Hanen et al., 1980). Pseudosciences often refer to "data" or "experimental findings," but many of these data do not actually exist, and other experiments are so poorly done that they can-

not be replicated and thus are useless (Radner & Radner, 1982).

Scientists have found evidence for a wide range of animal and human biological rhythms (Aschoff, 1981). But the biorhythm calculators sold in department stores, the daily columns in some newspapers, and the computer printouts available from vending machines are pure nonsense (Bainbridge, 1978). Why are biorhythms considered pseudoscientific when many other biological rhythms are accepted? There are several reasons. First, the idea of biorhythms is based on a series of unlikely and unsupported assumptions (Palmer, 1982): three *identical* cycles, of *precise* length, that begin *exactly* at birth, exist for *all* people and *influence their lives*. Each of the italicized points is highly questionable. No other known biological cycles are exact, or even near the precision required by biorhythms; a few *minutes'* variation in one of the cycles would make the biorhythm calculations useless, yet another cycle of similar length, the menstrual cycle, varies by many days among individual women. And there is no obvious biological reason why cycles should begin at birth (even apart from the problem of specifying which event in the birth process is the exact zero time).

But these objections pale beside the key one: Does it work? If these apparently shaky assumptions led to verifiable conclusions, we might be forced to look more closely. But careful attempts by outsiders to replicate the claims that biorhythms influence life events have failed (Hines, 1979). And when the claimants are asked to produce the original data and calculations for the theory, the data always seem to have been conveniently lost or destroyed (Palmer, 1982).

The popular appeal of biorhythms seems to lie in its oversimplified predictions for daily life, a kind of automated fortune teller or astrologer. The suggestions offered by newspaper biorhythm columns—"pace yourself; watch that temper; ponder choices carefully"— may be reasonable advice, but they clearly need not have anything to do with biological cycles.

The trappings of science do not a science make. And precise calculations of nonsense, by however powerful a computer, yield only printouts of nonsense (Helmers, 1979). Before you are taken in by biorhythms or any other pseudoscience, ask some hard questions about the logic and experimental support behind the proposal.

---

very peculiar behavior, you would note; there must be powerful reasons for their doing so.

And well there must be; but at the moment, human scientists can't tell you just what they are (Johnson, 1973; Pekkanen, 1982). Sleep may represent a kind of evolved safety mechanism, a way of keeping a diurnal species quiet in the dark so it doesn't stumble around and get into trouble. Or it may serve other, more subtle processes—or both. And it follows that if we don't know just what sleep does, then we can't explain the dramatic events within it that we call dreams (Webb & Cartwright, 1978).

Sleep researchers have only begun the process of solving this complex problem. So far, they have been concentrating on *what* happens in sleep and dreams, and now also know something of *how* it happens physiologically. But they are a long way from explaining *why*.

Observing a Night's Sleep One of the first tasks in exploring sleep is to develop a good description of a single night's sleep. Then you can seek a more general description of sleep as a process. Imagine that you are observing a sleeper and trying to find out what you can from the three measures of consciousness: physiological measures, the subject's verbal reports, and observation of overt behavior.

In arranging the situation, you first give the sleeper a comfortable bed and yourself a window overlooking it. Then you hook up at least three basic physiological measures: an EEG, an EOG, and an EMG (Orem & Barnes, 1980). Each of these is an electrical measure that is written out as a kind of graph (or "gram"), so that the E and G of each abbreviation stand for "electro . . . gram." The **EEG** is an **electro-encephalogram** (encephalo- means "head"); it is usually called simply a brainwave. The **EOG** is an **elec-**

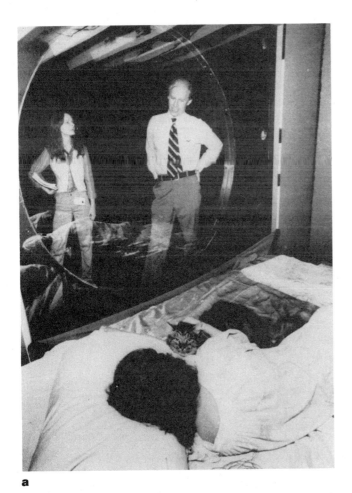

a　　　　　　　　　　　　　　**b**

Figure 7.4 ■ Observing a sleeper in the laboratory. (a) Electrodes are placed on the head and face for EEG, EMG, and EOG; other devices are used to measure breathing and heart beat. In the next room, this information is processed, displayed, and stored for future analysis. (b) The major form of display is a series of ink lines traced on a moving paper strip by a polygraph.

(UPI· photo)

trooculogram (oculo- means "eye"); it measures eye movements. The **EMG** is an **electromyogram** (myo- means "muscle"); it measures body muscle activity.

Figure 7.4

■　For experiental reports, you will wake the sleeper at different times and ask "What were you just doing?" Such wakings tend to interrupt sleep patterns, so it would actually take a number of nights' observations, with wakings at different points, to build up your data. But we will imagine that you can collect all of your data in one night.

Your sleeper lies down and closes his eyes. His waking EEG pattern of rapid, jumbled, small-amplitude waves begins to smooth out and slow down. His eyes· begin to drift around slowly and his body relaxes. If you question him now, he may not know whether he had just been asleep or not, so the experi-

ence of going to sleep seems to be a gradual one. This drifting transition state is called the **hypnogogic period:** the comparable transition from sleep back to waking is called the **hypnopompic period.** Both of these periods are altered states, ones in which people may have dreamlike imagery and in which they seem very suggestible. Emile Coué, a 19th-century French physician, chose these times as the times when people should tell themselves what they wanted to do or to be. They were to begin with Coué's famous general suggestion, "Every day, in every way, I'm getting better and better," then go on to specific suggestions concerning their particular problems.

As your sleeper drifts further asleep, you note a startling effect in his EOG traces: His eyes are drifting independently of each other, pointing first this way then that, in apparently random patterns (D. B. Co-

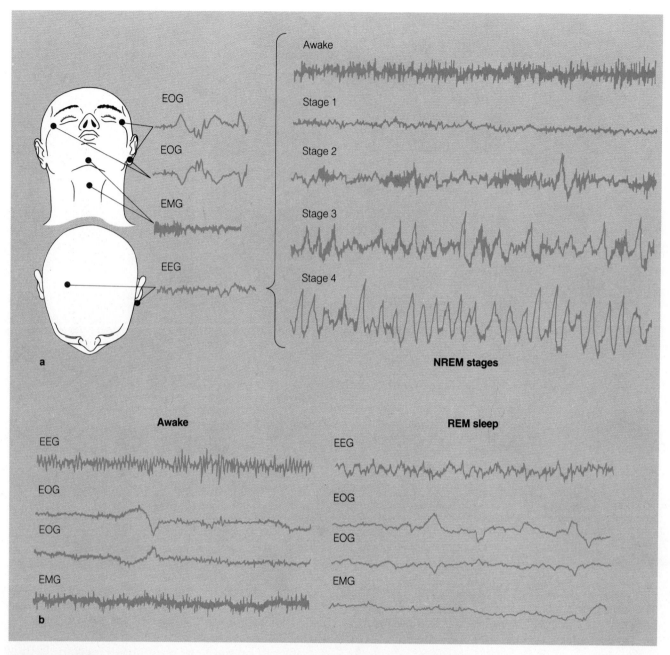

Figure 7.5 ■ Comparison of physiological measures for different types of sleep. (a) The NREM stages are represented in typical order of appearance; in reality each one gradually blends into the next. (b) REM is in some ways similar to waking but in others quite different; the EEG is more similar to waking than to that of any NREM stage and REMs are present, but the body muscles are deeply inhibited.

(a reproduced from *Some Must Watch While Some Must Sleep* by William C. Dement by permission of W. W. Norton & Company, Inc. Copyright © 1972, 1974, 1976 by William C. Dement.)

hen, 1979; Jacobs et al., 1971). His EEG shows that his brainwaves are becoming more synchronized, slower, and larger in amplitude, and special patterns are beginning to appear. Muscularly, he continues to relax. If you awaken him now, he may report casual quiet thoughts, much like what we call daydreaming: "I was thinking that tomorrow I'm going to. . . ." After per-

haps 45 minutes, you notice that the EEG is speeding up, becoming less synchronized, apparently reversing its course back toward waking. At this rate, by 90 minutes it seems like he'll be awake again. ■ Figure 7.5

After observing these changes, early researchers decided to break them down into four arbitrarily defined stages. Based on the common idea that we sink

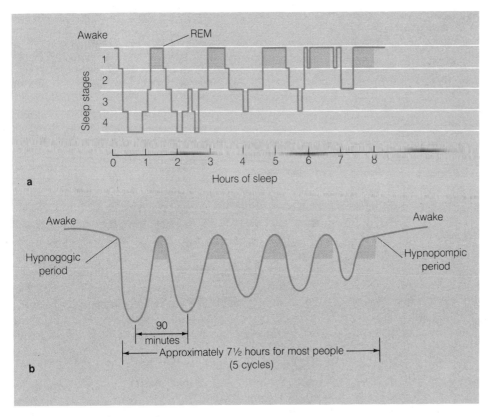

Figure 7.6 ■ Representations of a single night's sleep (for a young adult subject). (a) An actual pattern of sleep from one subject; changes from stage to stage seem abrupt because the EEG records must be scored either 1, 2, 3, or 4. (b) An idealized curve based on (a). The cycles of sleep become shallower as the night progresses, with the last REM period blending into waking. The hypnogogic and hypnopompic periods are transition zones in which the subject is neither fully awake nor quite asleep.

down into sleep, these **sleep stages** are numbered from 1 to 4, starting from waking, and are diagrammed as going down on the page (Rechtschaffen & Kales, 1968). ■ Figure 7.6

Your sleeper has thus gone from waking, through the hypnogogic state, and down through Stages 1, 2, 3, and 4. (The hypnogogic period is sometimes said to include all of this descending Stage 1; Schachter, 1976.) Now he is going back up through Stages 4, 3, and 2. Suddenly, as he reaches what was originally called "ascending Stage 1," new and dramatic changes occur. At first you think he has been jolted awake. His EEG goes to a rapid, small-amplitude, desynchronized wave like that of alert waking, and his eyes lock together again and dart about. His breathing and pulse both increase. You rush to the window overlooking his bed to see what has awakened him.

But he lies immobile, more quietly than before (Hobson et al., 1978). Far from being awake, he is strongly asleep; he will be as hard to awaken as if he were deep in Stage 4. If you look closely you can even see his eyes jerking about, but his lids are closed, and

if you lift one he sees nothing. You may also notice that he has a penile erection, and wonder if this strange activity has some sexual basis. These reactions seem so contradictory that you might even name this stage "paradoxical sleep" as early researchers did. Or you might simply label it after one of its most notable characteristics: **REM sleep,** for "rapid eye movements," letting all the rest of the stages be **NREM sleep,** for "non-REM" (Dement & Kleitman, 1957).

From the evidence of the EEG, EOG, and erection, your sleeper's central nervous system is substantially aroused; "inside," he is active and alert. But he is not receiving inputs from his senses; his eyes track imaginary objects, not real ones. And he is muscularly paralyzed, lest he try to carry out in fact what he thinks he is doing (Chase, 1981). If you succeed in waking the sleeper from this REM sleep, he will typically (about 80% of the time) report that he was dreaming (Dement, 1978). This is not the relaxed, casual daydreaming reports of other stages, but colorful, hallucinatory dreaming. He reports not that "I was thinking about . . . " but that "I was doing. . . . "

Surprisingly, the dream *content* he reports is likely to be quite ordinary; not the wonderful or horrifying dreams we sometimes remember, but routine activities with people he knows, and probably without sexual content. The erection, it seems, is simply a marker of autonomic nervous system arousal, not an indicator of sexual dreams. (A sleeping woman also shows evidence of apparent sexual arousal, although this is more difficult to observe; Asher, 1978.)

In perhaps 10 minutes, the REM period ends. The sleeper's breathing changes audibly, and he moves for the first time since REM began. Adjusting himself to a new position, he begins another 90-minute cycle. If you watch for the rest of the night, you may notice that this is also when he looks at the clock or goes to the bathroom. The end of REM, especially toward morning, comes close to the waking state; if he is going to awaken it will be at this point. This is also the time he may think briefly about the dream he has just had. If so, he may remember a bit of it in the morning, having dragged the memory into the edge of waking consciousness.

The sleeper finally awakens after about five cycles, with little or no memory of all the activity you watched. "Dream? I never dream," he may say, "I slept like a log." His only conscious memories may be of his thoughts as he entered the hypnogogic period and then of waking up, as if those 7-1/2 hours in between, including an hour or so of dreaming, had never existed.

As you drag yourself out of the lab with an armload of EEG, EOG, and EMG records, you may wonder—just as sleep researchers have wondered—"Just what is sleep?" "How does it work?" And most importantly, "Why do we sleep?"

What Is Sleep?   Sleep is a nearly universal behavior of animals. Even fish sleep, though they don't close their eyes, and the sleeping patterns of most mammals are quite similar to ours. In the absence of a human sleeper to observe, a pet or a zoo animal will do nicely as a subject. The REMs and the lack of body movement, except for occasional twitches that get through the muscular inhibition, are quite visible. Professional sleep researchers often use cats as sleep subjects because physiological measures of their sleep are nearly indistinguishable from those of humans.

Cats cannot tell us in words what they experience in dreams, but an ingenious research study has told us in another way. Cats with damage to the part of the brain stem that inhibits body movement during REM act out their dreams in full-fledged behavior (Morrison, 1983). They typically groom themselves, then get up and chase a mouse, but do both in a way that

shows they are actually dreaming. While grooming, they will ignore something stuck to them, for example, and while chasing the dream mice will ignore real ones. Further evidence relating this to REM sleep comes from the finding that REM-suppressing drugs stop these behaviors (Dixon, 1980).

Each day, people cycle through three major daily states of consciousness: usually about 16 hours waking, then about 8 hours alternating between NREM and REM sleep (roughly equivalent to "sleeping" and "dreaming"). There are clear differences between these states in all three languages: we experience them as different, their physiology is different, and our behavior in each state is different (Snyder & Scott, 1972). But for most of us, the experiences are the most interesting.

Psychologists believe that some kind of thought process continues 24 hours a day. It probably requires a complete cessation of organized neural activity in the cerebral cortex to eliminate all experiencing (as can result, for example, from epileptic attack, electroshock to the brain, or deep hypothermia.) Yet approximately a third of our lives is cut off from our waking experience, memory, and understanding, except for occasional fragmentary glimpses. What makes us unaware of each night's experiences is our inability to remember them because of what we may call a *memory barrier*. If you want to know last night's dreams, the memory barrier may seem unnecessary, but a little thought will show that it has probably evolved for our protection.

It is largely the continuity of remembered experience that makes you who you are and that allows you to operate in the world. You keep your social life organized by remembering who your friends are, when you last saw them, and what plans you made together. You survive and prosper to the extent that you avoid previously experienced dangers and seek out previously experienced opportunities. But if dream memories were not normally excluded, your life could be completely disrupted; you could *never* be sure of what you had really done and what you had only hallucinated.

It is probably a weakening of this memory barrier that accounts for one problem touched on earlier in the chapter: "pseudoinsomnia" patients report sleeping only a few hours when their physiology shows a normal eight hours (Mitler et al., 1975). It seems likely that they simply remember the thoughts they had while they were asleep, whereas the rest of us forget them.

This memory barrier has also led to some of the common misunderstandings of sleep and dreams. Most people think sleep is unconscious in the sense of being mentally inactive, but it is not. Many people

Exploring your own dreams

Although scientists are only beginning to understand how dreaming works, you can use what they have already discovered to learn about and control your own dreams.

Most people who wish to know more about their dreams begin with a dream diary; they place a pad, a pencil, and a light beside their bed at night, and tell themselves as they go to sleep that they want to record their dreams (Cartwright, 1977). The intent to write out their dreams seems to act as a hypnogogic-period suggestion, and some people will wake up at the end of a REM period and do so. This might be interesting if it works for you, but the next question is what your reported dreams mean. There may be some hidden message in them, as Freud suggested (Table 7.1, below), but if so no one can be sure what it is.

One of the most powerful criticisms of attempts to interpret the disguised meaning of dreams is that we lack objective criteria for assessing the interpretations. There is simply no way to determine objectively whether *any* particular interpretation is correct—or even whether it is better than other interpretations. Thus, when two dream analysts disagree, there is no way to tell if either is correct. Because no one can prove them wrong, many people confi-

dently offer dream interpretations; any newsstand has such books. But these are all pseudoscience at best. They may be fun to read, but don't depend on what they say.

The content of dreams does seem to be influenced by the preceding day's events—what Freud called *day residue*—perhaps because that is what most people think about as they go to sleep. Something you think about as you enter the hypnogogic period may continue to be the topic of both your NREM thoughts and your REM dreams. Some people claim that they can control the content of their dreams this way, by concentrating on some topic as they go to sleep. This may be possible, although there is as yet little evidence to support it.

Some creative people have even claimed to have solved difficult problems during sleep (Ghiselin, 1952). Some say they simply awakened in the morning with the solution; for others, the solution occurred in the course of a vivid dream and was remembered in those terms. Because we know that the evening's problem may be thought about, then hallucinated about, over and over during the night, these claims don't seem impossible. Unfortunately, researchers have found little evidence of any general ability to solve problems during sleep; if this is indeed possible, few of us know how to use it effectively (Cartwright, 1974).

One of the most interesting kinds

of dreams are **lucid dreams,** ones in which you *know* that you are dreaming. One psychologist reported a lucid dream in which he thought he was asleep and dreaming, but wasn't certain. Being a researcher, he set up an experiment to test his hypothesis, "If I'm dreaming, I can fly," he said, and suiting action to words, he lifted his legs and took off (Hilgard et al., 1975a). Researchers are now beginning to investigate lucid dreaming systematically. One of their hopes is to be able to teach subjects how to both have lucid dreams and report that they know they are dreaming; early reports suggest that some people may be able to do so (Galvin, 1982).

It may even be possible to combine several of these effects. You might be able to choose the topic for a lucid dream and then write it down afterwards, or at least wake up enough to be able to remember it the next morning. I once had an experience approaching this. I had lectured to two groups about sleep, and then had talked with participants about how much detail and color were included in dreams. That night I found myself in a lucid dream in which I marveled to myself; "Look at that detail! Look at that color!" And obviously I remembered it, though I no doubt have lost many details. (Roger Shepard, 1983, a psychologist whose work on visual imagery we discuss in Chapter 11, has reported a similar experience.)

think dreams are rare or brief, but subjects' dream reports suggest that dreams occur each 90 minutes of sleep and last many minutes. Most people think of dreams as vague and hazy, maybe even in black and white, as they are often portrayed in films and on television, but they are frequently reported to be detailed, concrete, and in color. (At least they are if you have ever seen color. Color blind people dream in the colors they see when awake; congenitally blind people dream in the senses they know, especially sound and touch.) But people also think that dreams are wild and exotic in content, and here the reality is less exciting; most dream reports concern ordinary activities, in the

same settings and with the same people as in everyday life (Hall & Van de Castle, 1966).

You can see how a memory barrier might account for the differences between what subjects in the lab report when they are awakened and what people believe about dreams. Forgetting detail could make dreams seem hazy and colorless, and forgetting most of the action could make them seem brief. It's even reasonable that if any dream were remembered, it would be the rare one that *is* wild or exotic. But there are some ways that people are attempting to find out more about their dreams. ■ Personal Application: Exploring Your Own Dreams

How Does Sleep Happen? There are two useful ways to describe how sleep happens. One is to look at *who* sleeps *how much* at different stages of life. The other is to look at what little is known of the neurological mechanisms that control sleep.

Cycles of sleeping and waking begin before birth. The relative amount of time the fetus spends in REM and NREM sleep is not well established, but the trend from birth to adulthood is clear (Roffwarg et al., 1966). A newborn spends 16 hours a day sleeping, 50% of it in REM sleep. This gradually tapers down to the adult average of about 20% REM of a total of about 7 hours. (The range of variations in adult sleep is about 8 ± 4, or about 4 to 12 hours.) As adults grow older they sleep fewer and fewer hours, apparently as a natural part of the sleep changes of a lifetime. In our culture, however, one of the myths about sleep is that you need 8 hours to stay healthy. Many older people fret about their lost sleep and may take heavy doses of drugs in an attempt to get the "normal" 8 hours, rather than sleeping only as much as they need to. ■ Figure 7.7

There are several mechanisms known to be responsible for parts of the sleep process, and almost certainly others not yet known. One important mechanism is the reticular activating system (RAS), a kind of consciousness switch (Chapter 2). As you lie down, close your eyes, and perhaps count sheep, you are deliberately moving toward minimal and monotonous sensory input, allowing the RAS to lower your alertness toward sleep. Any sudden noise wakes you up from this drift into the hypnogogic period by alerting the RAS and thus the rest of your brain. Other systems in the brainstem come into play to cross you over from "drowsy" to "asleep," and to lock you into the regular 90-minute sleeping cycles. At least one other mechanism, and perhaps more, comes into play with REM sleep. It is as if the RAS is driven back to active waking, while sensory input is blocked, body motor control is blocked, and hallucinated action is created.

Researchers are exploring the chemistry of sleep as well as its neurology. Some aberrations of sleep patterns, for example, are apparently related to problems of metabolism of serotonin, one of the body's major neurotransmitters (Jacobs, 1976). Researchers have even isolated a *sleep factor*, a chemical that can be taken from one sleeping animal and used to put another one to sleep (Pappenheimer, 1976). Recently, a similar sleep factor was identified in humans; if it could be manufactured, it might offer a natural sleeping drug without side effects (Maugh, 1982b).

Existing drugs interact with the chemistry of sleep in several ways. Many drugs, including both alcohol and various hypnotics or "sleeping pills," suppress REM sleep; hence, heavy drinking or reliance on barbiturates allows NREM but suppresses REM. It is ironic that drugs prescribed to make patients sleep have this effect because, of the two types of sleep, the body seems to need REM the most.

As we've already noted, if subjects (whether cats or people) are deprived of all sleep for a period of days, they become increasingly sleepy and eventually go to sleep standing up. But further investigation seems to show that the body has a specific need for REM sleep. In **REM-deprivation** studies, subjects are allowed to obtain NREM sleep but are awakened each time they reach REM. After a while they go directly to REM when they go to sleep, and it becomes increasingly difficult to keep them from it. If they are then allowed to sleep freely, they REM heavily for much longer than usual as if they were making up for the lost REM; this phenomenon is called **REM rebound.**

Because alcohol and other drugs suppress REM sleep, people who stop taking them may also experience a form of REM rebound. *Delirium tremens* (the DTs), a kind of hallucinatory episode combined with emotional arousal that can afflict long-term alcoholics after a day or so without alcohol, is now thought to be extreme REM rebound, a kind of waking nightmare. Patients who habitually use barbiturates for a long period of time may also experience horrible REM rebound nightmares when they try to reduce their dependency on the drug (Mitler et al., 1975).

It is also tempting to see schizophrenic hallucinations as the REM process "breaking through" into waking, as delirium tremens seems to be, but such suggestions for now remain largely speculative (Dement, 1968–1969). Perhaps if we really understood why anyone needs NREM *or* REM sleep, we would be better able to judge such speculations.

Why Do We Sleep? In asking why anyone sleeps, we encounter another paradox. The need for sleep that we show when sleep-deprived, and especially when REM-deprived, suggests that sleep *is required* (D. B. Cohen, 1979). But some people get along for long periods with relatively little sleep, suggesting that sleep is *not* truly necessary. How can this be? If biological mechanisms for NREM and REM sleep have evolved as part of our species' heritage, then the presence of such mechanisms is what requires sleep. If one person's mechanisms require 12 hours and another's require only 4 hours, then both are biological demands that must be met. Thus, the first person might become cranky and irritable on a regular 11 hours, but the second might feel the same effects from getting 3 hours of sleep. (Note that the need for sleep is clearly a biological one; in one well-controlled study, sleep-deprived rats developed numerous physical ailments, some of which were fatal; Rechtschaffen et al., 1983.)

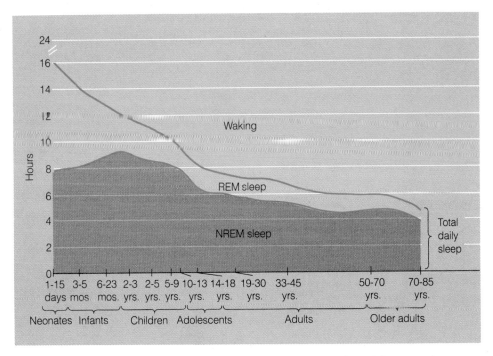

Figure 7.7 ■ The total amount of sleep and REM sleep decreases substantially as people age, and NREM sleep decreases somewhat.

(From "Ontogenetic Development of Human Sleep-Dream Cycle" by H. P. Roffwarg et al., *Science*, 1966, *152*, 604–609. Copyright 1966 by the American Association for the Advancement of Science. Used by permission.)

The traditional view is that sleep is a time for rest and repair, to recover from the events of the day. There is some support for this *restoration* view; sleep time increases following exercise, for example (Shapiro et al., 1981). But many researchers question whether restoration is the central reason for sleep (Drucker-Colin et al., 1979; Hartman, 1973). Cell repair, for example, goes on 24 hours a day, even though it reaches a peak at night. And other activity certainly goes on in sleep besides rest. NREM sleep may be restful, but REM sleep is clearly not; it is an active state that probably burns up substantial energy. If rest were the primary reason for a night's sleep, it would seem better to spend a few hours in NREM and then get up—or even simply to sit and rest for a few hours. Why have this repeated and lengthy cycle through both deep stages and active hallucinations?

One possibility is what can be called a hibernation theory. In the winter, a number of mammals enter a specialized form of long-term sleep called **hibernation.** During hibernation, the sleeping animal (a squirrel or bear, for example) wakes only infrequently—days or weeks apart—from a sleep so deep that all its body's metabolic processes are slowed dramatically (Rogers, 1981). The hibernation theory suggests that the elaborate mechanisms of sleep have evolved solely to keep us quiet in the dark. Animals hibernate to conserve energy and to remain out of trouble during the winter months. And both nocturnal and diurnal animals sleep for much the same purpose: to stay quiet and conserve energy during the period of time for which they are not well adapted. (The cones in our foveas that give us our precision daylight vision also make us nearly blind on a dark night.) It is, however, millions of years too late to observe the development of sleep, so this hypothesis is not easy to support or disprove. ■ Figure 7.8

And why have REM sleep? Researchers have proposed a number of possibilities. One suggests that REM maintains an activity level or tonus of the cerebral cortex (Ephron & Carrington, 1966). Another suggests that REM periods maintain the synchronization of our eyes. After an hour of random drifting in NREM an awakened sleeper's eyes are not well coordinated, but after a period of REM the eyes seem to have become resynchronized (Berger, 1969). Other theorists have suggested that REM is related to the sorting and storing of memories, particularly emotional memories (Chernik, 1972; Dewan, 1969). Again, this idea may have some merit, but raises some questions. Why, for example, does an infant spend more time in REM than an adult? One suggestion is that the large amount of REM in young organisms reflects the rapid growth rate of their brains (Roffwarg et al., 1966). According to this

Figure 7.8 ■ Animals in hibernation such as this dormouse, do not wake up even when handled. Some theorists argue that sleep serves a purpose similar to hibernation: to keep us quiet and using relatively little energy during a time when we are inefficient.

(Kim Taylor/Bruce Coleman, Inc.)

Table 7.1 ■ Freudian Dream Interpretation

Dream Concept	Dream Elements That Are Thought to Symbolize the Concept
Parents	Emperors, empresses, kings, queens
Children (brothers and sisters)	Small animals
Birth	Water
Death	Journey
Nakedness	Clothes, uniforms
Male genitals	Sticks, umbrellas, poles, trees, anything elongated, pointed weapons of all sorts
Erection	Balloons, airplanes, zeppelins, dreamer himself flying
Male sexual symbols	Reptiles, fishes, serpent, hand or foot
Female genitalia	Pits, hollow caves, jars, bottles, doors, ships, chests
Breasts	Apples, peaches, other fruit
Intercourse	Mounting a ladder or stairs, entering a room, walking down a hall or into a tunnel, horseback riding, and so forth.

Reprinted by permission from *Introduction to Psychology*, 3rd ed., by Dennis Coon. Copyright © 1983 by West Publishing Company. All rights reserved.

idea, these periods of active arousal and eye movement help develop mechanisms that will be needed later. The decrease of REM with age through childhood might then reflect the slowing growth rate of the brain. (Note that more than one of these proposals could be true; perhaps eye coordination or emotional memory storage are aided in adults after REM has already served its growth function.)

Another approach to REM sleep is to ask not about its mechanisms, but about possible functions of dream *content*. Freud (1900) suggested that dreams function to protect sleep by disguising aggressive or sexual thoughts that would otherwise awaken the sleeper. The apparent meaning of a dream, to Freud, was its "manifest content," but the dream's real meaning, called its **latent content,** was hidden through various processes. ■ Table 7.1

Freud's views of dreams have become widely known, but they have also been extensively criticized. Some dreams may indeed have hidden meanings for the human dreamer, but such explanations cannot explain REM in other species. If dreams do serve an interpretive function similar to what Freud described, their function must be an adaptation recently added to more basic physiological reasons that we share with other species (McCarley & Hobson, 1977).

One theory that attempts to address both the physiology of REM and the content of dreams is the **activation-synthesis** model (Hobson & McCarley, 1977). It suggests that the mechanisms of activation are basic

evolved ones that serve one or more physiological functions. But the synthesis of the cerebral activity into the content of dreams simply reflects our attempts to make sense of the activation (McDonald, 1981).

Sleep Problems

Sleep involves several separate mechanisms, and these can go wrong in various ways; sleep complaints are said to be the single most common symptom reported to physicians. Although many of these sleep problems afflict large numbers of people, their very existence has only recently been discovered and their cures remain unknown (Mendelson et al., 1977).

Approximately 30% of the population suffers from some form of **insomnia** (not being able to sleep). But there are also many **dysomnias** or abnormal patterns of sleep. A number of dysomnias occur in NREM sleep, the most common of which are sleepwalking and sleeptalking; they occur primarily in Stage 4, but why or how remains poorly understood (Mitler et al., 1975). Other common problems of NREM include bed wetting and teeth grinding, but the most disturbing are "night terrors," occasions when young children will scream as if in a nightmare. Often the parents will shake the child awake, only to find that he or she does not remember anything. Parents are now advised to ignore night terrors; children seem to grow out of

'IF IT WANTS TO DREAM, WE COULD GIVE IT SOME VAGUE, UNSTRUCTURED PROBLEM TO MULL OVER DURING THE NIGHT.'

© 1983 by Sidney Harris

them, and the experience itself is apparently not remembered, although being shaken awake by a frightened parent is.

One comparatively minor (but distressing) problem that seems to be related to REM mechanisms is sleep-onset paralysis, reported by perhaps 5% of the population. For someone with this problem, sinking into the hypnogogic period seems to activate the REM paralysis mechanism, almost as if this were the end of a previous REM period—but the person remains awake enough to sense the paralysis. The experience can be quite frightening; it often causes the person to jolt back awake, only to start all over again. Again, sufferers are advised to ignore the sensation as a harmless part of their personal sleep sequence.

Two more serious REM-related problems are narcolepsy and sleep apnea. **Narcolepsy** is a condition in which people suffer from sudden-onset sleep attacks; as many as 200,000 people in the United States may suffer from some degree of narcolepsy, many of them without realizing it. In the mildest forms, narcoleptics may simply "go blank" for a brief period and then continue as if nothing had happened, almost as if some switch mechanism for sleep had been briefly activated. Children with this degree of narcolepsy are often labeled inattentive and accused of daydreaming, but their problem is apparently a physiological one beyond their control. In more severe cases, narcoleptics actually fall asleep during the day, regardless of how well rested they are and often at inappropriate times and

places. In extreme cases of narcolepsy, the sleep attack is sudden and includes the full paralysis of REM; the sufferer goes directly from an active, often emotionally aroused state to a state of physical collapse, or **cataplexy.** Cataplexic attacks have occurred to people having sexual intercourse and to fire fighters climbing ladders.

The causes of narcolepsy are unknown, so you should not be surprised that the cure is unknown as well. (Some drugs are helpful, but these have undesirable side effects.) Some dogs also show inherited narcoleptic symptoms, however; researchers at Stanford University hope to use these dogs to study narcolepsy and to seek cures (Mitler et al., 1974). (They have found, for example, that these dogs show significantly lower levels of the neurotransmitter dopamine than do normal dogs; Mefford et al., 1983.) In the meantime, the dogs' very existence helps comfort many narcoleptics, who had been told for years that their problems must be psychological. ■ Figure 7.9

In **sleep apnea,** the sleeper ceases to breathe, seemingly as an aberration of REM muscular inhibition. Sleep apnea was first noted in the 1970s, in a middle-aged male who had complained of daytime tiredness and snoring that bothered his wife (Guilleminault et al., 1973). Researchers observing his sleep were astounded to see him stop breathing for several minutes; the resulting lack of oxygen and build-up of carbon dioxide then triggered deep reflexes and awakened him. He gasped back from the brink of death (causing the noises his spouse had considered snores), then slipped back to sleep—and stopped breathing again. He did this over 500 times per night. (Such "snores" have since been found to be so characteristic that tape recordings of them may be useful in diagnosing sleep apnea.) ■ Figure 7.10

Other sleep apnea patients were soon found, and the researchers then realized that the middle-aged patients they were seeing were the *survivors;* they had enlarged lungs and damaged hearts but were alive. It quickly became apparent that sleep apnea was a major cause of sudden infant death syndrome, or **SIDS** (unexplained sudden death of otherwise healthy infants, commonly called crib death) (Guilleminault et al., 1975). Research since has focused on what causes apnea in these infants and on how to spot potential cases early enough to prevent SIDS (Naeye, 1980). Genetic factors seem to be involved; new children in a family that has had one SIDS death seem much more likely to suffer from sleep disorders, including apnea (Harper et al., 1981). But environmental factors such as diet, cold viruses, or even minor food poisoning may also be involved (Simpson, 1980). Not all children with sleep apnea become adult victims, however. Many normal children show brief periods of apnea with no apparent

Figure 7.9 ■ Danielle, one of Stanford's narcoleptic dogs, shows the effects of a cataplexy attack: While barking excitedly, she slumps to the ground, eyes open but paralyzed. If the reason for her excitement is still present when she recovers, she may do the same thing again.

(Christopher Springmann/SFO)

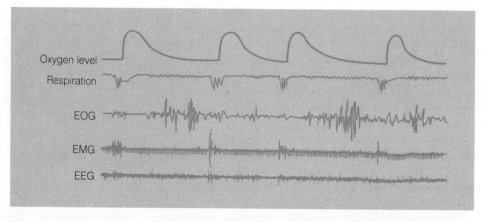

Figure 7.10 ■ Six minutes of records from a sleep apnea patient. Downward marks on the respiration trace indicate the chest movements of breathing. This sample is from a REM period; the eye movements (of one eye) can be seen in the EOG trace. The bursts of activity on the EMG trace show that the patient actually wakes up at about 90-second intervals, takes three quick breaths (shown by the respiration lines), and goes back to sleep. The breaths raise his oxygen level to near-normal, but as soon as he goes back to sleep the oxygen level falls sharply until it forces him to awaken again.

(Reproduced from *Some Must Watch While Some Must Sleep* by William C. Dement by permission of W. W. Norton & Company, Inc. Copyright © 1972, 1974, 1976 by William C. Dement.)

ill effects. Even those with severe cases, who are electronically monitored around the clock, often grow out of it.

The search continues for both cause and cure of sleep apnea. In the meantime, adults who suffer from it and who don't know it are at risk from a surprising source. People who complain of poor sleep are often given sleeping pills, which are typically nervous-system depressants. These pills could so depress the reflexes of a sleep apnea patient as to prove fatal—as could nonprescription depressants such as alcohol (Herbert, 1982b; Maugh, 1981c).

Now that researchers have developed some knowledge of sleep problems, people with sleep difficulties can be more effectively helped. But if patients are to receive effective treatment without being put at further risk, more information is obviously needed on how and why sleep happens.

HYPNOSIS AND MEDITATION

Techniques of consciousness alteration that could be called hypnotic or meditational have been developed independently in many cultures; something about the human nervous system seems to respond to certain ways of behaving with regular changes in consciousness. Both hypnosis and meditation are, at present, tricky to define and nearly impossible to explain. But the evidence is clear that both represent real phenomena that can have powerful effects on people.

Hypnosis

Hypnosis in particular is so elusive a phenomenon, when it is sought scientifically, that several well-known explorers of mind and behavior have given up on it—but others have taken it up again (Hilgard, 1971). **Hypnosis** is a systematic procedure for altering consciousness, usually carried out by one person (the hypnotist) to alter the consciousness of another (the subject); it is also the state of consciousness caused in the subject by such a procedure (Hilgard, 1975). A typical hypnotic procedure, as used in a research laboratory, begins with an *induction*, 10 or 15 minutes of verbal suggestions designed to create a passive, sleep-like (but waking) state. The resulting state of consciousness is then measured by a series of specific tasks drawn from the kinds of things that hypnotized subjects have been said to do. The number of tasks completed in a "hypnotic" way measures the subject's **susceptibility,** or responsiveness to hypnosis. ■ Table 7.2

Basic hypnosis measurement scales such as the one in Table 7.2 are heavily weighted with ideomotor ("thought-movement") tasks: The hypnotist has the subject extend an arm, for example, then suggests that it is getting heavy and measures whether the arm drops. A few tasks test other phenomena (Hilgard, 1965) including sensory hallucinations, temporary amnesia, and age regression ("You are now ten years old"). In posthypnotic suggestions, the subject is told that later, at a cue from the hypnotist, he or she will behave in a particular way. One task that implies a relationship between hypnosis and sleep is a "dream" suggestion ("Now go deeper asleep and have a dream about . . . "). The hypnotic state is *not* the same as sleep, by EEG and other criteria, but subjects do report dreamlike imagery and even show eye movements while "dreaming." After about 45 minutes and 12 tasks, the subject is "awakened," posthypnotic suggestions are tested, and the subject is made aware of all that has happened.

Under such experimental conditions, some evidence suggests substantial changes in consciousness,

Table 7.2 ■ Tasks in the Basic Hypnosis Measurement Scale

Item	Criterion of Passing
Postural sway	Falls without forcing
Eye closure	Eyes close without forcing
Hand lowering	Lowers at least 6 inches by end of 10 seconds
Arm immobilization	Arm rises less than 1 inch in 10 seconds
Finger lock	Incomplete separation of fingers at end of 10 seconds
Arm rigidity	Less than 2 inches of arm bending in 10 seconds
Moving hands together	Hands close as 6 inches
Verbal inhibition	Name unspoken in 10 seconds
Hallucination of fly	Any movement, grimacing, acknowledgment of effect
Eye catalepsy	Eyes remain closed at end of 10 seconds
Posthypnotic suggestion	Any partial movement response at signal
Amnesia	Recall of three or fewer items

From *Stanford Hypnotic Susceptibility Scales, Forms A and B*, by A. M. Weitzenhoffer and E. R. Hilgard, Stanford University Press, 1959. Reprinted by permission.

but other evidence suggests little change. Some subjects report feeling relaxed but bored; others seem to reach something like a controlled hypnogogic state, neither normal waking nor sleep, and are powerfully affected by the suggestions. Virtually all subjects remain aware of who and where they are—hypnosis is no more unconscious than is sleep—although some of the more responsive subjects do not remember what they did and may think that only a few minutes have passed. Between the extremes are a wide range of intermediate effects; as with most other consciousness variations, there is no sharp dividing line between "hypnotized" and "nonhypnotized."

Subjects who experience all of the suggested effects are called "high hypnotizables," and those who experience virtually none are "low hypnotizables." "Highs" and "lows" tend to be certain kinds of people, though why they are is little known (Hilgard, 1970). Highs are often humanities majors in college, lows science majors. Highs are often able to lose themselves in individual pursuits, both mental (such as reading) and physical (such as skiing), and lows are more likely to participate in group sports. Some, but not all, highs have been physically beaten as children. Highs may even be slightly genetically predisposed to be highs, but probably must learn how to utilize their potential skills through a variety of life experiences (Morgan et al., 1970).

Research in Hypnosis

The earliest explorations of hypnotic phenomena we would now call neither scientific nor research; the phenomenon wasn't even called hypnosis. It had first been suggested in the 1600s that humans could be "magnetized" like a bar of iron, and that this would improve their health. In the late 1700s, Franz Anton Mesmer began studying "animal magnetism," using a large tub of water with metal filings in it and iron rods sticking out of it (Sarbin, 1962). Curious visitors to his Paris establishment, often well-to-do women, sat around on cushions, touching the iron rods and listening to soothing music as Mesmer, dressed in flowing robes, passed among them. Periodically one would experience a "crisis," a kind of convulsive fit; after recovering, the person often felt better and Mesmer's treatments became popular. Suspicious citizens, however, questioned the activities at Mesmer's and the Royal Commission appointed to investigate denounced Mesmer as a charlatan. Its report included a not-so-subtle suggestion that the crises were sexual ones, encouraged by Mesmer's commanding presence and "magnetic passes" (repeated sweeping motions of the hands near the subject's body). As a result, Mesmer was banished from Paris.

Later researchers who tried to study "mesmerism" faced opposition. One English physician painlessly amputated the leg of a mesmerized patient in 1842, but his report was stricken from the records of the Royal Medical and Chirugical (Surgical) Society. Another English surgeon in India performed over 300 major operations using mesmerism as an analgesic (pain reliever), but the medical journals refused to publish his results.

Mesmerism finally did enter English medical journals, under the name *neurypnology* for "nervous sleep" (later simplified to *hypnology* and then *hypnosis*). It was becoming grudgingly accepted as a possible analgesic, but when nitrous oxide, ether, and chloroform were discovered the interest died down (Davis, 1982).

In the late 19th century, French investigators, most notably Jean Martin Charcot, began studying hypnosis as a treatment for abnormal behavior. When he described it as a phenomenon of the mentally ill, Charcot's work with hypnosis was readily accepted for publication.

In the 1880s, Freud came to France to learn about hypnosis. He used Charcot's methods on his own patients, and much of his early theory was based on this work. But Freud eventually became discouraged at his inability to get reliable results from hypnosis and after about 1900 abandoned the method. In the 1920s and 1930s, Clark Hull, now known for his comprehensive learning theory, attempted to study hypnosis with the first solidly scientific approach (Hull, 1933). Yet he also found it too confusing and elusive and gave up.

Only since the 1950s has hypnosis been subjected to careful, continued, scientific scrutiny. Although many questions remain, the phenomenon continues to be studied as a special kind of consciousness issue, one that may offer insights into other consciousness questions. One of the first and still foremost hypnosis research labs is at Stanford University. E. R. Hilgard, the founder and director, came to the study of hypnosis with a solid research background. Applying this to the questions of hypnosis, he noted that repeatable measurement of any phenomenon is an important first step in bringing it into the field of science; development of measurement scales was thus the lab's first task (Hilgard, 1965). These were then used to study a variety of phenomena.

Hilgard's neodissociation theory, a major product of the Stanford lab, grew out of his work in hypnotic pain relief. A standard laboratory pain technique is used in which subjects' arms are lowered into very cold (0 degrees C) water. As the pain mounts over the next 30 seconds or so, they report its severity at regular intervals. Hypnotized subjects who feel no pain from the cold water, according to their verbal reports, are then asked if some other part of themselves, a **hidden observer,** might know more (Hilgard et al., 1975b). If such a hidden observer is contacted, it frequently reports knowledge of some pain, though the pain is less than for the same subject when not hypnotized (Hilgard, 1978a). ■ Figure 7.11

The implications for a dissociated consciousness are obvious: For a hypnotized subject, the verbal report comes from one part of consciousness, the hidden observer's nonverbal report from another. These separate parts are the basis for neodissociation theory; they may represent consciousness splits in states other than hypnosis as well (Hilgard, 1973). ■ Figure 7.12

Research on practical uses of hypnotic effects has paralleled research on the effects themselves. One major use is the relief of pain for obstetrics, dentistry, or even major surgery (Hilgard & Hilgard, 1975). Physicians have become less enthusiastic about chemical analgesics because they do not work equally well for everyone and are often accompanied by serious side effects and aftereffects. Hypnotic analgesia is at least partially effective for perhaps half of the population (though only a small fraction can use it as the sole analgesic for surgery). Physicians have therefore made increasing use of hypnotic analgesia, either alone or in combination with small amounts of chemicals.

The other major contemporary use of hypnosis is in psychotherapy (Frankel & Zamansky, 1978). Even though Freud gave up on hypnosis, some psychoanalysts and other therapists use it. A newly developing use now making news is as a memory enhancer for witnesses, usually in connection with criminal cases

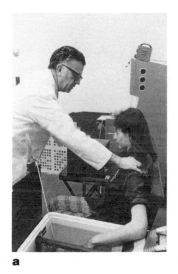

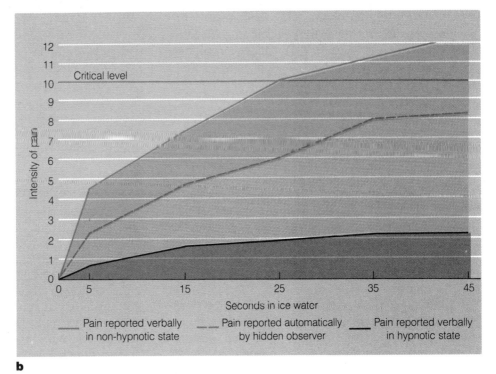

a

b

Figure 7.11 ■ A waking subject finds it very painful to put her hand into the cold water of this laboratory pain test. (a) Under hypnotic analgesia, however, she shows no facial expression of pain and reports little or no pain. (b) Pain reports rise over time in all three conditions, but they show interesting differences. The verbal report by a hypnotized subject rises to only a bit over 2 on the scale. The automatic key-pressing reports of the hidden observer indicate that it senses more pain, but less than the subject's waking report.

(**a,** E. R. Hilgard, Stanford University; **b,** graph from *Human Nature,* January 1978, accompanying the article "Hypnosis and Consciousness" by Ernest R. Hilgard. Copyright © 1978 by Human Nature, Inc. Reprinted by permission of the publisher.)

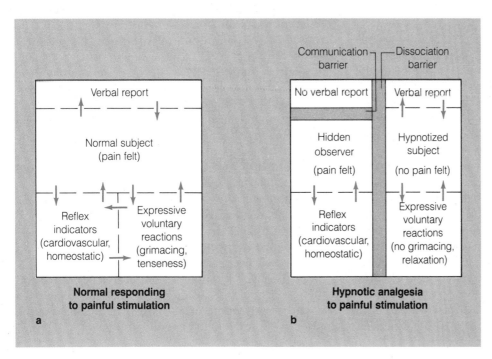

a **Normal responding to painful stimulation**

b **Hypnotic analgesia to painful stimulation**

Figure 7.12 ■ The hidden-observer results interpreted by the neodissociation theory of consciousness. (a) In the waking condition, physiological indicators, facial expression, and verbal reports all represent the same pain. (b) In the hypnotic-analgesia condition, the portion of the person's consciousness that provides verbal reports and facial expressions is cut off from the pain experience by some process represented here as a dissociation barrier. The hidden observer portion of consciousness is aware of the pain, but cannot verbally report it, as represented here by a communication barrier.

(Adapted from E. R. Hilgard, *Perspectives in Biology and Medicine,* Spring 1974, *17,* 301–316. Copyright © 1974 by the University of Chicago Press.)

(Block, 1976). The possibility of accidentally *creating* pseudomemories through the questioning remains strong, however (Hilgard, 1981). Hence, testimony given under hypnosis is usually inadmissible in court (even though nonhypnotic questioning may have a similar effect).

Meditation

Many cultures have developed traditional techniques for **meditation,** a clearing or emptying of the mind through a narrowly focused thought process (Golsman, 1977). Often meditation is part of a complex belief system, sometimes a religious one. A number of meditation techniques have been imported into the United States together with differing degrees of their belief systems.

Many meditation techniques, whatever their origin, share some common elements. Most, for example, use some device to allow the user to focus on nothing. Concentrating on nothing seems an impossible task; it's like telling someone *"Don't* think of an elephant." Meditation techniques get around this by providing a point of focus that is so unimportant or repetitive that it soon becomes essentially a focus on nothing. The meditator may stare at a blank wall, for example, or at a simple object such as a vase. In many cases, the meditator's own breathing is used as the focus.

In a meditation technique called Transcendental Meditation (TM), a special word or phrase called a mantra is used. An individual's mantra supposedly has deep personal meaning and is kept secret, but it probably functions simply as a sound that quickly loses meaning through repetition; it is likely that any word would serve equally well.

Herbert Benson, a researcher at Harvard who has done research on TM (Wallace & Benson, 1972), has been able to isolate the basic requirements for meditation from the religious belief system that surrounds TM. According to Benson (1975), meditation requires: (1) a quiet environment where you won't be interrupted; (2) a mental device on which to focus, such as a word or phrase; (3) a passive attitude, rather than an active striving one; and (4) a comfortable position. Regular use of this simplified meditation, he suggests, encourages a **relaxation response,** which he feels is the triggering of the parasympathetic portion of the autonomic nervous system (Benson et al., 1977; Hoffman et al., 1982). The crises of contemporary urban life may produce stress effects by triggering the sympathetic system's fight-or-flight response (see Chapter 2), he argues, but most people don't know how to rebalance themselves through the parasympathetic. Benson feels that his approach provides this balance.

PSYCHOACTIVE DRUGS

Drugs can also be used to alter consciousness. But where hypnosis and meditation use subjective experience to alter consciousness, drugs directly modify the underlying physiology. Some consciousness-altering drugs are exotic and uncommon, others are used everyday by almost everyone. (To an even greater extent than alcohol, caffeine and nicotine are our culture's drugs of choice; if you have not had a cup of coffee, a Coke, or a cigarette today, you are one of a distinct minority.)

Psychoactive drugs are drugs that cause mental effects (are "active" in the "psyche"); they directly alter the level of activity in one or more brain systems, causing increased or decreased activity in that system (Cooper et al., 1982). Many function by altering neural transmission at all synapses that use a particular neurotransmitter (Julien, 1981). Most such drugs fall into one of four major categories: (1) **depressants** reduce the level of nervous-system activity, (2) **stimulants** increase the level of nervous-system activity, (3) **hallucinogens** alter the perception of reality, and (4) **antipsychotics** relieve some symptoms of mental illness. We will examine some commonly used and abused drugs of the first three categories here; the fourth we will leave to Chapter 16. But first, we will look at some of the long-term effects of drug use that are common to many drugs.

Long-Term Drug Effects

When it receives regular doses of a psychoactive drug, the body adapts, attempting to maintain its physiology as close to its previous state as possible; it does so in different ways and with several consequences. One consequence is a buildup of **tolerance,** a kind of resistance, so that it takes more of the drug to achieve any effect (Mandel, 1973). Regular users of any drug typically require higher doses to feel an effect than nonusers do. (Marijuana is a notable exception.) Adaptation may also lead to **physical dependence,** a condition in which the drug is needed by the body because it has been built into regular body activity. A stimulant drug, for example, may come to be used instead of natural neurotransmitters; a normal level of activation will then depend on the presence of the drug. *Addiction* refers to the state of drug use where the user "must have" the drug; it can imply either physical dependence or **psychological dependence** (or, in many cases, both) (Dole, 1980).

A user who has built up physical dependence and then seeks to stop using the drug will experience **withdrawal** symptoms until the body readjusts to the absence of the drug. In general, withdrawal symptoms are opposite to the effect of the drug itself; withdrawal from a stimulant, for example, leaves the user relatively inactive or depressed. For long-term physical dependence, withdrawal may have to be gradual or the consequences—as with abrupt withdrawal from alcohol—can be fatal.

Other severe consequences, including fatalities, can result from combining drugs; the interactions of two or more drugs, simultaneously or alternated over time, can be very complex. Some drugs show **cross-tolerance,** where building up tolerance for one makes the user also tolerant for the other. But mixing other drugs may cause an effect much greater than a simple addition of their effects would suggest.

Virtually all psychoactive drugs have many effects, often on a number of body systems; the intended goal of a drug is the main effect and all others are **side effects.** But a main effect for one use may be a side effect for another. Unfortunately, physicians sometimes have to give a second drug to combat the side effects of the first one, and so forth. If a single physician carefully monitors the combination this may be acceptable; but frequently multiple drugs are prescribed by several physicians, each unaware of the others, or patients may mix prescription and over-the-counter drugs. In our society this happens all too often, especially to the elderly (R. J. Smith, 1979a).

One often-repeated claim about drug use is that use of a mild drug leads inevitably to use of a more serious one; although this progression frequently happens it does *not* seem to be inevitable. Physiological changes may have an effect; that is, people who develop a tolerance for one drug may move to a stronger one to achieve the desired effect. But a psychological explanation is more likely: People who seek unusual experiences through drugs are likely to begin with the weaker ones before trying the stronger ones. This by no means suggests that all who try weaker drugs will move to stronger ones.

Commonly Used and Abused Drugs

Most drugs used for medical purposes are depressants or stimulants; the hallucinogens may eventually be used medically, but are now primarily used illegally as recreational drugs (Brecher et al., 1972). All three categories are abused by some people, and all have potentially serious effects; extreme depression or stimulation is fatal, and excesses of hallucinogens can have severe and long-lasting psychological effects.
■ Figure 7.13

Depressants Several common drugs are depressants; commonly called "downers," they act to smooth and slow the nervous system. Tranquilizers are mild depressants used for their relaxing effect. PCP or "angel dust," once used as an animal tranquilizer but dropped because of its unpredictable effects, is now an illicit or street drug (Smith, 1978a). PCP causes some users to hallucinate and to become violent, while at the same time it eliminates pain and normal inhibitions: Users have jumped from windows believing they could fly and have broken handcuffs (and their wrists) when constrained. (Because it can cause hallucinations, PCP can also be classed as a hallucinogen.) Antihistamines are typically used to combat cold symptoms; then their depressant effects are side effects (the reason why cold tablets carry a warning not to drive or operate heavy machinery after taking them). But they are sometimes used in nonprescription sleeping tablets.

Sedatives and hypnotics are increasingly stronger depressants. The barbiturates, including Nembutal and Seconal, are sedatives (Adams, 1958). The best-known nonbarbiturate hypnotic is Quaalude (often called "ludes" as a street drug). Both sedatives and hypnotics are sometimes called sleeping pills, but as you've seen, this can be a misnomer; they simulate sleep rather than causing natural sleep. Sedatives and hypnotics are widely abused, legally and illegally.

Two recreational drugs, marijuana and alcohol, are also depressants. (Marijuana is actually unique in its properties: At lower dosages, it causes effects similar to the depressants but somewhat different, whereas higher dosages yield effects more like the hallucinogens; Julien, 1981.) Of these two, the illegal one, marijuana, appears to be less dangerous, but both have potentially serious side effects. Marijuana is a complex substance with many potentially active components (Miller, 1974). For most users it seems reasonably free from immediate dangers, despite the overblown rhetoric with which it has sometimes been combated (Grinspoon, 1969). Marijuana may even be useful medically in reducing the intraocular pressure of glaucoma and in relieving the nausea caused by anticancer drugs (Schultes, 1973). But neither its common illegal use nor this experimental use mean that marijuana is without risk. In large doses it can have an effect on hormonal balance, reducing the levels of the male hormone testosterone and thus of sperm count (Maugh, 1975). (In adolescents, whose hormone balance is critical, marijuana has sometimes seemed to trigger gynecomastia, which is breast development in males.) Other possible effects of long-term use may not yet be recognized.

All of the depressants can yield a minor euphoria, because the first neural circuits they depress are inhibitory ones and the reduced inhibitions cause a sense of euphoria. Hence small amounts of alcohol can be enjoyable. But alcohol is widely abused, and both the short-term and long-term effects are devastating

Figure 7.13 ■ Psychoactive drugs may be arranged on a continuum, ranging upward from a normal arousal level toward maximum stimulation or downward toward maximum depression of nervous-system activity level. The arrow at Hallucinogens indicates that these do not really lie on the activation/ depression dimension. (Note that any of the stimulants or depressants could be fatal in large enough doses; their placement here is based on usual doses.)

(Adapted from *Abnormal Psychology: Current Perspectives.* Copyright © 1972 by CRM Books. Reprinted by permission of the publisher, Random House, Inc.)

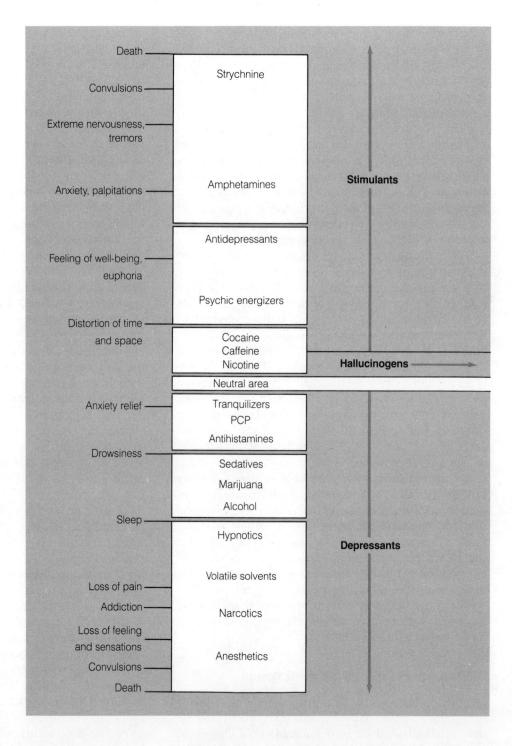

(Brown, 1982). People engaging in rapid-drinking contests can easily drink enough to kill themselves before they feel the full effects. Long-term drinking to excess damages various organs; it may destroy the liver and can cause a number of behavioral problems, including the severe memory loss associated with Korsakoff's syndrome (Oscar-Berman, 1980). Even small amounts seriously interfere with both physical coordination and emotional inhibition. The aggressive, belligerent drunk is a familiar character in both the media and reality, but the full effects of physical incoordination of even quiet drinkers is a social calamity. Excess alcohol intake is involved in over 50% of fatal driving accidents, and drunken drivers kill or injure 70 people a day in the United States. A similar percentage of those who commit murder (and many of the vic-

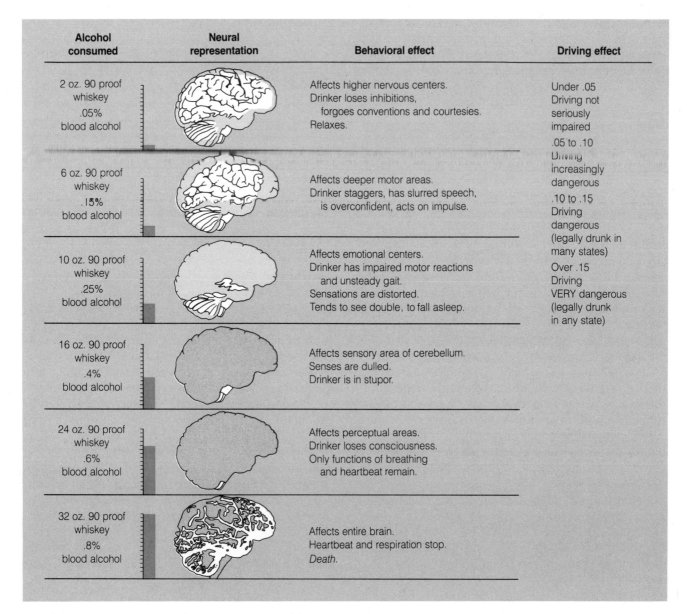

Alcohol consumed	Neural representation	Behavioral effect	Driving effect
2 oz. 90 proof whiskey .05% blood alcohol		Affects higher nervous centers. Drinker loses inhibitions, forgoes conventions and courtesies. Relaxes.	Under .05 Driving not seriously impaired
6 oz. 90 proof whiskey .15% blood alcohol		Affects deeper motor areas. Drinker staggers, has slurred speech, is overconfident, acts on impulse.	.05 to .10 Driving increasingly dangerous .10 to .15 Driving dangerous (legally drunk in many states)
10 oz. 90 proof whiskey .25% blood alcohol		Affects emotional centers. Drinker has impaired motor reactions and unsteady gait. Sensations are distorted. Tends to see double, to fall asleep.	Over .15 Driving VERY dangerous (legally drunk in any state)
16 oz. 90 proof whiskey .4% blood alcohol		Affects sensory area of cerebellum. Senses are dulled. Drinker is in stupor.	
24 oz. 90 proof whiskey .6% blood alcohol		Affects perceptual areas. Drinker loses consciousness. Only functions of breathing and heartbeat remain.	
32 oz. 90 proof whiskey .8% blood alcohol		Affects entire brain. Heartbeat and respiration stop. *Death.*	

Figure 7.14 ■ Behavioral effects of increasing levels of blood alcohol and legal limits for driving. (One California driver recently showed a level of .52%, the highest anyone could recall seeing; it could have been fatal in a person with less tolerance.)

(From *Eyewitness Series in Psychology* by Jozef Cohen, Rand McNally, Used by permission of the author.)

tims) are drunk. Many of those who fall asleep while smoking are also drunk, according to autopsy reports; this is a major cause of dwelling fires. ■ Figure 7.14

The depressant effect of solvents is incidental to their use as cleaning agents and bases for products such as paint and glue. Workers cleaning empty solvent tanks must wear special breathing equipment; without it, some have died from the fumes. Few solvents are used as street drugs, although some have been abused, as in glue sniffing.

The term *narcotics* basically refers to the opiates, drugs derived from the opium poppy. Opium has been used since at least 3000 B.C. for its analgesic and euphoric effects (Julien, 1981). In the early 1800s the primary active drug in opium was found to be morphine; recent research suggests that morphine derives its powerful effects by imitating naturally occurring brain chemicals, probably neurotransmitters, called endorphins (Wasacz, 1981). Further chemical refinement of morphine produces heroin, a semisynthetic drug that does not occur naturally. All of the opiates produce tolerance and strong physical and psychological dependence.

A number of synthetic narcotics have been developed in attempts to retain the analgesic properties of the opiates for medical use without the euphoric properties that result in abuse. Synthetic narcotics include Demerol and methadone, a drug widely used to treat opiate dependence. Methadone fulfills the user's physiological need for the opiate, usually heroin, but is less euphoric (Dole, 1980). Although the user remains physiologically dependent on a daily dose of methadone, the fact that methadone can be legally prescribed and is inexpensive helps the user avoid some of the problems associated with heroin use (such as committing crimes to pay for it).

Anesthetics are the strongest nervous-system depressants deliberately used. They are actually nervous-system poisons used in tightly controlled doses, and their effects must be monitored by a professional anesthesiologist. Even then there may be complications; coma or death occasionally occurs during routine surgery when a patient is unusually sensitive or monitoring is not perfect. Anesthetics are not usually abused, although nitrous oxide (laughing gas) can be.

Stimulants

Stimulants are the opposite of depressants; commonly called "uppers," they activate the nervous system (refer back to Figure 7.13). Stimulants are widely used, both legally and illegally, because they can make people feel better and work more productively.

By far the most common stimulants are nicotine in cigarettes and caffeine in coffee, tea, cola drinks, over-the-counter tablets (No-Doz), and even mixed with aspirin (Anacin). Nicotine and caffeine are generally benevolent stimulants, but even so must be treated with caution. Cigarette smoking, for example, is associated with sleep difficulties, probably because of nicotine's stimulant effects (Soldatos et al., 1980). And people who ingest too much caffeine can get "coffee nerves": they become edgy and irritable and find it difficult to sleep. If they cut down, they may develop headaches and other withdrawal symptoms (B. C. White et al., 1980).

Cocaine is derived from the leaves of the South American coca plant, which have been chewed by the Indians of the Andes as a stimulant and appetite reducer for at least 5000 years (Andrews & Solomon, 1975; Van Dyke & Byck, 1982). In small amounts cocaine is an effective stimulant with some euphoric

properties, which accounts for its wide recreational use. The coca leaf was an original ingredient in Coca-Cola. (Caffeine was introduced later as a substitute stimulant.) Freud was aware of cocaine's positive effects, for example, and wrote a number of favorable accounts of them (Byck, 1974). But Freud has been criticized for failing to see the potential dangers soon enough, both medical and social. Cocaine can be toxic in large doses, and when sniffed, as it frequently is, can eventually damage the nasal membranes or even destroy the sinus passages. But in general the greatest risk of cocaine use (apart from the legal consequences of using any illegal drug) seems to be the time, energy, and money devoted to its acquisition and consumption. (Cocaine dependence is so strong that monkeys will choose it over food, even after they have lost weight and begun to develop toxic effects; Aigner & Balster, 1978.)

Amphetamines, stimulants used medically to combat depression, are probably the most overprescribed class of drugs and one of the most widely abused. As street drugs they are often used to counteract the effects of hypnotics, and users can easily be trapped into a repeating cycle of "upper/downer/upper." The most extreme stimulant in Figure 7.13 is strychnine. It is the stimulant version of an anesthetic: a poison that can be medically useful if kept under very careful control.

Hallucinogens

Hallucinogens create their major effect through distortion rather than depression or stimulation (Barron et al., 1964). Where other drugs are downers and uppers, these might be considered "scramblers"; they typically distort users' perceptions and often their sense of time and emotional balance. Some, notably LSD (lysergic acid diethylamide), have been used experimentally as psychotomimetic drugs (meaning "psychosis imitating"), because their effects so imitate the perceptual and thought problems of a schizophrenic. ■ Notable Quote: An Experimental Experience with LSD

Many natural hallucinogens have been used by human cultures around the world. Psilocybin, extracted from Mexico's "magic mushroom," is a well-known example. (Even the active ingredient in catnip has a chemical structure similar to LSD.) It has even been suggested that the symptoms of possession that led to the 1692 witchcraft trials in Salem came from poisoning with ergot, a hallucinogenic fungus that grows on rye grain in damp conditions (Matossian, 1982).

Hallucinogens create hallucinations because they enter easily into the neurochemistry of the brain, perhaps in some way triggering the equivalent of waking dreams. If these effects were brief, mild, and predictable, they would be less dangerous than they are. But

An experimental experience with LSD

"After 40 minutes, I noted the following symptoms in my laboratory journal: slight giddiness, restlessness, difficulty in concentration, visual disturbances, laughing. . . . Later, I lost all count of time. I noticed with dismay that my environment was undergoing progressive changes. My visual field wavered and everything appeared deformed as in a faulty mirror. Space and time became more and more disorganized and I was overcome by a fear that I was going out of my mind. The worst part of it being that I was clearly aware of my condition. My power of observation was unimpaired. . . . Occasionally, I felt as if I were out of my body. I thought I had died. My ego seemed suspended somewhere in space, from where I saw my dead body lying on the sofa. . . . It was particularly striking how acoustic perceptions, such as the noise of water gushing from a tap or the spoken word, were transformed into optical illusions. I then fell asleep and awakened the next morning somewhat tired but otherwise feeling perfectly well."

Albert & Hoffman, in Julien, *A Primer of Drug Action* (1981). From Interim Drug Report of the Commission of Inquiry into the Nonmedical Use of Drugs, Information Canada, 1970.

LSD, a product of modern chemistry, is a remarkably potent drug; the functional dose is so small that it is easy to overdose. Even an "appropriate" dose may cause effects for eight hours or more. Furthermore, the effects themselves are unreliable; surrounding conditions are known to influence the content of the experience, but even an experienced user in comfortable surroundings may experience a horrifying "bad trip." Perhaps the most serious risks of LSD, however, are flashbacks, apparent drug effects that occur weeks or months after the drug was last taken. These flashbacks may be memories triggered in some way, or the drug may become stored in body tissues and later released, or there may have been permanent alterations to some synapses. They are among the least-understood consequences of LSD and their causes remain a mystery.

This chapter in general, and this last section in particular, has given you an insight into why psychologists study the nervous system. Whether sleep, meditation, or LSD flashbacks are the topic of concern, understanding human consciousness means understanding the workings of the nervous system. And

when it comes to manipulating your own consciousness, remember that you only have one nervous system and that it doesn't repair itself; if you harm it, you will have to live with the consequences. On the positive side, however, this also means that if you take care of it, it will take care of you. And what you provide it through learning it will give you back through memory—but these are topics for our next two chapters.

CHAPTER SUMMARY

1 Consciousness can be defined and studied in terms of the languages of experience, physiology, and overt behavior. Consciousness probably conveys some evolutionary advantages, but these are difficult to specify.

2 Consciousness can be further subdivided into vertical layers as Freud did, into parallel portions as Hilgard does, or into a variety of normal and altered states.

3 Many aspects of our physiology and consciousness vary along biological rhythms; the most studied are the 24-hour circadian cycle and the 90-minute ultradian cycle. Monthly and annual cycles are also important, but the study of "biorhythms" is actually a pseudoscience.

4 Sleep normally occurs at the same time within each 24-hour circadian period; distortion of this pattern can cause jet lag and problems in shift work. Within sleep, cycles of dreaming and other changes follow the ultradian cycle.

5 Both REM and NREM sleep (corresponding approximately to dreaming and sleeping) are required by our physiology. The reasons remain in debate, but a number of functions may be served simultaneously.

6 The mechanisms controlling REM and NREM can malfunction in various ways, yielding a number of problems of sleep; we are only beginning to understand many of them.

7 Hypnosis refers to both a procedure for altering consciousness and the results of that procedure. Hypnosis has been studied for some 200 years, but remains only partially understood.

8 Few meditative techniques have been carefully studied in the laboratory, but many share common procedures and probably lead to some common effects—perhaps the encouragement of the parasympathetic portion of the autonomic nervous system.

9 Psychoactive drugs alter consciousness by affecting the nervous system directly. Most such drugs lead to physical tolerance and dependence and thus to withdrawal symptoms if discontinued.

10 Depressants such as alcohol reduce nervous system activity; stimulants such as cocaine increase it. Hallucinogens such as LSD alter perception, and antipsychotics relieve some mental symptoms.

Further Readings

For general coverage of consciousness, see Ornstein's *The Psychology of Consciousness* (1977) or his edited collection *The Nature of Human Consciousness* (1973). Tart's collection *Altered States of Consciousness* (1972) is also broad-ranging in its coverage; Naranjo and Ornstein's *On the Psychology of Meditation* (1971) is more narrowly focused. Luce's *Body Time* (1971) is a highly readable review of biological cycles, and *The Clocks That Time Us* by Moore-Ede, Sulzman, and Fuller (1982) gives the latest research on circadian rhythms and clocks. General summaries of sleep research include Webb's *Sleep: The Gentle Tyrant* (1975) and Dement's *Some Must Watch While Some Must Sleep* (1978); D. B. Cohen's *Sleep and Dreaming* (1979) offers more detailed coverage of research. *Hypnosis for the Seriously Curious* by Bowers (1976) is a good summary; *Hypnosis at Its Bicentennial* is a collection of papers presented at an international research conference, edited by Frankel and Zamansky (1978). Hilgard discusses personal characteristics of high and low hypnotizables in *Personality and Hypnosis* (1970). For psychoactive drugs, see Julien's *A Primer of Drug Action* (1981).

Part IV

Abilities and Skills

A friend who knows of your interest in psychology arranges for you to visit a place where they train hundreds of performing animals for shows and events all over the country. "You'll like it," your friend says. "They use operant learning principles to teach all kinds of tricks." You haven't yet studied operant principles, but you keep your mouth shut and wait to see if you can understand what's going on anyway. You watch trainers putting several animals through their paces: a chicken dancing a jig in time to a country tune, a young pig pushing a supermarket basket, and a raccoon dropping a ball through a miniature basketball hoop. Each time the animals perform correctly, you notice, their trainers provide them with a bit of food as a reward. "So that's what operant conditioning means," you think. "It doesn't seem very complicated." You stop to discuss her work with the woman training the raccoon. "It's sometimes harder than it looks," she says. "You want to give enough food to be effective but not so much that they are soon satiated. You must also provide the food immediately, or its effects may be weakened. And sometimes it's better to let some performances go unrewarded. That way the animals learn persistence." Furthermore, she notes, at the training center they have discovered a further complexity. Some animals seem to have innate patterns of behavior that get in the way of their training. The raccoon does all right with the ball, but when they had it putting coins into a piggy bank they ran into trouble. "Raccoons in the wild manipulate small objects a lot, in the process of catching and eating food such as crawfish," she notes. "Maybe as a result, he seemed to like manipulating the coins so much that we couldn't get him to let go of them. So we gave up on the piggy bank." As you leave, you think about what you've seen and heard. Maybe when you actually study operant conditioning, you'll understand more.

As a species, we pride ourselves on our abilities to learn, to remember, and to use language. The most basic of these is the ability to learn, our topic for this chapter. Learning is intimately intertwined with memory because both refer to aspects of a single process. (What else do you retain through memory except learning?) We will look at memory later, however (Chapter 9); this separation is somewhat arbitrary but matches both historical and contemporary psychological usage. (Language is such a specialized ability that we will also consider it separately, in Chapter 10.)

Most species learn some of their behavior, but we rely on learning the most of all. In fact, it is difficult to point to any human behavior in which learning does *not* play an important role. In this chapter we will look at several kinds of learning that psychologists have described, starting with those we share with most species and working toward more exclusively human varieties. But first we must define the basic term. Just what is *learning?*

Chapter 8

Learning

DEFINING LEARNING

Learning is a central process in all human behavior and an especially important concept in psychology. But learning has its roots in the evolutionary utility of adapting behavior to particular environments; if we are to understand elaborate learning, we must begin with this concept of behavior adjustment.

Relatively simple organisms enter the world with many of their behaviors preprogrammed. Environmental stimuli can trigger one or more of these behaviors so the organism responds to the environment. In simple organisms the total set of possible behaviors is coded genetically, so in unusual environments they have no way of changing their behavior to deal with anything new. Caterpillars can safely follow each other in most circumstances, for example, but cannot adjust their following behavior. If their parade closes on itself, it can circle indefinitely. ■ Figure 8.1

More complex organisms, however, can adjust their individual behavior to their particular environment. They may use many genetically coded behaviors, but at least some details of their behaviors are learned through their success in dealing with the environment. Squirrels, for example, have innate behavior patterns for finding and eating food. Yet often much of what they must do in a particular environment to find and eat food efficiently is learned. One ethologist for example, studied squirrels raised in natural surroundings but without access to hazelnuts, which squirrels normally open easily and efficiently (Tinbergen, 1965). He found that these naive squirrels recognized the hazelnuts as food and attempted to open them, but that their initial attempts were quite clumsy; the shells they left were ragged and scarred. With successive attempts, however, the squirrels learned to open hazelnuts with increasing efficiency. Eventually they learned that hazelnuts have a natural groove that allows them to be quickly split down the middle, leaving the nutmeat intact. Thereafter, these squirrels were as efficient at eating hazelnuts as are wild ones. Such adaptive flexibility is one way of defining learning.

Some adaptive behaviors search out the necessities for individual survival, such as food and water, or species survival, such as mates. Other adaptive behaviors help avoid dangers, including predators, physically dangerous places, and poisonous foods. Learning is useful in all of these behaviors because it offers more flexibility than programmed behaviors.

There is a range of possibilities for learned adaptation, from a slight change in a programmed behavior to completely new behaviors. One simple adaptation is to perform an innate behavior in response to a different cue than the built-in one. Jackdaws (European blackbirds), for example, become very agitated at the sight of a predator carrying an injured jackdaw. In a behav-

ior called mobbing, they set up a great outcry and other nearby jackdaws join in (Curio et al., 1978). The tendency for jackdaws to mob in response to a flapping black object is innate: Ethologist Konrad Lorenz was mobbed when they saw him carrying his black bathing suit (1952). But mobbing allows them to identify new predators; Lorenz was thereafter avoided and screamed at by the local jackdaws.

More complex learning may involve refinement of existing behaviors, such as the way a squirrel learns to open hazelnuts. Elaborate learning can take this adaptation so far that virtually new behaviors are generated. No such behaviors can be *completely* new in the sense of being unconnected to the species' and the individuals' histories; each seemingly new behavior must develop from previous possibilities. But as adaptation builds on adaptation, a broad range of behaviors can be created. In our species with its cultural transmission of learned patterns, the cumulative effect is especially dramatic.

Today's learning is useful because it provides a guide for tomorrow's actions. But tomorrow will never be *exactly* the same as today. If learning is to guide behavior, the organism must balance the degree of similarity or difference in its environment. It should act similarly when situations are only slightly different, but not when situations are different in important ways.

In seeking to accommodate all these properties, psychologists define **learning** as a change in behavior, or the potential for behavior, that occurs as a result of environmental experience but is not the result of such factors as fatigue, drugs, or injury. Each component of this definition is important. "Change in behavior" is the basic element; but not everything an organism learns can be done at once, so the "potential for behavior" is added. That learning has taken place can only be known when the potential is demonstrated through behavior, but the learning can occur on one occasion and be demonstrated later. The phrase "as a result of environmental experience" eliminates innate behaviors, including those that appear years after birth through maturation. The final phrase in the definition excludes changes in behavior that result from experience but do not represent learning. The visual hallucinations of a fatigued driver or an LSD user, for example, are not the result of learning, nor are the consequences of illness or injury. Excluding such direct physiological changes from the definition does not mean that learning is not a physiological phenomenon, however. *All* behaviors, including learning, are based on physiology.

As an alternative to the term *learning*, and especially for the simpler forms of learning such as the jackdaws' mobbing, many psychologists use the term *conditioning*. Some theorists use both terms, others only one. In the balance of the chapter we will use either *learning* or *conditioning*, as seems appropriate to the particular discussion.

The two major categories of learning that we will look at first, classical and operant conditioning, were once thought to represent different *types* of learning based on distinctly different principles. Both classical and operant conditioning had been defined by the 1930s, and until sometime in the 1960s, learning theorists accepted this two factor approach (Rescorla & Solomon, 1967). Both types, however, were defined according to an *associationist* view of learning; they followed a line of thought that began with Aristotle but is most identified with the British "associationist" philosophers of the 18th and 19th centuries (Schultz, 1981). John Locke (1632–1704) had suggested that people learn by automatically associating stimuli that occur together, and by the early 1700s, the concept was well accepted. According to this view, the overall pattern of your associations represents all that you know about the world. Classical and operant approaches to learning were both based on the associationist view; they differed in what kinds of arrangements led to what kinds of association.

As researchers sought to clarify the characteristics of the two types of learning and to see when each was used, the distinctions between them became less clear (Staddon & Simmelhag, 1971; Terrace, 1973). Examples of learning outside narrowly defined laboratory experiments often seemed to combine the two types, for example, and careful examination of laboratory results showed operant effects in classical conditioning and vice versa (Davis & Hurwitz, 1977).

Since the 1960s, researchers have come to see classical and operant conditioning as different approaches to studying learning rather than different processes. And they are increasingly rejecting associationist interpretations of both approaches in favor of concepts based on the learning of information or knowledge.

We will first review these approaches as they were developed historically, using two Research Controversy boxes to point out the revisions. Then we will look at two other long-standing trends, social learning and cognitive learning, before noting how theorists are seeking to integrate all of them.

CLASSICAL CONDITIONING

Classical conditioning was called "classic" because it was the first form of learning to be carefully investigated; it was called "conditioning" because it was thought to be relatively simple, basic, and automatic. In fact, most organisms, even quite simple ones, can

Figure 8.1 ■ Caterpillars, genetically programmed to follow each other along branches, become trapped by that program when arranged in a circle; they will follow each other around the rim of this cup indefinitely.
Lilo Hess, LIFE Magazine, © 1948, Time, Inc.

show adaptation in behavior through classical conditioning—but in complex species the process is not as simple as it was once thought to be.

Classical conditioning is attributed primarily to the research of one man, **Ivan P. Pavlov** (1849–1936) (Cuny, 1965). Pavlov was a Russian research physiologist deeply engrossed in the study of digestion (for which he won a Nobel prize in 1904). To study the digestive effects of saliva he devised an apparatus that would restrain a dog while powdered meat was blown into its mouth; a tube inserted into its cheek brought out the saliva so that it could be measured. In about 1902, in the course of this research Pavlov noticed that dogs with previous experience in the harness sometimes began to salivate *before* they received the meat powder. At a time when animals were thought to be packages of instinctive responses, this raised the possibility of the dogs having *learned* to give a reflexive response to a new set of stimuli, those of the experimental situation.

Pavlov had not intended to look for animal learning, but he did notice this effect and knew what it implied. Pavlov was familiar with the developing field of psychology and he knew that concrete laboratory evidence of learning processes would be an important contribution to the new science. What he didn't know

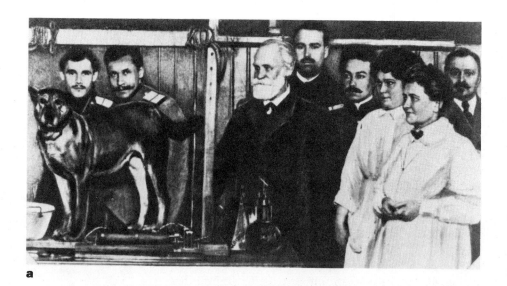

a

b

Figure 8.2 ■ (a) Ivan P. Pavlov (1849–1936), shown here with a research subject and some of his laboratory workers. (b) Pavlov's apparatus, used originally to study saliva in digestion and later to study classical conditioning. "We must count it an uncontested fact that the physiology of the highest part of the nervous system of higher animals cannot be successfully studied, unless we utterly renounce the untenable pretensions of psychology." (Pavlov, as quoted in Woodworth and Sheehan, 1964, p. 64).

(**a,** Culver Pictures)

was whether he wanted to align himself with this new and to him still highly questionable endeavor. But in the end Pavlov felt that he had to study what he had found; he spent the rest of his life exploring the variations of what we now call classical conditioning (Pavlov, 1927). ■ Figure 8.2

Overview of Classical Conditioning

Definitions and Time Sequences **Classical conditioning,** also called Pavlovian conditioning, is the process of pairing a neutral stimulus and a reflex-eliciting stimulus so that the neutral stimulus typically comes to elicit a version of the reflex. In less formal terms, it means that an organism can learn to respond to a new stimulus with an old response. What Pavlov originally noticed was that the dog responded with salivation to the stimulus of the experimental apparatus. Salivating in response to meat powder was an unlearned reflexive response for the dog, but salivating in response to being strapped into a harness was a learned or conditioned response. (Some psychologists feel that "condition*al*" is a better translation of

"PERHAPS, DR. PAVLOV, HE COULD BE TAUGHT TO SEAL ENVELOPES."

©1977 by Sidney Harris

Pavlov's concept, but we will stay with the most common usage, condition*ed*.)

Classical conditioning in natural circumstances may involve a mixture of stimuli. Pavlov's experimental apparatus, for example, was the source of many stimuli, any of which could have led to the observed salivation. But the simplest form of classical conditioning, and the way it is typically studied, involves two stimuli and variations of a single response. The first requirement is a stimulus that naturally induces some reflexive response, as meat powder induces salivation. This stimulus is called the **unconditioned stimulus (US)** and the natural response to it is called the **unconditioned response (UR).** In Pavlov's experiments the US might have been meat powder and its UR salivation.

Also necessary is a neutral stimulus, one that does not initially elicit the reflexive response. Because this neutral stimulus is to be conditioned, it is called the **conditioned stimulus (CS).** The version of the reflexive response that it comes to elicit through conditioning is called the **conditioned response (CR).** The CS might be a tone that would come to elicit a CR of salivation. Note that both the UR and the CR typically refer to similar behavior, in this case salivation. (We will note some exceptions to this principle later.) But the UR and CR often differ in detail; the number of drops of saliva for a CR may be less than for a UR, for example.

Learning experiments are often broken down into separate **trials,** each of which represents a separate learning episode. In classical conditioning each trial consists of presenting the US or the CS and measuring the response (by counting the drops of saliva, for example). Three kinds of trials are possible: (1) before conditioning, to be sure that the neutral stimulus is in fact neutral and that the US does produce a UR; (2) during conditioning, in which the CS is paired with the US; and (3) after conditioning, in test trials, to see if the conditioning has resulted in the CS yielding a CR. ■ Figure 8.3

Before conditioning, the CS presented alone should yield no response or an irrelevant one, and the US presented alone should yield a UR. During the repeated conditioning trials, the CS is closely paired with the US; typically this association leads to the CS gradually coming to elicit a CR. The most effective spacing is for the CS to precede the US slightly and then overlap it. Other sequences, such as terminating the CS before beginning the US, or putting the US before the CS (called *backward conditioning*), are possible but may be less effective. When enough paired trials have been run and conditioning has occurred, the previously neutral CS will then elicit a CR in the absence of the US.

Once a previously neutral stimulus has been conditioned it can be used to condition still other stimuli, a process called **second-order conditioning** (Rescorla, 1980). A tone that has come to elicit saliva, for example, might be paired with a light. The light could then come to elicit saliva without ever having been directly paired with meat powder. (The process cannot be continued indefinitely; only one or two levels beyond the original CS can be conditioned.)

Notice how classical conditioning fits our definition of learning: After conditioning, the learner behaves differently as a result of environmental experience, in a way that is not dependent on fatigue or other factors. When the learned behavior is not actually being tested, the effects of learning are still present but not visible to an observer; at these times they fit the "potential for behavior" part of the definition.

Reinforcement and Extinction So far we've looked only at the creation of a classically conditioned response. But if learning is to be adaptive to the environment, there must also be some way of eliminating the learned response when appropriate. In studying classical and operant conditioning, we will use the same two terms for strengthening and weakening learning, although their exact meanings will differ somewhat for the two forms of learning.

Reinforcement always means "strengthening" in learning, though the particular definition of reinforcement differs. In classical conditioning, reinforcement refers to the pairing of the US and CS. Thus a **reinforced trial** in classical learning is one where the US

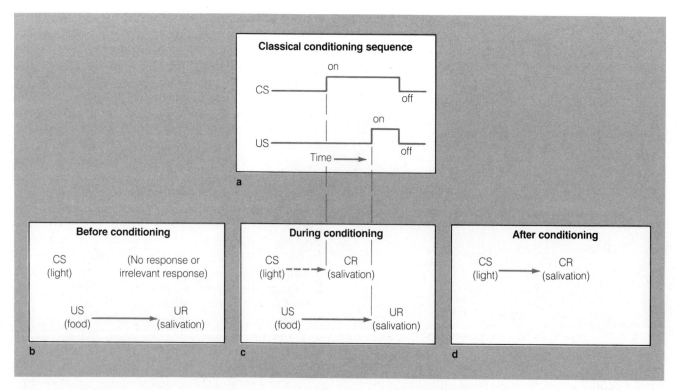

Figure 8.3 ■ (a) The most effective sequence for pairing the CS and US in classical conditioning is to have the CS precede and overlap the US. Some variations are possible but less effective. (b) Before conditioning begins, the CS should be neutral with respect to the CR; it can yield no response or some irrelevant response. The US should reliably yield the UR. (c) During conditioning, the time pairing shown in (a) causes the CS to begin to elicit the CR. (d) When conditioning is complete, the CS will reliably elicit a CR; the CR usually carries the same name as the UR (here *salivation*) but may differ in detail.

is present; its presence strengthens the learning. But consider what happens in a nonreinforced trial, one in which the US is not present.

Extinction is defined as an apparent weakening of learning as the result of a series of nonreinforced trials; in classical conditioning, this means a series of presentations of the CS without the US. Suppose that you have a good CR in response to the CS, but then present the CS over and over without ever again presenting the US. For the first few trials you will get a full CR. But as nonreinforced trial follows nonreinforced trial, the CS will weaken. After all, the only reason it is present in the first place is its history of pairings with the US. If those pairings cease, it will eventually go back to being a neutral stimulus. ■ Figure 8.4

In general, each nonreinforced trial reduces the effectiveness of the CS until it is once again a neutral stimulus. There are some complications, however. One complication occurs in the process of extinguishing a learned response. Suppose you use nonreinforced trials to extinguish a dog's learned salivation, so that by the end of the day the behavior seems gone. But if you test the dog the next day, it will again produce some

saliva and will have to go through another shorter period of extinction to get back to zero; this return of the supposedly extinguished response is called **spontaneous recovery.** Actually, the learning was not fully extinguished. Instead, the previous day's extinction curve represents a mixture of factors, including both extinction and fatigue. When the dog stopped responding the first day, it had not eliminated all effects of learning; it still had a residual to extinguish the next day.

Spontaneous recovery can have adaptive consequences in nature. If an animal responds in a way that once was adaptive and now isn't, it makes sense for the response to extinguish. But it can also be useful for the response to take several days to extinguish fully, lest the animal lose a valuable response too easily.

Another complication is the exact meaning of extinction. It probably represents largely conditioned inhibition, in which *non*responding becomes conditioned to the CS. According to this concept, the organism stops responding on the first series of extinction trials because two kinds of inhibition build up: conditioned inhibition, which is considered a further learning that is relatively permanent, and uncon-

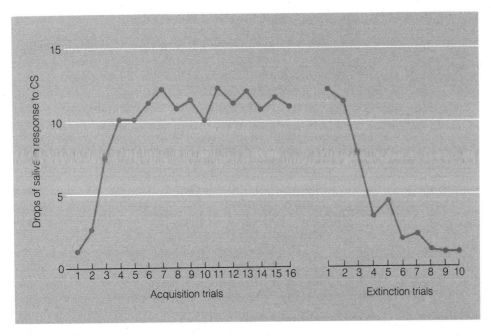

Figure 8.4 ■ The development and extinction of a conditioned salivation response. The drops of saliva counted are those that form after the CS begins and before the US, so they measure the CR only. The CR reaches a plateau of about 12 drops after 7 or 8 trials. Later, when the CS is presented alone in a series of extinction trials, the CR gradually diminishes. (Data from Pavlov, 1927.)

ditioned inhibition, a temporary form that dissipates with time. Thus spontaneous recovery represents the response strength left after unconditioned inhibition has dissipated.

Generalization and Discrimination Two opposing processes allow organisms to respond appropriately to situations similar to those that occurred in the past. **Generalization** is the tendency to respond to stimuli that are similar to the one originally used in conditioning, rather than only to identical stimuli. In classical conditioning, generalization means responding with a CR to stimuli similar to the CS. If the original CS is a tone, for example, the organism will respond nearly as much to a tone of slightly higher or lower pitch. Generalization is balanced by **discrimination,** the tendency not to respond to stimuli that are noticeably different from the original. A response that has been conditioned to a tone is not likely to appear in response to a light.

It is not always obvious, however, what *similar* and *different* mean in a given situation: How close in pitch does a tone have to be to be similar? In practice, what happens is that any organism generalizes along some dimension(s) that *it* finds similar. Stimuli that it finds identical will get equal responses: Differences in color for a light stimulus might be ignored by a color-blind subject, for example. Stimuli that the organism finds

quite similar will get nearly as much response, and more distant ones will get proportionately less. The pattern that results is called a **generalization curve;** it represents the subject's responsiveness to a range of stimuli. ■ Figure 8.5

Note that the breadth of the generalization curve is a measure of both generalization and discrimination. A broad curve indicates substantial generalization and little discrimination. A narrow curve indicates little generalization and finer discrimination. Together, generalization and discrimination balance the range of stimuli responded to as similar, expanding or narrowing that range as appropriate. You could get a dog in Pavlov's apparatus to be more discriminating, for example, through a controlled use of extinction. Remember that a tone paired with meat powder is conditioned; a tone presented without meat powder undergoes extinction. If you want the dog to respond only to a medium tone and not to a high or low one, you present a mixture of trials: reinforced medium-tone trials plus *non*reinforced high-tone and low-tone trials. You thus simultaneously condition a response to the medium tone and extinguish the generalized responses to high and low ones. The generalization curve will consequently narrow. With care, you could eventually squeeze the generalization curve to the limit of the animal's physical capacity to discriminate the stimuli.

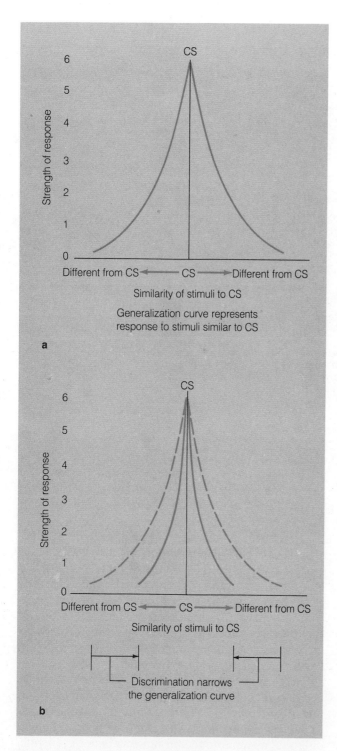

Figure 8.5 ■ (a) A generalization curve shows that the exact CS causes the greatest CR and similar stimuli cause lesser responses, depending on how similar they are. (b) Another narrower generalization curve, after a series of discrimination conditioning trials. These alternately present reinforced trials with the original CS and extinction trials with similar ones.

Applied Classical Conditioning

Classical conditioning has both natural uses, similar to those for which it presumably evolved, and applications that humans have devised. In the natural world, one likely use of generalization and discrimination is in directing eating behavior. Generalization might get an animal to eat something similar to what it ate before, whereas discrimination might be needed to keep it from eating something it shouldn't. Some butterflies, for example, are poisonous to birds. Initially birds generalize from one butterfly to another until they try a few poisonous ones; then they learn to discriminate by color and pattern, eating some butterflies and not others (Hiam, 1982).

This avoiding of potential poisons is one example of a special kind of classical conditioning. Called **aversion conditioning,** it represents conditioning an avoidance response, such as not eating or turning away, to a previously neutral or positive stimulus. Learning to avoid bad foods—as birds learn to discriminate among butterflies—is the most obvious example, but there are others (Eisner & Grant, 1981). Conditioned aversion to foods is characteristic of many species, although scavengers are most likely to have evolved special behaviors to avoid being poisoned. Rats, for example, eat only a small amount of any new food; if they become sick, even hours later, they will not eat that food again. This special conditioning protects them against the high probability of dangerous substances in their highly varied diet, especially because they do not have a regurgitative mechanism to get rid of poisons.

Animal aversion conditioning has many possible applications. Research has suggested, for example, that it might be used to teach wild coyotes not to eat sheep (Gustavson et al., 1974). Sheep carcasses would be laced with a drug that would make the coyotes sick and then left where coyotes would find them. Like birds with poisonous butterflies, the coyotes might never want to eat sheep again.

There are several known or suspected examples of naturally occurring classical conditioning in humans. It has been suggested that parents' cigarette smoke may act as a noxious US for children, for example, thus accidentally creating conditioned taste aversions for some foods. Classical conditioning is also used deliberately, most notably in psychotherapy. Often therapists seek to modify previous associations of emotional responses, for example, to eliminate an excessive fear by associating the fear stimuli with relaxation. Aversion conditioning has also been used to reduce troublesome behaviors such as alcoholism. Drinkers are given alcohol mixed with a drug that makes them sick, so the "sick" response will become conditioned to the taste of alcohol and to the stimuli associated with its consumption (Rimm & Masters, 1979).

Classical conditioning has one major shortcoming: It apparently does not provide for learning entirely new behaviors. But many current researchers are finding that classical conditioning is more than a passive association of two stimuli. It involves several subtle features that make it more adaptive in the natural environment but that were overlooked in earlier laboratory studies. In some cases it *can* result in new behaviors. ■ Research Controversy: Is Contiguity Enough?

OPERANT CONDITIONING

Operant conditioning is the term now most frequently used; this major alternative to classical conditioning was first called **instrumental conditioning.** Both terms refer to the learning of behaviors that operate on (have an instrumental effect on) the environment; such behaviors are typically more novel and more active than the responses of classical conditioning. *Operant* is Skinner's term; *instrumental* was used by **Edward L. Thorndike** (1874–1949), whose work forms the basis of operant conditioning (Joncich, 1968). Thorndike wrote the first monograph on animal learning (1898), and for nearly half a century his approach dominated learning theory.

In developing instrumental learning, Thorndike proposed three laws. The *law of readiness* addressed aspects of an organism's being prepared for learning (in several general senses). The *law of exercise* addressed practice effects. Neither of these remained a major component in his theory as it developed. But Thorndike's third law has remained the basis of operant principles (Postman, 1962b). This **law of effect** suggested that a behavior that was followed by a "satisfier" would be automatically "stamped in," or strengthened, whereas one that was followed by an "annoyer" would be automatically "stamped out," or weakened. The law of effect was revised over the years, and became a major element in Skinner's operant approach. (Psychologists who do not follow Skinner's lead prefer the term *instrumental learning;* Krantz, 1971. But we will stick with the more widely used *operant.*)

Another important theorist in the development of conditioning was **Clark L. Hull** (1884–1952) (Koch, 1954). Hull built an ambitious formal theory of learning, seeking to develop general but quantifiable laws (Hull, 1952; Hull et al., 1940). Hull and his collaborator and successor Kenneth Spence continued to refine his approach for many years (Logan, 1959), and many of his concepts remain in use (though the theory as a whole does not). One of the Hull's most important

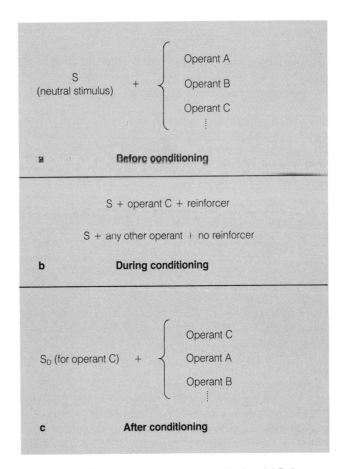

Figure 8.6 ■ The sequence of operant conditioning. (a) Before conditioning. A stimulus S may be followed by any of a number of operant behaviors; operant *A* is most probable, operant *B* less probable, and so forth. (b) During conditioning. In the presence of *S*, one of these operants, here operant *C*, is followed on each trial by a reinforcer. (c) After conditioning. The reinforced operant has become more probable in the presence of S. S has become a discriminative stimulus (S_D) for operant C; it sets the occasion for operant C to occur. (Operants A, B, or others can still occur, but are now less probable.)

ideas relates to why and how reinforcement works. Hull developed a concept of *drive reduction* to explain why a reinforcer such as food strengthens learning; the food is reinforcing, he said, because it reduces the hunger drive. This approach has influenced motivation theory as well as learning theory (Chapter 4).

Overview of Operant Conditioning

Definitions and Time Sequences   **Operant conditioning** describes a change in behavior that takes place because of the consequences following the behavior on previous occasions; its name emphasizes that the organism actively operates on the environment. ■ Figure 8.6

Is contiguity enough?

A key assumption of associative approaches has been that learning occurs through simple **contiguity**, or side-by-side pairing. In classical conditioning, this implies that the pairing of CS and US is enough to create conditioning. But recent studies have found problems with contiguity. First, conditioning seems to work only when the CS conveys useful *information* to the learner. Contiguity relationships that do not provide new information do *not* yield conditioning, whereas some useful relationships that are not contiguous do yield conditioning. Second, the conditioned response is an *adaptive* one, not just an imitation of the original unconditioned response.

The theorist most responsible for developing this approach to classical conditioning is Robert Rescorla. Contiguity is necessary but not sufficient for conditioning, he notes; the CS is conditioned only when it is a useful signal for what to expect concerning some biologically significant event (Rescorla, 1972). Rescorla has done most of his research in an arrangement called **CER** (conditioned emotional response) or **conditioned suppression** (1969). In a CER study, a CS paired with an aversive US such as a shock leads to a conditioned suppression of behavior. The CS acts as a warning, and the animal pauses and waits out the aversive event. Working with CERs, Rescorla has shown that classical conditioning is an adaptive use of information in several ways (Rescorla, 1972; Rescorla & Wagner, 1972). A response can be developed that has never been directly conditioned, for example. If a CS is never paired with shock, it comes to act as a safety signal that elicits a kind of fearlessness response (Rescorla, 1968).

Related work has been done by Kamin (1968), using the **blocking** effect: If a new CS is presented along with an existing CS, the existing CS seems to block the new one, which is not conditioned. Kamin and others point out that the blocked CS is not conditioned because it offers no useful new information (Mackintosh, 1975). To be conditioned, the CS has to offer something new, what Kamin (1969) calls a "surprise".

Another major line of research also suggests that animals are innately prepared to use some kinds of information more than others in classical conditioning (Garcia et al., 1972). In studying aversive conditioning, Garcia notes that innately appropriate stimuli can be conditioned over a lengthy time span, even when other stimuli have been present during the interim (Revusky & Garcia, 1970). A rat, for example, will associate sickness with a novel taste or odor experienced some time earlier, even if this means skipping more recent stimuli to do so. But it will *not* make the same association with a novel sound or light. The rat's evolutionary history has apparently prepared it for aversion conditioning to the stimuli of taste and smell (Palmerino et al., 1980). This relationship is called "belongingness"; animals will classically condition stimuli to responses when they belong together, as taste and sickness do (Barker et al., 1978).

That conditioning would take advantage of biologically useful information is perhaps not so surprising, but the extent to which it alters the response half of the conditioning is surprising. Siegel has shown that some drug-tolerance effects in rats are conditioned responses not to the drug itself but to the cues associated with it. If this relationship also holds true for humans, it could have implications for

medical uses of drugs. But the research has also shown that this tolerance occurs in a remarkable way: When conditioning is continued for long enough, the CR seems to anticipate the UR rather than imitating it.

Injections of insulin, for example, reduce blood-sugar levels, which can lead to dangerous shock (the cause of diabetic coma). Repeated pairings of a CS with insulin, however, develop a compensating CR of increased blood-sugar levels (Siegel, 1972). Similarly, repeated injections of morphine paired with a CS cause a rat to become more sensitive to pain. Thus the increased amounts of a drug needed to overcome drug tolerance may be in part the effect of learning (S. Siegel, 1977). Furthermore, the conditioned response is not limited to immediate cues such as the injection of the drug; it may become associated with environmental stimuli such as lights and sounds (Siegel et al., 1978). And the reversed CRs are not limited to drug effects; a study of fear conditioning using electric shock found a similar long-term effect. Where the shock elicited a heart-rate acceleration, the CS came to elicit a preparatory heart-rate deceleration (Obrist et al., 1972).

Taken together, these findings have led to several revisions of classical conditioning. They suggest it is an adaptive use of information requiring an element of surprise rather than simple contiguity. It works better for sets of stimuli and responses that belong together. And it responds adaptively to the anticipated situation, even if this means an opposite CR. Overall, these results have suggested a reframing of classical conditioning: What is learned is not "responses" but "information," and the information learned is that with biological significance for the species.

Before operant conditioning occurs, some stimulus may be followed by any one of a set of behaviors. (The stimulus can be a light or tone in a laboratory situation, but real-world situations typically contain many stimuli, making them harder to analyze.) The behaviors that follow the stimulus are called **oper-** **ants;** they are *not* limited to reflexive responses, as in classical conditioning, but can be any behavior that the organism is physically capable of. During conditioning, a rewarding stimulus or **reinforcer,** such as food (what Thorndike called a satisfier), is presented immediately following some operant. A reinforced trial—

stimulus plus operant plus reinforcer—increases the probability of that operant being performed in the future when that stimulus is present. (An operant can also be followed by an aversive stimulus, or **punisher.** This reduces its probability of being performed in the presence of the stimulus.)

The operant is not *caused* by the stimulus in the same way that a CS causes a CR, however. Instead, the stimulus has become a **discriminative stimulus (S_D);** it sets the occasion for the operant to occur. The previous history of consequences is what causes the operant to occur; the S_D says that now is an appropriate time for the operant because in the past it has been followed by a reinforcer. The ringing of a telephone, for example, is an S_D for humans. The ring doesn't cause the listener to answer the phone; it just says that now is the occasion to say hello, because this behavior has been followed in the past by someone being on the line.

Reinforcement, Punishment, and Extinction

Reinforcement in operant conditioning is the act of following an operant with a reinforcer; reinforcement strengthens the probability of the operant. Similarly, **punishment** is the act of following an operant with a punisher; it weakens the probability of the operant. (Reinforce*rs* and punishe*rs* are stimuli; when these stimuli follow an operant, the events are called reinforce*ment* and punish*ment*.) A single reinforcement or punishment, however, is not likely to have much effect on most operants. Operant conditioning usually includes a series of trials with consistent reinforcement or punishment in order to establish an effect.

Extinction in operant conditioning is still defined as the effect of a series of nonreinforced trials. But in operant terms, that means a series of occasions when the operant is *not* followed by a reinforcer. Suppose your telephone malfunctioned, so that whenever it rang and you answered, no one was there. You might keep answering for a while but with decreasing probability, letting more and more rings go unanswered until you eventually stopped answering.

It is important to recognize that, once learned, operants are not simply unlearned by either punishment or extinction. Instead, both punishment and extinction seem to superimpose new learning: learning *not* to offer a particular operant.

Thus the complete arrangement for operant conditioning is as follows. In the presence of a discriminative stimulus (S_D) an organism performs some operant behavior, which is followed by some consequence. Reinforcement increases the probability, and punishment decreases the probability, that the operant will occur the next time the S_D is present. Repeated performance of the operant without reinforcement leads to ex-

tinction. Once learned the operant is not unlearned, but may be replaced by other operants, including one of "not behaving."

Generalization and Discrimination Generalization and discrimination in operant conditioning have much the same meaning as in classical conditioning, but they apply to the behaviors an organism learns as well as to the stimuli that lead to them. In terms of stimuli, S_Ds are generalized and can be discriminated in much the same way as CSs. A rat may respond with a learned operant to a dim light after training with a bright one, for example, but if reinforcement never follows the dim S_D the rat soon discriminates between them. Similarly, as a child learns to answer the phone he or she may generalize to any phone, and then have to be taught not to answer phones at other people's houses, at stores, or in phone booths.

In terms of behavior, organisms also generalize across operants and can learn to discriminate them; employees must learn to answer a business phone with a more formal operant than they use to answer their home phones. The ability to generalize and discriminate in both S_Ds and operants offers an important flexibility in dealing with the natural world. The situation in which behavior is to occur (S_D) need not be identical to previous situations, only similar. If generalization across S_Ds is too broad, and behavior in some situations is not reinforced, extinction will occur for these and the S_D will be discriminated. Similarly, operant behavior need not always be identical. Instead it must get the job done; if the organism responds to an S_D with a variation of behavior and is still reinforced, the generalization of that operant is sustained. If the variant is repeatedly not reinforced, the operant is discriminated.

For a wild animal, operant conditioning can lead to a repertoire of learned behaviors that can be applied to a variety of situations. A squirrel, for example, is likely to have learned techniques for opening other nuts as well as hazelnuts, plus special techniques for pine cones, and so forth; the sight of one kind of nut is then an S_D for the appropriate technique. Animal trainers can deliberately use operant conditioning laws to generate new and even bizarre behavior: one pet squirrel was taught by its owner to water-ski behind a model speedboat. But such animal training works because operant conditioning has been generally adaptive over the millions of years of their evolution.

Measures of Operant Conditioning For measuring particular operant phenomena, such as the effect of reinforcing only occasional trials, two devices are especially helpful. The first is the **operant-conditioning chamber,** called a **Skinner box** by

Figure 8.7 ■ An operant-conditioning chamber, or Skinner box. In this chamber, designed for rats, the operant is bar pressing. The light above the bar acts as an S_D; a bar-press when it is lighted automatically releases a food pellet from the food storage magazine at the left, which rolls down the tube to the feeding tray beside the bar.

(Monkmeyer Press Photo Service)

most researchers (other than Skinner). This device simultaneously performs four key functions: It encloses the subject, simplifies the environmental cues, offers an arrangement for a single operant, and delivers reinforcers. ■ Figure 8.7

The operant chamber encloses the animal but allows it to move freely, unlike Pavlov's apparatus, which restrained the dogs. At the same time, it reduces the stimuli available; in an open research situation the subject could be surrounded by hundreds of stimuli, any of which might become an S_D. But the operant chamber typically uses a single light as a stimulus. The chamber also includes a single task suited to a particular experimental animal, and a remote-controlled reinforcer-delivery device. For pigeons, the operant is usually pecking a button (called a key); for a rat, it is usually pressing a bar with a forepaw. When the key or bar is energized, a key-peck or bar-press releases a food pellet. An audible click from the mechanism provides an immediate signal that reinforcement has occurred. (Reinforcement can be given or withheld according to some pattern, depending on the complexity of the associated hardware; many chambers are now controlled through computers. We will look at the effects of some patterns of reinforcement later.)

Typically, a rat is first allowed to become familiar with the box and to eat food out of the tray. Then the device is hooked up so that the bar releases a food pellet, but only when the light is on as an S_D. Once the rat learns the bar-press operant, the experimenter can study many other aspects of the situation. These include features of the learning process, such as generalization or extinction, and the effects of other variables, such as how hungry the rat is or whether it has been given a drug.

Before we go on, we may note one widely reported example of an incorrect generalization. In the 1940s, Skinner designed an improved baby crib: a temperature- and sound-controlled chamber raised off the floor to keep out drafts and to offer a better view of the room through Plexiglas walls instead of ordinary crib bars (Skinner, 1945). Skinner's second daughter was raised in this "aircrib" and he attempted to market it. It was unsuccessful, however, possibly because people generalized from the well-publicized Skinner box to the aircrib and assumed the crib required the baby to press a bar for supper. Rumors persist about the terrible effects this must have had; Skinner's daughter has been said to have been incurably insane or a suicide. In fact, she is a healthy artist living in London. (Skinner's elder daughter, herself a behavioral psychologist, has since raised her daughters in aircribs.)

The second useful device, the **cumulative recorder**, automatically charts the progress of condi-

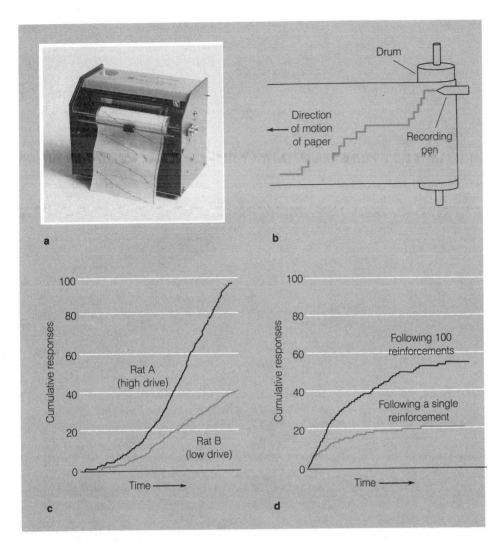

a

b

c

d

Figure 8.8 ■ Measuring operants with a cumulative recorder. (a) The cumulative recorder moves a strip of paper off a roll under a pen. (b) The pen moves upward one increment for each operant; if no operant occurs, the pen holds at that position, generating a horizontal line. When the pen reaches the end of its range, it automatically returns to the bottom of the paper; however, the true shape of the curve always rises because responses can only be added, not subtracted. (c) Cumulative curves for two rats with different degrees of hunger. The hungrier rat (A) obviously responds at a higher rate. (d) Cumulative curves during extinction. The animal that has received 100 reinforcements responds more often and for a longer time before reaching the horizontal level that indicates extinction (no further responses).

(**a,** Gerbrands Corporation; **b,** from *Introduction to Psychology,* 7th ed., by Ernest R. Hilgard et al., © 1979 by Harcourt Brace Jovanovich, Inc. Reprinted by permission of the publisher; **c** and **d,** adapted from *The Behavior of Organisms* by B. F. Skinner, Appleton-Century-Crofts, 1938. Reprinted by permission of the author.)

tioning or extinction by recording the addition of each new operant as it occurs, thus generating a **cumulative curve.** The overall shape of the cumulative curve indicates the general course of learning or extinction; the details can be analyzed later, if desired. ■ Figure 8.8

With this overview of operant conditioning, we can now look more carefully at how reinforcers and punishers are defined, some variations of reinforcement and punishment, and how completely new oper-

ants can be shaped and then linked together in behavior chains.

Reinforcement and Punishment

Defining Reinforcers and Punishers   A reinforcer is formally defined as any stimulus that increases the future probability of an operant that it immediately follows. More loosely, a reinforcer may be defined as something the organism will "work for," that is, change behavior in order to receive. These definitions may seem circular: Learning is strengthened by following it with a reinforcer, and the reinforcer is a stimulus that strengthens learning. The solution is to note the generality of reinforcers. A reinforcer defined on one occasion with one kind of operant will typically act as a reinforcer at other times and for other operants (Meehl, 1950). Similarly, a punisher is formally defined as an event that reduces the probability of behaviors it follows or, more loosely, one that the organism will "work" to escape from or avoid. Punishers also are usually general, applying to different occasions and different operants. For most organisms and most situations, for example, food is likely to be a reinforcer and electric shock a punisher. But a crucial aspect of both reinforcers and punishers is that they are always defined by their recipient. If food does not increase the probability of an operant, it is *not* a reinforcer, at least for that organism on that occasion. Similarly, if electric shock does not decrease the probability of an operant, it is not a punisher.

It is sometimes hard to know just what would be a reinforcer for some organism. One approach developed by Premack (1959) allows researchers to define and rank reinforcers for any organism, whether animal or person. First the organism is presented with all the stimuli to be classified; the ones that the organism approaches are reinforcers, the ones that it avoids are punishers. (This is close to an operational definition of how Thorndike described "satisfiers" and "annoyers".) To rank the reinforcers, how long the organism interacts with each is measured, assigning number 1 to the reinforcer on which the longest time was spent and so forth. **Premack's principle** then states that any stimulus on the list of reinforcers will be a reinforcer for any one lower on the list.

To see how the principle is applied, suppose you have a child whom you wish to encourage to read. You put the child in a room with dishes of food, toys, and books, and then observe that the child spends 20 minutes eating ice cream, 10 minutes playing with a toy, and no time with the books. Premack's principle tells you that either ice cream or the toy can be used to reinforce reading (and that ice cream can be used to reinforce playing with the toy, if you wish).

Before you can teach any organism with reinforcers, however, you must have some innate reinforcer with which to begin the process. Food, water, and sex are obvious **primary reinforcers** for many species; their reinforcing properties are built into the organism. Primary reinforcers are typically effective for all members of a species, though individual learning histories can alter them. But humans also seem to

work very hard for small rectangular pieces of dirty paper. Why should money also be a reinforcer?

Secondary reinforcers (or conditioned reinforcers) are those for which the reinforcing properties are learned through association with primary reinforcers. The click of the food magazine in a Skinner box comes to be a reinforcer in this way. Similarly, if a word such as *good* is repeatedly paired with smiles, touches, or food, it may come to have some of the positive effect of those reinforcers. Other secondary reinforcers seem to result from operant conditioning. Money, for example, has value to most people as an intermediate symbol for primary reinforcers, all of which can be purchased with it. (Note that punishers can also be characterized as primary or secondary. Just as *good* and *correct* can be secondary reinforcers, *bad* and *wrong* can be secondary punishers.)

Secondary reinforcers may not be as powerful as primary reinforcers in situations for which the primary reinforcers are appropriate; if you're really hungry, food may be a more effective reinforcer than money. But secondary reinforcers can be applied more generally than primary ones because they don't depend on any particular need. Some secondary reinforcers have such wide applicability that they are called *generalized reinforcers* (Skinner, 1953). Most people can be reinforced by money, for example, even when they are not hungry or thirsty or in need of other primary reinforcers. The ability to respond to money as a secondary reinforcer is not limited to humans, incidentally. Chimps will work hard to learn new tasks when reinforced by tokens, as long as these can later be exchanged for primary reinforcers (Kelleher, 1957).
■ Figure 8.9

Secondary reinforcers are often easier, cheaper, or more convenient to apply than primary ones and are not as dependent on the current needs of the organism. But secondary reinforcers also have a disadvantage: Being dependent on primary reinforcers, their value is subject to extinction without the continued presence of the primary reinforcers. If the Skinner box's click is never followed by a food pellet, if the word *good* is never followed by another reward, if the chimp's token or person's money can't buy anything, extinction will follow.

Types of Reinforcement and Punishment So far we have looked at three consequences that can follow an operant: presentation of a reinforcer, presentation of a punisher, or the absence of either (extinction). But two other possibilities exist. Removal of an existing reinforcer is another way to punish an operant, and removal of an existing punisher is another way to reinforce an operant. Apart from extinction, this provides four possible consequences that can follow an operant, two forms of reinforcement and two forms of punishment. ■ Table 8.1

Many people understand that positive reinforcement means something like a reward. But they think negative reinforcement must mean something like punishment. *It does not.* Remember that *reinforce* means "strengthen." So negative reinforcement must be something different from positive reinforcement that nevertheless strengthens learning. But why call it negative?

To understand the kinds of reinforcement and punishment, it is convenient to think of all the stimuli that could follow an operant as either reinforcers or punishers. Presenting a reinforcer (what we have been calling reinforcement) is more exactly direct or **positive reinforcement**. Removing a punisher that is already present is also a form of reinforcement—**negative reinforcement** (Skinner, 1953). It is reinforcement because it strengthens the operant it follows, but it is negative in that it removes an aversive stimulus rather than presenting a positive one. Negative reinforcement is like the old joke of hitting your head against a wall because it feels so good when you stop. (It is also sometimes called *escape*, for obvious reasons.)

Negative reinforcement requires that an aversive stimulus, or punisher, must first be present before it can be turned off. Hence negative reinforcement yields some of the undesirable consequences of punishers, such as emotional arousal. In general, these negative consequences argue against the use of negative reinforcement, but it is nevertheless extremely common in human affairs. One indicator that an apparent reward actually represents negative reinforcement is the sensation of relief that negative reinforcement engenders. Receiving a paycheck, for example, may be either a positive or a negative reinforcement. If it is money that you can go out and spend, it is positive reinforcement and is marked by a pleasurable sensation. But if you have already committed the money and must have it to avoid your creditors, the relief you feel when you get the check marks the situation as negative reinforcement. The check represents termination of the aversive stimulus of anxiety about the debt.

We have previously considered punishment to be the presentation of a punisher. But punishment can

Figure 8.9 ■ A chimpanzee inserts a token into a Chimp-o-Mat, a kind of vending machine that dispenses food in exchange for tokens. Because the tokens can be exchanged for the primary reinforcer of food, chimps will work to obtain them. The procedure is an obvious analogy to the human use of money.
(Yerkes Regional Primate Center)

also involve the removal of a reinforcer that is already present. There is no universally accepted term for this indirect form of punishment, but some psychologists call it **response cost,** on the grounds that a response (operant) will cost the removal of a reinforcer (Reese et al., 1978). In human terms, it's a fine, the kind of punishment commonly applied for a traffic violation; it extracts from the driver's wallet a quantity of those common generalized secondary reinforcers we call

Table 8.1 ■ Four Possible Consequences of an Operant

Stimulus	Reinforcer	Punisher
Presentation of stimulus	Presentation of a reinforcer = Positive reinforcement	Presentation of a punisher = Punishment
Removal of stimulus	Removal of a reinforcer = Response cost	Removal of a punisher = Negative reinforcement

money. (Jailing an errant driver would be the equivalent of presenting a punisher.)

These four outcomes offer four possible consequences that can follow any operant, two kinds of reinforcement and two kinds of punishment. Either reinforcment will raise the probability of the operant being repeated and either punishment will lower it; if none of these outcomes follow, the operant will be extinguished.

Using Reinforcement and Punishment Reinforcement for correct behavior is by far the best technique in any learning arrangement. It creates a positive emotional climate that does not interfere with efficient learning, and it can clearly specify the desired behavior. Extinction is the best system for reducing the frequency of old behaviors; the reinforcers for the undesirable behavior should be found and removed. Punishment should usually not be used if reinforcement or extinction can be used instead. Punishment is often unpleasant for the punisher as well as the punished, and it is also far less effective than reinforcement, in the long run, for changing behavior.

Punishment of an operant does not remove the reinforcement for undesirable behavior, but instead tries to counter it with an unpleasant event. The premise is that if the punishment is strong enough it will stop the behavior, despite whatever reinforcement has been maintaining it. Suppose an experimenter puts a mild electric current into the bar of a Skinner box, but leaves the reinforcer mechanism functional. If the rat presses, it is reinforced, but also gets a punishing shock to its paw. If the shock is unpleasant enough the rat will stop pressing the bar. It hasn't "unlearned" the bar-press, it has learned something new—that the bar is punishing. The original behavior will return in full strength if the rat finds out that the punishment is no longer present. In the meantime, if the rat gets hungry enough, it may press the bar anyway. Where extinction teaches additional behavior by *non-reinforcement*, punishment seeks to teach it by *countering* reinforcement.

Extinction may be frustrating, but most organisms tolerate it reasonably well; they go on to other activities and show few emotional behaviors. But the conflict generated by punishing a reinforced behavior can generate extreme emotional responses in many species. It may even yield neurotic behavior. A rat whose bar is electrified, for example, may begin to squeal, defecate, bite its own tail, or refuse to behave at all. Humans subject to punishment and reinforcement conflicts usually display it through a different set of behaviors, but their emotional response may be similar.

Thus a major problem with punishment is that it arouses unpleasant emotion in the recipient, which usually reduces the efficiency of learning. Another problem is that the negative emotion generated by punishment becomes classically conditioned to the circumstances, including the person who administers the punishment: A dog that has been regularly beaten will cringe when you lift a hand to pet it. A parent who uses repeated punishment may come to be a conditioned punisher and his or her presence or voice (CS) may arouse some of the same distress (CR) that the punishment (US) does.

Punishment is also inefficient as a guide to behavior. It indicates what behaviors should *not* be done, but offers no new behavior to replace them. "Don't do that" doesn't tell you what to do instead. Thus, punishment should be used only as an explicit guide to behavior that is *not* to be done; it is most appropriate when the behavior is dangerous or so disruptive that other behavior cannot easily be taught (Walters & Grusec, 1977). And it works best when combined with reinforcement of some alternate desirable behavior. Otherwise, the same conditions that generated the undesirable behavior in the first place are likely to reinstate it as soon as the punishment is no longer present.

Contingencies of Reinforcement An arrangement for a reinforcer or punisher to follow a particular operant regularly is called a **contingency.** The reinforcer or punisher is said to be **contingent** on the occurrence of the operant. As Table 8.1 shows, reinforcements and punishments are not differentiated by the kind of stimulus used but by the contingency between an operant and its immediate consequence. If reinforcements and punishments are random, they are unlikely to have much cumulative effect. Only when they are made contingent on a single behavior do they become powerful.

To be effective, reinforcements and punishments must also follow soon after the specific behavior that they are intended to influence. For some animal species, a few seconds delay may be too long for effective learning. Humans may tolerate longer delays but the most effective arrangement is still to minimize delay. Contingencies for humans can be more elaborate than those used with animals, however. Reinforcements and punishments can sometimes be delayed for a long time or applied according to complex rules. Learning to respond appropriately to delayed rewards is a part of growing up; young children respond well only to immediate and concrete rewards, but adults can respond to vague and distant ones. Often verbal rules speed the learning process by presenting the contingencies as a package; you can't tell a pigeon what the contingencies are, but you can tell a human subject.

Reinforcement and punishment may be either **intrinsic** (natural to a situation) or **extrinsic** (artificially related). Reinforcement or punishment is often intrinsically related to an operant, as when the search for food is reinforced by finding it or riding a bicycle carelessly is punished by the pain of skinned knees. Extrinsic reinforcement or punishment, however, is the consequence of deliberate human arrangements, as when some behavior is reinforced with pay or punished with a fine. In general the best contingencies are intrinsic ones. They are often more effective because they are naturally related and they continue to be available indefinitely. Often, in education or therapy with humans, one may have to apply extrinsic reinforcement (or punishment) to begin creating or changing a behavior. Ideally, though, when the behavior is established the extrinsic contingencies will be gradually removed and the intrinsic ones left to sustain the performance.

Reading, for example, is a self-reinforcing behavior because it is exciting and informative. However, this intrinsic reinforcement cannot reinforce *learning* to read. Reading is intrinsically reinforcing only when you can already read. Thus a teacher might use some extrinsic reinforcement contingency to encourage learning to read, perhaps using smiles, words of praise, or gold stars. But eventually the intrinsic reinforcement of reading should take over.

One possible risk in using extrinsic reinforcement is that under some circumstances it might detract from the power of the intrinsic reinforcement, a possibility called the **overjustification hypothesis** (Lepper & Greene, 1978; Lepper et al., 1973). This hypothesis suggests that being paid with extrinsic reinforcement can make an activity into work rather than play; when the extrinsic reinforcement is removed, the person may stop performing rather than being sustained by intrinsic reinforcement. Not everyone agrees that overjustification is a serious risk (see Feingold & Mahoney, 1975), but the possibility suggests caution in using extrinsic reinforcement.

Schedules of Reinforcement

Until now, we have referred to reinforcement as if it followed each and every operant of the type being reinforced. A failure to present reinforcement, we've noted, begins extinction. There are some intermediate patterns between 100% reinforcement and the 100% nonreinforcement of extinction, however. Any arrangement in which only some instances of the operant are reinforced is called **partial reinforcement.** The exact pattern by which some instances are reinforced and others not is called

the **schedule of reinforcement** (Ferster & Skinner, 1957). Partial-reinforcement schedules can be thought of as mixing the beginnings of extinction with regular reinforcement: A rat might press the bar several times without reinforcement but then be reinforced the next time.

Partial-reinforcement schedules are not as effective in teaching new behavior as is reinforcing every correct instance of the behavior. But once the behavior has been learned, partial reinforcement offers some significant advantages. It is cheaper and less likely to lead to satiation of the organism from too many reinforcers. Most important, though, it teaches resistance to extinction (Amsel, 1967). In effect, several unreinforced trials become S_Ds for continuing to behave (Capaldi, 1966). As a result the behavior does not extinguish as quickly in the absence of reinforcement. This phenomenon has especially important consequences for human learning if the behavior is not always going to be reinforced. It can be used to good advantage in teaching children and can also be a powerful controller of adult behavior, such as playing slot machines. ■ Figure 8.10

Partial-reinforcement schedules are of four basic types (although these can be combined into complex patterns). Reinforcement can be based on either the number of responses or the time interval since the last reinforcement, and the numbers or time intervals can be fixed or variable. **Fixed-ratio (FR) schedules** reinforce the next operant after some fixed number of unreinforced ones; *ratio* refers to the number of operants per reinforcement. A fixed-ratio schedule of 10 (FR 10), for example, means 9 unreinforced operants must occur before one is reinforced. **Variable-ratio (VR) schedules** reinforce the last operant of some average number, but the number of trials before reinforcement varies. A variable-ratio schedule of 10 (VR 10) means that a reinforcement is given, on the average, every 10th operant, but this might be after 2 operants one time and after 16 the next time.

Fixed-interval (FI) schedules reinforce the next response after a fixed time since the last reinforcement. A five-minute FI schedule (FI 5 '), for example, would not reinforce any operant within a five-minute period following the previous reinforcement. But after five minutes the next operant would be reinforced. **Variable-interval (VI) schedules** reinforce the next response after some average time interval, but the interval varies from one reinforcement to the next. On a five-minute VI schedule (VI 5 '), one reinforcement might come after one minute, the next after nine minutes. (Note that interval schedules never provide a reinforcer only because time has passed. The operant behavior must always occur to be reinforced.)

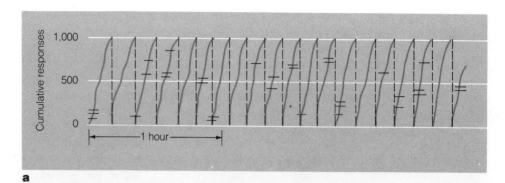

Figure 8.10 ■ Partial reinforcement schedules typically generate strong and sustained patterns of behavior. (a) This cumulative curve of a pigeon's pecking shows many thousands of responses without a break; each reset of the pen is 1000 responses. The reinforcements it received are indicated by the horizontal marks on the cumulative curve. (b) The intense play of slot machines is probably also the result of the partial reinforcement schedules on which they pay off. People will play them as fast as they can pull the lever, often for hours at a stretch, sometimes alternating two machines so they can play even faster.

(**a,** from *Introduction to Psychology*, 7th ed., by Ernest R. Hilgard et al., © 1979 by Harcourt Brace Jovanovich, Inc. Reprinted by permission of the publisher; **b,** Elliott Erwitt/Magnum Photos)

These four partial-reinforcement schedules have somewhat different effects, as shown by the different shapes of the cumulative curves that result from them. In general, ratio schedules generate faster rates of response than do interval schedules. Furthermore, in both ratio and interval schedules, variable schedules generate more consistent or regular rates of response: fixed-ratio schedules typically show brief pauses after each reinforcement, whereas fixed-interval schedules generate noticeable "scallops" in the response curve. ■ Figure 8.11

Shaping and Chaining To strengthen an existing operant, you simply wait for it to occur and reinforce it. But if the organism doesn't already perform that operant you must shape it. **Shaping** is a process of creating a new behavior by reinforcing successive approximations to it, almost like a sculptor shaping clay. You begin with the organism's repertoire of innate and previously learned operants and reinforce the one closest to the behavior you intend to shape. When the organism performs that behavior reliably, you pick only the examples most like what you want and rein-

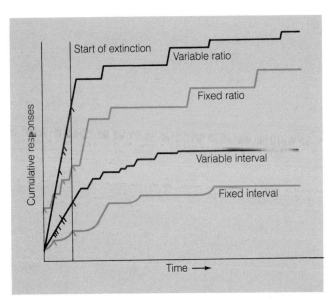

Figure 8.11 ■ The four different reinforcement schedules typically generate different cumulative curves. Fixed-interval schedules show a scalloped pattern, with a burst of responding at about the time of the next reinforcement followed by a period of no responding. Variable-interval schedules generate more rapid and consistent responses because the time of the next reinforcement is unpredictable. Fixed-ratio schedules yield a pattern of rapid responding until a reinforcement is obtained, followed by a pause before another rapid series. The most rapid and consistent response rate, and the one most resistant to extinction, is that of a variable-ratio schedule (the kind of schedule used for slot-machine payoffs).

(From *Psychology Today: An Introduction*, 2nd ed., by J. Braun et al., 1972. Copyright © 1972 by Random House, Inc. Reprinted by permission of the publisher.)

force those, repeating the process until you have shaped the desired behavior.

If you left a pigeon in a Skinner box with the reinforcing mechanism set to provide *non*contingent random reinforcement, what do you suppose might happen? Skinner found that individual pigeons "taught themselves" particular behaviors; one flapped its wings, another turned around and around to the left, and so forth (1948). Skinner called these actions **superstitious behaviors** in an analogy to human superstitions: A person wears a shirt and is strongly reinforced, so it's a "lucky shirt" (Gmelch, 1978). The idea was that something the pigeon did, like raising its wings, happened to precede a random reinforcement and thus was strengthened. If this happened a few times the pigeon might come to perform this behavior so frequently that further reinforcements would be assured and this operant would be learned as if it were on a partial-reinforcement schedule.

Shaping uses generalization and extinction as well as reinforcement. As the organism is reinforced, it gen-

eralizes to a set of behaviors rather than an exact one. From that set the experimenter chooses only some to reinforce, and the others extinguish. Shaping has long been used by animal trainers to create unusual behaviors in a number of species. A squirrel learning to open hazelnuts, for example, is shaped by natural circumstances, and the motorcycle-riding bears in Figure 8.12 were probably trained by shaping. ■ Figure 8.12

Ideally, then, creating a change in behavior by operant techniques consists of careful intensive reinforcing, by extrinsic reinforcers if necessary, of successive approximations to the desired behavior. Once the behavior is shaped, the intense and arbitrary reinforcement is gradually reduced to the minimum necessary to sustain performance, preferably to reinforcers that are intrinsic to the performance.

Behavior **chaining** consists of adding bits of additional behavior to an existing operant; it is a way of creating a lengthy behavior sequence that cannot be shaped as a single act (Skinner, 1938, 1953). Chaining starts with a single operant; once it is established, the opportunity to perform it can act as a secondary reinforcer for a simple preceding behavior. For example, once a rat has learned to climb a ladder to find food, the ladder being put in place is a secondary reinforcer for any preceding act that moves the ladder into place—such as pulling on a string. After the "pull-string" link is added to the "climb-ladder" link, another preceding behavior can be reinforced by its leading to the string. Each link is thus chained onto the beginning of the behavior sequence, and its strength is sustained by the reinforcement at the completion of the chain. Lengthy chains can be built up in this way, with a rat rapidly carrying out a complex series of behaviors lasting up to several minutes in return for a single reinforcement. ■ Figure 8.13

Chaining draws on the notion of shaping, but goes further. Each link of the chain may have to be shaped, for example, before being added. How much shaping is required and how complex a link is depends on the characteristics of the learner and the behavior being chained. Chaining has been used, for example, to teach retarded adults to dress themselves (Watson, 1968). Following the rule of backing up from the final step, the teacher dresses the person except for the last act, perhaps pulling down a sweater. When the learner can do that, he or she is reinforced. After several reinforced trials the learner has to perform the next preceding act, possibly pushing an arm through a sweater sleeve before pulling the sweater down and being reinforced. A few trials later both sleeves may be required, and so forth. Eventually, the person can carry out the complete chain of getting dressed.

As the principles of shaping and chaining were elaborated, it sometimes seemed that an animal could

Figure 8.12 ■ If you waited for two bears to get onto a motorcycle and ride away, you might have a long wait. But such behavior can be readily shaped, as shown by these members of the Moscow Circus.

(Ben Mancuso/Impact Photo)

be taught any behavior. But each species also has innate behavioral patterns. In recent years, researchers have begun studying what those innate patterns are, how strong they are, and what it takes to support or contradict them (Keil, 1981). Unfortunately, much of what we'd like to know about such issues remains unknown. In the meantime, the question of how flexible innate behavioral patterns are has led to a more careful assessment of animal learning studies. ■ Research Controversy: How Important Are Innate Constraints on Learning?

Applied Operant Conditioning

Animal training has been used for more serious purposes than amusement-park shows; animals are being trained to take over a wide range of human tasks where the animal's skills are appropriate. Operant techniques have also been applied in several areas of human learning, including behavioral therapy and education. Many people are even finding they can easily use operant principles in everyday life.

The intensity of response shown by the cumulative curve of Figure 8.10 suggests that pigeons will work

hard for small wages. And indeed they have been trained to do some unusual jobs. Soon, some humans may even owe their lives to hard-working pigeons—the Coast Guard has begun training pigeons to spot fliers downed at sea (Stark, 1981a). Carried in special observation pods beneath a helicopter, the pigeons search the seas for any sight of international orange, the color of the fliers' life jackets. (If they find it, they are reinforced. But lest their search behavior undergo extinction, they are also given reinforced practice sessions between searches.) Their wide range of vision and their attention to the task allows them to spot targets that human observers miss.

Other animals have also been trained as "employees" (Weingarten, 1981). Dogs have long been used to assist humans in herding sheep and tracking criminals, but operant training techniques are increasing the range of what they can do. In addition to seeing-eye dogs for the blind, hearing-ear dogs are being trained to assist the deaf; the dogs alert their owners to important sounds—the baby crying, the telephone ringing, even the owner's keys accidentally falling to the ground. Researchers are also teaching monkeys to act as hands for their paralyzed owners, even feeding them (Mack, 1981). If this experiment is

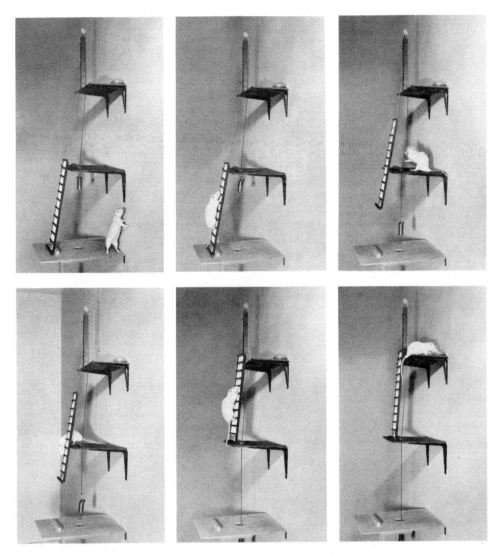

Figure 8.13 ■ A rat showing chained behavior. To reach its food dish on the second platform, it has to climb the ladder, then by pulling the string with paws and teeth raise the ladder until it can climb it again. The single reinforcement at the end is enough to sustain behavior chains several times longer than this, but they must be taught a bit at a time and the pieces linked together.

(Robert W. Kelley/LIFE MAGAZINE © 1952 Time, Inc.)

successful, monkeys could become useful assistants for people with impaired motor control.

The military also does research with animal "soldiers." One of the earliest suggestions was made during World War II. Skinner suggested that to reduce the risks to human pilots, a pigeon "pilot" could accurately guide a robot bomb by observing a screen and pecking so as to align the target in the center (1960). (The War Department never accepted the suggestion, however.) Current United States Navy research includes training porpoises and whales to retrieve spent practice torpedos (Monagan, 1982). The trainers would be well advised to be careful, however, lest their experiments literally blow up in their faces. In research during World War II, the Soviet army taught dogs to carry explosives under tanks. But the first time they tried their new weapon in battle, the dogs ran back under the Soviet tanks, accurately discriminating the $S_{D}s$ of these tanks on which they had been trained from the different German ones (Allman et al., 1982). A whole Soviet armored division is said to have been forced into hasty retreat.

The real value in laws of learning is not to teach squirrels to waterski or bears to ride motorcycles; it is primarily to understand, and perhaps assist, human learning (Hill, 1981). Operant conditioning plays a role in a broad range of human behaviors, especially those that are outside awareness or careful thought. Essentially the same rules used to teach a squirrel to waterski can teach a human to do so, or to do many other

RESEARCH CONTROVERSY

How important are innate constraints on learning?

As with classical conditioning, operant principles that were accepted for years are now being questioned and one major theme concerns the influence of innate behavior patterns on what is learned and how. The limitations imposed by innate learning or behavioral tendencies are usually termed **constraints on learning** (Hinde & Hinde, 1973; Shettleworth, 1972). One researcher has discussed such biological constraints in terms of **preparedness;** each species, he notes, is more prepared by its nature to learn some behaviors than others (Seligman, 1970; Seligman & Hagen, 1972).

Some of the first important work on biological constraints began with a re-examination of Skinner's report on superstitious behavior in pigeons (see p. 259). Brown and Jenkins (1968) noted that pigeons left long enough in the superstitious situation of non-contingent reinforcement eventually developed *pecking* behaviors, even if they had previously developed other superstitious behaviors (see also Staddon & Simmelhag, 1971). Brown and Jenkins argued that this reflected an innate relationship between pecking and food that overpowered the superstitious learning noted by Skinner. They called the phenomenon **autoshaping,** as the pigeon seems to shape its own responses to a behavior that is natural for it.

Autoshaping is so powerful that it can sometimes even contradict operant shaping. In autoshaping under noncontingent reinforcement, the pigeon's key-peck has no effect on its reinforcements. But if a key-peck is made to delay reinforcement, the pigeons still autoshape pecking—even though it causes them to receive fewer reinforcements (Williams & Williams, 1969). Thus, autoshaping does lead to a stereotyped behavior, but it is a behavior "prepared" by the evolutionary history of the species (Locurto et al., 1980). Autoshaping may also have intruded into operant studies with species other than pigeons (see, for example, Moore & Stuttard, 1979). ■ Figure 8.14

Other work on the relationship of biological constraints and operant learning has come from two professional animal trainers, one a former student of Skinner's. They used operant techniques to shape complex behaviors in animals for performing in shows; for example, they shaped a chicken's innate tendency to scratch into a dancing chicken act. But they could not teach some behaviors to some animals because the animals' natural behaviors intruded. Raccoons, with their dextrous handlike paws, could be taught to put one coin into a bank (though they tended not to let go of the coin). But when they were given two coins, they kept rubbing and handling them so long (a natural food-manipulation behavior) that the trainers gave up. In a play on Skinner's *Behavior of Organisms* (1938), they wrote a paper somewhat whimsically entitled "Misbehavior of Organisms" (1961), suggesting that some innate patterns are more powerful than operant training (Breland & Breland, 1961). The Brelands called this effect **instinctive drift;** the animals first seem to respond to the operant training, but then drift toward instinctive behaviors despite the reinforcement contingencies—perhaps because the behaviors themselves act as innate reinforcers. The "misbehavior" or instinctive-drift findings supplement those of autoshaping in determining the influence of innate factors in operant situations.

A third discovery has further explored innate constraints on learning. Bolles has studied negatively reinforced avoidance behaviors, in which an animal learns to avoid an aversive stimulus such as shock by some behavior that prevents the shock (1972). He has found that some avoidance behaviors are quickly learned, but others are learned slowly if at all. Bolles explains these findings in terms of **species-specific defense reactions (SSDRs),** innate defense behaviors characteristic of the species being tested (1970). Faced with the S_D that says a shock is due, a rat is likely to resort to an SSDR such as jumping or freezing. SSDRs are easily learned, according to Bolles, but learning to push a lever or other unnatural behavior to avoid danger may be difficult.

Taken together, these findings suggest that innate behavior tendencies can be powerful contributors to operant (as well as classical) learning. This has led some theorists to suggest an integration of ethology and behaviorism, two perspectives that until recently have rarely been associated (Fantino & Logan, 1979; Hinde, 1970). It has also led at least one behaviorist to suggest that these findings are an important revision to operant theory (Herrnstein, 1977a, 1977b). But Skinner has noted

things. Therapy based on learning theory—primarily on operant conditioning—is called **behavior modification** (Craighead et al., 1976; Kazdin, 1978).

One widely publicized application of behavior modification is Lovaas's work with autistic children (1977). Autistic children are seriously disturbed from birth; they probably suffer from a biological deficit of a kind as yet unknown. In the past many were institutionalized for life, often under physical restraint because of their self-destructive behavior. Experimental behavior-modification approaches, however, have made significant progress with some of them. At present, these children cannot be "cured," but a number are now able to live at home and even to attend school.

Some have learned to speak in this way, for example (Lovaas, 1977). For the boy shown in Figure 8.15, the apple picture is an S_D. When he offers the correct

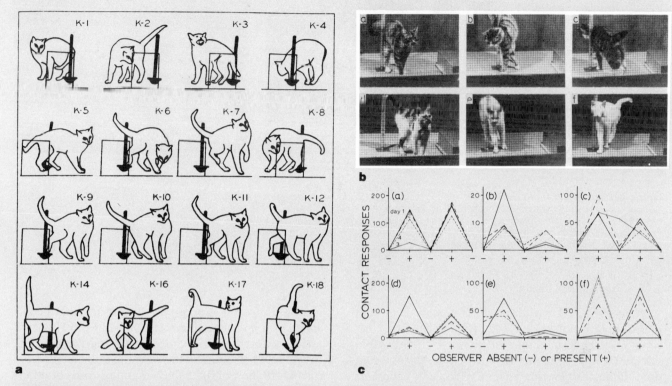

Figure 8.14 ■ A possible example of a species-specific behavior being mistaken for an operant or even autoshaping. (a) These drawings are from the research of learning theorist Edwin Guthrie, who thought they represented superstitious operants learned by cats as ways of escaping from a puzzle box. The vertical rod triggered release of the box door, and Guthrie's assumption was that escape from the box (negatively) reinforced the postures shown. (From Guthrie & Horton, 1946.) (b) Photos from recent research that claims Guthrie's cats were only showing a form of cat greeting behavior. These cats have *not* been reinforced, but rub against the post as a greeting in lieu of rubbing against the experimenter. (c) These curves show that the behavior in (b) occurs only when the observer is present—that is, the cats do not greet when no one is there.
(From B. Moore and S. Stuttard, "Dr. Guthrie and *Felis domesticus* or: Tripping Over the Cat," *Science*, 1979, *205*, 1031–1033. Copyright 1979 by the American Association for the Advancement of Science. Used by permission.)

that he never claimed organisms had no natural behavior tendencies (1977). Pigeon boxes differ from rat boxes precisely because these species differ in what they do easily. Others have suggested that, despite the observed differences between species, there are strong commonalities in learning laws across species (Bitterman, 1975). What Skinner and the operant researchers have focused on is the flexibility of behavior that does exist for complex species, and the rules that govern how behaviors are learned within this flexible range. Now researchers studying innate behaviors are looking for the possible constraints to this flexibility.

operant of choosing the apple drawing, he is reinforced with food. Later work will seek to teach him to generalize both S_D and operant, so apple S_Ds will be followed by apple operants as appropriate; partway through that process, he might have to respond to the apple picture with the spoken word *apple* for reinforcement to occur. ■ Figure 8.15

We noted earlier that punishment is useful primarily as an indicator of what *not* to do. Brief, mild punishment has been used in this way with some autistic children to eliminate repetitive self-destructive behavior (Bucher & Lovaas, 1968). Early research attempted to extinguish such behavior, but a child might hit her head against a wall thousands of times before the behavior extinguished—and might then start it again in a new room. Subsequently it has been found that a few brief punishments can often stop self-destructive behavior that has persisted for years.

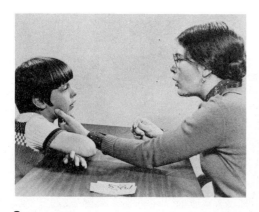

a   b   c

Figure 8.15 ■ Operant reinforcement used with an autistic child to teach him language. (a) The teacher holds the boy's head to get his attention as she shows him a picture of an apple. (b) He chooses the card with an apple drawing. (c) The teacher gives him a piece of candy as a reward (reinforcement). Similar training for each successive step has taught such children to make sounds, to shape words, and then to use the words appropriately.

(United Press International)

The therapy for autistic children now combines punishment, extinction, and reinforcement. Punishment in the form of mild electric shock may be used briefly to stop behavior that is self-destructive and time-filling, thus leaving a gap in which new behaviors can be taught by reinforcement. Less serious undesirable behaviors may be ignored, so as to extinguish them, or may be punished with the secondary punisher of "No!" which has been paired with the original shocks. Secondary verbal reinforcers are also used, with words such as *good* being paired with primary reinforcers such as food and then used alone to reinforce other behaviors (Lovaas & Newsom, 1976).

Some people are very critical of the concept of behavior modification, seeing it as a manipulative process that deprives people of "self-control." Their attitude, however, is in such striking contrast to the view held by its practitioners, that it is sometimes hard to believe that both groups are talking about the same process. Behavior modification is perceived by its practitioners as a rational use of the kind of learning (primarily operant) patterns that already exist. It may even be administered to oneself as a technique of self-control. (Behavior modification is discussed in more detail in Chapter 16.) ■ Personal Application: Modifying Others' Behavior

SOCIAL LEARNING

So far, we have been studying learning principles explored in animal research before being applied to humans. We turn now to a kind of learning that people are good at but animals do relatively little of. This third major form of learning, called **social learning** (or observational learning), is the learning of behavior from the observation of the behavior and rewards of others (Bandura, 1962). Social learning theory, as first described in Chapter 1, is usually said to have been founded by Albert Bandura (1977b). But like other developments in psychology, it has a longer history (Woodward, 1982). Dollard and Miller's work, beginning in the 1930s and 1940s, was one major predecessor (Dollard & Miller, 1941; Miller & Dollard, 1950). Bandura and other social-learning theorists accept both classical-conditioning and operant-conditioning principles, but they feel that observational learning must also be considered a major principle for humans.

Learning from Others

Social learning is not an exclusively human trait; many species, especially mammals, show some degree of learning from the behavior of others. Typically the young of the species observe their parents; this allows behaviors that the parents have learned, perhaps as naturally reinforced operants, to be continued by their young (Neuringer & Neuringer, 1974). Such learning has obvious evolutionary advantages, and presumably would be done by any species with enough brain size and complexity.

Social learning is an important contributor to the beginnings of cultural information. Something one individual learns can be repeated by others, whether in family units or in larger social groups. The washing of

Modifying others' behavior

There is a bumper sticker (printed by a student-created company) that neatly summarizes what behavioral modifiers think is going on:

SMILE . . . THANK YOU

Your behavior has just been modified

The request to "smile" is meant to represent an S_D and the "thank you" a reinforcer. If you did smile, the assumption is that the "thank you" slightly increased your probability of smiling—at least when asked to. Although "thank you" may be a weak reinforcer, it is true that people who smile at others thereby reinforce them. Random smiles may not reinforce any particular act, but if regularly applied, a series of smiles can be powerful. People with warm and ready smiles find others in their environment being nice to them because this has led in the past to those smiles, but people who seem always ready to punish with a frown will be avoided.

One study has shown what a smile can do and how necessary it is to have one (Gray et al., 1974). Researchers worked with problem children whose behavior did not fit their school's norms; each day the children attended a behavior modification class, then returned to their regular classes. Soon teachers began to report how effective the special class was at modifying the children's behavior. And their behavior had changed, but not in exactly the way the teachers thought—for the researchers were teaching these students how to alter *their teachers' behavior*. First, the children were taught to discriminate desirable (from their view) teacher behavior from undesirable. Then they were shown how to reinforce "good" teacher behavior and ignore or punish "bad" teacher behavior. When a teacher was helpful, the child might reinforce that by smiling and saying "It makes me feel good when you help me to understand." If the child felt a teacher was harsh, he or she might punish with "I can't learn when

you yell at me like that." The project was a resounding success: Teacher/student interactions were improved, students' self-images were strengthened, and some students even generalized the procedures to other students and to their parents.

Perhaps the most important principle demonstrated by this study is that all human social behavior is reciprocal: People who reward or punish others are themselves rewarded or punished by the behavior of those others. A feud is a classic reciprocal-punishment interaction, and a friendship is often a reciprocal-reinforcement one marked by a regular exchange of reinforcement, such as smiles, that both parties find agreeable. Skinner has noted that the situations most likely to lead to abuse of interpersonal power are those with the greatest imbalance between the participants (where reinforcers and punishers flow primarily one way); he cites as examples the military, mental hospitals, and schools (1976a). Teaching these problem children to use reinforcers and punishers partially balanced the teacher-student interaction.

Furthermore, in a mutually punishing situation, neither party may be to blame; the pattern requires two to play. Thus, a destructive interaction can be changed by changing the behavior of either participant. The first step in teaching the problem children to reinforce or punish teacher behavior was to ensure that they could accurately discriminate the difference. Their perception of classroom activity was checked by comparing it to that of an outside observer. One boy was found to be unable to discriminate teacher behavior accurately; for him, *any* teacher attention was punishing. Only after he was taught to discriminate could a teacher say anything to him that would be a reinforcer. This boy also had a smile that others found threatening or insolent rather than friendly. Before he could use it as a reinforcer, he had to be taught, by videotape and coaching, to smile in a way that others would find reinforcing.

This boy had been trapped in a reciprocal-punishment system with his teachers. Anything the teacher said he saw as a punisher; to the teacher, anything he did whether frown or smile—also tended to be a punisher. Once he could recognize favorable teacher behavior and could smile in a recognizably friendly way, the interaction became a reciprocal-reinforcement one. Overall, he and the other students *were* being taught to behave differently—but they were teaching their teachers to behave differently as well.

If you decide to try modifying your friends' behavior, you may feel embarrassed or phony at first. A good book can offer more information (for example, Reese et al., 1978), but there are several keys to doing it well. Always be honest, for one. Also try to offer a reinforcement contingency for desirable behavior and avoid punishment if possible. Be open about what you'd like to see happen, and maybe even offer an informal behavioral contract. Thus you might say "I'd like it better if you would . . ." (being honest and suggesting a desired behavior); "I'd be grateful if you'd try it that way" (offering reinforcement for a change in the desired direction); "I'd do . . . for you if you'd do this for me . . ." (offering a behavioral contract). After a few trials, you'll be surprised at how well it works—and how quickly you learn to do it automatically.

Some theorists have noted that you can use such techniques to modify your own behavior as well (Stuart, 1977). The procedures they suggest begin with similar operant arrangements. But because you have access to your own covert behavior and can apply covert reinforcement and punishment, their suggestions also include covert techniques. Some researchers have even suggested that behavioral self-control procedures can be useful in controlling states of consciousness, including getting to sleep and learning to meditate (Coates & Thoresen, 1977; Shapiro & Zifferblatt, 1976).

sweet potatoes by the Japanese macaque monkeys mentioned in Chapter 3, for example, is a culturally transmitted behavior invented by a single individual. (Our language includes implicit recognition of this process in the phrase "monkey see, monkey do.") Observing others' behavior, however, is rarely enough for learning the behavior in a fully efficient form to occur. Typically the observation of another's behavior provides the basic plan for attempting it, but practice and direct reinforcement/punishment contingencies must refine it for each individual (Skinner, 1974). Washing potatoes in the sea may not require much practice to be successful, but for a complex motor task, such as playing the piano, observation is probably only a first step and lengthy practice may be required.

Animals sometimes imitate each other, but they seem less able than humans to learn from reinforcements and punishments that others receive. Hunters have found, for example, that herd animals, which all run if one does, may ignore the sudden death of a neighbor. If no live animal showed alarm, for example, buffalo could be shot down, one after the other, without their neighbors seeming to notice.

Humans, of course, would notice! We learn a great deal from observing the behavior of others. When a teacher reinforces or punishes one child, for example, the others in the class also learn what is likely to be reinforced or punished. Reinforcement (or punishment) that is actively delivered to one person but has an effect on an observer is called **vicarious reinforcement** (or **vicarious punishment**) (Bandura, 1965). The observer's potential for a certain behavior is said to be strengthened by vicarious reinforcement and suppressed by vicarious punishment. Learning from observing others is called **modeling** (Bandura, 1971). A complete set of adult behaviors learned from others is called a role and the model for the behavior is a role **model**.

One way people learn so much from observing others' reinforcement and punishment is through language. "That could happen to me," for example, is an instruction to yourself to attend to and store what you see happening. Because we use language in this way, we can also go beyond direct observation, learning from another person's description of reinforcing or punishing events. We can learn to beware of devious behaviors based on Machiavelli's advice, even though he died hundreds of years before we were born.

The tendency to imitate a parent may very well be innate for a kitten, a coyote pup, or a human child. But in humans, learning from others' actions may itself be a learned operant. When a human child imitates a parent, several kinds of rewards or punishments may follow. The action may have intrinsic reinforcing or punishing consequences, such as the sweet taste of ice cream or the pain of a flame. And the parents may reinforce or punish specific behaviors. But parents also reinforce the general act of modeling. If a child is frequently rewarded for trying to imitate adult behavior, the tendency to imitate is strengthened.

This effect may even be powerful enough to overcome short-term punishments for particular imitations. Trying to play adult-style football, for example, can be painful and distressing for five-year-olds. But if they have generally been rewarded for imitating adults and doing as their parents ask, they may participate (Shah & Morris, 1978). As with other human behaviors, the kinds of learning involved are difficult to specify, but such children are obviously playing football because of previous learning and in doing so are contributing to their future behaviors. ■ Figure 8.16

The darker side of our society is taught in much the same way. Most people are aware that children of criminals may learn to be criminals. But we pay less attention to the effects of early experiences on ordinary people. Hunting, for example, is a traditional form of sport in our society, one that is often used to train young boys to be "men." But is it a form of training for aggression?

Overview of Social Learning

In general, social learning is based on operant learning but extends it in several ways (Bandura, 1974). Social learning theory notes that you can learn the general form of an operant by observing others perform it (even though a skilled performance requires practice and direct consequences). It also notes that the consequences you expect for certain behaviors can be learned from observing others (even though you may not receive the same consequences when you try it). Together, these observations broaden the range of possible operants you can try, and help direct your use of them. Social learning notes that packages of behaviors, even elaborate social interactions, may be similarly modeled. This offers individuals a way of efficiently acquiring complex behavioral patterns without observing each separate behavior, and it offers societies a way of perpetuating the roles demanded of their members.

The time sequences for social learning are the same as those for operant learning, but other learning relationships are added both before and after the operant sequence. Observation of a behavior performed by another and its consequences precedes actual operant trials of that behavior. Then, if a series of modeled operants has been successful, social learning notes that a general tendency to imitate has also been taught. Each complete learning sequence of observing, trying, and being reinforced seems to become a single trial for

Figure 8.16 ■ Role-play learning of play behavior—and not incidentally of sex roles. These very serious participants in the Midget Football Conference average five and six years old. They behave as they have seen models do, assisted by professional-quality uniforms and coaches. The modeled behavior is highly rewarded by their parents.

(© 1983 Billy Grimes from Black Star)

the more general operant of modeling. Each time someone successfully imitates another's behavior, the general tendency to imitate is strengthened.

Social learning also adds two other major emphases beyond those of operant learning. It emphasizes covert operant activities where both behavior and consequence may be invisible to an outside observer and it notes that learning can occur in the absence of performance.

Even though our basic definition of learning includes the potential for behavior, behavioral psychology has traditionally focused on demonstrated behavior. This makes good sense in studying a rat: Unless an experimenter gets a rat to demonstrate what it has learned, there's no evidence that the rat has learned. But humans can verbally report at least some of their covert activity. Whether these verbal reports are acceptable evidence has long been debated in psychology, but verbal reports imply that humans often learn things they don't easily display. Years of books, movies, and television, for example, have presented each person in our society with an astounding array of roles, including those of historical characters now long dead and hypothetical future ones. Yet few of us act out these roles; we are rarely Samurai warriors or space travelers once we become adults.

Social-learning theorists typically reflect psychology's emphasis on demonstrable evidence and thus seek ways to demonstrate human learning, but they also recognize that much learning may occur in the absence of performance. In a strict operant system, a behavior that had not yet occurred and been reinforced can't really have been learned. But the concept of observational learning suggests that learning *can* occur without behavior having been either performed or directly reinforced. Social-learning theorists thus focus not only on how a behavior is learned, but also on when and why it is performed. They have found, for example, that one function of a reinforcement contingency may be not to train a behavior, but simply to call for its performance (and perhaps polish that performance). Similarly, a punishment contingency may simply call for a behavior not to be performed, without either "unlearning" it or superimposing reverse learning.

To suggest that learning may occur without the behavior ever being performed is to admit that important covert activity is taking place. But social learning and some of its offshoots go even further, suggesting that a variety of operant details have covert counterparts. Some theorists, for example, have suggested that you can strengthen or weaken covert activity with self-applied covert reinforcement or punishment. For example, you can say to yourself "That was a good thing I just did" following an overt or covert act. Or you can punish an undesired covert act by thought stopping, a technique taught to patients troubled by intrusive or habitual thoughts: They are taught to tell themselves "No!" covertly when the unwanted thought intrudes (Meichenbaum, 1977).

Observational learning is a way of learning from more experiences than just your own, giving you a much larger repertoire of possible operants when faced with a new situation. A mental review of possible actions and their possible consequences might then provide an action that could be successful in a situation you had never before encountered. This is getting close to the notion of thinking about new possibilities.

Learning theory has thus moved from the kind of classical conditioning of reflexes that even very simple species can do, through the much more flexible operant learning, and through social or observational learning to include complex covert cognitive activity. It is only a small step from this point to cognitive learning.

COGNITIVE LEARNING

As learning theorists begin to incorporate more covert activity into their views, they move closer to the study of the cognitive processes, thinking and problem solving. But even cognitive psychology is based on learning. So to round out our look at the psychology of learning, let's consider two major historical approaches to cognitive learning that have influenced later work. One of these approaches derives largely from the Gestalt psychologists. The other approach, known as purposive behaviorism, included cognitive elements many years before social learning theory did. (We will consider the cognitive approach in more detail in Chapter 11.)

Gestalt Psychology and Insight

Although the Gestalt psychologists focused primarily on perception, they were also interested in what an organism, especially a person, did with that perception. In keeping with their emphasis on perceptual wholes or gestalts, they also looked for completion of whole patterns in thinking. Thus they emphasized the concept of **insight,** a sudden reorganizing of the elements of a problem into a new solution. Insight is essentially what psychologists interested in creativity call the "Aha!" experience. It often reflects prior effort to solve a problem, just as operant learning does (Harlow & Harlow, 1949). But insight differs from the operant concept of a gradually built-up response because it occurs suddenly in complete form. Before the "Aha!" the problem is not 33% or 66% or any percentage solved; it remains unsolved. After the solution is achieved through insight, it is present in full strength.

The Gestaltists saw insight as an all-or-nothing complete whole, but this reflected their overall perspective. Some behavioral psychologists have downplayed insight, seeing it as just the last step in a learning sequence—but that too represents a perspective. The truth is probably somewhere in between; let's look a bit more closely.

Wolfgang Köhler (1887–1967), one of the founders of Gestalt psychology, went to the Canary Islands to study chimpanzees in 1913. World War I broke out soon after and Köhler found himself with little to do but study chimps for the duration. His research was published in a classic book, *Mentality of Apes* (1925). By then, he was deeply involved and he stayed in the Canaries until 1920.

Köhler was especially interested in how the chimps solved problems. A typical problem was to show a chimp a banana outside the bars of its cage or hung from the ceiling, out of direct reach. Two forms of possible tools were provided: short sticks that could be fitted together to make a longer one, and boxes that could be stacked and climbed. Chimps were able to solve some problems relatively easily, such as using a single stick to pull the banana into the cage, if the stick lay in plain view beside the banana. But if the stick were in another part of the cage, or if two short sticks had to be put together, the problem was harder. When the chimps did solve it, the solution seemed to be of the "Aha!" variety; a chimp would go directly to the needed pieces and use them with dispatch. ■ Figure 8.17

In keeping with the basic Gestalt approach, Köhler interpreted the chimps' actions as a restructuring of the elements of the perceptual field. He felt that they showed an almost human-like understanding of the problem, but behavioral psychologists have argued that such behaviors are a natural form of chaining (similar to that shown in Figure 8.13).

When either chimps or humans show insightful learning, they often do achieve a solution suddenly and relatively completely. But careful observation often shows that the final solution came only at the end of a series of trial-and-error attempts. Several incorrect solutions may be close but inadequate, and the final insightful solution may combine them. Or the insightful solution may require adding one more piece to an existing solution, or generalizing an existing solution to a different problem. For a chimp to put two sticks together and pull in a banana, it had to have had prior experience with short sticks, for example. The insightful solution is thus not as completely new as it sometimes seems to be. It is a new step, based on extensive prior learning, much of which may have been more obviously reinforced-operant behavior.

Latent Learning and Cognitive Maps

A theory that combined the behavioral and cognitive approaches to learning was proposed by **Edward Chace Tolman** (1886–1959), an influential theorist whose work cannot be easily fitted into any of the traditions we've studied (MacCorquodale & Meehl, 1954). Initially trained as an engineer, he then took up behavioral psychology, and later studied under one of the founders of Gestalt psychology, Kurt Koffka. Tolman sought to combine his interests into a theory he called **purposive behaviorism,** for behavior directed to some purpose or goal (1959). His form of behaviorism had a whole-act quality taken from Gestalt psychology, and emphasized cognitive elements years before social learning would move in that direction. Yet Tolman studied this cognitive and purposive behavior not in humans, or even apes, but in rats (Tolman & Honzig, 1930a).

Tolman studied rats because Watson had used them and substantial data were being collected about them, and because they are cheap, tame, and easy to keep. As with other behaviorists, his real interest was people (Tolman, 1932), but he felt that even rats displayed purposive behavior and that this could be experimentally demonstrated. Behavior, Tolman said, "reeks of purpose" (Schultz, 1981, p. 242). The rat runs a maze, he felt, not because the reinforcement at the end "stamps in" maze running, but because the rat's purpose is to get to the goal box where the food is (Tolman, 1938). Purposefulness seems self-evident in humans; we often verbalize the purposes of our actions to ourselves or to others (though we may sometimes be mistaken about them). But a rat can't tell you its purpose as a human can.

Tolman wasn't arguing that the rat was conscious of its purpose; it made no difference to him whether it was or not. He just felt that a behavior's goal or purpose was a more accurate description of that behavior than a series of movements. More so than today, behaviorists in the first quarter of the century focused on the specific motor acts that made up a behavior. A successful maze run, they thought, was a series of right and left turns strung together, with each turn being made up of even smaller movements. But Tolman said that the rat was simply getting to the goal box, and he developed a number of ingenious experiments to demonstrate this.

Tolman showed that rats allowed to explore a maze without any food reinforcement in the goal box learned more than their performance demonstrated. Without food, their maze performance might get slightly better with trials, but not substantially. Yet when food was added they would suddenly show

Figure 8.17 ■ One of Köhler's chimpanzees demonstrates insightful problem solving. To reach the bananas, he piles up crates and climbs them. (Another chimp, lacking crates, once dragged an experimenter over and climbed him.) *"The solutions of such problems, when they came, appeared to come suddenly, as though a new 'configuration,' embracing the whole complicated means to the desired end, had suddenly sprung up in the animal's consciousness; it was exactly as though the appropriate action followed on a 'flash of insight,' and, as in the case of all insightful behavior, the insight remained a permanent possession, enabling its possessor to act at once appropriately on a subsequent occasion."* (Köhler, as quoted in Flugel and West, 1964, p. 206)

(Routledge and Kegan Paul)

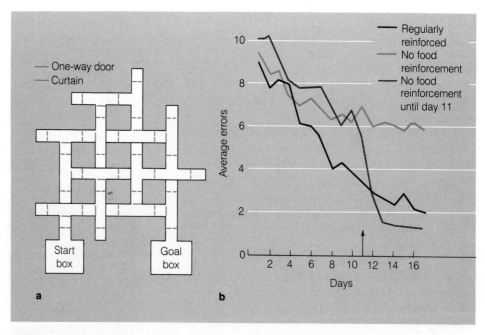

Figure 8.18 ■ Latent learning, as demonstrated by rats. (a) Some rats were allowed to explore the maze without any food reinforcement for 10 days; beginning on the 11th day, they were reinforced for reaching the goal box. A second group was always reinforced, and a third group was never reinforced. (b) The unreinforced group made some improvement over 16 days and the regularly reinforced group made substantial improvement. The curve for the latent-learning group is similar to the other unreinforced group for the first 10 days, but with reinforcement quickly catches up to the regularly reinforced one. In Tolman's view, the sharp change from Day 10 to Day 13 is a performance change rather than a learning change; it represents the appearance of learning that had been latent before being reinforced with food.

(**a,** from E. C. Tolman and C. H. Honzik, "Introduction and Removal of Reward and Maze Performance in Rats," University of California Publications in Psychology, *4* (1930), 17. Used by permission.)

much better performance. The phenomenon is called **latent learning;** Tolman said that the rat was learning all along, but didn't show that learning until reinforcement made it worthwhile. This work foreshadowed the learning/performance distinction that social learning theory emphasizes. ■ Figure 8.18

Tolman claimed that the maze-running rats, in addition to being purposive in seeking the goal box, also knew approximately where the goal box was. That is, they had a **cognitive map,** a kind of spatial representation that related the positions of the start box and the goal box. He showed, for example, that if a rat had reached a goal box by several turns it would take a more direct path to the box if one were offered (Tolman et al., 1946). To take a path never used over one previously reinforced does not make sense if the rat is learning mechanical path running. But it does make sense if the rat learns where the goal is. (Work on cognitive maps has also continued since Tolman; Olton, 1979.)

Ethologists would be less surprised by this idea than some of the early behaviorists were. Rats have made their homes in nearly as many different parts of the world as humans have, often living in burrows or out-of-the-way places and making their way to a variety of food locations each day. It is thus quite possible that Tolman's results reflect natural behavioral tendencies in the rat that are as easily developed as the pigeon's pecking or the cat's greeting. Rats might not have very useful cognitive maps for other kinds of problems.

Humans, of course, do use spatial and other conceptual frameworks to organize their experience. But they do so through more processes than we have so far examined. Humans arranged in a circle, for example, would learn to quit following each other, as the caterpillars of Figure 8.1 could not do. But they would also remember many details about the occasion for future reference (including how they came to be in such an unlikely situation). And they would no doubt talk about it to themselves and to each other. Before we can examine the range of human cognitive processes in more detail (Chapter 11), we must look at some aspects of memory and language (Chapters 9 and 10).

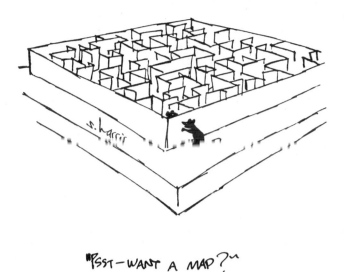

"PSST—WANT A MAP?"

©1983 by Sidney Harris

AN INTEGRATED LEARNING THEORY?

Throughout the first half of this century, learning theorists held out hope of finding a single theory or principle that could unify the study of learning for all species in all circumstances. Watson felt that classical conditioning would offer such an integrating principle when he called for a new psychology of behaviorism (Chapter 1). Skinner emphasized operant learning by reinforcement. Other learning theorists have also sought some single principle. But psychology came to the somewhat reluctant conclusion that it might have to accept two forms of learning—classical and operant.

In the meantime, two other approaches to behavior have been developing largely independent of learning theory: (1) the cognitive or information-processing approach to human thought, which we will examine further in Chapters 9 through 11; and (2) ethology, the branch of biology that looks at species-specific behaviors resulting from evolution (Chapters 1 and 3). The information-processing view has obvious implications for learning, but has not been a part of most learning theories. Ethologists have discussed such learninglike phenomena as imprinting (Hoffman & DePaulo, 1977), but learning theorists have considered their work to be so specialized as to be irrelevant.

Of the major theorists, only Tolman made a serious attempt to blend the objective behavioral approach with cognitive elements and even with some implications similar to those of ethology. Tolman's approach clearly suggested that the rat made appropriate use of information available to it, rather than simply having its responses stamped in. And his discussions of possible purposes that could be inferred from behavior were those meeting important survival needs—essentially an ethological view. But Tolman never pulled his theory together into a comprehensive and quantitative form. (MacCorquodale and Meehl did begin to do so in his behalf; 1953.) In fact, the trend has been to focus on smaller parts of the problem and not to try to build all-encompassing learning theories.

It remains to be seen whether an overall learning theory with one or a few principles can be pulled together; recent developments offer some signs that it might be possible. There is still a great deal of argument, but three trends seem to be emerging that might allow an integrated learning theory to be developed.

1 The boundary between classical and operant conditioning is softening, so that they are no longer thought to be entirely different forms of learning (Davis & Hurwitz, 1977). They often occur in combination, for example. ■Figure 8.19

2 Both classical and operant learning are being considered from a cognitive perspective, asking what information or knowledge is being learned in each case. (One current question in operant conditioning that we have not considered, for example, is whether reinforcers strengthen behaviors because of the information they provide; Buchwald, 1967; Cherfas, 1980; Egger & Miller, 1960; Estes, 1969.)

3 Both classical and operant learning are being considered from an ethological perspective, asking what biological utility they offer to a given species (as we saw in both Research Controversy boxes).

One possible result of current approaches would be a broad, integrative view of learning—not a single-principle form, but one that with a limited set of concepts allowed the study and comparison of many forms of learning. It would have to relate classical to operant learning, showing both how they are similar and how they differ. It would have to note the broad similarities in learning across species as well as the differences between them (Bailey & Bailey, 1980; Bitterman, 1975). It would have to describe what is learned in a way that accounts for both the information conveyed and how that information is translated into behavior (Wagner, 1976). And it would have to show how both the information used and the behaviors that result fit into the evolutionary history of that species (Menzel & Juno, 1982; Restle, 1975). No single person or small group may in fact build such a theory. But learning theorists and researchers as a large group are putting together all of those pieces; in a sense they are jointly building such a theory (Greeno, 1980; Kimble, 1981).

Figure 8.19 ■ Innate patterns and classical conditioning may interact in operant behavior. The key-peck on the left is typical of those when food is the reinforcer; that on the right is typical of those reinforced by water. The quite different beak positions resemble those of eating or drinking; it is as if the pigeon were eating or drinking the key. These innate patterns become classically conditioned to the key when the key-peck is reinforced as an operant.

(H. M. Jenkins and Bruce R. Moore. The form of the autoshaped response with food or water reinforcers. *Journal of the Experimental Analysis of Behavior*, 1973, *20*, 175. Copyright 1973 by the Society for the Experimental Analysis of Behavior.)

CHAPTER SUMMARY

1 The process of learning is one that allows organisms to adapt flexibly to local circumstances. Learning can be defined as a change in behavior or potential for behavior as a result of experience, though some further qualifications are necessary.

2 Two major forms of associative learning dominated research in the first half of this century: classical conditioning, as developed primarily by Pavlov, and operant or instrumental conditioning as developed by Thorndike, Hull, and Skinner.

3 In conventional classical conditioning, previously neutral stimuli are paired with stimuli that elicit reflexive responses and thereby come to elicit a learned version of those responses. Repeated trials without the original US lead to extinction.

4 Theorists have recently questioned several earlier interpretations of classical conditioning, suggesting that some biologically useful information must be conveyed if conditioning is to occur and that the conditioned response is adaptive to the situation, based on the information available.

5 In conventional operant conditioning, the future probability of a behavior that is followed by repeated reinforcement or punishment will be correspondingly increased or decreased. A series of nonreinforced trials will result in extinction.

6 Reinforcement and punishment can be defined in several ways, depending on the nature of the stimulus used and how it is applied. Reinforcements can also be given according to various schedules, and can be used so as to shape new behaviors and to chain them together.

7 Theorists have also questioned prior interpretations of operant conditioning, suggesting that innate constraints on what is easily learned and how are more important than had been previously thought.

8 Social learning theory, as developed by Dollard and Miller, Bandura, and others, is based largely on operant conditioning but emphasizes both social and cognitive factors in such concepts as modeling and vicarious reinforcement.

9 Cognitive learning itself has a substantial history, though it has not been the predominant trend. The Gestalt psychologists' work on insightful learning and Tolman's work in purposive behaviorism are major elements in this history.

10 Current suggestions for innate and cognitive or information interpretations in both classical and operant learning suggest that a broader and more eclectic learning theory may be required to encompass all kinds of learning. The direction of current approaches suggests Tolman's work but also draws from ethology.

Further Readings

For a review of the early work on learning, including that of Pavlov, Thorndike, Hull, and Tolman, see a text on the history of psychological thought, such as Schultz's *A History of Modern Psychology* (1981). A relatively brief and readable up-to-date treatment of learning theory, including the suggested revisions in both classical and operant approaches, is provided by Schwartz and Lacey's *Behaviorism, Science, and Human Nature* (1982). For more extensive coverage, see Schwartz's *Psychology of Learning and Behavior* (1978). Two major sources for detailed information are also two of the

most referenced books in psychology: *Hilgard and Marquis'
Conditioning and Learning* by Kimble (1961) and *Theories of
Learning* (1981) by Bower and Hilgard. Many of Skinner's
books are available; two especially useful ones are *About
Behaviorism* (1974) and the collection of papers *Cumulative
Record* (1972), named after a rat's cumulative record. A good
introduction to behavior modification, designed as an undergraduate text, is Reese, Howard, and Reese's *Human Behavior*
(1978). For self-control through behavior modification techniques, see Mahoney and Thoresen's *Self-Control: Power to the
Person* (1974). One somewhat unusual approach you might
find interesting is Hill's discussion of various real-world applications of learning theory, *Principles of Learning* (1981).

At a party you notice a familiar face and try to place it. "I know I know her," you think, "but who is she?" Only after you talk with her a while do you finally remember where and when you met her. A bit later, a friend asks you for another friend's phone number. "Let's see," you say. "It was 716-43 . . . , no . . . , 34 . . . , or was it 43 . . . , anyway, either 716-4307 or 716-3407." Still later, another student reminds you that you need to supply your social security number for the part-time work you've both been doing. "That's easy," you think, as you mentally say your number to yourself. Toward the end of the party, you are engaged in a lively discussion of foreign films and someone wonders which of Bergman's films had the scene with Death dancing away with the plague victims. "I know that," you say. "It was. . . ." and then you realize that it's on the tip of your tongue: you almost know what it is but can't quite reach it. "Search your memory," says someone, and you realize suddenly that you've been searching your memory all evening, in one way or another. Then, as you think about the images in the film, you remember that it is *Seventh Seal.* As the party breaks up, you think again about the memories you've searched for, the ones that have come easily and the ones you had to tease out. And you realize, in a sudden insight, that right now you're adding new memories, just as you have already added other memories during the party. You think of the years you've lived and the years stretching off into the future and wonder just how all those years of memories are stored so that you're usually able to remember what you want when you want.

Some people think of memory as a storeroom of miscellaneous facts. When we need a fact—such as the name of a movie—we rummage around in the storeroom to see if we can find it. If we can't find the fact, we say we've forgotten it. Then we may mean that we can't find it at this moment, even though we know that we know it. Or we may mean that we once knew it, but don't now. We use the word *forget* in both cases, but the differences are significant.

The everyday view of memory also tends to overlook its implicit uses: We may think of searching memory for a movie title but not realize that we have been using memory throughout the conversation. We have to remember what each person has said even to carry on a conversation, for example, and we must remember common social conventions about how to interact appropriately. In a conversation about movies, we must also remember what *movies* are and that we've seen the movie in question *before* we can begin to search for its title.

In this chapter, we will look at the processes and uses of memory as well as some of the unanswered

Chapter 9

Memory

questions about them. One of the most important of these questions is how best to conceptualize what memory does.

WHAT MEMORY DOES

Memory refers to the set of processes by which past experiences influence present actions. Psychologists have long thought of memory as associations among sensory elements, but now they see it more as an active information-processing system.

Ebbinghaus and Serial Associations

The pioneer in the objective, scientific study of memory was the German researcher **Hermann Ebbinghaus** (1850–1909). From about 1879 through 1885 Ebbinghaus explored memory, collecting an enormous amount of data (Ebbinghaus, 1885). One historian has called the book he published "perhaps the most brilliant single investigation in the history of experimental psychology" (Schultz, 1981, p. 74).

In the late 1800s, psychology was in its infancy; Ebbinghaus began his work the same year that Wundt founded the first psychology laboratory. Ebbinghaus's ideas about memory came from the philosophical tradition of associationism, which had also influenced learning theory (Chapter 8). The associationists proposed that the basic components of learning are sensory elements, which we link into perceptions by associating those that occur together. These combined associations we were said to remember (Schultz, 1981). So in his research Ebbinghaus sought to discover the rules by which the sensory elements were linked in the first place. To do so, he needed to study not the effects of prior learning, but the process of new learning.

These days, we might criticize Ebbinghaus for using primarily a single subject; practice effects over those years no doubt made that subject's memorization processes somewhat unusual. But as the subject was Ebbinghaus himself, we also have to admire his fortitude. Among other things, he memorized thousands of lists of **nonsense syllables,** consonant-vowel-consonant groups such as "NOL." Why did he choose nonsense syllables?

What Ebbinghaus needed, as any scientist does, was a simple model that captured the essence of the phenomenon to be explored. For Ebbinghaus, the problem was how to study human learning of verbal material without interference from previous learning.

To do so, he invented the nonsense syllable; it could be pronounced and learned as if it were a word, but had no previous meaning. (At least, Ebbinghaus thought it did not; similarities in sound or appearance between some of these and actual words were inevitable.)

Learning a string of nonsense syllables became Ebbinghaus's model of human verbal memorization. Such learning, where each item in the string is a cue to the next, is called **serial learning;** serial means "strung in a row." Serial learning can be done in several forms, but an approach often used by Ebbinghaus was the serial-anticipation technique: The first syllable is presented as a cue and the subject tries to remember the second one. Then the correct second one is presented; it acts as feedback of right or wrong, as further practice, and as a cue to the third syllable. Ebbinghaus used lists from a pool of over 2000 nonsense syllables he had created, presenting them with the aid of a metronome to regulate the timing. He kept track of how long it took him to learn these lists and how soon he forgot them. ■ Figure 9.1

Much of what Ebbinghaus found is still believed to be true. The best-known of his many findings is the now-classic **forgetting curve;** it shows that most forgetting occurs relatively soon after the learning experience, with less and less forgetting thereafter. Ebbinghaus was also the first to note a number of other effects, including ones related to the length of a memorized list. More elaborate models were needed, however, to describe all that memory does.

Encoding, Storage, and Retrieval

As Ebbinghaus tirelessly memorized lists of nonsense syllables, others were also beginning to explore memory. Soon memory came to be thought of as a series of three processes: putting in information, holding it in storage, and getting it back out. At first, it was believed new information was stored, held, and removed as if it had been locked in a storeroom. In recent years, models have become increasingly dynamic and fluid. In these information-processing models, stored information does not lie dormant but is actively manipulated.

The process of putting information into memory is **encoding,** meaning essentially to put into the proper form or code for storage and to store. Holding the encoded information for future use is **storage;** getting it back out of storage is **retrieval.** At first glance, this breakdown may not seem much more scientific than the everyday view. But even with this simple model you can be more specific than everyday language allows. Forgetting something that you know you still

a

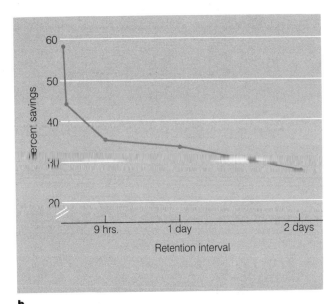

b

Figure 9.1 ■ (a) Hermann Ebbinghaus (1850–1909), the pioneer researcher in the psychology of memory (The Bettmann Archive). (b) Ebbinghaus's famous forgetting curve, one of the first quantitative summaries of human higher mental processes. (*Savings* indicates how much easier it is to relearn material after a period of forgetting; it is a standard measure of retention.) (After Ebbinghaus, 1885.)

know, for example, can be conceptualized as a retrieval failure, whereas more permanent forgetting may be a failure to encode or a loss from storage.

Just how useful these terms are, however, depends on the model in which they are used. In the storeroom model, encoding is seen as something like attaching a luggage claim check. The memory then lies in storage until a request acting as a claim number retrieves it. Although the model used in this chapter retains some of this flavor, it is based more on an information-processing approach.

The information-processing model gives all three terms more dynamic meanings (Zechmeister & Nyberg, 1982). Encoding includes applying a number of complex codes, more like a library cross-filing than a claim check. And rather than a simple labeling of the information, encoding includes reshaping it and combining it with existing information. And what is stored is not simply a discrete piece of new information, but a changed pattern of total information, one in which the new piece becomes part of a new whole. Finally, retrieval is not just recovery of a single piece of information. Instead, new pieces are continually being added to what is retrieved and this total is reencoded, so the pattern in storage changes with each retrieval.

Currently, only a dynamic approach such as information processing seems capable of capturing the essence of how people remember. But unfortunately,

none of the current models can adequately represent such a complex process. Thus current models are typically hybrid ones; they use encoding, storage, and retrieval as do the storeroom models, but they also seek to add some of the interplay of information-processing views. As psychologists investigate memory, they may devise a new model that more accurately describes its dynamics. In the meantime, most use a model that includes two forms of memory storage (Craik & Levy, 1976).

Two-Store Models

William James (1890) was probably the first psychologist to draw attention to the difference between what we usually call memory and the special system for storing something briefly and then letting it go (what you use between looking up a phone number and dialing it). But Brown (1958) and Peterson and Peterson (1959) were the first to demonstrate that *short-term memory* is distinctly different from ordinary memory. Peterson and Peterson, whose work led to the most follow-on research, asked subjects to remember trigrams, sets of three consonants such as "CRZ." This would be a trivial task, except that subjects were prevented from repeating the trigrams to themselves. The experimenter said the trigram, then immediately gave a three-digit number; the subject was asked to count

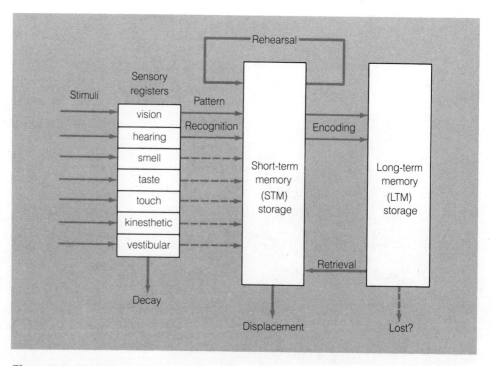

Figure 9.2 ■ The duplex model of memory. Incoming stimuli enter sensory registers where they remain in original form very briefly before they are either lost through decay or interpreted through pattern recognition into STM. (Dashed arrows indicate that all the sensory registers may be processing stimuli at the same time but do not necessarily do so.) Items in STM may also decay but are usually lost by displacement. Rehearsal can temporarily maintain items in STM, but only encoding into LTM can save them for later retrieval. (It is unknown whether items in LTM are ever truly lost, though we may fail to retrieve them for a number of reasons.)

backward by threes from that number until signaled to recall the trigram. Under these conditions, recall fell sharply from nearly 100% correct at immediate recall to around 10% only 18 seconds later.

This dramatic finding led to the development of models based on two distinct types of storage: **short-term memory (STM),** which lasts about 30 seconds, and **long-term memory (LTM),** which lasts for years (Broadbent, 1958). LTM is what you usually think of as memory, but STM is what you use between looking up a number and dialing it. STM is brief, limited in what it can hold to about as much as a phone number, and its contents can easily be lost (Deutsch & Deutsch, 1975). So for storing more information or for holding it longer, the information must be entered into LTM.

The **duplex model** of memory emphasizes the two processes of STM and LTM. Of its several versions, the most influential was proposed by Atkinson and Shiffrin (1968, 1971). The duplex model also includes a third element, called a sensory register, but the major emphasis is on STM and LTM. Figure 9.2 and Table 9.1 summarize the model. ■ Figure 9.2 ■ Table 9.1

According to the duplex model, incoming sensory information enters a very short-term storage system for each sense, the **sensory register.** This sensory information can either be passed on to STM or lost through a rapid fading called **decay.** As sensory information is passed to STM, it is altered from its initial form by a process of **pattern recognition** that interprets it in terms of some general pattern.

Once the patterned information enters STM, it can be lost, renewed, or stored. The process by which information is lost is **displacement,** or being pushed out of the limited storage area by other incoming information. Displacement is what you experience when you're trying to dial a newly looked-up phone number and someone asks you a question; if you pay attention to the question, it pushes the number out of STM. Information is renewed in STM by **rehearsal,** a kind of internal repetition (Postman, 1975). Rehearsal need not always be verbal, but often is; an example is repeating the phone number to yourself. Rehearsal can hold information in STM for longer than it would otherwise stay, so long as it is repeated every few seconds.

Table 9.1 ■ Summary of the Duplex Model

Feature	Sensory Registers	Short-term Memory (STM)	Long-term Memory (LTM)
Entry	From sense organs	Requires attention	Elaborative rehearsal
Maintenance	Not possible	Maintenance rehearsal	Organization
Format	Literal copy of input	Largely acoustic (some imagery and semantic)	Largely semantic (some auditory and visual)
Capacity	Large	Small (7 ± 2 items)	No known limit
Loss	Decay	Displacement (possibly decay)	Loss of accessibility by interference (possibly no loss)
Duration	1/4–2 seconds	Up to 30 seconds	Minutes to years
Retrieval	Pattern recognition	Automatic scanning	Retrieval cues used in search processes

Finally, information from STM can be encoded into LTM and stored. Only if it gets this far can you shift your attention and still retrieve the information when you return.

LTM is the storage system for all memories lasting longer than a few seconds, whether for an hour, a week, or many years. Once information is stored in LTM, some psychologists believe, it remains there, at least barring serious brain damage; others believe that some memory loss can occur (Loftus & Loftus, 1980). Usually, however, what we call forgetting is a failure of retrieval.

Besides memory storage, the duplex model also describes retrieval, or "remembering." (It is diagrammed in Figure 9.2 as an arrow from LTM back to STM.) The logic is that retrieval is like someone else giving you new information. Suppose someone asks for your phone number. You retrieve it from LTM, bringing it into awareness. After you've given the number, it fades from awareness. It is still in LTM and you can recall it again if you wish. But where was it when you thought about it, and what happened when you let go of it?

Presumably, what you retrieved was only a "copy" of the LTM phone number, so you don't have to encode the number again to keep it in LTM. But in some cases, the memory stored in LTM after it has been retrieved is different than it was before it was retrieved. This kind of complexity is putting the duplex model under stress, but the model is useful for explaining much of what happens in memory.

At least four lines of evidence have been widely quoted as support for the basic duplex model: duration differences, capacity differences, evidence from a memory task called free recall, and studies of the physiology of memory (Wickelgren, 1973). Each of these is currently under debate, but alternate views have not yet been demonstrated to be better explanations than the duplex model.

Duration differences between STM and LTM are striking. Without rehearsal or any attempt to memorize, information put into awareness quickly fades and disappears (usually in about 30 seconds). Yet once something is memorized, there seems to be no time limit on its retrieval. Elderly people may have retrieval problems, including those resulting from illness, but many can accurately recall events that occurred more than 50 years before. Obviously, many memories are not lost from LTM despite long time durations. In fact, some kinds of memory losses seem to affect recent memories more than older ones, as if LTM memories were strengthened over time (Squire et al., 1975).

Another line of evidence for the duplex model concerns **capacity,** or how much information can be held in memory (Shiffrin, 1976). The capacity of STM is extraordinarily limited, holding only about seven items. Yet the capacity of LTM seems virtually unlimited; memory experts have memorized large amounts of material daily for years without seeming to run out of storage capacity (Luria, 1968). Think about how much information is encoded in the memories of daily life. For a single brief interpersonal encounter, you store many details of sights, sounds, touches, smells, and so forth. To feed all that information to a computer would require substantial storage capacity, yet you can store many years worth of such detail without ever seeming to reach a capacity limit for LTM.

Recall is often used in everyday language as approximately equivalent to *remember*. In the psychology of memory, it is used with a modifier to specify a particular kind of remembering. **Free recall** means attempting to remember something, such as all the items of a previously presented list, in any order. ("Free" notes that the order is not important, unlike serial learning.) When free recall began to be studied, around the turn of the century, an interesting phenomenon was noticed. Subjects forgot more words from the middle of a list than from the beginning or end. This effect can be quantified by specifying each word's serial position in the original list, that is, whether it was the first word, the second one, and so forth. Suppose a list of words is read to a subject who listens until it is finished, then tries to remember the words. The probability of successfully recalling each word can be plotted according to its serial position in the presentation. Such a **serial position curve** shows a characteristic shape (Murdock, 1962). ■ Figure 9.3

If a list contains less than 20 words, the curve is U-shaped. For longer lists, the middle portion of the curve flattens out, but the ends remain the same (Figure 9.3a), indicating somewhat better recall for the first three or four words and significantly better recall for the last seven or so. The fact that the last words are recalled better is termed the **recency effect.** Improved recall for the early words is called the **primacy effect,** because these were entered into memory first.

Primacy and recency differences have long been considered strong evidence for an STM/LTM difference; the recency effect is related to STM and the primacy effect to LTM. (Monkeys show a similar curve of memory for photos, so this curve must reflect some general processes; Sands & Wright, 1980.) The last seven words in Figure 9.3a represent the capacity of STM, about seven items; because they are still present in STM, their immediate recall is more successful than for the other words. But if subjects must perform an intermediate task between presentation of the list and attempted recall, the last items cannot remain in STM and the recency effect disappears. The primacy effect occurs because the first few words entered into LTM can be rehearsed, and because they are new and different compared to their immediate surroundings, making them easier to remember later. The middle words all tend to interfere with each other in a kind of confusion effect, so they are harder to recall.

Physiological evidence also implies that STM is different from LTM. A piece of information stored in LTM has traditionally been called a memory **trace.** Just what any memory trace consists of, physiologically, remains largely unknown (Thompson, 1976). But STM traces and LTM traces do seem to be different: An STM trace is temporary, soon gone unless repeatedly rehearsed, whereas an LTM trace seems essentially permanent. Until relatively recently, there was thought to be another important difference: evidence from animal studies suggested that the LTM trace required a significant time to develop, or **consolidate,**

while the STM trace seemed immediate. At first, the consolidation time seemed to be as long as an hour, then perhaps a minute, and finally only 10 seconds (Duncan, 1949; Chorover & Schiller, 1965). But most recently, the findings that have seemed to demonstrate a consolidation effect have been said to be more likely to be retrieval effects (Lewis, 1979). So a time delay for LTM consolidation is no longer thought to be important, if it exists, and is no longer good evidence for a duplex model.

Some human memory problems also seem to support a duplex model. Humans show something like a consolidation failure after epileptic attacks or brain concussions: they typically have no memory for several minutes preceding the attack or injury. But now that the animal consolidation studies are being reinterpreted, these effects may be also. Other victims of accident or illness, or those subjected to experimental surgery, may show striking disruptions of memory. Some have apparently lost access to LTM storage, resulting in the generalized loss of memory called amnesia (Cermak, 1982). Others have apparently lost the ability to encode new traces into LTM; they can remember what they did up to the time of their injury, but not since (Scoville & Milner, 1957). But in both cases STM may be normal. This evidence still seems to support a duplex model, although it is being debated.

The combination of these several kinds of evidence—duration and capacity differences, primacy and recency effects in free recall, and physiological evidence—support the duplex model. But the model does have challengers.

An Alternative View: Levels of Processing

The model that has received the most attention as a possible competitor for the duplex model is the **levels-of-processing** model, which emphasizes three successively deeper or more complex levels at which incoming information can be processed (Craik & Lockhart, 1972). In this approach, the first or *physical* level represents processing of stimuli according to their physical structure; a printed letter or spoken word is processed at Level 1 simply as a shape or sound. The second or *acoustic* level represents processing stimuli deeply enough to recognize their basic pattern, typically their sound pattern or "name". A word is recognized at Level 2 as that word, but only in acoustic terms. Finally the *semantic* level represents processing deep enough to derive the word's conceptual meaning; only at Level 3 is the word understood. ■ Table 9.2

The levels-of-processing approach has had considerable appeal to psychologists: It seems intrinsically

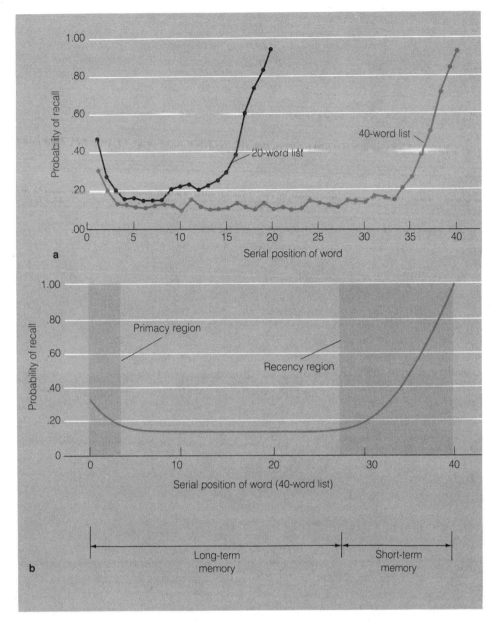

Figure 9.3 ■ (a) The serial position curve, based on free recall of word lists. The U-shape seen in the curve for the 20-word list flattens in the center for lists of 40 words or more, but the beginning and end remain similar. (b) A smoothed version of the results for the 40-word list, showing the regions where the primacy effect and the recency effect occur.

(Adapted from B. B. Murdock, Jr., *Journal of Experimental Psychology*, 1962, *64*, 482–488. Copyright 1962 by the American Psychological Association. Adapted by permission of the author.)

reasonable, and some studies have supported it. In one, for example, subjects were asked questions, immediately after the presentation of a word, that focused their attention at one of the three levels. "Is it in capital letters?" emphasized the first level, for example, "Does it rhyme with WEIGHT?" the second, and "Would it fit in the following sentence?" the third. The results supported the assumption that deeper processing leads to better recall; the third kind of question led to better recall than the second, which in turn was more effective than the first (Craik & Tulving, 1975).

But this model also has problems (Baddeley, 1978). Neither the concept of "depth" of processing nor the specific levels of processing can easily be operationally defined, so exact predictions are difficult to specify. But, in addition, some of the predictions that researchers made based on the model were not supported. Originally, for example, the model simply

Table 9.2 ■ Summary of the Levels-of-Processing Approach

Depth	Processing Level	Processing Function	Effect of Stimulus	
Shallow	1: Physical	Holds physical properties of original stimulus	*B*	*Apple*
	2: Acoustic	Processes only to sound of stimulus or its "name"	"Bee"	"Apple"
	3: Semantic	Processes the meaning of the stimulus	Second letter of alphabet	Red fruit, good to eat, ...
Deep				

stated that the deeper the level of processing, the better would be the memory and thus the better would be later retrieval. According to this, simple rehearsal would represent repetition at only a single level, which should not improve memory. But it does (T. O. Nelson, 1977). So some way of handling repetition at a single level must be included. Differences in retrieval strategies were also minimized in the original levels-of-processing model, but these have also turned out to be important. Later versions of the model have suggested that the initial depth of processing determines the *potential* memory strength; different techniques for retrieval then make differing uses of these potentials (Moscovitch & Craik, 1976).

The levels-of-processing approach continues to be revised and improved (Cermak & Craik, 1979). But as it incorporates concepts originally emphasized by the duplex model, such as rehearsal, it moves closer to it. In the meantime, users of the duplex model are adding distinctions based on levels of processing. The future may thus see a synthesis of the best parts of both models.

In the balance of the chapter, we will follow a time sequence within the duplex model, looking first at encoding, then at storage, then retrieval. But keep in mind as we do so that we are using a form of black-box model. Although the physiology of some structures or processes—such as a sensory register or rehearsal—may be partially understood, for others little may be known. Terms such as *STM* and *LTM* are only simplified representations of vastly more complex activities that correspond to no single brain location, structure, or process. So when you read that information "enters" a sensory register or STM can "hold" about seven items, keep in mind that this is only a verbal shorthand, not a literal description.

ENCODING INTO MEMORY

Before anything can be retrieved it must be in storage, and to be in storage it must first have been encoded. Although some of what we store is self-generated—we often remember our own thought processes, for example—it is conceptually easier to consider information brought in from the outside. So we begin with new information brought in through the senses; this goes first to the sensory registers.

Sensory Registers

A sensory register is a system for holding incoming sensory information just long enough for its pattern to be recognized. Each sense has its own sensory register. But as a species we pay most attention to two senses, vision and hearing; vision is our primary sense for general information, and hearing is the input channel for spoken language. Because vision and hearing are so important, most memory studies have used them as the input channels. And because language is so important, most studies have used language-based materials, whether presented as sights or sounds; these have ranged from nonsense syllables to complete prose passages. Some studies of nonlanguage visual materials have also been done, but comparatively little is known about memory for other sensory systems.

The visual sensory register is known as **iconic memory;** the representation of a visual input in the register is an **icon,** meaning a copy or image (Neisser, 1967; Long, 1980). Icons are *not* the same as the afterimages discussed in Chapter 6 (Coltheart, 1980), but just what and where they are is still being debated. Sakitt and her coworkers have suggested that the vis-

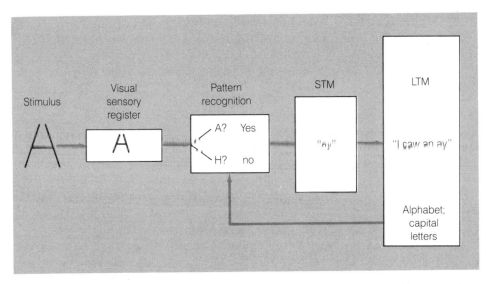

Figure 9.4 ■ The pattern recognition process (an expansion of the pattern-recognition arrows in Figure 9.2). For a stimulus in the sensory registers to be recognized it must be compared with appropriate LTM information.

ual sensory registers are in the rod cells of the retina (e.g., Sakitt & Long, 1979). Other evidence, however, suggests that the cones may also be involved, and the brain as well (Banks & Barber, 1977; McCloskey & Watkins, 1978). The auditory register is called **echoic memory;** a representation of a sound in the register is an **echo** (Crowder, 1976; Neisser, 1967). An icon lasts for about a quarter of a second, and an echo lasts a few seconds (Darwin et al., 1972; Haber & Standing, 1970). In this brief time before the icon or echo disappears, you must recognize it. If you do, the information goes into STM. (Any sensory information not moved to STM is lost through decay.)

In the duplex model, information reaching STM is thus recognized information. In levels-of-processing terms, it has reached Level 2 or 3. But how? Figure 9.2 shows only some arrows, but the step is quite complex. One major problem with a simple representation of pattern recognition is that it leaves out the role of LTM. For an icon or echo of a word to be recognized, it must be compared with the stored memories of what words look or sound like. Thus by the time a recognized word enters STM a form of retrieval from LTM has already occurred. ■ Figure 9.4

Short-Term Memory

Short-term memory is the center of the information-processing system. Information goes from it to LTM, but is also brought back to it when retrieved from LTM. Calling this central system "short-term" emphasizes

the duration of its storage, but STM is also called primary memory or immediate memory, because it receives information before LTM. Our focus here is on STM as an input way station between the very brief sensory registers and the virtually permanent LTM.

Encoding into STM Encoding is the process of coding information in STM and sending it on to LTM. Most of what we know about encoding concerns verbal material. Verbal inputs can be presented in an auditory form as speech, the form of language that our species has evolved to handle, or they can be presented in visual form to be read. Reading, a quite recent invention in the history of the species, is processed differently from speech. *Both* spoken and written words are coded in STM primarily in **acoustic codes** (according to their sound). Visually presented words are first translated to how they would sound, and the sound is then held in STM. If you look away from the page at the end of this sentence, for example, you may sense a residual of these words. But this residual will probably be more auditory (as if you had heard them) than visual (how they look on the page).

If you tried that exercise, you probably also retained a weak visual image of the page. And you no doubt understood the meaning of the suggestion, whether you tried the task or not. Researchers have found exactly this: Although acoustic codes are the most common form for STM verbal material, information can also be encoded as both **images** (representations of visual inputs) and **semantic codes** (according to meaning). Errors in recall from STM, for example, are typically acoustic; incorrect words are likely to be ones that *sound like* the actual word, whether the list was presented verbally or visually (Conrad, 1964). But deaf subjects, who do not use acoustic codes, tend to make imagery errors; their incorrect words *look like* correct ones. When hearing subjects have been instructed to pay attention to the meaning of the words, they tend to make semantic errors and include incorrect words with similar *meanings* to words on the list, even if these neither sound nor look alike (Shulman, 1972).

The levels-of-processing view offers a useful description of what is happening here. Words in STM are normally processed at Level 2, the acoustic level. Level-3 semantic processing takes greater effort and is usually not done unless there is good reason, such as the need to focus on a word's meaning. Errors made by the deaf, where Level 2 is not available, show that most of their information remains in a Level-1 visual code, but some may go directly to Level 3.

The study of visual imagery in STM is more recent, but it has been established that visual codes do exist (Posner et al., 1969; Shepard, 1978b). Visual STM probably also involves differences in coding similar to those of verbal STM, but these are harder to define and test, so less is known about them.

The Magic Number 7 and Chunking
One of the more striking aspects of memory is that STM seems limited to nearly exactly seven items, however this capacity is measured. This number became widely known through a review of many memory studies by George Miller (1956). Miller found that virtually all the studies available showed limits to STM, without rehearsal or practice, of 7 ± 2 (from 5 to 9 items). He was so taken by what he found that he called this STM limit the **magic number 7 ± 2.** Psychologists still don't know why it occurs, or at least why it seems so exact, but it continues to turn up in new studies (Broadbent, 1975). ■ Notable Quote: George Miller on the Magic Number 7 ± 2

You can easily experience this magic number for yourself. Have a friend help you with a version of the **memory-span** test (Dempster, 1981). Have your friend read a string of items, perhaps digits, at about one per second in a monotonous tone; when he or she stops, try to write down the string. (This version is called the digit-span test.) The most powerful effect will come if your friend begins with a string of four digits and progresses through strings of five, six, seven, eight, nine, and ten. (To avoid prior learning, have your friend create the strings.) The increase in difficulty at around seven is impressive, but what happens with longer lists is also informative. By eight or nine, you can feel the first items disappearing—

through displacement—as the last ones are read. By ten items, the task becomes so ridiculous that most people simply laugh and give up.

Once you've seen how impossible nine or ten digits are, try **chunking** them; that is, pull the separate digits into cohesive units or chunks. Your friend can create chunks merely by reading the digits in clusters: "3–1–6 . . . 8–7–2 . . . 5–9–4," for example, rather than "3–1–6–8–7–2–5–9–4." Words can also be chunked; the chunks might be names of theories or other sequences that you know well: *levels of processing, social learning theory, contingencies of reinforcement*, perhaps, rather than *of-contingencies-levels-theory-learning-social-of-processing-reinforcement*. Chunking greatly alters the number of items you can recall; nine digits or nine words that are nearly impossible alone become much easier when arranged into three chunks. But the magic number 7 still applies—to the number of chunks you can retain. (For substantial chunks, the limit may be somewhat lower than for simple items such as digits, more like five than seven or eight; Simon, 1974.) Obviously, the more you can squeeze into a chunk, the more total *information* you can hold in STM. But the information is still limited by that magic number.

One of the benefits of becoming an expert in any field is that you can hold more information per chunk and thus retain more total information. Chess masters, for example, can retain board patterns shown to them far more accurately than nonexperts—but only if the patterns represent meaningful games (Chase & Simon, 1973). The experts' memories for randomly arranged boards seem no better than nonexperts', but when the games are meaningful they apparently can chunk them, perhaps by standard patterns of offense or defense.

Maintenance Rehearsal, Decay, and Displacement
Once information is in STM, it will soon be lost unless it is rehearsed. Rehearsal is covert repetition of the information in STM. It is diagrammed in Figure 9.2 as an arrow that leaves STM, but then goes around and back into STM. To understand rehearsal, imagine that someone at a party tells you an important phone number; until you can find a pencil to write it down, you must retain it in memory. But not being a memory expert with quick ways of encoding into LTM, you'll soon lose the number unless you rehearse it. The process is something like repeating the number out loud to another person, except that you say it to yourself (Sperling & Speelman, 1970). The memory trace in STM is used to generate covert verbalization, which is like a new sensory input that you then remember. If you keep repeating it you can remember the number indefinitely. But if you have not entered it into LTM the least interruption will cause you to lose it. Levels-

of-processing theorists call this process **maintenance rehearsal;** it maintains the trace in STM, but only so long as it is continued (Craik & Lockhart, 1972).

If maintenance rehearsal ceases, the trace soon decays. But decay is rarely an important source of loss. Before the trace can decay, the number is likely to be displaced by other information. Paying attention to someone's question, for example, would eliminate the number from STM. STM decay takes up to 30 seconds, so in terms of time you could answer quickly and not experience decay. But the process of entering the question into STM displaces the number already there.

Displacement is actually the leading cause of loss from STM, because most of us take in new information more frequently than every 30 seconds. The root of the problem is the magic number 7 ± 2. Displacement begins when the critical five to nine items have filled STM to capacity and a single new item enters. The only way to avoid displacement is to push information on into LTM.

Long-Term Memory

Everything that tells you who you are and what you've done, or even what it means to be anybody, is represented in LTM—important personal information, school subjects, everyday knowledge about language and social customs, *everything*. If any part of it cannot be retrieved you may be in serious trouble, not knowing who you are, or what year it is, or what *dog* means. But even slight errors can cause trouble: wrong answers on an exam, calling one person by another's name, forgetting to keep an appointment, and so forth. Psychologists have proposed ways of distinguishing the various aspects of LTM, to focus on different issues. We cannot look at any of these in detail, but three of them are worth noting.

Tulving (1972) has proposed a distinction between *episodic* memory (what has happened to you and when) and *semantic* memory (factual, largely verbal, information). Such a distinction seems useful in studying amnesia patients, for example, who may forget who they are, yet remain able to make change or read a newspaper. Tulving's distinction also has important implications for memory research, most of which has studied episodic memory.

Flavell and Wellman (1977) have drawn our attention to several aspects of **metamemory,** or memory about memory. Metamemory includes all you know about the nature and processes of your own memory: knowing whether you already know something, knowing how hard it would be for you to learn something, or even knowing whether you are likely to be able to learn something. Metamemory, or "memory monitoring," can be surprisingly accurate, but requires substantial experience to develop (Hart, 1967; Wellman, 1977). We will note it occasionally below, in terms of the "knowing-you-know" experience.

Meacham and others are beginning to study *prospective* memory, which is remembering to do things at some time in the future rather than remembering things you have already done (Meacham & Leiman, 1982).

Encoding into LTM   Before any information can be retrieved, it must be encoded and kept until needed. Some information seems to be encoded and stored automatically, even when we wish it weren't. A horrifying experience, such as the assassination of President Kennedy, may be undesirably vivid in memory without any attempt having been made to remember it; such memories have been called "flashbulb" memories (Brown & Kulik, 1977). Brown and Kulik suggest that flashbulbs may be created by a specialized biological mechanism that says, in effect, "now print." But Neisser (1982b) has proposed that flashbulbs represent the summation of much rehearsal, and may even incorporate fabricated details that never happened.

Intentional memorization of less exciting information usually requires deliberate techniques. Probably the most important of such techniques concerns how the information is organized and packaged as it is encoded (Tulving & Bower, 1974). Successful retrieval requires retrieval cues in order to reach the stored

---

NOTABLE QUOTE:
George Miller on the magic number 7 ± 2

❝ My problem is that I have been persecuted by an integer. For seven years this number has followed me around, has intruded in my most private data, and has assaulted me from the pages of our most public journals. This number assumes a variety of disguises, being sometimes a little larger and sometimes a little smaller than usual, but never changing so much as to be unrecognizable. The persistence with which this number plagues me is far more than a random accident. There is, to quote a famous senator, a design behind it, some pattern governing its appearances. Either there really is something unusual about the number or else I am suffering from delusions of persecution. ❞
Miller, 1956, p. 91.

Figure 9.5 ■ Unorganized items are easier to encode and store if they can be organized somehow. (a) Here the items are organized around a schema of a school room, but any organizing schema will improve memory of the items. (b) Results of one study comparing recall success for organized and random conditions.

(**a** adapted from J. M. Mandler and R. E. Parker, *Journal of Experimental Psychology: Human Learning and Memory*, 1976, 2, 38–48. Copyright 1976 by the American Psychological Association. Adapted by permission of the author; **b** from G. H. Bower, *Cognitive Psychology*, 1970, 1, 18–46. Used by permission of Academic Press, Inc.)

information. If such cues are specifically associated with the material as it is encoded, later retrieval may be relatively easy. If no cues can easily be found, the information may remain stored but inaccessible.

Most study of LTM encoding has focused on verbal codes, but increasing attention is being given to visual codes. Paivio (1979) has even suggested a **dual-code theory** of LTM, suggesting that two semi-independent forms of LTM exist: one verbal and one visual. These two systems seem likely to reflect the functioning of the two cerebral hemispheres (as described in Chapter 2) (Bower, 1970a; Seamon & Gazzaniga, 1973).

An important way of developing retrieval cues is to organize the incoming material. One way to organize it is by forming chunks similar to those of STM; if you can retrieve the chunk, you get all of the information associated with it. But any system that can organize information can also help to encode it. Organizing systems are often based on verbal strategies, but can also use visual images (Mandler & Parker, 1976). ■ Figure 9.5

Still other organizing systems may also be used. Psychotherapists, for example, often find that some memories of their patients seem to be organized along emotional lines. Such memories are apparently related by the emotion the patient felt as the memory was encoded. (Try thinking how you felt when you were really embarrassed or really angry, and you are likely to recall some times when you felt that way.)

Elaborative Rehearsal and LTM We considered maintenance rehearsal earlier, noting that it could hold information in STM longer than it would remain otherwise. In the original duplex model of Atkinson and Shiffrin (1968, 1971), rehearsal was a single term, and was assumed to help encode material into LTM. One consequence of the levels-of-processing approach, however, has been to suggest a difference between two kinds of rehearsal (Craik & Watkins, 1973). Maintenance rehearsal doesn't seem to help improve encoding into LTM (Glenberg et al., 1977). For example, one man who had read a prayer nearly every day for 25 years, a total of about 5000 times, found that he still had not memorized it (Sanford, 1917). And most people cannot accurately describe—or even recognize—a Lincoln penny, despite daily practice (Nickerson, 1979). (Can you, without looking, say what is on each side?)

Many psychologists, however, believe that some kind of rehearsal *is* associated with encoding (Rundus, 1971). According to levels-of-processing theorists, rehearsal that is effective in encoding is **elaborative rehearsal,** in which you repeat the information but at the same time process it at Level 3 so as to elaborate its meaning (Craik & Lockhart, 1972). Where maintenance rehearsal makes use of LTM only to interpret the

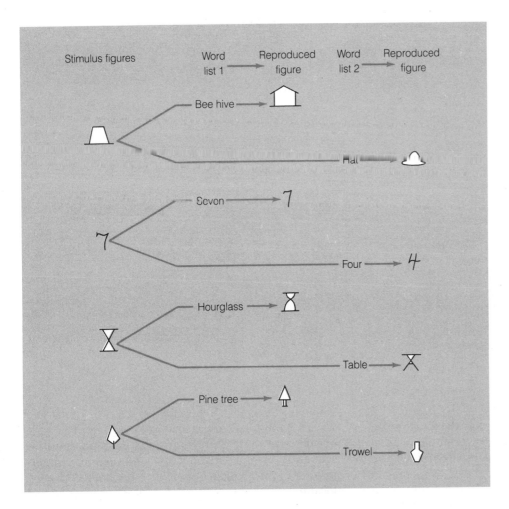

Figure 9.6 ■ Visual items are encoded partially by appearance, but this can be modified by verbal codes. Two groups of subjects were shown the same ambiguous shapes but given different names for them (word lists 1 and 2). Later, when they drew the shapes from memory, the drawings were modified in the direction of the names on their word list.

(Adapted from Carmichael et al., 1932.)

input to a Level-2 acoustic form, elaborative rehearsal uses LTM more extensively. It not only retrieves the Level-3 semantic meaning of the new input, but adds related words and ideas. In everyday language, elaborative rehearsal is a form of thinking about the material; the new input is thought about to elaborate its meaning, to interpret it in terms of what is already known, and so forth. In fact, it is at this elaborative rehearsal step that the greatest improvement in memory can be made. Chunking in STM is one form of elaborative rehearsal that can increase the information held and encoded to LTM. But more important is the role of elaborative rehearsal in creating retrieval cues to be used later.

One important aspect of elaborative rehearsal is the interaction of verbal and visual codes (Bower, 1972). We have a strong tendency to name and elaborate verbally all incoming material, a tendency that is often useful but can also be misleading. When a visual image is "named," the naming brings with it some characteristics of the general concept that it represents; these are added to and may even overcome the image itself. If a picture of an ordinary-seeming chair is presented and we name it as a chair, for example, we may be less likely to notice that this particular image is drawn with only three legs.

One early study demonstrated how verbal elaboration can affect the memory of visual images (Carmichael et al., 1932). Two groups of subjects were shown the same set of simple drawings, but were given different names for them. Later, when these subjects were asked to draw what they had seen, their drawings were biased in the direction of the names they had received. Although the original stimuli were clearly ambiguous, the remembered images were not. Psychologists have long argued about the processes by which such effects occur, however (Riley, 1962). The differences in the subjects' drawings could have resulted from their encoding the shapes as different when they were first seen. Or they could have resulted from using the name at the time of retrieval to clarify a weak visual memory. Or both processes might play a part. ■ Figure 9.6

People differ in the extent to which they use imagery elaboration (Paivio, 1969). In general, people seem to use much less imagery than semantic encoding, but

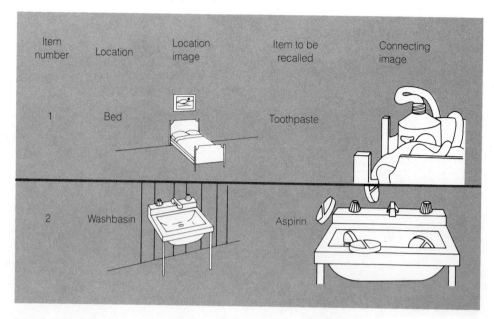

Figure 9.7 ■ Using the method of loci with a sequence of daily locations to remember items on a shopping list.

most can develop such imagery with practice. Although an imprecise image can bias the memory, in general, visual imagery offers a powerful aid to recall (Bower, 1972). Elaborative rehearsal techniques are thus important not only because they bias memories, but also because they offer the potential for greatly improving retrieval. A number of specialized techniques of elaborative rehearsal have long been used in this way.

Mnemonics Specialized techniques for improving encoding, and thus retrieval, are called mnemonic devices or simply **mnemonics.** Many mnemonics are purely verbal, a few are purely visual, and some are a mixture (Bower, 1973a).

You're probably familiar with some kinds of verbal mnemonics. One type is itself learned by rote; its benefit is that once learned it summarizes a large amount of information. "Thirty days hath September, April, June, and November . . ." is of this type; it uses meter and rhyme to help us remember how many days each month has. Another form of purely verbal mnemonic is the acronym, a word created out of separate letters that each stand for other words, as *M.A.S.H.* means "Mobile Army Surgical Hospital" (Bower, 1970b). Sometimes an acronym even becomes a word, as with *laser*, which stands for "light amplification by stimulated emission of radiation."

The **method of loci** is one of the oldest visual mnemonics; it uses a series of well-learned loci, or locations, as keys to remembering other things

(Bower, 1970a). To remember a series of items you visualize these locations, such as the rooms of a house or buildings along a street, one at a time in a standard sequence. At the same time, you mentally superimpose an image of an item to be remembered on each location. To remember the items you begin at the first location and mentally review the sequence. ■ Figure 9.7

The most effective mnemonics seem to be those that mix verbal and visual strategies. One of the best known of these is the **pegword** technique, in which previously memorized words act as pegs on which to hang other items (Bower, 1972). In one version, suitable for memorizing any ten items, you first learn a rhyming list for the numbers one to ten: "one is a bun, two is a shoe, . . ." and so forth. Then you combine an image of the first item with some "bun" image, the second with some "shoe" image, and so forth. Recalling the rhyming list is easy. And since the list is tied through images to the items you wish to remember, you retrieve these as well. (There are more complex techniques for longer lists; Higbee, 1977; Lorayne & Lucas, 1974.) ■ Figure 9.8

Mnemonics often seem cumbersome when described, yet work remarkably well. One such system for teaching foreign-language vocabulary is particularly effective (Atkinson, 1975). In this **keyword** method, the sound of the foreign word is used to create an image; for the Spanish word *pato* (pronounced "pot-o"), the image might be a cooking pot. This image is superimposed on another image that represents the

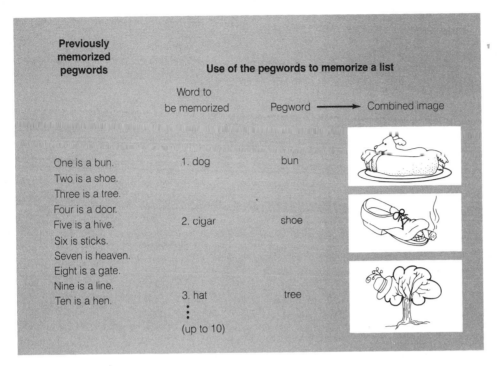

Previously memorized pegwords	Use of the pegwords to memorize a list		
	Word to be memorized	Pegword ⟶	Combined image
One is a bun.	1. dog	bun	
Two is a shoe.			
Three is a tree.			
Four is a door.			
Five is a hive.	2. cigar	shoe	
Six is sticks.			
Seven is heaven.			
Eight is a gate.			
Nine is a line.	3. hat	tree	
Ten is a hen.	⋮		
	(up to 10)		

Figure 9.8 ■ The pegword mnemonic technique. First memorize the ten rhyming pegwords. Then for any list of up to ten items to be memorized in sequence, create a visual image that links each item to be recalled with its pegword, using whatever imagery seems most appropriate and vivid.

word's meaning. In this case, *pato* means "duck," so the combined image might be a duck wearing a pot as a hat. In use, reading the word *pato* calls up the pot image, which carries the duck image, and *pato* thus means duck.

STORAGE IN MEMORY

Once input material has been encoded, it must remain in storage until needed and then be retrieved on demand if it is to be useful. In looking at storage, we will review two general issues: how the stored information is organized and what the physiological mechanisms of storage are. Hypotheses about the organization of memory are framed in black-box terms, just as we have done for STM or rehearsal. Hypotheses about the physiology of storage may be stated in such terms, but are also being explored in terms of neurons and RNA.

Organization of Storage

Organization of storage is obviously necessary if all the bits of knowledge that we accumulate are to be related to each other. Sometimes we encounter linkages we had been unaware of, as when a sight, a song, or an odor triggers some memory. It can sometimes be noted that such linkages are not random. One couple, for example, found themselves both thinking of a friend whom they had not seen in years. Then they realized that a song was playing in the background that had been popular when they last saw the friend. Even though neither of them had paid it much attention, the song retrieved associated memories of their friend. Some such automatic associations may be the cause of *involuntary memories*—those that seem to be retrieved out of the blue, without any intent to do so—though these have been little studied (Salaman, 1970).

There are many possible modes of storage—visual, auditory, emotional, and so forth—and many potential linkages between them; so far, psychologists have concentrated their studies on the organization of verbal memory. One general model suggests that verbal organization is hierarchical, with major concepts being further subdivided into smaller ones (Bower, 1970b). ■ Figure 9.9

This hierarchical pattern also has implications for encoding and retrieval. In learning the name of a new metal—*antimony*, for example—you would not have to learn all of its characteristics. Once you knew it was a metal, it would acquire the characteristics of metals. If you were asked "Does antimony float?" you would

"WHEN YOU'RE YOUNG, IT COMES NATURALLY, BUT WHEN YOU GET A LITTLE OLDER, YOU HAVE TO RELY ON MNEMONICS."

© 1978 by Sidney Harris—American Scientist Magazine

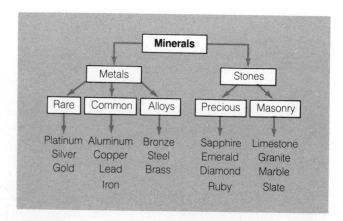

Figure 9.9 ■ A hypothetical conceptual hierarchy. In this case, the concept of *minerals* is more general than *metals* or *stones*, and each of these would be further subdivided.

(From G. H. Bower, *Cognitive Psychology*, 1970, 1, 18–46. Used by permission of Academic Press, Inc.)

probably say "no," because metals in general don't float. The hierarchical model also suggests that you could "search" memory through these categories. In trying to remember *antimony* you might note that it is a metal, not too common, but not valuable like gold, and so forth. You could add other cues, thinking of it as "anti-money," for example, and visualizing trying to spend it with no success. Then when you said "not valuable like gold" that might trigger the anti-money image and thus *antimony*.

It's clear that verbal memory involves linkages, and a hierarchy seems one way of representing them. But such a simple view does not do justice to the complexity of the actual connections. Collins and Quillian's (1969) **network model** of verbal memory has further specified some aspects of the hierarchical view: It relates major concepts, called *units*, to each other with *pointers*. Each unit has *properties*, descriptions that are also linked with pointers. ■ Figure 9.10

This network model lacks many aspects of real verbal memory but is specific enough to be useful. If you are asked whether a canary can sing, for example, your answer will be quicker than if asked whether it has skin. But why? The network model suggests a way of interpreting and quantifying such differences. *Can sing* is a property of the unit *canary*, and *has skin* is a property of the more general unit *animal*. If you enter the network with the word *canary*, you will thus reach the property *can sing* very quickly. *Can fly* as a property of birds in general, will take a bit longer to retrieve and *has skin* longer still. Such time measurements, called **reaction times (RT),** are useful in many information-processing studies.

The network model also implies another RT difference: From the arrangement of the model it follows that retrieving units should be faster than retrieving the properties associated with them. "A canary is a canary" will thus show the fastest response, with " . . . is a bird" and " . . . is an animal" taking longer; all three are faster than "a canary can sing."

In its present form, however, the network model does not predict some effects. One of these is the *typicality* effect: A sentence about a typical member at a given level in the hierarchy is answered faster than one about a nontypical member. A property of *bird*, such as "has feathers," will be retrieved faster for *canary* than for *penguin* or *ostrich*, even though the network model represents all three as one level down from *bird*. Both competing models and refinements of Collins and Quillian's model have been proposed (Collins & Loftus, 1975), and these will no doubt lead to further improvements. For now, the network model is useful, even though it cannot yet represent the complexity of real verbal memory.

Physiology of Storage

An understanding of the mechanisms of memory would have powerful implications—for developing possible chemical ways of improving our memories, for example. Unfortunately, relatively little is yet known about the physiology of memory, but reseachers continue to seek both its neurology and its molecular basis.

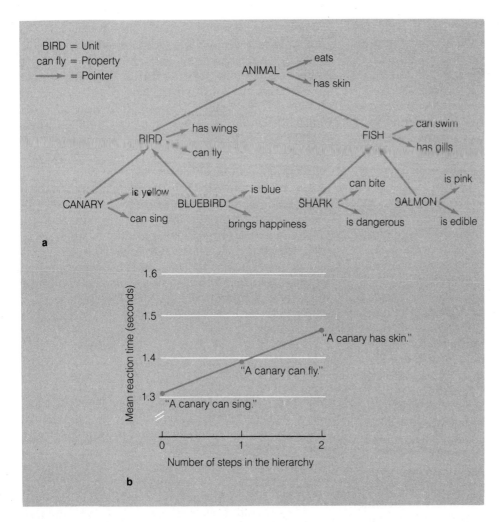

Figure 9.10 ■ (a) Part of a hierarchy in memory, as proposed by Collins and Quillian's network model (1969). Words in capitals, called *units*, are similar to the concepts in Figure 9.9, but the model also includes descriptive information or *properties* (words in lower case) and *pointers* to link them (arrows). (b) A plot of the time needed to decide whether a sentence is true or false (vertical scale) versus the number of steps in the hierarchy. "A canary can sing" is interpreted faster than the other statements, according to this model, because the other statements require moving to concepts at higher levels in the hierarchy.

(From A. M. Collins and M. R. Quillian, *Journal of Verbal Learning and Verbal Behavior*, 1969, *8*, 240–247. Used by permission of Academic Press, Inc.)

STM versus LTM STM and LTM have long been thought to represent different physiological processes. According to one proposal, the STM trace is the continuing activity in a **reverberating circuit,** a set of neurons so arranged that once stimulated they continue to self-stimulate (Hebb, 1949). In this model, more complex patterns represent interlocked sets of reverberating circuits, and the processes of encoding and storage in LTM result from some more permanent change in all the synapses that had been active in the reverberating circuits. The altered set of synapses rep-resents the LTM memory trace; if one of these synapses becomes activated, the overall pattern might be retrieved. According to this notion, elaborative rehearsal improves retrieval by adding other groups of neurons to the set, thus making the final pattern more distributed in the brain and offering more ways to retrieve it.

As a black-box model, this two-stage concept is a useful way of summarizing a variety of findings. As a physiological description, however, it is only a tentative proposal. The actual mechanisms of both STM and LTM remain unknown (Rosenzweig & Bennett, 1976). Where the patterns are located when memories involve many senses is one problem. There seems to be no specific memory area of the brain, so perhaps these memories are stored separately in the sensory areas. But then how are they linked together over the entire brain, and why don't they interfere with normal sensory processing? Another problem involves the unlimited capacity of LTM, which means that neurons must be involved in more than one memory. Even the billions of neurons we have are not enough for as many independent patterns as we can store memories.

RNA and Memory Molecules   Another line of research approaches memory problems from the molecular level. The genetic code in all species is carried in a library of DNA molecules within the nucleus of each cell (Chapter 3). Varieties of a related molecule, **RNA** (ribonucleic acid), then act as molecular messengers, carrying instructions from the DNA codes to other parts of the cell. When this relationship between DNA and RNA began to emerge in the 1950s, researchers wondered if RNA molecules could also play a role in memory. Early work suggested that the amount of RNA in rats' brains increased after they had been trained at some task, and a wide variety of experiments then examined the RNA of trained and naive animals of several species.

These experiments have been of several types (Jonas, 1974). In one approach, the brains of newly trained animals have been analyzed to see whether the amount of RNA or other molecules is different from that in untrained animals. Another approach has sought, using drugs, for example, to either improve or reduce RNA synthesis. A third approach has sought to transfer RNA extract from trained animals to naive ones to see if the memory also transferred. But results to date remain open to debate. Findings obtained by one laboratory are frequently not replicable by another one—often not even by the original lab at a later date. Analysis procedures are also complex and subject to many potential errors, but because these could affect either the first study or the attempts to replicate it, it's hard to tell whether an effect is real but elusive or simply an artifact. Until replicable results can be obtained, the role of RNA in memory, if any, remains unknown.

Emphasis has meanwhile shifted to smaller molecules than RNA, forms of proteins called peptides. These peptide molecules are made up of as many as 20 different amino acids, compared to the 4 used for DNA/RNA codes, so they have enough different combinations to encode enormous amounts of information—although it is not obvious how a molecule could be "retrieved" from LTM. One possibility might be a combination of neural circuits and molecules. One molecule would somehow facilitate action among one particular set of neurons and another molecule another set, perhaps by affecting the neurotransmitter produced or the sensitivity to it.

If memory is encoded through identifiable molecules, the finding will have important implications. If such a molecule could be created or extracted from others without damage (as we now take blood samples), you might be able to learn something by taking a pill or injection. Even if the molecules themselves could not be administered, drugs that aided or inhibited their synthesis might help you remember academic material, for example, or forget a painful event (Weingartner et al., 1981). But, to date, the drugs that aid memory in animals are often unreliable in their effects on humans, and some are dangerous (one of them is strychnine). Hence, their routine use is not likely to occur soon (Bartus, 1979).

RETRIEVAL FROM MEMORY

Memory traces, however they may be represented physiologically, are useful only if they can be retrieved. The term *retrieval* actually covers a number of phenomena. Recognizing a letter or word seems to be an automatic process that either works or doesn't. Remembering a face and a name, however, are different tasks, and remembering complex verbal material may be different still. Metamemory is also a separate task. You may remember that you know a word, for example, independently of being able to retrieve the word itself; thus the "knowing that you know" must be retrieved separately (Wellman, 1977).

Measuring Retrieval

Several kinds of evidence are used to measure retrieval, including free recall, recognition, and savings. What you think of as "remembering" is probably closest to free recall: retrieving items from LTM on the basis of minimal cues. We looked at free recall in the context of word lists, but it applies to many open-ended memory tasks: "Where were you two weeks ago at four in the afternoon?" might be a free-recall question asked of a defendant. Because of the relative scarcity of cues, free recall is the most difficult of the three common measures of memory. ■ Figure 9.11

Recognition is the easiest task; the original stimulus is presented, so you have maximum cues, and you must simply decide whether it is familiar (Mandler, 1980). Recognition scores vary, depending on how unique the presentation is; they can be very high for substantial periods of time, especially for visual recognition (Shepard, 1967). Recognition may work even when the trace is so weak that you no longer know that you know. A subject may claim to not remember anything, for example, yet if asked to guess an answer may do so correctly at a rate far higher than chance.

The method of **relearning,** or savings, asks the subject to relearn to the original level after some period of forgetting, and then measures how much faster the relearning was (Ebbinghaus, 1885; Nelson, 1978). The difference between the original learning and the relearning is the savings: If learning a list of nonsense syllables originally took 30 minutes but only 20 minutes to relearn a week later, the savings of 10 minutes implies a 33% retention of the original learning.

Free recall, recognition, and relearning are used with a variety of tasks. But for some tasks other measures are more appropriate. In retrieving information from STM, answers may be 100% correct, but the speed with which they are recovered may be informative. In searching LTM, retrieval may fail completely, yet the sequence of search and the related items retrieved may indicate how LTM is organized and how retrieval cues operate.

Scanning STM

You might not think retrieval applies to STM; it may seem as if the contents of STM are immediately present in consciousness. But there is a specialized form of retrieval from STM. Called **memory scanning** by Sternberg (1975), it refers to such tasks as deciding whether 3 was among several digits just read to you. To answer such a question, you "scan" the previous items, which are still in STM, to see if 3 was among them. Your answer may seem instantaneous, but it is not. Reaction times vary in regular ways and these have been used as an indicator of how scanning might work. Suppose someone read aloud to you a list of four items. He or she then reads a fifth item, and you must say "yes" if it was one of the four and "no" if it wasn't. A test stimulus such as this fifth item is called a *probe*; the question is how you scan the previous items and decide if the probe matches any of them.

You could compare all four against the probe simultaneously or could compare them one at a time. Experiments can demonstrate which possibility is more likely by comparing reaction times for lists of different sizes. Entering the memory set and the probe into STM should always take the same time, but the time taken in scanning would differ for the two possibilities. Scanning simultaneously would take the same time for five digits as for four, but scanning one at a

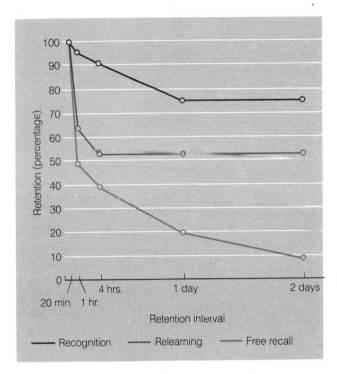

Figure 9.11 ■ Three different measures of memory. Free recall, the most difficult task, continues to show a drop in effective retrieval after two days. But the savings and recognition measures suggest that a relatively constant residual is left after about a day. The further loss in free recall may reflect a loss in retrieval cues rather than loss of the memory trace itself. (These cues are provided in the relearning and recognition tasks.)
(Adapted from Luh, 1922.)

time would take longer for each additional item. Results show that more time *is* needed for each additional item and thus that they are scanned one at a time. Ordinarily, the time differences between the two possibilities are not important because about 30 items can be scanned in a second. But such studies tell us something about how information is processed in STM.

Other research has examined the manipulation of visual images in STM (Posner et al., 1969; Shepard, 1978b). These show that visual imagery is used in STM, although the nature of the image remains in debate (Pylyshyn, 1981). (We will consider this research in more detail in Chapter 11 in the context of visual thinking.)

Searching LTM

Early in this chapter we noted that you might search your memory for an item such as a movie title. It's time to consider what that means in information-processing terms, both when the search is successful and when it fails. As noted earlier, some retrieval from LTM occurs in the pattern-recognition process. To recognize a pattern such as the letter *A*, for example, requires matching the visual input to the LTM trace representing *A*.

Such recognition/retrieval processes are not really what we usually mean by *remembering* or *searching memory*. These latter terms usually refer to deliberately seeking some stored fact. Many variables affect the deliberate LTM search/retrieval process, including external context, body state, specific cues, and the organization of LTM. Sometimes they work well, but sometimes they stop just short of the goal, leaving the item on the tip of the tongue. Let's see why.

Context   LTM traces are linked in many ways, so the more cues you have the more successful your search is likely to be (Tulving & Madigan, 1970). For many kinds of stored information, the original context of encoding offers cues for retrieval. In one study, for example, some subjects learned information underwater while others learned it on land. When tested later, subjects who learned underwater remembered more when underwater than when on land, and vice versa (Godden & Baddeley, 1975).

Such contextual cues can be used in their actual physical form, but are often effective even if used in an LTM-stored form. To remember where you misplaced your keys, for example, you can physically retrace your actions since you last had them; all of the sights and sounds around you will offer physical context cues. At the same time, you can try to recreate the mental or emotional context: "Let's see. I was feeling rushed and I ran over here and . . . ." The combination of contexts offers maximal cues, and you are likely to find the keys. But you can also mentally simulate the entire process without physically returning to the scene: "Let's see. I felt . . . and I walked . . . and I thought . . . ." As a consequence, you may find the keys in imagery rather than directly: "Oh yes, I remember they fell behind the desk and I was too busy to pick them up."

One study shows the value of such procedures (S. M. Smith, 1979). Subjects learned a list of 80 common words in a comfortably furnished lounge. The next day they were split into three groups for testing. A group tested in the same lounge remembered 18 of the words, but a second group tested in a different room—a stark, soundproof lab—remembered only 12. The third group, also tested in the lab, was first encouraged to remember what the lounge looked like. They remembered 17.2 words, essentially as many as those actually tested in the lounge.

Hypnotists often use such a conceptual-context approach when interviewing eyewitnesses to a crime or accident. The hypnotic procedure helps the witness relax and drift while the hypnotist suggests a recreation of the event. The hypnotized witness often reexperiences the event vividly and may be able to recover details that he or she could not remember before.

One specialized form of context is the internal context provided by a different body state. Usually, this means a drug-induced state; alcoholics, for example, often forget the next morning what they did when drunk the night before. Some of this may result from faulty encoding or even long-term brain damage. But it also may reflect the difference in context cues between a drunken state and a sober one. If the latter is true, the alcoholic should recall more of the night before when he or she gets drunk again; the similarity of context should offer more retrieval cues.

Tests of this notion of **state-dependent retrieval** have typically not used alcoholics because of their other physical and memory problems. Instead, they have used normal subjects compared in mildly drugged and normal (nondrugged) states (Eich, 1980). These studies show that retrieval is state-dependent: Subjects who learn when intoxicated can remember more when they are again intoxicated than when they are sober (Weingartner et al., 1976). The opposite also seems to hold true: Learning when sober does not carry over well into an intoxicated state. State-dependent effects seem to reflect differences in the cues used for retrieval. If enough other cues are available, the state-dependent effect disappears.

State-dependent learning has also been found with other physiological states; even differences in mood may be enough to affect recall (Bower, 1981). And state-dependent retrieval may explain the memory barrier that seems to block dream memories from waking recall (Chapter 7). It is probably not strong enough to be the sole explanation, but sleep is clearly a different physiological state and some state-dependent effects have been found for it (Evans et al., 1966).

Cues and Organization   In searching for LTM items that we should be able to find—those that we know we know—we can use either of the cues used in encoding, visual or verbal. Recognizing a person's face, for example, is primarily a visual task, especially if we don't know the person by name. Researchers have found that we can easily store and recognize hundreds, even thousands, of faces. But how? It can't be a pure image-matching system because faces are not static; each time you see a face, it looks somewhat different from before. So you presumably encode the image in some other way.

Researchers have been studying facial recognition with computer-simulation models. One such program accepts the values of 21 different facial features, such as thickness of eyebrows, then compares these values to compare the faces (Harmon, 1973). To

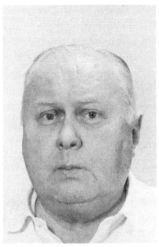

Figure 9.12 ■ Results of a computer program designed to study facial recognition (from Harmon, 1973). (a) The two faces judged by the program to be most similar from a group of 255 (all white males 20 to 50 years old). (b) The two faces judged by the program to be least similar. (Dr. Leon D. Harmon)

input a face, the computer aks for the value of the first feature; a human looking at a picture of the face chooses a value and types it in. When all values are in, the computer can search its memory of other faces, looking for a match. When this program was asked to find the two most similar faces in a set of 256, it first identified two different photos of the same subject, included by mistake; the human encoder had not noticed the duplication, but the program found it. For the remaining 255, the program identified a pair that seemed most similar and one that seemed least similar. Its choices seem reasonable to us, even without seeing all 255, but that alone is not evidence that the program is a good simulation of human facial recognition. Work continues on both improving this program and on other studies of human visual memory. ■ Figure 9.12

A different finding, however, suggests that facial recognition may be a specialized process, important in its own right but perhaps not a good model of visual encoding in general. An unusual memory loss has been found in a few brain-damaged patients: They fail to recognize any faces, even those of their spouses and children (Geschwind, 1979). They can still see and interpret faces; they can match frontal views to corresponding side views in pictures. And they can recognize people by their voices. The loss seems solely that of facial recognition. So specific a loss may imply that our species has evolved a specialized system for handling facial recognition. If this is true, it means that encoding and retrieval of other visual patterns may not follow the same rules as those for faces. (Visual recog-

nition for other than faces does seem to be quite efficient, however; Shepard, 1967.)

Tip-of-the-Tongue Phenomenon   Most of us have experienced the sensation of knowing that we know something but being unable to retrieve it; this has been called the **tip-of-the-tongue (TOT) phenomenon.** William James described the sensation, though its name has been applied more recently. ■ Notable Quote: William James on the Tip-of-the-Tongue Phenomenon

Brown and McNeill (1966) studied the TOT phenomenon by reading to subjects the definitions of uncommon words. Some subjects didn't know the words, others knew them immediately. Others, however, knew that they knew a particular word but couldn't quite retrieve it; they were experiencing the TOT state. These subjects and those in later TOT studies often knew many features of the target word, such as how many syllables it had (Koriat & Lieblich, 1974). They correctly identified the initial letter of the target word, for example, more than half the time. But apparently not enough cues were available, or perhaps not the necessary ones, to retrieve the target word. (This retrieval task is free recall. Given a list of words from which to recognize the target word, subjects would presumably have had no trouble doing so.) Note that TOT subjects knew whether they knew the word. The definition alone seemed to tell them that they knew an uncommon word even when they could not retrieve the word itself. And something like the TOT phenomenon also applies to visual items: Faces may trigger a sensation of familiarity even when you cannot retrieve the appropriate name (Yarmey, 1973). This is, in effect, the opposite of the finding noted earlier concerning recognition, that subjects sometimes can "guess" an answer that they don't know they know. In the TOT phenomenon, they know they know it, yet can't find it. These two examples tell us that "knowing you know," part of what is called metamemory, is somehow independent of the stored knowledge itself (Hart, 1967; Wellman, 1977).

Although the details are not understood, it seems that we automatically match inputs against LTM and produce "new" or "old" evaluations. But this matching process is not the same as actually retrieving the stored information used to make the match. It is likely that this matching process yields the sensation called **déjà vu,** the feeling that you've been in a place before or have had a conversation before. A partial match seems enough to trigger the feeling of knowing (Mandler, 1980). So it seems likely that something about the new place or conversation is similar enough to one that you *have* experienced to give a "familiar" output rather than an "unfamiliar" one.

VARIATIONS IN RETRIEVAL

Our information-processing mechanisms are remarkably rapid and accurate, but they are not perfect, so occasional errors (such as déjà vu) are to be expected. Our ordinary retrieval processes also create many

---

NOTABLE QUOTE:
William James on the tip-of-the-tongue phenomenon

❝Suppose we try to recall a forgotten name. The state of our consciousness is peculiar. There is a gap therein; but no mere gap. It is a gap that is intensely active. A sort of wraith of the name is in it, beckoning us in a given direction, making us at moments tingle with the sense of our closeness, and then letting us sink back without the longed-for term. If wrong names are proposed to us, this singularly definite gap acts immediately so as to negate them. They do not fit into its mold. And the gap of one word does not feel like the gap of another, all empty of content as both might seem necessarily to be when described as gaps.**❞**
James, 1890, vol. 1, p. 251.

---

kinds of distortions in information that is retrieved; they may even construct information that was never stored. Hence, for most of us, retrieved memories are only an approximation to the originally stored information. A few individuals, however, show that it is sometimes possible to recover information more exactly. We'll look at them after we consider the more usual distortions and constructions. Then we can consider forgetting as a failure of retrieval.

Constructive Memory

One important aspect of memory that can cause retrieval variations is called **constructive memory,** the constructing of patterns that were not originally stored in that form (Cofer, 1973). Constructive memory is an adaptive system, perhaps even necessary in a natural environment where the same exact situation is never encountered twice. But it can also cause problems because what we retrieve is different from what we stored. Constructive memory processes help us understand many aspects of the world, to read between the lines as it were; but what we read there may not be exactly what was written.

Inferences One major process in constructive memory is **inference,** deducing from evidence what must be true, even though it has not been stated directly. Researchers trying to program computers to understand language have found that humans often get more out of a sentence than is actually there. We infer what else must be true, using a wide variety of prior knowledge (Cofer, 1976). We use our knowledge of language conventions and social relationships, for example, so that a single sentence may allow us to infer what came before, what will come after, the education level and intent of the speaker, and other details. Suppose you are given the sentence "When Mary heard the bell on the ice-cream truck, she ran inside for her purse." Then if you are asked if Mary is a human female who intends to spend money on ice cream, you're likely to say "of course." But none of that is said in the sentence; you infer it from knowing about names, ice-cream trucks, money, and so forth.

Trying to hold an ordinary conversation with someone who did *not* make such inferences would be difficult; all the detail normally left unsaid would have to be made explicit. But the convenience of everyday inferences also causes retrieval problems. Not only do you infer things about Mary and the ice-cream truck, but you may *remember* them as having been said. In any conversation, what you remember is some mixture of what the other person actually said and what you inferred. If your inferences match the other speaker's intent, all is well; but if they don't, two peo-

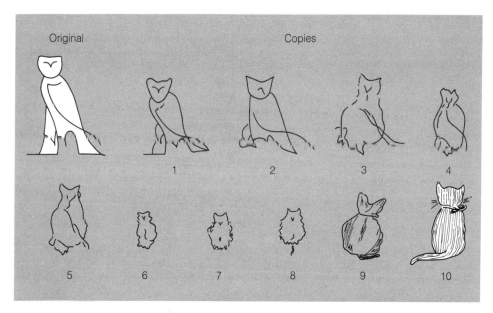

Figure 9.13 ■ Effects of the serial-reproduction memory task. The first of ten subjects saw the original stimulus, then reproduced it from memory a half-hour later. This reproduction was shown to Subject 2, and so forth. By the third reproduction the owl had lost much of its character; in the ninth and tenth it became a cat.

(From *Remembering* by F. C. Bartlett, Cambridge University Press, 1932. Used by permission.)

ple leave a conversation with two different memories of what was said.

One researcher compared John Dean's testimony in the Watergate scandal with audiotapes made at the time by President Nixon but only released after Dean's testimony was on record (Neisser, 1981). Neisser found that Dean's memories were *not* accurate regarding exactly what was said on a particular occasion—but they *were* accurate summaries of what was going on: who was, in general, thinking and saying what. This summarizing and pattern analyzing is what we are good at, Neisser argues. But in situations that demand exact recall, these same processes can get us into trouble.

In the process of encoding, for example, we use multiple cues. We are likely to use both visual appearance and verbal naming to encode a drawing that we want to remember. If these encoding techniques are both accurate, retrieval will be easier than if either code were used alone. But these encoding techniques may also distort what is stored and retrieved so it is different from the original. Such distortions have been studied in several ways. In the task called **serial reproduction,** for example, a drawing is shown to a subject, then removed and the subject draws it from memory (Bartlett, 1932). A second subject does the same with the first subject's drawing, and so forth. Such drawings go through a regular sequence, typically losing some details and gaining others. Self-

generated verbal codes probably play a part in this process. ■ Figure 9.13

Strictly verbal materials also become distorted in encoding and retrieval; as with vision, details may be omitted or new ones added. Bartlett, a pioneer in the field of memory for prose passages, noted this distortion (1932). Apparently because the cultural content of "The War of the Ghosts" was unfamiliar to subjects, it became distorted in a variety of ways in a single reproduction. ■ Figure 9.14

Problems of Eyewitness Testimony One area of society in which inaccurate retrieval is a major problem is eyewitness identifications. Some problems derive from our difficulty in matching visual memories with new visual inputs: matching a memory of a criminal with the appearance of a suspect, for example. Because of our general reliance on vision, we often consider such identifications to be strong evidence, but they are in fact highly flawed. Innocent defendants have been identified by several witnesses, only to have the identifications invalidated by conviction of the actual criminal (Buckhout, 1974). Though witnesses might find it easy to discriminate between an innocent defendant and the criminal if they are present together, they may not be able to encode the criminal's appearance and retrieve it accurately enough to discriminate that memory from the appearance of the innocent. ■ Figure 9.15

The War of the Ghosts

One night two young men from Egulac went down to the river to hunt seals, and while they were there it became foggy and calm. Then they heard war-cries, and they thought: "Maybe this is a war party." They escaped to the shore, and hid behind a log. Now canoes came up, and they heard the noise of paddles, and saw one canoe coming up to them. There were five men in the canoe, and they said:

"What do you think? We wish to take you along. We are going up the river to make war on the people."

One of the young men said: "I have no arrows."

"Arrows are in the canoe," they said.

"I will not go along. I might be killed. My relatives do not know where I have gone. But you," he said, turning to the other, "may go with them."

So one of the young men went, but the other returned home.

And the warriors went on up the river to a town on the other side of Kalama. The people came down to the water, and they began to fight, and many were killed. But presently the young man heard one of the warriors say: "Quick, let us go home; that Indian has been hit." Now he thought: "Oh, they are ghosts." He did not feel sick, but they said he had been shot.

So the canoes went back to Egulac, and the young man went ashore to his house, and made a fire. And he told everybody and said: "Behold I accompanied the ghosts, and we went to fight. Many of our fellows were killed, and many of those who attacked us were killed. They said I was hit, and I did not feel sick."

He told it all, and then he became quiet. When the sun rose he fell down. Something black came out of his mouth. His face became contorted. The people jumped up and cried.

He was dead.

Subject's Reproduction

Two youths were standing by a river about to start seal-catching, when a boat appeared with five men in it. They were all armed for war.

The youths were at first frightened, but they were asked by the men to come and help them fight some enemies on the other bank. One youth said he could not come as his relations would be anxious about him; the other said he would go, and entered the boat.

In the evening he returned to his hut, and told his friends that he had been in a battle. A great many had been slain, and he had been wounded by an arrow; he had not felt any pain, he said. They told him that he must have been fighting in a battle of ghosts. Then he remembered that it had been queer and he became very excited.

In the morning, however, he became ill, and his friends gathered round; he fell down and his face became very pale. Then he writhed and shrieked and his friends were filled with terror. At last he became calm. Something hard and black came out of his mouth, and he lay contorted and dead.

Figure 9.14 ■ "War of the Ghosts," used by Bartlett (1932) to investigate subjects' memory for prose, and one subject's reproduction of it.

(From *Remembering* by F. C. Bartlett, Cambridge University Press, 1932. Reprinted by permission.)

One recent line of research, the work of Loftus and her collaborators, has investigated other problems of eyewitness testimony (Loftus, 1980). This research has shown that inferences can affect retrieval when a witness is first questioned. In one study, subjects were shown a film of an automobile accident and then asked to estimate the speed of the cars (Loftus & Palmer, 1974). Most people are poor judges of a car's speed, so you might not expect accurate estimates. What was important, however, was how easily these estimates were changed by the words used in the question. All subjects were asked "About how fast were the two cars going when they _____?" with the final word being *contacted, hit, bumped, collided,* or *smashed.* Subjects estimated increasingly higher speeds depending on the wording of the question, with *smashed* yielding estimates nearly 10 miles an hour higher than *contacted.*

Those results show that the visual memory trace was affected at retrieval by the format of the question used to retrieve it. But a second study showed that the same question could also be a powerful modifier of further encoding and thus of retrieval at a later time. Subjects were questioned about broken glass a week after having been questioned with either *hit* or *smashed* (Loftus & Palmer, 1974). Of subjects who had originally been questioned with *smashed,* 32% remembered having seen broken glass—even though *no* broken glass had been shown. But only 14% of subjects questioned with *hit* reported broken glass. Questioning with the word *smashed* thus had a long-term influence on a detail of the memory that had not even been questioned.

Emotion and Retrieval It may also seem reasonable that we remember some things and not others because of their emotional values. But *reasonable* is not

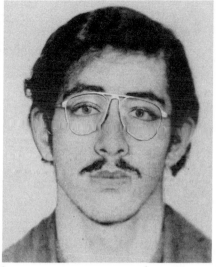

a   b   c

Figure 9.15 ■ An example of the problems of eyewitness identification. The men in (a) and (c) were both innocent but were picked out of police lineups by the victims of rapes and robberies committed by the man in (b). Only his later arrest and confession cleared them.

(From Buckhout, 1974; photos *The New York Times*.)

necessarily *true,* and little good experimental evidence on emotional memory distortion is available. There are several reasons for this. Much of the memory research to date has been done within an information-processing framework, which usually assumes "cold" (emotionless) processing. Humans do process some information unemotionally, but they may also add strong emotional "heat," which can interfere with efficient information processing; it's a truism that people don't think well when they are frightened or angry and that keeping "cool" may be a better way of managing the situation. In any case, psychologists currently know more about "cold" processes than "hot" ones.

Another reason for insufficient data on emotional distortion involves ethics. To study memory distortion by emotion, an experimenter would have to manipulate those emotions deliberately. But should any experimenter frighten or anger subjects for the sake of data? Some researchers argue "yes," but most are not convinced. Hence the relatively few studies have used weaker emotional arousal than the world outside the lab often does. (One study of the effects of mood variations indicates one way that weaker emotions can be incorporated into information-processing models; Bower, 1981.)

In the absence of experimental data, most of what is said about emotional distortion of memory derives from the work of Freud and other clinicians. Freud said that emotionally painful memories were **repressed**— pushed out of awareness as a way of reducing the emotional suffering they would otherwise cause. Repression is not a conscious or intentional act, but a motivated one carried out subconsciously. The person would not say "I'm going to forget that because it's painful," but would simply be unable to recall it. (Sometimes we deliberately block memories, but it's better to call that something else, perhaps *suppression.*)

The few emotion/memory experiments that have been done have been based on Freud's theory (MacKinnon & Dukes, 1962). Results of such studies have not provided strong support for repression. But because they have used weak emotions, the studies can't be taken as evidence against repression either. Provocative examples of emotional distorting or blocking of memories are easy to find—many have been reported by clinicians and other responsible observers— so the question is not whether it can happen. But these may be unusual or isolated examples. Because the concept of repression is hard to operationally define and test, the role it may play in ordinary memory processes remains unknown.

Stereotypes A special kind of inference results from **stereotypes,** which are expected familiar patterns. Stereotypes can concern anything, but some of the most important ones concern people; most of us have stereotypes about the kinds of people we are likely to encounter. Stereotypes can be useful time-savers for quickly sorting information, so long as the sorting is accurate. If we expect a preppie, a jock, a radical, or any other stereotyped person to behave in a particular way and they do, we have saved time and effort. But

Figure 9.16 ■ When a drawing like this was shown briefly to subjects, half reported that the black man was holding the razor. Apparently, previous stereotypes influence the process of encoding or retrieval.

(Redrawn from "Eyewitness Testimony" by Robert Buckhout, *Scientific American*, December 1974. Copyright © 1974 by Scientific American, Inc. All rights reserved. Used by permission.)

stereotypes can also mislead us, sometimes badly. If we expect certain behavior of a person we stereotype, we may "remember" that it occurred even when it didn't.

One researcher presented subjects with a series of drawings in which some stereotypical pattern was violated (Buckhout, 1974). One drawing showed a casually dressed white man threatening a well-dressed black man on a subway; the white man held a razor, a weapon associated in some people's stereotypes with black men. After having seen the picture briefly, approximately half the subjects "remembered" seeing a black man holding a razor, an effect attributed to their stereotypes biasing perception, encoding, or retrieval. ■ Figure 9.16

We saw in Chapter 6 that a picture is scanned point by point, rather than being perceived as a whole. This fact may help explain what happened in this study. If the razor were seen at one visual fixation and the faces at different ones, it might be easier for stereotypes to bias the reassembly of these fragments into a coherent whole. This hypothesis ties in with the idea

that constructive memory may make new wholes from various fragments.

Individual Differences

Memory processes are similar for most people, although variables such as IQ levels and age produce some differences (Craik, 1977; Eysenck, 1977; Hunt, 1978) and we all differ in the fine details (Underwood et al., 1978). But some people are much better than others at retrieval, and other people, often through accident or illness, are much worse.

The capability that you probably know as photographic memory is called by psychologists **eidetic imagery;** it refers to the ability to maintain visual images in STM, either new visual inputs or ones retrieved from LTM, in a manner so precise that they can be scanned almost as if looking at a picture (Haber & Haber, 1964).

People vary in the extent to which they can retrieve visual images, but those with the most extreme eidetic imagery can achieve truly surprising performances. One instructor at Harvard was able to remember half of a computer-generated random-dot matrix so precisely that when the other half was presented alone, she could overlap it with her eidetic image and see the resulting three-dimensional pattern (Stromeyer & Psotka, 1970) Such an image, with hundreds of dots in no apparent pattern, is virtually impossible to encode in any other way than as a photographic image. Attempts to find other such subjects have not been very successful, however, so she may represent an extreme case (Gummerman & Gray, 1971).

Children seem to have more eidetic imagery than adults. In one test, children were shown an illustration of the Cheshire Cat from *Alice in Wonderland;* then it was removed and the child was questioned about it. About 5% of the children showed evidence of eidetic imagery. One boy was able to count the number of stripes on the cat's tail (16) and accurately reported a number of other details (Leask et al., 1969).

The Harvard instructor made relatively little use of her eidetic imagery (though she would sometimes paint a remembered scene by first imaging it on the canvas, a sort of do-it-yourself version of painting by numbers). But many people do use both innate skills and learned techniques as professional memory experts, called **mnemonists** (Bower, 1973b). One of the most famous of these was Luria's subject S whose synesthesia, or blended senses, you read about in Chapter 5 (Luria, 1968). S's memorization skill was aided by his synesthesia, which automatically provided a wide range of cues for even the simplest of inputs: A person's name, for him, had a color, a shape, perhaps even a taste. But his memory seemed far beyond the ordinary, even apart from his synesthesia. He used a few mnemonics, including the method of loci, but he seemed not to have to do so. Where many professional mnemonists use extensive practice with specialized techniques, S seemed to remember anything he saw, indefinitely, virtually without change. Luria studied S for years, and sometimes would insert without warning a test on material ten or more years old; S always got them right.

In fact, S asked Luria to help him learn how to forget. After years of memorizing lists, all of which he still remembered, S was beginning to confuse one with another, a very specialized retrieval-cue problem. With Luria's help, S taught himself to block off the material deliberately at the end of a night's performance, so it would not be in the way later. Most of us struggle to remember more and forget less, but S's experiences remind us that forgetting is a useful pro-

cess that allows us to discard unused and outdated information. (Now if we could just get it to eliminate *only* useless information....) ■ Research Issue: Are Memory Experts Born or Made?

Retrieval Failures as Forgetting

We've already looked at some of the meanings of *forgetting:* displacement from STM, failure to encode into LTM, and the TOT state. But other kinds of retrieval failures best typify forgetting—those in which a memory is sought and simply not retrieved.

In the earliest storehouse notions of memory, simple decay was considered a primary cause of forgetting; the memory trace was thought to fade with time until it was unretrievable. Decay is still a useful concept for the sensory registers, and perhaps for STM. But it has long been recognized as a relatively minor, perhaps nonexistent, cause of forgetting from LTM (McGeoch, 1932).

In the associationist model, two forms of interference were used to explain most forgetting. These are still considered important, although with the development of various cognitive models there is growing disagreement about the extent to which any form of interference can adequately explain forgetting (Postman, 1976). These two forms of interference are named for the direction in which they occur. **Retroactive inhibition** works backward, when new information interferes with information already stored. **Proactive inhibition** works forward, when older stored information interferes with new inputs. Both reduce the effectiveness of retrieval (Keppel, 1968). ■ Table 9.3

Table 9.3 ■ Retroactive and Proactive Inhibition

	Retroactive Inhibition			
Experimental Group	Learn List A	Learn List B	Retention Interval	Test List A
Control Group	Learn List A	—	Retention Interval	Test List A
	Time			→
	Proactive Inhibition			
Experimental Group	Learn List A	Learn List B	Retention Interval	Test List B
Control Group	—	Learn List B	Retention Interval	Test List B
	Time			→

Are memory experts born or made?

The special abilities of mnemonists such as Luria's S have long been known, but researchers have paid surprisingly little attention to them (Brown & Deffenbacher, 1975). Their abilities have seemed too extraordinary to apply to generalized memory processes. But this is beginning to change as part of a general trend toward investigating real-life memory usage rather than specialized laboratory tasks (Neisser, 1982a).

S's synesthesia was apparently part of his biological makeup, whether genetic or the result of some unknown influence. But his was an unusual case. Researchers are finding that many professional mnemonists rely heavily on learned techniques and practice (Hunter, 1978).

One mnemonist whose capabilities may tell us about ordinary memory is Hunt and Love's subject VP (1972). VP was a gifted child, reading by the age of 3-1/2 and playing chess at 8. Intelligence tests confirm that he is exceptionally intelligent and that memory plays a strong role in his intelligence. But they do *not* indicate an extremely high level of memory skills; he scored at the 95th percentile in short-term retention. Further testing of VP has revealed that he has developed his skills to an exceptional degree, however, and soon adapts them to a new task. His initial digit span results were in the traditional 7 ± 2 range, for example. But he soon learned to chunk digits as he heard them, and easily increased his span to 17 digits. His performance on Bartlett's "War of the Ghosts" passage (Figure 9.14) was even more remarkable. He reproduced it with little distortion, even after six weeks. With tasks that require primarily visual coding, VP is less successful; he is a verbal mnemonist. Where S used his synesthesia as a basis for elaborate perceptual coding, VP uses his facility in several languages as a basis for most of his memory.

As S may have been born with his synesthesia, so VP may have been born with greater-than-usual language facility. But both developed their talents through hard work and practice. Interestingly, VP grew up within 35 miles of S's home, and both attended a school where rote memorization was the norm. Each seems to have learned ways of using their innate capabilities to cope with situational demands. Neisser (1982a) has noted that many individuals develop similar memory facility in response to their everyday tasks; because they do not typically use specialized mnemonics he calls them simply *memorists*, and includes several examples in his collection of natural-context memory.

Could more people develop these same abilities? Until recently, there was little experimental evidence related to this question. But Ericsson and Chase (1982) have shown that ordinary memory capacity may improve dramatically through learning. They described an average-intelligence undergraduate who, through practice, has gradually increased his digit span. Where VP reached 17 and the highest ever previously recorded was 18, he has reached 80. Furthermore, he did so without any coaching or instruction by Ericsson and Chase. They tested him repeatedly—an hour a day, three to five days a week, for 20 months—but the improvement seems to have been his own response to that testing.

Like VP, he developed rapid chunking techniques, utilizing various ways of coding and then combining chunks. But careful examination showed that he could still retain only about four large chunks in STM. In order to store that many digits he was rapidly encoding them into LTM. Cognitive psychologists had already noted evidence that some memory-span retrieval is from LTM, however, so that finding is not the most significant.

What Ericsson and Chase suggest *is* significant is that an individual of otherwise unexceptional talents could outperform the best mnemonists in history. As they point out, besides being flawed as a measure of pure STM, this memory-span test measures something that people do not usually do and thus rarely become skillful at. Ericsson and Chase suggest that the memory feats of the best mnemonists may be within many people's capacity if it were useful for them to learn these skills. They would probably agree with Neisser (1982a) that too much emphasis has been placed on laboratory tasks involving meaningless material. The true limits of human memory probably will be found only when people are tested on memory tasks that are important to them and in which they have a chance to develop their skills.

To understand the two directions of interference, consider the difficulties of remembering the correct meaning of a word. We can use a simplified example for illustration: the word *cell*. Suppose you have learned the biological meaning of *cell* and then go to a history class, where you learn that a medieval monk lived in a small room called a cell. You might have trouble learning this new meaning for *cell* because of interference from the old (biological) meaning; this would be proactive inhibition. Later, if you found yourself briefly confused in a biology class at the mention of *cell*, the effect would be retroactive inhibition; the newer (history) information would be interfering with the older (biology) information. In actuality, this

"I CAN'T REMEMBER THE LAST TIME I TREATED A CASE OF AMNESIA, AND I CAN'T EVEN REMEMBER IF I EVER DID TREAT ONE."

© 1983 by Sidney Harris

particular discrimination is unlikely to cause you much trouble. But both directions of interference are important sources of retrieval problems.

Retroactive inhibition was tested as early as the 1920s by having subjects learn material, then either sleep or carry out normal routines (Jenkins & Dallenbach, 1924). Researchers assumed that the various activities of ordinary waking would cause interference but that sleep over the same time would not. The findings did support this, though the benefits were soon lost once the sleeping subjects awakened and began to take in new information. Later research, however, has found the situation to be more complex: There does seem to be a benefit when sleep immediately follows the learning, but not if sleep is delayed (Ekstrand, 1972).

In the everyday world outside the lab, new inputs are continuously being added. These must retroactively interfere with some older memories. At the same time, some of the older memories may proactively interfere with new ones. (The problem that Luria's subject S encountered with too many old lists is a form of proactive inhibition.)

Amnesia means a generalized long-term loss of memory. It ordinarily refers to people who have forgotten the personal details of their lives but who retain more impersonal memories; they know language, so-

cial customs, and so forth. In general, they seem to show a separation of "memory for how" from "memory for what" (Cohen & Squire, 1980). Amnesia of this sort can result from many causes, including extreme emotional stress or physical injury (Cermak, 1982). Psychologists sometimes use the term to describe a type of motivated forgetting for which a patient needs therapy.

One kind of amnesia affects virtually all of us; *infantile amnesia* refers to the fact that most people cannot remember their early childhood experiences. Infantile amnesia is probably related to differences between early and later childhood in brain structure, coding strategies, or both, but it is currently little understood (Spear, 1979).

In studying memory, however, experimental psychologists prefer to focus on two kinds of amnesia in which nearly all memories are lost, apparently from physiological causes. Like the forms of interference, these are specified by the direction in which they operate. **Retrograde amnesia** is a general loss of memories for a past period of time. It often results from brain injury and extends backward from the time of injury. Sometimes only a few minutes are lost, but in other cases, the loss may extend back for months or years; sometimes memory gradually returns after the injury, but often it doesn't. Retrograde amnesia also results from illness that causes brain malfunction (Knight & Wooles, 1980). A common cause is Alzheimer's disease; it causes deterioration of the brain and a general loss of abilities, but one of the most notable symptoms is retrograde amnesia.

Physiological causes of retrograde amnesia are often thought to affect the stored traces of LTM. One report, however, suggests that some cases of brain damage may affect the retrieval mechanism instead. Here, the patient is thought to have retained his stored memories but is unable to retrieve them because of damage to the reticular activating system (RAS) (Goldberg et al., 1981). This study is among the first to suggest a physiological basis for retrieval; it argues that the arousal functions of the RAS (Chapter 2) include the activation of stored traces. This is too new a notion for there to be much evidence for or against it. In the meantime, a different kind of amnesia offers other insights into the processes and physiology of memory.

One of the most famous memory-loss patients is H.M. (Milner, 1959; Scoville & Milner, 1957). H.M. suffered from **anterograde amnesia,** a forward loss of memory in which he retained and could retrieve all of his old LTM traces but could not create new ones. Anterograde amnesia can also result from disease or injury; it is sometimes found in Korsakoff's syndrome, which is associated with chronic alcoholism (Butters & Cermak, 1980; Oscar-Berman, 1980). But the clearest case is H.M., because the tissue loss is known exactly: He had had experimental surgery to try to control his epilepsy, in which both the left and the right hippocampus were removed along with some associated structures.

After his surgery, H.M. apparently became trapped forever at one age and one point in time. He remembered his own past, details of world events, and so forth up until his operation, but seemed unable to learn anything since. After years of hospitalization, he did not recognize the doctors whom he saw daily, did not know where the bathroom was, and could read the same magazine indefinitely, never remembering that he had read an article once he finished it. His STM and maintenance rehearsal seemed normal and he could use these to hold a few items for hours if not interrupted, but nothing seemed to go on to LTM.

More subtle testing, however, has since suggested that H.M. and other such patients can learn some things. H.M., for example, could learn new motor skills. When tested on tasks such as tracing a figure while watching his hand in a mirror, he showed normal improvement—even though each time he tried the task he did not remember doing it before. ■ Figure 9.17

Initially, researchers thought that the hippocampus must be required for all new encoding to LTM

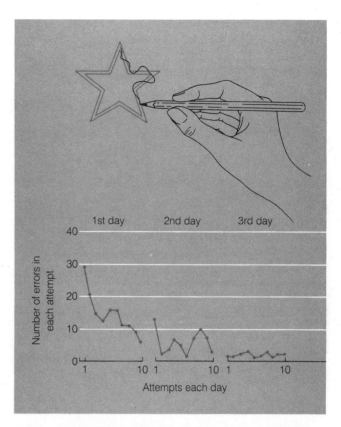

Figure 9.17 ■ Milner's patient H. M. showed profound anterograde amnesia for verbal material but was capable of learning new motor skills. In the test shown here, he had to draw between the two outlines of a star while observing his hand in a mirror. His scores, the number of times he went outside the lines, show typical improvement over three days, but each time he would claim never to have done the task before.

(From *Mechanics of the Mind* by C. Blakemore, Cambridge University Press, 1977. Reprinted by permission.)

because H.M. seemed unable to store anything without it. But the fact that he can store some tasks raises doubts about that interpretation. H.M.'s case implies that the hippocampus plays a major role in LTM, but it is not known whether the hippocampus loss prevents encoding or interferes with retrieval. In rats the hippocampus seems especially important in spatial memories (Olton, 1977). One pair of researchers has suggested that in humans the right hippocampus retains this spatial function, and the left hippocampus links words together in a kind of "semantic map" (O'Keefe & Nadel, 1978).

But H.M.'s ability to learn motor tasks despite re-

Improving your own memory

The features of memory described in this chapter suggest procedures for improving your own memory at each step from sensory register to retrieval (Cermak, 1976).

First you must get the information through a sensory register to STM. This includes some mechanical aspects, like pointing your eyes in the right direction, but most important is the attention process. If your attention shifts to a sight or sound outside the room, for example, you have just prevented the sights and sounds inside—a lecture, perhaps—from entering STM, and you won't remember them later. As attended information does enter STM, try to chunk it and elaborate on it as best you can to hold it and encode it into LTM.

Sometimes external memory aids can be useful in overcoming the limitations of STM (Harris, 1978). Taking notes is one technique for holding information outside LTM, and it can also help you encode the information into LTM. But the limited capacity of STM means that if you cannot control the rate of new input—as you cannot during a lecture, for example—the time it takes to write a note is time when you cannot be taking in new information. You can chunk information in some lectures as you listen and periodically make a brief summary note. But for lectures filled with detailed information,

you'll lose at least as much as you can write down; for these, a tape recorder might be worthwhile.

You may be able to encode some kinds of input to LTM through elaborative rehearsal—but you must take the time to do so. If you're introduced to someone, for example, try repeating his or her name out loud, and maybe even make some comment about it; this allows you to elaborate it before you go on with the conversation. If you hear the name once and immediately say something else, chances are that it will be gone for good, displaced from STM without a trace.

Try any other technique that helps you encode into LTM; the differences between the mnemonists S and VP tell us that no single technique is best for everyone. You will also probably be most successful if you develop different strategies for different kinds of tasks (Connor, 1977). In general, tell yourself that you intend to remember and practice developing quick visual and verbal cues (Lorayne & Lucas, 1974). Use specific mnemonics such as the method of loci or pegword techniques if apropriate, but your own associations may be equally effective (Bower, 1973a; Higbee, 1977). Try for vivid and unusual cues because they are distinctive, but also try to use the first ones that come to mind because these are already associated for you. Use both verbal and visual cues, perhaps thereby using the skills of both hemispheres. (Whatever associations you use, try not

to let them distort the meaning of what you are trying to remember, however; an instantly retrieved wrong concept may be as bad as none at all.)

For structured information, such as that in a textbook, use the text outlines, your own outlines, or even sketches or diagrams to arrange the patterns of your LTM storage. Don't study too long at one time; a series of separated sessions, called spaced practice, is better than a single long session (Glenberg, 1979). Practice retrieval at a time when it isn't critical, so you can add other cues or fill in the holes as necessary. Overlearning material by studying well past the point of minimally remembering it can also help when it comes to retrieval under stress, as on an exam. You might even try studying immediately before you go to sleep.

Finally, when it comes time for serious retrieval, as on an exam, use every cue you have. Recall your elaborated words or imagery and use your mnemonics. Use context cues by trying to remember yourself studying the material in your room or the library. Or use your informational hierarchies by finding something related to what you want and trying to move to the answer you need through associated concepts.

There will still be times when you can't remember something you want to; it happens to all of us. But if you follow these suggestions, you'll probably be surprised at how much you can remember.

---

moval of both the left and the right hippocampus requires a further interpretation. Perhaps motor memories are stored in a different location, or perhaps their encoding is so different that they are not affected in the same way as verbal and visual ones. Future physiological models of memory will have to explain H.M.'s problems, which raise as many questions as they answer (Wickelgren, 1979).

As you've seen, many aspects of memory remain in debate; this area of psychology is undergoing nearly continuous revision. But this does not mean it has nothing practical to offer you; on the contrary, what you've already studied in this chapter suggests many

ways of improving your own memory. ■ Personal Aplication: Improving Your Own Memory

---

CHAPTER SUMMARY

1 Memory is the process by which past experiences influence present behavior. It consists of three components: encoding, storage, and retrieval.

2 Most psychologists accept some form of two-store or duplex model of memory based on a short-term

memory (STM) and a long-term memory (LTM). One alternative model is that of levels of processing.

3 In a duplex model, incoming information enters sensory registers; it is held just long enough for pattern recognition to occur, in which the new information is matched to patterns derived from LTM.

4 Recognized information from the sensory registers then enters STM. There it will remain for only about 30 seconds or less unless rehearsal is used to hold it longer or displacement pushes it out sooner. Only about seven items can be kept in STM, although chunking can be used to increase the information in each item.

5 Information can also be encoded into LTM, primarily in verbal or visual codes. Elaborative rehearsal can be used to add other potential retrieval cues. A variety of mnemonics offer special techniques of encoding to aid later retrieval.

6 Studies of the physiology of memory have suggested both neural and molecular mechanisms of storage, but the actual nature of these remains largely unknown. Some drugs may be able to improve memory, but these do not appear practical for now.

7 STM can be scanned, but retrieval usually refers to recovery from LTM. A variety of cues may be used in searching memory. Searches are often successful, but sometimes result in partial retrieval (the tip-of-the-tongue state).

8 Constructive processes aid retrieval of general themes and patterns but can also result in inexact or distorted retrieval. Eyewitness testimony involves attempts at exact retrieval, but has been shown to be affected by constructive processes.

9 There are substantial individual differences in retrieval. Unusually efficient retrievals include eidetic imagery and the abilities of memory experts. Recent research, however, suggests that average individuals may be able to achieve substantial improvements in memory.

10 Forgetting usually means a failure to retrieve; amnesia is a long-standing and general problem in retrieval. Patients with anterograde amnesia are being studied to see why they seem able to retrieve old memories but not to encode new ones.

Further Readings

For a more detailed overview of memory processes than this chapter, see a good text such as Zechmeister and Nyberg's *Human Memory: An Introduction to Research and Theory* (1982) or Klatsky's *Human Memory: Structures and Processes* (1980). Several books mark particular trends in memory research and theory. Cognitive structures are the topic of *The Structure of Human Memory* by Cofer (1976). An important suggestion for synthesis of associationist views and cognitive ones is offered in Anderson and Bower's *Human Associative Memory* (1973). A cross-fertilization of clinical and laboratory findings is suggested in *Human Memory and Amnesia* by Cermak (1982). Neisser's collection *Memory Observed: Remembering in Natural Contexts* (1982), intended to encourage the study of real-life memory usage, includes some fascinating anecdotes as well as research papers. A number of other works look in more detail at particular aspects of what we have covered. These include Deutsch and Deutsch's *Short-Term Memory* (1975), Rosenzweig and Bennett's collection *Neural Mechanisms of Learning and Memory* (1976), and Paivio's *Imagery and Verbal Processes* (1979). Loftus's work is summarized in her *Eyewitness Testimony* (1980). For a summary of individual differences in memory, see Eysenck's *Human Memory: Theory, Research and Individual Differences* (1977). Luria's *The Mind of a Mnemonist* (1968) is a classic. Suggestions for improving your own memory are offered by Cermak's *Improving Your Memory* (1976) and Higbee's *Your Memory: How it Works and How to Improve It* (1977).

On a vacation trip in the West, you visit a friend at Stanford University. While there, you stop in a supermarket in nearby Palo Alto, California, to pick up some needed supplies. You are astounded to see a tall blonde young woman shopping while accompanied by what seems to be an ape. You edge closer for a better look and realize that it *is* an ape, and as best you can judge from your limited observations at the zoo, it's a gorilla. "I knew California was supposed to have some unusual people," you think. "But isn't that carrying it a bit far?" Later you ask your friend about it. "Oh, that was probably Penny Patterson," he suggests. "She's been training that gorilla—a female named Koko—for several years now, first as a graduate student, then as an independent researcher. Penny's been teaching Koko sign language. I hear she's getting pretty good at it—Koko, I mean—and knows several hundred signs." As you think back, you remember the woman making some movements that could be signs and talking to the gorilla, but you had been so surprised you hadn't noticed whether the gorilla signed back. "Koko makes up words of her own," your friend continues, "even, so I hear, lies and swears on occasion, all in sign language." "Terrific," you think to yourself. "Wait till I get back to school and tell them about this." But just to be sure that they'll believe you, you resolve to look up an article or two to take with you: a "talking" gorilla needs more evidence than just your telling about it.

While researchers such as Patterson study the possibilities of animal communication, elsewhere humans suffer terrible trials seeking to communicate because they have lost the capacity for language through accident or illness. Other humans produce such bizarre and fragmented speech that it is difficult to decide what, if anything, they are trying to communicate. What do all these examples have in common? Are humans the only species to use language? How do they do so? And what goes wrong when a human loses—or never develops—the capacity for language? Psychologists and other scientists interested in language by no means agree on the answers to such questions; on the contrary, there are fundamental disagreements on major issues. But some of what is generally agreed upon may surprise you. Our first task is to define language, so that we can begin to consider these and other questions.

Chapter 10

Language

DEFINING LANGUAGE

In defining language, we must examine its central features and uses. We also need to specify its input and output channels, so we can examine the relationships between speaking and writing, or between listening and reading, for example. We can also look, from an evolutionary or ethological viewpoint, at how the language of our species compares to the communications of other species.

What Is a Language?

Many of us use *language* and *speech* interchangeably. But does a person who writes but cannot speak have language? What about someone who uses only sign language? Such questions are not especially difficult to answer, but most people have not needed to draw such distinctions. In this chapter, however, we need to be as explicit as possible. For our purposes, we will define **language** as any set of symbols that can be sequenced according to particular rules so as to convey an indefinite number of meanings from one user of the language to another. This is a rather long definition, but each part is important.

First, "symbols" implies that not only words but also hand gestures, pictographs, mathematical signs, or other symbols may be the language elements. Animal calls might even be considered symbols in this sense— for example, if one call meant "danger" and another meant "water."

That the symbols are arranged "according to particular rules" is also important because the rules play a major role in conveying information. The rules for sequencing the words in a sentence, for example, are important in interpreting the meaning of the sentence. (To demonstrate this, try scrambling the word order in one of these sentences and let someone else try to make sense of it.) Typically, the rules of a language are *not* explicit. A language user may not be able to state them or even be aware that they exist. Instead, **implicit rules** are shown by the speech patterns of any native speaker of the language (Chomsky, 1980). For example, English speakers usually do not put verbs at the end of long sentences, but German speakers do. That children learn the implicit rules of a language can be shown by special tasks, such as giving them a meaningless word to pluralize (Berko, 1958). ■ Figure 10.1

The phrase "indefinite number of meanings" emphasizes the flexible and combinational qualities of a language. This requirement implies, for example, that a set of animal calls with fixed meanings is not a language, because the symbols cannot be combined and rearranged to yield new meanings.

That the meaning can be conveyed "from one user of the language to another" emphasizes that the major function of language is communication. (Language is also a major vehicle for thought, as we will see in Chapter 11.) Communication by language requires that one user follow a series of steps, which taken together are called language **production.** It then re-

quires the other user to take a different series of steps, all of which constitute language **comprehension.** The process by which children become able to produce and comprehend a language is called language **acquisition** (Moscowitz, 1978).

Note that the need for at least two users makes language a group activity. The originator of a new set of symbols might be able to manipulate them, even to think in them; but without at least one other user the major function of language, communication, would be impossible. A **natural language** is a human language developed over time and existing in a **language community,** a group of users within which children routinely learn to speak the language. English, French, and approximately 5000 others are thus natural languages. In contrast, computer languages, mathematics, formal logic, and other sets of symbols are *artificial languages* that have been created for special purposes. They have a group of users, but no native speakers.

The complete description of how the sounds of a language are related to its meaning is the **grammar** of the language (Bach, 1974). A grammar of English, for example, would seek to describe how any user generates or understands any "legitimate" or "well-formed" sentence. ("The boy ran home" is a legitimate English sentence; "The boy home ran" is not.) Note that a grammar is an ideal that can probably only be approximated. Partial grammars have been worked out for English and a few other languages, but a complete description is only a goal.

Most current grammars are considered to be sets of implicit rules for three aspects of language: phonology, syntax, and semantics. **Phonology** refers to the sounds of the spoken language (Hyman, 1975). **Syntax** refers to the way words are arranged to form sentences (Langendoen, 1970). **Semantics** refers to how meaning is conveyed by both words and sentences (Palmer, 1976).

Different aspects of language development and use are emphasized by different professionals. **Linguists** are most interested in **linguistic competence,** the language user's abstract knowledge about the structure of the language (Chomsky, 1968; Labov, 1980). Other specialists are more interested in how the language is used. **Sociolinguists,** for example, study such topics as how languages define social classes within a country, or some of the problems of a country with two official languages, such as Canada (Trudgill, 1974).

Psychologists who focus on language are called **psycholinguists;** they put more emphasis than linguists do on language *behaviors*, including how a child acquires a natural language and how children and adults use language (Danks & Glucksberg, 1980; Foss & Hakes, 1978). Psycholinguists are thus interested in

linguistic performance: how people use language in their everyday lives (Deese, 1978; Fillmore et al., 1979). Other psychologists are interested in language as part of some other specialty, as when cognitive psychologists examine language codes in memory. In general, psychologists interested in language are focusing increasingly on how meaning is communicated—which is the emphasis of this chapter (Elkind, 1981b).

That a language can generate completely new sentences is called **productivity.** Any language user can produce sentences that no other user has ever produced before, by stringing together a set of symbols in a legitimate but uncommon way. "The short fat green giraffe sat in the porch swing smoking a cigar," for example, may never have existed before. Its meaning may translate to a rather strange image, but you have no trouble decoding it because it combines English words according to the implicit rules of English.

Regularity of a language refers to the fact that strict rules govern the creation of sentences. Taken together, productivity and regularity mean that natural languages are enormously flexible. The productivity criterion says that any number of novel sentences can be created. The regularity criterion says that the creation of such novel sentences follows rules known to all native speakers, and thus these sentences can be comprehended.

Productivity and regularity are important in distinguishing a true language from any more limited set of symbols. Australian aborigines, for example, use a set of hand signs to aid them in cooperative hunting. But these are simply labels for the animals hunted and not a true sign "language," because there are no rules for constructing novel meanings, and thus no productivity or regularity. These signs do not have the flexibility that would allow users to create a unique utterance or to describe a unique event. (*Utterance* is used by linguists to refer to any language act; it is not limited to speech.)

In contrast, the sign language most often used by the deaf in this country, **American Sign Language** (**Ameslan** or **ASL**), is a true language (Hoemann, 1978; Siple, 1978). Like the aborigines' set of signs, Ameslan has some specific signs for common objects. It also has signs for common actions and abstract ideas, which adds to its flexibility. But most importantly Ameslan has rules for producing and interpreting new sequences that neither signer nor observer has ever seen before (Benderley, 1980a; Klima & Bellugi, 1978b). It can even be used for poetry (Klima & Bellugi, 1978a.) ■ Figure 10.2

One famous poem demonstrates both the productivity and regularity of English. In "Jabberwocky," Lewis Carroll (1872) produced a complete story that most English readers can read and feel they compre-

Figure 10.1 ■ Children who have learned the implicit rules of a language can apply them to words they have never heard. Whatever a "WUG" is, for example, two of them are obviously two "WUGs" to any English speaker because adding *s* to a noun typically pluralizes it (exceptions are learned later).

(Based on J. Berko, *Word*, 1958, *14*, 150–177. Used by permission.)

hend, even though many of the words for objects and actions are completely new. The meaning of *slithy*, for example, is unspecified, but it is obviously an adjective describing the plural noun *toves*—whatever they are. ■ Notable Quote: Lewis Carroll's "Jabberwocky"

Input and Output Channels

Our basic definition of language does not specify input or output channels. Normally, of course, hearing is the input channel and speaking the output one. But reading and writing use quite different physical channels to convey words. Gestures may convey meaning in a symbolic way without a direct correspondence to spoken words. In extreme cases, unusual input or output channels, such as touch or synthetic voices, may be used without disrupting the communication.

Hearing and speaking are natural input and output channels for language: Major areas of our brains have evolved to handle rapid and precise sound discriminations and to control facial and throat movements (Liberman, 1982; Lieberman, 1975). Yet we may be the only species on the planet to have evolved such skills. Even our closest biological relatives, the chimpanzees and gorillas, lack the sound-production structures and precision of motor control necessary to speak (Lenneberg, 1967; Lieberman et al., 1969).

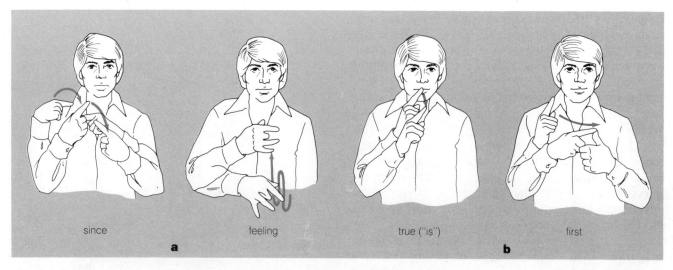

since · feeling · **a** · true ("is") · first · **b**

Figure 10.2 ■ (a) Hunting signs of Australian aborigines. They silently communicate which animals have been spotted, but cannot communicate other information. (b) American Sign Language (Ameslan) is a true language, with ways of describing objects or actions that are completely new. (Based on Frishberg, 1975.)

Vision and touch can also be used as input channels (as for reading or Braille), and hands can be used for output (to write or for sign language) (Schiefelbusch, 1980). But vision and hand use in the forms of reading and writing are such recent inventions that they have played virtually no role in the evolution of our species; they use arbitrary symbols devised by people biologically as advanced as we are. Although nearly all humans easily learn spoken language without instruction, many never learn to read well even with years of instruction (Tarnopol & Tarnopol, 1977). Speaking is apparently something our species does, whereas reading is something that many of us, but not all, can learn to do with some effort.

The earliest forms of writing were apparently simplified representations of actual objects; the earliest known examples are inventories of domestic animals and goods (Schmandt-Besserat, 1978). As writing developed, it simplified such representational symbols to more abstract ones. People still use a variety of representational sign systems, but most of these are not true languages. Some, like hobo signs, are used only by particular groups of people and some, like signal flags, can be combined into groups, but none has the regularity or productivity to be considered a language.
■ Figure 10.3

Many kinds of communication that form part of spoken language or accompany it are not easily represented in writing. One major example is the intonation pattern or "music" of speech. In some languages, such as Chinese, the same sound delivered at a higher or lower pitch changes the meaning; in that case the writ-

ten language must differentiate between them. In other languages, such as English, a few intonation patterns may be indicated in print, as the rising inflection of a spoken question is indicated by a question mark. But often the subtle information that intonation conveys is not easily coded in print.

The body can also be used to signal messages, either as part of speech or instead of it. Most cultures have some specific gestures with particular meanings. These are often obscene, as are a number of well-known finger gestures, but they include nonobscene ones such as applauding a performance (Morris, 1979). These gestures are typically very limited in number and not productive, however, so they add little to a given culture's language capabilities.

Another form of body movement that probably *is* important in face-to-face language communication, though its rules are poorly understood, is "body language." Body language includes elements of gaze, facial expression, body position, and movement that convey meaning (Cook, 1977). These often accompany speech, but sometimes are used alone. (If a message conveyed when a speaker is visible is in any way different than it would be if the speaker were hidden, then body language is conveying information.) Body language has long been the topic of popular treatments, but scientists have only recently begun to explore it (Birdwhistell, 1970; Hall et al., 1978; Knapp, 1980; Munter, 1982).

Language may still be possible for people who lack input or output channels of the kinds already noted. The most famous example is Helen Keller, who was

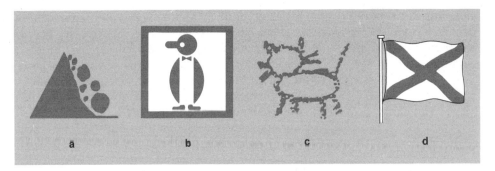

Figure 10.3 ■ Various symbol systems. None is a true language; they simply substitute a picture for a phrase. (a) Road sign for "falling rocks." (b) Shipping symbol for "keep frozen." (c) Hobo symbol for "kind lady lives here" (because kind ladies keep cats?). (d) Navy signal flag for "I need assistance."

deafened and blinded by illness at the age of 19 months. She had begun to comprehend the world before her illness, but was left a nonspeaking infant with neither the normal hearing input for speech nor a visual one for sign language. She was intelligent, yet had no communication channel but touch. An already literate person who had lost sight and hearing might be able to learn Braille, but how could you reach a child who had never developed any form of language?

Helen Keller was fortunate, however, in having a highly dedicated and resourceful teacher, Anne Sullivan. After many false starts, Sullivan was able to reach Keller by spelling words into her hand, a letter at a time. Once Keller realized that the pattern on her hand corresponded to events in the world, she couldn't wait to learn more (Keller, 1902). She graduated summa cum laude from Radcliffe, then spent her life working for the blind. Before she died in 1968, Keller had learned 6 languages, had written 11 books, and had become internationally known.

A recent technological breakthrough uses computers as a voice output for those who can neither speak nor write. Cerebral palsy sufferers, for example, frequently have normal or above-normal intelligence, yet brain damage may prevent them from controlling their bodies in a coordinated way. Because they cannot easily communicate, they are often treated as retarded, a major frustration for them. Various elements of current computer research are giving them a voice. The patient is given control of a portable minicomputer; as he or she enters words or letters, a small screen shows the entries. When a sentence is complete, another command causes the computer to "speak" the sentence, using a mechanical speech synthesizer. At present, the synthesized voice sounds rather strange but intelligible; because the speech synthesizer can put

NOTABLE QUOTE
Lewis Carroll's "Jabberwocky"

❝'Twas brillig, and the slithy toves
    Did gyre and gimble in the wabe:
All mimsy were the borogoves,
    And the mome raths outgrabe.

"Beware the Jabberwock, my son!
    The jaws that bite, the claws that catch!
Beware the Jubjub bird, and shun
    The frumious Bandersnatch!"

He took his vorpal sword in hand:
    Long time the manxome foe he sought—
So rested he by the Tumtum tree,
    And stood awhile in thought.

And, as in uffish thought he stood,
    The Jabberwock, with eyes of flame,
Came whiffling through the tulgey wood,
    And burbled as it came!

One, two! One, two! And through and through
    The vorpal blade went snicker-snack!
He left it dead, and with its head
    He went galumphing back.

"And has thou slain the Jabberwock?
    Come to my arms, my beamish boy!
O frabjous day! Callooh! Callay!"
    He chortled in his joy.

'Twas brillig, and the slithy toves
    Did gyre and gimble in the wabe:
All mimsy were the borogoves,
    And the mome raths outgrabe.❞

together anything entered, it is not limited to stock phrases. This allows patients to converse, something most of us take for granted but for them is a kind of mechanical miracle.

Language and Other Species

One line of language research looks at other species to see if their communication systems show languagelike attributes (Davis, 1978). Species as simple as insects have sometimes been described as having language, but the term is probably misused here (Hockett, 1960).

One of the ethologists who shared the Nobel Prize with Konrad Lorenz in 1973 was Karl von Frisch, best known for his work on the "dance language" of bees (1955, 1962, 1974). Von Frisch found that worker bees communicate to others by a particular pattern of movements the direction and approximate distance of a nectar source they have found. When the bee returns to the hive, it dances approximately in a figure-eight pattern, and the others then fly off in the correct direction.

This performance by bees is impressive and even, in a sense, what we have defined as language (J. L. Gould, 1975). The dance movements are symbols, they seem to be combined by rules, and they communicate from one user to another. The difficulty is with the "indefinite number of utterances" criterion. In the sense that the exact direction and distance need not be the same on two occasions, the bees' dance is a language. But the dance is always a variation of a single message: "food there." It is flexible in the direction specified, but is unable to convey other messages. So it is not what most people consider a language.

Many animal species have varying numbers of calls that convey a range of information, but these too lack the productivity and regularity of language. They are rather like innate versions of the aborigine's signs. Even when learning is possible, it seems only to vary a basic message, as some birds (and some primates) do in singing songs to claim territories (Marshall & Marshall, 1976). Incidentally, language need not be restricted to sound, although other animal communication systems, such as pheromone scent messages, seem equally limited in content and lacking in productivity (Sebeok, 1977; Wilson, 1972).

One of the few other mammals that possesses sound input and output flexible enough to be conceivably used for language is the dolphin. Several attempts have been made to communicate with dolphins—in English, in their own sounds, and in artificial compromise languages—with little success. Whether the dolphin's remarkable range of creaks, grunts, whistles, and sounds beyond our hearing is in fact a language remains unresolved (Parfit, 1980).

It seems unlikely that other nonprimate species can be taught to use language. Several species of birds—especially parrots and mynah birds—can learn human language sounds, but this seems to be pure sound imitation; the same birds also mimic such noises as windshield wipers. One ethologist, however, has recently claimed that her African gray parrot Alex can use language to name and describe objects (Page, 1982a). She claims that Alex's vocabulary includes 18 nouns, 4 colors, and 4 shapes and that Alex can combine these words appropriately and generalize to new objects. These behaviors, if true, suggest the rudiments of language. But it remains to be seen whether Alex can accomplish enough for us to consider his performance even minimal language.

Because the great apes are our closest biological relatives, scientists have tried to determine if they are capable of language. Beginning in the 1930s, researchers sought to teach chimps to speak (Kellogg, 1968). In the most successful of these efforts, a pair of researchers raised a chimp named Viki as if she were their own child, seeking to take advantage of the same environmental conditions that provide language samples and encouragement to a human child (Hayes & Hayes, 1951). But Viki learned to speak only four words (*Mama, Papa, cup,* and *up*), and had to hold her lips with her hands to be able to pronounce some of those.

On the basis of such results, researchers at first felt that chimps were incapable of even the most rudimentary language (Chomsky, 1968). But when they found that the great apes lack the structures and motor control to speak, they realized that speech was not a fair test of apes' language ability. In the late 1960s work shifted to use of either Ameslan or artificial symbolic languages that could be manipulated by hand. These have yielded much greater success.

The pioneer work was done by Beatrice and Allen Gardner. They realized that wild chimps use their hands in something like gestures, and recognized that this might be a different way to approach the question of language. They home-raised a 1-year-old female chimp named Washoe, beginning in 1966 (Gardner & Gardner, 1969, 1971). They taught her Ameslan through a combination of imitation, prompting, and molding (physically moving her hands into the correct positions). After 4 years Washoe had a vocabulary of 132 signs, and in using them she showed many of the characteristics of human children using language. She spontaneously combined as many as five signs. She overgeneralized some signs, using them in new situations where they were only marginally appropriate. She often made naming errors about similar objects—confusing a comb with a brush, for example. And she seemed able to produce novel but appropriate combinations, such as *water-bird* for a swan. Washoe did *not*

"Although humans make sounds with their mouths and occasionally look at each other, there is no solid evidence that they actually communicate with each other."

©1976 by Sidney Harris—American Scientist Magazine

seem to know the importance of word order, but word order is much less important in Ameslan than in English. ■ Table 10.1

Since the Gardners' work with Washoe, more than 20 chimp language projects have been undertaken, with varying degrees of success. The Gardners have since raised two chimps under more ideal conditions: The chimps were obtained when only a week old, trained by instructors fluent in Ameslan, and given even more human contact than was Washoe (Gardner & Gardner, 1978).

Several current projects are attempting to get chimps to use signs with each other, rather than solely with their human trainers. One chimp, Lucy, who was taught several hundred Ameslan signs, has been moved to a compound with other chimps, where she signs to other chimps and even to "her" pet cat. Washoe is also living with this group of chimps, which is being studied by Roger Fouts, a former student of the Gardners. Fouts reports that Washoe, who now knows about 200 signs, is actively teaching signs to her adopted "son" Loulis (Fouts et al., 1982). These are interesting developments, but it is not yet determined whether they represent the beginnings of a language community.

Several other chimps have also been taught Ameslan, although most are not as adept as Lucy. And one gorilla, Koko, has also learned somewhere between 300 and 800 signs. Koko has been trained since infancy (in 1972) by Penny Patterson (1978a, 1978b; Patterson

Table 10.1 ■ Some of Washoe's Ameslan Productions*

Washoe sorry	Out open please hurry	Clothes yours
Baby down	You me in	You hat
Go in	Gimme flower	Roger tickle
Hug hurry	More fruit	You more drink
Open blanket	Baby mine	Comb black

*Each English word represents a separate sign in Ameslan. (Based on Gardner & Gardner, 1971.)

& Linden 1981). Patterson talks to Koko and believes Koko comprehends speech. Patterson has recently obtained a computerized speech synthesizer for Koko, similar to the ones being developed for cerebral-palsy patients. Like Washoe, Koko shows a variety of behaviors that seem to indicate language use. She often combines signs in new ways (such as *finger-bracelet* for a ring and *eye-hat* for a mask). But Koko also does things that suggest she "thinks" in terms of these signs. She uses signs to express her own mood, for example, including *happy* and *sad*. She lies to conceal something she has done, like breaking a toy. She refers to both past and future events. And, even when she is alone, she signs to herself while looking at a picture book, like a child reading aloud. ■ Figure 10.4

Other researchers have developed artificial languages specifically for testing the linguistic competence of chimps. One such language was developed by David Premack (1971, 1976; Premack & Premack, 1972). It uses small plastic tokens of different colors and shapes,

Figure 10.4 ■ A well-known nonhuman user of Ameslan with her trainer. Koko, a gorilla, is being read the story of the three little kittens who lost their mittens by her trainer Penny Patterson. Koko, noting that the mother cat is angry and the kittens crying, signs *bad*.

(Ronald H. Cohn/The Gorilla Foundation)

which are formed into sentences by arranging them in a column on a board. Use of the tokens eliminates the need to interpret whether the Ameslan signs are performed correctly, and the rules for sequencing the tokens are more specific than are the word-order rules of Ameslan. Premack taught a chimp named Sarah to use this language, using Skinnerian shaping techniques. (To minimize human cues, Sarah was kept in a cage, unlike the home-raised chimps.) Sarah can handle many aspects of a language, such as negatives and quantifiers, but seems to be about equally successful at all of them; for human children some are much harder than others.

Another artificial language used with chimps was developed by Duane Rumbaugh. Called Yerkish (after the research center where it was developed, which in turn is named for a famous animal researcher, Robert Yerkes), it is a modified version of English that is represented by 75 colored panels connected to a computer. These can be pushed, according to a set of sequencing rules, to create a sentence. A chimp named Lana was taught to communicate with the computer or with a human by pushing the appropriate panels; a screen showed the replies (Rumbaugh, 1977; Rumbaugh et al., 1973). (The computer was hooked up 24 hours a day; Lana once asked "Please, machine, give tickle" in the middle of the night.) Lana showed many of the same languagelike abilities of the other chimps. She also used word order correctly—no doubt because the computer would not respond unless she did. Lana was unusual, however, in actively seeking new information: "Tim, give Lana name of this?" ■ Figure 10.5

In an interesting development from this research, both artificial chimp languages are now being explored as possible communication systems for retarded or autistic children, or others lacking spoken English (Deich & Hodges, 1975; Rock, 1979).

Since the beginnings of the Gardners' work, however, some linguists have remained unconvinced that the chimps or Koko are truly using language. In response to Premack's work with Sarah, Roger Brown, a well-known linguist, raised two objections (1973). In the "pigeon ping-pong problem," he compared Sarah's performance to Skinner's demonstration of shaping pigeon behavior (1962). The pigeon behavior was only superficially like human ping-pong, said Brown; perhaps Sarah's performance was similarly superficial. In the "Clever Hans problem," he drew an analogy between Sarah's "language" and the "arithmetic" skills of a horse by that name in the early 1900s. Clever Hans's skills turned out to reflect covert, apparently unconscious, cues given by its owner or other observers

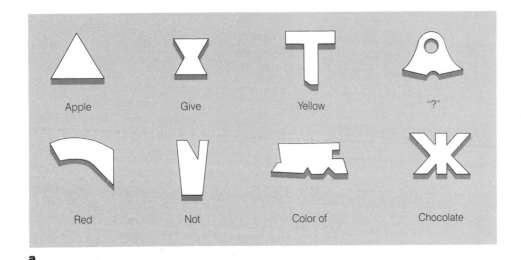

a

b

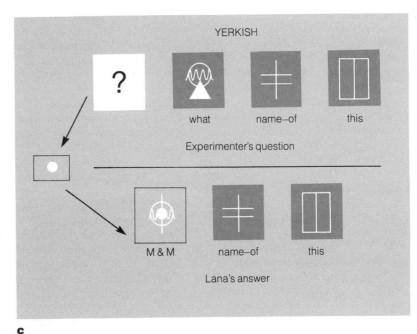

c

Figure 10.5 ■ Two artificial languages used with chimps. (a) In Premack's language, tokens are arranged on a board in sequences corresponding to sentences. The top set of four are a random sample of the available symbols; the bottom set say "Red (is) not (the) color of chocolate." (From Premack & Premack, 1972.) (b) Lana, shown with her computer keyboard. (c) A possible question and answer set in the Yerkish language. The question symbols would light up in sequence and Lana would press the answer keys in sequence.

(**b** and **c**, the Yerkes Primate Center)

(Pfungst, 1911). Brown suggested that the humans with Sarah could similarly cue her placement of the tokens.

Premack (1971) did one study in which a chimp was monitored by a person who did not know the rules of the language, and found only about a 10% decrease in the correctness of Sarah's performance. But Brown was not convinced. The similarity of the tasks to those previously practiced by Sarah could have led to her performance, he noted, without that performance really being a linguistic one.

Brown was a linguist, not a chimp researcher, however, and his criticisms were not accepted by the psychologists who did such research. Similar criticisms received widespread attention, however, when a psychologist who had studied an Ameslan-using chimp decided that its performance was not truly linguistic.
■ Research Controversy: Can Apes Really "Talk"?

RESEARCH CONTROVERSY

Can apes really "talk"?

Based on his own research and a review of the research of others, Herbert Terrace has claimed that the Ameslan use of all the apes is probably only elaborate operant conditioning. Terrace (1979) had studied a chimp called Nim (short for Neam Chimsky, after the famous linguist Noam Chomsky). As a former student of Skinner's, Terrace was trained to be very exacting in data analysis, so he undertook a detailed study of videotaped examples of Nim's signing. What he saw convinced him that Nim's performances could be more simply explained as imitation of the trainer's signs, with some variation. Terrace found that Nim both imitated and interrupted his trainers more than deaf children do. But most important, he found no appropriate use of word order when Nim used multiple signs—and thus no true sentences. The most controversial part of the study, however, was that Terrace and his associates also analyzed what filmed segments they could find of the work by the Gardners, Patterson, and Fouts—and claimed that their apes were not really showing language behavior either (Terrace et al., 1979).

Not surprisingly, the other researchers objected strongly, and the result was a flood of claims, counterclaims, and counter-counterclaims (Benderly, 1980b; B. T. Gardner, 1981). Terrace's major point is that productivity (with regularity) defines language, and that productivity is demonstrated only by the creation of acceptable sentences—which he does not believe has occurred. But a series of other points have been debated following his first papers, including how to treat the animals, how to test them, and how to analyze the data.

It seems a polarization is evolving between two approaches to the study of ape language, the naturalistic approach favored by the Gardners, Patterson, and Fouts, and the laboratory approach favored by Terrace, Premack, and Rumbaugh (Marx, 1980a). The former researchers, who see language as a social activity, rear their apes in as natural a setting as possible, play with them, blend language training with their daily activities, and accept the apes' use of sign in these circumstances as indicative of language behavior. The latter, who see the need for careful laboratory control of variables, tend to treat their apes as experimental subjects expected to learn a specific task to exacting specifications, and they seek to examine the evidence critically to rule out complex learning that lacks true understanding.

One basic disagreement concerns frame-by-frame analysis of filmed records. Terrace believes this offers greater precision. But the other group believes that making such films distracts both apes and trainers and that analyzing static frames distorts the movement-oriented nature of Ameslan. And the arguments have gotten more intense. Patterson has accused Terrace of overlooking or misinterpreting her published reports (1981), and the Gardners have threatened to sue Terrace if he includes tracings from their films in any more articles (Marx, 1980a). Terrace's group has dismissed some of Patterson's counterclaims as anecdotal and not real evidence; they have also accused the Gardners, Patterson, and Fouts of making misleading statements in interviews, rather than confining their remarks to the scientific journals (Seidenberg, 1980; Terrace, 1980). Each group has accused the other of inappropriate training methods and data analysis (Bazar, 1980). All in all, the debate has been rather more public and more heated than most in the scientific community.

But what of the issues? Can apes really "talk" (sign)? That still remains an open question. The answer will depend to some extent on the criteria chosen. The Gardners (1975) have noted that by some reasonable criteria Washoe showed language in 1967, although by others no ape would ever be able to do so. They suggest a criterion of similarity to human children; if the apes perform similarly—as the Gardners believe they do—then they are using language. Terrace has also used comparisons with human children, though he has been accused of being much more critical of the apes' productions than of the children's.

All sides seem to agree that much of the work to date offers only weak evidence concerning the possible syntactic abilities of apes. The emphasis has been on production more than comprehension, and most of that production has been of a labeling or naming variety. It is now agreed that apes can learn a number of names for objects and events. It is also generally accepted that they can use these labels to map concepts or thoughts they already have (Savage-Rumbaugh et al., 1980a). Wild chimps like to be tickled, for example, and encourage each other to do so; now they can sign "Come-tickle-hurry-tickle-please." But it is much less obvious whether they can comprehend more abstract uses of language.

In one attempt to demonstrate true symbolic communication in chimps, Sue Savage-Rumbaugh has taught two chimps, Sherman and Austin, to communicate in Yerkish (Savage-Rumbaugh et al., 1980b). But one of her reports was imitated nearly exactly, including its title, by Skinner and his co-workers; they showed similar communication between two pigeons, whimsically called Jack and Jill (Savage-Rumbaugh et al., 1978; Epstein et al., 1980).

It looks as if questions about the similarities and differences between human and ape language will be with us for some time. (Meanwhile, a new dimension is being added: whether chimps can solve problems—with or without the use of language. We will return to this work in Chapter 11.)

LANGUAGE ACQUISITION

How children acquire a natural language is open to many arguments. In considering how language acquisition takes place, we will look first at natural language communities, then at some nature/nurture issues.

Language Communities

All members of a language community by definition can communicate with each other. In a country the size of the United States, there are sometimes variations in pronunciation or local words that make communication difficult, but all United States English speakers belong to a single language community. (In contrast, New Guinea has approximately 700 language communities, none of which can understand the others. On a two-day canoe ride, a person may hear 10 different languages.)

Differences in regional accents are considered superficial, as are such word differences as *milkshake* (western United States) versus *frappe* (eastern United States) (Strebeigh, 1982). Differences greater than these, however, make communication increasingly difficult. A **dialect** is a variation on a language in which speakers of each dialect use enough different words and rules that communication is impeded. Dialects represent a kind of evolutionary drift in separated language communities: Living languages gradually change over time as living species are said to in Darwinian evolution. The result may be two dialects, both based on the same language but differing in details.

A "pidgin" is an artificial dialect, usually developed to aid communication among people from different natural language communities (DeCamp, 1971). In the several hundred years of European trade expansion around the world, for example, a trade pidgin grew up as a common language for sailors from different countries. Originally based on Portuguese, because Portugal was once the world trading power, this trade pidgin later added many Spanish and then English words while retaining some Portuguese syntax (Dillard, 1972). If a pidgin becomes the first language for some language community, so that children learn it as their only or primary language, it becomes more elaborated, with a more complex syntax; such a developed pidgin is called a creole (Bickerton, 1983).

This background is important to a current debate in psychology and education, the question of the status of so-called Black English.

Black English   **Black English** is a variation on what is usually called Standard English, the pattern used by the media in the United States and by most educated speakers. Since the days of slavery the differing speech patterns of some American blacks have frequently been considered "bad" English. But some linguists now argue that these language patterns are as regular as Standard English, and that Black English is thus a dialect of Standard English. Some have advocated that native speakers of this dialect be treated almost as if they spoke another language. Because reading is closely tied to speech, for example, it makes sense to read the language you speak, and readers have been developed that combine Black English and Standard English. ■ Table 10.2

Those who support the use of such readers say they can act as a transition to Standard English. The result, they say, will be people who are bidialectical (speak two dialects). Other linguists and educators say

Table 10.2 ■ A Sample of a Two-Dialect Reader

Black English	Standard English
Ollie big sister, she name La Verne.	Ollie's big sister is named La Verne.
La Verne grown up now, and she ain't scared of nobody.	La Verne is grown up. She isn't afraid of anyone.
But that don't mean she don't never be scared.	But that doesn't mean that she's never afraid.
The other day when she in the house, La Verne she start to screaming and hollering. Didn't nobody know what was the matter.	The other day while she was at home, La Verne started screaming and shouting. Nobody knew what the matter was.
Everybody been thinking that she be hurt.	Everybody thought that she was hurt.
So Big Momma run to the kitchen. Guess what Big Momma find?	Grandmother ran into the kitchen. Guess what Grandmother found?
La Verne been screaming 'cause she seen a bug. It wasn't no roach either 'cause La Verne, she ain't scared of no roach.	La Verne was screaming because she saw a bug. It wasn't a roach, because La Verne isn't afraid of roaches.
It was one of them big black water bugs. So Big Momma kill the bug and La Verne stop hollering.	It was a big water bug. Grandmother killed the bug, and La Verne stopped screaming.

From *Teaching Black Children to Read*, J. Baratz and R. W. Shuy (Eds.), Center for Applied Linguistics, Washington, D.C.

that Black English is not unified and consistent enough to be considered a dialect.

One linguist, however, has gone somewhat further. J. L. Dillard (1972) argues that Black English derives from two major sources in addition to English, both results of slavery. Some words of Black English, including ones that have entered Standard English—such as *jazz* and *banjo*—are African words. Other words and syntax rules are derived from trade pidgin, which the Africans learned during their transport by ship (because people captured from different tribes had no common language). This trade pidgin was kept as a common language once they arrived in this country, thus becoming a creole. Dillard points to such usages as *been* in the sentence "Everybody been thinking that she be hurt." This is not, he says, the English form, as in "I have been there," but a residual of the Portuguese *ben*, a marker indicating that an action is ongoing.

Such arguments have broad social as well as psychological implications (Feagans & Farran, 1982). The status of Black English and how it should be treated in the educational system are ongoing questions—one part of the broader issue of how to educate all United States children whose primary language is not English (John & Horner, 1970). The answers to such questions will influence how large numbers of citizens learn to communicate, to read, and perhaps even to think, as well as how they are defined in terms of social groups.

Bilingualism The issues surrounding Black English are important partially because of what we know about people who are **bilingual,** or speak two (or more) languages (Kolers, 1968). Most bilinguals are not equally competent in each language; they have one **first language,** which they learned at home, with their competence in other languages depending on such factors as when they learned each and under what circumstances (Macnamara, 1967). Being proficient enough in two languages to translate quickly and accurately between them is an exception rather than the rule. (Acting as a translator at the United Nations—listening in one language while simultaneously translating to and speaking the other—is so demanding that few can do it, and even those who can find it exhausting.)

Bilinguals who are equally proficient in two languages are usually native speakers of both. If their environment provides clearly demarcated language communities, children seem able to acquire two or more languages at the same time. If the grandchildren of immigrants always speak English at home but the grandparents' native language when they visit the grandparents' home, the children may acquire both languages. But if the cues that separate the language communities become blurred, the children may ac-

quire a nonexistent language, some composite of the separate languages they hear.

How extreme such mixing can be is illustrated by the well-publicized case of the Kennedy twins (Horowitz, 1978). Twins often develop a kind of two-person language community with a private code, or "twin language," which they soon give up in favor of the language used around them. The Kennedy twins, however, had been raised in a group that scrambled two languages. Their father was a former United States soldier, their mother a German national. When they married, they brought her mother, who spoke little English, to live with them. The twins were raised in a language community of one English speaker who added some German (father), one German speaker (grandmother), and one who regularly alternated and mixed the languages (mother). The language that the twins created not only combined English and German, it fluctuated in usage, with, for instance, a dozen or more ways of referring to a single item. They used their language to such an extent that they became unintelligible to others and were in danger of being institutionalized as retarded before two alert speech therapists figured out what they had done. They were taught Standard English and are now seemingly normal. ■ Figure 10.6

The Kennedy twins' case demonstrates many important features of language: how it is learned, how it can change with each generation of speakers, even how we often interpret intelligence through the language a person uses. Rarely does such an extreme example of twin language occur, but its existence alerts us to the many possible variations of human language.

Sex Differences Many human behaviors have been found to differ by sex, whether the causes are primarily nature or nurture ones. Language use is one such behavior; it turns out to be different for males and females in some surprising ways.

One speech therapist, Maureen O'Connor, uncovered some of these differences in the course of her work with transsexuals (Green, 1978). That a male transsexual would need to speak with a higher pitch as part of his transition to female is relatively obvious; women's voices are generally higher pitched than men's. But some other differences are less obvious. O'Connor finds that men and women have different intonation patterns, that their vocabulary and sentence structures differ, and that the body language accompanying speech differs.

O'Connor finds that female-to-male transsexuals experience few problems with the language differences, however; their female patterns are apparently acceptable in their new male role. But male-to-female transsexuals must change a number of strongly in-

Figure 10.6 ■ The Kennedy twins, Grace and Virginia, or "Poto" and "Cabengo" in their self-created twin language. Speech therapists eventually realized it was a mixture of English and German. "Eh pumpteen, eh come leek der here," Grace said to Virginia during an interview. "En ess listening on-tay-pay-tah" (meaning "Come look at this, but remember the tape recorder is still running"). (From Horowitz, 1978, p. 21)

(Union Tribune Publishing Company)

grained speech patterns to be accepted as female. For example, they must learn to use a rising inflection at the ends of many sentences, an intonation pattern characteristic of questions. The rising inflection is like saying "My statements are true (aren't they?)." She feels that this is indicative of a female role that is less assertive.

This therapist also notes that her work has made her more sensitive than most people to gender differences in language. But she is not alone in her concern with gender biases in language (Graham, 1973). Many people have observed that the conventional English usage of *he* and *his* when gender is unspecified inappropriately implies that all unspecified persons are males (Bodine, 1975; MacKay, 1980). Hence, APA and other organizations have developed guidelines for gender-neutral usage to avoid such implications (APA Publication Manual Task Force, 1977). The use of *he and she* in this text is one way in which many authors seek to avoid implicit stereotyping. The resulting forms occasionally become somewhat clumsy, as in "himself or herself," but it seems a small price to pay for a more gender-balanced language.

Nature/Nurture in Acquisition

Virtually all children acquire a natural language, but *which* language depends entirely on the language community in which they are raised. Adults can also learn new languages, but they seem to do so differently. How children acquire language and the differences, if any, between that process and adult language learning, are central issues in whether language is the result of nature or nurture. Of course, the answer must be some form of interaction, as it is in all versions of the nature/nurture question. But is the major bias in that interaction toward nature or nurture?

Lenneberg's Critical-Period View Erik Lenneberg (1967), a linguist, has argued that human language is a species-specific behavior with strong nature components. He notes, for example, that only severe brain damage or extreme deprivation prevents humans from acquiring a natural language. Virtually all brain-intact human children learn a natural language easily within a few years after birth, without specific training. Even humans with a developmental problem causing them to have brains smaller than a chimpanzee's still develop language in approximately normal fashion. And children who are unable to develop language through normal channels may still develop it in other ways. Deaf children have been said to invent sign languages of their own, for example, in order to express themselves (Goldin-Meadow & Feldman, 1977).

Furthermore, language acquisition seems to follow a common course, regardless of the language being learned or whether parents or others try to teach it. Linguists refer to common features of languages and language acquisition as **language universals,** and suggest that they may reflect innate structures and limitations (Greenberg, 1966). All natural languages consist of words that denote concepts, for example, and all create meaning by relating these concepts according to rules of syntax. The common sequence by which children acquire a natural language and the errors they make in doing so have also been seen as indicative of a universal process (Slobin, 1970).

Lenneberg argues that there is a critical period for language acquisition. Numerous prenatal *critical periods* exist, during which some body structure must develop if it is to develop at all (as we will see in Chapter 12). Language acquisition occurs postnatally over several years, and in other ways is not exactly comparable to the critical periods for body development. But Lenneberg says that the period of growth from infancy to adulthood involves a physiological structuring of key brain areas for both comprehension and production of language. When brain structuring ends at puberty, so does the childhood form of language acquisition, he feels. Adult language acquisition, according to Lenneberg, is then a different process, one based on our ability to learn new complex material of many kinds, and one that adds a new language by tying it to the naturally acquired first language.

Lenneberg's view incorporates both nature and nurture factors, but is strongly nature oriented. Nurture provides a natural language community, and the child's developing brain then builds in the ability to comprehend and to produce whatever language is spoken in that community.

In support of this critical-period view, Lenneberg offers three lines of evidence. Adults report that it is very difficult to learn a second language, and they may never speak it well. Yet children learn a first language without previous experience and seem able to quickly pick up a new one, as when they move to a new country. Children who learn language slowly, such as those with Down's syndrome, seem to make progress until puberty, and then reach their limit. And although adults who lose language through brain damage rarely recover it, children may recover completely if the loss occurs early enough for them to do so before puberty.

If correct, Lenneberg's interpretation has many implications, for both psychology and education. For instance, foreign languages ought to be taught in grade school or earlier, rather than in high school, and through natural conversation rather than a formal study of the rules of grammar. From a psychological viewpoint, because language is the basis of so much of our thought, a biological cutoff point at puberty has important implications. Children deprived of adequate natural-language inputs while growing up would be unable to learn much language as adults, and their thought processes would be severely limited.

Lenneberg's arguments, however, are far from universally accepted. The argument concerning recovery from brain damage seems to be a strong one. But more recent work with adults learning second languages suggests motivational and situational reasons why adults may usually be less successful than children. Apparently, well-motivated adults in the right environment, who take the time to practice, can learn a new language as well as children. Hence the extent to which children's language exposure affects their later thought remains in debate.

Skinner Versus Chomsky B. F. Skinner emphasizes a different view of language acquisition. In keeping with his general emphasis on the importance of learning, Skinner downplays all concepts of intellectual *development,* including language. Although a child's brain must be structured to make language learning possible, he argues, the learning itself is simply another form of reinforced behavior. Skinner suggests that all of our language behavior is shaped by the members of our language community. Language and other cognitive behaviors don't "develop," but are simply learned over years, becoming more complex as new learning builds on previous learning (Skinner, 1957).

In effect, Skinner turns Terrace's criticisms of the chimp language work upside down. Terrace argues that Koko and the chimps are *not* using language because they have simply learned a complex pattern of response to environmental cues. Skinner argues instead that the chimps *might be* using language, because he feels that humans using language are *also* responding to environmental cues on the basis of their learning history. (This was the overall conclusion stated in the Jack and Jill pigeon-language study noted in the Research Controversy box; Epstein et al., 1980.)

In contrast, Noam Chomsky, one of the country's foremost linguists, takes a position similar to Lenneberg's. Chomsky also believes that the predisposition to acquire a natural language is an innate tendency of human infants (1968, 1980). Chomsky has proposed that children have an innate *language-acquisition device* (LAD), a mechanism for processing whatever natural language they hear. Little more is needed for a child to acquire the implicit grammatical rules of a language, he notes, than simple exposure to some examples. Even if the adult utterances are not always complete or well formed, the child still extracts the underlying rules. Chomsky thus disagrees with Skinner on several grounds, and his criticisms of Skinner's position have been widely quoted.

It is not plausible, Chomsky asserts, that reinforcement for some utterances will teach a child to produce entirely new ones. Furthermore, he says, careful observations of adult–child interactions typically show more reinforcement for correct content than for correct form. Adults, in fact, often reinforce grammatically *incorrect* statements: They agree with the intended meaning (as when a child says "Mama isn't boy, he girl" and the parent answers "That's right") and fail to reinforce correct ones, or even disagree with correctly phrased ones, because they disagree with the intended meaning (as when a child says "There's the animal farmhouse" and the parent answers "No, that's a lighthouse") (Wingfield, 1979, p. 261). How can such a mixed reinforcement pattern ever teach children the implicit grammatical rules that they acquire? And finally, even when parents deliberately seek to teach correct rules, children often seem to fail to change their incorrect forms:

Child:	*My teacher holded the baby rabbits and we patted them.*
Mother:	*Did you say your teacher held the baby rabbits?*
Child:	*Yes.*
Mother:	*What did you say she did?*
Child:	*She holded the baby rabbits and we patted them.*
Mother:	*Did you say she held them tightly?*
Child:	*No, she holded them loosely.*

(Clark & Clark, 1977, p. 333)

A few of Chomsky's criticisms might be addressed by referring to known learning principles. If several similar utterances had been reinforced, for example, a new utterance of the same form might represent the generalization of an operant. Chomsky's other arguments (only some of which we have noted) are not easily countered, however, and many psychologists find Skinner's extreme nurture position regarding language a very weak one. (Chomsky's own views have also been criticized, however; Harman, 1982; Piattelli-Palmarini, 1980.)

It seems likely, based on the biological and linguistic evidence presented by Lenneberg and Chomsky, that human language acquisition has strong nature elements. Early language learning may even be nearly entirely nature based, something human infants do as a result of how their brains are wired. But as they grow older, details of the reinforcement patterns of their language communities may also contribute to their

acquisition (Nelson, 1975). By adulthood, further language learning might occur largely through operant principles. If some such synthesis turns out to be true, it would imply that Chomsky is most correct for infants but overlooks some important aspects of how the language community shapes language, especially as children get older. It would also imply that Skinner is mostly correct for adults but overlooks strong nature factors that shape a child's acquisition.

The Process of Acquisition

All children follow a similar sequence in acquiring a natural language. This sequence begins soon after birth, when they orient to the sounds of language in preference to other sounds. It continues through initial comprehension to early production, and finally, through refinement, to the adult pattern.

The newborn human infant seems ready to attend to the particular frequencies and speech patterns of a human voice. High-speed photography shows a pattern of small movements by which a normal infant "resonates" with the sounds of language (Condon & Sander, 1974). These movements probably represent the first step in language acquisition, one that sets the stage.

A general rule during the rest of acquisition is that comprehension typically precedes production. A child is able to understand both grammatical rules and pronunciation well ahead of the ability to produce them. This is often demonstrated when a parent adds grammatical details in repeating a child's speech. Children often show that they comprehend the correct forms, but still do not produce them, as we saw earlier. Similarly, the child may reject his or her own pronunciation if someone else offers it, showing that the child hears what it should be but cannot yet form the sound precisely: One linguist, for instance, spoke to a child who called his inflated plastic fish a *fis*. In imitation of the child's pronunciation, the observer said: "This is your *fis*?" "No," said the child, "my *fis*." He continued to reject the adult's imitation until he was told, "That is your fish." "Yes," he said, "my *fis*." (Berko & Brown, 1960, p. 531).

Throughout acquisition, the child generalizes what he or she has learned. These generalizations are often incorrect according to adult usage, however, and must be trimmed back by a process of discrimination. The generalization/discrimination balance applies to a variety of grammatical structures, but one of the most obvious is word meanings. A child who has learned a word for an object with several properties—a round red ball, for example—may generalize that word to other objects with any of those properties. If the word is *ball*, however, the child must learn to apply it only to other balls, and if the word is *red* it must be applied only to red things. Linguists call children's over-generalizations of words **over-extensions.** A young child often widely over-extends a word, applying it in ways that seem only remotely associated to an adult, before eventually narrowing its uses to appropriate ones. For example, *ball* may be used for anything round and *dog* for anything furry (Clark, 1975).

Another major rule is that the child's productions gradually increase in grammatical complexity. This is most obvious in sentence length. The child first produces one-word utterances, then two-word ones, and so forth. The first one-word forms are often labels for people and objects (*Dada*), but soon they are used (*down*) to represent more complex messages, such as descriptions or requests (Bloom, 1973). Two-word utterances are more clearly simple sentences (*See boy. Mommy sleep.*), although they still may require interpretation (*Allgone shoe. Byebye hot.*; Brown, 1973).

Most of the words used at the two-word stage are *content* words, such as names of objects and colors. More difficult for children are the *function* words that specify grammatical relationships, such as the prepositions *in* and *on*. Adults sometimes see such words as simple because they are small, but the concepts they represent are not so simple and children take some time to learn them. *In* for enclosures such as boxes and *on* for surfaces such as tables are learned first. But *on* for a box or *under* for a table are harder, and more complex notions such as *above, below,* or *in front of* are much harder. Asked to put a toy mouse *in* a box, for example, a one- or two-year-old child may comply correctly, but not do so if asked to put the mouse *on* the box (Clark & Clark, 1977).

Throughout acquisition, the child is acquiring the implicit rules of the language. Even when the child is wrong according to the adult usage, it is frequently because the child is using the rule. The incorrect verb form *holded*, for example, uses the general rule of "add *-ed* for past tense." The child is wrong only because *hold* is not a regular verb; its past tense is the irregular form *held*, and it must be learned as an exception to the general rule. The sequence in which children learn irregular forms is also a clear indicator that they are learning implicit rules. Typically, some of their first usages are exactly as they have heard the words used, so that *held* might be used correctly. As the child learns the implicit rule of adding *ed*, he or she then over-generalizes it, and errors such as *holded* occur. Later the form *held* returns, now used correctly as an exception to the rule (Cazden, 1968).

What the child acquires in a natural human language is a way of generating spoken sounds that convey a meaning to others (at least from the perspective of psychology; linguists would phrase it differently). In seeking to analyze how this exchange of meaning is accomplished, we will begin with production, then will turn to comprehension.

LANGUAGE PRODUCTION

We will focus on the production of speech, starting with the smallest units of sounds and words, then adding these up to form a sentence. Other forms of language production, such as signing or writing, share some features with speech, but differ on others. (In looking at comprehension we will use some reading examples, and in discussing the language areas of the brain we will note some of the ways in which non-speech language forms differ from speech.)

Sounds and Words

One of the earliest developments in speaking is the babbling stage, in which the child seems to practice the basic sounds in the language he or she hears: "ba-ba-ba," perhaps. Some linguists believe that babbling helps develop the articulatory programs for later speech (Kiparsky & Menn, 1977). Others feel it is simply muscular practice, little related to later speech (Ferguson & Garnica, 1975).

But even such simple sounds are made up of two components. You might think of them as a consonant (*b*) and a vowel (*a*), but to a linguist both are phonemes. A **phoneme** of any language is the smallest unit of *sound* that native speakers distinguish as meaningfully different from others. Many phonemes are similar in more than one language, but others are unique. (These unique phonemes cause the greatest pronunciation difficulties in learning a foreign language. Native speakers of Japanese, for example, have trouble distinguishing the English consonants *r* and *l* because these are not separate phonemes in Japanese.) Each language permits substantial variations in the pronunciation of some sounds without loss of meaning, but the defining characteristics of each phoneme must be maintained or meaning will be lost.

Note that phonemes are not equivalent to letters of the alphabet; English has only 26 letters but more than 40 major phonemes. The vowel *a*, for example, represents two different phonemes in the words *bat* and *bait*, and the consonant *c* represents different phonemes in *cake* and *ceiling*. Other phonemes, such as *sh*, are represented by two letters.

For most nonlinguists, however, the basic sound unit is the **syllable**, typically a vowel with a consonant in front, in back, or both. A syllable is both produced and understood as a unit. The major functional units a speaker works with in creating a sentence are syllables, which must be strung together in the correct sequence. One classic form of speech error suggests that syllables are organized into sequences as the sentence is created. In a **spoonerism,** two syllables are interchanged in an otherwise well-formed sentence so that a syllable intended to occur later in a sentence is inserted too early. (MacKay, 1970b). ■ Figure 10.7

An example of a spoonerism is "Let me sew you to your sheet," when the meaning is "Let me show you to your seat." Here, the first syllable of *seat* (the seventh word of the sentence) was inserted into what was intended to be *show* (the third word). For this kind of error to occur, the seventh word must already be in preparation when the third word is being spoken. This suggests that the words are assembled into a group at least several words long before any of them are spoken. The whole sentence may even be sequenced before the speaker begins saying it. Besides spoonerisms, many other types of speech errors have been described and collected (Fromkin, 1980). These offer interesting data for later interpretation, although neither linguists nor psychologists have been able to agree on the meaning of most of them (Fromkin, 1973; MacKay, 1972).

Syllables seem to be more basic units in putting together the spoken sentence than words. But words are important units in an earlier stage of the sentence creation: putting together the meaning. In the "short fat green giraffe" sentence, for example, *giraffe* is two syllables, but a single unit in terms of specifying an animal.

Some words are made up by adding special syllables to one end of a basic word root. Consider the words *smoke, smoking,* and *smoked.* In one sense these are three different words, but in another sense they are variants of one word, the verb *(to) smoke.* To deal with such combinations, linguists have specified another way of dividing words by meaning: The smallest unit of *meaning* in a language is a **morpheme;** a morpheme is often a word, but may also be a prefix or suffix, a grammatical marker attached to the front or back of a word. *Smoke* is both a word and a morpheme, but *smoking* and *smoked* consist of two morphemes: *smoke* plus either *-ing*, meaning the action is ongoing, or *-ed*, meaning it has ended. Such grammatical morphemes are known as inflections (Cazden, 1968). These two inflections are such common verb endings in English that they carry their meaning even when the basic verb they modify is unknown. In Carroll's "Jabberwocky," *whiffling* and *galumphing* obviously signify ongoing action, even if you've never seen anyone whiffle or galumph.

Carroll used other aspects of English grammar in creating this poem, however. He used word sequence

Figure 10.7 ■ The Reverend William Spooner, warden of New College, Oxford, in the early 1900s. His name has become the label for a speech error in which syllables are exchanged between one word and another, because he did this so often. The samples below are typical spoonerisms (from Clark & Clark, 1977). (The first, for example, really means "missed all my history lectures." To translate the others, say them aloud, then reverse key syllables.)

You have hissed all my mystery lectures.
I saw you fight a liar in the back quad; in fact, you have tasted the whole worm.
I assure you the insanitary spectre has seen all the bathrooms.
Easier for a camel to go through the knee of an idol.
The Lord is a shoving leopard to his flock.
Take the flea of my cat and heave it at the louse of my mother-in-law.

(Photo from The Bettmann Archive)

as a clue to meaning, for example. The combination of word endings and word sequence make *slithy toves* a descriptive phrase: *slithy* must be an adjective that describes the plural noun *toves*. Similarly their position in the sentence and the *did* in front of them make *gyre* and *gimble* present-tense verbs. In using such cues, Carroll was using more than phonemes or morphemes; he was using the rules of sentence structure.

Sentences

A complete sentence is more than just a string of phonemes and morphemes. It is a total structure, one in which the relationships among the parts are as meaningful as the parts themselves. There are several ways to interpret these larger relationships. We will look first at phrases, then at the propositions that lie behind them. Only then can we see just what a whole sentence really does.

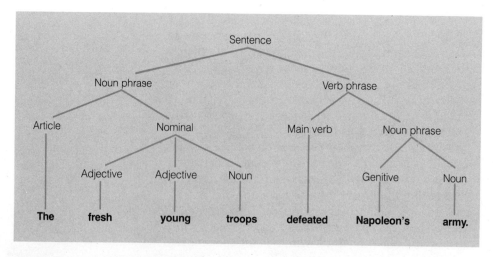

Figure 10.8 ■ Analysis of the surface structure of a sentence: It is made up of a noun phrase and a verb phrase, which are themselves made up of other components.

(From *Psychology and Language: An Introduction to Psycholinguistics* by Herbert H. Clark and Eve V. Clark, © 1977 by Harcourt Brace Jovanovich, Inc. Reprinted by permission of the publisher.)

Sentences can be broken down into **phrases,** sets of words smaller than a sentence that convey units of meaning. In our "unique" sentence, *a short fat green giraffe* is a noun phrase, and *sat in a porch swing* is a verb phrase. Most sentences consist of at least one noun phrase and one verb phrase, which can then be further subdivided. ■ Figure 10.8

The meaning of a sentence depends as much on the sequencing of the words and phrases within it as on the individual meanings of those words and phrases. Simple rearrangements of the sentence in Figure 10.8, for example, could yield "Napoleon's army defeated the fresh young troops" or "Napoleon's fresh young troops defeated the army."

The notion of propositions is somewhat more subtle. To a linguist, any word or phrase that specifies meaning is a **proposition;** it proposes that something is true (Fillmore, 1968). In Figure 10.8, for example, the single adjective *fresh* represents the proposition *the troops were fresh*. In the noun phrase *Napoleon's army*, the -*'s* morpheme represents the proposition *the army belonged to Napoleon*. The sentence thus represents a series of propositions collapsed into a compact form. Virtually all adult sentences include similar multiple propositions. These propositions could all be stated separately, but anyone who went around speaking in single propositions would be looked at strangely, to say the least. "The giraffe was short. The giraffe was fat. The giraffe was green. The giraffe sat," and so forth, is even stranger than our original sentence.

The simplest way of combining propositions is to use a conjunction, such as *and:* "Jane went out and George came in." But to say "The giraffe was short and the giraffe was fat" is to use unnecessary words. Natural languages also include **rewrite rules,** systems by which words can be put together into well-formed phrases. Here the rewrite rules of English allow us to drop some of the duplication and say "The giraffe was short and . . . fat." We can drop even more words if we also rearrange them: "The short fat giraffe." (Because one of the words we dropped was the original verb, this is no longer a complete sentence.)

The ways in which we are allowed to combine and rewrite propositions in English vary widely. Choosing one phrasing over another often carries additional meaning. Pronouns are often used to stand for particular people, for example, but using them implies that the referenced person is known to the listener: "The fresh young troops defeated his army" would be an appropriate version of the sentence in Figure 10.8 only if Napoleon were already known to be the topic of conversation. And "They defeated his army" would imply even more previous knowledge.

The total communication process by which one person's ideas are transmitted to another person goes as follows: In the production half, the speaker first generates an intended meaning to be communicated. He or she then develops a particular set of propositions and phrases with which to convey that meaning. Finally he or she must produce the pattern of sounds that correspond to the words.

In the comprehension half of communication, the listener must reverse the process, beginning with the sound string and going all the way back to meaning. If the meaning is not complicated and the speaker has been exceptionally careful, the comprehension process may be straightforward. But with complex meaning or less-than-perfect productions, the possibilities for errors in communication multiply.

LANGUAGE COMPREHENSION

Comprehension is in some ways like perception: Its apparent ease is the end product of substantial learning superimposed on innate tendencies and often carried out at a less than conscious level. Neither perception nor speech comprehension is simple, even though millions of people routinely accomplish both. In order to comprehend another's sentence, you must first rely on that speaker's following some basic principles. Then you must decode the sound stream into words that make up a sentence and interpret the propositions that this represents. Finally, you must interpret the sentence in some context, as part of a spoken conversation or a written passage.

Sometimes the context will be situational. A sentence may refer to a ball game you and another person are both watching, for example. (Learning to use such social-context cues is a part of learning a language; Krauss & Glucksberg, 1977.) Often, however, the context is provided by previous sentences, spoken or written. Comprehending a prose passage thus depends on the relationships among sentences in the same way that comprehending a sentence depends on the relationships among its words, phrases, and propositions. We will look at these points in order, beginning with two major principles, then moving from sound stream to prose passages.

Reality and Cooperative Principles

In all levels of comprehension, the listener or reader depends on the good will and skill of the language producer. The listener uses two major principles in comprehending another's production, the reality principle and the cooperative principle. In following the **reality principle,** listeners assume that productions to be comprehended do make sense. In following the **cooperative principle,** listeners assume that the speaker is trying to tell the truth, to tell them all they need to know and no more, and to be relevant, clear, and unambiguous (Grice, 1975). Taken together, these two principles help listeners rule out ambiguities, fill in gaps, and so forth. But they can be seriously mis-

leading if the speaker is not following them. The reality principle breaks down when speakers are unwilling or unable to produce utterances that make sense. (Workers in mental hospitals often minimize conversations with patients because they soon learn that patients do not always make sense.) The cooperative principle is more often misused deliberately—by advertisers, fortune tellers, magicians, and others. ■ Personal Application: Manipulation by Language

Comprehending Words, Sentences, and Prose

The first task of a listener is to interpret from a more-or-less continuous sound stream the words, phrases, and sentences that make it up. Then the underlying propositions can be extracted. In reading a printed passage, the words are separated for you, but in speech they often are not: Pauses between words may be no greater than pauses within them. You might think this would make the words in a sentence more difficult to identify than if they were presented separately. The children's phrase "I scream for ice cream" for example, seems to suggest that separating words out of a sound-stream could be confusing. But exactly the opposite is true.

Words and Concepts   This effect was noted by Pollack and Pickett (1964), who cut words out of a recording of normal speech and presented them separately; under these conditions, fewer than half the words were identifiable. Pollack and Pickett followed up by building tapes with more and more of the original passage following the words. They found that the more words the subjects were given, the more accurate was their identification. The effect was not gradual for any single word identification, however. Instead, the word remained unintelligible until some critical threshold was reached, when it immediately became clear. Word identification thus seems to be a form of perception; when enough features are available, perception occurs.

The separation of words as sounds and the interpretation of their meaning, it turns out, are closely linked processes. As early words in a sentence are identified, they provide cues that help predict what to expect next and thus aid in the identification of later words. Words that have multiple meanings, for example, cause relatively few decoding problems because context cues help guide you to the appropriate meaning. If you are discussing sleep, you are not likely to interpret the word *bed* as a river bed. But if you are discussing floods, the same word *bed* will be given the river interpretation.

Manipulation by language

Many people seek to manipulate our thoughts, emotions, or overt behaviors in some way, for a variety of reasons. Much of this manipulation is done through persuasive language. We recognize and accept persuasion in some forms, which are seen as legitimate communications. A debate or a scientific paper seeks to convince the listener or reader of the merits of a position through logic and data, for example, and many other forms of persuasive communication are considered equally acceptable.

Even acceptable persuasive communications take advantage of the subtle meanings of words, however, choosing those that will say more than they seem to on the surface. Advertising uses words and images to associate its products with the positive qualities that these words and images carry. In fact, this is so common in advertising that Chevrolet parodied itself a few years ago with singing commericals for "Baseball, hot dogs, apple pie, and Chevrolet." Political debates are notorious for their use of emotionally "loaded" words. The debate over abortion is one current controversy in which both sides use loaded words—such as *reproductive freedom* or *infanticide*—to describe the issues.

A notable historical example of manipulation through language comes from the 1925 Scopes trial, which concerned the teaching of evolution in the Tennessee public schools. The trial pitted the well-known politician and orator William Jennings Bryan against the noted trial lawyer Clarence Darrow. Of all the impassioned prose that came out of this clash of two strongly committed and bitterly opposed groups, one of the most biting passages was H. L. Mencken's description of Bryan, who was arguing the case against evolution. (Read it out loud to get the full effect.)

Once he had one leg in the White House and the nation trembled under his roars. Now he is a tinpot pope in the Coca-Cola belt and a brother to the forlorn pastors who belabor half-wits in galvanized iron tabernacles behind the railroad yards. . . . It is a tragedy, indeed, to begin life as a hero and to end it as a buffoon. (Quoted in Gould, 1981b, p.22)

Such a strong statement had little to do with the merits of the case (which Bryan in fact won). It was a deliberate attempt to use the power of sordid images to discredit what we would now call Bryan's image.

But at least Mencken's intention to persuade was obvious. Other forms of persuasive communication vary from sneaky to fraudulent. Advertising often seeks to manipulate through deliberate misuse of the cooperative principle (Harris, 1977). "The ingredient doctors recommend most," for example, is aspirin. If the advertiser were following the cooperative principle, the ad would say so instead of *seeming* to follow this principle while in fact concealing information. (It wants you to think it means some other mysterious ingredient, rather than plain old aspirin.) Such advertising claims have resulted in several federal cease-and-desist orders for pain-reliever manufacturers.

Even more manipulative are the procedures used by magicians and fortune tellers, sometimes as legitimate entertainment but too often as fraud. They do what is called "cold reading": appearing to interpret or read your past psychically with no previous knowledge of you (Hyman, 1977). In cold reading, the person who is being read plays by the rules of normal communication, being cooperative and helpful, while the reader manipulates him or her by breaking the rules (R. A. Schwartz, 1978).

The cold reader begins with a general statement that is likely to be true, based on the visible characteristics of the person. Depending on the reply, he or she continues on that topic or drops it, until the person being read has given up enough secrets to be impressed at how much the reader knows. "You're having some problems with a relative, I see." (Isn't everybody?) "Oh, you must mean Uncle Henry." "That's right, Uncle Henry." And so forth. By the time the person leaves, he or she is amazed by how much the reader knew about Uncle Henry—never realizing that he or she had provided all the information. The cold reader thus breaks the principle of cooperation (and to a lesser extent the reality principle) by deliberately phrasing remarks to draw out information while seeming to provide it and by concealing his or her lack of knowledge while claiming special knowledge.

In most conversations, the reality and cooperative principles are a good guide to communication. But when someone stands to gain your money, your vote, or other valuable consideration if they can change your mind, be careful. The two of you may not be playing by the same rules.

Warren and others later discovered a speech illusion that tells us how Pollack and Pickett's perceptual effect probably occurs. Warren took a recorded sentence, cut out one phoneme from within a word, and replaced it with a filler—a cough or tone. When asked if any sounds were missing from the resulting sentence, subjects said no. Even when told what to listen for, they could not locate the word from which the phoneme had been removed. Warren calls this the *phonemic restoration effect.* It apparently uses both syntactic and semantic constraints to fill in the appropriate phoneme that makes the word fit the sentence in which it occurs. One study, for example, used the sentence "It was found that the *eel was on the _____." (The * represents the filler sound.) When the last word was *axle*, the subjects heard "*eel" as "wheel." When it

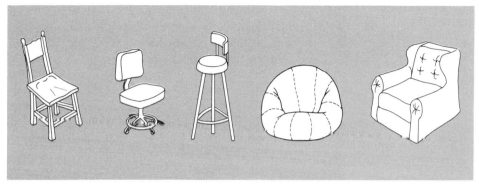

a

b

Figure 10.9 ■ Concepts. (a) *Chair* refers not to any specific chair but to the concept of chair as a portable structure for holding a person in a seated posture. (b) Even a rat can learn something similar to a basic concept. This one is learning the concept of *two;* first reinforced for choosing the two faces, it later chooses the two diagonal lines.

(**b**, © 1983 Frank Lotz Miller from Black Star)

was *shoe,* they heard "heel." For *orange,* they heard "peel," and for *table,* they heard "meal" (Warren & Warren, 1970). In this case only semantic information was varied, because all sentences were identical except for the meaning of the last word, and the semantic cue came *after* the missing phoneme. But subjects had no trouble restoring an appropriate phoneme for each sentence.

Thus even at the earliest stages of speech recognition, several aspects of language competence are already being used. Apparently, what happens in normal speech is that production errors, external noises, and other problems can interfere with some phonemes. But if we have enough information about what is being said, we can fill in the gaps. Thus Pollack and Pickett's subjects could interpret words in a string that they could not identify in isolation. However, we must have adequate information to fill in the gaps. People who have a hearing loss that eliminates some phonemes often make incorrect interpretations of what they hear, possibly because their interpretation mechanisms are working with too little information.

Word identification is only the beginning of mean-

ing interpretation, however. If you read "She sat down in a chair," you may easily identify the word *chair,* but what does it *mean?* The word *chair* does not communicate an exact visual image, as a photograph would. Instead, it offers a **concept,** a generalized idea that represents all such objects in the objective world, but is not the same as any of them. The actual chair could have had any of a variety of shapes, for example, none of which was specified. Lest you think this a simple notion, consider a couple of other problems. Is a stool a chair? Is the folding tripod used at sporting events a chair? Does a table become a chair if you sit on it? Trying to write an exact definition of even such a basic concept as *chair* is not easy. What then is the exact referent for such abstract concepts as *truth* or *fairness?* Even simple relative concepts such as *up* and *down* can be difficult to define exactly: they lose much of their ordinary meaning for an astronaut, for example. ■ Figure 10.9

A word's objective and specific meaning, what you find in a dictionary, is its **denotative** meaning. But the word's overtones or implications, which are often emotional ones, make up its **connotative** meaning; a

Table 10.3 ■ Some Ambiguous Sentences

Word ambiguity
1. California is a great state to live in despite its faults.
2. There is a fork in the road ahead.
3. To a waiter: "Do you have frog legs?"
4. Newspaper name: *The Chattanooga News-Free Press*

Sentence ambiguity
5. The car was stopped by the tree.
6. The magician made the prince a frog.
7. The police were ordered to stop drinking at midnight.
8. She missed the boat.
9. Norman Rockwell painted me on his front porch.
10. Jane reports that her neighbor had her second car stolen.
    a. Jane's neighbor was the victim of car theft for a second time.
    b. Jane's neighbor arranged the theft of Jane's old family jalopy.

    (and so forth)

From Moates & Schumacher, 1980

word's connotations may sometimes appear in a dictionary, but often do not. *Capitalism* and *fascism*, for example, have denotative meanings as ways of organizing groups of people, but they also carry powerful connotative meanings beyond their dictionary definitions.

Sentences and Passages Words convey some of the total meaning of any language production. But single words are limited in meaning. They only become elaborated into complex communication by the relationships among a series of them, in the form of sentences. Consider our sentence "The short fat green giraffe sat in the porch swing smoking a cigar." Here the first three words are two relative concepts and a color. (*Short* and *fat* do not describe exact sizes, only relative sizes.) In a series like this, the reader knows they all relate to the following noun and generates the composite of a "short fat green giraffe" even if he or she has never encountered this particular series before.

The verb form *sat* is then recognized as the past tense of *sit*. Because subject–verb is a usual sequence, the oddly colored giraffe is then mentally rearranged to an imitation of a human sitting posture. *In a porch swing* follows *sat* and obviously specifies the location of the seated giraffe. But correctly interpreting *smoking a cigar* is a more subtle process. The reader automatically uses it to modify *giraffe*, even though the phrase actually follows *porch swing*. Why not a porch swing smoking a cigar? It's hardly more outlandish than the giraffe image. Does the giraffe get the cigar because of subtle structural relationships in the sequence? Or is there some other kind of implicit rule, such as "attribute an action to a living creature before attributing it to an object"? These are the kinds of questions faced by those who would develop a grammar of English. Any useful explanation of how meaning is conveyed will have to be able to specify, for example, why the giraffe gets the cigar and not the porch swing.

In seeking to understand how anyone comprehends any sentence, psycholinguists use examples even more bizarre than the giraffe one. "Colorless green ideas sleep furiously" is an often-quoted example. This sentence is made up of English words put together into a legitimate sequence, yet it makes less sense than "Jabberwocky" because of its internal contradictions in meaning. Studying how people process such contradictions is one way of seeking how they extract meaning from sentences.

In some ways, sentences are easier to comprehend than shorter units, because more cues are available that can be cross-checked. But linguists have studied a number of **ambiguous sentences** whose words can represent two or more meanings (MacKay, 1970a). Ambiguous sentences cause comprehension problems because *different* underlying propositions may sometimes be rewritten to the *same* word or phrase. For example, the phrase "eating apples" in the sentence "They are eating apples" can represent people having lunch or a type of apple. Similarly, Sentence 10 in Table 10.3 has a total of eight meanings (Moates & Schumacher, 1980). ■ Table 10.3

The more elaborate the proposition, the more background information may be necessary to interpret it. Sometimes this results in comic failures of translation from one language to another. "Body by Fisher" is a traditional part of General Motors' advertising that is familiar to most Americans. But in translation for a foreign market, it became "Corpse by Fisher," a phrase that must have seemed out of place in an automobile ad.

Longer passages can be easier or harder to comprehend than sentences. More words can aid context and thus clarify meaning. But if the additional words are themselves ambiguous, they further deepen the confusion. Researchers have studied prose passages such as the following. See if you can tell what it means before knowing the context.

If the balloons popped, the sound wouldn't be able to carry, since everything would be too far away from the correct floor. A closed window would also prevent the sound from carrying, since most buildings tend to be well insulated. Since the whole operation depends on a steady flow of electricity, a break in the middle of the wire would also cause problems. Of course, the fellow could shout, but the human voice is not loud enough to carry that far. An additional problem is that a string could break on the instrument. Then there could be no accompaniment to the message. It is clear that the best situation would involve less distance. Then there would be fewer potential problems. With face to face contact, the least number of things could go wrong. (Bransford & Johnson, 1973, p. 394)

Some passages need only a verbal caption to set the context, but this one is made meaningful only by an illustration. It is typical of the description one person might give another when both could see the illustration, but without that visual aid it is almost unintelligible. ■ Figure 10.10

Thus, in interpreting lengthy passages you rely on a series of cues and processes. You identify words and begin to interpret them individually. As you build words into sentences, or sentences into passages, you summarize what you know and predict what is to follow. This usually works well, but if you encounter a word or sentence that doesn't fit you may have to go back and reorganize, or the later prose may not make sense. In reading a sentence such as "I was afraid of Ali's powerful punch, especially since it had already laid out many tougher men who had bragged they could handle that much alcohol" (Clark & Clark, 1977, p. 81), you can feel yourself stopping to reorganize your idea of what it means (Bever et al., 1973; Kolers, 1972). In all this, you rely on the reality and cooperative principles, assuming at each step that the input does make sense and that the speaker or writer is trying to help you comprehend the message. After that, how meaningful an exchange is depends on the skill of the participants.

Until now, we've considered these language processes in behavioral terms. The physiological basis of many of these steps remains unknown, but some parts are beginning to be understood. We look now at some of the brain areas important in language production and comprehension.

LANGUAGE AND THE BRAIN

Most language functions are controlled by the left hemisphere, though the right contributes the intonation patterns, or music, of speech. The arrangement in brain areas for right-handers is not the same as that for left-handers, however. We will look briefly at these topics before examining in more detail some language-related areas within the left hemisphere and how damage to these can affect language.

Hemisphere Differences

In written form, language offers only the cues to meaning that we have discussed in previous sections:

"You have a choice of three courses. You could increase speed somewhat and retain your comprehension, you could increase speed considerably and reduce comprehension, or you could increase speed tremendously and eliminate comprehension completely."

© 1977 by Sidney Harris—American Scientist Magazine

words, prefixes and suffixes, word order, and so forth. But spoken language includes another type of information in its intonation pattern. In the average right-handed person, virtually all language elements except intonation are controlled in the left hemisphere, with the "music" being added by the right hemisphere. (We will look at variations for some left-handers later.) In the newborn infant, neither hemisphere is complete, and the corpus callosum that joins them is even less complete. Within the first year of growth, both hemispheres seem to develop the beginnings of comprehension. But as the corpus callosum becomes complete enough to allow specialization, the left hemisphere develops the abilities of producing speech.

Reading is also packaged in the left hemisphere, with the visual inputs converted into their speech equivalents before being further processed. Some readers may be able to bypass part of the speech-translation step, called subvocalization. Speed-reading courses claim to teach how to do this, but some evidence suggests that suppression of subvocalization may reduce comprehension (Levy, 1978). Overall, the success of such courses is open to debate (Anderson, 1980).

If left-handed people were simply mirror images of right-handers, you could just substitute "left" for "right" in any description of brain function. But that is *not* the case. Most left-handers, for example, still have

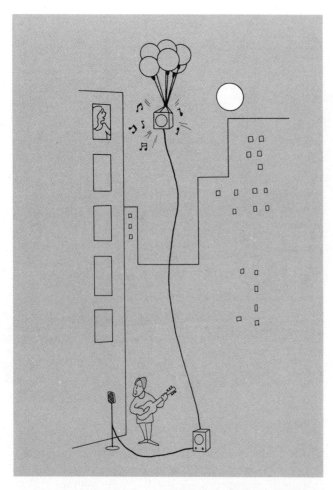

Figure 10.10 ■ Illustration that sets the context for the passage quoted in the text (pp. 328–329).

(From "Considerations of Some Problems of Comprehension" by J. D. Bransford and M. K. Johnson in W. G. Chase (Ed.), *Visual Information Processing*, Academic Press, 1973. Used by permission.)

their speech areas in the left hemisphere, just as right-handers do (Penfield & Roberts, 1959). Two researchers, Jerre Levy and Marylou Reid (1976), have suggested that the language hemisphere of a left-hander is indicated by the writing posture he or she uses. Those whose speech is in their left hemisphere, they argue, write in a reversed position, with the pencil pointed toward them as they write. Levy and Reid call these left-handers, who make up the majority, "hookers," because of this reversed or "hooked" position. According to Levy and Reid, the few left-handers who are not hookers have speech centers in their right hemisphere. They even suggest that a few right-handed hookers might be found, who would have right-hemisphere speech. (Not all researchers are convinced that Levy

and Reid are correct, however; Moscovitch & Smith, 1979.)

Whether or not hooking indicates which hemisphere the language is coming from, the pattern of brain organization for most left-handers is different from that for most right-handers—not just reversed, but qualitatively different. For left-handers, the dominant hemisphere, in terms of hand control, is *not* the same as the language hemisphere—as it is for right-handers. There is also substantially greater variation of arrangement in brain areas for left-handers, so that the arrangement for any particular left-hander is not easily predictable. Many left-handers also have some language capability in the right hemisphere, for example, although major control is in the left.

Cortical Language Areas

Within the speech hemisphere are two major areas involved in different aspects of speech. Any language input or output requires at least one of these, and often both. Still other brain areas are necessary for particular forms of input and output, such as hearing or writing. These areas are linked together by nerve tracts; when everything works well, they interact appropriately and language seems an integrated whole. But damage to these areas or to their connecting tracts can fragment the apparent integration of language, eliminating some aspects while sparing others. Reading can be lost, for example, without interfering with writing, leaving a patient able to write prose but immediately thereafter unable to read what he or she just wrote (Geschwind, 1972).

The first of the cortical language areas to be discovered was also the first cortical area of any type to be correctly specified. When the French physician, Paul Broca, identified **Broca's area** in 1861, he thought of it as *the* speech center. Now we know it as an important area in speaking, but *not* the most central one in comprehension or production. Broca had seen two patients who were unable to talk after strokes; upon autopsy, both were found to have suffered damage to an area below and in front of the face area of the motor-control strip. We now know that damage to Broca's area can eliminate the ability to produce spoken sentences, but a different area seems closer to being the center of language. In 1864, Carl Wernicke, through similar analyses of other patients, defined the area that now carries his name. **Wernicke's area** is both a language-interpretation area for inputs and a language-planning area for outputs. Speech inputs reach it from the adjacent auditory cortex, and speech outputs go forward from it to Broca's area along a nerve tract between them (Geschwind, 1979). ■ Figure 10.11

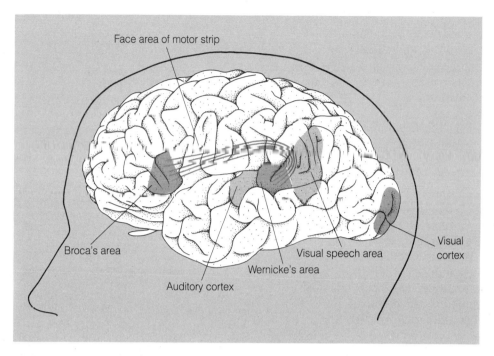

Figure 10.11 ■ Brain areas that cooperate to yield language performance. Another person's speech enters at the auditory cortex. Material read enters the visual cortex, then is interpreted into speech in the visual-speech area. Wernicke's area accepts both audio and visual inputs as speech. An answer is framed at Wernicke's area and sent forward to Broca's area, which creates the sound sequence. General commands for the sound sequence go to the face area of the motor strip, from which the detailed commands go to articulatory structures. (If the answer were written, commands would go to the hand area.) (Based on Geschwind, 1972.)

Consider the necessary sequence for a two-way communication, from the point of view of the second speaker. A voice input from Speaker 1 first reaches Speaker 2's ears and from there goes to the auditory cortex, where interpretation of the sound string begins. The sound string is further interpreted by Wernicke's area. If you need only repeat what you hear, the information can go directly from Wernicke's area to Broca's area. But for a meaningful reply, Wernicke's area must also communicate with other cortical areas, to retrieve memories and to plan the reply (Ojemann & Mateer, 1979).

Any reply is framed into a sentence plan by Wernicke's area, which sends it to Broca's area. Broca's area sequences the speech syllables for the reply, then sends commands, by way of the face area of the motor strip, to the speech articulators of mouth and throat. EEG recordings from the left side of the head show activity in preparation for speech as long as a half-second before any utterance; it apparently takes this long for the sequencing through Wernicke's and Broca's areas. During this time the missequencing of spoonerisms probably occurs, at Broca's area. The combination of Wernicke's and Broca's areas thus normally acts as an input-output mechanism. Wernicke's area helps in the transition to and from other areas of the cortex, but does not itself "understand" or "plan" speech: These functions require integration of numerous cortical areas.

Language performances frequently involve inputs or outputs other than speech. Several inputs can be visual, including sign language and reading. Of these, the brain arrangements for reading are best known (Gibson & Levin, 1975). (Sign-language integration may be different, especially for those who have never heard speech.) Reading also is interpreted through Wernicke's area, but it requires several additional steps before the input reaches there. First, through specific and precise learned eye movements we focus on a few words at a time. In this way, words are entered in sequence, as they are when spoken. Some problems in reading occur at this stage, because comprehension cannot exist unless inputs are presented appropriately (Carpenter & Just, 1980).

The visual input initially goes to the visual cortex, as does any other visual information. From there, the information moves forward through a visual-speech area into Wernicke's area (Figure 10.11). The translation at Wernicke's area and the consequent activation of Broca's area is what allows you to "hear" what you read. Even when you read to yourself, you are activating Broca's area, as if you were reading aloud. (If speed readers are successful in avoiding subvocalization, they probably are processing reading through Wernicke's area, but not passing the information on to Broca's area for speech planning.)

The functioning of these areas can be observed with a special technique (Lassen et al., 1978). A radioactive tracer is added to the blood; a monitor beside the skull senses the levels of radioactivity and feeds them to a computer, which displays the result as a grid of squares. The color of each square indicates how radioactive it is and thus to how much blood is flowing through that area of the cortex. Cortical blood flow changes depending on how active an area is, so you can see cortical areas light up in the computer display as they are used. The presentations for different forms of speech look quite different. For example, if a person is reading out loud and then begins to read silently, blood flow decreases to the auditory and facial control areas, and these immediately change color on the display.

Aphasias

Any loss of a language function from brain injury or disease is known as an **aphasia.** Specific kinds of loss have more specific names. A patient who cannot read, even though other functions remain, suffers from alexia; a patient who cannot write suffers from agraphia. Other aphasias can be equally selective, damaging or eliminating one function without necessarily affecting others. Some aphasias, for example, involve an inability to retrieve words, even when the patient knows them—an extreme version of the tip-of-the-tongue phenomenon. Others result in strange substitutions for some words rather than a prolonged search (Goodglass, 1980). ■ Figure 10.12 ■ Table 10.4

Two major types of aphasia are those resulting from damage to Broca's area and to Wernicke's area (H. Gardner, 1978; Geschwind, 1979). In **Broca's aphasia,** an expressive disorder, the patient either cannot speak at all or speaks only haltingly. With Wernicke's area still intact, a Broca's aphasia patient can understand inputs and can frame answers, but has trouble saying them. Whatever message he or she is able to produce, however, makes sense. Asked to describe a trip, the patient may say only "New York," but this answer will be appropriate.

Wernicke's aphasia is much more disruptive. If Wernicke's area is badly damaged, no form of meaningful language input or output may survive. Patients with Wernicke's aphasia can talk with normal speed and intonation, but what they say often makes little or no sense. Apparently Broca's area can still package speech sounds, but without Wernicke's area to plan a

Table 10.4 ■ Responses Given by an Aphasic Patient to Some Objects

Object	Response
Book	"Book, a husbelt, a king of prepator, find it in front of a car ready to be directed"
Candle	"Craft candlestick"
Drum	"Drum"
Rake	"Walking stick, would have been designed"
Dice	"Dice"
Scarecrow	"We'll call that a three minute resk witch, you'll find one in the country in three witches"
Anchor	"A martha argeneth"
Whale	"Ship painted, shoereen or a shoecream"

From *Brain Damage, Behavior, and the Mind* by Moyra Williams. Copyright 1979 by John Wiley & Sons. Reprinted by permission of John Wiley & Sons Ltd.

meaningful sentence, what results is confused at best, nonsense at worst. The patient may use empty words because the correct ones cannot be found—*thing* for any noun, for example. Or he or she may substitute words, sometimes related ones, such as *knife* for *fork,* sometimes unrelated ones, such as *hammer* for *paper.* Sometimes syllables will be combined to create words that do not exist—*pluver* or *flieber,* for example.

In most aphasias, damage affects speech mechanisms, rather than other cortical areas. But one noteworthy case demonstrates clearly that these areas are input/output mechanisms, and that the meaningful content of language must be received and generated by other areas (Geschwind, 1972). In this speech-isolation case, carbon-monoxide poisoning caused substantial brain damage before the patient was revived. The speech areas survived intact, as did the nerve tract between them, but they were almost totally isolated by destruction of surrounding cerebral areas.

The result was a patient who, in ordinary terms, no longer used language. In nine years of observation, she showed no evidence of comprehending anything said to her and never spoke spontaneously. Yet her speech mechanisms, if appropriately stimulated, did generate some kinds of automatic speech. They could repeat a whole sentence said to her, for example, apparently by translating from the spoken words back to motor commands for the same words. Yet no *person* seemed involved in the loop, only these isolated mechanisms. They were able to finish some standard phrases, once these were begun, such as "Roses are red, violets are blue. . . ." They were even able to learn new songs, ones written since her illness so that she could have had no previous memory of them. After a few repetitions, she would begin to sing along, and after a while she could finish the song alone.

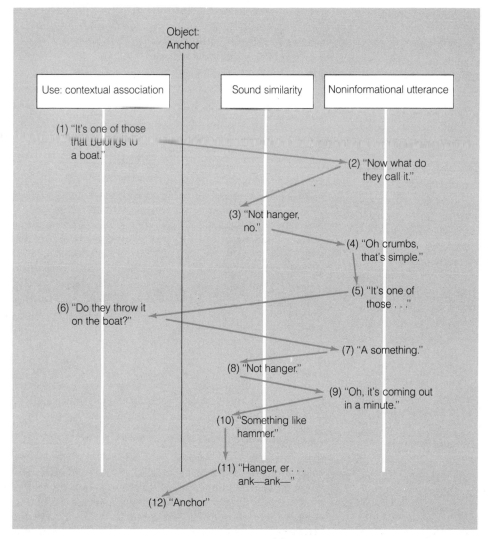

Figure 10.12 ■ The memory search that one aphasic patient went through in trying to retrieve the word *anchor* in response to seeing one.

(From *Human Learning and Memory: An Introduction* by A. Wingfield. Copyright © 1979 by Harper & Row, Publishers, Inc. Reprinted by permission of Harper & Row, Publishers, Inc.)

It's hard to know just how to describe such a patient. What "mind" was left of the original integrated person is nearly impossible to determine. So, in a sense, saying that the person could repeat phrases or learn songs is misleading. Yet it's also misleading to say that the speech mechanisms alone could do so. Also required were a variety of other connections, such as those to the ears and to the articulators, and perhaps to a remaining few areas of cortex—all of which used to be components of the person. In making us ask such questions, however, this case makes us more aware of how normal functioning depends on many components working together. To answer a question, or even to say the name of a seen object, is not a single act, in neurological terms. It is a lengthy sequence of acts, carried out over time and in different brain locations.

In this chapter we have focused on language as a means of communication. In examining this use of language, we have necessarily considered some aspects of language and thought, for they are inextricably linked. What else do you have to communicate but a thought? And what can an incoming communication do but arouse a thought? But we have not given much consideration to the use of language in extended private dialogues, or in specific forms of problem solving. These are among our topics in the next chapter. There we will see that language, although not the only mode of thought, is a central one. Talking to ourselves, it seems, is almost as important as talking to others.

CHAPTER SUMMARY

1 Language, as studied by psychologists, is a symbolic system for communication of meaning from one user to another. Its productivity allows the creation of unique statements, and its regularity allows these unique statements to be decoded.

2 Natural language channels for humans are speech and hearing, which have jointly evolved for efficient communication. In reading or writing or in unusual circumstances, other physical channels can be used.

3 Many species' behaviors have been investigated to see if they include some form of language. Most animal communication systems differ too much from what humans do to be considered language, but whether the apes can be taught some variation of language remains an open and hotly argued question.

4 The United States is primarily one language community, but many groups within it speak other languages or dialects. One of the more controversial issues is whether Black English is truly a distinct dialect.

5 Other language-community issues include how bilinguals learn and use their separate languages, what differences there are between male and female usage, and how to eliminate gender bias in phrasing.

6 The extent to which language acquisition reflects innate structures, and thus a critical period for acquisition, remains in debate; there is evidence for the importance of both nature and nurture factors.

7 Children acquire a natural language in a general sequence that is similar for most children and most languages, beginning with attention to the sounds they hear, then progressing through comprehension and production of increasingly complex forms.

8 Language comprehension depends on many factors, including the use by both speaker and listener of the cooperative and reality principles. Failure to follow these rules can seriously distort comprehension.

9 Comprehension of language depends on being able to hear or read the basic patterns and then to use both semantic and syntactical information to put together meaning.

10 Several different brain areas, primarily two in the left hemisphere, cooperate in language production and comprehension. Problems of aphasics offer some insight into how these areas function.

Further Readings

For more detailed coverage of all the issues of psycholinguistics, see Clark and Clark's *Psychology and Language* (1977). The problems faced by the deaf and their use of Ameslan are described in Benderly's *Dancing Without Music* (1980a). Books on the bee-language work and on each of the major ape projects are included in the references in that section; for a summary of animal language research, see *Eloquent Animals* by Davis (1978). *Black English* (1972) presents Dillard's arguments for the origins and structure of that dialect. For further exploration of the nature/nurture issues in acquisition, see Lieberman's *On the Origins of Language* (1975), Lenneberg's *Biological Foundations of Language* (1967), Skinner's *Verbal Behavior* (1957), and Chomsky's *Language and Mind* (1968). Many aspects of language acquisition, with examples, are presented in *A First Language* by Brown (1973), and *Spontaneous Apprentices* by Miller (1977) is a useful introduction. Warner and Gleitman's collection, *Language Acquisition* (1982), summarizes a variety of acquisition issues. Gibson and Levin have integrated research from many areas in *The Psychology of Reading* (1975). Fromkin's collection *Errors in Linguistic Performance* (1980) offers a variety of perspectives on language slips. For general discussion of the problems resulting from brain damage, including aphasias, see Gardner's *The Shattered Mind* (1975). Finally, for discussions of a variety of issues, see Lenneberg and Lenneberg's collection *Foundations of Language Development* (1975).

On a trip to the central computer facility to do some special homework for a programming class, you notice a stranger working busily at one of the terminals. A friend explains that it is a visiting researcher helping set up some projects involving "scripts." "For a play?" you ask. "No, not that kind of script," she says. "You know, computer scripts, sequences that tell the computer how the world works." "Oh yeah," you mumble, not really knowing but willing to go along. You ask her to introduce you, and the researcher tells you a bit of what's going on. "I've found that computers have a hard time understanding normal language," he notes. "No kidding," you think, remembering some of the problems you've had with learning to be as literal and exact as the machine seems to demand; but you hold your tongue and nod encouragingly. "We used to think that giving computers a dictionary and some grammatical rules would do it," he continued, "but it didn't. We found that humans add a great deal to any conversation by inferring things between the lines. For computers to understand, they also need to know the background information humans do." You imagine a computer in a crib, being raised and talked to as the language-learning chimps have been. But you only ask politely just how one goes about teaching a computer about the world. "You build up scripts," he says, "summaries of information about some common situation, such as eating at a restaurant. You must tell the computer that people first order, then eat, then pay, if you want it to understand dialogue involving restaurants." You agree, thank him, and get back to work. It still isn't obvious to you just why anyone *wants* to have a dialogue with a computer about restaurants, but at least you know what a script is.

We humans have long felt that our ability to think and solve problems sets us apart from the other animals and represents our highest achievement. But just what is thinking and how is it related to problem solving? Do humans think "naturally" or must they be taught to do so? Is it really true that no other species thinks? To illustrate principles that we'll come back to, let's look at two examples of thinking and problem solving.

The first problem is a verbal one; it simply requires you to comprehend the meaning of a complex statement: "If the puzzle you solved before you solved this one was harder than the puzzle you solved after you solved the puzzle you solved before you solved this one, was the puzzle you solved before you solved this one harder than this one?"

The second problem is primarily a visual one. Typical gears, like those in a mechanical clock or a car's transmission, are round wheels with alternating teeth and spaces on the periphery. As the gears rotate, each tooth of one gear fits into the space between two teeth

Chapter 11 ■ *Thinking*

Chapter 11

Thinking

of the other. Is it possible to arrange *square* gears so that they will stay continuously meshed? (The answer to the verbal problem is "yes"; we'll look at the square-gears problem later.)

DEFINING THINKING

Having learned something about the basic processes of learning, memory, and language, we can now explore thinking and problem solving. As usual, our first task is to define our topic. Given a working definition, we can go on to specify some of the ways in which we think and solve problems—even something of what it means to be creative.

Perspectives and Definitions

The major theoretical views of thinking in psychology have been the associationist view (which in contemporary form is a behavioral one), the Gestalt view, and the cognitive or information-processing view.

The associationist view, as noted in Chapter 8, suggests that events that are experienced together become associated with each other: A particular sight becomes associated with the particular sound that accompanied it, and remembering one leads to remembering the other. Thinking, in associationist terms, represents the hidden effect of such previous associations. Watson's early behaviorism avoided studying thinking because it could not be directly measured, so there has been little direct behavioral research on thinking. But some more recent behaviorists consider thinking to be a form of covert behavior, using verbal reports as indicators of covert activity (Maltzman, 1955; Meichenbaum, 1977).

The Gestalt view, as noted in Chapters 6 and 8, considered thinking to be a reorganization of conceptual wholes, or gestalts, typically through the sudden alteration called insight. Gestaltists also emphasized perception as a basis for thinking, but they focused on how perception and thinking were shaped by innate factors. They also emphasized the integrated quality of perception and thought, rather than seeking to break these into elements as the associationists did. Some thinking was **reproductive,** in which old associations were reproduced from memory, but **productive** thinking, in which new patterns were built by reorganizing old ones, was more important (Maier, 1940).

The cognitive perspective, however, has been for some time the most influential one in contemporary study of thinking: *cognition* essentially means "thought" (Weimer & Palermo, 1982). Cognitive theorists have accepted concepts from both the associationists and the Gestaltists, but have built them into

an information-processing framework. In the cognitive perspective, humans are seen as devices that take in information about the world, actively manipulate or process that information in a series of discrete steps, and generate behaviors directed toward some goal (Estes, 1978; Lachman et al., 1979). (The basic information-processing view also applies to comparatively simple organisms that do not think but do process information to yield behavior.) In processing information, humans use **schemata** (singular, **schema**), mental "structures" for managing the information (Neisser, 1967). There are schemata for perception, for thinking, and for verbal or other output. In this chapter we will consider a number of strategies for solving problems; these are all schemata. A subtraction schema, for example, structures the processing of problems presented in the form $X - Y = ?$

We will use a definition drawn largely from the cognitive view in which **thinking** is the active manipulation of information from both sensory input and memory. Thinking is a way of summarizing what is going on in the world, relating it to the particular observer or thinker, and making plans for future action based on what is found (Erickson & Jones, 1978). Some of the information processed in thinking is new information from the senses, but most of it is old information drawn from memory.

The importance of memory in thought has long been recognized, but each generation has tended to see the relationship in terms of its own technology (Roediger, 1980). The early associationists saw humans as blank slates on which the environment wrote. The current cognitive perspective draws heavily on computer technology; the information-processing view is basically an analogy to a computer's processing of information. Cognitive psychologists have developed many **computer-simulation models** of human thinking and problem solving (Boden, 1981; Simon, 1981b). We will note some of these throughout the chapter.

Verbal and Visual Modes

When we consider thinking, most of us do so in terms of verbal manipulations. Most studies in cognitive psychology have also emphasized verbal thinking. But thinking may also occur in visual or other perceptual modes.

Language is a common mode of human thought, but it is a relatively specialized and (in evolutionary terms) recent development. Thus, it is probably superimposed on more basic forms of perceptual thought. In a child, language develops later than perception, and thus is also a superimposed mode in each individual's development.

Because language is an abstract system that can generate an indefinite number of new combinations, it offers a very flexible mode of thought. People can easily talk about things they have never experienced perceptually, or even that no one has ever experienced perceptually. These nonperceptual ideas can be related to perceptual experiences *(a green giraffe)* or can be entirely abstract concepts *(equality, justice)*. This abstract capability of language is what makes it a useful vehicle for human thought.

But the perception-based modes of thought are also useful. They cannot do what language can, but they may be able to do things that language cannot. In fact, thinking seems to be possible in any of the sensory modes. However, we as a species emphasize some sensory modes more than others. Vision, for example, provides most of our environmental information and overrides most other senses in cases of conflict. Logically, then, visual thinking, or imagery, is our other major mode for thought (McKim, 1980b; Shepard, 1978a).

We should not, however, overlook the other sensory modes. Composers, for example, may hear music as they compose it—clearly a form of auditory thought (Mozart, 1789). A smell or taste may trigger associated thought in other modes; someone devising a new perfume or new food recipe may use primarily smell or taste modes. Touch, kinesthetic, and vestibular senses may be used by a creative dancer, gymnast, or other person who uses his or her body in new ways.

Surprisingly, perhaps, the touch, kinesthetic, and vestibular senses may even be useful in abstract thought and problem solving. Here they are used as analogies with other things. Some mathematicians, for example, report experiencing relationships in spatial or body-position terms; Einstein, in response to a letter asking about his thought processes, described them in "muscular" as well as visual terms. ■ Notable Quote: Albert Einstein on His Thought Processes

The overall effect that Einstein describes seems to be a spatial or even "body-in-space" form of thought, one that is intuitive and nonverbal. This effect sounds remarkably like a description of the right-hemisphere capabilities we discussed in Chapter 2. That words must be "sought for laboriously" at a later stage suggests a kind of translation from right-hemisphere imagery to left-hemisphere language. A verbal/visual (for Einstein, verbal/spatial) distinction is only the most obvious of the distinctions in thinking that seem related to hemisphere specialties. But remember that *seem* does not mean *are* and the roles of the two hemispheres in different types of thinking remain tentative at present. It is likely, however, that at least some differences in thinking reflect the brain's natural separation into two halves with separate skills.

Both psychologists and educators have noted the possibility that hemisphere thinking patterns depend on patterns of experience. For many years both had emphasized verbal thinking, but recently they have paid more attention to visual and other modes, partially as a result of the wide publicity given to split-brain findings. Such activities as art, music, and dance, once considered frills, may receive more emphasis in the future as ways of teaching right-hemisphere modes of thought (Samples, 1975).

Learning to Think

Thinking is something that virtually all humans do, but we require some learning to be able to think in even simple ways—and extensive training to think in others. Children even have to learn that an object *is* an object—what Piaget called object permanency (Chapter 12); they learn this through experience with objects and their properties. Yet sometimes even extensive experience may not yield correct thinking about the world. Children who have just seen a tilted bottle with water in it, for example, make serious errors in attempting to remember the angle of the water surface (Furth et al., 1974). In fact, many college students still cannot think accurately about the behavior of water, after many more years of experience (Thomas et al., 1973). ■ Figure 11.1

NOTABLE QUOTE
Albert Einstein on his thought processes

66 The words or the language, as they are written or spoken, do not seem to play any role in my mechanism of thought. The psychical entities which seem to serve as elements in thought are certain signs and more or less clear images which can be "voluntarily" reproduced and combined. . . . This combinatory play seems to be the essential feature in productive thought—before there is any connection with logical construction in words or other kinds of signs which can be communicated to others. . . . The elements [in thought] are, in my case, of visual and some of muscular type. Conventional words or other signs have to be sought for laboriously only in a secondary state, when the mentioned associative play is sufficiently established and can be reproduced at will. 99

Einstein, Letter to Jacques Hadamard, as quoted in Ghiselin, 1952, p.43.

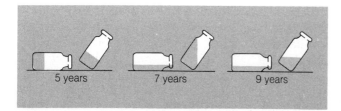

Figure 11.1 ■ Experience with the world is not necessarily enough to allow correct thinking about it. In general, older children make fewer and less extreme errors in simulating the position of the liquid in a tilted bottle—although at any age some subjects will make errors. (They apparently have not grasped the concept that because of gravity the water surface in the bottle will *always* be horizontal.)

Actually, you should not expect people to be able to think visually about complex problems without training and practice, any more than they can think verbally without it. Most people, for example, cannot accurately describe what the path of a ball will be after it is whirled in the air at the end of a string and released. Most expect it to continue in a curve after it is released, but basic study in physics shows that it will go straight (McCloskey, 1983). The square-gears problem posed at the beginning of the chapter also shows the utility of training in a particular mode of thought. Few people who have not seen a model like that shown in Figure 11.2a can visualize the arrangement of the gears shown there (Ferguson, 1977). The peculiar characteristics of a Möbius strip require even more experience (M. Gardner, 1978b). ■ Figure 11.2

Evolution and Uses of Thought

Until now, we haven't asked just what thought is good for, partially because we share the belief that it is useful. But it is worthwhile to ask that question explicitly, if only to clarify the different ways in which thinking can be useful.

In the simplest nervous systems, inputs are wired more or less directly to outputs. But with increasingly complex nervous systems, more and more neurons are devoted to information processing between input and output. Thought can be considered the information processing that takes place between sensory input and motor output. Even simple forms of thought would be useful for any adaptive organism, by allowing its behavior to be better adjusted to the environment as a whole, rather than simply a mechanical response to input. It is possible for complex behaviors to evolve without their possessors understanding them, as ethologists have shown is true for many species, for example, rattlesnakes (Dunkle, 1981). But if the brain capacity is available to handle complex information processing, this "thought" will be more efficient than

any direct response to the environment, even a complex one (Gould, 1982a). As processing increases in complexity, at some point thinking occurs (even though we cannot specify that point of transition).

The most basic and obvious use of simple thought is to represent the physical world in mental terms. To represent the world as a whole and respond to the overall perceptual pattern is a definite improvement over having single senses tied to particular behaviors. Another important step in the development of thought is for the thinker to represent itself in that perceived world. Once representations of world and self exist, they provide a base for the possibility of planning ahead or thinking about possibilities before they happen (Wicklund, 1979). And once the ability to consider possible alternative actions exists, it can be used to guide behaviors. Mentally manipulating and combining possibilities may lead to new behaviors. The more different possibilities can be sorted in memory, and the better the ways of combining and rearranging them, the more efficient will be the thought process.

This description of thought suggests that it has evolved in humans because it is a useful behavior. But it also suggests that some forms of thought may have evolved in other species. The question of whether animals have any form of self-awareness or thought, however, is thorny and often emotional. Many psychologists consider *any* speculation about the thought processes of nonhumans to be inappropriate. But other psychologists are willing to consider the possibility that an animal that pauses, looks around, and then acts has in some way thought about alternative actions or possible outcomes.

We can sense thoughts directly only in ourselves, of course, but it seems possible that other species do some of this. Acting as if our pets think as humans do is anthropomorphism (attributing human traits to nonhumans), and should be avoided. But acting as if they were unthinking machines, like automobiles, is equally ridiculous. We may never know just what an animal thinks about, if it does, but our evolutionary continuity with other species suggests possible parallels in cognitive functioning (Griffin, 1981). ■ Research Controversy: Do Animals Think? (p. 340)

VERBAL THINKING

Using a language for communication and thinking in that language are so closely intertwined that they are a single topic. But for convenience we considered language use as communication in Chapter 10; here we look more closely at language use in thought.

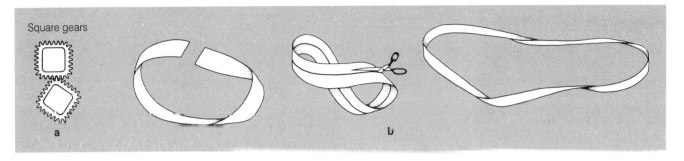

Square gears

a   b

Figure 11.2 ■ (a) The arrangement of square gears is logical when examined, but very hard to think about if you have never seen it. (b) A Möbius strip is even harder to consider visually. You can make one from a strip of paper by giving it a single twist and joining the ends. The result has only one edge and one surface, as you can demonstrate by tracing along the center; the line comes back to its starting point. Cutting the strip along this center line produces a single, longer, two-sided strip.

(**a,** from "Mechanical Movements" by W. M. Clark, 1929. Collection of the Newark Museum. Used by permission.)

Concept Formation

To have a concept means to respond to different stimuli (usually objects) as if they were the same: The concept of *dog*, for example, groups together a wide variety of animals. One major line of research in language and thought has been the study of how people form concepts. How does a child learn what is a *dog* and what is not? How does a college student learn what a *cognition* is?

Humans actually use two different kinds of concepts, intuitive natural ones and systematic scientific ones (Johnson-Laird & Wason, 1977). **Natural concepts,** such as *tree* or *fruit*, are developed quickly and easily, even without language; the verbal terms for natural concepts may simply be names for existing ideas. Even animals can develop natural concepts (Premack, 1978). Pigeons learn *tree* or *fish* relatively easily, for example (Herrnstein et al., 1976). They can even learn to discriminate Charlie Brown and the other "Peanuts" characters (Cerella, 1980). As we noted in Chapter 10, some researchers believe that current Ameslan use by apes merely names concepts the apes already have, such as *tickle*. Human children also seem to develop some concepts before they learn the words for them (Clark & Clark, 1977). In contrast, formal scientific concepts—such as *classical* and *operant conditioning* in psychology—may require extensive training; the process of acquiring expertise in any scientific field involves learning to use its concepts (Sokal, 1977).

How children acquire concepts has been studied primarily by psycholinguists; cognitive theorists have focused on adult learning. One approach, beginning in the 1950s, has been to devise artificial concepts based on lists of attributes and to see how subjects learn them (Bruner et al., 1956). Most psychologists now argue

that learning such artificial concepts involves developing and testing hypotheses. Levine (1975) has shown that subjects try one major hypothesis with two or three others held in reserve. If the primary hypothesis is disconfirmed, they choose an alternate hypothesis and test that one. (A possible sequence of hypothesis testing for a simple concept is shown in Figure 11.4a.) ■ Figure 11.4

In recent years, however, another approach to concept learning has been developed that focuses on the learning and use of natural concepts (or categories). Rosch and her colleagues (1973) note that natural categories more accurately reflect both the structure of the natural world and the thought processes of people seeking to understand that world. Rosch's view of natural categories emphasizes **prototypes,** central examples that typify the category (Rosch et al., 1976). For each category, some examples are closer to the prototype than others: A car is more a prototype *vehicle* than is an elevator, for example (Rosch & Mervis, 1975). ■ Table 11.1

Rosch (1973) finds that prototypes are important in thinking with language; they are learned quickly and serve as reference points for use of the categories. Prototypes can also usually be substituted for the category name in a sentence: In "A bird sat on the wire," *robin* is an acceptable substitute for *bird* but *penguin* is not. People also use prototypes in learning new concepts. Reed (1972), for example, studied how subjects learn to recognize certain types of drawings of faces. He found that they develop a prototype face summarizing the usual features of the category, even though they never see a face exactly like the prototype (see Figure 11.4b).

Do animals think?

The close physical similarities between humans and animals—especially other primates—have long implied that behaviors, including thinking, may also share similarities (Alcock, 1979). In nervous-system and sensory physiology, we find a general pattern of some shared physiology but some notable differences between ourselves and other primates. Looking at consciousness, the arguments about who is conscious or has a mind, are similar to those concerning primate language: Is what they're doing a weak version of what we do, or is it simply a learned trick with no real similarity to what we do?

No one really argues that other species think just as we do; obviously, much of our thought is based on language, which they do not have. But whether other forms of thought exist in animals is more arguable. Some psychologists argue that the evolutionary continuity of physiology, especially of nervous systems, implies a similar continuity of mind or thought. They accept

evidence of successful problem solving by animals as evidence of thought. Other psychologists point to animal studies in which problem solving occurs as a result of direct learning and argue that successful behavior does not necessarily imply either consciousness or thought.

These arguments, of course, reach their peak with consideration of our closest living relatives: If any other species has thought processes similar to ours, it is probably one of the great apes (Ferster, 1964; Menzel, 1973; Premack & Woodruff, 1978). Many psychologists are convinced that the several Ameslan-using chimps and the gorilla Koko are performing language acts, that is, using language meaningfully. They point to uses of Ameslan that seem akin to humans' uses of language outside of conversations. Koko, for example, often signs to herself, just as children talk aloud to themselves (Patterson & Linden, 1981).

Other studies with primates seem to demonstrate self-awareness more directly. A chimp is anesthetized, for example, and a red spot placed on its fore-

head; upon awakening, the chimp's responses to its image in a mirror seem to show that it is aware of having a different appearance from what it should (Gallup, 1979). But since the primate language work has been challenged by a pigeon that can "read" (Epstein et al., 1980), you should not be surprised to hear about a pigeon that has been taught to show "self-awareness" (Epstein et al., 1981). ∎Figure 11.3

These arguments over animal language, thought, or mind are somewhat controversial and are not likely to be resolved in the near future. But the recent swing toward recognizing covert activity in humans has led to increased interest in it in animals. You are likely to see references to the question of animal consciousness in the future, not only in psychology, but also as part of such issues as the use of animals in medical research, the slaughter of seal pups, whales, or porpoises, and the treatment of animals raised for meat (Singer, 1977).

a

b

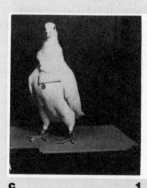

c   1

2

3

Figure 11.3 ∎ (a) Primates seem to engage in many kinds of problem solving even when there is no apparent reward for doing so. Here three monkeys work at opening various catches or locks, with obvious interest in the outcome. (b) Possible evidence for animal thought includes uses of Ameslan by apes for other than direct communication. The gorilla Koko, for example, often signs to herself. Here she signs "eye" when she sees a picture of a big-eyed frog in her picture book. (c) A pigeon shows trained "self-awareness" by using a mirror to observe a spot on its breast that it cannot see directly because of a bib. In (1), the spot is visible. In (2), the pigeon faces the mirror (not visible) at right. (When the pigeon leans forward, the bib covers the spot.) In (3) the pigeon pecks toward the position of the hidden spot, an act for which it will be rewarded.

(a, Harry F. Harlow, University of Wisconsin Primate Laboratory; **b,** Ronald H. Cohn/The Gorilla Foundation; **c,** R. Epstein et al., *Science* Vol. 212, pp. 695–696, 8 May 1981. Copyright 1981 by the American Association for the Advancement of Science/Photograph by R. Epstein.)

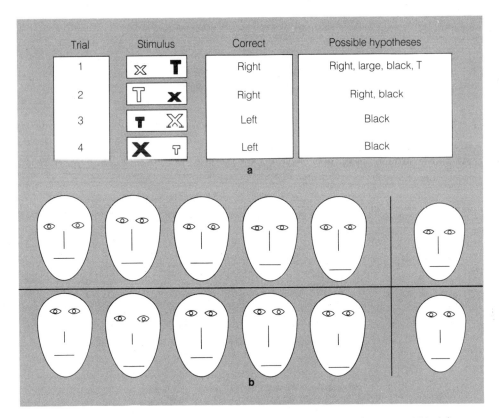

Figure 11.4 ■ Two studies in concept development. (a) In discovering the concept *black* from among the alternatives, subjects use information feedback on their choices to maintain or change hypotheses. (b) In discovering the concepts represented by the two rows of faces, subjects develop prototypes. Here the drawings on the right are the prototypes for each row. (The faces each differ slightly from the prototype, which thus represents an idealized summary of the concept.)

(**a**, adapted from M. Levine, *Journal of Experimental Psychology*, 1966, *71*, 331–338. Copyright 1966 by the American Psychological Association. Adapted by permission of the author; **b**, left from S. K. Reed and M. P. Friedman, *Memory and Cognition*, 1973, *1*, 157–163, © 1973 Psychonomic Society, Inc. Right from S. K. Reed, *Cognitive Psychology*, 1972, *3*, 382–407. Used by permission of Academic Press, Inc.)

	Prototype Ratings for Words in Three Categories[a]		
Rating[b]	Vehicle	Vegetable	Clothing
1	Car	Peas	Pants
2	Truck	Carrots	Shirt
3	Bus	String beans	Dress
4	Motorcycle	Spinach	Skirt
5	Train	Broccoli	Jacket
6	Trolley car	Asparagus	Coat
7	Bicycle	Corn	Sweater
8	Airplane	Cauliflower	Underwear
9	Boat	Brussel sprouts	Socks
10	Tractor	Lettuce	Pajamas
11	Cart	Beets	Bathing suit
12	Wheelchair	Tomato	Shoes
13	Tank	Lima beans	Vest
14	Raft	Eggplant	Tie
15	Sled	Onion	Mittens
16	Horse	Potato	Hat
17	Blimp	Yam	Apron
18	Skates	Mushroom	Purse
19	Wheelbarrow	Pumpkin	Wristwatch
20	Elevator	Rice	Necklace

[a]From E. Rosch and C. B. Mervis, *Cognitive Psychology*, *1*, 573–605. Used by permission of Academic Press, Inc.

[b]The words numbered 1 were rated most prototypical of the category; those numbered 20 were least prototypical.

Comprehension

We considered some aspects of language comprehension from the psycholinguistic point of view in Chapter 10. When cognitive psychologists study comprehension, they often use computer-simulation models. One of the most important findings from these models has been how much background information about the natural world is implicit in communication. Humans tend to share this background information, so it was overlooked until computer models demonstrated the need for it. The comment that someone "has" two hands, for example, is unambiguous to humans—apparently because of knowledge about their own bodies. For a computer to interpret such statements properly, it must be given that information explicitly. ■ Table 11.2

Much of the knowledge we use to comprehend language, however, concerns not objects, but events. One way of representing our knowledge of events is through **scripts,** plans or formats for standardized activities (Abelson, 1981; Schank & Abelson, 1977). A

Table 11.2 ■ A Sample Conversation with the SIR Simulation Program[a]

Person: Every boy is a person.

Computer Program: I UNDERSTAND.

A finger is part of a hand.

I UNDERSTAND.

Each person has two hands.

THE ABOVE SENTENCE IS AMBIGUOUS—PLEASE REPHRASE IT.[b]

There are two hands on each person.

I UNDERSTAND.

How many fingers does John have?

THE ABOVE SENTENCE IS AMBIGUOUS—BUT I ASSUME "HAS" MEANS "HAS AS PARTS."

I DON'T KNOW WHETHER FINGER IS PART OF JOHN.

John is a boy.

I UNDERSTAND.

How many fingers does John have?

HOW MANY FINGERS PER HAND?

Every hand has 5 fingers.

I UNDERSTAND.

How many fingers does John have?

THE ANSWER IS 10.

---

[a]From *The Thinking Computer: Mind Inside Matter* by B. Raphael. Copyright © 1976 by W. H. Freeman and Company. All rights reserved.

[b]*Has* might mean either "possesses" or "has attached as parts."

---

restaurant script, for example, notes that one usually follows a sequence that includes ordering, eating, and paying; if a person eats in a restaurant and leaves, we assume he or she has paid (Bower et al., 1979). For a computer to make that same assumption, it must be given the same script. ■ Table 11.3

Computer programs that simulate language comprehension are one subvariety of **artificial intelligence (AI),** the computer modeling of intelligent behavior (Waltz, 1982). Artificial intelligence has long focused on language use. In fact, one criterion for whether artificial intelligence has been achieved is Turing's test: If a human in one room cannot tell, by language communication alone, which of two other rooms contains another human and which a computer, the computer has artificial intelligence (Turing, 1950). When Turing devised this criterion, he thought of the communication as occurring through printed communication. But current artificial-intelligence research includes the development of programs to interpret natural human speech and to synthesize a verbal reply (Levinson & Liberman, 1981; Robinson, 1979).

Teaching computers to understand the natural world is a difficult process. Some researchers have created miniature, hypothetical "worlds" made up of information about a few objects and simple scripts for dealing with those objects. One of the best known is Terry Winograd's "blocks world" (1972). Through it, Winograd can examine how background knowledge is used for communication and thought. (When instructed to move one block, the program must "think about" what else to do to accomplish that move.) ■ Figure 11.5

One way of relating language as communication and as thought is in terms of control and self-control: Telling someone else what to do is a form of communication, but telling yourself what to do is a form of thought. Many communications—from "Please open your hymnals to number 99" to "Stick 'em up!"—are attempts at control by language. Like all forms of communication, however, these requests or commands must be understood if they are to be effective, and this understanding is already a form of thought. Obviously, "Stick 'em up!" does not work directly on your arms; it works because of your realization of the total situation, your danger, the demand being made, and so forth.

The process of self-direction or self-control is also often carried out with the help of language. If you pay attention to your own thought processes for a day or two, you'll almost certainly find examples of self-direction through covert speech. Children seem to learn to direct their behavior in this way as they learn language, first by speaking aloud and then by "turning down the volume" so the commands are audible only to themselves. And teaching them to direct their actions through covert speech is one way of teaching self-control (Meichenbaum, 1977). That thought occurs as subvocal speech can be shown by electrodes placed on the throat of speakers or on the hands of Ameslan users, which record low-level activity when people talk to themselves.

Thinking in Alternate Languages

One question about the relationship of communication and thought is whether you can think only about concepts that you have been taught to talk about. The **linguistic-relativity hypothesis,** proposed by the linguist Benjamin Whorf, claims that thinking is so dominated by language that people can only think about the world in terms of the concepts their language uses (Whorf, 1956). Thus, the thought patterns of the members of each language community would be similar but would differ from one language community to another.

Table 11.3 ■ Script Elements in Routine Events[a]

Going to a Restaurant	Attending a Lecture	Getting Up
Open door	ENTER ROOM	*Wake up*
Enter	*Look for friends*	Turn off alarm
Give reservation name	FIND SEAT	Lie in bed
Wait to be seated	SIT DOWN	Stretch
Go to table	Settle belongings	GET UP
BE SEATED	TAKE OUT NOTEBOOK	*Make bed*
Order drinks	*Look at other students*	*Go to bathroom*
Put napkins on lap	*Talk*	Use toilet
LOOK AT MENU	Look at professor	*Take shower*
Discuss menu	LISTEN TO PROFESSOR	*Wash face*
ORDER MEAL	TAKE NOTES	Shave
Talk	CHECK TIME	DRESS
Drink water	Ask questions	Go to kitchen
Eat salad or soup	Change position in seat	Fix breakfast
Meal arrives	Daydream	EAT BREAKFAST
EAT FOOD	Look at other students	BRUSH TEETH
Finish meal	Take more notes	Read paper
Order dessert	*Close notebook*	*Comb hair*
Eat dessert	*Gather belongings*	*Get books*
Ask for bill	Stand up	Look in mirror
Bill arrives	Talk	Get coat
PAY BILL	LEAVE	LEAVE HOUSE
Leave tip		
Get coats		
LEAVE		

[a]Items in all capital letters were mentioned by the most subjects, items in italics by fewer subjects, and items in lowercase letters by the fewest subjects. From G. H. Bower et al., *Cognitive Psychology*, 1979, 11, 177–220. Used by permission of Academic Press, Inc.

Whorf noted that languages develop different words to talk about important aspects of the environment. Eskimo, for example, has four words to distinguish different types of snow; English has only one and African languages typically have none. Furthermore, Whorf noted differences in the ways verb forms arrange the world. A verb in an American Indian language, for example, might mean something like "when pushed it resists and then bobs back"; this single concept might apply to a person's head or a fishing float.

In the strongest form of the linguistic-relativity hypothesis, people could not think about any concept not already coded by their language—but that is clearly an overstatement. The productivity of any natural language allows it to talk about completely new concepts, if only by combining phrases and coining new words. If it did not, we would be unable to talk about any new technology; but we can invent words as needed, like *television*.

A weaker form of the linguistic-relativity hypothesis suggests that the ready availability of concepts, including the words that name them, makes it much easier to think about them. If necessary, any English speaker can talk or think about more than one kind of snow—but an Eskimo could do it more easily, and an African only with some difficulty. Colin Turnbull, an anthropologist, reported (1962) that his description of

snow was translated into an African language, Ki Ngwana, as "water that had fallen from the sky, not like rain, but like white ashes, and which lay for month after month covering the land and even some of the buildings." The Africans, of course, didn't believe such a wild tale. Whether this weaker form of the linguistic-relativity hypothesis is an appropriate way to characterize thought remains undetermined.

People do think about environmental conditions that are important to them, and thus their languages have words for special environmental variations. In the long term, languages change to suit the needs of their users. Eskimos living in warmer climates would no longer need to make detailed discriminations about snow and their language would lose some of those words. In the short term, however, having a ready set of words can make the difference between thinking easily about a subject and becoming confused. Words act as an automatic chunking system, packaging a substantial amount of information into small chunks for easy manipulation. You could create a description of a kangaroo for someone who had never seen one, but it would be a great deal more cumbersome than simply saying "kangaroo" to someone who shares this word/concept with you.

It follows from the linguistic-relativity hypothesis that people who use several languages might be able to

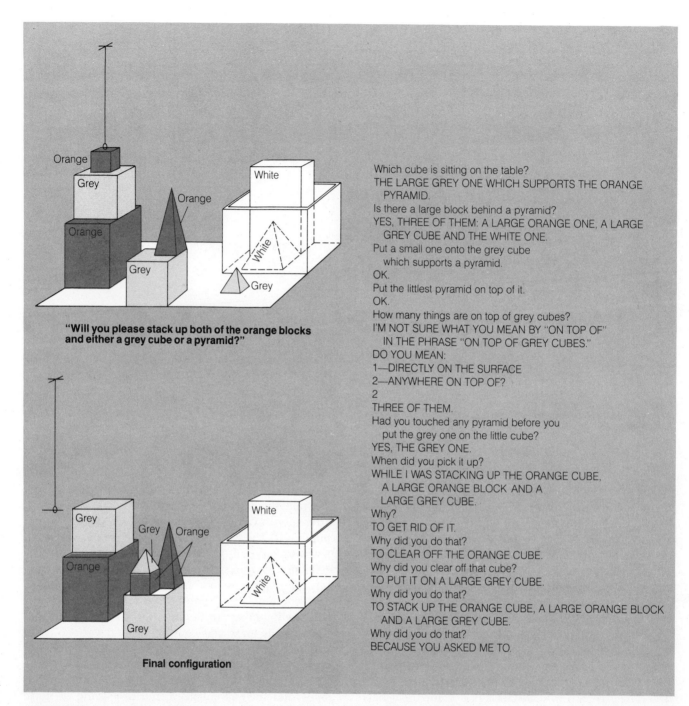

"Will you please stack up both of the orange blocks and either a grey cube or a pyramid?"

Final configuration

Which cube is sitting on the table?
THE LARGE GREY ONE WHICH SUPPORTS THE ORANGE
    PYRAMID.
Is there a large block behind a pyramid?
YES, THREE OF THEM: A LARGE ORANGE ONE, A LARGE
    GREY CUBE AND THE WHITE ONE.
Put a small one onto the grey cube
    which supports a pyramid.
OK.
Put the littlest pyramid on top of it.
OK.
How many things are on top of grey cubes?
I'M NOT SURE WHAT YOU MEAN BY "ON TOP OF"
    IN THE PHRASE "ON TOP OF GREY CUBES."
DO YOU MEAN:
1—DIRECTLY ON THE SURFACE
2—ANYWHERE ON TOP OF?
2
THREE OF THEM.
Had you touched any pyramid before you
    put the grey one on the little cube?
YES, THE GREY ONE.
When did you pick it up?
WHILE I WAS STACKING UP THE ORANGE CUBE,
    A LARGE ORANGE BLOCK AND A
    LARGE GREY CUBE.
Why?
TO GET RID OF IT.
Why did you do that?
TO CLEAR OFF THE ORANGE CUBE.
Why did you clear off that cube?
TO PUT IT ON A LARGE GREY CUBE.
Why did you do that?
TO STACK UP THE ORANGE CUBE, A LARGE ORANGE BLOCK
    AND A LARGE GREY CUBE.
Why did you do that?
BECAUSE YOU ASKED ME TO.

Figure 11.5 ■ An example of Winograd's "blocks world." The sentences in capitals are generated by the computer, which also portrays the current state of the blocks world visually on a screen. (The vertical lines topped by Xs in the visual display represent its way of lifting a block.) The program must make many inferences, as well as interpret propositions such as *on* and *in;* when alternate possibilities exist, as with *on top of,* it asks for clarification. (Note that Winograd's text and illustrations originally used the colors red, green, and blue. Labels have been changed to reflect the colors that appear here.)

(From *Understanding Natural Language* by T. Winograd. Copyright 1972 by Academic Press. Used by permission.)

think about things differently from those who know only one. Some bilinguals do seem to show different thought patterns when using different languages (Kolers, 1968), depending on when and how they learned the second language and other variables. Those who learned a second language in adulthood may never be able to think in it with the fluency of their first language. But those who develop early fluency in two languages seem to have a unified thought process, with language differences occurring only at the input or output stages. A single underlying concept has words in the two languages associated with it, but the concept is the basic thought mode (MacLeod, 1976).

In speaking aloud, some form of cognitive output switch is set for one language, and the ideas to be expressed are phrased in that language. (A comparable input switch controls processing of others' speech.) But the speaker can easily switch to the other language and continue, sometimes without noticing. For example, a bilingual hostess at a party in Montreal was talking to a guest in English. She told a joke that involved a French pun, then continued the conversation in French, apparently unaware that she had switched languages until she noticed the blank stares of some English-speaking guests. The psychologist to whom she was speaking has suggested that the pun put her output switch into the French mode until she remembered to put it back (Reynolds & Flagg, 1983).

Various artificial languages and notation systems are also important in thinking. Users of these gain the ability to think in ways that *no* natural language provides. The oldest and most universally useful artificial language is mathematics. Like other languages, it uses abstract symbols that stand for concepts and it sequences these symbols according to formal rules that convey meaning from one user to another. Other artificial languages include the patterns of formal logic and computer languages.

It is often useful not only to have several alternate languages for thinking but also to combine them. If you can think about a problem in several languages, simultaneously or in quick succession, you are more likely to solve it. One obvious combination is to mix the two major modes of thought, verbal and visual. This probably corresponds to thinking about the problem with both hemispheres. A film writer or director, for example, may think about visual qualities and dialogue more or less simultaneously, perhaps playing one against the other. Then, the "shooting" script may use a storyboard technique, with simple sketches to represent the flow of visual ideas and adjacent verbal notes to specify dialogue, camera settings, and so forth. The combination of thinking modes is more effective for this intrinsically mixed-mode task than is either alone.

© 1980 by Sidney Harris—created for *Discover*.

The ability to translate easily between languages is also important. In science, for example, the quantification of relationships is a basic procedure. This quantification often uses verbal names but mathematical specifications; laws of gravity, thermodynamics, and so forth, are names for mathematical relationships. The effect of a new front bumper shape on a car's aerodynamics, for example, can be discussed either in words or numbers. Those who know both languages, and can use either at will, can think about such problems in ways that those who use only words cannot (Hofstadter, 1982).

Thinking and External Notation

Most people mistakenly assume that all thinking must take place in the mind or brain. But the limited capacity of STM severely restricts how many things you can think about at once. Often it is difficult or impossible even to think about all aspects of the *problem* at once, much less to seek solutions.

One of the most significant advances of our species over others has been our invention of ways of storing and manipulating information outside our bodies. The use of external stores has a lengthy history, beginning with cave paintings and rock carvings and leading to elaborate notation systems and computer storage. External storage and the manipulations of it that can aid thinking are often done as writing, but they need not be. Sketching, for example, is a technique designed to externalize visual thought, and artists and architects often build rough models as a thinking aid. In fact, one reason why historians value artists' preliminary sketches and authors' original annotated manuscripts is that they offer an insight into the thought processes of their creators. The process by which Escher created prints such as "Belvedere" (Figure 6.27), for example, has been reconstructed by Ernst (1976) from Escher's preliminary sketches and notes.

Whatever the problem, the person who can externalize parts of it as necessary is more likely to be able to solve it. Different problems require different types and amounts of externalization, but most people should probably externalize more than they already do. Notes, sketches, models, and so forth are more likely to help than hinder most problem solving.

Most languages have formal notation systems to externalize thoughts framed in those languages. Writing or printing are notation systems that correspond to speech, and other notation systems aid thinking in other "languages." Mathematics has its own notation system (really systems, considering all the varieties). Another well-known notation system is that used for music. Neither playing nor composing music requires this notation system, any more than speaking requires you to know how to write. But those who do know the system find it a useful supplement to thought. There is even a notation system for writing down dance movements, called Labanotation.

Still other notation systems exist, and new ones continue to be created. Often these combine sketches and words or create new pictorial symbols to summarize complex verbal concepts. Their developers often refer to these as languages, but they typically fall somewhere between languages and notation systems. Using them may sometimes aid thinking, as a language does, but they are primarily a way of externalizing thoughts. ■ Figure 11.6

VISUAL THINKING

For most people, thinking is strongly identified with verbal thinking. Many do relatively little visual thinking and some even find it difficult to comprehend what nonverbal thought is like. This is especially true for college students, who have been selected largely for their verbal skill (and for professors, who make their living largely through verbal manipulation). Until the 1960s, when imagery became a respectable topic (Holt, 1964; Paivio, 1979), psychologists paid little attention to visual imagery as a form of thought. Before we note what they have found since then, let's try a couple of tasks that call for visual imagery.

The first task involves primarily visual thought, but you can use a few jotted notes to keep track of your thoughts. Imagine a $3'' \times 3'' \times 3''$ wooden cube, painted a solid color. Now mentally slice it in thirds horizontally so you have three layers, like layers of a cake. Then slice it in thirds across to give nine thin strips. Finally slice it in thirds along the last dimension, yielding 27 one-inch cubes. How many of those cubes are painted on three sides? How many on two sides? How many on one side? How many are not painted on any side? (Go ahead and think about it before going on. You need a break from reading.)

If you're like most people, you probably kept up an internal verbal commentary, even if you formed a good visual image: "Let's see. The corners will have 1-2-3 painted sides . . . ." And using both visual and verbal modes is often helpful in real problems. But if you're very verbally oriented, try assisting your weak visual thought in such problems and not overrunning it with words. (The answers are 8, 12, 6, and 1. If you have trouble seeing this, do some sketches or mark off a real cube and count.)

For the second task, imagine a map of your college campus and do a rough sketch of this image. Include buildings, landmarks, roads and paths, and so forth. Then compare it with a real map of your campus to see if your general proportions and relative locations are correct. (Don't be surprised if your map disagrees in some ways with the real map; we'll look later at why it might.)

In trying these tasks, you probably realized that imagining something is somewhat like perceiving it, but different. The various psychological views of thinking would agree, although all have begun their consideration of thinking by considering perception.

From Perception to Thought

To sense something is to take in a pattern of information; even relatively simple organisms can sense information important to their survival. But to perceive something means to go further, to put the pattern into a context of meaning—to understand it in some way—and that requires more information-processing capability in the nervous system. As we saw in Chapter 9, even pattern recognition involves active manipulation of incoming sensory information, including reference

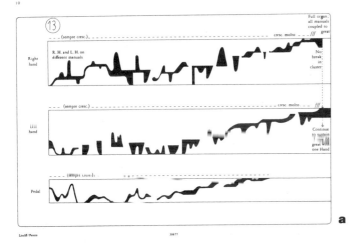

Figure 11.6 ■ Specialized notation systems for representing abstract concepts. (a) A music notation system developed by contemporary composer Gyoergy Ligeti. It represents one form of nonverbal activity (music) in terms of another form (visual shapes). (b) A pattern language invented by a group of architects. Symbols refer to attributes that a building should have; the symbol shown in detail means "windows near places where people spend more than a minute or two should all look out on areas of life." Desired patterns for a building are arranged in a "cascade," with patterns that influence other patterns placed higher up and arrows used to denote the most important relationships. This chart thus represents many things at once: building structure, people's activities, priorities, and so forth.

(**a**, © 1973 by Henry Litolff's Verlag, Frankfurt-am-Main. Reprint permission granted by C. F. Peters Corporation, New York; **b**, from *A Pattern Language Which Generates Multi-Service Centers* by C. Alexander et al. Copyright 1968 by Center for Environmental Structure. Used by permission.)

to previously learned patterns. Because it represents active processing of sensory data and remembered information, perception can be considered the basis of thinking.

One tool cognitive psychologists use to study visual perception and pattern recognition is computer simulation. This suggests that pattern recognition involves several steps, some of which involve the sensory systems. Visual simulation programs, for example, seek out lines and shapes in ways akin to the feature detectors in the human visual system (Chapter 6). Other steps involve comparisons with patterns stored in memory, a process similar to human use of LTM in pattern recognition (Chapter 9). But visual perception seems most obviously like thought in that each new visual pattern requires some manipulation for its meaning to be established. Even familiar objects or scenes are likely to be seen each time at different angles, in different light conditions, and so forth. Any process that depended on a direct match of input with memory would be unable to handle such variations. Instead, perception seems to be a best-estimate process—not simple matching, but a form of thought.
■ Figure 11.7

When an animal responds to stimuli in a way that shows it has recognized them—that is, shows the result of prior learning—we may argue over whether it has "thought about" the stimuli. Pigeons can recognize the letters of the alphabet, for example, and tend to confuse the same letters that humans do (Blough, 1982). But this isn't the same as human recognition of letters. Human recognition tasks typically involve the recovery of so much miscellaneous information along with the recognized pattern that it's hard *not* to think about what we perceive. If pattern recognition seems to be "only" memory and not really thinking, try visualizing an object you've seen, but in a somewhat different position. This clearly *depends* on memory, but is no longer the same as direct recovery of what you saw. This process of recognizing something that is not identical to a previous stimulus more obviously involves at least a simple variety of thinking.

Such pattern recognition has been studied by one of the psychologists most identified with visual-imagery research, Roger Shepard. Lynne Cooper and Shepard (1973), for example, presented subjects with two versions of the capital letter *R*, a correct version and a mirror image. Both versions were presented at various rotations from upright, and subjects were asked to say whether each letter was normal or a mirror image. To recognize upright letters is a simple recognition task. But to recognize letters that are rotated away from their upright position is somewhat harder and involves a kind of thinking: To know if a pattern presented

upside down is correct or backwards, you must first mentally rotate the image to an upright position.

Subjects in fact took differing amounts of time to recognize letters with different degrees of rotation. The pattern of the results suggested that subjects did rotate the letters mentally to upright before identifying them.
■ Figure 11.8

A follow-up study by Carpenter and Eisenberg (1978) showed that blindfolded subjects given letters to touch produced a pattern of reaction times similar to Cooper and Shepard's subjects. Even blind subjects seemed to rotate their tactile "image" of the letters in the same way.

Thus perception may be considered the beginning of thinking about the world. The more active information processing that must be done, and the more LTM information is brought to bear, the more we feel that thinking is taking place. At the limit of perceptual-based thinking, a simple stimulus can set off a lengthy chain of thought—as it may for a poet (Spender, 1946). It could be argued that such thinking is no longer tied to perception. But one line of research suggests that this is not the case.

Evidence from "interference" experiments demonstrates that any form of *imaging* (creating mental images) may also use the sensory system involved in that image. In one such experiment, subjects were asked to form a specific visual or auditory image (such as a volcano or the sound of a typewriter) (Segal & Fusella, 1970). As soon as subjects had formed the image, the researchers presented another sight or sound. Subjects had more trouble maintaining their imagery when the stimulus was in the same sensory mode as their image. A stimulus in the other mode caused relatively little interference. (The sight of a blue arrow interfered with subjects' visual images, for instance, but not their auditory ones.)

Thinking need not always include new sensory inputs. For someone deep in thought, current inputs may be largely unattended, with thought focused almost entirely on LTM-generated information. But even here perception has played some role. It has been active in the past, at least in storing the LTM information, and often in presenting the stimulus or problem that the thinker is now working on. And to the extent that images are used in the thinking, some perceptual systems are activated. Thus perception is always a part of the thinking process, and where one stops and the other begins is frequently not clear (Finke, 1980).

Manipulating Mental Images

When you tried the sliced-cube problem suggested earlier, you were drawing on memories—of cubes,

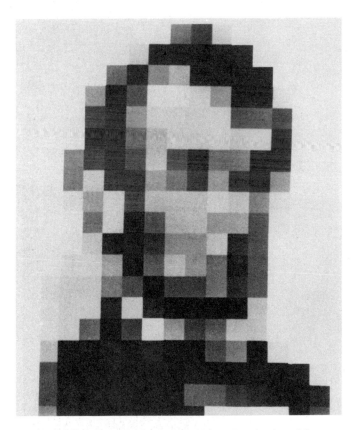

Figure 11.7 ■ A computer program designed to simulate vision first digitizes a picture, then analyzes it for sharp changes in intensity that may represent edges. It then fits these possible edges together to find shapes that fit its memory of possibilities. Even relatively degraded information can be enough to recognize familiar objects, as this version of a famous portrait illustrates.

(Courtesy of Bell Laboratories)

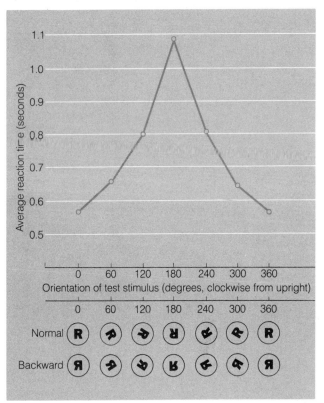

Figure 11.8 ■ When an incoming stimulus must be cognitively manipulated in order to be recognized, the process is a form of thinking. The time taken by such thinking depends on the amount of manipulation. Here rotated letters must be recognized as normal or backward. The time it takes to recognize them varies directly with the amount of mental rotation needed to bring them upright for comparison.

(From "Chronometric Studies of the Rotation of Mental Images" by L. A. Cooper and R. N. Shepard in W. G. Chase (Ed.), *Visual Information Processing*, Academic Press, 1973. Used by permission.)

painted surfaces, slicing into parts, and, of course, of counting. Even if you have never seen a painted cube sliced into 27 smaller cubes, the basic image still shouldn't be too hard to visualize. (In one survey, almost all respondents said they could generate visual and auditory images, and more than two-thirds said they could generate smell, taste, touch, and kinesthetic ones; McKellar, 1972.) But how did you decide how many faces were painted? To use a pure visual strategy, you would have had to "look at" the image of the sliced cube and count the faces. If you found yourself starting to do that and then jumped to logical statements—"Of course . . . all corners are three-sided, four on the top and four on the bottom"—you were mixing your strategies. (Whether you made this jump probably depends on your prior experience: Artists might find visualization the easiest, engineers might quickly switch to verbal rules, and so forth.)

If you *could* hold a pure visual image, however,

you couldn't see all of it at once. To examine a real cube, you would turn it over in your hand. The creative visual thinkers among you might have imagined a semitransparent cube, but it's probably easier to rotate the cube mentally. At that point, of course, you've added movement to the image.

Thinking of objects rotating in space is an obvious step beyond thinking of fixed objects, or of rotation in a single plane (as with Cooper and Shepard's rotated *R*s). Shepard has studied this kind of thought by presenting drawings of three-dimensional objects and asking if one can be rotated so as to exactly match the other (Shepard & Metzler, 1971). Such tasks are difficult to code verbally, and thus are presumably done almost entirely through imagery. Results for this task were similar to those for the *R*s; for rotation within one plane, the time needed to rotate figures varied directly with the number of degrees of rotation. ■ Figure 11.9

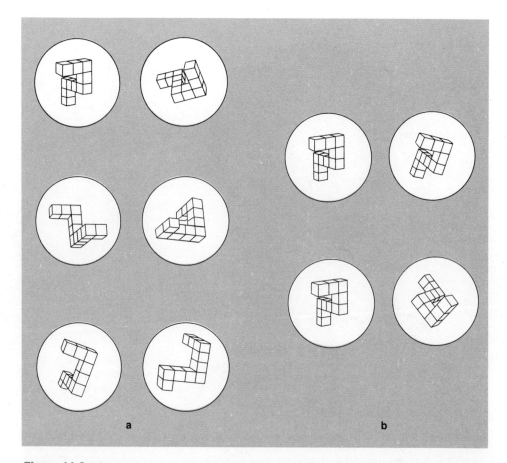

Figure 11.9 ■ Rotating images of three-dimensional objects is a more complex task than rotating letters, but also yields regular results. (a) Subjects were asked whether pairs such as these represented the same object; to answer required mentally rotating one and comparing it to the other. (Pairs 1 and 2 show the same object, but the objects in Pair 3 are different.) Note that the rotation can be in different planes; Pair 1 is rotated within the plane of the page, and Pair 2 requires rotation out of the page. (b) Pairs that rotated within the same plane were varied by degree of rotation.

(From R. N. Shepard and J. Metzler, "Mental Rotation of Three-Dimensional Objects," *Science*, 1971, *171*, 701–703. Copyright 1971 by the American Association for the Advancement of Science. Used by permission.)

Evidence that subjects' performance on this rotation task involves thought comes from performance on a similar task by pigeons (Holland & Delius, 1982). The pigeons' response times did *not* vary with angle of the stimulus; apparently they relied on some automatic process, such as humans use to recognize familiar forms in their usual orientations. (As a result, the pigeons were more efficient than humans for some angles; apparently thinking about a problem has its penalties as well as its rewards.)

A different approach to the study of imagery has been to ask subjects to hold a mental image of an object—such as a letter or a map—and to scan it; researchers then compare the results of the imagery scan to scanning the real object. For example, Brooks (1968) asked subjects to categorize the corners of cap-

ital letters (as top or bottom ones or as middle ones), a task requiring a sequential scan around the letter. Another important theorist and researcher in imagery, Steven Kosslyn, showed subjects a simple map, then asked them questions about the mental images they formed of the map (Kosslyn et al., 1978). Such studies have found that scanning the mental images seems in several ways to be like looking at the real object. A scan takes time in proportion to the distance it must cover, for example; in Kosslyn's map study, the time taken to move from a focus on one part of the map image to another part varied as if the subjects were moving their fixation point across a real map. ■ Figure 11.10

Another approach has asked subjects to compare some features of two images. In one series of experiments, Kosslyn (1975) asked subjects to imagine two

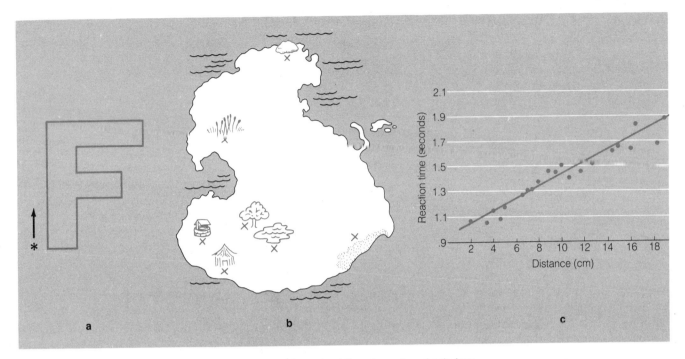

Figure 11.10 ■ Scanning mental images to answer questions about them is another simple form of thinking. (a) Subjects were asked to describe the corners on a mental image of a block letter, starting from one corner. They said "yes" for corners on top or bottom, "no" for corners in the middle. (A correct response here would be "yes, yes, yes, no, no, no, no, no, no, yes.") (b) Subjects were asked to form an image of this map after they had seen it once, then were asked to focus on a particular object in the image—the tree, for example. A few seconds later, a second object would be named and they would scan from the first spot to the second. (c) Times taken to scan the mental image varied as if the person were scanning the real map.

(a, From L. R. Brooks, *Canadian Journal of Psychology*, 22, 349–368. Copyright 1968 by Canadian Psychological Association. Used by permission; **b** and **c,** from L. M. Kosslyn, T. M. Ball, and B. J. Reiser, *Journal of Experimental Psychology: Human Perception and Performance*, 1978, 4, 47–60. Copyright 1978 by the American Psychological Association. Reprinted by permission of the publisher and author.)

specified animals and then asked questions about the images. If you imagine a fly next to an elephant, for example, the fly image is likely to be smaller than the elephant image. Thus questions about the fly image should take longer to answer than questions about the elephant image (because it's harder to "see" the fly). Kosslyn found that answering such questions does take longer. Other researchers have compared images of different sizes and shapes, with similar results (Moyer & Dumais, 1978a; Shepard & Chipman, 1970). All these studies suggest that scanning a mental image is much like scanning a picture.

People differ in the ease and quality of their imagery, as you might expect. Paivio (1978), for example, asked subjects to image clock faces that showed different times. The more similar the clock hands were on two clock images, the longer it took subjects to answer questions about them. ("Are the hands of a clock set at 4:10 closer together than those of a clock set at 9:23?" for example, was easier to answer than comparing one

set at 3:20 and one set at 7:25.) But using other tests Paivio also sorted subjects into "high-imagery" and "low-imagery" groups. Both groups showed the same pattern of relative difficulty for different clock settings, but the high-imagery subjects were substantially faster for all comparisons.

Although such studies offer convincing evidence for the use of images by subjects, psychologists do not agree on how those images are related to memory storage. The majority opinion is that proposed by Shepard (1978a): Mental images are generated from information stored in an **analog code**, or some picturelike form. But a counterargument has been offered by Pylyshyn (1973, 1981), who notes that use of images does not require information to be stored in spatial (analog) form. Pylyshyn proposes instead that information is stored in a **propositional code,** more like verbal statements than pictures. A number of experiments have sought to establish whether subjects use analog or propositional codes in generating images

(Anderson, 1978). Results have been mixed, but most have supported the use of analog codes (Kosslyn & Pomerantz, 1977; Reed, 1974; Shepard, 1978a).

Propositional codes may be used in addition to analog codes, however; people may rarely, if ever, store images in pure form. Remember from Chapter 9 that Paivio (1979) has suggested a dual code for memory. Just as you may have found it difficult to refrain from verbalizing mentally while imagining the painted cube, so we may routinely add verbal (propositional) codes to our perceptual memories. Then when we create an image, we may use whatever combination of codes provides the best image.

Idea Sketching

We noted earlier that notes or sketches, including standardized visual notation systems, may be an aid to thinking. Often, however, these notation systems are designed for exact specification in constrained circumstances. The three-view (front, top, side) drawings of machine parts used on blueprints, for example, are designed to summarize dimensions and guide construction. Because they are not very good at showing what the object would look like, they work best as a final step after an object has already been thought about. Such formal representations are the visual equivalent of formal prose.

But what is the visual equivalent of rough notes, shorthand, or outlines? One professor of design who has spent years teaching engineering students to think visually has some suggestions (McKim, 1980a). McKim advocates a process he calls **idea sketching,** drawing notes of visual thoughts somewhat as you would write notes of verbal thoughts. Idea sketches don't have to be polished, or even to mean anything to anyone else, to serve as efficient external storage for thoughts. In the sliced-cube problem, for example, you could sketch the middle slice, with the top slice pulled up away from it and the bottom one rotated so you could "see" it. Then you could count the faces more directly, checking each one off as you counted it.

Some conventional techniques for representing relationships can be considered standardized ways of idea sketching; they convey conventional messages yet still retain the necessary informality and flexibility. These include "exploded" drawings (as you might have created with the sliced cube), cross sections, wiring diagrams, and flowcharts. Of these, one of the most important and general techniques is the **flowchart,** which represents a series of activities as a set of boxes linked by lines or arrows. Flowcharts summarize relationships, not physical appearances. The flowchart in Figure 11.11c represents an industrial process, but though the boxes look somewhat like real objects, this is merely a convenience; the chart as a whole summarizes relationships, not objects. In psychology, as in many uses of flowcharts, the boxes may represent processes, like "sensory register," that have no visual appearance. ■ Figure 11.11

Drawing a map of your campus is actually a form of idea sketching more than a form of imaging a prior perception. Unless you've flown over the campus at high altitude, you've never seen the kind of relationships you're trying to draw. In fact, our **cognitive maps,** our mental representations of places we know, summarize different knowledge from printed maps. When people draw maps, they include psychological dimensions from their cognitive maps, as well as representations of actual physical relationships. You may exaggerate the size of areas you know well, for example. And the landmarks you add will be the ones important in your life, and not necessarily the most visible. When 200 students at one school were asked to do this task, those in each department tended to draw some of the buildings on campus—the ones in which that department held classes—accurately and in detail, while leaving out other buildings entirely (Saarinen, 1973).

Studying maps made in other times and cultures thus offers insight into the thought processes of those who drew the maps (Aziz, 1978). Map drawing has even been used to define how someone thinks about his or her town, and to compare differences in these thought patterns (Milgram et al., 1972). Los Angeles is many different places, for example, according to its residents' cognitive maps (Lynch, 1960). ■Figure 11.12

As with other formal operations, some adults never become very good at mentally representing information and others become exceptionally skilled. One chess player, for example, played 34 opponents at once, winning 24 and drawing the other 10—a performance that required continually updating maps of all 34 boards without ever seeing them—while at the same time planning further moves.

PROBLEM SOLVING

Having explored both verbal and visual forms of thinking, we turn to the topic of general problem solving. Here we will see that the most flexible thinking uses whatever combination of internal mode and external notation leads to a solution (Hayes, 1981; Newell & Simon, 1972).

Wallas (1926) made one of the earliest attempts to specify the processes of problem solving, suggesting that it occurred in four steps: preparation, incubation,

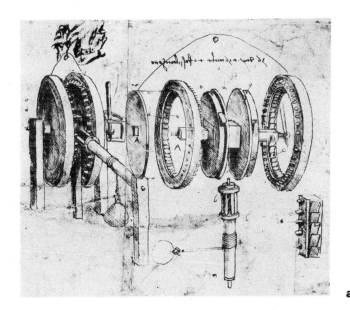

a

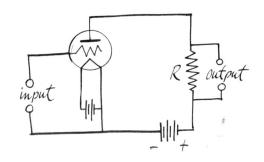

b

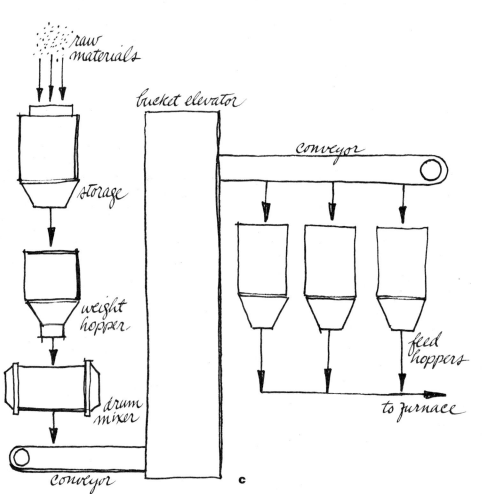

c

Figure 11.11 ■ Some conventional ways of sketching ideas. (a) When Leonardo da Vinci did this sketch—complete and exploded drawings of a weight-driven rachet—it was an innovative form of idea sketching. (b) These drawings, an approximate cross section of a vehicle and a wiring diagram, are increasingly more abstract representations of objects. (c) A flowchart is still more abstract, representing relationships rather than objects.

(a, University of Delaware Library. Used by permission; b and c, from *Experiences in Visual Thinking,* 2nd ed., by R. H. McKim, 1980, Brooks/Cole. Reprinted by permission.)

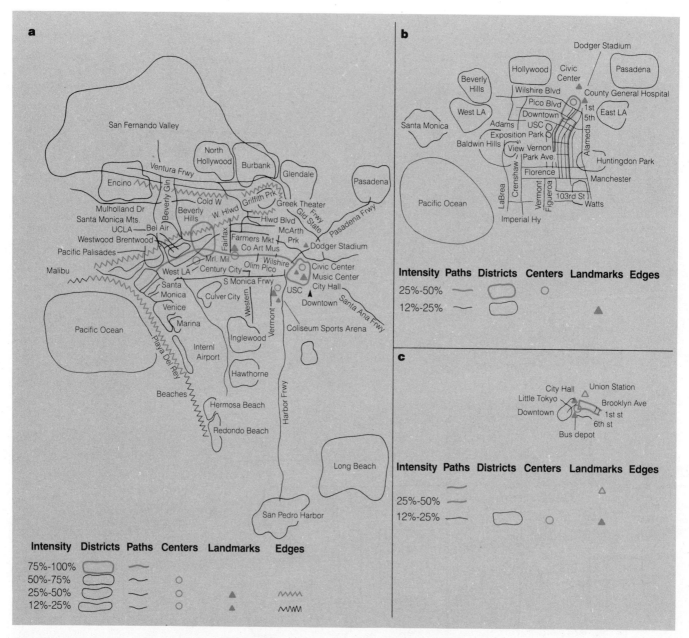

Figure 11.12 ■ Maps representing the mental images of Los Angeles held by different residents; details, dimensions, and accuracy presumably correspond to the ways in which these subjects think about their city. (a) The most complete map was drawn by a white middle-class resident of Westwood. (b) The map of a black resident of Avalon shows mostly local details, with both geographic and cultural information much more restricted. (c) The map of a Spanish-speaking resident of Boyle Heights indicates an extremely constricted view.

(From P. Orleans in *Science, Engineering, and the City*, Publication 1498, 103–117, National Academy of Engineering, 1967. Used by permission.

illumination, and verification. Preparation typically involves conscious hard work—sometimes years of it to become expert in a particular field, and often days or weeks of it on a particular problem. Incubation is an unconscious phase; it refers to a period in which the person consciously turns away from the problem and goes on about other business, yet apparently continues to work on it in ways that are out of normal awareness.

Illumination refers to the sudden awareness of a possible solution. It is a version of the insightful "Aha!" experience, shown in cartoons as a light bulb over a person's head. It may come when the person has not been consciously attending to the problem for some time, and may even have supposedly given up on it. Verification is a final, necessary conscious step. Having that subjective sense of "Aha!" is not solid evidence that the solution you've found is correct. It must be checked to see if it indeed works before the cycle is complete. (For an especially useful discussion of problem solving that reflects all of Wallas's steps, see Poincaré, 1913.)

Hemisphere differences may be relevant to Wallas's steps. Since reports from split-brain patients indicate that we are not usually aware of our right hemisphere's activities, the right hemisphere may be working on a problem during the incubation period. To say that the person attends to some other task may mean that the left hemisphere is attending to another task while the right continues to work on the problem.

If the right hemisphere is the source of some solutions developed through incubation, these solutions should be nonverbal, and often they are. A frequently reported example is Kekulé's solution to the chemical structure of benzene, a chain of atoms. It came to him in the form of a dream of a snake with its tail in its mouth. The answer represented by the snake image was that benzene has a ring structure, where the atoms on the ends of the chain are also attached together. This solution has the form of a right-hemisphere idea—not "Aha! It's a ring," but a visual image that represents something else. ■ Notable Quote: Friedrich Kekulé on His Discovery of the Benzene Ring

The Gestalt psychologists' influential early work on problem solving focused primarily on the sudden reorganization of a problem that is characteristic of insight (Scheerer, 1963). Köhler's (1925) studies of chimpanzee problem solving (Chapter 8) are among the best known of the Gestalt studies, but others examined various species and a wide variety of problems. The Gestaltists investigated problem solving in animals through arrangements such as the "Umweg" (detour) problem. An animal was placed in sight of food, but behind a screen; the insightful solution was to recognize that the food could be reached by going around

the screen. The more complex and adaptable its nervous system, the better the animal was at solving the problem. Chickens used a trial-and-error method, for example, eventually getting outside the screen but apparently without planning to do so; dogs solved the problem almost immediately, with the appearance of understanding where they needed to go. ■ Figure 11.13

The most influential contemporary model of problem solving, however, has been that of Newell and Simon (1972). They have been among the most outspoken advocates of artificial intelligence research as a tool for understanding human intelligence (Simon, 1981b). As Wallas noted, numerous aspects of human problem solving are unconscious, or not open to introspection. Newell and Simon suggest coping with this

---

NOTABLE QUOTE
Friedrich Kekulé on his discovery of the benzene ring

❝I turned my chair to the fire and dozed. Again the atoms were gamboling before my eyes. This time the smaller groups kept modestly in the background. My mental eye, rendered more acute by repeated visions of this kind, could now distinguish larger structures, of manifold conformations; long rows, sometimes more closely fitted together; all twining and twisting in snakelike motion. But look! What was that? One of the snakes had seized hold of its own tail, and the form whirled mockingly before my eyes. As if by a flash of lightning I awoke and I spent the rest of the night working out the consequences of the hypothesis. **❞**

Quoted in Lindzey et al., 1978, p. 343.

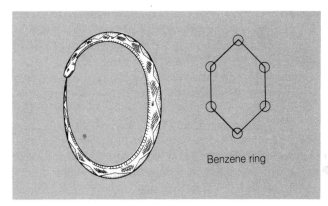

Benzene ring

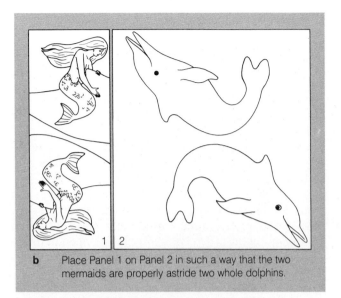

b Place Panel 1 on Panel 2 in such a way that the two mermaids are properly astride two whole dolphins.

Figure 11.13 ■ This problem can eventually be solved by trial and error, but many people solve it through insight. (The answer appears on p. 365, Figure 11.20.)

(© Stephen Stanley 1982)

difficulty through AI research. What we think we know about problem solving can first be programmed. If this does not yield solutions, the program can be revised until it works. Experimenters can then seek to discover if humans must also carry out those additional steps (Simon & Newell, 1971).

When ideas about possible human problem-solving steps are derived from the programs, they can be explored with human subjects in several ways. Various predictions can be tested quantitatively, for example. Newell and Simon have also asked subjects to report out loud what they are thinking as they solve problems (1972), but this method has not been widely adopted by other researchers.

In seeking to build a computer-simulation model of problem solving, Newell and Simon first gathered and analyzed what was known of human problem solving; their model assumes that limitations on people's storage capacity, storage time, and retrieval capabilities constrain their problem-solving abilities (Newell et al., 1958). (Would you have been able to solve the verbal problem on the first page of this chapter if it were read to you quickly rather than being written down?) But Newell and Simon also focused on the nature of different problems, saying that the *interaction* of the problem's demands with the problem solver's capabilities will determine whether the problem is solved.

Most of the problems they have investigated involve a series of choices between alternatives. The more choices to be made, and the more possibilities at each choice point, the harder the problem is. Newell and Simon refer to the available choices for a problem as the **problem space;** the task of the problem solver is to find the correct path through this problem space, from starting point to solution. In searching for the correct path, the problem solver uses (or processes) various forms of information, including the task instructions that define the problem, previous experience with similar or analogous tasks, plans or strategies stored in LTM, and information developed through working on the problem. Each of these four kinds of information can aid in solving the problem, but there are also potential difficulties with each of them. In reviewing problem-solving strategies we will note some of these difficulties.

Defining the Problem

Before a problem can be solved, it must be defined in such a way that work can proceed and a solution will be recognized when it is found. Even when a problem seems specific, it is important for the problem solver to be sure just what is needed. When the problem is less well defined, questioning may be even more important. Adams (1980) gave an example from aerospace research, where engineers spent months designing a system to reduce the shock of unfolding a special satellite panel in orbit. Finally someone thought to ask: "Do we need *any* shock-absorbing system?" The answer was no; all the work on designing a best system was unnecessary.

Other difficulties can occur if the would-be problem solver cannot understand the way the problem is presented. Simon and Hayes have described a problem of functional illiteracy, for example (1976). They note that people faced with printed instructions for assembling a device (put tab B under ring C while lifting lever D . . .) may be able to read the words yet not be able to interpret them.

One useful way of defining problems is in terms of the initial state, the final goal state, and various subgoals (Egan & Greeno, 1974). The initial state for assembling a bicycle, for example, might be the bicycle in a crate, and the goal state the bicycle ready to ride. Subgoals would include mounting the front wheel, the rear wheel, the handlebars, and so forth.

One difficulty in everyday problem solving, however, is that many tasks are **ill-defined problems,** not easily specifiable in terms of initial state, goal state, or subgoals (Reitman, 1964, 1965). (How much studying is enough to get an A on an exam?) When there are no

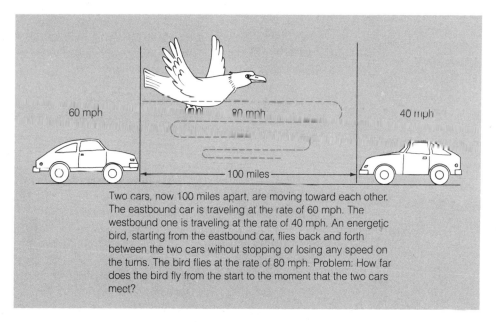

Two cars, now 100 miles apart, are moving toward each other. The eastbound car is traveling at the rate of 60 mph. The westbound one is traveling at the rate of 40 mph. An energetic bird, starting from the eastbound car, flies back and forth between the two cars without stopping or losing any speed on the turns. The bird flies at the rate of 80 mph. Problem: How far does the bird fly from the start to the moment that the two cars meet?

Figure 11.14 ■ This problem looks as if it could be represented verbally, visually, or mathematically. In fact, the mathematics needed to solve it is very simple. (Answer is on p. 365, Figure 11.20)

(Redrawn from *Introduction to Psychology*, 7th ed., by Ernest R. Hilgard et al., © 1979 by Harcourt Brace Jovanovich, Inc. Reprinted by permission of the publisher.)

exact specifications of goal state, as in composing music or designing a building, the problem is ill-defined. But problems can also be ill-defined because the initial state is not specified. "How do you teach a person to read?" is such a problem. The goal state, *reading*, can easily be specified, but without knowing more about the age, language skills, or intelligence of the initial state, the *person*, you cannot easily solve the problem. Furthermore, as Greeno (1976) has pointed out, the existence of well-defined initial and goal states still does not mean that people will establish well-defined subgoals. So it is best to consider the distinction between well-defined and ill-defined problems as a general one. In practice, at least some aspects of most ordinary problems may be ill-defined.

Another important aspect of specifying the problem is choosing a method of representing it—for example, in visual terms or in words. In many cases, the way a problem is represented may make the difference between solving it easily and not solving it at all (Schwartz, 1971). ■ Figure 11.14

Verbal thinking modes have often been emphasized over visual ones, but many problems are intrinsically visual, as in art or architecture. Other problems that could be solved verbally may be more easily solved visually or by a combination of visual and ver-

bal techniques. One well-known example concerns a monk climbing a mountain. One morning, the monk leaves his hut at the bottom of the mountain. All day he climbs the steep, narrow, and twisting path, stopping at various times to rest before reaching the shrine on top of the mountain at dusk. He spends all of the next day returning down the same narrow path. The problem is to show that there is a place on the path that he occupied at the same time of day on both days.

To solve this problem, you must first use verbal skills to define the problem, to be sure what is asked and—at least as important—what is not asked. Some people think they must *specify* the spot on the path, but that's impossible from the description; you need only show that some such spot exists. This can be done in at least three ways: in words, in equations or plots, and in mental images. Of these, imagery is by far the easiest approach, yet few people know how to use it. In contrast, the verbal logic is the most difficult approach, though the one most people try.

To solve it visually, just imagine the mountain at the dawn of Day 1, with the monk at the bottom. Then imagine the mountain at the dawn of Day 2, with the monk at the top. Then put the two mountains side by side and start both monks. Regardless of how fast the imagined monks climb up or down, they *must* reach a

"EVERY ONCE IN A WHILE MY RIGHT BRAIN THROWS SOMETHING IN."

© 1983 by Sidney Harris—American Scientist Magazine

point where the climbing one passes the descending one. That's your solution. You could also simply overlap the two imagined mountains, because it's the same mountain and same dawn-to-dusk interval. Then the climbing one would meet the descending one face-to-face as they passed through each other.

Other ways of solving this problem require performing similar analyses in different ways. The graphic solution requires some familiarity with that specialized approach, and arriving at the same solution verbally is somewhat harder. (It's hard even to *explain* the answer to someone else in words without using the imagery solution.)

Solving the Problem

There are many ways to solve problems, and most approaches will benefit from some organized plan. Planning means thinking ahead, deciding where you want to go, picking some intermediate steps that may help you get there, and deciding how to know when the plan is working or when it needs changing (Miller et al., 1960). If the original planning is well done, the problem-solving sequence may be straightforward.

Algorithms and Heuristics When problems are well defined, there may even be an exact procedure that will always yield an answer; such a procedure is called an **algorithm.** Solving the problem then consists of applying the algorithm until the answer is obtained. Procedures for addition or subtraction, for example, are algorithms. For most problems, algorithms do not exist—but useful strategies often do. A procedure that helps solve a problem (usually by reducing the number of alternatives to be considered) is called a **heuristic** (Reitman, 1964). Heuristics never guarantee a solution, but can be remarkably effective in aiding the search for one (Schoenfeld, 1979). There are many heuristics, but we will look only at two of the most important: working backward and means/end analysis.

In the **working backward** heuristic, you focus first on the goal state and ask what would be the last step before reaching that goal. Then you back up from there. Working backward is an especially useful heuristic in mathematics and other formal systems. In plane geometry, for example, working backward from the theorem toward the axioms greatly reduces the number of possible choices, compared to working forward. Newell and Simon have used the working-backward heuristic in a computer program called the **Logic Theorist,** designed to simulate how human subjects solve mathematical proofs (1972). When the Logic Theorist was tested on 52 classic theorems, it proved 38 of them, was unable to solve 1, and ran out of memory space to deal with the rest.

In using the **means/end** heuristic, you identify the goal state and the current state, and perform some action to reduce the difference between them (Greeno, 1978). (The goal is the end and whatever you can do to reduce the difference is the means.) After you have reduced the difference (moved closer to the goal), you assess the remaining difference and again try to reduce it. Most of us use the means/end heuristic frequently, without knowing it by name. Suppose you have to read an assignment on reserve in the library. You first look at your present status and compare it to the goal. If you are not in the library, you go there. Then you reassess and go to the reserve desk. Then you . . . and so forth. The fact that we carry out such step-by-step analyses frequently does not reduce the value of a means/end heuristic, however. It can be powerful. Newell and Simon have built a simulation model called the **General Problem Solver (GPS)** that is based on the means/end heuristic (1972). The GPS repeatedly applies the same two steps: (1) analyze the difference between the present state and the goal; (2) reduce the difference by applying some "operator" to change the current state. The GPS program has successfully solved a wide variety of problem types, including various

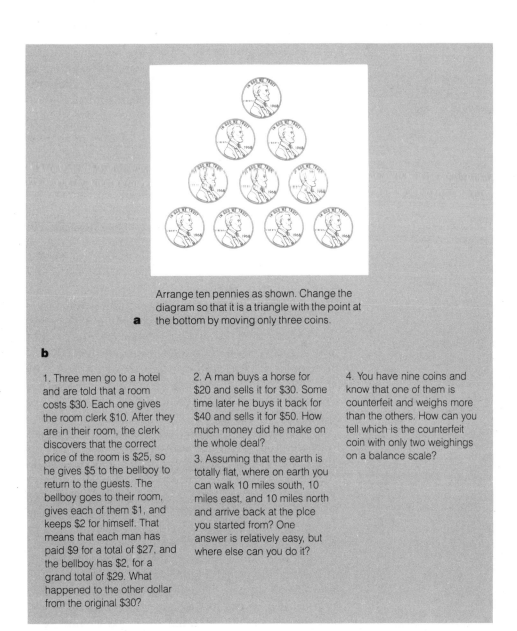

Arrange ten pennies as shown. Change the diagram so that it is a triangle with the point at the bottom by moving only three coins.

a

b

1. Three men go to a hotel and are told that a room costs $30. Each one gives the room clerk $10. After they are in their room, the clerk discovers that the correct price of the room is $25, so he gives $5 to the bellboy to return to the guests. The bellboy goes to their room, gives each of them $1, and keeps $2 for himself. That means that each man has paid $9 for a total of $27, and the bellboy has $2, for a grand total of $29. What happened to the other dollar from the original $30?

2. A man buys a horse for $20 and sells it for $30. Some time later he buys it back for $40 and sells it for $50. How much money did he make on the whole deal?

3. Assuming that the earth is totally flat, where on earth you can walk 10 miles south, 10 miles east, and 10 miles north and arrive back at the plce you started from? One answer is relatively easy, but where else can you do it?

4. You have nine coins and know that one of them is counterfeit and weighs more than the others. How can you tell which is the counterfeit coin with only two weighings on a balance scale?

Figure 11.15 ■ Logical strategies can be applied to problems of various types. (a) This problem is largely visual, but logical rules may be more useful than visual manipulations. (b) These problems can all be solved primarily through verbal logic. Yet visual images are often useful, as in Problems 3 and 4. (Answers are given in Figure 11.20, p. 365.)

grammatical analyses, logical proofs, and trigonometry problems.

A means/end heuristic will not work for problems in which you must temporarily go further from the goal to reach it eventually. But no heuristic guarantees a solution. In many problems, persistent application of the means/end heuristic will get the job done.

To solve the vast array of problems you may confront, you need not only some useful heuristics but also the ability to use them flexibly. Figure 11.15 provides a few exercises of different types for you to try.

As you do, pay attention to how you specify the problem and what strategies you use. ■ Figure 11.15

Thinking Biases There are many ways in which human problem solving becomes sidetracked through logical or conceptual errors (Nisbett & Ross, 1980). Some of the best-known ones were discovered by the Gestalt psychologists. One major thinking bias they noted is **functional fixedness,** the tendency to maintain the function we have assigned to objects and not see that they could serve other functions. If a pencil is

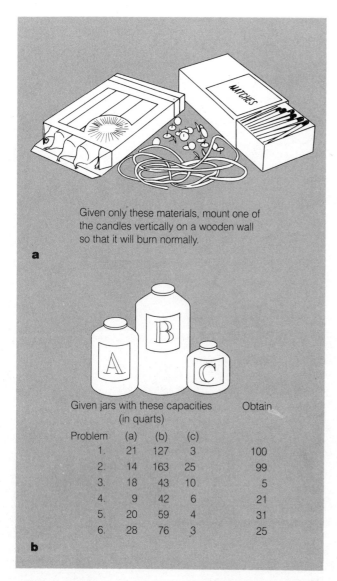

Given only these materials, mount one of the candles vertically on a wooden wall so that it will burn normally.

a

Given jars with these capacities (in quarts)   Obtain

Problem	(a)	(b)	(c)	
1.	21	127	3	100
2.	14	163	25	99
3.	18	43	10	5
4.	9	42	6	21
5.	20	59	4	31
6.	28	76	3	25

b

Figure 11.16 ■ Two classic problems illustrate problem-solving blocks noted by Gestalt psychologists. (a) Duncker's candle problem illustrates functional fixedness resulting from previous learning (1945). More people can solve the problem if the matches are presented separately from their box. (b) Luchins's water-jar problem illustrates mental set (1942). Even though the sixth task is easier than the first five, the pattern of solutions built up by the first five tends to prevent subjects from solving the sixth. (Answers are on p. 365, Figure 11.20)

(b, © Stephen Stanley 1982)

thought of solely as a writing tool, for example, its possible use as a prop, a weight, and so forth may be overlooked. Functional fixedness is an undesired form of **mental set,** the tendency to establish ways of doing something, including solving problems.

Mental sets can be important aids to perception and to more advanced problem solving, when they orient you correctly and thus speed the processes. If you have a "letter set," for example, you will be able to recognize letters flashed on a screen more easily than

if you have a "number set." Cues that help us take a set thus prepare us for problem solving of a particular kind. But the cues can sometimes lead us to adopt the wrong set, or the set can become so rigid that it blocks other possibilities. In that case, a process that is usually helpful becomes a harmful bias. Two classic problems illustrate difficulties caused by functional fixedness and mental set. ■ Figure 11.16

Duncker's candle problem (Figure 11.16a) is the classic example of functional fixedness. Duncker noted that in this case, providing the matches in a box seemed to block thinking of the box as a separate object for use in the problem; it was perceived simply as a container. People treated the box differently if it was empty at the beginning; then they recognized it as a possible part of the solution. (More recent research suggests that various small changes in the presentation of the problem can affect its solution; Weisberg & Suls, 1973.) Luchins's water-jar problem (Figure 11.16b) provides the classic example of mental set; it shows how quickly a set can develop and become rigid. By the time subjects have solved five problems with a similar strategy, they may fail to find what should be an easier approach to a sixth.

One important thinking bias that affects our ability to solve problems is the **availability trap;** if we can think of an example of something, it seems more likely than if we have no readily available example. Because we can think of words that begin with certain letters, for example, we know they are possible. But because we don't usually think of words by their second or third letters, we may not be able to find an example and we may thus seriously misjudge their likelihood. The availability trap is only one form of misjudging the probability of events. People tend to interpret *random,* for example, as not having any discernable sequence, and this leads to other thought errors. Any sequence of fifty-fifty probabilities is as likely as any other, but most people will judge regular sequences as less likely than irregular ones. (Several such thinking biases have been discussed by Kahneman & Tversky, 1972, 1973.)

One of the most general biases is the tendency to seek confirming evidence for hypotheses rather than disconfirming evidence. In a purely logical sense, disconfirmation of a hypothesis is as useful as confirmation. In fact, disconfirmation may offer more information about the hypothesis than confirmation does. Several versions of the four-card problem demonstrate this tendency to look for confirmation and not useful disconfirmation. In one form, subjects are shown cards with *E, J, 6,* and *7* showing on them. They are then asked to turn over only two cards to test the proposition "If a card has a vowel on one side, then it has an even number on the other." Obviously, they should turn over *E;* it must have an even number on the other side if the proposition is true. But which other card is useful?

Most people choose the 6, but this is wrong (Wason & Johnson-Laird, 1972). If it has a vowel it seems to confirm, and if it has a consonant it is irrelevant; hence, it doesn't matter what is on the other side. The important card is the 7, because if it has a vowel on the other side it disproves the proposition. People are better at this task when the problem is made more concrete, however: the same problem expressed in terms of stamps on letters was solved by 92% of subjects, compared to only 29% for the abstract form presented here (Johnson-Laird et al., 1972).

One book on creative thinking focuses on another thinking bias, blocking our own problem solving. In its second edition (Adams, 1980), the author reported further creative solutions to a problem in the first edition: how to draw four straight lines through a square pattern of nine dots (3 × 3) without lifting the pencil or retracing a line. The original solution involved breaking the thinking block that you have to stay within the boundaries of the pattern. But as other creative problem solvers worked on it, they raised other questions and broke other blocks, finding several *one*-line solutions. "Tear out the page," some said (going against a serious block for people who love books). Then you can fold it, or cut it up and retape it together, and draw a single line. You can even crumple it up and punch straight through it. But perhaps the most creative solution came from a 10-year-old girl, who took a direct and innovative approach: "I used a fat line," she wrote. "I[t] doesn't say you can't use a fat line.... P.S. acctually [sic] you need a very fat writing apparatice [sic]" (Adams, 1980, p. 31). She had questioned the concept of *line* more strongly than any of the others. Adams had not said the line had to be as small as the dots; everyone just assumed it did.

Such thinking biases have not been overlooked by people who would take advantage of others. Some people manipulate our thinking biases for entertainment, but others do so for less acceptable reasons.

■ Personal Application: Mental Magic

CREATIVITY AS PROBLEM SOLVING

The concept of creativity has long been used in a largely aesthetic or artistic sense. But defining creativity in solely aesthetic terms is neither practical nor appropriate. The first problem is that "beauty is in the eye of the beholder," but there are other difficulties. If merely producing something beautiful is creative, then nature or chance factors are creative. If painting any painting is creative, then chimpanzees and machines are creative—both have produced attractive art. Other people have so extended the concept of creativity as to render it valueless, arguing that everyone is creative if only they will let themselves be so. (This is meaningless because it is untestable. If someone suddenly becomes more creative, it argues that creativity was there all along. If people *never* do anything original, it just says that they are not using their innate creativity.)

Psychologists have wrestled with the question of creativity with only partial success (Taylor, 1975). There remains much less agreement about what constitutes creativity than about the elements of intelligence. Newell and Simon have suggested one possible definition of creativity as part of their research on problem solving (Newell et al., 1962). They propose four criteria for a creative solution to a problem: (1) it should be both novel and useful, (2) it should require rejecting previously accepted ideas, (3) it should result from intense motivation and persistence, and (4) it should result from clarifying a problem that was originally vague.

Not all psychologists accept the details of Newell and Simon's proposal, but many do believe that **creativity** can be usefully defined as flexible, innovative problem solving. As noted earlier, virtually all thought can be interpreted as problem solving. And whatever the nature or importance of the problem, there can be only three outcomes: it can remain unsolved, it can be solved in routine and predictable ways, or it can be solved creatively—in ways that are unique, especially adaptive, or "elegant" (simpler, cheaper, or otherwise more effective than other solutions). If the solution is aesthetically pleasing, so much the better, but whether it is creative rests on broader criteria. The problems themselves may be artistic but often are not: There are creative chemists, mathematicians, philosophers, mechanics—in fact, any field has creative people (Mansfield & Busse, 1981).

Note that the importance of a problem is *not* related to the creativity of its solution. Creativity can apply to a 10-minute problem solved for fun, or to the problems of everyday routine, just as it does to major aesthetic, technical, or national problems. Using a tennis racket to drain spaghetti, for example, might be a creative solution to an immediate problem.

Psychologists have long considered creativity a kind of giftedness. But if creativity simply represented high intelligence, there would be no need to define it separately. Instead, creativity is usually considered to differ in some ways from conventionally measured intelligence. (We will look at definitions and measures of intelligence in Chapter 14.) Creative thought is usually considered "divergent," for example, whereas most IQ tests require "convergent" thought.

Mental magic

Some people use our search for confirmation to our disadvantage. One of the most obvious ways this is done is in magic acts, much of which consist of setting up propositions so that what follows will be automatically taken by observers as confirming evidence. Many tricks could easily be shown to be impossible if audiences would look for ways of *disconfirming* what is claimed—but they don't. The class of magic that focuses on such tricks is known as mental magic, and magicians have used it to manipulate people for centuries (Kaye, 1975).

Mental magic includes reading minds, predicting the future, moving objects mentally, and so forth; these use some of the most subtle audience manipulations in the entire field of magic. To create these illusions, mental magic uses many of the principles and limitations of thought described in the last two chapters. One variety of mental magic that depends strongly on language manipulations is the process of cold reading already discussed in Chapter 10. But a number of other standard mental-magic techniques also illustrate limits to our ordinary thinking.

A classic example is the magician's *force:* A force is a procedure that *guarantees* that a particular choice will be made, at the same time convincing the chooser and the audience that the choice is free. There are hundreds of magicians' forces; they play some role in many forms of magic, but are especially useful in mental magic. Magicians' forces often rely on prepared objects, such as highly specialized decks of cards, pockets divided into segments, letter openers that can insert a prediction into a sealed envelope while opening it, and so forth.

But good magicians can perform several forces without any prepared equipment, because they can rely on normal thought processes of the observers. One of these thought processes is object constancy: A deck of cards slipped into a coat pocket and then brought out again is assumed by the audience to be the same deck, for example—but typically isn't. Another of these thought processes is our tendency to seek confirmation. And magicians may also use specialized memory techniques; they can do feats of memory or calculation that seem like magic using mnemonics.

That magicians rely on adult learned patterns of perception and thinking is reflected in the statement by a well-known magician and debunker of psychics known professionally as The Amazing Randi. Randi once remarked that "the people who are hardest to fool are children, because they look at what they're not supposed to look at. Scientists are pushovers" (Kaye, 1975, p. 45).

The latter part of Randi's quote also shows why magicians are being included in investigations of claims of paranormal mental powers. Uri Geller was investigated a few years ago by two physical scientists, used to studying objects that would not deliberately deceive them. They came away believing that Geller really had the power to bend keys and spoons mentally, impress his image on camera film, and so forth. But they had not taken the most elementary precautions against stage magic. Randi has caught Geller in such magic, can himself do all that Geller claims to do, and has a standing offer of $10,000 to anyone who can demonstrate *any* paranormal claims. Some have tried, but none have collected. To demonstrate how easy it is to fool investigators of psychic claims, Randi sent two teen-aged amateur magicians to one laboratory. In three years, their tricks were *always* accepted as real—even though Randi sent several letters to the researchers urging them to be careful of such deception and offering to show how it could be uncovered (Randi, 1983).

Trained magicians thus have a unique professional talent for investigating human behavior. Several psychologists are also amateur magicians and more are beginning to recognize this field as offering insight into behavior (P. R. Solomon, 1980). You may expect to see more about mental magic in the future—in newspapers, in classes, and perhaps even in professional journals.

To *converge* means to come together to a point, and to *diverge* means to spread out away from a point. These terms are also used to describe two different ways of thinking. **Convergent thought** is a narrowing from many alternatives down toward a single correct answer. **Divergent thought,** in contrast, is an expanding or widening of possibilities, a moving toward more remote choices (Dirkes, 1978). Convergent thought is typically used in problem solving and is typically measured by intelligence tests; it seeks *the* correct answer to a problem by eliminating alternatives. Divergent thought, however, is what is typically measured by creativity tests; it seeks to find new possible answers.

The convergent/divergent distinction seems readily interpretable in terms of hemispheres. The comparatively loose pattern searches of the right hemisphere seem more like divergent thought, and the verbal and sequential skills of the left hemisphere seem appropriate for convergent thought.

In seeking to measure the divergence of creative thought objectively, psychologists have developed a variety of tests (Barron, 1958). But a major problem with divergent tests is how to score them. Answers to "How many uses?" problems, for example, can be multiplied almost indefinitely. But one child might give 20 different and ingenious uses, and another might simply develop lists: "hit a person with it, hit a dog with it,

Consequences (Guilford, 1954)

Imagine all of the things that might possibly happen if all national and local laws were suddenly abolished.

Fable endings (Getzels and Jackson, 1962)

Write three endings for the following fable: a moralistic, a humorous, and a sad ending.

THE MISCHIEVOUS DOG

A rascally dog used to run quietly to the heels of every passerby and bite them without warning. So his master was obliged to tie a bell around the cur's neck that he might give notice wherever he went. This the dog thought very fine indeed, and he went about tinkling it in pride all over town. But an old hound said. . . .

Word association (Getzels and Jackson, 1962)

Write as many meanings as you can for each of the following words:

a duck
b sack
c pitch
d fair

Remote associations (Mednick, 1962)

Find a fourth word which is associated with each of these three words:

a rat—blue—cottage
b out—dog—cat
c wheel—electric—high
d surprise—line—birthday

Ingenuity (Flanagan, 1963)

As part of a manufacturing process, the inside lip of a deep cup-shaped casting is machine threaded. The company found that metal chips produced by the threading operation were difficult to remove from the bottom of the casting without scratching the sides. A design engineer was able to solve this problem by having the operation performed
_____ .

Product improvement (Torrance, 1966)

The subject is presented with a series of objects, such as children's toys or instruments used in his or her particular occupation, and asked to make suggestions for their improvement.

Pattern meanings (Wallach and Kogan, 1965)

The subject is shown a series of patterns of geometric forms (like the samples shown below) and asked to imagine all the things each pattern could be.

b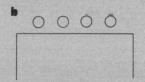

Common answer: "Table with things on top"

Unique answer: "Foot with toes"

Common answer: "Two igloos"

Unique answer: "Two haystacks on a flying carpet"

Figure 11.17 ■ (a) Some of the items that have been used to test creativity. The difficulty of scoring open-ended answers is a common problem with most such items. (b) These answers for pattern-meaning items seem clearly different, but they are no doubt especially striking. How different do such answers have to be to be considered creative?

(**a,** material from Guilford, 1954, is from J. P. Guilford, *Reports from the Psychology Laboratory,* University of Southern California, 1954. Used by permission; material from Getzels and Jackson, 1962, is from *Creativity and Intelligence Explorations with Gifted Students* by J. W. Getzels and P. W. Jackson, 1962, John Wiley & Sons. Used by permission; material from Mednick, 1962, is from S. A. Mednick, *Psychological Review* 1962, *69,* 220–232. Copyright 1962 by the American Psychological Association. Reprinted by permission of the author; material from Flanagan, 1963, is from J. C. Flanagan in C. W. Taylor and F. Barron (Eds.), *Scientific Creativity: Its Recognition and Development,* 1963, John Wiley & Sons. Reprinted by permission; material from Wallach and Kogan, 1965, is from *Modes of Thinking in Young Children* by M. A. Wallach and N. Kogan, 1965. Copyright © by Holt, Rinehart and Winston, Inc. Reprinted by permission of Holt, Rinehart and Winston, CBS College Publishing; material from Torrance, 1966, is copyright © 1966 by Personnel Press. Reprinted by permission of Scholastic Testing Service, Inc. from: *Torrance Tests of Creative Thinking: Verbal Forms A and B;* **b,** from Wallach and Kogan, 1965 [see above], by permission.)

hit a . . . ." The first behavior seems more creative than the second, but it implies that simply counting answers cannot be enough; they must be qualitatively rated as well. ■ Figure 11.17 ■ Notable Quote: A Creative Child on Possible Uses of a Newspaper)

Creativity involves more than how many answers can be generated (or even how unusual the answers are). To be truly creative, the answers must somehow meet the criteria of the problem. After all, any random answer is unusual; you want an unusual answer that is also relevant (Murray, 1959). Generally, only a logical analysis tells you whether a sudden insightful solution to an engineering, business, or other problem will actually work. Hence, both convergent and divergent thought are useful in creative problem solving. What is important is how much of which is applied when. Divergent thought is frequently useful in finding alternate possibilities relatively early in problem solving; convergent thought helps to select the best choice from among these possibilities. Application of the problem-solving skills we have discussed can sometimes yield solutions that are creative in many senses, including aesthetic ones. ■ Figure 11.18

For the sake of illustration, consider a practical problem. Suppose you were asked to design a bridge across a narrow gorge of a river. Roads run along both sides of the river, and the walls of the canyon rise sharply above them to rocky ridges. A conventional

Figure 11.18 ■ Creative product of a gifted individual. The title of the book *Inversions*, when inverted, becomes the author's name, Scott Kim—even though one form has ten letters and the other eight letters.

(From *Inversions* by S. Kim, McGraw-Hill Book Co., 1981. Used by permission.)

NOTABLE QUOTE
A creative child on possible uses of a newspaper

❝ You can read it, write on it, lay it down and paint a picture on it. If you didn't have covers, you could put it around you. You can burn it, put it in the garage and drive the car over it when you wash the car, lay it down and put your baby on it, put it on a busted window, put it in your door for decoration, put it in the garbage can, put it on a chair if the chair is messy. If you have a puppy, you put newspaper in its box or put it in your back yard for the dog to play with. When you build something and you don't want anyone to see it, put newspaper around it. Put newspaper on the floor if you have no mattress, use it to pick up something hot, use it to stop bleeding, or to catch the drips from drying clothes. You can use newspaper for curtains, put it in your shoe to cover what is hurting your foot, make a kite out of it, shade a light that is too bright. You can wrap fish in it, wipe windows, or wrap money in it and tape it [so it doesn't make noise]. You put washed shoes on newspaper, wipe eyeglasses with it, put it under a dripping sink, put a plant on it, make a paper bowl out of it, use it for a hat if it is raining, tie it on your feet for slippers. You can put it on the sand if you had no towel, use it for bases in baseball, make paper airplanes with it, use it as a dustpan when you sweep, ball it up for the cat to play with, wrap your hands in it if it is cold. ❞

Quoted in Zimbardo, 1980, p. 345.

solution is to bore tunnels through the sides of the gorge and reroute the approach roads through them, then sink pilings in the river and run a bridge across them. Could you develop a more creative solution?

A well-known engineer, T. Y. Lin, has offered an exceptionally creative solution, one that is practical—being simultaneously safer and cheaper than the conventional solution—and aesthetic (Davis, 1979). To achieve it, Lin first had to have a wide knowledge of his field, including the structural strengths of various materials and designs. He then questioned two major assumptions: that the bridge had to go straight across and that it had to stand on pilings. His solution rearranged the possibilities to break through both these blocks.

His bridge swept in a single smooth curve from bank to bank, suspended by a web of cables from the ridges. When the necessary calculations were checked, he found not only that it would cost millions of dollars less than a bridge on pilings, but that it would be less susceptible to earthquake and flood damage. These engineering criteria alone make his solution creative. But Lin's design, like many elegant solutions, also turns out to be aesthetically pleasing; his bridge has a breathtaking sweep, like contemporary sculpture on a grand scale. ■ Figure 11.19

When creative problem solving like Lin's is seen as a series of specifiable steps, it becomes less mysterious. But more importantly, it suggests ways of teaching those steps, and thus of teaching creativity (Olson, 1978.) Using the elements suggested in this chapter and the more detailed suggestions in the references will help you solve any problem more efficiently and more effectively.

Figure 11.19 ■ A model of Lin's proposed bridge.
(T. Y. Lin International)

CHAPTER SUMMARY

1 There have been several theories of thinking, but the current approach is based on information processing through cognitive schemata.

2 Humans think in several modes, with verbal and visual modes the most common, but they require both experience and specific training to do so well.

3 In more complex species, increasing amounts of information processing are done with perceived stimuli; at some point this information processing may be considered thinking. The ability to process the incoming stimuli and consider possible plans of action has obvious survival value, but it remains an open question whether any nonhuman species thinks.

4 Concept learning represents one basic form of verbal thinking; it can occur either through hypothesis testing or the development of prototypes.

5 Language comprehension has been studied with the aid of computer simulation models; these tell us that substantial background information is required for even simple communication.

11.13 Rotate the riders 90° so as to create two new porpoises.

11.14 The cars require exactly one hour to come together, so the bird flies 60 miles.

11.15 (a) Move the coins at each end of the bottom line to the end of the line second from the top, and then move the very top coin to the bottom of the diagram. The trick is to make the original bottom line into the two-coin line rather than moving the three coins at the top. This solution and an alternative one are diagrammed below.

(b) 1. The money is there, but the calculations have been totally confused by sometimes adding and sometimes subtracting. Each man paid $10 originally, *but* got back $1 so the total left to account for is $27. The hotel has $25 of that and the bellboy the other $2. You don't add the bellboy's money to the $27, you subtract it.

2. Twenty dollars. He made $10 on each transaction—the fact that it was the same horse is irrelevant. He paid a total of $60 and got a total of $80.

3. The north pole is one. Whichever way you walk first is south, east keeps you ten miles south of the pole, and ten miles north brings you back. We'll leave the other one for you to work on—.

4. Divide the coins into three groups of three coins each. Put one group on either side of the scale. If one side goes down, it has the counterfeit; if they balance, the remaining group contains the counterfeit. Whichever group is implicated, put one of the three coins on one side of the scale and another on the other side. If one side goes down, it holds the counterfeit coin; if they balance, the third coin is the one.

11.16 (a)

(b) 1. B − (A + 2C)
2. B − (C + 2A)
3. B − (A + 2C)
4. B − (A + 2C)
   or (A + 2C)
5. B − (A + 2C)
6. A + C

Figure 11.20 ■ Answers to puzzles and problems in Figures 11.13, 11.14, 11.15, and 11.16.
(11.13 and 11.16, Stephen Stanley)

6 Verbal thought is related to the particular language a person speaks, but not in as strongly constrained a way as proposed by the linguistic-relativity hypothesis. Multiple languages and external notation systems can offer more flexibility than a single language.

7 Most people are less accustomed to thinking visually, but they can learn to do so without much difficulty. Studies of visual thinking have examined imaging and rotating objects and the creation of mental maps. Idea sketching offers a way of externally storing such visual thoughts.

8 Problem solving requires first defining the problem, then solving it through a series of steps. Various heuristic strategies can reduce the number of steps and help assure a solution, although care is needed to prevent common oversights and biases from interfering with reaching a solution.

9 Creativity may be usefully defined as exceptionally able problem solving. This definition helps to understand the relationships between creativity in different fields and suggests how to improve your own creativity.

Further Readings

For more information on cognitive psychology, see a current text such as Anderson's *Cognitive Psychology and Its Implications* (1980), Matlin's *Cognition* (1983), or Reynold and Flagg's *Cognitive Psychology* (1983). Current research issues in visual imagery are presented in Block's collection *Imagery* (1981) and Kosslyn's *Image and Mind* (1980). Downs and Stea's *Maps in Minds* (1977) discusses cognitive maps. For visual thinking and idea sketching, see *Experiences in Visual Thinking* by McKim (1980a); various everyday uses of imagery are considered in Sommer's *The Mind's Eye* (1978). Computer models of thinking are discussed in *The Sciences of the Artificial* by Simon (1981a) and *Artificial Intelligence and Natural Man* by Boden (1977). Adams's *Conceptual Blockbusting* (1980) emphasizes how to avoid a variety of blocks to thought, and includes other helpful suggestions for problem solving. Ghiselin's collection *The Creative Process* (1952) offers some insight into the thought processes of well-known creative people. An information-processing view of creativity is presented in Gardner's *Art, Mind, and Brain* (1982a). Finally, for a well-presented set of problems to try your own skills on, see M. Gardner's *Aha! Insight* (1978a).

Part V

Development and Individual Differences

You visit a local school that has an arrangement with the psychology department allowing it to observe and test the children. In the first test you watch, a child stands before a table on which are two identical tall beakers half-filled with a bright red liquid. The young woman testing the child asks which beaker has more liquid. As the child answers that both have the same, you begin to get bored. "This really is what they mean by child's play," you think as you begin to look around for something more interesting. You hardly pay attention as the woman pours the red liquid from one of the beakers into a large shallow dish. You stifle a yawn as she asks the child, "Now which has more?" But you are startled when the child confidently points to the remaining tall beaker. "Are you sure?" asks the tester, but the child seems quite convinced. "What's wrong?" you wonder. "Is that child retarded? Anyone knows that pouring liquid from one beaker to another doesn't make it less or more liquid." But as you watch other such tests, you are forced to the realization that everyone does *not* know that—at least children don't seem to know it. "That is peculiar," you decide, "although I don't know whether I care." On your way out, you ask about the tests. "Those are Piagetian tests of conservation," she says, "tests that many people believe show a gradual progression in thought process over childhood." "Sounds reasonable," you decide, but it's her final remark as you leave that stays with you. "Some people also think that a similar developmental sequence is true of moral thinking—and that most college students are only about halfway through it."

Such findings are among those made by psychologists who study **development**: How a person goes from the genetic potential represented by a zygote to being some particular adult. All humans who have ever lived have been unique. Even monozygotic twins, whose genetic make up is identical, have different life experiences that help to make them different individuals. Developmental psychologists describe the interactions of nature and nurture influences that lead to each person's individuality. Developmental psychology has traditionally emphasized the period of life from birth to adolescence, but both prenatal development and changes throughout adult life are now included in what is called *life-span development* (Baltes et al., 1980; Baltes & Brim, 1980).

Developmental psychologists discuss their field in two ways, either moving by age periods throughout the life span or considering particular issues that cross several ages, such as cognitive development; we will take primarily an age-period approach. We will first consider prenatal development as a physiological structuring of the individual prior to birth. Then we will introduce the postnatal age periods used by developmental psychologists and five theoretical approaches to developmental issues. Finally, we will focus in succession on five age periods—infancy through

Chapter 12

Development

Prenatal Development
Zygote, Embryo, and Fetus
Critical Periods
Sequences and Stages in Postnatal Development
Developmental-Stage Theories
Social Learning as a Non-Stage Theory
Infancy
Physical Maturation
Research Controversy: Is Early Development Mostly the Product of Nature or Nurture?
Beginnings of Cognitive and Moral Development
Beginnings of Personality Development
Beginnings of Social Learning
Developmental Issue: Attachment
Childhood
Physical Growth
Cognitive and Moral Growth
Personal Application: Using Piaget's and Kohlberg's Theories in Teaching Children
Personality Growth
Social Learning Growth
Developmental Issue: Identification
Adolescence
Reaching Physical Adulthood
Reaching Cognitive and Moral Adulthood
Continued Personality Development
Continued Social Learning
Developmental Issue: Identity
Adulthood
Physical Adulthood
Cognitive and Moral Adulthood
Adult Personality
Adult Social Learning
Aging
Physical Aging
Personality Development throughout Life
Chapter Summary
Further Readings

old age—considering how the major theoretical perspectives describe each period.

PRENATAL DEVELOPMENT

Every individual begins with the fertilization of an ovum by a sperm, each carrying a sample of half the genes of the person from which they came. The resulting zygote, with its new combination of these genes, is limited in some ways and flexible in others. Some physical characteristics of the adult-to-be are relatively inflexibly specified, such as the overall body plan of any member of our species: one head, two legs, and so forth. (Even so, many characteristics, such as location and shape of major organs, vary more than you might think; Williams, 1978.) Other physical characteristics, such as adult height or lung capacity, are somewhat more flexible. But most human behaviors are much more flexibly specified, so finding a genetic contribution to any human behavior is difficult.

For many behaviors, the genetic potentials permit a vast range of possibilities. The language the adult speaks, as well as his or her view of the world and how to behave in it, are almost entirely the result of postnatal learning. Genetic codes specify the body's structural development and body structures provide the basis for behavior, so in that sense genetics limits behavior: No environmental training can teach language or cultural rules to a person whose brain structures are inadequate. But for reasonably intact individuals, *which* language and *which* culture they learn depends on experience. ■ Figure 12.1

Prenatal development consists almost entirely of physiological structuring of the developing zygote into a full-term fetus. The nine-month period from fertilization to birth is an exceptionally critical one for a person, but it is not a period about which developmental theorists argue. Prenatal development is largely the province of biology; the issues that psychologists emphasize begin with birth (Kessen, 1979). Hence we will briefly review prenatal development but not discuss any developmental theories until we are ready to consider postnatal development.

Zygote, Embryo, and Fetus

Each new human life begins with the fertilization of a single ovum by a single sperm. The mother's ovaries usually release only one ovum for the month, but the father's testes provide some 400 million sperm per ejaculation. Swimming at half a centimeter per minute, many sperm reach the egg, but generally only one penetrates its outer covering to fertilize it while it is still within one of the fallopian tubes leading from

ovary to uterus (Epel, 1977). The fertilized ovum, now called a **zygote,** divides and redivides as it travels, over three or four days, to the uterus. There it floats free for another three or four days, still dividing rapidly, before beginning to attach to the uterus. By the end of the first two weeks, the zygote is firmly implanted in the uterine wall and has developed three distinct layers of cells. The outer layer will become the skin, sense organs, and nervous system; the middle layer will become the heart, blood vessels, muscles, and skeleton; the inner layer will become the digestive system and related organs. The placenta, which transmits nourishment to the baby and takes away waste products, also develops during this phase.

During the next six weeks, the implanted zygote—now called an **embryo**—develops its major organs. Although the eight-week-old embryo is little more than an inch long, it has a recognizable brain, a heart that pumps blood, functioning kidneys, and an endocrine system that produces hormones. It even shows the beginnings of reflexive behavior, turning its head and opening its mouth if one of its hands touches its face, as it will in the sucking reflex when newborn (Newton & Modahl, 1978). ■ Figure 12.2

Bone cells begin to appear within the embryo during the ninth week; this event marks its transition to a **fetus,** which it is called until birth. For about 30 more weeks the fetus floats in the amniotic fluid that surrounds it as its body grows and its organs mature.

Critical Periods

Many important early embryological developments are time-sequenced exactly; a failure at one point will affect all later development (Tanner, 1978). Special times at which developmental events must occur, if they are going to be effective, are called **critical periods.** Limb growth, for example, occurs at one particular time in development; if anything interferes with limb development during this critical period, the limbs will never develop correctly. In the 1950s the drug thalidomide caused many limb abnormalities, including very short and missing limbs, because it interfered at this critical time (Taussig, 1962).

Various problems during prenatal development cause other birth defects. Some birth defects are genetic, reflecting an unfortunate combination of recessive genes or a mutation. But a child has also been subject to nine months of environmental shaping by the time it is born; both the normal uterine environment and anything introduced into it by the mother's bloodstream are environmental influences (Flanagan, 1962). A wide variety of common household and industrial substances are now suspected of causing birth defects that affect behavior; some of these may even

a

b

Figure 12.1 ■ Nature and nurture in two extended families. The similar appearance of the several generations in each family reflects both common genetics and common experiences. Some appearance aspects, such as facial features, are largely the result of nature; others, such as clothing, are entirely the result of nurture. If babies of these families were exchanged and each reared in the other family, some of their physical features would always be dissimilar to their "relatives," but their language, beliefs, and customs would be those of their adopted families.

(**a,** N. R. Farbman/Life Magazine © 1946 Time Inc.; **b,** Nina Leen/Life Magazine © 1948 Time Inc.)

affect the sperm, rather than later development (Kolata, 1978). One widely used substance, alcohol, may cause a cluster of birth defects (including mental retardation) called the fetal alcohol syndrome (Streissguth et al., 1980).

Birth defects of this sort, unlike mutations, are not directly transmittable to offspring; thalidomide-crippled individuals, for example, carry normal genes for limb development and may have normal children. But some physical problems of the mother may influence her ability to provide the ideal uterine environment and perhaps the later psychological environment as well. Maternal diet during pregnancy is thought to be especially important (Winick, 1981). Even the mother's diet when she was a child is important. A near-starvation diet, for example, which can stunt her body growth and minimize her adult height, may also cause her body to be a deficient environment for her developing child. It is possible that the child may then also be less intelligent than it could have been—even if *its* diet is ideal (Loehlin et al., 1975). Genetics, body structure, and environment thus interact in multiple ways and perhaps across generations.

Other interactions after birth may also be time dependent, but usually less critically; these are sometimes called sensitive periods. Language, for example, seems to require some early experience and practice. If children do not have an appropriate language environment during their early years, their language development—and with it their cognitive development in general—may never be normal (Curtiss, 1977; Lenneberg, 1967).

SEQUENCES AND STAGES IN POSTNATAL DEVELOPMENT

If all goes well during the prenatal period and the birth process, a new individual enters the world. Still neurologically incomplete, the newborn is as much as a year premature compared to the great apes (Gould, 1976). Therefore early postnatal development is partially a continuation of the physiological structuring of the prenatal period. But the newborn is complete

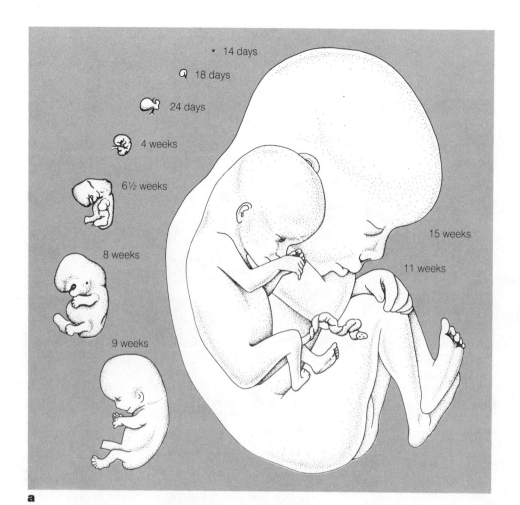

14 days

18 days

24 days

4 weeks

6½ weeks

8 weeks

9 weeks

15 weeks

11 weeks

a

b

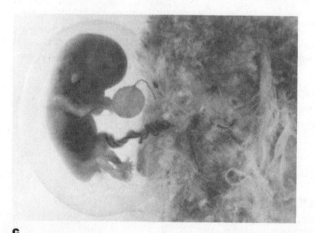

c

Figure 12.2 ■ (a) A sequence of human embryos. (b) The embryo at six weeks (front and rear), showing brain, spinal cord, and partially developed lungs. (c) At 8½ weeks, with more developed limbs and portions of skeleton. d) At 19½ weeks, the well-developed fetus sucks its thumb, one of the several reflexive movements possible by this time.

(**a,** from L. B. Arey, *Developmental Anatomy,* 7th ed., 1974. W. B. Saunders Company; **b** and **c,** from FROM CONCEPTION TO BIRTH: The Drama of Life's Beginnings by Roberts Rugh and Landrum B. Shettles with Richard N. Einhorn. Copyright © 1971 by Roberts Rugh and Landrum B. Shettles. Reprinted by permission of Harper & Row, Publishers, Inc.; **d,** © Lennart Nilsson, *A Child is Born,* Delacorte Press, New York)

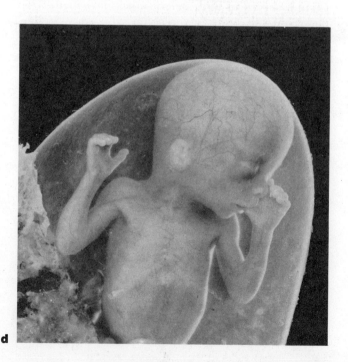

d

enough neurologically to notice and respond to environmental stimuli, from which it begins to learn about the world (Restak, 1982b).

The individual's life is traditionally divided into several time sequences. These mark major changes in the nature of development, even though their boundaries are sometimes hard to specify. We will consider five major sequences or periods in development: (1) infancy, from birth to about 18 months of age, during which nervous-system growth is completed, (2) childhood, from about 18 months to about age 13, during which the individual grows to adult size and acquires some of the most important learning, (3) adolescence, from about age 13 to about age 20, during which the individual acquires much of his or her adult identity; (4) adulthood; and (5) old age. Developmental psychologists often subdivide both the childhood and adulthood periods, but these major five are suitable for our purposes.

Developmental-Stage Theories

Four of the five approaches to development in this chapter are **stage theories;** each divides development into patterns of behavior called behavioral stages. Stage theories differ in how they define their stages, but all share some key assumptions (Bijou, 1968). Stage theories assume that patterns of behavior develop in a fixed sequence, with each more complex or more adultlike pattern following the preceding one in the same way for everyone. The stages may occur at different ages for different people and some people may never develop through all stages, but the stage *sequence* is considered universal. People are generally thought to move through each stage in order, without skipping stages. Stage theories also agree that behavior patterns are not exact and rigidly separated; people may sometimes behave as if they are in one stage and at other times as if they are in an earlier or later stage.

Each of the four stage theories that we will consider focuses on different aspects of behavior and each emphasizes different ages. Jean Piaget's theory of cognitive development emphasizes intellectual growth from infancy through adolescence (Flavell, 1973; Piaget & Inhelder, 1969). Although people can improve their cognitive skills in adulthood, Piaget has relatively little to say about adult cognitive development. Lawrence Kohlberg's theory of moral development grew out of Piaget's view and is in many ways similar to it except that Kohlberg focuses on cognitive processes in making moral decisions (Kohlberg, 1975).

Sigmund Freud's theory of psychosexual stages emphasizes childhood development, but is concerned with personality rather than cognition, especially those aspects of personality that are emotionally based and not fully conscious (Freud, 1933). Erik Erikson's theory of psychosocial stages is generally based on Freud's views, but focuses more generally on crises of life development (Erikson, 1963). It includes other aspects of early development than did Freud, and is more concerned with adult development. Table 12.1 summarizes these four stage theories; we will look at each in more detail and then contrast them with the major non-stage theory, the social-learning view. ■ Table 12.1

Piaget's Theory of Cognitive Development The Swiss biologist and psychologist **Jean Piaget** (1896–1980) is the person most associated with cognitive development (Elkind, 1974; 1981a). After earning a Ph.D. in biology at the age of 22, Piaget turned to the development of intelligence in children. "I was haunted," he said, "by the idea of discovering a sort of embryology of intelligence" (Leo, 1980). For 60 years he collected data and built up his theory of the development of cognitive processes in children. Others consider him a psychologist because of this work, but he thought of himself as a biologist. ■ Figure 12.3

Piaget's findings have revolutionized our understanding of how children think. Until Piaget, adults knew that children's thinking was different from that of adults but understood little about how it differed or how it eventually reached the adult pattern. Piaget's views are by no means universally accepted by developmental psychologists (for example, see Gelman, 1979), but they are probably as widely accepted as any single view within psychology.

Piaget's basic position is that our adult world view is not simply the direct result of environmental experience. Instead we construct our world and maintain its consistency largely through a kind of natural logic. We resist the effect of illusions or magic tricks because we know logically how things are supposed to be. But this adult logic must be built up gradually. Underlying premises on which our logic is based that now seem self-evident were only developed gradually as we grew up, according to Piaget. The fact that an object still exists even when it is out of sight, for example, seems so trivial that it escapes your notice as an adult; yet this **object permanence** is something an infant must learn (Bower, 1971). ■ Figure 12.4

In fact, Piaget's entire theory looks at how children learn to understand the underlying stability of the world despite varying sensory input from that world (Elkind, 1974, 1975). A key concept in all of his work is **conservation,** the reality of permanence in some feature of the world despite apparent change in that feature. Object permanence thus represents conservation of objects; later in development the child learns conservation of volume, weight, and so forth.

Table 12.1 ■ Summary of the Four Major Stage Theories

Stage	Age Period	Major Features	Cognitive Stage (Piaget)	Moral Stage (Kohlberg)	Psychosexual Stage (Freud)	Psychosocial Stage (Erikson)
Infancy	Birth at full term to about 18 months	Locomotion established; rudimentary language; social attachment	Sensorimotor	(Premoral)	Oral; anal	Trust versus mistrust
Early childhood	About 18 months to about 6 years	Language well established; sex typing; group play; ends with readiness for schooling	Preoperational	Punishment and obedience (Stage 1); reciprocity (Stage 2)	Anal; phallic	Autonomy versus doubt; initiative versus guilt
Late childhood	About 6 to about 13 years	Many cognitive processes become adult except in speed of operation; team play	Concrete operational	Good child (Stage 3)	Latency	Industry versus inferiority
Adolescence	About 13 to about 20 years	Begins with puberty, ends at maturity; attainment of highest level of cognition; independence from parents; sexual relationships	Formal operational	Law and order (Stage 4)	Genital	Identity versus role diffusion
Young adulthood	About 20 to about 45 years	Career and family development		Social contract (Stage 5)		Intimacy versus isolation
Middle Age	About 45 to about 65 years	Career reaches highest level; self-assessment; "empty-nest" crisis; retirement		Universal ethical principles (Stage 6)		Generativity versus stagnation
Old age	About 65 years to death	Enjoy family, achievements; dependency; widowhood; poor health				Integrity versus despair

Adapted from *Essentials of Psychology and Life*, 10th ed. by Philip G. Zimbardo. Copyright © 1980 Scott, Foresman and Company. Reprinted by permission.

Piaget divides cognitive growth into four major stages, corresponding approximately to age spans of birth–2, 2–7, 7–12, and 12–15 years. Adult development represents further refinement of the fourth stage, with no other major changes. Each of Piaget's stages is defined in terms of how the child in that stage understands the world. In the **sensorimotor stage** (birth–2 years), the infant comes to comprehend the physical world of separate permanent objects and to appreciate itself as both an object and a manipulator of objects.

The other three stages are defined in terms of **mental operations,** cognitive procedures that the child can carry out to mentally manipulate representations of the world. In the **preoperational stage** (2–7), the child cannot perform such operations. It thinks in direct and self-focused or **egocentric** terms, unable to adopt someone else's view. In the **concrete operational stage** (7–12), the child can perform mental operations involving physical objects, but cannot grasp abstract concepts. He or she can think of "three dogs and a pony" but not of "truth and justice."

Figure 12.3 ■ Jean Piaget (1896–1980). The Swiss biologist turned psychologist and originator of the stage theory of cognitive development. *"The psychological development that starts at birth and terminates in adulthood is comparable to organic growth. . . . Just as the body evolves toward a relatively stable level characterized by the completion of the growth process and by organ maturity, so mental life can be conceived as evolving toward a final form of equilibrium represented by the adult mind."* (Piaget, 1967, p. 3).

(© 1978 Yves de Braine from Black Star)

Figure 12.4 ■ In an infant who has not yet developed object permanence, out of sight is literally out of mind; the infant makes no attempt to seek a vanished object.

(Monkmeyer Press Photo Service)

Only upon reaching the **formal operational stage** (12–15) can the person appreciate abstractions, and with them formal logic, political satire, and other complex relationships that require the manipulation of abstract concepts. ■ Table 12.2

The cognitive abilities of a child· at each stage can be described in terms of the mental operations possible at that stage and the schemes used in these operations. A **scheme** to Piaget is a kind of mental structure that represents a general class of objects, events, or actions. (**Schemes** have often in the past been translated as "schemata" but current work suggests the new translation.) Schemes exist at all levels of abstraction and complexity; concepts such as "dog" or "law," for example, are schemes with different degrees of concreteness, and "tying your shoe" and "building a boat" are schemes with different degrees of complexity.

The process of moving from one stage to another, in Piaget's view, involves a balancing between two ways of managing schemes. When new perceptual inputs can be fitted in to existing schemes, the process is called **assimilation.** A child who sees a picture of a dog he or she has never seen before but can still identify as a dog has assimilated a new input to an existing scheme for "dog." When new inputs cannot be assimilated, however, they force a reorganization of existing schemes, called **accommodation** (Piaget, 1953). If reptiles lay eggs and mammals give birth to and suckle their young, what is a duck-billed platypus, a creature that lays eggs but suckles its young? Once you decide that it's an "egg-laying mammal," you have accommodated your scheme for mammal to incorporate the possibility of egg-laying.

We will note more about how Piaget's stages develop later, when we look at the relevant age periods. There you can see how each cognitive stage is closely tied to the overall development of the individual during that period.

Table 12.2 ■ Summary of Piaget's Theory of Cognitive Development

Stage (approximate ages)	Characterization
1 Sensorimotor (birth–2 years)	The infant is born with some innate reflexes, which form the basis of its exploration of the physical world. He or she begins with a totally body-centered view but through use of the senses gradually becomes aware of the external world beyond his or her body, including the separate objects within it.
2 Preoperational (2–7 years)	The young child acquires language, which permits symbolic representation of objects and events. He or she makes progress toward a less self-centered view, but concepts of space and time remain centered on the child and the present. In examining objects, he or she focuses on one property at a time: height *or* width, for example, but not both.
3 Concrete operational (7–12 years)	The older child begins to use logical reasoning, but this is still based primarily on "concrete," or realistic physical relationships. He or she becomes able to classify and number objects and to arrange them in series. He or she also achieves a number of forms of conservation, including number, mass, and weight.
4 Formal operational (12–15 years and up)	The adolescent begins to think in abstract terms, being able, for example, to consider complex issues of right and wrong or to discuss hypothetical events. He or she can solve a problem by systematically investigating a series of possible relationships and can work with a variety of subtle relationships, such as probability.

Kohlberg's Theory of Moral Development   One of Piaget's books (1932) concerning the moral development of the child was used by Harvard psychologist **Lawrence Kohlberg** (1927–   ) as a basis for his cognitive-developmental approach to morality. Kohlberg believes that the development of moral reasoning requires the development of cognitive reasoning but does not necessarily occur at the same pace (1973). Thus Kohlberg's stages of moral reasoning are less explicitly tied to ages of development than are Piaget's cognitive stages.

Although Kohlberg's approach is not a major theory of general developmental principles, it is the best-known and most influential theory of how moral thinking develops. Based on Piaget, Kohlberg's approach emphasizes moral thinking as exemplified by children's verbal reports concerning moral problems. One of the strongest criticisms of this approach is that what children *say* about a hypothetical moral dilemma may or may not be what they would *do* if faced with an actual situation (Blasi, 1980). Kohlberg answers such critics by noting findings that actual behavior does correlate with moral stage determined according to his scheme (1975). This argument reflects an ongoing disagreement within psychology between those who emphasize thought and verbal statements and those who feel actions speak louder than words. Each group has valid points to make, and full understanding of human behavior will require some integration of both views. But it is nevertheless important to recognize that Kohlberg's view focuses on the development of moral *thought*.

Kohlberg proposes three general levels of moral development, each of which is subdivided for a total of six stages. Like Piaget, he notes that early thought is extremely egocentric. To infants morality is irrelevant, and young children who do things adults would consider immoral are not malicious, simply incapable of thinking about anyone's needs but their own (Stages 1 and 2). As children's mental operations develop, they adopt conventional roles and maintain these for the sake of social stability (Stages 2 and 3). When they achieve formal operational thought, they are able to understand morality in more abstract terms, first as a democratic social contract, then as a function of pure ethical principles (Stages 5 and 6). ■ Table 12.3

We will also return to Kohlberg's stages as we examine the relevant age periods later.

Freud's Theory of Psychosexual Stages   Freud's theory is the basis of the psychoanalytic perspective (see Chapter 1), and has implications for several major areas in psychology. It is usually considered primarily a theory of personality, and we will consider it as such in Chapter 13. But it is also a stage theory of development.

According to Freud, a powerful life instinct, expressed primarily in a drive for sexual gratification, provides the energy behind (motivation for) much behavior throughout life (1935). This primarily sexual energy, called **libido,** must be harnessed and its expression controlled if the individual is to achieve a satisfactory adult role. According to Freud, the newborn infant is already a sexual being, although its sex drive has little focus. Freud's **psychosexual stages** of development seek to specify how the infant's diffuse sexual energy is focused or channeled at different ages, before reaching its mature expression in adult heterosexual behavior.

Freud proposed a series of five psychosexual stages: oral, anal, phallic, latency, and genital. The first

Table 12.3 ■ Summary of Kohlberg's Theory of Moral Development

Levels and Stages	Right Behavior	Reasons for Doing What Is Right
I. Premoral level		
Stage 1: Punishment and obedience	Doing what authorities specify as good or right behavior; obedience for its own sake;	To avoid punishment from parents or other authorities (or those who have superior power).
Stage 2: Reciprocity	Doing what satisfies one's own needs (and occasionally the needs of others); sharing equally with others.	To be fair, in the sense of reciprocity: "You scratch my back and I'll scratch yours".
II. Conventional level		
Stage 3: Good child	Doing what pleases or helps others and is approved of by them; conformity to stereotyped patterns of behavior; *intending* to do right becomes important.	To be a "good boy" or "good girl"; to behave as others do and as they want us to do.
Stage 4: Law and order	Doing one's duty; showing respect for authority and maintaining the existing social order for its own sake.	To obey what are seen as fixed laws or rules on which the social order depends.
III. Principled level		
Stage 5: Social contract	Doing what is constitutionally, democratically, or contractually agreed upon; contributing to further refinement of legal standards of conduct through the democratic process. (The official morality of the American government.)	To follow one's own personal values or opinions, but to do so within the boundaries of what is legal—not in the fixed "law and order" sense of Stage 4, but in recognition of the benefits to all citizens of legal constraints.
Stage 6: Universal ethical principles	Doing what matches self-chosen abstract principles; these principles are logical, consistent, and universal concepts of justice, human rights, and individual human dignity.	To keep one's commitment to self-chosen abstract principles; if these conflict with particular laws, then breaking those laws is a moral act.

Adapted from L. Kohlberg, "The Child as Moral Philosopher," Psychology Today. September 1968.

Table 12.4 ■ Summary of Freud's Theory of Psychosexual Development

Freud's Psychosexual Stages	Characterization
Oral Stage (birth–1 year)	Concern with receiving food passively and later with active biting behavior
Anal Stage (1–3 years)	Concern with bowel training, cleanliness, retaining and expelling feces
Phallic Stage (3–6 years)	Oedipal conflicts arise and must be resolved
Latency Period (6 years–puberty)	No interest in sexuality; same-sex friendships
Genital Stage (puberty up)	Lust blended with affection; adult role behavior

three stages are considered infantile or autoerotic because they focus sexual energy on the individual's own body. After a latency period, in which direct sexual expression is temporarily suspended, the focus turns outward to other people in the mature pattern. Table 12.4 summarizes the psychosexual stages. We will look at each of them briefly and describe them more fully at the relevant age period. ■ Table 12.4

The **oral stage** lasts throughout the first year and into the second. During this time, the infant's sexual pleasure is derived from oral activities: first from sucking, then, as its teeth come in, from biting. In this stage, the mouth is thus the prime **erogenous zone,** or body area responsive to sexual pleasure.

The **anal stage** begins in the second year and continues for a year or more. Freud believed that toilet training marks the developing child's first major encounter with social constraints on behavior. The child must learn during this stage both to retain and expel feces at appropriate times. Freud saw this as an early version of social training—to follow the rules and to postpone immediate demands—as well as a kind of sexual activity with the anus the key erogenous zone.

In the **phallic stage**, from about age 3 to about age 6, the child discovers its own genitals. (Freud's view tended to focus most directly on male experiences, with female ones being contrasted to these. The name of this stage refers to the phallus, or penis.) The child discovers masturbation, not only as a sexual act with the genitals as the erogenous zone, but as an individual act, one more independent of parents than the anal conflicts of the previous stage.

From about age 6 to puberty is a **latency period,** in which sexuality is not overtly related to any eroge-

nous zone. With puberty direct sexuality returns, this time directed outward rather than inward. This final **genital stage** marks the development of the adult pattern, with individuals focused on heterosexual interactions with others. The genitals remain the most directly involved area of the person's body, but the overall emphasis is no longer self-centered; it is relationship-centered.

It is important to understand that Freud meant all of these stages to represent general or personality development as well as specifically sexual development. The stage names refer to the key erogenous zones of those ages, but many stage behaviors are not explicitly sexual. The anal behavior of a two-year-old, for example, includes not only specific actions related to the retention or expulsion of feces, but other more generally retentive or expulsive behaviors: being neat, for example, or excessively disorderly.

These more general attributes of Freud's psychosexual stages mean that the stage descriptions characterize more of children's behaviors than a literal interpretation of the stage names might imply. But the stages also have implications for adult behavior. Freud believed that age alone is not enough to ensure passage to more advanced stages. Under some conditions, children may become static or **fixated** at one of these stages and never progress beyond it. Adults thus can also be characterized, according to the psychoanalytic perspective, as being oral, anal, or other personality types. Furthermore, even adults who *have* progressed to the genital stage can **regress** under some conditions, so their behavior becomes more like that of one of the earlier stages.

Erikson's Theory of Psychosocial Stages   **Erik H. Erikson** (1909–   ), although of Danish descent, was born and grew up in Germany and later moved to the United States, where he has done most of his work. While still in Germany Erikson became a psychoanalyst, and, as all psychoanalysts must, he underwent psychoanalysis. His analyst was Anna Freud, Sigmund Freud's daughter, and Erikson became a friend of the Freud family. After moving to the United States he spent many years teaching, including positions at Harvard, Yale, and Berkeley, before his retirement in 1970. Over these years Erikson developed and refined his own theory of developmental stages (1963). Although based on psychoanalytic principles, Erikson's approach puts less emphasis on sexuality than Freud's; Erikson instead emphasizes interactions between the individual and society. Thus his theory is psychosocial and Freud's is psychosexual. Furthermore, where Freud was concerned primarily with childhood development, Erikson has described developmental stages that continue throughout adulthood. ■ Figure 12.5

Erikson's theory identifies psychosocial crises or conflicts that mark different stages of life (Table 12.5). At each stage, the person's needs interact with those of society in some way. Erikson conceptualized the toilet-training issues of Freud's anal stage, for example, as representing a conflict between the child's autonomy on the one hand and shame or self-doubt on the other. This conflict arises out of the demand of society, represented by the parents, that the child develop correct elimination behavior. The central features of each stage are defined by what Erikson sees as the major conflict that must be resolved during that stage (Elkind, 1970). ■ Table 12.5

Social Learning as a Non-Stage Theory

The major non-stage view of development is social learning theory, one of the major perspectives in psychology (Chapter 1). Recall that social learning theorists believe humans learn most of their behaviors, often by observing other people's actions and the consequences of those actions. A social-learning view of development is thus of an individual gradually building up a repertoire of learned behaviors through experience in the world.

Social learning theorists believe that stage descriptions are misleading in that they seem to imply an innate or inevitable progression. These theorists agree that cognitive, moral, emotional, and social relationships typically become more complex and subtle from infancy to adulthood. But they feel that these changes represent the effects of repeated learning experiences and that little can be gained by arbitrarily dividing these learning sequences into formal stages (see, for example, Bandura & McDonald, 1963).

In some cases, disagreement between the social-learning view and stage theories is relatively minor. Piaget also believed that cognitive growth results largely from accumulated experience, for example, and Erikson emphasizes the role of social interaction at all stages. In other cases, however, the disagreements run deeper. Freud saw an inevitability in the sequence of early development, based on powerful innate instinct, whereas social learning theorists see many possibilities, depending on how a given culture defines and teaches sex roles. ■ Figure 12.6

Children raised under similar conditions may show similar behaviors, according to a social-learning view, but in a different culture might behave differently. Juvenile homosexual experience, for example, might easily interfere with the development of an unambiguous adult heterosexual role in a Victorian culture. But recent anthropological studies of a culture in which all young males routinely go through a period of

Figure 12.5 ■ Erik H. Erikson (1909–). Creator of the psychosocial approach, which is rooted in the psychoanalytic approach but emphasizes social variables and development throughout life. *"From the stages of life . . . such dispositions as faith, will power, purposefulness, competence, fidelity, love, care, wisdom—all criteria of vital individual strength—also flow into the life of institutions. Without them, institutions wilt; but without the spirit of institutions pervading the patterns of care and love, instruction and training, no strength could emerge from the sequence of generations. Psychosocial strength, we conclude, depends on a total process which regulates individual life cycles, the sequence of generations, and the structure of society simultaneously: for all three have evolved together."* (Erikson, 1970, pp. 79–80).
(Courtesy of the Harvard News Office)

homosexual behavior find no apparent problem with their developing an expected exclusively heterosexual orientation as adults (Herdt, 1980).

As we explore the developmental sequence throughout life we will follow a common pattern for each age period, looking first at physical characteristics, then at what these five theories of development emphasize for that period. (As we do, you may find it helpful to refer to the summary tables presented in this section.) Whether the theories agree or disagree about

a

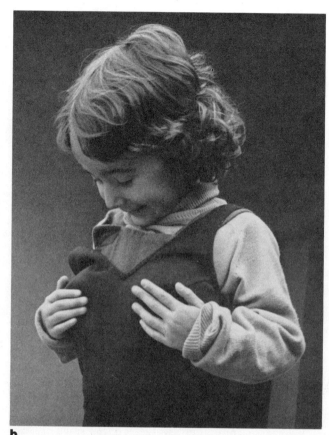
b

Figure 12.6 ■ Young children learn about adult roles, including sex roles, long before they become sexually active. A social-learning view of sex roles notes that adults both offer role models and reward role-play behavior.

(**a,** David Powers/Stock, Boston; **b,** Joanne Leonard/Woodfin Camp & Associates)

Table 12.5 ■ Summary of Erikson's Theory of Psychosocial Development

Stage (Approximate Ages)	Conflict	Description
1 Infancy	Basic trust versus mistrust	Parents must maintain an adequate environment—supportive, nurturing, and loving—so that the child develops basic trust.
2 Years 1–3	Autonomy versus shame or doubt	As the child develops bowel and bladder control, he or she should also develop a healthy attitude toward being independent and somewhat self-sufficient. If the child is made to feel that independent efforts are wrong, then shame and self-doubt develop instead of autonomy.
3 Years 3–5½	Initiative versus guilt	The child must discover ways to initiate actions on his or her own. If such initiatives are successful, guilt will be avoided.
4 Years 5½–12	Industry versus inferiority	The child must learn to feel competent, especially when competing with peers. Failure results in feelings of inferiority.
5 Adolescence	Identity versus role confusion	A sense of role identity must develop, especially in terms of selecting a vocation and future career.
6 Early adulthood	Intimacy versus isolation	The formation of close friendships and relationships with the opposite sex is vital to healthy development.
7 Middle adulthood	Generativity versus stagnation	Adults develop useful lives by helping and guiding children. Childless adults must fill this need through adoption or other close relationships with children.
8 Later adulthood	Ego integrity versus despair	An adult will eventually review his or her life. A life well spent will result in a sense of well-being and integrity.

From *Introduction to Child Development* by John P. Dworetzky. Copyright © 1981 by West Publishing Company. All rights reserved.

the characteristics of a particular age group, each retains its own focus. Sometimes these views can be combined, but other times their claims may be contradictory. Because of their general similarities, Piaget's and Kohlberg's views will be treated together, as will Freud's and Erikson's, noting the distinctions between these views. For some periods, a particular developmental issue will be considered; often these cut across theories or represent theoretical conflicts in interpretation.

INFANCY

Although physiological development actually begins nine months before birth, the newborn infant is often thought of as the beginning of a developmental sequence—we keep track of our ages as years from our *birth* day. Each theory of development begins with birth as well.

Physical Maturation

Infancy is a highly active period physiologically, with many body systems growing rapidly in order to reach the stage of completion exhibited by many other mammals at birth. Only as this growth rate slows in early childhood does complex human behavior, such as speech, begin. Because they are neurologically incomplete, it was long thought that infants must have little awareness or appreciation of the world around them. But recent work is uncovering some remarkably capable behaviors in infants, even newborns (Lipsitt, 1981). The view of what they can perceive and understand is continually being upgraded (L. B. Cohen, 1979; Cohen & Salapatek, 1975).

For an infant to develop normally, both input and output abilities must develop: The infant must be able both to perceive the world and to respond to it with some action.

Perceptual Development Psychologists have used a number of techniques to discover how perception develops and which aspects of perception are innate and which are learned. One well-known series of studies on depth perception used the **visual cliff,** a tablelike frame with a clear glass top and a checkerboard pattern underneath (Gibson & Walk, 1960). The checkerboard is close under the glass on the "shallow" side, then drops down to several feet below it on the "deep" side. ■ Figure 12.7

Both young animals and human infants have been tested on the visual cliff. Because the glass offers a solid supporting surface, an animal or infant operating only

Figure 12.7 ■ The visual cliff, designed to test depth perception. Young animals show depth perception by stopping at the cliff "edge" (or freezing if placed over the deep side). Human infants also perceive the depth; they will not cross the deep side even at their mother's urging.

(William Vandivert/*Scientific American*)

by touch should find no difference between the shallow and deep sides; a visual depth interpretation of the checkerboard pattern, however, might reasonably frighten or at least inhibit it. Results indicate that both young animals and infants *do* perceive the depth. If placed on the shallow side a kitten will walk about but will stop at the visual cliff "edge." When encouraged by its mother, an infant will crawl across the shallow side but will refuse to cross the deep side. If placed directly over the deep side, both animals and infants tend to "freeze" and remain immobile.

Neither animals nor infants can verbalize their experiences, but their actions tell us that they visually perceive the depth and seek to avoid it. The depth cues offered by the checkerboard pattern are therefore probably innate, or at least require relatively little experience; by the time the animals or infants are old enough to move about, they perceive the visual cliff as dangerous. Other depth cues, however, require more experience and practice (Gibson, 1970).

Research with infants has also sought to discover if they can perceive objects. Because human infants are relatively helpless for many months, it does not seem likely that they would be evolutionarily adapted to perceive a wide range of objects. But perception of one particular object—a human face—may be innate. Infants can see clearly only at a distance of about 18 inches; they have trouble trying to focus on either closer or more distant objects until their visual system has matured somewhat. But that distance is nearly ideal for perceiving their mothers' faces as they are held.

A classic series of studies investigated just what infants could see at that distance (Fantz, 1961). In these studies, the infant lay in a bed and looked straight up at a series of objects. (This position was used so that the infant's ability to hold its head up would not be a limiting factor in what it looked at.) The ability to perceive differences in the objects presented was indicated by the amounts of time the infant spent looking at them. ■ Figure 12.8

A number of different images have been tested, but of particular interest are three approximately face-shaped ones. Even the youngest infants tested looked at both the face and the scrambled face in Figure 12.8 more than the light/dark pattern. The light/dark pattern has the same percentage of light and dark as the face versions, so infants apparently prefer the more complex features. The face and scrambled face have the same complexity, however, so preference for the face seems to indicate innate recognition of the pattern. (If this is true, it may be why it is so easy for us to perceive faces in cartoons or in accidental patterns in the world.)

In the same way that infants seem predisposed to recognize a human face, they also seem predisposed to hear human speech and perhaps to smell human odors. Young infants orient to the sounds of any natural human language with a characteristic pattern of movements (Condon & Sander, 1974). They also can soon recognize and prefer their own mothers' voices (DeCasper & Fifer, 1980). This sorting of speech sounds from other sounds seems to be a necessary first step in learning language—a critical type of learning for humans because so much of our behavior, including thought, is language-related. Infants also soon recognize their own mother's odors and can pick them out from others (Macfarlane, 1978).

Much of early perceptual development thus seems to build on innate patterns. The objects seen, language heard, or odors smelled are provided by a particular environment. But the ability to attend to these and to process them meaningfully seem to have at least some innate basis.

Motor Development *Maturation* has an ordinary meaning of growing generally older and wiser. But to a developmental psychologist, **maturation** is a specific process by which physical growth alone results

in new behavior possibilities. Some behaviors, such as walking, are simply impossible for the newborn infant; it lacks the muscular coordination to sit up, much less walk. Walking is part of a sequence of motor development that occurs largely through maturation (Kelso & Clark, 1982). ■ Figure 12.9

Walking also requires practice, however. A child cannot simply be kept immobile until the age of 15 months and then be expected to walk. No amount of practice can make an infant walk before it is physically mature enough, but once it is physically mature relatively little practice is needed. This is shown by both natural and deliberate experiments. A kind of natural experiment occurs between cultures; in some cultures, infants are tightly strapped to their mothers' backs for several months, and in other cultures they play freely. Yet once removed from their mothers' backs, the strapped infants quickly catch up to the others. In controlled experiments, one of a pair of young identical-twins has been given special training and practice in some complex motor activity such as skating. This practice yields little long-term gain for the trained twin; the other twin soon catches up when given a chance.

The use of identical twins is necessary in such a study because of the normal differences in the rate of motor maturation. The bars in Figure 12.9 show the 25–90% ranges for each action, but nearly 25% of all infants achieved it still earlier and about 10% still later than shown. Note that charts such as Figure 12.9 are simply averages of what happens and not an ideal rate of development. A child developing faster or slower can still be perfectly normal, although statistically rare.

The largely physical maturation of perception and motor control provides increasingly flexible input and output systems for the infant. The theories of child development focus on what the infant does with these input and output systems. Although these theories focus mostly on nurture elements, some aspects of development other than perception and motor control may also have innate roots. In fact, one general trend in developmental psychology is toward more acceptance of maturational factors in cognitive and affective development (Kagan, 1976). ■ Research Controversy: Is Early Development Mostly the Product of Nature or Nurture?

Beginnings of Cognitive and Moral Development

For Piaget, the sensorimotor period, lasting from birth to about two years, is a time in which the infant must construct reality based on perceptual experience. The

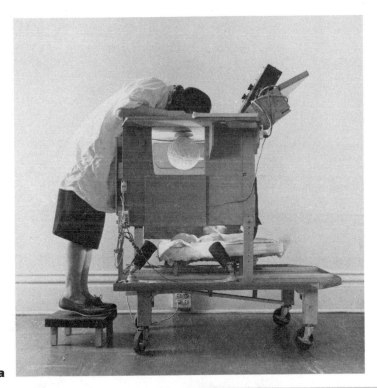

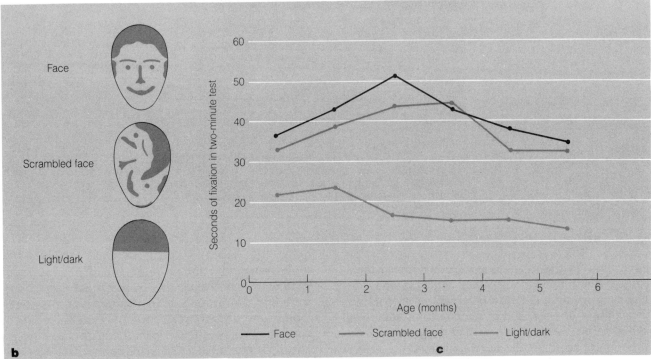

Figure 12.8 ■ Testing infants' ability to perceive faces. Reclining infants were shown a series of different colored blank globes, plus a spiral, a round version of a face, and three face-shaped images: a face, a scrambled face, and a simple light/dark version. The graph shows infants' interest in the face-shaped images, as measured by the amount of time they spent looking at each of them.

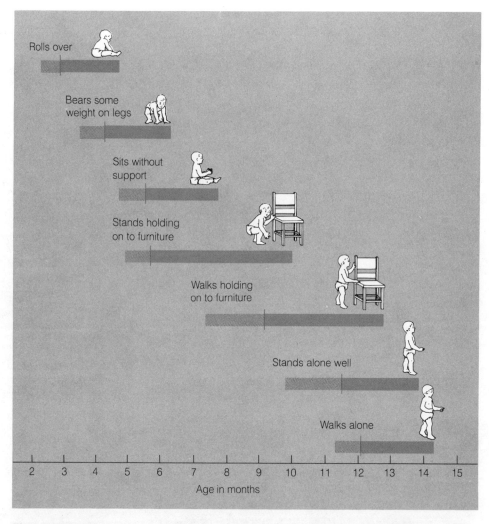

Figure 12.9 ■ Motor development follows a regular sequence, although the exact age for each action varies. The left end of the bar indicates when 25% of infants achieve that action, the vertical mark when 50% achieve it, the right end of the bar when 90% achieve it. The total range of ages at which each action is achieved is thus even greater than shown.

(Based on W. K. Frankenburg and J. B. Dodds, "The Denver Developmental Screening Test," *Journal of Pediatrics*, 1967, 71, 181–191. Used by permission.)

world outside the infant is not simply copied internally; rather, the world's often confused and conflicting sensory inputs must be organized into an understanding of objects that goes beyond superficial appearance (Piaget, 1954). A major step in this constructing of reality is the development of object permanence (Figure 12.4). Infants are pleased by the game of peek-a-boo, he said, because for them the face that appears and disappears is coming into and out of existence.

Piaget called this period a sensorimotor stage because he felt that the integration of the infant's developing sensory and motor skills were crucial in its construction of an objective world, one that can be both seen and touched. The infant begins the sensori-

motor stage with innate reflexes and a natural self-centeredness and ends it with substantial learned sensorimotor integration and a more object-centered world view. This construction of an external world of constant objects, within which the infant can move, is an important intellectual achievement, according to Piaget, one on which all later development depends (Tuddenham, 1966).

To Kohlberg, an infant is premoral, not capable of any moral thought, until it has progressed past Piaget's sensorimotor stage. (The thought processes developing during this stage, he believes, are the basis for the subsequent appearance of moral as well as cognitive thought, even though they have no direct moral content.)

Is early development mostly the product of nature or nurture?

Since the rise of behaviorism as a major perspective in United States psychology, much of psychological theorizing has emphasized learning. Watson's claim that infants are blank slates on which the environment can write has always been qualified, but nevertheless substantially accepted. In recent years, however, partially through the influence of the ethological view, psychologists have paid more attention to possible innate differences in human behavior patterns. We noted in Chapter 3 that one way of exploring the possibility of innate behavior patterns is to study identical twins reared separately (Rose, 1982). Another approach is to look for differences between racial or ethnic groups that might reflect differences in the gene pools of these groups.

Motor-development differences between racial groups have been known for some time. Australian aborigine newborns, for example, have strong necks and can support their own heads when held up, but neither Caucasian nor Japanese newborns can. There are also behavioral differences between groups. When a Caucasian infant is placed face down, for example, it tends to turn its head on one side, but a Japanese infant remains face down.

One researcher has explored these differences somewhat further to see if they imply other differences in later behavior (Freedman, 1979). Freedman compared newborn Chinese, Navaho, and Caucasian babies under several circumstances and found what he believes are characteristic differences among the groups. More importantly, he claims that these differences form a pattern that implies differences in later behavior. Freedman argues that social institutions that differ between cultural groups may be as much an effect of group differences as a cause of them. Navaho and Caucasian infants react differently to traditional Navaho cradle boards, for example; the Navaho infants remain calm when strapped to the boards, but Caucasian infants fight them.

Claims like Freedman's that genetic groups differ in later personality traits might be seen as strong "nature" claims. But, in fact, they point out the complexity of nature/nurture interactions. Freedman found some different responses in infants only a few days old; these responses do seem to represent innate differences (although prenatal differences, such as maternal diet, could conceivably be involved). But he also found differences in child-caretaking patterns in different ethnic groups. These, he feels, are both a result of the innate differences *and* a cause of further shaping of differences. As the infant grows, innate patterns and rearing patterns interact, so observed differences at all later ages are, as he puts it, "100% biological, 100% acquired" (Freedman, 1979, p. 39).

Beginnings of Personality Development

The first year of infancy represents Freud's oral stage. Where Piaget says that the sensing and touching of objects is important because of the mental representations these actions lead to, Freud's emphasis is on their emotional or motivational content. Sucking is not only an innate reflex that ensures nutrition (Blass & Teicher, 1980), it is an emotional need. A pacifier, a nipplelike object given to an infant to suck on, might thus satisfy an innate need for oral exploration. Adult behavior said to derive from the oral stage includes such directly oral activities as drinking, smoking, excessive eating, and nail-biting. It also includes other somewhat less obviously related personality characteristics, such as dependency, gullibility, and sarcasm.

The second year of a child's life begins Freud's anal stage. The parents' emphasis on toilet training combines with the intrinsic pleasure of gaining control over excremental functions to focus the young child on retaining or expelling feces. The anal stage, according to Freud, is the basis for personality traits associated with neatness, cleanliness, and retaining or expelling objects. Adult behaviors indicative of the anal stage can either be retentive ones, such as stinginess or stubbornness, or expulsive ones, such as violent destructiveness.

Erikson views the oral stage as a period in which the psychosocial crisis is one of trust versus mistrust. The degree to which the infant comes to trust the world, in Erikson's view, depends on the quality of care it receives. If the infant's needs are met quickly and it is fondled and talked to, the infant develops a sense of the world as a safe place and a sense of people as helpful and dependable. If the infant's care is inconsistent and uncaring, it comes to mistrust the environment, and this will affect all later stages of development.

Even if trust is established in the first year, however, this does not guarantee a lifetime of trusting relationships. The psychosocial crisis central to each of Erikson's stages is one that can recur in later stages. Thus the trust/mistrust problem is *central* to the first year, but can also recur (Elkind, 1970).

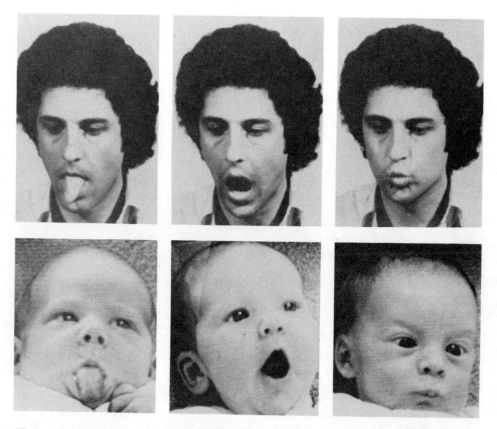

Figure 12.10 ■ Imitation of facial expressions by an infant. This seemingly simple task is actually a remarkably complex one, requiring both perceptual skills and motor control formerly thought beyond an infant's capabilities.

(A. N. Meltzoff and K. M. Moore, *Science*, Vol. 198, 7 October 1977, pp. 75–78. Copyright 1977 by the American Association for the Advancement of Science.)

Beginnings of Social Learning

Relatively little social learning can take place until the infant becomes neurologically complete enough to orient to, and learn from, others. Recent research suggests that something like social learning may occur relatively early, however: Infants may be able to imitate adult facial expressions that they see modeled. At first, this may not seem a surprising finding, but recall that infants must learn even that an object exists when it is out of sight, and that they understand most objects by handling or sucking them. In facial imitation, the infant must perceive the image of someone else's face and attempt to shape its own face in the same way. This seems a complex task for an infant, so perhaps it is a special kind of learning by observation that is in some way innately prepared (Meltzoff & Moore, 1977, 1983). ■ Figure 12.10

Developmental Issue: Attachment

All views of infancy and early childhood recognize the extreme physical dependence of the child on adult caretakers. But the various theories see dependency as having different effects on later development. Piaget saw adult caretakers as arrangers of the physical environment, as the child is learning to mentally construct a stable view of that environment. Freud saw suckling as an emotional need that, if frustrated, can cause problems in later life. Erikson says that infancy leads to a crisis of trust or distrust. Social learning sees the possibility of some limited learning by imitation.

Some early behaviorists felt that physical dependence leads to psychological dependence. Catering to a child's needs, Watson felt, would only spoil it. So where Erikson advocates immediate response to a child's needs to encourage trust, Watson advocated not responding, to minimize dependence. Watson also advocated early independence training to minimize the child's reliance on its parents (1928).

The major evidence against Watson's views came from ethology. Harlow's studies in the 1950s and 1960s showed that young monkeys cling to a "cloth mother," a terry-cloth-covered figure representing a mother monkey, even when they receive all their nourishment from a "wire mother" (Harlow, 1959). The young monkeys seemed to derive a contact comfort from this clinging that made them more secure. In

Figure 12.11 ■ An infant monkey clings for reassurance to its cloth mother in an experiment by Harlow. Even though the bottle mounted in the wire mother in the background provided their nourishment, young monkeys like this one tended to spend their time when not eating clinging to the terry-cloth figure.

(Harry F. Harlow/University of Wisconsin Primate Laboratory)

the presence of a strange object, the young monkey would rush to the cloth mother for security before venturing out to explore the intruder (Harlow et al., 1971). ■ Figure 12.11

A British psychiatrist, John Bowlby, suggested that the behavior of human infants and young children might parallel the monkey findings. He developed the concept of **attachment,** in which mother and infant develop special ties that comfort and support both of them (1973). Attachment is often said to begin with *bonding,* a close interaction between mother and child during the first hours or days after birth that links them together (for example, Marano, 1981). Some psychologists are critical of the emphasis on early bonding, however, even though they recognize that something like later attachment exists (Kagan, 1979).

Ainsworth and her colleagues have explored the concept of attachment through a procedure known as the "strange situation." Between the ages of about 6 and 18 months, children tend to become distressed when their mothers leave them alone, especially in an unfamiliar place. In examining the effect of attachment on this behavior, Ainsworth first observes the child's behavior in the unfamiliar situation when its mother is present. Then the mother leaves for a while; the child's behavior is observed both while she is gone and when she returns.

Children seem to show three major forms of attachment in this situation. "Securely attached" children are initially willing to explore the room, show little anxiety while their mother is away, and appear glad to see her when she returns. "Anxiously attached" children do not explore, show visible anxiety when alone, and are ambivalent to their mothers when they return, sometimes clinging to them and sometimes pushing them away. Still other children show "avoidant" behavior; they seem relatively unattached to their mothers, showing little distress when alone and little response when their mothers return. These differences seem related to parenting style. The mothers of securely attached infants are responsive and supportive, whereas those of avoidant children are unresponsive. Mothers of the anxiously attached are also insensitive, but not as rejecting as mothers of avoidant infants (Ainsworth, 1979).

Currently, many psychologists view the quality of early attachment as an important contributor to later personality. Rather than maternal care fostering unhealthy dependence, it seems to support later independence by contributing to a strong sense of security and self—or, in Erikson's terms, trust (Sroufe, 1979). But that care need not necessarily come from the mother (Etaugh, 1980). Although work on attachment initially focused on mothers, more recent work suggests that infants can become attached to fathers or other regular caretakers instead of or in addition to the mother. Even group care, as in Israel's kibbutzim, does not necessarily cause problems of attachment (E. Hall et al., 1982).

CHILDHOOD

The rapid physical growth and beginnings of psychological growth in infancy result in a young child able to move about in, and interact with, its physical and social environments. In the 10 to 12 years between infancy and puberty, children grow both physically and intellectually, from toddlers with minimal speech to persons on the verge of adulthood. In every culture childhood is the time for learning adult roles, often through play, before the culture requires actually carrying out adult roles (Shostak, 1978).

Physical Growth

After a rapid spurt in infancy, body growth stabilizes at a somewhat slower rate. Between age 1 and puberty at

"WHEN I WAS READY TO READ, THEY TAUGHT ME TO TIE MY SHOES — WHEN I WAS READY TO TIE MY SHOES, THEY TAUGHT ME TO READ."

© 1983 by Sidney Harris

about 12–14, boys and girls grow at a generally steady and equal rate (see Figure 12.16).

Maturation is less central in childhood than in infancy, but it continues to play some role in various achievements. The question of whether a particular child is physically mature enough for a particular task is typically discussed as the child's **readiness.** The discussion may concern physical, mental, emotional, or social readiness, but the issue is always whether the child is mature enough to begin some task. Choosing when a child should enter the sequence of formal schooling is a readiness decision, for example. Should a child who is just the legal age, but smaller than other children of that age, begin kindergarten? In another year that child will have missed out on a year of schooling, and might be said to have fallen behind age mates. But the child is also likely to be larger, better coordinated, and more socially adept, and thus more "ready" for school. Knowing when a child is ready for some activity is obviously not an easy task.

Cognitive and Moral Growth

Piaget called the period of early childhood (about ages 2–7) the preoperational stage. Young children, he felt, continue to learn how to construct the world and their own place in it, but they do not yet carry out mental operations. The preoperational child has thoughts about the world, but is incapable of thinking *logically* about it. The child's thinking is egocentric (self-centered) and animistic (believing that living forces move everything, including objects). One thing that led Piaget to begin his investigations, for example, was the reported belief of a child that the sun and moon followed him wherever he went. Piaget later found that such beliefs are common in young children (Elkind, 1969; Piaget, 1962).

During early childhood, the child establishes the bases for operational thought: extended experience with both objects and people, primitive forms of thought concerning objects, and basic language. An important form of thought that combines both object experience and language is conservation. In Piaget's scheme, conservation means holding constant, in one's constructed world, those attributes of the physical world that are in fact constant—even when they appear not to be.

Piaget's basic method of exploring children's thought was to ask them a question or pose a problem and then to analyze their answers, paying as close attention to their mistakes as to their correct answers. In a typical conservation problem for younger children, the researcher presents some quantity of objects—say a row of beads—and then manipulates it so that its appearance changes—perhaps spacing the beads farther apart. The watching children are then asked if the substance has changed in quantity. Until they achieve conservation, they will say that the row of beads contains more when the beads are spaced further apart. One of the best-known conservation tasks asks whether there is more liquid in containers of different shapes. ■ Figure 12.12

Not all psychologists agree that such a reply indicates the child's true cognitive abilities. In fact, not all even agree that childhood thought follows in a cumulative sequence from infancy (Kagan, 1978). But Piaget's views represent the most widely accepted position.

To Kohlberg, early childhood is the beginning of moral thought. The egocentrism of thought that Piaget has noted becomes, in Kohlberg's terms, Stage 1 moral thought: The direct consequences to a child of any action are what determine its goodness or badness. Kohlberg assesses the child's moral stage in the same way that Piaget assesses its cognitive stage—by evaluating the child's verbal response to a posed problem.

a

Figure 12.12 ■ Various procedures are used to test Piaget's concept of conservation of physical characteristics. (a) In testing conservation of mass, a tester may present two identical objects made of clay, then later reshape one and ask if both still contain the same amount of clay. (b) One of the best known tests examines conservation of liquid volume. (The answer "C contains more" indicates a lack of conservation.)

(Photo by Sybil Shelton/Peter Arnold, Inc.)

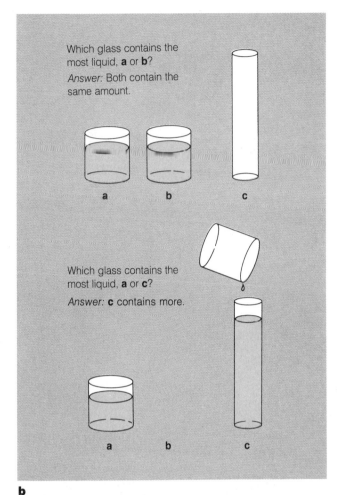

Which glass contains the most liquid, **a** or **b**?

Answer: Both contain the same amount.

a   b   c

Which glass contains the most liquid, **a** or **c**?

Answer: **c** contains more.

a   b   c

b

Note that, according to Kohlberg, the grounds used to make a decision are more important than the decision itself. Thus given the moral dilemma of whether a poor man should steal medicine for his dying wife, it is not important whether the child says yes or no; what is important is the logic behind the choice. "No, because someone would punish him" and "Yes, because his wife's relatives will be mad if he doesn't" might both constitute Stage 1 thinking.

In late childhood (from about age 7 to about age 11) the child begins to use logical mental operations, according to Piaget. Aided by an increasing sophistication of language, the child becomes capable of a variety of concrete operations, mental representations of physical objects and relationships. Several forms of conservation are achieved and the child can logically solve a variety of problems, as long as they concern physical objects. Another measure of the growing complexity of mental representation in later childhood is the ability to see alternate abstract representations in patterns made up of concrete objects (Elkind, 1974). ■ Figure 12.13

Achieving concrete operations also makes possible (but does not automatically lead to) Kohlberg's Stage 2 moral thinking. Morally correct behavior in Stage 2 is still largely egocentric, but occasionally includes the needs of others. Elements of fairness, reciprocity, and sharing are present, but these are always of a concrete nature ("you scratch my back and I'll scratch yours") rather than being concerned with loyalty, gratitude, or justice (Kohlberg, 1975).

Both Piaget's and Kohlberg's views have had impact on education. Kohlberg supports this use of his views, but Piaget was suspicious of it. ■ Personal Application: Using Piaget's and Kohlberg's Theories in Teaching Children

Personality Growth

To Freud, the important developments in early childhood are completing the anal stage and moving through the phallic stage. We considered the anal stage earlier. In the early phallic stage, the focus is on the child's own genitals and thus on awareness of self as male or female. At this same time, however, there is a general concern with male and female roles of others in the environment. This leads to two crucial problems, or "complexes," of the phallic stage.

In the **Oedipus complex,** the young boy develops a sexual interest in his mother and feels competitive aggression toward his father. (Oedipus was a character in Greek mythology who unknowingly killed his father and married his mother; to Freud,

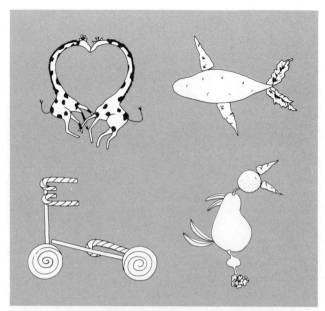

Figure 12.13 ■ Nursery-school-age children see only the parts that make up the whole—that is, they see the candy canes and lollipops but not the scooter. Kindergarteners and first graders see only the whole object (the scooter). From second grade on children are able to see both.

(From *Children and Adolescents: Interpretive Essays on Jean Piaget*, 2nd ed., edited by David Elkind. Copyright 1974 by Oxford University Press, Inc. Reprinted by permission.)

every young boy goes through a period of wanting to do the same.) But since the boy must recognize his father's much greater power, the Oedipus complex leads to another difficulty, the **castration complex;** the boy is said to become afraid that his father will cut off his genitals to punish him for competing for the sexual favors of the mother. These two related complexes are said to be resolved in an important development of the phallic stage, the boy's identification with the father. Identification relieves the fear of castration and indirectly gratifies the sexual desire for the mother. (The father has sexual relations with the mother, so by identifying with him in a sense the boy shares in them.)

Girls are said to go through a similar set of problems, but the formulation of these has been one of the most-criticized aspects of psychoanalytic theory. The female equivalent of the Oedipus complex is called the **Electra complex;** the young girl is said to develop a desire for sexual relations with her father. But where the Oedipus complex is marked by fear of losing the phallus (castration), the Electra complex is marked by a sense of already being deprived of one. This is called **penis envy,** and the girl is said to blame her mother for the loss. Again the resolution involves identification with the same-sex parent, in this case the mother.

Freud's formulation of the concept of penis envy has been widely attacked, both as an overly male-centered view and as being simply wrong. It clearly

reflects the largely male-centered view of his times. It is also, in fact, little supported by objective data—but objective data have not been obtained for most psychoanalytic concepts. (As we will note in Chapter 13, Karen Horney, one well-known psychoanalytic theorist, disagreed sharply with Freud's idea of penis envy.) Adult behavior traits said to have their origin in the phallic stage are seductiveness and competitiveness.

To Erikson, the beginning of the early childhood period, corresponding to Freud's anal stage, represents a crisis of autonomy versus shame. Encouraging the child's efforts, whether concerning elimination or other activity, helps develop a sense of autonomy; criticizing leads to shame and self-doubt. The psychosocial crisis corresponding to Freud's phallic stage is one of initiative versus guilt. Children who are free to engage in motor play develop physical initiative, and those whose questions are taken seriously and answered develop intellectual initiative. If motor activity and questions are discouraged, the consequence is guilt.

Late childhood (from about age 6 to about age 11) to Freud is a latency period; the young child's early concern with sex roles and sex play has lost intensity and the pubertal awakening of adult sexuality is yet to come. Children during this period are primarily interested in same-sex peer relations, with boys playing almost exclusively with boys and girls with girls. The behavior trait that develops during the latency period is **conscience,** the internalizing of parental moral and ethical demands.

During late childhood, Erikson says, the child becomes capable of deductive reasoning and of playing by formal rules. The psychosocial crisis of late childhood is one of industry versus inferiority. "Industry" describes a concern with the details of how things are made and how they work. If children in this 6–11 range are encouraged in their efforts to make practical things, whether building tree houses or cooking, then their sense of industry is supported. But if their efforts are seen as making a mess or are otherwise discouraged, the result is a sense of inferiority.

Because these are the beginning school years, age peers and school officials also play roles in the industry/inferiority crisis. (Here Erikson is moving beyond Freudian theory, which traditionally emphasized the home and family relationships.) The actions of peers and teachers can either sustain the home effects or contradict them. Unsuccessful school experiences can contribute to a sense of inferiority despite a supportive home; success can aid a sense of industry even for a child from a disparaging home (Elkind, 1970). Peer groups may also have positive or negative effects. Any supportive peer group encourages the child, but some peer groups share society's standards

Using Piaget's and Kohlberg's theories in teaching children

You might think you could apply Piaget's views to teach children such concepts as conservation more quickly. In fact, many teachers have thought the same and programs based on this concept are used in a number of schools. Piaget, however, did not support this idea. He believed that complex cognitive growth requires time and a myriad of experiences (Elkind, 1969). Thus, hurrying students through the stages probably would not work and in any case would be undesirable, because it would not provide as thorough a grounding in the early stages as more natural development. Educational researchers who have hoped to accelerate cognitive development have met with mixed success so far. Piaget is probably correct that a broad range of experiences contribute to cognitive growth; however, it is likely that the more such experiences education can provide, the

more impact it will have on cognitive growth.

Piaget's greatest positive influence on education may be the changed attitudes toward children's thought of all the teachers who have been exposed to his views (Elkind, 1969). For example, Piaget pointed out the importance of motor activity in young children's learning and their difficulty in dealing with abstract verbal concepts (Elkind, 1974). This observation in turn suggests the use of such sensorimotor-related teaching methods as those suggested by Maria Montessori (1966) or the colored rods for teaching arithmetic developed by Georges Cuisenaire (March, 1977). At the same time it argues against attempting to teach young children verbal and rule-oriented material, such as "new math"—an approach to arithmetic that met with limited success in the 1960s (Kolata, 1977a).

Educators have also looked at the idea of accelerating moral development. Kohlberg believes that even

relatively few adults achieve the highest stages of moral thought; thus the question also becomes how *far* can educators go in teaching moral thought. Kohlberg, like Piaget, believes that children can advance when exposed to logic only one stage higher than their own. They understand but reject the logic of earlier stages, and they do not comprehend the logic of stages more than one beyond their own (Kohlberg, 1975). This provides a logic for teaching moral thought: Present moral dilemmas and discuss them in increasingly sophisticated terms, beginning with the lowest stage represented within the class (Likona, 1977). This theoretically should help each child to advance at least one stage.

Unlike Piaget, Kohlberg himself has advocated the specific training of moral thinking (1972, 1975) and educators have designed both theoretical and applied techniques to do so (Adams, 1977; Duska & Whelan, 1975; Galbraith & Jones, 1976).

and encourage the development of conscience along conventional lines and others may be outspokenly antisociety. ■ Figure 12.14

Social Learning Growth

Social learning theorists agree that childhood is important to personality development, but they see no reason to divide learning into categories or stages. They see the child as a complex organism growing and learning in a predominantly social context. Some learning, as in isolated play, occurs through direct interaction of the child with the environment. But most learning occurs through contact with others, including siblings, peers, older children, and adults. All of these people are potentially important, and the relevance of each is partially determined by the others. If the family is an active and rewarding one, the child may be less likely to turn to antisocial peer groups for support.

One function of a society, according to the social-learning view, is to order and arrange the social-learning environments of the child. Required school attendance is only one example of how social rules

seek to teach the child particular behavior patterns. Often the potential power of peer and adult social groups is formally enlisted to teach the child how to behave as an adult. Religions seek to structure the child's future behavior by patterning the imitation of adults and by rewarding that imitation. Such groups as the "Hitler youth" of World War II Germany also adopted elaborate formal training. Although the principles of social groups may vary widely, the techniques for socialization of the children are quite similar.

Developmental Issue: Identification

A key element in the Freudian view of childhood development is **identification,** or internalizing the characteristics of a parent. Psychoanalytic identification is seen largely as a sexually motivated activity, a way of seeking gratification as well as of avoiding anxiety. Some adult behavior is viewed in the same way. "Identification with the aggressor," for example, is used to explain the behavior of some concentration camp or prison inmates who imitate the manner of

Figure 12.14 ■ Development of personality in later childhood depends on many factors, but peers play a powerful role, especially when organized into recognizable reference groups with specified standards of dress and behavior.

(Ed Lettau/Photo Researchers, Inc.)

their guards. This pattern is viewed as similar to the identification with the powerful same-sex parent that takes place in response to the Oedipus conflict. The child—or prisoner—is said to feel less threatened and more powerful by taking on the mannerisms of the threatening person.

The other theoretical perspectives agree that children learn from adults, but describe the learning process differently and put different emphases on it (Henderson, 1981). Neither Piaget's nor Kohlberg's theories emphasize any concept akin to identification. Erikson agrees that parents are important in the child's development, but puts less emphasis on direct internalizing of the parents' characteristics through identification. To Erikson, parents, peers, and others are all important because of their impact on the child at each psychosocial crisis.

The social-learning view does emphasize a concept similar to identification, but this concept, *imitation*, differs from psychoanalytic identification in several ways. Imitation is seen as a learning process more than a motivational one. That is, children imitate the behavior of parents and others because it offers some guide to action and because imitation is often rewarded—not because it satisfies hidden sexual motives or relieves anxiety over those motives. Some early forms of imitation, such as infants mimicking adult facial expres-

sions, might have biological preparation but most imitating is felt to be simply an effective way to learn about the world.

Developmental psychologists continue to argue about how and why something like identification or imitation occurs. They generally agree that parents are especially important in early childhood, when the family is the primary environment for the child; relationships developed within the family are then further elaborated in interactions with peers and others (Hartup, 1979; Bronfenbrenner, 1979). A longstanding emphasis on the mother's role is beginning to be complemented by studies of the father's influences (Lamb, 1979), although in some learning—such as language—fathers seem to play a minimal role (Bruner, 1978; McLaughlin, 1978).

An earlier emphasis on family relationships to the exclusion of other factors is also changing, however. More weight is being given to possible maturational (innate) factors (Kagan, 1976) and to ways in which the child influences the parents (Bell, 1979). Also changing is the view of variations from traditional two-parent families. Because a psychoanalytic view of identification requires the presence of both parents for healthy development, divorce has in the past been considered necessarily damaging for children. But some psychologists now believe that the conflicts of a disturbed marriage are much harder on children than are single-parent families (Hetherington, 1979).

Similarly maternal employment, formerly considered to rob the child of the critical presence of the mother, is now being considered less damaging and perhaps even useful. If children can learn from a variety of others, then providing other caretakers for part of the day exposes them to other adult roles. Identification with a working mother provides a role model likely to be of increasing importance as more women work outside the home for more of their lives than ever before. And even the father's role may be less stereotyped if he takes a more active part in child-rearing and care of the home (L. W. Hoffman, 1979).

ADOLESCENCE

Adolescence begins with puberty, the beginning of physical maturity, and ends with psychological maturity at about age 20. In all cultures, this is the time when children come of age and are officially accepted into the adult world (Bohannon, 1980). In so-called primitive cultures adolescence may be brief or nonexistent as a separate stage, with formal adulthood conveyed at puberty. In more industrialized societies, however, adolescence can be a prolonged and stormy period, with formal adulthood following physiological maturity by as much as ten years.

Reaching Physical Adulthood

Throughout childhood, boys and girls grow at about the same rate. But this changes at puberty, marked by the beginning of menstruation in females and the production of live sperm in males. First girls and then boys undergo a final growth spurt over three or four years before growth tapers off to zero with the achievement of adult stature. ■ Figure 12.15

As with motor development in infancy, individuals differ in the timing and amount of the pubertal growth spurt. The age of onset of puberty is affected by environmental factors, most notably the quality of diet. The age of first menstruation has been gradually falling for many years as the average diet improves, from about 16 in the early 1800s to under 13 in the 1980s (Bullough, 1981). This age is probably at or near the genetic limit and is unlikely to drop further. Individual genetic and environmental factors can affect the pubertal age somewhat while remaining within "normal" boundaries, however. Such environmental factors include diet and also exercise, at least for females. Rose Frisch, of Harvard's Center for Population Studies, has shown that for every year a young female

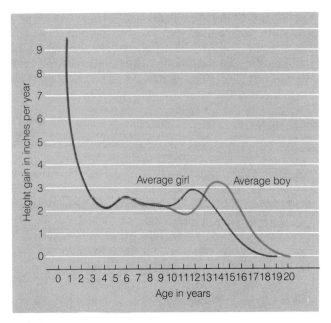

Figure 12.15 ■ Growth to physical adulthood shows a rapid growth rate in infancy, followed by a steady, somewhat slower growth rate until puberty. At puberty both sexes undergo a brief growth spurt before growth levels off at adult size. The pubertal growth spurt typically occurs earlier for girls than for boys, but varies by several years among different individuals.

(From N. Bayley, *Child Development*, 1956, *27*, 45–74. © Society for Research in Child Development. Used by permission.)

athlete is in training her first menstruation is delayed by five months ("Menarcheal Misunderstanding," 1981).

The range of individual differences and the average differences for the sexes mean that people of ages 10–15 vary widely in height and physical maturity. Some still seem like children while others seem to be young adults. Early in adolescence girls tend to be larger because they mature sooner, but by late adolescence most males reach and pass most females, yielding the average height differences found in adults.

Reaching Cognitive and Moral Adulthood

The last of Piaget's stages of cognitive development is the formal operational stage, which begins at about age 11 or 12 and reaches adult status within a few years. Piaget considered cognitive development throughout adolescence and adulthood as a further refinement of this stage. The formal operations that define adult thinking are mental manipulations according to abstract rules. Included in formal operations are such logical relationships as identity, negation, reciprocity, and correlation. (Identity is the mathematical relationship in which one item equals another. Negation states that something is "*not a* _____." Reciprocity implies any of several reciprocal relationships, such as the fact that "A equals B" means also that "B equals A." Correlation means that two variables change together in some way.) With them, a person can deal with problems of proportionality, probability, permutations, and combinations, which are all basically mathematical or logical concepts. But many people who have never studied the formal math or logic equivalents use the ideas behind these terms.

Unlike those still restricted to concrete operations, the adolescent capable of formal operations can deal with objects that have never existed and can manipulate them by arbitrary rules. Thus a college engineering class can be asked to design a chair for a hypothetical three-legged being living on a planet with twice earth's gravity. For someone who has achieved formal operations the task is challenging and enlightening; it helps show why our chairs are as they are and suggests how they might be improved. But a child functioning at the concrete level could never complete such a task. Similarly, a college logic class may teach the syllogisms of formal logic through such statements as "All oranges are elephants. Some elephants are Democrats. Are all oranges Democrats?" For those whose thinking is still in the concrete operational stage, such syllogisms are meaningless. Only formal operational thought allows a person to separate the form of an "all A are B" statement from its content.

Formal operational thought also allows people to consider the meaning of religious and philosophical concepts. The extended conversations about such topics in college reflect not only students' exposure to new ideas but the cognitive maturity that allows meaningful discussion of such abstract concepts.

Some people never solidly achieve formal operational thought. They may occasionally consider a problem in formal operational terms, but usually revert to concrete terms. College study in general helps to teach formal operations. One of the most frequently encountered findings of sociologists and others who sample public opinions is that the views of the college-educated typically differ from those who have not been to college. One way of characterizing the difference is in the degree of formal operational thought used in considering the questions asked.

Achieving at least some formal operational thought is a prerequisite for all of Kohlberg's last four moral stages. Only with the beginnings of formal operational thought are Stages 3 and 4 possible, and full development of formal operations is necessary for Stages 5 and 6. In no case, however, is achievement of the necessary cognitive development sufficient. Moral development to higher stages requires continued experience with other people's moral thought at higher stages. Without such experience, a person can achieve formal operational thought yet remain at an early moral stage.

If progression in moral thought continues, it can reach the two stages of conventional morality, Stages 3 and 4, in adolescence. Stage 3 in Kohlberg's scheme is based on interpersonal relationships. Stage 3 is often called the "good child" stage because it defines good behavior as that which pleases or helps others and is approved by them. A major element in Stage 3 moral development is conformity to a stereotypical image of right behavior.

Although not always specific to moral thinking, conformity to group norms is frequently noted as a general characteristic of adolescent behavior. Fads in clothes and language often produce a striking uniformity of appearance in this age group (along with a chance for others to assert themselves by not conforming). ■ Figure 12.16

With experience, those who have achieved formal operational thought can progress to Stage 4 moral thought, the law-and-order stage. The emphasis in Stage 4 is on orientation to authority, fixed rules, and the maintenance of the social order for its own sake. Right behavior consists of doing one's duty. (One high-school teacher found that his class easily adopted a totalitarian class pattern that he had devised to teach them about the Nazis; Jones, 1976.) Kohlberg believes that most American adults remain at the Stage 4 level, perhaps in part because most schools function as Stage 4 institutions (Kohlberg, 1975). He also finds, however, that more young people have reached the principled level (Stages 5 and 6) than was the case a generation ago—but also that more have remained at the preconventional level (Stages 1 and 2).

Continued Personality Development

Early adolescence, about ages 11 to 14, marks the last of Freud's stages, the genital stage. With the physiological maturation of puberty comes a reawakening of sexual interest after the latency period of late childhood. To develop a satisfactory adult orientation, the adolescent must integrate and subordinate the earlier oral, anal, and phallic *sensuality* into an overriding genital *sexuality*. Where the earlier stages were sexual in underlying motivation, they now become overtly sexual in the adult role. Although the stage name might seem to imply a selfish orientation, Freud meant the genital stage to have as its focus another young person of the opposite sex. Behavior traits he believed to be associated with the genital stage are intellectualization and aestheticism (the appreciation of beauty and other refined tastes).

a

b

c

Figure 12.16 ■ (a, b) Conformity to the standards of peer groups in adolescence often produces a remarkable uniformity in appearance and behavior. (c) In contrast, some people seek to assert their individuality by defying conformity of appearance.

(**a,** Mitchell Payne/Jeroboam; **b,** August Sander/Courtesy Sander Gallery Inc.; **c,** Ellis Herwig/Stock, Boston)

To Erikson, adolescence is characterized by mental as well as emotional and physical development. In this, his views are similar to both Piaget and Freud. Adolescents become able to think about other people's thinking and wonder what others think of them. They are able to conceive of ideal families, religions, and societies, and are often impatient with the inadequacies they see in existing institutions.

As impatient idealists, they often join one or another movement advocating rapid and dramatic change. They are the backbone of religious cults and of violent-revolution groups. More years of maturing will be necessary before the survivors of instant-change movements mellow into adults working within the system, as have some of the 1960s student radicals (Nassi, 1981).

The psychosocial crisis characteristic of adolescence is ego identity versus role confusion. This notion is so widely known that people who have never heard of Erik Erikson will describe themselves as undergoing an identity crisis (Elkind, 1970). Caught between childhood and adulthood, the adolescent seeks to establish an adult identity that will integrate what has gone before and will lead in an appropriate direction through what is yet to come.

Continued Social Learning

As with earlier age periods, the social-learning view interprets many of the adolescent life events differently from the other views. The social-learning view agrees that adolescent thought, including moral thought, is more elaborate than before and that adult identity, including sexual identity, is being established in adolescence. But social learning interprets these events as increasingly complex learning in an increasingly broad range of circumstances. Thinking is more elaborate, for example, not necessarily as a later stage but because it draws on all that has gone before.

Bandura has suggested (1982) that many of the important outcomes, as adolescence progresses into adulthood, occur by chance. Even though childhood and early adolescent experiences influence who a person becomes, Bandura argues, random factors play a major role in life development. These random factors include other people acting as models, rewards provided for imitative behaviors, and so forth. People become professionals of a certain kind, marry one person and not another, and in other ways structure their lives partly through chance factors—though prior learning may influence what they make of these factors. Thus a chance attendance at a particular lecture may cause a person to choose the topic of the lecture as a life career. One chance meeting may lead to romance and marriage, another to a job that becomes a life's work. The person must in each case be prepared to follow up on these events, but the events themselves are often unpredictable.

Developmental Issue: Identity

That adult identity is often critically shaped by the events of adolescence is obvious to virtually all theorists. But how to interpret this development of identity is less obvious. To Piaget, adolescence is a time of moving into adult thought—but identity as such is not specified. To Kohlberg, adolescent moral thought can move toward more adult patterns, but need not do so. To Freud, establishing an identity in adolescence is part of a sequence of motivated stages based partly on innate sexual urges. Erikson is the only stage theorist to

focus on the development of identity as a complex amalgam of thought, feeling, and behavior. No doubt that is why his term *identity crisis* has entered the popular vocabulary.

The social-learning view is in many ways similar to Erikson's. The social-learning view agrees that establishing an identity may be difficult, but not because it is an intrinsic crisis of adolescence. Social-learning theorists attribute the difficulty to the many opportunities offered by our society, coupled with the complex and often conflicting demands placed on adolescents. But in more traditional societies, where adolescents know, and expect to fulfill, an unambiguous adult role, a crisis is less expected. ■ Figure 12.17

ADULTHOOD

Adulthood, like the other age sequences, is both a biological and a social concept. Biologically it is specified by reproductive capacity. In some cultures social adulthood comes with biological maturity, but in most industrialized societies, adulthood follows some years of adolescence, and is marked by social and financial independence.

Our society's specification of when adulthood occurs is somewhat mixed: Young people can be soldiers several years before they can legally buy alcohol in many states, for example. The traditional age of 21 is often used, but subpopulations may mark the occasion in particular ways earlier or later—as graduating from high school or from medical school, for example.

Physical Adulthood

The end of adolescence marks the beginning of adulthood, which for the healthy can continue with relatively little change for 30 years or more. In evolutionary terms, however, early adulthood is the vital period. For any species, once the next generation has been conceived and raised to its own age of independence, the prior generation has done its part. Even if it required as much as 17 years for our ancestors to reach puberty, within a few years after that the children of the next generation would be old enough to stand a chance of survival. Thus a 25- or 30-year life span might be enough for a species such as ours to survive. Therefore, even what we now consider middle age is more a contemporary phenomenon than a historical one. For most of the history of our species, few people ever reached age 45.

Physically, the period of adulthood is a relatively constant one. Some reflexes slow down, but skilled performances typically improve with practice. So whether a person gets better or worse at some motor

a

b

Figure 12.17 ■ Adolescence and early adulthood are times of seeking a sense of identity and of developing relationships with the opposite sex. (a) An antiwar marcher symbolically states his identity as a seeker of peace by putting pink carnations in the rifles of Army guards at the Pentagon (1967). (b) Developing your own identity and personal relationships can be difficult in a crowded society.

(**a,** © Bernie Boston; **b,** Ralph Crane from Black Star) task depends on the particular demands of the task. A similar pattern exists for the physiology of cognitive performances. The speed of perceptual processes, and perhaps some thinking, slows somewhat with age, but mental skills developed through experience and practice often make up for it. Thus in raw physical prowess and speed of perceptual response, late adolescence or early adulthood marks a peak. But for any complex physical and mental activity, the trade-off of experience versus speed may yield a balance or even improvement for a number of years.

Cognitive and Moral Adulthood

Piaget said that most people achieve the last major stage in cognitive development in adolescence; thus cognitive development during adulthood is merely a refining of the content of formal operations.

Kohlberg's stages are less directly tied to age and less universally achieved than Piaget's. Piaget felt that most adults in the United States reach the formal operational stage; Kohlberg believes that most do *not* reach the upper two moral stages. (For convenience of presentation, Kohlberg's Stages 5 and 6 were shown in Table 12.1 as occurring in young adulthood and middle age, but this is not a very secure generalization. They may be achieved earlier or never.)

Kohlberg's Stages 5 and 6 are at what he calls the postconventional or principled level. They require fully elaborated formal operational thought, but may not occur even then. Our government is founded on postconventional morality—the Constitution is a Stage 5 document—but most people have not reached that level and pay only lip service to its institutions. As Kohlberg notes, whenever the Gallup Poll tries circulating the Bill of Rights as a petition, most people refuse to sign it (1975).

The Stage 5 morality of the Constitution has a social-contract, legalistic orientation. Right actions are defined in terms of both individual rights and standards that have been agreed upon by the whole society. Personal values and opinions are recognized as relative, rather than absolute, and the emphasis is thus placed on procedural rules for reaching consensus (or if necessary achieving compromise). The result is legalistic in its focus on socially created laws, but has gone beyond the rigid adherence to authority of the law-and-order Stage 4.

Right behavior in Stage 6 goes beyond official United States morality to universal ethical or moral principles. These principles (such as respect for the value of life and the dignity of the individual) are not agreed-upon by consensus, but exist as universal truths. The problem with Stage 6 is that people may see different universal principles, and having passed beyond social consensus they will have no way of reconciling their differences. Kohlberg recognizes this possibility, but is not bothered by it. His definition of moral thinking focuses not on the outcome at any stage, but on the type of thought. Referring to universal moral principles would thus always be Stage 6, even if two Stage 6 people claimed different principles to be true. (Kohlberg believes that Stage 6 people will all reach the *same* set of universal principles, based on a concern for all life, and so forth.)

It is worth noting that not all psychologists interested in morality agree with Kohlberg's stages—or even that any stage concept is necessary. For a review of other possibilities, see M. L. Hoffman (1979).

Adult Personality

Freud, like Piaget, offers no further formal stages beyond adolescence. Particular psychosexual stages are relevant in adulthood only to the extent that an adult's personality has been fixated at a pregenital stage or has regressed to that stage under stress. Based as it was on the observation of psychiatric patients, Freud's scheme has relatively little to say about the development of psychologically healthy adults.

One of Erikson's significant contributions is his concern with development beyond adolescence. His stages include separate ones for early adulthood and middle age, as well as a final stage of aging. To Erikson, early adulthood (about ages 20 to 45) is the period of courtship and early family life, a time of forming both close friendships and relationships with the opposite sex. The psychosocial crisis of early adulthood is one of intimacy versus isolation. This is also a time of achieving the identity sought in adolescence and of engaging in productive work.

Middle adulthood (about ages 45 to 65) to Erikson is the culmination of all that has gone before. If the psychosocial crises of prior stages have been successfully overcome, the person can use the developed identity as a secure base for *generativity*, a looking beyond self to the society and world as a whole and to the generations to come that will inhabit it. Those who fail to establish a sense of generativity remain self-centered, and to Erikson self-absorption leads to stagnation. Like Scrooge in Dickens's *A Christmas Carol*, the middle-aged adult who has not achieved generativity may become both selfish and greedy.

Adult Social Learning

The social-learning view remains as it has been throughout development, one of increasing layers of learning through social example and reward. In adulthood, people continue to carry out the roles they have seen others perform and those they have been rewarded for imitating. Chance factors continue to play a substantial role as people meet and marry, find jobs and homes, and rear children. Often the adult adopts a role that has been familiar for many years, perhaps in imitation of a parent; this is sometimes seen in the children of professionals who enter the same profession. (In our upwardly mobile society, the children of working-class parents are often urged to "better themselves" by taking up a more prestigious occupation.)

One factor that has in the past strongly limited both career and avocation choices has been the sex specification attached to them. It is still true that some professions and hobbies are much more the province of one sex than the other, but this is changing. People who successfully occupy roles formerly the exclusive province of the opposite sex act as models for others, both their own children and other people. ■ Figure 12.18

"You may wonder why I'm demanding money from you under the threat of violence. Perhaps a few words about myself will help explain matters. I was born to a middle-class family forty-two years ago. . . ."

AGING

The process of aging begins at birth, in one sense, but by aging we usually mean a set of degenerative changes that begin to be obvious in middle age and become increasingly evident with each passing year. The visible signs of aging are familiar to everyone, and the performance deficits, both motor and intellectual, are embedded in popular folklore. Yet, surprisingly, why aging occurs remains unknown. Even how it occurs is largely a mystery, though the causes of some of the more evident changes are known.

The demographic data tell us that the United States population as a whole is growing older each year. As the needs of this population become more obvious, psychologists and others have taken more interest in this final stage of life (Birren, 1970). Most people attribute any aberrational behavior of the elderly to "growing old," but psychologists and physicians are finding a variety of both psychological and physical causes of unusual behaviors (Patrusky, 1982).

Physical Aging

All species show consistent life spans when reared in a benevolent environment. Those lifetimes may be measured in a few days or many years, but healthy members of the same species live to similar ages. In the wild, most individuals die far earlier than their possible life span. But those who survive to old age become progressively more frail and weak until they die from accident, disease, or other environmentally induced

problems. Rarely is it possible to specify that death occurred directly from aging. At least a few species, however, show a genetically structured deterioration ending in death. The Pacific salmon, for example, ages and dies within a few days of spawning. And in the octopus, the optic gland produces a hormone that seems to cause rapid aging; removing the optic gland substantially increases the life span—at least in females (Wodinsky, 1977).

Humans are no different from other species in some of these characteristics. If they remain healthy, they live approximately 70 to 80 years—but comparatively few live much beyond this age, regardless of their previous health. *Average* life expectancy has increased enormously in the last hundred years, but the maximum life span does not seem to have increased appreciably. In short, *more* people get older—but they don't get any older than the oldest of their ancestors did (Hayflick, 1975). Whether a genetic program for aging exists in humans (as it does in the salmon) remains an open question (Lints, 1978). The gradual physical deterioration of aging may instead be a passive process, simply the result of accumulated biochemical errors and breakdowns in cellular regeneration (Timiras, 1978).

As humans age, they get slower and weaker in motor responses. They require less food and less sleep. (In fact, studies with animals suggest that a reduced

Figure 12.18 ■ Many contemporary adults are exploring life roles, whether as hobbies or professions, that were until recently thought appropriate only for the opposite sex.
(**a,** Cary Wolinsky/Stock, Boston; **b,** Ellis Herwig/Stock Boston)

diet throughout life, as long as it is above the starvation level, can defer the aging process and prolong life; Levin et al., 1981; Weindruck & Walford, 1982). The sensory capabilities of the elderly gradually decline so that they see and hear increasingly poorly (Sekuler, 1980). Their bodies shrink in height and they may suffer bone deterioration and deformities, such as "dowager's hump," a back problem that post-menopausal women sometimes suffer (Marx, 1980c). At least some genetic programming is present in these changes. Dowager's hump and many other problems of aging are caused by changes in hormone levels after the end of the reproductive period. (Women cease to be fertile at menopause and their ovaries drastically reduce hormonal output. At least some men continue to be fertile throughout their life, but their hormone output also decreases.) It's possible that some of these

changes can be reduced or eliminated by supplemental hormones (Marx, 1979; Landfield et al., 1981).

It is *not* true, however, that the aging brain necessarily deteriorates. The notion that you lose a certain number of neurons with each passing year has never been proved and is almost certainly not true (Diamond, 1976, 1978). The number of dendrite branches reduces somewhat with aging (Buell & Coleman, 1979) but at least some of this may result from a restricted or deprived environment. In some animal models, brain neurotransmitters such as acetylcholine seem to decrease with age (Gibson et al., 1981), but other research has suggested that this may be influenced by the amount of choline in the diet (Bartus et al., 1980). All in all it seems likely that the normal brain, although it may suffer somewhat from poor diet or restricted activity, survives very well.

Figure 12.19 ■ According to Erikson, the last stage of life is marked by a review of the person's accomplishments. But the aging adult need not withdraw from further activities in order to do so. A continuing involvement with children often brightens the lives of both children and the elderly.

Why then is senility thought to be so much a characteristic of old age? Most people fear becoming senile, yet many treat the physically infirm elderly as if they were all intellectually deficient. Senility, more technically called **senile dementia,** is not the consequence of normal aging but of degenerative diseases (Henig, 1981). These diseases most often strike the elderly, but are not limited to them. Some 3 million Americans now suffer from senile dementia (Katz, 1980).

The chief culprit is Alzheimer's disease; among its neurological indicators is a dense tangle of neural fibers and a shortage of an enzyme necessary to produce acetylcholine (Kolata, 1981b; Perl & Brody, 1980). Alzheimer's patients may lose more than 75% of the neurons in the basal forebrain, an area connected to the hippocampus (Whitehouse et al., 1982).

This may account for their severe memory loss. But research on Alzheimer's disease is difficult. Animal research is not sufficient, and direct research with patients is legally and ethically questionable because they have lost the comprehension necessary to give an informed consent (Kolata, 1982a).

Other factors can also contribute to apparent senility. One reversible source of mental confusion results from poor blood flow to the brain because of deposits in the arteries (Benditt, 1977). Poor diet and sleeping habits in some elderly, combined with the use of many prescription and over-the-counter drugs, can also produce confusion and memory problems (R. J. Smith, 1979a). People taking 20 or 30 different drugs a day are not uncommon. Any two drugs taken together may have different effects than either alone and drugs often affect the elderly differently, so the potential for problems is evident.

Personality Development throughout Life

Of the stage theorists, only Erikson offers a specific focus on aging. For him, this last stage is marked by a psychosocial crisis of integrity versus despair. An individual's life achievements are nearing completion and there is probably time for reflection. If the individual can look back on a fulfilled life, the consequence is a sense of integrity and achievement. If reflection shows a life of missed opportunities and failure, with no time left to begin anew, the consequence is despair. (And no doubt, although this is not Erikson's focus, a person's general physical health may contribute to a sense of well-being or despair.) ■ Figure 12.19

Social learning theorists point out that the continuity seen through adult life reflects the consistency of social modeling and rewarding patterns of a given society. In a culture where age is revered, growing old will be different than in a culture in which the elderly are a nonproductive drain on scarce resources. And within the culture, organized social groups continue to help structure the behavior of the old, just as they once provided guidance for the child.

The challenge for each of the theories of development that we have reviewed is to explain both the similarities among individuals at each stage of life and the differences between them. So far, no single theory can do that satisfactorily, but each offers some useful insight into how children become the adults they do and how those adults live out their lives. Perhaps the future will see a synthesis of these views that will offer a more complete picture.

CHAPTER SUMMARY

1 Each zygote is shaped into a particular newborn during the nine months of prenatal development. A series of critical periods exist for different body structures; development failures during these periods cannot be made up later.

2 Several major views of human development are stage theories, proposing some sequence of development stages through which individuals pass in becoming adults.

3 Stage theories include Piaget's cognitive-stage theory and Kohlberg's moral-stage theory developed from it, Freud's psychosexual-stage theory, and Erikson's psychosocial-stage theory.

4 Social learning theory offers, in contrast, a non-stage view of development as the result of accumulated learning.

5 Infancy is marked by rapid physical maturation. To stage theorists, infancy precedes or lays the groundwork for later stages. One developmental issue of infancy is the question of whether infants become attached to their caretakers and the later influences this may have.

6 Childhood is marked by a slower physical growth rate. It is also the time for beginning to acquire the behavioral patterns that will be useful as adults, but different theorists specify these patterns and their sequence in different ways. One developmental issue of childhood concerns the question of whether children identify with adults, and what role this plays in their later behavior.

7 Adolescence is the period of renewed physical growth that terminates in physical adulthood. It is also a time of coming of age socially, of adopting adult behavior patterns and being given adult responsibilities. One developmental issue of adolescence concerns the origins and meaning of a person's identity.

8 Adulthood reflects all that has gone before, as well as new changes as the individual matures and then ages.

Adult personality characteristics are specified differently by the different theories, just as previous stages have been defined differently.

9 Aging represents a generalized but gradual reduction of physical capacities. The mental problems implied in the term *senile* have many causes, but are by no means an inevitable part of aging.

Further Readings

Direct translations of Piaget are often difficult to read; for general coverage of his theory, see a summary such as Ginsberg and Opper's *Piaget's Theory of Intellectual Development* (1979). For a variety of approaches to the issues of moral development, see Lickona's edited collection *Moral Development and Behavior: Theory, Research and Social Issues* (1976). For Freud and Erikson, see the references in this chapter and in Chapter 13. Jacobson's *Developmental Neurobiology* (1978) and Tanner's *Fetus into Man; Physical Growth from Conception to Maturity* (1978) provide further details on physical growth. For the period of infancy, see Willemsen's *Understanding Infancy* (1979). For childhood in general, there are many good references. Among them are a special issue of the *American Psychologist* (October 1979) and texts such as Bijou's *Child Development: The Basic Stage of Early Childhood* (1976) or Hall, Perlmutter, and Lamb's *Child Psychology Today* (1982). For the approach of one well-known psychologist who sometimes disagrees with the views of stage theorists such as Piaget, see Kagan's works cited in this chapter or his *Understanding Children* (1971). One of the most cited books in psychology is *Carmichael's Manual of Child Psychology;* the third edition is by Mussen (1970). For adulthood and aging, see Kalish's *Late Adulthood: Perspectives in Human Development* (1975) or Huyck and Hoyer's *Adult Development and Aging* (1982). Aging issues in particular are the topic of the collection edited by Poon, *Aging in the 1980s: Psychological Issues* (1980).

After class you meet a friend for coffee. He seems a bit subdued, so you ask what's wrong. "I just came from psychology class," he says, "and they told us today that our personality tests were phonies. Too bad. I was really hoping it would help me figure out what I want to do with my life." Because you're not so sure of your own personality attributes, much less your future goals, you press him for details. "Well, we all took this personality test and then later we got back the psychologist's evaluation—at least that's what they told us. It said I was somewhat insecure, though I often tried not to show it, and a bunch of other stuff. Really seemed to describe me pretty well. I was thinking of asking the psychologist for more details. But then today my professor told us we all got the same description. 'It's a repeat of a well-known study,' she says. 'The descriptions were taken from astrology books and are designed to fit any average undergraduate.' Now I don't know any more about myself than before." "Interesting study," you think, but you don't say it. "Too bad," you comment. "But maybe you could take one of those tests that tell you what occupation you might like. I hear the Career Center gives them, and I was thinking of maybe taking one myself." He seems cheered a bit by the idea. You're really not very sure what a test like that could tell you—especially after hearing his story—but you resolve to follow up on it anyway.

Psychologists who study personality find that most people already have ideas about what personality means and can even describe how their friends usually behave. The task of psychologists, however, is to find out how much of what people think they know about personality is true and how much is false. They also seek to specify what is true for all people, not just a few friends. In studying how psychologists have done at this task, we must begin, as usual, by defining what we mean more exactly than everyday language requires.

DEFINING PERSONALITY

Just what is a personality? Does everyone have one—and only one? We think of personality as how people behave or what they are like, but people are often quite different in different contexts: A person may be a dutiful child at home, a strong leader at work, even a criminal in another context, and so forth. Is that one personality or many? (This question is not just an academic exercise. Acquaintances of patients with the pathological condition termed *multiple personality* are often unaware of the multiple lives; see Chapter 15.) These are only some of the questions that must be answered to define personality formally.

Personality

In general, psychologists define a **personality** as the total of a person's characteristic ways of dealing with the world. Some psychologists follow the behavioral tradition first popularized by Watson and define personality in terms of overt behaviors. Others refer to internal states or dispositions, which they infer from observed behavior.

These inferred dispositions potentially offer the same advantages in summarizing and predicting behavior as concepts such as hunger. But using inferred dispositions to define personality can also produce a kind of circular logic called the **nominal fallacy**, or *naming error*. Consider the personality trait of *honesty*. You watch a woman behave honestly, then say that she must be honest; the trait of honesty is thus inferred from behavior. Yet *honesty* may also be used to explain that same behavior: If asked why the woman behaved as she did, you say it is because she's honest. But you cannot explain what you saw merely by naming it. Honesty may in fact be a personality trait, but we must be careful how we define it and must always remember that it is inferred. If we allow our description, or name, to seem to be a cause, we commit the nominal fallacy. ■ Figure 13.1

Whenever we use behaviors to infer internal dispositions that are not directly measurable, we risk letting the name become an explanation. Most contemporary personality theorists are very careful in their definitions and use of inferred constructs; you should also be careful, in your study of these theories, to avoid the nominal fallacy.

Theories of Personality

A confusing mixture of information about personality comes from our parents, schools, religious institutions, the media, and other sources; we try to use it to understand what people are like and why. Psychologists call the result of our amateur attempts to make sense of this information **implicit personality theories** (Schneider, 1973). Everyone is likely to have ways of explaining people's behavior, but most people have not organized and formalized their personality theories; these remain implicit, showing up, for example, in answers to questions such as whether people are innately trustworthy or innately treacherous.

In contrast to implicit theories, formal personality theories are carefully thought out and then exactly and publicly stated; they are subject to more exacting criticism than are implicit theories. Furthermore, formal theories are put to scientific test through their ability to predict behavior. Each theory is used to generate testable predictions about behavior; the success or failure of those predictions is used to support or discredit the theory—rarely the case with implicit theories.

The task faced by each formal theory of personality is in a sense the task of all of psychology: to explain the behavior of any given human. Part of the explanation will focus on similarities among all humans, or among groups of them. Why do New Yorkers speak with a recognizable accent? Why do the Australian aborigines hunt with boomerangs? But the more exacting task, of psychology as a whole and of personality theorists in particular, is to explain the details of individual differences. No two New Yorkers speak in exactly the same way—voiceprints are as distinctive as fingerprints—and probably no two aborigines hunt in exactly the same way. Hence in describing personality and in explaining where it comes from theorists must account for group similarities *and* individual differences.

Part of the difficulty in formally defining personality is that there is much everyday knowledge about general behavioral tendencies. The cold reading done by magicians (Chapter 10), for example, is based on their knowledge of the concerns of most people: It doesn't take much insight to tell a person "Your sexual development has caused you some difficulty" or "You've had some trouble with money lately." In the research mentioned at the beginning of the chapter, a lengthy paragraph of such truisms was built of excerpts from newsstand astrology books; students who were led to believe it was a description of their personality were frequently impressed at how accurately it described them (Ulrich et al., 1963). In fact it did—but only in terms that were common to all college students; it told nothing about their particular personalities. It is useful to be able to state such generalities, but only as a first step. An effective personality theory must also be able to specify how each person in the group differs from the others and why.

This task is made more complex by the variation and flexibility of human behavior. People differ widely on a myriad of behaviors, yet each difference must be accounted for. And the same person changes over time, sometimes temporarily, sometimes permanently; these changes must also be explained by a theory of personality. In fact, the ideal personality theory would be able to tell you everything you ever wanted to know about any person's patterns of behavior. ■ Figure 13.2

Unfortunately, no current personality theory can do that. Each offers some leads toward a possible ideal theory, but each has drawbacks—and critics to point them out. It might seem that there should be more consensus than there is; psychologists have been working on personality theories for about 50 years and began with the accumulated wisdom of thousands more. But there are so many ways to approach the description and explanation of personality that it's difficult to compare different theories and reach decisive conclusions. In looking at some of the major approaches, about all we can do is point out some advantages and disadvantages of each approach and make a few suggestions about where they might go in the near future.

Assessment of Personality

If a theory of personality can describe what personalities are like, it may be able to measure them in some way. And, in fact, most personality theories do offer suggestions for the measurement, or **assessment,** of personality. Personality assessment is to some extent separate from personality theorizing, however. Some forms of assessment, for example, seek only to measure behaviors that imply other behaviors, without necessarily explaining where these behaviors come from or why they are related. Hence personality assessment is often discussed as a separate topic from personality theorizing. We will thus consider the various techniques of personality assessment only after we have discussed five major theoretical approaches. A particularly important form of assessment, intelligence testing, will be discussed in the next chapter.

Five Approaches to Personality

We will look at five general approaches to personality: Starting with some biological approaches and trait theories, we will then consider the personality-theory aspects of the psychoanalytic, behavioral, and humanistic perspectives. Some of these approaches include more than one recognized formal theory, but they share enough concepts to be grouped together. Since the task of personality theories is essentially the task of psychology as a whole, it should not surprise you to find that the major contemporary personality theories are related to the general perspectives first noted in Chapter 1. Only trait theories are not also a general perspective. Unlike theories in many areas of psychology, by the way, most personality theories are so identified with the names of the theorists who developed them that it makes sense to use these names to identify the theories, and not the formal names.

THE BIOLOGICAL APPROACH

The idea that different personality types are based on innate biological factors is one of the oldest views of personality. The proposals of such theories have often been utterly wrong, but as knowledge of biological and psychological processes has improved, so have biologi-

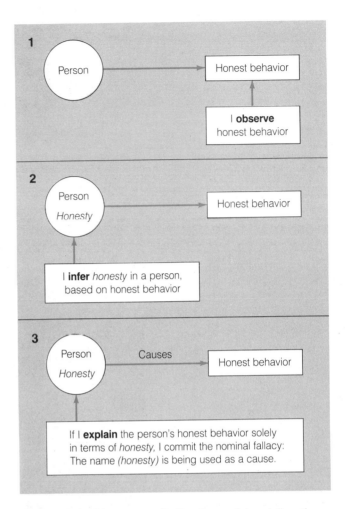

Figure 13.1 ■ Many personality theories use internal dispositions that are inferred from behavior, such as *honesty*. These are often useful summaries, but they can also easily lead to the nominal fallacy.

cal personality theories. Both the proposed mechanisms and ways of assessing them have changed over time, from views that now seem ludicrous to contemporary approaches based on genetic analysis and carefully observed behavior.

There have been at least three major biological approaches, focusing on body types, brain areas, and genetic influences. We'll look at them in that order.

Body Types

The suggestion that humans have a few basic body types and that each body type corresponds to a personality type dates at least to the Greek philosophers. The first modern attempt to develop a body-type classification scheme for personality analysis was that of Kretschmer (1925), who believed that he had isolated three body types: one tall and thin, one muscular, and

Figure 13.2 ■ The task of a personality theory is to explain how people come to behave in the ways they do, including why they are alike in some ways and different in others. What similarities and differences would you expect to find in the behavior of these people, and why? In answering such questions you use your own implicit personality theory as a guide.

(top left, Betsy Cole/Stock, Boston; top right, Frank Siteman/Stock, Boston; center left, J. Albertson/Stock, Boston; center right, Donald Dietz/Stock, Boston; bottom, Stock, Boston) one rounded and overweight. Kretschmer then sought to relate these body types to personality, primarily in terms of the major mental illnesses of his day. Kretschmer's work has had little direct impact on personality theory, but a few other psychologists have continued to explore the possible relationships of body type and personality. The best known of these is William Sheldon (1899–   ), whose theory is known as *somatotyping* (Sheldon & Stevens, 1942). Sheldon based his approach on three categories similar to Kretschmer's: Sheldon's *ectomorph* is thin and delicate, his *mesomorph* square and muscular, and his *endomorph* soft and rounded.

Sheldon also developed a three-part personality classification related to his somatotypes. He characterized the thin ectomorph as having a need for privacy and restraint, the athletic mesomorph a love of adventure and a lust for power, and the round endomorph a love of eating and physical comfort (Sheldon & Stevens, 1942). Sheldon's personality theory has never been very popular, although many people know something about his type categories and the behaviors supposedly associated with them. Sheldon has some supporters, who argue that his theory has not been given a fair chance (Lindzey, 1967). But critics argue that his theory is flawed in many respects (Humphreys, 1957), and few psychologists use it.

The initial appeal of such body-type theories is that they offer an apparently simple way of coding people that often seems to fit with everyday knowledge. But people do not fit exactly into a few types and coding schemes such as Sheldon's quickly become cumbersome: Because it assigns a 1 to 7 value on each of three types, his system actually offers a total of 343 different types rather than three. When the difficulties of similarly summarizing personality patterns are added, the theory's problems are magnified enormously. It may be that body type is in some way associated with personality, but no such relations have yet been clearly demonstrated. And if some association is demonstrated, it could as easily be a learned stereotype as an innate pattern: Endomorphs might learn to conform to society's view of jolly fat people, for example. (For an update of Sheldon's work and some other body-type theories, see Shontz, 1977.)

Brain Areas

Another very old view relates personality to the shape of the face and head. This view took several forms before it was replaced by the study of functional brain areas. *Physiognomy,* for example, sought to explain a person's *character* (what we now call *personality*) in terms of facial appearance. A high forehead supposedly indicated a noble character, a lower forehead and thick eyebrows indicated criminality, and so forth. Physiognomy was never a very scientific approach, and has long been discredited by serious investigators. But it seems to have a popular appeal, and books on versions of physiognomy still crop up (Brandt, 1980).

An approach that did seek to be scientific and that had lasting repercussions was **phrenology,** the "reading" of bumps on the head. Devised in the early 1800s by Franz Joseph Gall and J. G. Spurzheim, phrenology made several critical assumptions—all of which were wrong. First, phrenology adapted an existing notion of "faculties," mental attributes such as cautiousness, combativeness, hope, and self-esteem. Originally 27 such faculties were said to make up a person's character; others were added later. These faculties are not now considered useful ways of summarizing personality characteristics, so we could consider that first step to be wrong. Gall and Spurzheim also assumed that these faculties were located in particular brain areas and that the size of the areas reflected the strength of the faculty. That part is clearly wrong, too. Even if you consider hope, for example, to be a character trait, you cannot find it located at one spot in the brain. Their final incorrect assumption was that the shape of the outer surface of the skull accurately mirrored the shape of the brain. Based on this string of faulty assumptions, phrenologists claimed to assess a person's character by reading his or her bumps—running their hands over a person's skull, noting the projections, and estimating the strength of the corresponding faculties. Bump reading by traveling phrenologists became very popular in the 19th century (Davies, 1955). As with contemporary pseudosciences such as biorhythms (Chapter 7), phrenology was criticized by some but believed uncritically by many.

Phrenology would now be only another 19th-century curiosity except for the part it played in advancing the biological study of brain areas (Krech, 1962). Observation of the effects of brain injury had originally been one of Gall's inspirations, and even though his interpretation was wrong, its popularity spurred interest in investigating the brain areas responsible for behavior patterns. The discoveries of Broca's and Wernicke's language areas followed (Chapter 10), as did understanding of other critical areas.

The fact that brain damage could affect overall character as well as specific capabilities was first noted in the 1860s in the dramatic case of Phineas Gage. Gage was the young foreman of a railroad construction crew whose job included tamping down explosives with an iron bar. The explosive went off prematurely on one occasion, blowing the bar up and completely through the left side of Gage's head (Blakemore,

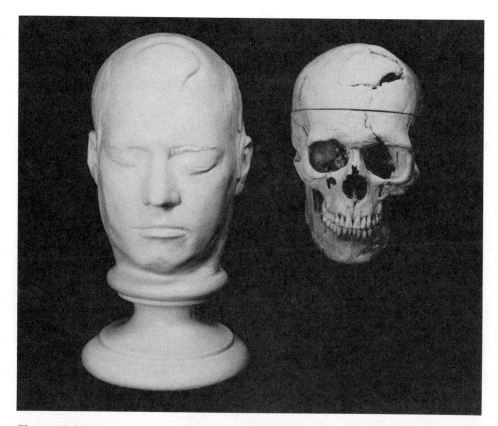

Figure 13.3 ■ The life mask and the skull of Phineas Gage, a 19th-century construction foreman whose personality seemed permanently altered when a $3\frac{1}{2}$-foot iron rod, driven by an explosion, passed upward completely through the left front of his head.

(Mr. A. Ley, Harvard Medical School, Boston)

1977). That Gage survived, without ever losing consciousness, was remarkable in itself, as the damage was quite severe. But it was not Gage's survival that earned him a place in history; it was the fact that his personality changed. The formerly responsible foreman became argumentative and untrustworthy; he spent the rest of his life drifting from place to place, often displaying his injury and the bar that caused it as a fairground attraction. ■ Figure 13.3

Some of Gage's personality changes may not have been the direct effects of his brain injury: He was no doubt frightened and upset by his near brush with death, he had a long convalescence in which to contemplate his life, and so forth. But the changes were widely reported as due to the brain injury, and his case strengthened the search for the brain areas associated with personality. That search still continues. One psychologist has written at length about his observations of the personality changes in brain-damaged patients, for example, and has advocated the study of such patients to other psychologists (Gardner, 1975).

Genetics

The idea that some personality factors might be innate also has a lengthy history. Beginning with the publication of Darwin's (1859) theory of evolution, the possible adaptive values of character traits began to be considered. These were initially thought to be the outward behavior that reflected **instincts,** or innate behavioral tendencies. Theorists such as McDougall (1908) listed the instincts that they believed characterized humans, just as biologists listed animal instincts. But the term *instinct* fell victim to the nominal fallacy, as theorists sought to use it as an explanation: "Birds fly south for the winter *because* they have an instinct to do so" or "People are aggressive *because* they have an aggressive instinct." Ethologists later adopted the more exact term *species-specific behavior*. But many psychologists merely dismissed instinct theories and sought other explanations, often learning-based ones, following Watson's lead.

As the principles of genetics became known, they

offered a physiological basis for what had been called instinctive behavior, and some psychologists began to examine whether personality traits might be inherited. The genetic basis of personality has never become a major theoretical area, but a few psychologists are studying genetic factors. Some have found evidence of temperament differences soon after birth, for example, that they believe contribute to later personality characteristics (Thomas et al., 1970). Others have compared the measured personality traits of twins, finding that identical twins have more similar traits than fraternal twins, as their greater genetic similarity would predict (Thompson, 1968). ■ Table 13.1

Twin studies have also played a substantial role in the study of intelligence, a characteristic many psychologists consider an important part of personality. We will look at some results of this work in Chapter 14. But few researchers have pursued the genetics of other personality attributes (McClearn, 1962). One who has is Cattell (1982), whose work in trait theory we will look at later. Another is Scarr, who has suggested that genetic patterns affect not only IQ but also such personality characteristics as vocational interests and even prejudices (Scarr & Weinberg, 1978). Some of the genetics and personality work that has been done is summarized in Loehlin and Nichols (1976). Perhaps the closest to a genetic personality theory has been the ambitious attempt by Thompson (1968) to develop an interactionist framework for integrating the past and any future findings of genetic and environmental influences.

THE TRAIT APPROACH

Defining Traits

A **trait** is a reasonably persistent attribute or characteristic of a person, usually expressed as an adjective: loyal or diligent, for example. How persistent an attribute must be is open to interpretation, but terms that obviously refer to short-term states are excluded. To describe a person as tall, graceful, or honest, for example, is to refer to different kinds of traits. Describing

that person as angry would normally not be a trait, because *angry* usually implies a short-term state. (It could be used as a trait, as in the phrase "angry young man," if it described a persistent condition.)

Obviously, many words are trait names. Allport and Odbert (1936) listed nearly 18,000 English words that they felt qualified as traits, and the author of one personality text found that approximately 7% of the 1000 most common English words were trait names (Cartwright, 1974). Cartwright also examined infrequently used words; using the criterion that the word must fit the sentence "The person is _____ ," he listed the first trait name for each letter of the alphabet in a list of infrequent words. The result gives a good idea of the full range of trait terms in English: "The person is abrasive, beefy, cataleptic, diabetic, egotistic, fleshless, ghoulish, happy-go-lucky, ill-mannered, lecherous, made-up, neurasthenic, openhanded, pharisaical, ritualistic, salacious, telepathic, un-American, vulpine, weak-kneed, yeasty, and zestful" (Cartwright, 1974, pp. 238–239).

The number of trait names in our language shows the widespread use of such terms to describe personality. A few well-chosen adjectives often seem to portray a person quite accurately, at least at first glance. But a closer look reveals many problems for the professional trait researcher. How many of these nearly 18,000 terms are really different and how many are merely synonyms? Are some more basic or important than others? Do the most important terms apply to all people all the time?

Each of the formal trait theories in psychology seeks its own answers to these and related questions. Typically some technique is used to obtain a short list of what are presumed to be key traits or dimensions. The dimension name actually refers to a pair of traits denoting the two ends of the dimension. *Honesty*, for example, is the name of the trait dimension that extends from extreme honesty to extreme dishonesty.

Ways are then established by which a person can be scored on each trait, and some summary of the person's personality is made, based on these scores. To be useful theoretically, such trait scores must be able to predict behavior at other times and in other situations

Table 13.1 ■ Correlations of Personality Traits for Twins

Twin Group	Number of Twins	Neuroticism	Self-sufficiency	Introversion	Dominance	Self-confidence	Sociability
Identical	= 55	.63	.44	.50	.71	.58	.57
Fraternal (same sex)	= 44	.32	.14	.40	.34	.20	.41
(opposite sex)	= 34	.18	.12	.18	.18	.07	.39

From W. R. Thompson, "Development and the Biophysical Bases of Personality" in E. F. Borgatta and W. W. Lambert (Eds.), *Handbook of Personality Theory and Research*, 1968, Rand McNally. Reprinted by permission of the author.

than those of the original trait assessment. But despite years of work by a number of trait theorists, it remains questionable whether any trait theory can offer useful predictions.

One major critic of trait theories, Walter Mischel (1968), suggested that perhaps seeking to measure traits was an inappropriate way of studying personality and that traits might never be able to describe personality precisely enough to have predictive value. There are two important criteria for a useful trait approach, according to Mischel. The first is that traits used should be **reliable,** that is, consistent over time for the same person: A person who scores high in honesty today should score similarly highly next week. But measured traits should also be consistent across situations. This is more an indicator of **validity,** or whether a test in fact measures what it claims to measure. (We will examine measures of reliability and validity in more detail in Chapter 14.) Mischel criticized trait theories in both of these areas.

Many psychologists were convinced by Mischel's arguments, but supporters of trait approaches rallied to prove him wrong (Fishbein & Ajzen, 1975). Mischel (1981a) now agrees that the reliability of traits has been better established since publication of his 1968 book. Indeed, impressive reliability has been demonstrated for some trait measures (Ajzen & Fishbein, 1977; Block & Block, 1980). But validity has not been well established. Whether the most honest person in one situation will also behave most honestly in another situation remains an open question. This person/situation debate pits those who believe that internal traits are the most important determiners of behavior against those who believe that external situations are; this debate continues to be a major unresolved controversy (Mischel, 1981b). ■ Research Controversy: Do Personality Traits or Situations Control Behavior?

Three Trait Theories

A number of psychologists have made trait analysis a major part of their life's work. Three of the most influential have been Gordon Allport, Raymond Cattell, and Hans Eysenck.

Allport   The first comprehensive and objective trait theory in psychology was that of **Gordon Allport** (1897–1967). Raised in Montezuma, Indiana, Allport has been described as an "all-American boy" (Abramson, 1980, p. 142). After college, he went to Europe and managed to obtain an interview with Freud in about 1919. As Allport (1968) later described the exchange, he was struck by how Freud's search for hidden motives caused him to overlook Allport's obvious ones. ■ Notable Quote: Allport on Freud's Interpretation of Motives

Later, as a personality theorist, Allport sought to avoid the kinds of interpretive problems he had seen in his visit with Freud. He set out to build an objective approach that would act as a framework for writing the life history of any individual. Basing his approach on the common assumption of personality traits, Allport set out to refine the general concept of a trait to a form that could be objectively defined and measured.

First he and Odbert (1936) investigated English trait names, finding, as noted earlier, nearly 18,000. Then they categorized these terms into several groups. According to Allport, real traits were generalized, consistent, stable modes of response to the environment. Other descriptive terms that he felt were *not* traits described temporary states of mind (e.g., *frantic*), character evaluations (e.g., *worthy*), or physical qualities (e.g., *tall*). Allport also put into a nontrait classification all terms referring to abilities and skills, such as *gifted,* although these are included in personality by many other theorists.

The remaining trait names offered a set of possible terms by which any individual's personality could be described. Each person, Allport (1961) believed, could be characterized by a very few *cardinal traits* and a limited number of *central traits*. Many other *secondary traits* might also describe that person, but would not distinguish him or her from other people.

Allport (1966a) always considered traits not as mere inferred constructs but as real nervous-system structures that played a dynamic role in behavior. Traits, he said, were "neuropsychic structures" that rendered different stimuli functionally equivalent insofar as responses to them were concerned (Allport, 1961). A trait of self-deprecation, for example, might cause a wide variety of events to be interpreted along similar lines, summarized something like "I made a mistake again." The quite different situations thus would be rendered functionally equivalent by the trait, in that the person treated the situations as if they were the same.

In his study of traits, Allport focused on describing the personality of a single person. In pursuing that goal he also made extensive use of first-person documents (Allport, 1942), and even published a book-long interpretation of 301 letters written by one woman over a 12-year span (Allport, 1965). Allport concluded from such research that each person's personality was a well-integrated whole; listing a person's traits was inadequate unless you also specified how they fitted together. He believed that each personality is a well-furnished system that brings many personal traits into each situation rather than simply responding to situational demands. In this, he clearly differed from theorists such as Mischel.

Allport also rejected Freud's emphasis on childhood events, arguing that events in the present were

RESEARCH CONTROVERSY

Do personality traits or situations control behavior?

A key assumption in the concept of personality is that people exhibit consistent patterns of behavior. If they did not, the term *personality* would have no meaning. Furthermore, these patterns of behavior must somehow arise from within the individual. They can represent prior learning from the environment, but must be internalized; we do not consider individual responses that arise primarily from current constraints to be personality traits. If a bank robber with a gun tells everyone in the bank to be quiet, we do not take their silence as indicative of a personality trait. Only when a person tends to say little regardless of the circumstances do we label him or her *taciturn*.

A major problem in trait theory has long been how to establish and measure the consistency in behavior that is assumed to exist. Each theory has sought to define basic traits so that a person's score on that trait consistently predicts other similar behavior. But virtually since the beginning of the trait approach it has been recognized that situational differences also influence how people behave. In a series of studies, for example, Hartshorne and May (1928) found that honesty in children as measured in one situation did not predict honest behavior in another situation very well: Lying did not necessarily correlate well with cheating, and neither correlated well with taking money left unattended. And behavior on a single dimension, such as lying, was not necessarily the same in interactions with peers as it was in interactions with adults.

Trait theorists have long sought to minimize situational effects on behavior by seeking newer and better ways to measure traits. They have continued to assume that the consistency is there, if they can only find the appropriate way to define and measure it. But Mischel's 1968 book attacked this basic assumption. Despite the efforts of trait theorists, he noted, the best studies reached only about .30 correlations between measured traits and predicted behavior. This .30 value, which explains only a small fraction of the observed variations in behavior, Mischel termed the **personality coefficient.** Its persistent low value, he claimed, was evidence that the basic assumption was faulty, not the measurement techniques. According to Mischel, the most important reason why people's behavior varies is that they find themselves in various situations. The apparent consistency of everyday behavior derives largely from a consistency of everyday situations, he said. The same people put into different situations ought to be expected to behave differently.

Mischel's arguments were widely accepted, especially by behaviorally oriented and social psychologists, who emphasize the effects of situational variables. But personality psychologists, most of whom believe in traits or other internal dispositions, only redoubled their efforts to find the consistency in people. Research since 1968 has yielded several tentative conclusions.

It does seem to be true that a variety of factors lead us as individuals to see more consistency in the people we know than may be the case. Our implicit personality theories lead us to expect consistency, and our tendency for cognitive consistency in general encourages us to find evidence for consistency in others' behavior. Furthermore, we typically encounter the people we know in similar situations each time, including the fact that we are always present. We don't know what those people are like in other situations when we are not around. Thus we are easily convinced that people have consistent personalities, whether they do or not.

But it also seems to be true that trait descriptions may prove to be useful and that better definitions and measurements of traits may yield better results than the .30 personality coefficient. Some researchers have suggested pooling the measures, for example (combining several examples of them and using the average). Such pooling substantially improves the consistency of the results (Epstein, 1979, 1980; Fishbein & Ajzen, 1975).

Another approach that may improve results is to look for consistency in different traits for different people, rather than using the same set of traits for all people. Bem and Allen (1974), for example, asked students to assess themselves as to which traits were consistently true for them. They found that students who described themselves as consistently friendly, for example, did behave consistently with respect to measures of that trait. Bem and Allen's results suggest that one reason for the persistent .30 personality coefficient is that each attempt to measure traits includes some people for whom the trait is consistent and others for whom it is not. Only by sorting on appropriate traits for these other subjects would you find their consistency.

Mischel (1981a) has admitted that pooling raises the reliability of measured traits, and that other procedures may improve predictability. But he has also suggested that another direction for further research, the exploration of cognitive approaches, may be more fruitful (Mischel, 1973, 1979). Cantor and Mischel (1979a), for example, worked on a new way of defining particular traits: Rather than using all possible equivalent measures of a trait such as friendliness, they looked for the measures that are most prototypical of the trait. Prototypicality is based on the work of cognitive psychologists who find, for example, that a robin represents a more typical bird for most people than an ostrich or penguin (Chapter 11). Similarly, some measures of friendliness may be more consistent because they are perceived by people as typically friendly behavior. Other possible measures may actually be inappropriate if they are not what most people have in mind by *friendliness*.

Other researchers have sought to reconcile trait and situational differences by looking primarily at the interactions between traits and situations (Bowers, 1973; Endler, 1977). Such research suggests that *honesty* or *friendliness* or other trait behavior depends most strongly on which people are in which situations rather than just the people or just the situations alone.

Perhaps such approaches will finally reconcile the trait/situation controversy.

most important. In his focus on the present, Allport developed the concept of **functional autonomy** of motives: Motives may have been learned in the past, but are now functionally autonomous, that is, operate in the present. Such motives can best be understood in terms of their present role, he felt, not in terms of their origins. This concept of functional autonomy of motives is often used by other theorists, in motivation as well as personality.

Allport anticipated later controversies and influenced later theorists in several other ways. He was the first personality theorist to emphasize objective, quantifiable techniques. His suggestion that different traits were important for different people anticipated one way of dealing with the trait/situation contro-

versy, as in the Bem and Allen study (1974). His emphasis on each individual's distinctiveness in some ways anticipated Carl Rogers's focus on the self. And his inclusion of self-consciousness as a relevant variable even anticipated the current inclusion of cognitive elements in personality.

Critics have suggested that Allport's emphasis on traits ignored important situational influences and that his focus on detailed analysis of an individual, often from personal documents, made his approach less objective than he claimed. But his influence as a theorist is not questioned. (For a review of Allport's work, see Evans, 1971.)

Cattell The first theorist to base a theory on formal mathematical analysis of trait dimensions was **Raymond Cattell** (1905–   ). Cattell was born and educated in England, where he first studied chemistry and physics; when he later turned to psychology, he brought to it a physical-sciences approach. His research on intelligence led to an invitation to Columbia University. After teaching at several universities in the United States, he established his own center, the Institute for Research on Morale and Adjustment in Boulder, Colorado.

Cattell's trait theory has been built around the use of **factor analysis,** a mathematical technique devised by Charles Spearman, the person responsible for many of the mathematical approaches in psychology. Factor analysis offers a way of analyzing a few common factors, or tendencies, from within a larger number of variables. Cattell also reviewed and categorized a large number of traits, seeking the most basic and useful ones, and developed a scheme for classifying them. Some traits are **surface traits** visible to any observer, he suggested, and others are **source traits,** the underlying structures actually responsible for the surface traits. Cattell's *constitutional traits* derived largely from heredity, and his *environmental traits* largely from learning. Several other categories divided traits in still other ways. Most of his work, however, focused on the development of a short list of source traits, using factor analysis of large clusters of surface traits (Cattell, 1950). He listed 16 basic source traits in descending order of importance. In accordance with the notion of a trait as a personality dimension, Cattell labeled these 16 traits by words representing the two ends of the dimension (see Figure 13.11).

Cattell has also maintained an interest in intelligence: His concepts of fluid and crystallized intelligence are discussed in Chapter 14. He has also gradually expanded his view of personality to incorporate situational, motivational, and genetic factors (Cattell, 1957, 1982).

Both Cattell's views and his factor-analytic approach have been influential, triggering the wide-

NOTABLE QUOTE
Allport on Freud's interpretation of motives

❝ Soon after I had entered the famous red burlap room with pictures of dreams on the wall, he summoned me to his inner office. He did not speak to me but sat in expectant silence for me to state my mission. I was not prepared for silence and had to think fast to find a suitable conversational gambit. I told him of an episode on the tram car on my way to his office. A small boy about four years of age had displayed a conspicuous dirt phobia. He kept saying to his mother, "I don't want to sit there . . . don't let that dirty man sit beside me." To him everything was *schmutzig* (filthy). His mother was a well-starched *Hausfrau,* so dominant and purposive looking that I thought the cause and effect apparent.

When I finished my story Freud fixed his kindly therapeutic eyes upon me and said, "And was that little boy you?" Flabbergasted and feeling a bit guilty, I contrived to change the subject. While Freud's misunderstanding of my motivation was amusing, it also started a deep train of thought. I realized that he was accustomed to neurotic defenses and that my manifest motivation (a sort of rude curiosity and youthful ambition) escaped him. For therapeutic progress he would have to cut through my defenses, but it so happened that therapeutic progress was not here an issue. **❞**

From G. Allport in *A History of Psychology in Autobiography,* Vol. 5, 1967, 383–384, E. G. Boring and G. Lindzey (eds.), Appleton-Century Crofts. Reprinted by permission of Irvington Publishers, Inc.

spread use of mathematical models in personality research and in other areas of psychology, including motivation (Cattell, 1966). Critics of Cattell have also focused on his use of factor analysis, however, arguing either that the basic data are questionable (Becker, 1960) or that his use of the technique is flawed. Cattell's approach has many imitators, but whether his 16 factors are really the basic traits—or even valid personality components at all—is still an open question.

Eysenck **Hans J. Eysenck** (1916–   ) has been both a serious personality theorist and a bit of a gadfly to the psychiatric establishment. Born in Germany, Eysenck later moved to England, where he attended college and has lived since. Like Cattell, he became interested in statistical approaches through Spearman's work. Eysenck received his Ph.D. in 1940 and was assigned to a hospital for the duration of World War II, where he saw large numbers of patients with symptoms deriving from wartime stresses. This experience interested him in the personality patterns that might lead to an ability to cope with continued stress.

Eysenck has developed a theory of personality traits that includes some elements obviously derived from his work with psychiatric patients. But he is also an iconoclast and critic of psychiatry. He is well known for his biting critiques of techniques that he considers less than fully objective, such as the projective tests for assessing personality that we examine later in the chapter. He has also achieved wide renown for his claim that psychotherapy is, in general, no more effective than no treatment at all (Eysenck, 1952, 1966b). Eysenck has seemed relatively unconcerned over the controversy this claim has created, taking himself no more seriously than he has taken what he considers the pretensions of some psychiatrists (Eysenck, 1972).

One thing Eysenck does take very seriously is psychology, both as an area for research and as a body of knowledge to be freely provided to anyone who might be interested. His popularly oriented books on intelligence and personality are not as controversial as his attacks on psychiatry, but they are viewed by some psychologists as unprofessional (Eysenck, 1966a; Eysenck & Wilson, 1976).

In building his personality theory, Eysenck used factor analysis to define what he believes to be a basic set of three factors and an intelligence factor. The first two factors, **neuroticism** and **psychoticism,** are largely derived from his work with 700 patients at the wartime hospital (Eysenck, 1947). (*Neurotic* is a term that has been used to describe psychiatric patients who remain in touch with reality while suffering from some form of anxiety; *psychotic* has been used to describe seriously disturbed patients who have lost touch with reality. See Chapter 15.)

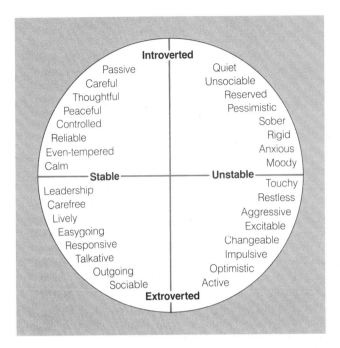

Figure 13.4 ■ Eysenck's framework for relating many personality traits to two key dimensions, introversion-extroversion and stability-instability.
(From *The Eysenck Personality Inventory* by H. J. Eysenck and S. B. G. Eysenck, Educational and Industrial Testing Service, 1963. Used by permission.)

Only the third dimension, **introversion-extroversion,** and the intelligence factor are conventional personality concepts. This third dimension describes a range from *introversion,* in which the person is focused inwardly, toward himself or herself, to *extroversion,* an orientation toward others and the external world. In studying nonpatient populatons Eysenck did not emphasize the psychoticism dimension, which applies mostly to the seriously disturbed, but he did use the neuroticism dimension. Together, the neuroticism and introversion-extroversion dimensions define a two-dimensional array offering a framework for other personality traits. Because of the psychiatric connotations of *neuroticism,* however, the label *stable-unstable* is often substituted (Eysenck & Eysenck, 1963). (Only those on the unstable end of the dimension are neurotic in the clinical sense.) ■ Figure 13.4

A person's personality structure, according to Eysenck (1960), is specified by his or her position on the two major dimensions and the intelligence factor. Subsidiary to this general description are personal habits and detailed specific responses. Eysenck also sought to define the dynamics of personality, drawing on other findings of experimental psychology as appropriate. We need not go into most of this, but it is worth noting that Eysenck considers his trait theory to be based on biology. In Eysenck's scheme learning may shape these factors, but the basic personality types are inherited (Eysenck, 1967).

The remaining three approaches—the psychoanalytic, behavioral, and humanistic ones—are basic perspectives that we first considered in Chapter 1 and have used in many chapters since. Hence only new elements or those of central relevance to personality will be explored here.

THE PSYCHOANALYTIC APPROACH

Freud has undoubtedly been one of the most influential theorists of human behavior to date. His psychoanalytic theory is simultaneously a theory of development, motivation, personality, and mental illness (1933, 1935, 1938). His procedure, psychoanalysis, is a specific form of psychotherapy, developed out of his experience with his patients (Jones, 1953–1957). Freud also had a number of followers, often referred to as **neo-Freudians**. Members of this group have expanded psychoanalytic theory by elaborating and modifying Freud's original proposals. Both Freud and his followers have had an important impact on theories of normal personality development.

Freud

The theoretical aspects of Freud's view of personality are actually an offshoot of his clinical practice. As Freud explored his patients' problems, he came to feel that all behaviors, no matter how seemingly insignificant, were motivated ones for all people. The title of one of Freud's books shows this perspective: *The Psychopathology of Everyday Life* (1901). This view of humanity as seen through its pathology has led to one major criticism of Freud: What may be true of disturbed people need not necessarily be true of normal ones.

Freud's view of motivation is basic to his approach to personality: He felt that the most important feature of human motivation was the need to suppress primitive instincts that humans share with animals (1935, 1938). Freud proposed two types of powerful innate motivations or instincts, those concerned with sex and aggression. He felt that these instincts, if unmodified, would dictate an unrestrained search for self-gratification, often to the detriment of others. Freud believed that it was a triumph of human society to have developed ways of teaching the young to restrain these instincts. External social rules against unrestrained sex and aggression were also needed, because childhood learning was not perfectly effective. But most behavior

that would be demanded by these innate instincts could be held in check by internalized rules. According to Freud, human cultures were thus precariously balanced systems for keeping in check the selfish motives of all of their members. Each member gave up some potential gains in exchange for greater safety. But societies must always be vigilant, he felt, lest the powerful instincts lying just below the surface of all humans erupt in wars or other violent acts.

Freud's views in their entirety are extremely elaborate and complex, but they are built up from a reasonably straightforward set of key ideas. Central to the psychoanalytic scheme is the concept that only a relatively small part of human mental activity is represented by conscious thought. Far more activity occurs at the preconscious and unconscious levels. **Preconscious** activities are processes that are not in consciousness at a given time but that can become conscious as needed: stored memories, for example. More important, however, are **unconscious** activities; these are largely a reservoir of instinctive urges, a biological residue of our evolution. Unconscious activities cannot directly enter consciousness, but can nevertheless influence behavior. The overall pattern has been compared to an iceberg, with the conscious level above water, the preconscious just below water, and the unconscious hidden in the depths.

Freud's view of how these levels interact in the adult personality is based on three inferred personality structures. The **id** is the representative of unconscious forces, the accumulation of the sex and aggression instincts. The id's impulses can be sensed but its mental workings are not available for conscious inspection. The **ego** is the largely conscious representative of rational thought. The newborn child reflects entirely id forces; the ego gradually develops through the child's interaction with the external world. The **superego** also develops through the child's experience; it represents the internalization of the parents' and society's prohibitions. Although Freud's idea was somewhat more complex, we can think of the superego as the conscience. ■ Figure 13.5

The interactions of these three elements of the adult personality determine behavior, according to Freud. The id selfishly presses its demands for action, with no regard for the consequences. It operates solely on the **pleasure principle,** seeking pleasure and avoiding pain, and functions through **primary process thinking,** which is irrational and highly motivated. Any evidence of such thinking suggests id forces at work. In contrast, the superego notes all of the reasons to restrain action. The more rational ego must then mediate between the conflicting demands of id and superego, seeking a course of action that will satisfy both. In doing so, the ego obeys the **reality**

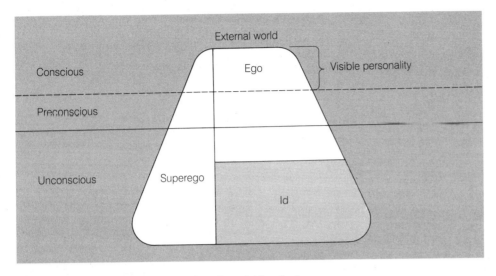

Figure 13.5 ■ Summary of Freud's view of mental functioning.
(Reprinted by permission from *Introduction to Psychology*, 3rd ed., by Dennis Coon. Copyright © 1983 by West Publishing Company. All rights reserved.)

principle, seeking to fit together id demands, superego limits, and the constraints of the external world through **secondary process thinking,** logical and realistic thinking that should be the primary pattern for a civilized person.

The adult pattern of interaction of id, ego, and superego represents the final outcome of the child's development through the series of psychosexual stages described in Chapter 12. Failure to progress to a higher stage leaves an adult **fixated** at one of the juvenile stages. An adult said to have an *anal personality*, for example, is fixated at the childhood anal stage: Such an adult would be excessively concerned with neatness, orderliness, and cleanliness. Under stress, adults might also **regress,** or return to an earlier stage.

A successful personality arrangement is one in which all the forces balance. The id's demands are perceived as the source of dynamic energy for all activity, termed **libido.** Ideal balance occurs when the ego can find an outlet for the libido that will satisfy the id while also meeting the limits of the superego. When this arrangement becomes unbalanced, however, problems result. An unrestrained id may produce a rapist or murderer, and an overly domineering superego may result in a person too inhibited to carry out daily activities. It is the task of society, acting through parents, to develop each child's ego and superego so as to balance the id and each other (Freud, 1930). It is the task of each adult to maintain that balance, and thus maintain mental health.

In the psychoanalytic view, one of the most important aspects of the adult personality is how it handles anxiety. The inherent conflict between id demands and superego constraints necessarily causes anxiety. A well-adapted personality deals effectively with this conflict and the potential anxiety in any of several ways, called **defense mechanisms** (Freud, 1946). One of the most effective is **sublimation,** the channeling of id demands into socially acceptable outlets. Both violent physical activity, such as boxing or automobile racing, and creative activity, such as painting, are considered socially acceptable ways of expressing id impulses. ■ Table 13.2

When the id/superego conflict is less well managed, however, problems occur. The anxiety may build noticeably, leading to an excessively anxious person. Or the id impulse may be **repressed,** pushed back into the unconscious and out of awareness; in this case, the anxiety will not be visible. Because the id impulses demand some channel of expression, however, they will continue to appear in disguised form in dreams, in slips of the tongue ("Freudian slips"), or in mental illness. ■ Table 13.3

Freud's views have been widely disseminated and extremely influential, in psychology and in many other fields. But have his ideas been supported by experimental tests? The short answer is that there have been far fewer careful experimental studies and far less support from those studies than the widespread belief in his views would suggest. A major review of the existing experimental studies found support for some of Freud's notions but not for others (Fisher & Greenberg, 1977). But the more elaborate answer requires that these results be put in context.

Freud was a clinician, not an experimenter. He felt that each person's personality dynamics are different and that well-concealed, powerful forces control them. These assumptions make Freud's system intrinsically

"VERY WELL, I'LL INTRODUCE YOU. EGO, MEET ID. NOW GET BACK TO WORK."

© 1983 by Sidney Harris

Table 13.2 ■ Defense Mechanisms

Denial of reality   Protecting self from unpleasant reality by refusal to perceive or face it

Fantasy   Gratifying frustrated desires by imaginary achievements

Repression   Preventing painful or dangerous thoughts from entering consciousness

Rationalization   Attempting to prove that one's behavior is "rational" and justifiable and thus worthy of self- and social approval

Projection   Placing blame for difficulties upon others or attributing one's own unethical desires to others

Reaction formation   Preventing dangerous desires from being expressed by adopting exaggerated opposed attitudes and types of behavior and using them as "barriers"

Displacement   Discharging pent-up feelings, usually of hostility, on objects less dangerous than those which initially aroused the emotions

Intellectualization (isolation)   Cutting off affective charge from hurtful situations or separating incompatible attitudes by logic-tight compartments

Undoing   Atoning for and thus counteracting immoral desires or acts

Regression   Retreating to earlier developmental level involving less mature responses and usually a lower level of aspiration

Identification   Increasing feelings of worth by identifying self with person or institution of illustrious standing

Compensation   Covering up weakness by emphasizing desirable trait or making up for frustration in one area by overgratification in another

Based on Anna Freud (1946) from *Abnormal Psychology and Modern Life*, 6th ed., by James C. Coleman et al. Copyright © 1980, 1976, 1972 by Scott, Foresman & Company, 1980. Reprinted by permission.

difficult to test. If what is true of one person may not be true of another, then combining data from a number of subjects is inappropriate. If the nature of the forces involved is well hidden, they may not be easily noted or measured. And if only powerful forces are involved, it may not be possible to test them experimentally, within ethical constraints. (There are obviously ethical limits to the anxiety that an experimenter could arouse, for example.) Hence the very limited experimental support available could be taken either as evidence that the theory has little validity, as it typically is by those who hold competing views (Skinner, 1954), or only as evidence that the theory is difficult to measure, as it typically is by Freud's supporters (Silverman, 1976).

One serious criticism of the psychoanalytic approach as a scientific proposal, however, is not easily countered by its supporters: It is said to be *overdetermined*, meaning that there are too many proposed possibilities, with no formal way to sort them out. Id impulses, for example, can be expressed directly; an aggressive impulse might cause aggressive behavior. But when they cannot be expressed directly, id impulses are said to be disguised; they may even be expressed as the opposite of the true impulse. Thus an aggressive impulse might be expressed as excessive concern for the oppressed, or a sexual impulse as an excessive demand for high moral standards. But this means that any overt behavior can be said to reflect exactly what it appears to, exactly the opposite, or anything in between. There is no formal statement in the theory to tell when a behavior is expressing the motive it seems to and when it is actually expressing the opposite; this is open to interpretation by each psychoanalyst.

Remember that any scientific theory must state its premises in a way that allows them to be tested empirically (Chapter 1). But the overdetermination of the psychoanalytic approach precludes any such test. Unless ways are developed to specify which motive will be expressed in which way, it may be impossible to test major aspects of psychoanalytic theory scientifically.

Neo-Freudians

The neo-Freudians, the psychoanalytic theorists who followed Freud, have increased the importance of the role of the ego as an active agent of self-control and have deemphasized the id. Freud's daughter Anna Freud, herself a psychoanalyst, contributed to this

Table 13.3 ■ Summary of Freud's Proposed Personality Structures

Structure	Basis	Level of Consciousness	Principle Followed	Process Used
Id	Instincts for sex and aggression	Unconscious	Pleasure principle	Primary process thinking
Ego	Learned behaviors in response to reality	Mostly conscious	Reality principle	Secondary process thinking
Superego	Learned social inhibitions	Partly conscious	—	—

trend with her book *The Ego and the Mechanisms of Defense* (1946). The neo-Freudians have also put more emphasis on the role of the larger society and continuing social influences (Munroe, 1955). The roles of id impulses and unconscious processes have been downplayed in favor of an ego developed out of interactions with others and operating in a social environment.

These changes in psychoanalytic thought by the neo-Freudians—who include Carl Jung, Alfred Adler, Erik Erikson, and Karen Horney—are similar to the arguments of theories developed since Freud first formulated his views. The focus on the ego is somewhat like the humanists' emphasis on "self" concepts; the focus on the role of society in ego development and action is similar to the behavioral approaches, especially social learning theory.

Jung **Carl Gustav Jung** (1875–1961) was a Swiss psychiatrist who became a close associate of Freud's soon after receiving his degree; their friendship, almost that of father and son, lasted for about six years before breaking up over their ongoing theoretical disputes. Jung's concern with mystical symbols did not fit with Freud's views and Freud's emphasis on sexuality was not shared by Jung. Where Freud saw the unconscious as a kind of dark force, bursting with forbidden impulses, Jung felt it to be more positive, a repository of accumulated wisdom of prior generations.

Jung's views included two forms of the unconscious (1968a). His *personal unconscious* was similar to Freud's preconscious, containing thoughts and memories that are not now conscious but could be. Jung's new contribution was the concept of a **collective unconscious** shared by all humans as an evolutionary heritage. Like Freud's unconscious, Jung's collective unconscious could influence behavior but could not directly enter consciousness. Patterns of images within the collective unconscious were termed **archetypes;** these are the common experiences of all people that have deep symbolic meaning, such as the rising of the sun (Jung, 1968b). Jung felt that these archetypes were the summary of our ancestors' experiences and were expressed in the similar myths and folklore of many cultures.

Jung's view, called *analytic psychology* to differentiate it from Freud's, has been popular primarily with nonscientists, to whom its mystical qualities appeal. But its concepts are extremely difficult, if not impossible, to validate scientifically and it is typically dismissed by scientific theorists and most psychologists. They argue that the proposal of a collective unconscious is a kind of Lamarckism, a concept of inheritance of acquired characteristics that has been discredited since Darwin (Chapter 3). They suggest that the cultural accumulation of common experiences adequately explains the existence of similar myths, and that the idea of a collective unconscious only obscures simpler processes.

Adler **Alfred Adler** (1870–1937), like Jung, was a young psychiatrist when he met Freud, and for a time he too worked closely with Freud. Adler also left after a few years to found his own school of thought, *individual psychology* (Adler, 1959). Adler wished to emphasize human desires for success and superiority rather than libido. In his view, the dominant force in humans is a striving for superiority, or often a compensating for inferiority. The particular direction in which each person strives for superiority is an individual one, but this goal is largely unconscious and only dimly understood by the person.

Adler's work has been overshadowed by Freud's and Jung's, but he has had substantial influence on other theorists—including both Allport and Maslow—as well as on popular concepts: The notion of the "inferiority complex" is his. His influence on other theorists, in fact, is so strong that some writers have suggested calling the later psychoanalytic theorists neo-Adlerians rather than neo-Freudians (Abramson, 1980).

Erikson **Erik H. Erikson** (1902–   ), whose theory of psychosocial stages we considered in Chapter 12, strongly emphasized the individual's interaction with a social environment; his views have been quite influential (Coles, 1970).

Erikson is also known for his psychoanalytic biographies of people he never met, such as Martin Luther (1963). This form of personality study through *psychohistory* was also practiced by Freud (e.g., Freud's psychohistory of Leonardo da Vinci; 1910). Another psychoanalyst was even hired by the United States government to do a study of Hitler during World War II that remained classified until recently (Langer, 1972). Psychohistories are provocative, but the validity of the interpretations they offer is far harder to demonstrate than that of interpretations of an actual patient—itself a difficult task—and the psychohistories have been strongly criticized (Stannard, 1980).

Horney   Karen Horney (1885–1952), the daughter of a Dutch mother and Norwegian father, was born and grew up in Germany, where she received her medical degree and became a psychoanalyst. In 1932, she immigrated to the United States. Horney's views (1953) focused on a concept of *basic anxiety*, the product of the intrinsic difficulties of life. According to Horney, the risk people face in coping with childhood experiences of isolation and helplessness is development of one of ten different *neurotic trends*, such as the neurotic need to exploit others.

Horney was one of the few analysts to suggest the possibility of self-analysis (1942). But she is best known for her objections to Freud's opinions on the psychology of women. As noted in Chapter 12, Freud's interpretation of women was centered around their supposed penis envy, deriving from their childhood discovery that they lacked this notable organ. He suggested a view of women's personalities that most psychologists today consider highly sexist as well as incorrect: Women, he felt, were more vain than men, more modest, more envious, more jealous, felt more inferior, and so forth. He traced virtually all of these presumed female traits back to penis envy.

It now seems easy to criticize these views. But remember that many aspects of Freud's views reflected the Zeitgeist in which he carried out his work; like any theorist, he incorporated at least some of his culture's (and gender's) views into his own. Horney was born nearly 30 years later than Freud and thus experienced a somewhat different Zeitgeist. But probably more important, she had a different view of her culture as a result of being a woman. As a psychoanalyst, she objected strongly to Freud's view of women on both biological grounds (it would not be evolutionarily reasonable for one sex to be programmed to want to be like the other) and cultural ones (some of the envy of women for men's roles was a rational response to a role-biased society). In retrospect, Horney's views on

women seem much more thoughtful and insightful than Freud's, but when she proposed them they were strongly resisted by the analysts—almost all of whom were male.

THE BEHAVIORAL APPROACH

We have already considered both Skinner's behaviorism and Bandura's social learning theory (especially in Chapters 1 and 8). Before briefly reviewing these approaches as personality theories, we note the earlier behavioral approach of Dollard and Miller.

Dollard and Miller

John Dollard (1900–1980) and **Neal Miller** (1909–   ) developed their theory of personality in the late 1940s (Dollard & Miller, 1950; Miller & Dollard, 1941). While at Yale, both became interested in Clark Hull's (1943) theory of learning, with its ambitious attempt to define objectively and quantify the learning process. They decided to see if Freud's exciting but loosely defined concepts could be adapted to a learning-theory framework. The theory they developed was based on four concepts: drive, cue, response, and reinforcement. Freud's instincts, as represented in the id, became for Dollard and Miller *primary drives*. These, in turn, were the basis for other *learned drives* (Miller, 1951). The combination of primary and learned drives provided the energy or motivation for behavior, and *cues* determined when, where, and which behavior would ensue. Any distinctive stimulus, in any sensory mode, could become a cue for some *response*, based on the learning history of the organism. Once the response had occurred, it could be followed by a *reinforcement*. If so, the response became more probable in the presence of the cues.

All organisms, according to Dollard and Miller, had a hierarchy of responses available, with different degrees of probability for each. If a high-probability behavior at the top of the hierarchy was blocked or unsuccessful, the next most likely response would occur. The effect of reinforcing a response would thus be to move it higher in the hierarchy by making it more probable. The overall effect was to allow an organism to adjust its range of behaviors to the environment, based on the success of those behaviors in producing reinforcement.

Dollard and, primarily, Miller sought to apply this approach to many psychoanalytic concepts (e.g., Miller, 1948b). The best-known work is Miller's (1944) analysis of conflict. Conflicts of several sorts play a major role in psychoanalytic theory, and Miller felt that a behavioral understanding of conflict would have broad application. He conceptualized conflict in terms of the probabilities of two responses to some object or event: approach and avoidance. Approaching an object, he felt, was a measurable indicator of liking or wanting the object, and moving away from it or avoiding it was an indicator of dislike. He then described several types of conflict, in which opposing tendencies had to be resolved in some way. An *approach-approach conflict* occurs when two desirable outcomes exist but choosing one prevents getting the other: keeping your money and buying a new car, for example. An *avoidance-avoidance conflict* represents a situation in which avoiding either of two undesirable outcomes brings you closer to the other. For example, studying might be an undesirable activity (not in psychology, of course) and getting a bad grade might be equally undesirable; avoiding either of these choices forces you toward the other.

According to Miller, both approach and avoidance tendencies become stronger as the organism moves closer to the goal; how rapidly the tendency changes he called a *goal gradient*. One of the ingenious results of this formulation was its ability to explain a particular phenomenon in learning. In some cases, a goal can be mixed, arousing both approach and avoidance tendencies. In such cases, the organism will often approach the goal but then stop some distance away, neither coming closer nor moving away. A wild animal may do this upon being offered food by a human, for example. It fears the person but wants the food, and may wind up, quivering, a foot away from the food, apparently unable either to advance or retreat. Clearly it is "in conflict."

Miller (1944) explained such outcomes by arguing that the avoidance gradient is steeper than the approach gradient. In his scheme, at far distances approach is the stronger tendency, and at near distances avoidance becomes stronger. The point where the two gradients intersect is the point where the organism stops. Furthermore, it will tend to stay there; if it moves further away the approach tendency becomes stronger, but if it moves closer the avoidance tendency becomes stronger. ■ Figure 13.6

Dollard and Miller's work has been very influential in psychology; most later behavioral theorists have drawn on their work in one way or another. They also discussed learning by imitation in a way that was a forerunner to modern social learning theory. And their interest in a behavioral approach to psychoanalytic concepts probably encouraged interest in those concepts among other experimentally oriented psychologists. Dollard and Miller have been criticized for using animal models, often rats, to study human personality. But they nevertheless originated many

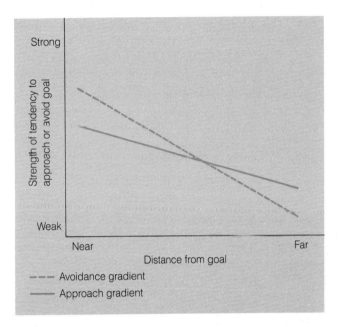

Figure 13.6 ■ Miller's resolution of the approach-avoidance conflict. The organism will tend to stop and remain at the point where the goal gradients intersect, because moving any closer will make the avoidance tendency stronger but moving any further away will make the approach tendency stronger. (Adapted from Miller, 1944)

notions about how behavior works that later behaviorists have found to be true of humans.

Skinner

Although not the only version of behaviorism, Skinner's approach is one of the best known and most controversial (Rachlin, 1976). All behaviorists emphasize overt, measurable behavior, but Skinner has insisted on limiting analysis to it. Internal activity, whether phrased in nervous-system terms or mental terms, is not an appropriate level of analysis, he feels. In this, Skinner is more extreme than many behaviorists, who are more willing to consider, for example, the possibility of thoughts as covert behavior (Meichenbaum, 1977). Skinner's view is often termed *radical behaviorism* because of his insistence on referring to environmental events in considering any behavior. His is virtually the only approach to personality to forego all inferred constructs and to rely only on observed behavior and contingencies of reinforcement. (Note, however, that Skinner has not developed his approach in detail as a personality theory.) ■ Table 13.4

Skinner refuses to consider internal activities partly because they are so difficult to measure. But he also believes that internal events such as thoughts or emotions are results of external events, not causes of them. For example, rather than saying that a farmer

Table 13.4 ■ The Personality of a Young Man Just Out of College, with Mentalistic Descriptions Reinterpreted in Behavioral Terms

Traditional Mentalistic Description	Behavioral Translation
He lacks assurance or feels insecure.	His behavior is weak and inappropriate.
He is dissatisfied or discouraged.	He is seldom reinforced and his behavior undergoes extinction.
He is frustrated.	Extinction is accompanied by emotional responses.
He feels uneasy or anxious.	His behavior has unavoidable aversive consequences that have emotional effects.
He has no sense of purpose or accomplishment.	He is rarely reinforced for doing anything.
He feels guilty or ashamed.	He has previously been punished for idleness or failure, which now evokes emotional responses.
He is disappointed in himself.	He is no longer reinforced by the admiration of others and the resulting extinction has emotional effects.
He becomes neurotic.	He engages in a variety of ineffectual modes of escape.

Adapted from Skinner, 1971.

has lost hope after several years of bad crops and thus does not plant again, Skinner says that the crop failure causes the later behavior of not planting. The experience of "losing hope" is simply a by-product of that sequence: It is an *effect* of crop failure rather than a *cause* of not planting. (For an extended discussion of this line of argument, see Skinner, 1971.) For a summary of Skinner's life and work, see some of his own works (1974, 1976b, 1978, 1979). For interpretations of his approach by others, see Evans (1968) or Nye (1979).

Bandura

Dollard and Miller discussed learning by imitation, as have other theorists, but contemporary social learning theory is most identified with Albert Bandura. As a personality theory, social learning theory shares some attributes with other approaches but brings its own unique focus (Bandura, 1962, 1977b; Bandura & Walters, 1963). The social learning approach is a form of learning theory, which implies both a conceptual emphasis on learning processes and a methodological emphasis on observable behavior and replicable results. In these aspects, it is similar to Dollard and Miller. But the "social" part of social learning theory suggests an emphasis on human learning in a social environment, in contrast to Dollard and Miller's frequent use of animal models.

Social learning theory also emphasizes the effects of reinforcement on learning. In this respect, it is akin to Skinner's view. But social learning theory suggests that both acts and reinforcements can be covert, carried out within the nervous systems of a single individual. And it considers reinforcement more important as a performance variable than a learning one (see Figure

13.7). These views are notable departures from Skinner's position.

The central focus of social-learning theory, as elaborated by Bandura and others, is on the process of **modeling,** the observation of some other person's actions and the learning from those actions, without the observer necessarily either performing the action or being rewarded for it (Bandura, 1971). Modeling is a more complex concept than simple imitation; it refers to abstractions about behavior, rather than exact duplications of behavior. A person could watch a model solve several moral dilemmas, for example, and then seek to resolve other dilemmas as he or she thinks the model would. Another subtlety of modeling is that actions can be combined from several models, so that the modeled behavior is not a direct imitation of any single model.

As Bandura has developed it, modeling involves four major processes (Bandura, 1977b). For observed behavior to be modeled successfully (reproduced at a later time), it must first be *attended* to; here characteristics of both the observed behavior and the observer are important. *Retention* (memory) processes must then ensure that the observed behavior is retained for later use. *Motor reproduction* processes govern whether the observer is physically able to perform the modeled action, and *motivational* processes offer the reason to do so. ■ Figure 13.7

The importance of modeling and associated concepts can hardly be overestimated. In a basic Skinnerian model, for any act to be learned it must be performed and then rewarded. This implies that any human learns only what he or she actually does and is reinforced for. By introducing the concept of **vicarious reinforcement,** social learning theory notes that a reward given to another person can have an effect on

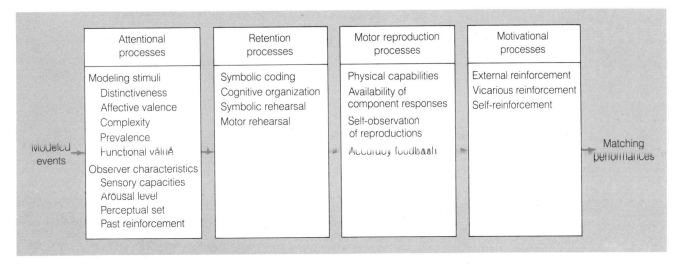

Figure 13.7 ■ The four component processes of modeling. Attentional processes determine whether the actions of a model will be perceived and noted. Retention processes govern whether the modeled acts will be retained. Reproduction of the modeled acts by the observer then depends on both physical constraints (motor reproduction processes) and motivational processes. The former control whether the act *can* be physically performed, the latter whether it *will* be performed.

(From *Social Learning Theory* by A. Bandura, © 1977. Reprinted by permission of Prentice-Hall, Inc., Englewood Cliffs, N. J.)

an observer. By adding the concept of **self-reinforcement,** it suggests that individuals can encourage their own actions by rewarding them. Both of these processes make learning a much more flexible concept than if overt action and external reinforcement were required in all cases.

Note that social learning theory sees reinforcement largely as a motivational process; it thus emphasizes a distinction between learning and performance. Figure 13.7 suggests that without some form of reinforcement an observed behavior may not be performed—even though it has been learned and retained. Only when reinforcement is offered for performance will the modeled behavior actually be reproduced. This learning/performance distinction is exceptionally important in the discussion of such issues as whether televised violence affects children (Chapter 18). It suggests that children who do not seem to imitate the violence they see may nevertheless have learned and stored such behavior. If this is true, it would take only an appropriate reinforcement, or the expectation of one, to cause them to be violent. In considering the effects of television, then, social learning theory says one must look deeper than whether children routinely act out what they see.

Social learning theory thus seeks to combine the benefits of a concentration on specific learned behavior with the utility of inferred constructs. Here the inferred constructs are not instincts or traits, but concepts related to the kind of learning that can be observed externally: for example, internal mediational processes—or "thoughts"—that are considered as self-generated stimuli. These can then be discussed as learned behaviors, even though they cannot be directly observed. Rather than seeking always to use externals, as in Table 13.4, a social learning theorist might accept a mental description such as "He feels that he is a failure." But the internal state would still be described as directly as possible, perhaps as "makes frequent covert self-deprecating statements" ("I always screw up, I'm no good," and so forth). A therapist who followed this approach might suggest making specific positive covert self-statements at regular intervals ("I'm doing better than yesterday, I at least improved in one respect," and so forth).

In a book that helped establish the anthropological concept of *cultural relativity* (that each culture has its own values and can only be understood in its own terms), Ruth Benedict (1934) suggested a culture could be considered as "personality writ large." Benedict meant that one could describe a culture as if it were a personality: as unusually passive or aggressive, for example. Social learning theory suggests that much of personality is "culture writ small"—that many of people's personality characteristics merely reflect the culture in which they were reared. Individual differences exist within any culture, of course, but these will differ from a baseline that is strongly specified by the culture. This is less obvious in a country with many subcultures, such as the United States. But historically some cultures have sought, often with considerable success, to rear their children toward some ideal mold for adulthood. One notable example was Nazi Germany. ■ Figure 13.8

Figure 13.8 ■ Adolf Hitler reviewing members of the Hitler Youth corps in 1935. The Hitler Youth were raised from childhood in a way that combined elements similar to the Boy Scouts, basic military training, and religious indoctrination. The combination, intended to instill dedication to Hitler and the Third Reich above all else, was among the most extreme forms of deliberate personality shaping yet attempted on a wide scale.

(The Bettmann Archive, Inc.)

Overall, social learning theory sees a person's personality as developing through a lifetime of interaction between the person and his or her environment, each of which influences the other (Bandura, 1974, 1978). This approach to personality is being explored by a number of theorists and it is likely to be an increasingly important viewpoint in the future. It offers a flexible framework for combining learning and current influences, for combining self and situation variables, for adding cognitive features, and so forth, while seeking to remain as objective and behaviorally focused as possible.

THE HUMANISTIC APPROACH

The humanistic approach (Buhler & Allen, 1972) is usually attributed to the independent approaches of two theorists, Abraham Maslow and Carl Rogers. Both emphasize concepts of the self and self-development, but they differ somewhat in how these concepts are defined and used.

Maslow

Maslow's views, like Freud's, were strongly influenced by his beliefs about human motivation, but his view of motivation differed radically from Freud's. Instead of powerful, innate, negative forces that must be kept in check, Maslow saw weak, innate, positive tendencies that must be nurtured (1968, 1970, 1971). Survival motives are the most powerful and most immediate motives, Maslow agreed; if you're starving, food will be of utmost importance. But then what? Maslow proposed his well-known **hierarchy of needs** to suggest how more exclusively human needs might appear after more basic needs were satisfied. ■ Figure 13.9

According to Maslow, all of the needs in the hierarchy are innate to humans, but those higher in the

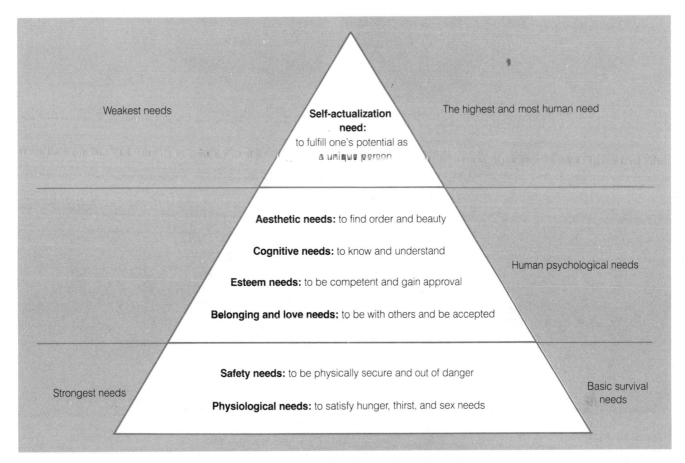

Weakest needs

Self-actualization need: to fulfill one's potential as a unique person

The highest and most human need

Aesthetic needs: to find order and beauty

Cognitive needs: to know and understand

Esteem needs: to be competent and gain approval

Belonging and love needs: to be with others and be accepted

Human psychological needs

Safety needs: to be physically secure and out of danger

Strongest needs

Physiological needs: to satisfy hunger, thirst, and sex needs

Basic survival needs

Figure 13.9 ■ Maslow's hierarchy of needs. Maslow proposed that humans share basic survival needs with animals; only if those are satisfied will a person seek to fulfill other more exclusively human needs. The most human of these is self-actualization, or becoming the best, most complete and fulfilled person you can be.

(After Maslow, 1970)

hierarchy are weaker; they only direct action when all earlier needs have been satisfied. Only when people have enough to eat and their physical safety is assured will they be motivated by a need to belong or a need for esteem. And only when they feel they belong and have high esteem can they seek to know and understand their world, or to create for pure esthetic pleasure. People who can achieve each of these goals in turn may eventually become the most competent, well-rounded, or **self-actualized** persons that it is possible for them to be. They would not be identical, of course, but each would be approaching his or her own best development.

Maslow's perspective on society is quite different from Freud's. In Maslow's scheme, society should help ensure that everyone can satisfy basic needs but should then allow them to develop further with as little interference as possible. Rather than maintaining social control over their instincts, as Freud felt was necessary, Maslow felt that society should encourage these weaker but higher motives. Maslow agreed that people can be as Freud described them—that they can commit unspeakably awful acts of violence, for example. But Maslow felt that the good acts of humans reflect the true nature of our species. The bad acts are not inevitable; they result when people are thwarted in their basic needs and hence are unable to function in accordance with higher motives. People might behave selfishly or violently because they had never progressed beyond the lowest level of the hierarchy, or because extreme need had caused them to revert to that level. But if given a chance, they would be self-actualizing.

In studying these relationships, Maslow focused not on patients, who by definition have psychological problems, but on the people whom he felt were the closest to self-actualization. These self-actualizers might not be perfect, he noted—they could be stubborn, irritating, vain, even ruthless—but each comes closer to his or her maximum potential than most people (Maslow, 1970). ■ Figure 13.10

Figure 13.10 ■ Albert Einstein and Eleanor Roosevelt were among the people identified by Maslow as self-actualizers. Neither was 100% successful at all tasks throughout life, but such an extreme criterion is not required.

(The Bettmann Archive, Inc.)

Rogers

Rogers, like Freud, developed his general theory out of his experiences with clinical patients. But Rogers's view nevertheless shares more of Maslow's optimism than Freud's pessimism. Rogers's view is also concerned with the development of self, but he approaches the concept of self differently than Maslow did (Evans, 1975a; Suls, 1982).

It seemed to Rogers that he was most successful as a therapist when he was being himself: not playing any special role, but simply responding to the patient. He also felt that he need not always try to work directly on a patient's specified problem. If he was content to be himself and encouraged the patient to do the same, he felt that progress came naturally and the patient was able to find his or her own solutions more easily. Rogers called this being *nondirective*. As he elaborated this view, he termed it **client-centered therapy** (Rogers, 1951). (The patient is referred to as a *client* to minimize the implicit connotations of mental illness in *patient*.) As he refined his therapy, he expanded his views to a more general theory of personality (Rogers, 1959, 1961).

Rogers's personality theory is a *person-centered theory* (Holdstock & Rogers, 1977) in several ways. First, it emphasizes a phenomenological approach, noting that each person's experienced world is unique, built up in part from that person's experiences. If a person's experiences have taught him or her that the world is a cruel place, it is *in fact* a cruel world that he or she inhabits because all of his or her experience is filtered through that view. Rogers's view is also person-centered in emphasizing self-actualization, though he defines it somewhat differently than Maslow did. To Rogers, to be self-actualizing is to strive toward *congruence* between one's concept of **self** (the set of beliefs about who and what one is) and one's experience. When a person's experience is at odds with the self, a state of *incongruence* exists, and the person may become a client.

Rogers's theory is thus a mixture of emotional and cognitive elements. None of these elements is specified operationally as exactly as experimental psychologists would wish, and in that sense Rogers's approach is less data-based than, for example, Skinner's. But Rogers has made a substantial effort to define his terms and to operationalize them to the extent possible. Overall, Rogers's approach is, as you might expect from its origins, partly a theory of therapy and partly a theory of personality. In both respects, it has been popular and influential, though its greatest influence has probably been in therapy (Chapter 16).

ASSESSING PERSONALITY

We all use our implicit personality theories to assess the personalities of people with whom we interact. We assess possible friends or roommates, professors, people seeking to sell us things, and many others. Formal personality assessment is less common, but it still is performed in a variety of situations. Job or college admission interviewers perform a kind of personality assessment, for example. Within the profession of psychology, most school psychologists and virtually all clinical psychologists frequently assess people's personalities.

The techniques used by assessors vary widely, depending on the assessor's training and the purpose of the assessment. There are two major reasons for assessing personality formally. First, the person assessed is to be selected or treated in some way; this includes employment interviews and psychiatric diagnostic interviews. A related use is to monitor people's progress, as employees might be given a follow-up interview or patients might be regularly monitored. A second reason for assessment is to define or test a personality theory; in this case, the assessment may be irrelevant to the people assessed. (If the theory is supported, however, the measurement might eventually be of practical use for selection or diagnosis.) To be meaningful, all assessment techniques should be both reliable and valid, but how reliability and validity are established varies with the user and the purpose. A clinician may be satisfied with a measure if further work with the patient seems to sustain the assessment. A theorist, however, may be content only with the most careful and quantitative measures of reliability and validity. (See Chapter 14 for further discussion of reliability and validity.)

In general, all measures of personality seek to put an individual in a standardized situation in which some responses are called for. The particular responses elicited are then assumed to reflect the personality of the person being assessed. There are three ways of doing this. **Observation techniques** use an outside observer, or *rater*, who judges some behavior of the person in a standard situation. Any situation could be used, but the most common technique is interviewing, with both the questions and the assessment of the answers structured in some way. **Self-report inven-**

tories ask the person to be assessed to take an active role in judging his or her own personality. This is often done through responding to statements such as "I prefer being alone to being with people." Both observation and self-report techniques may be used for theory purposes as well as selection and diagnosis. **Projective tests** ask the person to respond freely to a deliberately ambiguous stimulus; the pattern of responses is then interpreted by the rater. Projective tests are the most difficult to define or to score objectively. They are widely used by clinicians (especially psychoanalytically oriented ones) to assess patients, but their reliability and validity have not been established to the satisfaction of most experimentally oriented psychologists (Kaplan & Saccuzzo, 1982).

Future personality assessment will probably continue to rely on these three major types of techniques, although they will probably be refined as personality theories are further developed (Korchin & Schuldberg, 1981; Mischel, 1977).

Observation Techniques

The simplest and least-structured observation technique is the *unstructured interview,* in which a rater observes a person and then describes his or her personality. Such an interview may offer some ideas for further elaboration, but is too personal and too much the product of the rater to be useful in a scientific investigation. Furthermore, because no two personality descriptions include the same elements, they cannot be directly compared. These objections to unstructured observation are viewed less seriously by clinicians than by researchers, however. Unstructured interviews are commonly used in psychotherapy to assess a patient's condition: The clinician asks whatever questions seem relevant to the particular patient and the course of the interview, based on clinical experience. The intent in these cases is not to assess the patient on any formal scale, but to give the clinician an overall impression of the patient and his or her problems.

In most other uses of assessment, however, a more structured technique is used. The most common form of structured observation is the **structured interview,** in which the persons to be assessed are asked a standard set of questions and their answers are standardized. Formal interviews for employment or for college admission are of this type, as are the initial interviews of psychiatric patients in which a formal history is taken.

Another way of structuring observation is through the use of **rating scales,** in which the observed person's behavior is coded according to a prearranged format. Answers to a rating scale are often chosen from a few (perhaps five or seven) specified choices, such as *strongly disagree, weakly disagree,* and so forth. Rating scales can be used to assess behavior as it is being observed or to summarize prior observations, as a teacher might be asked to rate a child's behavior over a semester. Rating scales require two kinds of reliability checks. Normal reliability means that the same rater would rate the same behavior similarly if the action were repeated at a later date. But tests of **interrater reliability** check whether two or more raters watching the same behavior can rate it similarly. Until they can do so, the scores are not considered reliable.

Behavioral psychologists use structured counting systems to quantify particular actions. Rather than rating a child on some general impression of "sociability," for example, a behavioral psychologist might observe the children at recess and note on a special form the number of times the child spoke to another child, the number of times another child spoke to the one being assessed, and so forth. These observations are used for both therapeutic purposes and theory development.

Self-Report Inventories

Self-report assessment techniques call on the individual to report his or her own patterns of behavior. This seemed inherently reasonable to Allport, who suggested that "If we want to know how people feel, what they experience and what they remember, what their emotions and motives are like, and the reasons for acting as they do, why not ask them?" (quoted in Abramson, 1980, p. 263). But it's not that simple. People lie, for one thing, especially if they believe someone is assessing them on the basis of their answers. And even with the best of intentions, **response biases** may distort the person's answers. Most people, for example, tend to answer yes more than no, so a question phrased for a yes answer may be responded to more than a question that asks for the identical information but is phrased to require a no answer. Hence, formal self-report systems typically vary the form of questions and incorporate other checks on people's answers, seeking to eliminate both response biases and lying.

Behavioral self-reports also count specific actions, but ask the person to record his or her own behavior. To check for response bias, the person's own count is occasionally compared to an external observer's count of the same behavior.

Most self-report inventories, however, call for more interpretation by the person, although the interpretation is structured—as by having the person choose one of a few possible answers. In one approach, the **Q-sort** technique (Block, 1961), the person is given a deck of special cards, each of which carries a single descriptive personality statement such as "is productive; gets things done." The task is to sort them

into piles according to whether the rater agrees or disagrees with the statements. The Q-sort can be used to assess others, but is more often used to assess the person doing the sorting.

The most common form of self-report, however, is the **personality inventory,** in which the person answers a series of questions and the assessor evaluates the resulting total score. Personality inventories are used both to assess patients and to develop theories. Some test for a single personality trait, as in Wolpe and Lang's (1964) Fear Survey Schedule, developed in conjunction with behavioral therapy. Other inventories use multiple scales. After many questions have been answered, particular sets of questions are grouped together to provide separate ratings on a series of scales. One example drawn from theory building is Cattell's (1949) **Sixteen Factor Personality Questionnaire (16PF).** Answers to the questionnaire are used to develop separate ratings on the 16 factors Cattell feels characterize personality. As with any multi-factor scale, a **personality profile** can then be drawn in which the overall pattern of the person's responses is displayed graphically. If desired, similar profiles can be devised for groups of people by averaging their separate scores. ■ Figure 13.11

The best-known personality inventory is the **Minnesota Multiphasic Personality Inventory (MMPI)** (Hathaway & McKinley, 1967). The MMPI was not developed to fit any particular theory, but to identify people suffering from severe mental illness. It was devised by giving a large number of questions to hospitalized mental patients and to normal controls and comparing their answers. Any questions that were reliably answered differently by the patients were retained and the others were discarded. This approach is termed a **criterion-referenced** one, because the test is referenced to a criterion group, in this case the hospitalized patients.

Since the MMPI was first developed, subscales have been devised using a variety of criterion groups, including variations in normal personality types as well as different subcategories of patients. In addition, other questions scattered throughout the test can be combined into special validity scores. The various scales can be computer-scored to generate a profile for a particular test-taker that can be interpreted according to standardized criteria (Graham, 1978).

Projective Tests

Projective tests are so named because of their basic assumption that a person asked to interpret a deliberately ambiguous stimulus "projects," or inserts, his or her own thoughts into the description. Projective tests are claimed to reveal, with proper interpretation, even

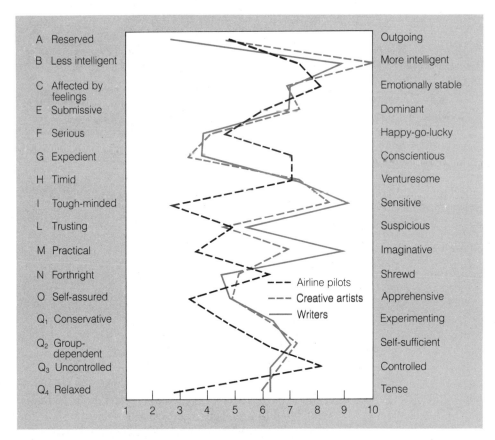

A	Reserved		Outgoing
B	Less intelligent		More intelligent
C	Affected by feelings		Emotionally stable
E	Submissive		Dominant
F	Serious		Happy-go-lucky
G	Expedient		Conscientious
H	Timid		Venturesome
I	Tough-minded		Sensitive
L	Trusting		Suspicious
M	Practical		Imaginative
N	Forthright		Shrewd
O	Self-assured		Apprehensive
Q₁	Conservative		Experimenting
Q₂	Group-dependent		Self-sufficient
Q₃	Uncontrolled		Controlled
Q₄	Relaxed		Tense

- - - Airline pilots
- - - Creative artists
——— Writers

1 2 3 4 5 6 7 8 9 10

Figure 13.11 ■ Personality profiles of three groups of professionals using Cattell's 16 personality factors. Each factor is expressed as a dimension, such as "reserved-outgoing." When scores on these dimensions are plotted, for an individual or a group, the result is a profile. Here the profiles show the three groups plotted to be similar in some factors, such as C or L, but quite different in others, such as I or Q4.

Adapted from *Handbook for the Sixteen Personality Factors*, copyright 1970 by the Institute for Personality and Ability Testing, Inc. Reproduced by permission of the copyright owner.)

deeply hidden personality characteristics. They are favored by psychoanalytically oriented therapists because they are thought to reveal even unconscious motives. But projective tests generate a wide variety of unstructured replies, and it is extremely difficult to interpret these systematically, or to test the validity of the interpretations. There have been some efforts to develop systems for structuring the interpretation, but they have not yet demonstrated adequate reliability for use by experimentalists. Neither have they shown much evidence of validity, although they continue to be widely used by clinicians (Kaplan & Saccuzzo, 1982).

The **Rorschach** projective test consists of a series of black and colored inkblot patterns (Rorschach, 1942), made by folding cards with ink on them to yield symmetrical figures. Herman Rorschach, the Swiss developer of the test, apparently experimented with thousands of such cards before settling on ten (Kaplan & Saccuzzo, 1982). In use, each of these ten cards is presented and the person taking the test is asked to describe what he or she sees. The examiner deliberately refrains from helping the test-taker structure the answers, so the length and type of answer will reflect the person's inner patterns. This lack of structure, however, results in a wide variety of answers, and despite the Rorschach's continued popularity with clinicians, there is little evidence that those answers can be meaningfully interpreted. (For a discussion of scoring categories, see Exner & Weiner, 1981.) ■ Figure 13.12

The **Thematic Apperception Test (TAT)** differs from the Rorschach in several ways, but as a projective test it shares the Rorschach's key assumption and suffers from some of the same problems of reliability and validity. Whereas the Rorschach was developed as a *clinical* assessment technique independent of any particular theory, the TAT was developed as a *personality* assessment technique based on Henry Murray's (1938) theory of needs. The TAT uses a series of 29 pictures of scenes (and one blank card). The scenes represent people in loosely structured situations so that subjects can

Figure 13.12 ■ Inkblots similar to those used in the Rorschach projective test. A patient's description of what he or she "sees" in such ambiguous patterns is thought to indicate otherwise-hidden personality conflicts or problems.

"RORSCHACH! WHAT'S TO BECOME OF YOU?"

© 1983 by Sidney Harris

interpret the scenes in terms of their own lives. Certain cards are considered appropriate for males and females and for different ages. The card in Figure 13.13, for example, might be given to a younger or older woman, who might be expected to project her feelings about her own mother or daughter. ■ Figure 13.13

The TAT is frequently used by personality theorists, but the Rorschach is not. In general, there are more and better scoring systems for the TAT, and the reliability and validity of the TAT are somewhat better established than they are for the Rorschach; however, many psychologists still consider them doubtful (Kaplan & Saccuzzo, 1982). Even Henry Murray, who devised the TAT, has expressed some reservations about its use: "The TAT is a kind of booby trap . . . ," he noted. "The patient reveals parts of himself when he composes a story to explain the picture. Then the psychologist may reveal parts of himself when he composes a formulation to explain the patient's story." (1968, p. 61).

One notable line of research that grew out of the TAT has been that on **achievement motivation,** the motive to achieve success (or to avoid failure). Achievement motivation was derived by McClelland and Atkinson from one of the 20 needs the TAT was devised to measure (McClelland et al., 1953). A great deal of work has followed the original specification, most of it done by Atkinson (e.g., 1974). But the concept of achievement motivation and its measurement based on a projective test has also been severely criticized by more experimentally oriented researchers (e.g., Entwisle, 1972), and it remains in debate.

Figure 13.13 ■ Card 12F from the TAT projective test. People are obviously represented in the TAT, but the situations portrayed are ambiguous enough to allow wide differences in interpretation.

An interesting, but also highly debated, offshoot of achievement motivation research has been the question of possible sex differences in the motive to *avoid* success, and the origins of any such sex differences (e.g., Sarason & Smith, 1971). In her doctoral dissertation, Horner (1968) studied this question by asking female students to write a story to go with the sentence: "After first-term finals, Anne finds herself at the top of her medical school class." (Note that this is a form of projective test, with the sentence as the ambiguous stimulus.) Horner found that 66% of female subjects wrote stories implying a fear of success—indicating the negative things that would happen to Anne, for example—compared to only 9% of male subjects given the sentence phrased with a male name. Horner's research sparked considerable follow-up work, but the results remain mixed (Tresemer, 1976). Women do often write such stories, but in some studies as many men have written them, so this may not be an actual sex difference. Other research has suggested

that the stories may only represent both males' and females' stereotypes of social roles, rather than indicating their own *motives*.

Overall, the different ways of assessing personality differ in origin, in form, in degree of reliability and validity, and in purpose. About all they share is that each seeks to specify something about the personality of the person being assessed. And almost always the testing and the purpose served are primarily those of someone other than the test-taker. Even when the outcome is relevant to the test-taker—as job applicant or patient, for example— someone else is actually directing the testing (the employer or therapist). There is one set of personality tests, however, that serve only the test-taker: the vocational interest tests designed to help people choose a profession. ■ Personal Application: Testing Your Own Vocational Interests

CHAPTER SUMMARY

1 A personality is a set of characteristic ways of dealing with the world, described in terms of overt behaviors or in inferred dispositions such as traits. Everyone has an implicit personality theory, but formal theories seek to be more exact and to be applicable to all people.

2 Earlier biological approaches have included some that are completely discredited, such as phrenology, and others that are little used today, such as somatotyping. Current biological approaches emphasize genetic factors.

3 A trait is a persistent personality attribute, such as honesty. There are many possible traits, and trait descriptions of personality are common. But there is substantial disagreement over whether improved ways of defining traits will overcome their limitations.

4 Gordon Allport used traits and first-person writings to define individuals' personalities. Raymond Cattell pioneered the use of factor analysis to find basic traits, specifying 16 of them. Hans Eysenck used factor analysis to specify a few trait dimensions, including neuroticism and introversion-extroversion.

5 Freud's psychoanalytic approach emphasizes the control of libido, based on sex and aggression instincts, through the interaction of three personality structures: the id, representing the instincts; the ego, representing rational thought; and the superego, representing society's prohibitions.

6 A number of neo-Freudian theorists, including Carl Jung, Alfred Adler, Erik Erikson, and Karen Horney, have revised and extended Freud's views. They have emphasized the ego and social forces more than Freud did, and the id and sexuality less. Horney was especially critical of Freud's views of women.

7 Behavioral approaches began with Dollard and Miller, who sought to specify Freud's concepts in learning-theory terms. Skinner has emphasized environmental factors and avoided all inferred dispositions. Bandura's social learning theory adds cognitive variables, empha-

PERSONAL APPLICATION

Testing your own vocational interests

Psychology is my second career. When, after ten years as a research engineer, I decided to return to school for my Ph.D. in psychology, one of the things I did was to go to a local testing psychologist's office and take an SVIB. The *Strong Vocational Interest Blank (SVIB)* was developed following World War I by K. E. Strong, Jr. He and his colleagues sought to analyze the different patterns of interests in the people who made up different professions. Using the same criterion-referenced approach used for the MMPI, Strong gave several hundred questions to successful professionals in a number of fields and developed scales that sorted for each profession. The questions dealt with general interests, likes, and dislikes, but each question was kept only if it usefully discriminated between groups.

By 1966, the version of the SVIB that I took included 399 items that offered interpretations in terms of 54 occupations for men; a separate form was available for 32 different occupations for women. Long-term reliability studies had by then already shown impressive results, even over a 20-year span. And validity tests had found the SVIB to be useful for predicting job satisfaction: Young people who scored similarly to the professionals already in a field were satisfied with that occupation when they entered it (Strong & Campbell, 1966).

The SVIB reports scores on a series of educational and occupational scales. In my case, it reported a high rating on tendency toward advanced education, a desirable result for someone about to devote four years to full-time education. In occupations, I scored very low on mortician, policeman, and others. My third-highest score was librarian, no doubt reflecting a somewhat compulsive tendency for organizing things as well as a love of books. My second highest was biologist, a profession for which I have a great deal of empathy. (Note that Chapter 3 of this text is a more "biological" chapter than most introductory psychology texts have.) And my highest score? Psychologist, of course. I was already commit-ted to graduate school, so I doubt I'd have changed if it had not been. But I do wish I had taken an SVIB 10 or 12 years earlier, when I was a rather confused undergraduate in engineering.

One anecdote does not demonstrate much. But the reliability and validity measures of the SVIB agree with my experience: It does seem to indicate patterns of interest that are important in choosing a profession. Your school counseling or career service, or a psychologist who specializes in testing, can give you the latest version, now called the **Strong-Campbell Interest Inventory (SCII)** (Campbell & Hansen, 1981). It includes 162 occupations, 99 of them added since 1977, and almost all of them scored for males or females. I'd suggest you try one. (Just one word of caution: the SCII says nothing about whether you can accomplish the work involved in a given profession, only that you think like the people already in that profession. There are also aptitude tests for different occupations, however, to answer this other question.) ■ Figure 13.14

---

sizing modeling and the difference between learning and performance.

8 Humanistic approaches include those of Maslow and Rogers. Maslow proposed a hierarchy of needs that suggests the most human motives are also the weakest, becoming applicable only when more basic needs are met; only then do people seek to become self-actualized. Rogers has emphasized other aspects of the self.

9 Personality assessment is done by various people for various ends. Assessment techniques include both observation of others and self-report inventories.

10 Different assessment techniques are preferred by different users. Structured techniques with demonstrated reliability and validity tend to be used by experimenters and theorists. Less-structured interview and projective techniques are used by clinicians, who value the insight they believe these offer.

Further Readings

For further elaboration of various issues in personality, see a good text, such as Mischel's *Introduction to Personality* (1981b). Specific theoretical approaches are presented in Nordby and Hall's very readable summary, *A Guide to Psychologists and Their Concepts* (1974). Interviews with some of the theorists we have discussed are included in Evans's *The Making of Psychology* (1976). More detailed and formal coverage of theories is provided by Hall and Lindzey in *Theories of Personality* (1978) and by Smith and Vetter in *Theoretical Approaches to Personality* (1982). Cattell has collected the available genetics research in *The Inheritance of Personality and Ability* (1982). For Allport's work, see Evans's *Gordon Allport* (1971). Hall's *A Primer of Freudian Psychology* (1954) is an easy-to-read introduction to Freud's views. For further discussion of Freud and the neo-Freudians, see Roazen's *Freud and His Followers* (1975). For Skinner's work, see his own *Reflections On Behaviorism and Society* (1978) or Nye's interpretation of his views, *What is B. F. Skinner Really Saying?* (1979). Maslow's views are presented in his *Motivation and Personality* (1970). For a comparison of the psychoanalytic, behavioral, and humanistic approaches, see Nye's *Three Psychologies* (1981). Finally, if you're interested in assessing your own personality, see Eysenck and Wilson's *Know Your Own Personality* (1976).

THE NEXT GROUP OF RESULTS ARE OCCUPATIONAL SCALES. THEY INDICATE HOW SIMILAR YOUR INTERESTS
ARE TO THE INTERESTS OF EMPLOYED PEOPLE IN VARIOUS OCCUPATIONS. THE AVERAGE WORKER SCORES ABOUT
50 ON THE SCALE WHICH IS BASED ON HER OR HIS OCCUPATION.

VERY SIMILAR 55+	SIMILAR 54-45	AVERAGE RANGE 44-26	DISSIMILAR 25-16	VERY DISSIMILAR 15-
58 PHYSICIAN	52 OPTOMETRIST	43 DENTAL HYGIENIST	25 SOCIAL WORKER	15 EXEC HOUSEKEEPER
	50 PSYCHOLOGIST	42 VETERINARIAN	23 BUYER	13 LANGUAGE TEACHER
	49 COLLEGE PROF.	42 DENTIST	23 GUIDANCE COUNS.	13 ELEM. TEACHER
	49 PHYS. THERAPIST	41 MATHEMATICIAN	23 RECREATION LEAD.	12 SOC. SCI TEACHER
	48 MEDICAL TECH.	41 ENGINEER	22 DENTAL ASSISTANT	10 SECRETARY
	46 DIETITIAN	40 ARTIST	21 CREDIT MANAGER	8 DEPT. STORE SALES
	46 PHARMACIST	40 SPEECH PATHOL.	21 BANKER	8 HOME ECON. TCHR.
		39 ACCOUNTANT	21 LIFE INS. AGENT	5 CHRISTIAN ED DIR
		38 MATH-SCI. TEACH.	21 ENGLISH TEACHER	3 ART TEACHER
		38 LANGUAGE INTERPR.	20 INSTRUM ASSEMBL.	1 BUSINESS ED TCHR
		37 LAWYER	19 INT. DECORATOR	
		37 MUSICIAN	17 LIC. PRAC. NURSE	
		37 ADVERTISING EXEC.		
		37 CHEMIST		
		35 COMPUTER PROGR.		
		35 ENTERTAINER		
		34 PHYS. ED. TEACHER		
		34 X-RAY TECHNICIAN		
		33 REPORTER		
		32 LIBRARIAN		
		31 OCCUP. THERAPIST		
		31 PHYSICIST		
		30 YWCA		
		29 REGISTERED NURSE		
		28 BEAUTICIAN		
		27 FLIGHT ATTENDANT		
		27 ARMY OFFICER		

* * * * * * * * * * * * * * * * * * * *

BELOW ARE YOUR HIGHEST OCCUPATIONAL SCALE SCORES. YOU SHOULD PAY PARTICULAR ATTENTION TO
THOSE OCCUPATIONS WHERE YOUR SCORES INDICATED THAT YOU HAD THE MOST SIMILAR INTERESTS. YOU WILL
HAVE THE BEST CHANCE OF FINDING SATISFACTION IF YOU DECIDE ON AN OCCUPATION WHERE YOUR INTERESTS
ARE SIMILAR WITH YOUR CO-WORKERS AND LESS CHANCE IF YOUR INTERESTS ARE DISSIMILAR. IF YOU RECORDED
THE SAME LIKES AND DISLIKES AS THE WORKERS, YOUR SCORE WILL BE HIGH FOR THAT OCCUPATION. IF YOUR
LIKE AND DISLIKE RESPONSES WERE DIFFERENT FROM THOSE OF PEOPLE IN THE OCCUPATION, YOUR SCORE WILL
BE LOW AND YOU WOULD NOT LIKELY BE STAISFIED IN THAT KIND OF WORK.

AS BEFORE, PAGE REFERENCES ARE GIVEN FOR THE OCCUPATIONAL OUTLOOK HANDBOOK (OOH), WHICH
PRESENTS ADDITIONAL INFORMATION ON EMPLOYMENT OPPORTUNITIES AND RELEVANT WORK SITUATIONS.
REFERENCES ARE ALSO LISTED FOR THE DICTIONARY OF OCCUPATIONAL TITLES (DOT) FOURTH EDITION-1975.
THE DOT GIVES DETAILED JOB DESCRIPTIONS OF THE DUTIES AND FUNCTIONS OF EACH OCCUPATION AND CAN BE
FOUND IN YOUR LOCAL LIBRARY OR PURCHASED FROM THE U.S. GOVERNMENT PRINTING OFFICE FOR $12.00.
THE FIRST DOT REFERENCE IS FOR PAGE NUMBER AND THE SECOND DOT REFERENCE IS FOR THE DOT CODE FOR
THAT PARTICULAR OCCUPATION.

YOUR HIGHEST SCORES APPEARED ON THE FOLLOWING SCALES AND INDICATE THE GREATEST DEGREE OF
SIMILARITY BETWEEN YOUR ANSWERS AND THOSE OF FEMALES IN THESE OCCUPATIONS--

```
58 PHYSICIAN---------PHYSICIANS DIAGNOSE, TREAT, AND ATTEMPT TO PREVENT PHYSICAL ILLNESSES. EIGHT
                     YEARS OF COLLEGE TRAINING, A ONE-YEAR RESIDENCY, AND A PASSING SCORE ON
     OOH 463-461     A STATE BOARD EXAMINATION ARE NECESSARY BEFORE AN INDIVIDUAL IS
     DOT 53-54       LICENSED TO PRACTICE MEDICINE. PERSONS INTERESTED IN THIS FIELD MUST BE
     DOT 070.010-.101 WILLING TO STUDY A GREAT DEAL THROUGHOUT THEIR CAREERS TO KEEP UP WITH
                     THE LATEST MEDICAL ADVANCES. HIGH MORAL STANDARDS, EMOTIONAL STABILITY,
                     A PLEASANT PERSONALITY, AND AN ABILITY TO MAKE DECISIONS IN EMERGENCIES ARE
                     ALSO IMPORTANT. DIFFERENT SPECIALTIES ARE OBSTETRICS, GYNECOLOGY, AND
                     SURGERY. THE EMPLOYMENT OUTLOOK FOR THIS FIELD IS EXPECTED TO BE VERY GOOD
                     THROUGH THE MID-1980S.

52 OPTOMETRIST------OPTOMETRISTS EXAMINE EYES AND PRESCRIBE CORRECTIVE LENSES AND TREATMENT. SIX
                    YEARS OF COLLEGE TRAINING AND A PASSING SCORE ON A STATE BOARD EXAMINATION
     OOH 459-461    ARE REQUIRED TO BE GRANTED A LICENSE. PERSONS INTERESTED IN THIS CAREER
     DOT 63         SHOULD HAVE BUSINESS APTITUDE, SELF-DISCIPLINE, AND AN ABILITY TO DEAL
     DOT 079.101    TACTFULLY WITH PATIENTS. RELATED OCCUPATIONS ARE OPHTHALMOLOGIST AND OPTI-
                    CIAN. EMPLOYMENT FOR THIS OCCUPATION IS EXPECTED TO GROW ABOUT AS FAST AS
                    THE AVERAGE FOR ALL OCCUPATIONS.

50 PSYCHOLOGIST------PSYCHOLOGISTS STUDY THE NORMAL AND ABNORMAL BEHAVIOR OF INDIVIDUALS AND
                     GROUPS TO UNDERSTAND AND EXPLAIN THEIR ACTIONS. PSYCHOLOGISTS TEACH, COUNSEL,
     OOH 528-531     OR DO EXPERIMENTAL RESEARCH. A MASTERS DEGREE IS THE MINIMAL REQUIREMENT
     DOT 48-49       FOR ENTRANCE INTO THIS FIELD, AND A PH.D. IS BECOMING INCREASINGLY
     DOT 045.061-.107 IMPORTANT. PERSONS CONSIDERING THIS FIELD MUST BE EMOTIONALLY STABLE,
                     MATURE, SENSIBLE, PATIENT, AND ABLE TO DEAL EFFECTIVELY WITH PEOPLE.
                     RELATED OCCUPATIONS ARE PSYCHIATRIST AND PSYCHOMETRIST. EMPLOYMENT IS
                     EXPECTED TO GROW FASTER THAN FOR MOST OCCUPATIONS.
```

Figure 13.14 ■ Excerpts from a computerized SCII interpretive report for Jean A.

(Reprinted by permission of NCS/Interpretive Scoring Systems. Adapted and reproduced by special permission of Consulting Psychologists
Press, Inc., Palo Alto, CA, 94306 as agent for Stanford University Press, from the Strong Campbell Interest Inventory Manual, Form T325 of the
Strong Vocational Interest Blank, copyright 1974, 1977, 1981 by the Board of Trustees of Leland Stanford Junior University.)

While visiting some married friends one day, you make the mistake of asking about their new baby. Since both mother and father are psychologists, it turns out they have thought more about their baby's future intelligence than most people, and they soon tell you more about it than you really needed to know. "We both do pretty well, so we felt the baby had a good start genetically," the mother says, "and I conceived while still in my 20s, so we knew that chances of some forms of retardation would be lower than if we waited. Then I avoided all alcohol throughout my pregnancy, took as few drugs as possible and then only those my doctor and I agreed were not likely to cause problems." You nod and smile, but she's not finished. "And, of course, I ate a balanced diet and took care of myself." You begin to wish you hadn't brought up the subject. The father then joins the discussion. "We took natural childbirth classes and arranged with our doctor to minimize drugs given to Patty during delivery. They also can affect the baby, you know." You smile again, and begin to edge for the door. "Now that she's born," Patty picks up, "we talk to her and hold her a lot, we have special mobiles hanging over her crib for visual stimulation, and we're buying special toys from that store that specializes in them." "Yes," says George. "We want to be sure to help maximize her intelligence by providing the best environment possible." You smile, agree, reach the door, and make your exit, even though they have much more to say. As you head home, you wonder: "Does all that really matter? If so, it's a wonder that most people are as intelligent as they are."

Think about what you mean when you say a person is intelligent, and you will see that *intelligence* must refer to some actual or potential behaviors (including the covert behaviors of thinking and problem solving). And at least some of these behaviors must cluster. If a person behaves intelligently at one time, you expect him or her to exhibit other intelligent behaviors. But what behaviors are the best general indicators of intelligence, and how can you measure them? Can you know the extent to which they are innate or learned, fixed or variable? Can you use the same kinds of measurements for different ages, to make educational and occupational decisions, and so forth? There are, in fact, so many such questions that it is difficult to keep track of them (Cronbach, 1975).

In this chapter we examine how the concept of intelligence has been defined and measured, from the beginnings of the intelligence test to some of the controversies that surround it today. A summary diagram will help keep track of the many issues involved in intelligence development and testing. ■ Figure 14.1

Intelligence

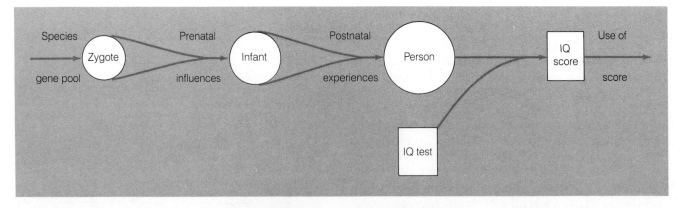

Figure 14.1 ■ The development and measurement of intelligence. Each person begins as a zygote, a sample of the species' gene pool. Prenatal influences interact with genetic potential to yield an infant at birth. Postnatal experiences interact with the growing child and adult and his or her intelligence always reflects all those factors. When that person takes an IQ test the interaction of the person's abilities and the test yields a score, which then can be used.

WHAT IS INTELLIGENCE?

Many psychologists consider intelligence tests to be one of the most successful applications of their discipline to date. Yet arguments over what intelligence really is—or if it is even a useful concept—are widespread, both in the popular media and within psychology. So before we look at the tests themselves, we need to consider what they seek to measure.

The Concept of Intelligence

We will adopt the definition offered by David Weschsler, the designer of some of the most widely used intelligence tests. Wechsler's general concept of **intelligence** is "the capacity of an individual to understand the world about him and his resourcefulness to cope with its challenges" (1975, p. 139). But Wechsler also says that the objective meaning of such a definition can be found in a cluster of measurable behaviors. Therefore, much of this chapter concerns the specification and measurement of behavioral clusters in the search for appropriate objective measures of intelligence.

Our summary of how intelligence develops and is measured (Figure 14.1) begins with the genetic history of the species. Each person begins as a zygote (fertilized egg), a single sample of the species' gene pool. Prenatal influences during gestation shape the developing fetus within the range of possibilities specified by its genes. The infant at birth thus reflects the net total of millions of years of evolution, a single genetic sample, and nine months of environmental shaping. Postnatal experiences continue to shape the developing child and

adult, yielding at any age a particular person who reflects all that has gone before.

IQ tests are constructed to measure the intelligence of some people under some circumstances. Under the best circumstances, an IQ test samples the person's intelligence—but for many reasons the sample may be imperfect. The score, whether a good or bad sample, is used by someone for some purpose. This use may be appropriate or inappropriate, depending on a variety of circumstances (Cole, 1981).

One of the problems you may have encountered in considering intelligence, especially if you have discussed it with others, is the mixing of different issues. One person may question whether intelligence is genetically influenced (Kamin, 1974); others may raise the problems faced by test takers who are socially disadvantaged (Cleary et al., 1975) or are not native English speakers (Olmedo, 1981). Still others may want to argue about whether test scores should be used to assign students to different ability groups (Reschly, 1981). Each of these issues is worth discussion, but they should not be confused with one another; each needs to be considered separately (R. J. Smith, 1979b).

We will use Figure 14.1 as a framework for considering these and other issues. But before we begin, let's briefly summarize some aspects of intelligence testing; later, we can consider test construction in more detail.

How Could You Test Intelligence?

Imagine for a moment that no intelligence tests exist and you have the inspiration to devise one. How might you go about it? Your first problem is to think about

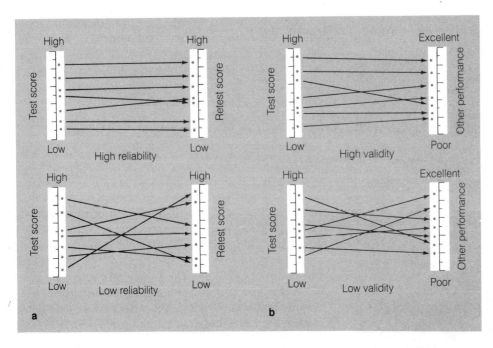

Figure 14.2 ■ How correlations indicate the extent of reliability or validity. (a) On a reliable test, people score about the same both times they take the test, yielding a high reliability coefficient. (b) On a valid test, people score about the same as they do on some criterion, yielding a high validity coefficient.

(From *Psychology Today*, 4th ed. Copyright © 1979 by Random House, Inc. Reprinted by permission of the publisher.)

what you want to measure until you can specify it narrowly enough to begin to measure it. Then you have to build a test to operationally define your concept. If problem solving seems to you to be intelligent behavior, you'd throw in a few problems. If social skills seem relevant, you'd have to decide how to test those. There are many decisions to make, but you could come up with a mixed set of problems—called **test items**—designed to measure intelligence. But then what?

Reliability and Validity   You won't know whether anyone can do the items until you give them to some people. So suppose you try them on a few friends. Unfortunately, that alone won't tell you much. For one thing, you won't know without repeated testing whether they score similarly each time. Until the test is **reliable**—gives repeated measures that are similar—you can go no further.

Giving the same people the same test more than once is one of the techniques psychologists use to assess reliability; it is called a **test–retest measure.** Another technique, called a **split-half measure,** is also useful for assessing internal reliability. If you have several items of each type, you can split each group of items in half to form two shorter tests. After your subjects take the complete test, you compute the scores separately for the two half-tests and compare them. If all your items really measure the same skills, any sub-

set of these items should give about the same results as any other subset. Thus the scores on one half of the items should be similar to the scores on the other half.

Reliability is a necessity before you can even ask what a test measures. But once your test is reliable, you must also ask if it is **valid**—if it measures what it claims to measure. It will be invalid if it turns out to measure some factor other than intelligence. Suppose, for instance, someone were so foolish as to propose that hat size measures intelligence because he or she felt it indicated how big people's brains are. Measures of hat size are quite reliable; they are easy to obtain and vary little from time to time (at least for adults). But they are not valid; they don't measure intelligence.

One basic type of validity is called **criterion validity:** You assess your new measure by comparing it to some existing measure, called the criterion. If you are developing a new test of a type that already exists, criterion validity may be sufficient. You would first check reliability by doing repeated tests and correlating the results. This correlation process yields a **reliability coefficient;** a high reliability coefficient shows that test takers get about the same scores each time, so you're measuring *something*. Then to measure validity you would correlate your test with the criterion. This yields a **validity coefficient;** a high validity coefficient indicates that test takers do about as well on the test as on the criterion. ■ Figure 14.2

Figure 14.3 ■ Alfred Binet (1857–1911), the French originator of the intelligence test. *"It seemed to us that it would be extremely useful to give a guide to future examination commissions: . . . It is necessary to guard against the judges who will compose them getting into the habit of leaving decisions to luck, based on subjective and hence uncontrollable impressions, which will be sometimes good, sometimes bad, and will give too large a part to the arbitrary, the capricious. . . . It will never be to one's credit to have attended a special school. We should at the least spare from this mark those who do not deserve it. . . . And finally, as a principle, we are convinced, and will not cease repeating, that one must introduce into the practical procedures [of testing] the precision and the exactitude of science every time one can, and one can almost always."* (Binet & Simon, 1905, pp. 163–164.)
(Photo from the Bettmann Archive, Inc.)

Criterion validity is limited in several ways. One major problem is that no criterion exists for any new concept. If you were the first to develop an intelligence test, for example, you could not use criterion validity to assess it. Another problem is that whatever new test you devise can at best be only as good a measure as the criterion. You cannot build a better test than the criterion, because by definition a better test would give different results from the criterion; you have no way of telling whether differences from the criterion represent improvements or errors.

Psychologists overcome the limitations of criterion validity by using a series of different criterion measures. None of these criteria measures exactly what the new test is designed to measure, but each defines a portion of it. This form of validity definition is called **construct validity;** it builds up the concept, or *construct,* from a set of separate measures (Campbell & Fiske, 1959). The use of construct validity is an ongoing process in which each additional comparison strengthens the definition of the test; it is almost like building and assessing a new theory. Thus, in a sense, construct validity is a series of criterion-validity measurements. In fact, one expert has suggested that *all* validity is construct validity and that criterion validity is simply a limited form (Cronbach, 1980).

Binet's Test   All current intelligence tests had their beginning in a task somewhat like the one just posed. But the task was more narrowly defined, so perhaps it did not seem as difficult as it might today. In 1881, the French government introduced the concept of education for all children. In doing so, they found that children of low ability, who had formerly been kept home by their parents, were unable to profit from the regular schooling; they would either have to be left out of the system or given special schooling. **Alfred Binet** (1857–1911) was asked to devise a test to predict which children would be unable to handle regular schooling, so they could be treated differently before they failed (Wolf, 1973). ■ Figure 14.3

Binet's task was somewhat easier than the general one posed earlier. He knew what people he had to deal with, and more important, he had a ready-made validity criterion: His test would be successful if it sorted a group of children in a way that matched their later success in school. It would take a few years to be sure he had such a test, but the criterion was clear. Years later, the test he and a co-worker devised was adapted as a general-purpose intelligence test (Binet & Simon, 1908).

Binet's original test sought to predict later school success using problems similar to those that the children would face in their schoolwork. He developed a series of questions of increasing difficulty so most five-year-olds could answer some, most six-year-olds those and others, and so forth. Binet thus established a set of questions that characterized the average ability of each age group. The child began with the easiest questions and progressed as far as he or she could. If a child successfully answered questions for the five-year-old level but not the six-year-old level, the child was assigned a **mental age (MA)** of five. Children who scored a mental age equal to their actual or **chronological age (CA)** were exactly on track. The six-year-old who could solve seven-year-old-level problems was considered advanced, the one who could only solve five-year-old-level problems retarded.

The IQ Binet himself did *not* combine mental and chronological age into an IQ score. But later a means of obtaining a single numerical indicator of a child's relative state of advancement or retardation was devised: dividing mental age by chronological age. As a result, an advanced six-year-old might score 8/6 = 1.33, a retarded one perhaps 4/6 = 0.67. To get rid of the decimal point, multiply by 100: 8/6(100) = 133 and 4/6(100) = 67. Then, for the average six-year-old whose mental age equaled his or her chronological age, the score would be 6/6(100) = 100. This resulting score was a particular kind of quotient, the **intelligence quotient (IQ).**

$$IQ = \frac{\text{mental age}}{\text{chronological age}} \times 100$$

Such an IQ computation worked fine for children, but assumed that each increasing year brings greater performance. We might wish this were so for adults, so we could all go on getting smarter each year, but it is not. Hence the term *IQ* is still used, but no major reputable test still uses the original ratio or quotient computation of MA over CA (Reschly, 1981). Subsequent tests have kept 100 as the average score and similar meanings for higher and lower scores, but have computed all scores in a new way. Contemporary IQ tests, for children as well as adults, now set 100 as the IQ score equivalent to an average performance for a tested group of subjects. Scores above and below 100 still signify greater or lesser intelligence, but they are computed by adding or subtracting IQ points for each standard deviation above or below the average score. (A standard deviation is a conventional measure of the amount of variation in a set of numbers. See Appendix.) On the contemporary version of Binet's test, for example, a person whose numerical score is one standard deviation better than the test average is assigned an IQ of 116.

This type of score is called a **deviation quotient.** Deviation quotients have several advantages. One important advantage is that they allow different age groups to be compared directly; an IQ of 100 always means "average" for any age group and values above and below 100 always have similar meanings. (In Binet's test each age group was computed separately, and the scores for different ages were not directly comparable.) Current IQ tests are designed to yield a normal distribution of scores, with most scores clustered between 90 and 110 and nearly all falling between about 60 and 140. ■ Figure 14.4

"YOU DID VERY WELL ON YOUR I.Q. TEST. YOU'RE A MAN OF 49 WITH THE INTELLIGENCE OF A MAN OF 53."

©1977 by Sidney Harris—American Scientist Magazine

With these basic ideas in mind, we can begin looking at the development and testing of intelligence (following the sequence of Figure 14.1). This discussion will frequently use *IQ* as a shorthand for "measured intelligence." But remember that *IQ* refers to specific ways of defining and measuring some human skills; it is not identical to all that one might mean by intelligence.

THE NATURE AND NURTURE OF INTELLIGENCE

As we first noted in Chapter 1, nature and nurture always interact, even though we may discuss them separately. And as first noted in Chapter 3, the reaction range is a useful concept for summarizing those interactions.

Reaction Ranges and Intelligence

People find it difficult to think in several dimensions at once. So, when considering the factors that lead to some human behavior, the temptation is to focus on only a few similar ones at a time: genetic conditions that can affect IQ, for example, or variations in parenting techniques. It's much harder to think of all factors at the same time: to ask how a particular genetic

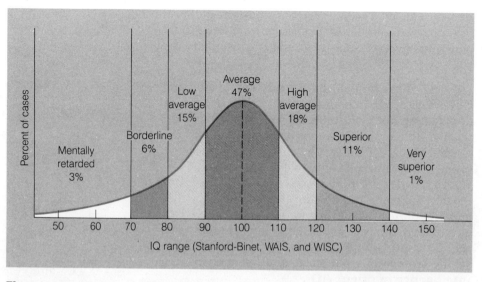

Figure 14.4 ■ IQ tests are designed to yield an approximately normal distribution of scores. The average of the distribution is set at 100, with each 16 IQ points equal to one standard deviation above or below that. Common descriptive labels for ranges of IQ are shown, together with the proportion of the total population that they represent; from 90 to 110 is considered average, and includes nearly half the population.

(From *Human Learning and Memory: An Introduction* by Arthur Wingfield. Copyright © 1979 by Harper & Row, Publishers, Inc. Reprinted by permission of Harper & Row, Publishers, Inc.)

background may interact with a particular parenting style, for example. Yet we must do so if we are to understand most human behaviors and certainly if we are to understand the development of intelligence (Willerman, 1979a, 1979b)—these interactions determine real outcomes, and thinking about the questions in simpler terms can only be misleading (Scarr & Weinberg, 1978).

One way of summarizing multiple factors in human development is the use of reaction ranges. Each person's **reaction range** for some structure or behavior is the range of possibilities allowed by that person's genetics. Environmental influences then shape the actual structure or behavior to some value within the reaction range. Figure 14.5 presents a hypothetical set of reaction ranges for intelligence. The relationships summarized here are generally accepted, although not all psychologists agree on the details. ■ Figure 14.5

Many relationships are summarized in Figure 14.5. Moving vertically from one curve to the next we see the difference between genotypes (genetic types) for a single kind of environment. Moving horizontally at a single IQ level we see that different genotypes can develop the same IQ if they are raised in different environments. Moving along a single reaction-range curve we see how sensitive IQ is to environmental differences for that genotype, and what the limits might be with an exceptionally enriched environment.

Several general conclusions can be drawn from this model:

1 The better the environment, the higher the IQ, for all genotypes.

2 If all individuals are reared in an identical environment, actual IQs will reflect the order of genotypes; Type C will have a higher IQ than Type B, for example.

3 If individuals come from varying environments, actual IQs may *not* be in the same order as genotypes: A Type C genotype from a deprived environment can have a lower IQ than a Type B reared in an enriched environment.

4 The greatest range of possibilities, in response to environmental variation, occurs for the highest genotype; this is shown by the vertical arrows at the right, which represent the reaction ranges. (An actual reaction range for intelligence might be approximately 30 IQ points.)

It is thus possible that a number of things about IQ which seem confusing or contradictory might all be true. Consider Figure 14.5 in light of the following questions. Does genetics control IQ? (Yes; see Types A through D.) Does environment control IQ? (Also yes; note the vertical arrows of the reaction ranges.) Can you say of two people that the person with the higher measured IQ has the higher genetic potential? (Not usually. Only if you know they have had equal envi-

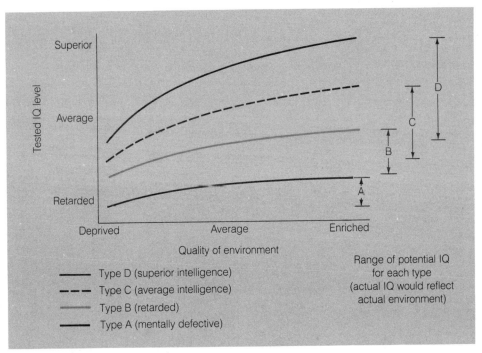

Figure 14.5 ■ Hypothetical reaction ranges for four different genotypes (genetic samples) show that environment and genetics both influence measured IQ.

(Adapted from I. I. Gottesman, "Genetic Aspects of Intelligent Behavior," in N. Ellis (ed.), *Handbook of Mental Deficiency: Psychological Theory and Research*, McGraw-Hill, 1963. Used by permission of N. Ellis.)

ronments can you say that; otherwise they could be like Type B in an enriched environment versus Type C in a deprived one.) As we consider the genetic and environmental influences on intelligence, keep these relationships in mind, and refer back to Figure 14.5 as necessary.

The Genetics of Intelligence

The evolution of a large brain and the intelligence it makes possible have been a major part of the evolution of our species. Because the course of a species' evolution is carried by its gene pool, intelligence, like other attributes, is genetically influenced. As noted in Chapter 3, heritability measures how much of the variation in a characteristic in a population results from genetic differences. The heritability of intelligence for the most-studied population, the white middle class in the United States, has been estimated to be as high as .85 or as low as .50 (Loehlin et al., 1975; Scarr, 1981a); this means that from nearly half to as much as three-quarters of the variation among individuals in this group results from genetic differences.

Remember that heritability estimates are always for populations, and can never tell us how important genetics has been for any single individual. A comparison of individual IQs, however, can sometimes tell

us something about genetics. One of the bases for the heritability figures just quoted is a comparison of individuals with differing degrees of genetic similarity. In a simple genetic model, the coefficient of genetic relationship between two individuals ranges from .0 for completely unrelated persons, through .50 for parent/child or sibling relationships, to 1.0 for identical (monozygotic) twins. When the IQs of individuals with differing degrees of relationship are correlated, the overall pattern is clear: The closer the genetic relationship, the higher the correlation in IQ (Bouchard & McGue, 1981). Correlations range from zero for unrelated persons reared apart to .85 for monozygotic twins reared together. This is strong evidence for genetic influences in intelligence. ■ Figure 14.6

But Figure 14.6 also reveals environmental effects. Consider the bottom two sets of values, both for genetically unrelated children. A strictly genetic model predicts a zero correlation for them. But their IQs are correlated at about .30, apparently from a family-environment effect. Or consider the top two lines. The IQs of monozygotic twins correlate far more highly than any other group, but also show the effects of environment by the differences between the correlations of those reared apart (.67) and together (.85). This is exactly what the reaction-range curves of Figure 14.5 suggest: Intelligence is the consequence of both genetics and environmental shaping.

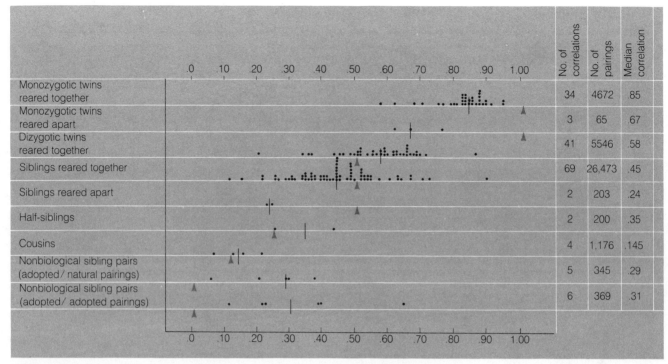

Figure 14.6 ■ Summary of IQ correlations for individuals with different degrees of relationships. The plotted points indicate the correlation values in different studies. The vertical lines indicate the median values of the studies, and the pointers indicate the theoretical values to be expected if intelligence were the result of a simple genetic relationship. The first line, for example, says that different studies found values for the IQ of monozygotic twins reared together varying from about .58 to about .95. The median value of all these studies was .85, and the theoretical value for a genetic model is 1.00. (Note that the chart does *not* include Burt's data, which are questionable in some respects; Hawkes, 1979.)

(From "Familial Studies of Intelligence: A Review," by T. J. Bouchard, Jr. and M. McGue, *Science*, 1981, *212*, 1055–1059. Copyright 1981 by the American Association for the Advancement of Science. Used by permission.)

Environmental Shaping of Intelligence

As we have seen, the zygote's genetic sample fixes the limits of a person's lifetime structural and behavioral development; it is that person's "nature." The range of possibilities may be broad or limited, but it is always the environment that selects within them to shape the outcome. *Given* type D genetics, for example, the person may be below average, a genius, or simply average entirely as the result of environment.

Everything in the Type D zygote's prenatal and postnatal environments—the total of "nurture"—has to be ideal for that person to reach the highest IQ potential. Unfortunately, however, neither prenatal nor postnatal environment is ever ideal. Hence, in noting prenatal and postnatal influences we will frequently consider environmental factors that can reduce intelligence. This is not because most environmental influences are negative, but because describing possible problems is more informative than simply saying that if all goes well a person will reach the upper limit.

For nine months after conception, the developing zygote's normal environment is its mother's body. If the maternal environment is close to ideal, the developing individual is buffered from outside influences and provided with ample nutrients. But the newborn's potential intelligence may be affected if the mother's diet is deficient, if she smokes, if she contracts certain illnesses, if she takes some drugs, or if she suffers injury. If its mother is an alcoholic, for example, the newborn may have fetal alcohol syndrome, a developmental deficiency that causes retardation (Streissguth et al., 1980).

One of the most dangerous times in a person's life is the transition from prenatal to postnatal environment. The evolution of our large brains has made the birth process a risky one for infants. Even with a number of mechanisms that help minimize birth damage, such as the infant's still-flexible skull, there is risk of brain damage from the birth itself and from anoxia (transient oxygen starvation) (Windle, 1969). Modern medicine has eased some of the problems, as with the use of cesarean sections for especially risky births. But it has also added problems; the drugs given to mothers often affect the infant for at least several days, and their long-term consequences are little known (Newton & Modahl, 1978).

If the newborn survives the birth process relatively intact, it enters a new and vastly wider environment. From the first slap on the bottom until death, the individual is subject to an awesome array of potential influences that can affect intelligence. Some postnatal environmental influences are also physiological, such as diet, drugs, disease, and injury. But a new major class of potential influences—the socializing or learning influences—also affect the individual's nervous system, although less blatantly.

The adult's intelligence is strongly influenced by the quantity and quality of childhood language experiences, for example (Lewis, 1976). Other important postnatal experiences include parental caretaking patterns, from ways of holding the newborn through techniques of punishing or encouraging the child. Extreme cases provide dramatic examples of the negative consequences of failure in caretaking. Psychologically disturbed parents have sometimes kept children in closets or tied to beds for years; such children are severely and often permanently retarded, despite attempts at therapy.

Less extreme variations in nurture influences are harder to detect because their effects are not so drastic, but some have been noted.

One question with major social implications now being investigated is whether the general IQ of large groups of people, perhaps even the populations of whole countries, can be deliberately increased by improving environmental conditions. One such study, done in Colombia, had encouraging results (McKay et al., 1978). Poland has sought to improve the conditions of large numbers of its children by raising them collectively (Firkowska et al., 1978). And Venezuela has embarked on an ambitious national campaign to raise the collective IQ of its citizens by improving all conditions that affect intelligence, from prenatal maternal nutrition through postnatal health and education (Walsh, 1981). The success of this national project will take years to determine, but a large proportion of the Venezuelans will no doubt be healthier and more intelligent than they would have been.

The result of a zygote's genetic nature and environmental nurture is a person with some set of abilities that might be characterized as intelligence. We will examine how that intelligence is measured a bit later. But first, following our summary in Figure 14.1, we can briefly examine the course of intelligence over a lifetime.

Intelligence over a Lifetime

As researchers have devised intelligence tests for a variety of populations, one trend has been to build special ones for very young children. The assumption has been that it's better to find potential problems as early as possible, leaving more time to remedy them. The latest tests of verbal ability have questions ranging down to the 2-year-old level. Tests for infants measure overt behaviors, such as following an object with the eyes or responding to directions (Bayley Scales of Infant Development, 1969).

Recently, researchers have attempted to measure some physiological indicator of brain activity directly. They have measured heart-rate response to toys presented in certain patterns, for example, or EEG measures in response to simple inputs. However, it will take some time to validate these intriguing physiological measures, because there is no currently accepted measure of infant intelligence to use as a criterion.

Measures of physical parameters at birth, such as length, do not predict IQ at age four well (Broman et al., 1975). And tests in the first few years, although reasonably reliable, may not be valid measures of later IQ; they do not necessarily correlate well with later tests (Shepard, 1976). This discrepancy may be primarily a measurement problem, with infant tests tapping different abilities than do later IQ tests. Or it may be that early intelligence is in fact relatively flexible and the measures are tapping actual changes over the early years.

After the first few school years, however, intelligence measures usually stabilize, although later changes of 5 or 10 IQ points are common (Loehlin et al., 1975). A plateau level of adult intelligence is reached by the late teens or early 20s. After that, IQ holds relatively constant, perhaps decreasing slightly, for many years. It was long thought that IQ dropped relatively steeply through middle age and beyond, but this depressing conclusion is now being revised on several grounds (Baltes & Schaie, 1976; Horn & Donaldson, 1976). ■ Figure 14.7

One problem in interpreting curves like that of Figure 14.7b is that they have frequently been drawn from cross-sectional data. **Cross-sectional studies** compare several different age groups within a population at the same time. If all other factors were constant, this curve would show what happens to a person over a lifetime. But other factors are rarely constant in a society like ours; dramatic changes occur rapidly. A more accurate way to study development over time is to do **longitudinal studies,** in which the same subjects are followed and studied as they age. Longitudinal

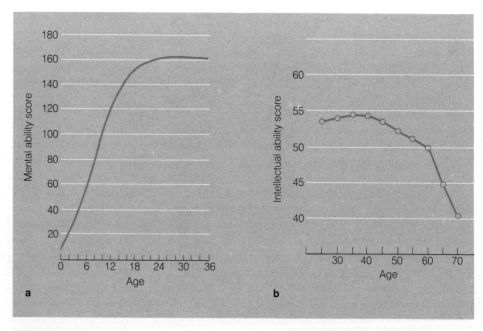

Figure 14.7 ■ (a) IQ continues to rise until the early 20s, then remains relatively stable during adulthood. (Based on a large-scale longitudinal study, using tests appropriate to the various ages with the scores adjusted to a single scale.) (b) Cross-sectional tests of populations typically show a decrease in intellectual ability after about age 40, but the data may be misleading. (The scale here is a common one used to compare different tests and is not calibrated in IQ points.)

(**a**, from N. Bayley, "Development of Mental Abilities," in P. Mussen (ed.), *Carmichael's Manual of Child Psychology*, Vol. 1. Copyright 1970 by John Wiley & Sons. Used by permission; **b**, from K. W. Schaie and C. R. Strother, *Psychological Review*, 1968, 70, 671–680. Copyright 1968 by the American Psychological Association. Reprinted by permission of the author.)

studies are complex and costly, however, and require years of work before the data are available.

For groups relatively close in age, cross-sectional data may not differ much from longitudinal data. Today's 13-year-olds in another year may not be very different from today's 14-year-olds. But across many years and major social changes, serious discrepancies can occur. Available 70-year-olds, for example, represent the survivors of a once larger population and have lived through major social changes. It is unlikely that they reflect what today's children will be like in another 60 years.

One major change that would be expected to depress the IQ curve is the improvement in education over the last 60 years. People who are 70 years old today attended school under quite different circumstances early in the century than today's students. Many current 70-year-olds may have had little schooling at all, much less some college, which is common today. (The same argument could be made regarding diet, medical care, and other variables.) Thus, today's older people may have lower IQs, but these may be the same values they have had for all of their adult lives, rather than reflecting a drop as they aged.

Changes that do occur with age might also be more important for certain IQ measures than for others: tests

of factors such as perceptual speed might show a drop, whereas tests that measured accumulated knowledge might show a continued rise. The overall curve would then depend on the particular set of test items used.

But still other changes that occur with age are probably the ones most relevant to the drop in Figure 14.7b. A wide variety of illnesses and other conditions can reduce intelligence, and many of these affect primarily older people. Thus, with each additional year of age beyond middle adulthood, the population includes more and more people whose intelligence is diminished by organic problems. This will inevitably depress the curve for the group as a whole, even if many of its members increase in IQ or show no loss. Figure 14.7b might be correct as a probability curve for the group without reflecting the actual course of any individual's IQ.

Obviously, longitudinal studies are needed if we are to assess these various possibilities properly. One ambitious long-term longitudinal study may help answer some of these questions—at least for the high-IQ segment of the population. The **Terman study** began with over 1500 gifted youngsters in 1921 and has followed them ever since (Oden, 1968; Terman, 1925). Most of the Terman subjects are now in their 70s, so we may soon have longitudinal data on this group for most of the range of Figure 14.7. We still will not know how well the outcome for this group represents the population as a whole, but it will be a start.

DEFINING INTELLIGENCE

Our discussion of the genetics and development of intelligence has been based on the assumption that something called *intelligence* not only exists but can be measured. It's now time to examine more closely some of the possible ways of defining and measuring intelligence.

You may have heard someone repeat the well-known remark that "intelligence is that which IQ tests measure." There is some truth to this, in that each IQ test may be considered a particular operational definition of intelligence. But this phrase can also imply that intelligence does not exist independent of IQ tests and this overstates the case. Some concepts of intelligence precede and underlie each test. You might think that these concepts would vary with each person, but one theorist has argued that they are widely shared in our culture, even by children (Sternberg, 1981b). All IQ tests are attempts to operationalize these underlying ideas of intelligence.

Before a test of intelligence can be developed, however, several major conceptual decisions must be made. We will look at three of these decisions: (1) whether intelligence is an achievement or an aptitude; (2) whether intelligence is general or specific; and (3) whether there are special types or patterns of intelligence.

Is Intelligence Achievement or Aptitude?

Achievement tests are designed to measure what someone has already accomplished. You are probably most familiar with academic exams, but society makes use of a wide range of achievement tests. Driver's license exams, for example, seek to measure acquired driving skills as well as knowledge of rules of the road. **Aptitude tests,** in contrast, are designed to measure what can be achieved in the future; they measure current abilities, but only because these will be useful in acquiring new skills. You almost certainly took one of the best-known aptitude tests: the Scholastic Aptitude Test (SAT). The SAT is intended to measure how well you might do on your college exams before you are admitted (Hargadon, 1981).

All tests must measure something the test taker can do today. Hence, the difference between aptitude and achievement tests depends on their *intent:* achievement tests seek to measure what you have done, aptitude tests to predict what you are capable of. The same test can even be both an achievement and an aptitude test. The final exam in an introductory chemistry class, for example, is an achievement test for that class, but could also be considered an aptitude test for advanced chemistry. In building an aptitude test, a crucial question is what current achievement can be measured that will be a useful predictor of some other future achievement.

Intelligence tests are both generalized aptitude tests and achievement tests. Their purpose is to predict future performance, and thus they can be considered generalized aptitude tests. But they inevitably call upon skills that reflect previous learning and in that sense must also be achievement tests. Many arguments about the uses of intelligence tests can be understood in this context. If all children have been equally exposed to language inputs, for example, the ones with the largest vocabularies presumably have the highest innate aptitude for vocabulary learning. Similarly, if all chemistry students read the text and attended classes, those with the highest grades probably have the most aptitude for chemistry.

But when all children have not had identical exposure, you cannot make the same assumption: A child with little language exposure cannot develop a large vocabulary, regardless of aptitude. So a vocabulary test given to a group of children with mixed language backgrounds taps both aptitude and exposure. The test clearly measures *achievement;* the child either knows a given word or does not. But whether achievement reveals aptitude may be arguable. (Obviously, if some students were sick and missed half the chemistry lectures, their final exam scores would not accurately reflect their aptitude for chemistry.) Such problems can be avoided by using items to which all children have had equal exposure. These can be very familiar concepts or ones so unique that none of the children has encountered them before.

Is Intelligence General or Specific?

One way of conceptualizing intelligence is as a very general trait, applicable to a wide range of problems. Many psychologists view it this way and IQ measures have been found to correlate with many behaviors. An alternate view of intelligence, however, is as a collection of separate, more specialized skills. These skills might still tend to cluster, so a person especially competent at one might be expected to be good at most others. But this separate-skills view also implies that some people might be much more "intelligent" in some ways than in others (Carroll & Horn, 1981).

Table 14.1 ■ Summary of Thurstone's Proposed Primary Abilities

Primary Ability	Ability indicated by
Verbal comprehension	Understanding word meanings, as in a vocabulary test
Word fluency	Using words rapidly and flexibly, as in solving verbal problems
Number	Using numbers, as in solving arithmetic problems
Space	Creating and manipulating mental representations of objects, as in deciding what an object would look like from another angle
Memory	Remembering previously presented information, such as word lists
Perceptual speed	Discriminating the details of a complex presentation rapidly and accurately, as in deciding if two drawings are identical or not
Reasoning	Discovering a general rule, based on a series of examples, as in deciding what the next number will be in a series such as 2, 4, 8 . . .

After Thurstone and Thurstone, 1963.

To the extent that different skills do correlate, then the question of whether there is one intelligence or many is of interest only to theorists and researchers. But because some measures of intelligence might give quite different results than others, the question becomes important for many people—both those who are tested and those who use the test results as a basis for making decisions, such as teachers.

Different theorists have proposed differing numbers of separate skills, from several to more than a hundred. One influential view was that of L. L. Thurstone (1877–1955), who proposed seven **primary mental abilities** (1938). ■ Table 14.1

Examining Thurstone's primary abilities, however, shows that other distinctions can easily be made. Is "verbal comprehension" as measured by single words the same as verbal comprehension of a page of prose? Is "memory" a unitary ability, or is memory for spatial relations different from memory for numbers or words? If you continued this exercise, you could develop a much longer list of potential skills. But it might be better to arrange the list to group types of verbal skills or types of memory together.

Another influential approach, J. P. Guilford's **structure-of-intellect model,** does just that. According to Guilford (1967), one important dimension of such a list is "operations," such as memory. Another dimension is "content," such as spatial figures or words. Memory for spatial figures and memory for words would thus be one operation (memory) applied to two kinds of content (figures and words). Finally, Guilford suggested a third dimension, "product," or what the outcome of the process is. Then he arranged

these three dimensions at right angles to each other. Overall, Guilford suggested 5 operations, 4 contents, and 6 products for a total of 120 separate intellectual skills (about two-thirds of which have been measured). ■ Figure 14.8

Guilford's model represents the greatest number of subskills that anyone has formally proposed. These are clearly too many for easy analysis and summary, and probably draw unnecessarily fine distinctions for most purposes. But the model is a useful way of conceptualizing the relationships involved, and reminds us that operations may be different from content or product. And it offers a ready-made system for drawing finer distinctions if it becomes necessary. In the development of a new test or in comparing two apparently similar tests, for example, Guilford's model might point to subtleties that could otherwise be overlooked.

Another influential approach, which sought to combine the concepts of intelligence as one ability and as several separate skills, was proposed by the English psychologist Charles Spearman (1863–1945). Spearman used the technique of factor analysis, which he developed, to analyze subjects' performances on different types of tests. Spearman found that a single factor seemed influential in a variety of tasks; he called it a **general intelligence factor (*g*).** But some differences between different types of tasks could not be explained by *g*: Some people did much better on numerical tasks, others on verbal tasks, and so forth. Spearman suggested that these differences reflected additional **specific factors (*s*)** (1927).

According to Spearman, then, each person has a general level of overall intelligence (*g*) that directs or

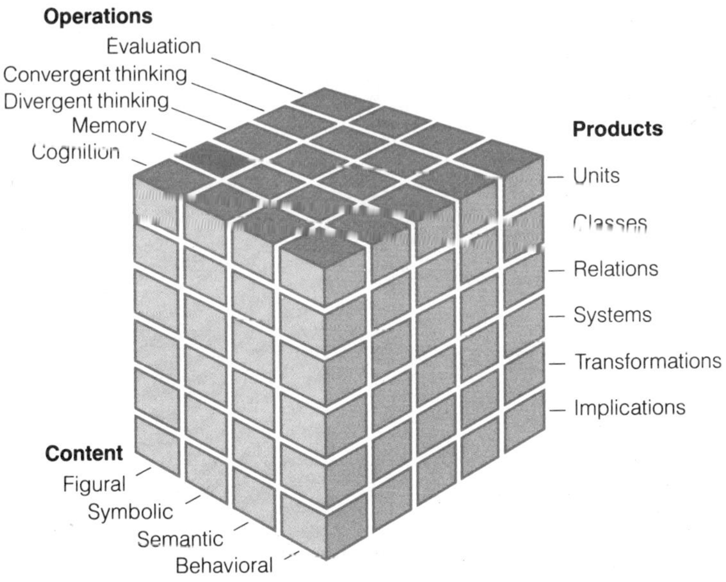

Figure 14.8 ■ Guilford's structure-of-intellect model of intelligence suggests that a total of 120 different special abilities can be distinguished. Each represents the intersection of three dimensions, or one small block in the diagram. The accented block, for example, represents a memory operation for a figural content to produce a unit product; it might be shown in the remembering of a particular shape.

(From J. P. Guilford, *American Psychologist*, 1959, *14*, 469–479. Copyright 1959 by the American Psychological Association. Reprinted by permission of the author.)

draws on a number of more specialized skills (*s*s). Most tests of intelligence measure *g*, so there are substantial correlations among tests. But different tests tap different *s*s. Thus no two tests will correlate perfectly, and subjects may do much better on some tests than on others, depending on particular *s* factors.

Each of these three models has influenced the development and interpretation of intelligence tests, and each tells us something about intelligence. Guilford noted some important distinctions and suggested that a large number of specialized skills may be involved. Thurstone suggested that for most purposes it may be enough to distinguish among a much smaller number of more generally defined abilities. And Spearman suggested that it may be useful to think of both a general overriding ability and a small number of separate skills. Some future theory may even integrate these points, with Guilford's many factors (or Spearman's *s*s) representing the finest level of detail, groups of these factors adding up to Thurstone's primary abilities, and finally being integrated by a general intelligence factor such as Spearman's *g*.

Are There Types of Intelligence?

Other theorists have suggested that intelligence can be thought of as being of different types (often only two types). These types sometimes overlap those discussed above, and other times point to different kinds of distinctions.

Most theorists agree, for example, that a basic difference exists between verbal and visual–spatial forms of intelligence. This distinction is found frequently and is one of the major differences claimed to exist between the sexes (for a summary, see Maccoby & Jacklin, 1974b). These sex differences may exist because of differential hormonal effects on the developing brain, which may cause differential development of the two cerebral hemispheres (Arnold, 1980). Whatever the source of these differences, any test of intelligence should be examined to see whether it measures verbal intelligence, visual–spatial intelligence, or both. ■ Figure 14.9

R. B. Cattell (1971) drew a somewhat different distinction, between **fluid intelligence,** the ability to

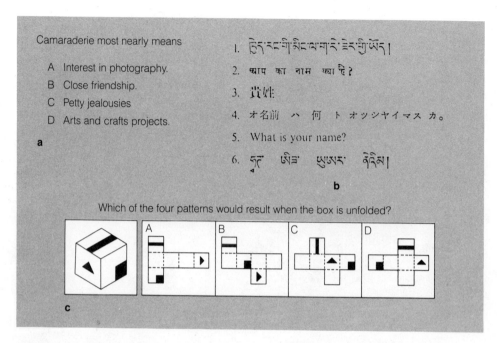

Figure 14.9 ■ One basic difference in IQ items is whether they are primarily verbal or visual-spatial. (a) This type of question seems a straightforward verbal definition. (b) The enormous amount of learning necessary even to read the question, however, is shown in an example such as this one: All questions here simply ask for your name. Question 1 is Tibetan, 2 is Hindi, 3 is Chinese, 4 is Japanese, and 6 is English written in Tibetan script. (c) This visual task also seems straightforward, but may require specialized experience to solve (correct answer is D).

judge novel situations and respond to them, and **crystallized intelligence,** the ability to recover old knowledge when appropriate to new occasions. The two kinds of intelligence are clearly related but not identical. It requires a high fluid intelligence, for example, to develop a high crystallized one. If a group of children were raised in common, you might expect those with the highest fluid intelligence to develop the largest vocabularies. But a high fluid intelligence cannot guarantee development of a high crystallized intelligence if the environment does not provide the necessary knowledge.

Furthermore, fluid intelligence depends on speed of processing, according to Cattell, and crystallized intelligence develops with experience. Thus fluid intelligence might decrease as a person ages and crystallized intelligence might increase. An older person might not learn a new word as fast as a younger person, but might have a much larger vocabulary. Thus tests emphasizing fluid abilities might be more likely to show a drop in intelligence with age, and those emphasizing crystallized abilities might be more likely to show an increase. In nature/nurture terms, fluid intelligence

should be more dependent on genetics and prenatal environment; development of crystallized intelligence should be more dependent on postnatal experience. (Not all theorists accept Cattell's fluid/crystallized distinction, however; Guilford, 1980.)

Still other distinctions could be drawn, though these have not yet made a significant impact on testing. One sociologist, for example, has criticized all intelligence tests for being too impersonal, and has suggested that measures of "social intelligence" be developed to complement them (Archer, 1980). Some psychologists have also suggested that an assessment of social or everyday competence is needed to supplement conventional IQ measures (Scarr, 1981b).

One way of synthesizing many of these distinctions is to think of intelligence in terms of information processing (Glaser, 1981; Sternberg, 1981c). An intelligent act is then one that is efficient in information-processing terms, and anything that affects the efficiency of information processing will affect intelligence. One information-processing approach to testing is to use Piaget's theory as a basis for tests (Tuddenham, 1970), but non-Piagetian models also exist.

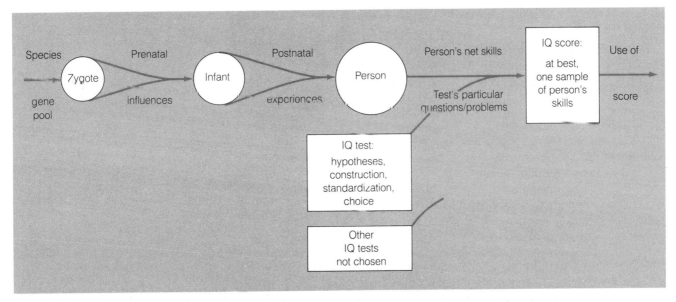

Figure 14.10 ■ Revision of Figure 14.1, emphasizing how particular tests interact with a person's skills to yield a score.

In general, an information-processing approach summarizes a person's intelligence as a set of cognitive skills. Some of these skills are more the product of nature (more fluid, in Cattell's terms), and others represent a store of retrievable environmental experiences in LTM (more akin to crystallized intelligence). All of a person's abilities, in response to any mode of testing, would constitute his or her intelligence. But the most that any practical intelligence test could hope to accomplish would be to sample the person's skills.

As we turn to the problems of developing tests to measure intelligence, it's wise to remember that intelligence tests only sample intelligence. The best tests offer a useful and informative sample, but still are likely to leave out parts of intelligence; other tests may be so limited a sample as to be misleading.

MEASURING INTELLIGENCE

There are several steps in obtaining an IQ score. The test to be used must be designed according to some underlying assumptions of what intelligence is. The test's reliability and validity must be demonstrated, and it must be standardized against some population. The test must then be chosen as the one to be used with some subject and must be administered to that subject according to the original test instructions

(Green, 1981). If everything in this sequence is done correctly, the resulting score will be a useful sample of that particular person's skills. But if any step in this sequence is not done correctly, the score may be grossly misleading. We will examine these steps in sequence. ■ Figure 14.10

Building a Test

Having read about some of the proposed distinctions among types of intelligence, you might now find the task of building a test more forbidding. How can you simultaneously measure both a single *g* and up to 120 specific factors? How can you test verbal and visual items, fluid and crystallized ones, impersonal and social ones? The answer is that you can't. Each test begins with a particular set of assumptions, not only about what intelligence is, but about the goals of that particular test. Testing a particular kind of ability in a limited population is more feasible than testing all skills of all people.

Suppose you assume that intelligence is a general trait and that verbal intelligence reflects it fully. Then your only problem is to develop some specific verbal items. But if you feel visual–spatial skills are different and also important, then you will also have to develop visual items and decide how many of each to include. Obviously, the more factors you try to cover, the more complex the task, and the sooner you will run into problems with test length. So you will always have to choose a limited sample of the possibilities that occur to you. To say that a particular test does not consider some kinds of intelligence is thus not a very powerful criticism; it almost inevitably will not (Carroll & Horn, 1981).

The question of who the test is designed for becomes increasingly important as you develop particular test items. Items in a Binet-type test were specifically developed for each age. You might not be that specific, but the approximate age of the population to be tested will be relevant, at least up to adulthood. Another relevant attribute of the subject population is their probable skill level. A test designed to sort for degree of retardation, for example, will be useless with more able populations, and a test designed to identify gifted children is inappropriate with a retarded group. Similar relationships exist for particular skills: You would not create a language-focused test for those with a language deficit or a spoken test for those with hearing problems.

Once you decide who you want to test and what the general framework of the test is to be, you can then design a test. If you are using verbal items, you must choose what type they are to be—word identifications, sentences, or prose passages. Exactly which words, sentences, or passages will you use, and how many items will there be? If you have several types of items, how will the scores be added up? For each item you include, you may reject hundreds of other possibilities.

Once your test is designed, you must decide if it is any good. So you **standardize** it by giving it to samples of your intended population and assessing the results. Besides checking reliability and validity, you see if a reasonable distribution has been obtained, and specify that distribution as part of the test's basic data. (A "reasonable" distribution usually means an approximately normal one, with the most frequent score in the middle and the other scores distributed evenly on both sides.)

If all this is successful, you might try to get others to use the test. You might first publish your results in a professional journal, where they would be subject to inspection and criticism by other specialists. Then you might offer the test to others, along with the many existing tests.

Existing Tests

The first test to use the IQ computation was the **Stanford-Binet Intelligence Scale** (Terman, 1916), translated into English and adapted by Stanford professor **Lewis M. Terman** (1877–1956). ■ Figure 14.11

Binet did not use a ratio IQ scale (MA/CA), preferring to score children simply in terms of the MA they

Figure 14.11 ■ Lewis M. Terman (1877–1956), the Stanford professor whose adaptation of Binet's scale became the Stanford-Binet, the first IQ scale. Terman also originated the continuing long-term longitudinal study of gifted children that is named after him. *"The assumption that it is easier to measure a part of one aspect of intelligence than all of it is fallacious in that the parts are not separate parts and cannot be separated by any refinement of experiment. . . . After many vain attempts to disentangle the various intellective functions, Binet decided to test their combined functional capacity without any pretense of measuring the exact contribution of each to the total product. It is hardly too much to say that intelligence tests have been successful just to the extent to which they have been guided by this aim."* L. M. Terman, *The Measurement of Intelligence*, 1916, p. 43.
(Stanford University Archives)

achieved (Binet & Simon, 1908). One psychologist has suggested that Binet would have "objected violently" to the calculation of an IQ as a generalized measure of intelligence (Tuddenham, 1974). But when Terman adopted Binet's measure as the basis of the Stanford-Binet, he added the concept of IQ originally proposed by a German psychologist in 1912.

The Stanford-Binet has been revised several times since its first version (Terman & Merrill, 1953). The most substantial, 1937 revision took 11 years to prepare (Terman & Merrill, 1953). During this time they wrote and pilot-tested hundreds of new items, standardized the best ones on 3000 children, and then took two years just to complete the statistics (Sears, 1979). The newest revision still uses the 1937 items, but with a new standardization on 2100 children, including nonwhites (Thorndike, 1973). The current version is largely verbal, though it includes memory, inference, and other operations, as well as some visual-motor skills. Items range from the two-year-old level to the adult level; an IQ value can be assigned for any age from $2 \frac{1}{2}$ onward. ■ Table 14.2

The other major intelligence measure is the Wechsler tests. These originated as a single test, but

Table 14.2 ■ Sample Items on the Stanford-Binet IQ Test

Age	Task
2	PICTURE VOCABULARY Examiner shows cards with pictures of common objects, such as a key, for child to name.
3	PICTURE MEMORIES Examiner shows a card with a picture of an animal, then another card with that animal plus others. Child is to remember the animal and find it on the second card.
4	COMPREHENSION Examiner asks "why" questions, such as "Why do we have houses?" Child is to answer appropriately.
5	DEFINITIONS Examiner presents vocabulary items, such as "ball", using the format "What is a _____ ?"
6	OPPOSITE ANALOGIES Examiner presents incomplete "opposites", using the format "A table is made of wood; a window of _____ ?"
7	SIMILARITIES Examiner asks for the similarities between pairs of objects, using the format "In what way are _____ and _____ alike?
8	VERBAL ABSURDITIES Examiner reads sentences with internal contradictions that child is to identify.
9	RHYMES Examiner gives a rhyming example, then asks for specific rhymes, such as "a color that rhymes with head".
10	FINDING REASONS Examiner asks for specific reasons, such as "two reasons why children should not be too noisy in school".
11	ABSTRACT WORDS Examiner asks child to define a series of abstract words, such as "compare".
12	PICTURE ABSURDITIES Examiner shows pictures with internal contradictions that child is to identify.
13	DISSECTED SENTENCES Examiner shows a card with the words of a sentence in scrambled order. Child must unscramble the sentence.
14	RECONCILIATION OF OPPOSITES Examiner asks how pairs of words are alike, using words usually considered opposite, such as winter and summer.
Adult	PROVERBS Examiner quotes a common proverb, such as "Great oaks from little acorns grow." Test-taker must correctly interpret the proverb's generalized meaning, not merely its literal one.

Stanford-Binet Test examples pertain to the 1973 edition, not to the forthcoming 4th edition to be published in 1985. Used with permission of Riverside Publishing Co.

have since been revised as separate adult and child versions: the **Wechsler Adult Intelligence Scale (WAIS)** (1981) and the **Wechsler Intelligence Scale for Children (WISC).** The WAIS and WISC were standardized on samples of the United States population (including nonwhites), based on census data. The **Wechsler Preschool and Primary Scale of Intelligence** was later added for children aged $4\frac{1}{2}$ to 6 (Sattler, 1982). ■ Table 14.3

The developer of these tests, David Wechsler (1896–1981), designed the original scale in an attempt to improve on the Stanford-Binet and other tests, especially for use with those who had language problems or other difficulties (Matarazzo, 1981). Several of the changes he introduced differentiate the Wechsler scales from the Stanford-Binet. One difference is that both the WAIS and the WISC have two subscales, a **verbal scale,** composed of items similar to Stanford-Binet items, and a **performance scale,** designed to assess abilities in which verbal skills are relatively unimportant. ■ Figure 14.12

The Wechsler scales are also scored differently from the Stanford-Binet. The two subscales have been separately standardized; a full-scale IQ can be computed from all items, but separate verbal and performance scores can also be computed. Furthermore, item types within each subscale can be separately scored; these are often plotted as a test **profile,** which gives a more detailed portrayal of a person's skills. ■ Figure 14.13

There are a number of other well-known general tests and many more specialized ones. The Primary Mental Abilities Test (1941), for example, was designed to assess five of Thurstone's ability factors. Of the tests focusing on a single type of problem, some use only verbal items, such as the Peabody Picture Vocabulary Test (Dunn, 1965), which presents picture cards and vocabulary words that must be chosen to define the pictures. Others use only performance items; the Porteus Maze Test, for example, consists entirely of maze problems (Docter, 1972).

Developing, choosing, and administering individual tests continues to be a major function of psychologists. But most people are more likely to take **group**

Table 14.3 ■ Summary of Items on the WAIS

Test	Description
Verbal Scale	
Information	Questions tap general range of information; for example, "How many nickels make a dime?"
Comprehension	Tests practical information and ability to evaluate past experience; for example, "What is the advantage of keeping money in a bank?"
Arithmetic	Verbal problems testing arithmetic reasoning.
Similarities	Asks in what way certain objects or concepts (for example, *egg* and *seed*) are similar; measures abstract thinking.
Digit span	Series of digits presented auditorily (for example, 7-5-6-3-8) are repeated in a forward or backward direction; tests attention and rote memory.
Vocabulary	Tests word knowledge.
Performance Scale (see Figure 14.12)	
Digit symbol	A timed coding task in which numbers must be associated with marks of various shapes; tests speed of learning and writing.
Picture completion	The missing part of an incompletely drawn picture must be discovered and named; tests visual alertness and visual memory.
Block design	Pictured designs must be copied with blocks; tests ability to perceive and analyze patterns.
Picture arrangement	A series of comic-strip-type pictures must be arranged in the right sequence to tell a story; tests understanding of social situations.
Object assembly	Puzzle pieces must be assembled to form a complete object; tests ability to deal with part/whole relationships.

a

b

Figure 14.12 ■ Items similar to those in the performance subscale of the WAIS.: (a) is an example of object assembly, and (b) illustrates picture completion.

(Simulated items from the Wechsler Scales. Courtesy of the Psychological Corporation.)

PART V ■ *Development and Individual Differences*

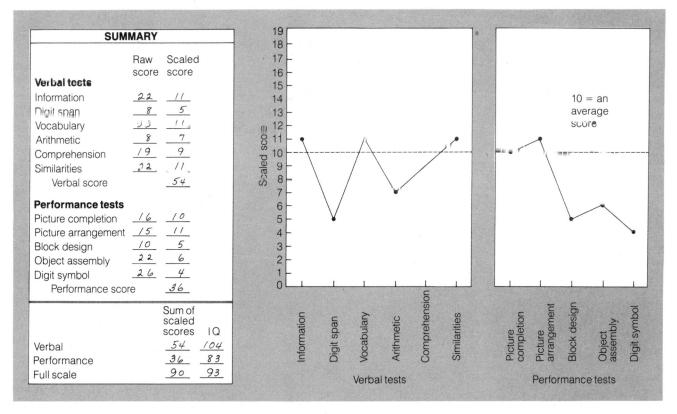

SUMMARY		
	Raw score	Scaled score
Verbal tests		
Information	22	11
Digit span	8	5
Vocabulary	33	11
Arithmetic	8	7
Comprehension	19	9
Similarities	22	11
Verbal score		54
Performance tests		
Picture completion	16	10
Picture arrangement	15	11
Block design	10	5
Object assembly	22	6
Digit symbol	26	4
Performance score		36

	Sum of scaled scores	IQ
Verbal	54	104
Performance	36	83
Full scale	90	93

Figure 14.13 ■ A test profile of a 16-year-old male, based on subscales of the WAIS. (The overall IQ score is a compromise across all subscales.)

tests, designed to be given to several people at once by a single test administrator. Group tests are typically paper-and-pencil tests, using standardized printed instructions, written answers, and systematic scoring techniques (frequently done by computer) to minimize the need for expert testers and individual test sessions. Group tests can measure several factors, but many concentrate on a single type of item. One test that can be given individually or to a group is the Goodenough-Harris Drawing Test; children are asked to draw a man or woman and their drawings are scored for detail and completeness according to standardized criteria (Dunn, 1972). Another individual or group test is the Progressive Matrices Test (Bortner, 1965), based on a single nonverbal item type, the choice of a block to complete a matrix. The task is thought to test perceptual logic relatively independent of schooling. ■ Figure 14.14

The development and widescale use of group tests owes its existence to World War I; without it, intelligence testing in the United States might have remained a professional activity of a few specialists. Terman published the Stanford-Binet in 1916. When the United States entered the war a year later, there was a sudden need to assess the abilities of large numbers of military recruits quickly. Within two years, the APA had helped the United States Army develop and administer two group scales, the Army Alpha test for literates and the Army Beta test for illiterates (Haney, 1981), to nearly 2 million recruits. This led to widespread familiarity with the tests and their use by civilians after the war. The 1930s saw a proliferation of group tests, and most general-purpose mental testing since then (often in schools) has been done with group tests, even though most experts still believe that individually administered tests are preferable (Fox, 1981).

One trend in testing that may combine the best features of individual and group tests is **tailored testing** by computers. Large numbers of possible questions would be developed and standardized, and the computer would select appropriate ones, neither too hard nor too easy, based on the testee's early responses (Recase, 1977). Another trend has been the search for direct physiological measures of information-processing abilities that would correlate with measured intelligence. A measure of pupil dilation during problem solving, for example, has been found to be related to SAT scores (Ahern & Beatty, 1979). Physiological measures are also being tested with physically handicapped children (Pines, 1982).

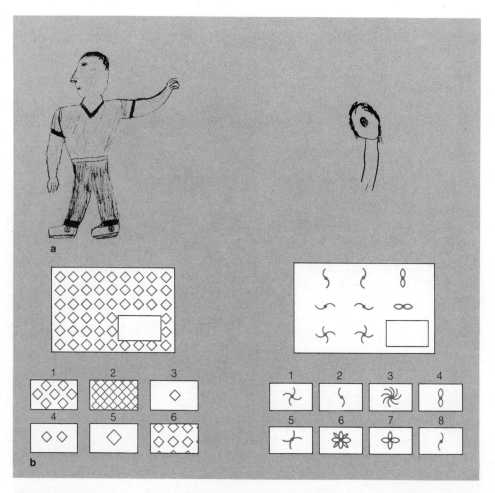

Figure 14.14 ■ Two nonverbal IQ tests. (a) Drawings done by two boys aged 10 years 9 months. According to the scoring criteria of the Goodenough-Harris Drawing Test, the first translates to an IQ of 110, the second to an IQ of 54. (b) Samples from the Progressive Matrices Test, a group test, demonstrate that tasks can be self-explanatory and items can still be relatively easier or more difficult.

(**a**, from *Children's Drawings as Measures of Intellectual Maturity* by Dale B. Harris, © 1963 by Harcourt Brace Jovanovich, Inc. Reproduced by permission of the publisher; **b**, from Raven's *Standard Progressive Matrices Test*. Reprinted by permission of J. C. Raven Limited.)

Using a Test

The best test possible cannot guarantee a meaningful score if it is inappropriately given. And even a correctly obtained score can be misinterpreted or misused. A prospective test user, such as a school psychologist asked to test a particular child, must first choose a test, then must administer and score it according to its instructions as well as federal, state, and other guidelines (Novick, 1981). Only then can the test user seek to interpret the outcome.

The test chosen should meet two criteria: It should fit the purpose, and it should have been standardized on a population similar to the child to be tested. If the test user wants to know how well the child is likely to

do in school, where language skills and previous learning are important, a Binet-style test might be best. If the child comes from a deprived environment— perhaps taken away from abusing parents by court order—a test that is less verbally dependent, such as a performance measure on the WISC, might be more useful. If a specific deficit is suspected, such as the reading problem known as dyslexia, a full WISC profile might be helpful. (Dyslexic children can be intelligent in many respects, yet read very poorly; Clark, 1973. Hence they might test as average if several subscales are averaged together, whereas a profile would show more clearly what they could and couldn't do.)

The test user would also try to match the child to

"What with the primary mental ability test and the differential aptitude test and the reading readiness test and the basic skills test and the I.Q. test and the sequential tests of educational progress and the mental maturity test, we haven't been learning *anything* at school."

© 1978 by Sidney Harris—American Scientist Magazine

the test's standardization group and keep any differences in mind for later interpretation of the score. Among the most important dimensions on which the test should match the child are general intelligence level and language skills. If the child is from some specialized population, the psychologist might look for a test standardized on a similar population: urban or rural, of particular ethnic background, and so forth. He or she probably could not match all important characteristics, but each one that is not matched is a potential source of error. A Zuni Indian child, for example, might score at the average 100 IQ level on a test standardized for white urban Americans but still have higher than average intelligence. The Zuni culture has traditionally downplayed personal competitiveness, and he or she might not have tried as hard as the children on whom the test was standardized.

Note that this matching of testee to test-standardization group is an important part of the test's validity. Validity is not independent of the person being tested; rather, the standardization procedure measures how well the test works for that kind of testee (Loehlin et al., 1975). Giving a test to an inappropriate testee invalidates the results.

Once a test has been chosen, it must be administered and scored exactly as described in its standardization data; any deviation can also invalidate the results. Giving more or less time for answers, prompting answers, or being personally warm or cold to the testee can alter the outcome, as can any scoring error.

If the test fits the child's background and the tester's purpose, and if it has been administered and scored appropriately, the result may be a reasonable sample of the testee's abilities. Only then does it make sense to interpret the score and use it for some purpose. ■ Figure 14.15

Figure 14.15 ■ A psychologist administers an IQ test to a child. It is critical that an appropriate test be used, that child and tester get along together, and that the tester carefully follow all the test's instructions for timing, scoring, and so forth, if the resulting score is to be useful.

(Abigail Heyman/Archive)

Even then, however, a test score can be used appropriately or inappropriately (Gordon & Terrell, 1981). Consider the child with a selective deficit such as dyslexia. Even if a test that matches the child's background is properly administered and scored, the score may be appropriate for some uses and not others. The child will score much lower on a test with strong reliance on reading than on tests that avoid the child's reading handicap. So the score may be a valid predictor of how the child will do on reading-based schoolwork but will not be a good general measure of the child's full range of abilities.

Similarly, a profile test given to a child recently taken from an abusing and otherwise limited home may give a valid description of the child's current abilities. But it may not be a valid measure of the child's growth potential. Most children don't change dramatically in IQ, so a valid test after about age eight or ten predicts later IQ reasonably well. But this does not necessarily hold for children whose circumstances change dramatically; after a few years in a greatly improved environment, a previously deprived child might score much higher than before. The first score might accurately reflect the child's low level of abilities when the test was taken, but treating this score as a long-term stable measurement would be wrong.

IQ tests are not a way of measuring some fixed hidden number called an IQ, but only one way of objectively assessing general behavioral tendencies (Wechsler, 1975). If decisions must be made about people—to keep them in one form of school or switch them to another, to offer them remedial help, and so forth—someone must make those decisions on the basis of whatever information they have. IQ tests may offer less-than-perfect information, yet still be more accurate than other assessments (Stanley, 1976c).

Children who hear poorly or are muscularly incompetent, for example, have often been mistakenly considered to be retarded. Hearing tests are now given as early as possible, to catch hearing problems before they inhibit intellectual development. And efforts are being made to reach the "trapped intelligence" of cerebral palsy (CP) sufferers, people who frequently cannot control their bodies well enough to speak or write. One CP victim was able to interact with an experimental intelligence test in the form of a computer program, by using his limited muscular control to punch the keys. He turned out to be very intelligent and has since designed dozens of other computer programs himself (Ray, 1980). In years past, he might never have had the chance to show what he could do.

If IQ tests are inappropriately used and are the basis for a wrong decision, they can be harmful. But carefully chosen tests offer a powerful tool for going past the sometimes superficial ways people judge each other to the skills within: a brilliant child of the "wrong" color or sex, or one whose looks, speech, or walk seems odd, may easily be mistakenly characterized by people—but not by an objective test.

In summary, there are many possible problems involved in the development and testing of intelligence. Some problems actually reduce intelligence from its maximum potential. There are also many potential problems in the measurement itself. ▪ Figure 14.16

EXTREMES OF INTELLIGENCE

There are no sharp breaks between normal intelligence and the extremes of gifted and retarded; each group shades gradually into the next (as in Figure 14.4). But the extremes of the distribution are sufficiently different that it makes sense to categorize and discuss them separately.

The Mentally Gifted

Those for whom all nature and nurture factors have gone well are the **gifted** (usually defined as the top few percent of the population on some IQ measure). Although a minority by definition, they have long been considered a valuable social resource: The Chinese may have used tests to discover talented individuals as early as 2200 B.C. (Fox, 1981). Modern study of the intellectually gifted began with Darwin's cousin Galton (1869), who first examined the heritability of high intelligence, using his own family and Darwin's as some of his subjects (see Chapter 3).

Most of what is known about the development of the gifted, however, comes from the Terman study, some 60 years in progress now and still under way. Terman began the study by seeking out children with IQs above 140, or approximately the top 1% of the population (Seagoe, 1975). The study began in 1921 with over 1500 subjects (Stanley, 1976b); numbers have decreased over the years through death or quitting participation, but substantial data have been collected on over 1000 (Terman, 1925). Periodic volumes update the status of the project as a whole (Oden, 1968; Sears, 1977) or of segments of it, as Sears and Barbee (1977) have done for the women.

The Terman study has provided some major conclusions about the gifted. The first noteworthy one is that not all of the gifted are obvious to their teachers. Most of Terman's sample was obtained by testing only the children referred by teachers, but to assess this method of selection he also tested all children in a few classes and compared the results to the referrals. Terman estimated that some teachers failed to notice 10–25% of the gifted in their classes and rated others as gifted who were not. In some cases, asking teachers simply to name the youngest children in their classes identified more of the gifted than asking them to name the brightest (presumably because the brightest children were promoted early, and the age difference was easier to identify than other signs of giftedness) (Fox, 1981).

The most widely quoted conclusion from the early years of the Terman study has been the debunking of the myth of the fragile, unpopular, clumsy intellectual. Terman's gifted children were both heavier at birth and generally healthier throughout childhood than their classmates (Oden, 1968). This implies that giftedness is not an isolated phenomenon or compensation for other weaknesses, but the reflection of a

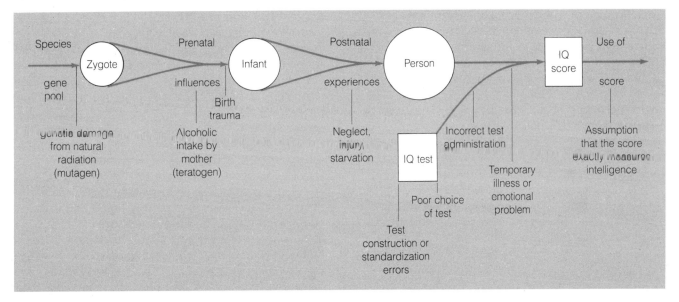

Figure 14.16 ■ Revision of Figure 14.1, emphasizing some of the problems that can affect the development of a person's abilities, the testing of those abilities, or the use of the resulting score.

generally high level of health and ability. The Terman children were also socially popular with their peers, contrary to the myth of unpopularity.

As adults, the Terman children were unusually successful in a wide range of occupations. As a group, they earned more advanced degrees, wrote more books, and in other ways were far more productive than an average group of this size. But not all were equally successful, even though all were similarly intelligent; some were failures and dropouts. High intelligence may be a necessary condition for advanced degrees and creative work, but is not a sufficient one (Albert, 1975). (Differences in family upbringing or other unknown factors must account for such performance differences among those of equal intellectual ability.)

For the first 50 years of the Terman study, general interest in the gifted of this country was relatively low; before 1971, only four states had laws defining giftedness. But a report to Congress in 1971 by the United States Commissioner of Education identified gifted children as a neglected national resource, and within the next seven years 38 more states adopted formal guidelines for identifying them (Fox, 1981). But how the gifted should be educated once they are identified is still a highly debated topic (Stanley, 1980). Options range from doing nothing, which may leave them bored or unproductive, to leaving them in the same grade while enriching their curricula, to advancing them a number of grades (Stanley, 1976a). Some exceptionally able children who have skipped grades have entered college very young; one recently graduated from college at 11.

Such extreme advancement was for long considered unwise. Stories were told of William James Sidis, a gifted youngster who entered Harvard at the age of 11 in 1909, but never lived up to that promise and died an obscure clerk. His case is now thought to reflect a variety of causes, however, and opinions about grade skipping are changing (Montour, 1977). No doubt the social lives of those advanced many years in school are somewhat distorted, but exceptionally intelligent children are unlikely to have conventional social lives in any case (Nevin, 1977). Telephone, video, and computer linkages have been suggested to provide communication among the few (45 known) "severely gifted" children (IQs over 180), so they can interact with intellectual peers (Holden, 1980b).

One major change in assessment of the gifted since Terman's study began is in the criteria used for definition. Terman's single criterion of a score over 140 on one primarily verbal IQ test would now be considered narrow by many experts and hopelessly limited by some (Sternberg, 1981a). Tests are now being developed to identify particular gifts. Identification and special schooling for the mathematically gifted, for example, is now well established, partly because of the ongoing Study of Mathematically Precocious Youth, begun in 1971 (Stanley, 1979). Other tests are being proposed and developed for identification of gifted underachievers and of the gifted within disadvantaged or racially or culturally different groups (Mercer & Lewis, 1978).

As work with the gifted has developed, controversy has arisen over the question of how giftedness and creativity are related. Because creativity draws on the full range of human problem-solving capabilities, many psychologists consider it as closely intertwined with giftedness, if not an integral part of it (Passow, 1981). One psychologist has argued that giftedness should be defined as higher-than-average levels of three traits: general ability, task commitment, and creativity (Renzulli, 1978). Several of the theoretical approaches to general intelligence have also been applied to creativity, and vice versa. Guilford, for example, has long been interested in creativity as part of the ways of thinking that make up his structure-of-intellect model (1967). Conversely, Torrance (1971) has argued that the Torrance Tests of Creative Thinking (1966) may be a better way of identifying the disadvantaged gifted than traditional intelligence measures.

The Mentally Retarded

The term *retarded* derives from Binet's concept that the less intelligent are similar to normal people of younger ages, but "retarded" in their mental growth. The mental growth of the retarded *is* slower than normal; however, they are never exactly the same as younger "normals" and are more limited in their eventual growth.

By definition, the **mentally retarded** are those who score below 70 on a standard IQ test and have problems in adapting their behavior to their environment. (A score alone is not sufficient, because different environments place different demands on people.) Based on this definition, about 3% of the United States population—about 6 million people—are retarded (Telford & Sawrey, 1981). The American Association on Mental Deficiency classifies them into four categories (Grossman, 1977). ■ Table 14.4

The great majority of retarded people are considered **mildly retarded;** they have IQs of 50–70. The mildly retarded can accomplish many normal activities if given the time to learn. They often progress through a number of years of regular schooling, though with increasing difficulty as they lag further behind. If referred by teachers and identified by individual IQ tests, they are often sent to special education classes (although there is growing opinion that they would do better staying in regular classes and getting extra help; Reschly, 1981).

The mildly retarded lack the abstract cognitive skills demanded in school (and measured by most intelligence tests). Under supportive conditions, however, they are able to speak, read, compute, and socially interact well enough to learn and hold a variety of paying jobs and to become self-supporting. They are slow to learn a job, but once it is learned are willing, able, and exceptionally reliable employees. (For a

first-person account of what it is like to be mildly retarded, see Bogdan & Taylor, 1976.)

More extremely retarded people differ in several ways from the mildly retarded: They generally have known biological anomalies, and their deficits are more permanent and more comprehensive. They have problems with social and other skills as well as academic abilities.

The **moderately retarded,** with IQs of 35–50, cannot survive in an ordinary classroom and require special education. With appropriate training in self-care and job skills, they can maintain some independence, perhaps living in a halfway house and working at a special shop such as those sponsored by charitable institutions. But they are unable to handle the demands of even menial jobs on their own. The **severely retarded,** with IQs of 20–35, can sometimes participate in special work, but only in the framework of institutional care. They can develop limited speech, but most of what they learn may be better considered habit training than education. Behavior modification techniques, requiring little active understanding or cooperation from the subject, are often used for this purpose (Thompson & Grabowski, 1977). The **profoundly retarded,** with IQs below 20, cannot achieve even these behaviors. Training is relatively ineffective, with speech and even toilet training frequently nonexistent, and they survive only with constant institutional care.

The retarded are not equally incapable in all intellectual abilities; as with other levels of intelligence, some are better on one kind of task than another. Occasionally there are extreme examples, however; called **idiot savants,** they are retarded in most respects, yet have a single unusual talent. Idiot savants are relatively rare, but several different types of abilities have been repeatedly found (Hill, 1974). Some are calendar calculators, who can rapidly tell the day of the week that any given date would fall on. (In one case, identical twins were found to share this ability.) Other idiot savants show isolated abilities in music or art.

Idiot savants pose difficult problems of interpretation. Were they children with an unusually gifted potential that was largely obliterated by unknown causes, leaving only these islands of ability? Just how are their strong specific abilities related to their weak general ones? Researchers do know that these special abilities tend to deteriorate as the idiot savant's general abilities get better. A recent article suggests that this may occur because as they are able to do more, they no longer can focus as single-mindedly on the previous skill (Restak, 1982a). It may be that the penalty for having a broad-ranging and flexible intelligence is the loss of some capability in more narrow specializations.

Table 14.4 ■ Characteristics of the Mentally Retarded

Category of Retardation	Causes	Estimated Incidence in U.S. Population	Education Possible	Life Adaptation Possible
Mild 50–70 IQ (equivalent to 8–12-year-old)	Many, often mixed and largely unknown	2.1% 4,200,000	Sixth grade maximum by late teens, special education helpful	Can be self-supporting in nearly normal fashion if environment is stable and supportive; may need help with stress
Moderate 35–50 IQ (equivalent to 6–8-year-old)	Typically biological brain damage of varying degrees and causes. Becomes increasingly obvious with very low groups.	0.6% 1,200,000	Second to fourth grade by late teens; special education necessary	Can be semi-independent in sheltered environment; needs help with even mild stress
Severe 20–35 IQ (equivalent to 3–6-year-old)		0.2% 400,000	Limited speech, toilet habits, and so forth with systematic training	Can help contribute to self-support under total supervision
Profound below 20 IQ (equivalent to 0–3-year-old)		0.1% 200,000	Little or no speech; not toilet trained; relatively unresponsive to training	Requires total care

Some 200 causes of retardation are known (Brewer & Kalalek, 1979). A problem during virtually any of the developmental steps in Figure 14.1 can decrease intelligence to the mildly retarded level, and few cases of mild retardation can be assigned a specific cause. Many mildly retarded individuals come from families in which possible contributing causes cluster, including poor nutrition and poor prenatal and postnatal care. (One study found that vitamin and mineral supplements increased the IQ of retarded children by an average of 10 points over several months; Harrell et al., 1981. If this finding is replicated, it will be of major importance in the care of the retarded.) Genetic factors may also contribute to mild retardation, but it is often not possible to separate them from environmental factors. Mild retardation has thus sometimes been labeled cultural-familial retardation, implying this cluster of possible causes. ■ Figure 14.17

With each increasing degree of deficit, the causes of retardation become more obvious; the profoundly retarded often suffer dramatically visible deficiencies. At the same time, there are fewer individuals in each category, partly because such severe problems are often fatal. Many of today's profoundly retarded, in fact, would have died in previous generations; they are kept alive only with difficulty and often have shortened life spans. Because of their common physical problems, it has been suggested that the lower three categories be termed **mentally deficient** rather than mentally retarded. Some of the common causes of mental deficiency include genetic problems and developmental abnormalities, such as those caused by drugs, poisons, or disease.

One of the best-known and most common causes of mental deficiency is **Down's syndrome;** it accounts for 10–20% of the severely retarded (Telford & Sawrey, 1981). First described in the late 1800s by Down, who termed it *mongolism* because of a characteristic eye fold and occasional yellowish skin tinge, Down's syndrome also produces other readily identifiable facial and body characteristics, including stubby fingers and a thick ridged tongue. ■ Figure 14.18

Down's syndrome is a genetic problem, the consequence of an extra 21st chromosome. This usually results from an incorrect cellular division in the process of creating an ovum, but as many as 25% of the cases may reflect problems with the sperm (Holmes, 1978). Though genetic, Down's syndrome is rarely inherited; it is a new problem each time it occurs. (Down's syndrome is inherited in about 2–5% of cases.) For reasons still unknown, the frequency of Down's syndrome increases sharply among older mothers: The incidence in mothers over 45 is about 1 in 40, compared to about 1 in 1500 for mothers aged 15–24 (Telford & Sawrey, 1981). But most Down's syndrome children are nevertheless born to younger mothers, because they have most of the children.

Many problems of early development can cause retardation, often as interactions of nature and nur-

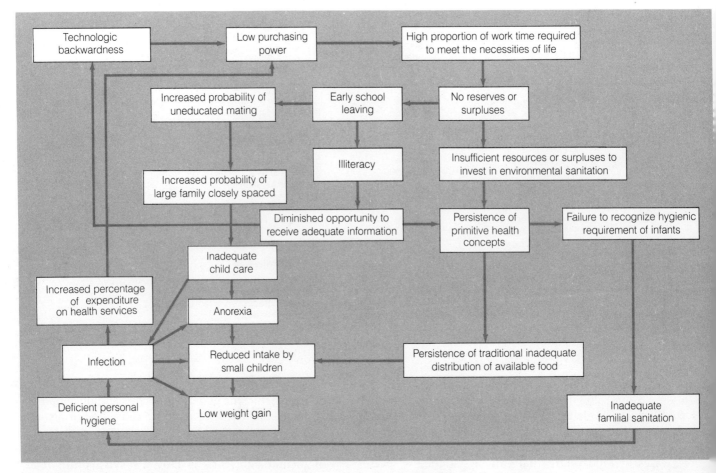

Figure 14.17 ■ Some of the relationships among biological and social factors that may contribute to cultural-familial retardation. Note that these factors are not independent but are complexly intertwined. Hence there is no particular entry point to the chart; begin at any point and it will lead to others.

(From *Progress in Human Nutrition*, Vol. 1, p. 84, Fig. 14 by S. Margen, The AVI Publishing Company, Inc., Westport, Connecticut, 1971. Used by permission.)

ture. Two illustrative examples are phenylketonuria (PKU) and cretinism. In PKU, a single recessive gene causes a lack of a liver enzyme. An ordinary diet will cause massive brain damage and retardation (80% of untreated cases have IQs below 40, 60% below 20). But if the diet from birth excludes the particular amino acid that cannot be digested, the individual can develop normally. (Tests of newborns for PKU are required in many locales.) In cretinism, lack of a thyroid hormone causes severe retardation and a characteristic coarse facial appearance. Some cases are genetic, but others result from a lack of adequate iodine in the diet. (In parts of the world where dietary iodine is scarce, as much as 4–7% of the population suffers from cretinism; "Thyroid gland and World Health," 1981.) Dietary cretinism can be minimized if sufficient iodine is present in food—one reason for iodized salt—and administering replacement hormone can allow those with genetic cretinism to develop normally (Telford & Sawrey, 1981).

The more that is learned about the causes of retardation, the more effective can be the ways of preventing it. Many possible causes of mild retardation can be addressed by social programs such as that being attempted in Venezuela. Retardation caused by diseases such as encephalitis may be prevented by preventing outbreaks of the disease. PKU and cretinism demonstrate how various environmental manipulations may prevent retardation, even in genetic syndromes, once the problem is understood. And as more is learned about other causes of mental deficiency, other interventions may be possible.

Understanding the causes of retardation has previously required detailed study of each condition. But one report (Marx, 1981) offers the possibility of a more general understanding of causes of retardation. It suggested that various kinds of environmental retardation may all cause the same type of damage: a brain-cell defect marked by abnormal dendritic spines. This same kind of cell abnormality may even occur in genetic

Figure 14.18 ■ A Down's-syndrome child.
(Bruce Roberts/Photo Researchers, Inc.)

retardation, such as Down's syndrome. If this is true, research could focus on this common damage and possible ways of avoiding or relieving it, rather than on studying each cause of retardation separately.

One of the important controversies concerning the retarded is how they are classified. Two somewhat different notions are now intermingled: (1) that there is a continuum of IQ scores; and (2) that the mentally deficient are different in important ways from the mildly retarded. One possibility is to consider the mildly retarded at the bottom of the normal IQ distribution, and the mentally deficient in a different system. If this change in classifying scheme were accompanied by new categories—perhaps *low academic aptitude* or *low classroom potential* instead of mildly retarded, for example—the negative implications of the current *retarded* label might be somewhat alleviated (Reschly, 1981).

The suggested category changes are part of a general trend to minimize institutionalization and max-

imize mainstreaming of a variety of groups, including the physically handicapped and mentally ill as well as the retarded (Zigler & Muenchow, 1979). Encouraging people with limited abilities to take on a broad range of responsibilities is likely to cause them substantial frustration and distress, however. Some psychologists are now suggesting special mental health services for this particular population of emotionally disturbed retarded (Reiss et al., 1982).

And not everyone is ready to accept the idea of cultural mainstreaming. One of the central issues concerns the right to rear children. "If the mentally retarded are able to work and live, they should be allowed the same rights as anyone else," according to one side of the argument. "But they make terrible parents and should not have children even if their problems are not inherited," says the other. As with other aspects of care for the retarded, court battles have ensued—for example, over whether a retarded couple should be allowed to rear their normal-IQ child.

By far the most controversial issue, however, has been the assignment of disproportionate numbers of minority children to classes for the mildly mentally retarded. This fact has been the basis of several widely publicized court cases. One case resulted in the banning of IQ tests for class reassignment in California; other decisions have led to strict racial quotas on assignment (Bersoff, 1981). These court cases can be said to reflect a general misunderstanding of what mild mental retardation means, as well as of what IQ tests do (Lambert, 1981). The issue is also one of statistical interpretation. In fact, 99% of blacks are *not* categorized as mildly retarded, compared to 99.5% of whites; the proportion of blacks assigned to special classes has been larger, but the actual percentages of both groups that have been so assigned are quite small (Reschly, 1981).

The school question is part of a much broader and even more heated social argument, however: whether there are intelligence differences between racial groups and, if so, whether these differences are genetic (Crawford, 1979). The understanding of nature/nurture interactions that you have acquired from this chapter should already have made you more sophisticated about these issues than most participants are. But within the many misunderstandings and misplaced arguments that surround these questions are some real issues, which should now make much more sense to you. ■ Research Controversy: Are There Racial Differences in Intelligence?

RESEARCH CONTROVERSY

Are there racial differences in intelligence?

Questions about the comparative intelligence of groups of people have been raised since the earliest days of the testing movement. The groups involved have varied, but one consistent theme has been that many of those found to be of lower intelligence have been of lower social status. Thus much recent controversy has used as a historical starting point some of the testing of immigrant groups (primarily European whites) of the 1920s and 1930s (Gould, 1981a; Kamin, 1982; see Herrnstein, 1982 for a critique of the media presentation of the controversy, however.)

Recent controversy has centered on racial and socioeconomic differences, mostly between blacks and whites, but including other ethnic and disadvantaged minorities. This focus began with an exchange of opposing views on the extent to which observed IQ differences were genetic (Jensen, 1969; Kagan, 1969) and has continued to be hotly argued (Herrnstein, 1973; Jensen, 1973; Kamin, 1974). The argument gained further heat when some of the data on genetic relationships published by Burt were shown to be almost certainly fraudulent (Hawkes, 1979; Hearnshaw, 1981). (Note that these data are *not* included in Figure 14.6.)

Currently, questions are also being raised about the findings concerning the relative intelligence of age groups and the differences in types of male/female thought. (There are no reported male/female IQ differences because most tests are so constructed that males and females score equally.)

An implicit—sometimes explicit—assumption in many discussions of these group differences has been that there are no real differences, only a use of tests by a controlling majority to demean a minority (Williams, 1974). No doubt the early testers were much less sophisticated than current ones, and may have shared with their society a belief that some groups were innately less able than others. And no doubt errors have been made in the assessing of both individuals and groups (Reschly, 1981). It seems more likely that a variety of factors led to these errors, rather than an implicit conspiracy against some groups, but the question of just how racist the early testers were draws a wide variety of opinion from current psychologists. (See, for example, the open letter by Hebb, 1978, in the *American Psychologist*, followed by a string of rebuttals and counterrebuttals in later issues.)

The issues involved in determining what group differences actually do exist, and why, are many and complicated. In one book designed to summarize all that was known about racial differences in intelligence, the authors note: "It seems unlikely that there has ever been a controversy that has involved a more complex tangle of ethical, public-policy, emotional, measurement, design, and inference issues than the attempt to determine the relative contribution of genetic and environmental variation to group differences in intellectual performance" (Loehlin et al., 1975, p. 7). The issues begin with how to operationally define the groups; the concept of *race*, for example, is far from a clear one. But they also include how to measure differences and, most difficult of all, what to make of any differences that are found.

Much of the measurement arguments have turned on the question of whether tests are culturally or ethnically biased (Flaugher, 1978). This question was first raised early in the study of testing. Noting the frequently reported lower intelligence of rural children, for example, one researcher developed alternate test forms, standardizing one on urban and one on rural children; she found that each group did poorly on the other's test (Shimberg, 1929). More importantly, however, the items on which they did well or poorly were not obvious to inspection. They apparently measured not superficial differences—*cow* versus *skyscraper*—but real differences in patterns of problem solving between the groups. Another researcher standardized on Pueblo Indian children a Draw-A-Horse Test, designed to parallel the Goodenough-Harris Drawing Test (Figure 14.14). Although Indian children typically scored lower than whites on the Goodenough-Harris test, white children averaged only a 74 on the Draw-A-Horse—borderline retarded by Indian standards (DuBois, 1939).

Since then, many attempts have been made to develop **culture-free** or **culture-fair tests,** ones that will measure intelligence without relying on items that differ between cultures (or ethnic subcultures). But developing and validating a new view of intelligence is a difficult and lengthy task, and to date no culture-free test is generally accepted.

One major effort to build a test that will reflect basic processing abilities more than accumulated verbal knowledge has been carried out over more than five years by Alan and Nadeen Kaufman (Herbert, 1982a). The Kaufmans have used concepts drawn from the work of Russian psychologist A. R. Luria and from split-brain research as the basis for their **Kaufman Assessment Battery for Children (KABC).** The KABC uses sequential and simultaneous items. Sequential items are designed to test children's abilities to handle a string of items; in the word-order task, for example, children hear a series of spoken words and must repeat them in order. (Such items presumably draw on left-hemisphere skills.) Simultaneous items are designed to test spatial reasoning and the ability to synthesize and integrate information; one such task asks children to identify a partial outline (such as that in Figure 6.2). (Such gestalt closure items presumably draw on right-hemisphere skills.)

The KABC has been subjected to over 40 validation tests, and does reduce the score difference between racial groups. Testing psychologists are mixed in their opinions of the KABC's potential, and the test may not be readily accepted. The KABC is the first individual intelligence test since the 1930s, however, and may become an important one.

In the meantime, it is easy to build

biased tests, the current equivalent of the Draw-A-Horse. Some of these, such as sociologist Adrian Dove's Chitling Test, have been done only to demonstrate how tests might be biased ("Taking the Chitling Test," 1968). It asks questions based on black slang, jazz musicians, dice, and how long to cook chitlins as a parody of what is perceived as white bias in existing tests.

Other serious attempts have been made to develop tests oriented to minority populations and to take social and medical factors into account (Mercer, 1979). One psychologist has argued that each minority group should be tested on its own terms (Garcia, 1981). No **culture-specific test** has been accepted as offering more useful information than broader-based existing tests (Cronbach, 1978).

A more subtle possibility than simple bias in test items is that different ethnic groups may have consistently different patterns of thought. The first major test of this **ethnic-profile hypothesis** was done in New York City (Lesser et al., 1965). It found, as did a similar study in Hawaii (Werner et al., 1968), generally consistent patterns within ethnic groups. (Oriental Americans, for example, tended to obtain higher numerical scores, and Caucasians tended to obtain higher verbal scores.) ■ Figure 14.19

Future standard tests may include some specific items designed for particular minority populations, typical profiles for particular ethnic groups, and so forth. But the issues at stake are not just testing ones. It now seems that virtually any test devised will result in differences between some groups. How are these differences to be interpreted? They may all reflect test errors or hidden problems, but what if they do not?

The primary reason for proposing black-standardized tests has been that blacks typically score lower on existing tests than whites in the United States (Kaplan & Saccuzzo, 1982). Theoretically, this difference could reflect hidden test bias, but research to date doesn't demonstrate that current IQ tests are racially biased. On the contrary, one national committee recently decided that the evidence suggested IQ tests are not racially biased (Holden,

1982). So what does the finding of racial differences imply if it is valid?

For one thing, the difference is not a major one for most purposes; mean differences between blacks and whites are about 15 IQ points. For another, it says nothing about why those differences exist. Some of the difference could be genetic, but any generalized difference in environment between blacks and whites could also contribute. Blacks as a group have been repeatedly found to have a less nutritious diet than whites, for example, and—possibly as a consequence—infants to be of lower birth weight (Loehlin et al., 1975). Genetically, many blacks also lack an enzyme that allows them to digest cow's milk, a major source of infant nutrition. Any or all of these (and numerous other) factors could contribute to slightly reduced intelligence in enough people to lower the entire curve.

The most important point, however, is that group differences say very little about any person. A person's race says virtually nothing about that person's intelligence. The full range of abilities exists within each race and that range is very much greater than the average difference between races. If you're looking for the gifted or the retarded, you must measure individuals—and all the evidence suggests that objective tests are less biased than human subjective assessment. Terman's teachers were less accurate at finding their gifted students than the tests, and more minority children might be considered retarded by their teachers, and fewer considered gifted, without tests than with them (Holden, 1982).

Remember that the basic intent of a test is to discriminate among people—but discrimination is not the same as bias (Reschly, 1981). The issues on which we should focus are those concerning the validity of the discrimination for a particular purpose (Messick, 1980). If members of one group then score slightly higher or lower than another, it may raise questions for further research, but it does not invalidate the measure. Each of us is a unique person, as well as a member of many groups by birth and choice. We are each defined by that total, not by membership in any one group.

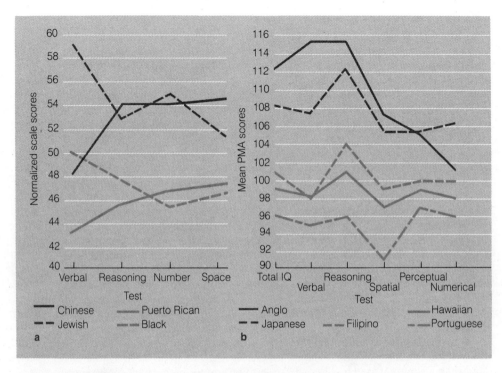

Figure 14.19 ■ Results from two studies that suggest different ethnic profiles of intelligence. (a) Score patterns of 320 middle- and lower-class New York City children. (Modified scales were used, to be as fair to subjects' backgrounds as possible, and tests were given in English or the native language, as appropriate. Lower-class children scored consistently lower in all groups; the results here are the average for both classes.) (b) Score patterns on Primary Mental Abilities test of 635 ten-year-old Hawaiian children classified according to ancestry.

(**a**, from G. S. Lesser et al., *Monographs of Society for Research in Child Development*, Vol. 30, No. 4, © 1965 by Society for Research in Child Development. Used by permission; **b**, from E. E. Werner et al., *Journal of Social Psychology*, 1968, 75, 43–59. Used by permission of The Journal Press.)

CHAPTER SUMMARY

1 Intelligence refers to the total ability to comprehend and deal with the world. It represents the end product of a series of interactions, in which a zygote is shaped throughout life by a series of influences.

2 Intelligence tests must be both reliable and valid. Earlier tests used an IQ score based on mental age divided by chronological age; current tests use the *IQ* term but compute it differently, based on the score distribution of a standardization group.

3 Genetic influences on intelligence are strong, but so are environmental influences. The concept of reaction ranges allows these two types of influence to be considered jointly.

4 Prenatal influences directly shape the developing fetus, allowing maximal development if all goes well. But a wide variety of drugs, hormones, poisons, and diseases can detrimentally affect the fetus. Postnatal influences include direct physiological ones but also many more subtle ones of rearing and education.

5 Intelligence tests are intended to be general-purpose aptitude tests, though they are often based on specific achievements. From several to several hundred separate skills may be involved. These vary on several dimensions, including a verbal/visual one.

6 Before intelligence can be measured, a test must be constructed of separate items and carefully standardized on some reference group. The best-known IQ tests are the Stanford-Binet and the Wechsler adult and child scales. A variety of other individual and group-administered tests exist for special purposes.

7 In measuring a person's intelligence, a particular test must be chosen, administered, and scored. For the score to be a reasonable sample of the person's intelligence, all of this must be done correctly, but even a valid score must be used appropriately.

8 Potential problems in the development of intelligence begin with the genetic sample and continue throughout life. Absence of factors such as nutrients or language, or presence of factors such as drugs or abuse, will reduce

intelligence. Different problems affect the measuring of intelligence, including errors in test choice, administration, scoring, or interpretation.

9 The mentally gifted represent the top few percent of the population. The Terman longitudinal study has shown them to be generally healthy and successful, contradicting the image of them as puny and withdrawn. Current work in creativity ties it closely to giftedness, either as one component in a general ability or as a special gift.

10 The mentally retarded make up the bottom 3% of the population. Most are mildly retarded, with IQs of 50–70; they can achieve relatively normal lives in supportive environments. Those who suffer more obvious organic damage, both genetic and environmentally induced, vary in maximum ability from limited self-care to total dependence.

11 Arguments about group differences in intelligence currently focus on racial differences, with many technical, ethical, and other issues interwoven. Observed differences among racial groups may represent a mixture of real differences and differences generated by the tests, but are in any case small compared to the range of differences within each group.

Further Readings

For more information on testing, see a current textbook, such as *Psychological Testing* by Kaplan and Saccuzzo (1982). The nature and nurture of intelligence is discussed in Willerman's *The Psychology of Individual and Group Differences* (1979b). For up-to-date coverage of a wide variety of testing issues, with extensive bibliographies, see the October 1981 special issue of the *American Psychologist* (available for purchase from the APA, Room 403, 1400 North Uhle Street, Arlington, Virginia 22201). A periodically updated summary of available tests is published in the *Mental Measurements Yearbook* (Buros, 1978). For various technical test issues, see the latest edition of one of the most frequently referenced books in psychology, *Psychological Testing* by Anastasi (1982). For the Terman study, see Seagoe's report on *Terman and the Gifted* (1975). Discussion of both the gifted and the retarded is included in Telford and Sawrey's *The Exceptional Individual* (1981). Loehlin, Lindzey, and Spuhler's *Race Differences in Intelligence* (1975) continues to be an excellent summary of the racial-differences issue; Scarr's *Race, Social Class, and Individual Differences in IQ* (1981) includes some newer research. Recent summaries of two positions on the source of racial differences are presented in Jensen's *Bias in Mental Testing* (1980) and Grover's *The Cognitive Basis of the Intellect* (1981).

As you go about your daily life, you probably notice a variety of behaviors that strike you as somewhat unusual, a bit peculiar, or downright weird. Magazine articles on hobbies describe people who collect empty beer cans, anything associated with old buses, or dozens of Edsels. A picture in the paper shows a jail inmate eating lightbulbs. An artist offers passersby the opportunity to electrocute him in the name of art. A soldier is arrested by military police after driving his tank over a row of parked cars. Police question a man they found talking to trees. A letter to Dear Abby describes a man who makes a mud puddle in his backyard and then wallows in it. ("Otherwise, he is perfectly normal," his wife says.) Some reports are macabre, others chilling in their violence and horror. A woman steals her daughter's body from the mausoleum and keeps it on a bed at home, tied up in pink ribbon. A young man, screaming that he has "sinned against God" by stepping on insects, chops off his left foot with two hatchets. Two young women set each other afire in search of a "beautiful" death.

All of these behaviors (and all are real examples) are abnormal by some standards. Some are abnormal by virtually everyone's standards. Psychologists have long sought to understand abnormal behavior and have made some progress in doing so, though questions still outnumber answers. In this chapter we will look at abnormal behaviors, including how they are classified and some of their known and suspected causes. In the next chapter we will examine how people with mental or behavioral problems are treated.

DEFINING AND CLASSIFYING ABNORMAL BEHAVIOR

At least three criteria can be used to define **abnormal behavior**: statistical frequency, social acceptability, and adaptiveness. The most direct definition is the *statistical* one: *Abnormal* literally means "away from the norm," so the less frequent the behavior the more abnormal it is. But many desirable behaviors are statistically infrequent and some undesirable behaviors, such as interpersonal violence, are unfortunately frequent. A *social acceptability* definition, in which *normal* is what a given society accepts, overcomes these difficulties (Ullmann & Krasner, 1975), but such a view is also arguable; what about societies such as Nazi Germany? The Germans who resisted the Nazi movement (many of whom died in doing so) can be seen as psychologically healthier than those who complied with Nazi expectations. Overall, the third possibility may be the best one: Behavior can be considered ab-

Chapter 15

Abnormal Psychology

normal if it is *maladaptive,* for both the individual and, ultimately, the society (Coleman et al., 1980) ■ Figure 15.1

We notice behaviors that are statistically unusual or that offend our sense of social propriety. But any such behavior can be more closely examined in terms of whether it is adaptive or maladaptive in that person's life. The behavior *in context* is what is important in defining abnormality, not the behavior itself.

When confronted by unusual behavior, we seek to put it into context so we will know what else to expect and how to respond. Suppose you encounter a nude man strolling down the street, for example; should you laugh, ignore him, turn and run, or . . .? If you knew his behavior was a prank, you might laugh. If you had reason to believe it reflected serious abnormality, you might avoid him; such people have attacked police officers. (In fact, only a small percentage of psychologically disturbed individuals are physically dangerous—but it is difficult, if not impossible, to specify *which* ones. Hence people who act "abnormally" are often seen as potentially dangerous.)

Accepted roles in a society offer expected behaviors that help us know how to interact with each other. Even strange behavior, if it fits an acceptable role, may not seem threatening. A tall man in medieval armor can stride down a street without attracting much attention, for example, when the behavior fits an acceptable context (advertising a new movie). The same behavior without the context might send passersby fleeing for cover. In judging another's unusual behavior, each of us can be said to compare it to a mental list of acceptable contexts: "It's a joke, a fraternity initiation, an advertising gimmick," and so forth. Only when we cannot fit the behavior into such a context do we call it *abnormal.* One adult dressing up to play cowboys and Indians may be abnormal, but when a group of respected businessmen get together on weekends to do the same thing, complete with a log fort, it is a social club and perfectly acceptable.

One of the most inclusive acceptable contexts for unusual, even bizarre, behavior is contemporary art. One artist, for example, prepared a demonstration in which he lay beside live wires and a bucket of water. If an observer had kicked over the bucket, the artist would have been electrocuted; the "art" lay in the tension of this situation. Another artist specialized in self-mutilation, which he photographed for display, eventually killing himself in the process. Most people would agree that he was abnormal. Yet within the context of art he was allowed to go about his self-destruction, and his photographs were put on exhibition (Hughes, 1972).

Behaviors that fall outside acceptable contexts are the focus of psychologists and others interested in abnormal behavior. Several of the major perspectives in psychology offer explanations for why people behave abnormally. We will look at these, but first we need to examine the overall concept of abnormality; one way to do so is in terms of the models used to define it.

Models of Abnormal Behavior

A *model* of abnormality is an overall description of abnormal behavior, including a proposed explanation of why such behavior occurs and suggestions for how to deal with it. It focuses attention on certain aspects of behavior and shapes the interpretation of that behavior.

The Demon Model   For most of recorded history, the primary model of abnormality was *demonic possession.* Early writings in numerous cultures attributed abnormal behaviors to a demon or spirit taking possession of the person. The afflicted person's only hope lay in the demon being driven out by a shaman or priest through exorcism; unfortunately, the person was sometimes tortured or killed in the process.

By the late 15th century, people came to believe that some possessions were deliberately encouraged by those possessed; these "witches" were tortured and killed in large numbers—most were beheaded or strangled, though some were burned alive (Zilboorg & Henry, 1941). A few people objected; Johann Weyer (1515–1588), for example, offered a point-by-point rebuttal of the witchcraft dogma, suggesting that witches were sick in mind or body. But Weyer was too far ahead of his time; he was attacked as Satan's representative and his works were banned. Witch hunting continued through the 16th and 17th centuries, in Europe and in the United States colonies. Even after the killing of witches ended, the demon model of abnormal behavior was common until well into the 19th century—and is not unknown today.

The Medical Model   The 18th century saw a flowering of numerous sciences, which greatly advanced human understanding of the physical world. At the same time a scientific approach to medicine identified many diseases: Key symptoms were first identified as indicators of an underlying disease, then patients with that disease were studied until the cause was identified and a cure found. In the 19th century, it began to seem possible that diseases of the brain might be responsible for abnormal behaviors.

PART V ■ *Development and Individual Differences*

Figure 15.1 ■ People engage in
many unusual behaviors, but just which
ones should be considered "abnormal"
is not always clear. (a) This man is indulging in an acceptable form of behavior, a hobby; he built this working
steam engine and track in his backyard. (b) This man may have a good
reason for his lack of clothing, but such
behavior can indicate a mental disorder.

(a, Richard Hartt, LIFE MAGAZINE, © Time, Inc.;
b, Wide World Photos)

A medical model, which remains the primary model today, replaced the demon model. The **medical model** sees abnormal behavior as the result of a mental disease or illness akin to a physical disease. This model is usually attributed to a German psychiatrist (a physician specializing in "mental diseases"), Emil Kraepelin (1856–1926); he established a system of classifying mental disease, based on clusters of symptoms, that is the basis of our present classification.

One of the early successes of the medical model was the identification of *general paresis,* an infection of the nervous system by syphilis that results in widespread brain deterioration, behavioral deterioration, and death. In 1825, observers had begun to suggest that some common behaviors in mental asylums were the result of a single disease. By 1905, the spirochete that causes syphilis had been discovered and by 1909 a cure had been found. Physicians thus became able to identify and treat one of the period's most common causes of abnormal behavior (Coleman et al., 1980). Encouraged by this success, most people interested in abnormal behavior adopted the medical model.

But critics have since objected to the medical model as a basis for defining *all* abnormal behavior. General paresis is the effect of an actual physical disease, they note. There are many such **organic causes** of abnormal behavior, including a wide variety of injuries, poisons, and diseases (Heilman & Valenstein, 1979; Snyder, 1980a). When such organic causes are discovered, they become part of conventional medicine. But should abnormal behaviors be considered the effect of "mental disease" even if no organic cause has been identified? A variety of nonorganic or **functional causes** of abnormal behavior have also been proposed, including emotional conflicts, inappropriate socialization, and faulty learning. When medical terms such as *symptom* or *disease* are applied to behaviors with functional causes, these are not medical terms but analogies. The overall framework is no longer medicine but a medical model, a pattern that is "as if" it were medicine. This as-if approach is the focus of controversy.

One obvious effect of the medical model is that it specifies who should do what with people exhibiting abnormal behavior. In the medical model, those who behave abnormally are displaying *symptoms;* they need to become *patients* of a *doctor* who will *diagnose* and *treat* their *mental disease,* in a *mental hospital* if necessary (Maher, 1966). But critics question whether the medical model is appropriate for a person who is simply behaving strangely because that's what he or she has learned to do. The most outspoken critic of the medical model has been psychiatrist Thomas Szasz, who has compared it to the demon model (1961). Witches of the late Middle Ages were identified by witch-hunters using a document called the *Malleus Maleficarum* (*Witches' Hammer*). Today's psychiatrists are contemporary witch-hunters, said Szasz: They are licensed by the state to identify those whom we cannot allow to retain their liberty, and they do so with the aid of classification systems that are today's *Malleus Maleficarum.* Szasz's view is extreme, but his criticisms have drawn attention to the implications of the medical model and encouraged the development of alternate models.

Alternate Models Several alternate models have been proposed in recent years; these typically reject the "disease" implications of the medical model, preferring to define abnormal behavior in terms of learned acts or simply as inappropriate for some social context without specifying its origin. Alternate models include ones based on a humanistic framework, sometimes called problems-in-living models, and several behavioral models. Skinner, for example, following the approach outlined in Chapter 13, feels that it is preferable just to describe abnormal acts, and that to attribute them to internal factors is unnecessary and unwarranted. To say a person who behaves strangely is mentally ill and then to explain the behavior as caused by a mental illness is to fall prey to the nominal fallacy, Skinner argues.

Such alternate models have been widely influential within psychology, and each view has its adherents. However, none has yet displaced the medical model within psychiatry; because psychiatrists are by training physicians, none seems likely to do so in the immediate future. But these alternate models have influenced psychiatrists nonetheless; for example, the latest classification scheme (called DSM-III) shows a new emphasis on psychosocial stresses and coping strategies—factors more a part of problems-in-living and behavioral models than traditional disease ones.

Causes of Abnormal Behavior

Known organic causes of abnormal behavior include genetic variations, early developmental problems, biological changes associated with aging, and a variety of diseases (including the slow viruses, which take years to develop fully and whose victims show few nonbehavioral signs of illness). Many forms of nervous-system injury, from birth trauma to war injuries, can also cause abnormal behavior.

When organic causes are known, a patient can be given whatever care is medically appropriate. But overlooked organic factors may play a role in many abnormal behaviors whose causes are assumed to be functional. In one study, 100 people undergoing psychiatric examination were given an extensive battery of medical tests that mental patients would not normally receive (Hall et al., 1980). Nearly half were found to have previously undiagnosed medical conditions relevant to their behavior problems. More than 60% of these showed rapid clearing of their mental symptoms with treatment of these conditions; under other circumstances, their illnesses might never have been diagnosed. This study involved mostly lower-income patients, and thus may have found more previously undiagnosed medical conditions than would be found in a middle- or upper-income group. But it nevertheless suggests that in the absence of detailed medical examinations symptoms of physical illness may be easily misinterpreted as signs of mental disease.

Other organic causes of behavioral symptoms no doubt exist that are not yet understood. One could carry this line of argument further and propose that all behavioral problems reflect biological aberrations, but this would be too extreme. Most psychologists believe that at least some socially undesirable or maladaptive behaviors reflect inappropriate learning in a healthy nervous system. (They do not agree, however, on just how these behaviors are learned and maintained, any more than they agree on how "normal" behaviors develop.)

One complexity is that organic and functional causes typically interact in several ways. Even when a known physical condition such as general paresis is present, different patients respond differently to it, either minimizing or enhancing the effects. Conversely, a problem that begins as a learned response to environmental stress may have later organic consequences. A person might become depressed because of the death of a close relative, for example, and respond by refusing to eat, exercise, or even leave his or her room. This pattern of response to grief might initiate organic changes that could contribute further to the abnormal behavior. Perhaps the most important form of interaction, however, is where both biological and psychological events must be present before abnormal behavior occurs. For example, in the case of schizophrenia, one of the most serious forms of abnormal behavior, genetic predispositions and environmental stressors seem to fit together to yield the problem. Someone who is genetically predisposed apparently is more likely to develop schizophrenia—but *only* if the environmental stress is severe enough.

Perspectives on Abnormal Behavior

In seeking the important causes of any abnormal behavior, a psychologist is likely to look for factors that he or she considers important in the development of normal behavior. As we have seen in previous chapters, the different perspectives in psychology focus on different events and times in a person's life and interpret these events differently in explaining behavior; this same pattern is true for understanding abnormal behavior. Of the seven major psychological perspectives, only the ethological view does not offer a well-defined approach to abnormal behavior. Some perspectives share enough features, however, that we can focus discussion on four approaches: the psychoanalytic, behavioral and cognitive, humanistic, and physiological approaches. We will review these approaches here and discuss their particular suggestions later in this chapter and in the next.

Freud's psychoanalytic view grew out of his therapeutic practice, and hence is basically a view of abnormality that can also be applied to normal development rather than vice versa. It is strongly associated with the medical model. The psychoanalytic view is that abnormalities are distortions of normal coping patterns: A poorly restrained id may result in inappropriate sexual or aggressive behavior; an excess of superego restraint may result in excessive guilt or overcontrolled behavior. In analyzing such patterns, Freud emphasized the concept of abnormal behaviors being "functional." He felt that these behaviors served the function of protecting the ego against anxiety and thus became established, even if they were maladaptive in other ways. Numerous other terms commonly used in discussing abnormal behavior are also derived from psychoanalytic theory, which for many years was regarded as *the* explanation of abnormal behavior. But the newest psychiatric classification scheme has moved away from some of Freud's categories, and incorporated elements suggested by other perspectives.

The behavioral perspective argues that abnormal behaviors develop according to the same rules of learning as normal behaviors. It rejects the medical model, agreeing with Rogers (Chapter 13) that a person whose behavior is maladaptive is not a patient with a mental illness, but a client with a behavior to be changed.

You might wonder if it matters whether a person is a patient or a client. In fact, such differences can strongly affect how behavior is interpreted. In one study, for example, traditional and behavioral therapists were asked to rate the adjustment of a person whom they saw being interviewed on videotape (Langer & Abelson, 1974). Some observers were told, correctly, that the person was a job applicant and others that the person was a patient. Behavioral therapists rated the person similarly in both conditions; apparently to them a patient was just another person. But traditional therapists tended to see the patient's behavior as less well adjusted; apparently the "patient" label

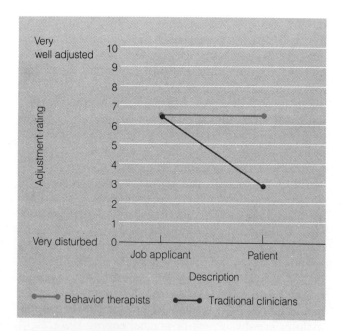

Figure 15.2 ■ Mean adjustment ratings given by therapists to a person whom they had seen being interviewed. Behavioral therapists were not influenced by the supposed "patient" status of the person (who was actually a job applicant), but the label altered the ratings given by traditional clinicians.

(Adapted from E. J. Langer and R. P. Abelson, *Journal of Consulting and Clinical Psychology*, 1974, *42*, 4–9. Copyright 1974 by the American Psychological Association. Adapted by permission of the author.)

biased their interpretation of the behaviors they observed. ■ Figure 15.2

The social-learning and cognitive views can be grouped with the basic behavioral perspective in this general review. A behavioral view of abnormal behavior typically draws on concepts from both Skinnerian behaviorism and social learning theory; concepts such as modeling and vicarious reinforcement, for example, come from social learning theory (Bandura, 1974). Many so-called cognitive views of abnormality can be considered variations on behaviorism (Wolpe, 1980); they tend to emphasize such behaviors as covert negative self-statements (for example: "I'll never do anything right; I don't deserve to live"). There are differences between cognitive and other behavioral views, however. For example, reinforcement tends to play a relatively minor role in most cognitive views (Davison, 1980), and some approaches emphasize primarily cognitive variables such as "irrational beliefs" (Ellis, 1962). But many aspects of cognitive theory have not yet been widely applied to abnormal behavior and a full-fledged cognitive approach to abnormality does not yet exist. Thus, cognitive and behavioral views are not yet as different from each other as they both are from other perspectives.

The humanistic view proposes that humans share a weak instinct toward self-actualization, rather than the strong instincts for sex and aggression proposed by the psychoanalytic view. To a humanist, abnormal behavior represents a distortion of the instinctive movement toward self-actualization. Maslow's version of humanism is unique in focusing on the best-adapted people (self-actualizers), rather than the worst (as Freud did) or on the entire spectrum (as behaviorism does). To Maslow, everyone who was not at or moving toward self-actualization was in that sense abnormal. But Maslow's view (1969), perhaps because it focuses on well-adapted people, has tended to be more influential as a personality theory than as an approach to abnormal behavior.

The humanistic view most associated with abnormal behavior is that of Rogers. Like Freud, Rogers developed his views of personality out of his experiences as a therapist. But Rogers reached very different conclusions about the nature of normality and abnormality than Freud did; Rogers agreed with Maslow that abnormal behavior represents a distortion of the natural growth of the self. Rogers's views, however, have emphasized therapy more than theoretical explanations of why abnormal behavior occurs; thus we will examine his approach in greater detail in Chapter 16.

The physiological perspective seeks explanations of abnormal behavior in terms of biological mechanisms, whether or not these are illnesses (Maugh, 1981a). It looks for such causes of abnormality as genetic variations or neurotransmitter deficits, as well as illnesses or injuries. Note that the biological perspective is *not* equivalent to the medical model, however; one can seek a biological cause for abnormal behavior in a client without necessarily using a model of mental illness.

Classification of Abnormal Behavior

Psychiatrists, clinical psychologists, social workers, and others who are charged by society with dealing with abnormal behavior use standardized schemes of diagnosing mental illness and classifying patients into categories. Substantial effort goes into building, updating, and applying such classification schemes. But why classify—wouldn't it be just as easy to deal with each person as an individual?

Why Classify?   One reason why classification is useful is a scientific one. Sorting or classifying portions of the total subject matter has contributed to the successes of most sciences. In geology, classification aided understanding of the different ways rocks form. In biology, classification aided understanding of life processes such as reproduction. Classification of abnormal behavior should also contribute to the understanding of such behavior.

A similar reason follows from the medical model. Medicine progressed through the identification of specific diseases, each with a particular cause, course of development, and outcome. Specific treatments were developed for particular diseases. A cough, for example, might be a symptom of any number of diseases, but rather than treating the cough, physicians seek to identify the disease causing the cough and treat that. In the medical model, classifying abnormal behavior (symptoms) into categories is seen as the first step in identifying a particular underlying mental disease so that specific treatments can be devised.

Even those who argue against the medical model typically accept the utility of some form of classification. Whatever the causes of abnormal behaviors, some way of grouping similar behaviors together is likely to be useful in understanding them, and thus in preventing or treating them.

Any useful classification scheme first has to discriminate "abnormal" behavior from "normal," then specify whatever subcategories are included. It will also probably include separate categories for problems that are *acute* (a single well-defined episode), *chronic* (persistent over years), or *episodic* (episodes of abnormality interspersed with episodes of normality). The test of any such classification scheme will be whether it increases understanding of the causes and treatments of abnormal behaviors. A few theorists have argued that the imprecision of existing classifications and the unreliability of diagnosing particular patients makes the entire process a waste of time. In one study, for example, psychiatrists were in agreement on diagnoses only about 40–60% of the time (Beck et al., 1962). Another study noted that knowing a person's diagnostic category did not provide much of an accurate prediction about that person's future behavior (Zigler & Phillips, 1961). But others argue to the contrary; that a task is difficult to accomplish, they say, is no reason to give up the attempt (Rimland, 1969).

DSM-III The pioneering effort of Emil Kraepelin, noted earlier, became the basis for later classifications including the current one. **DSM-III** is the third version of the *Diagnostic and Statistical Manual* (DSM) published by the American Psychiatric Association (1980). Each revision of DSM has provided significant improvements in how people are classified. The developers of DSM-III, for example, sought to define categories in ways that were less culture-specific than those of DSM-II, so that workers the world over could use the same classifications.

But each revision also gives up some categories that have become widely familiar. DSM-III has dropped the distinction between neuroses and psychoses that was a major feature of DSM-II, for example. (DSM-III still refers to some disorders as psychotic ones, but no longer uses the term *neurotic*.) You are still likely to encounter these terms, however, and should be familiar with them. In DSM-II, **neuroses** were disorders that were generally considered less severe; patients were said to remain in touch with reality, but to have difficulty managing anxiety. **Psychoses** were more severe disorders, typically with some break from reality.

Other major changes in DSM-III include rearranged and newly created categories, more explicit and detailed descriptions of each category, and ways of judging the patient's life stress and degree of coping. DSM-III is based on five factors, called *axes*. Axis I is the primary diagnosis, based on the observed behaviors (symptoms), and the other axes are supplementary. Axis II describes problems that develop early in children or are of long standing in adults. Axis III specifies physical illnesses known to be present, because these might be relevant either as causes or effects of behavior. Axes IV and V, which are optional, provide rating scales for judging how severe the stresses are in the patient's life and how well he or she seems to be coping with those stresses. ■ Table 15.1

DSM-III was tested extensively before publication and has shown generally good reliability (Spitzer et al., 1979). Even before it was published, however, psychologists were questioning its categories. Some are not convinced that axes IV and V incorporate enough psychosocial factors, for example (McLemore & Benjamin, 1979; Schacht & Nathan, 1977). Others consider some categories, such as the personality disorders, to be questionable (as we will note below). Those who reject the medical model of mental illness do not accept the DSM-III classification scheme, although generally it is well accepted (Smith, 1981). But no classification scheme will meet with universal approval. DSM-III promises significant improvements over DSM-II in ease and accuracy of classifying, and future versions can be expected to refine it further.

We will describe some of the major DSM-III categories in the balance of the chapter. Before we turn to these categories, however, a word of warning is in order. Students of abnormal psychology frequently experience an effect called the *medical student syndrome*. Knowing about this syndrome may help you avoid, or at least minimize, its effect. ■ Personal Application: Avoiding the Medical Student Syndrome

Table 15.1 ■ Summary of DSM-III Categories

Axis I, Clinical Syndromes

1. Disorders Usually First Evident in Infancy, Childhood, or Adolescence
   A. Mental retardation
   B. Attention deficit disorder
   C. Conduct disorder
   D. Anxiety and other disorders of childhood or adolescence: separation anxiety and avoidant disorders, . . . , elective mutism, . . .
   E. Eating disorders: anorexia nervosa, bulimia, pica, rumination disorder of infancy
   F. Stereotyped movement disorders: tics, Tourette's disorder
   G. Other disorders with physical manifestations: stuttering, enuresis, encopresis, sleepwalking disorder, sleep terror disorder
   H. Pervasive development disorders: infantile autism, childhood onset pervasive developmental disorder.

2. Organic Mental Disorders
   A. Organic brain syndromes: delirium, dementia, amnestic, delusional, hallucinosis, affective, personality
   B. Organic mental disorders: dementias arising in the senium and presenium, substance-induced organic mental disorders

3. Substance Use Disorders
   A. Substance abuse: alcohol, barbiturate, opioid, cocaine, amphetamine, phencyclidine, hallucinogen, *Cannabis*
   B. Substance dependence: alcohol, barbiturate, opioid, amphetamine, *Cannabis,* tobacco

4. Schizophrenic Disorders*
   A. Disorganized
   B. Catatonic
   C. Paranoid
   D. Undifferentiated
   E. Residual

5. Paranoid Disorders

6. Psychotic Disorders Not Elsewhere Classified
   A. Schizophreniform disorder
   B. Brief reactive psychosis
   C. Schizoaffective disorder

7. Affective Disorders
   A. Major affective disorders: bipolar disorder, major depression*
   B. Other specific affective disorders: cyclothymic and dysthymic disorders

8. Anxiety Disorders*
   A. Phobic disorders
   B. Anxiety states: panic disorder, generalized anxiety disorder, obsessive-compulsive disorder
   C. Posttraumatic stress disorder

9. Somatoform Disorders*
   A. Somatization disorder
   B. Conversion disorder

C. Psychogenic pain disorder
D. Hypochondriasis

10. Dissociative Disorders*
    A. Psychogenic amnesia
    B. Psychogenic fugue
    C. Multiple personality
    D. Depersonalization disorder

11. Psychosexual Disorders
    A. Gender identity disorders: transsexualism, gender identity disorder of childhood
    B. Paraphilias: fetishism, transvestism, pedophilia, exhibitionism, voyeurism, sexual masochism, sexual sadism, atypical
    C. Psychosexual dysfunctions: inhibited sexual desire; inhibited sexual excitement; inhibited female, male orgasm; premature ejaculation; functional dyspareunia; functional vaginismus
    D. Ego-dystonic homosexuality

12. Factitious Disorders

13. Disorders of Impulse Control Not Elsewhere Classified

14. Adjustment Disorder

15. Psychological Factors Affecting Physical Condition

16. Conditions Not Attributable to a Mental Disorder That Are a Focus of Attention or Treatment: malingering, borderline intellectual functioning, antisocial behavior, academic and occupational problems, uncomplicated bereavement, . . . , marital problem, parent-child problem, . . .

Axis II

1. Specific Developmental Disorders
   A. Developmental reading disorder
   B. Developmental arithmetic disorder
   C. Developmental language disorder
   D. Developmental articulation disorder

2. Personality Disorders: paranoid, schizoid, schizotypal, histrionic, narcissistic, antisocial, borderline, avoidant, dependent, compulsive, passive-aggressive*

Axis III, Physical Disorders and Conditions

Axis IV, Severity of Psychosocial Stressors

None, minimal, mild, moderate, severe, extreme, catastrophic

Axis V, Highest Level of Adaptive Functioning Past Year

Superior, very good, good, fair, poor, very poor, grossly impaired

*Included in this chapter.
(From *American Psychiatric Association, Diagnostic and Statistical Manual of Mental Disorders,* 3rd ed., 1980, Washington, D.C.: APA. Used by permission.)

Avoiding the medical student syndrome

The **medical student syndrome** refers to the experience of reading about a disease and beginning to think that you have that disease. Many symptoms of disease—coughs, headaches, sore muscles, rapid heartbeat, and so forth—can occur for various reasons, and other symptoms can easily be imagined: "Dry mouth? Perhaps my mouth *has* been unusually dry lately. I do remember licking my lips several times." The result is that medical students can read a list of the symptoms of some exotic disease and begin to think they are coming down with it.

A variation of the medical student syndrome occurs among psychology students as they read about patterns of abnormal behavior. Many abnormal behaviors, especially those formerly categorized as neuroses, are similar to behaviors of nearly all people. We all feel anxious or frightened at times, put off doing what we should do, make overly ambitious plans, or become depressed at temporary setbacks. Hence it is all too easy to recognize some of your own actions and, like the medical student, to wonder if you suffer from a particular mental disease.

But you almost certainly do not. Most of the abnormal patterns of behavior described in this chapter are abnormal not because they occur at all, but because they are more intense, more frequent, or more long-lasting than usual—so much more so that the person or someone else becomes disturbed or frightened by them. Some symptoms, such as hallucinations, are rare in everyday life, but can occur as the result of such factors as drugs or fatigue; hallucinating objects in the road is not uncommon for fatigued drivers on empty roads late at night, for example.

It is possible that some readers of this chapter do have problems for which professional help might be advisable. But they are probably already well aware of their problems. If everything about your life seemed at least tolerable, if not perfect, before you read this chapter, the odds are very high that you are normal. In fact, it would be unusual—though not abnormal in the sense of mental illness—if you did *not* find some of these behaviors familiar.

ANXIETY DISORDERS

Anxiety is a feeling of fear or apprehension (Gray, 1978). The DSM-III category of **anxiety disorders** includes subcategories in which anxiety is obviously present and others in which it is less obvious. Freud distinguished several kinds of anxiety, including *realistic anxiety* (the fear of actual danger) and *neurotic anxiety* (the fear that one's id impulses will get out of control). But Freud's distinctions are no longer drawn by many researchers and therapists.

Behavioral theorists note that anxiety, like hunger or honesty, is an inferred state that links observed variables (Davison & Neale, 1982). To them, anxiety is an inferred variable that links stimulus situations, self-reports, physiological changes, and overt behavior. For example, if a patient who is shown a photograph of a dog (stimulus) says that it causes anxiety (self-report), shows an accelerated heart rate (physiological change), and turns away from the photo (overt behavior), these events are linked by saying the patient is made anxious by dogs.

If all of the elements that imply anxiety were highly correlated, any of them would provide as good a measure as any other. But they are not always highly correlated; physiological measures in particular can change for other reasons (Lang, 1969b). Researchers and therapists thus generally use a combination of situation, self-report, and observed behavior to define anxiety. A researcher studying the effects of anxiety in a normal population might define anxiety in terms of a threatening situation, such as the threat of electric shock. In studying anxiety in a patient population, self-report or observation is usually used. The Taylor Manifest Anxiety Scale, for example, asks people to answer true or false to 50 items taken from the MMPI (Taylor, 1953). In Paul's Timed Behavioral Checklist for Performance Anxiety (1966), an observer counts the frequency of certain overt behaviors, such as hand tremors and voice quivers.

The first two anxiety disorders we will look at, phobias and anxiety states, were formerly classified as neuroses; however, the neurosis category was dropped from DSM-III, largely because it was an outgrowth of psychoanalytic theory rather than being merely descriptive. The neuroses were all said to reflect problems of managing anxiety, even when no anxiety seemed present; according to the psychoanalytic view, anxiety was sometimes not seen because the other behaviors were a successful defense against it. Now the presence or absence of anxiety is established by specific criteria.

Phobic Disorders

People with **phobic disorders** or **phobias** intensely fear some object or situation; that object or situation may be somewhat dangerous, as are dogs or heights, but the fear is out of proportion to the real danger and the person usually recognizes it as irrational. Common phobias include exaggerated fears of height, open space, closed space, germs, particular animals, and crowds (Marks, 1969). These fears are named by combining the Greek word for the feared object with *phobia* (derived from a frightening Greek God, Phobos); thus *claustrophobia* means "fear of closed places." The most common phobia is **agoraphobia,** a fear of open spaces and/or going away from home. Some agoraphobics become virtual prisoners in their own homes; if they try to leave, anxiety builds up with distance from home, and they retreat. ■ Patient Quote: Agoraphobia

Phobias are relatively common in the general population; their actual frequency depends on how severe the anxiety must be to be called a phobia. Most people are realistically apprehensive about heights, for example. In contrast, people so afraid of snakes that they cannot read a nature magazine for fear of encountering a picture of a snake are clearly phobic. But there is a substantial gray area between these extremes. One study, for example, found a rate of phobias of 7.7%—but only about 1 in 40 of these was severely disabling (Agras et al., 1969).

Theoretical views of phobias differ greatly. To psychoanalysts, the feared object or situation is a substitute for some other unconscious fear. In one well-known case, Freud (1909) interpreted the horse phobia of a boy called Little Hans as a fear of the boy's father; to acknowledge a fear of one's father is itself frightening, Freud suggested, and thus the fear was transformed. Psychoanalysts have considered the Little Hans case important (Jones, 1955), but critics have argued that Freud's 140-page interpretation is largely inference, based on little or no evidence (Wolpe & Rachman, 1960).

The behavioral interpretation of phobias is based on Mowrer's **two-factor theory** (1939, 1947): A fear is first developed through classical conditioning (the first factor); then various avoidant behaviors are learned through operant conditioning (the second factor). Mowrer's two-factor theory drew on Watson's work in classical conditioning. In one of the most famous reports in psychology, Watson had reported the creation of an artificial phobia in an 11-month-old boy called Little Albert (Watson & Rayner, 1920). Little Albert initially had no fear of a white rat, but when the rat was repeatedly paired with a frightening noise made by striking a metal bar, he became afraid of the rat and later of other furry objects. Some later attempts failed to replicate Watson's claims, leaving his results in some doubt.

The two-factor theory, however, accepts the idea that classical conditioning of a fear is the first step in a phobia. This fear provides the base for further operant learning. Exposure to cues related to the feared object generates anxiety. Turning away from or avoiding such cues reduces the anxiety and is thus negatively reinforced. (As noted in Chapter 8, removal of an aversive stimulus is negative reinforcement.) Phobic persons thereby teach themselves a wide range of phobic behaviors, each of which is reinforced by avoidance of the feared stimulus (Miller, 1948a). In the meantime, the original fear does not extinguish because there are no unreinforced trials—the feared stimulus is not repeatedly encountered.

The two-factor theory fits some phobias, but other factors are probably also involved. Social learning theorists, for example, have suggested that some fears may be acquired by modeling rather than by direct conditioning (Bandura & Rosenthal, 1966). And recent suggestions that classical conditioning of animals involves innate preparedness factors (Chapter 8) may also be relevant: Humans may develop some classical conditioning, and thus some phobias, more easily than others (Seligman & Hager, 1972). For example, subjects who experienced shock paired with pictures showed more conditioned arousal to snake pictures than to pictures of houses and faces (Öhman et al., 1975). (Other researchers remain unconvinced; I. M. Evans, 1976.)

Furthermore, some people may be more predisposed than others to become phobic, based on differences in the responsiveness of their nervous systems. In one study, people with high levels of arousal to shock developed conditioned reactions to pictures more readily than people with low levels of arousal (Hugdahl et al., 1977). Genetic factors may even be involved. Although little evidence specific to phobias exists, anxiety disorders in general seem to include genetic predispositions (Rosenthal, 1970).

Anxiety States

People with **anxiety states** experience anxiety that is not clearly associated with specific objects or events. In panic and generalized anxiety disorders, the major symptoms are those of the anxiety itself. In obsessive-compulsive disorders, anxiety is associated with repetitive thoughts or actions.

Panic and Generalized Anxiety Disorders People with **panic disorders** suffer from sudden intense **anxiety attacks,** in which they experience the aroused physiology of intense fear—rapid heart rate, labored breathing, dizziness, sweating, and trembling (Lader & Mathews, 1970). These anxiety attacks can be associated with particular situations, but often are not; attacks can occur without any apparent triggering stimulus. Anxiety attacks do not last long, but can occur frequently. Patients can also feel that they or the world are "not real," or that they are "going crazy" during anxiety attacks. To date, relatively little is known about the causes or development of panic disorders.

People with **generalized anxiety disorders** suffer from chronic anxiety that can grow intense at some times and fade at others, but without evident relationship to their environment; they typically worry about all sorts of actual or potential problems, but it is not clear whether worry causes their anxiety or is merely a way of trying to understand it. The chronic physiological arousal of this nonspecific anxiety, sometimes called *free-floating anxiety*, causes a variety of physical consequences: Sufferers are often restless and overreactive to stimuli, develop muscle cramps and twitches, and may show other difficulties, such as sleep disturbances.

The psychoanalytic view considers generalized anxiety the result of unconscious conflicts over id impulses. The ego cannot allow sexual or aggressive impulses to be expressed for fear they will be punished, but this source of anxiety is not consciously recognized. The dangerous impulses are repressed, but some of the fearfulness associated with the conflict enters consciousness.

The behavioral view argues that some stimuli must be triggering the generalized anxiety, even if they are unrecognized; a person made anxious by social contact, for example, might undergo varying degrees of anxiety throughout the day without connecting it to interpersonal encounters. One cognitive approach relates generalized anxiety to a feeling of helplessness or lack of control over life events. Humanistic theorists have not tried to explain specific disorders such as phobias or generalized anxiety, but in their view anxiety disorders generally reflect frustration arising from an inability to behave in self-actualizing ways.

Obsessive-Compulsive Disorder People with **obsessive-compulsive disorders** experience frequent, repetitive thoughts or impulses or carry out stereotyped behaviors that seem irrational and that they cannot control (Stern & Cobb, 1978). **Obsessions** are thoughts or impulses that continue to recur despite the person's avowed intent to avoid them; they may involve any topic, but often center on acts that the individual considers immoral, including sexual deviations, suicide, and murder (Akhter et al., 1975). Persons with obsessions are often afraid that they will actually carry them out, but in fact they rarely do so. **Compulsions** are behaviors that the person *does* feel compelled to carry out, even though they serve no useful purpose. But compulsive behaviors are not dramatic, as are those involved in obsessions; they are usually ritualistic, even trivial, acts such as walking in a certain way or washing one's hands repeatedly. A well-known literary example is the compulsive handwashing of Shakespeare's Lady Macbeth.

Most people experience minor obsessions or compulsions. A song you hear keeps running through your head or you have to go back to check whether you locked your door, even when you're sure you did. Other activities are sometimes called compulsive, as when a person is said to be a compulsive gambler. But obsessive-compulsive disorders differ from such ordinary behaviors in both frequency and intensity, commonly occurring many times each day despite the person's efforts to stop them. Even compulsive gamblers rarely carry out their actions the way true com-

---

PATIENT QUOTE
Agoraphobia

❝Let me assume that I am walking down University Drive by the Lake. I am a normal man for the first quarter of a mile; for the next hundred yards I am in a mild state of dread, controllable and controlled; for the next twenty yards in an acute state of dread, yet controlled; for the next ten, in an anguish of terror that hasn't reached the crisis of explosion; and in a half-dozen steps more I am in as fierce a panic of isolation from help and home and of immediate death as a man overboard in mid-Atlantic or on a window-ledge far up in a skyscraper with flames lapping his shoulders. The reader who can't understand why I have not merely whistled or laughed or ordered the phobias off my psychic premises, or who thinks that I must be grossly exaggerating a mere normal discomfort, like the initial dread in the dentist's chair, is not the reader for whom I am writing one line of this book. . . . It is as scientific a fact as any I know that my phobic seizures at their worst approach any limits of terror that the human mind is capable of in the actual presence of death in its most horrible forms.**❞**

Leonard, 1927, quoted in Kaplan, 1964.

---

pulsives do. One woman, for example, washed her hands over 500 times a day, even though this caused painful sores (Davison & Neale, 1982). True obsessive-compulsive disorders are relatively rare, making up less than 20% of anxiety disorders, or about 5% of all psychiatric patients (Ingram, 1961).

Mildly obsessive-compulsive behaviors can sometimes be adaptive, as when tasks require careful repetitive checking of details or unusual persistence despite setbacks. One professional mathematician, for example, spent a great deal of effort and considerable computer time to calculate the value of the square root of 2 to over a million decimal places ("The longest root," 1971). As is true of most abnormal behaviors, obsessive-compulsive acts begin to be a problem when they are *not* appropriate to a person's life. The more disruptive of time, energy, and social relationships the behaviors are, the more obviously abnormal they are.

Obsessive-compulsive behaviors seem to be techniques for handling anxiety. Most adult obsessive-compulsives, for example, were highly anxious as children (Kringlen, 1970) and their compulsive behaviors as adults are followed by temporary relief of anxiety (Hodgson & Rachman, 1972). But the source of the anxiety, and how it leads to obsessive-compulsive behavior, are described differently by different perspectives.

A psychoanalytic explanation says that obsessions and compulsions are ways of dealing with id impulses. Compulsive behavior is viewed as overcontrol of id impulses and obsessive thoughts are seen as id impulses that break through the person's inadequate defenses. A behavioral view begins with anxiety from any cause, then adds the second half of the two-factor theory: learning of new behaviors that reduce the anxiety (Meyer & Chesser, 1970). If appropriate behaviors are learned, they are considered normal (perhaps termed *persistent* or *careful*). But if inappropriate behaviors are learned, they are considered abnormal. A more cognitive approach suggests that obsessive-compulsives tend to overestimate the probability of undesirable events (Carr, 1974); the time and energy they spend avoiding possible negative consequences thus predisposes them to obsessive-compulsive behaviors.

STRESS AND PSYCHOPHYSIOLOGICAL DISORDERS

We noted earlier that the continued arousal in generalized anxiety disorders can lead to some physical symptoms. **Psychophysiological disorders** are problems in which the *primary* difficulty is some stress-related illness, such as ulcers. Psychophysiological disorders were once called *psychosomatic illnesses,* the *psych* referring to "mind" and the *somatic* to "body." The term means mind-body illnesses. It was sometimes misused to refer to imagined illnesses, but was actually intended to refer to real physical problems—not illnesses "in the mind" or imaginary, but those "caused by" the mind, that is, arising from mental activity rather than a disease agent such as a virus.

When the sympathetic nervous system is activated, body resources are mobilized for active behavior in the next few minutes: the fight-or-flight response (Chapter 2). If this arousal continues for more than a few minutes or recurs many times a day it can be devastating. Some wild animals, for example, become so aroused if captured that their hearts cannot withstand it; if kept captive, they may die in hours from the continued arousal. Many other species, including humans, seem able to survive continued stress but may develop a number of illnesses as a consequence.

Hans Selye (1976) called the body's reaction to continued sympathetic activation the *General Adaptation Syndrome (G.A.S.).* The G.A.S. is characterized by an initial period of crash activation that makes the organism more capable of coping (the fight-or-flight response). Selye considered this amount of stress positive; he called it *eustress* (Levine, 1971). If sympathetic arousal continues, the organism enters a plateau phase; it continues to cope but only by burning up energy reserves. This continued stress is not desirable—Selye (1974) called it *distress*—because it leads to a variety of problems when reserves are exhausted. If stress lasts long enough the organism collapses, and may possibly die, because of its decreased ability to respond to environmental demands and an increased vulnerability to disease (Richter, 1957).

In one well-known study of continued stress two monkeys were strapped into a pair of chairs each day, where they played one of two roles (Brady, 1968). One monkey was passively exposed to occasional electric shock, which it could neither prevent nor escape. The other was taught that it could prevent the shocks if it pressed a bar—but it had to do so every 20 seconds. If it grew tired or careless and 20 seconds elapsed, both monkeys received shocks. Within weeks, the continued vigilance necessary to avoid the shocks had given this "executive monkey" a bleeding peptic ulcer. The fact that stress caused the ulcers and not the shocks was indicated by the continued health of the other monkey. ■ Figure 15.3

Further work with rats has suggested that the nature of the stress and the response called for—especially whether the organism can take effective action and whether feedback about that action is immediate—affect whether ulcers will be induced. In one *predictability* study rats received shocks at irregular intervals that they could not avoid. Rats receiving a warning signal before each shock did *not* develop ulcers, but rats receiving no warning did (Weiss, 1972). Apparently what was most stressful was the unpredictability of the shocks.

In follow-up *coping* studies, one rat could postpone shock, as the executive monkey did; both it and another rat received shocks only if the first one made a mistake. Both rats received a warning signal, so predictability was not involved. In these studies the passive rat lost the most weight (a sign of stress in rats) and developed ulcers (Weiss, 1972). The important difference between the rat studies and the executive monkey results was explained in terms of how frequently the avoidance response had to be made and whether there was feedback showing that its response had indeed put off the shock. (The executive monkey was forced to respond frequently for extended periods and never received feedback as to its success in delaying the shock.)

Continued stress may also increase an organism's vulnerability to externally caused diseases. Stressed rats are less able to reject implanted tumors, for example, apparently because the stress has reduced the efficiency of their immune systems (Keller et al., 1981; Visintainer et al., 1982). If this is also true for humans, almost any illness might be made more probable, or its effects more severe, in a person subject to stress. Because many diseases may be affected by stress, DSM-III has no single category for psychophysiological disorders; Category 15 of axis I is used to indicate that a physical condition is involved and axis III is used to name the condition (see Table 15.1).

Attempts have been made to see if the effects of naturally occurring stresses on humans parallel the animal results, but so far the pattern of stress effects is not clearly established. Obviously, the same kind of studies cannot be done on humans as on rats, and the complexity of human behavior makes it difficult to sort out the factors in naturally stressful events (Janis & Mann, 1976). One approach, which has sought to quantify human life stresses, is the *Social Readjustment Rating Scale (SRRS)* (Holmes & Rahe, 1967). To build the SRRS, Holmes and Rahe asked people to estimate the relative stressfulness of various life events (whether desirable or not), using marriage as a basis for comparison; more stressful events were given higher values, less stressful ones lower values. ■ Table 15.2

To use the SRRS in assessing the effects of stress, the values for some specified time period in people's lives are added up and the scores are compared with their medical histories for that period. Critics of this approach have suggested that these life-stress dimen-

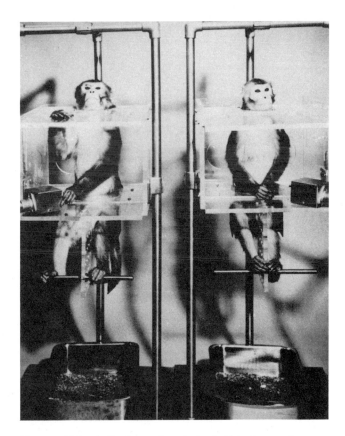

Figure 15.3 ■ In the "executive monkey" study, two monkeys received periodic electric shocks. For the monkey on the right all shocks were inescapable; vigilance and correct action by the "executive" on the left could prevent the shocks, however. The executive soon developed ulcers, a psychosomatic illness resulting from the continued stress of responsibility for the shocks.
(Division of Medical Audio-Visual Services, Walter Reed Army Institute of Research, Washington, D.C.)

sions are too simple, and that merely adding scores fails to consider important interactions among events (Rabkin & Struening, 1976). But the SRRS has been found to correlate with a number of physical problems, from heart attacks (Rahe & Lind, 1971) to colds (Holmes & Holmes, 1970).

Other studies of stress have found additional variables. Genetic variables may predispose some people to stress diseases, for example (Friedman & Iwai, 1976). A few people seem *not* to become ill under stress, perhaps because they have more of a sense of control (Pines, 1980). Too much occupational stress seems to cause problems, but some may actually enhance performance (Hall & Lawler, 1971). For example, pressure that is related to a specific task and can be controlled by performing or completing that task may in fact increase productivity and feelings of success. One stress effect, coronary heart disease, has been linked to a behavior pattern called the *type A personality*, in which people approach virtually all tasks in an aggressive and

Table 15.2 ■ The Social Readjustment Rating Scale

Rank	Life Event	Mean Value
1	Death of spouse	100
2	Divorce	73
3	Marital separation	65
4	Jail term	63
5	Death of close family member	63
6	Personal injury or illness	53
7	Marriage	50
8	Fired at work	47
9	Marital reconciliation	45
10	Retirement	45
11	Change in health of family member	44
12	Pregnancy	40
13	Sex difficulties	39
14	Gain of new family member	39
15	Business readjustment	39
16	Change in financial state	38
17	Death of close friend	37
18	Change to different line of work	36
19	Change in number of arguments with spouse	35
20	Mortgage over $10,000	31
21	Foreclosure of mortgage or loan	30
22	Change in responsibilities at work	29
23	Son or daughter leaving home	29
24	Trouble with in-laws	29
25	Outstanding personal achievement	28
26	Wife begins or stops work	26
27	Begin or end school	26
28	Change in living conditions	25
29	Revision of personal habits	24
30	Trouble with boss	23
31	Change in work hours or conditions	20
32	Change in residence	20
33	Change in schools	20
34	Change in recreation	19
35	Change in church activities	19
36	Change in social activities	18
37	Mortgage or loan less than $10,000	17
38	Change in sleeping habits	16
39	Change in number of family get-togethers	15
40	Change in eating habits	15
41	Vacation	13
42	Christmas	12
43	Minor violations of the law	11

From T. H. Holmes and R. H. Rahe, *Journal of Psychosomatic Research,* 1967, *11,* 213–218. Copyright 1967 Pergamon Press, Ltd. Reprinted with permission.

hurried way (Dembroski & MacDougall, 1982). And at least some stress effects may involve endorphins (Paulos & Tessel, 1982), the brain chemicals thought to be internally generated pain relievers (Chapters 2 and 5). Obviously numerous variables affect how people perceive stress and how they are affected by it.

SOMATOFORM DISORDERS

People with *somatoform disorders* complain of illness or pain when no evidence of physical disease can be found; they are not deliberately pretending, but sincerely believe that they suffer from some disease. (People who claim to be sick when they know they are not are malingerers, and are included in another category.) The major somatoform category is **conversion disorder;** people with conversion disorders display symptoms of some physical problem even though tests show nothing organically wrong. A person with a conversion disorder may claim to be blind, for example, and act blind in ordinary circumstances, yet score significantly *below* chance on a visual test—a result that can only be explained by the person actually seeing the test items and reporting them incorrectly (Theodor & Mendelcorn, 1973).

Sensory and motor symptoms are common in conversion disorder, but nearly any disease or symptom can be imitated. Several aspects of conversion disorders, however, often imply that the problem is not a true illness. Conversion disorders often appear suddenly in a person under severe stress, and may serve to relieve the stress. People with conversion disorders may also show a lack of concern with their problems, called *la belle indifférence:* Going blind or losing the use of one's legs should be a frightening and depressing event, but they may speak of it lightly and casually (Mucha & Reinhardt, 1970). Other consequences may also fail to fit the pattern of physical disease: "Paralyzed" limbs usually do not atrophy, and "blind" patients may move about without bumping into people.

Discriminating conversion disorders from true diseases remains difficult, however. People who suffer from physical disorders of taste and smell, for example, may complain that everything suddenly tastes disgusting, or that they keep smelling something bad. Because taste and smell disorders are not well understood, such complaints may erroneously be assumed to reflect a conversion disorder (Ziporyn, 1982). Other obscure symptoms, such as strange sensations or pains, may also be misdiagnosed. One study of a group of patients diagnosed as having conversion disorders found that nine years after the diagnosis, 60% had developed symptoms of or died from physical diseases—often diseases of the central nervous system (Slater & Glithero, 1965). Some diseases and deaths might have been expected in any such group, but this high percentage suggests that some of the complaints diagnosed as conversion disorders had in fact been early symptoms of physical disease. A later study of patients diagnosed as having conversion disorders found that 25% had physical problems that could contribute to their symptoms (Watson & Buranen, 1979).

Conversion disorder was one of the earliest patterns of abnormal behavior to be recognized. It was first called *hysteria,* after the Greek for "womb," because Hippocrates thought it occurred only in women and was caused by the uterus wandering around inside the body. That conversion disorders could often be temporarily, and sometimes permanently, relieved by hypnotic suggestion was discovered in early research on hypnosis; this was demonstrated for Freud by Charcot, the French physician who taught Freud how to use hypnosis. Freud came to believe that hysteria represented a way of "converting" massive anxiety into a physical symptom, and thus renamed hysteria *conversion reaction*. (Freud's term is used in DSM-III, but this need not imply agreement with Freud's proposed causes.)

Entire groups can sometimes be affected by hysteria; this phenomenon is usually called *mass hysteria*, although one recent book calls it *mass psychogenic illness* (Colligan et al., 1982). (Neither term is a DSM-III category.) Typically, some person in a group displays a symptom, then others develop it, until many in the group are affected in what is termed *hysterical contagion*. Numerous outbreaks in the Middle Ages included wild dancing or biting attacks; contemporary versions have usually involved vague symptoms such as itching, nausea, or fainting (Rosenwein, 1983).

Freud's view of conversion disorder was based on the Electra complex, in which a female child incestuously desires her father but represses that urge. (In Freud's time, conversion disorder was still thought of as exclusive to females.) Freud suggested that some event in a woman's life might reawaken her repressed feelings for her father and that the resulting anxiety could be converted into physical symptoms. Contemporary psychoanalytic theorists, however, have suggested other possibilities for both males and females. (Even today most cases seem to be females; Kroll, 1979. But this may reflect patterns of social stress, because male cases are not infrequent in groups of men under stress, as in war.)

A behavioral view of conversion disorders was presented by Ullmann and Krasner (1975). They suggested that the symptom "chosen" is one with which the patients have had some experience, either personally or through observation; this symptom is then adopted when some form of reinforcement is available to sustain it. Often negative reinforcement occurs through a reduction in life stress (as when a soldier avoids combat). But the symptom can also be positively reinforced (as through an insurance settlement for a "disabling" difficulty). Some evidence supports the idea that symptoms *are* familiar to patients; of a group of naval aviators who developed conversion disorders during their stressful flight training, 60% had parents with significant illnesses related to the organ affected in their case (Mucha & Reinhardt, 1970). But this alone does not demonstrate *why* a symptom was adopted.

The physiological perspective offers additional insight into conversion disorders. When symptoms are localized to one side of the body, as in a paralyzed arm or leg, it is more often the left side (Galin et al., 1977; Stern, 1977). This suggests that the right hemisphere is controlling the symptom in these cases. The right hemisphere has been characterized as less logical and more emotional than the left and as the body specialist. The use of a body symptom to escape emotional stress might thus be a right-hemisphere strategy; that the "person" is unaware that this strategy is being used may really mean that the left hemisphere is unaware of it. (This possibility is only speculative, but it does fit the observed data.)

DSM-III lists three other somatoform disorders. People with *psychogenic pain disorder* report ill-defined but severe and persistent pain, either in the absence of a definable medical condition or out of proportion to a defined condition. (*Psychogenic* means "psychologically caused.") The mechanisms of pain remain poorly understood, so it is possible that some such patients are suffering from pain of organic origin. But for many the pain seems to play the same role that conversion disorders do in reducing stress from other problems or in getting them out of difficult situations. People with *hypochondriasis* worry continually that they are falling ill with some major disease, although they are usually healthy. Early life experiences (such as parents who exaggerated any minor illness) may initiate hypochondriasis, and reinforcement (such as increased attention from others) may sustain it. People with *somatization disorders* also commonly seek doctors' appointments, but they also fake symptoms to obtain hospitalization; some have had repeated surgery for ills they did not actually have.

DISSOCIATIVE DISORDERS

People with **dissociative disorders** show a sudden and temporary dissociating of normal consciousness, identity, or memory. In extreme cases they may behave as two or more completely different people. The dissociative disorders are all relatively rare, but their sometimes dramatic separations raise such basic questions about normal integration of identity and behavior that they have received substantial attention from psychologists and psychiatrists as well as the popular media.

Multiple Personality

People with **multiple personality** disorder exhibit two or more distinct and often quite different alternating personalities. Periods of alternation are typically minutes or hours, though they can be longer. When one personality is "in charge" the person dresses, speaks, and behaves with ordinary consistency. But with each change in personality a different pattern emerges: One personality may smoke or drink and another not, one may dress conservatively and another flamboyantly. The extent to which the separate personalities are aware of each other's existence varies, as does the amount of internal communication. Some personalities are always aware of events, even when another personality is in charge. Others are aware of their existence only when they are in control and are unable to understand the frequent periods for which they have no memory. (Note that multiple personality is *not* a form of schizophrenia, as is often mistakenly thought. Although schizophrenia refers to a kind of split, as we will note later, the meaning is quite different.)

The inherent drama of a multiple personality case is obvious, and Thigpen and Cleckley's book *The Three Faces of Eve* (1954) captured public interest and was later made into a movie. But multiple personality cases are exceedingly rare—only about 100 have ever been reported—and some observers have questioned the authenticity of these reports. Multiple personalities have often been investigated at length by hypnotic techniques, and critics have raised the possibility that therapists have unknowingly contributed to the development of these personalities rather than uncovering them. (Some forms of dissociation can be easily established under hypnosis, as in the hidden observer research described in Chapter 7. Imagine what might be possible in hundreds of hours of hypnotherapy.)

Chris Sizemore, Thigpen and Cleckley's patient, has written that her case was even more complex than they reported (Sizemore & Pittillo, 1977). Several groups of 3 personalities rotated within her at different times—21 personalities in all—before she resolved what she hopes is her last trio. But self-reports are less reliable than clinical observations, so Sizemore's account offers no more demonstration of the reality of such cases than the original report. ■ Figure 15.4

More recently, however, some cases have been subjected to assessments that offer more solid evidence. In one case, each of the patient's three personalities was given Osgood's Semantic Differential, a standard personality measure (Jeans, 1976). The descriptions independently generated from the test closely matched those of the psychiatrist (Osgood et al., 1976). Other researchers have found notable differences in the EEG patterns of multiple personalities (Herbert, 1982c). Such evidence suggests that multiple personality can be a real phenomenon and can develop without therapist intervention.

Psychoanalytic and behavioral perspectives both recognize multiple personality as a highly exaggerated form of normal behavior—we all are somewhat differ-

© 1983 by Sidney Harris

ent people in different circumstances—which allows one personality to act in a way that the other personality need not feel responsible for. The primary personality may be tightly controlled and proper, and one of the alternate personalities may represent all the irresponsible, self-indulgent impulses that the primary personality does not permit. But the psychoanalytic and behavioral perspectives differ in their interpretations of how and why these different behavioral tendencies are packaged into distinct personalities. The psychoanalytic interpretation is based on repression, beginning with the forbidden Oedipal desires of childhood. The behavioral interpretation emphasizes the rewards offered by such behaviors, both in reduced stress and in "having your cake and eating it too," by being able to carry out multiple roles.

Because separate personalities are often unable to remember what has happened since they were last in control, a cognitive interpretation may also be relevant. Bower (1981) likened the memory gaps of the different personalities to state-specific memory effects (Chapter 9). He suggested that mood differences among the multiple personalities may act as state-specific memory cues, so that each personality remembers its own memories better than those of the other personalities.

Other Dissociative Disorders

There are several other dissociative disorders in which aspects of the self are lost or separated. People with

Figure 15.4 ■ Chris Sizemore, the woman called "Eve White" by Thigpen and Cleckley in *The Three Faces of Eve* (1954). She is shown with her own painting; it symbolizes the groups of three personalities that came and went over years of therapy before she reached what seems to her to be a stable resolution.

(Gerald Martineau/The Washington Post)

psychogenic amnesia temporarily lose the ability to recall important personal information through psychological causes; often the memory loss directly follows and obliterates some highly stressful event, such as a personal tragedy. The period covered by the amnesia may be only the preceding few days or the person's entire life history; memory can be recovered in hours or not for years. During the amnesia, episodes from the person's personal life are lost but general knowledge remains. The person may not know his or her age, name, or address, yet may show appropriate knowledge of money, social customs, and current events. Once memory returns, it seems to do so completely and the person is not likely to experience a recurrence.

People with **psychogenic fugue** also experience amnesia for personal history, but the amnesia is usually total and the person leaves home and behaves as if he or she were a different person. After a confused transitional period, the person may get a job under a new identity and continue in this new identity for years. (Media accounts of amnesia cases, in which a person is found wandering far from home, are more often descriptions of fugue than of psychogenic amnesia.)

People with **depersonalization** disorder suddenly lose their normal sense of self. They may feel that they are not real, that their body has become alien or distorted, or even that they are floating detached from their body. As with the other dissociative disorders, depersonalization experiences are likely to follow severe stress. Depersonalization most often occurs in adolescence or young adulthood, and thus may reflect problems in establishing an adult identity or possibly even physiological changes related to puberty. (Less severe depersonalization experiences are not uncommon among college freshmen, especially those far from their families and home environments for the first time.)

MAJOR AFFECTIVE DISORDERS

We turn now to disorders in which anxiety is not an obvious central feature. People with **major affective disorders** show wide variations in mood from extreme elation to extreme depression (Becker, 1977).

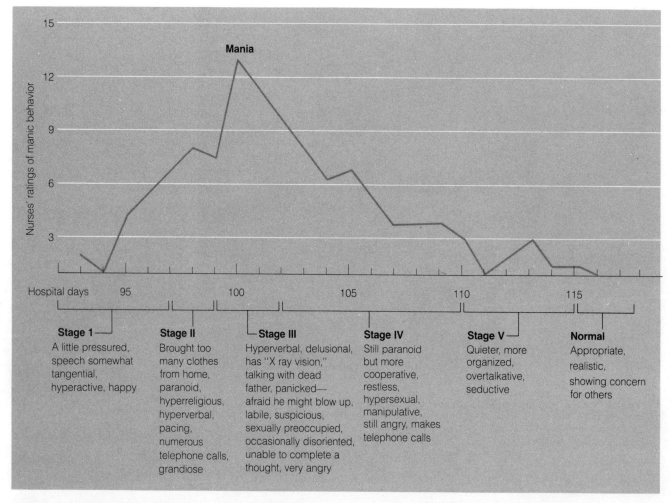

Figure 15.5 ■ Stages of a single manic episode in a hospitalized patient, showing characteristic swings of mood and activity level.

(Adapted from G. Carlson and F. K. Goodwin, *Archives of General Psychiatry*, February 1973, *28*, 221-228. Copyright 1973 by the American Medical Association. Used by permission.)

(*Affect* means "mood or emotion.") In the relatively rare bipolar disorder, both ends of the mood continuum are shown; more frequently, depression alone occurs.

Bipolar Disorder

People with **bipolar disorder** show swings in mood that include extremes of elation and depression. The episodes of elation include other behaviors that can be characterized as unusually active and irrationally optimistic. (The thought patterns in such an episode are sometimes called a "flight of ideas.") This syndrome of rapid, optimistic behavior is termed **mania**; a person behaving this way is described as *manic*. ■ Figure 15.5

People with bipolar disorder sometimes swing from one extreme directly to the other, but can also show periods of moderate mood between manic and depressive episodes. In depressive episodes, bipolar patients are depressed in activity as well as mood. Their manic states include rapid movement and ambitious plans, but their depressed states include slow movements, greater-than-usual amounts of sleep, and general pessimism. These characteristics suggest that some general activation level may be varying, rather than mood alone (Bunney et al., 1972). ■ Figure 15.6

Because the recurring "switches" in mood need not follow obvious environmental cues, researchers have emphasized possible biological causes, including genetics and biochemistry. One way of assessing whether a condition is genetically based is to compute the **concordance** rate, the percentage of other family members who show the condition. Researchers can compare, for example, concordance rates for identical

Characteristics of Depression

Mood
Is dejected, discouraged, sad, feels that all is hopeless. May be anxious, apprehensive, hostile. May think frequently of suicide.

Self-concept
Feels helpless, unworthy, sinful. Has reduced self-confidence and initiative. Complains of difficulty concentrating.

Activity Level
Diminished (or sometimes increased) levels of everyday activities, inlcuding eating, sex, work, and hobbies.

Appearance
Stooped posture, sad or blank facial expression, slow movements, limited and monotonic speech.

Physical Difficulties
Poor sleep, constipation, loss of energy, fatigue, weight loss.

Figure 15.6 ■ Depression is characterized by a variety of subjective experiences and overt behaviors.
(Lawrence Cameron/Jeroboam)

or monozygotic (MZ) and fraternal or dizygotic (DZ) twins. Twins of both types have environmental as well as genetic similarities. But the *difference* between the concordance rates for the two kinds of twins reflects genetic factors. (If environmental similarities account for a given amount of concordance, any extra for MZ twins is thought to represent the greater genetic similarity between them.) Such studies have found that bipolar disorder is genetically influenced: The concordance rate for MZ twins has been estimated to be 72%, compared to only 14% for DZ twins (Allen, 1976).

Note that even a strong genetic predisposition does not mean a person will inevitably show the disorder. Even a 72% concordance rate means that 28% of MZ twins of bipolars do *not* have similar problems. Furthermore, even in those who have the disorder, learned behavior or environmental events may contribute to the timing or severity of the mood swings.

Studies of patients' biochemistry has suggested that variation in levels of the neurotransmitter norepinephrine (NE) may be involved in both mania and depression (Schildkraut, 1965). No method is yet available to measure neurotransmitter levels in the brain directly, so the evidence for this *norepinephrine hypothesis* is indirect. Some evidence comes from the administration of drugs that are known to raise or lower NE levels. Drugs that raise NE levels also seem to raise mood levels; they can trigger a manic episode in a bipolar patient who is temporarily normal (Bunney et al., 1970) and can pull a depressed bipolar patient out of the depression (Cobbin et al., 1979). Other evidence comes from measuring levels of NE metabolites, chemical products that result from the breakdown of NE. If high or low NE levels are present, one would expect comparably high or low levels of NE metabolites—and low levels of NE metabolites *are* typically found in depressed patients.

Major Depression

Virtually everyone undergoes periods of depression in response to environmental stress, and more severe depressive episodes are one of the most common disorders. About 5–10% of men and 10–20% of women will suffer depression severe enough to be diagnosed as depressive at least once in their lives (Weissman &

PATIENT QUOTES
Differing degrees of depression

"Th.: Good morning, how are you today?

Pt.: (Pause) Well, okay I guess, doctor. . . . I don't know, I just feel sort of discouraged.

Th.: Is there anything in particular that worries you?

Pt.: I don't know, doctor . . . everything seems to be futile . . . nothing seems worth while any more. It seems as if all that was beautiful has lost its beauty. I guess I expected more than life has given. It just doesn't seem worth while going on. I can't seem to make up my mind about anything. I guess I have what you would call the "blues."

Th.: Can you tell me how your trouble started?

Pt.: I don't know . . . it seems like I have a lead weight in my stomach . . . I feel different . . . I am not like other people . . . my health is ruined . . . I wish I were dead.

Th.: Your health is ruined?

Pt.: . . . Yes, my brain is being eaten away. I shouldn't have done it . . . If I had any willpower I would kill myself . . . I don't deserve to live . . . I have ruined everything . . . and it's all my fault.

Th.: It's all your fault?

Pt.: Yes . . . I have been unfaithful to my wife and now I am being punished . . . my health is ruined . . . there's no use going on . . . (sigh) . . . I have ruined everything . . . my family . . . and now myself . . . I bring misfortune to everyone . . . I am a moral leper . . . a serpent in the Garden of Eden . . . why don't I die . . . why don't you give me a pill and end it all before I bring catastrophe on everyone. . . . No one can help me. . . . It's hopeless . . . I know that . . . it's hopeless.

The patient lay in bed, immobile, with a dull, depressed expression on his face. His eyes were sunken and downcast. Even when spoken to, he would not raise his eyes to look at the speaker. Usually he did not respond at all to questions, but sometimes, after apparently great effort, he would mumble something about the "Scourge of God." He appeared somewhat emaciated, his breath was foul, and he had to be given enemas to maintain elimination. Occasionally, with great effort, he made the sign of the cross with his right hand. The overall picture was one of extreme vegetativelike immobility and depression.**"**

(From J. C. Coleman et al., *Abnormal Psychology and Modern Life*, 6th ed. Copyright © 1980, 1976, 1972 by Scott, Foresman and Company. Reprinted by permission.)

Meyers, 1978). People with **major depression** show depression notably beyond ordinary levels, but without associated manic episodes. The severity of their depression ranges from somewhat more depressed than normal to a stuporous inactivity. Symptoms that may be present (though a patient may not show all of them) include sadness, appetite loss, sleep difficulties, shift in activity level (becoming lethargic or agitated), loss of pleasure in usual activities, loss of energy, feelings of worthlessness and self-blame, difficulty in thinking or concentrating, and thoughts of death or suicide. ■ Patient Quotes: Differing Degrees of Depression

A variety of findings suggest that major depression is not the same as the depressed cycles of bipolar disorder (DePue & Monroe, 1978). Many major depressives have disturbed sleep or insomnia rather than increased sleeping, some are agitated rather than lethargic, the age of onset is older than for bipolar disorder, and so forth. There are enough differences *among* major depressives, however, to suggest that this category may represent several different conditions. (DSM-III suggests that some patients can be differentiated by considering their depression to be psychotic if delusions or hallucinations are present.)

There is evidence of some genetic contribution to major depression, but to a lesser extent than in bipolar disorder: Concordance rates for MZ twins are about 40% and for DZ twins about 11% (Allen, 1976). The possibility that abnormal levels of NE are involved in depression was noted earlier; another theory suggests that a different neurotransmitter, serotonin, may be involved. Note, however, that variations in neurotransmitters may be associated with some disorder but not necessarily be the cause of that disorder. People behave quite differently when depressed, for example, and something about these behavioral differences could change their levels of neurotransmitter. In the case of the neurotransmitter hypotheses, drugs that are known to modify the neurotransmitters also modify the patient's depression; this suggests that the relationship is causal.

There are also a variety of psychological theories of depression (Akiskal & McKinney, 1975; Blaney, 1977). Freud's original view was based on an exaggeration of the depression that can develop when mourning the death of a loved one (1917). Later, as it became obvious that people could become depressed without loss of a loved one, a concept of *symbolic loss* was added that suggested interpersonal relations could be interpreted *as if* a loss of love had occurred. Following the loss of a loved one on whom the person was dependent, Freud suggested, a complex series of largely unconscious events occur. The result is a mixture of anger at the lost person for going away and guilt over

PART V ■ *Development and Individual Differences*

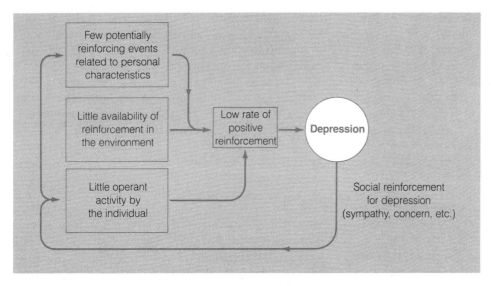

Figure 15.7 ▪ A behavioral model of depression that suggests how low levels of activity and reinforcement can sustain each other—and thus a depressed state.

(After P. H. Lewinsohn, 1974, in *Abnormal Psychology*, 3rd ed., by G. C. Davison and J. M. Neale. Copyright © 1982 by John Wiley & Sons. Used by permission.)

real or imaginary prior failures toward the lost person. This anger is turned inward, resulting in the symptoms of depression. Freud's concept of *anger turned inward* has been widely used by psychoanalysts; little research has been done on the concept, however, and what has been done has not supported it (e.g., Weissman et al., 1971).

A behavioral view of depression emphasizes loss of reinforcement (Eastman, 1976). In the death of a loved one, the many reinforcers provided by that person are removed and the period of mourning may remove still others, such as interaction with friends. Some friends may in fact reward a grieving role with sympathy and kindness, and thus help perpetuate it (Ullmann & Krasner, 1975). This *loss of reinforcement* view applies equally well to other life changes that may trigger depression, such as loss of a job or moving to a new town. These factors may combine to provide a self-perpetuating depressed role (Lewinsohn, 1974). Depressed people do report taking part in fewer pleasant events than do nondepressed people (Lewinsohn & Libet, 1972). But this evidence cannot be taken as strong support for Lewinsohn's model (Figure 15.7) for at least two reasons: It does not show that few reinforcers lead to depression rather than the opposite, and depressed people have been found to underestimate the reinforcers they do receive (Nelson & Craighead, 1977). ▪ Figure 15.7

A cognitive-behavioral model of depression is Seligman's (1975) **learned helplessness** approach. Seligman has shown that unavoidable failures can teach

animals to give up in the face of new threats, whereas prior successes can teach them to persist. Animals that give up are said to have learned a sense of helplessness that negatively affects their later behavior; a dog that has been subjected to inescapable shock, for example, may sit passively and accept shock that it could escape. Such animals also eat less, resulting in weight loss, and show decreased norepinephrine levels (as depressed humans do). Seligman originally proposed that people who become depressed are those who have learned that they cannot succeed, and who thus give up in the face of stress. Criticism of that proposal led to a refined and more cognitive version (Abramson et al., 1978) in which people are assumed to make attributions about the causes of their behavior, that is, to decide *why* it occurs (Weiner et al., 1972). People who are likely to become depressed are those who attribute their failures to enduring personal faults. In contrast, those who attribute failure either to temporary personal factors ("I was tired") or to outside factors ("The test was too hard") are unlikely to become depressed. Initial findings support this revised model. Depressed college students, for example, more often attributed their failures to personal attributes than did nondepressed students (Seligman et al., 1979). The attribution-oriented version of the learned helplessness model has attracted widespread professional attention, and may become the dominant psychological model of depression if further research supports it.

Aaron Beck (1967) developed an alternative cognitive model out of work with his own patients that has also been favorably received. Beck, a psychiatrist, felt that depressed people characteristically blame themselves much more for whatever setbacks they encounter than a normal person would. We all suffer less-than-successful events, but we interpret them in a variety of ways. Beck has argued that people inclined to depression interpret most of them in terms of self-blame and self-deprecation; these illogical thought patterns then result in the emotional symptoms of depression. Studies have found that depressed people do engage in self-blame (e.g., R. E. Nelson, 1977). But again this correlation does not demonstrate cause; self-blaming cognitions could make people depressed, as Beck has argued, or being depressed could make people blame themselves. In attempts to demonstrate cause, Beck and others have investigated whether changing the cognitions can affect the depression (Beck, 1976).

SCHIZOPHRENIC DISORDERS

People with **schizophrenic disorders** or **schizophrenias** experience serious distortions of reality. They may experience thinking distortions (such as delusions), perceptual distortions (such as hallucinations), and a variety of other symptoms. Schizophrenia is one of the most serious of the psychotic disorders; schizophrenics are the people most likely to be considered "mad" or "crazy." It is also one of the most common of the serious disorders: Schizophrenics make up about a quarter of all patients admitted to mental hospitals. Furthermore, schizophrenia is an enduring condition that is resistant to treatment; fewer schizophrenics are discharged, so about half of all mental hospital patients at any given time are schizophrenic.

Schizophrenic symptoms are recognized and considered abnormal in many cultures (Murphy, 1976), and were among the earliest to be recognized as indicating a mental disorder. The modern view of schizophrenia dates from an 1860 case description by Morel, a Belgian psychiatrist; he described the gradual deterioration in thought processes of a 13-year-old boy and named the disorder *demence precoce*, for progressive mental deterioration (*demence*) occurring at a young age (*precoce*). When Kraepelin devised his classification scheme in 1898, he included Morel's term in Latin (*dementia praecox*).

Eugen Bleuler, a Swiss psychiatrist, suggested a few years later that the common element in the many symptoms of dementia praecox was a splitting of associative bonds—between thought and speech, between thought and affect, and so forth. Bleuler also questioned both assumptions of the term *dementia praecox*; he felt that progressive deterioration need not always occur and that such problems need not begin in childhood. Bleuler thus renamed the disorder *schizophrenia* after the multiple associative "splits" he felt were more characteristic of it. (Remember, as we noted earlier, that schizophrenia does *not* imply a split between personalities.)

Bleuler's expanded definition allowed patients to be diagnosed as schizophrenic who would not have fitted Kraepelin's dementia praecox category. Subsequently more and more patients in the United States were diagnosed as schizophrenic: from 20% of admissions at one hospital in the 1930s to a peak of 80% in 1952 (Davison & Neale, 1982). Since the 1950s, though, fewer patients have been diagnosed as schizophrenic. DSM-III will probably further reduce the frequency of schizophrenic diagnosis, because it includes new categories for some patients formerly labeled schizophrenic.

Symptoms of Schizophrenia

There is no single symptom that characterizes all schizophrenics. They may exhibit virtually all the symptoms of the other disorders, as well as others to be described later (Neale & Oltmanns, 1980; Wynne et al., 1978). Schizophrenia is diagnosed when clusters of severe symptoms occur together in patterns specified by DSM-III, but only when deterioration follows a previously acceptable level of functioning. People who never develop acceptable functioning fall into other categories.

One of the major symptoms of schizophrenia is disordered language. Patients with mild speech disruption give the impression that attention difficulties or speech-production problems may be involved and their thoughts may not be seriously disturbed. Such patients may be able to speak relatively normally and to carry on a meaningful conversation, but may frequently change the subject, as if they are unable to keep their attention on any one topic for very long, or may show occasional misstatements or word peculiarities that do not prevent their primary message from being conveyed. Other patients show more extreme disruptions of speech patterns, which make their intended messages less and less obvious. In the severe forms, it becomes difficult to tell whether the patient has well-formed thoughts and cannot fit the words to them, or whether the words reflect equally distorted thoughts. ■ Patient Quotes: Schizophrenia

In schizophrenic speech, sentences are often fragmented and may seem entirely unrelated to previous topics. The speech includes *neologisms*, made-up words that mean nothing to anyone else, and *clang associations,* inappropriate words or phrases that rhyme with something already said. It may also show *perseveration,* repeated use of the same words or phrases, or *blocking,* sudden ending of speech before an idea is completed. In extreme forms, schizophrenic speech becomes so garbled that it has been called *word salad.* Researchers have sought to understand how and why such schizophrenic speech occurs, but with only limited success (Cohen et al., 1974; Rochester et al., 1977). ■ Figure 15.8

Dramatic speech disruptions have long been considered indicative of schizophrenia. But a major study, the International Pilot Study of Schizophrenia (IPSS), found that only about 10% of schizophrenics showed such speech symptoms (Sartorius et al., 1974). Disorders in thought, shown by the *content* of speech, were far more common. The IPSS study found that nearly all schizophrenics (97%) showed one important disruption of thought: a lack of insight into their own condition. They seemed not to understand where they were, why they were there, or that the things they said and did were considered unusual by others. Many (65%) also showed another major disruption of thought: a **delusion,** a belief considered untrue (and often bizarre) by other people. The majority of these delusions were of persecution; patients believed that people (or nonhuman entities) were plotting against them. Other relatively common delusions include the belief that someone is inserting thoughts into the patient's head or removing the patient's own thoughts, or broadcasting the patient's thoughts so that others may hear them (Mellor, 1970). Patients may also believe that external forces are causing strange sensations in their bodies or causing them to feel inappropriate emotions or to commit inappropriate acts.

Many schizophrenics also show disturbances in perception or attention. The most obviously abnormal perceptual distortions are hallucinations; the most common of these (74% of the IPSS group) are auditory—in particular, talking about the patient, frequently in disparaging terms (Mellor, 1970). Other perceptual disturbances include unusual body sensations and feelings that the world appears distorted or unreal. Extremes of sensory input are also noted, ranging from the world seeming colorless and drab to extreme sensory sensitivity. Some insight into what such patients experience may be obtained from their drawings or paintings. ■ Figure 15.9

Affective symptoms have long been included in schizophrenic diagnoses; common problems have included a reduction in emotional responsiveness, termed *blunted* or *flat affect,* and inappropriate emotional displays, such as laughing at news of a relative's death or becoming angry over nothing. But in DSM-

PATIENT QUOTES
Schizophrenia

❝ How old are you?"

"Why I am centuries old, sir."

"How long have you been here?"

"I've been now on this property on and off for a long time. I cannot say the exact time because we are absorbed by the air at night, and they bring back people. They kill up everything; they can make you lie; they can talk through your throat."

"Who is this?"

"Why, the air."

"What is the name of this place?"

"This place is called a star."

"Who is the doctor in charge of your ward?"

"A body just like yours, sir. They can make you black and white. I say good morning, but he just comes through there. At first it was a colony. They said it was heaven. These buildings were not solid at the time, and I am positive that this is the same place. They have others just like it. People die, and all the microbes talk over there, and prestigitis you know is sending you from here to another world. . . . I was sent by the government to the United States to Washington to some star, and they had a pretty nice country there. Now you have a body like a young man who says he is of the prestigitis."

"Why do you think people believe in God?"

"Uh, late, I don't know why, let's see balloon travel. He holds it up for you, the balloon. He don't let you fall out, your little legs sticking out down through the clouds. He's down to the smoke stack, looking through the smoke trying to get the balloon gassed up you know. Way they're flying on top that way, legs sticking out, I don't know, looking down on the ground, heck, that'd make you go dizzy you just stay and sleep you know, hold down and sleep there. The balloon's His home you know up there. I used to sleep outdoors, you know, sleep outdoors instead of going home. He's had a home but His not tell where it's at you know.❞

Top, White, 1932, p. 228; bottom, Chapman and Chapman, 1973, p. 3.

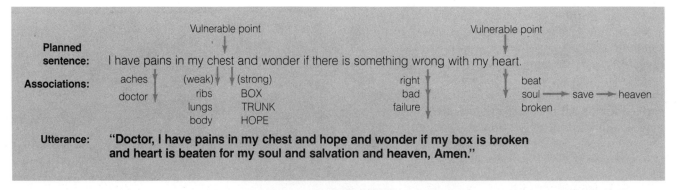

Figure 15.8 ■ This model of schizophrenic speech suggests that various associations to words and phrases offer the possibility of inappropriate intrusions at vulnerable points in a sentence.

(From B. Maher, "The Shattered Language of Schizophrenia," *Psychology Today*, November 1968. Reprinted from Psychology Today Magazine. Copyright © 1968 American Psychological Association.)

Figure 15.9 ■ Some drawings of cats, done by Louis Wain (1860–1939) in the 1920s over the course of his illness, suggesting the progressive distortions in perception and/or thought characteristic of schizophrenia.

(Derek Bayes, LIFE MAGAZINE, © 1964, Time, Inc.)

III, severe affective symptoms are considered signs of a newly specified category, *schizoaffective disorder.*

Motor disturbances are also characteristic of some schizophrenics. These include behaviors that are controlled but bizarre, such as peculiar facial expressions or ritualistic body movements, as well as extremes of activity from restless overactivity similar to that of mania to nearly total inactivity.

Most schizophrenics also show a disruption of ordinary activities, such as social relationships or employment. Some of this disruption of daily life results from their other symptoms; certainly many of these symptoms would put strains on any social relationship. The reason for other changes is less obvious: Schizophrenics often show very poor grooming and personal hygiene, for example, but it is not clear why.

Types of Schizophrenia

DSM-III discriminates among five subcategories of schizophrenia. **Disorganized schizophrenia** (formerly called hebephrenic schizophrenia) is characterized by a mixture of symptoms; one of the most notable is "silly" behavior, including inappropriate giggling and peculiar gestures. Speech often makes little or no sense and hallucinations and delusions are common. Normal inhibitions are often reduced or lost, and patients may become hostile or obscene, or smear their feces on the walls. This pattern represents a severe and widespread deterioration: Disorganized schizophrenics seem to become disturbed earlier, deteriorate further, and remain less responsive to treatment than any other schizophrenic subcategory.

Catatonic schizophrenia is characterized by extremes of motor activity, including excited, even violent, activity and stuporous inactivity. Patients can cycle between these extremes, but most show primarily one extreme or the other (Morrison, 1973). Catatonic patients who shift from one extreme to the other may do so suddenly and without warning; in the active state, they can be quite dangerous. The most common pattern, however, is the inactive one; some patients will hold a fixed position for hours or even days. During this time their immobility and glassy stare suggest a lack of contact with their surroundings, but some can later report in detail the events that occurred around them. While immobile, some catatonic patients may resist efforts to move them, but others will allow their limbs to be rearranged and will hold the new positions—a phenomenon termed *waxy flexibility.*
■ Figure 15.10

Paranoid schizophrenia is characterized by delusions, usually of persecution but also of grandeur (believing oneself to be a famous person) and others. The delusions are accompanied by a cluster of related

"THE COMPUTER CAN TALK TO TERMINALS ALL OVER THE COUNTRY. BENTLEY THINKS IT'S TALKING ABOUT HIM."

behaviors; paranoid schizophrenics are typically suspicious and often believe that what others are doing or saying, even what happens on television, is part of a plot against them. Paranoid schizophrenics can be dangerous; they sometimes attack people they believe to be a threat. Otherwise, apart from their particular delusions, they are often less disturbed than those in other subcategories. Speech and thought patterns continue to be relatively intact, for example, compared to the deterioration of disorganized schizophrenics. Persons with delusions but without hallucinations or other evidence of schizophrenia may be diagnosed as having a *paranoid disorder.* Some people with paranoid symptoms may even hold jobs and continue to function, although with their suspicions and peculiar ways they may be considered eccentric.

Undifferentiated schizophrenia is used to label patients whose symptoms are too mixed or changeable to fit clearly into one of the major types. Often patients considered undifferentiated are either in the process of becoming schizophrenic for the first time or are in a state of transition from one type to the other. **Residual schizophrenia** is the term used for schizophrenics who have largely recovered but still exhibit some symptoms.

a   **b**

Figure 15.10 ■ Two hospitalized schizophrenic patients: (a) a disorganized schizophrenic and (b) a catatonic schizophrenic.

(**a,** ©1983 Benyas-Kaufman from Black Star; **b,** Elinor S. Beckwith/Taurus Photos)

Causes of Schizophrenia

Research suggests that genetic, biochemical, and environmental factors are all important contributors to schizophrenia. The person who becomes schizophrenic probably is genetically predisposed to do so. That genetic predisposition probably results in biochemical differences, primarily in the nervous system. And the reasons why some predisposed individuals become schizophrenic and others do not are probably best described in terms of life stresses and learning.

Genetic Factors Studies of twins, family patterns, and adopted children all offer evidence for genetic predispositions to schizophrenia. Estimates of concordance rates differ substantially, depending on the definition used; including only twins who are both hospitalized as schizophrenics yields a lower concordance rate than including twins hospitalized with other psychotic diagnoses or milder schizophrenic symptoms without hospitalization (Gottesman &

Shields, 1982). But regardless of the definition of concordance, differences between types of twins still indicate a genetic predisposition. Data from a number of researchers around the world over the last several decades reveal that rates for MZ twins are several times greater than those for DZ twins (Rosenthal, 1970).

Children of schizophrenic parents often exhibit a wide variety of disorders (Rieder, 1973). Kringlen (1978), for example, found that 20% of the children of two schizophrenics developed schizophrenia; a total of 72% developed some abnormality. Studies of the children of schizophrenics who have been adopted and reared by others offer the strongest evidence for genetic factors because they separate out the effects of environment. Such studies find much higher frequencies of abnormality in the adopted children of schizophrenic parents than in control groups of other adopted children. In one study, for example, nearly 20% of 47 adopted children of schizophrenic parents were later diagnosed as schizophrenic, but none of 50 control subjects became schizophrenic (Heston, 1966). In other studies, when disorders similar to schizophrenia have been included the incidence has increased to as high as 30% (Rosenthal et al., 1971).

Biochemical Factors Research on the biochemistry of schizophrenics typically seeks to establish a difference between the levels of some body chemical in schizophrenics and controls. As noted earlier, however, merely finding such a difference is not enough; it could be a result rather than a cause of schizophrenia. A number of apparent differences in the biochemistry of schizophrenics have been found, but many were later shown to reflect methodological errors, such as using an inappropriate control group. In one case, for example, hospitalized schizophrenics were compared to nonhospitalized controls; the difference between them turned out to reflect hospitalization, not schizophrenia.

Contemporary studies have focused on the production and use of key neurotransmitters, especially dopamine (Snyder, 1978). The **dopamine hypothesis** proposes that schizophrenics have either an excess of dopamine or an excess of receptor sites for it (Davis, 1978). Evidence for the dopamine hypothesis includes the effects of several antipsychotic drugs. The relative effectiveness of such drugs in relieving schizophrenia is directly proportional to their effectiveness in blocking dopamine action at brain synapses. Some research suggests that they function by binding directly to the dopamine receptors (Turkington, 1983).

Other studies of the biology of schizophrenia have looked at brain structures. It has been found, for example, that schizophrenics are more likely to have had difficult births than are average persons, suggesting that at least some cases could reflect brain damage at birth (McNeil & Kaij, 1978). Both schizophrenics and their children show unusual EEG patterns (Greenberg, 1983b). CAT-scan studies (Chapter 2) have found that chronic schizophrenics have larger ventricles and more indications of brain atrophy than healthy individuals (Weinberger et al., 1979). Furthermore, patients with more enlarged ventricles are less responsive to antipsychotic drugs (Weinberger et al., 1980). (Evidence of disturbed dopamine activity has also been found in such brain-atrophied schizophrenics; van Kammen et al., 1983.)

One interesting physiological finding concerns hearing "voices"; patients' reports of voices were found to coincide with electrical activity in their vocal cords, apparently confirming earlier suggestions that the voices are the patients "talking to themselves" (McGuigan, 1966). (This does not tell *why* they do so, of course, or why they do not recognize that they are doing so.)

Environmental Factors The existence of a genetic predisposition is insufficient to determine whether a person will become schizophrenic. If genetic factors alone were sufficient, the concordance rate for MZ twins would be 1.0—but, as noted earlier, it is not. Hence some environmental factors must also be influential in determining who actually develops schizophrenia.

There has long been agreement that severe environmental stress can trigger schizophrenia in susceptible or vulnerable individuals (Neufeld, 1982). A relatively minor stress might trigger the disorder in a vulnerable individual, with greater stress needed for a more resistant individual. In the past, when a previously well-adapted person seemed to develop schizophrenia in "reaction" to the environment, the schizophrenia was termed **reactive.** When a person had shown a gradual deterioration from a young age, with no obvious unusual stress, the result was termed **process** schizophrenia—suggesting the result of some physiological "process" or illness. (*Process* and *reactive* referred to extremes of a continuum, not to two distinct categories.) Traditionally, the outlook for recovery was considered much more favorable for reactive schizophrenics, who might recover quickly once the precipitating stress was eliminated.

DSM-III, however, uses two new categories for the brief transient reactions that might earlier have been considered reactive schizophrenia: *brief reactive psychosis* and *schizophreniform disorder*. Only problems lasting longer than six months are now considered schizophrenias.

It has also been suggested that various long-term environmental factors might contribute to schizophrenia. Most such proposals have focused on the stresses and learning patterns within families. One of the earliest such suggestions was that children were made schizophrenic by the inappropriate treatment of cold and distant mothers (Fromm-Reichmann, 1948). Other proposals suggested that both parents were at fault, because of the way in which they treated the child—as in "double-bind" situations, where the child was wrong no matter what he or she did (Bateson et al., 1956). One psychiatrist not only argued that family problems could cause schizophrenia, but further argued that schizophrenia might be an adaptive way of working through the person's difficulties (Laing, 1964).

Strong objections have been raised to each of these proposals, however. Often they are supported only by anecdotal evidence or interpretations of a few case histories. When research has been done on family arrangements, it has often been methodologically weak (Fontana, 1966). And when unusual interactions *have* been found between parents and children, the pattern has seemed to occur only with the schizophrenic child and not with other children in the family (Mishler & Waxler, 1968). This has convinced many psychologists that any unusual patterns of parental behavior toward schizophrenic children are more likely the *result* of the child's schizophrenia than the cause of it (Liem, 1974).

One finding sometimes offered as evidence that generalized stress causes schizophrenia is that schizophrenia is more often diagnosed in patients of lower socioeconomic status (SES). One ten-year study found the rate of schizophrenia to be twice as great in the lowest as in the next-higher SES group (Hollingshead & Redlich, 1958). But this correlation alone does not indicate that the stresses of lower-SES existence cause schizophrenia. It is also possible that the progressive deterioration of behavior in schizophrenia causes a loss of social status through lost jobs and social relationships. (Evidence to date suggests that both directions of causation may occur; e.g., Turner & Wagonfield, 1967.)

It remains possible that long-term stresses or family patterns may contribute to schizophrenia in some individuals. But it is not yet clear just which patterns might have such effects or how. Furthermore, even if such patterns do exist, they can be only part of the picture. Many children who grow up in extremely stressful family situations, or with flagrantly psychotic parents, do *not* become schizophrenic.

It is also possible that one or more of these proposals is true, but only for *some* patients. It is generally believed that schizophrenia really consists of an unknown number of different disorders with similar symptoms. If a proposed environmental factor affects only one of these subcategories, it might not show up clearly when all subcategories are examined together. Such issues are one reason for seeking to classify patients more exactly.

ANTISOCIAL PERSONALITY DISORDER

Axis II of DSM-III includes a group of childhood disorders and a total of 11 **personality disorders,** patterns of inflexible and maladaptive personality traits that typically begin in adolescence or earlier and continue throughout adult life. Many mental health professionals, however, consider personality disorders to be of questionable utility for several reasons. The first criticism concerns the reliability of diagnosis; it was notably poor in earlier versions of DSM and has remained lower for preliminary tests of DSM-III than for most other categories. This low reliability is related to the ambiguous nature of personality disorders: in weak

form they seem similar to behaviors seen in normal people, whereas in strong form they seem similar to other DSM-III categories. *Paranoid, schizoid,* and *schizotypal* personalities, for example, seem like weak versions of schizophrenic or paranoid disorders. Another objection is that the personality disorders are based on trait theory. As discussed in Chapter 13, Walter Mischel and others have argued strongly that traits are an inappropriate way to categorize normal behavior. Those who agree with Mischel are not likely to find traits any more useful in defining abnormal behavior.

Of the 11 personality disorders, only one is generally regarded as a distinct and useful category. **Antisocial personality** is also known by two earlier terms, *sociopathic personality* and *psychopathic personality;* all three terms refer to people whose behavior is ethically or morally abnormal. Such people, usually called **sociopaths,** often appear well adjusted, even charming. But their adjustment has been characterized as a mask behind which they are shallowly selfish, apparently having no concern for other people and doing whatever their whims suggest (Cleckley, 1976). The impulsive behavior of sociopaths is frequently self-destructive in the long run, although they tend to view it as reasonable and can often escape the consequences of their acts by acting contrite and talking their way out of trouble. But their actions typically leave behind them a string of destroyed personal relationships, jobs, and sometimes lives.

A sociopath may commit a crime on impulse—even a major crime when little is to be gained—and show no real remorse if caught. Most of what is known about sociopaths comes from studies of those who have been imprisoned for such crimes. But a sociopath may also be a casual cheat, an expert in underhanded politics, a manipulative lover, or an employee who gives the boss an exploding cigar. All such patterns are characterized by impulsiveness and lack of concern for, or even understanding of, others' feelings. It has been estimated that 3% of adult males and 1% of adult females in the United States are sociopaths (Davison & Neale, 1982), but the characteristics of the noncriminal ones have been little studied to date.

One researcher, however, has devised an ingenious approach to finding noncriminal sociopaths for study (Widom, 1977). Widom placed a classified ad in a counterculture newspaper seeking "charming, aggressive, carefree people who are impulsively irresponsible but good at handling people and at looking after number one." In eight months, 68 people responded (45 male, 23 female). Of these, 28 (23 male, 5 female) were chosen for extensive testing; 68% fit the characteristics of sociopaths. Widom's technique may offer a way for future researchers to find and study other noncriminal sociopaths so that the category will not be as heavily weighted toward criminal behavior as it is now. ■ Patient Quotes: Noncriminal and Criminal Sociopaths

As with schizophrenia, proposed causes of antisocial personality include genetic, biochemical, and environmental factors. Studies of MZ and DZ twins and adopted children suggest that genetic factors predispose some people to antisocial personality (e.g., Cadoret, 1978). Research on the biology of sociopaths has discovered several differences between them and nonsociopaths. One well established but little understood difference is in EEG patterns. Numerous studies have found several types of abnormal EEGs in a third to a half of all sociopaths tested (Syndulko, 1978), but what these patterns may imply about the brain functions of sociopaths remains unknown.

The biological difference that has been the primary focus of research has been the level of autonomic arousal. Lykken (1957) hypothesized that sociopaths might be unusually low in anxiety and thus unconcerned about the possible negative consequences of their actions. In testing this **underarousal hypothesis,** Lykken found that sociopaths learned poorly in an avoidance-learning situation involving shock (unless they learned how to avoid it by taking some action, they received a shock). When shock was not involved, sociopaths and controls made the same number of errors. But when shock was involved, nonsociopaths sharply reduced their errors and sociopaths did not. This supported the underarousal hypothesis, suggesting that sociopaths' underactive autonomic nervous systems cause them to be less motivated to avoid punishment than are normal people. A further test of the underarousal hypothesis was added by Schachter and Latané (1964). They gave sociopaths and nonsociopaths injections of adrenalin to stimulate their autonomic nervous systems, then compared their performances in Lykken's learning task. To complete the comparison, both groups also received placebo injections that had no effect on the autonomic system. With the placebo injections, sociopaths were worse than controls in avoidance learning, as in Lykken's study. But with the adrenalin injections sociopaths did much better, suggesting that the additional arousal made them more responsive to the punishing shocks. For the nonsociopaths, the additional arousal was apparently too much for efficient learning and their performance was actually worse. ■ Figure 15.11

Sociopaths may not be unresponsive to all kinds of punishment, however; other studies have suggested that they do respond to punishment that is meaningful to them. When errors were punished by a money loss, for example, sociopaths learned an avoidance task as well as controls (Schmauk, 1970). Apparently money loss was a more real punishment than electric shocks.

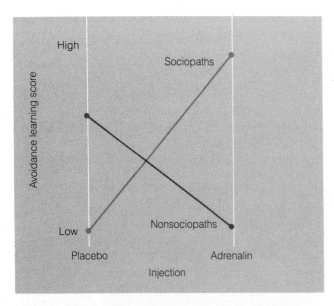

Figure 15.11 ■ Injections of adrenaline improved the avoidance learning of sociopaths but interfered with avoidance learning of nonsociopaths, thus supporting the hypothesis that sociopaths have underactive autonomic nervous systems.

(From S. Schachter and B. Latané, "Crime, Cognition, and the Autonomic Nervous System," Reprinted from the 1964 *Nebraska Symposium on Motivation* by permission of University of Nebraska Press. Copyright © 1964 by the University of Nebraska Press.)

Research on environmental factors in the development of antisocial personality has focused on family relationships. One major review of prior studies concluded that the important family elements were a lack of affection and severe parental rejection (McCord & McCord, 1964). Other studies have suggested that inconsistent patterns of parental rewards and punishments are involved, especially if these include letting children avoid punishment for wrongdoing by seeming to be sorry.

That children could learn some sociopathic patterns, such as lying to escape the consequences of an act, seems likely. But whether such learning actually plays a major role remains to be established. Many family studies have obtained data by asking family members about a person's childhood after the person was already known to be a sociopath, a method that is subject to many possible errors or biases in memory and thus is not a very reliable source of evidence. Overall, patterns of family interaction and the resulting socialization of children probably play some role in many disorders, including antisocial personality, just as they play a role in normal personality (Wiggins, 1968). But just *what* patterns cause *what* effects remains open to debate.

Sometimes the criminal behavior of sociopaths seems so far removed from ordinary sensibilities that they seem almost more mentally disturbed than schizophrenics. But sociopaths are usually not considered legally insane. This seeming contradiction is only one of many problems of integrating legal procedures with findings in psychology. We will look at some of these issues in Chapters 16 and 18.

CHAPTER SUMMARY

1 Abnormal behaviors can be defined in terms of statistical frequency and social acceptability, but are probably best defined in terms of adaptability. After many centuries of a demon model of abnormal behavior, the predominant model of the last hundred years has been the medical model, which likens patterns of abnormal behavior to diseases.

2 There are many known (and no doubt many still unknown) organic causes of abnormal behavior. Many other functional or psychological causes have been proposed; these may play a role in abnormal behavior, but the evidence for choosing among alternate proposals is not yet very strong.

3 Classification of abnormal behaviors (or mental disorders) is important both from a scientific perspective and in the medical model. The current classification scheme is called DSM-III.

4 Anxiety disorders include the phobias (which are irrational fears of objects or events), panic and generalized anxiety disorders (in which the fear is less obviously associated with particular cues), and obsessive-compulsive disorders (in which anxiety seems to be represented in intrusive thoughts and behaviors).

5 Continued stress probably contributes to a number of physical illnesses. Anxiety also seems to play a role in conversion disorders and other somatoform disorders, but in these the apparent physical disorder has no organic basis.

6 In the dissociative disorders, splits among aspects of normal consciousness or identity can lead to multiple independent personalities or to amnesia for personal identity (but none of these splits are the same as those in schizophrenia).

7 In the major affective disorders, the primary symptoms are extremes of mood. These may alternate from mania to depression in the bipolar disorders, or remain at the depressed end in major depression.

8 The schizophrenias include a number of subcategories, which in turn may actually represent other, as yet unspecified types. All schizophrenias represent serious splits within the individual that separate belief systems, perception, speech, affect, or other components from each other, yielding fragmented or distorted behavior.

9 The most notable of the personality disorders is antisocial personality, also called sociopathic or psychopathic personality. Sociopaths are superficially normal but lack understanding of others' emotions, and perhaps lack strong emotional responsiveness of their own. They

are selfish and uncaring in the extreme; some will murder on a whim, but others may never behave in criminal ways.

10 A similar pattern of causes is found for several major disorders: genetic predispositions, environmental learning, and environmental stress interact to yield the disorder.

Further Readings

For further information on all categories, see a good text such as Coleman, Butcher, and Carson's *Abnormal Psychology and Modern Life* (1980) or Davison and Neale's *Abnormal Psychology* (1982). For factors that contribute to mental disorders, there are more specialized offerings. Rosenthal's *Genetic Theory and Abnormal Behavior* (1970) summarizes genetic research and both Heilman and Valenstein's collection *Clinical Neuropsychology* (1979) and Snyder's *Biological Aspects of Mental Disorder* (1980a) discuss biological factors. Neufeld's collection examines *Psychological Stress and Psychopathology* (1982). Several collections of first-person accounts provide the patient's-eye views of symptoms and disorders. A classic collection is *The Inner World of Mental Illness* by Kaplan (1964); a recent collection is Peterson's *A Mad People's History of Madness* (1982). Landis and Mettler offer briefer excerpts arranged by symptoms in *Varieties of Psychopathological Experience* (1964). Stone and Stone's collection *The Abnormal Personality in Literature* (1966) includes some excerpts that are pure fiction and some that are probably first-person accounts pretending to be fiction. In terms of particular categories, see Marks's *Fears and Phobias* (1969). For multiple personality, see either Thigpen and Cleckley's *The Three Faces of Eve* (1954) or Sizemore and Pittillo's first-person view of the same case, *I'm Eve* (1977). Becker discusses the *Affective Disorders* (1977). For schizophrenia, see Neale and Oltmanns' *Schizophrenia* (1980) or Wynne, Cromwell, and Matthysse's collection *The Nature of Schizophrenia* (1978); a first-person account is Green's *I Never Promised You a Rose Garden* (1964). For antisocial personality, see McCord and McCord's *The Psychopath* (1964) or Cleckley's classic *The Mask of Sanity* (1976).

In browsing through a magazine, you notice an article on the problems of therapy for abnormal behavior. Glancing through it, you are struck by how many questions you have and how complex the problems seem to be. What are biological therapies and how do these relate to psychotherapies? What happens to a person who is picked up by the police because of his or her suspicious behavior? What goes on in the state mental hospital that you've driven by but never been in? As you continue to scan the article, you find you have more questions than answers. And you wonder if this is because you haven't studied the issues, or if there really is some confusion as to the best treatment for the disturbed.

In fact, there are many forms of therapy and substantial argument about the effectiveness of each of them—not to mention ethical issues about whether they should be used at all. You may or may not know someone who has had therapy for mental problems. But all over the country people who have been unable to cope with their problems alone are this minute being examined by various mental-health specialists. Some receive powerful drugs to alter their behavior. A few receive electric shock to their heads, perhaps even surgical alterations of their brains. Many talk about their problems with professional listeners. Others practice new behaviors under the guidance of professional behavior-changers. Still others learn to change the way they talk to themselves, under the guidance of cognitive specialists. Many of these troubled people and their professional helpers meet one-to-one, but some meet in groups, from families to groups of strangers. All of this activity is, in the medical-model term, *therapy* for abnormal behavior.

What, if anything, do all these activities have in common? How effective are they, and why? This chapter examines the various forms of therapy, seeking answers to these and related questions.

APPROACHES TO THERAPY

Therapy includes a number of different procedures carried out by different professionals in different settings. All therapies for abnormal behavior (or "mental illness") are attempts to help people who have problems ("patients") become less troubled and better adapted. These therapies all developed gradually, so understanding their history helps to understand their present forms. In contemporary therapy, one major factor in how patients are treated concerns whether they are hospitalized or are voluntary outpatients. Hence we begin with a brief history of approaches to

Chapter 16

Therapy

therapy, with an emphasis on the creation and development of mental hospitals. Then we turn to contemporary issues of commitment and treatment in hospitals, before moving to our main topic: forms of individual therapy (mostly with voluntary outpatients).

A major distinction in contemporary therapies is between biological therapies and psychotherapies. **Biological therapies** modify abnormal behavior through direct biological intervention; the techniques they use include electric shock, surgery, and drug therapy (sometimes termed *chemotherapy,* for "chemical therapy"). **Psychotherapies** use talk and other interpersonal behaviors to improve abnormal behavior without direct biological intervention. After looking at biological therapies and psychotherapies, we will end the chapter with a brief note on group therapies.

Historical Approaches

The earliest suggestions of "treatment" for mental illness are Stone Age skulls that show holes bored by stone tools, probably to release evil spirits thought to cause psychological problems. Surprisingly, some of these early "patients" survived this drastic process. ■ Figure 16.1

As we noted in Chapter 15, "treatment" of witches in the Middle Ages was usually fatal, often horribly so; saving the person's soul by driving out the demon was considered a higher goal than saving the person's life. But even then some disturbed people were treated more as patients than as witches, by being confined to hospitals, for example (Allderidge, 1979). By the 16th century many disturbed individuals were confined to asylums, public institutions that were combinations of hospital, workhouse, and jail.

The first hospital officially for mental patients was St. Mary of Bethlehem, a London priory that was converted to an asylum in 1547. This was not a hospital as we understand the term, however. Less severely disturbed patients were sent out to beg for their keep; more disturbed ones were kept inside, where they were a sort of human zoo. It was fashionable for the well-to-do to visit Bethlehem, where they paid a small fee to observe the disturbed and agitated inmates, physically tied down or moving restlessly about, often screaming or crying. The conditions in Bedlam, as it was popularly known, led to the use of the word *bedlam* to mean a place of noisy uproar and confusion. ■ Figure 16.2

Over the next two hundred years, large public hospitals were established in a number of countries. Conditions in all of them were much like Bedlam, with patients often chained to the walls of small, dark cells, sometimes so tightly that they could not lie down at

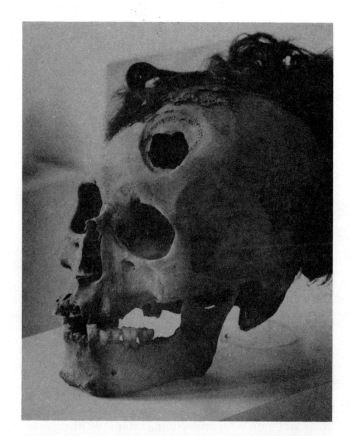

Figure 16.1 ■ A pre-Columbian skull with a partially healed hole, indicating that the "patient" survived for some time. (David Mangourian)

night. No one visited the cells except to provide minimal food, and the cells were never swept or cleaned.

The first major change in conditions occurred at the French hospital La Bicêtre in 1792, a few years after the early phase of the French Revolution. Perhaps inspired by the revolution, Philippe Pinel (1745–1826), the new head of La Bicêtre, undertook an experiment to "free" the patients. Their chains were removed, their rooms were cleaned, and they were allowed to go outside—some after 30 years in chains. Pinel's experiment marked the beginning of the **moral treatment** movement, in which patients were treated less as zoo animals and more as people who had lost their faculties through stress but who, with kindness, could regain them. A number of small therapeutic communities were created in which patients and staff lived together, seeking moral reeducation through trust, good food, and a calm environment. (At least one such community still exists, the Gheel colony in Belgium.)

Despite some notable successes, moral treatment never became the predominant approach. Most mental hospitals remained large anonymous institutions in which a variety of what we would consider harsh,

Figure 16.2 ■ Detail from a Hogarth engraving of Bedlam.
(The Granger Collection, New York)

even cruel, procedures functioned as therapy. Benjamin Rush (1745–1813), considered the founder of United States psychiatry, campaigned for humane treatment of the mentally ill, but this meant something different in the late 1700s than it does now. Rush's therapy often involved bleeding his patients, frightening them by convincing them they were about to die, and restraining them in various devices.

Several developments of the 18th and 19th centuries interacted to maintain the large hospitals and to inhibit the development of moral treatment communities. One such influence was, ironically, a movement intended to improve the lot of mental patients: the **mental hygiene** movement begun by Dorothea Dix (1802–1887). Dix was a former schoolteacher who in 1841 began teaching in a women's prison. Appalled at the conditions, she began a nationwide campaign to get better treatment for prisoners and mental patients. Dix's efforts over the next 40 years raised millions of dollars, most of which went to building large mental hospitals; she is credited with establishing 32 of them (Coleman et al., 1980). Her efforts greatly improved physical conditions for untold numbers of patients, but at the same time perpetuated the large-hospital approach. The medical model also supported hospitalization. If medicine might soon develop biological cures for many "mental diseases," what better place to treat patients than in a hospital?

By the beginning of the 20th century, the pattern was well established. People who behaved inappropriately in ways that others could not overlook were typically shipped off to regional mental hospitals, there to await the cures that everyone hoped would be forthcoming. Unfortunately, such cures were not soon found, and the mental hospitals were often little better than warehouses for the disturbed. Although conditions improved in the four hundred years following the founding of Bedlam, even in the early 1950s most of the energy of hospital personnel was directed toward confining the often violent patients and seeing to their own safety (Coleman et al., 1980). ■ Figure 16.3

Commitment and Hospitalization

Any person who comes, or is brought by others, to a psychotherapist for evaluation of abnormal behavior will be examined or *assessed:* his or her problem will be analyzed, including the factors that may have led to it

Figure 16.3 ■ Mental hospital scene in the 20th century. Before the development of drug therapies, many agitated patients had to be locked in cells or tied to their beds for their own safety as well as that of more passive patients.

(Jeff Albertson/Stock, Boston)

Table 16.1 ■ Court Decisions Establishing Basic Rights of Mental Patients

Right to treatment

In 1972 a U.S. District Court in Alabama ruled, in the case of *Wyatt* v. *Stickney*, that a mentally ill or mentally retarded individual had a right to receive treatment. Since the decision, the State of Alabama has increased its budget for treatment of mental health and mental retardation by 300%.

Freedom from custodial confinement

In 1975 the United States Supreme Court upheld the principle that patients have a right to freedom from custodial confinement if they are not dangerous to themselves or others and if they can safely survive outside of custody. In *Donaldson* v. *O'Connor*, the defendants were required to pay Donaldson $10,000 for having kept him in custody without providing treatment.

Right to compensation for work

In 1973 a United States District Court ruled in the case of *Souder* v. *Brennan* (Secretary of Labor) that a patient in a nonfederal mental institution who performed work must be paid according to the Fair Labor Standards Act. (A 1976 Supreme Court ruling nullified the part of the lower court's decision dealing with state hospitals, but the ruling still applies to private facilities.)

Right to legal counsel at commitment hearings

The State Supreme Court in Wisconsin decided in 1976 in the case of *Memmel* v. *Mundy* that an individual had the right to legal counsel during the commitment process.

Right to live in a community

In 1974, the United States District Court decided, in the case of *Stoner* v. *Miller*, that released state mental hospital patients had a right to live in "adult homes" in the community.

Right to refuse treatment

Several courts have decided and some states have passed laws permitting patients to refuse certain treatments, such as electroconvulsive therapy and psychosurgery.

Right to less restrictive treatment

In 1975 a United States District Court, in the case of *Dixon* v. *Weinberger*, established the right of individuals to receive treatment in less restrictive facilities than mental institutions.

Adapted from J. C. Coleman et al., *Abnormal Psychology and Modern Life*, 6th ed., Copyright © 1980, 1976, 1972 by Scott, Foresman and Company. Reprinted by permission.

and its probable future course, with or without treatment. A person who meets certain criteria may be **committed,** placed in a mental hospital, for short-term observation or long-term treatment. Some patients voluntarily commit themselves, but others are committed involuntarily. Much of the concern about involuntary commitment centers on legal issues more than strictly therapeutic ones: Who can be committed, and how can their rights be protected without undue risk to other people from mentally ill people who are dangerous? Once patients are committed, other legal issues are raised, such as whether a committed patient has a right to treatment or to refuse some forms of treatment.

Commitment   Most involuntary patients are committed through the process of *civil commitment*, a legal procedure applicable to a person whose sanity has been questioned even though he or she may not have committed a crime. (We will look at criminal commitment a bit later.) State laws vary and are regularly modified, but in general a person deemed by psychiatrists to be *both* mentally ill *and* dangerous to self or others can be involuntarily committed (Schwitzgebel & Schwitzgebel, 1980). In emergency situations, as when a violent person is brought in by police, a temporary commitment is possible, usually on the signatures of two physicians. This temporary hold may range from 24 hours to several weeks. Longer-

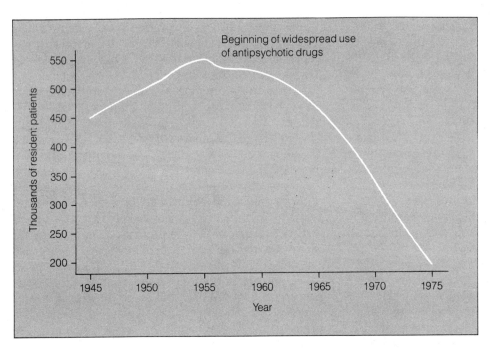

Figure 16.4 ■ Number of patients in government mental hospitals in the United States. The dramatic fall in patient populations after 1956, which occurred despite a rising general population, was caused by the discovery and widespread use of antipsychotic drugs.

term commitment requires a formal hearing before a judge or jury, during which the state must show convincing evidence of imminent dangerousness as well as the presence of mental illness. The person subject to commitment may resist it with the aid of an attorney and defense witnesses.

If the person is committed, he or she is typically sent to a state mental hospital, though there are also Veterans' Administration hospitals and mental wings in conventional hospitals (where short-term patients are typically sent for observation). Once committed, patients may be released on the decision of staff psychiatrists or may petition the courts to direct their release on any of several grounds that have been established by court decisions. ■ Table 16.1

People were not always so well protected; early in this century, commitment was often appallingly easy and frighteningly long-term. Some of the abuses this permitted came to light in the "sweep" of the mental hospitals in the 1950s that followed the discovery of antipsychotic drugs. Patients were examined carefully, sometimes for the first time in many years, to see if the new drugs would help. It was found that some had been institutionalized because their heirs wanted their money, because their parents couldn't control them or afford to feed them, because they spoke only an obscure foreign language, and so forth. Publicity about such examples—some of which were documented by one of psychiatry's foremost critics, Thomas Szasz (1963, 1982)—contributed to an ongoing series of

changes in the rules of commitment through legislation and court decisions (see Table 16.1). ■ Figure 16.4

The key element in civil commitment is the concept of dangerousness (Shah, 1978). Extreme advocates of patients' rights, such as Szasz, have argued that no one should be institutionalized for what he or she *might* do. But any society seeks to protect its citizens, and the rights of patients must be balanced against the rights of possible victims of violence. There has been a great deal of argument over whether the mentally disturbed are likely to be violent and whether psychiatrists can predict their violence (Monahan, 1978). Unfortunately, there are not enough data to answer either question conclusively.

Many released mental patients *have* committed violent acts, but these have been primarily persons with criminal records predating their mental problems (Monahan, 1981). Patients without criminal records seem to be less violent than the average person, but this may also be misleading. There is no way to know whether those who were committed would otherwise have committed crimes; perhaps they are nonviolent after release because they have changed while institutionalized. It is clear that some agitated emergency patients are dangerous when committed, but the long-term dangerousness of mental patients in general remains in debate. The increasing legal constraints on commitment are partially designed to prevent assessments of dangerousness from being made too easily.

Hospitalization   Other legal issues deal with what can or should be done in the way of treatment *after* a person is committed. Despite optimistic expectations early in this century, biological therapies have had only limited success. Drugs that relieve some symptoms have allowed many patients to be released and have thus eased hospital overcrowding. In other cases, the symptoms have been reduced only enough to yield quieter patients—a significant benefit in reducing the "snake pit" quality of wards, but not a therapy that brings further improvement. And psychotherapy has made little impact, if only because of the ratio of patients to staff psychiatrists, which may be hundreds, even thousands, to one. However dedicated the staff, such ratios allow only rare contact between psychiatrist and patient. The 1972 right-to-treatment court decision (noted in Table 16.1) was a response to such a situation, where one psychiatrist was responsible for 2000 patients. The *Wyatt* v. *Stickney* ruling said that when patients are committed to a mental hospital, they have a right to expect treatment, not merely warehousing. (In contrast, another decision allows patients to refuse treatment if they prefer; White & White, 1981.) But most patients still spend little time in anything that could be called psychotherapy (Rosenhan, 1973); they merely pass the time as best they can.

One of the concepts of moral treatment was that the environment itself was to be a kind of therapy (Bockhoven, 1963). Unfortunately, the mental hospital environment can have more undesirable than desirable influences. For some people, the mental hospital can be a refuge, an asylum in the beneficial sense. There they can relax and try to collect their thoughts, away from the stresses of their regular lives (Braginsky et al., 1982). But such people seem to be the exceptions. The operations of a mental hospital necessarily lead to loneliness, enforced idleness, and massive regimentation (Goffman, 1961), which affect many patients negatively. Such factors can even lead to a pattern of adaptation called the **hospitalization syndrome,** which leaves patients *less* able to live in a nonhospital environment. ■ Figure 16.5

As many large public hospitals are shut down, for the problems we have noted or because of limited funds to maintain them, many maladapted patients are being sent back "to the community" for treatment (Kiesler, 1982). This process of **deinstitutionalization** means that maladapted ex-patients may have no one to watch out for them; many lead a precarious existence on the fringes of society, often literally sleeping in the streets (Bassuk & Gerson, 1978; Holden, 1978).

Even if patients resist the hospitalization syndrome, their status as institutionalized patients often causes nonpatients to see them as maladapted. If patients continually seek release, they may be considered too aggressive or not yet aware of their problems; but if they do not, they may be seen as too passive. This was one of the most striking findings of David Rosenhan and several others who deliberately had themselves admitted to mental hospitals as schizophrenic "pseudopatients" (Rosenhan, 1973). Once in the hospital, they never again claimed to hear voices (the symptom they reported in order to be admitted) or otherwise behaved abnormally. Yet they found that virtually anything they did was likely to be considered further evidence of their abnormality. They were *never* recognized as sane by staff members, partially because the staff spent little time with them. One psychiatrist, for example, had a lengthy conversation with Rosenhan on the night of his admittance, apparently thinking him to be another staff member. (Rosenhan is a professor of psychology and law.) Yet when the psychiatrist learned Rosenhan was a patient, he never again spoke more than a word or two to him. Even the ward nurses and attendants, whose duties included observing the patients, perceived their actions through the filter of knowing them to be patients. All the pseudopatients, for example, kept notes on their experiences for later analysis, but no staff member ever read these notes—although in at least one case the comment "writing behavior" was added to a pseudopatient's file.

Other patients, however, often realized that the pseudopatients were not mentally ill and even guessed that they were studying the hospital. In light of this difference between staff and patients, it is interesting to speculate whether the continued close contact and occasional genuine personal concern of other patients may be one of the few truly therapeutic aspects of mental hospitals: It is not uncommon for ex-patients to describe how much they were helped by other patients.

Criminal commitment occurs when a person has committed a crime but is found *insane* rather than guilty. Here again the problems are mostly legal and philosophical. One beneficial effect of the medical model is its implication that people are not personally responsible for their peculiar behaviors. If people cough or limp because of disease, they are not accused of doing so deliberately; thus people who behave strangely because of "mental disease" ought to be similarly excused. But when this logic is applied to criminal behavior some people question it, and the insanity plea has come under increasing criticism, especially in well-publicized murder cases. ■ Research Controversy: Should Insanity Be a Defense?

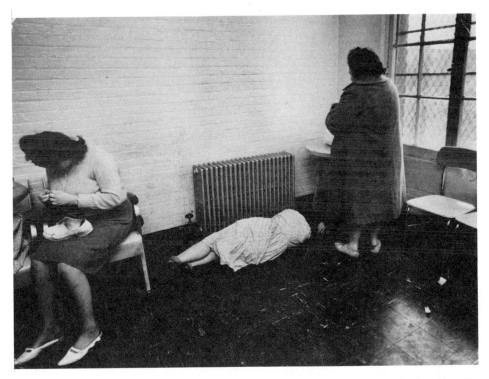

Figure 16.5 ■ Even the best public mental hospitals can be lonely places. It's difficult to know if such scenes reflect the patients' original problems or a long-term hospitalization syndrome.
(Ken Heyman)

BIOLOGICAL THERAPIES

A number of biological techniques have long been proposed as therapies for abnormal behavior. In recent years, these proposals have included special diets, electrically induced sleep, blood cleansing by dialysis, modification of sleep/waking cycles (for depression), and even plastic surgery—for example, facial repairs to aid a patient's self-image. But few of these have had much influence. The three primary biological therapies in the 20th century have been electroconvulsive shock, psychosurgery, and drugs.

As we consider these therapies, there are several points worth remembering. First, the effectiveness of a biological therapy does not indicate that the problem is primarily biological. Biological therapies may be as useful for a problem of psychological or functional origin as for one of biological origin. Note also that all three biological therapies are powerful interventions. When they work, they can offer dramatic and lasting gains, but they also carry strong risks, including death. In deciding whether to use such powerful techniques, responsible clinicians always seek to balance the risks against the potential benefits—or the risks of no therapy (such as suicide).

Electroconvulsive Therapy

One early success of conventional medicine was Pasteur's discovery that inoculation by a weak form of a disease could sometimes prevent the disease; inoculations have been standard practice ever since. Similarly, the first cure for general paresis involved the use of malaria. Such early successes at fighting disease by noxious counteragents may have contributed to the use of treatments for mental disease that strongly stressed the body (Coleman et al., 1980). Remember that Rush favored blood-letting and frightening his patients; other early psychiatrists used devices that spun patients around or suddenly flipped them upside down, all apparently in hopes of shocking them to their senses.

This trend led to the use of convulsive therapy—that is, induced convulsions. Originally, therapists tried insulin-coma therapy. Insulin is a hormone that regulates blood sugar; too much of it causes convulsions, coma, and eventually death. The therapy, developed by a Viennese psychiatrist in 1932, involved hour-long comas terminated by glucose injections (Coleman et al., 1980). A few patients briefly improved, but in general insulin coma showed little therapeutic value and was dropped. Therapists then tried

RESEARCH CONTROVERSY

Should insanity be a defense?

One aspect of our judicial system that stirs controversy out of all proportion to the number of cases involved is the use of insanity as a criminal defense. It is legally possible for a defendant to plead "not guilty by reason of insanity" to a crime that everyone agrees he or she has committed and, if the legal tests of insanity are met, to leave the courtroom free (or, more likely, to go to a mental hospital rather than prison). But very few defendants successfully do so. The insanity defense has been controversial over its nearly 150-year history because of a few widely publicized cases, not because large numbers of cases are involved. The first successful insanity defense and a later controversial one both involved the attempted assassination of major public figures.

The first case was that of Daniel M'Naghten, who, while suffering from paranoid delusions, attempted to assassinate Queen Victoria's prime minister but shot and killed the minister's secretary instead. In 1843, a British court found M'Naghten not guilty and thereby established the *M'Naghten rules:* A defendant was not guilty by reason of insanity if he could be shown to be suffering from "a defect of reason, from disease of the mind, as not to know the nature and the quality of the act he was doing, or, if he did know it, that he did not know he was doing what was wrong" (Bazelon, 1974, p. 20). Queen Victoria asked the House of Lords to review this decision; they upheld it. Insanity has since remained a controversial defense in English, and subsequently United States, law.

Two major revisions have since broadened the legal concept of **insanity.** To the M'Naghten rules of "not knowing what" or "not knowing it was wrong," some states added "irresistible impulse": knowing that an action was wrong but being unable to avoid doing it. In 1972, a new description first proposed by the American Law Institute was adopted. It stated that "A person is not responsible for criminal conduct if at the time of such conduct as the result of mental disease or defect he lacks substantial capacity either to appreciate the wrongfulness of his conduct or to conform his conduct to the requirements of the law" (Bazelon, 1974, p. 21). (Note how this phrasing added to the ambiguity of the definition: *Lacks substantial capacity* means that a person need be only partially unable to understand or behave appropriately, and *appreciate* means not only to understand but to fully grasp the meaning of actions.)

A more recent controversy over the insanity defense involved John W. Hinckley, Jr., the young man who shot President Reagan and several others, supposedly to demonstrate his devotion to the actress Jodie Foster. Hinckley, whom we first encountered in Chapter 1, pleaded not guilty by reason of insanity and, after the jury heard conflicting psychiatric testimony, was acquitted. Perhaps because our recent political history has included several assassinations of public figures, his acquittal caused public outrage. Lawyers for several of the victims even considered suing his former psychiatrist for failing to commit him or to warn others he was dangerous (Press, 1983). Adding insult to injury, Hinckley wrote a series of apparently rational letters to the media, defending the jury's decision. In a full-page article in *Newsweek,* Hinckley calmly discussed his case; apart from his reference to Foster as his "girlfriend"—he had only phoned her, and she had asked him not to do so again—he sounded rational. ∎ Notable Quote: John Hinckley on His Successful Insanity Defense

As Hinckley noted, his case has led to renewed efforts to eliminate the insanity defense. But he didn't make clear some of the legal ambiguities that have led to such suggestions. Much of the controversy derives from the fact that insanity is a legal term, not a psychological or psychiatric one; it corresponds to *no* DSM-III category or concept. Psychologists or psychiatrists who testify in insanity cases must first decide what they think about the accused's state of mind in their own terms, then must try to translate these into the different criteria of legal insanity. Predictably, they are often able to interpret the same findings to fit either defense or prosecution positions.

Note, for example, that by most interpretations of legal criteria a criminal sociopath is *not* insane; only if a judge or jury could be convinced that this sociopath lacked "substantial capacity" to "appreciate" could he or she be found insane. According to the other criteria, sociopaths are quite sane: They usually know what they are doing, know that it is socially and legally wrong, and are not irresistibly compelled to act. (Part of the controversy about Hinckley has been whether he is a schizophrenic or a sociopath.) The ambiguity of translating a DSM-III concept such as *antisocial personality* into legal *insanity* was demonstrated in one case in which a noted psychiatrist testified in court on a Friday afternoon that a sociopath was *not* suffering from a "mental disease." On Monday, based on a policy change, the administrators of the psychiatrist's hospital said that sociopathy *was* a mental disease (Smith, 1978b).

Public argument over the insanity defense will probably continue, and the defense may even be prohibited. As a result of the Hinckley case, for example, the American Psychiatric Association has officially suggested that lawyers not request, and psychiatrists not provide, testimony in terms of legal insanity (Herbert, 1983b).

other convulsion-inducing techniques. In 1938 two Italian psychiatrists tried applying current directly to the head; the result was an artificial epileptic attack, including motor convulsions so powerful that some patients broke their own vertebrae—but some also showed dramatic improvement, especially from severe depression. Their approach, in somewhat modified form, is now known as **electroconvulsive therapy (ECT)** (sometimes colloquially called "shock treatment").

In the contemporary form, patients are given muscle-relaxant drugs to inhibit the motor effect of the seizures and are carefully monitored by an attending physician. Then a 70- to 130-V current is passed between electrodes on opposite sides of the head for a fraction of a second. The resulting seizure results in unconsciousness, from which the patient awakens a few minutes later with no memory of the seizure. Patients are often briefly confused after one shock and may show general disorientation and memory problems with repeated shocks. (Contemporary treatment rarely uses over a dozen shocks, although hundreds per patient were sometimes administered in the past.) The memory problems usually clear within a few months after the last shock, but may persist for some people (Squire et al., 1975). ■ Figure 16.6

Receiving ECT seems a horrible fate to many people. A 1982 referendum in Berkeley, California, actually prohibited ECT, although that decision was later stayed by the courts (Cunningham, 1983). But for those who are severely depressed, ECT is often strikingly effective (Klerman, 1972), and it can be useful for some other disorders, though not as reliably. No one can say *how* or *why* ECT works, however; the prevailing view is that it may in some way alter the availability or use of neurotransmitters (Fink, 1979). One report has suggested that ECT may increase production of endorphins, but further research is needed to explain the relationship between the endorphin increase and mood improvement (Greenberg, 1983a).

A variation on the conventional technique is *unilateral ECT,* the application of shock to only one side of the brain (typically the right). Unilateral ECT yields less memory loss (Squire & Slater, 1978), but most psychiatrists who use ECT still use it bilaterally (American Psychiatric Association, 1978). The effectiveness of unilateral ECT to the right hemisphere may be related to that hemisphere's proposed role in emotional responsiveness and other body functions—and the reduction in memory loss may mean that *loss* is confined to the right hemisphere, whereas most memory *tests* are left-hemisphere oriented.

NOTABLE QUOTE
John Hinckley on his successful insanity defense

❝I don't feel guilty for being found not guilty by reason of insanity. It was the proper verdict and, although I was surprised by it, my fragile conscience is clear of useless guilt. . . .

Perhaps the [public uproar over the verdict] is for the belief that a person can shoot the president of the United States and not be punished for it. To hell with the mental state of the defendant; throw him in jail, so say the disgruntled masses. I can only respond with a shake of my head and the wish that society will someday show some compassion for its disturbed outcasts. Sending a John Hinckley to a mental hospital instead of prison is the American Way. . . .

The defense doctors found me to be delusional, psychotic, schizophrenic and perhaps the most alienated young man they had ever examined. On the other hand, despite evidence to the contrary, the prosecution doctor said I merely had some personality problems and deserved to be punished with imprisonment. The jury thought long and hard about everything they saw and heard and acquitted me. . . . .

To abolish the insanity defense would be a travesty of justice. Now we have the proposal by legislators that a not-guilty-by-reason-of-insanity verdict should be changed to a guilty-but-mentally-ill combination. The advocates of this idea want the disturbed defendant to be treated for his illness and, once he is cured, to be sent to prison to be punished for his crimes. . . .

Let's leave the insanity defense alone and accept the fact that, every once in a while, someone is going to use this 'defense of last resort' and win with it. I was acquitted not because of my parents' money, or my attorneys, or the black jury; I was found not guilty by reason of insanity because I shot the president and three other people in order to impress a girl.❞

From *Newsweek,* September 20, 1982, p. 30. Copyright 1982 by Newsweek, Inc. All rights reserved. Reprinted by permission.

Psychosurgery

The early history of **psychosurgery**—surgery with the specific intent of altering behavior—is even more unattractive than that of ECT. Based solely on a report of surgery on two chimpanzees, in 1936 Portuguese psychiatrist Antonio Moniz developed the **prefrontal lobotomy,** in which connections are severed between the prefrontal areas (in the forehead) and the rest of the brain in order to achieve a calming effect. Moniz's procedure quickly became popular and he was awarded the Nobel Prize for Medicine in 1949. (Not everyone was as pleased with the operation as the Nobel Committee. When he received the award Moniz had retired, having been shot by one of his lobotomy patients; Valenstein, 1973.)

In the United States, Moniz's lobotomy (the *prefrontal* was often dropped) was championed by Walter Freeman (Shutts, 1981). Freeman claimed to have performed or supervised over 3500 lobotomies, many of them in his office under local anesthesia (Freeman, 1959). The tool of choice was an ice pick; in one common form of the operation, it was driven through the back of the eye socket with a hammer, then swung from side to side to cut the nerve tracts. Between the 1930s and the 1950s, many thousands of lobotomies were performed on a wide range of patients, including children. Some improved, but many others suffered a wide range of side effects, including seizures, a general slowing of behavior, shallow or absent affect, and even death in some cases (Barahal, 1958).

In the mid-1950s the number of lobotomies dropped to nearly zero. Contemporary psychosurgery is much less frequent, the expected outcome is much more exactly targeted, and the procedures cause damage only to very small and selected areas (Valenstein, 1980). All psychosurgery remains controversial, but a congressionally sponsored study—originally expected to condemn psychosurgery—found substantial support for it, often among former patients (Culliton, 1976). The sudden drop in lobotomies after 20 years of widespread use, however, was not caused by awareness of their damaging effects. It was the result of the breakthrough in the most widely used form of biological therapy: drugs.

Drug Therapy

The most significant biological therapy to date has been the use of drugs to relieve mental problems. This is far from the perfect solution in most cases, but its impact on mental problems in the past 30 or 40 years has been remarkable: Drugs have led to greater changes in treatment than any other development since the Stone Age (with the possible exception of the

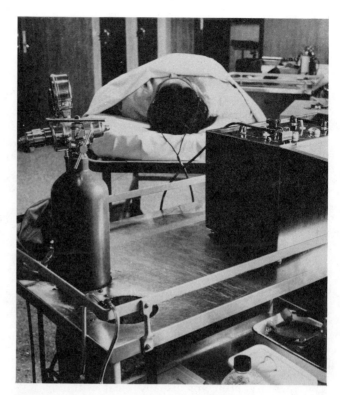

Figure 16.6 ■ A patient being prepared for ECT. Note the electrodes on the patient's head and wires leading to the shock generator at the right.

(St. Louis Post Dispatch/Black Star)

medical model that led to their use). Dramatic decreases in lobotomies and in the number of hospitalized mental patients (Figure 16.4) are among the consequences of the discovery of the **antipsychotics,** drugs that relieve a variety of psychotic symptoms. Three other widely used classes of therapeutic drugs have also been developed: antidepressants, lithium (for mania), and antianxiety drugs (Ray, 1978). ■ Table 16.2

The first antipsychotic drug to be used successfully was reserpine, a compound derived from a root long used in India to treat a variety of what we would call mental illnesses. Research in the early 1950s found that reserpine has a calming effect but also several side effects, including low blood pressure. The true breakthrough came with the development in the mid-1950s of the phenothiazines, beginning with chlorpromazine. A number of pharmaceutical companies soon developed variations on chlorpromazine, all with similar names and properties. More recently several other classes of antipsychotic drugs have been developed, but the phenothiazines remain the most widely used.

The antipsychotic drugs are sometimes called *major tranquilizers* because they reduce the agitation of

Table 16.2 ■ Drugs Used in Treating Mental Disorders

Class	Generic Name	Trade Name	Used to Treat	Effects
Antipsychotic phenothiazines	chlorpromazine thioridazine promazine trifluoperazine prochlorperazine perphenazine fluphenazine	Thorazine Mellaril Sparine Stelazine Compazine Trilafon Prolixin	Psychotic (especially schizophrenic) symptoms such as extreme agitation, delusions, and hallucinations; aggressive or violent behavior.	Somewhat variable in suppressing psychotic symptoms. Side effects, such as dry mouth, are often uncomfortable. In long-term use may produce motor disturbances such as tardive dyskinesia.
butyrophenones	haloperidol	Haldol		
thioxanthenes	thiothixine chlorprothixene	Navane Taractan		
Antidepressant tricyclics	imipramine amitriptyline nortriptyline protriptyline doxepin	Tofranil Elavil Aventyl Vivactil Sinequan	Relatively severe depressive symptoms, especially of psychotic severity and unipolar type.	Somewhat variable in alleviating depression, and effects may be delayed up to three weeks. Multiple side effects, some dangerous. Use of MAO inhibitors requires dietary restrictions.
monoamine oxidase (MAO) inhibitors	isocarboxazid phenelzine tranylcypromine	Marplan Nardil Parnate		
Antimanic (bipolar)	lithium carbonate	Eskalith Lithane Lithonate Lithotabs Phi-Lithium	Manic episodes and some severe depressions, particularly recurrent ones or those alternating with mania.	Usually effective in resolving manic episodes, but highly variable in effects on depression. Multiple side effects unless carefully monitored; high toxicity potential.
Antianxiety *(minor tranquilizers)*	diazepam chlordiazepoxide flurazepam oxazepam clorazepate	Valium Librium Dalmane Serax Tranxene	Nonpsychotic problems in which anxiety and tension are prominent features; also used as anticonvulsants and sleep inducers.	Somewhat variable in achieving tension reduction. Side effects include drowsiness and lethargy. Dependence and toxicity are dangers.

Adapted from J. C. Coleman et al., *Abnormal Psychology and Modern Life*, 6th ed. Copyright © 1980, 1976, 1972 by Scott, Foresman and Company. Reprinted by permission.

disturbed schizophrenics. But the term is somewhat misleading; they are chemically different from the tranquilizers used to combat anxiety, and in fact are ineffective against anxiety. Furthermore, the antipsychotics should not be considered a cure; they are symptom suppressors, effective only as long as patients continue to take them (Berger, 1978). But they *are* quite effective at symptom suppression. One carefully controlled study found them to be substantially more effective than several other therapies, including psychoanalysis and ECT; furthermore, psychoanalysis together with drugs was no more effective than drugs alone (May, 1968). These results also held in a five-year follow-up (May et al., 1976).

The antipsychotics are far from a complete success, however: They are not a cure and are not helpful for all patients. They may even be harmful for some, although why patients respond differently is not yet understood (Neale & Oltmanns, 1980). Furthermore, even when the antipsychotics are effective they cause a number of undesirable side effects, including dry mouth, blurred vision, and muscular stiffness. After prolonged use, even more severe side effects occur: muscular control problems that resemble Parkinson's disease. One particular pattern of involuntary, jerky mouth and face movements, called *tardive dyskinesia*, has until recently been considered permanent, although there is now reason to believe that it can be overcome (Kolata, 1979). Both the benefits and side effects of the antipsychotics seem to result from their influences on the neurotransmitter dopamine, so it is difficult to both maintain the benefits and reduce the side effects. (One report has suggested that the drugs most effective against schizophrenia bind directly to dopamine receptors and thus block them; Turkington, 1983.)

Many schizophrenics can be released from mental hospitals because antipsychotic drugs reduce their overt symptoms, but the symptom reduction does not make them normal, and their social adjustment is often marginal. When, for a lack of organization or a dislike of the side effects, they fail to take their maintenance doses, they often have to be readmitted. The result has sometimes been a "revolving door," although some progress has been made in reducing the frequency of readmission through follow-up care after release, including halfway houses and outpatient therapy (Hogarty et al., 1974).

There are two classes of **antidepressants;** they have similar effects in the brain, but through somewhat different mechanisms. The tricyclics block reuse of the neurotransmitters norepinephrine and serotonin, thus holding them at the synapses longer. The MAO inhibitors reduce the effectiveness of MAO (monoamine oxidase), the enzyme that normally breaks down norepinephrine and serotonin, again leading to more available transmitters. The tricyclics are much more widely used than the MAO inhibitors, both because they are more effective and because the MAO inhibitors carry some severe risks (Morris & Beck, 1974): MAO inhibitors are naturally toxic and can cause damage to body organs. They can even be fatal in combination with certain foods, including beer, some cheeses, and chicken livers. Ingredients in these foods act as neurotransmitters, and with MAO inhibited can lead to overstimulation of the heart (McGeer, 1971).

As with the antipsychotics, the antidepressants also have some undesirable side effects and do not work equally well on all patients. (Patients considered possible candidates for ECT are those for whom none of the antidepressants is effective.) The antidepressants also do not provide a cure; patients who stop taking them usually relapse (Klerman, 1975). But when they work, the antidepressants do restore fully normal behavior.

One of the most effective drug therapies is **lithium,** a basic chemical element that relieves mania (Tosteson, 1981). Lithium is given in the form of lithium carbonate, a simple inorganic salt. Lithium seemed so unlikely to be effective when it was first proposed that its use in the United States was delayed until its utility was widely demonstrated elsewhere. Lithium relieves about 70% of manic states and some

cases of bipolar depression. An overdose of lithium can be fatal, so it must be carefully monitored, but in low doses it has few notable side effects. Furthermore, lithium is perhaps the only true preventive therapy: Bipolar patients who maintain a regular dosage often completely block manic episodes (Davis, 1976). Unfortunately, lithium may also block *all* extremely pleasurable or euphoric experiences (Honigfeld & Howard, 1978).

The most widely used—and abused—therapeutic drugs are the **antianxiety drugs,** also known as *minor tranquilizers:* More prescriptions are written for Valium, for example, than for any other drug. Many of the antianxiety drugs are strongly addictive and can also easily be fatal, accidentally or intentionally (they are a common mode of suicide), when used singly or in combination with other drugs (alcohol magnifies the effect of some). Even taken in moderation, the antianxiety drugs can have undesirable side effects, such as drowsiness and lethargy. They can be useful for patients who suffer from powerful and debilitating anxiety, but the astounding number prescribed reflects far more use than seems necessary or reasonable.

PSYCHOTHERAPIES

Although hospitalized patients remain an important focus of contemporary psychotherapy, many approaches have been developed for working with non-hospitalized persons. A few are preventive, seeking to reduce mental illness before it occurs, but most seek to help people who already have problems. We will discuss the range of contemporary psychotherapies before examining some of them in more detail, noting: (1) who psychotherapists are, in terms of their titles, training, and occupations; (2) what psychotherapists believe and how their beliefs influence their actions; and (3) how effective psychotherapies are, according to researchers, and some of the problems of such research.

Who Psychotherapists Are

The popular image of a psychotherapist is that of a psychiatrist, who is often thought to be a psychoanalyst—as if all these terms were synonymous. In fact, a number of different professional specializations exist; the specialists have different degrees and training and hold different jobs, even though they often interact with patients in similar ways.

A **psychiatrist** has completed an M.D. degree, then taken a residency in mental diseases rather than some other subspecialty (Light, 1980). Psychiatrists are theoretically qualified to practice medicine (depending

508 _____ *PART V ■ Development and Individual Differences*

on local licensing limits) but rarely do so. Because of their medical degrees, psychiatrists can prescribe drugs and ECT; because of their strong links to the medical model, they are often the only psychotherapists allowed to commit patients or to be heads of mental hospitals. (One ongoing controversy centers on payments to psychiatrists but not other psychotherapists by medical insurance carriers; American Psychological Association, 1980.)

Psychologists who specialize in psychotherapy are called **clinical psychologists.** Many hold Ph.D. degrees based on research training, but some are graduates of specialized programs aimed at clinical work that may give a Psy.D. degree (Walsh, 1979). **Counseling psychologists** also have typically followed a program with less emphasis on research, although they may have obtained either an M.A. or a Ph.D. (Smith, 1982). Counseling psychologists generally work with people whose problems are within or at the boundaries of "normal" behavior in such settings as school counseling centers (Janis, 1982).

A **psychoanalyst** is defined by specialized training beyond the major academic degree: a psychoanalyst has met the requirements of a psychoanalytic training program, including being psychoanalyzed. Freud felt that psychoanalysts (often abbreviated to *analysts*) need not be physicians, and many early analysts held no advanced degrees. More recently, many psychoanalytic training institutes have accepted only psychiatrists, although some accept holders of other degrees (most often the Ph.D.). Thus not all psychoanalysts are psychiatrists, nor vice versa.

Psychotherapists in private practice are usually either psychiatrists or clinical psychologists. But several other specialists play a role in therapy, especially in mental hospitals. A **psychiatric social worker** may have any of several degrees, followed by training in a mental-health setting. Others whose duties include activities that could be considered psychotherapy are psychiatric nurses and occupational therapists. In large hospitals, one or more of each of these specialists may work together as a therapeutic team, and both inside and outside the hospital they may be assisted by other paraprofessionals, people with less-specialized training. ■ Table 16.3

A different kind of professional who is usually *not* a therapist, but whose work is relevant to mental health, is the professional researcher. Researchers studying abnormal behavior and the ways of treating it may be psychiatrists, psychologists, neurologists, biochemists, or others (Kietzman et al., 1975). Some researchers may see patients, primarily to test the effectiveness of existing therapy or to develop a new approach (e.g., Bandura et al., 1969). Others may do laboratory research with animal models or biochemical processes.

Table 16.3 ■ Professionals and Paraprofessionals in Psychotherapy

Professional

Psychiatrist
M.D. degree with internship plus residency training (usually three years) in a psychiatric hospital or mental-health facility.

Clinical psychologist
Ph.D. in psychology with both research and clinical skill specialization or Psy.D. in psychology (a professional degree with more clinical than research specialization), plus one-year internship in a psychiatric hospital or mental-health center.

Counseling psychologist
Ph.D. in psychology plus internship in a marital or student counseling setting; normally, the counseling psychologist deals with adjustment problems not involving mental disorder.

Psychoanalyst
M.D. or Ph.D. degree plus intensive training in theory and practice of psychoanalysis.

Psychiatric social worker
B.A., M.S.W., or Ph.D. degree with specialized clinical training in mental-health settings.

Psychiatric nurse
R.N. in nursing plus specialized training in care and treatment of psychiatric patients. M.A. and Ph.D. in psychiatric nursing is possible.

Occupational therapist
B.S. in occupational therapy plus internship training with physically or psychologically handicapped, helping them make the most of their resources.

Paraprofessional

Community mental health worker
Capable person with limited professional training who works under professional direction (especially crisis intervention).

Alcohol or drug-abuse counselor
Limited professional training but trained in the evaluation and management of alcohol- and drug-addicted persons.

Pastoral counselor
Ministerial background plus training in psychology. Internship in mental-health facility as a chaplain.

Adapted from J. C. Coleman et al., *Abnormal Psychology and Modern Life*, 6th ed. Copyright © 1980, 1976, 1972 by Scott, Foresman and Company. Reprinted by permission.

Psychotherapists' Belief Systems

Of the categories discussed, only *psychoanalyst* indicates the professional has particular beliefs about abnormal behavior. A clinical psychologist, for example, can approach abnormal behavior from any of the perspectives in psychology, depending on his or her training and experience. But what a therapist believes about the causes of abnormal behavior is important in how he or she approaches it.

Both the procedures ("modes") and the related views on ethics ("morals") of any psychotherapy are closely tied to its theoretical beliefs (London, 1964). What seems ethical or moral to one kind of psychotherapist may very well seem unethical to another—*not* because either is unethical according to universally accepted standards, but because differing belief systems have different ethical implications.

Consider how any particular problem should be approached. If a person is bothered by smoking cigarettes and consults a psychotherapist for help, what is the most ethical way for the therapist to proceed? If the therapist believes that this "patient's" smoking is only a "symptom" of a deeper emotional problem, the *only* ethical course is to seek out the deeper problem—through an analysis of the person's personal history, emotional relationships, and so forth. For this therapist, seeking to reduce smoking without treating the "real" problem would be unethical, something like giving cough drops for tuberculosis. But a psychotherapist who believes that the smoking may be only a troublesome habit will behave quite differently. Then the *only* ethical course is to seek to change the "behavior" that the "client" wants changed (assuming the change is not illegal or immoral). This therapist would seek to deal directly with the smoking, not as a symptom but as *the* problem. In this belief system, delving into the client's emotional makeup and life history would be an unethical intrusion.

In categorizing such different beliefs, London (1964) distinguished between insight and action therapies. **Insight therapies** seek to help patients understand their own psychological functioning by achieving insight (becoming aware of the motives, patterns of childhood learning, and current situations that influence their behavior), primarily through verbal exchanges between patient and therapist. Particular forms of insight therapy emphasize different events and structure the verbal exchanges differently, but the overall pattern is similar. The major insight therapies are the psychoanalytic and humanistic ones.

In contrast, **action therapies** seek to alter directly the behaviors that cause people to come to the therapists, primarily through some form of action or nonverbal behavior (although verbal exchange also occurs). The clients' actions in therapy may involve making lists, watching films, drinking alcohol (in therapy for alcoholism), role-playing new behaviors, and others. The therapists' may include administering reinforcement or participating in role-play, for example. The action therapies we will consider are the behavioral therapies and some related but more cognitively oriented approaches.

Overall, to understand the approach of a given mental-health professional, you would need to know both the form and the content of the person's training: the academic degree, the type of institution, whether his or her belief system was insight or action oriented, and just what it holds to be true about people. Knowing that one person had a Ph.D. degree with a biological focus from a behavioral school, for example, and another had a Psy.D. degree with a humanistic focus from a professional-psychology school would help you

to predict their views on various aspects of psychotherapy.

But your predictions would still be only approximations. Practicing therapists, unlike theory builders or researchers, have no strong reasons to remain conceptually "pure." They often combine elements from several approaches, using them all at once or selecting different approaches for different patients or symptoms. Such combined approaches are termed **eclectic** (Garfield & Kurtz, 1974). Even approaches normally considered as different and as opposed as psychoanalytic and behavioral ones have been combined by some therapists (Wachtel, 1977). We will discuss "pure" psychotherapies, but these are somewhat of an abstraction; real therapists are usually more eclectic.

Research on Psychotherapy Effectiveness

A controversial topic in therapy concerns research on psychotherapy's effectiveness. Therapists who already believe in their school of therapy find research projects on effectiveness to be at best a waste of time and at worst ethically objectionable (when they use a control group that does not receive therapy). People who question the effectiveness of current therapies, however, believe that continuing to use unproven methods is itself a waste of time or ethically objectionable (in taking time and charging money for a procedure that has not been shown to work). These arguments are not easily resolved.

Drug therapies for abnormal behaviors are automatically subjected to experimental verification, as are drugs for other purposes. The Food and Drug Administration (FDA) requires experimental evidence that any proposed new drug is both safe *and* effective for the purpose intended before it can be sold. But psychotherapies have not been subject to any such rules. Psychotherapists must meet local licensing criteria in order to practice, but the procedures they use need not have been shown to be *either* safe or effective. Some psychologists and others have argued that they should be.

You might wonder why extensive research should be necessary. It might at first seem reasonable that the thousands of active therapists, their patients, and the patients' relatives should be able to tell us about the effects of therapy. But personal reports from any or all of these groups are suspect.

Satisfied therapists are not a reliable source of unbiased data because they have too much at stake. After many years of study to achieve their status and trying their best with patients, they are all too likely to see improvement where there is none. Even if a patient is not improving, the therapist can always say, "Think how much worse that person would have been without therapy." Without knowing what the patient's behavior would have been in other circumstances, this interpretation cannot be disproved. A variety of other factors also influence the therapist's perceptions, including the fact that patients who are not doing well may terminate therapy, leaving the therapist to interact only with the ones who are improving.

Satisfied patients are also weak evidence for therapeutic success. Many people have trouble assessing their own behavior accurately and psychiatric patients as a group are likely to be even less successful. Furthermore, there are reasons for them to see improvement in themselves whether or not it has occurred. They may exaggerate their problems when they first seek help, for example, in order to justify doing so. Then, after spending considerable time and money, they may minimize their remaining problems—both to justify having spent the time and money and to justify terminating therapy.

The patients' relatives, friends, and employers are probably more accurate judges of progress than either therapists or patients. But they can still only judge progress, not whether that progress was the direct result of the therapy.

In fact, one of the most serious difficulties in assessing psychotherapy effectiveness is that many (perhaps most) people with psychological problems get better over time, even without formal therapy. This effect is termed **spontaneous remission;** it presumably reflects one or more unspecified positive influences, from a change in diet to informal psychotherapy from friends (Cowen, 1982). From a patient's viewpoint the high incidence of spontaneous remission is a positive finding, but from a scientific viewpoint it makes assessment of any psychotherapy much more difficult: Any effective therapy must not simply lead to improvement, but must yield significantly *more* improvement than spontaneous remission.

For all these reasons, controlled research is necessary to establish whether any form of psychotherapy is effective (Lambert, 1979). Since the 1970s psychotherapy has seen "almost an explosion" of research on effectiveness (Singer, 1981, p. 119), but the research has many difficult problems (Kazdin, 1980). Neither patients nor therapists are identical, so individual differences can always cloud the outcome. Psychotherapy often takes months or even years—during which some patients drop out and others are subject to many influences besides the therapy. If the proposed therapy is considered experimental, informed-consent requirements can be difficult to meet, especially with patients whose understanding of their situation is marginal.

But a key problem is the need for a randomly assigned placebo control group. It is well known that

"I BELIEVE I HAVE A NEW APPROACH TO PSYCHOTHERAPY, BUT, LIKE EVERYTHING ELSE, IT FIRST HAS TO BE TESTED ON MICE."

© 1983 by Sidney Harris

behavioral manipulations can have placebo effects, that is, lead to changes that reflect the patient's belief in the procedure rather than the procedure itself (Chapter 1). To be truly effective, a psychotherapy must be more powerful than a similar placebo. (If any person who looked like a therapist and spoke reassuringly could get the same results, why have therapists spend years in training?) But deliberate use of ineffective placebo "therapies" is considered questionable, perhaps even unethical, by some therapists (O'Leary & Borkovec, 1978). The major problem is the same as it is in medicine when an effective treatment has already been demonstrated. To withhold that treatment from some patients and give them a placebo instead is unethical. For psychotherapists who believe their procedures are effective, randomly assigning one group of patients to an intentionally ineffective placebo is similarly unethical.

Consequently, many studies do not use placebo controls. Instead, they compare the effectiveness of one psychotherapy to another form, or to a drug, or sometimes to a "wait-list" control group: would-be patients who are not currently receiving any therapy (Garfield & Bergin, 1978). Studies that do use placebo controls often offer therapy to the placebo group at the end of the study; if several therapies have been compared, the placebo group receives the one that has been shown to be most effective.

Results of research on effectiveness remain open to various interpretations (Garfield, 1981). Just as therapists' belief systems can lead them to see improvement in their patients, so can it lead to a favorable interpretation of ambiguous research findings. One major comparison of behavioral and psychoanalytic therapies, for example, yielded results that could be said to favor the behavioral approach *or* the psychoanalytic approach *or* no treatment, depending on the interpretation (Davison & Neale, 1982; Sloane et al., 1975). It thus remains unclear just how effective any of the psychotherapies are, or what their relative advantages might be—although more sophisticated research may improve that situation. ■Research Controversy: Do Psychotherapies Work?

INSIGHT THERAPIES

Many therapies that derive from different theoretical perspectives and see themselves as following different procedures can nevertheless be grouped as insight therapies on the basis of common assumptions and procedures (London, 1964). Insight therapies assume that all behaviors reflect underlying motives, that abnormal behaviors represent aberrations in the expression of these motives, and that effective change in abnormal behaviors requires an understanding of those motives. Insight procedures seek to achieve insight almost entirely through talk, most of which is generated by the patient or client. The insight therapist's role is to remain relatively hidden (in psychoanalysis, literally out of sight), offering little talk, few specific suggestions, and little information about his or her own private life. The therapist seeks in this way to focus the patient's attention inward; this looking into oneself is what is meant by insight.

Of the many insight therapies, two are most important and probably most unlike each other: the psychoanalytic and humanistic therapies.

Psychoanalytic Therapies

The earliest form of insight therapy is Freud's psychoanalysis. Many other insight therapies derive from it, and psychoanalysis itself has changed over time and is practiced somewhat differently by different analysts. Hence, when we say *psychoanalysis* we really mean a cluster of related therapies. As noted in earlier chapters, psychoanalysis was developed originally as therapy and was not derived from a theory of personality. The psychoanalytic views of motivation, child development, and personality that we have already noted are all derived from Freud's (and the neo-Freudians') clinical practice. ■Figure 16.8

Freud's view of abnormal behavior was that childhood conflicts between id impulses and social constraints, or their internalized superego equivalents, were handled by repression. Once a conflict was repressed, it was frozen in that form, in a pattern one analyst has likened to the Ice Age mammoths occasionally found frozen in Siberian glaciers (Wachtel, 1977). These frozen conflicts can remain active, however, unconsciously influencing adult behavior and leading to the symptoms of mental illness. Psychoanalysis seeks to uncover these repressed childhood conflicts, to let the patient see them for what they were then, and to help the patient work through them in the present to reach a more balanced integration of id and superego. In seeking this resolution, the patient must work back past layers of newer memories and patterns of anxiety avoidance (called *defenses*) to reach the hidden childhood conflicts. Psychoanalysis seeks to achieve this end through five key processes: (1) free association, (2) dream analysis, (3) analysis of resistance, (4) transference, and (5) interpretation.

In a typical psychoanalytic session, the analyst remains quiet, seated just behind and out of sight of the patient, who in traditional psychoanalysis reclines on a couch. The patient's task is to **free associate:** to say whatever comes to mind without any attempts to edit, regardless of how embarrassing, trivial, or irrelevant it may seem. Freud believed that all thoughts were associated and that each new thought was connected to the previous one, even if the connections were not evident. Free association was designed to follow a chain of thought to see where it led, in hopes of uncovering some clue to the roots of the patient's problems.

In **dream analysis,** the patient remembers as many dreams as possible and reports them to the analyst, who helps the patient discover the hidden meanings of the dreams. The plot of each dream is thought to represent the patient's conflicts with the real meaning disguised; the forces of repression are thought to function even in sleep.

During therapy, the patient may show **resistance** toward the analyst, an apparent reluctance to continue. This resistance may take the form of not talking, of not remembering any dreams, or even of forgetting a therapy appointment. To the analyst, resistance is a sign that the patient is getting close to some repressed conflict and thus encountering stronger defenses that try to keep the conflict hidden. Hence he or she will seek to follow up the topic being discussed when resistance occurs.

As analysis continues, the patient may show signs of **transference,** the transferring to the analyst of attitudes or emotional responses once held toward a parent: Expressions of anger toward the analyst, for example, may be taken as evidence of transference of

Do psychotherapies work?

The opening salvo in an ongoing battle over the effectiveness of psychotherapies was Eysenck's (1952) claim that psychoanalysis (then the prevailing form of psychotherapy) *didn't work,* that is, was no more effective than the rate of spontaneous remission. Supporters of psychoanalysis soon rallied to its defense and Eysenck's claim was widely criticized on various grounds (e.g., Meltzoff & Kornreich, 1970). But other researchers have repeated and defended Eysenck's claim (e.g., Ervin, 1980). Points made by both sides are supported by evidence, but to date that evidence remains limited in enough respects to allow these conflicting interpretations. New approaches are needed to resolve whether any particular psychotherapy—or psychotherapy in general—"works."

One major new approach was developed by Smith and Glass (1977). In a procedure they called **meta-analysis,** they analyzed the results of 375 different controlled studies of therapeutic effectiveness, seeking to see if all psychotherapy combined was more effective than no psychotherapy. (*Meta-* indicates something larger than the term it modifies; this was meta-analysis because it analyzed the total of many separate analyses.) Smith and Glass's approach was more sophisticated than

many prior analyses, but it has still not resolved the controversy.

Smith and Glass reported that psychotherapy *is* demonstrably more effective than no psychotherapy: The average therapy patient, they noted, is better off than 75% of the people in untreated control groups. Predictably, psychotherapy supporters accepted the new finding as finally laying Eysenck's criticisms to rest (Singer, 1981). Equally predictably, critics pointed to what they saw as methodological flaws and to the relative weakness of the claimed effect (Rimland, 1979). "Better than 75%" sounds more impressive than it really is, critics noted; the average person would be better off than 50% of the control group, by definition, even without treatment. Smith and Glass's own findings show a displacement of the distribution by only about two-thirds of one standard deviation. ■ Figure 16.7

In a reanalysis of some of Smith and Glass's data, Landman and Dawes (1982) found that Smith and Glass's statistical assumptions did not yield inflated values, as some critics had charged; if anything, they somewhat reduced the estimated effectiveness. But Landman and Dawes left open a number of other criticisms of the studies that provided data for the meta-analysis. So arguments over effectiveness will continue.

A new dimension was added to these arguments in 1979, with hearings in the United States Senate concerning whether psychotherapy should be eligible for Medicare payments. Members of the Senate demanded evidence of effectiveness of psychotherapy if public money was to be spent on it (Marshall, 1980a).

Such evidence may be available in a few years, thanks to a federal commitment to major research on effectiveness. The first project funded was to cost over $3 million and to run for three years, comparing the effect on depression of two types of psychotherapy and one drug (Kolata, 1981a). But this is considered only a pilot test to see if large-scale studies are feasible. If they are, it may require another 10 to 20 years (and millions of dollars) before more complete results are in.

Until that happens, therapists of various theoretical backgrounds will continue to "treat patients" or "help clients," assuming that the effectiveness of their approach will eventually be demonstrated. In the meantime, about all that can be said with certainty is that most psychotherapies seem to help somewhat with the less severe problems, but few if any help much with serious disorders such as schizophrenia (Marshall, 1980b).

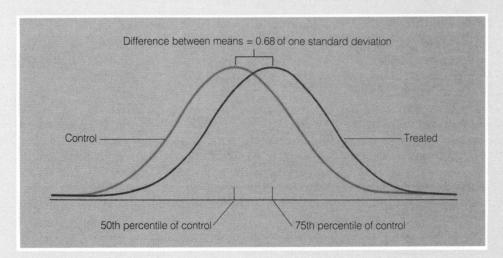

Difference between means = 0.68 of one standard deviation

Control — Treated

50th percentile of control — 75th percentile of control

Figure 16.7 ■ Smith and Glass's (1977) meta-analysis of 375 controlled studies of effectiveness showed that psychotherapy improves the average patient by about two-thirds of a standard deviation.

(From M. L. Smith and G. V. Glass, *American Psychologist,* 1977, 32, 752–760. Copyright 1977 by the American Psychologist Association. Reprinted by permission of the author.)

Figure 16.8 ■ Freud's office. Note the couch for the patient and Freud's chair behind it.
(Historical Pictures Service, Chicago)

childhood hostility toward a parent. Transference is viewed by analysts as a sign of progress, and is encouraged. In fact, one reason the analyst remains out of sight is to be a more ambiguous figure and thus encourage transference. The opposite of transference, however, called **countertransference,** is to be avoided; the analyst must not respond to the patient in anger or in other ways that represent the analyst's own emotional responses. (The need to recognize and avoid countertransference is a major reason all analysts must themselves undergo analysis.)

When the analyst begins to see a pattern in the patient's free associations and dreams, he or she begins to offer **interpretation** of the patient's behaviors, suggesting what the behaviors "really" mean. The analyst thereby seeks to encourage insight, but must be careful not to offer interpretations too soon or too strongly, lest the patient reject them. Freud originally suggested that analysis sessions occur five days a week, perhaps for years. Most psychoanalysts do not see their patients this frequently, but for therapy to continue for many years is not uncommon. Furthermore, an analyst who follows Freud's advice always refrains from offering direct advice on current decisions, and seeks to keep the patient from becoming too comfortable—lest the patient become complacent and thus fail to achieve insight (Freud, 1919). (Because many variations on

classic psychoanalysis have been developed, these descriptions may not exactly reflect the practices of all analysts.)

After all this effort, does psychoanalysis "work"—that is, does it cure the problems that led patients to enter therapy in the first place? Analysts answer that both patients and therapists stay in therapy because they know it works (e.g., Appelbaum, 1982). Yet even most analysts (though not all) agree that psychoanalysis is of little use with schizophrenics or other patients who are unable to communicate effectively (Feinsilver & Gunderson, 1972). Analysis works best, they note, with relatively well-educated and verbal patients whose problems are not too severe (Luborsky & Spence, 1978).

But critics refuse to accept even these limited claims of effectiveness. They point out that controlled studies have not demonstrated the effectiveness of psychoanalytic therapy over placebos or other forms of therapy (e.g., Prochaska, 1979). Psychoanalysis or other insight therapies may yield insight, critics suggest, but this means merely learning to talk about problems in the same framework as the therapist (Levy, 1963). Psychoanalytic patients have psychoanalytic insights, humanistic patients have humanistic insights, and so forth (Marmor, 1962). Furthermore, say the critics, insight is the therapist's goal, not the

patient's; patients come to be helped with their problems, not to learn to talk about them (London, 1964).
■ Notable Quote: Perry London on the Limited Value of Insight

Humanistic Therapies

The other major group of insight therapies are the **humanistic therapies,** approaches offered by humanistic theorists that emphasize self-actualization through the exercise of free will (Ellis, 1973). Humanist therapists see themselves as offering a warm, supportive, and encouraging environment within which a client can make his or her own decisions. They do not think of the people they help as sick patients who must be made well, but as innately good and self-actualizing people who have lost their way and need help in finding it again.

The major form of humanistic therapy is Carl Rogers's **client-centered** approach. Like Freud, Rogers based a general theory of personality on his own experiences as a therapist. Rogers began to offer his approach as an alternative to psychoanalysis in the 1940s. In the years thereafter, he continued to refine it, gradually deemphasizing particular procedural techniques and emphasizing personal characteristics of the therapist. It is especially important, Rogers (1966) has noted, for the therapist to be *genuine* or *congruent,* able to convey support for the client honestly.

Rogers's approach emphasizes talk, primarily by the client, to develop insight and, consequently, improvement in the client's problems. But the details of client-centered therapy differ notably from psychoanalysis: Rogers's system is based on different beliefs about human nature, so the therapist's actions and the nature of the expected insight also differ.

As noted in previous chapters, Rogers believes that human nature is characterized by an innate but weak tendency toward self-actualization. Under supportive conditions, each person seeks to maximize his or her capabilities, becoming well-adapted and happy in the process. But problems ensue, according to Rogers, when people become too concerned with how others view them and consequently begin to deny aspects of their true selves. The task of therapy is to help a person rediscover his or her true *self* and become comfortable with it (Holden, 1977). A basic tool of the therapist in this task is **unconditional positive regard;** the therapist seeks to convince the client of his or her worth and of the therapist's support, regardless of what the client has done or said. (Some of the client's *actions* may be disavowed, but not the client as a valuable person.) Unconditional positive regard is important, in Rogers's scheme, because he feels that the client's problems reflect the *conditional* regard of others: "I'll love you *if* you behave correctly."

A Rogerian therapist encourages the client to talk about his or her emotional problems, then responds with two levels of **empathy,** the accepting and clarifying of the client's expressed emotions. In early stages of therapy, the therapist uses primary empathy, responding to the client's statements by rephrasing the emotional content of what the client just said. As therapy progresses, the therapist begins to include a more advanced form of empathy, responding to emotions that the therapist thinks may lie behind the client's statements (Egan, 1975). In offering both forms of empathy the therapist seeks to respond in terms of the client's **phenomenological world,** the pattern of how things seem to the client. If the client states something the therapist thinks is factually incorrect, the

---

NOTABLE QUOTE:

Perry London on the limited value of insight

❝ For most of the problems of most people, it seems generally to be the case that the achievement of insight, however detailed and precise, into their motivations, however unconscious, does not by itself solve their problems, reduce their symptoms, or change their lives in any but a gross intellectual or economic sense. . . .

Most modern Insight therapists . . . are likely to rationalize the use of insight more in terms of [these] somewhat indirect effects. 'True, achieving insight will not necessarily solve all problems or remove all symptoms,' they say, 'but what it will do is put the patient in a position where he can now control his behavior if he is sufficiently motivated to do so.'

When the connection between insight and symptoms is loosened, as it is here, it may be proper to 'successfully' terminate treatment with symptoms still present, or conversely, to say that treatment is a failure even with all the symptoms gone unless insight has somehow been achieved. The first case is akin to saying that the treatment cured everything except what bothered the patient in the first place, while the second says that it does not matter if the patient is well unless he is also educated.❞

From *The Modes and Morals of Psychotherapy* by Perry London, 1964, Holt, Rinehart and Winston, pp. 60, 61, 62. Reprinted by permission of the author.

---

therapist does not contradict the client but responds "It seems to you that. . . . "

Rogerian therapists assume that the client can make appropriate decisions and needs to be encouraged to make them; hence the therapist never gives advice about how to behave. For this reason, Rogers's approach has also been termed *nondirective* therapy. But this term is not used much any more, perhaps in recognition that therapy necessarily involves some directing—even if it is toward making one's own decisions.

Rogers has long encouraged the analysis of therapy effectiveness; he was one of the earliest proponents of such research. But evidence for the effectiveness of client-centered therapy remains inconsistent (Parloff et al., 1978). Some critics suggest that part of the difficulty is Rogers's reliance on clients' self-reports as the data for improvement; this reliance is consistent with Rogers's beliefs, but such responses are subject to a variety of biases. As with other insight therapies, client-centered therapy is probably most appropriate for well-educated and verbal persons whose problems are relatively mild. One widely noted study by Rogers and others demonstrated the possibility of building empathic relationships with schizophrenics, but this did not seem to make them less schizophrenic (May, 1974; Rogers et al., 1967).

ACTION THERAPIES

In marked contrast to the insight therapies are the action therapies, which seek different outcomes for different reasons. Where insight therapists seek insight as both a necessary and sufficient therapeutic goal, action therapists see insight as largely irrelevant. Instead, they emphasize specific learned behavior; to them, the client's original problem is inappropriate behavior and the desired outcome of therapy is appropriate behavior. But it is the events of therapy that give action therapies the name: Both client and therapist are *active*, often in several ways. The client not only talks but also role-plays, carries out procedures to relax physically, watches or imagines particular scenes, and so forth. The therapist not only talks but also participates in role-play, manipulates reinforcers, directs the course of relaxation or imagery, and so forth.

Action therapies developed largely as applications of research findings rather than from therapeutic practice, and action therapists maintain a scientific/academic approach that sets them apart from many insight therapists (Kanfer & Phillips, 1970; Kazdin, 1978). (Most of the people who originated action therapies were originally trained as insight therapists. But

as they sought to improve their effectiveness, they developed other forms of therapy.)

London used the term *action therapy* to emphasize what therapists do (1964); we have adopted it for the same reason. But the term preferred by action therapists is **behavioral therapy,** which emphasizes the intent to develop appropriate behavior (Rimm & Masters, 1979; Schwartz, 1982). Early behavioral therapists often referred to their approach as **behavior modification,** and some still prefer this term (Bandura, 1969; Leitenberg, 1976; Ullman & Krasner, 1965). But *behavior modification* has been closely identified with procedures based on classical and operant learning. As newer and broader approaches have incorporated social learning theory and cognitive elements, the more general term *behavioral therapy* has become common (Davison & Stuart, 1975).

Behavioral Therapies

Behavioral therapists differ somewhat among themselves but share theoretical beliefs that contrast sharply with those of the insight therapists. In explaining abnormal behavior, insight therapists emphasize past events that have carried over into the present, with the assumption that the history of these events must be reexamined in detail before present difficulties can be overcome. Behavioral therapists also assume that current problems derive from past events, but their focus is almost entirely on why the problems currently exist. They assume that current behaviors are maintained by current situation-behavior relationships, primarily current patterns of reinforcement. Hence in seeking to change problem behaviors they focus on modifying current behavior and reinforcements, with little or no concern for past relationships.

The only major distinction we will draw among the behavioral therapies is between those that emphasize direct procedures, involving overt behaviors and reinforcement (discussed in this section), and those that add substantial covert or cognitive elements (discussed in the next section). Direct procedures have both advantages and limitations compared to procedures that incorporate cognitive elements. Direct procedures are effective, for example, with people who are nonverbal, low in intelligence, or uncooperative. They can thus be used with clients who are difficult to reach with other psychotherapies, including retarded or very young children and withdrawn or nonverbal schizophrenics. Direct procedures have disadvantages, however, for some kinds of problem behaviors, especially with people who *are* verbal and cooperative.

Therapies Based on Classical Conditioning The primary behavioral-therapy approach based on classical conditioning is **counterconditioning,** which seeks to replace an inappropriate response to some stimulus with a more appropriate response through repeated presentations of that stimulus in situations that elicit the appropriate response. Usually the inappropriate response is anxiety and the appropriate response is relaxation. The intent of counterconditioning for a person with a dog phobia, for example, would be to replace fear responses to dog-related stimuli with relaxation responses.

The best-known form of counterconditioning is Joseph Wolpe's **systematic desensitization** (1969), which uses special techniques to develop a highly relaxed state, then presents a sequenced series of frightening stimuli. This sequence, called a **hierarchy,** begins with the weakest situation that the client thinks would arouse fear and then lists increasingly fearful stimuli. In use, the first item on the hierarchy is presented after the client is deeply relaxed, perhaps by hypnosis or by a special muscular-relaxation sequence pioneered by Jacobson (1974). If the client can remain relaxed in the presence of the first stimulus on the hierarchy, the therapist moves to the next. If the client begins to experience anxiety at any point, the stimulus is removed and the client is helped to relax again.

The stimuli on the hierarchy can be presented in real form, in simulated form through slides, films, or tapes, or solely through the client's imagining them. Real stimuli are thought to be better for encouraging transfer to everyday situations (Wilson & O'Leary, 1980), but for reasons of convenience or practicality, filmed or imagined stimuli are often used. Slides of dogs are more convenient to manipulate than live dogs, for example, but a fear of flying may require cues that are difficult to manipulate; these could be imagined. Use of stimulus representations such as slides has the advantage that several clients with the same problem can be aided at one time. ■ Figure 16.9

A client is exposed to one or more hierarchy situations for about a half hour, two or three times a week. To help ensure that the effects will transfer to everyday situations, the therapist usually gives the client further homework, suggestions for use of similar techniques in real situations (Davison, 1968). Some clients also find that the relaxation techniques are useful in generally relieving anxiety, in addition to their use with hierarchy items (Goldfried & Trier, 1974).

Experimental tests have typically found systematic desensitization to be effective. Even when the desensitization is done through imagery, for example, the anxiety reduction transfers to everyday situations (Goldfried & Davison, 1976). In one of the more extensive tests of any psychotherapy, systematic desensitization was compared to insight therapy and to an attention-placebo control group (Paul, 1966). Subjects

"LEAVE US ALONE! I AM A BEHAVIOR THERAPIST! I AM HELPING MY PATIENT OVERCOME A FEAR OF HEIGHTS!"

© 1983 by Sydney Harris

in this latter group received therapists' attention, listened to tapes, and took placebo pills. Paul even had the systematic desensitization carried out by insight therapists who were taught to do so, to control for the possibility that therapist enthusiasm might influence the outcome. The results showed that systematic desensitization subjects improved much more than the other two groups, even though both insight *and* the placebo treatment yielded significant improvement. (There was no difference between insight therapy and the placebo treatment.) Furthermore, these results held in a two-year follow-up (Paul, 1967).

Note that systematic desensitization by means of imagined fear stimuli requires some cognitive activity (the imagery). But the basic procedure is considered to be classical conditioning, and is considered most effective when real stimuli are used. The cognitions are a convenient shortcut and are not integral to the procedure. A behavioral therapist could hypothetically construct a hierarchy based solely on a patient's responses to differing stimuli, then apply these stimuli when the client was relaxed, without requiring either verbal cooperation or imagery. Hence the systematic desensitization procedure is considered more direct than cognitive. (Wolpe has also pointed out that cognitions themselves may be considered behaviors; 1978.)

Figure 16.9 ■ Several clients undergoing systematic desensitization for their fear of dogs.
(The New York Times News Service)

A more dramatic—and ethically questionable—form of counterconditioning begins with the strongest possible fear stimulus rather than the weakest. In **flooding,** the client is asked to imagine the worst item on the hierarchy of possibilities. **Implosion therapy** goes even further, with the therapist verbally suggesting grossly magnified forms of the feared object, especially as these relate to what psychoanalysts consider universal basic fears (Stampfl & Levis, 1973). Once the feared situation is imagined, it is held for an hour or more, until the client is no longer frightened—through sheer exhaustion, if nothing else. The logic is that the non-fear at the end of the session will become conditioned to the formerly fearful stimulus. Both flooding and implosion therapy are used only experimentally and only by a few practitioners. There is some evidence they can be effective (Barrett, 1969; Meyer et al., 1975), but most therapists consider them inappropriate because of the stress they put on clients.

Another form of counterconditioning seeks to create the opposite effect of systematic desensitization. **Aversion therapy** is intended to *cause* the client to be anxious in response to a stimulus in cases where prior approach behaviors are defined as the problem. Aversion therapy has been used, for example, with alcoholics and with clients whose sexual preferences are considered inappropriate, such as fetishists or child molesters. In aversion therapy, the desired object or a representation of it is presented, together with an elec-

tric shock, a nausea-inducing drug, or other stimulus that induces avoidance. After a series of such pairings, a conditioned aversion can be built up that will help the client avoid the stimuli that cause problems.

There are several difficulties with aversion therapy. Results are mixed, with some procedures more effective than others (Wilson & O'Leary, 1980). A number of ethical objections have also been raised, mostly having to do with what someone considered inappropriate use of the procedure. There have been objections to its use with homosexuals, for example, even when the clients were voluntarily seeking to alter their own sexual arousal patterns. And some uses of aversion therapy with prison inmates have been widely criticized and, in some cases, legally prohibited.

Lest aversion therapy be considered totally useless, however, we can note one study in which it probably saved a child's life (Lang & Melamed, 1969). A nine-month-old baby had been hospitalized several times for chronic vomiting and rumination (regurgitating and rechewing food), and was in critical condition when aversion therapy began. The therapy utilized one-second shocks to the leg whenever signs of potential vomiting began. After two one-hour sessions, most vomiting ceased and the child began to gain weight. Within three weeks, he went home with no further traces of the behavior. Such cases demonstrate how direct procedures can be used on those who cannot verbally cooperate.

Therapies Based on Operant Conditioning Operant techniques also offer ways of reducing inappropriate behaviors and increasing appropriate ones. Most forms of operant therapy emphasize training new behaviors through reinforcement, but there are also specialized uses of extinction and punishment. One long-term research project using all three procedures is Ivar Lovaas's work with autistic children (Lovaas, 1977). **Autistic children** are strangely unresponsive to other people; they typically do not develop speech and they spend much of their time contemplating mechanical devices or their own bodies, which they move in stereotyped ways. (*Autistic* means "focused inward upon the self.") Some autistic children are self-destructive, biting their arms or banging their heads against a wall, so they must be physically restrained 24 hours a day; some must be tied to their beds.

In his initial work with autistic children, Lovaas sought to let their self-destructive behavior extinguish. This was sometimes effective, but only after thousands of self-inflicted blows. Furthermore, the effect might not generalize; once in a new location, the child might begin self-damaging again and require further extinction trials. In exasperation at one such child, Lovaas resorted to an unscientific behavior and spanked her. Remarkably, the behavior ceased briefly. When it started again, Lovaas spanked her again, and soon the damaging behavior ceased (Lovaas, 1977).

Lovaas soon substituted electric shock for spanking, both because it is easier to apply immediately and because it is less likely to injure the child. Rarely are more than a few such shocks necessary to terminate self-destructive behavior—though *why* the shocks should be more punishing than the self-destructive behavior itself is unknown. Freed from the constraining effects of their destructive behaviors, the children can be tub-bathed, sometimes for the first time in years, and otherwise cared for more normally. Then work can begin on shaping appropriate behaviors, primarily with positive reinforcement. Initial work teaches the child to attend to the therapist, then language and other behaviors are gradually shaped. Autistic children remain quite unlikely to become normal, even with extensive therapy, but some have made substantial progress, including limited speech and attendance at special schools. ■ Figure 16.10

Lovaas's work has occasionally been criticized by nonbehaviorists, who understand only that he has given electric shocks to young children. But those few shocks have allowed the children to be unstrapped from their beds, to be with their families, and to begin to live lives closer to normal ones. Lovaas has argued that until we can discover a better way to help them, these procedures are in the children's best interests. Other behaviorists agree, and some have made further

points. Skinner has noted, for example, that the greatest benefit a therapist can offer an institutionalized patient is to help the patient learn the skills necessary to leave the mental hospital (Skinner, 1976a).

For those better able than autistic children to understand their therapy, behavioral therapists often discuss possible procedures and explain in detail what will be done. Sometimes reinforcement contingencies are then formalized in a **behavior contract,** an agreement that explicitly states what behaviors will be reinforced. A more elaborate version of behavioral contracting is Ayllon and Azrin's **token economy** plan (1968), in which appropriate behaviors earn tokens that can then be "spent" for various reinforcers. Experimental token economies have been widely used in mental hospitals, where typically all patients in a ward participate. Tokens are earned for such behaviors as self-grooming, joining in social events, or helping clean the ward. They can be spent for various desired benefits, such as sleeping late, movies, snacks, and so forth. Even highly regressed schizophrenics have made significant progress under such conditions. The effectiveness of token economies was demonstrated by temporarily eliminating the reinforcement contingencies after behavioral improvements have been obtained (Ayllon & Azrin, 1965). If the improvements were a function only of new activities and increased attention, they should have continued. But Figure 16.11 shows that they reverted to their former level when the contingencies changed, indicating that the new behaviors were being sustained by the reinforcement contingencies. ■ Figure 16.11

Many other forms of direct intervention have been successful in teaching a number of behaviors to a variety of populations, including retarded, handicapped, and psychotic children and adults. But behavioral therapies for people who are better able to cooperate have begun to incorporate a range of additional cognitive elements.

Cognitive-Behavioral Therapies

A major trend in behavioral theory in recent years has been the development of **cognitive-behavioral** approaches, views that share behaviorism's emphases on learned behavior but also make use of covert behaviors (Mahoney, 1977). Several of the cognitive-behavioral approaches use a suggestion first made by John Watson: They consider thinking to be a form of "self-talk," which they seek to understand and change (see Chapter 1).

The best-known behavioral approach that incorporates cognitive elements is social learning theory.

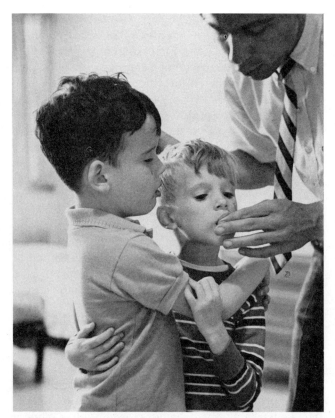
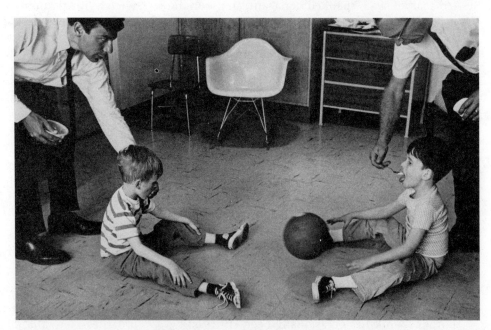

Figure 16.10 ■ Behavioral therapy with autistic children using both immediate food reinforcement and affection. These boys are being taught to interact with each other, which autistic children do not do on their own.

(Photos by Allan Grant, courtesy of Dr. Ivar Lovaas)

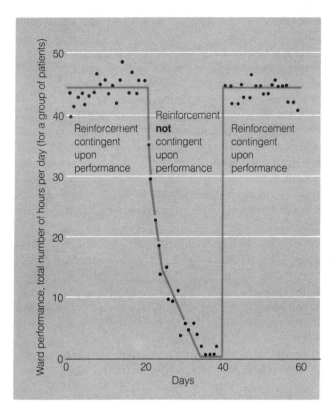

Figure 16.11 ■ When tokens were given to a group of patients for self-grooming and doing chores, these behaviors were maintained at a high rate. When reinforcement was withdrawn for these behaviors, they dropped back to zero. Reinstituting the reinforcement contingency restored them.

(Adapted from T. Ayllon and N. Azrin, *Journal of the Experimental Analysis of Behavior*, 1965, 8, 357–383. Copyright 1965 by the Society for the Experimental Analysis of Behavior. Reprinted by permission.)

We will look at some of its suggestions for therapy before noting several other cognitive-behavioral approaches.

Social Learning Theory   Social learning theory is not usually considered a cognitive-behavioral approach. It is more a transition form between the strictly external approach favored by Skinner and the cognitive-behavioral approaches. Social learning theory emphasizes overt behavior, just as Skinner has, but goes further in suggesting how such behavior may be learned. A major element in social learning theory, as noted in previous chapters, is the concept of *modeling:* It suggests that a person can learn from merely watching the behavior of another (Bandura & Walters, 1963). Social learning theory is thus somewhat cognitive in that modeling implies some covert or cognitive activity on the part of the observer/learner.

The therapeutic approach derived from social learning theory similarly emphasizes overt behavior,

but accepts some covert activity in seeking that behavior, especially the covert activity involved in modeling (Bandura, 1967). Social learning therapists use a number of forms of modeling, including live demonstrations or filmed representations. One series of studies, for example, used filmed representations of medical situations, including surgery and dental work, to help people get over fears of such situations (Melamed et al., 1975). Some therapists even use **covert modeling,** in which the client *imagines* watching a model behave (Kazdin, 1975). In covert modeling, clients might even imagine themselves behaving more effectively. Modeling is also a major part of role-play therapy: The behavioral therapist acts out a more appropriate action for a situation in which the client has difficulty (Lazarus, 1971).

Social learning therapists agree, however, that overt behavior is both a goal and a necessary element in therapy (Bandura, 1977a). Cognitive learning by modeling is not an end in itself, but a way of helping the client perform similar behaviors. In role-play, for example, the therapist's behavior provides a possible role for the client, but it is the client's active practicing of the role that is important. The therapist and client may exchange roles repeatedly until the client not only cognitively "understands" the role, but can carry it out effectively.

Modeling as therapy originally used only live or filmed representations of successful behavior. A person with a fear of dogs, for example, would be exposed to scenes of other people behaving fearlessly with dogs (Bandura & Menlove, 1968). But later studies added various forms of active participation by the client. One frequently cited study compared the effectiveness of two forms of modeling and another therapy in relieving fears of snakes (Bandura et al., 1969). Subjects were first divided into four matched groups. One control group received no treatment and a second group received standard systematic desensitization. The third group received a "symbolic modeling" treatment: They watched a film of a subject handling a snake while they tried to remain relaxed. As in systematic desensitization, if subjects felt themselves becoming anxious they stopped the film until they could again become relaxed. The fourth group received a mixed "live modeling with participation" treatment: They watched as another person handled a snake and encouraged them to come closer and even to touch the snake if they could. ■ Figure 16.12

The control group showed little change and the systematic desensitization resulted in considerable improvement (as measured by how much closer subjects could come to a snake after the study). But symbolic modeling was more effective, and live modeling

Figure 16.12 ■ The most effective therapeutic procedure found in one major study of snake phobias was a mixture of modeling and guided participation, somewhat like the procedure being used here to help zoo visitors overcome their reluctance to approach snakes.

(Judy Howard)

with participation the most effective of all. Later studies have shown modeling to be useful in a variety of problems, especially when combined with reinforced practice of the modeled behavior—even with groups normally difficult to help, such as hospitalized schizophrenics (Bellack et al., 1976).

One major study of the effectiveness of social-learning therapy was even done in a ward of long-term, regressed schizophrenics, the "most severely debilitated institutionalized adults ever studied systematically" (Davison & Neale, 1982, p. 595). In this study, by Paul and Lentz (1977), one ward of a new mental hospital was set up as a social-learning ward, using the token economy plan as a basis but adding modeling and other features. The social-learning ward was then compared to two other treatments. Another ward of the new hospital was set up according to the principles of **milieu therapy,** a contemporary variant of moral treatment in which social relationships among patients and staff are structured to aid recovery (Jones, 1953). The arrangements in both the social-learning and milieu wards structured about 85% of the patient's time. For a control group, a conventional

ward at another hospital was used; it structured only about 5% of patients' time.

Paul and Lentz followed the patients in these three wards for four and a half years. In that time, both of the special wards showed notable gains over the conventional ward; 10% of the social-learning patients and 7% of the milieu patients were discharged and none of those in the conventional ward were. In addition, however, the social-learning patients who were discharged to specialized community placements, such as halfway houses, were much more likely to successfully remain in these situations than were patients from either the conventional or milieu wards.

Other Cognitive-Behavioral Therapies Several other therapeutic approaches are more clearly cognitive than social learning theory (Mahoney, 1974). These approaches emphasize specific forms of cognition, and directly changing these cognitions, more than social learning theory does, and they emphasize overt behavior somewhat less. (Cognitive change is expected to result automatically in behavioral change.)

One therapy that has long existed outside of conventional therapy is now seen as a cognitive-behavioral therapy. **Rational-emotive therapy,** devised by Albert Ellis (1977), suggests that people guide their lives by cognitive propositions about how the world works. Ellis has argued that people can unknowingly state impossible rules to themselves, thereby causing themselves to become disturbed or depressed. He has described a number of such irrational beliefs, including that one must be competent to be worthwhile and that it is easier to avoid difficulties than to face them. According to Ellis, people behave as if they were saying these beliefs to themselves: "I must win everyone's love or I'm a failure." When life experiences do not match up to such extreme expectations, mental problems ensue. A rational-emotive therapist tries to get the client first to accept the view that real events do not count as much as one's attitude toward them. Then the therapist seeks to aid the client to discover his or her own irrational beliefs and modify them. The approach is considered *rational-emotive* because of the underlying assumption that if appropriate cognitions (rational thoughts) can be developed, appropriate emotions will follow.

Aaron Beck's **cognitive restructuring** approach was also developed to alter self-defeating cognitions of depressed clients (Beck et al., 1979). But Beck's views differ from those of Ellis in several respects. Beck does not expect to find variations of a small number of self-defeating beliefs, as Ellis does, but feels that people develop highly individual beliefs. Beck also puts more emphasis on the client's actively restructuring his or her own cognitions, with less specific suggestion from the therapist. Beck encourages each client to seek his or her own self-defeating beliefs, and when one is identified, to test out alternate, more adaptive, beliefs in everyday encounters. Beck's approach has already been shown to be more effective than a commonly used antidepressant drug (Rush et al., 1977). Perhaps because of this success, it is one of the two psychotherapies to be compared in the major federally sponsored study described earlier.

Donald Meichenbaum's (1977) **self-instructional** technique teaches children and adults how to direct both their overt actions and their covert thoughts through (covert) self-talk. Most of us learn how to direct ourselves with self-talk, Meichenbaum suggests, whether we are directing overt behavior ("Careful, . . . slowly, . . . don't drop it. . . . ") or covert behavior ("Don't worry about that now. It'll work out."). Meichenbaum's approach has been successfully used in a variety of situations, including helping hyperactive children to be less impulsive and helping college students to be less anxious about taking tests (Meichenbaum, 1972).

The variety and range of behavioral therapies offer therapists the possibility of picking particular approaches for particular problems. A well-educated depressed patient, for example, might be treated with Beck's cognitive restructuring procedure; more direct operant techniques might be used with a disturbed child. One behavioral therapist, Arnold Lazarus (1981), has formalized a kind of behavioral eclecticism; in **multimodal therapy,** the therapist develops an individualized treatment profile for each client, using techniques drawn for a wide range of behavioral therapies—or even insight therapies, if appropriate. ■ Table 16.4

Lazarus's approach is one more indication that some of the many conceptual and methodological splits that have characterized therapy may be resolved in the future (Goldfried, 1980). As behavioral therapists include cognitive features for certain problems, they move closer to insight therapists. As insight therapists seek experimental verification of the efficacy of their procedures and pay more attention to how their patients or clients behave based on their insights, they move closer to behavioral therapists. If those developments truly represent a trend, as they seem to, future therapy may become fully eclectic, with therapists choosing from a number of experimentally verified techniques the ones that best suit the client's difficulties. In the meantime, cognitive-behavioral techniques can also offer a new approach to self-control. ■ Personal Application: Self-Control through Cognitive-Behavioral Techniques

GROUP THERAPIES

Nearly all the psychotherapies we have noted involve one-to-one relationships between a single therapist and a single patient or client; exceptions include systematic desensitization applied to more than one person at a time and the token economies. Any form of therapy, such as these last two, in which a group of clients or patients is treated in common, could be termed group therapy. But in fact the term **group therapy** is usually reserved for approaches in which the group interactions are the central focus of the therapy, rather than being merely a physical or economic convenience. ■ Figure 16.13

Table 16.4 ■ Treatment Profile for a Patient in Multimodal Therapy

Modality	Problem	Proposed Treatment
Behavior	Frequent crying Negative self-statements	Nonreinforcement Positive self-talk assignments
Affect	Unable to express overt anger Absence of enthusiasm and spontaneous joy Emptiness and aloneness	Role-playing Positive imagery procedures General relationship building
Sensation	Out of touch with most sensual pleasures Frequent lower back pains	Sensate-focus method Orthopedic exercise
Imagery	Distressing scenes of sister's funeral	Desensitization
Cognition	Irrational self-talk: "I am evil," "I must suffer," "I am inferior."	Deliberative rational disputation and corrective self-talk
Interpersonal relationships	Childlike dependence Easily exploited and submissive	Specific self-sufficiency assignments Assertion training

Adapted from A. A. Lazarus, *Journal of Nervous and Mental Diseases*, 1973, *156*, 404–411. © 1973 by The Williams & Wilkins Co. Used by permission.

Self-control through cognitive-behavioral techniques

Some theorists have suggested that you can use behavioral techniques to modify your own behavior (Stuart, 1977). The behavioral self-control procedures they suggest begin with operant arrangements similar to those used to change others' behavior. But because several of the cognitive-behavioral approaches involve active manipulation of cognitions by the client, often in situations encountered in daily life, it is also logical that these cognitive approaches could contribute to teaching self-control practices (Mahoney & Arnkoff, 1978).

Various cognitive-behavioral techniques for self-control have in fact been developed. Among the best known approaches is that of Carl Thoresen and Michael Mahoney, who have written several guides to self-control through cognitive-behavioral techniques (e.g., Mahoney & Thoresen, 1974). You have access to your own covert behavior and can apply covert reinforcement (or punishment), they note, and thus their suggestions for self-control include covert techniques. They suggest that you can not only change your behavior in various ways (as in stopping smoking, dieting or improving study habits) but also that you can do so in large part through covert techniques (such as covertly verbally reinforcing an appropriate act: "Good for me. If I can keep that up, I'll soon have it.").

As noted in our discussion of operant techniques in Chapter 8, some researchers believe that behavioral self-control procedures can be useful in controlling states of consciousness, including getting to sleep and learning to meditate (Coates & Thoresen, 1977; Shapiro & Zifferblatt, 1976). Thoresen has suggested that the logical end point of such developments is to use behavioral self-control techniques to encourage self-actualization; he calls his view *behavioral humanism* (Thoresen, 1972). As you've seen, humanistic approaches suggest that eliminating obvious behavioral problems is only the beginning of self-actualization. Thoresen thus suggests that you not only seek to change bad habits, but that you use the specific techniques he and Mahoney describe to help yourself become the person you would like to be in other ways.

Group therapy has become popular since World War II, and is now widely practiced in a number of forms. One of the earliest of these is an insight-oriented approach called **psychodrama;** participants interact with each other in highly emotional, often confrontational, ways, as if they were playing dramatic roles on a stage. Emotional responses of a gentler sort are the focus of humanistically oriented **encounter groups** (or sensitivity groups), in which participants share their emotional feelings about each other (Rogers, 1970). **Assertiveness training** groups have a behavioral focus: They model and role-play appropriate ways to stand up for one's rights without being either too passive or too aggressive.

In addition, there are other specialized forms of group therapy, such as marital or family therapy in which a family is treated as a whole, in recognition of the close web of relationships that bind family members to each other (Margolin, 1982). Special-problem groups such as Alcoholics Anonymous meet to share common problems and helpful suggestions.

Group therapies seem to offer numerous advantages. Some allow a single therapist to interact with more people than he or she could treat individually, reducing the individual cost or allowing mental hospital patients to see their therapist more often. Other group therapies offer the possibility of directly learning better ways of getting along in social groups, or of coping with a common problem. Unfortunately, however, the research results on group therapies have been the poorest in all of therapy. There are few appropriately controlled studies to indicate whether *any* of these groups is accomplishing its task. (What there is, as you might expect by now, comes primarily from the behaviorally oriented groups.) It is possible that one or more of the group therapies do in fact offer what they claim to offer, but for the most part this remains to be demonstrated. Some attempts to obtain effectiveness data have been initiated, however, so the group therapies may eventually be among the demonstrated possibilities open to the eclectic therapist.

CHAPTER SUMMARY

1 Therapies are of two major types: biological therapies, such as drugs, and psychotherapies. Psychotherapies can be further subdivided into insight therapies, in which talk is the major procedure and self-understanding the major goal, and action therapies, in which active behaviors are both procedures and goals.

2 Contemporary mental hospitals derive from large public asylums of the 16th century. Major changes in these asylums occurred in the 18th century with the development of moral treatment, and in the 20th century with the development of antipsychotic drugs.

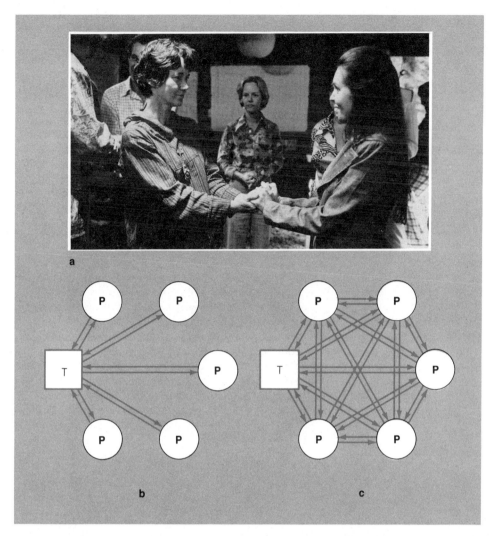

Figure 16.13 ▪ (a) A group therapy session. (b) Group therapy sometimes consists of a series of one-to-one interactions between therapist (T) and patients (P). Other group members listen and may offer support, but do not contribute substantially to interactions other than their own. (c) Group therapy is usually arranged so that all participants interact with each other, to teach patients how to interact in social groups.

(© Karen R. Preuss 1977/Jeroboam)

3 People whose behaviors get them into difficulty may be committed if they are assessed as both mentally ill and dangerous. Once committed, they must convince the staff that they are no longer mentally ill in order to obtain release—although after some time in the hospital, some become adapted and no longer are willing or able to function outside.

4 There are three major biological therapies. Electroconvulsive therapy (ECT) and psychosurgery are each effective for some patients who cannot be helped in other ways, but these therapies are not used in the manner or to the extent that they once were. Drug therapies, although rarely cures, have been responsible for major changes in the number and condition of institutionalized patients since the mid-1950s.

5 Psychotherapy is carried out by several types of professional and paraprofessional workers, including psychiatrists and clinical psychologists. Psychotherapists differ in the type and extent of their professional education and in their beliefs about the causes of abnormal behavior.

6 A continuing argument surrounds the question of whether psychotherapies are effective, but both conceptual and methodological difficulties inhibit easy answers. At present, it seems as if psychotherapies are more effective than no therapy, although the extent of their effects remains in debate.

7 Psychoanalytic and humanistic approaches, notably Rogers's client-centered therapy, are the major insight therapies. Psychoanalysis was for many years *the* psychotherapy and remains the image many people have of therapy, despite the fact that there are few data to indicate its effectiveness. Rogers has been more interested in research on effectiveness than have psychoanalytic therapists, but the data for the effectiveness of client-centered therapy remain limited.

8 The predominant action therapies, the behavioral therapies, have been successful with a range of clients, including those unable to cooperate in insight therapy. Therapies based on classical conditioning include systematic desensitization; those based on operant conditioning include token economies. Lovaas's work with autistic children illustrates the behavioral view of treatment ethics, in which developing the client's skills is the highest goal.

9 The other action therapies, the cognitive-behavioral approaches, include social-learning therapy (which adds modeling and other cognitive elements to operant techniques) and several others: Ellis's rational-emotive therapy, Beck's cognitive restructuring, and Meichenbaum's self-instructional approach. Cognitive-behavioral techniques can also be used for self-control.

10 A number of group therapies are widely used for different goals, but there is little evidence that these are effective in fulfilling their claims.

Further Readings

For general coverage of all therapeutic issues, see a contemporary text of abnormal psychology, such as Coleman, Butcher, and Carson's *Abnormal Psychology and Modern Life* (1980) or Davison and Neale's *Abnormal Psychology* (1982). London's insight/action distinction is presented in *The Modes and Morals of Psychotherapy* (1964); the book is somewhat dated, but the distinctions offer a useful framework for comparing psychotherapies. For special issues concerning commitment, see Monahan's *The Clinical Prediction of Violent Behavior* (1981), Szasz's critique of commitment in *Law, Liberty, and Psychiatry* (1963), or Goffman's sociological analysis of some aspects of mental hospitals in *Asylums* (1961). Rosenhan's article "On Being Sane in Insane Places" (1973) gives a first-person view of the hospitalization experience as it appears to a pseudopatient. Legal issues in commitment and otherwise are discussed in *Law and Psychological Practice* (1980) by Schwitzgebel and Schwitzgebel. Types of biological therapies are the topics of Fink's *Convulsive Therapy* (1979), Valenstein's *The Psychosurgery Debate* (1980), and Ray's *Drugs, Society and Human Behavior* (1978). For various psychotherapies, see the texts noted earlier or Garfield and Bergin's collection, *Handbook of Psychotherapy and Behavior Change* (1978). Psychotherapy effectiveness is discussed in Rachman and Wilson's *The Effects of Psychological Therapy* (1980). For specialized topics, note Lovaas's *The Autistic Child* (1977), Ayllon and Azrin's *The Token Economy* (1968), and Mahoney and Thoresen's *Self-Control: Power to the Person* (1974).

Part VI

Social Issues and Applications

Seeking a way to earn a few extra dollars, you notice an advertisement in the local paper asking for subjects for a psychology experiment. You decide to try it. The experimenter explains, to you and another subject, that the experiment concerns the effects of punishment on learning. You and the other subject will draw lots to see who will be the "teacher" and who will be the "learner." The learner will attempt to memorize a list of word pairs, so he or she can respond to the first word of each pair with the correct second word. The teacher will present the test words and, if the learner makes an error, will apply a brief electric shock to the learner. You are relieved to find that the random drawing makes you the teacher. After you are given a brief sample shock from the apparatus, you watch the learner being strapped into a chair—"to prevent excessive movement during shock," the experimenter says. Then you are taken into the adjoining room and seated before a long row of switches and an intercom to the learner's room. As the experiment proceeds, you are expected to punish each error with a shock of increasingly higher voltage, always using the next switch in the row. Soon the learner begins to cry out with each shock, then screams in pain, and finally refuses to answer. If you heed the experimenter's demands to continue, the learner eventually falls completely silent—perhaps, you think, from a heart attack. Only when you push the last switch, or when you absolutely refuse to continue, do you discover that you have *not* been participating in a learning study at all. Instead it has been a study of compliance, testing how long you would continue to obey the experimenter. The "learner" is in fact a confederate of the experimenter and has received no shocks.

This arrangement is not imaginary; it was used in one of the best-known and most controversial experiments in social psychology (Milgram, 1963, 1965). Compliance is only one of the topics social psychologists study, and Milgram's experiments placed unusual and controversial demands on his subjects (many cried and trembled even as they continued to apply the shocks). But this experiment nevertheless typifies some aspects of social psychology. As psychology, it focused on individual behavior, that of the "teacher." But as *social* psychology, it emphasized influences on behavior from conflicting social pressures, empathy for the other subject versus the experimenter's demands. You probably believe that you would soon refuse to continue if you were really in Milgram's study. But his results show that most people, including college students, will press every switch!

Social psychology is the study of human behavior that occurs within, or is influenced by, social groups. It concerns how we perceive ourselves and others, how we develop attitudes toward people or

Social Processes

events, and how we function within various social contexts. In seeking answers to such questions that will be relevant to real issues, social psychologists often use realistic experimental situations. But they sometimes must resort to deceptive explanations of the research, as Milgram did, to obtain realistic behavior from subjects (who might change their actions if they knew the experiment's true intent). Social psychologists must also sometimes cause their subjects psychological discomfort in attempts to understand everyday behavior in socially significant situations.

To know that people will comply with an experimenter's trivial request, for example, tells little about why people will torture or kill each other when told to do so. Milgram's study, with its dramatic and stressful procedures, is ethically debatable but tells us more about the power of social demands than a weaker situation would. In fact, Milgram's original concern was why German citizens went along with Nazi leaders during World War II, and his findings are still applicable to the use and abuse of authority. During the Vietnam War, for example, Lieutenant Calley and the soldiers in his squad explained why they followed orders to massacre women and children at My Lai in terms much like those used by Milgram's subjects: "I had no other choice. It was my duty. Other people in my place would do the same," and so forth.

This chapter examines basic social processes, looking at how we perceive ourselves and others and at how our attitudes are formed and changed and how they influence our behavior. Then, we consider the individual in group settings; we return to Milgram's study as we look at group membership and group conflict. Chapter 18 concludes the text with some important applications of social psychology, including prosocial (altruistic) behavior, aggression, courtroom issues, and environmental influences.

SOCIAL COGNITION

We have already noted the increasing influence in psychology of the information-processing approach: Cognitive models are being applied to consciousness, learning, memory, language, and thought (Chapters 7–11). They are also becoming increasingly important in the study of social behavior; **social cognition** is the study of how we perceive ourselves and others, especially what behaviors we expect from members of various social groups (Higgins et al., 1981; Rosenberg & Kaplan, 1982).

Perceiving Ourselves

Psychologists have long recognized that we monitor and analyze our own behavior (James, 1890), and have noted that self-perception is closely related to our perceptions of others. Charles Horton Cooley (1902), for example, discussed three aspects of our **self-concept:** how we think other people perceive us, how we think they judge us, and how we react to that judgment. Cooley coined the phrase *looking-glass self* to emphasize that we see ourselves as we think others see us. Contemporary social psychologists note that we use our self-concepts to help guide our behavior, both to help us perceive ourselves as consistent and to present ourselves to others as we wish them to see us (Goffman, 1959). ■ Notable Quote: William James on the Self

Self-Schemas Cognitive psychologists often describe human information processing in terms of **schemas,** organized cognitive structures about objects or events. College students, for example, have object schemas such as "my car" and event schemas such as "lecture class." Many schemas concern social interactions; these help us organize incoming information and arrange our behavior in response to social situations (Taylor & Crocker, 1981).

Hazel Markus has suggested that people also organize and explain their experiences in terms of **self-schemas,** cognitive generalizations we use to summarize our personal experiences; these help guide how we think about ourselves and how we behave (Markus, 1977). According to Markus, each person develops self-schemas for important behaviors; students have self-schemas about classroom performance, for example, but nonstudents do not. Some self-schemas are rare, such as a schema for deep-sea diving; others are nearly universal, such as a **gender schema** for one's sense of self as male or female. A person's total set of self-schemas can be considered his or her self-concept (Markus et al., 1982).

Gender Schemas and Androgyny Chapter 4 noted that the gender label assigned at birth and the gender-differentiated rearing that follows assignment have powerful effects on each person's gender identity or gender schema. Assignment and rearing also significantly influence gender role, one of many **role schemas** that shape people's behavior. Other role schemas include student, son or daughter, friend, or employee; each role schema summarizes the cues that elicit it (such as the presence of parents) and the behaviors needed to fulfill it. Like all schemas, role schemas help us simplify our information processing and allow us to adjust our behavior to a situation quickly and automatically.

Unfortunately, the rapid and automatic processing made possible by schemas can also lead to biases in thought and action. **Stereotypes** are oversimplified and overgeneralized schemas that can bias our percep-

Figure 17.1 ■ Stereotypes of roles appropriate to social groups have long constrained who can do what—but perhaps such stereotypes, including racial and gender ones, are beginning to be broken.

(Suzanne Szasz/Photo Researchers)

tion of reality. Later, we will look at stereotyped views of social groups and prejudiced behavior toward those groups. But stereotypes also apply to gender groups: men and women. Substantial current research seeks to discover how sex-role stereotypes develop and are maintained, and how they influence the way people view themselves and others (Broverman et al., 1972). ■ Figure 17.1

Eleanor Maccoby and Carol Jacklin's (1974b) review of sex difference studies (described in Chapter 4) found many gender stereotypes to be myths. Other stereotypes, such as greater aggression in males and better verbal skills in females, were well supported by data. Still other gender-role differences remained possible but undemonstrated, such as a greater propensity for child care in females. Maccoby and Jacklin, who are developmental psychologists, wanted to identify actual behavioral differences. But social psychologists concerned with sex differences have also been interested in people's concepts of ideal behavior. To examine

these, social psychologists have compared people's general gender schemas to their self-schemas. One major finding is that people's actual behaviors often do not correspond to their generalized gender schemas. The generalized schemas seem to be more stereotypes than accurate assessments (Frieze et al., 1978). ■ Table 17.1

Researchers have approached the study of gender self-schemas in several ways. Most have compared individuals' self-schemas to the gender stereotypes. But several researchers have felt that traditional gender stereotypes are misleading in understanding others; instead, they use for comparison the concept of **androgyny,** a gender role that incorporates positive features of both male and female stereotypes.

One major approach is that of Sandra Bem, who has specified androgyny as a balance between extremes of masculine and feminine behavior (1974, 1981a, 1981b). To Bem, androgyny is defined as a self-report of little difference between the number of masculine and feminine traits; a high androgynous person could have many traits of both types or few of them. A different approach is taken by Janet Spence and her associates. Spence lists masculine and feminine characteristics separately, and any person can be high or low on any of these characteristics. To Spence, a high-androgynous individual is simply one who incorporates many elements from both lists and a low-androgynous individual incorporates few elements from either list (Spence & Helmreich, 1981). To compare the two views, note that Bem would rate people who reported few masculine or feminine traits as being high in androgyny, just as if they reported many of each type. But to Spence, having few of each gender-coded trait is low androgynous.

Markus has followed Spence's approach; she has found that people can be divided into four categories on the basis of their self-schemas. Some people's self-schemas are strongly masculine and some are strongly feminine. But high-androgynous subjects identify with both masculine and feminine schemas and low-androgynous subjects identify with neither (Markus et al., 1982). ■ Figure 17.2

The findings of Bem, Spence, and Markus agree that some form of androgyny is more adaptive than traditional, rigidly stereotyped roles. One finding that supports the desirability of androgynous roles is that high-androgynous subjects ranked themselves higher in self-esteem than did other subjects (Spence et al., 1975). This finding strengthens the argument that further reducing sex-role stereotypes will benefit everyone.

Self-perception Most research on self-concept examines subjects' responses to questions chosen by the experimenters. This approach fits a scientific model, in which the experimenter carefully controls the experimental conditions but it means experimenters cannot know how subjects would have described their self-concepts if free to do so. When researchers in one study simply asked sixth-grade students to describe themselves, their responses were different from answers to the usual questions of experimenters (McGuire & Padawer-Singer, 1976). Most studies have asked people about their self-esteem—in effect, how good or bad they think they are. But only 10% of the students described themselves in such evaluative terms. Their responses fell into eight major categories, including descriptions of activities and people significant to them. (Older subjects, of course, might describe themselves differently.)

A long-standing assumption in traditional self-concept research is that humans think about their behavior and plan what they do. But some researchers question the extent to which our behavior is planned. In a series of studies Ellen Langer (1978) has demon-

"A WOMAN OBSTETRICIAN! WHAT DO WOMEN KNOW ABOUT THAT SORT OF THING?"

© 1983 by Sidney Harris

strated that people are often not aware of their behaviors, and that many actions, even social ones, are carried out **mindlessly** (by automatic routines). *Not exercising conscious control of our actions is the norm*, she says; conscious deliberation only occurs under special circumstances. Langer has drawn on the concept of behavioral *scripts*, sequences that describe how common actions normally proceed (Abelson, 1981; Schank & Abelson, 1977). (See Chapter 11.) Humans naturally develop scripts for all routine activities, she argues, and use these scripts to guide their behavior automatically whenever they can. They attend to their behavior only when they encounter a novel situation or when the scripted behavior becomes unusually effortful, is interrupted, or leads to unusual consequences (Langer, 1978).

One study illustrates several of these points (Langer et al., 1978). Confederates asked people waiting in line at a copy machine if they could go ahead of them. The request was phrased in one of three ways: (1) without explanation, (2) with an appropriate explanation ("because I'm in a rush"), and (3) with a placebo explanation ("because I have to make copies"). Not surprisingly, the unexplained request was more often refused than the one with an appropriate explanation. However, the placebo explanation was just as effective

Table 17.1 ■ Comparison of Sex Stereotypes with Actual Findings

	Stereotype*	Strength of Finding
Aggression	Males aggressive; females not at all aggressive.	1. Strong consistent differences in physical aggression. 2. Inconsistent findings with indirect aggression.
Dependency	Females submissive and dependent; males dominant and not at all dependent.	Weak differences, which are more consistent for adults than for children.
Nurturance	Females tactful, gentle, and aware of feelings of others; males blunt, rough, and not at all aware of feelings of others.	Moderate differences on some measures. Overall, findings are inconclusive.
Emotionality	Females emotional and very excitable in a minor crisis; males not at all emotional nor excitable in a minor crisis.	Moderate differences on paper-and-pencil measures. Overall, findings are inconclusive.
Verbal skills	Females very talkative; males not at all talkative.	Moderate differences on some measures, especially for young children.
Math skills	Males like math and science very much; females dislike math and science very much.	Moderate differences on problem-solving tests, especially after adolescence.

*Note: Source for stereotypes: Broverman et al., 1972.

Adapted from *Women and Sex Roles: A Social-Psychological Perspective* by I. Frieze, J. Parsons, P. Johnson, D. Ruble, & G. Zellman, 1978. Used by permission of W. W. Norton and Company, Inc.

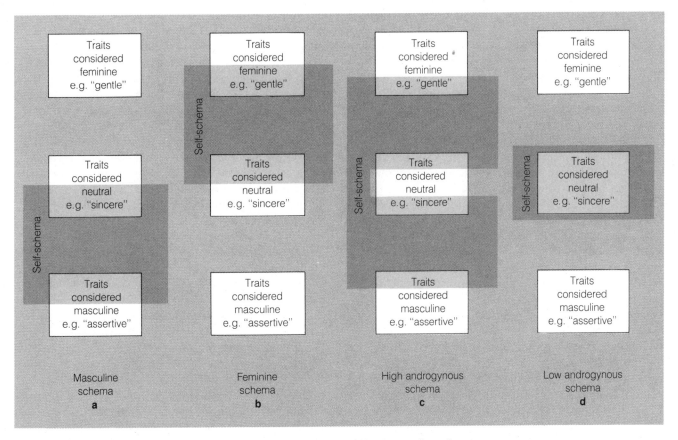

Figure 17.2 ■ Four types of self-schema. (a) Subjects with a strong traditional masculine orientation include stereotypical masculine elements in their self-schemas, but not feminine ones. (b) Subjects with a strong traditional feminine orientation show the opposite pattern, including feminine elements but not masculine ones. (c) High androgynous subjects include both masculine and feminine elements in their self-schemas. (d) Low androgynous subjects include neither masculine nor feminine elements. (Adapted from Markus et al., 1982.)

as the appropriate one. Langer (1978) suggested that the placebo explanation triggered a "favor X + reason Y—comply" script, even though the reason was meaningless (*everyone* was there to make copies). But when confederates asked to make 20 copies rather than 5, the placebo request was rejected as often as the unexplained one. Only when faced with the greater "effort" (anticipated long delay), Langer argued, did subjects actually think about the meaning of the explanation, and only then was their action *mindful*. Even though compliance with the placebo request required substantial information processing, it was carried out at a mindless level.

Nisbett and Wilson (1977) have also shown that subjects can be unaware of the causes of their own behavior. In a number of studies, they manipulated subjects' behavior, then asked them why they behaved as they did. They might, for example, expose subjects to a description of a beach scene and sometime later ask them to name a common detergent. The subjects would be likely to name Tide. But if those who named Tide were asked why, they would only answer that it is a popular brand. Subjects frequently showed no awareness that their behavior had been manipulated, falling back on conventional explanations of why people behave in such ways.

These findings suggest that people often don't pay attention to their own actions; even when they do, they may fail to perceive the causes of their actions. If true, this has several important implications, both for research and for behavior in general. If social psychologists assume people routinely think about their actions and they do not, for example, the research cannot accurately represent reality. (This may not have been noticed before because laboratory experiments are novel situations for most subjects, and hence they will be self-aware in them; Langer, 1978.) Langer's view also suggests that people who live routine lives may become less and less aware of their actions as routine scripts carry them through the day. This may be especially true of people with substantial experience who are now in limited surroundings, such as elderly patients in nursing homes. Such patients may be made more aware, and thereby healthier and happier, by asking them to make even simple choices such as which day to see a movie (Langer & Rodin, 1976).

Other researchers accept that people vary in how closely they observe and analyze their behavior, but are not willing to accept conclusions as extreme as those of Langer or Nisbett and Wilson. Robert Wicklund (1975, 1979), for example, has tried to find out when and why people think about their behaviors and has examined the effects self-awareness can have on those behaviors. Wicklund has suggested that people can consider their own behavior with an **objective self-awareness,** just as they would carefully examine some external event. But people will be objectively self-aware, and their behaviors will agree with their self-concepts, *only* when they pay attention to both their behavior and the relevant aspects of their self-concepts.

In one study demonstrating the effect of self-awareness, Carver (1975) first identified via a questionnaire two groups of subjects, some who supported punitive measures to enhance learning (called *high-punitive*) and some who opposed punitive measures (*low-punitive*). Later in the semester, these subjects participated in a learning experiment in which they supposedly administered shocks to another subject. They were allowed to choose the intensity of the shock, and their choices were considered a measure of their actual punitiveness. In the basic procedure, there was no difference in the shock intensities chosen by subjects who had described themselves as high-punitive and low-punitive. But when subjects faced a mirror during the experiment, the high-punitive ones chose higher shock levels. Apparently seeing themselves in the mirror encouraged self-awareness and then they behaved more in keeping with their previous statements.

One theoretical approach that we will return to later in the chapter focuses on how people develop their self-schemas under conditions of limited awareness. Daryl Bem's (1972) **self-perception theory** states that when people *do* try to understand why they behave, they do so by observing their own overt behavior, just as they would observe the behavior of another person. Self-perception theory argues that people always seek to explain their behaviors, but because they don't know the actual reasons they use the same conventional explanations they would use to assess another person's behavior.

Self-perception theory contradicts common ideas about how we understand ourselves. The conventional view is that we derive self-perception from direct access to our thoughts and sensations. Thus we should know we are hungry by sensations from our stomach or elsewhere in the body. But self-perception theory says we often rely instead on the same external cues that are available to outside observers. If you see someone else eating at a party, says Bem, the explanation is "That person must be hungry." Likewise, if you notice yourself eating, you say "I must be hungry."

Individuals vary in the extent to which they are aware of their own actions, just as they vary in many other respects. Mark Snyder (1979) has studied such differences among people in terms of whether they are high or low in *self-monitoring*. **High self-monitors,** according to Snyder, are particularly sensitive to the social cues offered by other people, and use these cues to monitor (regulate and control) their own social behavior. In contrast, **low self-monitors** are not as aware of situational cues, have a less-varied repertoire of social skills, and are less flexible in adapting to differing situations. High self-monitors tend to agree with statements such as "In order to get along and be liked, I tend to be what people expect me to be rather than anything else," whereas low self-monitors tend to agree with statements such as "I find it hard to imitate the behavior of other people" (Snyder, 1974, p. 531).

According to Snyder, differences in people's level of self-monitoring affect their behavior in all social circumstances. A high self-monitor in a social situation asks "Who does this situation want me to be and how can I be that person?" (Snyder, 1979, p. 102). A low self-monitor in a social situation asks "Who am I and how can I be me in this situation?" (Snyder, 1979, p. 103). High self-monitors behave differently in different situations, and thus seem less consistent when personality traits are measured. Low self-monitors behave more similarly across various situations, and thus seem more consistent when measured in personality traits. As we saw in Chapter 13, the question of traits versus situations has been a controversial issue in personality theory. Snyder's approach promises to help in understanding personality by identifying which people might exhibit cross-situationally variable behavior and which ones might exhibit cross-situationally consistent behavior (Gabrenya & Arkin, 1980).

Perceiving Others

Another traditional area of research within social psychology concerns **person perception,** including how we characterize other people, how we explain their actions, and how we evaluate them as possible friends or enemies.

Forming Impressions   We tend to form impressions of other people quickly and automatically, often on the basis of very limited information. These impressions are typically self-consistent and similar to those formed by other observers in the same situation. Given a brief description of a person, subjects can usually extrapolate what they think that person is like in other ways. They may even do so from a quick glance at a picture. ■ Figure 17.3

But psychologists have learned that the apparent simplicity of these judgments and the agreement among observers is misleading. Impression formation is subject to a variety of *cognitive biases*, some of which are only beginning to be understood. The internal consistency of our impressions, for example, is often achieved by selectively biasing the information to make it seem consistent. And the agreement among observers is more likely to represent shared cultural stereotypes than accuracy.

For many years, psychologists considered impression formation in terms of trait theory (Chapter 13). Subjects might be given several trait labels describing a hypothetical person and asked to describe what else would be true of that person. In general, people have seemed to average these traits in arriving at an overall assessment: A person described using two positive traits and one negative one has been perceived in a generally positive way, reflecting the average of the three traits (Anderson, 1965). One notable exception, however, involves **central traits;** these are traits usually associated with a number of others, such as the evaluative traits *warm* or *cold*. When a central trait is included in the list, it tends to be much more influential than the others in altering the overall impression. In a classic study, Solomon Asch (1946a) gave subjects a list of seven traits: *intelligent, skillful, industrious, determined, practical,* and *cautious,* plus either *warm* or *cold*. Subjects described the people represented by these two lists quite differently; the difference between *warm* and *cold* was far more influential than the difference between other, less-central traits.

The tendency for some traits to bias the perception of others has been termed a **halo effect** when the trait is positive and a **negative halo effect** when it is negative. In the halo effect, a person who has a very positive trait is assumed to have other desirable traits. In the negative halo effect, a person with a very negative trait is assumed to have other negative traits. These halo effects apply to physical appearance as well as to behavioral traits. Other things being equal, people tend to attribute more positive traits to physically attractive people and fewer positive traits to physically unattractive people (Dion et al., 1972). (See Table 17.3 below.)

The set of rules by which people combine traits has been termed an **implicit personality theory** (Rosenberg & Sedlak, 1972). As part of their socialization, people learn to assess each other in particular ways. Each person's experiences are unique, and thus so is each person's implicit personality theory. But broad aspects of implicit personality theories are often widely shared by members of social groups. It is these shared beliefs that often result in observer agreement about someone, entirely apart from whether the observers are accurate in their assessment.

As the concept of personality traits began to be questioned (Chapter 13), so did the use of traits in impression formation. In this area, as in several others in social psychology, recent models have been cognitive, emphasizing how people process information about each other. These cognitive models have re-

a   b

Figure 17.3 ■ Do you think you know what these two people are like? Why? If you think they differ in opinions and behavior, you are forming an impression based on appearance only; this strategy can sometimes be useful but can also easily be incorrect.

(**a**, © Peter Menzel/Stock, Boston; **b**, Tim Carlson/Stock, Boston)

framed some of the old questions in terms of cognitive schemas. When a person quickly forms an impression of someone else, for example, cognitively oriented social psychologists say the person is drawing on a general schema, such as *lawyer, athlete,* or *secretary.* As the observer learns more about the person, the general schema gives way to one developed to fit this person only. Where initial predictions about the person would be based on what a *lawyer* is like, later ones would be based on what *Sally* or *George* is like.

One contemporary approach takes these ideas a step further. Nancy Cantor and Walter Mischel (1977, 1979a) have argued that the concept of **prototype** can be as usefully applied to person perception as to object perception. Cantor and Mischel base their approach on Eleanor Rosch's (1973) concept of prototypes in object categories (Chapter 11). Rosch has noted that the category *chair,* for example, is cog-

nitively represented not by an exact list of attributes, but by a general *family resemblance* (Rosch et al., 1976). Any particular chair is recognized most easily when it is most like the ideal or prototype chair. The less like the prototype, the harder it is for a chair to be recognized as a chair. Rosch has also noted that categories are arranged in hierarchies from more abstract to more detailed ones. Usually, she suggested, people find it easiest to think and talk in terms of middle-level categories, for example, *chair* rather than the more abstract *furniture* or the more detailed *kitchen chair.*

Cantor and Mischel adapted Rosch's prototype/category approach to impression formation by developing three levels of categories to describe persons. They found that both the notion of prototypes and the use of medium levels of abstraction are appropriate to how people form impressions of others. Cantor and Mischel have continued this line of research, seek-

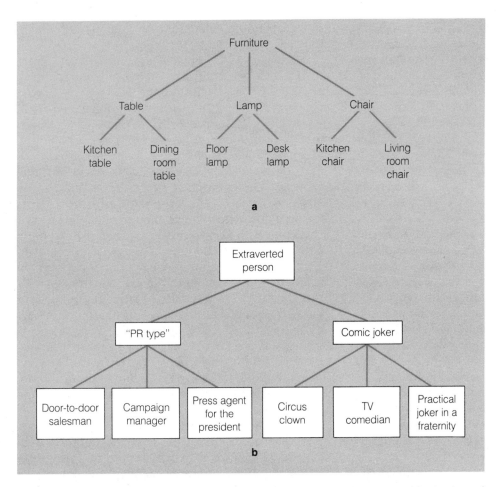

Figure 17.4 ■ Prototypes in person perception. (a) A representation of the concept *furniture*, as proposed by Rosch: middle-level entries, such as *chair*, are easiest to think and talk about; *furniture* is too general and *kitchen chair* too specific. (b) Cantor and Mischel's representation of extroverted personality types. As with object categories, middle-level entries are easiest to use.

(Adapted from N. Cantor and W. Mischel, "Prototypes in Person Perception," in L. Berkowitz (Ed.), *Advances in Experimental Social Psychology, 12,* 3–52, 1979. Used by permission of Academic Press, Inc.)

ing to discover, for example, whether people always use similar levels of description or whether they vary the level to suit the particular task. Also note that people's prototypes can as easily be in error about other people as their implicit personality theories can be. The concept of prototype seems a useful way of describing what people do, but they still may not do it accurately. Cantor and Mischel (1979b) believe that prototypes actually reflect some interaction between real characteristics of the people assessed and concepts added by the person doing the assessing. ■ Figure 17.4

Other cognitive researchers have reexamined biases in impression formation. David Hamilton (1979), for example, has analyzed how people develop and use stereotypes of social groups. Two of the major biases Hamilton has discussed are cue salience and illusory correlations. **Cue salience** refers to the greater impact

that some cues or types of information exert in our impression formation (Taylor & Fiske, 1978). Salient cues are often physical: race, sex, age, mode of dress, physical handicap, and so forth. The more distinctive such cues are, the greater is their impact in impression formation. A single female in a group of males or a single black in a group of whites tends to be characterized more on the basis of sex or race than such a person in a more mixed group (Taylor et al., 1977).

Illusory correlations are subjective assessments of group/behavior correlations that are made by observers when in fact no true correlations exist (Crocker, 1981). Illusory correlations are thought to result from the salience of two kinds of cues: the characteristics of the people being observed and the characteristics of their behavior. Those people who are unusual in a group will be noticed more than other people. And extreme or unpleasant behaviors will be noticed more than other behaviors. Thus the combinations most likely to be noticed and remembered are unusual people behaving in extreme or unpleasant ways. Even if all members of a group behave unpleasantly with the same frequency, the observer will tend to notice and remember when a distinctive minority group member does so. The result is an illusory correlation: The observer sees the distinctive minority member and the extreme behavior as occurring together more often, when in fact this does not happen. Such illusory correlations may importantly contribute to incorrect stereotypes about minority members of social groups (Hamilton, 1981).

Leslie McArthur (1982) has discussed at length how cognitive processes could develop and maintain stereotypes based on any visible physical difference among groups, such as race, sex, or physical handicap. As McArthur noted, such stereotypes influence how people treat each other, creating self-fulfilling prophecies; if people expect a minority person to behave in a certain way, the minority person may in fact do so (Snyder et al., 1977; Word et al., 1974). McArthur also discussed an old cognitive bias called the primacy effect. The **primacy effect** refers to the fact that early information will be easily accepted, as in the formation of impressions, whereas later information may be rejected or modified if it does not match the first impression (Luchins, 1957). Taken together, the current understanding of impression formation's many biases suggests that, as McArthur has said, "We stereotype people who look different because we look at them differently" (1982, p. 204).

Attribution Theory   Other research in social psychology has examined how people explain the causes of another person's behavior. This issue is often expressed in terms of how people attribute behaviors to certain causes (Nisbett & Ross, 1980). **Attribution theory,** an influential theory originally proposed by Fritz Heider (1958), was the dominant social psychological approach throughout the 1960s and 1970s, before yielding to views based on social cognitions (Harvey & Weary, 1981; Kelley & Michela, 1980). Currently, attribution theory is a collection of similar approaches offered by different theorists.

In general, according to attribution theorists, observers attribute others' behaviors to internal and/or external causes in predictable, but not necessarily accurate, ways. *Internal causes* are inferred dispositions, such as traits, motives, emotions, or skills; you see a person eating, and infer that he or she is hungry. *External causes* include anything in the environment outside the person whose behavior is being examined, such as rewards, punishments, role limitations, and so forth; a person may in fact be eating to gain weight for a wres-

tling match or in deference to the person who cooked the food.

Heider's (1958) original approach to attribution theory has been called a naive or common-sense approach to causal attribution. Heider proposed that people seek to explain their environment, especially the actions of other people, by finding a *sufficient reason* for an action (Jones & Davis, 1965). In seeking these reasons, observers look for any effects of the action that the actor could have foreseen and deliberately achieved. Observers then attribute the cause of the action to the observer's *intention* to create these effects. Suppose one person shoots another. First the observer checks for both *knowledge* and *ability* on the part of the person doing the shooting. If that person could not have known the gun was loaded or does not have the ability to hit a target (as in the case of a young child), the shooting is attributed to accident. But if both knowledge and ability are present, the observer then examines the effects of the shot. If the incident involved a policeman shooting a fleeing murder suspect, the attribution would be to the intent to carry out police duties. If it involved a person shooting a spouse after an argument, the attribution might be to anger and an intent to kill.

Heider's approach suggested that people use complex calculations about the world to interpret what they see, looking not only at actions but also at the effects of those actions and the presumed knowledge and ability of the actor. But Heider's original formulation was not precise enough to allow careful experimental tests of his ideas. Jones and Davis (1965) later refined and formalized Heider's approach in terms of correspondent inferences. According to Jones and Davis, observers are likely to make inferences about the cause of some action when the actor's intention is seen as "corresponding" to the behavior and its effect. Attributing the behavior to the actor's intentions and general dispositions to behave was termed making a **correspondent inference.**

People are likely to make correspondent inferences, said Jones and Davis, according to three major criteria: (1) noncommon effects, (2) social desirability, and (3) freedom of choice. *Noncommon effects* are distinctive outcomes of an action that do not follow alternative actions. If the only way a fleeing suspect could be stopped was for a police officer to shoot, "stopping the suspect" would be a noncommon effect and the observer would attribute the shooting to it. But if there had been several ways to stop the suspect, the observer would look for a reason why the officer chose shooting rather than another action. *Socially desirable* acts that everyone might attempt tell little about the actor, whereas socially undesirable actions are presumed to reflect an internal disposition. When a person is smiling and sociable at a party, where everyone is supposed to be friendly, observers will not attribute the smiling to a friendly disposition. But if a person behaves rudely under those circumstances, the observer will attribute that to a general trait of rudeness. Similarly, if the actor is perceived as having little *free choice* in a behavior, the act will not be attributed to a disposition. But if the actor is seen as having free choice, acts will lead to inferences about dispositions.

Jones and Davis (1965) suggested that actions will be attributed to internal dispositions when there are few noncommon effects among possible alternate actions, when social desirability is low, and when freedom of choice is high. (In all cases, these are as perceived by the observer. The observer may or may not be accurate, but will make attributions on the basis of what he or she *thought* was true for the actor.) Jones and Davis's correspondent inferences model generated a great deal of research in the 1960s and 1970s, much of it supporting their proposals, and the model has since been extended and refined (Jones & McGillis, 1976).

Another major variant of attribution theory was proposed by Kelley (1967), who suggested that observers pay attention to three possible causes for actions: (1) persons (dispositions), (2) entities (environmental objects or stimuli), and (3) times (occasions or situations). In attributing an action to one of these causes, observers are assumed to attend to the distinctiveness, consistency, and consensus associated with these possible causes. Behavior is *distinctive* when it is rare or occurs in few situations. It is *consistent* when it occurs in many different situations. And it is high in *consensus* when most people act that way in a similar situation. According to Kelley, attributions will be made to personal dispositions of the actor when behavior is low in distinctiveness, high in consistency, and low in consensus (McArthur, 1972). (This means the actor behaves this way frequently and in different situations, even when most people do not.)

A third major theoretical approach to attribution is that of Weiner and his associates (Weiner et al., 1972). Weiner examined how people attribute success or failure of an action in terms of two dimensions: *internal/external* and *stable/unstable*. Observers are said to attribute behaviors to one of four categories based on these dimensions, depending on how the observers interpret the situation. The internal/external dimension used by Weiner and his associates has been typical of attribution theories. But his addition of the stable/unstable distinction focuses attention on the difference between different types of internal and external attributions. To attribute behavior to an actor's *stable* disposition or ability, for example, is to expect the same behavior on future occasions. But to attribute it to unusual effort

TABLE 17.2 ■ Classification Scheme for the Perceived Determinants of Achievement Behavior

Stability	Locus of Control	
	Internal	External
Stable	Ability	Task difficulty
Unstable	Effort	Luck

Based on Weiner, 1974.

on this occasion (an internal *unstable* cause) is to imply that the behavior may not occur the next time. ■ Table 17.2

These three major theoretical approaches to attribution have all emphasized how observers assess the causes of other people's behaviors. But Bem's self-perception theory, discussed earlier, has also been an important source of attribution research. According to Bem (1972), actors may also make attributions about their own behaviors similar to attributions they make about other people.

Attribution Biases   Research on attribution has uncovered several regular biases in how people attribute the causes of their own and other people's behavior. A variety of these biases arise from the way we usually process information. As noted in Chapter 11, people tend to make certain consistent errors in information processing, such as seeking confirming, rather than disconfirming, evidence. Cognitive biases that yield attribution biases include the tendencies to be more swayed by a few vivid examples than by statistical information and to retain the original view of a relationship even when it is later shown to be incorrect.

The fact that some cues take precedence over others in making attributions has been discussed by Taylor and Fiske (1978) in terms of the salience of these cues. Taylor and Fiske also noted that we frequently tend to make attribution judgments quickly and with little thought—what they call "off the top of the head"—rather than in the careful and calculating fashion implied by Jones and Davis (1965) or Kelley (1967).

Another type of attribution bias derives from the difference between our knowledge of ourselves and our perspective on our own actions versus our knowledge of and perspective on other people. One such bias is **false consensus,** the tendency to assume that most other people behave as we do. One study that demonstrated this asked students to wear a large sign reading "Eat at Joe's"; subjects who agreed to do so estimated that 62% of their peers would also agree, whereas subjects who refused estimated that 67% would also refuse (Ross et al., 1977).

A major attribution bias based on differences in perspective is the **actor-observer difference** suggested by Jones and Nisbett (1972). They noted that observers tend to attribute their own actions to situational factors but tend to attribute others' actions to personal dispositions (Watson, 1982).

The attribution bias that has generated the most research and discussion, however, is the **fundamental attribution error.** This is the tendency to overestimate the importance of internal dispositions as causes of behavior and to underestimate the importance of situational causes (Ross, 1977). If we see a person behave in a manner that seems friendly, aggressive, or honest, for example, we are likely to attribute that behavior to a personal tendency (disposition) to be friendly, aggressive, or honest. In doing so, we tend to overlook situational reasons for these behaviors: The apparently friendly person may be trying to sell something, the apparently aggressive person may be an undercover police officer, and the apparently honest one may know his or her behavior is being observed.

Many studies have confirmed the existence of the fundamental attribution error (Jones, 1979), although some researchers have questioned whether this tendency is important enough to be called *fundamental* and whether it is always an *error* (Harvey & McGlynn, 1982; Harvey et al., 1981). But others have supported the concept (Reeder, 1982). Whether correctly named or not, the fundamental attribution error is an important and pervasive bias in how people interpret the causes of their own and each other's actions.

It is a common finding in attribution research that people tend to take credit for their own successes (attribute them to their own internal dispositions) but blame outside factors for their failures (attribute them to external causes) (Weary & Bradley, 1978). Because logically we should be as responsible (or not responsible) for our failures as for our successes, this is another attribution bias. Initially, researchers identified this as an ego-enhancing motivational bias: People claim their successes but not their failures because it helps them feel good about themselves (Jones & Nisbett, 1972).

But Lee Ross and some other researchers have challenged this introduction of motivational explanations (Miller & Ross, 1975; Ross, 1977). They argued that cognitive interpretations alone are enough to explain the different attributions concerning success and failure. People normally *intend* and *expect* to succeed, they noted. Thus successes fit expectations and are seen as following directly from internal dispositions, most specifically the intent to succeed. But failures are unintended and unexpected, and thus must logically reflect some other influence than the actor's own dis-

positions. Other researchers, however, have continued to argue that motivational bias better explains the total pattern of findings (Weary Bradley, 1978), and the explanation of this bias remains unresolved (Harvey & Weary, 1981).

Interpersonal Behavior

Social psychologists are interested in many aspects of how people interact with each other. We will consider interaction patterns in groups later. In this section, we examine social psychologists' views of two aspects of individual interactions: loneliness and interpersonal attraction.

Loneliness Loneliness is a relatively new topic in experimental social psychology, athough it has long been of interest to psychotherapists. But loneliness has come to be recognized as an extremely common and serious problem. One national study, for example, found that more than a quarter of all Americans—the equivalent of 50 million people—reported recently feeling lonely (Weiss, 1973). ■ Figure 17.5

Loneliness is now defined as an aversive subjective experience resulting from a deficiency in social relationships (Perlman & Peplau, 1982). The aversiveness of being lonely can range from mild discomfort to severe pain. "Subjective experience" is used in the definition because the number and quality of actual social interactions are less important than the perception of whether they are adequate; some people are not lonely even when alone and others are lonely in a crowd. Thus, social deficiency does not depend simply on how many social contacts a person has but on the quality of those contacts, particularly the number of close or intimate contacts, as contrasted to the person's expectations (Peplau & Perlman, 1982). Several measurement scales have been developed to assess loneliness. Perhaps the best known is the UCLA Loneliness Scale (Russell et al., 1980), which assesses both the cognitive beliefs concerning social contacts and the emotional tone associated with these contacts.

Occasional transient loneliness is common—perhaps universal. Research is usually concerned with severe or long-lasting loneliness. Researchers also distinguish between *situational* loneliness resulting from some change in social circumstances (such as a spouse's death or a move to a different part of the country) and *chronic* loneliness. Some researchers believe that situational loneliness can become chronic unless something or someone intervenes to prevent it (Perlman & Peplau, 1982).

Loneliness results from the interaction of personal characteristics and situations. Sometimes situations are most important. People who have few social con-

Figure 17.5 ■ More than a quarter of all Americans report some loneliness. Who is lonely and why are topics now being explored by some social psychologists.
(© 1983 Leif Skoogfors/Woodfin Camp & Associates)

tacts of any sort, or few that can be expected to yield friendships, may be lonely despite their willingness and ability to interact socially. A forest ranger may live alone in the woods, an elderly person may be confined to his or her room by illness, or a student with a heavy course load may spend most of his or her time studying. All may feel lonely largely as a result of situational factors.

But many people are apparently lonely more because of personal characteristics than situational ones. Personal characteristics associated with loneliness include low self-esteem, shyness, and self-consciousness (Perlman & Peplau, 1982). In demographic terms, more loneliness is reported by adolescents than other age groups, and by widowed than by divorced people, who in turn report more loneliness than those never married. Loneliness is, not surprisingly, least common among those currently married. Socioeconomic status and ethnic group membership may also influence loneliness; it has repeatedly been found to be greater for lower-income groups (e.g., Weiss, 1973) and may be lower among specific ethnic or racial groups, though little evidence has been obtained to date (Dunn & Dunn, 1980).

Sex differences are not usually found on the UCLA Loneliness Scale, but men do report less loneliness in response to direct questions than do women. This may reflect a difference in willingness to report loneliness, however, rather than different experiences. When

questioned, men seem to comply with a social expectation that they *should* be less lonely, and therefore report lower levels than women, even though their experiences are no different (Borys et al., 1982).

Researchers have identified several patterns of behavior that differ between lonely and nonlonely persons. Lonely subjects are *low self-disclosers,* for example; in conversations with persons of the opposite sex, they begin with a low degree of intimate self-disclosure and maintain that nonintimate level throughout the conversation (Solano et al., 1982). In contrast, nonlonely subjects (especially males) reserve the less intimate levels for same-sex conversations. Nonlonely subjects of both sexes typically begin an opposite-sex conversation with a personal disclosure, then gradually escalate the level of intimacy in small increments.

Lonely subjects are also low in various other social skills, including a set of skills termed *partner attention.* Lonely subjects seem less aware of others and more self-absorbed in social encounters; they ask fewer questions and make fewer statements about the other person than do nonlonely subjects (Jones et al., 1982). This low level of social attention and social reinforcement may lead to rejection by others.

We need to know much more about the causes of loneliness if it is to be cured or prevented, but research has already suggested several possibilities for reducing loneliness. One of the benefits of a "social-skills" approach, for example, is that it may be possible to teach people the skills they lack. When lonely subjects were taught to use partner attention in social interactions, they reported significant reductions in loneliness (Jones et al., 1982).

Interpersonal Attraction Interpersonal attraction is one of the oldest topics in social psychology. Research began soon after World War II with studies of who became friends with whom, then later expanded to include romantic attachment and love. Researchers have described a number of variables that affect interpersonal attraction. We will consider three of the most powerful: proximity (physical closeness), similarity, and physical attractiveness.

One of the earliest and best-known studies in social psychology was an investigation of friendship patterns in student housing by Festinger, Schachter, and Back (1950). They found a powerful *proximity* effect in friendship choices: Residents generally became friends with the people living closest to them, even though all had been randomly assigned to rooms. Asked to name the people they often saw socially, residents specified next-door neighbors 41% of the time, those two doors away 22%, and those at the end of the hall 10%. Similar results were found in a new suburban community where all houses were similar and residents moved in at about the same time; nearly all participants at social events, as reported in the local paper's social column, lived very close to each other (Whyte, 1956).

Later research (for example, Priest and Sawyer, 1967) continued to find a proximity effect. Patterns of friendship are strongly influenced by how closely people are placed together. In one of the more striking studies, Segal (1974) examined friendship patterns that developed in a group of state police trainees. The trainees were always lined up alphabetically at the academy; after six weeks, most listed as friends other trainees whose names were very close to theirs in alphabetical order. ■ Figure 17.6

Other variables that have been explored may be related to physical closeness. The closest people are also most likely to become familiar, are most likely to be interacted with, and may be seen as most predictable; all of these variables are known to increase liking. Overall, physical closeness seems a powerful determiner of who will come to like whom; the variables of familiarity, interaction, and predictability describe particular aspects of *how* closeness leads to liking.

Work in the 1960s added *similarity* as another major determinant of friendship (Berscheid & Walster, 1969). One researcher who studied college dormitory friendship patterns was able to control experimentally how roommates were assigned (Newcomb, 1961). Newcomb arranged roommate assignments for one dormitory so that some roommate pairs were similar to each other and some were dissimilar. Even though all pairs were physically close, only the similar ones tended to become friends. (Note that similarity might be a more powerful variable in many situations than it probably was in the proximity studies noted earlier; all students in one dorm or police trainees in one class are probably similar in many respects.)

Researchers have investigated in the laboratory similarities on a number of other dimensions, including attitudes toward various topics. Some have also used **field studies,** experiments conducted in natural settings, often with people who never know that they have been experimental subjects. One field study, for example, explored friendship by investigating the existing friendship patterns of high-school students to see what characteristics friends might share (Kandel, 1978). Kandel found the greatest similarity on four sociodemographic characteristics: grade in school, sex, race, and age. Nearly everyone's best friends were other students of the same grade and sex, and most were of the same race and age. These results are not very surprising on a number of grounds: School grade and age determine physical closeness, and sex and race are visible indicators of membership in important social groups.

What was surprising was the pattern of similarities in other variables. Many variables you might expect to be important were very low in similarity, including parents' education, parents' income levels, and students' career orientation. The greatest similarities were in use of illegal drugs, especially marijuana and LSD; these similarities were far more predictive of friendships than several dozen other variables (apart from the four demographic ones). Note that these data do not say whether drug users become friends or friends convince each other to share drug use. It is likely that both processes play some role, with similar behaviors leading to friendship and friendship encouraging further similarity. (Both of these factors were present in Newcomb's 1961 study.)

A third major variable that affects friendship, and becomes especially important in patterns of dating and marriage, is *physical attractiveness* (Berscheid & Walster, 1974b). Definitions of what attributes are physically attractive are in large part determined by a person's culture: chipped teeth, body scars, artificially elongated heads, and bound feet are among the characteristics that have been deemed attractive in different cultures (Garfield, 1982). But given a culture's definition of physical attractiveness, those people who meet the definition are most desired as friends, lovers, and mates.

In fact, the variable of physical attractiveness affects almost all aspects of how a person is perceived by

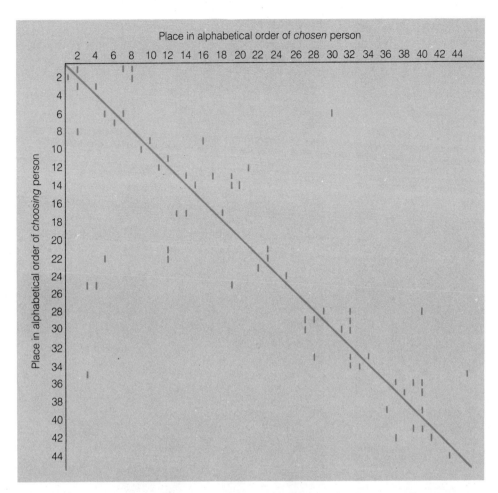

Figure 17.6 ■ The matrix of friendship choices in state police trainees. Most named as their best friends others very close to themselves in alphabetical sequence, apparently because they were seated in alphabetical order during training and thus were physically close together. (This diagram is similar to a correlation scatter plot, but because individuals could not choose themselves as friends, there are no entries directly on the diagonal line.)

(From M. W. Segal, *Journal of Personality and Social Psychology, 30*, No. 5, 1974, 654–657. Copyright 1974 by the American Psychological Association. Reprinted by permission of the author.)

others. In a well-known report entitled "What Is Beautiful Is Good," Dion and her associates (1972) noted that physically attractive people were rated as having a wide range of socially desirable traits and were expected to be more competent and happier. Only in rare cases did this halo effect of attractiveness break down: The physically attractive were *not* expected to be better parents, for example. In contrast, physically unattractive people were characterized negatively, reflecting the negative halo effect. ■ Table 17.3

It is obvious, however, that not everyone can find an exceedingly attractive partner; by definition, many more people are average than unusually attractive. Researchers have wondered how people arrange their patterns of dating and mating in terms of each other's attractiveness. One possibility might be that people seek partners who are about as attractive as they are.

Table 17.3 ■ The Halo and Negative Halo Effects

Trait Rating Assigned by Subjects[a]	Attractive Person	Average Person	Unattractive Person
Social desirability of personality	65.39	62.42	56.31
Occupational status	2.25	2.02	1.70
Marital competence	1.70	.71	.37
Parental competence	3.54	4.55	3.91
Social and professional happiness	6.37	6.34	5.28
Total happiness	11.60	11.60	8.83
Likelihood of marriage	2.17	1.82	1.52

[a]The higher the number, the more socially desirable, the more prestigious an occupation, and so on, the stimulus person is expected to possess.

Adapted from K. Dion et al., *Journal of Personality and Social Psychology,* 1972, *24*, 285–290. Copyright 1972 by the American Psychological Association. Adapted by permission of the authors.

Figure 17.7 ■ People tend to choose partners who are similar to themselves in many respects, including degree of physical attractiveness.

(left, Fredrik D. Bodin/Stock, Boston; top right, Jean-Claude Lejeune/Stock, Boston; bottom right, Stock, Boston)

But when Walster and her colleagues (1966) tested this *matching hypothesis,* they found it didn't hold. In their "computer-dating" study, subjects who were randomly matched sought further dates solely on the basis of their dates' physical attractiveness, regardless of their own attractiveness.

Other researchers have since found that both dating and engaged couples *are* similar in attractiveness, however (e.g., Murstein, 1972). It thus seems that people may initially seek the most attractive dates, but in the long run they settle for dates and mates who are similar to themselves in degree of physical attractiveness. (Remember that similarity also increases liking.) ■ Figure 17.7

The questions of friendship and attraction lead toward the concept of romantic love. But comparatively little research has been done on how liking leads to loving. Researchers who have studied this include Zick Rubin (1973, 1974) as well as Ellen Berscheid and Elaine Walster (1974a), whose research, you may recall from Chapter 1, Senator William Proxmire thought was unnecessary or inappropriate and thus deserving of his Golden Fleece award. Romantic love is likely to be influenced by many of the same factors that influence friendship, but the additional factors that lead to the intensity and focus that characterize love are not yet known.

ATTITUDES

Attitudes have often been defined by social psychologists in terms of three factors: cognitive *beliefs* about a person or object, affective or evaluative *feelings* about

One-item Rating Scale

How much do you like the church?

not at all ___ ___ ___ ___ ___ ___ ___ very much

  1   2   3   4   5   6   7

Likert Scale

For each statement, check the extent to which you agree.
1.   I believe that the church is the greatest institution in America today.
(+2) ____ strongly agree
(+1) ____ moderately agree
(0) ____ neutral
(−1) ____ moderately disagree
(−2) ____ strongly disagree
2.   The church represents shallowness, hypocrisy, and prejudice.
(−2) ____ strongly agree
(−1) ____ moderately agree
(0) ____ neutral
(+1) ____ moderately disagree
(+2) ____ strongly disagree

Thurstone Scale (Adapted from Thurstone & Chave, 1929)

Check the statements with which you agree:
____ 1. I enjoy the church because there is a spirit of friendliness there. (3.3)
____ 2. I respect any church members' beliefs, but I think it is all "bunk." (8.8)
____ 3. I think the organized church is an enemy of science and truth. (10.7)
____ 4. I believe in what the church teaches but with mental reservations. (4.5)
____ 5. I feel that church services give me inspiration and help me to live up to my best during the following week. (1.7)
____ 6. I feel the need for religion but do not find what I want in any one church. (6.1)

Figure 17.8 ■ Three types of scales for measuring attitudes.

(From *Attitudes and Persuasion: Classic and Contemporary Approaches* by Richard E. Petty and John T. Cacioppo. © 1981 Wm. C. Brown Publishers, Dubuque, Iowa. All rights reserved. Reprinted by permission.)

that person or object, and *behavior* toward that person or object. Some psychologists have suggested that all three of these components together make up an attitude (Freedman et al., 1981). But perhaps the most common contemporary definition equates an **attitude** with the evaluative or feeling component. Beliefs are closely related, in that they influence the development and maintenance of attitudes. And behavior is closely related, because attitudes often lead to behaviors that reflect the attitudes—although just how closely attitudes and behavior are related is a major area of research (Petty & Cacioppo, 1981). A person might have a set of beliefs about Chevrolets, for example, including correct facts about their size and shape as well as some incorrect beliefs. But the person's attitude toward Chevrolets is his or her general and enduring evaluation of them as good or bad cars. The question

of whether attitudes determine behavior would then focus on whether the person's attitude was related to the purchase of a Chevrolet.

Measurements of attitudes vary in complexity from one-item scales that ask how much a person or object is liked, through Likert scales, which ask for the degree of agreement with statements about the person or object, to Thurstone scales, complex scales that assign point values to various statements about the person or object (Thurstone & Chave, 1929). These methods of assessing attitudes vary in reliability and in difficulty of construction and use. But the one-item rating scale is reliable enough to be widely used; the more complex scales are more precise, but often such precision is unnecessary. ■ Figure 17.8

Attitudes have long been a major topic of research in social psychology. Relatively little of this research has been devoted to attitude formation, though psychologists generally assume that attitudes are learned through a variety of experiences. Most research has focused on attitude change, beginning with a series of attempts during World War II to modify the attitudes of both military personnel and civilians. The most active area of current research, however, is the study of how behavior is related to attitudes.

Attitude Formation

It is comparatively easy to evaluate attitudes; people can often express how much they like or dislike something in simple terms (Staats et al., 1962). But the sources of these attitudes are complex and subtle. Researchers have demonstrated that attitudes can be learned by several of the forms of learning described in Chapter 8: classical, operant, and observational.

Classical conditioning studies have shown that pairing an object with a stimulus that elicits an unpleasant response will result in a more negative attitude toward the object. When words were paired with electric shocks, for example, the words alone came to be described in more negative terms (Staats et al., 1962). Attitudes can even be conditioned by pairing with other stimuli that have already been conditioned through second-order conditioning (Staats & Staats, 1958). Subjects saw nonsense syllables on a screen as they heard words that already elicited favorable or unfavorable reactions (such as *beauty* or *ugly*); as a result, they developed comparable attitudes toward the nonsense syllables.

Interest in operant learning of attitudes derived from Greenspoon's (1955) well-known experiment in which he increased the number of plural nouns used in conversation by reinforcing them with a murmured "mm-hmmm." Hildum and Brown (1956) used similar verbal reinforcement of subjects' positive or negative attitude statements about their college and found that this increased the number of positive or negative statements. Verbal statements alone do not demonstrate that attitudes have changed, of course, but later research has shown that similar operant techniques do result in stable attitude change (e.g., Insko, 1965).

Observational learning of attitudes has also been demonstrated. As with other forms of observational learning, what models actually do may be more important than what they say. For example, children who saw adult models advocate either charity or greed, and also saw them behave charitably or greedily when asked for a donation, were more influenced by the action than by the words (Rushton, 1975).

The complexity of attitude learning has been shown by studies that indicate the possibility of *vicarious classical conditioning*, that is, classical conditioning through observation. In one such study, subjects watched a model wince in apparent pain at a series of supposed electric shocks, though the model actually received no shocks. After repeated pairings of a CS tone and the model's painful expression, the observers themselves came to show painlike facial expressions in response to the tone (Vaughn & Lanzetta, 1980).

Such findings show that people form attitudes toward other people or objects through a variety of learning experiences, including second-order conditioning or vicarious classical conditioning. They suggest that we can form attitudes toward people or events with which we have no direct experience—simply because they are associated with other things we like or dislike or because someone else likes or dislikes them (Petty & Cacioppo, 1981).

Attitude Change

Studies of attitude change have been based on a number of different theoretical approaches, but in general the theories have been either motivational or informational in format. We will consider these types of theories separately.

Motivational Theories   Most motivational approaches assume that people's attitudes have cognitive components and that they are motivated to keep these cognitions balanced or consistent (Abelson et al., 1968). Such approaches include Heider's balance theory and Festinger's cognitive dissonance theory.

Fritz Heider's (1958) **balance theory** proposed that the relationship between two or three key elements—such as a subject or person (*p*), some other person (*o*), and an object or event (*x*)—can be either balanced or unbalanced. An unbalanced relationship

among elements motivates people to alter the relationship toward balance. Relations among the elements are stated in terms of whether each person likes or dislikes the other elements. If both people like each other and also the object, the relationship is balanced: Sue likes Lee, Lee likes Sue, and both like a democratic form of government. Various imbalances can also exist, however, and they motivate change: Sue likes Lee and Lee likes Sue, but Lee likes a democratic government and Sue, a Communist, does not. In this case Lee might either change his mind about Sue or about governments, but Heider's theory implies the motivation to seek *some* balanced resolution. ■ Figure 17.9

Leon Festinger's (1957) **cognitive dissonance theory** focuses on paired relationships between specific cognitions within a single individual. Two cognitions that do not fit are *dissonant* and this misfit motivates change toward a better fit, or being *consonant*. Cognitive dissonance theory has generated more research than any other theory of attitudes, perhaps more than any other theory in social psychology. Some of its implications are quite surprising and, although years of research have suggested a narrower range of application than originally proposed, it remains a major approach to attitude change (Wicklund & Brehm, 1976).

In Festinger's theory, two cognitions are consonant if one follows from the other. They can also be neutral if one has no relationship to the other. But when they are dissonant—that is, when one implies the opposite of the other—the person is motivated toward consonance. Consonance can be achieved in several ways, especially by changing one of the cognitions.

The most surprising implications for attitude change follow when one cognition is that the person has behaved in a particular way and the other is an attitude toward that behavior. If a person were somehow to behave in a way contrary to his or her attitude, dissonance theory suggests that the attitude might change to be consonant with the behavior. The longstanding view of attitudes was that they caused behavior, not vice versa, so this has been a revolutionary idea.

One type of finding that has supported dissonance theory concerns people faced with a decision between two nearly equal alternatives. Researchers have found that once a choice is made, people raise their opinion of the chosen alternative and lower their opinion of the rejected alternative (Younger et al., 1977). According to cognitive dissonance theory, knowing that the alternative you chose has some flaws causes dissonance and you will discount its flaws. Knowing that the alternative you rejected has advantages also causes dissonance and you will discount its advantages. The

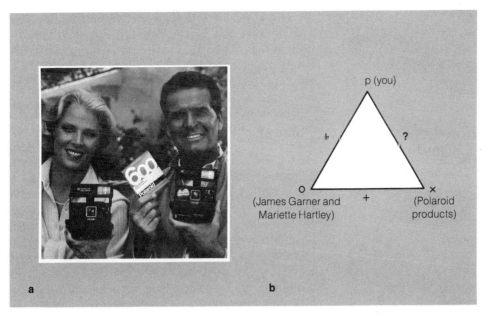

a   b

Figure 17.9 ■ Balance theory applied to advertising. The reader is *p*, the celebrities are *o*, and the camera is *x*. The ad says the celebrities like the camera and the advertiser expects the reader to have or to form a positive attraction to the celebrities. To balance the set of three, the reader would then develop a positive attitude toward the camera.

(Photo courtesy of the Polaroid Corporation)

result is a *postdecisional spreading* between attitudes toward the two alternatives, causing them to appear more unlike each other than they did before the choice was made. Suppose you initially cannot decide whether to buy the blue slacks or the brown ones. After you choose the brown ones, they will seem more clearly superior than they did before you chose them, because you now emphasize their advantages and the disadvantages of the blue ones.

A more surprising outcome concerns the effects of behavior that goes against existing attitudes but seems to have **insufficient justification.** The classic insufficient-justification study was done by Festinger and Carlsmith (1959). They convinced subjects who had just spent time at an insufferably boring task to tell later subjects how interesting the task was. Some subjects were paid $1 to talk to later subjects and others were paid $20. Subjects' cognitions "I thought this was boring" and "I said this was interesting" were thus dissonant. The $20 fee, however, was sufficient justification to make the first two statements consonant: "I'm willing to tell a white lie for $20." But $1 was apparently insufficient justification for the dissonance; the $1 subjects thus reduced their dissonance by changing their attitudes toward the task, deciding that it was actually rather interesting.

The insufficient-justification effect was later found in other studies, all of which initially seemed to pose a paradox: Reinforcement theory says people will like something more when they receive *more* reward, but these results suggested they would like it more when they receive *less* reward. Further research has shown that both effects occur, with particular details of the arrangement being critical for the insufficient-justification effect. Dissonance leading to attitude change occurs only when the person feels responsible for the dissonant elements and when the consequence is negative. ("I did it freely, and it had a negative effect, so I must have felt strongly about doing it.") A person who believes that he or she had no choice will not change attitudes. And if the outcome is favorable, it seems to balance the cognitions. ("I did something I don't believe in, but for a good cause.")

Many other studies have explored when and how dissonance is created and what effects it may have on attitudes (Wicklund & Brehm, 1976). Although some limits have been discovered, dissonance theory often predicts well what people will do. One aspect of dissonance theory that has only been tested recently, however, is the extent to which the motivational effects of dissonance are akin to physiological motivations such as hunger or thirst (Chapter 4). One study, however, used psychophysiological measures to demonstrate for the first time that cognitive dissonance leads to a generalized body arousal, as other motives do (Fazio & Cooper, in press).

Figure 17.10 ■ In seeking to appear to be credible communicators, people may associate themselves with objects, such as the flag, that are positively perceived and symbolize power.

(W. McNamee/Woodfin Camp & Associates)

Informational Theories An alternate approach to attitudes that also has a long history is an informational or cognitive approach. The major informational approach has been the **message-learning** approach developed by Carl Hovland and others (1953) at Yale. (This approach is also known as the *Yale school*.) Hovland's view of attitude change focused on persuasive communications designed to change someone's attitudes. It separated and examined important aspects of the communication's *source*, the *message* itself, the *recipient* (or target) of the message, and the *channel* of communication. These measurable independent variables were thought to influence such mediating processes as paying attention to the message, comprehending the message, yielding to the persuasion, and retaining the changed attitude. An effective message would change the recipient's attitude and probably also change beliefs and behaviors related to that attitude.

The source of a persuasive communication can be a person, a group, or an institution. Researchers have studied the influence of **source factors** by giving different subjects the same message but attributing it to different sources (e.g., Kelman & Hovland, 1953). One important source variable is **communicator credibility,** or overall believability. In general, people are more likely to accept a persuasive communication from a high-credibility source than one from a low-credibility source. Credibility effects are more likely to be found when the issue is not personally relevant or significant to the recipient, however. (This is something like "This person should know, and it doesn't make much difference to me, so I'll accept it.") The recipient may judge a communicator to be credible because he or she is an expert, is perceived as trustworthy, or for other reasons. Expertise is a more important factor when extreme changes in attitude are called for; apparently only special knowledge can justify an extreme claim. Other relevant source factors include attractiveness, similarity to the recipient, and power over the recipient. (The power variable is unusual because it is likely to cause overt compliance without true attitude change.) ■ Figure 17.10

Message factors investigated by the Yale school typically concerned structural features of the message: the emotional tone, the type of conclusion, and so forth. Relevant message factors include the comprehensibility of the message (if it cannot be understood, it will not cause attitude change), the number of arguments (more are better, until people get bored), and whether to draw the conclusion or leave it to the listener to do so (leave it to the listener, if you are sure he or she will draw that conclusion). One review suggested another important message factor, the quality of the arguments themselves: Petty and Cacioppo (1981) suggested that some inconsistencies in the findings on message factors may reflect unnoticed differences in the quality of the persuasive arguments used in different studies.

The style of presentation can also be important. Humor helps only some presentations but a rapid and fluent delivery is almost always effective. Another important variable is the timing of the message, but the effect is somewhat complex. If two opposing arguments are presented, as in a trial or before an election, which sequence is more effective depends on details of the timing (Miller & Campbell, 1959). In some cases, the first message will be more effective (a primacy effect), but in other cases, the second will be more effective (a recency effect). (Note that the primacy and recency effects here are not identical to similarly named memory effects discussed in Chapter 9, but they are related; in both memory and message presentation, the first and last items have an advantage.)

One widely studied message factor is fear arousal. A classic study by Janis and Feshbach (1953) found a low-fear condition most effective, but some later studies found high-fear messages most effective (e.g., Leventhal, 1970). Further research suggests that high fear arousal (as in advertising that suggests smoking cigarettes will kill you) will be effective when the message includes three elements: strong arguments for a negative consequence, arguments that the negative consequence is highly likely if the recommendations are not accepted, and strong assurances that accepting the recommendations will eliminate the negative consequence. ■ Figure 17.11

Important **recipient factors** include age, intelligence, and self-esteem. Children become more persuasible as they get older, up to about the age of eight; after that they become gradually less persuasible until they become adults, with little change thereafter. Intelligent recipients comprehend a message more easily but are also more likely to resist it; level of intelligence thus interacts with the complexity of the message (McGuire, 1968). In general, people with lower self-esteem are more persuasible. Women are generally more persuasible than men (Cooper, 1979). This may be because women's socialization has traditionally encouraged cooperation whereas men's has encouraged independence, or it may be because most of the messages used in the studies have been of more interest to men; people with little prior interest in or knowledge of a topic are more easily persuaded (Eagly et al., 1981).

A more recently developed approach that complements the Yale school is the **cognitive response approach;** it assumes that the importance of source, message, and recipient variables lies in the cognitive responses they lead to (Petty & Cacioppo, 1981). According to cognitive response theory, the recipient generates cognitive arguments for or against the message, depending on aspects of both the message and the recipient. If something about the message or its presentation suggests it is seeking to convince the recipient for ulterior motives (as in advertising), the recipient may think of counterarguments as a defense. If the message comes from someone who is trying to help (such as a physician), the recipient may think of supporting arguments.

These internal cognitions are crucial to attitude change; whatever encourages the recipient to argue in favor of the message will aid persuasibility. Researchers have noted, for example, a phenomenon termed **inoculation:** presenting weak arguments against the advocated position and then countering them (McGuire, 1964). (The analogy is to medical inoculation: presenting a weakened form of a disease to develop antibodies against it.) Cognitive-response researchers

Mark Waters was a chain smoker. Wonder who'll get his office?

Too bad about Mark. Kept hearing the same thing everyone does about lung cancer. But, like so many people, he kept right on smoking cigarettes. Must have thought, "been smoking all my life... what good'll it do to stop now?" Fact is, once you've stopped smoking, no matter how long you've smoked, the body begins to reverse the damage done by cigarettes, provided cancer or emphysema have not developed. Next time you reach for a cigarette, think of Mark. Then think of your office—and your home.
American Cancer Society

Figure 17.11 ■ An ad based on fear arousal.
(American Cancer Society)

now include inoculation in a group of effects termed **forewarning** effects. Anything that warns a recipient that someone is about to try to change his or her mind, they say, will generate a rehearsal of counterarguments that will help resist persuasion (Petty & Cacioppo, 1977).

Cognitive response theory and other self-persuasion approaches have provided insights into aspects of attitude change that had not been understood before. But they are probably best considered as supplements to the earlier views. Petty and Cacioppo (1981) suggested that a blending of self-persuasion and other approaches holds the most promise for the future. (Self-persuasion analyses might help researchers understand *why* particular source, message, or recipient factors were effective, for example.)

Attitudes and Behavior

Early attitude theorists operated under the assumption that attitudes would automatically be reflected in behavior. One of the first important challenges to this idea was raised in a famous study by LaPiere (1934). LaPiere, a Caucasian, toured the United States with a young Chinese couple; they stayed at 66 hotels or motels and ate at 184 restaurants. Despite a strong anti-Oriental prejudice at that time, all but one of the hotels and motels let them in and all the restaurants served them. Yet when LaPiere wrote these same places six months later, asking if they would admit Chinese, 92% of the 128 who replied said they would not. This near-total disagreement between actual behavior and verbal reply was long interpreted as strong evidence that attitudes (as measured by the letters) need not reflect behaviors (as measured by actually admitting the guests).

Other studies reported similar findings and the controversy in personality theory over whether traits (a concept similar to attitudes) predict behaviors added fuel to the fire. (See Chapter 13.) In 1969, a major research review suggested that "it is considerably more likely that attitudes will be unrelated or only slightly related to overt behavior than that attitudes will be closely related to actions" (Wicker, 1969, p. 65). Wicker later suggested that "it may be desirable to abandon the attitude concept" (1971, p. 29). Many psychologists accepted these views, and research in attitudes and attitude change diminished.

More recently, however, interest in attitudes has revived. Schuman and Johnson (1976), for example, argued that some of the criticisms were overstated and that any expectation that general attitudes would always predict specific behavior was naive. They suggested that a more appropriate direction for future research would be to ask more narrow and specific questions. As Fazio and Zanna (1981, p. 165) put it, "Under what conditions do what kinds of attitudes held by what kinds of individuals predict what kinds of behavior?" In defense of at least limited utility of attitudes, Schuman and Johnson (1976) cited the results of a study of voting behavior: Kelley and Mirer (1974) found, in an analysis of four presidential elections, that preelection attitudes accurately predicted voting behavior for more than 85% of subjects.

Contemporary researchers offer several ways of improving the fit between attitudes and behavior. Some suggestions are methodological; various experimental flaws in earlier research may have reduced the size of attitude/behavior relationships. Fishbein and Ajzen (1972; Ajzen & Fishbein, 1980), for example, suggested that a similar level of specificity is needed for both attitude and behavior. If the behavior to be explored is cheating on a test, for example, then the attitude measured must be toward cheating on tests, not some general attitude toward dishonesty. Fazio and Zanna (1981) also noted that attitude/behavior correlations will be stronger when subjects have had direct experience with the behavior in question.

Fishbein and Ajzen's suggestion is only one part of their overall recommendations for attitude theory. They have developed a new theoretical view of attitudes and behavior called the **theory of reasoned action** (Fishbein, 1980; Fishbein & Ajzen, 1975, 1981). It fits a number of external and internal variables together mathematically to yield both attitudes and behaviors. The single best predictor of behavior is the person's *intention*, they argued, which is in turn a function of the person's attitude and *subjective* norm (the assessment of how others will view the action). ■ Figure 17.12

THE INDIVIDUAL IN GROUP SETTINGS

Our focus so far has been on how social psychologists view aspects of individual behavior that may be influenced by other people. It's now time to turn to some characteristics of *social groups*, collections of people who consider themselves in some way alike or members of a group as distinguished from nonmembers. We will focus on three aspects of group processes: social influences that yield conformity or obedience, processes within groups that make them influential, and relationships between groups.

Social Influences

The influence of groups on individuals is a classic topic in social psychology (Allen, 1965). One of the earliest important studies (Sherif, 1935, 1936) used the autokinetic effect, in which a stationary light in a dark room seems to make small irregular movements (Chapter 6). Subjects were asked to judge the extent of these movements both alone and in a group. In the group, they changed their judgments to conform more closely to what other group members (actually confederates of the experimenter) reported. Because the perceived movements were actually illusions, subjects seem to have used group norms to help judge what they saw.

The key development that led to many studies of *compliance* to group demands was the work of Solomon Asch (1951). Instead of using an ambiguous effect, Asch showed subjects simple visual stimuli that were virtually impossible to misjudge: Subjects stated which of three lines matched another line, with all four available for comparison. Subjects were highly accurate in choosing the correct lines if there was no social pressure toward misjudgments. But when each subject was seated with a group of Asch's confederates, who unanimously chose an incorrect alternative, about a third of

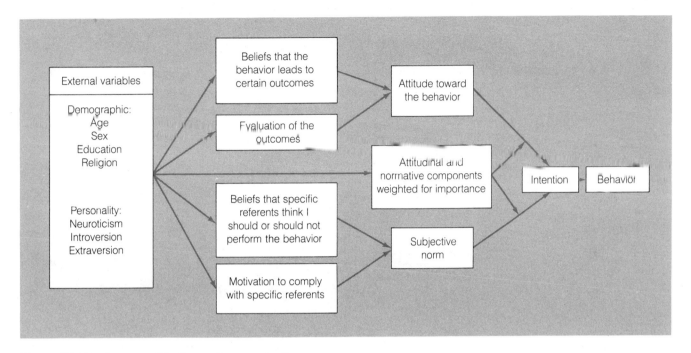

Figure 17.12 ■ Summary of the theory of reasoned action.

(Reprinted from the 1979 *Nebraska Symposium on Motivation* by permission of University of Nebraska Press and M. Fishbein. Copyright © 1980 by the University of Nebraska Press.)

the subjects also chose the obviously incorrect answer (Asch, 1951, 1956).

Asch's results indicate a social **compliance** effect, a yielding to group norms even when the individual believes differently. Few of Asch's subjects actually doubted their own judgments, but many were willing to go along with the group—even though they were not specifically requested to do so. (Instructions simply asked for an individual judgment of line length.) Many later studies have confirmed and extended the Asch findings (e.g., Crutchfield, 1955).

Research on compliance effects since Asch's study have examined the effects of numerous variables, including whether the subject's response is given publicly or privately and the effect of early compliance or independence on later responses. In general, a public response is more likely to be compliant than a private one: The more subjects must give the response out loud, face-to-face with the confederates, the greater is the compliance. Early responses, whether compliant or independent, also seem to create a behavioral commitment toward compliance or independence. Subjects who comply early tend to continue to comply and those who resist early tend to continue to resist.

Characteristics of the confederate group, such as its attractiveness to the subjects, its size, and the unanimity of its reports, have also been studied. Attractive groups produce both greater compliance and private

changes in belief (Allen, 1965). Groups other than the experimental one may also play a role in the outcome, as subjects often report considering what some personally important *reference group* (such as friends or family) would think before making their decision. Hence apparent independence in the experimental situation may in fact mean the subject is following a different group's norm.

A group need not be large to produce conformity. As group size increases from one other person to three, or perhaps four, conformity typically rises sharply but larger groups do not add to compliance and may even reduce it. The unanimity of the other group members is also important regardless of group size: If one other group member fails to conform, the subject is much less likely to conform. A single confederate who always gave the correct answer reduced conformity in Asch's (1951) study from 35% to only 5%. If the other holdout switches to conforming answers, however, subjects soon conform also. Overall, compliance to expressed group opinions is a common and powerful effect in these studies, although a variety of factors raise or lower the extent of compliance (Allen, 1965).

The next major addition to the compliance research came with Stanley Milgram's (1963, 1965) obedience study, described at the beginning of the chapter. Rather than studying compliance to an implicit group norm, Milgram examined **obedience** to an explicit

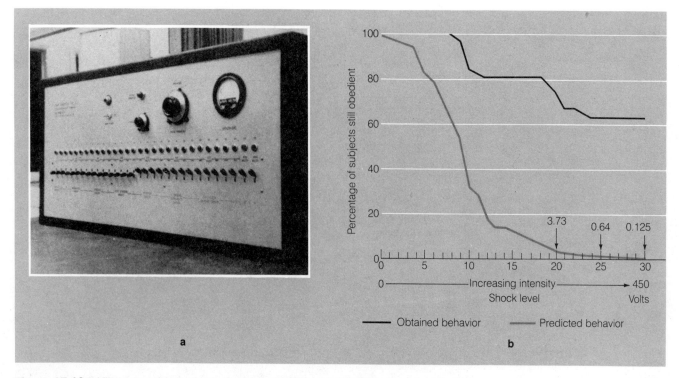

a

b

— Obtained behavior   — Predicted behavior

Figure 17.13 ■ Milgram's experiment on compliance. (a) The control panel for the "shock generator." Each time the subject (supposedly) applied a shock, he or she was to use the next switch, which supposedly applied 15 volts greater shock. (From the film "Obedience," distributed by New York University Film Library; copyright 1965 by Stanley Milgram.) (b) Estimates of behavior compared to real behavior in Milgram's study. The curves must begin at 100%, indicating that all subjects begin the sequence. They decrease as subjects refuse to obey further, so the height of a curve at any time represents the percentage of subjects still obeying.

(**a**, copyright 1965 by Stanley Milgram. From the film OBEDIENCE, distributed by the Pennsylvania State University Audio Visual Service; **b**, from S. Milgram, "Some Conditions of Obedience and Disobedience to Authority," *Human Relations*, 1965, *18*, 57–76. Reprinted by permission of the author.)

demand made by a representative of the group. He wanted to know how long subjects would continue to follow the requests of an experimenter and administer shocks to a "learner."

His results—that most people would continue to obey the experimenter until the end—ran counter to the estimates of both amateurs and professionals. College students, psychologists, and others to whom Milgram described the experiment all estimated that few if any people would continue to the end. But in both the original study and numerous replications, under differing conditions and with different types of subjects, most people *did* obey (Milgram, 1974). ■ Figure 17.13

Milgram's study has been widely criticized both within and outside psychology. There have been objections to the methodology, to the interpretation of the results, and to the ethics of even doing such a study. Milgram (1974, 1977) has countered many of these criticisms, but the study and its meaning remain

highly controversial. ■ Personal Application: Would You Electrocute Someone If I Asked You To?

Group Processes

Research such as Asch's shows that people will often comply with group norms, even when the group is a new one for them and the demand for compliance is only implicit. Milgram's research shows that most people will obey explicit demands from accepted social groups, even when they go against strongly held personal beliefs such as not hurting someone else. Until recently, however, there had been few attempts to integrate these and a variety of other social-influence findings so that they could be compared in a single theoretical framework.

Social Impact Theory   One researcher has proposed a theoretical view that could aid such integration. Bibb Latané's (1981) theory of **social impact**

Would you electrocute someone if I asked you to?

One of the most notable aspects of the Milgram findings is their discrepancy with our beliefs about ourselves. It's far easier for us to believe that people remote in space and time—such as citizens of Nazi Germany in the 1940s—would comply with orders to harm others than it is to believe that we or our friends would do so. The feeling "I wouldn't do that" is a common reaction among people first exposed to Milgram's work, including most college students.

But remember that college students also predicted that few people would obey. And the finding that people *expect* low obedience is as commonly replicated as the fact that most people actually do obey. Although many psychologists have questioned Milgram's findings, none has offered convincing evidence that the findings are wrong or not appropriate to other circumstances.

So let us consider what Milgram's findings mean if they *are* correct and if they *do* indicate general tendencies. If Milgram is right, you probably would comply with the shock situation if I asked you to, despite your feeling now that you would not. This seems an exceptionally depressing idea. Is there a brighter way to view it? I think there is.

Milgram's findings tell us that most people go along with duly constituted authority in situations they consider legitimate. The "learner" being shocked was supposed to be a paid voluntary subject who would not be physically damaged by the shocks, painful though they might be. And the real subject thought he or she might as easily have been the "learner" as the "teacher." These findings alone tell us only that people will go along with social groups, even at some personal cost, in seemingly legitimate situations—a behavior that is necessary if social groups are to survive. It says that we have to be careful of what goals and methods our social groups adopt, but some obedience may be necessary for smooth-running societies.

Another relevant point is that some subjects did not obey. And in variations of the study it was found that the example of one other disobedient confederate was enough to reduce the level of obedience sharply. This says that there are ways of resisting even strong forces toward obedience and that the examples of a few people can help others disobey. Future research may be able to define better what differentiates those who obey from those who do not. Variables already known to reduce obedience include putting the learner physically close to the subject, providing more feedback on the learner's distress, increasing the learner's social status, and reducing the experimenter's authority. The moral belief stage of the subject, as assessed by Kohlberg's system (see Chapter 12), is also relevant.

A finding from another area of research, concerning who will help in a crisis, suggests that simply having thought about such issues beforehand and having resolved to behave differently may change a person's response to a crisis. (We will explore this research in Chapter 18.) If a similar effect is true for obedience, then the fact you have just read about Milgram's research may make it *less* likely that you would electrocute someone if I asked you to.

---

suggests that the effects of a group on individual behavior are a function of three features of the group: its *strength* (salience or importance), its *immediacy* (closeness in space or time), and the *number* of group members present. These three variables are multiplied to yield the total effect on the person who is the target of group influence. Latané sees his proposal as a kind of *psychosocial law*, akin to the psychophysical laws of perception (Chapter 5). He has suggested a number of possible applications of his proposed law, using findings from a wide range of studies of group influence.

One application was a replication of Asch's research using high-school students (Gerard et al., 1968). Where Asch found increasing conformity when up to about three conforming confederates were used, this study found increasing effects with up to about seven confederates. Latané plotted the increase in conformity for each additional confederate and found it fitted a power function, as he had predicted: The first confederate had the greatest impact and each succeeding one had less impact. (The power function is the same relationship commonly found in perceptual scaling; the logarithmic relationships in the Weber-Fechner law in Chapter 5 describe a power function.)

One study that confirmed all three proposed variables examined how much newspaper space students assigned to various hypothetical news stories. Playing the role of editor, students assigned space to stories according to the importance they felt these had as news. The status of the people in the stories was varied to examine the effect of the strength variable: An incident might be reported as happening either to professors or secretaries, for example. The immediacy was varied by locating the stories in either a nearby city or a distant one. The number of people in each story was also varied. Subjects were influenced by each of these variables in ways predicted by social impact theory (Latané, 1981). Note that the space a news story gets is not a measure of compliance; rather it is intended to measure the total social impact on the subjects. It is this social impact that Latané argued allows comparison of diverse studies on a common basis.

One aspect of group influence not yet well integrated into social impact theory is the *minority influence,* the effect of people who offer alternate suggestions from those proposed by the majority. Traditionally, researchers look at the power of the majority, and social impact theory is one way of quantifying majority power. But when a minority view will become influential has not been widely studied (Tajfel, 1982).

Groupthink A specialized approach to group dynamics has been offered by Irving Janis (1972). He suggested that some kinds of groups are susceptible to **groupthink,** an effect that leads to a number of cognitive and behavioral biases. Through groupthink, Janis argued, a group of highly intelligent and competent persons may make faulty decisions that none of the participants might have accepted if acting alone. The processes of groupthink are best described through an example. One of the most interesting in Janis's book concerns the United States' backing of an abortive attempt by Cuban exiles to invade Castro's Cuba in 1961. This ill-fated attack at the Bay of Pigs was such a disaster that "Bay of Pigs" was for a time a synonym for failure. Fourteen hundred exiles landed on April 17, 1961, and within two days all were either killed or captured. (Twelve hundred survivors were later ransomed by the United States.)

According to Janis, President John F. Kennedy and a group of distinguished advisors authorized this debacle because they made several major assumptions, all of which could have been easily shown to be wrong. They assumed that no one would know of the United States' involvement, that the Cuban air force was ineffectual, that the exiles had high morale, and so forth. These assumptions seem so clearly wrong in retrospect that Janis felt the official explanation—that a new president simply went along with an existing plan—is inadequate.

Janis suggested instead that a small group (here the president and his advisors) can suffer several forms of bias that constitute groupthink. They can develop an illusion of invulnerability, in which as the "good guys" they think they can get away with almost anything. People may not express their doubts, feeling that questioning the group is disloyal. This produces an illusion of unanimity, in which each member suppresses his or her doubts because the rest of the group appears unanimous. When the group is lead by a suave and forceful leader, the group may become docile, willing to allow the leader to manipulate the way in which the group interacts. These and other aspects of groupthink, according to Janis, make such groups highly vulnerable to bad decisions. Janis's view is interesting, but has not

been tested enough to see how general these effects are.

Group Polarization One effect of group processes that has received a great deal of research attention and does seem to have general effects is the *group polarization* effect. **Group polarization** is the tendency for group discussion to move individual members' opinions or attitudes more toward the average opinion of the group. Group polarization research grew out of an effect originally termed the *risky shift* phenomenon. Risky shift referred to the tendency of a group of subjects asked to take some form of risk (such as how much to gamble on a game) to accept a much higher or lower risk than the individuals forming the group do alone. In other words, when subjects discuss the question as a group they shift toward a more extreme decision. As research explored the risky shift phenomenon, however, situations were found in which the group decision was *less* risky, so the more general term *group polarization* is now preferred.

Lamm and Myers (1978) have done an extensive review of group polarization, the circumstances under which it occurs, and possible theoretical explanations of it. Two of the more probable explanations are those that emphasize informational and social-comparison factors. The *informational* view suggests that polarization results because group discussion will bring out new arguments (information) in favor of the action to be taken. If most of the group is in favor of taking a risk, for example, each person in the group will hear other arguments in favor of risk taking that he or she might not have thought of. The group members thus act to persuade each other to take even more risk than they would have taken on their own.

An alternate possibility emphasizes *social comparison,* the tendency to compare oneself to others in the group and to try to behave favorably in their view. Thus if the group favors taking risks, the individual may wish to demonstrate how good he or she can be at taking risks—and thus move toward a more risky position. But if the group takes a conservative position, the individual may wish to demonstrate conservatism and will take less risk than he or she would otherwise have. Both views have substantial research support, and both may contribute to group polarization.

Group Productivity A final point regarding group processes is the *group productivity* question: whether groups can solve problems more effectively than individuals working alone (Hill, 1982). There is no question that several people can usually come up with more or better answers than *one* of them working alone—but the correct comparison is between the same people working alone or in a group. If there were

Figure 17.14 ■ A white antibusing demonstrator using a flag as a weapon against a black man being held by other demonstrators, in a 1976 confrontation in Boston. The attacker thus ironically uses, to express intergroup hatred, a symbol of a group that theoretically includes both men. (Wide World Photos)

a positive group effect through the interactions among them, ten people working together should produce more than the same ten people working separately. But Gayle Hill's (1982) review suggested that this does not usually happen. Group performance is typically better than that of any average individual, but not better than that of the best individual in the group. (This implies that group gains come from the input of the most talented members.) In some cases, there can even be a negative effect: Solutions offered by the most talented members may be overlooked or rejected by the more-numerous, less-talented individuals. Hill's findings thus support a proposal by Steiner (1972) that there can be a *process loss* in groups by which group interaction reduces productivity.

In-Group and Out-Group Relations

Our final major topic concerns relationships between groups. This topic's implications for such intergroup issues as race relations have significant practical importance. The tendency for different ethnic or racial groups to band together and reject others is by no means unique to the United States; it is a widespread tendency wherever such groups exist. And it is not a new topic in the United States; group differences based on religious or other identifications have long been common. But the 1954 Supreme Court decision outlawing school segregation has led to many bitter confrontations, primarily between blacks and whites. ■ Figure 17.14

Understanding the sources of such antagonisms might allow us to develop more effective means of combatting them. In exploring these topics we will look first at the circumstances that help create and sustain patterns of in-groups ("us") and out-groups ("them"). Then we will note some suggestions for reducing intergroup conflicts.

Group Differentiation Marilynn Brewer (1979) offered a combined cognitive-motivational analysis of intergroup relations. She noted a number of forces that shape groups and their perceptions of each other, but we will discuss only a few of these.

The earliest view of intergroup relations was a functionalist view, which suggested that the development of an **in-group,** a group with which people strongly identify, serves two functions: It helps support the in-group members and justifies exploiting members of all other groups, or **out-groups.** Development of in-groups and out-groups was thought to grow from and further encourage a natural competition for scarce resources that each group sought to claim. Research

"The way I see it, you can't trust anyone over nine."

Figure 17.15 ■ Two members of Germany's Greens environmental party (foreground) elected in 1983 to the West German parliament. Their appearance is an obvious contrast to that of other parliament members (background).
(Wide World Photos)

has shown that intergroup competition can sharpen or intensify group conflict, but competition does not seem necessary for the development of conflict. Merely knowing that another group exists is sometimes enough to trigger derogatory comments toward it.

A number of other variables also contribute to differentiation of groups. One important factor is perceived similarity among in-group members and dissimilarity between in-group and out-group members. Such similarity/dissimilarity contrasts can occur on various dimensions; the more salient the dimension, the more influential it is likely to be in establishing in-groups versus out-groups. Highly visible differences between groups, such as those between races or between males and females, are thus obvious candidates for group-membership criteria. ■ Figure 17.15

The violence directed toward some out-groups (as in Figure 17.14) leaves the impression that bias against the out-group must be a major part of in-group/out-group relations. But Brewer's (1979) review suggested that this is not always the case. Most studies have found the major effect of in-group/out-group differentiation to be a bias in favor of the in-group, which need not include an opposite bias against the out-group. When an out-group *is* treated negatively, forces other than group differentiation must also be at work.

Brewer suggested that this finding may offer help with a different kind of social problem, the kind in which small individual acts add up to cause harm at the social level. It is notoriously difficult to get people to cooperate in solving such problems—cleaning up the environment, for example—when each individual sees his or her own cost more clearly than the overall social benefit. Brewer suggested that the satisfaction achieved from belonging to and supporting an in-group might be used to sustain appropriate actions toward such problems. (The Sierra Club represents one form that Brewer's suggestion might take.)

Reducing Group Conflict   In another major review of intergroup relations, Henri Tajfel (1982) noted other ways by which groups may come to be differentiated, emphasizing cognitive variables and theories that apply such concepts as prototypes and illusory correlations. One of the more interesting aspects of Tajfel's review, however, concerns ways of reducing group conflict. Unfortunately, as Tajfel noted, great strides have not yet been made in understanding how to reduce intergroup discrimination or conflict. But three trends in contemporary research seem to offer possibilities: intergroup cooperation, intergroup personal contact, and multigroup membership.

Just as *intergroup* competition can accentuate differences, many studies suggest that *intergroup cooperation* can reduce them—but there are qualifications. Intergroup cooperation will be most effective when it can generate a genuine sense of a new total group, rather than two discrete groups that are cooperating temporarily. The strength of identity of the prior groups is important here: Groups that have had strong separate identifications in the past are less likely to merge through cooperative effort.

Many studies have also explored the effects of increasing *interpersonal contact* between members of separate groups. In-group/out-group differentiations typically result in little interpersonal contact between members of separate groups, and this is thought to encourage derogation of out-group members. Perhaps if they could be seen as people similar to in-group members, they would be less likely to become objects of scorn or hatred. Research in interpersonal contact suggests that only some kinds of contact are helpful, however; the contact should minimize differences and maximize similarities, or it may perpetuate intergroup distinctions. Unfortunately, recent research on interpersonal contact has not yielded very optimistic conclusions. The existing distinctions between racial and ethnic groups seem quite resistant to change.

The third possibility for reducing group conflict is *multigroup membership*, creating and emphasizing a variety of groups with differing memberships that overlap so as to reduce the salience of any single group. Besides being a member of a racial group, for example, a person is likely to be a member of groups defined by sex, age, religion, profession, and so forth. Research results are only suggestive so far, but emphasizing such overlapped categories may help reduce the value of a single grouping by race or ethnic identity.

CHAPTER SUMMARY

1 Social psychology is the study of behavior that occurs in or is strongly influenced by groups. A major trend in this field is that of social cognition, applying cognitive approaches to how we perceive ourselves and others.

2 A cognitive approach to self-concept suggests that people develop self-schemas, summaries of attributes of oneself akin to schemas about objects or other people.

3 One key aspect of self-schemas is their gender specification. Some researchers have suggested that traditional male and female gender schemas be replaced with androgynous ones.

4 Some researchers question any cognitive approach that requires complex processing of routine events. They warn that at least some of our actions may be more mindless than many models suggest.

5 Attribution theory studies how people attribute causes of actions to internal dispositions or external factors. Several attribution biases have been noted, including a fundamental attribution error: to attribute too much influence to dispositions and too little to situations.

6 Studies of interpersonal behavior have examined such topics as loneliness and who is attracted to whom.

7 A major part of social psychology has long been the study of attitudes, enduring evaluations of persons or objects. Attitude change has been studied through the Yale school's message-learning approach and more recently through the cognitive response approach.

8 A major part of research on the individual in group settings has explored conformity to group norms and obedience to explicit demands of group representatives. A striking finding has been that more people are more obedient than is generally believed.

9 A variety of group processes have been explored. One approach that seeks to summarize how these affect individuals is social impact theory.

10 Relations between in-groups and out-groups are a topic with substantial practical applications, most obviously to race relations. Several different procedures offer some promise for reducing intergroup conflict, but further work is needed if these are to be effective in reducing strongly established group conflicts.

Further Readings

An easy-to-read general introduction to social psychology is Aronson's *The Social Animal* (1980). For more complete coverage of all the topics in this chapter see a good text, such as Penrod's *Social Psychology* (1983) or Freedman, Sears, and Carlsmith's *Social Psychology* (1981). Carlsmith, Ellsworth, and Aronson's *Methods of Research in Social Psychology* (1976) focuses on the research methodology used. Recent trends in cognitive explanations are the topic of Hastorf and Isen's *Cognitive Social Psychology* (1982). How we perceive others is the focus of *Person Perception* (1979) by Schneider, Hastorf, and Ellsworth and *Perspectives on Attributional Processes* (1981) by Harvey and Weary. The loneliness research is summarized in Peplau and Perlman's *Loneliness* (1982). Rubin focuses on interpersonal attraction as representative of social psychological research in *Liking and Loving* (1973). Attitudes and attitude change are examined at length in Petty and Cacioppo's *Attitudes and Persuasion* (1981). For Milgram's research, see *The Individual in a Social World* (1977). Janis's views of the Bay of Pigs and other such decision errors are described in *Victims of Groupthink* (1972).

You've agreed to fill out a questionnaire on your opinions of urban life; you expect it to be boring, but it's something different to do and you will receive a small fee for it. When you show up for your session, the receptionist directs you to a room down the hall. As you enter, two other people are already working quietly on their questionnaires, so you take a seat and begin working. After a while, something catches your eye. Looking up, you see white smoke curling through ventilation slots in the door from an adjoining room. Your first impulse is to jump up, but as you look around, you see that the others in the room are ignoring the smoke. One meets your glance, shrugs, and continues with the questionnaire. "Maybe they know something I don't," you think. "Maybe I'm overreacting." You return to the questionnaire, but the smoke begins to make you uncomfortable. Again you glance around, trying to decide whether it's really smoke, not just steam. Another person coughs, but doesn't look up. "Maybe it *is* an experiment," you think; "Maybe it's truth gas designed to make us fill in the questionnaires honestly." Finally, several minutes after you first noticed it, you can stand the smoke no longer; it fills the room, obscuring your questionnaire, and is still coming through the door. You go out to the receptionist and somewhat apologetically report the smoke. Only then do you find out that this has been a psychology experiment. The others in the room were confederates of the experimenter, and the questionnaires were only a cover. The real experiment concerned whether you would report the smoke and when. You're glad you did report it, but you wonder whether you would have done so sooner if the others hadn't been there.

In earlier chapters we explored the development and behavior of individuals in a variety of ways, looking at nature and nurture variables, questions of motivation, perceptual inputs, and learning. We examined how people use language, how they think, and what might be meant by intelligence. We looked at issues concerning their personalities and behavioral problems, as well as therapies designed to help them. In Chapter 17, we turned from the focused study of the individual to a broader view of the individual within social groups.

This chapter concludes our look at individuals in groups by examining some of the social issues that concern us all. Studying how the presence of other people will affect a bystander's actions in an emergency (as in the "smoke-filled room" study just described) is only one of many research areas for social psychologists interested in practical applications of their science. We will examine some of these areas under three major headings: prosocial behavior (primarily helping other people), aggression (one of the

Social Issues and Applications

most troublesome of antisocial behaviors), and applied research—on courts, the environment, and public health.

PROSOCIAL BEHAVIOR

Prosocial behavior is any positive human behavior that sustains societies, including cooperation, charity, and other forms of helping (Wispé, 1972). The term *prosocial* was first used in the 1950s to describe types of aggression that are helpful to societies, such as parents disciplining children or police arresting criminals. Since the 1960s, however, *prosocial* has been applied primarily to benevolent actions that sustain societies, to people helping others in non-painful ways.

Helping behaviors include all forms of prosocial behavior that contribute to the well-being of others, from making them feel better to saving their lives. The helping person may help someone else for any reason, including an obviously selfish one: Many people help others because they are paid to do so, or receive other clear benefits. But paid helping seems easy to interpret through reinforcement theories. Of greater interest to social psychologists studying prosocial behavior have been helping behaviors that seem to have no obvious gain to the helper (Staub, 1978, 1979). Some helping behaviors in fact have obvious costs or risks to the helper.

Altruistic behaviors are those forms of helping in which the costs or risks to the helper are more obvious, or apparently stronger, than any potential gains (Rushton, 1980; Rushton & Sorrentino, 1981). Early definitions of altruistic behaviors specified *no* gain to the helper, but that seems too extreme a view (Rosenhan, 1972). Current approaches to **altruism** (the performance of altruistic behaviors) accept at least the covert reward of feeling good about the act (Wispé, 1978). Some even suggest that people balance their probable costs with possible gains when they perform altruistic acts. Overall, however, when minimal rewards are likely compared to the costs or risks, the behavior is altruistic. When the rewards are more obvious and stronger, the behavior is helping but not altruistic (Macaulay & Berkowitz, 1970).

Two examples may make the distinction clearer. Suppose a person rescued the drowning dog of an obviously wealthy owner from a wading pond in summer. The small cost and risk and the potential monetary reward from a grateful owner make the behavior, although clearly a helping one, not very altruistic. But consider a real alternate example. On his way home from work on a snowy day in 1982, a Washington, D.C., man found himself at the site where

an airliner had crashed into a river. A woman passenger struggled in the icy water as other passersby watched. He immediately dove in and saved her life, an act that cost him a painful chilling and could have cost him his life. Now *that's* altruism. (Even though he must have known others would applaud his action—he received a medal for it—the possible praise seems weak compared to the risk of his life. In general, as long as rewards play no role in the decision to act, an action is altruistic, whatever the rewards that later follow.) ■ Figure 18.1

Naming altruism has been far easier than explaining it, however. Whether on evolutionary grounds or on developmental or reinforcement ones, altruism has posed a puzzle. *Why* do some people accept costs and run risks—and sometimes die—to help others, including people they have never met?

Theories of Altruism

Altruism has been approached in several ways, including some outside of psychology. We will consider four major views—the evolution of innate tendencies, learning, social rules of conduct, and situational factors. One major difference among these approaches is the extent to which they emphasize internal or external constraints: factors within the altruistic person or factors outside the person (in social groups or the immediate situation) that influence the act. The first approach we consider, which comes from outside psychology, emphasizes internal factors developed through evolution.

Sociobiology   The sociobiological view of altruism, which has received substantial attention in recent years, was proposed by E. O. Wilson. **Sociobiology** is the study of social behaviors in various species that have evolved through natural selection. It grew out of Wilson's (1975) book, which emphasized the evolution in nonhuman species of a wide variety of social behaviors.

This proposal has been highly controversial, with the strongest criticisms concerning the smallest portion of the book: his suggestion that human social behaviors, including altruism, might have genetic bases. Because people have long considered altruistic acts to be the most noble and most human of behaviors, his suggestion that they are simply a part of the species' heritage has been widely attacked. Many people reject Wilson's work as a too-easy intuitive leap from insects to humans. The sociobiological view of altruism is not so easily dismissed, however. Wilson's points are not drawn entirely from insects and may have some relevance to humans. Thus, although this view has not

Figure 18.1 ■ This Pulitzer-Prize-winning photograph depicts a definitive act of altruism: seeking to resuscitate a man who had received a severe electrical shock, despite the continued threat of shock. (This attempt was successful.)

(Florida Times-Union/Jacksonville Journal. © 1983 Florida Publishing Company)

played much part in social psychology, we should at least briefly note the arguments. ■ Notable Quote: E. O. Wilson on Human Altruism

Wilson described many behaviors that involved a risk to, or even the certain death of, one individual in order to help another. In social insects such as ants and bees, for example, worker or soldier castes often exist; individuals of these types characteristically sacrifice themselves in defense of the group. Thus, honeybee workers that sting an intruder will die, because their stingers remain embedded in the intruder and are torn from their bodies. If self-sacrifice could evolve in other social species, why not in humans?

Critics such as Donald Campbell (1979), however, have noted that the self-sacrificing worker or soldier insects are sterile, while members of the species who can reproduce are not self-sacrificing, but competitive. Campbell argued that potential reproducers always seek to perpetuate themselves, not to sacrifice themselves so that others may reproduce. Self-sacrifice would eliminate their altruistic genes from the gene pool.

But altruism in the animal kingdom is not limited to sterile insect castes. Some mother birds will lead a predator away from their nest by pretending to be injured and making themselves an inviting target. Some mammals also show altruistic behaviors, as when prairie dogs give alarm cries to warn of predators. Such altruistic acts place the actors in greater danger than if they did not perform these acts. A simple view of evolution by survival would expect any behavior that reduced an individual's chance of survival to be less "fit" and thus to be eliminated. How could such life-threatening behaviors become established in a population?

The key to this puzzle, argued Wilson (1975), is that altruistic behaviors typically aid the survival of relatives, who share some of the genes of the altruistic individual. Overall, whether genes that influence altruism are retained will depend on how much the acts reduce the survival of all individuals carrying them. If

Figure 18.2 ■ One major view of altruism emphasizes modeling and reinforcement of altruistic acts, such as firefighting. (For children who do not directly participate, as here, television might be a source of altruistic modeling.)

(© Jill Freedman/Archive Pictures, Inc.)

members of a family run some risk in exchange for a greater gain in family survival, then the altruistic genes will be transmitted. Even if some individuals die in altruistic behavior, their saved relatives can pass on the same genes.

Wilson and others carried out calculations, based on estimates of shared genetics, risks, and survival rates, suggesting how altruism might become established. But such calculations have not convinced their critics, especially when it comes to human behavior. Campbell (1979), for example, argued that individual survival has been more important than altruism in human evolution, and that the innate tendency for humans is thus competitive and self-serving. Instead, Campbell suggested that *cultural* evolution established human altruism. The advantage of altruism to a society means that the society will do its best to teach and support altruism—in opposition to genetic selfishness.

Some of the arguments surrounding the sociobiological view of altruism are clearly relevant to psychology. If cultural evolution is responsible for altruism, for example, social psychologists should be able to specify how particular societies teach and sustain altruistic behaviors (Grusec, 1981).

Modeling and Reinforcement One major psychological approach to altruism is based on the idea that

we learn altruistic behaviors in the same way as other behaviors: by modeling the desired behaviors and reinforcing them when they occur (Bandura, 1977b). When people behave altruistically, for example, their heroic acts are often publicized as models, and other people may offer them a variety of benefits.

One study demonstrated effects of both modeling and reinforcement (Midlarsky et al., 1973). Sixth-grade girls were allowed to win money at a pinball game, then were encouraged to donate some of it to needy children. How to play the game was demonstrated by a model, who after winning behaved in one of three ways: kept all her winnings (*selfish*), ignored them (*neutral*), or donated them (*charitable*). When the subjects played the game, the model offered praise (*social reinforcement*) for any donations.

Both social reinforcement and modeling increased the altruistic behavior of donating. Reinforcement alone was shown by the effect of the neutral model: When the neutral model reinforced donating, subjects gave twice as much of their winnings as when she did not. Modeling alone was even more effective: Subjects who had seen the charitable model donated almost all of their winnings, even when they were not socially reinforced. The selfish model, however, caused a more subtle effect. Merely observing the selfish model did *not* reduce altruism; with no social reinforcement, subjects still donated as much as when they saw the neutral model. But social reinforcement by the selfish model backfired. When the model was selfish, yet tried to reinforce altruism, subjects actually donated *less.* Apparently "Do as I say, not as I do" is a very poor way to encourage altruism.

A study by Grusec and Skubiski (1970) also supported the effectiveness of modeling. Children observed a model play a game and donate half the winnings to charity. When the children then played the game alone, they also donated. (They were observed through a one-way mirror, so their behavior could not be a response to the model's presence.) However, when the model merely described but did not perform the desired behavior, the children were no more altruistic than others who saw no model. Thus, it is not enough for the model to offer information about the appropriate behavior; the model must actually carry out the behavior. Apparently "Do as I say" is not enough either; the key is "Do as I do." ■ Figure 18.2

Note that both modeling and reinforcement are external factors, even though their effects may only be noted subsequently. That is, a subject who donates to charity after having seen a model do so is showing the delayed effects of an external factor. Even when a person self-reinforces an altruistic act, the self-reinforcement was learned from prior external reinforcement (Aronfreed, 1968).

Social and Personal Norms Another set of influences for altruism that begin as external factors and then become internalized are **social norms**—rules of conduct established and maintained within societies to guide the correct behavior of all members. Social norms may be important legal and moral guidelines, such as "Thou shalt not steal," or relatively trivial ones, such as those that specify appropriate clothing for formal wear. Each society has a range of social norms that are taught to all children and sustained among adults through social sanctions: People who steal go to jail and people who wear jeans to formal parties are likely to be laughed at or even refused admittance.

When social norms are accepted and internalized by individual members of the society, they become **personal norms.** Such personal norms will continue to affect behavior even in the absence of the original social group. A person whose standards of proper conduct were internalized in one social group may continue to follow those standards in other countries and in later years, rather than adopting the local or current social norms (Schwartz, 1977).

Social norms are shared by a group, but personal norms may be chosen from a variety of groups or even created by the person. You may have learned personal norms about etiquette from one group, norms about

honesty from another, and so forth. Thus each person's behavior differs somewhat from every other person's, even if all people are conforming to their own personal norms.

Approaches to altruism that emphasize social or personal norms are called *normative views* (Schwartz & Howard, 1981). Considerable altruism research has focused on two proposed social norms, for *reciprocity* and for *social responsibility.* Gouldner (1960) claimed that the predominant social norm in our culture is the **norm of reciprocity.** This norm includes the demands that people should help those who have helped them and that they should not injure those who have helped them. (It permits injuring those who have injured them.) The reciprocity norm is central to social existence, argued Gouldner, because it encourages a variety of helping behaviors and discourages antisocial ones. If a person helps another, the helped person is indebted and must seek to repay the debt by offering help of similar kind and amount. The idea of reciprocal debts encourages cooperation on tasks too large for one person to handle and thus helped sustain such actions as community barn raisings on the American frontier. And the fact that repayment should be approximately equal sets up a desirable state of ambiguity over who is indebted to whom. If you do me a favor and I do you one, have I done enough or do I still owe you? Or have I done too much and now you owe me? So long as such ambiguity exists, we are likely to keep doing favors for each other, without ever being sure that we're even.

Other theorists have proposed related views. Homans (1961), for example, suggested that people weigh the personal costs and rewards associated with altruism and always assess the possibility that they might be helped later by those they help—or, conversely, that if they fail to help when they can, others might fail them later. This is similar to Campbell's (1979) suggestion about cultural evolution. Campbell argued that it is in society's interest to offer social rewards for altruism and social sanctions for failures to act altruistically. A person faced with the possibility of altruistic behavior would know of the possible rewards or sanctions and thus might behave altruistically.

A number of studies have supported Gouldner's concept of a reciprocity norm, showing that children do learn and use such a norm and that adults in various cultures seem to apply it in various ways (Gergen et al., 1975). Staub and Sherk (1970), for example, found that children who were given candies by another child in one situation reciprocated by sharing a crayon with that child in another situation. The more candies they received in the first encounter, the more willing they were to share. Adults have similarly been shown to reciprocate favors (e.g., Berkowitz, 1968).

If people really do keep track of past and probable future reciprocity, altruistic behavior *is* rewarded, so defining altruism so that it excludes gain becomes questionable. The other major proposed social norm, however, better fits our definition of altruism.

Berkowitz has proposed a **norm of social responsibility,** which calls for helping any dependent person, regardless of whether that person can or will reciprocate. According to the social-responsibility norm, people should help those who are unable to care for themselves—the very young and very old, the sick, and so forth. But they should also help even competent others to the extent that some of the others' well-being is dependent on them. Berkowitz and Daniels (1963), for example, showed that subjects would work hard in a laboratory task to help out another subject whose evaluation as a "supervisor" was dependent on their production. The norm of social responsibility is thus broader than mere responsibility for the helpless. It is more of a "pull your own weight" or "shoulder your own burden" norm, one that says whenever others depend on our playing our part, we must do our best to live up to that expectation.

Research examining a variety of personal norms has often focused on what actually determines whether altruistic behavior will occur: Is it enough to have an appropriate norm, or must that norm be made relevant in some way? Schwartz (1977) has proposed that cognitive awareness of a personal norm is necessary but not sufficient for altruistic behavior. In Schwartz's model, activation of a norm causes a sense of obligation to act, but the person then defends against this obligation in various ways. One defense is to reinterpret the situation: "Maybe it isn't really an emergency." Another is to blame the victim: "He's in difficulty because he was stupid and stupid people deserve to lose." If such a defense succeeds, the person will not act. Thus whether a person actually behaves altruistically is a product of awareness of an emergency, personal norms, and defenses against those norms.

Normative theories of prosocial behavior also have problems, however. First, enough social guidelines exist that a norm can be proposed for almost any behavior: If a person helps, he or she is following a "Help thy neighbor" norm; if not, he or she is following a "Take care of yourself" norm. Furthermore, personal norms are by definition different for different people and it is hard to define them except by the behaviors they are said to cause. When you add the possibility of defense, as in Schwartz's model, the situation becomes even foggier: Even if a person can be shown to have a norm, he or she is not expected always to act according to it. Researchers emphasizing such criticisms have sought other causes of altruistic behavior in the external situations in which behavior occurs.

Situational Factors The most prominent situational approach has been that of Bibb Latané and John Darley (1970), whose research began in response to a particular murder case. A young New York woman named Kitty Genovese was killed as she screamed, fought with her attacker, and cried for help over a span of several hours. At least 38 people heard or saw portions of her murder, yet none of them intervened in any way—not even to call the police (Rosenthal, 1964). The consequent publicity aroused a nationwide surge of theorizing and argument; Kitty Genovese's name became synonymous with all that people thought was wrong with our society.

When Latané and Darley first began their research, they thought of the Genovese case in terms of "bystander apathy." But it soon became obvious that apathy was an inappropriate term. There are a variety of reasons why bystanders may not act in an emergency; it is rarely if ever because they are apathetic (Clark & Word, 1974). Latané and Darley thus have more recently discussed their work in terms of **bystander intervention,** asking when and why a witness to a crime or other emergency will take action, whether that action is merely helping (as in phoning the police) or truly altruistic (as in risking his or her own life). ■ Figure 18.3

One of the first of Latané and Darley's (1968) studies of bystander intervention was the now classic "smoke-filled room" described at the beginning of this chapter. Most subjects who saw the smoke while alone in the room promptly reported it: 12 of 24 subjects did so within two minutes, 18 within four minutes. But when they were with two confederates who did not act or with two other real subjects, many subjects failed to report the smoke and those who did often waited much longer. Of 24 subjects studied in groups of three, only one reported the smoke within four minutes and only three within six minutes. Clearly, having others present drastically reduced reporting of the possible emergency. But why?

Latané and Darley found through later interviews that subjects seemed unaware of the influence of the other people. Instead they offered hypothetical reasons why the smoke might not have been an emergency, including the possibility that it was steam, not smoke, or even that it was a truth gas (both possibilities that should also have disturbed them). Latané and Darley concluded that the presence of others who did not act influenced how the subjects interpreted the situation. It was not that subjects were influenced not to act in an emergency; rather, they were less likely to

Figure 18.3 ■ Although we may not physically shield our sight of those needing help, most of us are influenced by a variety of situational factors that cause us either not to recognize an emergency or not to intervene in one we do recognize.

(TK /Photo Researchers)

recognize that it *was* an emergency. Latané and Darley called this effect **pluralistic ignorance.**

Latané and Darley (1970) then explored the influence of others when there could be no question that an emergency existed. In one study, subjects heard the experimenter apparently fall and hurt her ankle in an adjoining room; in another, subjects who thought they were participating in a group discussion over intercoms heard someone they thought was another subject have an epileptic attack. In both studies, the presence of others again greatly reduced the likelihood of the subject taking any action, even though the problem was clear. As part of the supposed discussion in the second study, for example, subjects were aware of the other subject's (supposed) epilepsy, and all later said they recognized the situation as an emergency. Thus pluralistic ignorance could not explain the substantial differences between helping behavior of subjects who believed only they had heard the attack compared with subjects who believed they were one of several subjects who heard it. This effect is called **diffusion of responsibility;** if a person is only one of several people who can help, the responsibility for action is spread among all of them. Ironically, this means that a person in trouble may be less likely to be helped if several people are present than if only one person is present.

Latané and Darley (1970) combined these and other observations into a five-step model of bystander intervention. The initial step is noticing that something is happening. If the bystander never notices an event, there can be no question of considering it an emergency. But if an event is noticed and pluralistic ignorance or other factors prevent the bystander from recognizing it as an emergency, he or she will fail to act (and not recognize the failure). Even if a situation is recognized as an emergency, diffusion of responsibility may still inhibit action. (It should be noted, however, that in some circumstances, the presence of many people may actually encourage some of them to act; Schwartz & Clausen, 1970.) Finally, the bystander must be able to specify a useful form of assistance and must be able to implement that assistance. If strength is needed, for example, and the bystander is strong, the intervention can be direct; but if the bystander is not strong, he or she must call someone else. The bystander will intervene only if all steps yield affirmative answers. A "no" at any step terminates the process before any intervention. ■ Figure 18.4

Who Helps Whom?

A different approach to the study of helping behaviors, including altruism, has been to examine the personal characteristics of those who help and those who are helped.

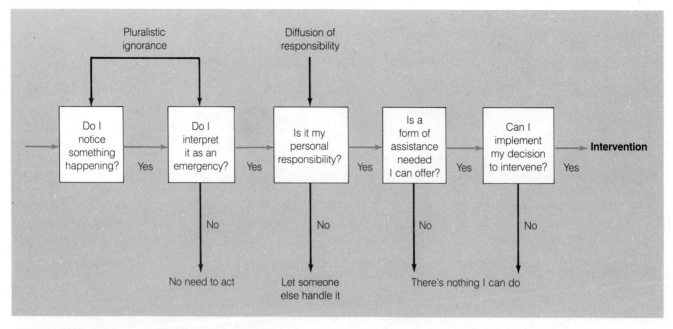

Figure 18.4 ■ Latané and Darley's model of bystander intervention suggests that a person will offer help only if he or she progresses through five steps from first noticing an event to implementing a decision to intervene, even if not consciously aware of all these steps. Pluralistic ignorance can cause the person not to notice or appreciate the emergency. Diffusion of responsibility can cause the person not to intervene even when the emergency is obvious.

(Based on Latané and Darley, 1970)

Who Helps?   Social psychologists have long sought to define personality characteristics associated with helping, with little success. As noted in Chapter 13, psychologists' definitions of personality in general have encountered many difficulties, so problems with defining an altruistic personality are not surprising (Rushton, 1981). One study, for example, administered a battery of personality tests to college students who were later placed in a variety of helping situations (Gergen et al., 1972). Some personality traits did seem to be associated with particular forms of helping, but there were no consistent relationships between personality traits and a general tendency to help.

Instead of examining student subjects in laboratory situations, Huston and his colleagues (1981) interviewed people who had intervened in real-life episodes, often at great risk to themselves (84% were injured in doing so). These interveners were in general somewhat taller and heavier than would be expected of a randomly chosen group, and tended to have had more training for emergencies than most people, including lifesaving or police training. Even though their specific training was often irrelevant to the intervention they performed, learning how to intervene in one type of emergency seemed to have influenced intervening in another. Another experiential factor that

occurred more often than would be expected by chance was experience as a victim; this may have helped them recognize emergencies or encouraged them to take responsibility for action by creating empathy with the victim (Batson & Coke, 1981).

Short-term changes in mood or emotion also affect the tendency to help. Isen and her colleagues (1976), for example, found that people who were in a good mood caused by some unexpected benefit (such as finding a dime in a phone booth) were more likely to help someone else. But the effect was quite short-lived, fading to zero within 20 minutes. Short-term guilt can also encourage helping (Carlsmith & Gross, 1969). Apparently the good feeling that helping provides is especially desirable when a person is feeling guilty about having not helped (or having harmed) someone else. Other negative moods can also increase helping, although the effects are not as reliable as for guilt (Weyant, 1978).

People are also made more likely to help by a very ordinary process—asking them. In a field study, a person left a bookbag unattended in the library and another stole a wallet from it (Shaffer et al., 1975). When bystanders had been asked by the bag's owner to watch it, 64% sought to stop the thief. Without the request, only 14% did.

Figure 18.5 ■ Prosocial behavior, including the willingness to befriend children of different racial or ethnic backgrounds, can be strengthened by television programs such as "Sesame Street" or "Mr. Rogers' Neighborhood."

(Bill Eppridge, LIFE MAGAZINE © 1967 Time Inc.)

Who Gets Help?   Most research on who gets helped has focused on two characteristics: People tend to receive help if they are similar to the helpers or are considered attractive by them. One field study of similarity, for example, compared males and females whose mode of dress characterized them as "hippie" or "straight" (Emswiller et al., 1971). Both hippies and straights were more likely to help someone (by lending them a dime for a phone call) when they appeared to be similar (also hippie or straight) than when they appeared to be different. This effect was similar for both females and males (unlike many other studies of helping).

As noted in Chapter 17, attractiveness is often an important variable in social interactions. It is not surprising, then, that several studies have found that attractiveness encourages helping (e.g., Benson et al., 1976). At least one such study probably measured something besides simple altruism, however. Pomazal and Clore (1973) did a field study on how often hitchhikers were picked up. They found that male drivers stopped more often than females and that female hitchhikers were picked up more often than males. (Studies of helping often find that females receive more help than males and males give more help than females; these behaviors fit social stereotypes.) But fe-

males were picked up much less frequently when they wore a knee brace or arm sling. These additions had originally been expected to increase their dependency and thus their chances of being picked up (according to the social responsibility norm). Instead, it seemed to have made them less attractive. Flirtatious remarks were often made by male drivers who picked up female hitchhikers without braces or slings, suggesting that this form of helping behavior "may have had little to do with altruism" (Pomazal & Clore, 1973, p. 161). Such flirtatious behavior was not found when the braces or slings were worn, suggesting that the lower rate of helping in those cases was perhaps a better measure of altruism. (Note that, by a stringent definition, picking up a hitchhiker would be considered only helping, not altruism.)

Increasing Prosocial Behavior

Because prosocial behavior is by definition desirable for societies, we would expect societies to find ways of developing and maintaining it. Social psychologists have studied possible ways of increasing prosocial behavior, many focusing on the mass media, primarily television. Such children's shows as "Sesame Street" aim to increase prosocial behavior as well as factual learning: counting to ten or defining a word may be in the foreground, but such prosocial issues as interracial equality are also presented through modeling. A major national review of research on television's effects found that such presentations can increase prosocial behavior in children (NIMH, 1982). ■ Figure 18.5

One chapter of this wide-ranging report for the National Institute of Mental Health (NIMH) focused on possible benevolent effects: increasing imagination, creativity, and prosocial behavior. The authors divided prosocial behaviors into three types: altruism, friendly behavior, and self-control. Studies have found, they noted, that shows such as "Sesame Street" can increase children's tendency to play with others who are racially or culturally different from themselves (Gorn et al., 1976). Of most relevance to our discussion, however, are their findings on altruism.

The studies reviewed by NIMH agreed that "children who watch altruistic behavior on television become more altruistic themselves" (NIMH, 1982, p. 48). Similar results were obtained from programs specially designed for a particular study and from regular commercial programs. Six- to nine-year-old children, for example, imitated a charitable model seen on a special videotape. And five-year-old children gave up points toward a prize in exchange for helping a puppy in distress after watching an altruistic "Lassie" episode (Sprafkin et al., 1975). Children who watched "Mister Rogers' Neighborhood" (a series that stresses cooperation and friendship) for four weeks became more

Will your behavior change after reading this chapter?

In line with our questions about television programs and research on other media influences, it seems only reasonable to ask whether this discussion of altruism will have an effect on your behavior. Unfortunately, there is little direct research on this topic, and some of it suggests that simply reading about altruism may not change behavior. But there is reason to believe that studying helping behavior sometimes leads to more actual helping behavior.

One of the key findings of Latané and Darley (1970), as well as of other researchers, is that cognitive factors play a substantial role in altruistic or helping behavior. Latané and Darley's concept of pluralistic ignorance specifically points to a cognitive effect: the presence of others who are not helping influences whether a situation is defined as an emergency. Your study of the pluralistic ignorance effect, however, has made new additions to your own cognitive structures. It is reasonable to expect these new additions to play a role in future situations.

Subjects in Latané and Darley's studies often seemed confused about whether to define a situation as an emergency. If you were in a similar state of confusion or ambiguity, you might find yourself remembering the Latané and Darley studies and deciding to act. Is the smoke in the next block from a burning house or just someone's burning trash? In the past, your response might have been: "It must be trash, or someone would have called the fire department." Now it might occur to you that *you* could be that someone, and you might act, either to go and see or to call immediately.

Schwartz (1977) noted how personal norms are sorted and defended against to yield helping or nonhelping. Now that you know of Schwartz's work, you may think about your own personal norms differently—either in terms of your norms or in terms of your defenses. If you notice a possible emergency but find yourself saying "But I'm busy; someone else will help," perhaps you will remember Schwartz's defenses or Latané and Darley's diffusion of responsibility and choose to act instead.

Although it is anecdotal evidence and thus only suggestive at best, I can note an example of how the research has affected me. Before I read and began to teach about bystander-intervention work, I tended to assume, when other people had already stopped, that an automobile breakdown or accident on a busy freeway must already have been reported. Now I always take the next exit and call the Highway Patrol. I have discovered that sometimes the problem has already been reported, but quite often it has not. I have yet to be faced with a dangerous emergency that would more strongly test my altruism—such as the incidents reported by Huston and associates (1981)—but helping on the freeway, either by stopping to give aid or calling for help if others have stopped, has become a personal norm. And once in a while I do hear myself saying "Not now; I'm too busy. Someone else will." Then I think about the issues I've just described, and offer help.

No one can or should tell you when to risk a dangerous intervention. I personally would *not* jump on a gun-wielding holdup man, as one Berkeley, California, woman did. But at least for those forms of intervention where the cost to you is tolerable, I hope you will be more likely to intervene now than you might have been before reading this chapter.

---

prosocial; gains were even greater if the prosocial program viewing was followed by training through role playing (Friedrich & Stein, 1975). (For a representative study of prosocial influences that used "The Waltons," see Baron and associates, 1979.)

Although most studies have focused on children, some have examined the effects of televised prosocial behavior on adults. The NIMH review, for example, noted a study in which watching prosocial programs led to a better mood and less hurtful behavior (such as getting angry) in married adult men.

One specialized form of media intervention for adults that might be expected to play a role in altruism, but has been little studied, is the effect of psychology textbooks such as this one on the behavior of students—including you. ■Personal Application: Will Your Behavior Change After Reading This Chapter?

AGGRESSIVE BEHAVIOR

We turn now to aggression, which is characteristically antisocial rather than prosocial behavior. Acts of aggression between people, small groups, and whole societies fill our daily news, and few of us have not experienced at least some acts of aggression. In Chapters 1 and 16 we discussed John Hinckley, the would-be assassin of President Reagan. The government's failure to keep track of Hinckley and to prevent his attempt is more understandable when you realize that the Secret Service list of possible presidential assassins has some 60,000 names!

Not surprisingly, psychologists have long been interested in what aggression is, what causes it, and what we can do about it (e.g., Baron, 1977; Berkowitz, 1969; Zillman, 1979). But attempts to study aggression

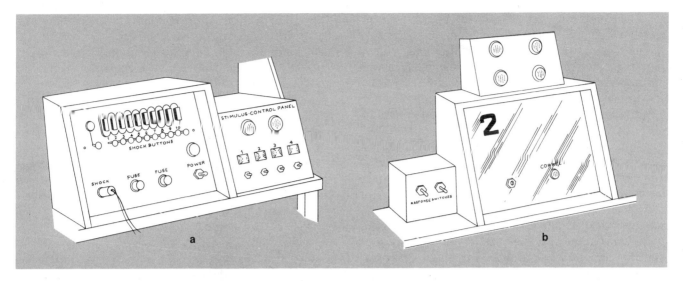

Figure 18.6 ■ The Buss aggression machine is a common laboratory measure of tendency to aggress. In this early version of the machine, (a) shows the subject's control panel and (b) the panel supposedly used by the target of the aggression (actually a confederate of the experimenter).

(From *The Psychology of Aggression* by A. H. Buss, 1961, John Wiley & Sons. Used by permission of the author.)

have often been limited by problems of definition and measurement. *Aggression* can mean many different things. Behaviors commonly described as aggressive include violent crimes, nursery school children hitting each other, a person destroying an unreliable car, and the making of sarcastic remarks. It has not been easy for psychologists to agree on what such behaviors have in common or, once defined, how they can be studied.

Defining and Measuring Aggression

Here, we define **aggression** as behavior intended to harm another person who does not wish to be harmed. (This definition is a variation of one proposed by Baron and Byrne, 1982.) Having *behavior* in our definition means that aggression cannot be used as an explanation for actions: One cannot say a harmful act results from a trait of aggression when aggression is defined as the act itself. Saying aggression is *intended to harm* excludes pain or damage caused for good ends (such as that inflicted in caring for bad burns), but includes failed attempts to harm (such as attempted murder when the gun misfires). (Operationally defining a person's intentions is sometimes difficult, of course.) Specifying *another person* eliminates acts, such as shooting one's television set, that may be noisy and violent, but are better considered an emotional outburst than aggression. (Destroying another person's property would be aggression if the intent was to cause suffering

to the owner.) Finally, noting that the victim must *not wish to be harmed* eliminates voluntary participation in violent acts (in masochism, for example).

The next question is how to measure aggression. In analyzing actual events, a variety of measures of inflicted injury can be used; crime statistics, for example, offer data that could be examined. But in experiments, the measure of aggression must assess *intent* to harm without permitting real harm. One measure widely used by social psychologists is the Buss aggression machine. This device, designed by Arnold Buss (1961), is similar to the apparatus used by Stanley Milgram to test subjects' compliance (described in Chapter 17). It supposedly delivers painful shocks to an unseen person in an adjoining room when the subject operates its controls. In fact, no shocks are given, but the intensity and length of shock that the subject calls for can be used as a quantitative measure of aggression. ■ Figure 18.6

A wide variety of other measures have also been used, some quite ingenious. Kulik and Brown (1979), for example, used a device built into a telephone to measure how hard the subject slammed the phone when frustrated. (According to our definition, force directed toward a telephone is not itself aggression. Nevertheless, it could be used as a measure of aggression if it is shown to correlate with aggression directed toward people.)

All such laboratory measures of aggression have been criticized, however, on several grounds. One objection is that causing subjects to be aggressive is intrinsically unethical, even when their supposed aggression actually injures no one. Subjects are themselves injured, critics suggest, by being shown how aggressive they are. Researchers who use laboratory experiments, however, believe that the benefits of the knowledge such experiments can provide outweigh what they see as relatively low costs to volunteer subjects.

A different objection grows out of the ethological perspective. Ethologists argue that species should be studied by observing their "natural" behavior. Similar suggestions for the observation of human behavior, including aggressive behavior, have pointed out that laboratory experiments, whether with aggression machines or slammed phones, lack *ecological validity*. That is, the situations are so artificial that their results cannot tell us about "natural" human aggression. Berkowitz and Donnerstein (1982), however, argued that such ethological criticisms miss the point of doing controlled research. All that is needed, they claimed, is a situation to which the subject assigns a meaning similar to the meaning of a real situation. If the assigned meaning is similar, the behavior will also be similar and thus meaningful. In concrete terms, a subject may be frustrated in the lab by an artificial arrangement. But if the subject responds to that frustration as he or she would to everyday frustrations, then the laboratory measurement is useful. And whether or not responses to a laboratory situation are similar to those in natural situations is something that can be tested. Any measure that is treated similarly can then be taken as a meaningful indicator of what the subjects would do in other circumstances.

The major objections to experiments on aggression can be summarized as suggesting that they are too realistic for the good of subjects and that they are not realistic enough for the answers to mean much. But psychologists who do experiments on aggression counter these arguments by noting that relatively weak situations that do not overly distress subjects *can* tell us about real aggression. However, the extent to which the experimental measure reflects more serious aggression must always be experimentally established.

Theories of Aggression

Theories of aggression, in effect, approach the Kitty Genovese case by asking not why the bystanders failed to intervene but why she was murdered in the first place. A complete understanding of human aggression would require several different levels of explanation. It would first have to explain aggression by humans in general. (Is there something in our genes that causes us to be aggressive?) Then it would have to explain different rates and forms of aggression among different groups of people. (Anthropologists have described cultures in which aggression is almost literally unthinkable, and others in which it is commonplace and expected.) Finally, it would have to explain any single act of aggression: Why this particular act by this person in this situation?

Psychologists address all three levels of explanation, but have emphasized the third one; the behavior of individuals is always the central focus of psychology. Species-wide explanations are of some interest to psychologists who hold an ethological perspective. Social psychologists, of course, are interested primarily in the group factors. We will look at three major approaches that emphasize different causes and try to explain different aspects of aggression. As we first noted in Chapter 1, at least some of the differences between these views may be merely differences of emphasis—but other differences may be true disagreements.

Biological Views Several theories of aggression propose biological explanations. Freud (1920, 1930), for example, proposed that an aggressive instinct is an innate characteristic of all humans. He then accounted for individual differences in rate and form of aggression through an interaction of learned behaviors with this innate instinct. According to Freud, overt aggression is only one possible consequence of the aggressive instinct. Depending on how the individual's personality has been shaped by life experiences, the aggressive instinct could be suppressed or turned toward more acceptable channels, but it will always be present.

Konrad Lorenz (1966), the founder of ethology, compared human aggression to behaviors found in other species. According to Lorenz, there are several types of aggression in animals, all of which serve some useful survival purpose. When unrestrained aggression would be more harmful than helpful, he argued, inhibitions on aggression have also evolved. Some animal aggression is directed toward other species: Predators are aggressive toward prey, and many species meet outside threats with aggression. A trapped individual may attack, a mother may attack to save her young, or specially assigned members of some social species may attack to defend the group as a whole. In these cases, aggression need not be restrained.

But aggression also plays a major role within many species, as when males fight among themselves for territory or for females. Animals may also show prosocial aggression, ways of disciplining the young or maintaining dominance hierarchies. Such within-group aggression must be restrained for the good of the species. In all such cases, argued Lorenz, these species have evolved behaviors that inhibit aggression. Fight-

Figure 18.7 ■ Two male Thompson's gazelles engaging in the formalized combat typical of many animal species. Such stylized aggression is matched by formal defeat or submission cues that terminate the aggression. If humans have innate aggression tendencies or inhibitions, however, these are difficult to specify within the wide range of learned aggression patterns seen in different people.

(ANIMALS ANIMALS/Kojo Tanaka)

ing males of predator species tend not to use their most deadly weapons on each other, and when one male gains an advantage the other often escapes by behaving in some recognizably submissive way. In the case of humans, argued Lorenz, our ancestors' comparative inability to kill each other meant that such inhibitory behaviors never needed to evolve. However, now that we have weapons we use them indiscriminately, unlike the more restrained lion or wolf. ■ Figure 18.7

E. O. Wilson (1975), the originator of sociobiology, distinguished eight different forms of animal aggression. Animal species often are capable of several of these forms, which they use selectively according to situational cues. Wilson further suggested a relationship between human aggression and competition for resources; he proposed that humans also have innate tendencies toward aggression—perhaps of several different types.

Lorenz's views have met with substantial criticism (e.g., Montague, 1976). Some critics quarrel with his interpretations of other species' behavior, but most focus on his suggestions concerning humans. It is not clear that our ancestors were less deadly than other species; even without the most primitive weapons, other primates, including chimpanzees, can and do kill each other (Horn, 1978). Interpersonal violence dates back at least to the damaged Neandertal skull men-

tioned in Chapter 3, and there is no reason to believe that such violence began with the Neandertals. Critics of both Lorenz and Wilson have argued that cultural influences are far more important determiners of human aggression (for example, Leakey & Lewin, 1977a). Whatever potential for aggression we may inherit as a species, they have suggested, is culturally overridden and repackaged into forms to fit current circumstances. In most cases, cultural forces teach and support nonaggression. But when prosocial aggression is necessary, as in warfare, cultural processes teach and sustain it.

A somewhat different biological approach focuses on the brain structures (primarily the limbic system) that control aggression (Moyer, 1976; Valzelli, 1980). This approach is related to that of Lorenz and Wilson in that we can presume that biological structures for aggression evolved, but the application of this view differs. A focus on biological mechanisms is primarily adapted by physiological psychologists or physicians who seek to understand and control outbursts of illogical and uncontrollable aggression—what Mark and Ervin (1970) have termed the *episodic dyscontrol syndrome*. As we noted earlier, people suffering from such outbursts may be candidates for psychosurgery.

A biological approach also notes that some drugs can affect levels of aggression. In one study, for example, large doses of alcohol substantially increased aggression and large doses of THC (the active ingredient in marijuana) slightly decreased aggression (Taylor et al., 1976). (It has been estimated that more than half of all murders, rapes, and violent assaults are committed while the perpetrators are drunk.)

The Frustration-Aggression Hypothesis   Most social psychologists have not used biological theories in studying aggression. Instead they have emphasized various forms of culturally transmitted learning (although some say these interact with innate tendencies). One major view of aggression is the **frustration-aggression hypothesis,** first formalized by Dollard and his colleagues (1939). This view, which has led to much social psychology research, proposes that a tendency to aggression is an innate response to frustration, although the actual occurrence and pattern of aggressive behavior may depend on learned patterns of response to situational cues.

The original formulation of the frustration-aggression hypothesis proposed that frustration (the blocking of an action toward a goal) always results in aggression and that aggression is always the result of frustration (Dollard et al., 1939). This proposal was soon revised by one of the original authors, however. In Miller's (1941) version, frustration always leads to the instigation of aggression, but situational factors, such as a learned inhibition or a fear of retaliation, can prevent actual aggressive behavior.

Considerable research has supported some aspects of the frustration-aggression hypothesis, but has also somewhat narrowed its scope and led to further revisions (Berkowitz, 1978). One study, for example, found that not all arbitrary thwartings yielded aggression; those that reduced behavioral freedom of action yielded more aggression than other thwartings (Worchel, 1974). The study that used phone-slamming as a dependent measure found that cognitions could influence aggression that had been initiated by frustration: Kulik and Brown (1979) found that frustration was more likely to lead to aggression if the subject believed that the person responsible for the frustration caused it deliberately and without good reason.

Other psychologists have challenged the importance of the frustration-aggression hypothesis. Bandura (1973), for example, suggested that frustration might be a source of arousal—but that frustration-induced arousal, like other types of arousal, could have a variety of outcomes. According to Bandura, whether aggression actually occurs is more the result of learned patterns of behavior triggered by environmental cues. Aggression might be made more likely by frustration-induced arousal, he

suggested, but the key factors are the learned patterns and the cues that specify them. (Note that this general view is similar to Schachter's two-factor theory of emotion described in Chapter 4, in which generalized arousal can yield different emotions depending on how it is interpreted.)

Even supporters of the frustration-aggression model have added more emphasis on situational cues. Berkowitz, for example, noted that weapons can act as cues to increase aggression, even when they supposedly play no direct role in the experiment; in one study, a rifle and pistol lying on a table in the experimental room sharply increased the aggressive behavior of subjects (Berkowitz & LePage, 1967). Other situational cues can also contribute to aggression, including any cues that remind a subject of prior painful experiences or prior reinforcements for aggression (Berkowitz, 1978).

In a revision of the frustration-aggression hypothesis, Berkowitz (1978) proposed that the important aspect of frustration is that it is psychologically painful; he suggested that any painful event, whether psychologically or physically painful, might yield aggression. This new proposal is tentative, but offers promise of integrating frustration research with other causes of aggression. Animals subjected to such painful stimuli as shock often become aggressive, for example. And some of the differences between types of frustration may be explained by how psychologically painful each type is.

The frustration-aggression hypothesis has thus gradually been transformed from the all-inclusive 1939 proposal of Dollard and his colleagues to part of a broader perspective: Frustration and other events can cause pain, pain and other events can yield arousal, and arousal in the presence of situational cues for aggression can lead to overt aggression.

Findings that do not fit easily into a direct frustration-aggression model might be integrated into such a broader model. Cognitive interpretations of events, for example, could be considered as the processing of cues for aggression. In one study, subjects who were aware that an opponent *intended* to be aggressive toward them became more aggressive themselves (Epstein & Taylor, 1967). Other studies have found that urban riots are directly related to ambient temperature. Baron and Ransberger (1978) described the phenomenon as having a curvilinear relationship to temperatures; they felt that most riots occurred at high, but not peak, temperatures. Carlsmith and Anderson (1979), however, reanalyzed the data and showed that the relationship is linear: The hotter it gets, the more likely people are to riot. This increase in aggression could be considered to be caused by the pain (discomfort) of the higher temperatures.

a

b

Figure 18.8 ■ Modeling and reinforcing aggression are powerful techniques for teaching it. (a) Research with modeled aggression toward inflated Bobo dolls showed that children often closely imitated adult patterns. (b) This 1944 *Life* photograph of a community fox-kill demonstrates how social groups can both model and reinforce particular patterns of violence.

(**a,** by permission of A. Bandura. From the film *Social Learning of Aggression through Imitation of Aggressive Models;* **b,** Wallace Kirkland, LIFE MAGAZINE © 1944 Time Inc.)

Modeling and Aggression   A modeling view based on Bandura's (1973, 1977b) and others' work is perhaps the most important approach to aggression in psychology today. This modeling approach notes that aggressive behaviors are typically both demonstrated and reinforced (at least vicariously). ■ Figure 18.8

In a series of well-known studies, Bandura and his colleagues (1961, 1963) examined the effects on children's behavior of adult aggression toward an inflated Bobo doll, a standing plastic figure with a weighted bottom that returns upright if knocked down. Children first saw adult models hit, kick, and throw the Bobo dolls in particular ways. Later, when the children were allowed to play with the Bobo dolls (in a different location and with the adult model not present) they often closely imitated the adult patterns of aggression, including the sounds—"pow"—that had accompanied them (Bandura et al., 1961). (According to our definition, striking the doll is not real aggression, but, like slamming the phone, can act as a laboratory measure of the tendency to act aggressively.) A further study demonstrated that the models need not be live; similar results were obtained from filmed demonstrations (Bandura et al., 1963).

Other social learning theorists have explored various aspects of aggression. Gerald Patterson (1976), for example, examined the patterns of coercive interaction in families, in which a child's aggression interacts with his or her parents' aggression so that each sustains the other. But probably the most widely explored and cited aspects of the modeling view have been the suggestions that filmed acts of aggression serve as effective models. The significance of such findings for the mass media, especially television, is obvious and far-reaching. We will turn to those implications in the next section.

But first it may be worthwhile to look at a single notable act of aggression from the perspective of various theories. Even though the causes of aggression vary from person to person, and even from incident to incident, an attempt to apply these approaches to a single case can serve as a review and help demonstrate that each approach may be useful in some instances. ■ Research Issue: What Caused Charles Whitman to Become the Texas Tower Sniper?

Aggression and the Media

Research on the effects of media violence on real aggression is one of the most rapidly expanding areas of research in social psychology and communications. The ten-year review by the NIMH (1982), mentioned earlier in the context of prosocial effects, also examined violence and aggression.

Televised Violence   The 1982 NIMH report followed one done ten years earlier by an advisory committee for the United States Surgeon General's office (1972). The 1972 report focused primarily on the impact of television violence; its conclusion was that available research suggested televised violence could contribute to aggressive behavior, agreeing with the 1969 findings of a National Commission on the causes and prevention of violence (Baker & Ball, 1969). ■ Figure 18.10

Following these two reports, both governmental agencies and researchers began to scrutinize television violence. The result was widespread public awareness of the possible impact of televised violence, accompanied by substantial argument over the tentative conclusions of the national commissions. Many social psychologists accepted these conclusions, although some remained unconvinced (Kaplan & Singer, 1976). But despite some concerned citizens groups and some congressional discussions, violence on television remained essentially constant over the years 1972 to 1982.

The 1982 NIMH report was far more blunt in its conclusions. After noting that some researchers still claimed no direct effects, it concluded "according to

many researchers, the evidence accumulated in the 1970s seems overwhelming that televised violence and aggression are positively correlated in children. The issue now is what processes produce the relation" (NIMH, 1982, p. 38).

Not surprisingly, supporters of the television industry have continued to argue that no effects have been demonstrated. The NIMH report was quickly criticized by a research group sponsored by the American Broadcasting Companies (Walsh, 1983). This self-serving report was critiqued by the authors of the NIMH report, who wrote of "the dreadful basket of alleged research analyses done by ABC . . . replete with carefully worded misinterpretations, omissions of large bodies of evidence, and sheer misstatements of fact" (quoted in Walsh, 1983, p. 804).

As the NIMH report noted, most researchers believe that televised violence directly contributes to actual aggression. Even a major field study funded by the Columbia Broadcasting System agreed: Teenaged London boys said they were more likely to engage in "serious violence" after watching televised violence (Belson, 1978). Research studies exploring these effects have emphasized modeling, as first suggested by the Bobo-doll work. One major longitudinal study showed that the correlations between watching violence and aggressive behavior were best explained by observational learning (Lefkowitz et al., 1977).

Other research has explored specific variables that contribute to the modeling of violence. In the laboratory, the most powerful effects are found with the youngest children, some of whom begin to imitate what they see on television as early as two years old. This suggests the possibility of a powerful cumulative effect after years of exposure. (However, news reports show that specific violent incidents are often duplicated by both children and adults within days after their showing, suggesting that some effects can be immediate.) Seeing models rewarded for violence is even more powerful than simply seeing the violent acts, a finding relevant to the widespread use of violence by television's heroes.

Field studies using actual media productions typically agree with and extend the laboratory results. One study examined the effects of violent movies on juvenile delinquents and found similar increases in aggression in both United States and Belgian delinquents, suggesting that such results are not exclusive to our culture (Parke et al., 1977).

What about Catharsis?   One argument proposed in favor of televised violence is that it might be good for people to "let out" their aggression through observing violence. Both violent crimes on TV and aggressive sports such as boxing have been defended in this way.

RESEARCH ISSUE

What caused Charles Whitman to become the Texas Tower Sniper?

One night in 1966, Charles Whitman, seemingly a responsible young family man, murdered both his mother and his wife. He then packed a supply of guns, ammunition, and food to the top of an observation tower on the campus of the University of Texas in Austin. For several hours he fired at anyone he could see, killing 14 and injuring 31 before two policemen entered the tower and shot him to death. The notes Whitman left and the autopsy results give us some clues to his motives. But different views of aggression offer different ways of assessing this evidence. ■ Figure 18.9

An ethologist might note that most aggression in primate species is carried out by males either competing for mates or defending against predators (Bernstein & Gordon, 1974). The idea that human males have a greater tendency to aggression than females is among the best established sex differences to date (Maccoby & Jacklin, 1974b). Hence the fact that Whitman was a male might be relevant (although of course women also commit murder; Jones, 1980).

But why *this* male and why *these* acts, at *this* time? One answer might be biological. Whitman himself requested that an autopsy be performed "to see if there is any visible physical disorder," partially because he had "had some tremendous headaches." The autopsy could not be conclusive because of brain damage caused by the bullets that killed him, but evidence was found of a possible brain tumor in his limbic system (Mark & Ervin, 1970). A physiological psychologist might note that such a tumor could have triggered aggressive attacks in Whitman (Moyer, 1976).

A psychoanalyst might emphasize the stress Whitman reported at the separation of his parents and the hatred he expressed toward his father. The psychoanalyst might further note that Whitman killed his mother first, and crushed her hand with its wedding rings, before killing his wife. These murders, in which father and mother, self and wife, love and hatred are all mixed up, might be considered by the psychoanalyst to be the basic crime, with the sniper episode simply a way of passively committing suicide thereafter. (Whitman expected to die, as indicated by references to his autopsy and insurance policy.)

A frustration-aggression theorist might pay special attention to the problems in Whitman's life just before this episode, seeking evidence of mounting frustration at his inability to cope with them.

A cognitive psychologist might be interested in Whitman's attempts to make sense of his environment as well as of his own thoughts and impulses (Blumenthal et al., 1972). Throughout the notes quoted in Figure 18.9 Whitman analyzed his own problems and made rational plans, both for his crimes and for the later disposal of himself and his resources. "It was after much thought that I decided to kill my wife," he wrote, even though he admitted that "I cannot rationally pinpoint any specific reason for doing this." Unquestionably, his cognitions and their outcome were abnormal, but they nevertheless played a role in what he did and how he did it. Some part of Whitman knew that what he was doing was wrong and wished not to do it: He wrote of not understanding himself and of fighting a "mental turmoil." But unfortunately that more rational side lost the fight.

A modeling view of Whitman would seek clues in his prior history of modeled and reinforced aggression. A social learning theorist would look at the patterns of culture within which Whitman grew up and lived (Bandura, 1973). Whitman had years of experience with guns and had long been exposed to violence in the contemporary news and entertainment media (Berkowitz, 1978; Eron, 1982). He was a trained military man and expert marksman who had been taught to kill efficiently. Furthermore, he no doubt knew of many other people who had sought a way out of personal problems through murder and suicide, and he was familiar with the military role of sniper. This doesn't tell us just why he chose to follow this role, however; most soldiers with similar backgrounds and knowledge don't commit multiple murder. Other factors must also have been involved.

So why did Charles Whitman do what he did? Probably for some combination of these reasons and others. He was male and perhaps carried some aggressive remnants of our evolutionary history as a consequence. He was raised in a society with both role models and direct rewards for aggression and he was trained to kill. He was frustrated and distressed over his own marriage problems and over the divorce of his parents. He may have had a brain tumor. He himself knew most of this, sought to understand it, and sought help for what he could not overcome alone.

Eventually, Whitman committed a series of atrocities, but he did so for all these reasons in conjunction, not because of any single one in isolation. A different person in his circumstances, or Whitman in other circumstances, would probably have behaved differently—but this time, the outcome was the Texas tower sniper, dead at age 25 along with 16 other victims. The more we can learn about such aggressive acts, the more able we will be to help people overcome the tendencies to commit such acts.

Sunday, July 31, 1966, 6:45 P.M.

I don't quite understand what it is that compels me to type this letter. Perhaps it is to leave some vague reason for the actions I have recently performed. [At this point, Whitman had harmed no one; his wife and mother were elsewhere in the city, still alive.]

I don't really understand myself these days. I am supposed to be an average reasonable and intelligent young man. However, lately (I can't recall when it started) I have been a victim of many unusual and irrational thoughts. These thoughts constantly recur, and it requires a tremendous mental effort to concentrate on useful and progressive tasks. In March when my parents made a physical break I noticed a great deal of stress. I consulted a Dr. Cochrum at the University Health Center and asked him to recommend someone that I could consult with about some psychiatric disorders I felt I had. I talked with a Doctor once for about two hours and tried to convey to him my fears that I felt come [sic] overwhelming violent impulses. After one session I never saw the Doctor again, and since then I have been fighting my mental turmoil alone, and seemingly to no avail. After my death I wish that an autopsy would be performed on me to see if there is any visible physical disorder. I have had some tremendous headaches in the past and have consumed two large bottles of Excedrin in the past three months.

It was after much thought that I decided to kill my wife, Kathy, tonight after I pick her up from work. . . . I love her dearly, and she has been as fine a wife to me as any man could ever hope to have. I cannot rationally pinpoint any specific reason for doing this. I don't know whether it is selfishness, or if I don't want her to have to face the embarrassment my actions would surely cause her. At this time, though, the prominent reason in my mind is that I truly do not consider this world worth living in, and am prepared to die, and I do not want to leave her to suffer alone in it. I intend to kill her as painlessly as possible. . . .

Monday, 8-1-66, 12:30 A.M.
To Whom It May Concern:

I have just taken my mother's life. I am very upset over having done it. However, I feel that if there is a heaven she is definitely there now. And if there is no life after, I have relieved her of her suffering here on earth. The intense hatred I feel for my father is beyond description. . . .

Friends interrupted. 8-1-66, Mon., 3:00 A.M.
Both Dead.

I imagine it appears that I brutally killed both of my loved ones. I was only trying to do a good thorough job.

If my life insurance policy is valid please see that all the worthless checks I wrote this weekend are made good. Please pay off all my debts. I am 25 years old and have never been financially independent. Donate the rest anonymously to a mental health foundation. Maybe research can prevent further tragedies of this type.

Charles J. Whitman

Give our dog to my in-laws, please. Tell them Kathy loved "Schocie" very much. . . .

Figure 18.9 ■ Charles Joseph Whitman, the Texas tower sniper, and excerpts from his notes.

(Photo UPI; excerpts from Bruce Porter, "The Many Faces of Murder," *Playboy* Magazine, October 1970.)

Figure 18.10 ■ Children at play: an example of the kind of behavior that televised violence probably encourages, raising significant questions about the content of both news and entertainment programs.
(© Richard Kalvar/Magnum)

"CONTRARY TO THE POPULAR VIEW, OUR STUDIES SHOW THAT IT IS REAL LIFE WHICH CONTRIBUTES TO VIOLENCE ON TELEVISION."

Reproduced by Special Permission of PLAYBOY Magazine; Copyright © 1977.

Such arguments derive from the psychoanalytic concept of **catharsis,** the supposed release of pent-up aggressive instinct in nondamaging ways. Aggressive urges supposedly accumulate to form a psychic pressure that must somehow be relieved. In this view, observing violence can act as a safety valve for the built-up pressures, thus reducing the instinctual aggressive urges. The frustration-aggression hypothesis, which was in large part based on Freud's views, also adopted the concept of catharsis.

As noted earlier, the views of differing psychological perspectives can sometimes be integrated. But catharsis is not such an issue. The predictions made by psychoanalytic and modeling perspectives are clearly opposed: Catharsis says that watching violence will reduce aggression and modeling says it will increase it. The research evidence bearing on this issue is equally clear. The NIMH report stated it succinctly: "Since practically all the evidence points to an increase in aggressive behavior, rather than a decrease, the theory [of catharsis] is contradicted by the data" (1982, p. 40).

An extensive review of the evidence on catharsis by Geen and Quanty (1977) reached a similar conclusion. Geen and Quanty pointed out that some studies had found initial aggression led to a reduction of further aggression, as predicted by catharsis. But they felt that these examples were better explained by arousal of anxiety and subsequent inhibition of aggression than by cathartic reduction of the tendency to aggress.

"At present," they said, "we must conclude that the notion of catharsis has not been confirmed, that reductions in aggression . . . might be more parsimoniously explained in terms of active inhibition, and that in the absence of such inhibitions the expression of aggression increases the likelihood of further such behavior" (Geen & Quanty, 1977, p. 33).

Aggressive Pornography Another form of media aggression that social psychologists have recently begun to study is aggressive pornography: filmed or other presentations in which (usually) women are the target of physical coercion or abuse in conjunction with explicit sexual activity (Malamuth & Donnerstein, 1982).

Some feminists have long held that all pornography represents a kind of aggression toward women (e.g., Lederer, 1980). But research has not always found a tendency for pornography to increase aggression; a national Commission on Obscenity and Pornography (1970) concluded, after reviewing the research then available, that there was no evidence pornography had antisocial effects. In recent years, however, coercive or aggressive pornography, which was not common prior to the Commission's report, has increased; such material may contribute to actual aggression toward women. (There is also violent homosexual pornography, but most research has focused on that featuring male coercion of women.)

Research on aggressive pornography has found a number of complex interactions among characteristics of the viewer, the pornography, and subsequent situations (Malamuth & Donnerstein, 1982), but some general findings seem to be emerging. It seems clear, for example, that "normal" male subjects (as opposed, for example, to convicted rapists) are less aroused by rape scenes in which the victim is portrayed as nonconsenting and distressed than by those in which the victim is portrayed as being responsive to the aggressive advances. It is also clear that seeing portrayals of what could be called "consenting rape" makes it more likely that subjects will accept the *rape myth*—the concept that women really desire to be taken by force (Malamuth & Donnerstein, 1982).

Furthermore, research indicates that aggressive pornography does increase the tendency for males to act aggressively toward women (but not toward other men). Some evidence suggests that these effects can even be caused by aggressive portrayals other than hard-core ones. R-rated movies in which the primary content is not sex or violence, but which present a rape with a later positive outcome, may lead to a greater acceptance of sexual violence and of the rape myth (Malamuth & Check, 1981). (It should be noted, considering our earlier discussion, that movies of this type are shown on television.)

APPLIED RESEARCH

In this last section, we look at three areas in which psychological research (primarily that of social psychologists) is being applied. First we consider some of the many courtroom issues in which psychology has played or could play a role; our focus on juries also includes studies of how juries use eyewitness testimony. Then we examine a growing field in social psychology, influences of the environment, especially the crowded urban environment. Finally, we look at some research that could be considered a prosocial activity: using social psychology findings to improve public health.

Psychology in the Courtroom

Since the early days of this century, some psychologists have explored the roles psychology might play in the courtroom (Munsterberg, 1908). But they were relatively few and lawyers paid little attention to them until the 1970s. Then several social scientists did some volunteer work in conjunction with well-publicized "political" trials, beginning with that of a well-known

antiwar activist (Hans & Vidmar, 1982). The result was a dramatic surge of interest in both research and application of results. Research psychologists now study a variety of issues concerning psychology and the law (Bartol, 1983; Kerr & Bray, 1982; Loftus & Monahan, 1980). Companies that claim to help lawyers choose juries and conduct their cases also do a thriving business, but much of this work is of questionable value, according to research psychologists (Hunt, 1982).

Both the research and the applied work have raised many new questions while seeking to answer old ones. There are practical questions, such as how effective the expensive consulting companies really are; research indicates that their recommendations may produce no better results than the lawyers' intuitions alone. There are other research questions, such as why some jury members vote as they do. And there are ethical and even philosophical questions, such as whether seeking to choose jury members who will favor the defendant is an unwarranted intrusion into the jury process, or whether studying biases in jury decision-making questions the entire process of trial by jury (Hunt, 1982). We will look briefly at a few of these issues.

Selecting Juries Although there are many local variations, the general process of selecting a jury goes as follows (Hans & Vidmar, 1982). Citizens selected from some pool, often voter registration lists, are brought to court as potential jurors. The lawyers and sometimes the judge question potential jurors about possible biases that could affect their decision, in a process called *voir dire*. Potential jurors may be rejected through one of two forms of challenge. Lawyers can reject any number of potential jurors for cause, if they can show evidence of potential biases: Jurors who are relatives of the defendant, for example, or who admit to biases, are excused. Lawyers can also reject a fixed number of jurors through peremptory challenges, for whatever reason they wish. Defense lawyers try to eliminate jurors biased against the defendant and prosecutors try to eliminate those biased toward the defendant. Hypothetically, this should result in an unbiased jury.

Consulting social scientists (psychologists, sociologists, and others) contribute to both forms of challenge. Usually detailed community surveys are obtained that seek to define the characteristics of "good" and "bad" jurors (those who will tend to favor or oppose the side paying for the survey). Research has shown that various aspects of a case, including the type of crime and the age, sex, and race of defendant, can affect the outcome, and that people respond differently to these factors in different areas of the country. Thus the ideal jurors for a trial must be determined for a particular case, rather than relying on previously obtained general tendencies.

Before surveys were developed, lawyers used various rules of thumb for choosing jury members. These suggested that demographic characteristics—primarily age, sex, race, and occupation—affected jurors' decisions in certain kinds of trials. Psychological research, however, has shown that these rules of thumb are often wrong. Zeisel and Diamond (1978), for example, studied lawyers' use of peremptory challenges by arranging for dismissed jurors also to hear the trial and vote after it was over. By comparing the votes of these "shadow jurors" to the actual juries, they could see how the peremptory challenges had influenced the trials' outcomes. Zeisel and Diamond found that some attorneys used challenges effectively, but others did not. Overall, results with the original jurors would typically have been the same as with the replacement jurors; in only 2 or 3 of 12 trials was the verdict likely to have been different. In these cases, the jury was less likely to convict; the defense lawyers seemed to do a better job than the prosecutors.

However, the most sophisticated research studies suggest that using personality or demographic variables to predict outcomes is of limited value (Hans & Vidmar, 1982). Studies using as many as 23 predictor variables have only been able to account for about 10% of the variance in juror decisions (Hepburn, 1980; Moran & Comfort, 1982; Penrod, 1980). This means that if jurors were actually split fifty-fifty for and against the defendant, you could guess with a 50% probability of being correct that any particular juror should be challenged. With the use of many predictor variables, you might be able to specify correctly how 65% of jurors would vote. In fact, many paid consultant studies may be even less useful because they often rely on measures with less demonstrated utility than those noted—including clinical judgment, handwriting analysis, and "body language" (Saks, 1976a, 1976b).

Future research may improve the use of predictor variables, including demographic, attitudinal, and personality ones. But a major limitation on such research is the fact that jurors do as they are supposed to and base some substantial part of their decision on the evidence! Thus, the study of other variables can at best specify only a portion of why a decision is made. Finding the variables that help tip the scales slightly may be valuable to lawyers, especially in cases involving millions of dollars, but jury-choice research is intrinsically limited from the point of view of understanding trial decisions.

Other research on juries may offer more promise for improving an attorney's chances at trial. Testing alternate trial strategies on mock juries, for example, has shown promise. In such research, alternate trial strategies are used in presenting the case to different groups of subjects playing the roles of jurors. The presentation that results in the most favorable decisions in these mock trials is then used in the actual trial (Hunt, 1982).

Eyewitnesses Problems with eyewitness testimony have been among the earliest concerns of psychologists interested in legal issues. Munsterberg (1908), for example, described the results of a staged crime in a 1902 university class, in which observers disagreed about many aspects of the brief event. Cognitive psychologists have recently renewed interest in issues of perception and memory in eyewitnesses, as we saw in Chapter 9 (Loftus, 1979).

Social psychologists have also begun to study eyewitness issues, primarily how information from these witnesses should be used in the courtroom. In some cases, researchers from cognitive and social specialties have cooperated in examining the issues (for example, Penrod et al., 1982; the authors include Steven Penrod, a social psychologist, and Elizabeth Loftus, a cognitive psychologist). This cooperation is useful in studying problems such as the use of police line-ups, in which a possible suspect or photograph of a suspect is presented to a witness along with other nonsuspects. Some aspects of line-up biases are best considered perceptual or memory ones, such as how facial features are processed and recalled. Other aspects of line-ups are best considered social-persuasion situations, such as the arrangement by which a police officer presents the situation to the witness (Malpass & Devine, 1981).

Psychologists have discovered a variety of features of eyewitness accounts that can bias their accuracy (some of which were noted in Chapter 9). But controversy has arisen over how these findings should enter the judicial process. Some writers have urged that psychologists not be called as expert witnesses on eyewitness testimony until we know more about how jurors interpret eyewitness accounts (McCloskey & Egeth, 1983a, 1983b). If jurors are already adequately skeptical, they have argued, psychologists' testimony should not be needed. Eyewitness researchers who have specifically examined jurors' and attorneys' beliefs, however, have found that some biases are known to them but many are not (Deffenbacher & Loftus, 1982). (College students, incidentally, were generally better informed than other citizens *or* attorneys.) They consequently argue that psychologists' testimony is sorely needed to prevent misuses of potentially unreliable eyewitness reports (Loftus, 1983a, 1983b).

Should the Supreme Court base its decisions on social-science research?

For hundreds of years of English common law and nearly 200 years of United States law, the rules for juries were that 12 persons must reach a unanimous verdict. Then in 1970 the Supreme Court allowed that juries could be smaller and in 1972 that they need not return a unanimous verdict. A brief review of how these decisions were made and what has happened since highlights what psychologists can contribute to legal decisions—if they are permitted to do so.

In its precedent-setting decisions on jury size and rules, the Supreme Court cited supporting research studies. But observers found that the Court had failed to use the best research available and had misinterpreted some of what it did use. The studies cited were said to be a mixture of speculative writings, references irrelevant to the issues, and studies whose conclusions did not support the Court's logic. The scientific and scholarly community was predictably critical of these oversights (Saks, 1982).

In 1975, the Supreme Court reaffirmed its new size rule, this time citing four studies that were relevant—but were also so riddled with methodological errors as to be worthless (Saks, 1977). More criticism followed. Researchers who did more carefully controlled studies found that the results contradicted the Court: Decision making in juries of 6 in fact differs in several notable ways from that in juries of 12. Smaller juries are less likely to "hang" (be unable to reach a decision), for example, indicating a possibly greater tendency to convict a defendant when there is a reasonable doubt (Roper, 1980). Researchers found that non-unanimous decision-making rules also lead to numerous differences in how juries reach their decisions, in opposition to the Court's assumption. These differences include how long it takes, how jurors communicate, and how confident they feel (Saks, 1982).

Somewhat after the fact, the Supreme Court learned to do its homework. When in 1978 it refused to accept juries smaller than 6, its decision reflected extensive knowledge of the research that had followed its earlier decisions. "The opinion," according to one observer, "reads like a *Psychological Bulletin* article" (Saks, 1982, p. 335).

Thus we are left with an interesting paradox. On the basis of little or no evidence, the Supreme Court accepts a major change in a procedure hundreds of years old. Subsequently it quotes extensively from empirical research in a decision reaffirming the change—even though much of the quoted research argues against the change! Only in a third case does the Court begin to base its decisions on appropriate research. One can only hope that in the future the Supreme Court will consider the research evidence *before* making such major changes.

Jury Size and Decision Rules There have been several proposed and actual innovations in courtroom practice in recent years (Saks, 1982). Two notable innovations have been allowed by Supreme Court decisions: the reduction of permissible jury size from 12 to 6 people and the change of required decision rules from unanimity to two-thirds or five-sixths majorities. These innovations were both based on arguments that could very well be operationalized and studied by psychologists. Yet the Supreme Court decisions themselves preceded such studies, and the studies since have often contradicted the Court's logic (Saks, 1982). It seems that social psychologists could play a valuable role in aiding such decisions, but the Court has only recently begun to realize this. ■ Research Controversy: Should the Supreme Court Base Its Decisions on Social-Science Research?

Environmental Psychology

The study of environmental influences on behavior is implicit in many perspectives of psychology. The environment shapes a species through life or death, and provides all the nurture variables that shape each individual's development. But **environmental psychology** as a subspecialty of psychology focuses on the *built environment*—the specific arrangements of cities and their contents, from furniture to traffic planning (Sommer & Ross, 1958). Some psychologists have been interested in environmental psychology issues, such as the effects of noise or crowding, for at least 30 years. But as with the other topics in this chapter, interest has greatly expanded in recent years (Bell et al., 1978; Stokols, 1977). The first text of environmental psychology, for example, was published in 1974 (Ittelson et al., 1974).

Practically any aspect of the built environment that contributes to the quality of life can be studied, and many have been. One thrust of environmental research that we will not explore in detail is the effect of noise as a stress-inducing variable. In general, the findings from this research show that people adapt well to short-term noise and somewhat less well to long-term noise; especially troublesome are irregular, unpredictable noises over which the person has no control (Glass & Singer, 1972). We will look briefly at two aspects of space utilization in the built environment: the questions of territoriality and crowding. ■ Figure 18.11

Figure 18.11 ■ The built environment includes many factors that can be supportive or destructive to the people living in it. Such obvious differences as are shown here are also correlated with other powerful factors, however, such as differences in education, diet, and medical care. Hence it is difficult to assess the direct effects of the built environment alone.

(left, © George Malave 1980/Stock, Boston; right, Stock, Boston)

Territoriality A significant feature of urban life is its allocation of space. For much of the history of our species, population density was probably measured in square miles per person. Contemporary free-roaming primate troops, such as chimpanzees or baboons, cover large areas to find enough food to support themselves. But in contemporary cities population density reaches astounding levels: Stanley Milgram (1970) estimated that a person in downtown Manhattan could encounter 220,000 people within a 10-minute walking radius. Such high densities raise a variety of space-utilization issues. Some of these involve the immediate space around each person, what Sommer (1969) and others call **personal space.** Other issues involve particular spaces that a person owns or has rights to, such as an office, a car, or a home; these are often called personal *territories.* Obviously both personal-space and personal-territory issues are related to overall urban crowding (Altman, 1975). But the issues studied under these concepts are somewhat different.

One approach to territoriality is ethological, such as that popularized by Robert Ardrey (1966). Many animals do establish and defend personal territories; the red-winged blackbird, for example, uses its wing patches and distinctive call as territory defense cues. But human territories do not seem to be established or defended in anything like the well-defined species-specific patterns seen in animals. On the contrary, humans show wide differences in how much personal space they establish as their own and how they interact with the space of others. These differences include both cultural and individual variations, and are thus probably largely learned (Altman & Chemers, 1980). ■ Figure 18.12

Human territories also vary in a number of ways not seen commonly, if at all, in animals. A person's territory can be his or her home, somewhat like an animal's territory, but it can also refer to several different areas, such as work or school territory, whereas animals only have home territories. Territory can also refer to temporarily established spaces, in a library or on a bus, for example: One study examined how people establish their territorial rights to coin-operated games in an arcade (Werner et al., 1981).

One of the first to study how people establish and use personal space was E. T. Hall (1859), who called this topic *proxemics.* Later researchers have not retained Hall's term, but have found support for his concepts. It was Hall who suggested, for example, that people in "contact cultures," such as Arab ones, regularly maintain much smaller personal spaces than people in European-style cultures (as in Figure 18.12). Hall also noted a number of other relationships. People generally use smaller personal distances as they know each other better or are attracted to each other, for example. (If you observe people at a party or other social situation, you can often tell something about their relationship by how close together they are.)

Arrangements of the built environment can have significant social impact. One classic example concerns

a **b**

Figure 18.12 ■ There are both cultural and individual differences in desired personal space. (a) In contact cultures, such as those of Arab countries, people typically interact at much closer distances than in European-style cultures. (Shown are vendors in Kuwait.) (b) In the United States, people usually maintain greater personal distances and some prefer not to interact closely when they don't have to.
(**a,** Bruno Barbey/Magnum; **b,** Ken Graves/Jeroboam)

the architectural arrangement of public-housing tracts. Many of these large projects for low-income residents were built in the last 30 or 40 years, often at enormous cost. But planners have only gradually realized that some architectural arrangements work much better than others for such tracts, and that the differences may relate to territoriality.

It has been suggested, for example, that low-rise buildings arranged around small entryways to a few units may have less crime and vandalism than high-rise buildings in which all living quarters open off common corridors (Newman, 1972). According to this argument, people who look out on an entryway used by relatively few people consider the entry part of their territory and seek to protect it. Loitering strangers are noticed and if necessary the police are called. In high-rise buildings, however, windows typically look away from the central entries and units open off long anonymous corridors. Inhabitants cannot easily observe the corridors and, according to Newman, do not consider them part of their own territory.

Such corridors and elevators do often become a "no-man's-land," used for violent crime, drug dealing, and public toilets—although a variety of other reasons for this have also been proposed. One well-publicized example is the Pruitt-Igoe project in St. Louis; it was built in the 1950s as a model project, but by the late 1960s its problems had become so bad that the city could neither maintain its units properly nor get people to live in them. The multi-million-dollar, 2800-unit

project was hence subjected to an extreme form of renovation—it was dynamited. ■ Figure 18.13

Crowding Personal space and territoriality are obviously related to crowding, but specific research on its possible negative effects was inspired by a widely noted study of crowding in rats (Calhoun, 1962). Calhoun created an artificial environment for rats in a 10-by-14-foot room divided into four pens. Each pen could comfortably hold 12 adult rats, but the total population was allowed to increase to 80, nearly twice the 48 that the room could reasonably hold; physical arrangements and rat dominance patterns further increased the density in some pens. Over 16 months of observation, this crowding resulted in dramatic distortions of normal rat social behavior. Some rats became hyperactive, others apathetic or withdrawn. Pathological behaviors among male rats ranged from sexual deviations (mounting other males or ignoring females) to cannibalism. Many female rats miscarried, died after giving birth, or failed to care for their young; infant mortality in some pens reached 96% (Calhoun, 1962). To many social psychologists, such behavioral disturbances seemed strikingly similar to aberrant behaviors noted in crowded human cities, and a number of research projects sought to relate measures of human crowding to measures of behavioral pathology (Altman, 1978).

Later research has found that crowding does not always cause such negative effects, even for animals

Figure 18.13 ■ The Pruitt-Igoe project in St. Louis meets an early end through dynamite after vandalism and crime, possibly related to its spatial arrangements, rendered it uninhabitable.
(United Press International Photo)

(Freedman, 1979, 1980). But attempts to find out just what effects crowding does have on humans have faced a number of difficulties. Some early studies did find correlations between such crowding measures as number of people per acre or average household size and such pathology measures as juvenile delinquency and infant mortality (e.g., Schmitt, 1966). But it soon became apparent that human crowding effects could not so easily be measured. One problem was methodological: The most crowded areas were also those whose inhabitants were the poorest and had the least education, worst diet, and so forth. If pathologies were found, they could result from any combination of these variables, so many social psychologists turned to laboratory studies (Baum & Epstein, 1978; Freedman, 1975).

Another problem is that crowding for humans is probably more a result of cognitive interpretation than of simple numbers. We have already noted cultural differences in personal space; these are related to cultural differences in what people consider crowded. Furthermore, people in cities move about through a number of settings in which density varies widely. A bus or elevator may be densely packed, a street somewhat crowded, and an office or home relatively empty. People often voluntarily join extremely high-density groups for particular purposes, such as at ball games or the beach. ■ Figure 18.14

When crowding does cause problems for humans, the critical variable is probably not crowding as such

but stress caused by crowding. However, physical crowding is not related to stress in any simple way (Stokols, 1972). Even in nonurban cultures, people may adopt high-density living arrangements but these may cause them no stress (Draper, 1973). Some studies have distinguished between *spatial density* (how much personal space each person has) and *social density* (how many different people each person routinely encounters). Even then the relationships are not obvious. Sometimes high spatial density induces a sense of crowding, sometimes high social density does. (A combination of both is most likely to yield a sense of crowding.)

Social psychologists seeking to understand crowding have offered several views of why undesired crowding is aversive. Some believe crowding is troublesome when it invades privacy and reduces people's sense of personal space (Altman, 1975). Others suggest that the key is loss of the sense of control; in one study, merely having the option to leave a crowded room reduced the stress, even when the option was not used (Sherrod, 1974). It is even possible that a sense of low control, if continued over some time, can result in a generalized sense of helplessness. One study of college dormitories compared suite-design dormitories, in which only a few residents shared a bath and lounge, with corridor-design dormitories, in which many people shared baths and lounges (Baum et al., 1978). Students in the corridor dorms not only felt more crowded, but showed more stress and less willingness

Figure 18.14 ■ Crowding is only aversive in some situations. People often voluntarily cluster in very high densities for particular purposes, as on this beach.

(Peter Vandermark/Stock, Boston)

to engage in social interaction in another situation, and in general seemed to feel more helpless.

Researcher Jonathan Freedman (1975) has proposed a different interpretation of crowding: that it intensifies whatever other response tendencies people already have. People who tend to be outgoing or shy might become hyperactive or withdrawn if crowded, people who are already somewhat aggressive might become more so, and so forth.

The question of whether crowding has consequences for humans akin to those of Calhoun's rats remains unresolved. It is likely, however, that future answers will require noting a number of different factors, including crowding of what kind, for whom, and for how long.

Public Health

One of the most recent ways to use social psychology research is to increase public health (Matarazzo, 1980). One writer (Taylor, 1978) suggested five areas in which such research could play a role: (1) etiology (discovering behavioral or social causes of illness), (2) prevention (changing behavior so as to reduce chances of developing illness), (3) management (seeking aid and helping to control an illness), (4) treatment (controlling symptoms, especially pain), and (5) delivery (arranging for people who need it to obtain care).

In studying etiology, for example, psychologists have found that behavioral and social factors such as stress, depression, feelings of helplessness, diet, smoking, and life-style can contribute to physical illness. Studies of illness prevention have used attitude-change techniques to alter risk factors associated with heart disease, such as smoking, excessive drinking, and obesity. Research on self-control techniques has been applied to development of self-management strategies for patients. In the treatment area, research has shown that patients cope better with pain if they are first given a realistic idea of what to expect. Finally, psychologists have helped integrate patient and staff needs into the design of health-care delivery systems that are more convenient and comfortable for all participants.

As a specific example of the work in this area, we may look briefly at some prevention research, concerned with reducing heart-disease risk factors in general and smoking in particular. This research shows both the difficulties and potential promise of public health research.

In one major project, researchers at Stanford University carried out what they called the *Three-Community Study*, an attempt to use mass-media techniques to reduce risk factors for heart disease (Maccoby & Alexander, 1979). Three small California towns were chosen; one received no treatment, as a control group, and the other two were both subjected to intensive media campaigns for a three-year period. One of the towns also received intensive counseling for persons most seriously at risk. The study was difficult,

"I FIND THAT AS LONG AS YOU AVOID EYE CONTACT, YOU HARDLY REALIZE THERE IS A CROWD."

© 1983 by Sidney Harris

time consuming, and expensive. New problems kept cropping up, including the need to develop media presentations in Spanish for the substantial minority of Spanish speakers in these towns. There were also problems arising from the unusual nature of the program, which fell somewhere between a field study and a nonexperimental public health project. Researchers interested in tighter control criticized the multirisk approach, which sought to improve dietary habits, reduce smoking, and change other factors all at once. People interested primarily in intervention questioned the need for controls and the extensive collection and analysis of data. But in the end the study successfully demonstrated, for the first time, that major health changes can be achieved through mass media alone. It found that the media alone took longer to be effective than media plus personal intervention, but after two years were nearly as effective (and of course much more practical). The study became a landmark effort, not only for cardiovascular disease prevention but for prevention in general, with public agencies in numerous states and foreign countries becoming interested in similar projects (Maccoby & Alexander, 1979).

Other less extensive projects have focused on a single major risk factor, smoking. One review of this research described a number of approaches to the reduction of smoking, including ones based on psychotherapy, behavior modification, and attitude change (Leventhal & Cleary, 1980). Unfortunately, the authors concluded that much of this intervention was not very successful; initial high rates of quitting were found with many techniques, but many people in all programs soon returned to smoking.

This somewhat pessimistic conclusion has been contradicted by Stanley Schachter (1982), however. He noted that many people do quit smoking and wondered whether the results reported by Leventhal and Cleary represented a special population of difficult cases. When he interviewed nearly all members of two populations (the Psychology Department at Columbia University and the population of a small New York town), Schachter found that many of them had quit smoking successfully—at least two or three times as many as in most research studies. Schachter thus argued that results such as Leventhal and Cleary's grossly underestimate people's ability to quit smoking. By looking only at self-selected subjects who come to therapists for help, he noted, psychologists have focused on people who found it unusually difficult to quit. Programs aimed at the general population need not necessarily expect the weak results found with these self-selected cases.

Finally, we may note a different approach, one that recognizes the difficulty of anyone quitting smoking who has already made it a habit. A three-year field investigation using filmed models showed that it is possible to decrease the number of high-school students who take up smoking in the first place (Evans et al., 1981).

Overall, research to date suggests that approaches drawn from traditional research areas of psychology can be effective in various areas of public health. Furthermore, existing research techniques or modifications of them can assess the effectiveness of health-care interventions. Health care thus may be added to altruism, aggression, legal procedures, and urban crowding as an applied problem to which psychologists can contribute both knowledge and skills.

CHAPTER SUMMARY

1 Prosocial behaviors are those that help and support other people in social groups. The most studied form of prosocial behavior is altruism, helping others when substantial costs or risks are incurred and no obvious gains are obtained in return.

2 The sociobiological view of altruism compares it to self-risking or self-sacrificing behaviors in social animals. But

psychologists emphasize more specifically human patterns, including those that are learned through modeling or are in response to social or personal norms.

3 Questions of who helps whom suggest that helpers are not easily characterized by personality variables, but that being prepared for emergency intervention of any kind may increase the tendency to help. People who are more likely to be helped are those who are similar to the helpers or attractive to them.

4 Prosocial behaviors can be increased in the same way as other behaviors, that is, by techniques of modeling and reinforcement. Mass-media programs that include helping themes can help increase prosocial behaviors in children.

5 Aggression can be defined as behavior intended to harm an unwilling victim. It has often been measured in the laboratory by the Buss aggression machine, but can be measured by any laboratory variable that correlates with real aggression.

6 Aggression in humans may be related to aggressive patterns in animals and is one likely outcome of frustration, but psychologists emphasize that learned patterns determine the mode and rate of aggression.

7 Modeled aggression is an important contributor to learned aggression, a finding that has led to extensive research on media violence. A national summary of this research finds that televised violence does generally increase aggression. A variant of this research finds that aggressive pornography may increase aggression toward females.

8 Psychologists have contributed to court decisions in several ways, although not always in time to influence Supreme Court decisions. As more is discovered about eyewitness biases, some psychologists are arguing for a greater role as expert witnesses, to point out such biases.

9 The built environment influences behavior in numerous ways, but much environmental research has focused on issues of personal space, territoriality, and crowding. Crowding can be aversive, but simple measures of people per unit of space are probably not as important as culturally based cognitive interpretations of crowded situations.

10 Psychological knowledge and research techniques offer promise in studying and improving public health, although such potentially cost-effective techniques as mass-media campaigns are difficult and expensive to study.

Further Readings

For general issues, see the social psychology texts suggested at the end of Chapter 17. Prosocial issues are presented in Rushton's *Altruism, Socialization, and Society* (1980) and two collections—one edited by Rushton and Sorrentino, *Altruism and Helping Behavior* (1981), the other edited by Wispé, *Altruism, Sympathy, and Helping* (1978). The bystander-intervention research is described in Latané and Darley's *The Unresponsive Bystander* (1970). The sociobiological view of both altruism and aggression is presented in Wilson's *Sociobiology* (1975). Physiological structures and possible biological problems are discussed by Moyer in *The Psychobiology of Aggression* (1976). For a summary of the NIMH survey of television's influence on both altruism and aggression, see Volume 1 of *Television and Behavior* (1982). Baron's *Human Aggression* (1977) presents one social psychologist's view of aggression. Bandura's view is given in *Aggression* (1973). For a review of legal issues, see Bartol's *Psychology and American Law* (1983) or the collection edited by Kerr and Bray, *The Psychology of the Courtroom* (1982). Environmental issues are considered in a text, *Environmental Psychology* (1978) by Bell, Fisher, and Loomis, and in a collection edited by Stokol, *Perspectives on Environment and Behavior* (1977). For an introduction to personal space and territoriality, see Sommer's *Personal Space* (1969). A variety of issues concerning territoriality and crowding are presented in Altman's *The Environment and Social Behavior* (1975). Crowding is the focus of Freedman's *Crowding and Behavior* (1975) and the collection edited by Baum and Epstein, *Human Response to Crowding* (1978). The August 1982 issue of the *American Psychologist* includes a number of articles on issues in psychology and public health.

Any science can begin with general observations of its subject matter. But if those observations are to lead to more than anecdotes, they must be quantified. Only when phenomena can be counted or measured can they be examined with the precision that allows small changes to be noted. And only quantification according to standardized measurement scales allows different observers to compare their separate observations. Thus when the Stanford Hypnosis Laboratory began its research in the 1950s (Chapter 7) development of measurement scales was a major priority. Once such scales were created, the hypnotizability of different subjects could be directly compared and the relative effectiveness of procedures designed to change hypnotizability could be explored. Furthermore, researchers at different laboratories could compare their findings because they could obtain quantified results based on common procedures.

The numerical procedures that allow phenomena to be measured and results compared are called **statistics**. This appendix will introduce you to the major categories of statistics used in psychology, to give you a basic familiarity with what they are intended to do and why they are necessary. It will *not* teach you how to compute any of them, however. That role is best left to statistics classes and to the summary "cookbooks" designed to remind users how to compute common statistics. Rather than show you the computations, this appendix summarizes the logic behind statistics and the reasons for using them. It is this logic that is central to understanding statistics, not the computations themselves.

Chapter 1 also discusses some statistics including a discussion of correlation. That information is not duplicated here. We focus instead on two major categories of statistics with somewhat different purposes, one type that describes data and one type that aids the interpretation of data.

Basic to all quantitative analyses is a set of numbers that measure some phenomenon of interest. Each number is a datum; more than one are **data**. A set of numbers to which the various statistics are applied is often called a data base. A data base is often a set of measurements taken during an experiment or the collection of information reported during interviews. In psychology, for example, the data base might be expressed in terms of IQ scores, experienced pain, frequency of anxiety attacks, or many other forms. Once the data are obtained they are interpreted with the help of various statistics.

Descriptive statistics describe aspects of the data base through other numbers, noting how many subjects behave in some way, how frequently a particular behavior occurs, and so forth. Given data on student sleep habits, for example, you could ask how many

Appendix

Statistics in Psychology

Descriptive Statistics
Numbers and Scales
Distributions and Curves
Measures of Central Tendency
Measures of Variation
Inferential Statistics
Populations and Samples
Proof and Disproof
Statistical Significance
Further Readings

students get less than eight hours of sleep a night. The answer would be a single descriptive statistic, one of many that could be computed from the same data.

Inferential statistics go beyond simple description; they estimate what else is probably true about some relationship being investigated through the data. One important function of inferential statistics is to help investigators decide whether data from a particular group of subjects probably also represent some larger population. If 20 of 25 subjects were to remember better with the help of mnemonics (Chapter 9), for example, are we justified in saying that most students will? We can never know with certainty, of course, without testing all students—an obviously impossible task. But under certain statistical circumstances we can infer from the data on some students what is probably true about students in general.

DESCRIPTIVE STATISTICS

Any description is a summary of the major characteristics of whatever is being described. Usually we think in terms of a verbal description of a physical object: "The text you are holding is a rectangular solid object. . . ." But data are sets of numbers. How can we usefully describe them? We can't just say: "This is a page of numbers. . . ." That describes the page, not the meaning of the numbers on it. Descriptive statistics are ways of conveying the important qualities, the meaning, of a set of numbers. Like any description they offer both advantages and disadvantages. They have the advantage of summarizing and simplifying what they describe, and thus they help us understand and remember it. But this summarizing and simplifying carries a risk. If descriptive statistics are misinterpreted they may offer a description that is misleading, perhaps completely wrong.

In looking at descriptive statistics we begin with some basic uses of numbers to describe events. Then we note three common types of descriptive statistics, those that describe the shape of the data, its central tendency, and its variation.

Numbers and Scales

The numbers that make up any data base are measurements on some scale, or quantification system. IQ scores, for example, are expressed in terms of a specialized scale on which 100 is an average performance (Chapter 14). But pain reports are on a different kind of scale, and the two scales cannot be compared: No degree of pain is numerically comparable to some IQ score. To know which statistics are appropriate for which kinds of scores you need to know a bit about different kinds of scales. Psychologists use four different kinds: nominal, ordinal, interval, and ratio scales. Each has advantages, but they vary in the extent to which they can be analyzed statistically.

Nominal means "in name," and **nominal scales** are those in which numbers merely act as names for observations. Nominal scales can be convenient but they cannot be manipulated statistically. The numbers on football jerseys, for example, are a kind of nominal scale; they name the players, but the number *50* has no particular statistical relationship to the number *10*. (It may have some relationship, depending on how numbers are assigned, but it is not, for example, five times better to have.) In psychology, a nominal scale might be used in assigning numbers to certain types of responses. A Type 2 response could then be a brief way to describe a behavior. But two Type 2s would not add up to a Type 4.

If something is "in order" it occurs in a given sequence, as when people are assigned to seats in alphabetical order. **Ordinal scales** use a sequenced numerical order, although the meaning of each interval need not be the same. The pain-report scale used in the hidden observer study (Chapter 7), for example, was an ordinal scale. According to the instructions given to subjects, a pain of "10" was to be greater than one of "9," which was greater than one of "8." But the additional pain represented by a rise from 9 to 10 was not necessarily the same as that at any other interval, such as the increase from 2 to 3 or from 8 to 9. Hence, if a subject reported a pain of 4 on one occasion and 8 on another, this did not say that he or she felt twice the pain the second time.

Interval scales are ordinal scales in which the intervals are known to be equal. When your body temperature is measured on the Fahrenheit scale, for example, two degrees of fever is twice as much as one degree. But the Fahrenheit scale still lacks one important property, and this keeps it from being as flexible as it could be. Outside temperature measured on the Fahrenheit scale often goes below zero. When this happens, readings cannot be compared as ratios; you might think that 90° F is twice as hot as 45° F, but how much hotter is 90° F than −10° F?

To be able to compare any value on a scale to any other value in a ratio, the scale must begin with a zero that represents none of the measured activity. Such scales are called **ratio scales**; only ratio scales are subject to the full range of statistical analyses. A set of numbers from a ratio scale often constitutes the data base for a psychology study. How often some behavior occurs, for example, comes from a ratio scale that begins with zero: It is not possible to do something less often than zero.

Distributions and Curves

We turn now to ways of describing the shape of data. Initially, it may not seem reasonable that a set of numbers can even have a shape. People, yes, and objects—but numbers? The answer to this apparent paradox lies in turning the original or raw data into some form of visual presentation; it is the graphic display that actually has a shape.

There are many forms of graphic display. One basic form is the **frequency histogram**, which uses vertical bars drawn to heights that represent the frequency of some event (the number of times it occurs). Suppose, for example, a researcher has measured the IQs of all the children in a small town. In the IQ data there would be some frequency of scores for each IQ level: perhaps 53 scores at an IQ of 100, 47 at 105, and so forth. We could describe the overall shape of the data by any display that showed how the IQ frequencies are distributed. To display the data in a frequency histogram, we would choose some IQ intervals and count up the number of scores within each interval. The intervals would define the number of bars used and the frequencies would define their heights. The smaller the interval chosen, the more bars there would be and the more detailed would be the histogram.

■ Figure A.1

A different but related display is the **frequency polygon**. It is generated by marking a point at the height of each bar in the center of the interval represented by the bar and then connecting the points by straight lines (Figure A.1d). As the size of the intervals is made smaller there will be more points, and the frequency polygon will begin to look more like a plotted curve.

A **plot** is another graphic display of the relationship between two sets of numbers. In any plot, a horizontal x-axis and a vertical y-axis are labeled with scales representing the two quantities to be plotted. (In plotting experimental findings, dependent variables are typically plotted on the y-axis.) To plot each point, you go out the x-axis (to the right) to the appropriate value for the point being plotted, then up the y-axis to the appropriate value; there you place your point. Figure A.2a shows a point plotted that represents

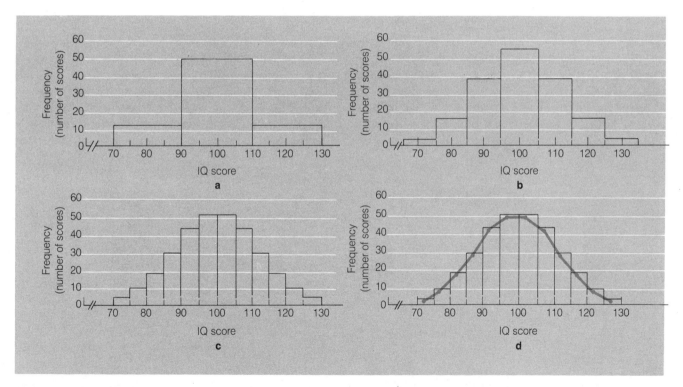

Figure A.1 ■ Frequency histograms and frequency polygons are related displays of data. (a) An extremely simple frequency histogram, drawn with such broad frequency intervals (70–90, 90–110, 110–130) that the shape of the data is nearly obliterated. (b) and (c) As increasingly smaller frequency intervals are used, the shape of the data becomes clearer. (d) A frequency polygon is created by connecting points that represent the values of each bar in the frequency histogram.

$x = 100, y = 53$, or 53 scores of 100 in the IQ distribution. ■ Figure A.2

When a smooth line is drawn to fit the plotted points, the result is called a **curve** (even though many "curves" are actually straight lines). Figure A.2b shows the curve that might result if all the IQ data were plotted; here the x-axis represents IQ and the y-axis represents frequency, that is, how many people had that particular IQ. (Note that this curve is the smoothed form of a frequency polygon with intervals of one IQ point.) The shape in Figure A.2b is called the **normal curve**, or bell-shaped curve. Basically, the normal-curve shape of Figure A.2b tells you that most subjects have IQs in the middle range, with a few spread out toward each end to give the bell shape its flare at the bottom.

The overall distribution of any data base is called a **frequency distribution**. The normal curve is a display of a particular type of frequency distribution called the **normal distribution**. A normal distribution is typically found for IQs and for other measurements of a population in which most people cluster around some central value, with some falling above and some below. The details of this particular distribution are well known and many of the manipulations that can be done with data are based on the characteristics of a normal distribution. It is known, for example, what percentage of the total population falls under the normal curve at any point out from its center (see Figure A.5 later in the appendix).

Not all variables will be normally distributed, however. Consider the frequency distribution that might be found for yearly income in a country with only two socioeconomic classes, a large group of poor peasants and a much smaller group of wealthy landowners. The shape in Figure A.3a shows graphically what we just noted in words, that there are two groups of separated scores. Such a shape is **bimodal**; we'll note why in a minute. But because this is not a normal distribution, it also says that we cannot apply further statistical techniques that can be used with a normal distribution. ■ Figure A.3

A less extreme example of a nonnormal distribution might be obtained from a more industrialized country with a substantial middle class and fewer people with increasingly high incomes. As plotted in Figure A.3b, this shape looks rather like a normal distribution but is a bit distorted, or skewed. In fact, it is technically called a **skewed distribution**. (Skewed distributions are described in terms of the direction of the "tail" of the distribution; Figure A.3b shows a distribution that is skewed right.) Skewed distributions are not as different from normal ones as bimodal distributions are, and obviously the less skew, the more they become like normal distributions. But a distribution skewed as badly as Figure A.3b would have to be treated as nonnormal.

Data can have other shapes, of course, but these are enough for our purposes. A surprising range of variables about humans turn out to fit the normal distribution well: Usually most of us are in the middle, with a few off to each side.

Measures of Central Tendency

Once the shape of the data is known to be at least something like a normal distribution, we can then look more closely at the middle of the curve and seek to describe it statistically. Measures of **central tendency** do this quantitatively; they describe in a summary sta-

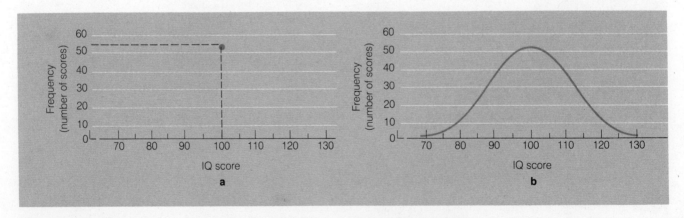

Figure A.2 ■ (a) The points of a plot are located by moving out the x-axis to the location that corresponds to the value of the point, then going up to the y-axis value. This point shows 53 scores at an IQ value of 100. (b) When all the points are plotted and a smooth line fitted to them, the result is a curve. When plotted, IQ distributions typically show this shape, called a normal or bell-shaped curve.

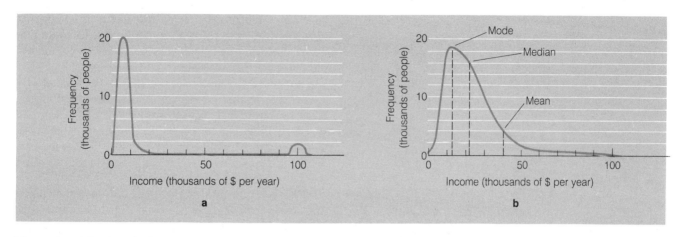

Figure A.3 ■ Two hypothetical nonnormal distributions. (a) A bimodal curve, such as might result if everyone in a population had either a low income or a high income. (b) A skewed curve, such as might result if there were a large group with moderate incomes and increasingly few people at the higher incomes.

tistic where the center of the distribution tends to be. At least one of the three measures of central tendency is already known to you. You probably call it the *average*, which is part of its full name of arithmetic average, but it is also known as the *mean*, the term most psychologists prefer. The other two measures of central tendency have similar-looking names—the *mode* and the *median*—which makes them more confusing than they might be otherwise. One of the useful characteristics of a normal distribution is that all three measures of central tendency give the same result, but for skewed or other nonnormal distributions they can be quite different.

The **mean**, or arithmetic average, is computed by adding all of the separate values (IQ scores in our earlier example) and dividing by the number of scores. For symmetrical distributions, including normal ones, this gives the center score (100 IQ score in Figure A.2b). But for skewed distributions the mean may not be as good a measure of central tendency as some other statistic. In our hypothetical two-class country of Figure A.3a, for example, the mean would yield an average income of perhaps $40,000. However, *no one* in that country actually earns $40,000, so this is certainly not what we mean by *average* in the sense of "common." For such a shape we need a better measure.

The **mode** is specifically the "most common" value—the number that appears most frequently in a distribution. In Figure A.3a the mode corresponds to the peak of the peasant distribution, which is a common income and thus somewhat more representative than the mean. But this mode completely ignores the wealthy portion of the population and thus does not truly represent the complete curve. We described the shape of this curve earlier as *bimodal*. Now you see

why: It really has two modes, or common values, one representing each of the two income classes. Once a plot has shown the curve to be bimodal, we can easily find the two modes thus represented: The modes for these two groups would be the most common incomes above and below some middle point.

Our third measure, the median, describes central tendency in still a different way. The **median** is the score that has as many scores above it as below it. What makes this measure useful is its applicability to a skewed distribution. In the distribution of Figure A.3b, for example, the computed mean would be pulled well toward the right, perhaps to $45,000, by the few very high incomes; but the mode, at perhaps $13,000, is not very representative of the whole shape either. The median would give the income of the person who was in the middle position, with as many people earning more money as earning less. This value, perhaps $25,000, would probably be the best one to use as a measure of central tendency for the entire distribution.

Most psychologists usually obtain normal distributions and thus report means, but you might encounter mode or median in special circumstances. Now that you know the difference, by the way, you might also listen for mistakes made by those who don't. It's not uncommon to hear a radio commentator, for example, read a report that clearly specifies *median* and in the next sentence refer to the *average*. In casual discussion, this might not matter, but for anything you really want to understand it may matter a great deal.

Measures of Variation

Now we have the shape of the distribution and its central tendency. What more do we want to know? Let's assume that we have a normal distribution; the

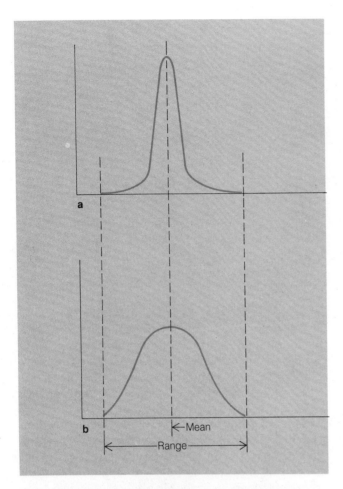

Figure A.4 ■ Two normal distributions with the same mean. Because they also have the same range, the difference between their shapes will only be shown by the standard deviation, which is substantially larger for (b) than for (a).

criteria that define the distribution as normal still do not tell us how "fat" or "skinny" it is. Both distributions of Figure A.4, for example, are normal and both have the same mean, but their shapes or spreads are obviously different; we need a measure that tells us this quantitatively. Such a measure is called a **measure of variation** because it tells how far most scores vary from the mean. It should tell us that the distribution in Figure A.4b has more variation than that in A.4a. ■ Figure A.4

Two measures of variation frequently used by psychologists are the range and the standard deviation. The **range** is simply the difference between the highest and lowest scores—that is, how wide a range they cover. If the highest IQ obtained was 150 and the lowest 50, the range would be 150 − 50 = 100. The range is an exceptionally simple measure to compute, but unfortunately it is not very useful. Nearly all scores might have been between 80 and 120, for example, but the *maximum* difference computed by the range

would not tell us that. If we used only the range to describe this distribution to someone else it would not be very informative. (Figures A.4a and A.4b, for example, have the same range.)

We need a measure that tells us the "usual" or "common" degree of variation that the distribution has. The **standard deviation** provides such a measure; it estimates the usual, common, or "standard" deviation from the mean. The more scores that are distributed away from the mean, the greater the standard deviation.

The computation of the standard deviation takes into account how many scores are included and how much each of them deviates from the mean. It translates this information into a single number that summarizes how variable or distributed the set of scores is. For a normal distribution, the mathematical relationships are such that six standard deviations—three above the mean and three below it—include virtually all (99.7%) of the scores in the distribution. For many purposes, however, four standard deviations (two above and two below the mean) include most (95%) of the scores. Because most of the scores fall near the mean in a standard distribution, even two standard deviations (one above and one below the mean) include approximately two thirds of the scores. ■ Figure A.5

A person who knows the properties of the standard deviation can use the mean and standard deviation of any distribution to help interpret a score within it. Suppose a score on a psychology exam was 75. How good is that? If the mean of the exam is 60, you know it's at least better than the mean—but you don't know how much better. If the standard deviation is 5, a score of 75 is three standard deviations above the mean, or one of the highest scores in the distribution. But if the standard deviation is 15, then 75 is only one standard deviation above the mean, and thus not nearly as high in the distribution.

A common way of assessing scores uses this logic to establish a special kind of score based on the mean and the standard deviation. A **standard score** replaces the actual numerical score with one that says how far that score fell above or below the mean for the group, expressed in standard deviations (Figure A.5b). An exam score that is one standard deviation above the mean for that exam would translate to a standard score of +1.0. Changing to standard scores is especially helpful in comparing scores from different distributions when the range of the distributions differs greatly. Suppose the mean scores on two psychology exams, for instance, were both 70 out of 100, but one exam showed a range of 20 to 100 and the other only 50 to 70. A raw score of 70 is obviously a lot better on

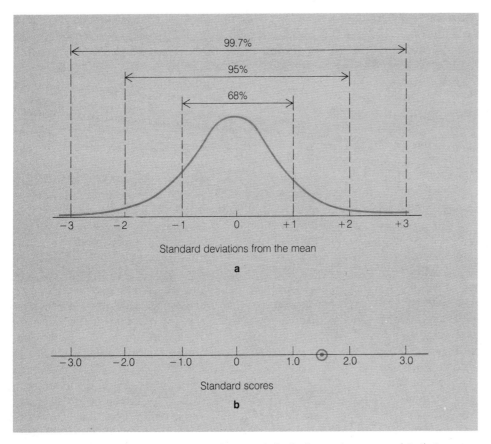

Figure A.5 ■ Because the characteristics of a normal distribution are known, any data that are found to be normally distributed can be analyzed by a number of statistics. The percentage of the total scores that fall under any portion of the distribution is known, for example; 69% of the scores fall between −1 and +1 standard deviations, about 95% between −2 and +2, and virtually all between −3 and +3. (b) Standard scores are created by translating the raw score into some number of standard deviations above or below the mean. The marked point here, for example, represents a score that is 1½ standard deviations above the mean. If it were a representation of IQ scores, it would correspond to an IQ of 124 (100 + 1.5 × the standard deviation of 16).

the second exam—it is the best score in the class. Translating a 70 on each exam into standard scores would show this numerically by yielding perhaps +0.5 versus +3.0. The standard score translation might be even more useful for other scores. How good a 60 is on each exam, for example, is not obvious from the ranges alone—but it would be if restated in standard scores.

Published reports of psychological research usually provide the mean and standard deviation for any distribution that is discussed. With a little practice you will find these a useful shorthand, a way of describing a whole set of numbers with a few numbers. They can be, in short, descriptive statistics. But other numbers are used to suggest what you can infer from these data.

INFERENTIAL STATISTICS

Describing what was actually found in a study is only the first step in interpreting the results. Researchers also use various inferential statistics to help draw correct inferences about the phenomenon being studied. One of the most important inferences is the extent to which any sample of subjects can be said to represent the overall population from which it comes.

Populations and Samples

One major problem in any research study is how to specify the larger group to which the results apply. Remember that rarely does any researcher care only about how the particular subjects in the study are affected. The subjects are almost always intended to represent much larger groups—ideally, all humans. The rules by which researchers can legitimately make such inferences, however, are rather exactly specified. The most central rule is that results can only be inferred for those larger populations from which the subjects were randomly sampled.

Any group of subjects may be considered a sample of some larger group. But only certain ways of obtaining that sample allow researchers to generalize their results to that larger group, called a **population**. Researchers must first define the appropriate population—who they wish their subjects to represent. Although researchers would like their results to apply to all people, inferential statistics allow them only to generalize to the specific population from which their subjects were selected. (In psychological research, when this population isn't white rats it is often first-year psychology students; many universities include subject participation as a course requirement—as you may already know.) It is also essential that the **sample** of subjects from the defined population be drawn randomly if later procedures are to have meaning. Each subject must be selected without bias, usually through a prearranged mathematical procedure, so that all members of the population have an equal chance of being in the sample. This ensures that the sample does not differ in any regular or biased way from the population.

Technically, researchers are allowed to generalize their results *only* to the population from which their subjects were randomly selected. In fact, because even students have rights, including the choice of which studies they wish to participate in, volunteer subjects are often accepted. The researchers simply never know the exact extent to which these subjects actually represent other students—or other nonstudents. However, even if they did randomly sample the school's subject pool, other students at the same school who hadn't volunteered to take the class that puts students into the pool would not be represented. And even if all students at the school were required to take the class, students at other schools, much less all humans in general, still wouldn't be represented. Whatever the population sampled, there will always be larger groups to which researchers will wish to generalize. Technically this is going beyond what researchers are allowed to do, however, so they typically phrase such extrapolations with caution: "Thus it may be that people in general. . . ."

To summarize, actual findings are obtained from a small group that represents a sample of some larger population. Investigators can legitimately infer statistically that the population will have the same characteristics as the sample, but only if the subjects were randomly sampled from the population. Further inferences about other groups are less secure and are often expressed only as possibilities.

Proof and Disproof

Some inferential statistics are ways of disproving some hypothesis. But before we look at them it's worthwhile considering the whole concept of disproof a bit more closely than in Chapter 1. On first consideration, it may seem that the way to test any proposed relationship empirically is to look for evidence that proves it, or as scientists say "supports" it. (*Proof* is a more absolute term, more appropriate within an exactly specified system such as geometry than in an empirical science where all facts are considered tentative.) Instead, in what seems initially to be a paradox, the correct scientific approach calls for setting up an arrangement that looks for **disproof**, or lack of support. Let's see why the arrangement for disproof not only makes sense but also is necessary.

One of the reasons the scientific method protects us against ourselves is that our natural tendency in thinking is to seek support or confirmation (Chapter 11). But solid confirmation only comes from situations in which it is *possible* that *disproof* can happen. This is a thorny concept, but let's see if an example helps. Suppose some hypothetical sect claims that its true believers never die. One of the members is currently elderly and sick, so you feel that their claim will soon be tested and perhaps disproved. But when death ensues, their response is, "Gee, and all along I thought Louise was a true believer—right up to the end." Hypothetically, such a sect could continue to believe its claim indefinitely, even as each of its members dies. Why doesn't a death disprove the belief? The key is that *true believer* is not defined ahead of time, so no real disproof is possible. Instead, the death is simply taken as proof that the person was not a true believer. Only *if* the sect first agrees that George is a true believer, and that his living or dying will be an acceptable test of the proposal, can his death be disproof of their proposition.

The paradox, remember, is that the test of a hypothesis must be so arranged that disproof is possible, even if the researcher fully expects that it won't happen. Only in this way is the test a valid one. This is sometimes described as making the hypothesis **falsifiable**, arranging so that it will be shown to be false if it really is. Consider another example. Suppose a person claims that behind you stands a ghost that mimics your every move. Is that notion testable? That all depends. What would be necessary to test this hypothesis? You say you don't see it in a mirror. "Ghosts don't show in mirrors," the person answers. You whirl around quickly and it's not there. "Ghosts are very fast." Your friends don't see it. "Not everyone can see this ghost." What are you left with? Essentially, the other person claims the ghost is there and you can't demonstrate that it's not. But the problem is the other person's, not yours. The other person has no right to claim it's there unless he or she offers a test that could possibly show the ghost not to be there if it isn't. Unless he or she offers the possibility of disproof, you need not pay any attention to the claim. (It is because of this logic that scientists often ignore the claims of pseudo-sciences.)

Scientists who believe that they understand some phenomenon may set out to test their belief through an experiment. As described in Chapter 1, they generally examine the effect of some treatment on an experimental group compared to the performance of an untreated control group. Their hypothesis—that the experimental treatment is effective—is subject to disproof if the behavior of the experimental group does not differ significantly from that of the control group. In contrast, the hypothesis is supported if the experimental group is significantly different from the control group. If that happens, the results are said to disprove the **null hypothesis**, the proposal that the experimental treatment is *not* effective. Hence, any experimental result is considered in terms of disproof of some hypothesis. Results that are *not* statistically significant tend to disprove the experimental hypothesis. Results that *are* statistically significant tend to disprove the null hypothesis.

Statistical Significance

Quantification, the expression of events numerically, has so long been recognized as part of the scientific method that anyone who wishes to convince anyone else typically seeks to do so with detailed numbers. Unfortunately, numbers may seem convincing even if their legitimacy is questionable. Social psychologists have shown, for example, that numbers that "look scientific" often greatly increase the impact of a message; for example, students are much more likely to believe astrological descriptions of themselves when these are based on very detailed birth information than when identical descriptions are based on less precise information. Obviously, many numbers offered us by various sources have little validity and ought never to be believed. For example, such misuse of legitimate aspects of the scientific method is a defining characteristic of pseudosciences, such as astrology or "biorhythms" (Chapter 7).

But the question of whether data should be believed still exists when there is no question of fraud. Even a researcher who has been extremely careful in the observing, correlating, or experimenting that has generated a data base must still question what those data really mean. Otherwise, he or she may be taken in not by fraud but by chance events, what we could call an accidental finding. Here everyday assessment techniques turn out to be seriously flawed and the researcher must apply carefully developed objective techniques to assess results. There are many ways in which our everyday thought processes misinterpret the world, but the best summary for our purpose is twofold: We are terrible at estimating the probability that an event will happen, and we seek confirmation rather than disproof.

As an example of our difficulties in probability estimation, consider an experience many people have had. A small group of people begin to discuss birthdays and two of them discover that they have the same birthday. "Isn't that a remarkable coincidence?" they say. But is it? How likely do you think it is that two or more people in your introductory psychology class have the same birthday? What about a smaller class: Would you be surprised to find a match of birthdays in a class of 40? Many people would, but you shouldn't be; the chances are nearly 9 in 10 that *any* group of 40 people will include 2 with the same birthday. In fact, the chances are better than 50% even for groups as small as 25 and approach 100% for groups larger than 50. Technically, the probability can never exactly equal 100% because we are considering probabilities and these do not guarantee the outcome. But if your class has 60 or more people, there are almost certainly 2 or more students whose birthdays match. ■ Figure A.6

Our tendency to seek out and accept apparent confirmation is another powerful cognitive bias that easily misleads us (Chapter 11). Frequently, for example, we accept a single event that occurs as if it were proof of something when it is just a random occurrence. Consider the situation when you dream that something may happen. If your dream prediction comes true you may be impressed, perhaps even a bit frightened. But how many people make how many predictions—and about how likely events? In fact, we frequently make predictions that *don't* come true, but we simply forget them and go on. The one that fits, even if hundreds have not, is the only one we notice and remember. "That's scary," you may say, "I knew so and so was calling before I answered the phone." Not really. There are only a limited number of people who will call you, and most calls will be from an even smaller group; sooner or later, you almost certainly will think of the right person just before answering. But it's only evidence of how you process information, not that you are psychic.

Now suppose a psychologist tries a number of approaches without success before finding some result

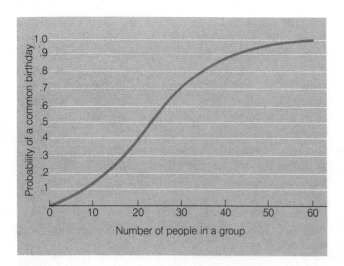

Figure A.6 ■ Because there are only 365 possible birthdays (excluding leap years), the more people you get together in a group the greater the chance that two or more of them will share a birthday. But most people do not appreciate how probable the chance of a shared birthday is for even relatively small groups. As shown, the chances approach 100% (a probability of 1.0) for groups of 60 and are quite high even for smaller groups.

that seems to confirm her hypothesis. Can she believe that she has finally located the answer? Or is she "capitalizing on chance"—taking advantage of an accident? Not even trained scientists can be relied upon to assess this correctly without special techniques, though their training may prevent the worst sort of errors that untrained individuals make. These specialized techniques are called tests of **statistical significance**; they mathematically calculate the probability that a particular finding might occur by chance. Only if the outcome of research is unlikely to occur by chance is the scientist justified in believing it. But such calculations can be complex.

Suppose you encounter a family with 13 sons and no daughters, for example. Is this an unusual finding or an expected one? The answer is "It depends." The odds against such a family are more than 8000 to 1 and thus they are definitely uncommon in everyday experience. But if you were to *look* for such families, checking data nationwide, the more you looked the more probable it would be that you would find one. On the average, you might expect to find 1 such family in every 8000; this means that in millions of families, you're almost certain to find a number with 13 sons. Thus on a national basis such a family is virtually inevitable, rather than unusual. Obviously, only careful procedures and statistical computations, ones that include how many people were looked at and how, can tell how unusual any given research finding is.

What researchers really need to know, however, is whether a finding is unusual enough to be believable. One complexity of statistical-significance calculations is that they simply estimate probabilities. But researchers must make a yes-or-no decision, that is, they must decide whether they have good data or chance results. What has to be added to make this decision is a specific value of probability that will be the accepted cutoff point. For psychology the cutoff point customarily accepted is the **.05 level**: Any consequence more likely than .05 (5 chances in 100) to have occurred by chance must be rejected. The odds that it was simply a chance finding are too high, and a researcher cannot legitimately interpret or publish such results. But note that the result could still be a chance one even if the calculated probability is less than .05. It just is more than 95% likely to be real and less than 5% likely to be chance.

It is, of course, possible to get even more significant findings: .01 (1 chance in 100) is usually the next level reported, but you will sometimes see .001, or odds of only one in 1000 that the result reflects chance. If you look up any of the original studies cited in this text you will find some probability value reported for any data that is discussed; it will usually appear as a footnote such as "$p < .05$," indicating that the probability of chance results has been calculated as less than .05.

What such probability computations mean can be expressed in terms of sampling a population. Just as the subjects examined in a study are a sample of some population, so the mean values of the data obtained from the experimental group and the control group are two different samples of that population mean. The null hypothesis states that any difference between the obtained means is only a chance difference reflecting nonmeaningful differences in the two samples. In order to reject the null hypothesis, the researcher must show that the differences between experimental-group and control-group means are greater than any accidental differences that could reasonably be expected.

If a researcher had lots of time and money, he or she could run many control groups and examine the differences among them. For the experimental treatment to be considered effective, the experimental group's mean would have to differ from these control means more than they differed from each other. Researchers, however, rarely have that much time and money. Fortunately, the statistical significance computations provide a way to estimate a similar result; they estimate what those other sample means would have been like, based on the characteristics of the actual data obtained. A .05 significance value, for example, estimates that if 100 samples of the actual mean were taken by using 100 control groups, only 5 would vary by as much from the population mean as the experimental group did. The other 95 would not vary as much. So the experimenter knows that there is a

5% chance that he or she has chance results and a 95% chance that the experimental group is actually different. This doesn't guarantee that the observed difference is real, but it makes it 95% probable.

Remember, however, that these probability computations only report the likelihood that the numbers are real or believable (Chapter 1). The significance of the results in terms of their importance must always be determined in other ways. This problem is made worse by a convention among scientists to use only *significance* as a shorthand word, when they mean *statistical significance*. Whenever you read about research that mentions significant or nonsignificant findings, remember that the importance of the findings rests on different grounds. Even inferential statistics are only aids to interpretation. In the long run, it is the human user of statistics who must figure out what they really mean.

Further Readings

For further exploration of statistics in psychology, see a statistics text oriented to the behavioral sciences such as Wright's *Understanding Statistics* (1976) or Pagano's *Understanding Statistics in the Behavioral Sciences* (1981). Specialized statistics concerning IQ or other testing are included in Kaplan and Saccuzzo's *Psychological Testing* (1982). An integrated discussion of statistics and their role in experimental design is presented in Jaccard's *Statistics for the Behavioral Sciences* (1983).

BIBLIOGRAPHY

Abelson, R. P. (1981). Psychological status of the script concept. *American Psychologist, 36*, 715–729.

Abelson, R. P., Aronson, E., McGuire, W. J., Newcomb, T. M., Rosenberg, M. J., & Tannebaum, P. E. (1968). *Theories of cognitive consistency: A sourcebook.* Chicago: Rand McNally.

Abramov, I., Gordon, J., Hendrickson, A., Dobson, V., & LaBossiere, E. (1982). The retina of the newborn human infant. *Science, 217*, 265–267.

Abramson, L. Y., Seligman, M. E. P., & Teasdale, J. D. (1978). Learned helplessness in humans: Critique and reformulation. *Journal of Abnormal Psychology, 87*, 49–74.

Abramson, P. R. (1980). *Personality.* New York: Holt, Rinehart & Winston.

Acton, E. M., & Stone, H. (1976). Potential new artificial sweetener from study of structure-taste relationships. *Science, 193*, 584–586.

Adams, D. (1977, March). Building moral dilemma activities. *Learning,* pp. 44–46.

Adams, E. (1958, January). Barbiturates. *Scientific American,* pp. 60–64.

Adams, J. L. (1980). *Conceptual blockbusting: A guide to better ideas* (2nd ed.). New York: W. W. Norton.

Adelson, J. (1982, April). Still vital after all these years. *Psychology Today,* pp. 52–59.

Adler, A. (1959). *The practice and theory of individual psychology.* Totowa, NJ: Littlefield Adams.

Adler, N. T. (Ed.). (1981). *Neuroendocrinology of reproduction.* New York: Plenum Press.

Agranoff, B. W., & Davis, R. E. (1974). More on seasonal variations in goldfish learning. *Science, 186*, 65.

Agras, S., Sylvester, D., & Oliveau, D. (1969). *The epidemiology of common fears and phobias.* Unpublished manuscript. [Cited in Davison & Neale, 1982]

Ahearn, S., & Beatty, J. (1979). Pupillary responses during information processing vary with scholastic aptitude test scores. *Science, 205*, 1289–1292.

Aigner, T. G., & Balster, R. L. (1978). Choice behavior in rhesus monkeys: Cocaine versus food. *Science, 201*, 534–535.

Ainsworth, M. D. S. (1979). Infant-mother attachment. *American Psychologist, 34*, 932–937.

Ajzen, I., & Fishbein, M. (1977). Attitude-behavior relations: A theoretical analysis and review of empirical research. *Psychological Bulletin, 84*, 888–918.

Ajzen, I., & Fishbein, M. (1980). *Understanding attitudes and predicting social behavior.* Englewood Cliffs, NJ: Prentice-Hall.

Akhter, S., Wig, N. N., Varma, V. K., Pershad, D., & Verma, S. K. (1975). A phenomenological analysis of symptoms in obsessive-compulsive neurosis. *British Journal of Psychiatry, 127*, 342–348.

Akil, H., Richardson, D. E., Hughes, J., & Barchas, J. D. (1978). Enkephalin-like material elevated in ventricular cerebrospinal fluid of pain patients after analgetic focal stimulation. *Science, 201*, 463–465.

Akiskal, H. S., & McKinney, W. T., Jr. (1975). Overview of recent research in depression: Integration of ten conceptual models into a comprehensive clinical frame. *Archives of General Psychiatry, 32*, 285–305.

Albert, R. S. (1975). Toward a behavioral definition of genius. *American Psychologist, 30*, 140–151.

Alcock, J. (1979). *Animal behavior: An evolutionary approach* (2nd ed.). Sunderland, MA: Sinauer Associates.

Allderidge, P. (1979). Hospitals, mad houses, and asylums: Cycles in the care of the insane. *British Journal of Psychiatry, 134*, 321–324.

Allen, G. W. (1967). *William James.* New York: Viking Press.

Allen, M. G. (1976). Twin studies of affective illness. *Archives of General Psychiatry, 33*, 1476–1478.

Allen, V. L. (1965). Situational factors in conformity. In L. Berkowitz (Ed.), *Advances in experimental social psychology* (Vol. 2, pp. 133–175). New York: Academic Press.

Allman, W. F., Hamer, B., & Tierney, J. (1982, January/February). Dog mines and bat bombs. *Science 82,* p. 86.

Allport, G. W. (1942). *The use of personal documents in psychological science.* New York: Social Science Research Council.

Allport, G. W. (1961). *Patterns and growth in personality.* New York: Holt, Rinehart & Winston.

Allport, G. W. (Ed.). (1965). *Letters from Jenny.* New York: Harcourt Brace Jovanovich.

Allport, G. W. (1966a). Traits revisited. *American Psychologist, 21*, 1–10.

Allport, G. W. (1966b). William James and the behavioral sciences. *Journal of the History of the Behavioral Sciences, 2*, 145–147.

Allport, G: W. (1968). *The person in psychology: Selected essays.* Boston: Beacon Press.

Allport, G. W., & Odbert, H. S. (1936). Trait-names: A psycho-lexical study. *Psychological Monographs, 47*(211), 1–171.

Altman, I. (1975). *The environment and social behavior: Privacy, personal space, territory, crowding.* Monterey, CA: Brooks/Cole.

Altman, I. (1978). Crowding: Historical and contemporary trends in crowding research. In A. Baum & Y. M. Epstein (Eds.), *Human response to crowding* (pp. 3–29). Hillsdale, NJ: Lawrence Erlbaum.

Altman, I., & Chemers, M. (1980). *Culture and environment.* Monterey, CA: Brooks/Cole.

American Psychiatric Association. (1980). *Diagnostic and statistical manual of mental disorders* (3rd ed.). Washington, DC: Author.

American Psychiatric Association Task Force on Electroconvulsive Therapy. (1978). *Report: Electroconvulsive therapy.* Washington, DC: American Psychiatric Association.

American Psychological Association. (1975). *A career in psychology.* Washington, DC: Author.

American Psychological Association. (1980). Brief of American Psychological Association as amicus curiae. *American Psychologist, 35*, 1028–1043.

American Psychological Association. (1981). Ethical principles of psychologists. *American Psychologist, 36*, 633–638.

American Psychological Association. (Annual). *Graduate studies in psychology.* Washington, DC: Author.

American Psychological Association Publication Manual Task Force. (1977). Guidelines for non-sexist language in APA journals: Publication manual change sheet 2. *American Psychologist, 32*, 487–494.

Amoore, J. E. (1970). *Molecular basis of odor.* Springfield, IL: Charles C Thomas.

Amoore, J. E., Johnston, J. W., Jr., & Rubin, M. (1964, February). The stereochemical theory of odor. *Scientific American,* pp. 42–49.

Amsel, A. (1967). Partial reinforcement effects on vigor and persistence. In K. W. Spence & J. T. Spence (Eds.), *The psychology of learning and motivation: Advances in research and theory* (Vol. 1, pp. 1–65). New York: Academic Press.

Anastasi, A. (1982). *Psychological testing* (5th ed.). New York: Macmillan.

Anderson, J. R. (1978). Arguments concerning representations for mental imagery. *Psychological Review, 85,* 249–277.

Anderson, J. R. (1980). *Cognitive psychology and its implications.* San Francisco: W. H. Freeman.

Anderson, J. R., & Bower, G. H. (1973). *Human associative memory.* Washington, DC: V. H. Winston.

Anderson, N. H. (1965). Averaging versus adding as a stimulus-combination rule in impression formation. *Journal of Experimental Psychology, 70*, 394–400.

Anderson, W. F., & Diacumakos, E. G. (1981, July). Genetic engineering in mammalian cells. *Scientific American*, pp. 106–121.

Andersson, B. (1971). Thirst—and brain control of water balance. *American Scientist, 59*, 408–415.

Andrews, G., & Solomon, D. (Eds.). (1975). *The coca leaf and cocaine papers.* New York: Harcourt Brace Jovanovich.

Appelbaum, S. A. (1982). Challenges to traditional psychotherapy from the "new therapies." *American Psychologist, 37*, 1002–1008.

Archer, D. (1980). *How to expand your S.I.Q. (social intelligence quotient).* New York: M. Evans.

Ardrey, R. (1966). *The territorial imperative.* New York: Atheneum.

Arkes, H. R., & Garske, J. P. (1982). *Psychological theories of motivation* (2nd ed.). Monterey, CA: Brooks/Cole.

Arkin, A. M., Antrobus, J. S., & Ellman, S. J. (Eds.). (1978). *The mind in sleep: Psychology and psychophysiology.* New York: Halsted Press.

Arnold, A. P. (1980). Sexual differences in the brain. *American Scientist, 68*, 165–173.

Aronfreed, J. (1968). *Conduct and conscience: The socialization of internalized control over behavior.* New York: Academic Press.

Aronson, E. (1980). *The social animal* (3rd ed.). San Francisco: W. H. Freeman.

Asch, S. E. (1946a). Forming impressions of personality. *Journal of Abnormal and Social Psychology, 41*, 258–290.

Asch, S. E. (1946b). Max Wertheimer's contribution to modern psychology. *Social Research, 13*, 81–102.

Asch, S. E. (1951). Effects of group pressure upon the modification and distortion of judgments. In H. Guetzkow (Ed.), *Groups, leadership, and men* (pp. 177–190). Pittsburgh: Carnegie Press.

Asch, S. E. (1955, November). Opinions and social pressure. *Scientific American*, pp. 31–35.

Asch, S. E. (1956). Studies of independence and submission to group pressure: I. A minority of one against a unanimous majority. *Psychological Monographs, 70*(9, Whole No. 417).

Ascher, L. (1978, August). Measuring women's sex arousal during sleep. *Psychology Today*, pp. 20, 24.

Aschoff, J. (Ed.). (1981). *Handbook of behavioral neurobiology: Vol. 4. Biological rhythms.* New York: Plenum Press.

Atkinson, J. W. (1974). Strength of motivation and efficiency of performance. In J. W. Atkinson & J. O. Raynor (Eds.), *Motivation and achievement* (pp. 193–218). Washington, DC: V. H. Winston.

Atkinson, R. C. (1975). Mnemotechnics in second-language learning. *American Psychologist, 30*, 821–828.

Atkinson, R. C., & Shiffrin, R. M. (1968). Human memory: A proposed system and its control processes. In K. W. Spence & J. T. Spence (Eds.), *The psychology of learning and motivation: Advances in research and theory* (Vol. 2, pp. 89–115). New York: Academic Press.

Atkinson, R. C., & Shiffrin, R. M. (1971, August). The control of short-term memory. *Scientific American*, pp. 82–90.

Attneave, F. (1971, December). Multistability in perception. *Scientific American*, pp. 62–71.

Axelrod, J. (1974, June). Neurotransmitters. *Scientific American*, pp. 58–71.

Axelrod, R., & Hamilton, W. D. (1981). The evolution of cooperation. *Science, 211*, 1390–1396.

Ayala, F. J. (1978, September). The mechanisms of evolution. *Scientific American*, pp. 56–69.

Ayllon, T., & Azrin, N. H. (1965). The measurement and reinforcement of behavior of psychotics. *Journal of the Experimental Analysis of Behavior, 8*, 357–383.

Ayllon, T., & Azrin, N. H. (1968). *The token economy: A motivational system for therapy and rehabilitation.* New York: Appleton-Century-Crofts.

Aziz, B. N. (1978, August). Maps and mind. *Human Nature*, pp. 50–59.

Bach, E. (1974). *Syntactic theory.* New York: Holt, Rinehart & Winston.

Bachrach, A. J., Erwin, W. J., & Mohr, J. P. (1965). The control of eating behavior in an anorexic by operant conditioning techniques. In L. P. Ullmann & L. Krasner (Eds.), *Case studies in behavior modification* (pp. 153–163). New York: Holt, Rinehart & Winston.

Baddeley, A. D. (1978). The trouble with levels: A reexamination of Craik and Lockhart's "Framework for memory research." *Psychological Review, 85*, 139–152.

Bahill, A. T., & Stark, L. (1979, January). The trajectories of saccadic eye movements. *Scientific American*, pp. 108–117.

Bailey, R. E., & Bailey, M. B. (1980). A view from outside the Skinner box. *American Psychologist, 35*, 942–946.

Bainbridge, W. S. (1978, Spring/Summer). Biorhythms: Evaluating a pseudoscience. *Skeptical Inquirer, 2*, 40–56.

Baird, L. C. (1980). Cube or hexagon? *American Scientist, 68*, 602.

Baker, P. F. (1966, March). The nerve axon. *Scientific American*, pp. 74–82.

Baker, R. K., & Ball, S. J. (Eds.). (1969). *Violence and the media: A staff report to the National Commission on the Causes and Prevention of Violence.* Washington, DC: U.S. Government Printing Office.

Bakker, R. T. (1975, April). Dinosaur renaissance. *Scientific American*, pp. 58–78.

Baltes, P. B., & Brim, O. G., Jr. (Eds.). (1980). *Life-span development and behavior.* New York: Academic Press.

Baltes, P. B., Reese, H. W., & Lipsitt, L. P. (1980). Life-span developmental psychology. *Annual Review of Psychology, 31*, 65–110.

Baltes, P. B., & Schaie, K. W. (1976). On the plasticity of intelligence in adulthood and old age: Where Horn and Donaldson fail. *American Psychologist, 31*, 720–725.

Bandura, A. (1962). Social learning through imitation. In M. R. Jones (Ed.), *Nebraska Symposium on Motivation* (Vol. pp. 211–269). Lincoln, NE: University of Nebraska Press.

Bandura, A. (1965). Vicarious processes: A case of no-trial learning. In L. Berkowitz (Ed.), *Advances in experimental social psychology* (Vol. 2, pp. 1–55). New York: Academic Press.

Bandura, A. (1967, March). Behavioral psychotherapy. *Scientific American*, pp. 78–86.

Bandura, A. (1969). *Principles of behavior modification.* New York: Holt, Rinehart & Winston.

Bandura, A. (Ed.). (1971). *Psychological modeling: Conflicting theories.* New York: Lieber-Atherton.

Bandura, A. (1973). *Aggression: A social learning analysis.* Englewood Cliffs, NJ: Prentice-Hall.

Bandura, A. (1974). Behavior theory and the models of man. *American Psychologist, 29*, 859–869.

Bandura, A. (1977a). Self-efficacy: Toward a unifying theory of behavioral change. *Psychological Review, 84*, 191–215.

Bandura, A. (1977b). *Social learning theory.* Englewood Cliffs, NJ: Prentice-Hall.

Bandura, A. (1978). The self system in reciprocal determinism. *American Psychologist, 33*, 344–358.

Bandura, A. (1982). The psychology of chance encounters and life paths. *American Psychologist, 37*, 747–755.

Bandura, A., Blanchard, E. B., & Ritter, B. (1969). Relative efficacy of desensitization and modeling approaches for inducing behavioral, affective, and attitudinal changes. *Journal of Personality and Social Psychology, 13*, 173–199.

Bandura, A., & McDonald, F. J. (1963). The influence of social reinforcement and the behavior of models in shaping children's moral judgments. *Journal of Abnormal and Social Psychology, 67*, 274–281.

Bandura, A., & Menlove, F. L. (1968). Factors determining vicarious extinction of avoidance behavior through symbolic modeling. *Journal of Personality and Social Psychology, 8*, 99–108.

Bandura, A., & Rosenthal, T. L. (1966). Vicarious classical conditioning as a function of arousal level. *Journal of Personality and Social Psychology, 3*, 54–62.

Bandura, A., Ross, D., & Ross, S. (1961). Transmission of aggression through imitation of aggressive models. *Journal of Abnormal and Social Psychology, 63*, 572–582.

Bandura, A., Ross, D., & Ross, S. A. (1963). Imitation of film-mediated aggressive models. *Journal of Abnormal and Social Psychology, 66,* 3–11.

Bandura, A., & Walters, R. H. (1963). *Social learning and personality development.* New York: Holt, Rinehart & Winston.

Banks, W. P., & Barber, G. (1977). Color information in iconic memory. *Psychological Review, 84,* 536–546.

Barahal, H. S. (1958). 1000 prefrontal lobotomies: Five-to-ten-year follow-up study. *Psychiatric Quarterly, 32,* 653–678.

Baran, S. J., Chase, L. J., & Courtright, J. A. (1979). Television drama as a facilitator of prosocial behavior: "The Waltons." *Journal of Broadcasting, 23,* 277–284.

Bard, P. (1934). On emotional experience after decortication with some remarks on theoretical views. *Psychological Review, 41,* 309–329.

Barker, L. M., Best, M. R., & Domjan, M. (Eds.). (1978). *Learning mechanisms in food selection.* Waco, TX: Baylor University Press.

Baron, R. A. (1977). *Human aggression.* New York: Plenum Press.

Baron, R. A., & Byrne, D. (1982). *Exploring social psychology* (2nd ed.). Boston: Allyn & Bacon.

Baron, R. A., & Ransberger, V. M. (1978). Ambient temperature and the occurrence of collective violence: The "long, hot summer" revisited. *Journal of Personality and Social Psychology, 36,* 351–360.

Barrett, C. L. (1969). Systematic desensitization versus implosive therapy. *Journal of Abnormal Psychology, 74,* 587–592.

Barron, F. (1958, September). The psychology of imagination. *Scientific American,* pp. 150–170.

Barron, F., Jarvik, M. E., & Bunnell, S., Jr. (1964, April). The hallucinogenic drugs. *Scientific American,* pp. 29–37.

Bartlett, F. C. (1932). *Remembering: A study in experimental and social psychology.* Cambridge: Cambridge University Press.

Bartol, C. R. (1983). *Psychology and American law.* Belmont, CA: Wadsworth.

Bartus, R. T. (1979). Physostigmine and recent memory: Effects in young and aged nonhuman primates. *Science, 206,* 1087–1089.

Bartus, R. T., Dean, R. L., Goas, J. A., & Lippa, A. S. (1980). Age-related changes in passive avoidance retention: Modulation with dietary choline. *Science, 209,* 301–303.

Bassuk, E. L., & Gerson, S. (1978, February). Deinstitutionalization and mental health services. *Scientific American,* pp. 46–53.

Bateson, G., Jackson, D. D., Haley, J., & Weakland, J. (1956). Toward a theory of schizophrenia. *Behavioral Science, 1,* 251–264.

Batson, D., & Coke, J. S. (1981). Empathy: A source of altruistic motivation for helping? In J. P. Rushton & R. M. Sorrentino (Eds.), *Altruism and helping behavior: Social, personality, and developmental perspectives* (pp. 167–188). Hillsdale, NJ: Lawrence Erlbaum.

Baum, A., Aiello, J. R., & Calesnick, L. E. (1978). Crowding and personal control: Social density and the development of learned helplessness. *Journal of Personality and Social Psychology, 36,* 1000–1011.

Baum, A., & Epstein, Y. M. (Eds.). (1978). *Human response to crowding.* Hillsdale, NJ: Lawrence Erlbaum.

Bayley, N. (1969). *Manual: Bayley scales of infant development.* New York: Psychological Corporation.

Bayley, N. (1970). Development of mental abilities. In P. Mussen (Ed.), *Carmichael's manual of child psychology* (Vol. 1, pp. 1163–1209). New York: John Wiley.

Bazar, J. (1980, January). Catching up with the ape language debate. *APA Monitor,* p. 4.

Bazelon, D. L. (1974, June). Psychiatrists and the adversary process. *Scientific American,* pp. 18–23.

Beach, F. A. (1975). Behavioral endocrinology: An emerging discipline. *American Scientist, 63,* 178–197.

Beach, F. A. (Ed.). (1977). *Human sexuality in four perspectives.* Baltimore: Johns Hopkins University Press.

Beal, M. F., Kleinman, G. M., Ojemann, R. C., & Hockberg, F. H. (1981). Gangliocytoma of third ventricle: Hyperphagia, somnolence and dementia. *Neurology, 31,* 1224–1227.

Beck, A. T. (1967). *Depression: Clinical, experimental and theoretical aspects.* New York: Harper & Row.

Beck, A. T. (1976). *Cognitive therapy and the emotional disorders.* New York: International Universities Press.

Beck, A. T., Rush, A. J., Shaw, B. F., & Emery, G. (1979). *Cognitive therapy of depression.* New York: Guilford Press.

Beck, A. T., Ward, C. H., Mandelson, M., Mock, J. E., & Erbaugh, J. K. (1962). Reliability of psychiatric diagnosis: II. A study of consistency of clinical judgments and ratings. *American Journal of Psychiatry, 119,* 351–357.

Beck, J. (1975, August). The perception of surface color. *Scientific American,* pp. 61–75.

Becker, J. (1977). *Affective disorders.* Morristown, NJ: General Learning Press.

Becker, W. C. (1960). The matching of behavior rating and questionnaire personality factors. *Psychological Bulletin, 57,* 201–212.

Békésy, G. von. (1957, August). The ear. *Scientific American,* pp. 66–78.

Békésy, G. von. (1960). *Experiments in hearing.* New York: McGraw-Hill.

Bell, A. P., & Weinberg, M. S. (1978). *Homosexualities: A study of diversity among men and women.* New York: Simon & Schuster.

Bell, A. P., Weinberg, M. S., & Hammersmith, S. K. (1981). *Sexual preference: Its development in men and women.* Bloomington, IN: Indiana University Press.

Bell, P. A., Fisher, J. D., & Loomis, R. J. (1978). *Environmental psychology.* Philadelphia: W. B. Saunders.

Bell, R. Q. (1979). Parent, child, and reciprocal influences. *American Psychologist, 34,* 821–826.

Bellack, A. S., Hersen, M., & Turner, S. M. (1976). Generalization effects of social skills training in chronic schizophrenics: An experimental analysis. *Behavior Research and Therapy, 14,* 391–398.

Belsky, J. (1980). Child maltreatment: An ecological integration. *American Psychologist, 35,* 320–335.

Belson, W. (1978). *Television violence and the adolescent boy.* London: Saxon House.

Bem, D. J. (1972). Self-perception theory. In L. Berkowitz (Ed.), *Advances in experimental social psychology* (Vol. 6, pp. 1–62). New York: Academic Press.

Bem, D. J., & Allen, A. (1974). On predicting some of the people some of the time: The search for cross-situational consistencies in behavior. *Psychological Review, 81,* 506–520.

Bem, S. L. (1974). The measurement of psychological androgyny. *Journal of Consulting and Clinical Psychology, 42,* 155–162.

Bem, S. L. (1981a). The BSRI and gender schema theory: A reply to Spence and Helmreich. *Psychological Review, 88,* 369–371.

Bem, S. L. (1981b). Gender schema theory: A cognitive account of sex typing. *Psychological Review, 88,* 354–364.

Benderly, B. L. (1980a). *Dancing without music: Deafness in America.* New York: Doubleday.

Benderly, B. L. (1980b, July/August). The great ape debate: Can gorillas and chimps use language or not? *Science 80,* pp. 60–65.

Benditt, E. P. (1977, February). The origin of atherosclerosis. *Scientific American,* pp. 74–85.

Benedict, R. (1934). *Patterns of culture.* Boston: Houghton Mifflin.

Bennett, W., & Gurin, J. (1982, March). Do diets really work? *Science 82,* pp. 42–50.

Benson, H. (1975). *The relaxation response.* New York: William Morrow.

Benson, H., Kotch, J. B., Crassweller, K. D., & Greenwood, M. M. (1977). Historical and clinical considerations of the relaxation response. *American Scientist, 65,* 441–445.

Benson, P. L., Karabenick, S. A., & Lerner, R. M. (1976). Pretty pleases: The effects of physical attractiveness, race, and sex on receiving help. *Journal of Experimental Social Psychology, 12,* 409–415.

Benzer, S. (1973, December). Genetic dissection of behavior. *Scientific American*, pp. 24–37.

Berger, P. A. (1978). Medical treatment of mental illness. *Science, 200*, 974–981.

Berger, R. J. (1969). Oculomotor control: A possible function of REM sleep. *Psychological Review, 76*, 144–164.

Berko, J. (1958). The child's learning of English morphology. *Word, 14*, 150–177.

Berko, J., & Brown, R. (1960). Psycholinguistic research methods. In P. H. Mussen (Ed.), *Handbook of research methods in child development* (pp. 517–557). New York: John Wiley.

Berkowitz, L. (1968). Responsibility, reciprocity, and social distance in helpgiving: An experimental investigation of English social class differences. *Journal of Experimental Social Psychology, 4*, 46–63.

Berkowitz, L. (Ed.). (1969). *Roots of aggression*. Chicago: Aldine.

Berkowitz, L. (1978). Whatever happened to the frustration-aggression hypothesis? *American Behavioral Scientist, 21*, 691–708.

Berkowitz, L., & Daniels, L. R. (1963). Responsibility and dependency. *Journal of Abnormal and Social Psychology, 66*, 429–436.

Berkowitz, L., & Donnerstein, E. (1982). External validity is more than skin deep: Some answers to criticisms of laboratory experiments. *American Psychologist, 37*, 245–257.

Berkowitz, L., & LePage, A. (1967). Weapons as aggression-eliciting stimuli. *Journal of Personality and Social Psychology, 7*, 202–207.

Berlyne, D. E. (1960). *Conflict, arousal and curiosity*. New York: McGraw-Hill.

Berlyne, D. E. (1966, August). Conflict and arousal. *Scientific American*, pp. 82–87.

Bernstein, I. S., & Gordon, T. P. (1974). The function of aggression in primate societies. *American Scientist, 62*, 304–311.

Berscheid, E., & Walster, E. H. (1969). *Interpersonal attraction*. Reading, MA: Addison-Wesley.

Berscheid, E., & Walster, E. H. (1974a). A little bit about love. In T. L. Houston (Ed.), *Foundations of interpersonal attractiveness*. New York: Academic Press.

Berscheid, E., & Walster, E. H. (1974b). Physical attractiveness. In L. Berkowitz (Ed.), *Advances in experimental social psychology* (Vol. 7, pp. 157–215). New York: Academic Press.

Bersoff, D. N. (1981). Testing and the law. *American Psychologist, 36*, 1047–1056.

Bever, T. G., Garritt, M. F., & Hurtig, R. (1973). The interaction of perceptual processes and ambiguous sentences. *Memory & Cognition, 1*, 277–286.

Bickerton, D. (1983, July). Creole languages. *Scientific American*, pp. 116–122.

Bijou, S. W. (1968). Ages, stages, and the naturalization of human development. *American Psychologist, 23*, 419–427.

Bijou, S. W. (1976). *Child development: The basic stage of early childhood*. Englewood Cliffs, NJ: Prentice-Hall.

Bindra, D. (Ed.). (1980). *The brain's mind: A neuroscience perspective on the mind-body problem*. New York: Gardner Press.

Binet, A., & Simon, T. (1905). Sur la nécessité d'établir un diagnostic scientifique des états inférieurs de l'intelligence. *L'Année Psychologique, 11*, 163–190.

Binet, A., & Simon, T. (1908). Le developpement de l'intelligence chez les enfants. *L'Année Psychologique, 14*, 1–90.

Bingham, R. (1982, April). On the life of Mr. Darwin. *Science 82*, pp. 34–39.

Binkley, S. (1979, April). A timekeeping enzyme in the pineal gland. *Scientific American*, pp. 66–71.

Birdwhistell, R. L. (1970). *Kinesics and context: Essays on body motion communication*. Philadelphia: University of Pennsylvania Press.

Birren, J. E. (1970). Toward an experimental psychology of aging. *American Psychologist, 25*, 124–135.

Bishop, J. A., & Cook, L. M. (1975, January). Moths, melanism, and clean air. *Scientific American*, pp. 90–99.

Bitterman, M. E. (1975). The comparative analysis of learning: Are the laws of learning the same in all animals? *Science, 188*, 699–709.

Bizzi, E. (1974, October). The coordination of eye-head movements. *Scientific American*, pp. 100–106.

Blakemore, C. (1977). *Mechanics of the mind*. Cambridge: Cambridge University Press.

Blaney, P. H. (1977). Contemporary theories of depression: Critique and comparison. *Journal of Abnormal Psychology, 86*, 203–223.

Blasi, A. (1980). Bridging moral cognition and moral action: A critical review of the literature. *Psychological Bulletin, 88*, 1–45.

Blass, E. M., & Teicher, M. H. (1980). Suckling. *Science, 210*, 15–22.

Block, E. B. (1976). *Hypnosis: A new tool in crime detection*. New York: David McKay.

Block, J. (1961). *The Q-sort method in personality assessment and psychiatric research*. Springfield, IL: Charles C Thomas.

Block, J. H., & Block, J. (1980). The role of ego-control and ego-resiliency in the organization of behavior. In W. A. Collins (Ed.), *The Minnesota symposium on child psychology* (Vol. 13, pp. 39–101). Hillsdale, NJ: Lawrence Erlbaum.

Block, N. (Ed.). (1981). *Imagery*. Cambridge, MA: MIT Press.

Bloom, L. (1973). *One word at a time: The use of single word utterances before syntax*. The Hague: Mouton.

Blough, D. S. (1961, July). Experiments in animal psychophysics. *Scientific American*, pp. 113–122.

Blough, D. S. (1982). Pigeon perception of letters of the alphabet. *Science, 218*, 397–398.

Blumenthal, A. L. (1977). Wilhelm Wundt and early American psychology: A clash of two cultures. *Annals of the New York Academy of Sciences, 291*, 13–20.

Blumenthal, M. D., Kahn, R. L., Andrews, F. M., & Head, K. B.. (1972). *Justifying violence: Attitudes of American men*. Ann Arbor: University of Michigan, Institute for Social Research.

Boag, P. T., & Grant, P. R. (1981). Intense natural selection in a population of Darwin's finches (*Geospizinae*) in the Galapagos. *Science, 214*, 82–84.

Bockhoven, J. (1963). *Moral treatment in American psychiatry*. New York: Springer.

Boden, M. A. (1977). *Artificial intelligence and natural man*. New York: Basic Books.

Boden, M. A. (1981). *Minds and mechanisms: Philosophical psychology and computational models*. Ithaca, NY: Cornell University Press.

Bodine, A. (1975). Androcentrism in prescriptive grammar: Singular "they," sex-indefinite "he," and "he or she." *Language in Society, 4*, 129–146.

Bodis-Wollner, I., Atkin, A., Raab, E., & Wolkstein, M. (1977). Visual association cortex and vision in man: Pattern-evoked occipital potentials in a blind boy. *Science, 198*, 629–631.

Bogdan, R., & Taylor, S. (1976). The judged, not the judges: An insider's view of mental retardation. *American Psychologist, 31*, 47–52.

Bogen, J. E. (1975, Spring). Educational aspects of hemispheric specialization. *UCLA Educator, 17*, 24–32.

Bohannon, P. (1980, September/October). Culture by numbers. *Science 80*, pp. 28–32.

Bolles, R. C. (1970). Species-specific defense reactions and avoidance learning. *Psychological Review, 77*, 32–48.

Bolles, R. C. (1972). The avoidance learning problem. In G. H. Bower (Ed.), *The psychology of learning and motivation: Advances in research and theory* (Vol. 6, pp. 97–145). New York: Academic Press.

Bolles, R. C., & Faneslow, M. S. (1982). Endorphins and behavior. *Annual Review of Psychology, 33*, 87–101.

Bonner, J. T. (1980). *The evolution of culture in animals*. Princeton, NJ: Princeton University Press.

Boring, E. G. (1950a). *A history of experimental psychology* (2nd ed.). Englewood Cliffs, NJ: Prentice Hall.

Boring, E. G. (1950b). The influence of evolutionary theory upon American psychological thought. In S. Persons (Ed.), *Evolutionary thought in America* (pp. 267–298). New Haven, CT: Yale University Press.

Boring, E. G. (1953). A history of introspection. *Psychological Bulletin, 50*, 169–189.

Boring, E. G. (1961). Fechner: Inadvertent founder of psychophysics. *Psychometrika, 26*, 3–8.

Boring, E. G. (1963). *History, psychology and science*. New York: John Wiley.

Borkowski, J. G., & Anderson, D. C. (1977). *Experimental psychology: Tactics of behavioral research.* Glenview, IL: Scott, Foresman.

Bortner, M. (1965). Review of the progressive matrices test. In O. K. Buros (Ed.), *The sixth mental measurements yearbook* (pp. 764–765). Highland Park, NJ: Gryphon Press.

Borys, S., Perlman, D., & Goldenberg, S. (1982, May). *Sex differences in loneliness.* Paper submitted for presentation at the annual meeting of the Midwestern Psychological Association, Minneapolis, MN.

Bouchard, T. J., Jr., & McGue, M. (1981). Familial studies of intelligence: A review. *Science, 212,* 1055–1059.

Bower, G. H. (1970a). Analysis of a mnemonic device. *American Scientist, 58,* 496–510.

Bower, G. H. (1970b). Organizational factors in memory. *Cognitive Psychology, 1,* 18–46.

Bower, G. H. (1972). Mental imagery and associative learning. In L. W. Gregg (Ed.), *Cognition in learning and memory* (pp. 51–88). New York: John Wiley.

Bower, G. H. (1973a). Educational applications of mnemonic devices. In K. O. Doyle, Jr. (Ed.), *Interaction: Readings in human psychology.* Boston: D. C. Heath.

Bower, G. H. (1973b, October). Memory freaks I have known. *Psychology Today,* pp. 64–65.

Bower, G. H. (1981). Mood and memory. *American Psychologist, 36,* 129–148.

Bower, G. H., Black, J. B., & Turner, T. J. (1979). Scripts in memory for text. *Cognitive Psychology, 11,* 177–220.

Bower, G. H., & Hilgard, E. R. (1981). *Theories of learning* (5th ed.). Englewood Cliffs, NJ: Prentice-Hall.

Bower, T. G. R. (1971, October). The object in the world of the infant. *Scientific American,* pp. 30–38.

Bower, T. G. R. (1976, November). The visual world of infants. *Scientific American,* pp. 38–47.

Bowers, K. S. (1973). Situationism in psychology: An analysis and critique. *Psychological Review, 80,* 307–336.

Bowers, K. S. (1976). *Hypnosis for the seriously curious.* Monterey, CA: Brooks/Cole.

Bowlby, J. (1973). *Attachment and loss: Vol. 1. Attachment; Vol. 2. Separation.* New York: Basic Books.

Brady, J. V. (1958, October). Ulcers in "executive" monkeys. *Scientific American,* pp. 95–100.

Brady, R. O. (1976). Inherited metabolic diseases of the nervous system. *Science, 193,* 733–739.

Braginsky, B. M., Braginsky, D. D., & Ring, K. (1982). *Methods of madness: The mental hospital as a last resort.* Lanham, MD: University Press of America.

The Brain. (1979). [Articles from the September 1979 issue of *Scientific American.*] San Francisco: W. H. Freeman.

Brandt, A. (1980, December). Face reading: The persistence of physiognomy. *Psychology Today,* p. 90–96.

Bransford, J. D., & Johnson, M. K. (1973). Consideration of some problems in comprehension. In W. G. Chase (Ed.), *Visual information processing* (pp. 383–438). New York: Academic Press.

Brecher, E. M., & Consumer Reports Editors (Eds.). (1972). *Licit and illicit drugs: The Consumers' Union report on narcotics, stimulants, depressants, inhalants, hallucinogens, and marijuana.* Boston: Little, Brown.

Breland, K., & Breland, M. (1961). The misbehavior of organisms. *American Psychologists, 16,* 681–684.

Brenner, D., Lipton, J., Kaufman, L., & Williamson, S. J. (1978). Somatically evoked magnetic fields of the human brain. *Science, 199,* 81–83.

Brewer, G. D., & Kakalik, J. S. (1979). *Handicapped children: Strategies for improving services.* New York: McGraw-Hill.

Brewer, M. B. (1979). In-group bias in the minimal intergroup situation: A cognitive-motivational analysis. *Psychological Bulletin, 86,* 307–324.

Bricke, J. (1974). Hume's associationist psychology. *Journal of the History of the Behavioral Sciences, 10,* 397–409.

Brindley, G. S. (1963, October). After-images. *Scientific American,* pp. 84–93.

Broadbent, D. E. (1958). *Perception and communication.* New York: Pergamon Press.

Broadbent, D. E. (1975). The magic number seven after fifteen years. In A. Kennedy & A. Wilkes (Eds.), *Studies in long term memory* (pp. 3–18). New York: John Wiley.

Broman, S. H., Nichols, P. L., & Kennedy, W. A. (1975). *Preschool IQ.* Hillsdale, NJ: Lawrence Erlbaum.

Bronfenbrenner, U. (1979). Contexts of child rearing; Problems and prospects. *American Psychologist, 34,* 844–850.

Brooks, L. R. (1968). Spatial and verbal components of the act of recall. *Canadian Journal of Psychology, 22,* 349–368.

Broverman, I. K., Vogel, S. R., Broverman, D. M., Clarkson, F. E., & Rosenkrantz, P. S. (1972). Sex-role stereotypes: A current appraisal. *Journal of Social Issues, 28,* 59–79.

Brown, E., & Deffenbacher, K. (1975). Forgotten mnemonists. *Journal of the History of the Behavioral Sciences, 11,* 342–349.

Brown, F. A., Jr. (1972). The "clocks" timing biological rhythms. *American Scientist, 60,* 756–766.

Brown, I. (1982, Summer). Alcohol: Servant or master? *Stanford Magazine,* pp. 26–32.

Brown, J. (1958). Some tests of the decay theory of immediate memory. *Quarterly Journal of Experimental Psychology, 10,* 12–21.

Brown, P. L., & Jenkins, H. M. (1968). Auto-shaping of the pigeon's key-peck. *Journal of the Experimental Analysis of Behavior, 11,* 1–8.

Brown, R. (1973). *A first language: The early years.* Cambridge, MA: Harvard University Press.

Brown, R., & Kulik, J. (1977). Flashbulb memories. *Cognition, 5,* 73–99.

Brown, R., & McNeill, D. (1966). The "tip of the tongue" phenomenon. *Journal of Verbal Learning and Verbal Behavior, 5,* 325–337.

Bruch, H. (1978). *The golden cage: The enigma of anorexia nervosa.* Cambridge, MA: Harvard University Press.

Bruner, J. S. (1978, September). Learning the mother tongue. *Human Nature,* pp. 42–49.

Bruner, J. S., Goodnow, J. J., & Austin, G. A. (1956). *A study of thinking.* New York: John Wiley.

Bryant, V. M., Jr., & Williams-Dean, G. (1975, January). The coprolites of man. *Scientific American,* pp. 100–109.

Bucher, R., & Lovaas, O. I. (1968). Use of aversive stimulation in behavior modification. In M. R. Jones (Ed.), *Miami Symposium on the prediction of behavior, 1967: Aversive stimulation* (pp. 77–145). Coral Gables, FL: University of Miami Press.

Buchwald, A. M. (1967). Effects of immediate versus delayed outcomes in associative learning. *Journal of Verbal Learning and Verbal Behavior, 6,* 317–320.

Buckhout, R. (1974, December). Eyewitness testimony. *Scientific American,* pp. 23–31.

Buell, S. J., & Coleman, P. D. (1979). Dendritic growth in the aged human brain and failure of growth in senile dementia. *Science, 206,* 854–856.

Buhler, C., & Allen, M. (1972). *Introduction to humanistic psychology.* Monterey, CA: Brooks/Cole.

Bullock, T. H., Orkand, R., & Grinell, A. (1977). *Introduction to nervous systems.* San Francisco: W. H. Freeman.

Bullough, V. L. (1981). Age at menarche: A misunderstanding. *Science, 213,* 365–366.

Bunge, M. (1980). *The mind-body problem: A psychobiological approach.* New York: Pergamon Press.

Bunney, W. E., Goodwin, F. K., & Murphy, D. L. (1972). The "switch process" in manic-depressive illness. *Archives of General Psychiatry, 27,* 312–317.

Bunney, W. E., Murphy, D. L., Goodwin, F. K., & Borge, G. F. (1970). The switch process from depression to mania: Relationship to drugs which alter brain amines. *Lancet, 1,* 1022.

Buros, O. (Ed.). (1978). *The eighth mental measurements yearbook.* Highland Park, NJ: Gryphon Press.

Buss, A. H. (1961). *The psychology of aggression*. New York: John Wiley.

Butler, R. A. (1954, February). Curiosity in monkeys. *Scientific American*, pp. 70–75.

Butters, N., & Cermak, L. S. (1980). *Alcoholic Korsakoff's syndrome: An information-processing approach to amnesia*. New York: Academic Press.

Butzer, K. W. (1977). Environment, culture, and human evolution. *American Scientist, 65*, 572–584.

Buys, D. (1982). New hope for the deaf. *Friendly Exchange, 2* (2), 18–19.

Byck, R. (Ed.). (1974). *Cocaine papers by Sigmund Freud*. New York: Stonehill.

Cadoret, R. J. (1978). Psychopathology in adopted-away offspring of biologic parents with antisocial behavior. *Archives of General Psychiatry, 35*, 176–184.

Cagan, R. H., & Kare, M. R. (Eds.). (1981). *Biochemistry of taste and olfaction: Papers from a symposium, Philadelphia, April 1980*. New York: Academic Press.

Cain, W. S. (1977). Differential sensitivity for smell: "Noise" at the nose. *Science, 195*, 796–798.

Cain, W. S. (1979). To know with the nose: Keys to odor identification. *Science, 203*, 467–470.

Calcium blockers given after CPR may save brains denied blood up to an hour. (1982, January 18). *Medical World News*, pp. 11–12, 24.

Calhoun, J. B. (1962, February). Population density and social pathology. *Scientific American*, pp. 139–148.

Callahan, P. S. (1974). *The magnificent birds of prey*. New York: Holiday House.

Campbell, D. P., & Hansen, J. C. (1981). *Manual for the SVIB-SCII Strong-Campbell interest inventory* (3rd ed.). Stanford, CA: Stanford University Press.

Campbell, D. T. (1979). Comments on the sociobiology of ethics and moralizing. *Behavioral Science, 24*, 37–45.

Campbell, D. T., & Fiske, D. W. (1959). Convergent and discriminant validation by the multitrait-multimethod matrix. *Psychological Bulletin, 56*, 81–105.

Campos, J. J., & Sternberg, C. R. (1981). Perception, appraisal and emotion: The onset of social referencing. In M. Lamb and L. Sherrod (Eds.), *Infant social cognition* (pp. 273–314). Hillsdale, NJ: Lawrence Erlbaum.

Cannon, W. B. (1927). The James-Lange theory of emotions: A critical examination and an alternate theory. *American Journal of Psychology, 39*, 106–124.

Cantor, N., & Mischel, W. (1977). Traits as prototypes: Effects on recognition memory. *Journal of Personality and Social Psychology, 35*, 38–48.

Cantor, N. & Mischel, W. (1979a). Prototypes in person perception. In L. Berkowitz (Ed.), *Advances in experimental social psychology* (Vol. 12, pp. 3–52). New York: Academic Press.

Cantor, N., & Mischel, W. (1979b). Prototypicality and personality: Effects on free recall and personality impressions. *Journal of Research in Personality, 13*, 187–205.

Capaldi, E. J. (1966). Partial reinforcement: An hypothesis of sequential effects. *Psychological Review, 73*, 459–477.

Caplan, D. (Ed.). (1980). *Biological studies of mental processes*. Cambridge, MA: MIT Press.

Carey, S., & Diamond, R. (1977). From piecemeal to configurational representation of faces. *Science, 195*, 312–314.

Carlen, P. L., Wilkinson, D. A., Holgate, R., & Wortzman, G. (1978). Reversible cerebral atrophy in recently abstinent chronic alcoholics measured by computerized tomography scans. *Science, 200*, 1076–1078.

Carlsmith, J. M., & Anderson, C. A. (1979). Ambient temperature and the occurrence of collective violence: A new analysis. *Journal of Personality and Social Psychology, 37*, 337–344.

Carlsmith, J. M., Ellsworth, P. C., & Aronson, E. (1976). *Methods of research in social psychology*. Reading, MA: Addison-Wesley.

Carlsmith, J. M., & Gross, A. E. (1969). Some effects of guilt on compliance. *Journal of Personality and Social Psychology, 11*, 232–239.

Carlson, G., & Goodwin, F. K. (1973). The stages of mania: A longitudinal analysis of the manic episode. *Archives of General Psychiatry, 28*, 221–228.

Carmichael, L., Hogan, H. P., & Walter, A. A. (1932). An experimental study of the effects of language on the reproduction of visually perceived form. *Journal of Experimental Psychology, 15*, 73–86.

Carpenter, P. A., & Eisenberg, P. (1978). Mental rotation and the frame of reference in blind and sighted individuals. *Perception and Psychophysics, 23*, 117–124.

Carpenter, P. A., & Just, M. A. (1980). Cognitive processes in reading: Models based on readers' eye fixations. In A. M. Lesgold & C. A. Perfetti (Eds.), *Interactive processes in reading* (pp. 177–213). Hillsdale, NJ: Lawrence Erlbaum.

Carr, A. T. (1974). Compulsive neurosis: A review of the literature. *Psychological Bulletin, 81*, 311–319.

Carroll, J. B., & Horn, J. L. (1981). On the scientific basis of ability testing. *American Psychologist, 36*, 1012–1020.

Carroll, L. (1872, 1964). *The jabberwocky and more nonsense*. New York: Dell.

Cartwright, D. S. (1974). *Introduction to personality*. Chicago: Rand McNally.

Cartwright, R. D. (1974). Problem solving: Waking and dreaming. *Journal of Abnormal Psychology, 83*, 451–455.

Cartwright, R. D. (1977). *Night life: Explorations in dreaming*. Englewood Cliffs, NJ: Prentice-Hall.

Carver, C. S. (1975). Physical aggression as a function of objective self-awareness and attitudes toward punishment. *Journal of Experimental Social Psychology, 11*, 510–519.

Casey, K. L. (1973). Pain: A current view of neural mechanisms. *American Scientist, 61*, 194–200.

Cates, J. (1970). Psychology's manpower: Report on the 1968 national register of scientific and technical personnel. *American Psychologist, 25*, 254–263.

Cattell, R. B. (1949). *Manual for forms A and B: Sixteen personality factor questionnaire*. Champaign, IL: Institute for Personality and Ability Testing.

Cattell, R. B. (1950). *Personality: A systematic, theoretical, and factual study*. New York: McGraw-Hill.

Cattell, R. B. (1957). *Personality and motivation, structure, and measurement*. New York: Harcourt Brace Jovanovich.

Cattell, R. B. (Ed.). (1966). *Handbook of multivariate experimental psychology*. Chicago: Rand McNally.

Cattell, R. B. (1971). *Abilities: Their structure, growth, and action*. Boston: Houghton Mifflin.

Cattell, R. B. (1973, July). Personality pinned down. *Psychology Today*, pp. 40–46.

Cattell, R. B. (1982). *The inheritance of personality and ability: Research methods and findings*. New York: Academic Press.

Cavalli-Sforza, L. L. (1974, September). The genetics of human populations. *Scientific American*, pp. 80–89.

Cazden, C. B. (1968). The acquisition of noun and verb inflections. *Child Development, 39*, 433–448.

Cerella, J. (1980). The pigeon's analysis of pictures. *Pattern Recognition, 12*, 1–16.

Cermak, L. S. (1976). *Improving your memory*. New York: McGraw-Hill.

Cermak, L. S. (Ed.). (1982). *Human memory and amnesia*. Hillsdale, NJ: Lawrence Erlbaum.

Cermak, L. S., & Craik, F. I. M. (Eds.). (1979). *Levels of processing in human memory*. Hillsdale, NJ: Lawrence Erlbaum.

Chapanis, A. (1953, April). Psychology and the instrument panel. *Scientific American*, pp. 74–82.

Chapman, L. J., & Chapman, J. P. (1973). *Disordered thought in schizophrenia*. New York: Appleton-Century-Crofts.

Chase, M. H. (1978, August). The secret life of neurons. *Psychology Today*, p. 104.

Chase, M. H. (1979, November). Every 90 minutes a brainstorm. *Psychology Today*, p. 172.

Chase, M. H. (1981, November). The dreamer's paralysis. *Psychology Today*, p. 108.

Chase, W. G., & Simon, H. A. (1973). Perception in chess. *Cognitive Psychology, 4*, 55–81.

Chedd, G. (1981, January/February). Who shall be born? *Science 81*, pp. 32–41.

Cherfas, J. J. (1980). Signals for food: Reinforcers or informants? *Science, 209*, 1552–1553.

Chernik, D. A. (1972). Effect of REM sleep deprivation on learning and recall by humans. *Perceptual and Motor Skills, 34*, 283–294.

Chomsky, N. (1968). *Language and mind*. New York: Harcourt Brace Jovanovich.

Chomsky, N. (1980). *Rules and representations*. New York: Columbia University Press.

Chorover, S. L., & Schiller, P. H. (1965). Short-term retrograde amnesia in rats. *Journal of Comparative and Physiological Psychology, 59*, 73–78.

Clark, E. V. (1975). Knowledge, context, and strategy in the acquisition of meaning. In D. P. Dato (Ed.), *Georgetown University round table on languages and linguistics, 1975* (pp. 77–98). Washington, DC: Georgetown University Press.

Clark, H. H., & Clark, E. V. (1977). *Psychology and language: An introduction to psycholinguistics*. New York: Harcourt Brace Jovanovich.

Clark, M., & Agrest, S. (1975, July 28). Sonar for the blind. *Newsweek*, p. 69.

Clark, R. D., III, & Word, L. E. (1974). Where is the apathetic bystander? Situational characteristics of the emergency. *Journal of Personality and Social Psychology, 29*, 279–287.

Clark, R. W. (1980). *Freud: The man and the cause—a biography*. New York: Random House.

Clark, W. C., & Yang, J. C. (1974). Acupunctural analgesia? Evaluation by signal detection theory. *Science, 189*, 1096–1098.

Clarke, L. (1974). *Can't read, can't write, can't talk too good either*. New York: Walker.

Cleary, T. A., Humphreys, L. G., Kendrick, S. A., & Wesman, A. (1975). Educational uses of tests with disadvantaged students. *American Psychologist, 30*, 15–41.

Cleckley, J. (1976). *The mask of sanity* (5th ed.). St. Louis: Mosby.

Coates, T., & Thoresen, C. (1977). *How to sleep better: A drug-free program for overcoming insomnia*. Englewood Cliffs, NJ: Prentice-Hall.

Cobbin, D. M., Requin-Blow, B., Williams, L. R., & Williams, W. O. (1979). Urinary MHPG levels and tricyclic antidepressant drug selection. *Archives of General Psychiatry, 36*, 1111–1115.

Cofer, C. N. (1973). Constructive processes in memory. *American Scientist, 61*, 537–543.

Cofer, C. N. (Ed.). (1976). *The structure of human memory*. San Francisco: W. H. Freeman.

Cohen, B. D., Nachmani, G., & Rosenberg, S. (1974). Referent communication disturbances in acute schizophrenia. *Journal of Abnormal Psychology, 83*, 1–14.

Cohen, D. (1979). *J. B. Watson: The founder of behaviorism. A biography*. Boston: Routledge & Kegan Paul.

Cohen, D. B. (1979). *Sleep and dreaming: Origins, nature and functions*. New York: Pergamon Press.

Cohen, L. B. (1979). Our developing knowledge of infant perception and cognition. *American Psychologist, 34*, 894–899.

Cohen, L. B., & Salapatek, P. (Eds.). (1974). *Infant perception: From sensation to cognition* (2 vols.). New York: Academic Press.

Cohen, N. J., & Squire, L. R. (1980). Preserved learning and retention of pattern-analyzing skill in amnesia: Dissociation of knowing how and knowing what. *Science, 210*, 207–210.

Cole, N. S. (1981). Bias in testing. *American Psychologist, 36*, 1067–1077.

Coleman, J. C., Butcher, J. N., & Carson, R. C. (1980). *Abnormal psychology and modern life* (6th ed.). Glenview, IL: Scott, Foresman.

Coles, R. (1970). *Erik H. Erikson: The growth of his work*. Boston: Little, Brown.

Colligan, M. J., Pennebaker, J. W., & Murphy, L. R. (Eds.). (1982). *Mass psychogenic illness: A sociological analysis*. Hillsdale, NJ: Lawrence Erlbaum.

Collins, A. M., & Loftus, E. F. (1975). A spreading-activation theory of semantic processing. *Psychological Review, 82*, 407–428.

Collins, A. M., & Quillian, M. R. (1969). Retrieval time from semantic memory. *Journal of Verbal Learning and Verbal Behavior, 8*, 240–247.

Coltheart, M. (1980). Iconic memory and visible persistence. *Perception and Psychophysics, 27*, 183–228.

Commission on Obscenity and Pornography. (1970). *The report of the Commission on Obscenity and Pornography*. New York: Bantam.

Condon, W. S., & Sander, L. W. (1974). Neonate movement is synchronized with adult speech: Interactional participation and language acquisition. *Science, 183*, 99–101.

Conner, W. E., & Masters, W. M. (1978). Infrared video viewing. *Science, 199*, 1004.

Connor, J. M. (1977). Effects of organization and expectancy on recall and recognition. *Memory & Cognition, 5*, 315–318.

Conrad, R. (1964). Acoustic confusions in immediate memory. *British Journal of Psychology, 55*, 75–84.

Cook, M. (1977). Gaze and mutual gaze in social encounters. *American Scientist, 65*, 328–333.

Cooley, C. H. (1902). *Human nature and the social order*. New York: Charles Scribner's.

Cooper, H. M. (1979). Statistically combining independent sources: Meta-analysis of sex differences in conformity research. *Journal of Personality and Social Psychology, 37*, 131–146.

Cooper, J. R., Bloom, F. E., & Roth, R. H. (1982). *The biochemical basis of neuropharmacology* (4th ed.). New York: Oxford University Press.

Cooper, L. A., & Shepard, R. N. (1973). Chronometric studies of the rotation of mental images. In W. G. Chase (Ed.), *Visual information processing* (pp. 75–176). New York: Academic Press.

Coppinger, L., & Coppinger, R. (1982, April). Livestock-guarding dogs that wear sheep's clothing. *Smithsonian*, pp. 65–73.

Corballis, M. C., & Beale, I. L. (1976). *The psychology of left and right*. Hillsdale, NJ: Lawrence Erlbaum.

Coren, S., & Girgus, J. S. (1978). *Seeing is deceiving: The psychology of visual illusions*. Hillsdale, NJ: Lawrence Erlbaum.

Cowan, W. M. (1979, September). The development of the brain. *Scientific American*, pp. 106–117.

Cowen, E. L. (1982). Help is where you find it: Four informal helping groups. *American Psychologist, 37*, 385–395.

Cowles, M., & Davis, C. (1982). On the origins of the .05 level of statistical significance. *American Psychologist, 37*, 553–558.

Craig, J. C. (1977). Vibrotactile pattern perception: Extraordinary observers. *Science, 196*, 450–452.

Craighead, W. E., Kazdin, A. E., & Mahoney, M. J. (1976). *Behavior modification: Principles, issues, and applications*. Boston: Houghton Mifflin.

Craik, F. I. M. (1977). Age differences in human memory. In J. E. Birren & K. W. Schaie (Eds.), *Handbook of the psychology of aging* (pp. 384–420). New York: Van Nostrand Reinhold.

Craik, F. I. M., & Levy, B. A. (1976). The concept of primary memory. In W. K. Estes (Ed.), *Handbook of learning and cognitive processes: Vol. 4. Attention and memory* (pp. 133–175). Hillsdale, NJ: Lawrence Erlbaum.

Craik, F. I. M., & Lockhart, R. S. (1972). Levels of processing: A framework for memory research. *Journal of Verbal Learning and Verbal Behavior, 11*, 671–684.

Craik, F. I. M., & Tulving, E. (1975). Depth of processing and the retention of words in episodic memory. *Journal of Experimental Psychology: General, 104*, 268–294.

Craik, F. I. M., & Watkins, M. J. (1973). The role of rehearsal in short-term memory. *Journal of Verbal Learning and Verbal Behavior, 12*, 599–607.

Craske, B. (1977). Perception of impossible limb positions induced by tendon vibration. *Science, 196*, 71–73.

Cravioto, J. (1971). Infant malnutrition and later learning. *Progress in Human Nutrition, 1*, 80–96.

Crawford, C. (1979). George Washington, Abraham Lincoln, and Arthur Jensen: Are they compatible? *American Psychologist, 34*, 664–672.

Crawshaw, L. I., Moffitt, B. P., Lemons, D. E., & Downey, J. A. (1981). The evolutionary development of vertebrate thermoregulation. *American Scientist, 69*, 543–550.

Crick, F. H. C. (1979, September). Thinking about the brain. *Scientific American*, pp. 181–188.

Crisp, A. H., Palmer, R. L., & Kalucy, R. S. (1976). How common is anorexia nervosa?: A prevalence study. *British Journal of Psychiatry, 128*, 549–554.

Crocker, J. (1981). Judgment of covariation by social perceivers. *Psychological Bulletin, 90*, 272–292.

Crompton, A. W., & Parker, P. (1978). Evolution of the mammalian masticatory apparatus. *American Scientist, 66*, 192–201.

Cronbach, L. J. (1975). Five decades of public controversy over mental testing. *American Psychologist, 30*, 1–14.

Cronbach, L. J. (1977). *Educational Psychology* (3rd ed.). New York: Harcourt Brace Jovanovich.

Cronbach, L. J. (1978). The BITCH test (black intelligence test of cultural homogeneity): A review. In O. K. Buros (Ed.), *The eighth mental measurements yearbook* (Vol. 1, pp. 249–250). Highland Park, NJ: Gryphon Press.

Cronbach, L. J. (1980). Validity on parole: How can we go straight? In W. B. Schrader (Ed.), *New directions for testing and measurement: No. 5. Measuring achievement: Progress over a decade*. San Francisco: Jossey-Bass.

Crowder, R. G. (1976). *Principles of learning and memory*. Hillsdale, NJ: Lawrence Erlbaum.

Crutchfield, R. (1955). Conforming and character. *American Psychologist, 10*, 191–198.

Crutchfield, R. S., & Krech, D. (1962). Some guides to the understanding of the history of psychology. In L. Postman (Ed.), *Psychology in the making: Histories of selected research problems* (pp. 3–27). New York: Alfred A. Knopf.

Culliton, B. J. (1976). Psychosurgery: National commission issues surprisingly favorable report. *Science, 194*, 299–301.

Cunningham, S. (1983, March). Superior court restarts electroshock in Berkeley. *APA Monitor*, p. 17.

Cuny, H. (1965). *Ivan Pavlov: The man and his theories*. New York: Paul S. Eriksson.

Curio, E., Ernst, U., & Vieth, W. (1978). Cultural transmission of enemy recognition: One function of mobbing. *Science, 202*, 899–901.

Curtis, H. (1979). *Biology* (3rd ed.). New York: Worth.

Curtiss, S. (1977). *Genie: A psycholinguistic study of a modern-day "wild child."* New York: Academic Press.

Czeisler, C. A., Moore-Ede, M. C., & Coleman, R. M. (1982). Rotating shift work schedules that disrupt sleep are improved by applying circadian principles. *Science, 217*, 460–463.

Czeisler, C. A., Weitzman, E. D., Moore-Ede, M. C., Zimmerman, J. C., & Knauer, R. S. (1980). Human sleep: Its duration and organization depend on its circadian phase. *Science, 210*, 1264–1267.

Dahlberg, C. C., & Jaffe, J. (1977). *Stroke: A doctor's personal story of his recovery*. New York: W. W. Norton.

Daly, M., & Wilson, M. (1978). *Sex, evolution, and behavior*. North Scituate, MA: Duxbury Press.

Danks, J. H., & Glucksberg, S. (1980). Experimental psycholinguistics. *Annual Review of Psychology, 31*, 391–417.

Darwin, C. (1859). *On the origin of species by means of natural selection*. London: J. Murray.

Darwin, C. (1871). *The descent of man and selection in relation to sex*. New York: Appleton.

Darwin, C. (1872). *The expression of emotions in man and animals*. London: J. Murray.

Darwin, C. T., Turvey, M. T., & Crowder, R. G. (1972). An auditory analogue of the Sperling partial report procedure: Evidence for brief auditory storage. *Cognitive Psychology, 3*, 255–267.

Davidson, J. M. (1981, July). The brain/the orgasmic connection. *Psychology Today*, p. 91.

Davidson, J. M., & Davidson, R. J. (Eds.). (1980). *The psychobiology of consciousness*. New York: Plenum Press.

Davies, J. D. (1955). *Phrenology: Fad and science: A 19th-century American crusade*. New Haven, CT: Yale University Press.

Davis, A. B. (1982). The development of anesthesia. *American Scientist, 70*, 522–528.

Davis, D. (1979, July 30). Spans to set spirits soaring. *Newsweek*, pp. 80–83.

Davis, F. (1978). *Eloquent animals: A study in animal communication*. New York: Coward, McCann & Geoghegan.

Davis, H., & Hurwitz, H. M. B. (Eds.). (1977). *Operant-Pavlovian interactions*. New York: Halsted Press.

Davis, J. M. (1976). Overview: Maintenance therapy in psychiatry: II. Affective disorders. *American Journal of Psychiatry, 133*, 1–13.

Davis, J. M. (1978). Dopamine theory of schizophrenia: A two-factor theory. In L. C. Wynne, R. L. Cromwell, & S. Matthysse (Eds.), *The nature of schizophrenia: New approaches to research and treatment*. New York: John Wiley.

Davison, G. C. (1968). Systematic desensitization as a counterconditioning process. *Journal of Abnormal Psychology, 73*, 91–99.

Davison, G. C. (1980). And now for something completely different: Cognition and little r. In M. J. Mahoney (Ed.), *Psychotherapy process: Current issues and future directions* (pp. 203–209). New York: Plenum Press.

Davison, G. C., & Neale, J. M. (1982). *Abnormal psychology* (3rd ed.). New York: John Wiley.

Davison, G. C., & Stuart, R. B. (1975). Behavior therapy and civil liberties. *American Psychologist, 30*, 755–763.

Dawkins, R. (1976). *The selfish gene*. New York: Oxford University Press.

DeCamp, D. (1971). Introduction: The study of pidgin and creole languages. In D. H. Hymes (Ed.), *Pidginization and creolization of languages* (pp. 13–39). Cambridge: Cambridge University Press.

DeCasper, A. J., & Fifer, W. P. (1980). Of human bonding: Newborns prefer their mothers' voices. *Science, 208*, 1174–1176.

Deese, J. (1978). Thought into speech. *American Scientist, 66*, 314–321.

Deffenbacher, K. A., & Loftus, E. F. (1982). Do jurors share a common understanding concerning eyewitness behavior? *Law and Human Behavior, 6*, 15–30.

Deich, R. F., & Hodges, P. M. (1975, May). Learning from Sarah. *Human Behavior*, pp. 40–42.

deLacoste-Utamsing, C., & Holloway, R. L. (1982). Sexual dimorphism in the human corpus callosum. *Science, 216*, 1431–1432.

Delgado, J. M. R. (1967). Social rank and radio-stimulated aggressiveness in monkeys. *Journal of Nervous and Mental Disease, 144*, 383–390.

Delgado, J. M. R. (1969). *Physical control of the mind: Toward a psychocivilized society*. New York: Harper & Row.

Dembroski, T. M., & MacDougall, J. M. (1982). Coronary-prone behavior, social psychophysiology, and coronary heart disease. In J. R. Eiser (Ed.) *Social psychology and behavioral medicine* (pp. 39–62). New York: John Wiley.

Dement, W. C. (1968–1969). A new look at the third state of existence. *Stanford M.D., 8*(1), 2–8.

Dement, W. C. (1978). *Some must watch while some must sleep*. New York: W. W. Norton.

Dement, W., & Kleitman, N. (1957). Cyclic variations in EEG during sleep and their relation to eye movements, body motility, and dreaming. *Electroencephalography and Clinical Neurophysiology, 9*, 673–690.

Dempster, F. N. (1981). Memory span: Sources of individual and developmental differences. *Psychological Bulletin, 89*, 63–100.

DePue, R. A., & Monroe, S. M. (1978). Learned helplessness in the perspective of the depressive disorders: Conceptual and definitional issues. *Journal of Abnormal Psychology, 87*, 3–20.

Derêgowski, J. B. (1972, November). Pictorial perception and culture. *Scientific American*, pp. 82–88.

Derêgowski, J. B. (1980). *Illusions, patterns and pictures: A cross-cultural perspective*. New York: Academic Press.

Dethier, V. G. (1971). A surfeit of stimuli: A paucity of receptors. *American Scientist, 59*, 706–715.

Dethier, V. G. (1976). *The hungry fly: A physiological study of the behavior associated with feeding*. Cambridge, MA: Harvard University Press.

Dethier, V. G. (1977). The taste of salt. *American Scientist, 65*, 744–751.

Dethier, V. G. (1978). Other tastes, other worlds. *Science, 201*, 224–228.

Deutsch, D. (1975, October). Musical illusions. *Scientific American*, pp. 92–104.

Deutsch, D., & Deutsch, J. (1975). *Short-term memory*. New York: Academic Press.

Dewan, E. M. (1969). *The programming (p) hypothesis for REM*. Bedford, MA: Air Force Cambridge Research Laboratories.

Diamond, M. C. (1976). Anatomical brain changes produced by environment. In J. McGaugh & L. Petrinovich (Eds.), *Knowing, thinking, and believing* (pp. 215–224). New York: Plenum Press.

Diamond, M. C. (1978). The aging brain: Some enlightening and optimistic results. *American Scientist, 66*, 66–71.

Dickerson, R. E. (1978, September). Chemical evolution and the origin of life. *Scientific American*, pp. 70–86.

Dillard, J. L. (1972). *Black English: Its history and usage in the United States*. New York: Random House.

Dion, K., Berscheid, E., & Walster, E. (1972). What is beautiful is good. *Journal of Personality and Social Psychology, 24*, 285–290.

Dixon, B. (1980, June). Pet dreams. *Omni*, p. 18.

Dirkes, M. A. (1978). The role of divergent production in the learning process. *American Psychologist, 33*, 815–820.

Dobelle, W. H., Mladejovsky, M. G., & Girvin, J. P. (1974). Artificial vision for the blind: Electrical stimulation of visual cortex offers hope for a functional prosthesis. *Science, 183*, 440–444.

Dobzhansky, T. (1960, September). The present evolution of man. *Scientific American*, pp. 206–217.

Docter, R. F. (1972). Review of the Porteus maze test. In O. K. Buros (Ed.), *The seventh mental measurements yearbook* (Vol. 1, pp. 751–753). Highland Park, NJ: Gryphon Press.

Dole, V. P. (1980, December). Addictive behavior. *Scientific American*, pp. 138–154.

Dollard, J., Doob, L. W., Miller, N. E., Mowrer, O. H., & Sears, R. R. (1939). *Frustration and aggression*. New Haven, CT: Yale University Press.

Dollard, J., & Miller, N. E. (1950). *Personality and psychotherapy: An analysis in terms of learning theory and culture*. New York: McGraw-Hill.

Dörken, H., & Webb, J. T. (1981). Licensed psychologists on the increase, 1974–1979. *American Psychologist, 36*, 1419–1426.

Downs, R. M., & Stea, D. (1977). *Maps in minds: Reflections on cognitive mapping*. New York: Harper & Row.

Draper, P. (1973). Crowding among hunter-gatherers: The !Kung bushmen. *Science, 182*, 301–303.

Drucker-Colin, R., Shkurovich, M., & Sterman, M. B. (Eds.). (1979). *The functions of sleep*. New York: Academic Press.

DuBois, P. H. (1939). A test standardized on Pueblo Indian children. *Psychological Bulletin, 36*, 523.

Duncan, C. P. (1949). The retroactive effect of electroshock on learning. *Journal of Comparative and Physiological Psychology, 42*, 32–44.

Duncker, K. (1945). On problem solving. *Psychological Monographs, 58* (5, Whole No. 270).

Dunkle, T. (1981, October). A perfect serpent. *Science 81*, pp. 30–35.

Dunkle, T. (1982, April). The sound of science. *Science 82*, pp. 30–33.

Dunn, E. F., & Dunn, P. C. (1980). Loneliness and the black experience. In J. Hartog, J. R. Audy, & Y. A. Cohen (Eds.), *The anatomy of loneliness*. New York: International Universities Press.

Dunn, J. A. (1972). Review of the Goodenough-Harris drawing test. In O. K. Buros (Ed.), *The seventh mental measurements yearbook* (Vol. 1, pp. 352–353). Highland Park, NJ: Gryphon Press.

Dunn, L. M. (1965). *Expanded manual for the Peabody picture vocabulary test*. Minneapolis, MN: American Guidance Service.

Duska, R., & Whelan, M. (1975). *Moral development: A guide to Piaget and Kohlberg*. Paramus, NJ: Paulist/Newman Press.

Eagly, A. H., Wood, W., & Fishbaugh, L. (1981). Sex differences in conformity: Surveillance by the group as a determinant of male nonconformity. *Journal of Personality and Social Psychology, 40*, 384–394.

Eastman, C. (1976). Behavioral formulations of depression. *Psychological Review, 83*, 277–291.

Eaton, G. G. (1976, October). The social order of Japanese macaques. *Scientific American*, pp. 97–106.

Ebbinghaus, H. E. (1885). *Memory: A contribution to experimental psychology* (H. A. Ruger & C. E. Bussenues, Trans.). New York: Teachers College, Columbia University.

Eccles, Sir J. (1965, January). The synapse. *Scientific American*, pp. 56–66.

Egan, D. E., & Greeno, J. G. (1974). Theory of rule induction: Knowledge acquired in concept learning, serial pattern learning, and problem solving. In L. W. Gregg (Ed.), *Knowledge and cognition* (pp. 43–103). Hillsdale, NJ: Lawrence Erlbaum.

Egan, G. (1975). *The skilled helper*. Monterey, CA: Brooks/Cole.

Egger, M. D., & Miller, N. E. (1963). When is a reward reinforcing? An experimental study of the information hypothesis. *Journal of Comparative and Physiological Psychology, 56*, 132–137.

Eggers, H. M., & Blakemore, C. (1978). Physiological basis of anisometropic amblyopia. *Science, 201*, 264–266.

Ehrhardt, A. A. (1979). In H. L. Vallet & I. H. Porter (Eds.), *Genetic mechanisms of sexual development* (pp. 473–483). New York: Academic Press.

Ehrhardt, A. A., & Meyer-Bahlburg, H. F. L. (1981). Effects of prenatal sex hormones on gender-related behavior. *Science, 211*, 1312–1318.

Ehrlich, P., & Ehrlich, A. (1981). *Extinction: The causes and consequences of the disappearance of species*. New York: Random House.

Eibl-Eibesfeldt, I. (1970). *Ethology: The biology of behavior*. New York: Holt, Rinehart & Winston.

Eibl-Eibesfeldt, I. (1972). *Love and hate: The natural history of behavior patterns*. New York: Holt, Rinehart & Winston.

Eich, J. E. (1980). The cue-dependent nature of state-dependent retrieval. *Memory and Cognition, 8*, 157–173.

Einstein, A. (1952). Letter to Jacques Hadamard. In B. Ghiselin (Ed.), *The creative process: A symposium* (pp. 43–44). Berkeley, CA: University of California Press.

Eisner, T., & Grant, R. P. (1981). Toxicity, odor aversion, and olfactory aposematism. *Science, 213*, 476.

Ekman, P. (1973). *Darwin and facial expression: A century of research in review*. New York: Academic Press.

Ekman, P., Friesen, W., & Ellsworth, P. (1972). *Emotion in the human face*. New York: Pergamon Press.

Ekstrand, B. R. (1972). To sleep, perchance to dream (about why we forget). In C. P. Duncan, L. Sechrest, & A. W. Melton (Eds.), *Human memory: Festschrift in honor of Benton J. Underwood* (pp. 59–82). New York: Appleton-Century-Crofts.

Elkind, D. (1969, May 26). Giant in the nursery—Jean Piaget. *The New York Times Magazine*.

Elkind, D. (1970, April 5). Erik Erikson's eight ages of man. *The New York Times Magazine*.

Elkind, D. (1974). *Children and adolescents: Interpretive essays on Jean Piaget* (2nd ed.). New York: Oxford University Press.

Elkind, D. (1975). Perceptual development in children. *American Scientist, 63*, 533–541.

Elkind, D. (1981a). Obituary: Jean Piaget (1896–1980). *American Psychologist, 36*, 911–913.

Elkind, D. (1981b). Recent research in cognitive and language development. In L. T. Benjamin, Jr. (Ed.), *The G. Stanley Hall lecture series* (Vol. 1, pp. 61–80). Washington, DC: American Psychological Association.

Ellis, A. (1962). *Reason and emotion in psychotherapy*. New York: Lyle Stuart.

Ellis, A. (1973). *Humanistic psychotherapy*. New York: McGraw-Hill.

Ellis, A. (1977). The basic clinical theory of rational-emotive therapy. In A. Ellis & R. Grieger (Eds.), *Handbook of rational-emotive therapy*. New York: Springer.

Ellis, W. D. (1967). *A source book of gestalt psychology*. New York: Humanities Press.

Emswiller, T., Deaux, K., & Willits, J. E. (1971). Similarity, sex, and requests for small favors. *Journal of Applied Social Psychology, 1*, 284–291.

Endler, N. S. (1977). The role of personality-situation interactions in personality theory. In D. Magnusson & N. S. Endler (Eds.), *Personality at the crossroads: Current issues in interactional psychology*. New York: Halsted Press.

Entwisle, D. R. (1972). To dispel fantasies about fantasy-based measures of achievement motivation. *Psychological Bulletin, 77*, 377–391.

Epel, D. (1977, November). The program of fertilization. *Scientific American*, pp. 129–138.

Ephron, H. S., & Carrington, P. (1966). Rapid eye movement sleep and cortical homeostasis. *Psychological Review, 73*, 500–526.

Epps, G. (1982, January/February). The brain biologist and the mud leech. *Science 82*, pp. 34–41.

Epstein, C. J., & Golbus, M. S. (1977). Prenatal diagnosis of genetic diseases. *American Scientist, 65*, 703–711.

Epstein, R., Lanza, R. P., & Skinner, B. F. (1980). Symbolic communication between two pigeons (*Columba livia domestica*). *Science, 207*, 543–545.

Epstein, R., Lanza, R. P., & Skinner, B. F. (1981). "Self-awareness" in the pigeon. *Science, 212*, 695–696.

Epstein, S. (1979). The stability of behavior: On predicting most of the people much of the time. *Journal of Personality and Social Psychology, 37*, 1097–1126.

Epstein, S. (1980). The stability of behavior: II. Implications for psychological research. *American Psychologist, 35*, 790–806.

Epstein, S., & Taylor, S. P. (1967). Instigation to aggression as a function of degree of defeat and perceived aggressive intent of the opponent. *Journal of Personality, 35*, 265–289.

Epstein, S. M. (1967). Toward a unified theory of anxiety. In B. A. Maher (Ed.), *Progress in experimental personality research* (Vol. 4, pp. 1–89). New York: Academic Press.

Erickson, J. R., & Jones, M. R. (1978). Thinking. *Annual Review of Psychology, 29*, 61–90.

Ericsson, K. A., & Chase, W. C. (1982). Exceptional memory. *American Scientist, 70*, 607–615.

Erikson, E. H. (1963). *Childhood and society* (rev. ed.). New York: W. W. Norton.

Erikson, E. H. (1970). The life cycle: Epigenesis of identity. In H. E. Fitzgerald & J. P. McKinney (Eds.), *Developmental psychology: Studies in human development*. Homewood, IL: Dorsey Press.

Ernst, B. (1976). *The magic mirror of M. C. Escher*. New York: Random House.

Eron, L. D. (1982). Parent-child interaction, television violence, and aggression of children. *American Psychologist, 37*, 197–211.

Erwin, E. (1980). Psychoanalytic therapy: The Eysenck argument. *American Psychologist, 35*, 435–443.

Estes, W. K. (1969). Reinforcement in human learning. In J. T. Tapp (Ed.), *Reinforcement and behavior* (pp. 63–94). New York: Academic Press.

Estes, W. K. (1978). The information-processing approach to cognition: A confluence of metaphors and methods. In W. K. Estes (Ed.), *Handbook of learning and cognitive processes* (Vol. 5, pp. 1–18). Hillsdale, NJ: Lawrence Erlbaum.

Etaugh, C. (1980). Effects of nonmaternal care on children: Research evidence and popular views. *American Psychologist, 35*, 309–319.

Evans, I. M. (1976). Classical conditioning. In M. P. Feldman & A. Broadhurst (Eds.), *Theoretical and experimental bases of the behavior therapies* (pp. 73–112). New York: John Wiley.

Evans, J. F., Gustafson, L. A., O'Connell, D. N., Orne, M. T., & Shor, R. E. (1966). Response during sleep with intervening waking amnesia. *Science, 152*, 666–667.

Evans, R. (1972). E. B. Titchener and his lost system. *Journal of the History of the Behavioral Sciences, 8*, 168–180.

Evans, R. I. (1968). *B. F. Skinner: The man and his ideas*. New York: E. P. Dutton.

Evans, R. I. (1971). *Gordon Allport: The man and his ideas*. New York: E. P. Dutton.

Evans, R. I. (1975a). *Carl Rogers: The man and his ideas*. New York: E. P. Dutton.

Evans, R. I. (1975b). *Konrad Lorenz: The man and his ideas*. New York: Harcourt Brace Jovanovich.

Evans, R. I. (1976). *The making of psychology: Conversations with creative contributors*. New York: Alfred A. Knopf.

Evans, R. I., Rozelle, R. M., Maxwell, S. E., Raines, B. E., Dill, C. A., & Guthrie, T. J. (1981). Social modeling films to deter smoking in adolescents: Results of a three-year field investigation. *Journal of Applied Psychology, 66*, 399–414.

Evarts, E. V. (1979, September). Brain mechanisms of movement. *Scientific American*, pp. 146–156.

Exner, J. E., & Weiner, I. B. (1981). *The Rorschach: A comprehensive system: III. Assessment of children and adolescents*. New York: John Wiley.

Eysenck, H. J. (1947). *Dimensions of personality*. London: Kegan Paul.

Eysenck, H. J. (1952). The effects of psychotherapy: An evaluation. *Journal of Consulting Psychology, 16*, 319–324.

Eysenck, H. J. (1960). *The structure of human personality*. New York: Macmillan.

Eysenck, H. J. (1966a). *Check your own IQ*. Middlesex, England: Penguin Books.

Eysenck, H. J. (1966b). *The effects of psychotherapy*. New York: International Universities Press.

Eysenck, H. J. (1967). *The biological basis of personality*. Springfield, IL: Charles C Thomas.

Eysenck, H. J. (1972). *Psychology is about people*. New York: Library Press.

Eysenck, H. J., & Eysenck, S. B. G. (1963). *The Eysenck personality inventory*. London: University of London Press.

Eysenck, H. J., & Wilson, G. (1976). *Know your own personality*. Middlesex, England: Penguin Books.

Eysenck, M. W. (1977). *Human memory: Theory, research and individual differences*. New York: Pergamon Press.

Fantino, E., & Logan, C. A. (1979). *The experimental analysis of behavior: A biological perspective*. San Francisco: W. H. Freeman.

Fantz, R. L. (1961, May). The origin of form perception. *Scientific American*, pp. 66–72.

Favreau, O. E., & Corballis, M. C. (1976, December). Negative aftereffects in visual perception. *Scientific American*, pp. 42–48.

Fazio, R. H., & Cooper, J. (in press). Arousal in the dissonance process. In J. T. Cacioppo & R. E. Petty (Eds.), *Social psychophysiology*. New York: Guilford Press.

Fazio, R. H., & Zanna, M. P. (1981). Direct experience and attitude-behavior consistency. In L. Berkowitz (Ed.), *Advances in experimental social psychology* (Vol. 14, pp. 161–202). New York: Academic Press.

Feagans, L., & Farran, D. C. (Eds.). (1982). *The language of children reared in poverty: Implications for evaluation and intervention. Papers from a conference, Chapel Hill, N.C. May 1980*. New York: Academic Press.

Feigl, H. (1960). Mind-body, *not* a pseudo problem. In S. Hook (Ed.), *Dimensions of mind* (pp. 24–36). New York: New York University Press.

Fein, J. M. (1978, April). Microvascular surgery for stroke. *Scientific American*, pp. 59–67.

Feingold, B. D., & Mahoney, M. J. (1975). Reinforcement effects on intrinsic interest: Undermining the overjustification hypothesis. *Behavior Therapy, 6*, 367–377.

Feinsilver, D. B., & Gunderson, J. G. (1972). Psychotherapy for schizophrenics—is it indicated? *Schizophrenia Bulletin, 1*, 11–23.

Fender, D. H. (1964, July). Control mechanisms of the eye. *Scientific American*, pp. 24–33.

Fenton, M. B., & Fullard, J. H. (1981). Moth hearing and the feeding strategies of bats. *American Scientist, 69*, 266–275.

Ferguson, C. A., & Garnica, O. K. (1975). Theories of phonological development. In E. H. Lenneberg & E. Lenneberg (Eds.), *Foundations of language development: A multidisciplinary approach* (Vol. 1, pp. 153–180). New York: Academic Press.

Ferguson, E. S. (1977). The mind's eye: Nonverbal thought in technology. *Science, 197*, 827–836.

Ferster, C. B. (1964, May). Arithmetic behavior in chimpanzees. *Scientific American*, pp. 98–106.

Ferster, C. B., & Skinner, B. F. (1957). *Schedules of reinforcement*. New York: Appleton-Century-Crofts.

Festinger, L. A. (1957). *A theory of cognitive dissonance*. Stanford, CA: Stanford University Press.

Festinger, L., & Carlsmith, J. M. (1959). Cognitive consequences of forced compliance. *Journal of Abnormal and Social Psychology, 58*, 203–210.

Festinger, L., Schachter, S., & Back, K. (1950). *Social pressures in informal groups: A study of human factors in memory*. New York: Harper & Row.

Fillmore, C. J. (1968). The case for case. In E. Bach & R. T. Harms (Eds.), *Universals of linguistic theory* (pp. 1–90). New York: Holt, Rinehart & Winston.

Fillmore, C. J., Kempler, D., & Wang, W. S.-Y. (Eds.). (1979). *Individual differences in language ability and language behavior*. New York: Academic Press.

Fink, M. (1979). *Convulsive therapy: Theory and practice*. New York: Raven Press.

Finke, R. A. (1980). Levels of equivalence in imagery and perception. *Psychological Review, 87*, 113–132.

Firkowska, A., Ostrowska, A., Sokolowska, M., Stein, Z., Susser, M., & Wald, I. (1978). Cognitive development and social policy. *Science, 200*, 1357–1362.

Fishbein, M. (1980). A theory of reasoned action: Some applications and implications. In M. M. Page (Ed.), *Nebraska Symposium on Motivation* (Vol. 27, pp. 65–116). Lincoln, NE: University of Nebraska Press.

Fishbein, M., & Ajzen, I. (1972). Attitudes and opinions. *Annual Review of Psychology, 23*, 487–544.

Fishbein, M. & Ajzen, I. (1975). *Belief, attitude, intention and behavior: An introduction to theory and research*. Reading, MA: Addison-Wesley.

Fishbein, M., & Ajzen, I. (1981). On construct validity: A critique of Miniard and Cohen's paper. *Journal of Experimental Social Psychology, 17*, 340–350.

Fisher, A. E. (1964, June). Chemical stimulation of the brain. *Scientific American*, pp. 60–68.

Fisher, S., & Greenberg, R. P. (1977). *The scientific credibility of Freud's theories and therapy*. New York: Basic Books.

Fjerdingstad, E. J. (1974). Seasonal changes in goldfish learning? *Science, 183*, 1321.

Flanagan, G. L. (1975). *The first nine months of life* (rev. ed.). New York; Simon & Schuster.

Flanagan, J. C. (1963). The definition and measurement of creativity. In C. W. Taylor & F. Barron (Eds.), *Scientific creativity: Its recognition and development*. New York: John Wiley.

Flaugher, R. L. (1978). The many definitions of test bias. *American Psychologist, 33*, 671–679.

Flavell, J. H. (1973). *The developmental psychology of Jean Piaget*. New York: Van Nostrand Reinhold.

Flavell, J. H., & Wellman, H. M. (1977). Metamemory. In R. V. Kail, Jr. & J. W. Hagen (Eds.), *Perspectives on the development of memory and cognition* (pp. 3–33). Hillsdale, NJ: Lawrence Erlbaum.

Flugel, J., & West, D. (1964). *A hundred years of psychology*. New York: Basic Books.

Fodor, J. A. (1981, January). The mind-body problem. *Scientific American*, pp. 114–123.

Follett, B. K., & Follett, D. E. (Eds.). (1981). *Biological clocks in seasonal reproductive cycles: Proceedings of a symposium, Bristol, England, March, 1980*. New York: Halsted Press.

Fontana, A. (1966). Familial etiology of schizophrenia: Is a scientific methodology possible? *Psychological Bulletin, 66*, 214–228.

Foss, D. J., & Hakes, D. T. (1978). *Psycholinguistics*. Englewood Cliffs, NJ: Prentice-Hall.

Fouts, R. S., Hirsch, A. D., & Fouts, D. H. (1982). Cultural transmission of a human language in a chimpanzee mother/infant relationship. In H. E. Fitzgerald, J. A. Mullins, & P. Page (Eds.), *Psychological perspectives: Child nurturance series* (Vol. 4). New York: Plenum Press.

Fox, L. H. (1981). Identification of the academically gifted. *American Psychologist, 36*, 1103–1111.

Fox, R., Aslin, R. N., Shea, S. L., & Dumais, S. T. (1980). Stereopsis in human infants. *Science, 207*, 323–324.

Fox, R. E., Barclay, A. G., & Rodgers, D. A. (1982). The foundations of professional psychology. *American Psychologist, 37*, 306–312.

Fox, R., Lehmkuhle, S. W., & Bush, R. C. (1977). Stereopsis in the falcon. *Science, 197*, 79–81.

Frankel, F. H., & Zamansky, H. S. (Eds.). (1978). *Hypnosis at its bicentennial: Selected papers*. New York: Plenum Press.

Franken, R. E. (1982). *Human motivation*. Monterey, CA: Brooks/Cole.

Frankenburg, W. K., & Dodds, J. B. (1967). The Denver developmental screening test. *Journal of Pediatrics, 71*, 181–191.

Fraser, A. B. (1981, January). To see a dazzling festival of light, just raise your eyes. *Smithsonian*, pp. 72–79.

Fraser, A. B., & Mach, W. H. (1976, January). Mirages. *Scientific American*, pp. 102–111.

Freedman, D. G. (1979, January). Ethnic differences in babies. *Human Nature*, pp. 36–43.

Freedman, J. L. (1975). *Crowding and behavior*. San Francisco: W. H. Freeman.

Freedman, J. L. (1979). Reconciling apparent differences between responses of humans and other animals to crowding. *Psychological Review, 86*, 80–85.

Freedman, J. L. (1980). Responses of humans and other animals to variations in density. *Psychological Review, 87*, 327–328.

Freedman, J. L., Sears, D. O., & Carlsmith, J. M. (1981). *Social psychology* (4th ed.). Englewood Cliffs, NJ: Prentice-Hall.

Freeman, W. (1959). Psychosurgery. In S. Arieti (Ed.), *American handbook of psychiatry* (Vol. 2, pp. 1521–1540). New York: Basic Books.

French, J. D. (1957, May). The reticular formation. *Scientific American*, pp. 54–73.

Fretz, B. R., & Stang, D. J. (1980). *Preparing for graduate study in psychology: Not for seniors only!* Washington, DC: American Psychological Association.

Freud, A. (1946). *The ego and the mechanisms of defence*. New York: International Universities Press (C. Bains, Trans.). (Original work published 1936)

Freud, S. (1900, 1953). The interpretation of dreams. In J. Strachey (Ed. and Trans.), *The standard edition of the complete psychological works of Sigmund Freud* (Vols. 4–5). London: Hogarth Press.

Freud, S. (1901, 1960). The psychopathology of everyday life. In J. Strachey (Ed. and Trans.), *The standard edition of the complete psychological works of Sigmund Freud* (Vol. 6, pp. 1–289). London: Hogarth Press.

Freud, S. (1905, 1953). Fragment of an analysis of a case of hysteria. In J. Strachey (Ed. and Trans.), *The standard edition of the complete psychological works of Sigmund Freud* (Vol. 7, pp. 7–122). London: Hogarth Press.

Freud, S. (1909, 1955). Analysis of phobia in a five-year-old boy. In J. Strachey (Ed. and Trans.), *The standard edition of the complete psychological works of Sigmund Freud* (Vol. 10, pp. 5–147). London: Hogarth Press.

Freud, S. (1910, 1957). Leonardo da Vinci and a memory of his childhood. In J. Strachey (Ed. and Trans.). *The standard edition of the complete psychological works of Sigmund Freud* (Vol. 11, pp. 63–137). London: Hogarth Press.

Freud, S. (1917, 1957). Mourning and melancholia. In J. Strachey (Ed. and Trans.), *The standard edition of the com-*

plete psychological works of Sigmund Freud (Vol. 14, pp. 243–258). London: Hogarth Press.

Freud, S. (1919, 1955). Lines of advance in psycho-analytic therapy. In J. Strachey (Ed. and Trans.), *The standard edition of the complete psychological works of Sigmund Freud* (Vol. 17, pp. 159–168). London: Hogarth Press.

Freud, S. (1920, 1955). Beyond the pleasure principle. In J. Strachey (Ed. and Trans.), *The standard edition of the complete psychological works of Sigmund Freud* (Vol. 18, pp. 7–64). London: Hogarth Press.

Freud, S. (1930, 1961). Civilization and its discontents. In J. Strachey (Ed. and Trans.), *The standard edition of the complete psychological works of Sigmund Freud* (Vol. 21, pp. 64–145). London: Hogarth Press.

Freud, S. (1933, 1963). New introductory lectures on psycho-analysis. In J. Strachey (Ed. and Trans.), *The standard edition of the complete psychological works of Sigmund Freud* (Vol. 22, pp. 1–182). London: Hogarth Press.

Freud, S. (1935). *A general introduction to psychoanalysis* (rev. ed.) (J. Riviere, Trans.). New York: Liveright.

Freud, S. (1938). *The basic writings of Sigmund Freud* (A. A. Brill, Ed. and Trans.). New York: Modern Library.

Friedman, R., & Iwai, J. (1976). Genetic predisposition and stress-induced hypertension. *Science, 193,* 161–162.

Friedrich, L. K., & Stein, A. H. (1975). Pro-social television and young children. The effects of verbal labeling and role playing on learning and behavior. *Child Development, 46,* 27–38.

Frieze, I., Parsons, J., Johnson, P., Ruble, D., & Zellman, G. (1978). *Women and sex roles: A social-psychological perspective.* New York: W. W. Norton.

Frisby, J. (1980). *Seeing: Illusion, brain and mind.* New York: Oxford University Press.

Fromkin, V. A. (Ed.). (1973). *Speech errors as linguistic evidence.* The Hague: Mouton.

Fromkin, V. A. (Ed.). (1980). *Errors in linguistic performance: Slips of the tongue, ear, pen, and hand. Papers from a meeting, Vienna, 1977.* New York: Academic Press.

Fromm-Reichmann, F. (1948). Notes on the development of treatment of schizophrenics by psychoanalytic psychotherapy. *Psychiatry, 11,* 263–273.

Fuchs, F. (1980, June). Genetic amniocentesis. *Scientific American,* pp. 47–53.

Furth, H. G., Ross, B. M., & Youniss, J. (1974). Operative understanding in reproductions of drawings. *Child Development, 45,* 63–70.

Gabrenya, W. K., Jr., & Arkin, R. M. (1980). Self-monitoring scale: Factor structure and correlates. *Personality and Social Psychology Bulletin, 6,* 13–22.

Gaither, N. S., & Stein, B. E. (1979). Reptiles and mammals use similar sensory organization in the midbrain. *Science, 205,* 595–597.

Galbraith, R., & Jones, T. M. (1976). *Moral reasoning: A teacher's handbook for adapting Kohlberg to the classroom.* Minneapolis, MN: Greenhaven Press.

Galin, D., Diamond, R., & Braff, D. (1977). Lateralization of conversion symptoms: More frequent on the left. *American Journal of Psychiatry, 134,* 578–580.

Gallup, G. G., Jr. (1979). Self-awareness in primates. *American Scientist, 67,* 417–421.

Galton, F. (1869). *Hereditary genius: An inquiry into its laws and consequences.* London: Macmillan.

Galvin, R. M. (1982, August). Control of dreams may be possible for a resolute few. *Smithsonian,* pp. 100–107.

Garcia, J. (1981). The logic and limits of mental aptitude testing. *American Psychologist, 36,* 1172–1180.

Garcia, J., McGowan, B. K., & Green, K. F. (1972). Biological constraints on conditioning. In M. E. P. Seligman & J. L. Hager (Eds.), *Biological boundaries of learning* (pp. 21–44). New York: Appleton-Century-Crofts.

Gardner, B. T. (1981). Project Nim: Who taught whom? *Contemporary Psychology, 26,* 425–426.

Gardner, B. T., & Gardner, R. A. (1971). Two-way communication with an infant chimpanzee. In A. M. Schrier & F. Stollnitz (Eds.), *Behavior of nonhuman primates* (Vol. 4, pp. 117–184). New York: Academic Press.

Gardner, H. (1975). *The shattered mind: The person after brain damage.* New York: Alfred A. Knopf.

Gardner, H. (1978, March). The loss of language. *Human Nature,* pp. 76–84.

Gardner, H. (1982a). *Art, mind, and brain: A cognitive approach to creativity.* New York: Basic Books.

Gardner, H. (1982b, June). The music of the hemispheres. *Psychology Today,* pp. 91–92.

Gardner, L. I. (1972, July). Deprivation dwarfism. *Scientific American,* pp. 76–82.

Gardner, M. (1978a). *Aha! Insight.* San Francisco: W. H. Freeman.

Gardner, M. (1978b, August). Mathematical games: A Möbius band has a finite thickness and so it is actually a twisted prism. *Scientific American,* pp. 12–16.

Gardner, M. (1979). *The ambidextrous universe: Mirror asymmetry and time-reversed worlds* (rev. ed.). New York: Charles Scribner's.

Gardner, M. (1981). *Science: Good, bad and bogus.* Buffalo, NY: Prometheus Books.

Gardner, R. A., & Gardner, B. T. (1969). Teaching sign language to a chimpanzee. *Science, 165,* 664–672.

Gardner, R. A., & Gardner, B. T. (1975). Early signs of language in a child and chimpanzee. *Science, 187,* 752–753.

Gardner, R. A., & Gardner, B. T. (1978). Comparative psychology and language acquisition. *Annals of the New York Academy of Science, 309,* 37–76.

Garfield, E. (1982, August 23). Putting your best face forward: The social psychology of physical attractiveness. *Current Contents,* 5–11.

Garfield, S. L. (1981). Psychotherapy: A 40-year appraisal. *American Psychologist, 36,* 174–183.

Garfield, S. L., & Bergin, A. E. (Eds.). (1978). *Handbook of psychotherapy and behavior change: An empirical analysis* (2nd ed.). New York: John Wiley.

Garfield, S., & Kurtz, R. (1974). A survey of clinical psychologists: Characteristics, activities, and orientations. *Clinical Psychologist, 28,* 7–10.

Garner, W. R. (1970). Good patterns have few alternatives. *American Scientist, 58,* 34–42.

Gazzaniga, M. S. (1970). *The bisected brain.* New York: Appleton-Century-Crofts.

Gazzaniga, M. S. (1972). One brain—two minds? *American Scientist, 60,* 311–317.

Gazzaniga, M. S. (1975, Spring). Review of the split brain. *UCLA Educator, 17,* 9–12.

Gazzaniga, M. S. (1981). 1981 Nobel prize for physiology or medicine. *Science, 214,* 517–518.

Gazzaniga, M., & LeDoux, J. E. (1978). *The integrated mind.* New York: Plenum Press.

Geen, R. G., & Quanty, M. B. (1977). The catharsis of aggression: An evaluation of a hypothesis. In L. Berkowitz (Ed.), *Advances in experimental social psychology* (Vol. 10, pp. 1–37). New York: Academic Press.

Gelb, A. (1929). Die "Farbenkonstanz" der Sehding. *Handbook Norm. Path. Phys., 12,* 594–678.

Gelman, R. (1979). Preschool thought. *American Psychologist, 34,* 900–905.

Gerard, H. B., Wilhelmy, R. A., & Connolley, E. S. (1968). Conformity and group size. *Journal of Personality and Social Psychology, 8,* 79–82.

Gergen, K. J., Ellsworth, P., Maslach, C., & Seipel, M. (1975). Obligation, donor resources, and reactions to aid in three cultures. *Journal of Personality and Social Psychology, 31,* 390–400.

Gergen, K., Green, M., & Metzer, K. (1972). Individual orientations to prosocial behavior. *Journal of Social Issues, 28,* 105–130.

Geschwind, N. (1972, April). Language and the brain. *Scientific American,* pp. 76–83.

Geschwind, N. (1979, September). Specializations of the human brain. *Scientific American,* pp. 158–168.

Getzels, J. W., & Jackson, P. W. (1962). *Creativity and intelligence: Explorations with gifted students.* New York: John Wiley.

Ghiselin, B. (Ed.). (1952). *The creative process: A symposium.* Berkeley, CA: University of California Press.

Giacometti, L. (1978, November). Thumbs up. *Human Nature*, pp. 40–47.

Gibson, E. J. (1970). The development of perception as an adaptive process. *American Scientist, 58,* 98–107.

Gibson, E. J., & Levin, H. (1975). *The psychology of reading.* Cambridge, MA: MIT Press.

Gibson, E. J., & Walk, R. D. (1960, April). The visual cliff. *Scientific American,* pp. 64–71.

Gibson, G. E., Peterson, C., & Jenden, D. J. (1981). Brain acetylcholine synthesis declines with senescence. *Science, 213,* 674–676.

Gilbert, W., & Villa-Komaroff, L. (1980, April). Useful proteins from recombinant bacteria. *Scientific American,* pp. 74–94.

Gilchrist, A. L. (1979, March). The perception of surface blacks and whites. *Scientific American,* pp. 112–124.

Gillam, B. (1980, January). Geometrical illusions. *Scientific American,* pp. 102–111.

Ginsburg, H., & Opper, S. (1979). *Piaget's theory of intellectual development* (2nd ed.). Englewood Cliffs, NJ: Prentice-Hall.

Gintzler, A. R. (1980). Endorphin-mediated increases in pain threshold during pregnancy. *Science, 210,* 193–195.

Glaser, R. (1981). The future of testing: A research agenda for cognitive psychology and psychometrics. *American Psychologist, 36,* 923–936.

Glass, D. C., & Singer, J. E. (1972). *Urban stress.* New York: Academic Press.

Glenberg, A. M. (1979). Component-levels theory of the effects of spacing of repetitions on recall and recognition. *Memory & Cognition, 7,* 95–112.

Glenberg, A., Smith, S. M., & Green, C. (1977). Type I rehearsal: Maintenance and more. *Journal of Verbal Learning and Verbal Behavior, 16,* 339–352.

Glickstein, M., & Gibson, A. R. (1976, November). Visual cells in the pons of the brain. *Scientific American,* pp. 90–98.

Gmelch, G. (1978, August). Baseball magic. *Human Nature,* pp. 32–39.

Godden, D. R., & Baddeley, A. D. (1975). Context-dependent memory in two natural environments: On land and underwater. *British Journal of Psychiatry, 66,* 325–331.

Goffman, E. (1959). *The presentation of self in everyday life.* New York: Doubleday.

Goffman, E. (1961). *Asylums: Essays on the social situation of mental patients and other inmates.* Chicago, IL: Aldine.

Gogel, W. C. (1978, May). The adjacency principle in visual perception. *Scientific American,* pp. 126–139.

Goldberg, E., Antin, S. P., Bilder, R. M., Jr., Gerstman, L. J., Hughes, J. E. O., & Mattis, S. (1981). Retrograde amnesia: Possible role of mesencephalic reticular activation in long-term memory. *Science, 213,* 1392–1394.

Goldfoot, D. A., Westerborg-Van Loon, H., Groeneveld, W., & Koos Slob, A. (1980). Behavioral and physiological evidence of sexual climax in the female stump-tailed macaque (*Macaca actoides*). *Science, 208,* 1477–1479.

Goldfried, M. R. (1980). Toward the delineation of therapeutic change principles. *American Psychologist, 35,* 991–999.

Goldfried, M. R., & Triver, C. S. (1974). Effectiveness of relaxation as an active coping skill. *Journal of Abnormal Psychology, 83,* 348–355.

Goldin-Meadow, S., & Feldman, H. (1977). The development of language-like communication without a language model. *Science, 197,* 401–403.

Goldstein, E. B. (1984). *Sensation and perception* (2nd ed.). Belmont, CA: Wadsworth.

Goldstein, T. (1980). *Dawn of modern science: From the Arabs to Leonardo da Vinci.* Boston: Houghton Mifflin.

Goleman, D. (1977, October). Split-brain psychology: Fad of the year. *Psychology Today,* pp. 89–90, 149, 151.

Goleman, D. (1978, November). Special abilities of the sexes: Do they begin in the brain? *Psychology Today,* pp. 48–59, 120.

Goleman, D. (1982, March). Staying up: The rebellion against sleep's gentle tyranny. *Psychology Today,* pp. 24–35.

Golsman, D. (1977). *The varieties of meditative experience.* New York: E. P. Dutton.

Goodglass, H. (1980). Disorders of naming following brain injury. *American Scientist, 68,* 647–655.

Gordon, B. (1972, December). The superior colliculus of the brain. *Scientific American,* pp. 72–82.

Gordon, E. W., & Terrell, M. D. (1981). The changed social context of testing. *American Psychologist, 36,* 1167–1171.

Gordon, J. W., & Ruddle, F. H. (1981). Mammalian gonadal determination and gametogenesis. *Science, 211,* 1265–1271.

Gorn, G. J., Goldberg, M. E., & Kanungo, R. N. (1976). The role of educational television in changing the intergroup attitudes of children. *Child Development, 47,* 277–280.

Gottesman, I. I. (1963). Genetic aspects of intelligent behavior. In N. R. Ellis (Ed.), *Handbook of mental deficiency: Psychological theory and research* (pp. 253–296). New York: McGraw-Hill.

Gottesman, I. I., & Shields, J. (1982). *Schizophrenia: The epigenetic puzzle.* Cambridge: Cambridge University Press.

Gould, J. L. (1975). Honey-bee recruitment: The dance-language controversy. *Science, 189,* 685–693.

Gould, J. L. (1980). The case for magnetic sensitivity in birds and bees (such as it is). *American Scientist, 68,* 256–267.

Gould, P., & White, R. (1974). *Mental maps.* New York: Penguin Books.

Gould, S. J. (1975, May). The child as man's real father. *Natural History,* pp. 18–22.

Gould, S. J. (1976, February). Human babies as embryos. *Natural History,* pp. 22–26.

Gould, S. J. (1977). *Ever since Darwin: Reflections in natural history.* New York: W. W. Norton.

Gould, S. J. (1978, November). The panda's peculiar thumb. *Natural History,* pp. 20–30.

Gould, S. J. (1979a, May). Mickey Mouse meets Konrad Lorenz. *Natural History,* pp. 30–36.

Gould, S. J. (1979b, June/July). Our greatest evolutionary step. *Natural History,* pp. 40–44.

Gould S. J. (1979c, October). Shades of Lamarck. *Natural History,* pp. 22–28.

Gould, S. J. (1980). *The panda's thumb: More reflections in natural history.* New York: W. W. Norton.

Gould, S. J. (1981a). *The mismeasure of man.* New York: W. W. Norton.

Gould, S. J. (1981b, October). A visit to Dayton. *Natural History,* pp. 8–22.

Gould, S. J. (1982a, January). The guano ring. *Natural History,* pp. 12–19.

Gould, S. J. (1982b, February). Nonmoral nature. *Natural History,* pp. 19–26.

Gould, S. J. (1983). *Hen's teeth and horse's toes.* New York: W. W. Norton.

Gouldner, A. W. (1960). The norm of reciprocity: A preliminary statement. *American Sociological Review, 25,* 161–178.

Graham, A. (1973). The making of a nonsexist dictionary. In B. Thorne & N. Henley (Eds.), *Language and sex: Difference and dominance.* Rowley, MA: Newbury House.

Graham, F. A., Leavitt, L. A., Strock, B. D., & Brown, J. W. (1978). Precocious cardiac orienting in a human anencephalic infant. *Science, 199,* 322–324.

Graham, J. R. (1978). The Minnesota Multiphasic Personality Inventory (MMPI). In B. B. Wolman (Ed.), *Clinical diagnosis of mental disorders: A handbook* (pp. 311–331). New York: Plenum Press.

Grant, P. R. (1981). Speciation and the adaptive radiation of Darwin's finches. *American Scientist, 69,* 653–663.

Gray, F., Graubard, P. S., & Rosenberg, H. (1974, March). Little brother is changing you. *Psychology Today,* pp. 42–46.

Gray, J. A. (1978, July). Anxiety. *Human Nature,* pp. 38–45.

Green, B. (1978, February 16). Teaching a man to sound female: Speech therapy for transsexuals. *San Francisco Chronicle,* p. 34.

Green, B. F. (1981). A primer of testing. *American Psychologist, 36,* 1001–1011.

Green, H. (1964). *I never promised you a rose garden.* New York: Holt, Rinehart & Winston.

Green, R. (1974, February). Children's quest for sexual identity. *Psychology Today,* pp. 45–51.

Greenberg, J. (1983a). Findings shed light

on how ECT works. *Science News, 123,* 325.

Greenberg, J. (1983b). Pre-psychosis: Key in brain waves? *Science News, 123,* 341.

Greenberg, J. H. (1966). *Language universals.* The Hague: Mouton.

Greeno, J. G. (1976). Indefinite goals in well-structured problems. *Psychological Review, 83,* 479–491.

Greeno, J. G. (1978). Nature of problem solving abilities. In W. K. Estes (Ed.), *Handbook of learning and cognitive processes* (Vol. 5, pp. 239–270). Hillsdale, NJ: Lawrence Erlbaum.

Greeno, J. G. (1980). Psychology of learning, 1960–1980: One participant's observations. *American Psychologist, 35,* 713–728.

Greenspoon, J. (1955). The reinforcing effect of two spoken sounds on the frequency of two responses. *American Journal of Psychology, 68,* 409–416.

Gregory, R. L. (1966). *Eye and brain: The psychology of seeing.* New York: McGraw-Hill.

Gregory, R. L. (1968, November). Visual illusions. *Scientific American,* pp. 66–76.

Gregory, R. L. (1970). *The intelligent eye.* New York: McGraw-Hill.

Grice, H. P. (1975). Logic and conversation. In P. Cole & J. L. Morgan (Eds.), *Syntax and semantics: Vol. 3. Speech acts* (pp. 41–58). New York: Seminar Press.

Griffin, D. R. (1981). *The question of animal awareness: Evolutionary continuity of mental experience* (rev. ed.). New York: Rockefeller University Press.

Grings, W. W., & Davison, M. E. (1978). *Emotions and bodily responses: A psychophysiological approach.* New York: Academic Press.

Grinspoon, L. (1969, December). Marijuana. *Scientific American,* pp. 17–25.

Gross, C. G. (1973). Inferotemporal cortex and vision. *Progress in Physiological Psychology, 5,* 77–123.

Grossman, H. (Ed.). (1977). *Manual on terminology and classification in mental retardation.* Washington, DC: American Association on Mental Deficiency.

Grover, S. C. (1981). *The cognitive basis of the intellect: A response to Jensen's bias in mental testing.* Lanham, MD: University Press of America.

Grusec, J. E. (1981). Socialization processes and the development of altruism. In J. P. Rushton & R. M. Sorrentino (Eds.), *Altruism and helping behavior: Social, personality, and developmental perspectives* (pp. 65–90). Hillsdale, NJ: Lawrence Erlbaum.

Grusec, J. E., & Skubiski, S. L. (1970). Model nurturance, demand characteristics of the modeling experiment, and altruism. *Journal of Personality and Social Psychology, 14,* 352–359.

Guilford, J. P. (1954). *A factor analytic study across the domains of reasoning, creativity*

and evaluation: I. Hypothesis and description of tests (Reports from the Psychology Laboratory). Los Angeles: University of Southern California.

Guilford, J. P. (1959). Three faces of intellect. *American Psychologist, 14,* 469–479.

Guilford, J. P. (1967). *The nature of human intelligence.* New York: McGraw-Hill.

Guilford, J. P. (1980). Fluid and crystallized intelligence: Two fanciful concepts. *Psychological Bulletin, 88,* 406–412.

Guillemin, R., & Burgus, R. (1972, November). The hormones of the hypothalamus. *Scientific American,* pp. 24–33.

Guilleminault, C., Eldridge, F. L., & Dement, W. C. (1973). Insomnia with sleep apnea: A new syndrome. *Science, 181,* 856–858.

Guilleminault, C., Peraita, R., Souquet, M., & Dement, W. C. (1975). Apneas during sleep in infants: Possible relationship with sudden infant death syndrome. *Science, 190,* 677–679.

Gummerman, K., & Gray, C. R. (1971). Recall of visually presented material: An unwonted case and a bibliography for eidetic imagery. *Psychonomic Monograph Supplements, 4*(10).

Gurin, J. (1979, November/December). Chemical feelings. *Science 80,* pp. 28–33.

Gustavson, C. R., Garcia, J., Hankins, W. G., & Rusiniak, K. W. (1974). Coyote predation control by aversive conditioning. *Science, 184,* 581–583.

Guthrie, E. R., & Horton, G. P. (1946). *Cats in a puzzle box.* New York: Reinhart Press.

Haber, R. N. (1978). Visual perception. *Annual Review of Psychology, 29,* 31–59.

Haber, R. N. (1980). How we perceive depth from flat pictures. *American Scientist, 68,* 370–380.

Haber, R. N., & Haber, R. B. (1964). Eidetic imagery: I. Frequency. *Perceptual and Motor Skills, 19,* 131–138.

Haber, R. N., & Standing, L. G. (1970). Direct estimates of apparent duration of a flash followed by visual noise. *Canadian Journal of Psychology, 24,* 216–229.

Haley, J. (Ed.). (1967). *Advanced techniques of hypnosis and therapy: Selected papers of Milton H. Erikson, M.D.* New York: Grune & Stratton.

Hall, C. S. (1954). *A primer of Freudian psychology.* New York: New American Library.

Hall, C. S., & Lindzey, G. (1978). *Theories of personality* (3rd ed.). New York: John Wiley.

Hall, C. S., & Van de Castle, R. L. (1966). *The content analysis of dreams.* New York: Appleton-Century-Crofts.

Hall, R. C. W., Gardner, E. R., Stickney, S. R., LeCann, A. F., & Popkin, M. K. (1980). Physical illness manifesting as psychiatric disease: II. Analysis of a state hospital inpatient population. *Archives of General Psychiatry, 37,* 989–995.

Hall, D. T. , & Lawler, E. E., III. (1971).

Job pressures and research performance. *American Scientist, 59,* 64–73.

Hall, E., Perlmutter, M., & Lamb, M. (1982). *Child psychology today.* New York: Random House.

Hall, E. T. (1959). *The silent language.* New York: Fawcett.

Hall, J. A., Rosenthal, R., Archer, D., DiMatteo, M. R., & Rogers, P. L. (1978, May). Decoding wordless messages. *Human Nature,* pp. 68–75.

Hall, J. G., Sybert, V. P., Williamson, R. A., Fisher, N. L., & Reed, S. D. (1982). Turner's syndrome—clinical genetics conference. *Western Journal of Medicine, 137,* 32–44.

Hamilton, D. L. (1979). A cognitive-attributional analysis of stereotyping. In L. Berkowitz (Ed.), *Advances in experimental social psychology* (Vol. 12, pp. 53–84). New York: Academic Press.

Hamilton, D. L. (1981). Illusory correlation as a basis for stereotyping. In D. L. Hamilton (Ed.), *Cognitive processes in stereotyping and intergroup behavior* (pp. 115–144). Hillsdale, NJ: Lawrence Erlbaum.

Handler, P. (1979). Basic research in the United States. *Science, 204,* 474–479.

Hanen, M. P., Osler, M. J., & Weyant, R. G. (Eds.). (1980). *Science, pseudoscience and society.* Waterloo, Ontario: Wilfred Laurier University Press.

Haney, W. (1981). Validity, vaudeville, and values: A short history of social concerns over standardized testing. *American Psychologist, 36,* 1021–1034.

Hans, V. P., & Vidmar, N. (1982). Jury selection. In N. L. Kerr & R. M. Bray (Eds.), *The psychology of the courtroom* (pp. 39–82). New York: Academic Press.

Hargadon, F. (1981). Tests and college admissions. *American Psychologist, 36,* 1112–1119.

Harlow, H. F. (1959, June). Love in infant monkeys. *Scientific American,* pp. 68–74.

Harlow, H. F. (1973). *Learning to love.* San Francisco: Albion.

Harlow, H. F., Harlow, M. K., & Suomi, S. J. (1971). From thought to therapy: Lessons from a primate laboratory. *American Scientist, 59,* 538–549.

Harman, G. (Ed.). (1982). *On Noam Chomsky: Critical essays* (2nd ed.). Amherst, MA: University of Massachusetts Press.

Harmon, L. D. (1973, November). The recognition of faces. *Scientific American,* pp. 70–82.

Harper, R. M., Leake, B., Hoffman, H., Walter, D. O., Hoppenbrouwers, T., & Hodgeman, J. (1981). Periodicity of sleep status is altered in infants at risk for the sudden infant death syndrome. *Science, 213,* 1030–1032.

Harrell, R. F., Capp, R. H., Davis, D. R., Peerless, J., & Ravitz, L. R. (1981). Can nutritional supplements help mentally retarded children? An exploratory study. *Proceedings of the National Academy of Sciences, 78,* 574–578.

Harris, J. E. (1978). External memory aids. In M. M. Gruneberg, P. E. Morris, & R. N. Sykes (Eds.), *Practical aspects of memory*. London: Academic Press.

Harris, J. E. (1978). External memory aids. In M. M. Gruneberg, P. E. Morris, & R. N. Sykes (Eds.), *Practical aspects of memory*. London: Academic Press.

Hart, J. T. (1967). Memory and the memory-monitoring process. *Journal of Verbal Learning and Verbal Behavior, 6,* 685–691.

Hartman, E. L. (1973). *The functions of sleep*. New Haven, CT: Yale University Press.

Hartman, E. L. (1978, December). L-tryptophan: The sleeping pill of the future? *Psychology Today*, p. 180.

Hartshorne, H., & May, M. A. (1928). *Studies in deceit*. New York: Macmillan.

Hartup, W. W. (1979). The social worlds of childhood. *American Psychologist, 34,* 944–950.

Harvey, J. H., & McGlynn, R. P. (1982). Matching words to phenomena: The case of the fundamental attribution error. *Journal of Personality and Social Psychology, 43,* 345–346.

Harvey, J. H., Town, J. P., & Yarkin, K. L. (1981). How fundamental is "the fundamental attribution error"? *Journal of Personality and Social Psychology, 40,* 346–349.

Harvey, J. H., & Weary, G. (1981). *Perspectives on attributional processes*. Dubuque, IA: W. C. Brown.

Haseltine, F. P., & Ohno, S. (1981). Mechanisms of gonadal differentiation. *Science, 211,* 1272–1278.

Hasler, A. D., Scholz, A. T., & Horrall, R. M. (1978). Olfactory imprinting and homing in salmon. *American Scientist, 66,* 347–355.

Hassett, J. (1978, March). Sex and smell. *Psychology Today*, pp. 40–45.

Hassett, J. (1980, December). Acupuncture is proving its points. *Psychology Today*, pp. 81–89.

Hastorf, A. H., & Isen, A. M. (Eds.). (1982). *Cognitive social psychology*. New York: Elsevier.

Hathaway, S. R., & McKinley, J. C. (1967). *Minnesota Multiphasic Personality Inventory, revised manual*. New York: Psychological Corporation.

Hawkes, N. (1979). Tracing Burt's descent to scientific fraud. *Science, 205,* 673–675.

Hay, R. L., & Leakey, M. D. (1982, February). The fossil footprints of Laetoli. *Scientific American*, pp. 50–57.

Hayes, J. R. (1981). *The complete problem solver*. Philadelphia: Franklin Institute.

Hayes, K. J., & Hayes, C. (1951). Intellectual development of a home-raised chimpanzee. *Proceedings of the American Philosophical Society, 95,* 105–109.

Hayflick, L. (1975, Spring/Summer). Why grow old? *Stanford Magazine*, pp. 36–43.

Hearnshaw, L. S. (1981). *Cyril Burt, psychologist*. New York: Random House.

Hearst, E. (Ed.). (1979). *The first century of experimental psychology*. Hillsdale, NJ: Lawrence Erlbaum.

Hebb, D. O. (1949). *The organization of behavior*. New York: John Wiley.

Hebb, D. O. (1955). Drive and the C.N.S. (conceptual nervous system). *Psychological Review, 62,* 243–254.

Hebb, D. O. (1978). Open letter: To a friend who thinks the IQ is a social evil. *American Psychologist, 33,* 1143–1144.

Hechinger, N. (1981, March). Seeing without eyes. *Science 81*, pp. 38–43.

Heidbreder, E. (1933). *Seven psychologies*. New York: Appleton-Century-Crofts.

Heidbreder, E. (1969). Functionalism. In D. L. Krantz (Ed.), *Schools of psychology* (pp. 35–70). New York: Appleton-Century-Crofts.

Heider, F. (1958). *The psychology of interpersonal relations*. New York: John Wiley.

Heilman, K., & Valenstein, E. (Eds.). (1979). *Clinical neuropsychology*. New York: Oxford University Press.

Heimer, L. (1971, July). Pathways in the brain. *Scientific American*, pp. 48–60.

Held, R. (1965, November). Plasticity in sensory-motor systems. *Scientific American*, pp. 84–94.

Heller, H. C., Crawshaw, L. I., & Hammel, H. T. (1978, August). The thermostat of vertebrate animals. *Scientific American*, pp. 102–113.

Helmers, C. (1979, November). Is pseudo-science done by computer pseudo-computer-science? *Byte*, pp. 6–9.

Henderson, R. W. (Ed.). (1981). *Parent-child interaction: Theory, research, and prospects*. New York: Academic Press.

Henig, R. M. (1981). *The myth of senility*. New York: Doubleday.

Henle, M. (1978). Gestalt psychology and gestalt therapy. *Journal of the History of the Behavioral Sciences, 14,* 23–32.

Hepburn, J. R. (1980). The objective reality of evidence and the utility of systematic jury selection. *Law and Human Behavior, 4,* 89–102.

Herbert, W. (1982a). Intelligence test: Sizing up a newcomer. *Science News, 122,* 280–281.

Herbert, W. (1982b). Sleeping pills and apnea linked in elderly. *Science News, 121,* 421.

Herbert, W. (1982c). The three brains of Eve: EEG data. *Science News, 121,* 356.

Herbert, W. (1983a). Hormone aberration-anorexia link found. *Science News, 123,* 340–341.

Herbert, W. (1983b). Shrinking the insanity defense. *Science News, 123,* 68.

Herdt, G. H. (1980). *Guardians of the flutes: Idioms of masculinity*. New York: McGraw-Hill.

Herkenham, M., & Pert, C. (1980). In vitro autoradiography of opiate receptors in rat brain suggests loci of opiatergic pathways. *Proceedings of the National Academy of Sciences, 77,* 5532–5536.

Heron, W. (1957, January). The pathology of boredom. *Scientific American*, pp. 52–69.

Herrnstein, R. J. (1973). *IQ in the meritocracy*. Boston: Little, Brown.

Herrnstein, R. J. (1977a). Doing what comes naturally: A reply to professor Skinner. *American Psychologist, 32,* 1013–1016.

Herrnstein, R. J. (1977b). The evolution of behaviorism. *American Psychologist, 32,* 593–603.

Herrnstein, R. J. (1982, August). IQ testing and the media. *Atlantic Monthly*, pp. 68–74.

Herrnstein, R. J., Loveland, D. H., & Cable, D. (1976). Natural concepts in pigeons. *Journal of Experimental Psychology: Animal Behavior Processes, 2,* 285–302.

Herron, J. (Ed.). (1979). *Neuropsychology of left-handedness*. New York: Academic Press.

Hess, E. H. (1956, July). Space perception in the chick. *Scientific American*, pp. 71–80.

Heston, L. L. (1966). Psychiatric disorders in foster home reared children of schizophrenic mothers. *British Journal of Psychiatry, 112,* 819–825.

Hetherington, E. M. (1979). Divorce: A child's perspective. *American Psychologist, 34,* 851–858.

Hiam, A. W. (1982, April). Airborne models and flying mimics. *Natural History*, pp. 42–49.

Higbee, K. L. (1977). *Your memory: How it works and how to improve it*. Englewood Cliffs, NJ: Prentice-Hall.

Higgins, E. T., Herman, P., & Zanna, M. P. (Eds.). (1981). *Social cognition: The Ontario symposium*. Hillsdale, NJ: Lawrence Erlbaum.

Hildum, D. C., & Brown, R. W. (1956). Verbal reinforcement and interviewer bias. *Journal of Abnormal and Social Psychology, 53,* 108–111.

Hilgard, E. R. (1965). *Hypnotic susceptibility*. New York: Harcourt Brace Jovanovich.

Hilgard, E. R. (1969). Pain as a puzzle for psychology and physiology. *American Psychologist, 24,* 103–113.

Hilgard, E. R. (1971). Hypnotic phenomena: The struggle for scientific acceptance. *American Scientist, 59,* 567–577.

Hilgard, E. R. (1973). A neodissociation interpretation of pain reduction in hypnosis. *Psychological Review, 80,* 396–411.

Hilgard, E. R. (1975). Hypnosis. *Annual Review of Psychology, 26,* 19–44.

Hilgard, E. R. (1977a). *Divided consciousness: Multiple controls in human thought and action*. New York: John Wiley.

Hilgard, E. R. (1977b). Neodissociation theory of multiple cognitive control systems. In G. E. Schwartz & D. Shapiro (Eds.), *Consciousness and self-regulation:*

Vol. 1. Advances in research. New York: Plenum Press.

Hilgard, E. (1978a, January). Hypnosis and consciousness. *Human Nature*, pp. 42–49.

Hilgard, E. R. (1978b). Pain perception in man. In R. Held, H. W. Leibowitz, & H.-L. Teuber (Eds.), *Handbook of sensory physiology: Vol. 8. Perception.* Berlin: Springer Verlag.

Hilgard, E. R. (1978c). States of consciousness in hypnosis: Divisions or levels? In F. H. Frankel & H. S. Zamansky (Eds.), *Hypnosis at its bicentennial: Selected papers* (pp. 15–36). New York: Plenum Press.

Hilgard, E. R. (1980). Consciousness in contemporary psychology. *Annual Review of Psychology, 31*, 1–26.

Hilgard, E. R. (1981, Spring). Hypnosis gives rise to fantasy and is not a truth serum. *Skeptical Inquirer, 5*, 25.

Hilgard, E. R., Atkinson, R. C., & Atkinson, R. L. (1975a). *Introduction to psychology* (6th ed.). New York: Harcourt Brace Jovanovich.

Hilgard, E. R., & Hilgard, J. R. (1975). *Hypnosis in the relief of pain.* Los Altos, CA: William Kaufmann.

Hilgard, E. R., Morgan, A. H., & Macdonald, H. (1975b). Pain and dissociation in the cold pressor test: A study of hypnotic analgesia with "hidden reports" through automatic keypressing and automatic talking. *Journal of Abnormal Psychology, 85*, 218–224.

Hilgard, J. R. (1970). *Personality and hypnosis: A study of imaginative involvement.* Chicago: University of Chicago Press.

Hill, A. L. (1974). Idiot savants: A categorization of abilities. *Mental Retardation, 12*(6), 12–13.

Hill, G. W. (1982). Group versus individual performance: Are N + 1 heads better than one? *Psychological Bulletin, 91*, 517–539.

Hill, W. F. (1981). *Principles of learning: A handbook of applications.* Sherman Oaks, CA: Alfred.

Hilts, P. (1980a, January/February). Bulldozers, bassoons, and silicone chips. *Science 80*, pp. 77–79.

Hilts, P. (1980b, December). The clock within. *Science 80*, pp. 60–67.

Hinckley, J. W., Jr. (1982, September 20). The insanity defense and me. *Newsweek*, p. 30.

Hinde, R. A. (1970). *Animal behavior: A synthesis of ethology and comparative psychology.* New York: McGraw-Hill.

Hinde, R. A., & Hinde, J. S. (Eds.). (1973). *Constraints on learning.* New York: Academic Press.

Hines, T. M. (1979, Summer). Biorhythm theory: A critical review. *Skeptical Inquirer, 3*, 26–36.

Hirst, W., Neisser, U., & Spelke, E. (1978, June). Divided attention. *Human Nature*, pp. 54–61.

Hobson, J. A., & McCarley, R. W. (1977). The brain as a dream state generator: An activation-synthesis hypothesis of the dream process. *American Journal of Psychiatry, 134*, 1335–1348.

Hobson, J. A., Spagna, T., & Malenka, R. (1978). Ethology of sleep studied with time-lapse photography: Postural immobility and sleep-cycle phase in humans. *Science, 201*, 1251–1253.

Hochberg, J. E. (1957). Effects of the gestalt revolution: The Cornell symposium on perception. *Psychological Review, 64*, 73–84.

Hochberg, J. E. (1962). Nativism and empiricism in perception. In L. Postman (Ed.), *Psychology in the making: Histories of selected research problems* (pp. 255–330). New York: Alfred A. Knopf.

Hochberg, J. E., & Brooks, V. (1978). Art and perception. In E. C. Carterette & H. Freedman (Eds.), *Handbook of perception* (Vol. 10). New York: Academic Press.

Hockett, C. F. (1960, September). The origin of speech. *Scientific American*, pp. 89–96.

Hodgson, R. J., & Rachman, S. J. (1972). The effects of contamination and washing on obsessional patients. *Behavior Research and Therapy, 10*, 111–117.

Hoemann, H. W. (1978). *Communicating with deaf people: A resource manual for teachers and students of American Sign Language.* Baltimore, MD: University Park Press.

Hoffman, H. S., & DePaulo, P. (1977). Behavior control by an imprinting stimulus. *American Scientist, 65*, 58–66.

Hoffman, J. W., Benson, H., Arns, P. A., Stainbrook, G. L., Landsberg, L., Young, J. B., & Gill, A. (1982). Reduced sympathetic nervous system responsivity associated with the relaxation response. *Science, 215*, 190–192.

Hoffman, L. W. (1979). Maternal employment: 1979. *American Psychologist, 34*, 859–865.

Hoffman, M. L. (1979). Development of moral thought, feeling and behavior. *American Psychologist, 34*, 958–966.

Hofstadter, D. R. (1982, May). Number numbness, or why innumeracy may be just as dangerous as illiteracy. *Scientific American*, pp. 20–34.

Hogarty, G. E., Goldberg, S. C., Schooler, N. R., & The Collaborative Study Group. (1974). Drug and sociotherapy in the aftercare of schizophrenic patients: III. Adjustment of nonrelapsed patients. *Archives of General Psychiatry, 31*, 609–618.

Holden, C. (1975). Lie detectors: PSE gains audience despite critics' doubts. *Science, 190*, 359–362.

Holden, C. (1977). Carl Rogers: Giving people permission to be themselves. *Science, 198*, 31–35.

Holden, C. (1978). The plight of the "deinstitutionalized" mental patient. *Science, 200*, 1366.

Holden, C. (1979). Paul MacLean and the triune brain. *Science, 204*, 1066–1068.

Holden, C. (1980a). Identical twins reared apart. *Science, 207*, 1323–1328.

Holden, C. (1980b). A new visibility for gifted children. *Science, 210*, 879–882.

Holden, C. (1980c, November). Twins reunited. *Science 80*, pp. 54–59.

Holden, C. (1981). The politics of paleo-anthropology. *Science, 213*, 737–740.

Holden, C. (1982). NAS backs cautious use of ability tests. *Science, 215*, 950.

Holdstock, T., & Rogers, C. R. (1977). Person centered theory. In R. Corsini (Ed.), *Contemporary personality theories.* Itasca, IL: F. E. Peacock.

Holland, V. D., & Delius, J. D. (1982). Rotational invariance in visual pattern recognition by pigeons and humans. *Science, 218*, 804–806.

Hollingshead, A. B., & Redlich, F. C. (1958). *Social class and mental illness: A community study.* New York: John Wiley.

Holmes, L. (1978, October). How fathers can cause the Down syndrome. *Human Nature*, pp. 70–72.

Holmes, T. H., & Rahe, R. H. (1967). The social readjustment scale. *Journal of Psychosomatic Research, 11*, 213–218.

Holmes, T. S., & Holmes, T. H. (1970). Short-term intrusions into the life style routine. *Journal of Psychosomatic Research, 14*, 121–132.

Holt, R. R. (1964). Imagery: The return of the ostracized. *American Psychologist, 19*, 254–264.

Holt, S., Ford, M. J., Grant, S., & Heading, R. C. (1981). Abnormal gastric emptying in primary anorexia nervosa. *British Journal of Psychiatry, 139*, 550–552.

Holtzman, J. D., & Gazzaniga, M. S. (1982). Dual task interactions due exclusively to limits in processing resources. *Science, 218*, 1325–1327.

Homans, G. C. (1961). *Social behavior: Its elementary forms.* New York: Harcourt Brace Jovanovich.

Honigfeld, G., & Howard, A. (1978). *Psychiatric drugs: A desk reference* (2nd ed.). New York: Academic Press.

Hook, E. B., & Porter, I. H. (Eds.). (1981). *Population and biological aspects of human mutation: Papers from a symposium, Albany, N.Y., 1980.* New York: Academic Press.

Hopson, J. L. (1979, March). We may follow our noses more often than is now realized. *Smithsonian*, pp. 78–85.

Horn, J. C. (1978, July). The Gombe chimps: A slight case of murder. *Psychology Today*, p. 18.

Horn, J. L., & Donaldson, G. (1976). On the myth of intellectual decline in adulthood. *American Psychologist, 31*, 701–719.

Horner, M. S. (1968). *Sex differences in achievement motivation and performance in competitive and noncompetitive situations.* Unpublished doctoral dissertation, University of Michigan.

Horney, K. (1942). *Self-analysis*. New York: W. W. Norton.

Horney, K. (1953). *Collected works of Karen Horney* (2 vols.). New York: W. W. Norton.

Horowitz, J. (1978, April 2). Breaking the code that binds: Kennedy twins leaving secret language world. *Los Angeles Times*, Part VII, pp. 1, 20–23.

Hounshell, D. A. (1981, January). Two paths to the telephone. *Scientific American*, pp. 156–163.

Hovland, C. I., Janis, I. L., & Kelley, H. H. (1953). *Communication and persuasion*. New Haven, CT: Yale University Press.

Howells, W. W. (1960, September). The distribution of man. *Scientific American*, pp. 112–127.

Hubel, D. H. (1963, November). The visual cortex of the brain. *Scientific American*, pp. 54–62.

Hubel, D. H. (1979, September). The brain. *Scientific American*, pp. 38–47.

Hubel, D. H., & Wiesel, T. N. (1962). Receptive fields, binocular interaction, and functional architecture in the cat's visual cortex. *Journal of Physiology, 160*, 106–154.

Hubel, D. H., & Wiesel, T. N. (1979, September). Brain mechanisms of vision. *Scientific American*, pp. 130–144.

Hubert, H. B., Fabsitz, R. R., Feinleib, M., & Brown, K. S. (1980). Olfactory sensitivity in humans: Genetic versus environmental control. *Science, 208*, 607–609.

Hudspeth, A. J. (1983, January). The hair cells of the inner ear. *Scientific American*, pp. 54–64.

Hugdahl, K., Fredrikson, M., & Öhman, A. (1977). Preparedness and arousability as determinants of electrodermal conditioning. *Behavior Research and Therapy, 15*, 345–353.

Hughes, R. (1972, December 18). The decline and fall of the avant-garde. *Time*, pp. 111–112.

Hull, C. L. (1933). *Hypnosis and suggestibility: An experimental approach*. New York: Appleton-Century-Crofts.

Hull, C. L. (1943). *Principles of behavior*. New York: Appleton-Century-Crofts.

Hull, C. L. (1952). *A behavior system: An introduction to behavior theory concerning the individual organism*. New Haven, CT: Yale University Press.

Hull, C. L., Hovland, C. I., Ross, R. T., Hall, M., Perkins, D. T., & Fitch, F. G. (1940). *Mathematico-deductive theory of role behavior*. New Haven, CT: Yale University Press.

Humphrey, N. (1982). Consciousness: A just-so story. *New Scientist*, 474–477.

Humphreys, L. G. (1957). Characteristics of type concepts with special reference to Sheldon's typology. *Psychological Bulletin, 54*, 218–228.

Hunt, E. (1978). Mechanics of verbal ability. *Psychological Review, 85*, 109–130.

Hunt, E., & Love, T. (1972). How good can memory be? In A. W. Melton & E. Martin (Eds.), *Coding processes in human memory* (pp. 237–260). Washington, DC: V. H. Winston.

Hunt, M. (1982, November 28). Putting juries on the couch. *The New York Times Magazine*.

Hunter, I. M. L. (1978). The role of memory in expert mental calculations. In M. M. Gruneberg, P. E. Morris, & R. N. Sykes (Eds.), *Practical aspects of memory*. New York: Academic Press.

Huston, T. C., Ruggiero, M., Conner, R., & Geis, G. (1981). Bystander intervention into crime: A study based on naturally-occurring episodes. *Social Psychology Quarterly, 44*, 14–23.

Hutchinson, J. B. (Ed.). (1978). *Biological determinants of sexual behavior*. New York: John Wiley.

Huxley, H. E. (1965, December). The mechanism of muscular contraction. *Scientific American*, pp. 18–27.

Huyck, M. H., & Hoyer, W. J. (1982). *Adult development and aging*. Belmont, CA: Wadsworth.

Hyman, L. M. (1975). *Phonology: Theory and analysis*. New York: Holt, Rinehart & Winston.

Hyman, R. (1977, Spring/Summer). "Cold reading": How to convince strangers that you know all about them. *Zetetic [Skeptical Inquirer], 1*, 18–37.

Ingram, I. M. (1961). The obsessional personality and obsessional illness. *American Journal of Psychiatry, 117*, 1016–1019.

Insko, C. A. (1965). Verbal reinforcement of attitude. *Journal of Personality and Social Psychology, 2*, 621–623.

Isaac, G. (1978, April). The food-sharing behavior of protohuman hominids. *Scientific American*, pp. 90–108.

Isen, A. M., Clark, M., & Schwartz, M. F. (1976). Duration of the effect of good mood on helping: "Footprints on the sands of time." *Journal of Personality and Social Psychology, 34*, 385–393.

Ittelson, W. H., Proshansky, H. M., Rivlin, L. G., & Winkel, G. H. (1974). *An introduction to environmental psychology*. New York: Holt, Rinehart & Winston.

Iversen, L. L. (1979, September). The chemistry of the brain. *Scientific American*, pp. 118–129.

Jaccard, J. (1983). *Statistics for the behavioral sciences*. Belmont, CA: Wadsworth.

Jackson, D. (1980, October). Reunion of identical twins raised apart, reveals astonishing similarities. *Smithsonian*, pp. 48–56.

Jacobs, B. L. (1976, March). Serotonin: The crucial substance that turns dreams on and off. *Psychology Today*, pp. 70–71.

Jacobs, B. L., & Trulson, M. E. (1979). Mechanisms of action of LSD. *American Scientist, 67*, 396–404.

Jacobs, G. H. (1981). *Comparative color vision*. New York: Academic Press.

Jacobs, L., Feldman, M., & Bender, M. B. (1971). Eye movements during sleep: I. The pattern in the normal human. *Archives of Neurology, 25*, 151–159.

Jacobson, E. (1974). *Progressive relaxation* (3rd ed.). Chicago: University of Chicago Press.

Jacobson, M. (1978). *Developmental neurobiology*. New York: Plenum Press.

James, W. (1884). What is emotion? *Mind, 19*, 188–205.

James, W. (1890). *The principles of psychology*. New York: Henry Holt.

James, W. (1902, 1961). *The varieties of religious experience: A study in human nature*. New York: Macmillan.

James, W. (1981). *The principles of psychology* (3 vols.). Cambridge, MA: Harvard University Press.

Janis, I. L. (1972). *Victims of groupthink: A psychological study of foreign-policy decisions and fiascos*. Boston: Houghton Mifflin.

Janis, I. L. (Ed.). (1982). *Counseling on personal decisions: Theory and research on short-term helping relationships*. New Haven, CT: Yale University Press.

Janis, I. L., & Feshback, S. (1953). Effects of fear-arousing communications. *Journal of Abnormal and Social Psychology, 48*, 78–92.

Janis, I. L., & Mann, L. (1976). Coping with decisional conflict. *American Scientist, 64*, 657–667.

Jarvik, L. F., Klodin, V., & Matsuyama, S. S. (1973). Human aggression and the extra Y chromosome: Fact or fantasy? *American Psychologist, 28*, 674–682.

Jeans, R. F. I. (1976). An independently validated case of multiple personality. *Journal of Abnormal Psychology, 85*, 249–255.

Jenkins, H. M., & Moore, B. R. (1973). The form of the autoshaped response with food or water reinforcers. *Journal of the Experimental Analysis of Behavior, 20*, 163–181.

Jenkins, J. G., & Dallenbach, K. M. (1924). Obliviscence during sleep and waking. *American Journal of Psychology, 35*, 605–612.

Jensen, A. R. (1969). How much can we boost IQ and scholastic achievement? *Harvard Educational Review, 39*, 1–123.

Jensen, A. R. (1973). *Educability and group differences*. New York: Harper & Row.

Jensen, A. R. (1980). *Bias in mental testing*. New York: Free Press.

Jerison, H. J. (1973). *Evolution of the brain and intelligence*. New York: Academic Press.

Jerison, H. J. (1976, January). Paleoneurology and the evolution of mind. *Scientific American*, pp. 90–101.

Johanson, D. C., & Edey, M. A. (1981). *Lucy: The beginnings of humankind*. New York: Simon & Schuster.

Johansson, G. (1975, June). Visual motion perception. *Scientific American*, pp. 76–87.

John, V. P., & Horner, V. M. (1970). *Early childhood bilingual education.* New York: Modern Language Association of America.

Johnson, L. C. (1973). Are stages of sleep related to waking behavior? *American Scientist, 61,* 326–338.

Johnson-Laird, P. N., Legrenzi, P., & Legrenzi, M. S. (1972). Reasoning and a sense of reality. *British Journal of Psychology, 63,* 395–400.

Johnson-Laird, P. N., & Wason, P. C. (1977). An introduction to the scientific study of thinking. In P. N. Johnson-Laird & P. C. Wason (Eds.), *Thinking: Readings in cognitive science.* Cambridge: Cambridge University Press.

Johnston, V. S., & Chesney, G. L. (1974). Electrophysiological correlates of meaning. *Science, 186,* 944–946.

Jonas, G. (1974). The memory molecules: Can learning be chemically transferred? In J. D. Alexander (Ed.), *Nature/science annual* (pp. 18–27). New York: Time-Life Books.

Joncich, G. (1968). *The sane positivist: A biography of Edward L. Thorndike.* Middletown, CT: Wesleyan University Press.

Jones, A. (1980). *Women who kill.* New York: Holt, Rinehart & Winston.

Jones, A. P., & Friedman, M. I. (1982). Obesity and adipocyte abnormalities in offspring of rats undernourished during pregnancy. *Science, 215,* 1518–1519.

Jones, D. G. (1981). Ultrastructural approaches to the organization of central synapses. *American Scientist, 69,* 200–210.

Jones, E. (1953–1957). *The life and works of Sigmund Freud* (3 vols.). New York: Basic Books.

Jones, E. E. (1979). The rocky road from acts to dispositions. *American Psychologist, 34,* 107–117.

Jones, E. E., & Davis, K. E. (1965). From acts to dispositions: The attribution process in person perception. In L. Berkowitz (Ed.), *Advances in experimental social psychology* (Vol. 2, pp. 219–266). New York: Academic Press.

Jones, E. E., & McGillis, D. (1976). Correspondent inferences and the attribution cube: A comparative reappraisal. In J. H. Harvey, W. J. Ickes, & R. F. Kidd (Eds.), *New directions in attribution research* (Vol. 1, pp. 389–420). Hillsdale, NJ: Lawrence Erlbaum.

Jones, E. E., & Nisbett, R. E. (1972). The actor and the observer: Divergent perceptions of the causes of behavior. In E. E. Jones, D. E. Kanouse, H. H. Kelley, R. E. Nisbett, S. Valins, & B. Weiner (Eds.), *Attribution: Perceiving the causes of behavior* (pp. 79–94). Morristown, NJ: General Learning Press.

Jones, M. (1953). *The therapeutic community.* New York: Basic Books.

Jones, R. (1976, May/June). You will do as directed. *Learning,* pp. 20–26.

Jones, W. H., Hobbs, S. A., & Hockenbury, D. (1982). Loneliness and social skill deficits. *Journal of Personality and Social Psychology, 42,* 682–689.

Jonides, J., Irwin, D. E., & Yantis, S. (1982). Integrating visual information for successive fixations. *Science, 215,* 192–194.

Julesz, B. (1965, February). Texture and visual perception. *Scientific American,* pp. 38–48.

Julesz, B. (1974). Cooperative phenomena in binocular depth perception. *American Scientist, 62,* 32–43.

Julesz, B. (1975, April). Experiments in the visual perception of texture. *Scientific American,* pp. 34–43.

Julien, R. M. (1981). *A primer of drug action* (3rd ed.). San Francisco: W. H. Freeman.

Jung, C. G. (1968a). *Analytic psychology: Its theory and practice.* New York: Pantheon Books.

Jung, C. G. (1968b). *Man and his symbols.* New York: Dell.

Kagan, J. S. (1969). Inadequate evidence and illogical conclusions. *Harvard Educational Review, 39,* 274–277.

Kagan, J. S. (1971). *Understanding children.* New York: Harcourt Brace Jovanovich.

Kagan, J. (1976). Emergent themes in human development. *American Scientist, 64,* 186–196.

Kagan, J. (1978, January). The baby's elastic mind. *Human Nature,* pp. 66–73.

Kagan, J. (1979). Family experience and the child's development. *American Psychologist, 34,* 886–891.

Kahneman, D., & Tversky, A. (1972). Subjective probability: A judgment of representativeness. *Cognitive Psychology, 3,* 430–454.

Kahneman, D., & Tversky, A. (1973). On the psychology of prediction. *Psychological Review, 80,* 237–251.

Kalish, R. A. (1981). *Late adulthood: Perspectives in human development* (2nd ed.). Monterey, CA: Brooks/Cole.

Kalmus, H. (1952, May). Inherited sense defects. *Scientific American,* pp. 64–70.

Kamin, L. J. (1968). "Attention-like" processes in classical conditioning. In M. R. Jones (Ed.), *Miami symposium on the prediction of behavior, 1967: Aversive stimulation* (pp. 9–31). Coral Gables, FL: University of Miami Press.

Kamin, L. J. (1969). Predictability, surprise, attention, and conditioning. In B. A. Campbell & R. M. Church (Eds.), *Punishment and aversive behavior* (pp. 279–296). New York: Appleton-Century-Crofts.

Kamin, L. J. (1974). *The science and politics of I.Q.* Hillsdale, NJ: Lawrence Erlbaum.

Kamin, L. J. (1982). Mental testing and immigration. *American Psychologist, 37,* 97–98.

Kan, Y. W., & Dozy, A. M. (1980). Evolution of the hemoglobin S and C genes in world populations. *Science, 209,* 388–391.

Kandel, D. B. (1978). Similarity in real-life adolescent friendship pairs. *Journal of Personality and Social Psychology, 36,* 306–312.

Kandel, E. R. (1979, September). Small systems of neurons. *Scientific American,* pp. 60–70.

Kanfer, F. H., & Phillips, J. S. (1970). *Learning foundations of behavior therapy.* New York: John Wiley.

Kanizsa, G. (1976, April). Subjective contours. *Scientific American,* pp. 48–52.

Kaplan, B. (Ed.). (1964). *The inner world of mental illness.* New York: Harper & Row.

Kaplan, R., & Singer, R. (1976). Violence and viewer aggression: A reexamination of the evidence. *Journal of Social Issues, 32,* 35–70.

Kaplan, R. M., & Saccuzzo, D. P. (1982). *Psychological testing: Principles, applications, and issues.* Monterey, CA: Brooks/Cole.

Karp, L. E. (1978, October). Genetic crossroads. *Natural History,* pp. 8–21.

Katchadourian, H. A., & Lunde, D. T. (1980). *Fundamentals of human sexuality* (3rd ed.). New York: Holt, Rinehart & Winston.

Katz, B. (1980, November). The struggle against senility. *Discover,* pp. 62–64.

Kaufman, L., & Rock, I. (1962, July). The moon illusion. *Scientific American,* pp. 120–130.

Kaye, M. (1975). *The handbook of mental magic.* New York: Stein & Day.

Kazdin, A. E. (1975). Covert modeling, imagery assessment, and assertive behavior. *Journal of Consulting and Clinical Psychology, 43,* 716–724.

Kazdin, A. E. (1978). *History of behavior modification: Experimental foundations of contemporary research.* Baltimore, MD: University Park Press.

Kazdin, A. E. (1980). *Research design in clinical psychology.* New York: Harper & Row.

Keerdoja, E., Robinson, C., & Clausen, P. (1980, March 3). Karen Ann Quinlan still lingers on. *Newsweek,* p. 14.

Keesey, R. E. (1980). A set-point analysis of the regulation of body weight. In A. J. Stunkard (Ed.), *Obesity.* Philadelphia: W. B. Saunders.

Keesey, R. E., & Powley, T. L. (1975). Hypothalamic regulation of body weight. *American Scientist, 63,* 558–565.

Keil, F. C. (1981). Constraints on knowledge and cognitive development. *Psychological Review, 88,* 197–227.

Kelleher, R. T. (1957). A multiple schedule of conditioned reinforcement with chimpanzees. *Psychological Reports, 3,* 485–491.

Keller, H. (1902, 1954). *The story of my life.* New York: Doubleday.

Keller, S. E., Weiss, J. M., Schleifer, S. J., Miller, N. E., & Stein, M. (1981). Suppression of immunity by stress: Effect of a graded series of stressors on lymphocyte stimulation in the rat. *Science, 213,* 1397–1400.

Kelley, H. H. (1967). Attribution theory in social psychology. In D. Levine (Ed.), *Nebraska Symposium on Motivation* (Vol. 15, pp. 192–238). Lincoln, NE: University of Nebraska Press.

Kelley, H. H. (1972). Causal schemata and the attribution process. In E. E. Jones, D. E. Kanouse, H. H. Kelley, R. E. Nisbett, S. Valins, & B. Weiner (Eds.), *Attribution: Perceiving the causes of behavior* (pp. 151–174). Morristown, NJ: General Learning Press.

Kelley, H. H., & Michela, J. L. (1980). Attribution theory and research. *Annual Review of Psychology, 31,* 457–501.

Kelley, S., & Mirer, T. W. (1974). The simple act of voting. *American Political Science Review, 68,* 572–591.

Kellogg, W. N. (1968). Communication and language in the home-raised chimpanzee. *Science, 162,* 423–427.

Kelman, H. C., & Hovland, C. I. (1953). "Reinstatement" of the communicator in delayed measurement of opinion change. *Journal of Abnormal and Social Psychology, 48,* 327–335.

Kelso, J. A. S., & Clark, J. E. (Eds.). (1982). *The development of movement control and coordination.* New York: John Wiley.

Kempe, R. S., & Kempe, C. H. (1978). *Child abuse.* Cambridge, MA: Harvard University Press.

Kennedy, J. M. (1983). What can we learn about pictures from the blind? *American Scientist, 71,* 19–26.

Keppel, G. (1968). Retroactive and proactive inhibition. In T. R. Dixon & D. L. Horton (Eds.), *Verbal behavior and general behavior theory* (pp. 172–213). Englewood Cliffs, NJ: Prentice-Hall.

Kerr, N. L., & Bray, R. M. (Eds.). (1982). *The psychology of the courtroom.* New York: Academic Press.

Kessen, W. (1979). The American child and other cultural inventions. *American Psychologist, 34,* 815–820.

Kety, S. S. (1979, September). Disorders of the human brain. *Scientific American,* pp. 172–179.

Keynes, R. D. (1958, December). The nerve impulse and the squid. *Scientific American,* pp. 83–90.

Keynes, R. D. (Ed.). (1979). *The Beagle record: Selections from the original pictorial records and written accounts of the voyage of H.M.S. Beagle.* Cambridge: Cambridge University Press.

Kiesler, C. A. (1982). Mental hospitals and alternative care. *American Psychologist, 37,* 349–360.

Kiesler, C. A., & Lowman, R. P. (1980). Hutchinson versus Proxmire. *American Psychologist, 35,* 689–690.

Kietzman, M. L., Sutton, S., & Zubin, J. (Ed.). (1975). *Experimental approaches to psychopathology.* New York: Academic Press.

Kim, S. (1981). *Inversions.* New York: McGraw-Hill.

Kimble, G. A. (1961). *Hilgard and Marquis' conditioning and learning* (2nd ed.). New York: Appleton-Century-Crofts.

Kimble, G. A. (1981). Biological and cognitive constraints on learning. In L. T. Benjamin, Jr. (Ed.), *The G. Stanley Hall lecture series* (Vol. 1, pp. 7–60). Washington, DC: American Psychological Association.

Kimmel, A. J. (1979). Ethics and human subjects research: A delicate balance. *American Psychologist, 34,* 633–635.

Kimura, D. (1973, March). The asymmetry of the human brain. *Scientific American,* pp. 70–78.

Kimura, M. (1979, November). The neutral theory of molecular evolution. *Scientific American,* pp. 98–126.

Kinsbourne, M. (1981, May). The brain/sad hemisphere, happy hemisphere. *Psychology Today,* p. 92.

Kinsbourne, M. (1982). Hemispheric specialization and the growth of human understanding. *American Psychologist, 37,* 411–420.

Kinsey, A. C., Pomeroy, W. B., & Martin, C. E. (1948). *Sexual behavior in the human male.* Philadelphia: W. B. Saunders.

Kinsey, A. C., Pomeroy, W. B., & Martin, C. E. (1953). *Sexual behavior in the human female.* Philadelphia: W. B. Saunders.

Kiparsky, P., & Menn, L. (1977). On the acquisition of phonology. In J. Macnamara (Ed.), *Language learning and thought.* New York: Academic Press.

Klatsky, R. L. (1980). *Human memory: Structures and processes* (2nd ed.). San Francisco: W. H. Freeman.

Klein, R., & Armitage, R. (1979). Rhythms in human performance: $1\frac{1}{2}$ hour oscillations in cognitive style. *Science, 204,* 1326–1328.

Klerman, G. L. (1972). Drug therapy of clinical depressions. *Journal of Psychiatric Research, 9,* 253–270.

Klerman, G. L. (1975). Drug therapy of clinical depressions—current status and implications for research on neuropharmacology of the affective disorders. In D. F. Klein & R. Gittelman-Klein (Eds.), *Progress in psychiatric drug treatment.* New York: Bruner/Mazel.

Klima, E., & Bellugi, U. (1978a, October). Poetry without sound. *Human Nature,* pp. 74–83.

Klima, E. S., & Bellugi, U. (1978b). *The signs of language.* Cambridge, MA: Harvard University Press.

Klineberg, O. (1938). Emotional expression in Chinese literature. *Journal of Abnormal and Social Psychology, 33,* 517–520.

Klotz, I. M., Haney, D. N., & King, L. C. (1981). Rational approaches to chemotherapy: Antisickling agents. *Science, 213,* 724–731.

Kluger, M. J. (1979). *Fever: Its biology, evolution, and function.* Princeton, NJ: Princeton University Press.

Knapp, M. L. (1980). *Essentials of nonverbal communication.* New York: Holt, Rinehart & Winston.

Knight, R. G., & Wooles, I. M. (1980). Experimental investigation of chronic organic amnesia: A review. *Psychological Bulletin, 88,* 753–771.

Koch, S. (1954). Clark L. Hull. In W. Estes, S. Koch, K. MacCorquodale, P. E. Meehl, C. G. Mueller, Jr., & W. N. Schoenfeld (Eds.), *Modern learning theory* (pp. 1–176). New York: Appleton-Century-Crofts.

Kohlberg, L. (1968, September). The child as a moral philosopher. *Psychology Today,* pp. 24–30.

Kohlberg, L. (1972, December). Understanding the hidden curriculum. *Learning,* pp. 10–14.

Kohlberg, L. (1973). *Collected papers on moral development and moral education.* Cambridge, MA: Harvard University, Center for Moral Education.

Kohlberg, L. (1975). The cognitive-developmental approach to moral education. *Phi Delta Kappan, 56,* 670–677.

Kohler, I. (1962, May). Experiments with goggles. *Scientific American,* pp. 62–85.

Köhler, W. (1925). *The mentality of apes.* New York: Harcourt Brace Jovanovich.

Kolata, G. B. (1977a). Aftermath of the new math: Its originators defend it. *Science, 195,* 854–857.

Kolata, G. B. (1977b). Sexual dimorphism and mating systems: How did they evolve? *Science, 195,* 382–383.

Kolata, G. B. (1978). Behavioral teratology: Birth defects of the mind. *Science, 202,* 732–734.

Kolata, G. B. (1979). Mental disorders: A new approach to treatment? *Science, 206,* 36–38.

Kolata, G. B. (1981a). Clinical trial of psychotherapies is under way. *Science, 212,* 432–433.

Kolata, G. B. (1981b). Clues to the cause of senile dementia. *Science, 211,* 1032–1033.

Kolata, G. B. (1982a). Alzheimer's research poses dilemma. *Science, 215,* 47–48.

Kolata, G. B. (1982b). Grafts correct brain damage. *Science, 217,* 342–344.

Kolb, B., & Taylor, L. (1981). Affective behavior in patients with localized cortical excisions: Role of lesion site and side. *Science, 214,* 89–91.

Kolers, P. A. (1964, October). The illusion of movement. *Scientific American,* pp. 98–106.

Kolers, P. A. (1968, March). Bilingualism and information processing. *Scientific American,* pp. 78–86.

Kolers, P. A. (1972, July). Experiments in reading. *Scientific American,* pp. 84–91.

Kollar, E. J., & Fisher, C. (1980). Tooth induction in chick epithelium: Expression of quiescent genes for enamel synthesis. *Science, 207,* 993–995.

Korchin, S. J., & Schuldberg, D. (1981). The future of clinical assessment. *American Psychologist, 36*, 1147–1158.

Koriat, A., & Lieblich, I. (1974). What does a person in a "TOT" state know that a person in a "don't know" state doesn't know? *Memory & Cognition, 2*, 647–655.

Kosslyn, S. M. (1975). Information representation in visual images, *Cognitive Psychology, 7*, 341–370.

Kosslyn, S. M. (1980). *Image and mind.* Cambridge, MA: Harvard University Press.

Kosslyn, S. M., Ball, T. M., & Reiser, B. J. (1978). Visual images preserve metric spatial information: Evidence from studies of image scanning. *Journal of Experimental Psychology: Human Perception and Performance, 4*, 47–60.

Kosslyn, S. M., & Pomerantz, J. R. (1977). Imagery, propositions, and the form of internal representations. *Cognitive Psychology, 9*, 52–76.

Kowler, E., & Martins, A. J. (1982). Eye movements of preschool children. *Science, 215*, 997–999.

Krantz, D. L. (1971). The separate worlds of operant and non-operant psychology. *Journal of Applied Behavior Analysis, 4*, 61–70.

Krashen, S. D. (1975, Spring). The major hemisphere. *UCLA Educator, 17*, 17–23.

Krauss, R. M., & Glucksberg, S. (1977, February). Social and nonsocial speech. *Scientific American*, pp. 100–105.

Krech, D. (1962). Cortical localization of function. In L. Postman (Ed.), *Psychology in the making: Histories of selected research problems* (pp. 31–72). New York: Alfred A. Knopf.

Kretschmer, E. (1925). *Physique and character.* New York: Harcourt Brace Jovanovich.

Kringlen, E. (1970). Natural history of obsessional neurosis. *Seminars in Psychiatry, 2*, 403–419.

Kringlen, E. (1978). Adult offspring of two psychotic parents, with special reference to schizophrenia. In L. C. Wynne, R. L. Cromwell, & S. Matthysse (Eds.), *The nature of schizophrenia: New approaches to research and treatment.* New York: John Wiley.

Kroll, P., Chamberlain, P., & Halpern, D. (1979). The diagnosis of Briquet's syndrome in a male population. *Journal of Nervous and Mental Disease, 169*, 171–174.

Kubovy, M., & Pomerantz, J. R. (Eds.). (1981). *Perceptual organization.* Hillsdale, NJ: Lawrence Erlbaum.

Kulik, J. A., & Brown, R. (1979). Frustration, attribution of blame, and aggression. *Journal of Experimental Social Psychology, 15*, 183–194.

Labov, W. (1980). *Locating language in time and space.* New York: Academic Press.

Lachman, R., Lachman, J. L., & Butterfield, E. C. (1979). *Cognitive psychology and information processing: An introduction.* Hillsdale, NJ: Lawrence Erlbaum.

Lackner, J. R., & Graybiel, A. (1979). Parabolic flight: Loss of sense of orientation. *Science, 206*, 1105–1108.

Lader, M., & Mathews, A. (1970). Physiological changes during spontaneous panic attacks. *Journal of Psychosomatic Research, 14*, 377–382.

Laing, R. D. (1954). Is schizophrenia a disease? *International Journal of Social Psychiatry, 10*, 184–193.

Lamb, M. E. (1979). Paternal influences and the father's role: A personal perspective. *American Psychologist, 34*, 938–943.

Lamberg, L. (1980, July/August). Soothing burns. *Science 80*, pp. 83–85.

Lambert, M. J. (1979). Psychotherapy outcome research. *American Psychologist, 34*, 91.

Lambert, N. M. (1981). Psychological evidence in *Larry P. v Wilson Riles:* An evaluation by a witness for the defense. *American Psychologist, 36*, 937–952.

Lamm, H., & Myers, D. G. (1978). Group-induced polarization of attitudes and behavior. In L. Berkowitz (Ed.), *Advances in experimental social psychology* (Vol. 11, pp. 145–195). New York: Academic Press.

Lancaster, J. (1978, February). Carrying and sharing in human evolution. *Human Nature*, pp. 82–89.

Landfield, P. W., Baskin, R. K., & Pitler, T. A. (1981). Brain aging correlates: Retardation by hormonal-pharmacological treatments. *Science, 214*, 581–584.

Landis, C., with Mettler, F. A. (Ed.). (1964). *Varieties of psychopathological experience.* New York: Holt, Rinehart & Winston.

Landman, J. T., & Dawes, R. M. (1982). Psychotherapy outcome. *American Psychologist, 37*, 504–516

Lang, P. J. (1969). The mechanics of desensitization and the laboratory study of human fear. In C. M. Franks (Ed.), *Behavior therapy: Appraisal and status* (pp. 160–191). New York: McGraw-Hill.

Lang, P. J., & Melamed, B. G. (1969). Case report: Avoidance conditioning therapy of an infant with chronic ruminative vomiting. *Journal of Abnormal Psychology, 74*, 1–8.

Lange, C. (1885, 1922). One leuds beveegelser. (I. A. Haupt, Trans.) In K. Dunlap (Ed.), *The Emotions.* Baltimore: Williams & Wilkins.

Langendoen, D. T. (1970). *Essentials of English grammar.* New York: Holt, Rinehart & Winston.

Langer, E. J. (1978). Rethinking the role of thought in social interaction. In J. Harvey, W. Ickes, & R. Kidd (Eds.), *New directions in attribution research* (Vol. 2, pp. 35–58). Hillsdale, NJ: Lawrence Erlbaum.

Langer, E. J., & Abelson, R. P. (1974). A patient by any other name . . .; Clinician group differences in labeling bias. *Journal of Consulting and Clinical Psychology, 42*, 4–9.

Langer, E., Blank, A., & Chanowitz, B. (1978). The mindlessness of ostensibly thoughtful action: The role of "placebic" information in interpersonal interaction. *Journal of Personality and Social Psychology, 36*, 635–642.

Langer, E. J., & Rodin, J. (1976). The effects of choice and enhanced personal responsibility: A field experiment in an institutional setting. *Journal of Personality and Social Psychology, 34*, 191–198.

Langer, W. (1972). *The mind of Adolf Hitler.* New York: Basic Books.

Langman, V. A. (1982, January). Giraffe youngsters need a little bit of maternal love. *Smithsonian*, pp. 95–103.

LaPiere, R. T. (1934). Attitudes versus action. *Social Forces, 13*, 230–237.

Lassen, N. A., Ingvar, D. H., & Skinhøj, E. (1978, October). Brain function and blood flow. *Scientific American*, pp. 62–71.

Latané, B. (1981). The psychology of social impact. *American Psychologist, 36*, 343–356.

Latané, B., & Darley, J. M. (1968). Group inhibition of bystander intervention in emergencies. *Journal of Personality and Social Psychology, 10*, 215–221.

Latané, B., & Darley, J. M. (1970). *The unresponsive bystander: Why doesn't he help?* New York: Appleton-Century-Crofts.

Lavie, P., & Kripke, D. F. (1975, April). Ultradian rhythms: The 90-minute clock inside us. *Psychology Today*, pp. 54–56, 65.

Lazarus, A. A. (1971). *Behavior therapy and beyond.* New York: McGraw-Hill.

Lazarus, A. A. (1973). Multimodal behavior therapy: Treating the BASIC ID. *Journal of Nervous and Mental Disease, 156*, 404–411.

Lazarus, A. A. (1980). *The practice of multimodal therapy.* New York: McGraw-Hill.

Lazarus, R. S. (1982). Thoughts on the relations between emotion and cognition. *American Psychologist, 37*, 1019–1024.

Leakey, R. E., & Lewin, R. (1977a, November). Is it our culture, not our genes, that makes us killers? *Smithsonian*, pp. 56–65.

Leakey, R. E., & Lewin, R. (1977b). *Origins.* New York: E. P. Dutton.

Leask, J., Haber, R. N., & Haber, R. B., (1969). Eidetic imagery in children: II. Longitudinal and experimental results. *Psychonomic Monograph Supplements, 3* (Whole No. 35).

Lederer, L. (Ed.). (1980). *Take back the night: Women on pornography.* New York: William Morrow.

Lefkowitz, M. M., Eron, L. D., Walder, L. O., & Huesmann, L. R. (1977). *Growing up to be violent: A longitudinal study of the development of aggression.* New York: Pergamon Press.

Lehrman, D. S. (1964, November). The reproductive behavior of ring doves. *Scientific American*, pp. 48–54.

Leitenberg, H. (Ed.). (1976). *Handbook of behavior modification and behavior therapy*. Englewood Cliffs, NJ: Prentice-Hall.

Lenneberg, E. H. (1967). *Biological foundations of language*. New York: John Wiley.

Lenneberg, E. H., & Lenneberg, E. (Eds.). (1975). *Foundations of language development: An interdisciplinary approach* (2 vols.). New York: Academic Press.

Leo, J. (1980, September 29). From mollusks to moppets. Jean Piaget: 1896–1980. *Time*, p. 55.

Leonard, W. E. (1927, 1964). The locomotive god. In B. Kaplan (Ed.), *The inner world of mental illness* (pp. 311–322). New York: Harper & Row.

Lepper, M. R., & Greene, D. (Eds.) (1978). *The hidden costs of reward: New perspectives on the psychology of human motivation*. Hillsdale, NJ: Lawrence Erlbaum.

Lepper, M. R., Greene, D., & Nisbett, R. E. (1973). Undermining children's intrinsic interest with extrinsic rewards: a tentative test of the "overjustification" hypothesis. *Journal of Personality and Social Psychology, 28*, 129–137.

Leshner, A. (1978). *An introduction to behavioral endocrinology*. New York: Oxford University Press.

Lesser, G. S., Fifer, G., & Clark, D. H. (1965). Mental abilities of children from different social-class and cultural groups. *Monographs of the Society for Research in Child Development, 30* (No. 4).

Lester, H. A. (1977, February). The response to acetylcholine. *Scientific American*, pp. 106–117.

Lettvin, J. Y. (1981). 1981 Nobel prize for physiology or medicine. *Science, 214*, 518–520.

Lettvin, J. Y., Maturarana, H. R., McCulloch, W. S., & Pitts, W. H. (1959). What the frog's eye tells the frog's brain. *Proceedings of the Institute of Radio Engineers, 47*, 1940–1951.

Levenkron, S. (1978). *Best little girl in the world*. New York: Warner Books.

Levenkron, S. (1982). *Treating and overcoming anorexia nervosa*. New York: Charles Scribner's.

Leventhal, H. (1970). Findings and theory in the study of fear communications. In L. Berkowitz (Ed.), *Advances in experimental social psychology* (Vol. 5, pp. 119–186). New York: Academic Press.

Leventhal, H., & Cleary, P. D. (1980). The smoking problem: A review of the research and theory in behavioral risk modification. *Psychological Bulletin, 88*, 370–405.

Levin, P., Janda, J. K., Joseph, J. A., Ingram, D. K., & Roth, G. S. (1981). Dietary restriction retards the age-associated loss of rat striatal dopaminergic receptors. *Science, 214*, 561–562.

Levine, F. M. (Ed.). (1975). *Theoretical readings in motivation: Perspectives on human behavior*. Chicago: Rand McNally.

Levine, J. S., & MacNichol, E. F., Jr. (1982, February). Color vision in fishes. *Scientific American*, pp. 140–149.

Levine, M. (1966), Hypothesis behavior by humans during discrimination learning. *Journal of Experimental Psychology, 71*, 331–338.

Levine, M. A. (1975). *A cognitive theory of learning*. Hillsdale, NJ: Lawrence Erlbaum.

Levine, S. (1971, January). Stress and behavior. *Scientific American*, pp. 26–31.

Levinson, S. E., & Liberman, M. Y. (1981, April). Speech recognition by computer. *Scientific American*, pp. 64–76.

Levy, B. A. (1978). Speech processes during reading. In A. M. Lesgold, J. W. Pellegrino, S. D. Fokkema, & R. Glaser (Eds.), *Cognitive psychology and instruction* (pp. 123–151). New York: Plenum Press.

Levy, J., & Reid, M. (1976). Variations in writing posture and cerebral organization. *Science, 194*, 337–339.

Levy, L. H. (1963). *Psychological interpretation*. New York: Holt, Rinehart & Winston.

Lewin, R. (1981a). Ethiopian stone tools are world's oldest. *Science, 211*, 806–807.

Lewin, R. (1981b). Lamarck will not lie down. *Science, 213*, 316–321.

Lewin, R. (1981c). Protohuman activity etched on fossil bones. *Science, 213*, 123–124.

Lewin, R. (1981d). Seeds of change in embryonic development. *Science, 214*, 42–44.

Lewin, R. (1982). How did humans evolve big brains? *Science, 216*, 840–841.

Lewinsohn, P. H. (1974). A behavioral approach to depression. In R. J. Friedman & M. Katz (Eds.), *The psychology of depression: Contemporary theory and research*. New York: John Wiley.

Lewinsohn, P. H., & Libet, J. M. (1972). Pleasant events, activity schedules and depression. *Journal of Abnormal Psychology, 79*, 291–295.

Lewis, D. J. (1979). Psychobiology of active and inactive memory. *Psychological Bulletin, 86*, 1054–1083.

Lewis, J. (1982). *Something hidden: A biography of Wilder Penfield*. New York: Doubleday.

Lewis, M. (Ed.). (1976). *Origins of intelligence: Infancy and early childhood*. New York: Plenum Press.

Lewontin, R C. (1978, September). Adaptation. *Scientific American*, pp. 212–230.

Lewy, A. J., Wehr, T. A., Goodwin, F. K., Newsome, D. A., & Markey, S. P. (1980). Light suppresses melatonin secretion in humans. *Science, 210*, 1267–1269.

Liberman, A. M. (1982). On finding that speech is special. *American Psychologist, 37*, 148–167.

Lickona, T. (Ed.). (1976). *Moral development and behavior: Theory, research and social issues*. New York: Holt, Rinehart & Winston.

Lickona, T. (1977, March). How to encourage moral development. *Learning*, pp. 37–43.

Lieberman, P. (1975). *On the origins of language: An introduction to the evolution of human speech*. New York: Macmillan.

Lieberman, P., Klatt, D. H., & Wilson, W. H. (1969). Vocal tract limitations on the vowel repertoires of rhesus monkey and other non-human primates. *Science, 164*, 1185–1187.

Liem, J. H. (1974). Effects of verbal communications of parents and children: A comparison of normal and schizophrenic families. *Journal of Consulting and Clinical Psychology, 42*, 438–450.

Light, D. (1980). *Becoming psychiatrists: The professional transformation of self*. New York: W. W. Norton.

Lindzey, G. (1967). Behavior and morphological variation. In J. N. Spuhler (Ed.), *Genetic diversity and human behavior* (pp. 227–240). Chicago: Aldine.

Lindzey, G., Hall, C. S., & Thompson, R. F. (1978). *Psychology* (2nd ed.). New York: Worth.

Lints, F. A. (1978). *Genetics and aging*. Basel: S. Karger.

Lipsitt, L. P. (Ed.). (1981). *Advances in infancy research* (Vol. 1). Norwood, NJ: Ablex.

Llinás, R. R. (1975, January). The cortex of the cerebellum. *Scientific American*, pp. 56–71.

Locurto, C. M., Terrace, H. S., & Gibbon, J. (Eds.). (1980). *Autoshaping and conditioning theory*. New York: Academic Press.

Loehlin, J. C., Lindzey, G., & Spuhler, J. N. (1975). *Race differences in intelligence*. San Francisco: W. H. Freeman.

Loehlin, J. C., & Nichols, R. C. (1976). *Heredity, environment and personality*. Austin, TX: University of Texas Press.

Loewenstein, W. R. (1960, August). Biological transducers. *Scientific American*, pp. 98–108.

Loftus, E. F. (1979). *Eyewitness testimony*. Cambridge, MA: Harvard University Press.

Loftus, E. F. (1983a). Silence is not golden. *American Psychologist, 83*, 564–572.

Loftus, E. F. (1983b). Whose shadow is crooked? *American Psychologist, 38*, 576–577.

Loftus, E. F., & Fries, J. F. (1979). Informed consent may be hazardous to health. *Science, 204*, 11.

Loftus, E. F., & Loftus, G. R. (1980). On the permanence of stored information in the human brain. *American Psychologist, 35*, 409–420.

Loftus, E., & Monahan, J. (1980). Trial by data: Psychological research as legal evidence. *American Psychologist, 35,* 270–283.

Loftus, E. F., & Palmer, J. C. (1974). Reconstruction of automobile destruction: An example of the interaction between language and memory. *Journal of Verbal Learning and Verbal Behavior, 13,* 585–589.

Logan, F. A. (1959). The Hull-Spence approach. In S. Koch (Ed.), *Psychology: A study of a science* (Vol. 2, pp. 293–358). New York: McGraw-Hill.

London, P. (1964). *The modes and morals of psychotherapy.* New York: Holt, Rinehart & Winston.

Long, G. M. (1980). Iconic memory: A review and critique of the study of short-term visual storage. *Psychological Bulletin, 88,* 785–820.

The longest root. (1971, October 25). *Time,* p. 59.

Lorayne, H., & Lucas, J. (1974). *The memory book.* New York: Stein & Day.

Lorenz, K. Z. (1952). *King Solomon's ring.* New York: Thomas Y. Crowell.

Lorenz, K. Z. (1958, December). The evolution of behavior. *Scientific American,* pp. 67–78.

Lorenz, K. Z. (1965). *Evolution and modification of behavior.* Chicago: University of Chicago Press.

Lorenz, K. Z. (1966). *On aggression.* New York: Harcourt Brace Jovanovich.

Lorenz, K. Z. (1974). Analogy as a source of knowledge. *Science, 185,* 229–234.

Lovaas, O. I. (1977). *The autistic child: Language development through behavior modification.* New York: Halsted Press.

Lovaas, O. I., & Newsom, C. D. (1976). Behavior modification with psychotic children. In H. Leitenberg (Ed.), *Handbook of behavior modification and behavior therapy* (pp. 303–360). Englewood Cliffs, NJ: Prentice-Hall.

Luborsky, L., & Spence, D. P. (1978). Quantitative research on psychoanalytic therapy. In S. L. Garfield & A. E. Bergin (Eds.), *Handbook of psychotherapy and behavior change: An empirical analysis* (2nd ed.). New York: John Wiley.

Luce, G. G. (1971). *Body time.* New York: Bantam.

Luchins, A. (1957). Primacy-recency in impression formation. In C. Hovland (Ed.), *The order of presentation in persuasion* (pp. 33–61). New Haven, CT: Yale University Press.

Luchins, A. S. (1942). Mechanization in problem-solving: The effects of Einstellung. *Psychological Monographs, 54*(Whole No. 248).

Ludel, J. (1978). *Introduction to sensory processes.* San Francisco: W. H. Freeman.

Luh, C. W. (1922). The conditions of retention. *Psychological Monographs 31*(3, Whole No. 142).

Lunde, D. T. (1976). *Murder and madness.* San Francisco: San Francisco Book Co.

Luria, A. R. (1968). *The mind of a mnemonist: A little book about a vast memory* (L. Solotaroff, Trans.). New York: Basic Books.

Luria, A. R. (1970, March). The functional organization of the brain. *Scientific American,* pp. 66–78.

Lykken, D. T. (1957). A study of anxiety in the sociopathic personality. *Journal of Abnormal and Social Psychology, 55,* 6–10.

Lynch, K. (1960). *The image of the city.* Cambridge, MA: MIT Press.

Macaulay, J. R., & Berkowitz, L. (Eds.). (1970). *Altruism and helping behavior.* New York: Academic Press.

Maccoby, E. E., & Jacklin, C. N. (1974a, December). Myth, reality and shades of gray: What we know and don't know about sex differences. *Psychology Today,* pp. 109–112.

Maccoby, E. E., & Jacklin, C. N. (1974b). *The psychology of sex differences.* Stanford, CA: Stanford University Press.

Maccoby, N., & Alexander, J. (1979). Reducing heart disease risk using the mass media: Comparing the effects on three communities. In *Social and psychological research in community settings: Designing and conducting programs for social and personal well-being* (pp. 69–100). San Francisco: Jossey-Bass.

MacCorquodale, K., & Meehl, P. E. (1953). Preliminary suggestions as to a formalization of expectancy theory. *Psychological Review, 60,* 55–63.

MacCorquodale, K., & Meehl, P. E. (1954). Edward C. Tolman. In W. K. Estes, S. Koch, K. MacCorquodale, P. E. Meehl, C. G. Mueller, Jr., & W. N. Schoenfeld, *Modern learning theory* (pp. 177–266). New York: Appleton-Century-Crofts.

Macfarlane, A. (1978, February). What a baby knows. *Human Nature,* pp. 74–81.

Mack, S. (1981). Novel help for the handicapped. *Science, 212,* 26–27.

MacKay, D. G. (1970a). Mental diploplia: Towards a model of speech perception at the semantic level. In G. B. Flores d'Arcais & W. J. M. Levelt (Eds.), *Advances in psycholinguistics* (pp. 76–100). Amsterdam: North-Holland.

MacKay, D. G. (1970b). Spoonerisms: The structure of errors in the serial order of speech. *Neuropsychologia, 8,* 323–350.

MacKay, D. G. (1972). The structure of words and syllables: Evidence from errors in speech. *Cognitive Psychology, 3,* 210–227.

MacKay, D. G. (1980). Psychology, prescriptive grammar, and the pronoun problem. *American Psychologist, 35,* 444–449.

MacKinnon, D. W., & Dukes, W. F. (1962). Repression. In L. Postman (Ed.), *Psychology in the making: Histories of selected research problems* (pp. 662–744). New York: Alfred A. Knopf.

Mackintosh, N. J. (1975). A theory of attention. *Psychological Review, 82,* 276–298.

MacLean, P. D. (1970). The limbic brain in relation to the psychoses. In P. Black (Ed.), *Physiological correlates of emotion* (pp. 129–146). New York: Academic Press.

MacLeod, C. M. (1976). Bilingual episodic memory: Acquisition and forgetting. *Journal of Verbal Learning and Verbal Behavior, 15,* 347–364.

MacLusky, N. J., & Naftolin, F. (1981). Sexual differentiation of the central nervous system. *Science, 211,* 1294–1303.

Macnamara, J. (1967). The bilingual's linguistic performance—a psychological overview. *Journal of Social Issues, 23,* 58–77.

MacNichol, E. F., Jr. (1964, December). Three-pigment color vision. *Scientific American,* pp. 48–56.

MacVicar, B. A., & Dudek, F. E. (1981). Electrotonic coupling between pyramidal cells: A direct demonstration in rat hippocampal slices. *Science, 213,* 782–785.

Maher, B. A. (1966). *Principles of psychopathology: An experimental approach.* New York: McGraw-Hill.

Maher, B. A. (1968, November). The shattered language of schizophrenia. *Psychology Today,* pp. 30–33, 60.

Mahoney, M. J. (1974). *Cognition and behavior modification.* Cambridge, MA: Ballinger.

Mahoney, M. J. (1977). Reflections on the cognitive-learning trend in psychotherapy. *American Psychologist, 32,* 5–13.

Mahoney, M., & Arnkoff, D. (1978). Cognitive and self-control therapies. In S. Garfield & A. Bergin (Eds.), *Handbook of psychotherapy and behavior change: An empirical analysis* (2nd ed.). New York: John Wiley.

Mahoney, M. J., & Thoresen, C. E. (1974). *Self-control: Power to the person.* Monterey, CA: Brooks/Cole.

Maier, N. R. F. (1940). The behavior mechanisms concerned with problem solving. *Psychological Review, 47,* 43–53.

Malamuth, N. M., & Check, J. V. P. (1981). The effects of mass media exposure on acceptance of violence against women: A field experiment. *Journal of Research in Personality, 15,* 436–446.

Malamuth, N. M., & Donnerstein, E. (1982). The effects of aggressive-pornographic mass media stimuli. In L. Berkowitz (Ed.), *Advances in experimental social psychology* (Vol. 15, pp. 103–136). New York: Academic Press.

Malpass, R. S., & Devine, P. G. (1981). Guided memory in eyewitness identification. *Journal of Applied Psychology, 66,* 343–350.

Maltzman, I. (1955). Thinking: From a behaviorist point of view. *Psychological Review, 66,* 367–386.

Mandel, A. J. (1973). Neurobiological barriers to euphoria. *American Scientist, 61,* 565–573.

Mandler, G. (1980). Recognizing: The judgment of previous occurrence. *Psychological Review, 87,* 252–271.

Mandler, J. M., & Parker, R. E. (1976). Memory for descriptive and spatial information in complex pictures. *Journal of Experimental Psychology: Human Learning and Memory, 2,* 38–48.

Mansfield, R. S., & Busse, T. V. (1981). *The psychology of creativity and discovery: Scientists and their work.* Chicago: Nelson-Hall.

Marano, H. E. (1981, February). Biology is one key to the bonding of mothers and babies. *Smithsonian,* pp. 60–69.

March, R. (1977, November). Georges Cuisenaire and his rainbow rods. *Learning,* pp. 81–88.

Margolin, G. (1982). Ethical and legal considerations in marital and family therapy. *American Psychologist, 37,* 788–801.

Margules, D. L. (1979, October). Obesity and the hibernation response. *Psychology Today,* p. 136.

Mark, V. H., & Ervin, F. R. (1970). *Violence and the brain.* New York: Harper & Row.

Marks, C. E. (1981). *Commissurotomy, consciousness and unity of mind.* Cambridge, MA: MIT Press.

Marks, I. M. (1969). *Fears and phobias.* New York: Academic Press.

Marks, L. E. (1978). *The unity of the senses.* New York: Academic Press.

Markus, H. (1977). Self-schemata and processing information about the self. *Journal of Personality and Social Psychology, 35,* 63–78.

Markus, H., Crane, M., Bernstein, S., & Siladi, M. (1982). Self-schemas and gender. *Journal of Personality and Social Psychology, 42,* 38–50.

Marler, P., & Griffin, D. R. (1973). The 1973 Nobel prize for physiology or medicine. *Science, 182,* 464–466.

Marmor, J. (1962). Psychoanalytic therapy as an educational process: Common denominators in the therapeutic approaches of different psychoanalytic "schools." In J. H. Masserman (Ed.), *Science and psychoanalysis: Vol. 5. Psychoanalytic education* (pp. 286–299). New York: Grune & Stratton.

Marshall, E. (1980a). Psychotherapy faces test of worth. *Science, 207,* 35–36.

Marshall, E. (1980b). Psychotherapy works, but for whom? *Science, 207,* 506–508.

Marshall, G. (1976). *The affective consequences of "inadequately explained" physiological arousal.* Unpublished doctoral dissertation, Stanford University.

Marshall, J. T., Jr., & Marshall, E. R. (1976). Gibbons and their territorial songs. *Science, 193,* 235–237.

Marshall, N. K. (1982, February). The brain: A chilling effect. *Psychology Today,* p. 92.

Marx, J. L. (1978). Restriction enzymes: Prenatal diagnosis of genetic disease. *Science, 202,* 1068–1069.

Marx, J. L. (1979). Hormones and their effects in the aging body. *Science, 206,* 805–806.

Marx, J. L. (1980a). Ape language controversy flares up. *Science, 207,* 1330–1333.

Marx, J. L. (1980b). Gene transfer given a new twist. *Science, 208,* 386–387.

Marx, J. L. (1980c). Osteoporosis: New help for thinning bones. *Science, 207,* 628–630.

Marx, J. L. (1981). Cell defect in mental retardation. *Science, 211,* 1409.

Marx, J. L. (1982). Transplants as guides to brain development. *Science, 217,* 340–342.

Maslach, C. (1979). The emotional consequences of arousal without reason. In C. E. Izard (Ed.), *Emotions in personality and psychopathology* (pp. 565–590). New York: Plenum Press.

Maslow, A. H. (1968). *Toward a psychology of being.* New York: Van Nostrand Reinhold.

Maslow, A. H. (1969). Toward a humanistic biology. *American Psychologist, 24,* 734–735.

Maslow, A. H. (1970). *Motivation and personality* (2nd ed.). New York: Harper & Row.

Maslow, A. H. (1971). *The farther reaches of human nature.* New York: Viking Press.

Masters, W. H., & Johnson, V. E. (1966). *Human sexual response.* Boston: Little, Brown.

Masters, W. H., & Johnson, V. E. (1970). *Human sexual inadequacy.* Boston: Little, Brown.

Masters, W. H., & Johnson, V. E. (1975). *The pleasure bond: A new look at sexuality and commitment.* Boston: Little, Brown.

Matarazzo, J. D. (1980). Behavioral health and behavioral medicine: Frontiers for a new health psychology. *American Psychologist, 35,* 807–817.

Matarazzo, J. D. (1981). Obituary: David Wechsler (1896–1981). *American Psychologist, 36,* 1542–1543.

Matin, L., Picoult, E., Stevens, J. K., Edwards, M. W., Jr., Young, D., & MacArthur, R. (1982). Oculoparalytic illusion: Visual field dependent spatial mislocations by humans partially paralyzed by curare. *Science, 215,* 198–201.

Matlin, M. (1983). *Cognition.* New York: Holt, Reinhart & Winston.

Matossian, M. K. (1982). Ergot and the Salem witchcraft affair. *American Scientist, 70,* 355–357.

Maugh, T. H., II. (1975). Marihuana: New support for immune and reproductive hazards. *Science, 190,* 865–867.

Maugh, T. H., II. (1981a). Biochemical markers identify mental states. *Science, 214,* 39–41.

Maugh, T. H., II. (1981b). A new understanding of sickle cell emerges. *Science, 211,* 265–267.

Maugh, T. H., II. (1981c). To sleep, perchance to gasp. . . . *Science, 214,* 214.

Maugh, T. H., II. (1982a). The scent makes sense. *Science, 215,* 1224.

Maugh, T. H., II. (1982b). Sleep-promoting factor isolated. *Science, 216,* 1400.

May, P. R. A. (1968). *Treatment of schizophrenia: A comparative study of five treatment methods.* New York: Science House.

May, P. R. A. (1974). Psychotherapy research in schizophrenia—another view of present reality. *Schizophrenia Bulletin, 1,* 126–132.

May, P. R. A., Tuma, A. H., Yale, C., Potepan, P., & Dixon, W. J. (1976). Schizophrenia—a follow-up study of results of treatment: II. Hospital stay over two to five years. *Psychiatry, 33,* 481–486.

Mayr, E. (1974). Behavior programs and evolutionary strategies. *American Scientist, 62,* 650–659.

Mayr, E. (1977). Darwin and natural selection. *American Scientist, 65,* 321–327.

Mayr, E. (1978, September). Evolution. *Scientific American,* pp. 46–55.

McArthur, L. A. (1972). The how and what of why: Some determinants and consequences of causal attribution. *Journal of Personality and Social Psychology, 22,* 171–193.

McArthur, L. Z. (1982). Judging a book by its cover: A cognitive analysis of the relationship between physical appearance and stereotyping. In A. H. Hastorf & A. M. Isen (Eds.), *Cognitive social psychology.* New York: Elsevier.

McCarley, R. W., & Hobson, J. A. (1977). The neurobiological origins of psychoanalytic dream theory. *American Journal of Psychiatry, 134,* 1211–1221.

McClearn, G. E. (1962). The inheritance of behavior. In L. Postman (Ed.), *Psychology in the making: Histories of selected research problems* (pp. 144–252). New York: Alfred A. Knopf.

McClelland, D. C., Atkinson, J. W., Clark, R. W., & Lowell, E. L. (1953). *The achievement motive.* New York: Appleton-Century-Crofts.

McCloskey, M. (1983, April). Intuitive physics. *Scientific American,* pp. 122–130.

McCloskey, M., & Egeth, H. E. (1983a). Eyewitness identification: What can a psychologist tell a jury? *American Psychologist, 38,* 550–563.

McCloskey, M., & Egeth, H. E. (1983b). A time to speak, or a time to keep silence? *American Psychologist, 38,* 573–575.

McCloskey, M., & Watkins, M. J. (1978). The seeing-more-than-is-there phenomenon: Implications for the locus of iconic storage. *Journal of Experimental Psychology: Human Perception and Performance, 4,* 553–565.

McCord, W., & McCord, J. (1964). *The psychopath: An essay on the criminal mind.* New York: Van Nostrand Reinhold.

McDonald, M. C. (1981). The dream debate: Freud vs. neurophysiology. Does dream theory need revision. *Science News, 119,* 378–380.

McDougall, W. (1908). *An introduction to social psychology.* London: Methuen.

McEwen, B. S. (1976, July). Interaction between hormones and nerve tissue. *Scientific American,* pp. 48–58.

McFarland, R. A. (1975). Air travel across time zones. *American Scientist, 63,* 23–30.

McGeer, P. (1971). The chemistry of mind. *American Scientist, 59,* 221–229.

McGeoch, J. A. (1932). Forgetting and the law of disuse. *Psychological Review, 39,* 352–370.

McGill, T. E., Dewsbury, D. A., & Sachs, B. D. (1978). *Sex and behavior.* New York: Plenum Press.

McGuigan, F. J. (1966). Covert oral behavior and auditory hallucinations. *Psychophysiology, 3,* 421–428.

McGuire, W. J. (1964). Inducing resistance to persuasion: Some contemporary approaches. In L. Berkowitz (Ed.), *Advances in experimental social psychology* (Vol. 1), 192–229.

McGuire, W. (1968). Personality and susceptibility to social influence. In E. F. Borgatta & W. W. Lambert (Eds.), *Handbook of personality theory and research.* Chicago: Rand McNally.

McGuire, W. J., & Padawer-Singer, A. (1976). Trait salience in the spontaneous self-concept. *Journal of Personality and Social Psychology, 33,* 743–754.

McKay, H., Sinisterra, L., McKay, A., Gomez, H., & Lloreda, P. (1978). Improving cognitive ability in chronically deprived children. *Science, 200,* 270–278.

McKellar, P. (1972). Imagery from the standpoint of introspection. In P. W. Sheehan (Ed.), *The function and nature of imagery.* New York: Academic Press.

McKim, R. H. (1980a). *Experiences in visual thinking* (2nd ed.). Monterey, CA: Brooks/Cole.

McKim, R. H. (1980b). *Thinking visually: A strategy manual for problem solving.* Belmont, CA: Wadsworth.

McKinney, F. (1976). Fifty years of psychology. *American Psychologist, 31,* 834–842.

McKusick, V. A., & Ruddle, F. H. (1977). The status of the gene map of the human chromosomes. *Science, 196,* 390–405.

McLaughlin, B. (1978, December). Second look: The mother tongue. *Human Nature,* p. 89.

McLemore, C. W., & Benjamin, L. S. (1979). Whatever happened to interpersonal diagnosis?: A psychosocial alternative to DSM-III. *American Psychologist, 34,* 17–34.

McNeil, E. (1967). *The quiet furies.* Englewood Cliffs: NJ: Prentice-Hall.

McNeil, T. F., & Kaij, L. (1978). Obstetrical factors in the development of schizophrenia: Complications in the births of preschizophrenics and in reproduction by schizophrenic parents. In L. C.

Wynne, R. L. Cromwell, & S. Matthysse (Eds.), *The nature of schizophrenia: New approaches to research and treatment.* New York: John Wiley.

Meacham, J. A., & Leiman, B. (1982). Remembering to perform future actions. In U. Neisser (Ed.), *Memory observed: Remembering in natural contexts* (pp. 327–336). San Francisco: W. H. Freeman.

Mednick, S. A. (1962). The associative biases of the creative processes. *Psychological Review, 69,* 220–232.

Meehl, P. E. (1950). On the circularity of the law of effect. *Psychological Bulletin, 47,* 52–75.

Mefford, I. N., Baker, T. L., Boehme, R., Foutz, A. S., Ciaranello, R. D., Barchas, J. D., & Dement, W. C. (1983). Narcolepsy: Biogenic amine deficits in an animal model. *Science, 220,* 629–632.

Meichenbaum, D. H. (1972). Cognitive modification of test-anxious college students. *Journal of Consulting and Clinical Psychology, 39,* 370–380.

Meichenbaum, D. H. (1977). *Cognitive-behavior modification: An integrative approach.* New York: Pelnum Press.

Meisel, R. L., & Ward, I. L. (1981). Fetal female rats are masculinized by male littermates located caudally in the uterus. *Science, 213,* 239–242.

Melamed, B. G., Hawes, R. R., Heiby, E., & Glick, J. (1975). Use of filmed modeling to reduce uncooperative behavor of children during dental treatment. *Journal of Dental Research, 54,* 797–801.

Mellor, C. S. (1970). First rank symptoms of schizophrenia. *British Journal of Psychiatry, 117,* 15–23.

Meltzoff, A. N., & Moore, M. K. (1977). Imitation of facial and manual gestures by human neonates. *Science, 198,* 75–78.

Meltzoff, A. N., & Moore, M. K. (1983). Newborn infants imitate adult facial gestures. *Child Development, 54,* 702–709.

Meltzoff, J., & Kornreich, M. (1970). *Research in psychotherapy.* New York: Atherton.

Melzack, R. (1961, February). The perception of pain. *Scientific American,* pp. 41–49.

Melzack, R. (1970, October). Phantom limbs. *Psychology Today,* pp. 63–68.

Melzack, R. (1973). *The puzzle of pain.* New York: Basic Books.

Melzack, R. (1974). Shutting the gate on pain. *Science Year, 1975,* pp. 56–67.

Menarcheal misunderstanding. (1981, October). *Scientific American,* pp. 93–94.

Mendelson, W. B., Gullin, J. C., & Wyatt, R. J. (1977). *Human sleep and its disorders.* New York: Plenum Press.

Mental Health Law Project. (1976). *Summary of activities* (Vol. 2, No. 2).

Menzel, E. W. (1973). Chimpanzee spatial memory organization. *Science, 182,* 943–945.

Menzel, E. W., Jr., & Juno, C. (1982). Marmosets (*Saguinus fuscicollis*): Are

learning sets learned? *Science, 217,* 750–752.

Mercer, J. R. (1979). *SOMPA, system of multicultural pluralistic assessment: Technical manual.* New York: Psychological Corporation.

Mercer, T. B., & Lewis, J. G. (1978). Using the system of multicultural assessment (SOMPA) to identify the gifted minority child. In A. Y. Baldwin, G. H. Gear, & L. J. Lucito (Eds.), *Educational planning for the gifted: Overcoming cultural, geographic and socioeconomic barriers.* Reston, VA: Council for Exceptional Children.

Merton, P. A. (1972, May). How we control the contraction of our muscles. *Scientific American,* pp. 30–37.

Messick, S. (1980). Test validity and the ethics of assessment. *American Psychologist, 35,* 1012–1027.

Meyer, V., & Chesser, E. S. (1970). *Behavior therapy in clinical psychiatry.* Baltimore: Penguin.

Meyer, V., Robertson, J., & Tatlow, A. (1975). Home treatment of an obsessive-compulsive disorder by response prevention. *Journal of Behavior Therapy and Experimental Psychiatry, 6,* 37–38.

Michael, C. R. (1969, May). Retinal processing of visual images. *Scientific American,* pp. 104–114.

Miczek, K. A., Thompson, M. L., & Shuster, L. (1982). Opioid-like analgesia in defeated mice. *Science, 215,* 1520–1522.

Midlarsky, E., Bryan, J. H., & Brickman, P. (1973). Aversive approval: Interactive effects of modeling and reinforcement on altruistic behavior. *Child Development, 44,* 321–328.

Miles, L. E. M., Raynal, D. M., & Wilson, M. A. (1977). Blind man living in normal society has circadian rhythms of 24.9 hours. *Science, 198,* 421–423.

Milgram, S. (1963). Behavioral study of obedience. *Journal of Abnormal and Social Psychology, 67,* 371–378.

Milgram, S. (1965). Some conditions of obedience and disobedience to authority. *Human Relations, 18,* 57–76.

Milgram, S. (1970). The experience of living in cities. *Science, 167,* 1461–1468.

Milgram, S. (1974). *Obedience to authority: An experimental view.* New York: Harper & Row.

Milgram, S. (1977). *The individual in a social world.* Reading, MA: Addison-Wesley.

Milgram, S., Greenwald, J., Kessler, S., McKenna, W., & Waters, J. (1972). A psychological map of New York City. *American Scientist, 60,* 194–200.

Miller, D. T., & Ross, M. (1975). Self-serving biases in the attribution of causality: Fact or fiction? *Psychological Bulletin, 82,* 213–215.

Miller, G. A. (1956). The magical number seven, plus or minus two: Some limits on our capacity for processing information. *Psychological Review, 63,* 81–97.

Miller, G. A. (1969). Psychology as a means of promoting human welfare. *American Psychologist, 24,* 1063–1075.

Miller, G. A. (1977). *Spontaneous apprentices: Children and language.* New York: Seabury Press.

Miller, G. A. (1980, January). Giving away psychology in the 80's. *Psychology Today,* pp. 38–50, 97–98.

Miller, G. A., Galanter, E., & Pribram, K. (1960). *Plans and the structure of behavior.* New York: Holt, Rinehart & Winston.

Miller, L. I. (Ed.). (1974). *Marijuana: Effects on human behavior.* New York: Academic Press.

Miller, N., & Campbell, D. T. (1959). Recency and primacy in persuasion as a function of the timing of speeches and measurements. *Journal of Abnormal and Social Psychology, 59,* 1–9.

Miller, N. E. (1941). The frustration-aggression hypothesis. *Psychological Review, 48,* 337–342.

Miller, N. E. (1944). Experimental studies of conflict. In J. M. Hunt (Ed.), *Personality and the behavior disorders* (Vol. 1, pp. 431–465). New York: Ronald Press.

Miller, N. E. (1948a). Studies of fear as an acquired drive: I. Fear as motivation and fear-reduction as reinforcement in the learning of new responses. *Journal of Experimental Psychology, 38,* 89–101.

Miller, N. E. (1948b). Theory and experiment relating psychoanalytic displacement to stimulus-response generalization. *Journal of Abnormal and Social Psychology, 43,* 155–178.

Miller, N. E. (1951). Learnable drives and rewards. In S. S. Stevens (Ed.), *Handbook of experimental psychology* (pp. 435–472). New York: John Wiley.

Miller, N. E., & Dollard, J. (1941). *Social learning and imitation.* New Haven, CT: Yale University Press.

Miller, W. A., Ratliff, F., & Hartline, H. K. (1961, September). How cells receive stimuli. *Scientific American,* pp. 222–238.

Milner, B. (1959). The memory deficit in bilateral hippocampal lesions. *Psychiatric Research Reports, 11,* 43–58.

Milner, B. (Ed.). (1975). *Hemispheric specialization and integration.* Cambridge, MA: MIT Press.

Mischel, W. (1968). *Personality and assessment.* New York: John Wiley.

Mischel, W. (1973). Toward a cognitive social learning reconceptualization of personality. *Psychological Review, 80,* 252–283.

Mischel, W. (1977). On the future of personality assessment. *American Psychologist, 32,* 246–254.

Mischel, W. (1979). On the interface of cognition and personality: Beyond the person-situation debate. *American Psychologist, 34,* 740–754.

Mischel, W. (1981a). Current issues and challenges in personality. In L. T. Benjamin, Jr. (Ed.), *The G. Stanley Hall lecture series* (Vol. 1, pp. 81–99). Washington, DC: American Psychological Association.

Mischel, W. (1981b). *Introduction to personality* (3rd ed.). New York: Holt, Rinehart & Winston.

Mishler, E. G., & Waxler, N. E. (1968). *Interaction in families: An experimental study of family processes and schizophrenia.* New York: John Wiley.

Mitchell, G. D. (1979). *Behavioral sex differences in nonhuman primates.* New York: Van Nostrand Reinhold.

Mitler, M. M., Boysen, B., Campbell, L., & Dement, W. (1974). Narcolepsy, cataplexy in female dogs. *Experimental Neurology, 45,* 332–340.

Mitler, M. M., Guilleminault, C., Orem, J., Zarcone, V. P., & Dement, W. C. (1975, December). Sleeplessness, sleep attacks, and things that go wrong in the night. *Psychology Today,* pp. 45–50.

Mittwoch, U. (1981). Whistling maids and crowing hens—hermaphroditism in folklore and biology. *Perspectives in Biology and Medicine,* 595–606.

Moates, D. R., & Schumacher, G. M. (1980). *An introduction to cognitive psychology.* Belmont, CA: Wadsworth.

Monagan, D. (1982, March). CIA seals. *Science 82,* p. 80.

Monahan, J. (1978). Prediction research and the emergency commitment of dangerously mentally ill persons: A reconsideration. *American Journal of Psychiatry, 135,* 198–201.

Monahan, J. (1981). *The clinical prediction of violent behavior.* Rockville, MD: National Institute of Mental Health.

Money, J. (1980). *Love and love sickness: The science of sex, gender difference, and pair-bonding.* Baltimore, MD: Johns Hopkins University Press.

Money, J., & Ehrhardt, A. A. (1972). *Man & woman, boy & girl: The differentiation and dimorphism of gender identity from conception to maturity.* Baltimore, MD: Johns Hopkins University Press.

Montagna, W. (1965, February). The skin. *Scientific American,* pp. 56–66.

Montague, A. (1976). *The nature of human aggression.* New York: Oxford University Press.

Monte, C. F. (1975). *Psychology's scientific endeavor.* New York: Praeger.

Montessori, M. (1966). *The secret of childhood* (M. J. Costelloe, Trans.). Notre Dame, IN: Fides.

Montour, K. (1977). William James Sidis, the broken twig. *American Psychologist, 32,* 265–279.

Monty, R. A., & Senders, J. W. (Eds.). (1976). *Eye movements and psychological processes.* New York: Halsted Press.

Moore, B. R., & Stuttard, S. (1979). Dr. Guthrie and *Felis domesticus* or: Tripping over the cat. *Science, 205,* 1031–1033.

Moore-Ede, M. C. (1982, September). What hath night to do with sleep? *Natural History,* pp. 22–24.

Moore-Ede, M. C., Sulzman, F. M., & Fuller, C. A. (1982). *The clocks that time us: Physiology of the circadian timing system.* Cambridge, MA: Harvard University Press.

Moran, G., & Comfort, J. C. (1982). Scientific juror selection: Sex as a moderator of demographic and personality predictors of impaneled felony juror behavior. *Journal of Personality and Social Psychology, 43,* 1052–1063.

Morell, P. (Ed.). (1977). *Myelin.* New York: Plenum Press.

Morell, P., & Norton, W. T. (1980, May). Myelin. *Scientific American,* pp. 88–116.

Morgan, A. H., Hilgard, E. R., & Davert, E. C. (1970). The heritability of hypnotic susceptibility of twins: A preliminary report. *Behavior Genetics, 1,* 213–224.

Morris, D. (1979, October). Gestures. *Natural History,* pp. 114–121.

Morris, J. (1974). *Conundrum.* New York: Harcourt Brace Jovanovich.

Morris, J. B., & Beck, A. T. (1974). The efficacy of antidepressant drugs. *Archives of General Psychiatry, 30,* 667–674.

Morrison, A. R. (1983, April). A window on the sleeping brain. *Scientific American,* pp. 94–102.

Morrison, J. R. (1973). Catatonia: Retarded and excited types. *Archives of General Psychiatry, 28,* 39–41.

Moscovitch, M., & Craik, F. I. M. (1976). Depth of processing, retrieval cues, and uniqueness of encoding as factors in recall. *Journal of Verbal Learning and Verbal Behavior, 15,* 447–458.

Moscovitch, M., & Smith, L. C. (1979). Differences in neural organization between individuals with inverted and noninverted handwriting postures. *Science, 205,* 710–713.

Moscowitz, B. A. (1978, November). The acquisition of language. *Scientific American,* pp. 92–108.

Moskowitz, H. W., Kumaraiah, V., Sharma, K. N., Jacobs, H. L., & Sharma, S. D. (1975). Cross-cultural differences in simple taste preferences. *Science, 190,* 1217–1218.

Mourant, A. E., Kopéc, A. C., & Domaniewska-Sobczak, K. (1978). *The genetics of the Jews.* New York: Oxford University Press.

Mowrer, O. H. (1939). A stimulus-response analysis of anxiety and its role as a reinforcing agent. *Psychological Review, 46,* 553–565.

Mowrer, O. H. (1947). On the dual nature of learning—a reinterpretation of "conditioning" and "problem-solving." *Harvard Educational Review, 17,* 102–148.

Moyer, K. E. (1976). *The psychobiology of aggression.* New York: Harper & Row.

Moyer, R. S., & Dumais, S. T. (1978). Mental comparisons. In G. H. Bower (Ed.), *The psychology of learning and motivation: Advances in research and theory* (Vol. 12, pp. 117–155). New York: Academic Press.

Mozart, W. A. (1789, 1970). A letter. In P. E. Vernon (Ed.), *Creativity* (pp. 55–56). Middlesex: Penguin.

Mrosovsky, N., & Sherry, D. F. (1980). Animal anorexias. *Science, 207,* 837–842.

Mucha, T. F., & Reinhardt, R. F. (1970). Conversion reactions in student aviators. *American Journal of Psychiatry, 127,* 493–497.

Muller-Schwarze, D., & Silverstein, R. M. (1980). *Chemical signals: Vertebrates and aquatic invertebrates.* New York: Plenum Press.

Munroe, R. (1955). *Schools of psychoanalytic thought.* New York: Henry Holt.

Munsterberg, H. (1908). *On the witness stand.* New York: Doubleday.

Munter, M. (1982, Summer). Beyond words. *Stanford Magazine,* pp. 46–49.

Muntz, W. R. A. (1964, March). Vision in frogs. *Scientific American,* pp. 110–119.

Murdock, B. B., Jr. (1962). The serial position effect of free recall. *Journal of Experimental Psychology, 64,* 482–488.

Murphy, J. M. (1976). Psychiatric labeling in cross-cultural perspective. *Science, 191,* 1019–1028.

Murray, H. A. (1968, September). A conversation with Henry A. Murray: The psychology of personality. (Interview by M. H. Hall) *Psychology Today,* pp. 56–63.

Murray, H. A. (1938). *Explorations in personality.* New York: Oxford University Press.

Murray, H. A. (1959). Vicissitudes of creativity. In H. H. Anderson (Ed.), *Creativity and its cultivation* (pp. 96–118). New York: Harper & Row.

Murstein, B. I. (1972). Physical attractiveness and marital choice. *Journal of Personality and Social Psychology, 22,* 8–12.

Musacchia, X. J., & Jansky, L. (Eds.). (1981). *Survival in the cold: Hibernation and other adaptations: Proceedings of a symposium, Prague, July, 1980.* New York: Elsevier.

Mussen, P. H. (1970). *Carmichael's manual of child psychology* (3rd ed., 2 vols.). New York: John Wiley.

Myers, R. H., & Shafer, D. A. (1979). Hybrid ape offspring of a mating of gibbon and siamang. *Science, 205,* 308–310.

Naeye, R. L. (1980, April). Sudden infant death. *Scientific American,* pp. 56–62.

Napier, J. (1980). *Hands.* New York: Pantheon Books.

Naranjo, C., & Ornstein, R. (1971). *On the psychology of meditation.* New York: Viking Press.

Nassi, A. J. (1981). Survivors of the sixties: Comparative psychosocial and political development of former Berkeley student activists. *American Psychologist, 36,* 753–761.

National Association for Mental Health. (1979, March 23). Bulletin No. 103.

National Institute of Mental Health. (1982). *Television and behavior: Ten years of scientific progress and implications for the eighties.* Washington, DC: U.S. Government Printing Office.

Nauta, W. J. H., & Feirtag, M. (1979, September). The organization of the brain. *Scientific American,* pp. 78–105.

Naylor, H. (1980). Reading disability and lateral asymmetry: An information-processing analysis. *Psychological Bulletin, 87,* 531–545.

Neale, J. M., & Oltmanns, T. F. (1980). *Schizophrenia.* New York: John Wiley.

Nebes, R. D. (1975, Spring). Man's socalled "minor" hemisphere. *UCLA Educator, 17,* 13–16.

Neisser, U. (1967). *Cognitive psychology.* New York: Appleton-Century-Crofts.

Neisser, U. (1968, September). The processes of vision. *Scientific American,* pp. 204–214.

Neisser, U. (1976). *Cognition and reality: Principles and implications of cognitive psychology.* San Francisco: W. H. Freeman.

Neisser, U. (1981). John Dean's memory: A case study. *Cognition, 9,* 1–22.

Neisser, U. (Ed.). (1982a). *Memory observed: Remembering in natural contexts.* San Francisco: W. H. Freeman.

Neisser, U. (1982b). Snapshots or benchmarks? In U. Neisser (Ed.), *Memory observed: Remembering in natural contexts* (pp. 43–48). San Francisco, W. H. Freeman.

Nelson, K. (1975). Individual differences in early semantic and syntactic development. *Annals of the New York Academy of Sciences, 263,* 132–139.

Nelson, R. E. (1977). Irrational beliefs in depression. *Journal of Consulting and Clinical Psychology, 45,* 1190–1191.

Nelson, R. E., & Craighead, W. E. (1977). Selective recall of positive and negative feedback, self-control behaviors, and depression. *Journal of Abnormal Psychology, 86,* 379–388.

Nelson, T. O. (1977). Repetition and depth of processing. *Journal of Verbal Learning and Verbal Behavior, 16,* 151–172.

Nelson, T. O. (1978). Detecting small amounts of information in memory: Savings for non-recognized items. *Journal of Experimental Psychology: Human Learning and Memory, 4,* 453–468.

Neufeld, R. W. J. (Ed.). (1982). *Psychological stress and psychopathology.* New York: McGraw-Hill.

Neuringer, A., & Neuringer, M. (1974). Learning by following a food source. *Science, 184,* 1005–1008.

Neutra, M., & Leblond, C. P. (1969, February). The Golgi apparatus. *Scientific American,* pp. 100–107.

Nevin, D. (1977, October). Young prodigies take off under special program. *Smithsonian,* pp. 76–81.

Newcomb, T. M. (1961). *The acquaintance process.* New York: Holt, Rinehart & Winston.

Newell, A., Shaw, J. C., & Simon, H. A. (1958). Elements of a theory of human problem solving. *Psychological Review, 65,* 151–166.

Newell, A., Shaw, J. C., & Simon, H. A. (1962). The process of creative thinking. In H. E. Gruber, G. Terrell, & M. Wertheimer (Eds.), *Contemporary approaches to creative thinking* (pp. 63–119). New York: Atherton.

Newell, A., & Simon, H. A. (1972). *Human problem solving.* Englewood Cliffs, NJ: Prentice-Hall.

Newman, E. A., & Hartline, P. H. (1982, March). The infrared "vision" of snakes. *Scientific American,* pp. 116–127.

Newman, O. (1972). *Defensible space.* New York: Macmillan.

Newton, N., & Modahl, C. (1978, March). Pregnancy: The closest human relationship. *Human Nature,* pp. 40–49.

Nichol, S. E., & Gottesman, I. I. (1983). Clues to the genetics and neurobiology of schizophrenia. *American Scientist, 71,* 398–404.

Nickerson, R. S., & Adams, M. J. (1982). Long-term memory for a common object. In U. Neisser (Ed.), *Memory observed: Remembering in natural contexts* (pp. 163–175). San Francisco: W. H. Freeman.

Nisbett, R., & Ross, L. (1980). *Human inference: Strategies and shortcomings of human judgments.* Englewood Cliffs, NJ: Prentice-Hall.

Nisbett, R. E., & Wilson, T. D. (1977). Telling more than we can know: Verbal reports on mental processes. *Psychological Review, 84,* 231–259.

Nordby, V. J., & Hall, C. S. (1974). *A guide to psychologists and their concepts.* San Francisco: W. H. Freeman.

Noton, D., & Stark, L. (1971, June). Eye movements and visual perception. *Scientific American,* pp. 34–43.

Novick, M. R. (1981). Federal guidelines and professional standards. *American Psychologist, 36,* 1035–1046.

Novin, D., Wyrwicka, W., & Bray, G. A. (Eds.). (1976). *Hunger: Basic mechanisms and clinical implications.* New York: Raven Press.

Nye, R. D. (1979). *What is B. F. Skinner really saying?* Englewood Cliffs, NJ: Prentice-Hall.

Nye, R. D. (1981). *Three psychologies: Perspectives from Freud, Skinner, and Rogers* (2nd ed.). Monterey, CA: Brooks/Cole.

Obrist, P. A., Sutterer, J. R., & Howard, J. L. (1972). Preparatory cardiac changes: A psychobiological approach. In A. H. Black & W. F. Prokasy (Eds.), *Classical conditioning II: Current research and theory* (pp. 312–340). New York: Appleton-Century-Crofts.

Oden, M. H. (1968). The fulfillment of promise: 40-year followup of the Terman gifted group. *Genetic Psychology Monographs, 77,* 3–93.

Öhman, A., Erixon, G., & Löfberg, I. (1975). Phobias and preparedness: Phobic versus neutral pictures as conditioned stimuli for human autonomic responses. *Journal of Abnormal Psychology, 84,* 41–45.

Ojemann, G., & Mateer, C. (1979). Human language cortex: Localization of memory, syntax, and sequential motor-phoneme identification systems. *Science, 205,* 1401–1403.

O'Keefe, J., & Nadel, L. (1978). *The hippocampus as a cognitive map.* New York: Oxford University Press.

Olds, J. (1956, October). Pleasure centers in the brain. *Scientific American,* pp. 105–116.

Olds, J., & Milner, P. (1973). Positive reinforcement produced by electrical stimulation of septal area and other regions of rat brain. In E. S. Valenstein (Ed.), *Brain stimulation and motivation: Research and commentary* (pp. 69–80). Glenview, IL: Scott, Foresman.

O'Leary, K. D., & Borkovec, T. D. (1978). Conceptual, methodological, and ethical problems of placebo groups in psychotherapy research. *American Psychologist, 33,* 821–830.

Olmedo, E. L. (1981). Testing linguistic minorities. *American Psychologist, 36,* 1078–1085.

Olson, R. W. (1978). *The act of creative thinking: A practical guide.* New York: Harper & Row.

Olton, D. S. (1977, June). Spatial memory. *Scientific American,* pp. 82–98.

Olton, D. S. (1979). Mazes, maps, and memory. *American Psychologist, 34,* 583–596.

Omenn, G. S. (1978). Prenatal diagnosis of genetic disorders. *Science, 200,* 952–958.

Orem, J., & Barnes, C. D. (Eds.). (1980). *Physiology in sleep.* New York: Academic Press.

Ornstein, R. E. (Ed.). (1973). *The nature of human consciousness: A book of readings.* San Francisco: W. H. Freeman.

Ornstein, R. E. (1977). *The psychology of consciousness* (3rd ed.). New York: Harcourt Brace Jovanovich.

Ornstein, R. E. (1978, May). The split and the whole brain. *Human Nature,* pp. 76–83.

Oscar-Berman, M. (1980). Neuropsychological consequences of long-term chronic alcoholism. *American Scientist, 68,* 410–419.

Osgood, C. E., Luria, Z., & Smith, S. W., II. (1976). A blind analysis of another case of multiple personality using the semantic personality technique. *Journal of Abnormal Psychology, 85,* 256–270.

Oster, G. (1973, October). Auditory beats in the brain. *Scientific American,* pp. 94–102.

Pagano, R. R. (1981). *Understanding statistics in the behavioral sciences.* St. Paul, MN: West.

Page, J. (1982a, March). Call me Ishmael. *Science 82,* pp. 88–89.

Page, J. (1982b, January/February). A dog's worst friend. *Science 82,* pp. 90–92.

Paivio, A. (1969). Mental imagery in associative learning and memory. *Psychological Review, 76,* 241–263.

Paivio, A. (1978). On exploring visual knowledge. In B. S. Randhawa & W. E. Coffman (Eds.), *Visual learning, thinking, and communication.* New York: Academic Press.

Paivio, A. (1979). *Imagery and verbal processes.* Hillsdale, NJ: Lawrence Erlbaum.

Palmer, F. R. (1976). *Semantics: A new outline.* Cambridge: Cambridge University Press.

Palmer, J. D. (1982, October). Biorhythm bunkum. *Natural History,* pp. 90–99.

Palmer, J. D., & Goodenough, J. E. (1978, December). Mysterious monthly rhythms. *Natural History,* pp. 64–69.

Palmerino, C. C., Rusiniak, K. W., & Garcia, J. (1980). Flavor-illness aversions: The peculiar roles of odor and taste in memory for poison. *Science, 208,* 753–755.

Pappenheimer, J. R. (1976, August). The sleep factor. *Scientific American,* pp. 24–29.

Parfit, M. (1980, October). Are dolphins trying to say something or is it all much ado about nothing? *Smithsonian,* pp. 73–81.

Parke, R. D., Berkowitz, L., Leyens, J. P., West, S. G., & Sebastian, R. J. (1977). Some effects of violent and nonviolent movies on the behavior of juvenile delinquents. In L. Berkowitz (Ed.), *Advances in experimental social psychology* (Vol. 10, pp. 135–172). New York: Academic Press.

Parker, D. E. (1980, November). The vestibular apparatus. *Scientific American,* pp. 98–111.

Parlee, M. B. (1978, April). The rhythms in men's lives. *Psychology Today,* pp. 82–91.

Parloff, M. B., Waskow, I. E., & Wolfe, B. E. (1978). Research on therapist variables in relation to process and outcome. In S. L. Garfield & A. E. Bergin (Eds.), *Handbook of psychotherapy and behavior change: An empirical analysis* (2nd ed.). New York: John Wiley.

Partridge, B. L. (1982, June). The structure and function of fish schools. *Scientific American,* pp. 114–123.

Passow, A. H. (1981). The nature of giftedness and talent. *Gifted Child Quarterly, 24,* 5–10.

Patrusky, B. (1982, January/February). What causes aging? *Science 82,* p. 112.

Patterson, F. (1978a). Conversations with a gorilla. *National Geographic, 154,* 438–465.

Patterson, F. (1978b). Linguistic capabilities of a lowland gorilla. In F. C. C. Peng (Ed.), *Sign language and language acquisition in man and ape: New dimensions in comparative psycholinguistics.* Boulder, Colorado: Westview Press.

Patterson, F. G. (1981). Ape language. *Science, 211,* 86–87.

Patterson, F., & Linden, E. (1981). *The education of Koko.* New York: Holt, Rinehart & Winston.

Patterson, G. R. (1976). Aggressive child: Victim and architect of a coercive system. In E. J. Marsh, L. A. Hammerlynch, & L. C. Handy (Eds.), *Behavior modification and families.* New York: Bruner/Mazel.

Paul, G. L. (1966). *Insight versus desensitization in psychotherapy.* Stanford, CA: Stanford University Press.

Paul, G. L. (1967). Insight versus desensitization in psychotherapy two years after termination. *Journal of Consulting Psychology, 31,* 333–348.

Paul, G. L., & Lentz, R. J. (1977). *Psychosocial treatment of chronic mental patients: Milieu versus social learning programs.* Cambridge, MA: Harvard University Press.

Paulos, M. A., & Tessel, R. E. (1982). Excretion of β-phenethylamine is elevated in humans after profound stress. *Science, 215,* 1127–1129.

Pavlov, I. P. (1927). *Conditioned reflexes: An investigation of the physiological activity of the cerebral cortex.* New York: Oxford University Press.

Pawelek, J. M., & Körner, A. M. (1982). The biosynthesis of mammalian melanin. *American Scientist, 70,* 136–145.

Pekkanen, J. (1982, June). Why do we sleep? *Science 82,* p. 86.

Penfield, W. (1958). *The excitable cortex of conscious man.* Springfield, IL: Charles C Thomas.

Penfield, W. (1975). *The msytery of the mind.* Princeton, NJ: Princeton University Press.

Penfield, W., & Rasmussen, T. (1950). *The cerebral cortex of man.* New York: Macmillan.

Penfield, W., & Roberts, L. (1959). *Speech and brain mechanisms.* Princeton, NJ: Princeton University Press.

Penrod, S. (1980, May). *Evaluating social scientific methods of jury selection.* Paper presented at the meeting of the Midwestern Psychological Association, St. Louis, MO.

Penrod, S. (1983). *Social psychology.* Englewood Cliffs, NJ: Prentice-Hall.

Penrod, S., Loftus, E., & Winkler, J. (1982). The reliability of eyewitness testimony: A psychological perspective. In N. L. Kerr & R. M. Bray (Eds.), *The psychology of the courtroom* (pp. 119–168). New York: Academic Press.

Peplau, L. A., & Perlman, D. (Eds.). (1982). *Loneliness: A sourcebook of current theory, research, and therapy.* New York: John Wiley.

Perl, D. P., & Brody, A. R. (1980). Alzheimer's disease: X-ray spectrometric evidence of aluminum accumulation in neurofibrillary tangle-bearing neurons. *Science, 208,* 297–299.

Perlman, D., & Peplau, L. A. (1982, August). *Loneliness research: Implications for interventions.* Paper presented at the American Psychological Association annual meeting.

Perlman, E. (1980, July/August). Walking on thin air. *Science 80*, pp. 89–90.

Petersen, D. (Ed.). (1982). *A mad people's history of madness*. Pittsburgh, PA: University of Pittsburgh Press.

Peterson, L. R., & Peterson, M. J. (1959). Short-term retention of individual verbal items. *Journal of Experimental Psychology, 58*, 193–198.

Pettigrew, J. D. (1972, August). The neurophysiology of binocular vision. *Scientific American*, pp. 84–95.

Petty, R. E., & Cacioppo, J. T. (1977). Forewarning, cognitive responding, and resistance to persuasion. *Journal of Personality and Social Psychology, 35*, 645–656.

Petty, R. E., & Cacioppo, J. T. (1981). *Attitudes and persuasion: Classic and contemporary approaches*. Dubuque, IA: C. Brown.

Pew, T. W., Jr. (1979, December). Biofeedback seeks new medical uses for concept of yoga. *Smithsonian*, pp. 106–114.

Pfeiffer, J. (1980, June). Current research casts new light on human origins. *Smithsonian*, pp. 91–103.

Pfungst, O. (1911). *Clever Hans (the horse of Mr. Van Osten)*. New York: Holt.

Phelps, M. E., Kuhl, D. E., & Mazziotta, J. C. (1981). Metabolic mapping of the brain's response to visual stimulation: Studies in humans. *Science, 211*, 1445–1448.

Phillips, D. P. (1978). Airplane accident fatalities increase just after newspaper stories about murder and suicide. *Science, 201*, 748–750.

Piaget, J. (1932, 1965). *Moral judgment of the child* (2nd ed.). New York: Free Press.

Piaget, J. (1954). *Construction of reality in the child*. New York: Basic Books.

Piaget, J. (1962). *Play, dreams and imitation in childhood*. New York: W. W. Norton.

Piaget, J. (1966). *Origins of intelligence in children*. New York: International Universities Press.

Piaget, J. (1968). *Six psychological studies* (D. Elkind, Ed.). New York: Random House.

Piaget, J., & Inhelder, B. (1969). *Psychology of the child*. New York: Basic Books.

Piattelli-Palmarini, M. (Ed.). (1980). *Language and learning: The debate between Jean Piaget and Noam Chomsky*. Cambridge, MA: Harvard University Press.

Pickard, G. E., & Turek, F. W. (1982). Splitting of the circadian rhythm of activity is abolished by unilateral lesions of the suprachiasmatic nuclei. *Science, 215*, 1119–1121.

Pietsch, T. W., & Grobecker, D. B. (1978). The compleat angler: Aggressive mimicry in an antennariid anglerfish. *Science, 201*, 369–370.

Pilbeam, D. (1978, June). Rearranging our family tree. *Human Nature*, pp. 38–45.

Pines, M. (1978, November). Modern bioengineers reinvent human anatomy with spare parts. *Smithsonian*, pp. 50–57.

Pines, M. (1980, December). Psychological hardness: The role of challenge in health. *Psychology Today*, pp. 34–44, 98.

Pines, M. (1982, May). The IQ's connected to the heartbeat. *Science 81*, pp. 70–71.

Plutchik, R. (1980). *Emotion: A psychoevolutionary synthesis*. New York: Harper & Row.

Plutchik, R., & Kellerman, H. (Eds.). (1980). *Emotion: Theory, research and experience: Vol. 1. Theories of emotion*. New York: Academic Press.

Poincaré, H. (1913, 1952). Mathematical creation. In B. Ghiselin (Ed.), *The creative process: A symposium* (pp. 33–42). Berkeley, CA: University of California Press.

Pollack, I., & Pickett, J. M. (1964). Intelligibility of excerpts from fluent speech: Auditory versus structured context. *Journal of Verbal Learning and Verbal Behavior, 3*, 79–84.

Pomazal, R. J., & Clore, G. L. (1973). Helping on the highway: The effects of dependency and sex. *Journal of Applied Social Psychology, 3*, 150–164.

Pomerantz, J. R., & Kubovy, M. (1981). Perceptual organization: An overview. In M. Kubovy & J. R. Pomerantz (Eds.), *Perceptual organization* (pp. 423–456). Hillsdale, NJ: Lawrence Erlbaum.

Poon, L. W. (Ed.). (1980). *Aging in the 1980s: Psychological issues*. Washington, DC: American Psychological Association.

Porter, B. (1970, October). The many faces of murder. *Playboy*, pp. 97–98, 209–220.

Posner, M. I., Boies, S. J., Eichelman, W. H., & Taylor, R. L. (1969). Retention of visual and name codes of single letters. *Journal of Experimental Psychology, 79*(1, Whole part 2).

Postman, L. (Ed.). (1962a). *Psychology in the making: Histories of selected research problems*. New York: Alfred A. Knopf.

Postman, L. (1962b). Rewards and punishments in human learning. In L. Postman (Ed.), *Psychology in the making: Histories of selected research problems* (pp. 331–401). New York: Alfred A. Knopf.

Postman, L. (1975). Verbal learning and memory. *Annual Review of Psychology, 26*, 291–335.

Postman, L. (1976). Interference theory revisited. In J. Brown (Ed.), *Recall and recognition* (pp. 157–181). New York: John Wiley.

Premack, A. J., & Premack, D. (1972, October). Teaching language to an ape. *Scientific American*, pp. 92–99.

Premack, D. (1959). Toward empirical behavior laws: I. Positive reinforcement. *Psychological Review, 66*, 219–233.

Premack, D. (1971). Language in chimpanzee? *Science, 172*, 808–822.

Premack, D. (1976). *Intelligence in ape and man*. Hillsdale, NJ: Lawrence Erlbaum.

Premack, D., & Woodruff, G. (1978). Chimpanzee problem-solving: A test for comprehension. *Science, 202*, 532–535.

Press, A. (1983, March 7). When can a shrink be sued? *Newsweek*, p. 77.

Prewitt, K. (1981). Usefulness of the social sciences. *Science, 211*, 659.

Priest, R. F., & Sawyer, J. (1967). Proximity and peership: Bases of balance in interpersonal attraction. *American Journal of Sociology, 72*, 633–649.

Pritchard, R. M. (1961, June). Stabilized images on the retina. *Scientific American*, pp. 72–78.

Prochaska, J. O. (1979). *Systems of psychotherapy*. Homewood, IL: Dorsey Press.

Provine, W. B. (1973). Geneticists and the biology of race crossing. *Science, 182*, 790–796.

Pylyshyn, Z. W. (1973). What the mind's eye tells the mind's brain: A critique of mental imagery. *Psychological Bulletin, 80*, 1–24.

Pylyshyn, Z. W. (1981). The imagery debate: Analogue media versus tacit knowledge. *Psychological Review, 88*, 16–45.

Rabkin, J. G., & Struening, E. L. (1976). Life events, stress, and illness. *Science, 194*, 1013–1020.

Rachlin, H. (1976). *Introduction to modern behaviorism* (2nd ed.). San Francisco: W. H. Freeman.

Rachman, S. J., & Wilson, G. T. (1980). *The effects of psychological therapy* (2nd ed.). New York: Pergamon Press.

Radner, D., & Radner, M. (1982). *Science and unreason*. Belmont, CA: Wadsworth.

Rafferty, J. F. (1983, March–April). Watching the biological clock. *Harvard Magazine, 85*, 26–29.

Rahe, R. H., & Lind, E. (1971). Psychosocial factors and sudden cardiac death: A pilot study. *Journal of Psychosomatic Research, 15*, 19–24.

Raloff, J. (1982). Occupational noise—the subtle pollutant. *Science News, 121*, 347–350.

Randi, J. (1983, Summer). The project alpha experiment: Part 1. The first two years. *Skeptical Inquirer, 7*, 24–33.

Ranucci, E. R., & Teeters, J. L. (1977). *Creating Escher-type drawings*. Palo Alto, CA: Creative Publishing.

Raphael, B. (1976). *The thinking computer: Mind inside matter*. San Francisco: W. H. Freeman.

Ratkevich, R. P. (1977). *Dinosaurs of the southwest*. Albuquerque, NM: University of New Mexico Press.

Ray, K. (1980, July/August). Trapped intelligence. *Science 80*, pp. 82–83.

Ray, O. S. (1978). *Drugs, society and human behavior* (2nd ed.). St. Louis, MO: Mosby.

Ray, W. J., & Ravizza, R. (1981). *Methods toward a science of behavior and experience*. Belmont, CA: Wadsworth.

Recase, M. D. (1977). Procedures for computerized testing. *Behavior Research Methods and Instrumentation, 9*, 148–152.

Rechtschaffen, A., Gilliland, M. A., Bergmann, B. M., & Winter, J. B. (1983). Physiological correlates of prolonged sleep deprivation in rats. *Science, 221,* 182–183.

Rechtschaffen, A., & Kales, A. (Eds.). (1968). *A manual of standardized terminology, techniques and scoring system for sleep stages of human subjects.* Washington, DC: U.S. Government Printing Office.

Reed, S. K. (1972). Pattern recognition and categorization. *Cognitive Psychology, 3,* 383–407.

Reed, S. K. (1974). Structural descriptions and the limitations of visual images. *Memory & Cognition, 2,* 329–336.

Reeder, G. D. (1982). Let's give the fundamental attribution error another chance. *Journal of Personality and Social Psychology, 43,* 341–344.

Reese, E. P., Howard, J., & Reese, T. W. (1978). *Human behavior: Analysis and application* (2nd ed.). Dubuque, IA: W. C. Brown.

Reeves, W. (1958). *Body and mind in western thought.* Baltimore, MD: Penguin.

Regan, D. (1979, December). Electrical responses evoked from the human brain. *Scientific American,* pp. 134–146.

Regan, D., & Beverley, K. I. (1979). Visually guided locomotion: Psychophysical evidence for a neural mechanism sensitive to flow patterns. *Science, 205,* 311–313.

Regan, D., & Beverley, K. I. (1982). How do we avoid confounding the direction we are looking and the direction we are moving? *Science, 215,* 194–196.

Regan, P., Beverley, K., & Cynader, M. (1979, July). The visual perception of motion in depth. *Scientific American,* pp. 136–151.

Reiss, S., Levitan, G. W., & McNally, R. J. (1982). Emotionally disturbed mentally retarded people: An underserved population. *American Psychologist, 37,* 361–367.

Reitman, W. R. (1964). Heuristic decision procedures, open constraints, and the structure of ill-defined problems. In M. W. Shelley & G. L. Bryan (Eds.), *Human judgments and optimality.* New York: John Wiley.

Reitman, W. R. (1965). *Cognition and thought: An information processing approach.* New York: John Wiley.

Remorseless killer sentenced to death. (1972, February 2). *Palo Alto Times,* p. 6.

Rensberger, B. (1981, October). Facing the past. *Science 81,* pp. 40–51.

Renzulli, J. S. (1978, –). What makes giftedness? Reexamining a definition. *Phi Delta Kappan, 60,* 180–184, 261.

Reppert, S. M., & Schwartz, W. J. (1983). Maternal coordination of the fetal biological clock in utero. *Science, 220,* 969–971.

Reschly, D. J. (1981). Psychological testing in educational classification and placement. *American Psychologist, 36,* 1094–1102.

Rescorla, R. A. (1968). Probability of shock in the presence and absence of CS in fear conditioning. *Journal of Comparative and Physiological Psychology, 66,* 1–5.

Rescorla, R. A. (1969). Pavlovian conditioned inhibition. *Psychological Bulletin, 72,* 77–94.

Rescorla, R. A. (1972). Informational variables in Pavlovian conditioning. In G. H. Bower (Ed.), *The psychology of learning and motivation: Advances in research and theory* (Vol. 6, pp. 1–46). New York: Academic Press.

Rescorla, R. A. (1980). *Pavlovian second-order conditioning.* Hillsdale, NJ: Lawrence Erlbaum.

Rescorla, R. A., & Solomon, R. L. (1967). Two-process learning theory: Relationships between Pavlovian conditioning and instrumental learning. *Psychological Review, 55,* 151–182.

Rescorla, R. A., & Wagner, A. R. (1972). A theory of Pavlovian conditioning: Variations in the effectiveness of reinforcement and nonreinforcement. In A. H. Black & W. F. Prokasy (Eds.), *Classical conditioning II: Current theory and research* (pp. 64–99). New York: Appleton-Century-Crofts.

Restak, R. M. (1982a, May). Islands of genius. *Science 82,* pp. 62–67.

Restak, R. M. (1982b, January/February). Newborn knowledge. *Science 82,* pp. 58–65.

Restle, F. (1975). *Learning: Animal behavior and human cognition.* New York: McGraw-Hill.

Revusky, S., & Garcia, J. (1970). Learned associations over long delays. In G. H. Bower (Ed.), *The psychology of learning and motivation: Advances in research and theory* (Vol. 4, pp. 1–84). New York: Academic Press.

Reynolds, A. G., & Flagg, P. W. (1983). *Cognitive psychology* (2nd ed.). Boston: Little, Brown.

Richards, W. (1971, May). The fortification illusions of migraines. *Scientific American,* pp. 88–96.

Richman, D. P., Stewart, R. M., Hutchinson, J. W., & Caviness, V. S., Jr. (1975). Mechanical model of brain convolutional development. *Science, 189,* 18–21.

Richter, C. P. (1957). On the phenomenon of sudden death in animals and man. *Psychosomatic Medicine, 19,* 191–198.

Rieder, R. O. (1973). The offspring of schizophrenic parents: A review. *Journal of Nervous and Mental Disease, 157,* 179–190.

Riesen, A. H. (1950, July). Arrested vision. *Scientific American,* pp. 16–19.

Riggs, L. A. (1976). Human vision: Some objective explorations. *American Psychologist, 31,* 125–134.

Riley, D. A. (1962). Memory for form. In L. Postman (Ed.), *Psychology in the making: Histories of selected research problems* (pp. 402–465). New York: Alfred A. Knopf.

Rimland, B. (1969). Psychogenesis versus biogenesis: The issues and the evidence. In S. C. Plog & R. B. Edgerton (Eds.), *Changing perspectives in mental illness.* New York: Holt, Rinehart & Winston.

Rimland, B. (1979). Death knell for psychotherapy? *American Psychologist, 34,* 192.

Rimm, D. C., & Masters, J. C. (1979). *Behavior therapy: Techniques and empirical findings* (2nd ed.). New York: Academic Press.

Ritter, R. C., Slusser, P. G., & Stone, S. (1981). Glucoreceptors controlling feeding and blood glucose: Location in the hindbrain. *Science, 213,* 451–453.

Roazen, P. (1975). *Freud and his followers.* New York: Alfred A. Knopf.

Robinson, A. L. (1979). Communicating with computers by voice. *Science, 203,* 734–736.

Robinson, D. N. (1982). Cerebral plurality and the unity of self. *American Psychologist, 37,* 904–910.

Robinson, F. P. (1970). *Effective study* (4th ed.). New York: Harper & Row.

Rochester, S. R., Martin, J. R., & Thurston, S. (1977). Thought-process disorder in schizophrenia: The listener's task. *Brain and Language, 4,* 95–114.

Rock, I. (1974, January). The perception of disoriented figures. *Scientific American,* pp. 78–85.

Rock, I. (1975). *An introduction to perception.* New York: Macmillan.

Rock, I. (1981, March). Anorthoscopic perception. *Scientific American,* pp. 145–153.

Rock, I., & Harris, C. S. (1967, May). Vision and touch. *Scientific American,* pp. 96–104.

Rock, M. A. (1978, July). Gorilla mothers need some help from their friends. *Smithsonian,* pp. 58–63.

Rock, M. A. (1979, April). Keyboard symbols enable retarded children to "speak." *Smithsonian,* pp. 91–96.

Rodin, J. (1978, February). The puzzle of obesity. *Human Nature,* pp. 38–47.

Rodin, J. (1981). Current status of the internal-external hypothesis for obesity: What went wrong? *American Psychologist, 36,* 361–372.

Roediger, H. L. (1980). Memory metaphors in cognitive psychology. *Memory & Cognition, 8,* 231–246.

Roffwarg, H. P., Muzio, J. N., & Dement, W. C. (1966). Ontogenetic development of the human sleep-dream cycle. *Science, 152,* 604–619.

Rogers, C. R. (1951). *Client-centered therapy: Its current practice, implications and theory.* Boston: Houghton Mifflin.

Rogers, C. R. (1959). A theory of therapy, personality, and interpersonal relationships, as developed in the client-centered framework. In S. Koch (Ed.), *Psychology: A study of a science* (Vol. 3, pp. 184–256). New York: McGraw-Hill.

Rogers, C. R. (1961). *On becoming a person: A therapist's view of psychotherapy.* Boston: Houghton Mifflin.

Rogers, C. R. (1966). Client-centered therapy. In S. Arieti (Ed.), *American handbook of psychiatry* (Vol. 3, pp. 183–200). New York: Basic Books.

Rogers, C. R. (1970). *Carl Rogers on encounter groups.* New York: Harper & Row.

Rogers, C. R., Gendlin, G. T., Kiesler, D. V., & Truax, C. B. (1967). *The therapeutic relationship and its impact: A study of psychotherapy with schizophrenics.* Madison, WI: University of Wisconsin Press.

Rogers, L. (1981, October). A bear in its lair. *Natural History,* pp. 64–70.

Rolls, B. J., Wood, R. J., & Rolls, E. T. (1980). Thirst: The initiation, maintenance and termination of drinking. In J. M. Sprague & A. N. Epstein (Eds.), *Progress in psychobiology and physiological psychology* (Vol. 9). New York: Academic Press.

Roper, R. T. (1980). Jury size and verdict consistency: "A line has to be drawn somewhere?" *Law and Society Review, 14,* 987–995.

Rorschach, H. (1921). *Psychodiagnostik.* Bern: Bircher.

Rosch, E. H. (1973). Natural categories. *Cognitive Psychology, 4,* 328–350.

Rosch, E. H., & Mervis, C. B. (1975). Family resemblances: Studies in the internal structure of categories. *Cognitive Psychology, 7,* 573–605.

Rosch, E. H., Mervis, C. B., Gray, W. D., Johnson, D. M., & Boyes-Braem, P. (1976). Basic objects in natural categories. *Cognitive Psychology, 8,* 382–439.

Rose, R. (1982). Separated twins: Data and their limits. *Science, 215,* 959–960.

Rosenberg, M., & Kaplan, H. B. (1982). *Social psychology of the self-concept.* Arlington Heights, IL: Harlan Davidson.

Rosenberg, S., & Sedlak, A. (1972). Structural representations of implicit personality theory. In L. Berkowitz (Ed.), *Advances in experimental social psychology* (Vol. 6, pp. 235–297). New York: Academic Press.

Rosenfeld, A. (1981a, October). The adoptees union. *Science 81,* pp. 20–23.

Rosenfeld, A. (1981b, December). The heartbreak gene. *Science 81,* pp. 46–50.

Rosenhan, D. L. (1972). Learning theory and prosocial behavior. *Journal of Social Issues, 28,* 151–163.

Rosenhan, D. L. (1973). On being sane in insane places. *Science, 179,* 250–258.

Rosenthal, A. M. (1964). *Thirty-eight witnesses.* New York: McGraw-Hill.

Rosenthal, D. (1970). *Genetic theory and abnormal behavior.* New York: McGraw-Hill.

Rosenthal, D., Wender, P. H., Kety, S. S., Welner, J., & Schulsinger, F. (1971). The adopted-away offspring of schizophrenics. *American Journal of Psychiatry, 128,* 307–311.

Rosenwein, R. E. (1983). Affliction in the workplace. *Science, 220,* 838–841.

Rosenzweig, M. R. (1961, October). Auditory localization. *Scientific American,* pp. 132–142.

Rosenzweig, M. R., & Bennett, E. L. (Eds.). (1976). *Neural mechanisms of learning and memory.* Cambridge, MA: MIT Press.

Rosenzweig, M. R., & Leiman, A. L. (1982). *Physiological psychology.* Lexington, MA: D. C. Heath.

Ross, J. (1976, March). The resources of binocular perception. *Scientific American,* pp. 80–86.

Ross, L. (1977). The intuitive psychologist and his shortcomings: Distortions in the attribution process. In L. Berkowitz (Ed.), *Advances in experimental social psychology* (Vol. 10, pp. 173–220). New York: Academic Press.

Ross, L., Greene, D., & House, P. (1977). The false consensus effect: An egocentric bias in social perception and attribution processes. *Journal of Experimental Social Psychology, 13,* 279–301.

Roth, E. F., Jr., Friedman, M., Ueda, Y., Tellez, I., Trager, W., & Nagel, R. L. (1978). Sickling rates of human AS red cells infected in vitro with *Plasmodium falciparum* malaria. *Science, 202,* 650–652.

Routtenberg, A. (1978, November). The reward system of the brain. *Scientific American,* pp. 154–164.

Rubin, Z. (1973). *Liking and loving: An invitation to social psychology.* New York: Holt, Rinehart & Winston.

Rubin, Z. (1974). Lovers and other strangers: The development of intimacy in encounters and relationships. *American Scientist, 62,* 182–190.

Ruch, J. C. (1978). A study of self-hypnosis, with implications for other self-control procedures. In F. H. Frankel & H. S. Zamansky (Eds.), *Hypnosis at its bicentennial: Selected papers* (pp. 131–144). New York: Plenum Press.

Rumbaugh, D. M. (Ed.). (1977). *Language learning by a chimpanzee: The LANA project.* New York: Academic Press.

Rumbaugh, D. M., Gill, T. V., & von Glasersfeld, E. C. (1973). Reading and sentence completion by a chimpanzee (pan). *Science, 182,* 731–733.

Rundus, D. (1971). Analysis of rehearsal processes in free recall. *Journal of Experimental Psychology, 89,* 63–77.

Rusak, B., & Groos, G. (1982). Suprachiasmatic stimulation phase shifts rodent circadian rhythms. *Science, 215,* 1407–1409.

Rush, A. J., Beck, A. T., Kovacs, M., & Hollon, S. D. (1977). Comparative efficacy of cognitive therapy and pharmacotherapy in the treatment of depressed outpatients. *Cognition Therapy and Research, 1,* 17–39.

Rushton, J. P. (1975). Generosity in children: Immediate and long-term effects of modeling, preaching and moral judgment. *Journal of Personality and Social Psychology, 31,* 459–466.

Rushton, J. P. (1980). *Altruism, socialization and society.* Englewood Cliffs, NJ: Prentice-Hall.

Rushton, J. P. (1981). The altruistic personality. In J. P. Rushton & R. M. Sorrentino (Eds.), *Altruism and helping behavior: Social, personality, and developmental perspectives* (pp. 251–266). Hillsdale, NJ: Lawrence Erlbaum.

Rushton, J. P., & Sorrentino, R. M. (Eds.). (1981). *Altruism and helping behavior: Social, personality, and developmental perspectives.* Hillsdale, NJ: Lawrence Erlbaum.

Rushton, W. A. H. (1962, November). Visual pigments in man. *Scientific American,* pp. 120–132.

Rushton, W. A. H. (1975, March). Visual pigments and color blindness. *Scientific American,* pp. 64–74.

Russell, D., Peplau, L. A., & Cutrona, C. E. (1980). The revised UCLA Loneliness Scale: Concurrent and discriminant validity evidence. *Journal of Personality and Social Psychology, 39,* 472–480.

Russell M. J. (1976, April 8). Human olfactory communiction. *Nature,* pp. 520–522.

Russett, C. E. (1976). *Darwin in America: The intellectual response, 1865–1912.* San Francisco: W. H. Freeman.

Saarinen, T. F. (1973). The use of projective techniques in geographic research. In W. H. Ittelson (Ed.), *Environment and cognition.* New York: Seminar Press.

Sackeim, H. A., Gur, R. C., & Saucy, M. C. (1978). Emotions are expressed more intensely on the left side of the face. *Science, 202,* 434–436.

Sagan, C. (1974). *Broca's brain: Reflections on the romance of science.* New York: Random House.

Sakitt, B., & Long, G. M. (1979). Spare the rod and spoil the icon. *Journal of Experimental Psychology: Human Perception and Performance, 5,* 19–30.

Saks, M. (1976a). The limits of scientific jury selection: Ethical and empirical. *Jurimetrics Journal, 17,* 3–22.

Saks, M. J. (1976b, January). Scientific jury selection. *Psychology Today,* pp. 48–57.

Saks, M. J. (1977). *Jury verdicts: The role of group size and social decision rule.* Lexington, MA: D. C. Heath.

Saks, M. J. (1982). Innovation and change in the courtroom. In N. L. Kerr and R. M. Bray (Eds.), *The psychology of the courtroom* (pp. 325–383). New York: Academic Press.

Salaman, E. (1970). *A collection of moments: A study of involuntary memories.* London: Longman.

Samples, R. E. (1975, February). Learning with the whole brain. *Human Behavior,* pp. 16–23.

A sampling of a ghetto reader. (1972, August 7). *Time,* p. 46.

Sands, S. F., & Wright, A. A. (1980). Primate memory: Retention of serial list items by a rhesus monkey. *Science, 209,* 938–940.

Sanford, E. C. (1917, 1982). Professor Sanford's morning prayer. In U. Neisser (Ed.), *Memory observed: Remembering in natural contexts* (pp. 176–177). San Francisco: W. H. Freeman.

Sarason, I. G., & Smith, R. E. (1971). Personality. *Annual Review of Psychology, 22,* 393–446.

Sarbin, T. R. (1962). Attempts to understand hypnotic phenomena. In L. Postman (Ed.), *Psychology in the making: Histories of selected research problems* (pp. 745–785). New York: Alfred A. Knopf.

Sartorius, N., Shapiro, R., & Jablonsky, A. (1974). The international pilot study of schizophrenia. *Schizophrenia Bulletin, 2,* 21–35.

Satinoff, E. (1978). Neural organization and evolution of thermal regulation in mammals. *Science, 201,* 16–22.

Sattler, J. M. (1982). *Assessment of children's intelligence and special abilities.* Boston: Allyn & Bacon.

Savage-Rumbaugh, E. S., Rumbaugh, D. M., & Boysen, S. (1978). Symbolic communication between two chimpanzees (*Pan troglodytes*). *Science, 201,* 641–644.

Savage-Rumbaugh, E. S., Rumbaugh, D. M., & Boysen, S. (1980a). Do apes use language? *American Scientist, 68,* 49–61.

Savage-Rumbaugh, E. S., Rumbaugh, D. M., Smith, S. T., & Lawson, J. (1980b). Reference: The linguistic essential. *Science, 210,* 922–925.

Scarr, S. (1981a). *Race, social class, and individual differences in IQ.* Hillsdale, NJ: Lawrence Erlbaum.

Scarr, S. (1981b). Testing for children: Assessment and the many determinants of intellectual competence. *American Psychologist, 36,* 1159–1166.

Scarr, S., & Weinberg, R. A. (1978, April). Attitudes, interests and IQ. *Human Nature,* pp. 29–36.

Schacht, T., & Nathan, P. E. (1977). But is it good for psychologists? Appraisal and status of DSM-III. *American Psychologist, 32,* 1017–1025.

Schachter, D. L. (1976). The hypnogogic state: A critical review of the literature. *Psychological Bulletin, 83,* 452–481.

Schachter, S. (1971). Some extraordinary facts about obese humans and rats. *American Psychologist, 26,* 129–144.

Schachter, S. (1979). The interaction of cognitive and physiological determinants of emotional states. In L. Berkowitz (Ed.), *Advances in experimental social psychology* (Vol. 12, pp. 49–80). New York: Academic Press.

Schachter, S. (1982). Recidivism and self-cure of smoking and obesity. *American Psychologist, 37,* 436–444.

Schachter, S., & Latané, B. (1964). Crime, cognition, and the autonomic nervous system. In D. Levine (Ed.), *Nebraska Symposium on Motivation* (Vol. 12, pp. 221–273). Lincoln, NE: University of Nebraska Press.

Schachter, S., & Singer, J. E. (1962). Cognitive, social, and physiological determinants of emotional state. *Psychological Review, 69,* 379–399.

Schaie, K. W., & Strother, C. R. (1968). A cross-sequential study of age changes in cognitive behavior. *Psychological Bulletin, 70,* 671–680.

Schank, R., & Abelson, R. (1977). *Scripts, plans, goals, and understanding.* Hillsdale, NJ: Lawrence Erlbaum.

Scheerer, M. (1963, April). Problem-solving. *Scientific American,* pp. 118–128.

Schiefelbusch, R. L. (Ed.). (1980). *Nonspeech language and communication: Analysis and intervention.* Baltimore, MD: University Park Press.

Schildkraut, J. J. (1965). The catecholamine hypothesis of affective disorders. *American Journal of Psychiatry, 122,* 509–522.

Schmandt-Besserat, D. (1978, June). The earliest precursor of writing. *Scientific American,* pp. 50–59.

Schmauk, F. J. (1970). Punishment, arousal, and avoidance learning in sociopaths. *Journal of Abnormal Psychology, 76,* 443–453.

Schmidt-Nielsen, K. (1981, May). Counter-current systems in animals. *Scientific American,* pp. 118–128.

Schmitt, F. O., Dev, P., & Smith, B. H. (1976). Electrotonic processing of information by brain cells. *Science, 193,* 114–120.

Schmitt, F. O., Worden, F. G., Adelman, G., & Dennis, S. G. (Eds.). (1981). *The organization of the cerebral cortex: Proceedings of a colloquium.* Cambridge, MA: MIT Press.

Schmitt, R. C. (1966). Density, health and social disorganization. *American Institute of Planners Journal, 32,* 38–40.

Schneider, D. (1974, July). The sex-attractant receptor of moths. *Scientific American,* pp. 28–35.

Schneider, D. J. (1973). Implicit personality theory. *Psychological Bulletin, 79,* 294–309.

Schneider, D. J., Hastorf, A. H., & Ellsworth, P. C. (1979). *Person perception* (2nd ed.). Reading, MA: Addison-Wesley.

Schneider, S. F. (1981). Where have all the students gone?: Positions of psychologists trained in clinical/services programs. *American Psychologist, 36,* 1427–1449.

Schoenfeld, A. H. (1979). Explicit heuristic training as a variable in problem-solving performances. *Journal for Research in Mathematics Education, 10,* 173–187.

Schoolman, H. M., & Bernstein, L. M. (1978). Computer use in diagnosis, prognosis, and therapy. *Science, 200,* 926–931.

Schultes, R. E. (1973, August/September). Man and marijuana. *Natural History,* pp. 59–82.

Schultz, D. P. (Ed.). (1970). *The science of psychology: Critical reflections.* New York: Appleton-Century-Crofts.

Schultz, D. (1981). *A history of modern psychology* (3rd ed.). New York: Academic Press.

Schuman, H., & Johnson, M. P. (1976). Attitudes and behavior. *Annual Review of Sociology, 2,* 161–207.

Schwartz, A. (1982). *The behavior therapies: Theories and applications.* New York: Free Press.

Schwartz, B. (1978). *Psychology of learning and behavior.* New York: W. W. Norton.

Schwartz, B., & Lacey, H. (1982). *Behaviorism, science, and human nature.* New York: W. W. Norton.

Schwartz, G. E. (1975). Biofeedback, self-regulation, and the patterning of physiological processes. *American Scientist, 63,* 314–324.

Schwartz, G. E., Fair, P. L., Salt, P., Mandel, M. R., & Klerman, G. L. (1976). Facial muscle patterning to affective imagery in depressed and nondepressed subjects. *Science, 192,* 489–491.

Schwartz, J. H. (1980, April). The transport of substances in nerve cells. *Scientific American,* pp. 152–171.

Schwartz, R. A. (1978, Fall). Sleight of tongue. *Skeptical Inquirer, 3,* 47–55.

Schwartz, S. H. (1971). Modes of representation and problem solving: Well evolved is half solved. *Journal of Experimental Psychology, 91,* 347–350.

Schwartz, S. H. (1977). Normative influences in altruism. In L. Berkowitz (Ed.), *Advances in experimental social psychology* (Vol. 10, pp. 221–279). New York: Academic Press.

Schwartz, S. H., & Clausen, G. T. (1970). Responsibility, norms, and helping in an emergency. *Journal of Personality and Social Psychology, 16,* 299–310.

Schwartz, S. H., & Howard, J. A. (1981). A normative decision-making model of altruism. In J. P. Rushton & R. M. Sorrentino (Eds.), *Altruism and helping behavior: Social, personality, and developmental perspectives* (pp. 189–212). Hillsdale, NJ: Lawrence Erlbaum.

Schwitzgebel, R. L., & Schwitzgebel, R. K. (1980). *Law and psychological practice.* New York: John Wiley.

Scoville, W. B., & Milner, B. (1957). Loss of recent memory after bilateral hippocampal lesions. *Journal of Neurology, Neurosurgery, and Psychiatry, 20,* 11–19.

Scriver, C. R., Laberge, C., Clow, C. L., & Fraser, F. C. (1978). Genetics and medicine: An evolving relationship. *Science, 200,* 946–952.

Seagoe, M. V. (1975). *Terman and the gifted.* Los Altos, CA: William Kaufmann.

Seaman, B., & Seaman, G. (1977). *Women and the crisis in sex hormones.* New York: Rawson Associates.

Seamon, J. G., & Gazzaniga, M. S. (1973). Coding strategies and cerebral laterality effects. *Cognitive Psychology, 5,* 249–256.

Searcy, W. A., & Yasukawa, K. (1983). Sexual selection and red-winged blackbirds. *American Scientist, 71,* 166–174.

Sears, P. S., & Barbee, A. H. (1977). Career and life satisfactions among Terman's gifted women. In J. C. Stanley, W. C. George, & C. H. Solano (Eds.), *The gifted and the creative: A fifty-year perspective* (pp. 28–65). Baltimore, MD: Johns Hopkins University Press.

Sears, R. R. (1977). Sources of life satisfaction in gifted men. *American Psychologist, 32,* 119–128.

Sears, R. R. (1979). Obituary: Maud Merrill James (1888–1978). *American Psychologist, 34,* 176.

Sebeok, T. A. (Ed.). (1977). *How animals communicate.* Bloomington, IN: Indiana University Press.

Segal, M. W. (1974). Alphabet and attraction: An unobtrusive measure of the effect of propinquity in a field setting. *Journal of Personality and Social Psychology, 30,* 654–657.

Segal, S. J., & Fusella, V. (1970). Influence of imaged pictures and sounds on detection of visual and auditory signals. *Journal of Experimental Psychology, 83,* 458–464.

Seidenberg, M. (1980, March). Signing apes: What evidence? [Letter to the editor]. *APA Monitor,* p. 3.

Sekuler, R., & Ball, K. (1977). Mental set alters visibility of moving targets. *Science, 198,* 60–62.

Sekuler, R., Hutman, L. P., & Owsley, C. J. (1980). Human aging and spatial vision. *Science, 209,* 1255–1256.

Sekuler, R., & Levinson, E. (1977, January). The perception of moving targets. *Scientific American,* pp. 60–73.

Selfridge, O. G. (1955). Pattern recognition and modern computers. *Proceedings of Western Joint Computer Conference, 1955.* New York: Institute of Electrical and Electronics Engineers.

Selfridge, O. G. (1959). Pandemonium: A paradigm for learning. In *Mechanisation of thought processes* (Vol. 1, 511–526). London: Her Majesty's Stationery Office.

Seligman, M. E. P. (1970). On the generality of the law of learning. *Psychological Review, 77,* 406–418.

Seligman, M. E. P. (1975). *Helplessness: On depression, development, and death.* San Francisco: W. H. Freeman.

Seligman, M. E. P., Abramson, L. V., Semmel, A., & Von Baeyer, C. (1979). Depressive attributional style. *Journal of Abnormal Psychology, 88,* 242–247.

Seligman, M. E. P., & Hagen, J. L. (Eds.). (1972). *Biological boundaries of learning.* New York: Appleton-Century-Crofts.

Selye, H. (1974). *Stress without distress.* Philadelphia: J. B. Lippincott.

Selye, H. (1976). *The stress of life* (rev. ed.). New York: McGraw-Hill.

Senden, M. V. (1960). *Space and sight.* New York: Free Press.

Shaffer, D. R., Rogel, M., & Hendrick, C. (1975). Intervention in the library: The effect of increased responsibility on bystanders' willingness to prevent theft. *Journal of Applied Social Psychology, 5,* 303–319.

Shaffer, L. S. (1977). The golden fleece: Anti-intellectualism and social science. *American Psychologist, 32,* 814–823.

Shah, D., & Morris, H. (1978, December 4). Peewee football. *Newsweek,* pp. 129–131.

Shah, S. A. (1978). Dangerousness: A paradigm for exploring some issues in law and psychology. *American Psychologist, 33,* 224–238.

Shakow, D., & Rapaport, D. (1964). *The influence of Freud on American psychology.* New York: International Universities Press.

Shapiro, C. M., Bortz, R., Mitchell, D., Bartel, P., & Jooste, P. (1981). Slow-wave sleep: A recovery period after exercise. *Science, 214,* 1253–1254.

Shapiro, D. H., Jr., & Zifferblatt, S. M. (1976). Zen meditation and behavioral self-control: Similarities, differences, and clinical applications. *American Psychologist, 31,* 519–532.

Shashoua, V. E. (1973). Seasonal changes in the learning and activity patterns of goldfish. *Science, 181,* 572–574.

Shashoua, V. E. (1974). Seasonal changes in goldfish learning? *Science, 183,* 1321.

Sheldon, W. H., & Stevens, S. J. (1942). *The varieties of temperament: A psychology of constitutional differences.* New York: Harper & Row.

Shen, B. S. P. (1975). Science literacy. *American Scientist, 63,* 265–268.

Shepard, R. N. (1967). Recognition memory for words, sentences, and pictures. *Journal of Verbal Learning and Verbal Behavior, 6,* 156–163.

Shepard, R. N. (1978a). Externalization of mental images and the act of creation. In B. S. Randhawa & W. E. Coffman (Eds.), *Visual learning, thinking, and communication.* New York: Academic Press.

Shepard, R. N. (1978b). The mental image. *American Psychologist, 33,* 125–137.

Shepard, R. N. (1983, June). The kaleidoscopic brain. *Psychology Today,* pp. 62–68.

Shepard, R. N., & Chipman, S. (1970). Second-order isomorphism of internal representations: Shapes of states. *Cognitive Psychology, 1,* 1–17.

Shepard, R. N., & Metzler, J. (1971). Mental rotation of three dimensional objects. *Science, 171,* 701–703.

Shepard, W. (1976). Valued behaviors. *Science, 192,* 669–670.

Sherif, M. (1935). A study of some social factors in perception. *Archives of Psychology, 27*(No. 87).

Sherif, M. (1936). *The psychology of social norms.* New York: Harper.

Sherrod, D. R. (1974). Crowding, perceived control, and behavioral after-effects. *Journal of Applied Social Psychology, 4,* 171–186.

Shettleworth, S. J. (1972). Constraints on learning. In D. S. Lehrman, R. A. Hinde, & E. Shaw (Eds.), *Advances in the study of behavior* (Vol. 4, pp. 1–68). New York: Academic Press.

Shevrin, H., & Dickman, S. (1980). The psychological unconscious: A necessary assumption for all psychological theory? *American Psychologist, 35,* 421–434.

Shiffrin, R. M. (1976). Capacity limitations in information processing, attention, and memory. In W. K. Estes (Ed.), *Handbook of learning and cognitive processes: Vol. 4. Attention and memory* (pp. 177–236). Hillsdale, NJ: Lawrence Erlbaum.

Shimberg, M. E. (1929). An investigation into the validity of norms with special reference to urban and rural groups. *Archives of Psychology,* No. 104.

Shipman, P. (1979, November–December). What are all these bones *doing* here? *Harvard Magazine,* pp. 42–46.

Shontz, F. C. (1977). Constitutional theories of personality. In R. Corsini (Ed.), *Current personality theories.* Itasca, IL: F. E. Peacock.

Shorey, H. H. (1976). *Animal communication by pheromones.* New York: Academic Press.

Shostak, M. (1978, June). Memories of a !Kung girlhood. *Human Nature,* pp. 80–88.

Shulman, H. G. (1972). Semantic confusion errors in short-term memory. *Journal of Verbal Learning and Verbal Behavior, 11,* 221–227.

Shulman, R. G. (1983, January). NMR spectroscopy of living cells. *Scientific American,* pp. 86–93.

Shutts, D. (1982). *Lobotomy: Resort to the knife.* New York: Van Nostrand Reinhold.

Sidtis, J. J., Volpe, B. T., Holtzman, J. D., Wilson, D. H., & Gazzaniga, M. S. (1981). Cognitive interaction after staged callosal section: Evidence for transfer of semantic activation. *Science, 212,* 344–346.

Siegel, R. K. (1977, October). Hallucinations. *Scientific American,* pp. 132–140.

Siegel, R. K., & West, L. J. (1975). *Hallucinations: Behavior, experience, and theory.* New York: John Wiley.

Siegel, S. (1972). Conditioning of insulin-induced glycemia. *Journal of Comparative and Physiological Psychology, 78,* 233–241.

Siegel, S. (1977). Morphine tolerance acquisition as an associative process. *Journal of Experimental Psychology: Animal Behavior Processes, 3,* 1–13.

Siegel, S., Hinson, R. E., & Krank, M. D. (1978). The role of predrug signals in morphine analgesic tolerance: Support for a Pavlovian conditioning model of tolerance. *Journal of Experimental Psychology: Animal Behavior Processes, 4,* 188–196.

Silverman, L. H. (1976). Psychoanalytic theory: The reports of my death are greatly exaggerated. *American Psychologist, 31,* 621–637.

Simmons, J. A., Fenton, M. B., & O'Farrell, M. J. (1979). Echolocation and pursuit of prey by bats. *Science, 203,* 16–21.

Simon, H. A. (1974). How big is a chunk? *Science, 183,* 482–488.

Simon, H. A. (1980). The behavioral and social sciences. *Science, 209,* 72–78.

Simon, H. A. (1981a). *The sciences of the artificial* (2nd ed.). Cambridge, MA: MIT Press.

Simon, H. A. (1981b). Studying human intelligence by creating artificial intelligence. *American Scientist, 69,* 300–309.

Simon, H. A., & Hayes, J. R. (1976). Understanding complex task instructions. In D. Klahr (Ed.), *Cognition and instruction* (pp. 269–285). Hillsdale, NJ: Lawrence Erlbaum.

Simon, H. A., & Newell, A. (1971). Human problem solving: The state of the theory in 1970. *American Psychologist, 26,* 145–159.

Simpson, L. L. (1980, January). Deadly botulism. *Natural History,* pp. 12–24.

Singer, J. L. (1981). Clinical intervention: New developments in methods and evaluation. In L. T. Benjamin, Jr. (Ed.), *The G. Stanley Hall lecture series* (Vol. 1, pp. 101–128). Washington, DC: American Psychological Association.

Singer, P. (1977). *Animal liberation.* New York: Avon Books.

Siple, P. (Ed.). (1978). *Understanding language through sign language research.* New York: Academic Press.

Sizemore, C. C., & Pittillo, E. S. (1977). *I'm Eve.* New York: Doubleday.

Skinner, B. F. (1938). *The behavior of organisms: An experimental analysis.* New York: Appleton-Century-Crofts.

Skinner, B. F. (1945, 1972). Baby in a box. In B. F. Skinner (Ed.), *Cumulative record: A selection of papers* (3rd ed., pp. 567–573). Englewood Cliffs, NJ: Prentice-Hall.

Skinner, B. F. (1948). "Superstition" in the pigeon. *Journal of Experimental Psychology, 38,* 168–172.

Skinner, B. F. (1953, 1965). *Science and human behavior.* New York: Macmillan.

Skinner, B. F. (1954). A critique of psychoanalytic concepts and theories. *Scientific Monthly, 79,* 300–305.

Skinner, B. F. (1957, 1968). *Verbal behavior.* Englewood Cliffs, NJ: Prentice-Hall.

Skinner, B. F. (1960). Pigeons in a pelican. *American Psychologist, 15,* 28–37.

Skinner, B. F. (1962). Two "synthetic social relations." *Journal of the Experimental Analysis of Behavior, 5,* 531–533.

Skinner, B. F. (1963). Behaviorism at 50. *Science, 140,* 951–958.

Skinner, B. F. (1968). *The technology of teaching.* Englewood Cliffs, NJ: Prentice-Hall.

Skinner, B. F. (1971). *Beyond freedom and dignity.* New York: Alfred A. Knopf.

Skinner, B. F. (Ed.). (1972). *Cumulative record: A selection of papers* (3rd ed.). Englewood Cliffs, NJ: Prentice-Hall.

Skinner, B. F. (1974). *About behaviorism.* New York: Random House.

Skinner, B. F. (1975). The steep and thorny way to a science of behavior. *American Psychologist, 30,* 42–49.

Skinner, B. F. (1976a, January–February). The ethics of helping people. *The Humanist.*

Skinner, B. F. (1976b). *Particulars of my life.* New York: Alfred A. Knopf.

Skinner, B. F. (1977). Herrnstein and the evolution of behaviorism. *American Psychologist, 32,* 1006–1012.

Skinner, B. F. (1978). *Reflections on behaviorism and society.* Englewood Cliffs, NJ: Prentice-Hall.

Skinner, B. F. (1979). *The shaping of a behaviorist.* New York: Alfred A. Knopf.

Skinner, B. F. (1981). Selection by consequences. *Science, 213,* 501–504.

Slater, E., & Glithero, E. (1965). A follow-up of patients diagnosed as suffering from hysteria. *Journal of Psychosomatic Research, 9,* 9–13.

Sloane, R. B., Staples, F. R., Cristol, A. H., Yorkston, N. J., & Whipple, K. (1975). *Psychoanalysis versus behavior therapy.* Cambridge, MA: Harvard University Press.

Slobin, D. I. (1970). Universals of grammatical development in children. In G. B. Flores d'Arcais & W. J. M. Levelt (Eds.), *Advances in psycholinguistics* (pp. 174–186). Amsterdam: North-Holland.

Smith, B. D., & Vetter, H. J. (1982). *Theoretical approaches to personality.* Englewood Cliffs, NJ: Prentice-Hall.

Smith, D. (1981). Unfinished business with informed consent procedures. *American Psychologist, 36,* 22–26.

Smith, D. (1982). Trends in counseling and psychotherapy. *American Psychologist, 37,* 802–809.

Smith, M. L., & Glass, G. V. (1977). Meta-analysis of psychotherapy outcome studies. *American Psychologist, 32,* 752–760.

Smith, R. J. (1978a). Congress considers bill to control angel dust. *Science, 200,* 1463–1466.

Smith, R. J. (1978b). The criminal insanity defense is placed on trial in New York. *Science, 199,* 1048–1052.

Smith, R. J. (1979a). Study finds sleeping pills overprescribed. *Science, 204,* 287–288.

Smith, R. J. (1979b). Truth-in-testing attracts diverse support. *Science, 205,* 1110–1114.

Smith, S. M. (1979). Remembering in and out of context. *Journal of Experimental Psychology: Human Learning and Meaning, 5,* 460–471.

Snyder, F., & Scott, J. (1972). The psychophysiology of sleep. In N. S. Greenfield & R. A. Sternbach (Eds.), *Handbook of psychophysiology* (pp. 645–708). New York: Holt, Rinehart & Winston.

Snyder, M. (1974). The self-monitoring of expressive behavior. *Journal of Personality and Social Psychology, 30,* 526–537.

Snyder, M. (1979). Self-monitoring processes. In L. Berkowitz (Ed.), *Advances in experimental social psychology* (Vol. 12, pp. 85–128). New York: Academic Press.

Synder, M., Tanke, E. D., & Berscheid, E. (1977). Social perception and interpersonal behavior: On the self-fulfilling nature of social stereotypes. *Journal of Personality and Social Psychology, 35,* 656–666.

Snyder, S. H. (1977, March). Opiate receptors and internal opiates. *Scientific American,* pp. 44–56.

Snyder, S. H. (1978). Dopamine and schizophrenia. In L. C. Wynne, R. L. Cromwell, & S. Matthysse (Eds.), *The nature of schizophrenia: New approaches to research and treatment.* New York: John Wiley.

Snyder, S. H. (1980a). *Biological aspects of mental disorder.* New York: Oxford University Press.

Snyder, S. H. (1980b). Brain peptides as neurotransmitters. *Science, 209,* 976–983.

Sokal, R. R. (1977). Classification: Purposes, principles, progress, prospects. In P. N. Johnson-Laird & P. C. Wason (Eds.), *Thinking: Readings in cognitive science* (pp. 185–198). Cambridge: Cambridge University Press.

Solano, C. H., Batten, P. G., & Parish, E. A. (1982). Loneliness and patterns of self-disclosure. *Journal of Personality and Social Psychology, 43,* 524–531.

Soldatos, C. R., Kales, J. D., Scharf, M. B., Bixler, E. O., & Kales, A. (1980). Cigarette smoking associated with sleep difficulty. *Science, 207,* 551–553.

Solomon, P. R. (1980, February). Perception, illusion, and magic. *Teaching of Psychology, 7,* 3–8.

Solomon, R. L. (1980). The opponent-process theory of acquired motivation: The costs of pleasure and the benefits of pain. *American Psychologist, 35,* 691–712.

Solomon, R. L., & Corbit, J. D. (1974). An opponent-process theory of motivation. I. Temporal dynamics of affect. *Psychological Review, 81,* 119–145.

Solso, R. L. (1979). Twenty-five years of recommended readings in psychology. *American Psychologist, 34,* 703–705.

Sommer, R., (1969). *Personal space: The behavioral basis of design.* Englewood Cliffs, NJ: Prentice-Hall.

Sommer, R. (1979). *The mind's eye: Imagery in everyday life*. New York: Delacorte.

Sommer, R. & Ross, H. (1958). Social interaction in a geriatric ward. *International Journal of Social Psychiatry, 4*, 128–133.

Spear, N. E. (1979). Experimental analysis of infantile amnesia. In J. F. Kihlstrom & F. J. Evans (Eds.), *Functional disorders of memory*. Hillsdale, NJ: Lawrence Erlbaum.

Spearman, C. (1927). *The abilities of man*. London: Macmillan.

Spence, J. T., & Helmreich, R. L. (1981). Androgyny versus gender schema: A comment on Bem's gender schema theory. *Psychological Review, 88*, 365–368.

Spence, J. T., Helmreich, R., & Stapp, J. (1975). Ratings of self and peers on sex role attributes and their relation to self-esteem and conceptions of masculinity and femininity. *Journal of Personality and Social Psychology, 32*, 29–39.

Spender, S. (1970). The making of a poem. In P. E. Vernon (Ed.), *Creativity* (pp. 61–76). Middlesex: Penguin. (Original work published 1946)

Sperling, G., & Speelman, R. G. (1970). Acoustic similarity and auditory short-term memory: Experiments and a model. In D. A. Norman (Ed.), *Models of human memory* (pp. 151–202). New York: Academic Press.

Sperry, R. W. (1956, May). The eye and the brain. *Scientific American*, pp. 48–52.

Sperry, R. W. (1964, January). The great cerebral commissure. *Scientific American*, pp. 42–62.

Sperry, R. W. (1968). Hemisphere deconnection and unity in conscious experience. *American Psychologist, 23*, 723–733.

Sperry, R. (1982). Some effects of disconnecting the cerebral hemispheres. *Science, 217*, 1223–1226.

Spitzer, R. L., Forman, J. B. W., & Nee, J. (1979). DSM-III field trials: I. Initial interrater diagnostic reliability. *American Journal of Psychiatry, 136*, 815–817.

Sprafkin, J. M., Liebert, R. M., & Poulos, R. W. (1975). Effects of a prosocial example on children's helping. *Journal of Experimental Child Psychology, 20*, 119–126.

Springer, S. P., & Deutsch, G. (1981). *Left brain right brain*. San Francisco: W. H. Freeman.

Squire, L. R., & Slater, P. C. (1978). Bilateral and unilateral ECT: Effects on verbal and nonverbal memory. *American Journal of Psychiatry, 135*, 1316–1320.

Squire, L. R., Slater, P. C., & Chase, P. M. (1975). Retrograde amnesia: Temporal gradient in very long-term memory following electroconvulsive therapy. *Science, 187*, 77–79.

Sroufe, L. A. (1979). The coherence of individual development: Early care, attachment, and subsequent developmental issues. *American Psychologist, 34*, 834–841.

Staats, A. W., & Staats, C. K. (1958). Attitudes established by classical conditioning. *Journal of Abnormal Social Psychology, 57*, 37–40.

Staats, A. W., Staats, C. K., & Crawford, H. L. (1962). First-order conditioning of meaning and the parallel conditioning of a GSR. *Journal of General Psychology, 67*, 159–167.

Staddon, J. E. R., & Simmelhag, V. L. (1971). The "superstition" experiment: A re-examination of its implications for the principles of adaptive behavior. *Psychological Review, 78*, 3–43.

Stampfl, T. G., & Levis, D. J. (1973). *Implosive therapy: Theory and technique*. Morristown, NJ: General Learning Press.

Stanley, J. C. (1976a). The case for extreme educational acceleration of intellectually brilliant youths. *Gifted Child Quarterly, 20*, 66–75.

Stanley, J. C. (1976b). The study of the very bright. *Science, 192*, 668–669.

Stanley, J. C. (1976c). Test better finder of great math talent than teachers are. *American Psychologist, 31*, 313–314.

Stanley, J. C. (1979). The second d: Description of talent (further study of the intellectually talented youths). In N. Colangelo & R. T. Zaffrann (Eds.), *New voices in counseling the gifted*. Dubuque, IA: Kendall/Hunt.

Stanley, J. C. (1980). On educating the gifted. *Educational Researcher, 9*, 8–12.

Stannard, D. E. (1980). *Shrinking history: On Freud and the failure of psychohistory*. New York: Oxford University Press.

Stapp, J., Fulcher, R., Nelson, S. D., Pallak, M. S., & Wicherski, M. (1981). The employment of recent doctorate recipients in psychology 1975 through 1978. *American Psychologist, 36*, 1211–1254.

Stark, E. (1981a, September). Pigeon patrol. *Science 81*, pp. 85–86.

Stark, E. (1981b, November). 3-D comes back. *Science 81*, pp. 100–102.

Starr, R. H., Jr. (1979). Child abuse. *American Psychologist, 34*, 872–878.

Staub, E. (1978–1979). *Positive social behavior and morality* (2 vols.). New York: Academic Press.

Staub, E., & Sherk, L. (1970). Need for approval, children's sharing behavior, and reciprocity in sharing. *Child Development, 41*, 243–252.

Steiner, I. D. (1972). *Group process and productivity*. New York: Academic Press.

Stent, G. S., & Weisblat, D. A. (1982, January). The development of a simple nervous system. *Scientific American*, pp. 136–146.

Stern, D. B. (1977). Handedness and the lateral distribution of conversion reactions. *Journal of Nervous and Mental Disease, 164*, 122–128.

Stern, R. S., & Cobb, J. P. (1978). Phenomenology of obsessive-compulsive neurosis. *British Journal of Psychiatry, 132*, 233–234.

Sternberg, R. J. (1981a). A componential theory of intellectual giftedness. *Gifted Child Quarterly, 25*, 86–93.

Sternberg, R. J. (1981b). People's conceptions of intelligence. *Journal of Personality and Social Psychology, 41*, 37–55.

Sternberg, R. J. (1981c). Testing and cognitive psychology. *American Psychologist, 36*, 1181–1189.

Sternberg, S. (1975). Memory scanning: New findings and current controversies. *Quarterly Journal of Experimental Psychology, 27*, 1–32.

Stevens, C. F. (1979, September). The neuron. *Scientific American*, pp. 48–59.

Stevens, S. S., & Warshofsky, F. (1965). *Sound and hearing*. New York: Time-Life Books.

Stjärne, L., Hedqvist, P., Lagercrantz, H., & Wennmalm, Å. (Eds.). (1981). *Chemical neurotransmission. 75 years. Papers from a conference*. New York: Academic Press.

Stoddard, D. M. (Ed.). (1980). *Olfaction in mammals: Proceedings of a symposium, London, November 1978*. New York: Academic Press.

Stokols, D. (1972). On the distinction between density and crowding: Some implications for future research. *Psychological Review, 79*, 275–277.

Stokols, D. (Ed.). (1977). *Perspectives on environment and behavior*. New York: Plenum Press.

Stone, A. A., & Stone, S. S. (Eds.). (1966). *The abnormal personality through literature*. Englewood Cliffs, NJ: Prentice-Hall.

Strebeigh, F. (1982, April). Hot on the trail of the elusive *moots* and *woolies*. *Smithsonian*, pp. 101–108.

Streissguth, A. P., Landsman-Dwyers, S., Martin, J. C., & Smith, D. W. (1980). Teratogenic effects of alcohol in humans and laboratory animals. *Science, 209*, 353–361.

Stromeyer, C. F., III., & Psotka, J. (1970). The detailed texture of eidetic images. *Nature, 225*, 346–349.

Strong, E. K., Jr., & Campbell, D. P. (1966). *Manual for Strong Vocational Interest Blank*. Stanford, CA: Stanford University Press.

Stuart, R. B. (Ed.). (1977). *Behavioral self-management: Strategies, techniques and outcome*. New York: Bruner/Mazel.

Stunkard, A. J. (Ed.). (1980). *Obesity*. Philadelphia: W. B. Saunders.

Suedfeld, P. (1975). The benefits of boredom: Sensory deprivation reconsidered. *American Scientist, 63*, 60–69.

Suls, J. (Ed.). (1982). *Psychological perspectives on the self*. Hillsdale, NJ: Lawrence Erlbaum.

Sun, M. (1980). Panel asks "When is a person dead?" *Science, 209*, 669–670.

Surgeon General's Scientific Advisory Committee on Television and Social Behavior. (1982). *Television and growing up: The impact of television violence*. Washington, DC: U.S. Government Printing Office.

Syndulko, K. (1978). Electrocortical investigations of sociopathy. In R. D. Hare & D. Schalling (Eds.), *Psychopathic behaviour: Approaches to research* (pp. 145–156). New York: John Wiley.

Szasz, T. S. (1961). *The myth of mental illness*. New York: Harper & Row.

Szasz, T. S. (1963). *Law, liberty, and psychiatry*. New York: Macmillan.

Szasz, T. S. (1982). The psychiatric will. *American Psychologist, 37*, 762–770.

Szucko, J. J., & Kleinmuntz, B. (1981). Statistical versus clinical lie detection. *American Psychologist, 36*, 488–496.

Tajfel, H. (1982). Social psychology of intergroup relations. *Annual Review of Psychology, 33*, 1–39.

Takahashi, J. S., & Zatz, M. (1982). Regulation of circadian rhythmicity. *Science, 217*, 1104–1111.

Taking the chitling test. (1968, July 15). *Newsweek*, pp. 51–52, 72.

Talbot, R. E., & Humphrey, D. R. (Eds.). (1979). *Posture and movement*. New York: Raven.

Tanner, J. M. (1978). *Fetus into man: Physical growth from conception to maturity*. Cambridge, MA: Harvard University Press.

Tanner, J. M. & Taylor, G. R. (1965). *Growth*. New York: Time-Life Books.

Tarnopol, L., & Tarnopol, M. (Eds.). (1977). *Brain function and reading disabilities*. Baltimore, MD: University Park Press.

Tart, C. T. (Ed.). (1972). *Altered states of consciousness: A book of readings* (2nd ed.). New York: John Wiley.

Taussig, H. B. (1962, August). The thalidomide syndrome. *Scientific American*, pp. 29–35.

Taylor, I. A. (1975). A retrospective view of creativity investigation. In I. A. Taylor & J. W. Getzels (Eds.), *Perspectives in creativity* (pp. 1–36). Chicago: Aldine.

Taylor, J. A. (1953). A personality scale of manifest anxiety. *Journal of Abnormal and Social Psychology, 48*, 285–290.

Taylor, S. E. (1978). A developing role for social psychology in medicine and medical practice. *Personality and Social Psychology Bulletin, 4*, 515–523.

Taylor, S. E., & Crocker, J. (1981). Schematic bases of social information processing. In E. T. Higgins, C. P. Herman, & M. P. Zanna (Eds.), *Social cognition: The Ontario symposium* (Vol. 1, pp. 89–134). Hillsdale, NJ: Lawrence Erlbaum.

Taylor, S. E., & Fiske, S. T. (1978). Salience, attention, and attribution: Top of the head phenomena. In L. Berkowitz (Ed.), *Advances in experimental social psychology* (Vol. 11, pp. 249–288). New York: Academic Press.

Taylor, S. E., Fiske, S. T., Close, M., Anderson, C., & Ruderman, A. J. (1977). *Solo status as a psychological variable: The power of being distinctive*. Unpublished manuscript, Harvard University. [Cited in Hamilton, 1979]

Taylor, S. P., Vardaris, R. M., Rawtich, A. B., Gammon, C. B., Cranston, J. W., & Lubethin, A. I. (1976). The effects of alcohol and delta-9-tetrahydrocannabinol on human physical aggression. *Aggressive Behavior, 2*, 153–161.

Telford, C. W., & Sawrey, J. M. (1981). *The exceptional individual* (4th ed.). Englewood Cliffs, NJ: Prentice-Hall.

Teresi, D. (1978, November). The real bionic man. *Omni*, p. 44–49, 138–139.

Terman, L. M. (1916). *The measurement of intelligence*. Boston: Houghton Mifflin.

Terman, L. M. (1925). *Genetic studies of genius: I. Mental and physical traits of a thousand gifted children*. Stanford, CA: Stanford University Press.

Terman, L. M. (1932). Autobiography. In C. A. Murchison (Ed.), *A history of psychology in autobiography* (Vol. 2, pp. 297–331). Worcester, MA: Clark University Press.

Terman, L. M., & Merrill, M. A. (1953). Tests of intelligence. B. 1937 Stanford-Binet scales. In A. Weider (Ed.), *Contributions toward medical psychology: Theory and psychodiagnostic methods* (Vol. 2, pp. 510–521). New York: Ronald Press.

Ter-Pogossian, M. M., Raichle, M. E., & Sobel, B. E. (1980, October). Positron-emission tomography. *Scientific American*, pp. 171–181.

Terrace, H. S. (1973). Classical conditioning. In G. S. Reynolds, C. Catania, & B. Schard (Eds.), *Contemporary experimental psychology*. Chicago: Scott, Foresman.

Terrace, H. S. (1979). *Nim: A chimpanzee who learned sign language*. New York: Alfred A. Knopf.

Terrace, H. (1980). Signing apes: What evidence? [Letter to the editor]. *APA Monitor*, p. 3.

Terrace, H. S., Petitto, L. A., Sanders, R. J., & Bever, T. G. (1979). Can an ape create a sentence? *Science, 206*, 891–902.

Teuber, H. L., Battersby, W. S., & Bender, M. B. (1960). *Visual field defects after penetrating missile wounds of the brain*. Cambridge, MA: Harvard University Press.

Teuber, M. L. (1974, July). Sources of ambiguity in the prints of Maurits C. Escher. *Scientific American*, pp. 90–104.

Thacher, M. (1978, August). Flunking 20/20. *Human Behavior*, pp. 52–55.

Theodor, L. H., & Mendelcorn, M. S. (1973). Hysterical blindness: A case report and study using a modern psychophysical technique. *Journal of Abnormal Psychology, 82*, 552–553.

Thigpen, C. H., & Cleckley, H. M. (1954). *The three faces of Eve*. Kingsport, TN: Kingsport Press.

Thomas, A., Chess, S., & Birch, H. G. (1970, August). The origin of personality. *Scientific American*, pp. 102–109.

Thomas, H., Jamison, W., & Hummel, D. D. (1973). Observation is insufficient for discovery that the surface of still water is invariantly horizontal. *Science, 181*, 173–174.

Thompson, C. I. (1980). *Controls of eating*. Jamaica, NY: Spectrum.

Thompson, R. F. (1976). The search for the engram. *American Psychologist, 31*, 209–227.

Thompson, R. F., Hicks, L. H., & Shvyrok, V. B. (Eds.). (1980). *Neural mechanisms of goal-directed behavior and learning*. New York: Academic Press.

Thompson, T., & Grabowski, J. (Eds.). (1977). *Behavior modification of the mentally retarded* (2nd ed.). New York: Oxford University Press.

Thompson, W. R. (1968). Development and the biophysical bases of personality. In E. F. Borgatta & W. W. Lambert (Eds.), *Handbook of personality theory and research* (pp. 149–214). Chicago: Rand McNally.

Thoresen, C. E. (1972, April). Behavioral humanism. Stanford, CA: Stanford Center for Research and Development in Teaching.

Thorndike, E. L. (1898). Animal intelligence: An experimental study of the associative processes in animals. *Psychological Review, Monograph Supplement, 2* (No. 8).

Thorndike, E. L. (1911). *Animal intelligence: Experimental studies*. New York: Macmillan.

Thorndike, E. L. (1913). *Educational psychology: The psychology of learning* (Vol. 2). New York: Teachers College.

Thorndike, R. L. (1973). *Stanford-Binet intelligence scale, form L-M, 1972 norms tables*. Boston: Houghton Mifflin.

Thurstone, L. L. (1938). Primary mental abilities. *Psychometric Monographs* (No. 1).

Thurstone, L. L., & Chave, E. J. (1929). *The measurement of attitude*. Chicago: University of Chicago Press.

Thurstone, L. L., & Thurstone, T. G. (1963). *SRA primary abilities*. Chicago: Science Research Associates.

The thyroid gland and world health. (1981). *Science News, 119*, 215.

Timiras, P. S. (1978). Biological perspectives on aging. *American Scientist, 66*, 605–613.

Tinbergen, N. (1965). *Animal behavior*. New York: Time-Life Books.

Titchener, E. B. (1921). Wilhelm Wundt. *American Journal of Psychology, 32*, 161–178.

Tolman, E. C. (1932). *Purposive behavior in animals and men*. New York: Appleton-Century-Crofts.

Tolman, E. C. (1938). The determiners of behavior at a choice point. *Psychological Review, 45*, 1–41.

Tolman, E. C. (1959). Principles of purposive behavior. In S. Koch (Ed.), *Psychology: A study of a science* (Vol. 2, pp. 92–157). New York: McGraw-Hill.

Tolman, E. C., & Honzik, C. H. (1930a). "Insight" in rats. *University of California Publications in Psychology, 4*, 215–232.

Tolman, E. C., & Honzik, C. H. (1930b). Introduction and removal of reward, and maze performance in rats. *University of California Publications in Psychology, 4*, 257–275.

Tolman, E. C., Ritchie, B. F., & Kalish, D. (1946). Studies in spatial learning: I. Orientation and the short-cut. *Journal of Experimental Psychology, 36*, 13–24.

Torrance, E. P. (1966). *Torrance tests of creative thinking, verbal forms A and B.* Princeton, NJ: Personnel Press.

Torrance, E. P. (1971). Are the Torrance tests of creative thinking biased against or in favor of "disadvantaged groups"? *Gifted Child Quarterly, 15*, 75–80.

Tosteson, D. C. (1981, April). Lithium and mania. *Scientific American*, pp. 164–174.

Towe, A., & Luschei, E. (Eds.). (1981). *Handbook of behavioral neurobiology: Vol. 5. Motor coordination.* New York: Plenum Press.

Tresemer, D. (1976). The cumulative record of research on "fear of success." *Sex Roles, 2*, 217–236.

Trinkaus, E. (1978, December). Hard times among the Neanderthals. *Natural History*, pp. 58–63.

Trinkaus, E., & Howells, W. W. (1979, December). The Neanderthals. *Scientific American*, pp. 118–133.

Trudgill, P. (1974). *Sociolinguistics: An introduction.* Baltimore, MD: Penguin.

Tuddenham, R. D. (1966). Jean Piaget and the world of the child. *American Psychologist, 21*, 207–217.

Tuddenham, R. D. (1970). A "Piagetian" test of cognitive development. In W. B. Dockrell (Ed.), *On intelligence* (pp. 49–70). London: Methuen.

Tuddenham, R. D. (1974). Fame and oblivion. *Science, 183*, 1071–1072.

Tulving, E. (1972). Episodic and semantic memory. In E. Tulving & W. Donaldson (Eds.), *Organization of memory* (pp. 382–403). New York: Academic Press.

Tulving, E., & Bower, G. H. (1974). The logic of memory representations. In G. H. Bower (Ed.), *The psychology of learning and memory: Advances in research and theory* (Vol. 8, pp. 265–301). New York: Academic Press.

Tulving, E., & Madigan, S. A. (1970). Memory and verbal learning. *Annual Review of Psychology, 21*, 437–484.

Turing, A. M. (1950). Computing machinery and intelligence. *Mind, 59*, 433–450.

Turkington, C. (1983, April). Drugs found to block dopamine receptors. *APA Monitor*, p. 11.

Turnbull, C. M. (1961). *The forest people: A study of the Pygmies of the Congo.* New York: Simon & Schuster.

Turnbull, C. M. (1962). *The lonely African.* New York: Simon & Schuster.

Turner, R. J., & Wagonfield, M. O. (1967). Occupational mobility and schizo-phrenia. *American Sociological Review, 32*, 104–113.

Tversky, A., & Kahneman, D. (1974). Judgment under certainty: Heuristics and biases. *Science, 185*, 1124–1131.

Tyron, R. C. (1940). Genetic differences in maze-learning ability in rats. *Intelligence: Its nature and nurture. 39th yearbook of the National Society for the Study of Education* (pp. 111–119).

Ullmann, L. P., & Krasner, L. (Eds.). (1965). *Case studies in behavior modification.* New York: Holt, Rinehart & Winston.

Ullmann, L. P., & Krasner, L. (1975). *A psychological approach to abnormal behavior* (2nd ed.). Englewood Cliffs, NJ: Prentice-Hall.

Ulrich, R. E., Stachnik, T. J., & Stainton, N. R. (1963). Student acceptance of generalized personality interpretations. *Psychological Reports, 13*, 831–834.

Underwood, B. J., Boruch, R. F., & Malmi, R. A. (1978). A composition of episodic memory. *Journal of Experimental Psychology: General, 107*, 393–419.

Unger, R. K. (1979). Toward a redefinition of sex and gender. *American Psychologist, 34*, 1085–1094.

Uttal, W. R. (1973). *The psychology of sensory coding.* New York: John Wiley.

Valenstein, E. S. (1973). *Brain control.* New York: John Wiley.

Valenstein, E. S. (Ed.). (1980). *The psychosurgery debate: Scientific, legal, and ethical perspectives.* San Francisco: W. H. Freeman.

Valentine, J. W. (1978, September). The evolution of multicellular plants and animals. *Scientific American*, pp. 140–158.

Valzelli, L. (1980). *Psychobiology of aggression and violence.* New York: Raven Press.

Van Dyke, C., & Byck, R. (1982, March). Cocaine. *Scientific American*, pp. 128–141.

van Kammen, D. P., Mann, L. S., Sternberg, D. E., Scheinin, M., Ninan, P. T., Marder, S. R., van Kammen, W. B., Reider, R. O., & Linnoila, M. (1983). Dopamine-β-hydroxylase activity and homovanillic acid in spinal fluid of schizophrenics with brain atrophy. *Science, 220*, 947–977.

van Lawick-Goodall, J., & Hamburg, D. A. (1974, Spring/Summer). Gombe east Gombe west. *Stanford Magazine*, pp. 66–70.

Vaughan, E. D. (1977, October). Misconceptions about psychology among introductory students. *Teaching of Psychology, 4*, 138–141.

Vaughn, K. B., & Lanzetta, J. T. (1980). Vicarious instigation and conditioning of facial expressive and autonomic response to a model's expressive display of pain. *Journal of Personality and Social Psychology, 38*, 909–923.

Veit, P. G. (1982, March). Gorilla society. *Natural History*, pp. 48–58.

Visintainer, M. A., Volpicelli, J. R., & Se-ligman, M. E. P. (1982). Tumor rejection in rats after inescapable or escapable shock. *Science, 216*, 437–439.

von Frisch, K. (1955). *The dancing bees.* New York: Harcourt Brace Jovanovich.

von Frisch, K. (1962, August). Dialects in the language of the bees. *Scientific American*, pp. 78–87.

von Frisch, K. (1974). Decoding the language of the bee. *Science, 185*, 663–668.

Wachtel, P. (1977). *Psychoanalysis and behavior therapy: Toward an integration.* New York: Basic Books.

Wade, N. (1980). Court says lab-made life can be patented. *Science, 208*, 1445.

Wade, N. (1981). Gene therapy caught in more entanglements. *Science, 212*, 24–25.

Wagner, A. R. (1976). Priming in STM: An information-processing mechanism for self-generated or retrieval-generated depression in performance. In T. J. Tighe & R. N. Leaton (Eds.), *Habituation: Perspectives from child development, animal behavior, and neurophysiology.* Hillsdale, NJ: Lawrence Erlbaum.

Waid, W. M., Orne, E. C., Cook, M. R., & Orne, M. T. (1981). Meprobromate reduces accuracy of physiological detection of deception. *Science, 212*, 71–73.

Waid, W. M., & Orne, M. T. (1982). The physiological detection of deception. *American Scientist, 70*, 402–409.

Wald, G. (1950, August). Eye and camera. *Scientific American*, pp. 32–41.

Walker, J. (1982, April). "Floaters": Visual artifacts that result from blood cells in front of the retina. *Scientific American*, pp. 150–158.

Wallace, R. K., & Benson, H. (1972, February). The physiology of meditation. *Scientific American*, pp. 84–90.

Wallach, H. (1959, July). The perception of motion. *Scientific American*, pp. 56–60.

Wallach, H. (1963, January). The perception of neutral colors. *Scientific American*, pp. 107–116.

Wallach, M. A., & Kogan, N. (1965). *Modes of thinking in young children.* New York: Holt, Reinhart & Winston.

Wallas, G. (1926). *The art of thought.* New York: Harcourt.

Walsh, J. (1979). Professional psychologists seek to change roles and rules in the field. *Science, 203*, 338–340.

Walsh, J. (1981). A plenipotentiary for human intelligence. *Science, 214*, 640–641.

Walsh, J. (1983). Wide world of reports. *Science, 220*, 804–805.

Walster, E., Aronson, V., Abrahams, D., & Rottmann, L. (1966). Importance of physical attractiveness in dating behavior. *Journal of Personality and Social Psychology, 4*, 508–516.

Walters, G. C., & Grusec, J. E. (1977). *Punishment.* San Francisco: W. H. Freeman.

Waltz, D. L. (1982, October). Artificial intelligence. *Scientific American*, pp. 118–133.

Wanner, E., & Gleitman, L. R. (Eds.). (1982). *Language acquisition: The state of the art.* New York: Cambridge University Press.

Warga, C. (1980, November). Beneficial mutations. *Science 80,* pp. 100–102.

Warren, J. V. (1974, November). The physiology of the giraffe. *Scientific American,* pp. 96–105.

Warren, R. M., & Warren, R. P. (1970, December). Auditory illusions and confusions. *Scientific American,* pp. 30–36.

Wasacz, J. (1981). Natural and synthetic narcotic drugs. *American Scientist, 69,* 318–324.

Washburn, S. L. (1978a, September). The evolution of man. *Scientific American,* pp. 194–208.

Washburn, S. L. (1978b). Human behavior and the behavior of other animals. *American Psychologist, 33,* 405–418.

Washburn, S. L., & Moore, R. (1974). *Ape into man.* Boston: Little, Brown.

Wason, P. C., & Johnson-Laird, P. N. (1972). *Psychology of reasoning: Structure and content.* Cambridge, MA: Harvard University Press.

Wasserman, G. S., Felsten, G., & Easland, G. S. (1979). The psychophysical function: Harmonizing Fechner and Stevens. *Science, 204,* 85–87.

Watson, D. (1982). The actor and the observer: How are their perceptions of causality different? *Psychological Bulletin, 92,* 682–700.

Watson, G. C., & Buranen, C. (1979). The frequency and identification of false positive conversion reactions. *Journal of Nervous and Mental Disease, 167,* 243–247.

Watson, J. B. (1913). Psychology as the behaviorist views it. *Psychological Review, 20,* 158–177.

Watson, J. B. (1919). *Psychology from the standpoint of a behaviorist.* Philadelphia: J. B. Lippincott.

Watson, J. B. (1925). *Behaviorism.* New York: W. W. Norton.

Watson, J. B. (1928). *Psychological care of the infant and child.* New York: W. W. Norton.

Watson, J. B., & Rayner, R. (1920). Conditioned emotional reactions. *Journal of Experimental Psychology, 3,* 1–14.

Watson, L. S., Jr. (1968). *How to use behavior modification with the mentally retarded.* Columbus, OH: Mimeographed training manual. [Cited in Reese et al. 1978]

Weary Bradley, G. (1978). Self-serving biases in the attribution process; A reexamination of the fact or fiction question. *Journal of Personality and Social Psychology, 36,* 56–71.

Webb, W. B. (1975). *Sleep: The gentle tyrant.* Englewood Cliffs, NJ: Prentice-Hall.

Webb, W. B. (1981). The return of consciousness. In L. T. Benjamin, Jr. (Ed.), *The G. Stanley Hall lecture series* (Vol. 1, pp. 129–152). Washington, DC: American Psychological Association.

Webb, W. B., & Cartwright, R. D. (1978). Sleep and dreams. *Annual Review of Psychology, 29,* 223–252.

Wechsler, D. (1975). Intelligence defined and undefined: A relativistic appraisal. *American Psychologist, 30,* 135–139.

Wechsler, D. (1981). *Wechsler adult intelligence scale-revised.* New York: Psychological Corporation.

Weimer, W. B., & Palermo, D. S. (Eds.). (1982). *Cognition and the symbolic processes* (Vol. 2). Hillsdale, NJ: Lawrence Erlbaum.

Weinberger, D. R., Bigelow, L. B., Kleinman, J. E., Klein, S. T., Rosenblatt, J. E., & Wyatt, R. J. (1980). Cerebral ventricular enlargement in chronic schizophrenia. *Archives of General Psychiatry, 37,* 11–13.

Weinberger, D. R., Torrey, E, F., Neophytides, A. N., & Wyatt, R. J. (1979). Lateral cerebral ventricular enlargement in chronic schizophrenia. *Archives of General Psychiatry, 36,* 735–739.

Weindruch, R., & Walford, R. L. (1982). Dietary restriction in mice beginning at 1 year of age: Effect on life-span and spontaneous cancer incidence. *Science, 215,* 1415–1418.

Weiner, B. (1974). *Achievement motivation and attribution theory.* Morristown, NJ: General Learning Press.

Weiner, B., Frieze, I., Kukla, A., Reed, L., Rest, S., & Rosenbaum, R. M. (1972). Perceiving the causes of success and failure. In E. E. Jones, D. E. Kanouse, H. H. Kelley, R. E. Nisbett, S. Valins, & B. Weiner (Eds.), *Attribution: Perceiving the causes of behavior* (pp. 95–120). Morristown, NJ: General Learning Press.

Weingarten, P. (1981, June–July). When animals work for man. *National Wildlife,* pp. 14–15.

Weingartner, H., Adefris, W., Eich, J. E., & Murphy, D. L. (1976). Encoding-imagery specificity in alcohol state-dependent learning. *Journal of Experimental Psychology: Human Learning and Memory, 2,* 83–87.

Weingartner, H., Gold, P., Ballenger, J. C., Smallberg, S. A., Summers, R., Rubinow, D. R., Post, R. M., & Goodwin, F. K. (1981). Effects of vasopressin on human memory functions. *Science, 211,* 601–603.

Weintraub, P. (1980, December). Wired for sound. *Discover,* pp. 50–51.

Weisberg, R., & Suls, J. M. (1973). An information-processing model of Duncker's candle problem. *Cognitive Psychology, 4,* 255–276.

Weiss, J. M. (1972, June). Psychological factors in stress and disease. *Scientific American,* pp. 104–113.

Weiss, R. (1973). *Loneliness: The experience of emotional and social isolation.* Cambridge, MA: MIT Press.

Weissman, M. M., Klerman, G. L., & Paykel, E. S. (1971). Clinical evaluation of hostility in depression. *American Journal of Psychiatry, 128,* 261–266.

Weissman, M. M., & Meyers, J. K. (1978). Affective disorders in a U.S. urban community. *Archives of General Psychiatry, 35,* 1304–1310.

Weitzenhoffer, A. M., & Hilgard, E. R. (1959). *Stanford hypnotic susceptibility scale, forms A and B.* Palo Alto, CA: Consulting Psychologists Press.

Wellman, H. M. (1977). Tip of the tongue and the feeling of knowing experiences: A developmental study of memory monitoring. *Child Development, 48,* 13–21.

Werblin, F. S. (1973, January). The control of sensitivity in the retina. *Scientific American,* pp. 70–79.

Werner, C. M., Brown, B. B., & Damron, G. (1981). Territorial marking in a game arcade. *Journal of Personality and Social Psychology, 41,* 1094–1104.

Werner, E. E., Simonian, K., & Smith, R. S. (1968). Ethnic and socioeconomic status differences in abilities and achievement among preschool and school-age children in Hawaii. *Journal of Social Psychology, 75,* 43–59.

Wernick, R. (1980, January). One-eyed jacks, like the rest of us, aren't that wild. *Smithsonian,* pp. 63–71.

Wertheimer, M. (1979). *A brief history of psychology* (rev. ed.). New York: Holt, Rinehart & Winston.

Wetzel, R. (1980). Applications of recombinant DNA technology. *American Psychologist, 68,* 664–675.

Weyant, J. M. (1978). Effects of mood states, costs, and benefits on helping. *Journal of Personality and Social Psychology, 36,* 1169–1176.

White, B. C., Lincoln, C. A., Pearce, N. W., Reeb, R., & Vaida, C. (1980). Anxiety and muscle tension as consequences of caffeine withdrawal. *Science, 209,* 1547–1548.

White, D. (1981, September). Pursuit of the ultimate aphrodisiac. *Psychology Today,* pp. 9–12.

White, K. D., Post, R. B., & Leibowitz, H. W. (1980). Saccadic eye movements and body sway. *Science, 208,* 621–623.

White, M. D., & White, C. A. (1981). Involuntarily committed patients' constitutional right to refuse treatment. *American Psychologist, 36,* 953–962.

White, T. (1981). Primitive hominid canine from Tanzania. *Science, 213,* 348–349.

White, W. A. (1932). *Outlines of psychiatry* (13th ed.). New York: Nervous and Mental Disease Publishing.

Whitehouse, P. J., Price, P. L., Struble, R. G., Clark, A. W., Coyle, J. T., & DeLong, M. R. (1982). Alzheimer's disease and senile dementia: Loss of neurons in the basal forebrain. *Science, 215,* 1237–1239.

Whorf, B. L. (1956). *Language, thought and reality.* Cambridge, MA: MIT Press.

Whyte, W. H., Jr. (1956). *The organization man.* New York: Simon & Schuster.

Wickelgren, W. A. (1973). The long and the short of memory. *Psychological Bulletin, 80,* 425–438.

Wickelgren, W. A. (1979). Chunking and consolidation: A theoretical synthesis of semantic networks, configuring in conditioning, S-R versus cognitive learning, normal forgetting, the amnesic syndrome, and the hippocampal arousal system. *Psychological Review, 86,* 44–60.

Wicker, A. W. (1969). Attitudes versus action: The relationship of verbal and overt behavioral responses to attitude objects. *Journal of Social Issues, 25,* 41–78.

Wicker, A. W. (1971). An examination of the "other variables" explanation of attitude-behavior inconsistency. *Journal of Personality and Social Psychology, 19,* 18–30.

Wickler, W. (1973). *The sexual code: The sexual behavior of animals and men.* New York: Doubleday.

Wicklund, R. A. (1975). Objective self-awareness. In L. Berkowitz (Ed.), *Advances in experimental social psychology* (Vol. 8, pp. 233–275). New York: Academic Press.

Wicklund, R. A. (1979). The influence of self-awareness on human behavior. *American Scientist, 67,* 187–193.

Wicklund, R. A., & Brehm, J. W. (1976). *Perspectives on cognitive dissonance.* Hillsdale, NJ: Lawrence Erlbaum.

Widom, C. S. (1977). A methodology for studying noninstitutionalized psychopaths. *Journal of Consulting and Clinical Psychology, 45,* 674–683.

Wiggins, J. (1968). Inconsistent socialization. *Psychological Reports, 23,* 303–336.

Wightman, F. L., & Green, D. M. (1974). The perception of pitch. *American Scientist, 62,* 208–215.

Willemsen, E. W. (1979). *Understanding infancy.* San Francisco: W. H. Freeman.

Willer, J. C., Dehen, H., & Cambier, J. (1981). Stress-induced analgesia in humans: Endogenous opioids and naloxone-reversible depression of pain reflexes. *Science, 212,* 689–691.

Willerman, L. (1979a). Effects of families on intellectual development. *American Psychologist, 34,* 923–929.

Willerman, L. (1979b). *The psychology of individual and group differences.* San Francisco: W. H. Freeman.

Williams, D. R., & Williams, H. (1969). Auto-maintenance in the pigeon: Sustained pecking despite contingent nonreinforcement. *Journal of the Experimental Analysis of Behavior, 12,* 511–520.

Williams, M. (1979). *Brain damage, behavior, and the mind.* New York: John Wiley.

Williams, R. J. (1978, June). Nutritional individuality. *Human Nature,* pp. 46–53.

Williams, R. L. (1974). Scientific racism and I.Q.: The silent mugging of the black community. *Psychology Today,* pp. 32–41.

Wilson, E. O. (1963, May). Pheromones. *Scientific American,* pp. 2–11.

Wilson, E. O. (1972, September). Animal communication. *Scientific American,* pp. 52–60.

Wilson, E. O. (1975). *Sociobiology: The new synthesis.* Cambridge, MA: Harvard University Press.

Wilson, E. O. (1978, November–December). Altruism. *Harvard Magazine,* pp. 23–28.

Wilson, G. T., & O'Leary, K. D. (1980). *Principles of behavior therapy.* Englewood Cliffs, NJ: Prentice-Hall.

Wilson, J. D., George, F. W., & Griffin, J. E. (1981). The hormonal control of sexual development. *Science, 211,* 1278–1284.

Wilson, J. R. (1964). *The mind.* New York: Time-Life Books.

Winchester, A. M. (1976). *Heredity, evolution and humankind.* St. Paul, MN: West Publishing.

Windle, W. F. (1969, October). Brain damage by asphyxia at birth. *Scientific American,* pp. 76–84.

Wingfield, A. (1979). *Human learning and memory: An introduction.* New York: Harper & Row.

Winick, M. (1981, January). Food and the fetus. *Natural History,* pp. 76–81.

Winograd, T. (1972). *Understanding natural language.* New York: Academic Press.

Wispé, L. G. (1972). Positive forms of social behavior: An overview. *Journal of Social Issues, 28*(3), 1–19.

Wispé, L. G. (Ed.). (1978). *Altruism, sympathy, and helping: Psychological and sociological principles.* New York: Academic Press.

Witelson, S. F. (1976). Sex and the single hemisphere: Specialization of the right hemisphere for spatial processing. *Science, 193,* 425–427.

Witelson, S. F. (1977). Developmental dyslexia: Two right hemispheres and none left. *Science, 195,* 309–311.

Witkin, H. A., Mednick, S. A., Schulsinger, F., Bakkestrøm, E., Christiansen, K. O., & Goodenough, D. R. (1976). Criminality in XYY and XXY men. *Science, 193,* 547–555.

Witkop, C. (1975, October). Albinism. *Natural History,* pp. 48–59.

Wittig, M. A., & Petersen, A. C. (Eds.). (1979). *Sex related differences in cognitive functioning: Developmental issues.* New York: Academic Press.

Wodinsky, J. (1977). Hormonal inhibition of feeding and death in *Octopus:* Control by optic gland secretion. *Science, 198,* 948–951.

Wolf, T. H. (1973). *Alfred Binet.* Chicago: University of Chicago Press.

Wolman, B. W. (Ed.). (1982). *Psychological aspects of obesity: A handbook.* New York: Van Nostrand Reinhold.

Wolpe, J. (1969). *The practice of behavior therapy.* New York: Pergamon Press.

Wolpe, J. (1978). Cognition and causation in human behavior and its therapy. *American Psychologist, 33,* 437–446.

Wolpe, J. (1980). Cognitive behavior and its roles in psychotherapy: An integrative account. In M. J. Mahoney (Ed.), *Psychotherapy process: Current issues and future directions* (pp. 185–201). New York: Plenum Press.

Wolpe, J., & Lang, P. J. (1964). A fear survey schedule for use in behavior therapy. *Behaviour Research and Therapy, 2,* 27–30.

Wolpe, J., & Rachman, S. J. (1960). Psychoanalytic "evidence," a critique based on Freud's case of little Hans. *Journal of Nervous and Mental Disease, 131,* 135–147.

Wong, R. (1976). *Motivation: A biobehavioral analysis of consummatory activities.* New York: Macmillan.

Woods, P. J. (Ed.). (1979). *The psychology major.* Washington, DC: American Psychological Association.

Woodward, W. R. (1972). Fechner's panpsychism: A scientific solution to the mind-body problem. *Journal of the History of the Behavioral Sciences, 8,* 367–386.

Woodward, W. R. (1982). The "discovery" of social behaviorism and social learning theory, 1870–1980. *American Psychologist, 37,* 396–410.

Woodworth, R. S., & Sheehan, M. R. (1964). *Contemporary schools of psychology* (3rd ed.). New York: Ronald Press.

Worchel, S. (1974). The effect of three types of arbitrary thwarting on the instigation to aggression. *Journal of Personality, 42,* 300–318.

Word, C. H., Zanna, M. P., & Cooper, J. (1974). The non-verbal mediation of self-fulfilling prophecies in interracial interaction. *Journal of Experimental Social Psychology, 10,* 109–120.

Wright, R. L. D. (1976). *Understanding statistics: An informal introduction for the behavioral sciences.* New York: Harcourt Brace Jovanovich.

Wurtman, J. J., & Wurtman, R. J. (1979). Sucrose consumption early in life fails to modify the appetite of adult rats for sweet foods. *Science, 205,* 321–322.

Wurtman, R. J. (1975, July). The effect of light on the human body. *Scientific American,* pp. 69–77.

Wurtz, R. H., Goldberg, M. E., & Robinson, D. L. (1982, June). Brain mechanisms of visual attention. *Scientific American,* pp. 124–135.

Wynne, L. C., Cromwell, R. L., & Matthysse, S. (Eds.). (1978). *The nature of schizophrenia: New approaches to research and treatment.* New York: John Wiley.

Yarmey, A. D. (1973). I recognize your face but I can't remember your name: Further evidence on the tip-of-the-tongue phenomenon. *Memory & Cognition, 1,* 287–290.

Yellott, J. I., Jr. (1981, July). Binocular depth inversion. *Scientific American,* pp. 148–159.

Young, R. W. (1970, October). Visual cells. *Scientific American*, pp. 80–91.

Younger, J. C., Walker, L., & Arrowood, A. J. (1977). Postdecision dissonance at the fair. *Personality and Social Psychology Bulletin, 3*, 284–287.

Yunis, J. J. (1976). High resolution of human chromosomes. *Science, 191*, 1268–1270.

Yunis, J. J., & Prakash, O. (1982). The origin of man: A chromosomal pictorial legacy. *Science, 215*, 1525–1530.

Zahoric, D. M., Maier, S. F., & Pies, R. W. (1974). Preferences for tastes paired with recovery from thiamine deficiency in rats: Appetitive conditioning or learned safety? *Journal of Comparative and Physiological Psychology, 87*, 1083–1091.

Zajonc, R. B. (1980). Feeling and thinking: Preferences need no inferences. *American Psychologist, 35*, 151–175.

Zechmeister, E. B., & Nyberg, S. E. (1982). *Human memory: An introduction to research and theory*. Monterey, CA: Brooks/Cole.

Zeisel, H., & Diamond, S. (1978). The effect of peremptory challenges on jury and verdict: An experiment in a federal district court. *Stanford Law Review, 30*, 491–531.

Zigler, E., & Muenchow, S. (1979). Mainstreaming: The proof is in the implementation. *American Psychologist, 34*, 993–996.

Zigler, E., & Phillips, L. (1961). Psychiatric diagnosis and symptomatology. *Journal of Abnormal and Social Psychology, 63*, 69–75.

Zilboorg, G., & Henry, G. W. (1941). *A history of medical psychology*. New York: W. W. Norton.

Zillman, D. (1979). *Hostility and aggression*. Hillsdale, NJ: Lawrence Erlbaum.

Zimbardo, P. G. (1980). *Essentials of psychology and life* (10th ed.). Glenview, IL: Scott, Foresman.

Ziporyn, T. (1982). Taste and smell: The neglected senses. *Journal of the American Medical Association, 247*, 277–285.

Zuckerman, M., Buchsbaum, M. S., & Murphy, D. L. (1980). Sensation seeking and its biological correlates. *Psychological Bulletin, 88*, 187–214.

Zuckerman, Sir S. (1957, March). Hormones. *Scientific American*, pp. 76–87.

Zurif, E. B. (1980). Language mechanisms: A neuropsycholinguistic perspective. *American Scientist, 68*, 305–311.

Zwislocki, J. J. (1981). Sound analysis in the ear: A history of discoveries. *American Scientist, 69*, 184–192.

Exner, J. E., 427
Eysenck, H. J., 413–414, 430, 513
Eysenck, M. W., 300, 306
Eysenck, S.B.G., 413

Faneslow, M. S., 52, 171
Fantino, E., 262
Fantz, R. L., 382, 383
Farnsworth, P. N., 98
Farran, D. C., 318
Favreau, O. E., 188
Fazio, R. H., 547, 550
Feagans, L., 318
Fechner, G., 13
Fein, J. M., 65
Feingold, B. D., 257
Feinsilver, D. B., 514
Feirtag, M., 53
Feldman, H., 319
Fender, D. H., 193
Fenton, M. B., 142
Ferguson, C. A., 322
Ferguson, E. S., 338
Ferster, C. B., 257, 340
Feshback, S., 549
Festinger, L. A., 542, 546, 547
Fifer, W. P., 382
Fillmore, C. J., 309, 324
Fink, M., 505, 526
Finke, R. A., 348
Firkowska, A., 441
Fishbein, M., 410, 411, 550, 551
Fisher, A. E., 43
Fisher, C., 101
Fisher, G. H., 196, 204
Fisher, J. D., 586
Fisher, S., 18, 415
Fiske, D. W., 436
Fiske, S. T., 537, 539
Flagg, P. W., 345, 366
Flanagan, G. L., 370
Flanagan, J. C., 363
Flaugher, R. L., 460
Flavell, J. H., 285, 373
Flugel, J., 269
Fodor, J. A., 11
Follett, B. K., 215
Follett, D. E., 215
Fontana, A., 491
Foss, D. J., 308
Fouts, R., 313
Fox, L. H., 451, 454, 455
Fox, R. E., 4, 199, 203
Frankel, F. H., 230, 238
Franken, R. E., 109, 138
Frankenburg, W. K., 384
Fraser, A. B., 147, 148, 182
Freedman, D. G., 385
Freedman, J. L., 545, 557, 583, 584, 586
Freeman, W., 506
French, J. D., 61
Fretz, B. R., 37
Freud, A., 416–417
Freud, S., 16–18, 28, 213, 226, 230, 236, 373, 374, 376–378, 379, 385, 389, 390, 394, 396, 398, 412,

414–416, 417, 418, 474, 479, 484–485, 512–514, 570
Friedman, M. I., 118
Friedman, R., 477
Friedrich, L. K., 568
Fries, J. F., 8
Friesen, W., 138
Frieze, I., 531, 533
Frisby, J., 155, 156, 174, 209
Frisch, R., 393
Fromkin, V. A., 323, 334
Fromm-Reichmann, F., 491
Fuchs, F., 96
Fullard, J. H., 142
Fuller, C. A., 238
Furth, H. G., 337
Fusella, V., 348

Gabrenya, W. K., Jr., 535
Gage, P., 407–408
Gaither, N. S., 61
Galbraith, R., 391
Galin, D., 479
Gall, F. J., 407
Gallup, G. G., Jr., 44, 212, 340
Galton, F., 97, 100, 454
Galvin, R. M., 223
Garcia, J., 250, 461
Gardner, B. T., 44, 312–313, 316, 334
Gardner, E., 169
Gardner, H., 66, 67, 73, 77, 155, 332, 366, 408
Gardner, L. I., 75
Gardner, M., 67, 218, 338, 366
Gardner, R. A., 312–313, 316, 334
Garfield, E., 542
Garfield, S. L., 510, 511, 526
Garner, W. R., 177
Garnica, O. K., 322
Garske, J. P., 138
Gazzaniga, M. S., 68, 69, 70, 71, 72, 73, 77, 286
Geen, R. G., 577
Gelb, A., 184
Geller, U., 362
Gelman, R., 373
Genovese, K., 564
Gerard, H. B., 553
Gergen, K. J., 563, 566
Gerson, S., 502
Geschwind, N., 66, 295, 330, 331, 332
Getzels, J. W., 363
Ghiselin, B., 223, 366
Giacometti, L., 88
Gibson, A. R., 146
Gibson, E. J., 331, 334, 381
Gibson, G. E., 400
Gilbert, W., 99
Gilchrist, A. L., 186
Gillam, B., 205
Ginsburg, H., 402
Gintzler, A. R., 171
Girgus, J. S., 179
Glaser, R., 446
Glass, D. C., 580
Glass, G. V., 513

Gleitman, L. R., 334
Glenberg, A. M., 286, 305
Glickstein, M., 146
Glithero, E., 478
Glucksberg, S., 308, 325
Gmelch, G., 259
Godden, D. R., 294
Goffman, E., 430, 502, 526
Gogel, W. C., 202
Golbus, M. S., 96
Goldberg, E., 304
Goldfoot, D. A., 122
Goldfried, M. R., 517, 523
Goldin-Meadow, S., 319
Goldstein, E. B., 174, 209
Goldstein, T., 4
Goleman, D., 68, 74, 217
Golsman, D., 232
Goodall, J., 87
Goodenough, J. E., 215
Goodglass, H., 332
Goodwin, F. K., 482
Gordon, B., 146
Gordon, E. W., 453
Gordon, J. W., 125
Gordon, T. P., 575
Gottesman, I. I., 103, 439, 490
Gould, J. L., 142, 312
Gould, P., 354
Gould, S. J., 81, 82, 87, 89, 90, 105, 121, 326, 338, 371, 460
Gouldner, A. W., 563
Grabowski, J., 456
Graham, A., 319
Graham, F. A., 60
Graham, J. R., 426
Grant, P. R., 80, 84
Grant, R. P., 248
Gray, C. R., 301
Gray, F., 265
Gray, J. A., 473
Graybiel, A., 180
Green, B., 318
Green, B. F., 447
Green, D. M., 158
Green, H., 495
Green, R., 128
Greenberg, J., 491, 505
Greenberg, J. H., 320
Greenberg, R. P., 18, 415
Greene, D., 257
Greeno, J. G., 271, 356, 357, 358
Greenspoon, J., 545
Gregory, R. L., 150, 174, 186, 197, 206, 209
Grice, H. P., 325
Griffin, D. R., 25, 44, 338
Grings, W. W., 131
Grinspoon, L., 233
Grobecker, D. B., 82
Groos, G., 216
Gross, A. E., 566
Gross, C. G., 191
Grossman, H., 456
Grover, S. C., 463
Grusec, J. E., 256, 562, 563
Gruvson, J. E., 256
Guilford, J. P., 363, 444, 445, 446, 456
Guillemin, R., 74

Guilleminault, C., 227
Gummerman, K., 301
Gunderson, J. G., 514
Gurin, J., 52, 118, 171
Gustavson, C. R., 248
Guthrie, E. R., 263

Haber, R. B., 300
Haber, R. N., 175, 197, 283, 300
Hagen, J. L., 262, 474
Hakes, D. T., 308
Haley, J., 75
Hall, C. S., 223, 430
Hall, C. W., 469
Hall, D. T., 477
Hall, E., 387, 402
Hall, E. T., 581
Hall, J. A., 130, 310
Hall, J. G., 124
Hamburg, D. A., 87
Hamilton, D. L., 537, 538
Hamilton, W. D., 89
Hammersmith, S. K., 138
Handler, P., 4
Haney, W., 451
Hans, V. P., 578
Hansen, J. C., 430
Hargadon, F., 443
Harlow, H. F., 121, 122, 268, 340, 386–387
Harlow, M. K., 268
Harman, G., 321
Harmon, L. D., 294, 295
Harper, R. M., 227
Harrell, R. F., 457
Harris, C. S., 206
Harris, D. B., 452
Harris, J. E., 305
Harris, R. J., 326
Hart, J. T., 285, 296
Hartline, P. H., 147
Hartman, E. L., 52, 225
Hartshorne, H., 411
Hartup, W. W., 392
Harvey, J. H., 538, 540, 557
Haseltine, F. P., 125
Hasler, A. D., 142
Hassett, J., 166, 171
Hastorf, A. H., 557
Hathaway, S. R., 426
Hawkes, N., 460
Hay, R. L., 84
Hayes, C., 312
Hayes, J. R., 352, 356
Hayes, K. J., 312
Hayflick, L., 399
Hearnshaw, L. S., 460
Hearst, E., 8, 38
Hebb, D. O., 116, 291, 460
Hechinger, N., 61, 178, 180, 206
Heidbreder, E., 12, 14
Heider, F., 538, 546
Heilman, K., 468, 495
Heimer, L., 43
Hein, A., 208
Held, R., 206, 208
Heller, H. C., 112
Helmers, C., 218
Helmholtz, H. von, 186
Helmreich, R. L., 532

Amnesia (*cont.*)
general social information is retained; when personal identity is lost and the person establishes a new life, mental health professionals call it a fugue state. 303–304, 481

Amniocentesis A technique for obtaining, testing, and karyotyping tissue samples from a fetus that can determine if some birth defects or genetic diseases will be present. 96

Amphetamines, 236

Amplitude The vertical height of the measurement of one peak of a wave, such as a sound wave. 158

Amygdala Limbic system structure involved in the patterning of aggressive behavior, therefore sometimes surgically lesioned to reduce violent outbursts. 61

Analog code A picturelike form of storage of information that can be used to generate mental images, according to most theorists of memory storage. 351

Analogous parts Body parts of different species that have evolved independently from different ancestors but function similarly, such as the panda's sesamoid-bone "thumb" and the human thumb. 82–83

Anal personality, 415

Anal stage Freud's second stage of psychosexual development, from about age 1 to 3, during which toilet training marks the child's first major encounter with social constraints on behavior. 378, 385

Analysis by synthesis The brain's tendency to make the best compromise of multiple inputs in building a perception, with some perceptual cues given more weight than others. 207

Analyst, 509

Analytic psychology, 417

Androgen-insensitivity syndrome, 126, 127

Androgens Hormones considered to be male ones because they are produced in quantity by the testes; they may also be produced, in smaller amounts, by the ovaries. 125

Androgyny A gender role incorporating the positive features of both male and female role stereotypes; defined somewhat differently by different theorists, such as Bem and Spence. 531–532

Anencephalic infants, 60

Anesthetics, 236

Angel dust, 57, 233

Animal research, 33, 191, 476–477, 582

Animals:
    evolution of, 80–84
    human beings versus, 9–10
    language and, 312–316
    mating of, 123–124
    minds of, 44
    nervous systems of, 41–43
    thinking and, 340

Animistic, 388

Anorexia nervosa A life-threatening medical problem usually affecting teenage females who avoid eating for "nervous"

reasons, even when reporting strong hunger. 118, 120

Anterograde amnesia A forward loss of memory in which old long-term memory traces are retained and can be retrieved but new ones cannot be created; the case of H. M. is the best-known example. 304

Antianxiety drugs Widely used and abused therapeutic drugs, effective in treating debilitating anxiety but often with undesirable side effects; also called minor tranquilizers. 507, 508

Antidepressants Drugs that relieve the symptoms of, but do not cure, depression; the more common ones are the tricyclics, which alter the functioning of neurotransmitters, and others are the tricyclics and the MAO inhibitors, both of which affect neurotransmitter utilization at synapses. 507, 508

Antipsychotics Psychoactive drugs that relieve some symptoms of mental illness. 232, 506–508

Antisocial personality Most useful of the DSM-III subcategories of personality disorder, referring to those whose impulsive behavior is ethically or morally abnormal, often despite a well-adjusted appearance; also called *sociopathic personality* or *psychopathic personality*. 492–494

Anvil One of the three small bones of the middle ear. 161

Anxiety A feeling of fear or apprehension, which may range from mild to severe. 418, 473

Anxiety attacks Short-lasting but sometimes frequent intense experiences of the aroused physiology of fear (rapid heart rate, labored breathing, sweating, and trembling), characteristic of panic disorders. 474–475

Anxiety disorders A DSM-III category that includes disorders in which anxiety is obviously present and others in which it is less obvious, includes phobic disorders, anxiety states, and obsessive-compulsive disorders; some of these disorders were formerly classified as neuroses. 473–476

Anxiety states Experiences of anxiety that are not clearly associated with specific objects or events; these states include panic, generalized anxiety disorders, and obsessive-compulsive disorders. 474–476

Aphasia Any loss of a language function from brain injury or disease. 332–333

Applied research Research that seeks to develop applications of what has been understood through basic research. 4

Approach-approach conflict, 419

Aptitude tests Tests intended to predict what a person may be able to accomplish in the future, with training and practice; they frequently measure current accomplishments, but only to be used in predicting future performance. 443

Archetypes Patterns of images within Jung's collective unconscious that represent the common experiences of all people that have deep symbolic meaning;

supposedly the summary of our ancestors' experiences as expressed in the similar myths and folklore of many cultures. 417

Arousal, optimal, 116

Artificial intelligence (AI) The computer modeling of intelligent behavior, including the simulation of language comprehension. 342

Artificial languages, 308

ASL. *See* American Sign Language

Aspartate, 52

Assertiveness training Group therapies with a behavioral focus designed to model and role-play appropriate ways to stand up for one's rights. 524

Assessment In personality research, any of a number of techniques, usually based on particular theories, for measuring a person's personality attributes.

Assimilation In Piaget's theory, the process of fitting new perceptual input into existing schemes. 375

Associationist view of learning, 243

Attachment Bowlby's concept of special ties between mother and child that comfort and support both of them, beginning with bonding in the first few hours of life. 386–387

Attention, and perception, 181, 182

Attitudes Enduring general evaluations or feelings about something, often closely related to cognitive beliefs about and behavior toward the person or object. 544–550
    behavior and, 549–550
    changes in, 546–549
    formation of, 545–546

Attraction, interpersonal, 542–544

Attribution biases, 539–540

Attribution theory Originally proposed by Heider, now a collection of similar approaches in social psychology stressing that observers attribute the behavior of others to internal and/or external causes in predictable, but not necessarily accurate, ways. 538

Audition, 155. *See also* Hearing

Auditory illusions, 179

Auditory nerve The nerve that transmits coded sound information from the hair cells of the organ of Corti to the brain. 162–165

Autokinetic effect The "self-moving" effect whereby a fixed light in a darkened environment appears to move. 208

Autistic children Children who are focused inward and are extremely unresponsive to others, probably as the result of some biological deficit; operant therapy can cure some of the self-destructive stereotyped behaviors. 519, 520

Autonomic system The portion of the peripheral nervous system that carries commands to body organs, divided into the sympathetic and parasympathetic command systems. 54, 62, 63

Autoshaping The development of some operants rather than others in circumstances of no reinforcement or reinforcement of different operants; proposed as the consequence of "natural" behavioral tendencies of particular species, as a pigeon, for example, tends to autoshape pecking rather than other operants. 262

Availability trap A thinking bias that leads us to misjudge the probability of events: If we can think of an example of something it seems more likely than something for which we have no readily available example. 360

Average evoked potential An average of the changes in brain waves evoked by presentation of a particular stimulus, used to measure brain's response to the stimulus. 44

Aversion conditioning A kind of classical conditioning of an avoidance response to a previously neutral or positive stimulus, such as learning to avoid foods that taste similar to ones that have been paired with becoming sick. 248

Aversion therapy A form of counter-conditioning designed to increase anxiety in response to a stimulus where prior approach behaviors are considered the problem, such as pairing electric shock or a nausea-inducing drug with alcohol to cure alcoholism; aversion conditioning used deliberately as therapy. 518

Avoidance-avoidance conflict, 419

Axes, 471

Axon A specialized projection of a neuron that carries information to other neurons. 47, 51

Backward conditioning, 245

Balance theory Heider's motivational theory of attitude change proposing that the relationships between a person and some other person, object, or event can either be balanced or unbalanced (motivating change in the situation toward a balanced resolution). 546, 547

Bandura, Albert Founder of social learning theory who felt that behaviorism's emphasis on overt behavior was limited and instead looked at covert behavior and at human learning by observing the behavior of others and its consequences. (1925–). 24, 28, 264, 266, 379, 396, 420–421, 470, 474, 509, 516, 521, 562, 572, 573, 575, 586

Barbiturates, 224, 233

Basic research Research that seeks to understand underlying rules or mechanisms. 4

Basilar membrane One wall of the tympanic canal in the cochlea, flexed by the pressure waves of sound; the organ of Corti is attached to it and is thus also flexed by the sound waves. 162, 163

Behavior:
  abnormal, 465–471
  aggressive, 568–578
  attitudes and, 549–550
  brains and, 41–47
  causes of, 11–12
  covert, 20
  interpersonal, 540–545

overt, 20
  personality traits and, 411
  prosocial, 560–568
  technology of, 5

Behavioral genetics The study, by both biologists and psychologists, of how behaviors are genetically transmitted. 99–101

Behavioral humanism A view proposed by Carl Thoresen that turns the specific methodology developed by behaviorism toward the goal of humanism, aiding self-actualization. 27, 524

Behavioral therapy A psychother-apeutic method emphasizing specific learned behavior over insight and defining the client's original problem as inappropriate behavior to be changed during therapy into appropriate behavior by role-playing, relaxation techniques, and so on, with the active participation of the therapist. 516–519

Behavior contract A behavioral-therapy technique in which an explicit agreement is made between the client and the therapist regarding the behaviors to be reinforced. 519

Behaviorism A school of psychology that emphasizes the study of overt, measurable behavior and believes that behavior is largely the product of learning, primarily through reinforcement and punishment. 19–22
  basic concepts of, 20–21
  focus of, 21–22
  founders of, 19–20
  personality and, 418–422
  purposive, 269
  radical, 419–420

Behavior modification Therapy based on learning theory, primarily on operant conditioning, more commonly known as behavioral therapy; also, an early term for action or behavioral therapy, no longer preferred by some psychologists because of the term's close association with classical and operant learning proce-dures. 262–264, 265, 516

Biases, 359–361, 535, 539–540

Bilingual A person who speaks two (or more) languages and is likely to be equally proficient in both only if they are both native languages for the speaker. 318

Bimodal distribution A nonnormal frequency distribution in which there are two groups of separated scores. 592, 593

Binet, Alfred Developer of a test to predict school success, which later became a general-purpose intelligence test, and of the concept of mental age versus chronological age. (1857–1911) 436–437, 448

Binge-purge syndrome, 120

Binocular depth cues Visual indicators of depth that can only be used by two eyes working together; two important ones are binocular disparity and convergence. 199–202

Binocular disparity The difference between the two images of a single

object that are created by a person's eyes; these different images are fused by the brain into a perception of a single object, but the disparity of the images is a cue to the distance of that object. 199, 201

Binocular fusion The process by which the brain integrates the two images produced by binocular disparity into a total perception in depth that is different from the image seen by either eye. 201–202

Biochemistry, and schizophrenia, 491

Biofeedback The amplification of a measure of body functioning to help the person learn to control that function. 10, 11

Biological clocks Innate biological mechanisms that act as "clocks" for timing various biological cycles; such clocks can be more precisely synchron-ized by environmental information, notably light. 216

Biological cycles, 214–216

Biological therapies Techniques for modifying abnormal behavior through direct biological intervention, including the use of electric shock, surgery, and drug therapy. 498, 503–508
  drug therapy, 506–508
  electroconvulsive therapy, 503–505, 506
  psychosurgery, 506

Biology, and aggression, 570–572

Biorhythms, 218

Bipedalism, 87–89

Bipolar disorder Affective disorder characterized by a full range of mood swings from extremes of elation, or mania, to depression. 482–483, 508

Birth defects, 370–371

Black box In engineering, any device that responds to a particular input with a particular output: The analogy in psychology is to the psychophysics approach to the mind/body problem, wherein the performance characteristics of an organism are measured without asking what goes on inside the organism. 176, 190

Black English A manner of speaking used (with some local variations) by many black Americans; it is considered by some people to be merely an irregular set of variations on Standard English, but some linguists consider it to be a dialect derived from an earlier creole that in turn grew from combining African languages and trade pidgin. 317–318

Blindsight, 61

Blind spot An area of the retina near the center of the back of the eye where there are no visual receptors and thus no light sensing; blood vessels enter the eye at this point and the optic nerve exits; also called the optic disc. 151, 157

Blocking In classical conditioning, an effect whereby the presence of an existing CS seems to block the conditioning of a new CS in the same situation; blocking is thought to be avoided only if a new CS offers additional information about the environment, or a "surprise." 250, 487

"Blocks world," 342, 344
Body, versus mind, 10–11
Body language, 130
Body types, 405–407
Bonding, 387
Braille A raised-dot alphabet for the blind; one example of the possible uses of touch information in comprehending the world. 170
Brain The cluster of structures in a nervous system within which central processing takes place; in higher organisms, it lies within the skull, with inputs brought to it from sense organs and outputs sent from it to muscles and glands; developmentally, the elaboration of the front (head) end of the neural tube. 53, 59–74, 75
   aggression and, 571
   of animals, 41–43
   areas of, 65–67, 407–408
   behavior and, 41–47
   cerebellum, 59
   cerebrum, 55, 63–74
   hearing and, 164–165
   hemispheres of, 53, 64, 67–74, 75, 131, 329–330
   language and, 329–333
   personality and, 407–408
   sexual development and, 126–127
   study of, 43–47
Brain damage, 44, 45, 407–408
Brain scan, 44–45
Brainstem The oldest and most basic of the inner core or "reptilian brain" structures that contains basic survival mechanisms, such as those that keep the heart beating and the lungs breathing; may sustain these activities even in the case of "brain death" of higher brain centers. 59–61
Brief reactive psychosis, 491
Brightness One of three psychological dimensions of color, resulting from the overall amount of light that reaches the eye. 149, 186
Broca's aphasia An expressive disorder resulting from damage to Broca's area of the brain, in which the patient either cannot speak at all or speaks haltingly but appropriately. 332
Broca's area An area of the brain in the frontal lobe, usually the left; a crucial center for speech production. 66–67, 330–332
Bulimia, 120
Buss aggression machine, 569
Bystander intervention A research approach to helping behavior, seeking to understand when and why a witness to a crime will take action, whether a merely helping action such as phoning the police or an altruistic one that may risk the bystander's own life. 564, 566

Caffeine, 236
Cannon-Bard theory A theory of emotion proposing that stimuli to the thalamus result in simultaneous signals to arouse the body and to begin overt action. 134

Capacity The amount of information that can be held in memory; the capacity of short-term memory is limited to about seven items, but the capacity of long-term memory is virtually unlimited. 279
Cardinal traits, 410
Carrier In genetics, a person who carries the recessive gene for a characteristic although expressing the form specified by the dominant gene. 92
Case history A detailed compilation of data about a single individual; for a mentally disturbed patient it will include events and behaviors in the past having a bearing on the patient's current condition. 30
Castration complex Freudian concept of a key problem in the phallic stage, developing from the Oedipus complex, of fear of punishment by the father cutting off his genitals. 390
Cataplexy An extreme form of narcolepsy, in which the sleep attack includes the muscular paralysis associated with REM and the patient slumps to the ground. 227, 228
Catatonic schizophrenia One of the five DMS-III subcategories of schizophrenia, characterized by extremes of motor activity but most commonly by extreme fixed immobility. 489
Catharsis In psychoanalytic theory, the release of pent-up aggressive instincts in nondamaging ways; this concept has been used to defend televised violence as a release valve. 574, 577
CAT scan, 44, 46
Cattell, Raymond Developer of the factor-analytic technique of analyzing and classifying traits as well as the concepts of fluid and crystallized intelligence. (1905–) 409, 412–413, 426, 427, 430, 445–446
Cells:
   complex, 189, 191
   hypercomplex, 189, 191
   simple, 189
Central nervous system (CNS) The portion of the nervous system encased by bone: the brain and the spinal cord. 53–54
Central tendency Statistical summary of where the center of a normal distribution tends to be, measured by the mean, the mode, and the median. 592–593
Central traits Traits that are usually associated with a number of others, so that they carry more weight in a trait description than do less central traits; consequently, the presence of a central trait, such as *warm*, in a trait description can strongly bias the impression someone gets of the person being described. 410, 535
CER. *See* Conditioned emotional response
Cerebellum A brain structure located at the back of the cerebrum that smoothes and integrates motor commands to the muscles; the "little brain." 59
Cerebral cortex The outer layer of the cerebrum where its synapses occur and thus where actual communication within the cerebrum takes place: "gray matter." 64

Cerebral hemispheres The two halves of the cerebrum, each controlling the opposite side of the body and each having its own pattern of skills and modes of thought. 53, 64, 67–74, 75
Cerebral vascular accidents (CVAs), 65
Cerebrum The most recently evolved or "new mammalian" brain, what we may tend to think of as *the* brain; physically, the outermost brain layer, the complexity of which in humans makes consciousness possible. 55, 63–74
Chaining An operant conditioning process of adding bits of additional behavior to an existing operant to create a lengthy behavior sequence that cannot be shaped as a single act. 259, 261
Childhood, 387–393
   cognitive growth in, 388–389
   identification and, 391–393
   moral growth in, 388–389
   personality growth in, 389–391
   physical growth in, 387–388
   social learning in, 391
   teaching methods and, 391
Chlorpromazine, 506, 507
Chromosomal abnormalities, 94–95
Chromosomes The structures within the nucleus of every cell (23 pairs in all human cells except the specialized reproductive cells, the ova and sperm) that carry the genes. 91, 92, 124–125
Chronological age (CA) Calendar age, regardless of mental development. 436
Chunking Pulling together of separate items to be remembered into related "chunks" so that there are fewer total items to be recalled; a way of reducing the limitation of 7 ± 2 items in short-term memory. 284
Circadian cycle An approximately 24-hour biological cycle involving numerous physiological and behavioral changes, occurring in many species. 214
Civil commitment, 500–501
Clang associations, 486–487
Classical conditioning The process of pairing a neutral stimulus and a reflex-eliciting stimulus so that the neutral stimulus comes to elicit a version of the reflex; also called Pavlovian conditioning. 243–249
   applied, 248–249
   overview of, 244–247
   therapies based on, 516–518
   vicarious, 546
Client-centered therapy Rogers's nondirective therapy, a major form of humanistic therapy, in which the negative implications of the label *patient* are avoided by use of the term *client*; clients are encouraged to be themselves and progress naturally toward finding their own solutions to problems, seeking congruence between their sense of self and their experience. 23, 424, 515
Clinical psychologist A psychologist specializing in psychotherapy, holding a Ph.D. based on research training or a Psy.D. degree based on a more applied program. 509
CNS. *See* Central nervous system
Cocaine, 236
Cochlea Fluid-filled, spiral-shaped

structure of the inner ear that contains the sound transducers. 162

Coefficient of correlation (r) A summary of the degree of relationship between two variables that expresses what is displayed in a scatter plot; the higher the value between 0 and 1 the stronger the relationship (less scatter in the plot). 31

Cognitive-behavioral therapies Therapies utilizing behaviorism's emphasis on learned behavior but adding an emphasis on covert behaviors; the best known is social learning theory, although some other forms are more cognitively focused. 519–523, 524

Cognitive behaviorism View proposed by Donald Meichenbaum and others that retains a behavioral focus but permits exploration of covert behaviors, such as covert speech as a help in self-direction: "OK, now I need to attach this part to that one. . . ." 27

Cognitive biases, 535

Cognitive demon, 190, 193

Cognitive development:
    in adolescence, 393–394
    in adulthood, 398
    in childhood, 388–389
    in infancy, 382–384
    Piaget's theory of, 373–376

Cognitive dissonance theory Festinger's theory of the motivational effects of cognitions that do not "fit," that is, are *dissonant*; dissonant cognitions motivate some action to reduce the dissonance, including changes in behavior, attitudes, or cognitions. 546

Cognitive learning, 268–270

Cognitive map A mental representation of a known physical location; to Tolman an animal's cognitive maps were an important part of purposive behaviorism and to cognitive psychologists human cognitive maps are representative of various psychological dimensions as well as physical ones. 270, 352

Cognitive perspective An information-processing focus on how human thinking develops and functions and on the (possibly) uniquely human functions of thinking, problem solving, and creativity. 24–25

Cognitive–response approach A theory of attitude change proposing that the recipient of a communication generates cognitive arguments for or against a message, depending on aspects of both the message and the recipient; the recipient may think of counterarguments to advertisements and supporting arguments for a doctor's message. 549

Cognitive restructuring A cognitive-behavioral therapy developed by Aaron Beck to help clients alter their highly individual self-defeating beliefs by actively restructuring their own cognitions. 522–523

Collective unconscious Jung's concept of universal archetypes shared by all humans as an evolutionary heritage; like the Freudian unconscious, it can influence behavior but not directly enter consciousness. 417

Color, 145, 148–149

Color blindness The inability to make all the color distinctions that most people do. 124, 187

Color circle An arrangement of the colors we perceive into a circular pattern in which complementary colors are opposite each other. 149

Color constancy The automatic perceptual assumption that objects remain their original color despite changes in amount or color of illuminating light. 184

Color contrast, 187

Color perception, 186–188

Color solid A simultaneous representation of the three psychological dimensions of color (hue, brightness, and saturation); what we perceive as the richest colors are the hues of high saturation and medium brightness around the circumference. 149

Commission on Obscenity and
    Pornography, 577

Commitment Placement in a mental hospital for short-term observation or long-term treatment, either voluntary or involuntary; the latter usually requires that the patient be certified by psychiatrists as both mentally ill and dangerous to self and others. 500–501, 502

Committed, 500

Communicator credibility In the message-learning approach, how credible the source of a message seems to be, as viewed by the recipient of the message; credible communicators are more likely to be believed and their messages heeded. 548

Compensation, 416

Complementaries Colors opposite each other on the color circle: If lights of these colors (such as red/green) are mixed we perceive a neutral gray. 149

Complex cells Cerebral cortex visual cells that are sensitive to shape and movement and can respond to a combination of information from the simple cells. 189, 191

Compliance A social effect on behavior, the yielding to group norms even when the individual believes differently. 551

Compulsions Behaviors that a person feels compelled to carry out, even though they serve no useful purpose. 475–476

Computer-simulation models Models of human thinking and problem solving in the form of programs designed for computers; if such a program generates outputs that are akin to those of humans, it is considered a potentially useful simulation of human activity for further research. 336

Concept A generalized idea that represents all examples of a given class of object, event, and so on, but is not the same as any of them; for example, *dog*, *three*, *green*, and *truth* are all concepts that have wide applicability. 327
    natural, 339

Concept formation, 339–341

Concordance rate The percentage of other family members who show a condition, used to assess whether a condition is genetically based. 482–483

Concrete operational stage The third Piagetian developmental stage, from age 7 to 12, in which a child can perform mental operations involving physical objects but cannot grasp abstract concepts. 374, 388–389

Conditioned emotional response (CER) *See* Conditioned suppression

Conditioned response (CR) The version of the reflexive response that the conditioned response comes to elicit through classical conditioning. 245

Conditioned stimulus (CS) The neutral stimulus that does not initially elicit a reflexive response but in classical conditioning is conditioned to do so. 245

Conditioned suppression A conditioned suppression of behavior resulting from pairing of a conditioned stimulus with an aversive unconditioned stimulus such as a shock; the conditioned stimulus seems to act as a warning and the conditioned emotional response (CER) as an adaptive response to the warning. 250

Conditioning, 242–264
    aversion, 248
    backward, 245
    classical, 243–249, 516–518
    contiguity in, 250
    instrumental, 249
    operant, 249–262, 519
    second-order, 245

Cones One of the two types of transducers in the eye; cones are less sensitive to light than rods but provide color vision in strong enough light (such as daylight). 150–152, 153

Conflict, types of, 418–419

Confounded variables Variables that jointly change prior to some event of interest, so that which one (if any) actually caused the event cannot be determined without further research. 32–33

Congruence, 424

Connotative meaning A word's overtones or implications, often emotional ones. 327–328

Conscience In Freud's view, a behavior trait that develops during the latency period marked by the internalizing of parental moral and ethical demands. 390. *See also* Moral development

Consciousness A process of experiencing the external and internal environment in ways that separate immediate stimuli from immediate responses; the ability to process and "understand" stimuli rather than merely respond to them. 15, 211–237
    altered states of, 214–237
    definition of, 211–212
    divisions of, 213
    drugs and, 232–237
    functions of, 212–213
    hypnosis and, 229–232
    meditation and, 232
    sleep and, 214–228
    states of, 214

Conscious processes In the Freudian division of consciousness into three

Conscious processes (*cont.*)
levels, the ones that are in awareness at a given time, corresponding closely to what most people think of as consciousness. 213

Consent, informed, 8

Conservation The holding constant, in one's constructed world, of features or attributes of the physical world despite apparent changes in them, a key Piagetian concept. 373, 388

Consolidation The process by which new memories have been said to lead to permanently stored traces in long-term memory; in recent years the question whether consolidation time is actually required and, if so, how much has come under increasing scrutiny. 280

Constancies, perceptual, 183–186
  color, 184
  generalized object, 185–186
  location, 184, 185
  shape, 184–185
  size, 183, 184, 185

Constitutional traits, 412

Constraints on learning The limits to operant conditioning that may be imposed by innate learning or behavioral tendencies, a topic of some controversy in learning theory. 262

Constructive memory The constructing of patterns of information that were not originally stored in that form, an adaptive system that can cause helpful or confusing variations in memory retrieval. 296–300

Construct validity A way of assessing a test's validity by comparing it to multiple separate criteria, none of which is adequate alone, but the group of which taken together are a definition of the characteristic to be tested. 436

Contiguity Simple "side-by-side" association; in classical conditioning, long thought to be the necessary and sufficient pattern for conditioning, but now questioned by researchers who propose additional factors such as the information value or "belongingness" of the conditioning arrangement. 250

Contingency An arrangement for reinforcement or punishment to follow a particular operant regularly; the reinforcement or punishment is said to be contingent on the performance of the operant. 256–257

Contingent, 256

Contralateral, 68

Control, 4

Control group The group in a scientific experiment that is affected by all factors exactly as is the experimental group except for what is hypothesized to be the critical part of the procedure; the group is thus usually given a placebo drug or therapy instead of the experimental treatment. 34–35

Convergence The turning inward of the eyes that offers a binocular cue to the closeness of an object through feedback from the eye muscles. 199, 201

Convergent thought A narrowing down from many alternatives toward a single correct answer, typically used in problem solving and measured by intelligence tests. 362

Conversion disorder A somatoform category of mental disorder in which symptoms of some physical problem are shown even though tests indicate there is nothing organically wrong. 478–479

Conversion reaction, 479

Cooperative principle The usual assumption by a listener that a speaker is trying to tell the truth, to tell all that is needed to be known and no more, and to be relevant, clear, and unambiguous. 325

Coprolites, 84

Cornea The clear front of the eye through which light first passes; often considered merely a "window," it is actually a fixed-shape lens that provides much of the eyes' total focusing. 149

Corpus callosum The band of tissue joining the two halves of the cerebrum; the tissue severed in split-brain operations. 64, 68–69, 73

Correlation A statistical technique for describing how closely related two sets of numbers are; it is useful in exploring relationships, but it can never tell *why* the numbers are related. 29, 30–32
  coefficient of, 31

Correspondent inference An attribution by an observer of an individual's behavior to the actor's intentions and general dispositions to behave; whether this will happen depends on the presence of noncommon effects, the social desirability of the behavior, and whether the individual is seen as having a free choice in behaving. 538–539

Cortex, 59

Cortical blindness Blindness in a portion of each eye resulting from damage to the occipital cortex, in which other portions of the brain help correct for missing information caused by the blind spots. 155

Counseling psychologist A psychologist holding an M.A. or Ph.D. degree who generally works with people whose behavior is within "normal" boundaries. 509

Counterconditioning A behavioral-therapy approach based on classical conditioning that seeks to replace an inappropriate response to some stimulus with a more appropriate one, usually replacing anxiety with relaxation. 517–518

Countertransference Transferring of a psychoanalyst's emotional responses onto a patient; to help avoid this phenomenon, psychoanalysts are required to undergo psychoanalysis as part of their training. 514

Courtroom, psychology of, 578–580

Covert behavior Nonobservable behavior, measurable only indirectly. 20

Covert modeling A cognitive-behavioral therapy technique in which clients imagine watching a model exhibit a behavior or imagine themselves behaving more effectively, as opposed to the usual techniques of modeling in which the target behavior actually occurs. 521

Cranial nerves, 56

Creativity For many psychologists, equivalent to flexible, innovative problem solving in any field. 361–364

Credibility, 548

Cretinism, 458

Criminal commitment, 502

Criterion-referenced approach Any technique of test building in which the measure of quality is the extent to which results match an existing criterion; in personality theory, the approach utilized in building the MMPI, in which the criteria are the answers given by a group of people of some known dimension, such as mental patients; only questions answered differently by the criterion group are retained. 426

Criterion validity A basic type of test validity that judges a new measure by comparing it to an existing criterion measure. 435, 436

Critical periods Particular times during prenatal development at which developmental events must occur if they are to be effective; sometimes refers to postnatal periods during which some developmental event must occur if it is to happen normally. 370–371

Cross-cueing, 69–70

Cross-sectional studies Studies of some factor, such as intelligence, that compare several different age groups within a population at a given time. 441

Cross-tolerance An effect of some drugs whereby the tolerance built up to one drug makes the user tolerant to another; thus a higher dosage of the second drug is needed to attain a desired effect. 233

Crowding, 582–584

Crystallized intelligence Cattell's concept of the ability to recover old knowledge when appropriate to new occasions, as opposed to fluid intelligence. 446

Cue salience A major cognitive bias, referring to the greater impact that some cues or types of information, often physical ones, exert on impression formation. 537

Cultural evolution The refinement and transmission of information outside of physiology; culture has become the primary mode of adaptation for humans and it sets us apart from our precultural ancestors more than do biological changes. 89–91

Cultural relativity, 421

Culture-fair tests Intelligence assessment tools that attempt to avoid reliance on items that differ among cultures or ethnic subcultures; also called culture-free tests. 461

Culture-free tests Another name for culture-fair tests. 461

Culture-specific tests Tools for the assessment of intelligence that attempt to correct for cultural bias by being written separately for various minority populations, taking social and medical factors into account. 461

Cumulative curve The shape of the data generated by a cumulative recorder, indicating the general course of learning or extinction. 253

Cumulative recorder In operant conditioning, a device that automatically charts the progress of conditioning or extinction by recording each new operant as it occurs. 252–253

Curiosity, 116

Curve A smooth line connecting plotted points in a graphic data display, sometimes actually made up of a series of straight lines. 592

Dark adaptation Process by which the light receptors in the eye (rods and cones) regain their maximum sensitivity in the dark, following prior exposure to light; a two-step process in which cones adapt first but remain less sensitive to weak light than rods. 152

Darwin, Charles The British biologist whose theory of evolution by natural selection revolutionized our view of the origins of species—including our own—and whose work forms the basis of most study of evolution since. (1806–1882) 10, 80–81, 105, 124, 130, 408

Data In statistical analysis, a set of numbers that measure some phenomenon of interest; each number represents a datum, more than one are data, and the set of numbers to which the various statistics are applied is the data base. 589

Day residue, 223

Death instinct One of the two basic powerful instincts, according to psychoanalytic theory, reflected primarily in various forms of aggression. 18

Decay A fading of information from some memory store solely because time has passed; a usual source of loss from the sensory registers and a potential source of loss from short-term memory, but no longer felt to play an important role in loss from long-term memory. 278

Decibels (db) Units of measurement of loudness that measure a sound wave's maximum pressure (above atmospheric pressure); increases on the scale are geometric, so "10 db louder" means a sound 10 times greater in intensity. 160

Defense mechanisms In the psychoanalytic view, the means used by a well-adapted personality to deal with the potential anxiety caused by the conflict between id demands and superego constraints (can become abnormal if carried to extreme lengths). 415, 416

Deinstitutionalization Process of returning mental patients back to their communities as large hospitals are shut down, for financial or other reasons, which often means maladapted ex-patients lack both adequate treatment and basic necessities. 502

Déjà vu The sensation of having had an experience before, possibly caused by the process of automatically matching inputs

against long-term memory to produce "new" or "old" evaluations. 296

Delirium tremens, 224

Delusion A major disruption of thought, often seen in schizophrenics, in which a belief is held that is considered untrue (and often bizarre) by others. 487

Dementia praecox, 486. *See also* Schizophrenic disorders

Demerol, 236

Demonic possession, 466

Dendrites Branches projecting from neurons that receive information from other neurons. 47, 51

Denial of reality, 416

Denotative meaning A word's objective and specific meaning, such as a dictionary definition. 327

Deoxyribonucleic acid. *See* DNA

Dependent variables The measures of the outcome of an experimental procedure, such as the reduction of pain in a drug study. 35

Depersonalization A dissociative disorder characterized by a sudden loss of the normal sense of self, usually following severe stress; less severe symptoms are not uncommon in college students away from home for the first time. 481

Depressants Psychoactive drugs that reduce the level of nervous-system activity. 232, 233–236

Depression, major, 483–486

Deprivation dwarfism, 74

Depth perception, 192–202, 203–206

Descriptive statistics Numerical techniques for describing aspects of a data base, for example, noting how many subjects behave in some way, how frequently a particular behavior occurs, and so forth. 589, 590–595

central tendency, 592–593
curves, 592
distributions, 592
graphic displays, 591–592
numbers, 590
scales, 590
variation, 593–595

Desensitization, systematic, 517, 518

Determinism The view that behavior is fully determined by natural laws akin to those of chemistry or physics. 9

Development To psychologists, all aspects of the process of going from genetic potential to being some particular adult, especially in the period from birth on. 369–401

adolescence, 393–396
adulthood, 396–399
aging, 399–401
childhood, 387–393
infancy, 381–387
postnatal, 371–381
prenatal, 370–371

Developmental causes Nature and nurture factors that have acted over the course of a person's lifetime to make him or her the person he or she is at any given time. 11–12

Developmental-stage theories, 373–379
cognitive, 373–376
moral, 374, 376, 377

psychosexual, 374, 376–378
psychosocial, 374, 378–379, 380

Deviation quotient A contemporary form of calculation of IQ in which the basis for the IQ number is *not* mental age divided by chronological age, but is calculated in terms of how many standard deviations above or below the norm for a reference group a person's score on the test is. 437

Diagnostic and Statistical Manual. See DSM-III

Dialect A variation on a language in which speakers of each dialect use enough different words and rules that communication is impeded. 317

Diet:
aging and, 399–400
birth defects and, 371
mental retardation and, 458

Diethylstilbestrol (DES), 126

Difference threshold The smallest difference between two stimuli that will allow them to be sensed as different. 145

Diffusion of responsibility The effect on bystander intervention of the presence of others who can help, which seems to lessen the responsibility of each individual to act. 565

Discrimination In classical conditioning, the tendency of organisms not to respond to stimuli that are notably different from the CS; in operant conditioning, the tendency for organisms not to emit an operant in the presence of stimuli that are different from the original S_D *or* the tendency not to emit operants that are different from the original one.
in classical conditioning, 247
in operant conditioning, 251

Discriminative stimulus (S_D) A stimulus that sets the occasion for an operant to occur in conditioning (rather than causing the operant) because in the past it has been followed by a reinforcer. 251

Disorganized schizophrenia One of the five DSM-III subcategories of schizophrenia, characterized by a mixture of symptoms including inappropriate giggling and peculiar gestures, loss of normal inhibitions, meaningless speech, and hallucinations and delusions; disorganized schizophrenics generally become disturbed earlier and remain less responsive to treatment than those in other categories. 489

Displacement The process by which information is lost, or pushed out of the limited storage area of short-term memory by other incoming information. 278, 416

Disproof Lack of support for a hypothesis in an experiment; an experiment must be designed so that disproof is possible if the hypothesis is not true because only then will support of the hypothesis be meaningful. 596–597

Dissociative disorders Rare conditions in which a person shows a sudden and temporary dissociating of normal con-

Dissociative disorders (cont.)
sciousness, identity, or memory, including the extreme of behaving as two or more separate people (multiple personality). 479–481
Distribution, 592, 593
Diurnal Adapted evolutionarily for being active primarily during the day (as humans are); diurnal organisms have a basic circadian cycle of about 25 hours that is synchronized to 24 by the effects of daylight. 216
Divergent thought An expanding or widening of possibilities or moving toward more remote choices, the type of thought typically measured by creativity tests. 362
Dizygotic (DZ) twins Fraternal twins, genetically only siblings because they develop from separate zygotes. 92
DNA Abbreviation for deoxyribonucleic acid, the double-spiral molecule that forms the basis of all genes. 91–92
recombinant, 99
Dollard, John Codeveloper with Neal Miller of a behavioral approach to personality. (1900–1980) 264, 418–419, 572
Dominant gene A gene that overrides an alternate form, as when a person heterozygous for blue and brown eyes has brown eyes because that gene is dominant. 92
Dopamine, 52
Dopamine hypothesis The proposal that schizophrenics have either an excess of dopamine or an excess of receptor sites for it, with the further implication that this excess of dopamine is a cause of their symptoms (although the excess of dopamine could itself be caused by some other factor); evidence suggests antipsychotic drugs are effective with schizophrenia in proportion to their effectiveness in blocking dopamine, which supports the hypothesis. 491
Doppler effect The apparent change in pitch of a moving object—a steady pitch as an object approaches a listener with an abrupt drop to a lower pitch as it passes—caused by changes in the frequencies of the sound waves as received at the ear. 159
Double-blind test Procedure for guarding against bias in experimental results by having experimenters who observe or interact with subjects be unaware of ("blind" to) which subjects are receiving the experimental treatment and which the placebo; since subjects are also unaware, the procedure is "double-blind." 35
Double language view A contemporary monist position that it might be convenient to use mental terms in some situations and body (or brain) terms in others, but maintaining that these refer to the same kind of activity. 11, 44, 45
Dowager's hump, 400
Down's syndrome A common genetic cause of mental deficiency, which results from incorrect cellular division, causes readily identifiable facial and body

characteristics, and is the cause of 10–20% of severe retardation. 95, 98, 457, 459
Dream analysis One of the five key processes of psychoanalysis: remembering, reporting, and trying to find the meaning hidden in the plots of the patient's dreams, in order to understand the conflicts thought to be represented but disguised. 512
Dreams, 223, 226
Drift, 84
Drinking circuits The neural and hormonal linkages among tissues, organs, and the nervous system whose activity is what biologically corresponds to thirst; closely tied into the hypothalamus. 112, 113
Drive In the need-drive view of motivation, the general energizing of body activity that results from a tissue need. 112, 418
Drug dependence, 232
Drugs:
    aggression and, 571–572
    neurotransmitters, 52–53, 236
    See also Psychoactive drugs
Drug therapy, 506–508
Drug tolerance, 232
Drug withdrawal, 232–233
DSM-III The current third version of the *Diagnostic and Statistical Manual* published by the American Psychiatric Association, which provides the standards for specifying and categorizing (diagnosing, in the medical model) abnormal behaviors. 471, 472
Dual-code theory A theory of long-term memory suggesting that there are two semi-independent encoding and storage systems, verbal and visual. 286
Dualists Those who believe that mind and body are different and somehow influence each other; this is commonly accepted in our culture. 11
Duncker's candle problem, 360
Duplex model A major model of memory emphasizing the two processes of short-term and long-term memory as well as sensory registers. 277–280
Dwarfism, 74–75
Dyslexia Syndrome of problems in reading and coordination involving left/right distinctions, possibly caused by a failure of left and right sides of the brain to develop the normal pattern of specialization. 67
Dysomnias Abnormal patterns of sleep, including sleepwalking, sleeptalking, and "night terrors" in young children. 226

Ear, 161–165
    accessory structures of, 161–162
    auditory nerves, 162–165
    inner, 162
    middle, 161–162
    outer, 161
    transducers of, 162
Ear canal Tubular portion of the ear just inside the head that helps to amplify incoming sound waves. 161

Eardrum Flexible membrane between the outer and middle ear that is set in motion by air vibrations and in turn causes vibrations in the bones of the middle ear. 161
Ebbinghaus, Hermann Pioneer in the scientific study of memory, whose best-known finding is the forgetting curve. (1850–1909) 276, 277, 293
Echo A representation of sound in echoic memory, lasting a few seconds. 283
Echoic memory The auditory sensory register. 283
Eclectic approaches Combinations of various psychotherapeutic approaches, including seemingly opposing ones such as psychoanalytic and behavioral approaches, as used by practicing therapists, rather than the conceptually "pure" approaches of theoreticians and researchers. 510
Ecological validity, 570
Ectomorph, 407
Ectotherms, 110
Education, 391
EEG. *See* Electroencephalogram
Effect, law of, 249
Ego In psychoanalytic theory, one of three basic elements whose interrelationships determine personality development, through the child's interaction with the external world; the rational agent that seeks compromise between id demands and superego constraints. 18, 414
Egocentric Self-focused and unable to adopt someone else's view, as is a child in the Piagetian preoperational phase. 374, 388
Eidetic imagery The ability to maintain visual images in short-term memory, either new inputs or ones retrieved from long-term memory, in a manner so precise they can be scanned; also called photographic memory. 300–301
Elaborative rehearsal Repetition of material combined with processing at the deepest level of memory to elaborate its meaning for encoding and thus to improve later recall from long-term memory. 286–287
Electra complex The female equivalent of the Oedipus complex, in which the castration complex is replaced by penis envy. 390
Electroconvulsive therapy (ECT) Treatment for severe depression using convulsions induced by electric shock to the head; commonly called shock treatment. 503–505, 506
Electroencephalogram (EEG) A means of measuring the brain's function by charting electrical potential measured at points on the scalp; commonly known as brain wave. 43–44, 46, 218–219, 220, 221
Electromyogram (EMG) A measurement of body muscle activity, useful in assessing stages of sleep, especially REM. 219
Electrooculogram (EOG) A measurement of eye movement, useful in

assessing stages of sleep, especially REM. 219

Embryo An implanted human zygote at the third to ninth weeks of development; at eight weeks the embryo is slightly more than an inch long but has a recognizable brain, a heart that pumps blood, functioning kidneys and endocrine system, and the beginnings of reflexive behavior. 370

EMG. *See* Electromyogram

Emotions Affective experiences, that is, those causing body arousal and having meaning or value to the experiencer. 107–109, 130–137
    autonomic system and, 62
    biological factors in, 109
    cognitive factors in, 109
    controlling, 137
    definition of, 108
    experiencing, 130
    expressing, 130–131, 132, 133
    learning factors in, 109
    lie detection and, 135–136
    manipulating, 137
    memory and, 298–299
    survival through, 107–108
    theories of, 131, 134–135

Empathy In client-centered therapy, the accepting and clarifying of the client's expressed emotions. 515

Empiricist theories Theories that emphasize nurture factors, suggesting that some behavior, such as perception, is largely learned. 175–176

Encoding The process of putting information in the proper form or code for storage in memory. 276, 282–289

Encounter groups Humanistically oriented therapy groups in which the participants share their feelings about each other; also called sensitivity groups. 524

Endocrine glands, 74

Endocrine system The set of specialized glands that secrete hormones, usually directly into the bloodstream. 41, 74–76

Endomorph, 407

Endorphins A class of neurotransmitters with a chemical similarity to morphine that seem to be natural pain relievers; short for "endogenous (internal) morphines." 52, 171, 236

Endotherms, 110

Environment:
    intelligence and, 440–441
    schizophrenia and, 491–492

Environmental psychology A subspecialty of psychology focusing on the built environment—the specific arrangement of cities and their contents, from furniture to traffic planning, and how these influence behavior. 580–584

Environmental traits, 412

EOG. *See* Electrooculogram

Epilepsy, 49, 62

Episodic dyscontrol syndrome, 571

Erikson, Erik H. Developer of the theory of psychosocial stages of development, which stresses interactions between the individual and society and identifies psychosocial crises or conflicts that mark different stages of life. (1902–   ) 373,

374, 378–379, 380, 385, 386, 390, 392, 395, 396, 398, 401, 417–418

Erogenous zone A body area responsive to sexual pleasure; an important concept in Freud's definition of psychosexual stages. 378

Estrogen One of the best known and most important of the hormones; produced by the ovaries and normally considered to be "female," it is also produced in much smaller amounts by the testes. 125

Ethics, 7–8

Ethnic-profile hypothesis The possibility that different ethnic groups might have consistently different patterns of thought, independent of overall intelligence. 461

Ethological perspective The psychological perspective, based on the ethological view in biology, that emphasizes how humans evolved as a species and what that evolution implies about behavior. 25, 26

Ethology, 25, 26

Eugenics The deliberate breeding of humans selected for desirable characteristics. 97

Events, perception of, 209

Evolution The process by which the characteristics of all species change to keep them fitted to their environment; the major unifying principle of modern biology. 79–91
    human cultural, 89–91
    human physical, 84–89
    processes of, 80–84
    theory of, 10

Evolutionary tree A conceptual tool for summarizing evolutionary relationships: Its roots are the early life forms and each branch is a separate species splitting off from the others. 84–85, 86

Excitatory synapses Synapses at which the effect of the neurotransmitter is to make the postsynaptic neuron more likely to fire. 49, 50

Exercise, law of, 249

Expectation, and perception, 182–183

Experimental group The group in a scientific experiment that receives the procedure hypothesized to be effective. 34

Experimental method The basic procedure in the scientific method; a way of discovering the causes of events of interest by controlling all but a few key variables (the independent variables) and then measuring the effects of those variables (by measuring dependent variables). 32–36

Experimental treatment The procedure or treatment in an experiment, such as a drug or therapy, hypothesized to be effective. 34

Extinction In psychology, an apparent weakening of learning as a result of a series of nonreinforced trials: In classical conditioning, a series of presentations of the conditioned stimulus without the unconditioned stimulus in which the conditioned stimulus eventually becomes neutral; in operant conditioning, the

nonreinforced trials are a series of occasions when the operant is *not* followed by reinforcement. In evolutionary theory, the dying out of a species without leaving direct descendants. 81
    in classical conditioning, 246, 247
    in operant conditioning, 251, 256

Extrinsic Artificially related to a situation; extrinsic reinforcements and punishments are consequences of deliberate human arrangements. 257

Extroversion, 413

Eye, 149–155
    accessory structures of, 149–150
    accommodation of, 149–150
    optic nerves of, 152–155
    transducers of, 150–152

Eye color, 92, 93

Eyewitness testimony:
    problems of, 297–298, 299
    psychology of, 579

Eysenck, Hans J. Developer of a factor-analytic personality theory based on three personality dimensions (neuroticism, psychoticism, and introversion-extroversion) and an intelligence factor; known to psychotherapists for his view that psychotherapy may be generally no more effective than no treatment at all. (1916–   ) 413–414, 430, 513

Facial expressions, 131, 132, 133

Factor analysis, 412–413

False consensus The tendency to assume that most other people behave as we do when it is not necessarily true; a type of attribution bias. 539

Falsifiability The quality of a prediction that enables it to be tested experimentally. If a prediction is falsifiable, the experiment will show it to be incorrect if it is so; if an experiment does not show a falsifiable prediction to be wrong, it supports or confirms the hypothesis. 33, 596

Families, inbreeding of, 95–96

Fantasy, 416

Farsighted Being able to see clearly only for relatively distant objects, a common vision problem caused by an eyeball that is too short from front to back so that the lens cannot focus the images of near objects. 150

Feature detectors Specialized visual cells found in several animal species and presumably occurring in humans that are responsive to particular complex aspects of a visual stimulus, such as a line, angle, or shape; the further along the sequence of visual processing, the more complex these would be, with line and angle detectors, for example, being summarized by shape detectors. 189

Features, perception of, 188–193

Fechner, Gustav Early psychologist whose recognition of the mathematical lawfulness of mental phenomena marked the beginning of scientific psychology. (1801–1887) 13

Feedback loops In homeostatic motivations, the arrangement of sensors and effector mechanisms so that change in sensed information is "fed back" to cause a change in effector action. 111

Fertilization, 92

Fetal alcohol syndrome, 371

Fetus Human zygote from the ninth week after conception until birth, with the beginning of the period marked by the point at which the embryo develops bone cells. 370

Field studies Experiments that are conducted in natural settings rather than laboratories, often using people who do not know they have been experimental subjects. 542

Fight-or-flight response The survival mechanism by which the sympathetic system activates the internal organs, presumably as a preparation for fighting or fleeing. 54, 116, 117

Firing The sending of a single electrochemical pulse by a neuron along its axon; a neuron conveys information in terms of the rate at which it fires. 47

First language The native language one learns at home. 318

Fixated Being static and not progressing beyond one of the first four Freudian stages of psychosexual development. 378, 415

Fixed-interval (FI) schedules Partial-reinforcement schedules of operant conditioning that reinforce the next operant after a fixed time since the last reinforcement. 257

Fixed-ratio (FR) schedules Partial-reinforcement schedules of conditioning that reinforce the next operant after some fixed number of unreinforced ones. 257

Flooding A controversial form of counterconditioning in which the therapist presents the strongest, rather than the weakest, fear-evoking stimulus on the patient's hierarchy. 518

Flowchart A technique for visual representation of relationships (including psychological processes) representing a series of activities as a set of boxes linked by lines or arrows. 352

Fluid intelligence Cattell's concept of the ability to judge and respond to novel situations, as opposed to crystallized intelligence. 445–446

Focusing Bending of light waves by a lens (of an eye or camera) to bring them together to a point behind the lens. 149

Food, and taste, 167. *See also* Diet; Hunger; Obesity

Forewarning effects In the cognitive-response theory of communication persuasibility, those effects (like inoculation) that warn the recipient of a message that someone is about to try to change his or her mind, which will generate a rehearsal of counterarguments to help resist persuasion. 549

Forgetting curve Ebbinghaus's discovery that forgetting occurs relatively soon after a learning experience, with less and less forgetting thereafter. 276

Formal operational stage The fourth Piagetian developmental stage, usually from age 12 to 15, when a person becomes able to appreciate abstractions, formal logic, and other complex relationships that require manipulation of abstract concepts. 375, 393–394

Fortification illusions, 192

Fossils, 80, 81, 84, 85

Fovea Area of the retina at the center of the back of the eye having a dense concentration of cones and no covering layer of blood vessels, thus providing the most precise vision (in daylight); to "look at" something means to point the fovea at it. 151–152

Fraternal twins, 92

Free association One of the five key processes of psychoanalysis: saying whatever comes to mind during a therapy session without any attempts to edit, so that the chain of thought will lead toward the root of the problem. 512

Free-floating anxiety, 475

Free recall The attempt to remember something, such as items on a list, but in any order (unlike the sequenced recall of serial learning); often used as a type of laboratory test for memory, one that is more akin to everyday memory than is serial learning. 279–280

Free will The freedom of humans to choose to behave as they wish. 9

Frequency A measure of how often some event occurs; in hearing, the rate at which a sound wave cycles from one peak of compression or expansion to the next, expressed in terms of Hertz (Hz) or full cycles per second. 156

Frequency distribution The overall distribution of any data base. 592

Frequency histogram A graphic display of data using vertical bars drawn to heights that represent the frequency of some event (the number of times it occurs) for several groups. 591

Frequency polygon A graphic display of data related to the frequency histogram wherein points on the bars that represent intervals are connected by straight lines; as the intervals become more frequent and there are more points, the polygon will look more like a plotted curve. 591

Freud, Sigmund The founder and developer of psychoanalysis, whose ideas have strongly influenced 20th-century scientific and popular thinking. (1856–1939) 16–18, 28, 213, 226, 230, 236, 373, 374, 376–378, 379, 385, 389, 390, 394, 396, 398, 412, 414–416, 417, 418, 474, 479, 484–485, 512–514, 570

Freudian psychoanalysis, 414–416

Freudian slips, 415

Frontal lobe The portion of the cerebrum in the forehead, involved in making and carrying out plans; the rearmost portion contains the motor strip, for body control; often disconnected in early psychosurgery to reduce aggressive behavior. 65, 66

Frustration-aggression hypothesis A major view of aggression that proposes that a tendency to aggression is an innate response to frustration, although the actual occurrence and pattern of aggressive behavior may depend on learned patterns of response to situational cues. 572

Functional autonomy Allport's concept that motives, although learned in the past, are functionally autonomous; they operate in the present and are best understood in terms of their present role. 412

Functional causes Nonorganic causes of abnormal behavior, such as emotional conflicts, inappropriate socialization, or faulty learning. 468

Functional fixedness The tendency to maintain, mentally, the function assigned to objects and not see that they could serve other purposes, a major thinking bias noted by Gestalt psychologists. 359–360

Functionalism An early American school of psychology focusing on individual differences that asked what function consciousness serves (primarily in terms of aiding survival). 14

Fundamental attribution error The tendency to overestimate the importance of internal dispositions as causes of behavior and to underestimate the importance of situational causes; a major attribution bias. 540

Galapagos Islands, 80

Gamma-aminobutyric acid (GABA), 52

Ganglion cells, 152, 154

Gate-control theory A major theory of the interpretation of pain sensations suggesting that pain sensory messages are carried to the brain by one type of axon; another type of axon that runs down from the brain to synapse with the first type supposedly interrupts the flow of pain messages to the brain, "closing the gate." 171

Gender identity The sense of self as male or female, including both sexual and culturally coded sex-role behaviors. 128

Gender role The full set of behaviors that society expects of members of each sex, including many that are not relevant to reproduction. 128

Gender schema A self-schema for one's sense of self as male or female. 530–532, 533

Gene pool The total of all the genes in the living members of a species, representing all of the current genetic possibilities for that species. 94

General Adaptation Syndrome (G.A.S.), 476

General intelligence factor (g) Spearman's single intellectual factor that seemed influential on a variety of tasks in factor analysis of intelligence, supplemented by specific factors (s). 444

Generalization In classical conditioning, the tendency of organisms to respond to stimuli that are somehow similar to the CS; in operant conditioning, the tendency for organisms to emit an operant in the presence of stimuli that are similar to the original S_D *or the* tendency to emit operants that are similar to the original one.

    in classical conditioning, 247
    in operant conditioning, 251

Generalization curve The pattern of a subject's response to a range of stimuli; the breadth of the curve is a measure of both generalization and discrimination (a broad curve implying generalization and a narrow one implying discrimination). 247

Generalized anxiety disorders Disorders characterized by chronic, nonspecific (free-floating) anxiety; the typical pattern of worry about a variety of problems may be a cause of the anxiety or an attempt to understand it. 475

Generalized object constancy The combination of perceptual constancies that make up the tendency to perceive the environment in terms of stable, solid, predictable objects. 185–186

Generalized reinforcers, 254

General Problem Solver (GPS) A computer-simulation model of problem solving that uses the two-step process of the means/end heuristic. 358–359

Generativity, 398

Genes Specialized molecular structures that store and transmit codes for body processes, and thus the results of a species' evolution, from one generation to the next. 91–94
    dominant, 92
    recessive, 92

Gene splicing, 99

Genetic counseling Specific information and advice to potential parents about their own genetic characteristics and therefore the possible consequences for their offspring; often provided when some family history of genetic disease is known. 98

Genetic diseases, 96–97

Genetic engineering Correction or replacement of a faulty gene or other genetic manipulation intended to alter the structure or behavior of an organism. 99

Genetics, 91–104
    behavioral, 99–101
    chromosomes, 91, 92
    DNA, 91–92
    genes, 91–94
    intelligence and, 439
    manipulations of, 97–99
    nature/nurture interaction and, 101–104
    personality and, 408–409
    schizophrenia and, 490–491
    variations in, 94–96

Genitals The body structures used in intercourse and the last reproductive structures to develop prenatally; in the absence of an androgen the previously neutral structures will develop into female genitals and in the presence of testosterone they develop as male. 125–126

Genital stage Final Freudian stage of psychosexual development, from puberty to adulthood, during which direct sexuality returns and is focused outward to others, becoming relationship-centered. 378, 394

Genotype The genetic pattern that a person inherits, no matter what characteristics are expressed; it includes those recessive traits for which the person is a carrier. 92, 103

Gestalt psychology School of psychology founded in Germany that focuses on organized "wholes" in perception rather than the individual elements that make them up. 176–177, 268

Gifted Those who are in the top few percent of the population on an IQ measure as a result of nature and nurture factors going well. 454, 456

Gland A body organ that secretes a chemical, such as sweat or a hormone. 74

Glutamate, 52

Glycine, 52

Goal gradient, 419

Gonads The sex glands: the male testes or female ovaries. 125

Grammar The complete description of how the sounds (or other symbols, in a nonspoken language such as Ameslan) of a language are related to its meaning; a set of implicit rules for three aspects of language—phonology, syntax, and semantics. 308

Group conflict, reduction of, 556–557

Group differentiation, 555–556

Group polarization The tendency for group discussion to move individual members' opinions toward the average opinion of the group: more risky if the group favors risk-taking, less risky if the group is conservative. 554

Group processes, 552–555

Group productivity, 554–555

Group survival motives, 118–122
    parenting, 118, 121
    sexual, 121–122

Group tests Tests designed to be given to several people at once by a single administrator, generally paper-and-pencil tests using standardized instructions, written answers, and systematic scoring techniques. 449–451

Group therapy Psychotherapy in which group interactions are the central focus; potentially useful, but with few controlled studies to demonstrate effectiveness. 523–524, 525

Groupthink The effect of a group on individual thinking, as suggested by Janis; the cognitive and behavioral biases of the group may lead a group of highly competent persons to make faulty decisions that none of the participants would have made if acting alone. 554

Gustation, 165, 167. *See also* Taste

Hair cells Transducers in the cochlea (in the organ of Corti) and in the semi-circular canals that are the transducers for the senses of hearing and part of the vestibular sense. 162, 164

Hallucinations "Incorrect" perceptual experiences that differ strikingly from what other people would experience in the same sensory situation. 180, 182

Hallucinogens Psychoactive drugs that alter the perception of reality. 232, 236–237. *See also* Psychoactive drugs

Halo effect The tendency for some central traits to bias an individual's perception of another positively; a person with a very positive physical or behavioral trait is assumed to have other desirable traits. 535, 543

Hammer One of the three small bones of the middle ear. 161

Hearing The sense (technically called *audition*) that extracts information from vibrations in the air (or water) brought to an ear; an important sense for humans because it is the natural input channel for speech. 155–165
    auditory nerves to brain, 162–165
    cochlea's transducers, 162
    ear's accessory structures, 161–162
    restoration of, 163
    sound and, 155–161

Hedonism The tendency to do what is pleasurable and avoid what is painful; one of the earliest theories of human motivation. 108

Height, 102–103, 104

Helping behaviors All forms of prosocial behavior that contribute to the well being of others, from making them feel better to saving their lives. 560

Hemoglobin, 87

Hemophilia, 96

Hering grid, 192

Hering theory Early theory of color perception, still partially accepted, proposing that light receptors are all the same but that analyzers organize information from the receptors in terms of opponent processes: for example, the more blue an analyzer reports the less yellow it will report (a similar process applies to red/green, whereas black and white can mix to yield gray). 186, 187

Heritability The proportion of the variation of a trait in a particular population that is attributable to genetics; it is a relative index that changes with environmental changes, and refers only to a population as a whole, never to individuals. 104

Hermaphrodites Rare individuals with one testis and one ovary who develop the characteristics of both sexes. 125, 127

Hertz (Hz) Unit of measurement used to describe sound waves; one Hz is one cycle of compression/expansion per second. 156, 158

Heterosexuals Individuals who are erotically responsive primarily or only to the opposite sex; heterosexuality is usually considered the biologically "normal" orientation. 128

Heterozygote advantage The advantage that a heterozygote for a particular characteristic has over a homozygote when that trait may be lethal or harmful to the homozygote fully expressing the characteristic but advantageous to the heterozygote partially expressing it; one sickle-cell gene, for example, seems to offer protection against malaria. 97

Heterozygous Having the pair of genes for some characteristic be of different types, such as having one gene for blue

Heterozygous (*cont.*)
eyes and one for brown. 92

Heuristic A procedure that helps solve a problem, usually by reducing the number of alternatives to be considered; it differs from an algorithm in that no heuristic *guarantees* a solution. 358–359

Hibernation Specialized form of long-term sleep in which the metabolism of the sleeping animal (such as a bear or squirrel) slows dramatically, keeping the animal out of trouble and conserving energy in winter; some theorists liken ordinary sleep to a kind of short-term hibernation. 225

Hidden observer A dissociated aspect of a hypnotized subject's consciousness that may provide different reports of a subject's experience than the subject does ordinarily; in pain research, for example, the hypnotized subject may verbally report zero pain, but the hidden observer may indicate some pain; such research may be relevant to other altered or dissociated states of consciousness. 230

Hierarchy In systematic desensitization, the sequence of increasingly frightening stimuli presented to the patient, generally in simulated form (slides, films, tapes) or through the client's imagining them, but if practical in real form to create the most effective classical conditioning. 517

Hierarchy of needs Maslow's categorization of innate human needs, which suggests that the more exclusively human needs will appear only after more basic needs are satisfied; the basic goals include good and physical safety, whereas self-actualization is at the top of the hierarchy. 422–423

High self-monitors Individuals who are much more aware of their own actions than low self-monitors because they are particularly sensitive to the social cues offered by others, which they use to regulate and control (monitor) their own behavior. 534

Hippocampus Limbic-system structure involved in the storage of new memories, especially verbal ones. 61

Histogram, frequency, 591

Homeostasis The maintaining of a body variable within allowable boundaries by feedback loops that sense and correct deviations of the variable. 110–112

Homologous parts Body parts of different species that differ in form but have evolved from a common ancestor, such as the forefeet of most mammals compared to the human hand. 82, 83

Homo sapiens neandertalensis, 85
Homo sapiens sapiens, 85

Homosexuals Individuals who are erotically responsive primarily or only to their own sex; female homosexuals are also known as lesbians. 128

Homozygous Having the pair of genes for some characteristic be of the identical type, such as both being the gene for blue eyes. 92

Homunculus From the Latin for "little man," used in the context of brain function to mean a charting of the sensory and motor strips showing the relationship of areas of the cortex to the corresponding body parts. 66

"Hopkins beast," 42

Hormones Chemicals secreted by a gland inside the body that will affect a specific function such as growth or behavior. 74

pubertal, 127
sexual development and, 125, 126
sleep and, 216

Horney, Karen A neo-Freudian who developed biological and cultural objections to Freud's views of women and suggested the possibility of self-analysis; she also formulated the concept of basic anxiety as a response to the difficulties of coping with life, which may result in any of ten neurotic trends. 390, 418

Hospitalization, 499–502

Hospitalization syndrome Pattern of adaptation to the conditions of loneliness, enforced idleness, and regimentation in mental hospitals that leaves patients less able to live in a nonhospital environment. 502

Hospitals, 498–499

Hue The name we usually use to identify a color, such as "red"; one of the three psychological dimensions of color. 149

Hull, Clark L. Learning theorist who sought to build a comprehensive quantifiable theory; although his theory as a whole is little used, many of its elements have long been influential, such as the concept of drive reduction as an explanation of why a reinforcer has the effect it does. (1884–1952) 230, 249, 272, 418

Human evolution:
cultural, 89–91
physical, 84–89

Humanism "Developing flower" view of innately positive human nature needing only a nonpunishing environment to grow and self-actualize; proposed by Maslow as a "third force" and supplemented by the work of Rogers and others. 22–24

basic concepts of, 22–23
focus of, 23–24
founders of, 22, 23

Humanistic therapies A major group of insight therapies that emphasize self-actualization through the exercise of free will; especially client-centered therapy. 515–516

Hunger In the need-drive view of motivation, the drive that arises from the need for food, which in turn develops from food deprivation. 112, 113–115

Hybrid A mixture of different plant or animal varieties; the offspring are often larger and stronger than either parent (hybrid vigor). 96

Hypercomplex cells Cerebral cortex visual cells that combine information from the complex cells and may respond only to a light pattern of a particular shape, movement, and location. 189, 191

Hypnogogic period The drifting transitional state from waking to sleeping, during which people may experience dreamlike imagery and seem to be more responsive to suggestion. 219

Hypnology, 231

Hypnopompic period The drifting transitional state from sleep back to waking, during which people may experience dreamlike imagery and seem to be more responsive to suggestion. 219

Hypnosis A systematic procedure for altering consciousness or the state of consciousness caused in the subject by such a procedure; usually involves verbal suggestions for a passive, relaxed state given by one person (the hypnotist) to another. 229–232

Hypnosis movement scale, 229
Hypnotics, 233
Hypochondriasis, 479

Hypothalamus Limbic-system structure involved in the control of the autonomic system and the endocrine glands; central to the direction of motivated behaviors. 62, 74–75, 108

hunger and, 115, 119
sleep and, 216

Hypothesis A tentative statement of what some relationship might be: the first step in the experimental method. 33–34

Hypovolemic thirst A thirst resulting from extracellular fluid loss, such as blood loss from a wound. 113

Hysteria, 478–479
Hysterical contagion, 479

Icon The representation of a visual input in iconic memory, lasting about a quarter of a second. 282

Iconic memory The visual sensory register. 282

Id In psychoanalytic theory, one of three basic elements, the interrelationships of which determine personality development; the repository of the instinctive forces, it seeks selfish gratification. 18, 414

Idea sketching A process of drawing notes of visual thoughts as an aid to efficient external storage for thoughts; the visual equivalent of written notes for verbal thoughts. 352, 353

Identical twins, 92, 101

Identification Internalizing the characteristics of a parent, a key element in the Freudian view of childhood development. 391–393, 416

Identity, 396
Identity crisis, 396

Idiot savants Persons who are mentally retarded in most respects but have a single unusual talent in music, art, mathematics, or some other task. 456

Ill-defined problems Problems that are not easily specifiable in terms of initial state, goal state, or subgoals; at least some aspects of most ordinary problems are ill-defined, causing difficulties in everyday problem solving. 356–357

Illusions Both sensory inputs that tend to yield incorrect perceptual hypotheses and the incorrect perceptions that result; illusions commonly affect most people similarly. 179–180, 197, 201, 204, 205–206

Illusory correlations Subjective assessments of group/behavior correlations made by observers when no true correlations actually exist—a major cognitive bias. 537–538

Image In perception, a representation of what is in front of the lens of an eye or camera; in the eye, an upside-down image is focused on the retina. 149

Images Mental representations of sensory experience, usually but not exclusively visual representations; in memory, one type of code that is usually visual and in cognitive psychology, one way of thinking that is often visual but can be in other sensory modes. 283, 348–352

Imitation, 392

Implicit personality theories Universal amateur attempts to make sense and formulate theories of personality from the confusing mixture of information from parents, schools, the media, and other cultural institutions as well as from a person's unique experiences. 404, 535

Implicit rules Speech patterns shown by any native speaker of a language that show the speaker is using the rules of a language without necessarily being aware they exist. 308

Implosion therapy An extreme form of counterconditioning in which the patient holds in the imagination a grossly magnified version of the feared stimulus until no longer frightened. 518

Impossible objects Drawings that combine inconsistent perceptual cues to represent three-dimensional objects that cannot exist. 202–203

Impressions, formation of, 535–538

Imprinting Ethological concept of the tendency of some species to identify a sound-making object nearby at their birth as "mother." 25, 26

Inbreeding The breeding of close genetic relatives, which increases the chances that carriers of a maladaptive trait will have offspring who are homozygous for the problem, and thus expresses it. 95–96

Incentive A stimulus having some value that makes an organism approach or avoid it; a good-tasting food is a positive incentive and a bad-tasting food is a negative one. 115–116

Incongruence, 424

Independent variables The measures of the experimental treatment, such as the strength of drugs in a study administering them. 35

Individual psychology, 417

Infancy, 381–387
    attachment in, 386–387
    cognitive development in, 382–384
    moral development in, 382–384
    nature/nurture controversy and, 385
    personality development in, 385
    physical maturation in, 381–382
    social learning in, 386

Infantile amnesia, 303

Inference Deducing from evidence what must be true even though it has not been stated directly; a major process in constructive memory. 296–297

Inferential statistics Statistics that go beyond the descriptive to estimate what else is probably true about some relationship being investigated through the data; especially useful in helping investigators decide whether data from a particular group of subjects might also represent some larger population. 590, 595–599
    populations, 596
    proof and disproof, 596–597
    samples, 596
    statistical significance, 597–599

Informational theories, of attitude change, 548–549

Information processing In humans, the taking in of information through the senses and processing of it to yield behavior. 24

Informed consent, 8

Infrared radiation, 147

In-group In the theory of intergroup relations, a group with which people identify strongly, which helps support the in-group members and justifies exploiting members of all other groups, or out-groups. 555–556

Inhibition:
    proactive, 301
    retroactive, 301–303

Inhibitory synapses Synapses at which the effect of the neurotransmitter is to make the postsynaptic neuron less likely to fire. 49, 50

Inner core The portion of the brain that evolved first, with behaviorally primitive responses that serve basic survival needs; the "reptilian brain." 54

Inner ear The inner portion of the ear, containing the fluid-filled cochlea and semicircular canals. 162

Inoculation A technique of persuasibility that works like medical inoculation (which presents a body with a weakened form of a disease to help it form antibodies): presenting weak arguments against a person's own position and then countering them so as to strengthen the person's resistance to counterarguments. 549

Insanity As originally defined in British and U.S. law, the inability to know the nature and quality of an act being committed; some states have added the concept of "irresponsible impulse" and the current legal definition includes the idea of a lack of "substantial capacity . . . to appreciate the wrongfulness" of actions.
    as a legal defense, 504, 505

Insight The sudden and complete solving of a problem through a perceptual reorganization; described by the Gestalt psychologists as one aspect of their general emphasis on perceptual wholes (gestalts). 268, 269

Insight therapies Psychotherapies, including psychoanalytic and humanistic ones, that seek to help patients understand their psychological functioning through insight gained by verbal exchanges between patient and therapist. 510, 512–516
    humanistic, 515–516
    psychoanalytic, 512–514

Insomnia Inability to sleep normally, some form of which is experienced by about 30% of the population. 226

Instinctive drift The tendency of some organisms subject to operant conditioning to begin to exhibit "natural" behaviors in addition to or instead of the operants that are being extrinsically reinforced. 262

Instincts Innate behavioral tendencies; the concept was once a major one in personality theory but is now little used, having been recognized as strongly subject to the nominal fallacy; currently inborn tendencies are explored by ethologists as species-specific behaviors and by psychologists as genetic predispositions. 408–409

Institutionalization, 499–502

Instrumental conditioning Thorndike's term for what Skinner has called operant conditioning; still used by some psychologists as a preferred term to operant conditioning. 249. *See also* operant conditioning

Insufficient justification effect A provocative finding under some conditions of cognitive dissonance in which paying subjects *less* causes *more* attitude change; the classic finding was the $1/$20 study, in which subjects who were paid only $1 to tell a lie (apparently "insufficient justification") changed their opinion in the direction of believing the lie whereas subjects paid $20 did not. 547

Insulin, 250

Intellectualization, 416

Intelligence As defined by Wechsler, an individual's capacity to understand the world and the capacity to cope with the challenges it presents, demonstrated by measurable behaviors. 433–461
    artificial, 342
    concept of, 434
    crystallized, 446
    defining of, 443–447
    environment and, 440–441
    extremes of, 454–460
    fluid, 445–446
    genetics of, 439
    measurement of, 447–454
    race and, 460–461
    reaction ranges and, 437–439
    testing of, 434–437, 447–454
    types of, 445–447

Intelligence quotient (IQ) A number that reflects a person's score on some intelligence test; originally calculated as mental age divided by chronological age multiplied by 100, but now based on 100 as the mean for some normative group, with scores above or below that mean being recomputed on a common basis so that scores from different tests all use the same (IQ) scale. 437, 438, 439, 440, 442

Interaction The interlocking of two causative factors so that both must be present in appropriate quantities for some outcome to occur; for example, both light and water are necessary for plant growth. (Also used as a nonspecialized term meaning only combining in some way.) 10

International Pilot Study of Schizophrenia (IPSS), 487

Interpersonal attraction One of the oldest topics in social psychology, including friendships and romantic attachments; interpersonal attraction is strongly influenced by such variables as physical proximity, similarity, and physical attractiveness. 542–544

Interpersonal behavior, 540–545

Interpretation One of the five key processes of psychoanalysis: offering a patient suggestions of what a pattern seen by the analyst in free associations and dreams indicate the patient's behaviors might mean; the interpretations are offered carefully to encourage insight and to avoid the patient's rejecting the interpretation. 177–180, 514

Interrater reliability A check of a technique's accuracy that measures whether two or more raters watching the same behavior can rate it similarly. 426

Interval scales Ordinal scales in which the intervals between items are known to be equal, such as a temperature scale. 590

Interviews, 425

Intrinsic Natural to a situation; in connection with reinforcement or punishment, refers to contingencies that are naturally related to operants, as when finding food reinforces the search for food or when the pain of injury punishes careless behavior. 257

Introspection In psychology, the reporting of all sensory elements that make up perception; no longer used because of the problem of defining the elements of perception. 13–14

Introversion-extroversion One of Eysenck's personality dimensions, assessing a range of traits from an inward focus on the self (introversion) to an orientation toward others and the external world (extroversion). 413

Involuntary memories, 289

Ipsilateral, 68

IQ, 437, 438, 439, 440, 442. *See also* Intelligence, Intelligence quotient

Iris A ring-shaped, muscularly controlled structure lying behind the cornea of the eye and providing the eye's "color," such as blue or brown; the iris expands or contracts to control the light passing through the opening at its center (the pupil). 149

Isolation, 416

James, William One of the first and most important of the American psychologists. (1842–1910) 14–15, 131, 134, 177, 277, 296, 530, 531

James-Lange theory A theory of emotion proposing that the conscious experience of emotion *follows* a response to a stimulus: We are afraid because we run, rather than running *because* we are afraid (of a predator, for example). 134

Jargon, 28

Jet lag A cluster of symptoms in which people feel mildly ill and are behaviorally inefficient after a flight to a distant locale; actually caused by a disruption of their bodies' circadian cycles subsequent to a sudden time change, not by the flight itself. 217

Jung, Carl Gustav A neo-Freudian who developed the concept of the collective unconscious in addition to a personal unconscious; he differed from Freud in seeing the unconscious as a positive rather than a dark force and his analytic psychology did not share Freud's stress on sexuality. (1875–1961) 417

Juries, psychology of, 578–579

Just noticeable difference (JND) The amount of change required from one stimulus to another that will make them distinguishable; the JND depends on the level of stimulation already present, so the more intense the existing stimulus is the larger the change must be to be noticeable. 145

Karyotype A specialized graphic display of photographs of an individual's chromosomes, used to locate damaged or missing chromosomes and thus potential problems. 91

Kaufman Assessment Battery for Children (KABC) A new intelligence test based on sequential and simultaneous items that seek to assess the "process" skills of the left and right hemispheres, comparatively independent of accumulated verbal knowledge; potentially important test that may be especially useful in minimizing racial or cultural bias, but not yet widely accepted. 461

Keyword method Mnemonic technique for teaching foreign vocabulary in which the sound of the foreign word is used to create an image that is combined with an image of the word's meaning in one's native language. 288

Kinesthesia, 170

Kinesthetic illusion, 179–180

Kinesthetic sense The proprioceptive sense that monitors the position of limbs and joints and the tension of the muscles (also called kinesthesia). 142

Klinefelter's syndrome A condition in which an individual is born with an extra sex chromosome (XXY pattern); such a person has a generally male body type but other characteristics, including amount of body hair and muscle distribution, are intermediate between male and female. 124

Kohlberg, Lawrence Psychologist whose theory of moral development is a cognitive-developmental approach to the development of moral reasoning and thinking, as exemplified by children's verbal reports concerning moral problems. (1927–) 373, 374, 376, 377, 384, 388–389, 391, 394, 396, 398

Köhler, Wolfgang A founder of Gestalt psychology who studied problem-solving in chimpanzees, interpreting their actions as a restructuring of the elements of their perceptual field. (1887–1967) 176, 268, 355

Korsakoff's syndrome, 234

Labanotation, 346

Language Any set of symbols that can be sequenced according to particular rules so as to convey an indefinite number of meanings from one user of the language to another. 307–333

  acquisition of, 308, 317–322
  artificial, 308
  brain and, 329–333
  channels of, 309–312
  comprehension of, 308, 325–329
  definition of, 307–308
  manipulation by, 326
  natural, 308
  other species and, 312–316
  production of, 308, 322–325

Language acquisition The process by which children become able to produce and comprehend a language (the process by which adults learn language is thought to be rather different). 308, 317–322

Language-acquisition device (LAD), 320

Language community A group of users of a natural language within which children routinely learn to speak the language. 308, 317–319

Language comprehension A series of steps taken together after a first user has engaged in language production to complete communication by language. 308, 325–329, 341–342

Language hemisphere, 73

Language production A series of steps taken together that one user follows to communicate by language. 308, 322–325

Language productivity, 309

Language regularity, 309

Language universals Common features of languages and language acquisition that may reflect innate structures and limitations. 320

Latency period Freud's fourth stage of psychosexual development, from age 6 to puberty, in which sexuality is not overtly related to any erogenous zone. 378

Latent content According to Freud, the hidden but real meaning of a dream. 226

Latent learning Phenomenon of learning without reinforcement that is not exhibited until the reinforcement is presented, emphasized by Tolman as part of purposive behaviorism: Rats exploring a maze with no food reinforcement show a slight improvement in maze performance and suddenly show a marked improvement when food is added. 269–270

Lateral hypothalamus (LH) A portion of the hypothalamus that is a way station for the processing of hunger information, formerly thought to receive sensory signals indicating a body need for food and to turn on hunger. 115, 118, 119

Law of effect The most important of the laws proposed by Thorndike in developing instrumental learning whereby a behavior that is followed by a "satisfier" will be stamped in or strengthened and one followed by an "annoyer" will be stamped out or weakened. 249

Learned drives, 148

Learned helplessness A view of Seligman's, based on animal research, that suggests people who experience setbacks can learn to feel helpless in the face of adversity and to not fight to overcome it; as a cognitive-behavioral explanation of depression, the latest version suggests that the people most likely to become depressed are those who attribute their failure to enduring personal faults. 485

Learning Defined by psychologists as a change in behavior, or the potential for behavior, that occurs as a result of environmental experience but is not the result of such factors as fatigue, drugs, or injury; sometimes also called conditioning. 241–271
    classical conditioning, 243–249
    cognitive, 268–270
    definition of, 242–243
    innate constraints on, 262
    latent, 269–270
    operant conditioning, 249–264
    serial, 276
    social, 264–268

Learning theory An alternate term for the behavioral approach to behavior, emphasizing the ways in which humans as well as animals learn from the environmental consequences of their actions. 19, 271. *See also* Behaviorism

Lens Any optical device for focusing light; in the eye, the structure just behind the pupil that acts to focus incoming light on the retina, whose shape is muscularly adjustable to allow focusing of objects at different distances. 149

Leprosy, 170

Lesbian, 128

Lesion An area of damage or structural change in tissue; in psychology, lesions in the brain are used to study the relationships between particular brain areas and particular behaviors. 43

Level of $p < .05$. 36, 598

Levels-of-processing model A model of memory emphasizing three successively deeper or more complex levels at which incoming information can be processed; stimuli are processed first according to their physical structure, then by their basic patterns, and finally at a level deep enough for an understanding of the conceptual meaning; developed as a competitor of the duplex model but so far more of a source of ideas for incorporation into the duplex model. 280–282

Libido The Freudian concept of a powerful life instinct whose primarily sexual energy (which stems from id

demands) must be harnessed and its expression controlled if individuals are to achieve satisfactory adult roles. 125, 376, 415

Lie detection, 135–136

Life expectancy, 399

Life instinct One of the two basic powerful instincts, acording to psychoanalytic theory, reflected primarily in a drive for sexual gratification. 18

Life-span development, 369

Light The environmental information processed in vision; the visible spectrum is only a narrow band of the full range of the natural radiation, and some species perceive other wavelengths. 147–149

Limbic system The middle brain layer, superimposed on the inner core, thought to be the center of emotion; the "old mammalian" brain. 54, 61–62, 166

Linguistic competence A language user's abstract knowledge about the structure of the language or ability to produce and comprehend the language correctly, independent of what he or she wishes to say. 308

Linguistic performance How people use language in their everyday lives, a major interest of psycholinguistics. 309

Linguistic-relativity hypothesis Whorf's theory of the relationship of communication and thought proposing that thinking is so dominated by language that people can only think about the world in terms of the concepts used in their language. 342–343

Linguists Students of language development and use who emphasize linguistic competence, interested in how people use language forms but not what they use the language for—the structure rather than the content. 308

Lithium A chemical that relieves mania and some bipolar depression, and thus is an effective drug therapy for bipolar affective patients. 507, 508

Lobotomy, 66, 506

Location constancy The automatic perceptual assumption that we and the objects we see remain in their appropriate locations despite movement on the retina as we move our heads. 184, 185

Loci, method of, 288

Logic Theorist A computer program designed to simulate how human subjects solve mathematical proofs using the working-backward heuristic. 358

Loneliness The aversive subjective experience resulting from a deficiency in social relationships; an extremely serious and common problem, it has long been of interest to psychotherapists and is now a topic in experimental social psychology. 540–542

Longitudinal studies Studies of development over time in which the same subjects are followed and studied as they age. 441–442

Long-term memory (LTM) The second of the two types of memory storage proposed in two-store models; LTM

holds information for years, it can hold an indefinite amount of information, and its contents are lost only slowly if ever; information reaches LTM from short-term memory (STM). 278–279, 285–289
    retrieval from, 293–294
    storage of, 291–292

Looking-glass self, 530

Lorenz, Konrad Founder of ethology; took the position that behavior (like body structures) aids survival of a species and thus the typical behavior of a species represents the end product of evolution. (1904–) 25, 26, 28, 82, 83, 142, 242, 312, 570–571

Loudness A psychological dimension of hearing: The greater the amplitude of a sound wave, the louder the sound we hear. 158, 160

Low self-monitors Individuals who are not as aware as high self-monitors of situational cues, have a less-varied repertoire of social skills, and are less flexible in adapting to new situations. 535

LSD, 236–237

Luchins' water-jar problem, 360

Lucid dreams Ones in which the dreamer is aware that he or she is dreaming. 223

Ludes, 233

Mach reversible-card illusion, 205, 206

Magic, 362

Magic number 7±2 The number of items—from 5 to 9—to which the capacity of short-term memory is limited. 284, 285

Maintenance rehearsal Covert repetition of material that maintains a memory trace in short-term memory as long as it is continued, but that may not improve later recall from long-term memory. 285

Major affective disorders Mental disorders in which anxiety is not an obvious central feature, characterized by wide variations in mood from extreme elation to extreme depression; usually depression alone occurs. 481–486

Major depression Depression notably beyond ordinary levels but not associated with manic episodes, ranging in severity from somewhat more depressed than normal to a stuporous inactivity. 483–486

Major tranquilizers, 506–507

Mania A syndrome of rapid, optimistic behavior, shown at one extreme of bipolar disorder. 482, 508

Manipulation, by language, 326

MAO inhibitors, 52, 507, 508

Maps, 352, 354
    cognitive, 270, 352

Marijuana, 232, 233

Masculinization, 126

Maslow, Abraham Developer of humanistic perspective in psychology as a "third force" alternative to psychoanalysis and behaviorism; he

Mazlow, Abraham (*cont.*) focused on successful rather than disturbed people in building his theory of personality and motivation. (1908–1970) 22–23, 28, 422–423, 430, 470

Mass hysteria, 479

Maternal instinct, 121

Mating, 123–124

Maturation In developmental psychology, the specific process by which physical growth alone results in new behavior possibilities; as when growth of bones, muscles, and the nervous system make walking possible. 382. *See also* Development

Mean The arithmetic average, computed by adding all separate values or scores and dividing by the number of these values. 593, 594

Means/end heuristic A problem-solving technique in which the goal state and current state are identified, and step-by-step actions are planned to reduce the difference between them. 358, 359

Measures of central tendency, 592–593

Measures of variation A measure of how far the values on a frequency distribution vary from the mean. 593–595

Media, and aggression, 574–578

Median The value on a frequency distribution that has as many scores above it as below it. 593

Medical model The primary model of abnormal behavior, which defines it as the result of a mental disease or illness analogous to a physical disease. 467–468

Medical student syndrome The experience of studying a mental or physical disease and beginning to think you have that disease, often caused by seeing common experiences as if they were the "symptoms" of the disease. 471, 473

Meditation Any of a number of forms of mental control or discipline, often a clearing or emptying of the mind through a narrowly focused thought process. 232

Melanin, 93, 94

Memory, 275–305
  constructive, 296–300
  echoic, 283
  encoding into, 276, 282–289
  iconic, 282
  improvement of, 305
  involuntary, 289
  long-term, 278–279, 285–289, 291–292
  processes of, 276–282
  retrieval from, 276, 292–305
  short-term, 277, 278, 283–285, 291–292
  storage in, 276, 289–292
  two-store models of, 277–280
  variations in retrieval from, 296–305

Memory barrier, 222–223

Memory capacity, 279

Memory experts. *See* Mnemonists

Memory molecules, 292

Memory scanning A specialized form of retrieval from short-term memory in which, for example, a three-digit list might be read and the subject then asked if "3" was one of them. 293

Memory-span test Test for the recollection of a series of items presented once, which will generally be limited to the magic number 7±2 because most people process such lists in short-term memory. 284

Memory trace, 280

Menopause, 400

Menstruation, 393

Mental age (MA) The level of a child's intellectual development based on the skills possessed by normative groups of children at various ages. 436

Mental hygiene movement Movement begun by Dorthea Dix in the mid-19th century to improve physical conditions for prisoners and mental patients; it was successful in doing so, but through the establishment of many large mental hospitals, which have since been criticized on other grounds. 499

Mentally deficient A suggested alternative term for those who are in the lower three categories of mental retardation, emphasizing the likelihood that they suffer from various biological deficits. 457

Mentally gifted, 454–456

Mentally retarded Those who score below 70 on a standard IQ test and have problems in adapting to their environment. 456

Mental magic, 362

Mental operations Piaget's concept of cognitive procedures that can be carried out to manipulate representations of the world mentally. 374

Mental retardation, 456–460
  causes of, 457–459
  characteristics of, 457
  classification of, 459
  degrees of, 456
  education and, 459, 460
  mainstreaming and, 459

Mental set The tendency to establish ways of doing something, including problem solving; it can be an important aid to perception or a harmful bias blocking alternatives. 360

Mesomorph, 407

Message factors In the message-learning approach, qualities of the message itself that affect how persuasive it will be; these include the emotional tone and type of conclusion as well as comprehensibility and number and quality of the arguments themselves. 548–549

Message-learning approach An informational or cognitive approach to attitude change that focuses on persuasive communications designed to change attitudes, separating and examining aspects of the communication's source, the message itself, the recipient, and the channel of communication; also known as the Yale school. 548

Meta-analysis The analysis of the results of many separate studies of psychotherapy, in an attempt to determine if all psychotherapy combined is more effective than no therapy. 513

Metamemory Memory abut memory, including all a person knows about the nature and processes of his or her own memory. 285

Methadone, 236

Method of loci One of the oldest visual mnemonics, using a series of well-learned loci (locations) as keys to remembering other things. 288

Middle ear Portion of the ear between the eardrum and the cochlea containing the hammer, anvil, and stirrup, three tiny bones that are set in motion by the movement of the eardrum and then amplify the sound and transmit the vibrations to the inner ear. 161–162

Mildly retarded Those mentally retarded individuals with IQ scores between 50 and 70, who can perform many normal activities if given the time to learn. 456

Milieu therapy A contemporary variant of moral treatment, used in hospital settings, in which the social relationships among patients and staff are structured to aid recovery. 522

Miller, Neal With John Dollard, developer of a behavioral approach to personality; their learning theory was based on primary drives that are the basis for learned drives and on the additional concepts of cue, response, and reinforcement. (1909–) 264, 271, 418–419, 474, 572

Mind/body problem An old philosophical problem, now a central one in psychology, concerned with what the relationship is between mind and body; answers that they are fundamentally different are *dualist* and answers that they are different views of a single process are *monist*. 10–11, 44–45, 176

Mindlessness Carrying out behaviors by automatic routines, without the conscious planning and control that has traditionally been assumed to precede most human actions. 532

Minnesota Multiphasic Personality Inventory (MMPI) The best-known personality inventory, designed to identify persons suffering from mental illness; subscales have been developed that apply to variations in normal personality types, and the scales can be computer-scored to generate a profile for a particular test-taker that can be interpreted according to standardized criteria. 426

Minor tranquilizers, 507, 508

M'Naghten rules, 504

Mnemonics Specialized techniques, such as acronyms, for improving the encoding and retrieval of material in memory, primarily in long-term memory. 288–289

Mnemonists Professional memory experts who use both innate skills and learned techniques. 301, 302

Mode The most common value in a frequency distribution. 593

Model In experimental methodology, a simplified form of the problem under study; in psychology, the behavior or physiology of an animal species may serve as a model for the more complex human equivalent. In social learning theory, a person whose behavior is observed and imitated by another; when an extensive set of behaviors (a role) is involved, the person may be called a role model. 24, 32, 266

Modeling The process of learning through observation of another person's behavior and its consequences; a central concept in social learning theory. 24, 420
aggression and, 573–574
altruism and, 562–563
social learning and, 24, 266, 267, 420
as therapy, 521

Models In social learning theory, persons whose actions are imitated by observers; reinforcement and punishment of the model have vicarious effects on the observer.

Moderately retarded Those mentally retarded individuals with IQ scores of 35–50, who can be trained to maintain some independence but require special education. 456

Mongolism. *See* Down's syndrome

Monists Those who believe that mind and body are a single unified system. 11

Monocular depth cues Aspects of the visual scene that can indicate depth even to a person seeing with one eye; these may be based on optical rules, the position of the eyes in relation to other objects, and typical patterns found in the environment. 197–199, 200

Monozygotic (MZ) twins Identical twins, genetically identical because they result from the splitting of a single zygote. *See also* Twins. 92, 101

Moral development:
in adolescence, 394
in adulthood, 398
in childhood, 388–389
in infancy, 384
Kohlberg's theory of, 374, 376, 377

Moral treatment A movement begun at the end of the 18th century in which mental patients were to be treated kindly and taught by example to live normally in small therapeutic communities; at least one such community still exists, but the general movement was overwhelmed by the growth of the large regional mental hospitals. 498

Morpheme The smallest unit of meaning in a language, which may be a whole word, a prefix, or a suffix. 323

Morphine, 235–236

Motivation The reason any behavior occurs; the forces or processes that initiate the behavior, direct it, and contribute to its strength. 108
limbic system and, 62
perception and, 181–182
projective tests and, 428–429

Motivational theories, of attitude change, 546, 547

Motives The factors that initiate and direct behavior toward particular goals, such as hunger, which initiates food-seeking behavior. 107–130
biological factors in, 108
cognitive factors in, 109
current issues in, 109
definition of, 108

functional autonomy of, 412
for group survival, 118–122
for intermediate-term survival, 112–115
interpretation of, 412
learning factors in, 109
for long-term survival, 115–118
sexual, 121–122
for short-term survival, 109–112
beyond survival, 129–130
survival through, 107–108

Motor development, 382

Movement perception, 208

Müller-Lyer illusion, 205, 206

Multimodal therapy Development of an individualized treatment profile for each client proposed by Lazarus, using techniques from the wide range of behavioral therapies and from insight therapies. 523

Multiple personality A disorder in which one person exhibits two or more distinct and often quite different alternating personalities; these splits in personality are not the same as the associative splits of schizophrenia. 403, 479–480, 481

Muscular control, 56–59

Mutations Changes in the DNA structure of a gene, caused by natural or human-generated factors, that become new entries in the gene pool; they may be lethal, neutral, or advantageous. 94–96

Myelin sheath Layer of white fatty tissue that surrounds and insulates the axons of most human neurons; by causing the firing to "jump" between breaks in the sheath (nodes of Ranvier), it speeds up the rate of conduction of the action potential along the axon. 47–48

Naming error, 404

Narcolepsy A condition of sudden-onset sleep attacks, ranging from briefly going blank to falling suddenly into REM sleep, complete with muscular paralysis (cataplexy). 227, 228

Narcotics, 235–236

National Institute of Mental Health (NIMH), 567, 574, 577

Nativist theories Theories that emphasize nature factors, suggesting that some behavior, such as perception, is largely native or innate. 175

Natural concepts Intuitive concepts that are developed quickly and easily, even without language, and can even be learned by animals—such as *tree*. 339

Natural language A human language developed over time and existing, or having once existed, in a language community. 308

Natural selection theory, 80–81

Nature/nurture problem The question of whether behavior is the result of innate factors (heredity) or of environmental factors (learning). 10, 101–104
early development and, 385
intelligence and, 437–443

Neandertals An early subvariety of our species who had, their remains show, the

power to kill other humans with weapons as well as to care for the helpless and honor the dead; they may be a direct ancestor of or a parallel branch to *Homo sapiens sapiens*. 85–86

Nearsighted Being able to see clearly only for relatively close objects, a common vision problem caused by an eye that is too long from front to back so that the lens cannot focus the images of distant objects. 149–150

Need In the need-drive view of motivation, a tissue deficit that accumulates over time, such as the need for oxygen, water, or food. 112, 422–423

Negative afterimage A pattern of the same shape, but in the complementary color, of a brightly colored object seen after staring at it for a while and then looking at a neutral surface. 188

Negative halo effect The tendency for some traits to bias an individual's perception of another negatively; a person with a very negative physical or behavioral trait is assumed to have other negative traits. 535, 543

Negative reinforcement Removal of a punisher that is already present; this strengthens an operant that it follows, and thus is a form of reinforcement, but it does so in a "negative" way by removing an aversive stimulus rather than presenting a positive one. 255

Nembutal, 233

Neodissociation theory Hilgard's theory of a side-by-side division of consciousness, rather than a levels analogy such as Freud's, wherein the consciousness that solves a problem may be different from the one that reports the solution but is not necessarily lower. 213, 230, 231

Neo-Freudians Followers of Freud who have expanded psychoanalytic theory by modifying and elaborating his original proposals, including Jung, Adler, Erikson, and Horney. 18, 414, 416–418

Neologisms, 486

Neomammalian brain, 55

Nerves The components of the peripheral nervous system that either bring information to the central nervous system or transmit commands from it; each is made up of bundles of axons similar to telephone cables. 54

Nerve tract Bundle of axons that conveys information within the brain in the way that nerves do outside the brain; in perception, each sensory system includes a nerve tract that transmits information, in the form of action potentials, from the transducers to the cortex. 144

Nervous system The organization of nerve cells in the body comprising the brain, spinal cord, and peripheral nerves. 41–74
autonomic system, 54, 62, 63
behavior and, 41–47
brain, 41–47, 59–74, 75
brainstem, 59–61
central, 53–54
cerebellum, 59
cerebral cortex, 63–67

Nervous system (*cont.*)
divisions of, 53–54
endocrine system, 74–76
functions of, 54–55
limbic system, 61–62
muscular control and, 56–59
neurons, 47–50
neurotransmitters, 50–53
peripheral, 54
spinal cord, 55–56
synapses, 50

Network model A proposed model of verbal memory that suggests it is arranged as if major concepts were units, related to each other and to the properties that describe them by linkages called pointers; in the model, answering a question about a word entails entering the network and following pointers until the answer is found. 290

Neural tube Tubular structure that develops in the embryo and later becomes the central nervous system: the head end of the tube elaborates into the various brain structures and the remainder becomes the spinal cord. 53–54

Neuromuscular junctions, 57

Neurons Specialized cells that make up the nervous system, interconnected with each other at the synapses. 47–50

Neuroses Mental disorders that were generally considered less severe, with patients suffering from anxiety but remaining in touch with reality; no longer a category under DSM-III. 471

Neurotic anxiety, 473

Neuroticism One of Eysenck's personality factors, related to the psychiatric concept of neurotic behavior in that one end of his neuroticism dimension is similar to the anxious behavior of neurotics; to minimize the clinical implications, the dimension is sometimes called *stable/unstable* rather than neuroticism. 413

Neurotic trends, 418

Neurotransmitter Chemical released at synaptic knobs in response to the arrival of an action potential; the means of conveying from one neuron to the next the information represented by the firing of the first neuron. 50–53

Neurypnology, 230

Night vision, 151, 152, 153

Nitrous oxide, 236

NMR, 45–47

Nocturnal Adapted evolutionarily for being active primarily at night; nocturnal organisms have a basic circadian cycle of about 23 hours. 216

Nodes of Ranvier The breaks in the myelin sheath insulating most human axons; when the neuron fires, the "jumping" from node to node results in more rapid conduction of the action potential down the axon. 48

Noise. *See* Sound

Nominal fallacy A form of circular logic, also called the naming error, by which a description or *name* of a behavior is seen as the *cause* of that behavior. 404

Nominal scales Quantification systems

in which numbers merely act as names for observations, and thus have no relationship that can be manipulated statistically; one example is numbers given to team members. 590

Nondirective therapy, 516

Nonsense syllables Consonant-vowel-consonant groups with no apparent meaning (such as *NOL*), used by Ebbinghaus to study human learning of verbal material without interference from previous learning. 276

Norepinephrine, 52

Norepinephrine hypothesis, 483

Normal curve The bell-shaped curve of the plotted relationship of the normal distribution of data. 592

Normal distribution A particular frequency distribution, plotted as the normal curve, wherein most data cluster around the middle; typically found for such measurements as IQs within a population. 592

Norm of reciprocity A social norm that includes the demand that people should help as well as not injure those who have helped them. 563–564

Norm of social responsibility A social norm that calls for helping any dependent person, regardless of whether that person can or will reciprocate—such as the sick or the very young and old. 564

Norms, 563–564

Nose, 165–166

Nosebrain, 54, 166

Notation, 345–346, 347

NREM sleep All sleep stages other than REM sleep. 221

Nuclear magnetic resonance (NMR) imaging, 45–47

Null hypothesis The proposal that an experimental treatment is *not* effective; results that are statistically significant disprove the null hypothesis. 597

Obedience In social psychology, the questions of whether a subject will obey a direct command to perform some act, especially one he or she might be expected to disagree with; the extent of obedience is seen as a measure of the power of the group represented by the experimenter in coercing individual behavior; the best-known study of obedience is Milgram's shock study. 551–552

Obesity, motivation for, 109, 110, 115, 116–117

Objective self-awareness Objective thinking about one's own behaviors and conforming of these behaviors to one's self-concepts that an individual can achieve only by paying attention both to behavior and the relevant aspects of his or her self-concepts. 534

Object permanence The realization that an object still exists when it is not in sight, one of the things Piaget pointed out that infants must learn as a basis of adult world view. 373

Objects:

impossible, 202
perception of, 202–206

Observation techniques Ways of assessing personality that use an outside observer or rater to judge some behavior of the subject in a standard situation, usually a structured interview. 29–30, 425–426

Obsessions Thoughts or impulses that continue to recur despite the avowed intent to avoid them; they often center on acts the individual considers immoral and fears that he or she will carry out, although the acts rarely are committed. 475–476

Obsessive-compulsive disorders Disorders characterized by repetitive, intrusive thoughts or impulses and stereotyped behaviors that seem irrational and uncontrollable. 475–476

Occipital lobe The portion of the cerebrum at the back of the head; processes visual information. 65

Oedipus complex Freudian concept of a key problem in the phallic stage wherein a young boy develops sexual interest in his mother and competitive aggression toward his father. 389–390

Old mammalian brain, 54

Olfaction The technical term for *smell*. *See also* Smell. 165–166

Olfactory bulbs Structures within the skull, just above the nose and beneath the brain, that collect information from the transducers for smell in the olfactory mucosae and pass the information via olfactory tracts to the limbic system and frontal cortex. 166

Olfactory mucosa Mucous membrane in the nasal passages that traps molecules in the air to which the receptor cells respond with action potentials that travel to the brain, which recognizes them as smells. 165

Olfactory tracts Parallel tracts from the olfactory bulbs that carry sensed information about smell to the limbic system and the frontal lobe. 166

Operant conditioning Skinner's term for what Thorndike called instrumental conditioning, the learning of behaviors that operate on (have an instrumental effect on) the environment; as a learning process, a change of behavior that occurs because of the (positive or negative) consequences that have followed prior instances of the behavior. 249–264
applied, 260–264
measures of, 251–253
overview of, 249–253
reinforcement and punishment in, 253–260
therapies based on, 519

Operant-conditioning chamber A device for operant conditioning that encloses the subject, simplifies the environmental cues, offers an arrangement for a single operant, and delivers reinforcers; also called a Skinner box. *See also* Skinner box. 251

Operants Particular behaviors that are emitted in response to discriminative stimuli (S_Ds) and "operate on" the environment; also, the behaviors that are learned through operant conditioning, which can be any act the organism is physically capable of performing, thus offering greater learning flexibility than the reflexive responses learned in classical conditioning. 250

consequences of, 255

Operational definition The definition of every relevant variable and key aspect of a study in terms of the operations or procedures necessary to obtain it. 34

Opiates, 235–236

Opium, 235

Opponent-process theory A theory of emotion proposed by Solomon that suggests each emotion is matched by an opposite emotion and that activation of any emotion is followed somewhat later by automatic activation of its opposite, allowing an organism to cope better with emotionally arousing circumstances. In perception, another name for the Hering theory of color perception. 135, 186

Optic chiasma Junction of the optic nerves at which information from the left half of each retina (right visual field) is channeled to the left hemisphere of the brain and vice versa. 155, 156

Optic nerves, 152–155

Optimal arousal A model of motivation proposing that both too much and too little drive are undesirable to an organism, causing it to be less efficient in various behaviors. 116

Oral stage Freud's first stage of psychosexual development, from birth to about age 1, during which sexual pleasure is derived from sucking and biting. 378, 385

Ordinal scales Quantification systems using a sequenced numerical order but not necessarily having the same distance between each item on the scale. 590

Organic causes Causes of a behavior or condition (especially abnormal behavior) that stem from actual physical circumstances, such as injuries, poison, or disease. 468–469

Organ of Corti Inner-ear structure containing the hair cells; the location at which incoming vibrations are finally turned into action potentials in the sense of hearing. 162, 164

Orienting response A response to sudden increases or decreases in sensory input that temporarily improves all the senses and increases attention; activated through the RAS. 61

Osmotic thirst Thirst resulting from changes in cell-wall structure that occur when the cells are low in water content; when this information reaches the thirst center in the central nervous system, water-finding and consuming behavior is stimulated. 113

Otoliths Tiny crystals or "ear stones" attached to the hair cells in the vestibular sacs that sense gravity and provide information to the brain about the position of the head. 171

Outer ear The external portion of the ear and the ear canal just inside the head. 161

Out-groups All groups not part of the in-group. *See also* In-group. 555–556

Oval window Area in the ear where the stirrup is attached to the cochlea and where sound waves in the air become pressure waves in the fluid of the vestibular canal. 162

Over-extensions Children's over-generalizations of a word before eventually narrowing its use to an appropriate one, such as calling anything furry a dog. 322

Overjustification hypothesis Proposal in operant conditioning that a possible risk in using extrinsic reinforcement in conditioning is that it might detract from the power of intrinsic reinforcement. 257

Overt behavior Behavior that is observable by others and thus directly measurable. 20

Overtones Higher frequencies, in addition to the dominant part of a sound wave, that give distinctive detail to a sound. 159–160

Ovotestes, 125

Ovum The reproductive cell produced by the female, containing half the needed number of chromosomes; collectively, these "eggs" are known as ova. 92

Oxygen need, 110

$p < .05$ level The specific value of probability that is the accepted cutoff point in psychology: A significance level of .05 in experimental findings means that any consequence more likely than .05 (5 chances in 100) to have occurred by chance must be rejected because the odds are too high that it was a chance occurrence, rather than a result of the proposed treatment. 36, 598

Pain, 170, 171

Paleomammalian brain, 54

Pandemonium model, 190

Panic disorders Anxiety disorders characterized by sudden intense anxiety attacks that may or may not be associated with a particular situation. 474–475

Papillae, 167

Paranoid schizophrenia One of the five DSM-III subcategories of schizophrenia, characterized by suspicion and delusions of persecution or of grandeur but relatively intact speech and thought patterns. 489

Parasympathetic system The portion of the autonomic nervous system that signals the internal organs to resume normal functioning after a sympathetic system mobilization. 54, 62

Parenting, 118, 121

Parietal lobe The portion of the cerebrum in the top center area of the head that processes taste and touch information. 65

Partial reinforcement A schedule of reinforcement in operant conditioning wherein only some instances of the operant are reinforced, mixing the beginnings of extinction with regular reinforcement. 257, 258

Passages, 328–329

Pattern recognition A process of alteration of the initial form of sensory information in terms of a general pattern as it is passed on from the sensory registers to short-term memory. 278

Paul's Timed Behavioral Checklist for Performance Anxiety, 473

Pavlov, Ivan P. Russian research physiologist who won a Nobel prize for his work on digestion; his discovery in the course of this work that dogs could learn to give a reflexive response to a new set of stimuli became the basis for the study of classical conditioning. (1849–1936) 19, 243–245, 272

PCP, 57, 233

Pecking behaviors, 262

Pegword technique A mnemonic mixing verbal and visual techniques in which previously memorized words act as pegs on which to hang other items. 288

Penfried, Wilder Canadian neuro-surgeon whose years of work in the surface of the human brain provided some of the basis for the physiological perspective in psychology. (1891–1976) 26, 28, 43, 61, 67, 75, 330

Penis envy Controversial Freudian concept of sense of deprivation in young girls of the penis and blaming of the mother for the loss as punishment for desire for her father. 390

Peptides, 52

Perception The additional processing and adding of meaning to sensations, drawing on memories, predictions, and information from more than one sense, such as the perception of a colored object rather than the sensation of an isolated patch of color. 142, 175–209

Ames room and, 206, 207
analysis by synthesis, 207
attention and, 181, 182
brightness and, 186
color and, 186–188
constancies in, 183–186
of depth, 197–202, 203–206
of events, 209
expectation and, 182–183
of features, 188–193
general principles of, 177–183
gestalt principles of, 176–177
interpretation and, 177–180
motivation and, 181–182
of movement, 208
of objects, 202–206
of others, 535–540
physiological limits of, 180–181
questions in, 175–176
of self, 532–535
of shapes, 193–197
to thought, 346–348

Perceptual development, 381–382

Perceptual hypothesis A tentative interpretation of sensory input that may or may not be confirmed by further information; we continually create and test these hypotheses without realizing it. 179

Performance scale A subscale of the Wechsler intelligence scales that assesses abilities in which verbal skills are

Performance scale (*cont.*)
relatively unimportant. 449
Peripheral nervous system All the neurons outside the central nervous system. 54
Perseveration, 487
Personality The total of a person's characteristic ways of dealing with the world; behavioral psychologists define personality in terms of overt behaviors and others refer to internal states or dispositions inferred from observed behavior. 403–431
    behavior approach to, 418–422
    biological approach to, 405–409
    brain and, 407–408
    defining of, 403–405
    genetics and, 408–409
    humanistic approach to, 422–425
    multiple, 403
    psychoanalytic approach to, 414–418
    theories of, 404–405, 406
    trait approach to, 409–414
    type A, 477–478
Personality assessment, 405, 425–429
    observation techniques in, 425–426
    projective tests in, 425, 426–429
    self-report inventories in, 425, 426
Personality coefficient Mischel's term for what he saw as the inevitably low correlations between measured traits and predicted behavior (around .30), however measured, based on prior research, and which he felt was reflective of the basic inadequacy of a trait approach to personality. 411
Personality development:
    in adolescence, 394–396
    in adulthood, 398, 401
    in childhood, 389–391
    in infancy, 385
Personality disorders DSM-III category of 11 patterns of inflexible and maladaptive personality traits; considered a more questionable category than many others in DSM-III, with only the antisocial personality pattern generally accepted. 492–494
Personality inventory The most common self-report technique of personality measurement, in which the subject answers a series of questions and the assessor evaluates the resulting total score. 427
Personality profile A graphic display of an overall personality pattern drawn from the answers to a multi-factor assessment scale. 426
Personal norms Social norms that have become accepted and internalized by individual members of a society; these norms continue to affect behavior even in the absence of the original social group. 563
Personal space The immediate space around each person; how much is needed to prevent negative effects of crowding varies among cultures. 581–582
Personal unconscious, 417
Person-centered theory, 424
Person perception An area of social psychology concerned with how we characterize others, how we explain their

actions, and how we evaluate them as potential friends or enemies. 535–540
Perspective One of several major approaches in psychology; each perspective is based on a set of beliefs about human behavior that guide how users of that perspective study behavior. Major contemporary perspectives include psychoanalysis, behaviorism, humanism, and social learning theory, as well as the cognitive, physiological, and ethological perspectives. 15
Pesticides, 82
PET scan, 45
Phallic stage Freud's third stage of psychosexual development, from about age 3 to 6, during which the child discovers its own genitals and becomes more independent of its parents. 378, 389–390
Phantom limb pain, 171
Phenomenological world The pattern of how things seem to an individual; client-centered therapists try to respond to clients in terms of this pattern rather than contradicting them. 515
Phenomenology The view that each person lives in a subjective world that is partially his or her own construction and that the world differs as different people perceive it; a major element in Rogers's form of humanism. 23
Phenothiazines, 506, 507
Phenotype What the body actually expresses out of all the inherited characteristics; for example, a phenotypic description might specify brown eyes, even though the person's genotype also includes the gene for blue eyes.
Phenylketonuria. *See* PKU
Pheromones Scent messages that are a major form of communication for many species' survival and mating behaviors; their role, if any, in human motivation remains largely unknown. 166–167
Phi phenomenon The perception of apparent motion of fixed lights flashing on and off, which forms the basis for moving-light signs and movies; first studied by Gestalt psychologists. 208
Phobias Intense fears of some object or situation (also called phobic disorders). 474
Phobic disorders *See* Phobias
Phoneme The smallest unit of sound that native speakers of a language distinguish as meaningfully different from others, sometimes unique to one language. 322
Phonemic restoration effect, 326
Phonology The study of, or a resulting description of, the sounds of a spoken language. 308
Phrases Sets of words smaller than a sentence that convey units of meaning; for example, *a short fat green giraffe* is a noun phrase. 324
Phrenology A 19th-century attempt at studying personality scientifically by relating mental attributes to various bumps on the head; based on faulty assumptions, this nevertheless led to the investigation of brain areas responsible.

for behavior patterns. 407
Physical dependence A state of body adaptation to some regularly used drug, in which the drug becomes necessary to maintain normal body functioning; the physical definition of "addiction." 232. *See also* Psychological dependence
Physical development:
    in adolescence, 393
    in adulthood, 396–398
    aging and, 399–401
    in childhood, 387–388
    in infancy, 387–388
Physical level of memory, 280
Physiognomy, 407
Physiological perspective Focus on the mechanisms of behavior, primarily the brain and key glands, in determining why people behave as they do; investigates the "body" half of the mind/body problem. 26–27
Physiological psychologist, 4
Physiology. *See* Brain; Nervous system
Piaget, Jean Biologist and psychologist whose theory of cognitive development revolutionized the understanding of how children think and how they learn to understand the underlying stability of the world despite varying sensory input. (1896–1980) 337, 373–375, 376, 379, 382–384, 388, 389, 391, 393, 396, 398
Pineal hormones, 216
Pinna The visible external portion of the ear, which aids in collecting and channeling sound waves. 161
Pitch A psychological dimension of hearing: The greater the frequency of a sound wave, the higher the pitch we hear. 158
Pituitary gland The "master gland" inside the skull. The anterior lobe of the gland regulates growth and produces many hormones, including those directing the output of other glands; the posterior lobe receives hormones and chemical releasing factors from the hypothalamus. 74
PKU Abbreviation for phenylketonuria, a condition causing severe mental retardation because the lack of an enzyme needed for digestion of some foods leads to a buildup of toxic products in the brain; children put on a special diet from birth will still have the genetic fault but retardation will not develop. 99, 458
Placebo A presumably ineffective procedure given to a control group; the classic placebo, the sugar pill, may actually have a powerful effect in relieving pain, so a control drug or procedure must be carefully selected to have no effect. 34–35
Place principle Concept of different places or areas of the basilar membrane of the inner ear responding to different sound frequencies; one of the coding systems for auditory nerve transmission to the brain. 162–163, 164
Pleasure center A region of the hypothalamus that plays a major role in many motives and was once thought to be the physical seat of the pleasure/pain rule of hedonism. 108

Pleasure principle In Freud's theory, the guiding principle for the id, by which it seeks pleasure and avoids pain, regardless of other consequences. 414

Plot A graphic display of the relationship between numbers, with a horizontal x-axis and a vertical y-axis representing the two quantities to be plotted. 591–592

Pluralistic ignorance The effect on bystander intervention of the presence of others who do not act, whereby the subject is less likely to recognize that the situation is an emergency. 565

Polygraph An all-purpose laboratory instrument that can record several physiological measures simultaneously; when used as a lie detector it records such variables as rates of respiration and pulse, pulse amplitude, and skin resistance (although the utility of the traces in determining a subject's truthfulness remains in debate). 135–136

Ponzo illusion, 197, 201

Population The total group that the selection of subjects for an experiment is drawn from and thus is intended to generalize to or represent. 34, 596

Pornography, 577–578

Positive afterimage A "ghost" image in the original colors seen briefly after looking at a brightly colored area for a while and then at a neutral surface. 187–188

Positive reinforcement Presentation of a reinforcer; this strengthens an operant that it follows (technically increases the future probability of that operant in similar circumstances—those with similar S_Ds); to be contrasted to negative reinforcement, which also strengthens an operant, but does so differently. 255

Positron emission tomography (PET) scan, 45

Postnatal development, 371–381

Postsynaptic membrane The second half of a synapse: the portion of the surface of a dendrite or cell body at which neurotransmitter is received. 50, 51

Postural reflex, 59

Preconscious processes In the Freudian division of consciousness into three levels, the stored memories that are available to consciousness on demand but are not currently in awareness. 213, 414

Prefrontal lobotomy Psychosurgery in which connections between the prefrontal areas and the rest of the brain are severed to achieve a calming effect; no longer commonly performed. 66, 506

Premack's principle An approach to specifying what will reinforce any organism that arranges the organism's preferred activities in a hierarchy and suggests that the opportunity to engage in any activity on the list will reinforce any other activity lower on the hierarchy (initially less preferred). 254

Prenatal development, 370–371

Preoperational stage The second Piagetian developmental stage, from age 2 to 7, in which a child cannot perform mental operations but thinks in direct egocentric terms. 374

Preparedness A proposed biological constraint on learning imposed by the innate greater preparedness of each species to learn some behaviors more easily than others. 262

Presynaptic membrane The first half of a synapse: the portion of the surface of a synaptic knob from which neurotransmitter is released. 50, 51

Primacy effect A cognitive bias whereby early information will be easily accepted, as in impression formation, whereas later information that does not match the first impression may be rejected or modified: In memory research, the fact that the first items on a list are remembered better than items in the middle; in attitude change, the fact that the first arguments may have a stronger effect on a person's attitude than later arguments. 280, 538

Primary drives, 418

Primary mental abilities A set of seven skills proposed by Thurstone as the basis for all intelligent behavior. 444

Primary process thinking In Freud's theory, the irrational and highly motivated form of thinking that characterizes the id at work trying to implement the pleasure principle. 414

Primary reinforcers Innate reinforcers whose reinforcing properties are built into an organism, such as food, water, and sex. 254

Primates, 86–89, 90

Proactive inhibition A form of interference working forward to cause a failure of memory retrieval when older stored information interferes with new inputs. 301

Problem definition, 356–358

Problem solving, 352–361
  creativity as, 361–364
  thinking biases and, 359–361

Problem space All of the available choices for a problem solver at various stages from the beginning of a problem to its solution; the task of the problem solver is to find the correct path through this problem space, from starting point to solution, using (or processing) various forms of information. 356

Process schizophrenia Early term for schizophrenia developing gradually with no obvious stress as a cause, as if it were a physiological process or illness; not a category in DSM-III. 491

Productive thinking Thinking in which new patterns are built by reorganizing old ones, important to Gestalt theory; according to Gestalt psychology, one of two basic forms of thought. 336

Productivity In linguistics, the potential of a language to generate any number of completely new sentences that can be understood by another user. 309

Profile The plotting of scores on separate item types in a test (such as one of the Wechsler intelligence tests) to give a more detailed portrayal of a subject's skills. 449

Profoundly retarded Those mentally retarded individuals with IQ scores below 20 who cannot be trained to most tasks and who cannot survive without institutional care. 456

Projection, 416

Projective tests Personality assessment techniques that ask the subject to respond freely to a deliberately ambiguous stimulus; the rater then interprets the pattern of responses; two of the best-known ones are the Rorschach and the TAT. 425, 426–429

Proof, 596–597

Proposition In linguistics, a word or phrase that specifies meaning; it proposes that something is true. 324

Propositional code A view of information storage, proposed counter to the idea of the analog code, in which the form of stored information is more like verbal statements than pictures. 351–352

Proprioception The "sixth sense," including the kinesthetic and vestibular senses, that responds to changes primarily within rather than outside the body to give it a sense of where it is and what it is doing (also called the proprioceptive senses). 142, 170–174

Prosocial behavior Any positive human behavior that sustains societies, including cooperation, charity, and other forms of helping. 560–568

Prosthetic devices, 59

Prototypes In Rosch's view of concept learning, central examples of objects or persons that typify a category; in each category some examples are closer to the prototypes than others. 339, 536–537

Pseudohermaphrodites Individuals whose inappropriate prenatal hormones cause a mixed pattern of development; often shortened to "hermaphrodites," although this is technically inaccurate. 125

Pseudoinsomnia, 222

Pseudosciences Proposed claims about the world, often about human behavior, that mimic some of the appearance of true sciences but lack the underlying rigor—for example, "biorhythms," which seeks to associate itself with scientific research on biological cycles but in fact is not supported by replicable data. 218

Psilocybin, 236

Psychiatric social worker A person who has been trained in a mental-health setting such as a mental hospital but may or may not have an advanced degree. 509

Psychiatrist A psychotherapist who has an M.D. degree and has taken a residency in mental diseases, and who therefore can prescribe drugs and ECT and can commit patients to mental hospitals. 508–509

Psychoactive drugs Drugs that affect consciousness and behavior, often through effects on the synapses of the nervous system. 52–53, 182, 232–237
  depressants, 233–236
  hallucinogens, 236–237
  long-term effects of, 232–233
  stimulants, 236

Realistic anxiety, 473

Reality, denial of, 416

Reality principle In Freud's theory, the guiding principle for the ego, by which it seeks to reconcile the conflicting demands of id and superego; in linguistics, the usual assumption by a listener that language productions to be comprehended do make sense. 325, 414–415

Reasoned action, theory of, 550

Recall, 279–280. *See also* Memory, retrieval from

Recency effect In memory research, the fact that the last (most recent) items on a list are remembered better than items in the middle; in attitude change, the fact that the last (most recent) arguments may have a stronger effect on a person's attitude than earlier arguments. 280

Receptors The specialized sites on the postsynaptic membrane that receive and respond to sensed information by generating action potentials. *See also* Transducers 50–51, 144

Recessive gene A gene that is over-ridden by a dominant gene; the characteristic will be expressed if there is no dominant gene for that characteristic present, as when a person is homozygous for blue eyes and thus has that eye color. 92, 93

Recipient factors In the message-learning approach, influences on the persuasibility of a communication that stem from aspects of the recipient, such as age, intelligence, gender role, self-esteem, and level of prior interest in the subject of the communication. 549

Reciprocity, norm of, 563–564

Recognition The most sensitive measure of retrieval from memory, tested by showing subjects the previously learned material and asking them if it is familiar. 292

Recombinant DNA technology Gene splicing, or insertion of a new gene into the middle of a chromosome that did not have it before; has been used to cause bacteria to manufacture human hormones and may be used to modify human genetic diseases. 99

Reference group, 551

Reflection In perception, the fact that light waves bounce off objects in predictable ways; this allows us both to see the objects and to assess where they are located in space. 147

Reflexes:

postural, 59

spinal, 56, 58

Regress, 415

Regression In Freud's theory, the return to behavior characteristic of an earlier psychosocial stage, typically in response to stress. 416

Regression, 416

Regularity In linguistics, the strict rules of a language, known to all native speakers, governing the creation of sentences. 309

Rehearsal A kind of internal repetition by which information in short-term memory is renewed; theorists have proposed different types, including maintenance rehearsal and elaborative rehearsal. 278

elaborative, 286–287

maintenance, 285

Reinforced trial In classical conditioning, a trial in which the unconditioned stimulus is present to strengthen learning. 245–246

Reinforcement Any of several ways of strengthening learning: in classical conditioning refers to the pairing of US with CS, which strengthens the conditioned response to the CS; in operant conditioning refers to the following of an operant with either the presentation of a positive reinforcer or the removal of a negative reinforcer.

of altruism, 562–563

in classical conditioning, 245–246, 247

contingencies of, 256–257

loss of, 485

negative, 255

in operant conditioning, 251

partial, 257

positive, 255

schedules of, 257–260

self-, 420–421

types of, 254–256

use of, 256

vicarious, 24, 266, 420

Reinforcer A stimulus that will increase behavior if it is presented immediately following the behavior; food, for example, is a reinforcer for a hungry organism. 21, 250, 253–254

generalized, 254

primary, 254

secondary, 254

Relaxation response Benson's term for activation of the parasympathetic portion of the autonomic nervous system, claimed by him to be the common effect of various meditation procedures, including a simplified version he proposes. 232

Relearning A measure of retrieval from memory, tested by comparing the difference in the rate of learning material the first time and on subsequent occasions; the improvement, called savings, indicates the presence of some residual effect of the first learning. 293

Reliability Requirement of any assessment measure that it give repeated measures that are similar or that it be consistent over time for the same characteristic in the same person. 410, 435–436

Reliability coefficient A specialized coefficient of correlation that serves as a measure of the reliability of a test, showing that test takers get about the same scores each time the test is administered. 435

REM-deprivation studies Studies in which sleepers are awakened as they reach REM stage; these suggest that the body has a specific need for REM sleep, no matter how much sleep of other stages is had. 224

REM rebound The phenomenon of much longer periods of REM sleep in the sleep cycles of those who have been deprived of this stage, such as experienced by people in REM-deprivation studies or those who stop long-term use of alcohol or barbiturates (which are REM suppressors). 224

REM sleep A specialized sleep stage characterized by dreaming, rapid eye movements (hence REM), and physiological signs of sexual arousal; because a sleeper in this stage shows central nervous system arousal but muscular paralysis it has also been called paradoxical sleep. 221, 224, 225–226

Repression Unconsciously motivated concealment of motives or memories to avoid confronting consciously emotionally disturbing thoughts. 18, 299, 415, 416

Reproductive thinking Thinking in which old associations are reproduced from memory; according to Gestalt psychology, one of two basic forms of thought. 336

Reptilian brain, 54

Research:

applied, 4

basic, 4

in courtroom, 578–580

environmental, 580–584

public health, 584–585

See also Animal research

Reserpine, 506

Residual schizophrenia One of the five DSM-III subcategories of schizophrenia, used for those who have largely recovered but still exhibit some symptoms. 489

Resistance An apparent reluctance to continue psychoanalysis, taking such forms as forgetting appointments or not talking during them, thought to occur when the patient is getting close to some repressed conflict; analysis of resistance is one of the five key processes of psychoanalysis. 512

Response:

conditioned, 245

relaxation, 232

unconditioned, 245

Response biases, 426

Response cost Indirect punishment by removal of a reinforcer; the response (operant) will cost the removal of the reinforcer, such as the punishment of a fine for a traffic violation costing a quantity of reinforcers in the form of money. 255–256

Response biases Common answering tendencies, such as the tendency to respond yes rather than no regardless of question content, which distort certain assessment techniques such as self-report inventories.

Responsibility, diffusion of, 565

Resting potential, 49

Reticular activating system (RAS) A network of nerve connections in the brainstem, connected to many brain structures, that responds to sudden sensory changes by triggering an orienting response. 61, 224

Retina The light-sensitive layer of cells at the back and sides of the eye, on which the lens focuses an image; receptors in the retina (rods and cones) alter the light information to action potentials that are recombined by other cells in the retina before being sent up the optic nerves to the cortex. 149, 150–152, 154

Retrieval Getting back encoded information out of storage in memory. 276, 292–305
  context and, 294
  emotion and, 298–299
  failures in, 301–305
  individual differences in, 300–301
  from long-term memory, 293–294
  measurement of, 292–293
  from short-term memory, 293
  state-dependent, 294
  variations in, 296–305

Retroactive inhibition A form of interference working backward to cause a failure of memory retrieval when new information interferes with information already stored. 301–303

Retrograde amnesia A general loss of memories for a past period of time, often resulting from brain injury and extending backward from the time of the injury. 303–304

Reverberating circuit A tentative proposed physiological process in which the short-term memory trace is a set of neurons so arranged that once stimulated they continue to self-stimulate, more complex patterns represent interlocked sets of reverberating circuits, and the processes of encoding and storage in long-term memory result from some more permanent change in all the synapses that had been active in the reverberating circuits. 291

Rewrite rules Systems in natural languages by which words can be put together into well-formed phrases, typically by beginning with a series of propositions and combining or "rewriting" them. 324

Rhinencephalon, 54

Risk exercise, 137

RNA Short for ribonucleic acid, a molecule that acts as a molecular messenger, carrying instructions from the DNA codes in the nucleus to other parts of the cell; because of its relationship to DNA its role in memory has been sought, so far inconclusively. 292

Rods One of the two types of transducers in the eye; the rods are extremely sensitive to light and are useful for night vision but do not sense variations in color, as cones do. 150–152, 153

Rogers, Carl Major humanist theorist and developer of the client-centered form of psychotherapy. (1902–) 22–24, 28, 424–425, 470, 515–516, 524

Role schemas Those schemas that shape people's behavior, such as gender role, social and job roles, and kinship roles. 530

Rorschach A projective test (thought to reveal deeply hidden personality characteristics) in which subjects' responses to inkblot patterns are analyzed to assess inner personality patterns. 427, 428

Round window Structure at the lower end of the tympanic canal of the cochlea; pressure waves of sound cause it to vibrate, dissipating the energy of the waves back into the air of the middle ear after their information has been sensed by the hair cells of the organ of Corti. 162

Saccades Short, quick eye movements that move the point of gaze from one visual fixation to another; in reading these move the eyes from one set of words to the next, whereas in viewing a complex stimulus they move from one important feature to another, thus generating a scan path. 203

Sample The group of subjects drawn randomly from the defined population that will be used in an experiment. 142, 596

Sampling In perception, the process of selecting useful information and ignoring the rest of the vast total amount of information; every species has evolved senses that allow each organism to be most sensitive to useful information. 142

Satiety center, 113

Saturation One of the three psychological dimensions of color, resulting from the proportion of the light reaching the eye that is of a particular wavelength; a highly saturated color is seen as a strong color with little neutral gray. 149

Savants, 456

Scales, 590

Scan path The path followed by a person's gaze as he or she looks at a complex visual stimulus; the scan path tends to return frequently to portions of the stimulus that are visually or emotionally significant. 203

Scatter plot A plot of two sets of numbers that are in some way related, such as the scores on two tests by the same people; the amount of "scatter" of the plotted points is a visual indication of the degree of relationship that is expressed numerically as the coefficient of correlation. 30–31

Schedule of reinforcement The exact pattern of operant conditioning by which some instances of an operant are reinforced and others are not; can be of fixed-ratio, variable-ratio, fixed-interval, or variable-interval type. 257–260

Schema Organized cognitive structure about objects or events; the term is used to describe human information processing by cognitive psychologists, who pluralize it as *schemata*, but as social psychologists have adapted the concept (as in self-schemas) they have begun to use the English plural, *schemas*. 530

Schemata, 336

Scheme In Piaget's theory, a kind of mental structure that represents a general class of objects, events, or actions —similar, but not identical, to the Piagetian term *schema*. 375

Schizophrenias Mental disorders characterized by serious thinking, perceptual, or other distortions of reality, among the most common and serious of the mental disorders; the schizophrenic symptoms are splits of the associative bonds between thought and speech, between thought and affect, and so on (also called schizophrenic disorders); not the same as the splits seen in multiple personality. 486–492
  causes of, 490–492
  symptoms of, 486–489
  types of, 489

Schizophrenic disorders *See* Schizophrenias

Schizophreniform disorder, 491

Scholastic Aptitude Test (SAT), 443

School(s) of psychology A major theoretical movement in psychology with a name, a founder, and a group of followers. 14–15

Science A structured form of study and a range of phenomena based on the several elements of the scientific method, including quantification and repeatable, demonstrable results. 4, 9

Scientific method, 4

Scripts A way of representing knowledge of events through plans or formats for standardized activities, developed in the study of computer-simulation models of language. 341

Seconal, 233

Secondary process thinking In Freud's theory, the logical and realistic thinking that characterizes the ego's attempts to implement the reality principle; ideally the primary pattern of thinking for a civilized person.

Secondary reinforcers Reinforcers whose reinforcing properties are learned through association with primary reinforcers; also called conditioned reinforcers. 254

Secondary sex characteristics The physiological characteristics, other than the reproductive organs, that develop at puberty as a result of a burst of hormones from the gonads and that distinguish male from female, such as differences in distribution of body fat, muscle, and hair. 127

Secondary traits, 410

Second-order conditioning The process of using a conditioned stimulus as if it were an unconditioned one, for the purpose of conditioning another neutral stimulus; in Pavlov's procedure, for example, a tone that had been made a CS by pairings with meat powder might be then paired with a light (in the absence of meat powder). 245

Sedatives, 233

Seizures, 49, 62

Selective breeding The process of choosing the members of the current generation of a species that show desired characteristics and mating them in order to produce subsequent generations with these characteristics. 80

Selective pressure The process by which the environment shapes, by the life and death of the members of species, the features of all the species inhabiting it: A trait is "selected for" if it aids survival, enabling the individual and the species to reproduce; it is "selected against" if it inhibits survival. 81

Self The concept and set of beliefs one has about who and what one is, a central concept in Rogers's approach. 23, 424, 531

Self-actualization According to the humanistic psychology of Maslow and Rogers, the innate human tendency to develop maximally the capacities for love, self-expression, creativity, and other positive values. 22, 23
Self-actualize, 22, 23

Self-actualized persons Those who are motivated primarily by the self-actualization motive at the top of Maslow's hierarchy of needs and are thus competent, well-rounded, and near the peak of their individual potential. 22, 423, 424

Self-concept The total of a person's set of self-schemas, including nearly universal ones such as a gender schema and highly individualized ones for important behaviors. 530

Self-instructional technique A cognitive-behavioral technique developed by Meichenbaum that teaches adults and children to direct both their overt actions and their covert thoughts through (covert) self-talk. 523, 524
Self-monitors, 534–535
Self-perception, 532–535

Self-perception theory Daryl Bem's view that self-understanding is based on the same external cues used to assess the actions of others; when people attempt to understand why they behave, they do so by observing their own overt behavior just as they observe that of others rather than by analyzing their own thoughts and sensations. 534

Self-reinforcement Social-learning concept that individuals can encourage their own actions by reinforcing them, overtly or covertly. 420–421

Self-report inventories Personality measurement techniques in which the persons to be assessed take active roles in judging their own personalities. 425, 426

Self-schemas Cognitive generalizations summarizing personal experiences, used to guide how we think about ourselves and how we behave. 530, 533

Semantic codes Means by which information is coded in memory in the form of meaning (primarily meaning as usually expressed in words); in short-term memory, a semantic code for some input would store what the input meant, rather than, for example, its visual appearance: the meaning of "apple" might be remembered, but not whether it was "apple" or "APPLE." 283
Semantic level of memory, 280

Semantics The ways in which meaning is conveyed by both words (or other symbols, in nonspoken languages) and sentences. 308

Semicircular canals Fluid-filled sensory structures in the inner ear for the vestibular sense. 162

Senile dementia Technical term for the memory problems and mental confusion that are usually called senility; caused not by aging alone but also by various degenerative diseases and conditions that can affect younger people too, such as Alzheimer's disease. 401

Sensation The basic experiences provided by sensory systems such as the single visual sensation of a patch of color; part of the process of perception. 141–174
    hearing, 155–165
    proprioception, 142, 170–174
    smell, 165–167
    taste, 167, 168
    touch, 167–170
    vision, 147–155, 156, 157

Sensorimotor stage The Piagetian developmental stage from birth to 2 years of age, during which the infant comes to comprehend the physical world as separate permanent objects and to appreciate itself as both an object and a manipulator of objects. 374, 384

Sensory adaptation The tendency for a sensory system to respond less to stimuli that continue without change. 146

Sensory deprivation Extreme reduction of sensory input, used in experiments that initially seemed to indicate a lack of solid sensory input for interpretation produces mental confusion and hallucinations, although some researchers have questioned these results. 180

Sensory registers In the duplex model of memory, very short-term storage systems for each sense from which sensory information is either passed on to short-term memory or lost through decay. 278, 279, 282–283
Sensory sampling, 142

Sensory system The set of structures that, working together to sample one type of environmental information to be processed by the brain, make up each sense; includes accessory structures, transducers or receptors, and nerve tracts. 142–147
    function of, 144–146
    integration of, 146–147
    structures of, 144
Sentences, 323–325, 328–329

Serial learning Any of several types of laboratory tests of memory in which subjects seek to memorize lists of items (usually words) and then to recall them in order. 276

Serial position curve The plot of the probability of remembering each item on a list in free recall, showing that subjects tend to remember the first and last items better than those in the middle. 280, 281

Serial reproduction A task demonstrating distortions in memory encoding by having one person reproduce a drawing from memory, a second person draw the first person's drawing from memory, and so forth; the drawings go through a typical sequence of losing some details and gaining others. 297
Serotonin, 52

Set point The ideal value for a body variable maintained by the process of homeostasis, such as ideal body temperature. 111–112

Severely retarded Those mentally retarded individuals with IQ scores of 20–35, who can sometimes participate in special work and develop limited speech, but only in the framework of institutional care. 456
Sex assignment, 127
Sex differences, 128–129
    language and, 318–319
    loneliness and, 541
Sex-drive hormones, 125

Sex-linked characteristics Traits, such as color blindness, that are coded by genes on the portion of the arm of the X chromosome that is missing from the Y; recessive genes of this sort are expressed more in males than in females. 124
Sexual development, 124–129
Sexuality, and psychoanalysis, 17
Sexual motivation, 121–122

Sexual selection The selecting of some mates and not others, often based on physical or behavioral traits characteristic of one sex in a species; an important mechanism of evolution. 123–124

Shape constancy The automatic perceptual assumption that an object retains a uniform shape despite the retinal patterns that change as, for example, the object is seen from different angles. 184–185
Shapes, perception of, 193–197

Shaping A process of creating a new behavior by reinforcing successive approximations to it, beginning with the organism's repertoire of innate and previously learned operants and reinforcing the one closest to the target behavior. 258–259
Shock treatment, 503–505, 506

Short-term memory (STM) One of the two types of memory storage proposed in two-store models, STM holds information about 30 seconds, can only hold about seven items, and its contents can easily be lost; the information must be entered into long-term memory (LTM) for further storage. 277, 278, 283–285
    retrieval from, 293
    storage of, 291–292

Sickle-cell anemia A widespread genetic disease affecting primarily blacks of African descent, in which the red blood cells sometimes assume a distorted shape that interferes with normal blood flow causing both pain and tissue damage. 96–97, 98

Side effects All effects of a drug other than its intended main effect, including effects that may occur when drugs are taken in combination. 233

SIDS Short for sudden infant death syndrome, the unexplained death of otherwise healthy infants, otherwise

of the cerebral hemispheres. 67–74

Split-half measure Means of judging a test's reliability, especially its internal reliability, by splitting each group of items so scores on the two halves can be compared; if all items measure the same skills, results on each half should match. 435

Spontaneous recovery The return of a supposedly extinguished learned response in classical conditioning (after some time has passed since the extinction trials). 246

Spontaneous remission The tendency of many persons with psychological problems to get better over time without formal therapy, posing a serious problem in assessing the effectiveness of psychotherapies. 511

Spoonerism A classic form of speech sequencing error in which two syllables are interchanged in an otherwise well-formed sentence, showing that the later word was already in preparation when the first incorrect one was spoken. 323

S-R (stimulus-response) position A way of referring to the behavioral perspective; the view of an environmental stimulus causing a response is more characteristic of Watson than of later behavior theorists such as Skinner. 20

Stage sequence, 373

Stage theories Approaches to development that assume that patterns of behavior develop in a fixed sequence, with each more complex or more adultlike pattern following the preceding one in the same way (although not necessarily at the same age for everyone). 373–379

Standard deviation A statistical measure that estimates the usual or common deviation away from the mean on a frequency distribution. 594

Standardize To assess a proposed test by giving it to a sample of the intended population, assessing reliability and validity and seeing if an appropriate distribution of scores has been obtained. (if the test is to be published, such standardization data are an integral part of the test). 448

Standard score A score used to replace the actual numerical score on a frequency distribution that says how far that score fell above or below the mean for that group, expressed in standard deviations. 594–595

Stanford-Binet Intelligence Scale The first major IQ test, based on Binet's early work but adding the calculation of IQ (mental age divided by chronological age), which Binet did not use, and developed by Terman at Stanford University; in revised form, it remains one of the most used IQ tests. 448, 449

Stanford Hypnosis Laboratory, 230, 589

State-dependent retrieval Long-term memory retrieval that is better when the subject is in the same state (for example, mildly drugged) when remembering as

when originally learning; this may represent the effect of similarity in context cues on retrieval. 294

State of consciousness A set of values on one or more experiential or physiological dimensions; for example, an "alert, focused waking state" can be described in terms of the degree of alertness and focus, expressed either as what each feels like to the experiencer or in terms of physiological activity. 214

Statistical significance A way of assessing whether a research finding is probably an accurate assessment of some relationship or a chance outcome. Tests of statistical significance estimate the probability that a given result is a chance finding and scientists must then choose how great a risk to take; in psychology, the probability that the finding is only chance must be less than .05 (5 percent). 35–36, 597–599

Statistics, 589–599
   descriptive, 589, 590–595
   inferential, 589, 595–599

Stereochemical theory Theory of how olfactory transducers code information about smell that proposes that the shapes of receptor sites match the shapes of particular molecules; when a molecule fits into a site it would activate associated neurons, acting in various combinations to give our full range of smells. 165

Stereoscopes, 202

Stereotypes Expected familiar patterns (often types of people whom we characterize in some way, such as "preppie" or "jock") that result in a special kind of inference; in social psychology, oversimplified and overgeneralized schemas that can bias the perception of reality. 299–300, 530–531, 533

Stimulants Psychoactive drugs that increase the level of nervous-system activity. 232, 236

Stimulus:
   ambiguous, 182, 183
   conditioned, 245
   discriminative, 251
   unconditioned, 245

Stirrup One of the three small bones of the middle ear. 161

Storage Holding encoded information in memory for future use. 276, 289–292
   organization of, 289–290
   physiology of, 290–292

Stress, and anxiety disorders, 476–478

Strokes, 65

Strong-Campbell Interest Inventory (SCII) A criterion-referenced test containing a series of educational and occupational scales, a useful and reliable tool for predicting job satisfaction. 430, 431

Strong Vocational Interest Blank (SVIB), 430

Structuralism An early school of psychology, founded by Wundt, that searched for the structure of consciousness and the basic elements of perception through introspection. 14

Structured interview The most

common form of structured observation technique for personality assessment, in which the persons to be assessed are asked a standard set of questions and their answers are standardized, as in the formal employment interview. 425

Structure-of-intellect model Guilford's model of intelligence, dividing it into a number of skills, operations, and contents that interact to produce 120 separate intellectual subskills. 444, 445

Stuttering, 73–74

Sublimation In the psychoanalytic view, a defense mechanism that works by channeling id demands and impulses into socially acceptable outlets. 415

Subtractive A mixture of color in which each object absorbs, or subtracts, from the light that strikes it all of the spectrum but its own color; thus a mixture of complementary colors will yield black, as all colors have been absorbed. 149

Sudden infant death syndrome (SIDS), 227

Superego In psychoanalytic theory, one of three basic elements, the interrelationships of which determine personality development; the internalized representative of society's constraints on behavior, it seeks to prohibit id activity. 18, 414

Superfemale, 124

Supermale Individual born with an extra Y chromosome (XYY pattern), showing tall and well-muscled male body development and sometimes mild retardation; whether XYYs are more aggressive and prone to violence is an unresolved issue. 124–125

Superstitious behaviors Behaviors learned through noncontingent random reinforcement as if it were on a partial-reinforcement schedule; for example, an accidental reinforcement might strengthen the wearing of the particular shirt that was worn on that occasion. 259

Suppression, 299

Suprachiasmatic nuclei (SCN), 216

Supreme Court, 580

Surface traits, 412

Surveys Observational technique by which large numbers of people representing a particuar population answer questions; the answers are then summarized statistically. 29

Survival motives, 109–122
   group, 118–122
   individual, 109–118
   intermediate-term, 112–115
   long-term, 115–118
   short-term, 109–112

"Survival of the fittest." See Evolution

Susceptibility In hypnosis research, degree of responsiveness to hypnosis, measured by the number of tasks a subject completes in a "hypnotic" way. 229

Syllable For nonlinguists, the basic sound unit of a language; typically a vowel with a consonant in front, in back, or both. 322–323

Sympathetic system The portion of the

Sympathetic system (*cont.*)
autonomic nervous system that activates
the body's internal organs to prepare for
violent, rapid physical activity. 54, 62
Synapses The junctions between
neurons, at which the axons of one
neuron transmit information to the
dendrites or cell body of another neuron
by means of neurotransmitters. 47, 50, 51
    excitatory, 49, 50
    inhibitory, 49, 50
Synaptic cleft Gap between presynaptic
and postsynaptic membranes across
which the neurotransmitter travels. 50,
51
Synaptic knobs Specialized ends of
axons where the information represented
by the neurons firing is passed, by means
of synapses, to other neurons. 47, 50, 51
Synesthesia A blending of information
in the senses in which one (or more)
sensory system code overlaps into
another, as in experiencing a "color" of a
sound. 145
Syntax The way words (or other
symbols, in nonspoken languages) are
arranged to form sentences. 308
Systematic desensitization The
best-known form of counterconditioning,
in which a sequence or hierarchy of
increasingly frightening stimuli are
presented to a patient in a deeply relaxed
state so the client can learn to remain
relaxed in the presence of increasingly
stronger stimuli. 517, 518

Tabula rasa From the Latin for "blank
slate"; an earlier philosophical proposal
that human behavior was entirely
learned—the child at birth was a "blank
slate"—that Watson adapted as part of
his theory of behaviorism. 20
Tailored testing Testing adjusted by
computer to be most appropriate for the
individual subject, combining the best
features of individual and group
tests. 451
Tardive dyskinesia, 407
Taste The sense (technically called
gustation) that extracts information in the
form of molecules from liquids placed in
the mouth; one of the chemical senses
(together with smell). 165, 167, 168
Taste buds Structures located in ridges,
or papillae, around the sides of the
tongue containing transducers that
receive taste information from molecules
in solutions in the mouth. 167
Taylor Manifest Anxiety Scale, 473
Tay-Sachs disease A fatal genetic
disease resulting from a single gene
mutation that causes the lack of an
enzyme and thus the buildup of harmful
deposits in brain cells; affects primarily
Jews of eastern European ancestry. 96
Technology of behavior A set of
practical rules that may be applied to
concrete problems of behavior. 5
Television, and aggression, 574–577
Temperature, and sleep, 216, 217
Temperature control, 110

Temporal lobe The portion of the
cerebrum beneath the temple that
processes auditory information. 65
Terman, Lewis M. Translator and
revisor of Binet's original intelligence
test, which he adapted into the
Stanford-Binet Intelligence Scale, and
the originator of the Terman study.
(1877–1956) 442, 448, 451, 454, 455
Terman study A long-term longitudinal
study of intelligence in over 1500 gifted
persons that started in 1921 when they
were children and is still following the
same group. 442–443
Territories, 581–582
Test items In measuring intelligence,
problems presented on a test that will
assess relevant skills or behavior. 435
Testosterone One of the best known of
the androgens, or "male" sex hormones;
it is actually produced by both ovaries
and testes and seems to be the "libido"
or sex-drive hormone for both sexes. 125
Test–retest measure Means of judging
a test's reliability by giving the same test
over again to the same people at different
times. 435
Tests In psychology, techniques for
measuring characteristics of people in a
standardized way so their performance
can be numerically compared to the
results for other test takers. 30
    achievement, 443
    aptitude, 443
    culture-fair, 461
    culture-free, 461
    culture-specific, 461
    design of, 447–448
    group, 449–451
    intelligence, 434–437, 447–454
    projective, 425, 426–429
    tailored, 451
    use of, 452–454
Thalamus A structure at the top of the
reptilian brain that relays inputs from the
sensory systems to the cerebrum. 61
Thematic Apperception Test (TAT) A
personality assessment technique based
on a theory of needs using pictures of
loosely structured scenes to evoke
interpretations from subjects that will
reveal their needs and feelings; one of
the major projective tests. 427–428
Theory A formal statement of what is
believed to be true about a class of
problems, summarizing separate facts
into laws and directing the search for
further laws. 16
Theory of natural selection Darwin's
proposal that natural forces could shape a
variety of species from a common
ancestor by a process similar to selective
breeding. 80–81
Theory of reasoned action A
theoretical view of attitudes and behavior
considering both external and internal
variables; it proposes that the single best
predictor of behavior is a person's
intention, which is in turn a function of
the person's attitude and subjective norm
(the assessment of how others will view
the action). 550
Therapy, 497–524

    action, 516–523
    approaches to, 497–502
    biological, 498, 503–508
    client-centered, 23, 424, 515
    group, 523–524
    insight, 512–516
    psycho-, 498, 508–512, 513
Thinking In the cognitive view, the
active manipulation of information from
both sensory input and memory; a way
of summarizing what is going on in the
world, relating it to the particular
observer or thinker, and making plans
for future action based on what is
found. 336
    in alternate languages, 342–345
    animals and, 340
    biases in, 359–361
    computer-simulation models of, 336
    concept formation and, 339–341
    convergent, 362
    definition of, 336
    divergent, 362
    external notation and, 345–346, 347
    language comprehension and, 341–342
    learning of, 337–338
    perception to, 346–348
    productive, 336
    reproductive, 336
    uses of, 338
    verbal, 336–337, 338–346
    visual, 336–337, 346–352
Thirst In the need-drive view of
motivation, the drive that results from the
need for fluid, a basic motive of most
species. 112–113
Thirst center, 113
Thorndike, Edward L. Learning
theorist whose work in instrumental
conditioning laid the groundwork for
Skinner's and others' work in operant
conditioning by stating his law of effect:
that behaviors followed by a "satisfier"
would be "stamped in" or learned.
(1874–1949) 249, 254, 272
Three-Community Study, 584–585
3-D movies, 202
Threshold:
    absolute, 144–145
    difference, 145
Threshold potential, 49
Thrill seekers, 137
Timbre The texture of a sound, caused
by the interpretation by the ear and brain
of the complexity of frequencies that
make up sounds. 159
**Tip-of-the-tongue (TOT) phenom-
enon** The sensation of knowing that we
know something but being unable to
retrieve it from memory, part of
metamemory and apparently independent
of the stored knowledge itself. 295–296
Token economy A form of group-
applied behavioral contracting in which
tokens are given to reward appropriate
behaviors, and these can then be "spent"
on reinforcers such as snacks; particularly
useful in situations such as hospital
wards. 519, 521
Tolerance A developed resistance to the
effects of a drug that has been taken
regularly, caused by the body's
adaptation to the drug's effects; it means

that a regular drug user may have to take increasingly large doses to maintain the same level of effect. 232

Tolman, Edward Chace Student of both behavioral and Gestalt schools of psychology and developer of the theory of purposive behaviorism. (1886–1959) 269, 270, 271, 272

Tongue, 167

Touch, 167–170

Trace The effect of some piece of information, such as a sensation or thought, that is said to be what is stored in long-term memory; the trace must represent some physiological change in the nervous system, but what the change is has not yet been specified. 280

Trait A reasonably persistent attribute or characteristic of a person, usually expressed as an adjective such as *honest* or *loyal*; which terms are and which are not trait names has been decided differently by various trait theorists. 409–414

Trait theories, 410–414

Tranquilizers, 506–507, 508

Transcendental Meditation (TM), 232

Transducers Specialized cells of the sensory systems that respond to sensed information by generation action potentials, "transducing" or altering the form of the information (see also Receptors). 144

    of ear, 162

    of eye, 150–152

    of nose, 165–166

    of skin, 169

    of tongue, 167

Transference One of the five key processes of psychoanalysis: the transferring of attitudes and emotions once held toward a parent onto the analyst, encouraged as a sign of progress and aided by keeping the psychoanalyst out of the patient's sight. 512–514

Transsexuals Individuals whose gender identity seems opposite to their physiology and who may seek surgery to change their sex. 128, 129

Trials Separate learning episodes in a learning experiment; in classical conditioning each trial consists of presenting the US or the CS and measuring the response. 245

Tricyclics, 507, 508

Trisomy 21, 95

Triune brain, 54, 55

Trust, 385

Tryptophan, 52

Turner's syndrome A condition in which a female is born with one missing sex chromosome (XO pattern), resulting in a normal female appearance but the possibility of various physical problems. 124

Twins, 92

    antisocial personality and, 493

    behavior of, 102

    concordance rates of, 483

    depression in, 484

    intelligence and, 409

    in research, 101

    schizophrenia in, 490

Two-factor theory A theory of emotion proposed by Schachter that suggests both body arousal and cognitive interpretations are important in determining the experienced emotion; in behavioral theory, an interpretation of phobias that suggests the fears are first developed through classical conditioning and that then the avoidant behaviors are learned through operant conditioning. 134–135, 474

Type A personality, 477–478

UCLA Loneliness Scale, 540, 541

Ultradian cycle A 90-minute biological cycle marking regular changes in sleep patterns and possibly in waking activity. 215

"Umweg" problem, 355

Unconditional positive regard A basic tool of Rogers's client-centered therapy, offered as an attempt to convince a client of his or her innate worth and of the therapist's support, regardless of what the client has done or said. 515

Unconditioned response (UR) The natural response to an unconditioned stimulus, such as the dogs' salivation in Pavlov's experiments. 245

Unconditioned stimulus (US) A stimulus that naturally induces some reflexive response, such as the meat powder in Pavlov's experiments that induced salivation in dogs. 245

Unconscious, 414, 417

Unconscious motives The psychoanalytic term for those motives of which we have never been aware and those we have repressed. 18

Unconscious processes In the Freudian division of consciousness into three levels, the memories that are not available for conscious recall but that can affect behavior through dreams, mannerisms, or slips of speech; largely a reservoir of instinctive urges. 213

Underarousal hypothesis Proposal that sociopaths are unusually low in anxiety and thus unconcerned about the possible negative consequences of their actions, supported by results of some task-learning tests. 493

Undifferentiated schizophrenia One of the five DSM-III subcategories of schizophrenia, including those patients whose symptoms are too mixed or changeable to fit into another category or who are in a transition state. 489

Undoing, 416

Unilateral ECT, 505

Unstructured interview, 425

Vagus nerve, 56

Validity Requirement of any assessment technique that it actually measure the factor it claims to measure. 410, 435–436

Validity coefficient A specialized coefficient of correlation that serves as a measure of the validity of a test, showing that test takers get comparable scores on the test and on some criterion. 435

Variable Any measurable dimension of the world that varies over time. 32

    confounded, 32–33

    control of, 34–35

    dependent, 35

    independent, 35

Variable-interval (VI) schedules Partial-reinforcement schedules of operant conditioning that reinforce the next operant after some average time interval, varying from one reinforcement to the next. 257

Variable-ratio (VR) schedule Partial-reinforcement schedules of operant conditioning in which only the first operant after some average number of operants is reinforced but the actual number of operants before reinforcement varies for each instance of reinforcement. 257

Variation, 593–595

Ventricles, 54

Ventromedial hypothalamus (VMH) A portion of the hypothalamus that is a way station for the processing of hunger information, formerly thought to receive sensory signals from food intake and to turn off hunger. 115, 118, 119

Verbal scale A subscale of the Wechsler intelligence scales that assesses verbal abilities. 449

Verbal thinking, 336–337, 338–346

Vesicles Packets of stored neurotransmitter that rupture to spill the chemical into the synaptic cleft. 50, 51

Vestibular sacs Chambers at the base of the semicircular canals of the inner ear that sense the position of the head with respect to gravity. 171, 172

Vestibular sense The proprioceptive sense that responds to gravity and accelerations of the head via information from vestibular sensors within and at the base of the semicircular canals of the inner ear. 142, 170–174

Vicarious classical conditioning, 546

Vicarious punishment Social learning view that people can learn from the negative consequences that follow another person's behaviors; a punishment thus has a direct effect on the person whose behavior is reinforced and a vicarious effect on an observer. 24, 266

Vicarious reinforcement Social learning view that people can learn from the positive consequences that follow another person's behaviors; a reinforcement thus has a direct effect on the person whose behavior is reinforced and a vicarious effect on an observer. 24, 266, 420

Vision The sense that extracts information from the form of radiation we call light; probably the most-relied-on sense for humans and the sense that tends to be given precedence if information from vision and other senses is in conflict. 147–155

    eye's accessory structures, 149–150, 157

    light and, 147–149

    optic nerves to brain, 152–155, 156

    retina's transducers, 150–152

Vision (*cont.*)
touch and, 170

Visual cliff A device for studying depth perception—a glass top covering both a shallow area and a lowered one—that shows human infants perceive depth through visual clues, not just by touch. 381

Visual field The total area that you can see; the left visual field, all you can see to the left, is processed by the right cerebral hemisphere, and vice versa. 67

Volley principle Concept of a group of neurons in the auditory nerves firing as a sequenced group in order to provide a frequency code for transmission of sound information to the brain, for sounds with frequencies greater than the response frequencies of the hair cells. 163–164

Watson, John B. Founder of behaviorism; his approach was to ask what useful purpose a behavior served and to examine only behaviors that could be directly observed. (1878–1958) 19–20, 21, 28, 386, 474

Weber–Fechner law The relationship between sensations and physical stimuli that Fechner derived from Weber's law: $P = K \log I$, or (perceived intensity) = (a constant) $\times$ (logarithm of stimulus intensity), which describes the sensitivity of a sensory system in terms of the physical energy needed to activiate it. 145

Weber's constant The value of the constant proportional increase for any level of stimulus intensity required for one just noticeable difference; the process is the same for every sensory system but the value of the constant differs for each. 145

Weber's law The general statement regarding Weber's constant that, for sensory system response, a constant fractional increase in physical intensity of a stimulus is needed to produce each just noticeable difference. 145

Wechsler Adult Intelligence Scale (WAIS) A major intelligence measure, standardized on the U.S. population, that includes separate performance and verbal scales. 449, 450, 451

Wechsler Intelligence Scale for Children (WISC) An intelligence measure for children similar to the WAIS for adults. 449

Wechsler Preschool and Primary Scale of Intelligence An intelligence measure for young children aged $4\frac{1}{2}$ to 6 similar to the WAIS and the WISC. 449

Weight. *See* Anorexia nervosa; Obesity

Wernicke's aphasia An expressive disorder caused by damage to Wernicke's area of the brain, in which the patient speaks with normal speed and intonation but makes little or no sense. 332

Wernicke's area An area of the brain in the temporal lobe, usually the left; a crucial center for interpretation and planning of language. 67, 330–332

White noise A combination of all sound frequencies that sounds like a hiss rather than a tone; can be used to mask irregular sounds. 160

Withdrawal The process of readjusting the body away from physical dependence on some drug; a variety of symptoms (usually the opposite of the drug's effects) mark withdrawal from different drugs, some of them potentially fatal. 232–233

Working-backward heuristic A problem-solving technique that works by focusing on the goal state and working backward from the last step before reaching that goal and each step before that, greatly reducing the number of possible choices compared to working forward. 358

Wundt, Wilhelm Founder of the first psychology laboratory in 1879. (1832–1920) 12, 13–14, 176

X chromosome The X-shaped chromosome always transmitted from the mother and sometimes also from the father; a human zygote with two X chromosomes will be female. 124

Y chromosome The chromosome that, when transmitted by the father, determines a human zygote will be male; because the father can transmit either an X or a Y, it is always the sperm that determines the genetic sex of a child. 124

Young–Helmholtz theory Early theory of color perception, still partially accepted, that proposes three different types of color receptors (red, green, and blue) with different color sensations resulting from combining separate signals in the brain. 186, 187

Zeitgeist A German word meaning "spirit of the times"; it notes that innovations occur in a historical context and that, in some contexts, a particular innovation (such as the invention of the telephone or the founding of psychology) is inevitable. 13

Zygote The fertilized ovum, containing a full set of chromosomes—half from the mother and half from the father. 93, 370